W9-CJR-643

100 GREAT KINGS, QUEENS and Rulers of the World

100 GREAT KINGS, QUEENS and RULERS OF THE WORLD

Edited by John Canning

WITHDRAWN
FROM THE RODMAN PUBLIC LIBRARY

RODMAN PUBLIC LIBRARY

TAPLINGER PUBLISHING COMPANY
NEW YORK

First published in the United States in 1968 by
TAPLINGER PUBLISHING CO., INC.
New York, New York

Copyright © 1967 by the Hamlyn Publishing Group Ltd.
All rights reserved. Printed in the U.S.A.

SECOND PRINTING

No part of this book may be reproduced or transmitted in any form or by any means, electronic or mechanical, including photocopy, recording, or any information storage and retrieval system now known or to be invented, without permission in writing from the publisher, except by a reviewer who wishes to quote brief passages in connection with a review written for inclusion in a magazine, newspaper or broadcast.

Library of Congress Catalog Card Number: 68-23429

ISBN 0-8008-5775-5

923.1
C225

NOV 5 '73 A-1

NOV 5 '73

RODMAN PUBLIC LIBRARY

Contents

CONTENTS

CONTENTS

CONTENTS

100 GREAT KINGS, QUEENS and Rulers of the World

Editor's Note

"THE BENEFITS of a good monarch are almost invaluable, but the evils of a bad monarch are almost irreparable," wrote Walter Bagehot in his classic study of the English Constitution. He was, of course, referring to the constitutional monarchy, but what applies to the constitutional monarch applies even more to the despot.

In this volume I have presented a personal selection of great kings and queens, the word "great" implying no moral judgement but used as a simple descriptive label for those whose significance for good or bad has been considerable. Most of them exercised absolute or near-absolute power, for the emergence of the constitutional monarch is a comparatively recent phenomenon. Bagehot, referring to the latter, says he has three rights: the right to be consulted, the right to encourage, the right to warn. And he adds that a king of sense and sagacity would want no others. For the rest he represents in his person all the dignified trappings of the state and is invested by his subjects with an almost mystical aura. He is the head of society. Even George III was a "consecrated obstruction".

However, by a unique combination of circumstance and national character the only major country with this type of effective yet controlled system was Britain, and it is significant that it is the only great nation in which royalty has survived to the present day (and even strengthened its position). Since Bagehot's time the great dynasties of Hohenzollern, Habsburg and Romanov have crumbled and vanished.

I have also included rulers who seemed to partake wholly or to a large extent in the royal mystique. Thus there is a certain resemblance between, say, Pericles, on the one hand, and Franklin D. Roosevelt and John F. Kennedy on the other. Pericles was almost the physical and spiritual embodiment of fifth-century Athens; Roosevelt and Kennedy, though their executive powers were not as great, nevertheless embodied to a quite extraordinary degree (as can any great American President) the sense of unity and purpose of their nation. All were performing a quasi-royal function.

The position of General de Gaulle is another case in point. Few Frenchmen throughout France's long history can so self-consciously have associated themselves with *la Gloire*, and his majestic and lofty utterances might well have been envied by *Le Roi Soleil*.

Conversely where this quasi-royal function is not involved, as in societies where the executive and the dignified aspects of the state are separated—modern Britain for instance—I have not included statesmen who were undoubtedly great rulers: Gladstone, Disraeli, Lloyd George and Winston Churchill, for example. I have deliberately excluded also Hitler, Mussolini and Stalin. These have all been treated in earlier volumes of this series, and I felt that the space available should go to other interesting modern figures who have had a crucial influence on our age.

A word on method. For the sake of consistency, I have used anglicizations of names throughout. Also, where confusion might arise owing to the fact that a selected king has the same designation as another I have sought to clarify the matter by qualifying in the chapter heading the one being presented. Thus William I (the Conqueror); Philip II (King of Spain, Naples and Sicily); and Peter I (the Great).

JOHN CANNING
August, 1967

CHEOPS

(Reigned *c*. 2900–*c*. 2875 B.C.)

YES, HE certainly left his mark on the world, that Egyptian king or Pharaoh whose name was Khufu—or, as the Greeks transliterated it, Cheops. So far as we know (and in fact we do not know very much about him) he was not a great warrior, he made no far-spreading conquests, he showed no particular concern for the welfare of his people, he framed no code of laws for their guidance nor did he enlarge the bounds of knowledge or inspire the practice of new arts. And yet he made sure that he would be remembered when most of the dynasties have long since slipped into oblivion. He built himself a tomb. . . .

And what a tomb! There it stands today, some five miles from the west bank of the Nile, near the Arab village of Al-Gizah on the edge of the narrow trench that is the Land of Egypt: there it stands, the most stupendous mass of masonry that has ever been put together by human hands, the nearest approach to a man-made mountain that the world affords. We know it as the Great Pyramid; but Khufu, the man who gave the orders for its construction and saw to its completion, called it *Ikhet*, which in the tongue of the ancient Egyptians means "the Glorious". He chose the name well for something that is still "glorious" after the lapse of not far short of fifty centuries.

Nearly five thousand years have passed into history since Khufu reigned as Pharaoh at Memphis, if we may accept the dates commonly assigned to his reign of 2900 to 2875 or thereabouts before Christ. This means that the Pyramid was already very old when Joseph rode past it, as he must often have done when pursuing his official business as the Pharaoh's vizier; indeed, it would have appeared as ancient to Joseph as Westminster Abbey appears to us. No doubt he often stopped to view it, as it glowed in the burning sun or at night thrust its cone into the star-spattered sky. He must have pondered on its history, and thought of the mighty monarch who had built it; and perhaps he inquired of the priests who in the adjacent temple maintained a daily ritual of prayer and praise in honour of their royal founder.

When Joseph saw it, the Pyramid was bigger and higher than it appears today, since in the course of centuries some twenty or thirty feet of the outer casing have been stripped away to be used in the building of the forts and gimcrack palaces of Cairo. Nothing remains of the inscribed slabs of smooth limestone or polished granite which originally enclosed it as in a skin. But even so, the statistics are impressive. The Pyramid is about 450 feet high, and it stands on a base of 755 feet each way, covering an area of $12\frac{1}{2}$ acres. It has been calculated that more than two million three hundred thousand blocks of stone are incorporated in its huge frame, each weighing two and a half tons, and that in all there are over eighty-five million cubic feet of masonry still remaining after the depredations of time and the even more destructive man. And this monstrous construction was—not a temple to match the majesty of the gods, not a palace to exhibit the magnificence of a king, not a centre of imperial government, or an arsenal, or even the strongpoint of a system of national defence—not any of these things, but, as already stated, a tomb.

How Khufu's heart must have rejoiced as from his palace windows he watched it growing day by day, rising ever higher above the plain! It was not the joy of construction that drove him to it. He was not impelled by any urge to build the most magnificent, the greatest, of all the works of man. But it made him feel *safe*. Against what? Not the common run of enemies: he had nothing to fear from them, whether they attacked from Nubia in the south or from Syria or Arabia across the Red Sea—his armies were quite capable of taking care of *them*. But there was one foe that no armour was proof against, that no legions of soldiers could put to flight—the sting and stab of death. He knew, and needed no reminder from the priests, that even Pharaohs were mortal just as other men, and that the day must come when all his pomp and panoply of power would drop away and he would become a corpse.

This need not be the end of him, however: there was a way of dodging the finality of death, of keeping the dread spectre at bay, if not for all time at least for a time beyond measuring! There were sacred texts that showed how this might be done, formulae known to the priests and the initiated few, procedures that were powerful to preserve the spirit when it had quitted the body. The theology of ancient Egypt is a most strange and wonderful thing, and we shall never be able to understand it in all its profundities and complexity, but it would seem that it was believed that so long as something of the body was preserved, so long would the spirit be allowed by the gods to continue to share their life in the world beyond the setting sun. Hence the tremendous pains taken by the Pharaohs and other great ones to secure their corpses from decay, by the weird process of mummification, after which they were hidden away in places which even the most determined and venturesome of tomb-robbers would find it impossible to violate.

In the great age of the Pyramid-builders, the age of the Fourth Dynasty of the Egyptian kings, it was the practice to bury the Pharaoh in a chamber carved out of the solid rock beneath the pyramid's centre. The construction of this pyramid-tomb became the chief object and interest of each new ruler when he ascended the throne, and to it he caused to be devoted the treasure and the labour-power of all his dominions. He began it when he became king, he continued the work through his reign, and he hoped for nothing so much as that it might be finished before death overtook him. For if it were completed in time, it would provide him with a last resting-place in which *something* of his personality might continue in being.

When the Pharaoh died, his corpse was given over to the corps of official embalmers, who carried out the gruesome process according to the sacred, time-honoured formulae. On the day of burial the body became the centre of a series of elaborate ceremonies embodying occurrences in the life of the god-king Osiris who had been killed but through magical processes had been brought to some sort of life again, and was enabled to bestow a similar measure of immortality on those who worshipped him and were mummified as he had been. The royal mummy was conveyed to the pyramid, to where in its side a shaft had been left open, leading down to the tomb-chamber in the underlying rock. Down this the mummy was lowered, and laid on its left side in a fine coffin of cedar-wood, which again was deposited in a massive sarcophagus of granite or limestone. Food and drink were left beside it, as well as a selection of toilet articles, a magic wand, and a number of amulets for protection against the horrid serpents and other enemies of the dead. Then the deep shaft leading to the burial chamber from the outer air was filled to the top with sand and gravel, and carefully sealed up so that not a sign remained of its existence.

This, or something like this, was what Khufu—or Cheops, to use the name by which he is generally known—had in mind when early on in his reign he gave orders for the construction of the Great Pyramid. As he sat on his throne he must often have thought of the end of all this mighty work—this vast expenditure of materials and labour, this direction of a nation's economy to a single object. And what was the end he envisaged? Nothing other than a small chamber, deep in the ground beneath the mightiest building ever made by human hands, in which his mummified body might lie on and on, snug and warm, while his spirit roamed among the palm-trees and rivulets of the Land of the Blessed!

More than two thousand years after Cheops's death and mummification, that inquisitive old Greek Herodotus visited Egypt, and of course he was shown, as tourists have always been shown, the Pyramid that covered the great king's tomb. He asked the priests of his acquaintance to tell him what they knew of him, and they hastened to oblige. What they had to tell was not complimentary, and it would seem that they bore Cheops a grudge. He had plunged into every kind of wickedness . . . he had given orders, as soon as he came to the throne, that no more sacrifices should be made to the gods and that all the temples should be closed. . . . Not content with these sacrilegious acts he (and here Herodotus must have pricked up his ears and got his wax-tablets ready) had conscripted all the people to work on a particular project of his own. This was the construction of a monster pyramid that he intended for his tomb. Herodotus took careful note of all that was told him, and in due course he included it in the history that he was writing.

A hundred thousand labourers were employed on the job, working in gangs of ten thousand, each gang working for three months at a time. Ten years were consumed in quarrying the stone. The principal quarries were on the farther side of the Nile, and the massive blocks were dragged along a specially constructed roadway to the river; and at high water, when the flats were flooded, they were floated across the valley to the base of the pyramid hill. Here an enormous stone ramp or causeway had been constructed—a labour that had taken ten years, resulting in something that was hardly less remarkable than the pyramid itself. Up this incline the blocks were dragged to the plateau on which the pyramid was to stand, and where more workmen had been engaged for years in excavating the subterranean tomb-chamber. Twenty years were occupied in building the pyramid itself. "It is composed of polished stones, none less than thirty feet long, and jointed with the greatest exactness"—so exact that the joints are in some cases of one ten-thousandth of an inch.

Of exceptional interest is Herodotus's explanation of the way in which the pyramid was raised stage by stage. After the first rows of blocks had been laid, a bank or platform of earth was raised against the wall, and up this the blocks for the next layers were dragged or hoisted with the aid of machines made of heavy timbers.

When this part of the work had been completed, another ramp or platform was built, and more machines were brought into action—or, as Herodotus is careful to state, they may have lifted the first set of machines and used them over again. "I should relate it in both ways," he says, "just as it was related to me." Then he goes on to tell us that he had been shown an inscription on the pyramid, written in the Egyptian characters (i.e. hieroglyphics), stating "how much was expended in radishes, onions, and garlic, for the workmen; which the interpreter, as well I remember, reading the inscription, told me amounted to one thousand six hundred talents of silver. And if this really be the case, how much more was probably expended in iron tools, in bread, and in clothes for the workmen!"

Ever on the alert for an interesting story, however fanciful, Herodotus adds that he had been told that Cheops ran out of money before the work was completed, and "descended to such a degree of infamy that he prostituted his own daughter in a brothel, and ordered her to exact—they did not say how much; but she exacted a certain sum of money, as much as her father had ordered her, and at the same time asked every man who came in to her to give her a stone towards an edifice which she had designed as a monument to herself . . . and of these stones they said the pyramid was built that stands in the middle of the three, in front of the great pyramid. . . ."

As already indicated, very little is known of Cheops apart from his Great Pyramid. He was not, it seems, of royal birth, but came of a noble family in Middle Egypt. Very likely he was a protégé of Seneferu, the first king of the IVth Dynasty, whom he followed upon the throne, and it is recorded that among the ladies of his harem was one who had been a favourite of Seneferu. He may have had his successes as a warrior and a statesman, but it is significant that the inscriptions that have come to light bearing his name are mostly in districts where his quarrying operations were carried on. He was not the inventor of the pyramid, but he set the model that his successors copied, and his own pyramid is the greatest and noblest of this very special form of construction. And our admiration for the monument, so writes the great American Egyptologist Professor Breasted, "should not obscure its real and final significance; for the Great Pyramid is the earliest and most impressive witness surviving from the ancient world to the final emergence of organized society from prehistoric chaos and local conflict, thus coming for the first time completely under the power of a far-reaching and comprehensive centralization effected by one controlling mind".

This was Cheops's achievement in the light of History, but when we remember what he himself had in mind we must arrive at the saddest of conclusions. The day came at length when the Khalif Mamoun, a medieval ruler of Egypt, inflamed by tales of immense wealth buried in the great Pharaoh's tomb, after spending an enormous fortune in breaking into the solid structure at length succeeded in forcing an entrance and penetrating the complex of passages to the underground chamber in which the royal mummy should have been deposited. Within it stood a splendid sarcophagus of red granite. It was without a lid—and it was empty.

HAMMURABI

(Reigned *c.* 1790–*c.* 1750 B.C.)

JUST LOOK at his letter, lying here in this case in the British Museum. You didn't know it was a letter? It looks like a piece of brick? Well, so it does, and in fact it is made of a lump of baked clay. But those marks on it that look like scratches—they are letters in the cuneiform (wedge-shaped) script of the ancient Babylonians, and it is a letter written getting on for four thousand years ago, by a king of Babylonia to one of his trusted servants.

Hammurabi was the king's name, and he was the sixth king in what is called the first dynasty of Babylon—the dynasty which was founded by a certain Samuabum and was continued by Sumulailum, Zabum, Apil-Sin, Sin-muballit (he was Hammurabi's father) and so in a quaint-sounding succession until the last of that particular line, whose name is given as Samsuditana. About most of them we know very little, but they belonged to the Semites, the race to which Jews and Arabs also belong, and seem to have established their rule in the middle portion of the Mesopotamian plain some time before 2000 B.C. There were already people in the land when they arrived, but they seem to have got on with them fairly well to begin with and were allowed to build cities, of which Babylon was the chief. To the south of them were the Sumerians, who were in a much more advanced state of civilization, dwelling in city-states of which the most important were Larsa, Erech, Isin, Eridu, and, most famous of all, Ur of the Chaldees as the Bible calls it. In course of time rivalries developed between the land of Akkad, as the region round Babylon was called, and the land of Sumer, and when Hammurabi came to the throne he inherited a war with Rim-Sin, king of Larsa. After a long and hard struggle, he won it; he took Rim-Sin captive, and put an end to Larsa as an independent state.

When this was we cannot be sure. Until recently it used to be generally stated that Hammurabi reigned about 2000 B.C., although some authorities put it some hundreds of years earlier, and some perhaps two or three hundred years later. It now seems most likely that he reigned at Babylon from about 1790 to 1750 B.C. Whenever it was, it was a very long time ago, and yet his reign is exceedingly well documented, what with the large number of tablets and inscriptions that have been preserved. Not least among these is the collection of letters in the British Museum, addressed by King Hammurabi to a certain Sin-idinnam, who seems to have been a trusted official of some kind. They are on a great variety of subjects, short and sometimes sharp in their wording, and absolutely clear. Most of them convey the king's instructions in matters of official business. Each letter—written on a small clay tablet—was enclosed in a clay envelope, inscribed with the address of the official for whom it was intended; the envelopes were thrown away when the recipient broke them open, but in a few instances small portions of the envelope still adhere to the letters. Both letter and envelope were baked in an oven before dispatch, and the envelope was dusted with dry powder to prevent it sticking to the letter that was put into it.

In the collection are some scores addressed by Hammurabi to Sin-idinnam, and in nearly all the latter is told to do something or the other. He is to order the dwellers on the Damanum canal to clean and clear it out within the current month, he is to arrest eight officials who have refused to do what they were told and to send them to Hammurabi in Babylon, he is to investigate a charge of theft of corn that has been brought against a man named Awel-ili by a man with the even stranger-sounding name of Awelu-tummumu, he is to send forty-seven shepherds to Babylon to give an account to the king of the flocks under their charge, he is to take steps to prevent certain fishermen from fishing in prohibited waters, he is to look into a dispute between a landlord and a tenant about the payment of rent for a plot of land, he is to make arrangements for a certain number of slaves to be provided on a particular day, he is to take on more sheep-shearers to get the job done in time, he is to appoint this man and is to give that other man the sack . . .

"Why haven't you sent Enubi-Marduk to me at Babylon as I ordered," demands Hammurabi; "as soon as you get this, tell him to start at once, and to travel day and night, and let him make sure that he arrives speedily." Time and again Sin-idinnam is enjoined to pay particular attention to the state of the banks of the Euphrates and of the canals dependent on it—a matter of the utmost importance in a land relying so largely on irrigation for its subsistence. Then there are letters dealing with the matter of the Goddesses—or rather, the images of the Goddesses—of Emutbalum, a district in the Elamite country to the east which had been recently raided by the Babylonian forces.

From what can be made out, it would appear that the "goddesses" had been captured and carried away in triumph to Babylon. But then the Babylonians had met with reverses, and the pious Hammurabi and his priestly advisers would very naturally assume that the goddesses themselves were angry at the insult that had been offered to them in being detained in a foreign land against their will. So Hammurabi took steps to have them returned to their own country. "Thus saith Hammurabi unto Sin-idinnam," runs the first letter; "behold, I am dispatching unto thee the officers Zikir-ilisu and Hammurabi-bani, that they may bring hither the goddesses of the country of Emutbalum. Thou shalt cause the goddesses to travel in the processional boat as in a shrine, that they may come to Babylon. And the temple women (their female attendants or priestesses) shall follow after them. For the food of the goddesses thou shalt provide . . . sheep, and thou shalt take on board provisions for the maintenance of the temple-women on the journey until they reach Babylon. And thou shalt appoint men to draw the tow-ropes, and chosen soldiers, so that they may bring the goddesses to Babylon in safety. Let them not delay, but make haste to reach Babylon." Sin-idinnam did as he was ordered, and then in a further letter he is told to arrange for the "goddesses" to be entrusted to troops under the command of one Inuhsamar, who would "bring them in safety", by which presumably is meant they would be returned to their shrines in Emutbalum, after which he might rest assured that he would be able to overcome the enemy with "the troops that are in thy hand".

Not only are there numerous letters from Hammurabi in the collection but many other documents, concerned in the main with legal and commercial transactions, and including deeds recording the buying and selling of houses and lands, leases of house-property, the hiring of slaves and labourers, the loan of money, the dissolution of business partnerships, the adoption of children, marriage contracts, bills of divorce, and so on. These in themselves are indications that the people over whom King Hammurabi ruled had attained a quite high state of civilization, an order of things to which many generations must have contributed. This conclusion is amply confirmed by the Code of Laws with which Hammurabi's name is indissolubly connected.

"Hammurabi's Code" is inscribed in ancient Babylonian characters on a pillar of black basalt that was discovered by French archaeologists in 1902, when they were excavating the remains of the ancient Persian city of Susa. The pillar was in several pieces when unearthed, but they were joined together and the restored monument has been for many years one of the most valued treasures of the Louvre Museum, in Paris; a very fine copy is in the British Museum in London. Originally the pillar may have been erected in the temple at Sippara (not far from the modern city of Baghdad), where it stood for perhaps a thousand years, until a king of Elam sacked Sippara and carried it away to Susa as a trophy. Then at some later date Susa in turn fell to a conqueror and was laid in ruins; Hammurabi's column was buried beneath piles of rubble until at length it was disinterred by the French archaeologists at the beginning of this century.

The pillar (or *stele*, to use the technical term for such a monument) is 7 feet 4 inches in height and 2 feet in diameter. On the upper part is carved in relief a picture of Hammurabi standing before the god Shamash, the Sun-god who in the Babylonian pantheon was also the god of justice in heaven and on earth. Shamash is seated on his throne; he is wearing a horned head-dress, symbolical of divine power, and from his shoulders rise flames of fire. Hammurabi is dressed in a long robe and is standing in the traditional attitude of worship with his right arm bared and raised; it is generally stated that he is receiving his "laws" from the god, but this is unlikely, since in the text the claim is made that they were originated by the king himself. (This claim is not strictly true, however; Hammurabi was a codifier rather than an originator, and the Code was based upon laws and customs that had acquired the sanctity of long tradition.)

The "laws" are engraved on the lower part of the pillar. There are 282 of them, and there were perhaps another thirty-five, but these were in the lower part of the column and have been erased, it is assumed, by the Elamite conqueror who wanted the room for an inscription of his own (which, however, was never added). They are preceded by an introduction, in which we are told that "Anu the King of the Gods, and Bel the Lord of Heaven and Earth had delighted the flesh of mankind by calling me, the renowned prince, the god-fearing Hammurabi, to establish justice in the earth, to destroy the base and wicked, and to hold back the strong from oppressing the weak . . ." Then follow more lines of eulogy, in which Hammurabi is styled among many other things the hero king, the wise and prudent ruler, the guardian of the city, the renowned potentate who has filled his people when there was dearth in the land, the far-seeing one who has provided them with pasture and drinking-water, the impetuous bull who overthrows his enemies, the grave of his foes, the promulgator of justice, the exalted one who humbles himself before the great gods. . . . "When Merodach (the god of Babylon) had instituted me governor of men, to conduct and to direct them, then it was that I established Law and Justice in the land, for the good of all the people. . . ."

Then follow the "laws", and it is noticeable that they do not seem to be arranged in any sort of order, and it would also seem that they cannot compose the whole Code since there are some very obvious gaps in the enactments. Thus punishment is prescribed for a man who steals from a temple or a "great house", but nothing is said about thefts from ordinary citizens. It may be that the laws given on the pillar are those about which there was most doubt, or perhaps they were those in most frequent demand, and there were many other rules of behaviour which were so generally accepted that there was no need to have them inscribed in this most public and permanent fashion. However this may be, the Code is the most complete and valuable collection of ancient laws to come down to us.

The Code opens with the enactment that "if a man has laid a curse upon another man, and it is not justified, then the layer of the curse shall be slain". This may strike us as decidedly harsh, but it is to be noted that capital punishment rather than fines or imprisonment is most frequently prescribed. Thus a man who has given false evidence in a lawsuit shall be slain, and likewise the thief above mentioned, a man who has broken into a house ("he shall be slain before the breach he has made, and there buried"), a receiver of stolen goods, a man who has harboured a runaway slave instead of restoring him to his owner, and a man who goes to help in putting out a fire and seizes the opportunity of making off with some of the householder's goods ("That man shall be thrown into the same fire"). A woman who kills her husband because she has become enamoured of another man shall be impaled on a stake. If disaffected persons happen to meet in a wineseller's, and she does not seize and take them to the "great house", she shall be slain.

Trial by some form of ordeal is provided for in certain cases. "If a married woman is found lying with another male, they shall both be bound and thrown into the river," runs one clause; but "if the finger is pointed against a man's wife because of another male, and she has not been found lying with him, then she shall plunge for her husband into the holy river"—in which case if she floated she was found innocent, but if she sank—well, she was obviously guilty and fully deserved her fate. Similarly, when a man has had "a spell thrown over him" he shall plunge into the holy river; if the holy river seize him, the layer of the spell shall take his house, but if he emerges safe and sound, the layer of the spell shall be slain, and he who plunged into the holy river shall take *his* house.

Coming now to domestic relations, a man may divorce his wife if she should prove barren, but he must return her dowry before sending her back to her father's house. If a wife mismanages her home and neglects her husband, all he has to do is to say "thou art divorced", and she must return to her father without her dowry; but a man is not permitted to divorce his wife just because he has got tired of her, but must maintain her as long as she lives. Several laws show a real concern for the woman. Thus a wife who has developed a deep aversion for her husband and says, "Thou shalt not possess me", may take her dowry and go back to her father, always provided she has given her husband no other cause for complaint. It is also recognized that a woman whose husband has been taken prisoner in the wars, and she is left destitute, may take up with another man, although if the first man should be released and return home she must go back to him.

Another group of enactments illustrates the old rule about "an eye for an eye". Thus, "if a man has destroyed the eye of a freeman, his own eye shall be put out". "If a man has knocked out the teeth of a man of the same rank, his own teeth shall be knocked out." But here class distinctions enter into the picture, for if the victim is a man of inferior rank or a slave, he or his master is to receive financial compensation only. That the practice of surgery was a dangerous occupation is illustrated by such a "law" as this: "If a doctor has treated a severe wound with a metal knife, and has caused the man to die, or has opened a man's tumour with a metal knife and destroyed the man's eye, his hands shall be cut off." Not long before the end of the Code is this pithy pronouncement: "If a mad bull meet a man in the highway and gore him, and kill him, that case has no remedy." So we come to the last one of all: "If a slave shall say to his master, 'Thou art not my master,' his master shall cut off his ear."

Then comes the epilogue, in which Hammurabi writes, "These are the judgments of justice which Hammurabi, the mighty king, has established, conferring upon the kingdom a sure guidance and a gracious rule. If a man heed not my words that I have written on this pillar, if he has scorned my malediction, nor feared the curse of God; if he has annulled the law that I have given, or altered my words . . . may Anu, the Father of the Gods, extinguish his glory, shatter his sceptre, may he curse his end!"

THOTHMES III

(Reigned 1501-1447 B.C.)

THE OBELISK on the Thames Embankment in London which is called "Cleopatra's Needle" has nothing to do with Cleopatra, but was set up with another obelisk in the temple of Ra in Heliopolis by Thothmes III about one thousand and four hundred years before Cleopatra reigned. Mr. R. Engelbach, in his book *Problem of the Obelisks*, wondered what Thothmes III's feelings would have been "had he known that one (obelisk) would be taken to a land of whose existence he never dreamed (the U.S.A.) and that the other would fall into the hands of what was then a savage people; and, after undergoing such vicissitudes as ship-wreck and injuries from a German air-bomb, would still be standing, though thousands of miles away, after a lapse of nearly 3,500 years?" Not very far away from the obelisk, in the British Museum, is the giant head of Thothmes III, dignified and inscrutable.

Thothmes III, XVIIIth Dynasty, is considered to have been the greatest Pharaoh of the New Empire period and by some to have been the greatest in Egyptian history. He reigned for fifty-four years from 1501 to 1447 B.C. or, as recent authorities argue, from 1504 to 1450 B.C. He fought seventeen campaigns in Syria and maintained Egypt as the greatest military state of the time; his grandfather, Thothmes I, had been the first to militarize Egypt and send expeditions into Western Asia to make sure that there should be no repetition of the invasion of the Hyksos, who set up their own kings in Egypt. That invasion had left terrible and humiliating memories for the Egyptians so that Thothmes I and his grandson, Thothmes III, were regarded as heroes; the latter left annals of many of his campaigns inscribed on the walls of the great temple to the God Ammon at Karnak and on the walls of his tomb.

Thothmes III was an energetic and forceful man, becoming Egypt's great warrior Pharaoh, but for the first twenty-two years of his reign he was kept in the background by his co-regent, Queen Hatshepsut, who was probably both his step-mother and his aunt. She was, as far as is known, the first woman to rule as Pharaoh claiming divine origin; this was done by other Pharaohs, including

Thothmes III when he ruled alone. There was almost certainly a party which supported Queen Hatshepsut and one which supported Thothmes III, but there does not seem to have been any serious trouble in the kingdom, even though it was very unorthodox to have a woman as ruler, and they got round this by pretending that she was a man. In nearly all the representations of her as Pharaoh, wearing the double crown of Upper and Lower Egypt, she is shown as a man, sometimes with a beard, though there is one relief in which she is dressed as a woman; male pronouns are used in describing her, but sometimes there is confusion between the masculine and the feminine.

Ineni, the architect who built the first tomb in the valley, which came to be known as the Valley of the Tombs of the Kings, states in an inscription that Thothmes III followed his father Thothmes II "as King of the Two Lands, having become ruler upon the throne of the one who begat him . . . the Divine Consort, Hatshepsut, carried on the affairs of the Two Lands according to her own ideas. Egypt was made to work in submission to her, who was the excellent off-spring of the God and who came forth from him". Some authorities think that Hatshepsut and Thothmes III were married, but this seems unlikely since he married her daughter Merytra Hatshepsut, who became his Great Royal Wife and mother of his successor Amenophis II.

There is little information about Thothmes III during the reign of Hatshepsut and he is hardly mentioned in the inscriptions on obelisks and monuments which she had erected during her lifetime. He must have deeply resented his position, for when he ruled as sole Pharaoh, not only was her name erased from her monuments but those of her architect, Senmut, and of other officials were removed from their monuments. Thothmes III "hated her with a deadly hatred", wrote Wallis Budge, and is surprised that more of Queen Hatshepsut's monuments were not destroyed, though other authorities have expressed surprise that so great a man as Thothmes should have shown his resentment in this way.

It is no discredit to Thothmes III that he remained in the background during the reign of Hatshepsut, for she was a most able woman and he may, indeed, have held her in some admiration. She was already in a powerful position when he became co-regent as a young prince following his father's death. She was probably co-regent with her father, Thothmes I, towards the end of his life after his royal wife had died. His son, Thothmes II, who succeeded, is believed to have been a rather effeminate character and was the son of a secondary wife, so that to give him the royal power, which was considered so essential to a ruler by the Ancient Egyptians, he was married to his half-sister, Hatshepsut; purity of descent was reckoned through the female, rather than the male, line. Queen Hatshepsut's titles were "King's daughter, King's Sister, God's Wife and King's Great Wife" and she was certainly the ruler. By Thothmes II she had two daughters, Neferura, who died young, and Merytra; Thothmes III was the son of a secondary wife, Aset or Isis, so that when his father, Thothmes II, died, Queen Hatshepsut was officially made co-regent because she was of royal blood.

Queen Hatshepsut had, therefore, been in control of the government during her husband's reign of about thirteen years and by her talents and gifts she had won over to her able civil servants. Thothmes III, therefore, could do little except fret in the background; she was much too powerful and popular as a ruler to be overthrown by a palace revolution.

During her reign Egypt had peace and prosperity and the people of Syria and Palestine, conquered by her father, Thothmes I, continued to pay their tributes. She sent an expedition to the Land of Punt, which is now Somaliland, to do barter with the people of the country and bring back gold, skins and animals, but principally to bring back myrrh, which was used as incense at the ceremonies in the temples. The story is told in detail in delightful bas-reliefs on the walls of the beautiful funerary temple, dedicated to the Gods Amen-Ra and Hathor at Der el-Bahri in the Valley of the Tomb of the Kings. She died in middle age, worn out perhaps by the task of ruling a great kingdom. Her body has not been found in spite of all the elaborate arrangements she made at her funerary temple of Der el-Bahri.

The story of Queen Hatshepsut is important to the story of Thothmes III, since twenty-two years of his reign had passed by without his being able to display his talents to the full. It is a tribute to his character that he kept himself ready to rule the kingdom on the departure of the queen and that he did not become an embittered and angry young man. How well prepared he was is shown by the rapidity with which he led the Egyptian army on his first campaign in Palestine and Syria in the first or second year that he had assumed full power as Pharaoh.

On the death of the great queen the peoples of Syria and Palestine had revolted and refused to pay the tributes which they had done since the conquests of Thothmes I. It was a formidable revolt by well-armed and powerful peoples formed into a league under the

King of Kadesh whose territory lay by the Orontes river. "Behold," it is stated in the Annals, "from Yeraza (northern Judea) to the marshes of the earth (the Euphrates) they had begun to revolt against His Majesty." These Annals of Thothmes III's seventeen campaigns are inscribed on the walls and obelisks in the temple of the God Ammon at Karnak and in the Pharaoh's tomb. The King of Kadesh, who was a redoubtable warrior, and was backed by many peoples, including the powerful King of Mitanni to the east of the Euphrates, had heard little of Thothmes III and probably thought that he was a nonentity.

In April, 1479 B.C., or about that year, Thothmes III left with his army from a fortress (later known as el Kantara) on the borders of Sinai, and took the army in nine days the one hundred and sixty miles to Gaza, and then on to Yehem on the southern slopes of Mount Carmel. The King of Kadesh had advanced south from the Orontes river in Syria, collecting troops of his allies on the way, and they waited for the Egyptians near Megiddo with a well-equipped army. Their soldiers were well trained and they had developed chariot warfare, probably before the Egyptians had, and, indeed, the peoples of Syria were in some respects more advanced than the Egyptians. It was clearly going to be an important battle and the result would be watched closely in Asia and elsewhere to see if Egypt was to remain the dominant power or whether there would be great changes.

Thothmes III, who was new to warfare, summoned a Council of his generals. Among the official annals of the campaigns there is an excellent account of this Council and of subsequent events, "the earliest full description of any decisive battle" states Sir Alan Gardiner in *Egypt of the Pharaohs*. It is also of great interest as giving for the first time an insight into the character of the Pharaoh, who shows himself, even before his first battle, to have been a born commander. There were three roads the army could take to reach the enemy drawn up before Megiddo; two of them were easy routes and the most likely ones to be followed by a large army with chariots, tents and baggage, while the other was a difficult track over Mount Carmel. The generals advised strongly against the difficult track: "How should we go by this road which is narrow and risky . . . will not horse have to come behind horse and man behind man? Shall our vanguard be fighting, while our rear-guard is still halted over yonder in Aaruna and cannot get into action?" Pharaoh did not take their advice; he must have realized that the enemy would be expecting the Egyptian army to advance by the easier road and have disposed their troops accordingly. It should be stated, however, that the official reports often show the Pharaoh to have been right and his generals wrong.

The Egyptian army led by Thothmes came through the pass without incident and the first stage of the battle was already won, for the Syrians were taken by surprise and had to reassemble their army to deal with the Egyptians who were in a strong position. Thothmes's boldness and the leisurely way he camped before the battle impressed the Egyptian army and caused consternation among the Syrians, who were defeated. The townsmen of Megiddo shut their gates in panic so that the army could not escape into the city though some of the leaders got in—"the people of the city . . . lowered clothing to pull them up within the walls".

Thothmes wanted to attack immediately while there was still confusion, but the Egyptian army was busy looting. "Then we captured their horses, their chariots of gold and silver were made spoil; their champions lay stretched out like fishes on the ground. The victorious army of His Majesty went round counting their shares. . . . Now if only the army of His Majesty had not given their heart to plundering the things of the enemy, they would have captured Megiddo at this moment."

The result was that the Egyptian army had to settle down to a siege of Megiddo and the King of Kadesh escaped from the city to stir up further trouble for the Egyptians in the future; but the opportunity to throw off the Egyptian yoke was lost by this first big defeat, for there was never again the same unity; on his subsequent campaigns Thothmes was able to deal with his opponents piece-meal. When Megiddo surrendered Thothmes showed magnanimity by granting terms and forbidding any killing. At the same time the city was despoiled and a long list is given of the plunder which showed how rich was this part of Western Asia. Thothmes returned to Egypt in triumph after a successful campaign lasting six months; there were ceremonies at the Temple of Amon at Karnak which was enriched with enemy spoils; hostages were brought from Syria and some were trained with the object that they should go back to their country as willing vassals.

While Thothmes was away on his many campaigns in Western Asia, Egypt was ably ruled by his Prime Minister, Rekhmara, who has left an account on his tomb of what he considered were the duties of a just Prime Minister, and he seems to have followed these precepts. It is probable that Thothmes enjoyed the military life which was very much freer for him than the life at Thebes with its ceremonies and rigid etiquette. He made sure that he lived comfortably on his expeditions; there is a stele in the Louvre on which Antef, the King's herald, describes how he used to go ahead with the advance guard and prepare a suitable palace or building for the Pharaoh's reception, so that when Thothmes arrived he found it "equipped with everything that is desired in a foreign country, I had made it better than the palaces of Egypt, purified, cleansed, set apart . . ."

The soldiers, too, seemed to have liked this rich country where there was plenty of plunder; in Phoenicia the annals state that "the army of His Majesty was drunk and anointed with oil every day as at a feast in Egypt". Thothmes had a collection made of the plants and animals, which were brought as an offering to the temple at Karnak and are recorded in bas-reliefs in a chamber which came to be called the "Botanic Gardens".

He made good use of his sea-power and formed bases in the coastal towns from which he could strike inland to capture cities such as Kadesh. The King of Kadesh continued to fight back and had shown his resourcefulness during the siege of his city by sending out a mare from Kadesh to cause confusion among the Egyptian chariots drawn by stallions, as they stood in battle array, but one of Thothmes's trusted captains, Amenemhab, dashed out and killed the mare before she reached the stallions.

On his eighth campaign in the thirty-third year of his reign Thothmes crossed the Euphrates at the "great bend" near Carchemish (fifty miles north-west of Aleppo) and attacked the King of Mitanni in Naharin—the Land of the Two Rivers (Euphrates and Tigris)—thus "extending the boundaries of Egypt". He then marched south to Niy, which he captured, and went elephant hunting; the story of how the Pharaoh's life was saved is recounted by Captain Amenemhab on his tomb at Thebes: "He hunted 120 elephants for the sake of their tusks. I engaged the largest which was among them, which fought against His Majesty; I cut off his hand (trunk) while he was alive before His Majesty, while I stood in the water between two rocks."

No country of the Near East had attained so large an empire or so much power as Egypt under Thothmes III. Rich tributes came yearly from Western Asia; Nubia paid tribute and there was a campaign there in the fiftieth year of his reign; the trade, which had been restarted by Queen Hatshepsut with the Land of Punt was maintained by Thothmes, and there were exchanges with the peoples of Crete and Cyprus. It was a period in history when war was profitable and Egypt's treasury was filled to overflowing, much of which enriched Thebes, the city of his beloved God Ammon. Thothmes added a colonnade of forty granite columns and almost as many pillars; on the walls of the temple were cut the names of the peoples he had conquered; repairs and additions were made to temples at Heliopolis, Memphis, Abydos, Denderah and Coptos. Thotmes died in the fifty-fourth year of his reign, loved and respected; his body was found in Queen Hatshepsut's temple of Der el Bahri in 1881 and lies in the Cairo Museum.

AKHNATON

(Reigned *c.* 1380–*c.* 1360 B.C.)

NOTHING MORE delightful has come out of Ancient Egypt than the wall paintings and sculptures showing the young King Akhnaton with his consort, the beautiful Queen Nefertiti, with the little princesses who were their daughters. There is a simplicity about them, a charming realism, a domestic intimacy that is altogether lacking in the art that went before and most of what followed. Thus in one we may see the king and queen in a fond embrace, the queen sitting on her husband's knee; and in another the king is sitting on a chair with the queen on a cushion opposite him, and the daughters, according to their age, climbing on to his lap or standing or sitting beside the royal pair. Then here is one showing them in their chariot, and Nefertiti is reaching up as though to kiss the king, while their little daughter, the Princess Mertaton, who is just tall enough to see over the chariot's side, shows an eager interest in the pair of prancing horses. And here in a vivacious fresco are two of the princesses, naked save for their bead necklaces, fondling one another as they sit on cushions at the feet of their parents.

Appealing as they are, it must be acknowledged that they are not the pretty-pretty pictures that royal portrait painters have been generally commissioned to produce. They are not in the least stylized but bear all the signs of being true to life. But this is understandable enough when we are told that the king who commissioned the portraits assumed as one of his royal titles, as soon as he came to the throne, "He who lives in Truth".

When he became king it was in succession to his father Amenhotep III, and to begin with he himself bore the name of Amenhotep. This was in 1380, or it may have been 1375 B.C., and he is supposed to have reigned about twenty years. How old he was at the time of his accession is a matter in dispute; some authorities hold that he was a boy not yet in his teens, while others are of the opinion that he was already a young man.

The XVIIIth Dynasty to which he belonged furnished Egypt with some of her greatest and most successful sovereigns. Amenhotep III had had a long reign of thirty-six years, and he bequeathed to his son a realm that was prosperous and well-governed, and so extensive that it is more deserving of the name of empire than of kingdom. But the fourth Amenhotep was a very different man from his father, who had well earned his title of Amenhotep the Magnificent.

From the beginning of his reign he was much under feminine influence, at first that of his mother Queen Tiy and then on his marriage that of his wife, Queen Nefertiti, in addition, and of course the royal ladies had their own circle of courtiers and chosen counsellors. This is understandable enough when we remember his extreme youth, but as he grew older he showed a marked preference for the peaceful joys of his palace over the risks and ardours of military campaigning. Very clearly he was not cut out for the rougher tasks of kingmanship; which was a pity, since a period of instability had set in on the Egyptian frontiers in Africa and Asia. The governors in the outlying provinces were exposed to such pressures that they had great difficulty in holding their own, and to their imploring messages for assistance the young Pharaoh seems to have turned an almost deaf ear. He was not really interested in such things. Not politics but religion was what concerned him most. As Professor Breasted explains the situation, the philosophizing theology of the priests was of more importance to him than all the provinces of Asia; and so, instead of gathering the army so sadly needed in Syria, where the Hittites were overrunning the Egyptian defences, he immersed himself heart and soul in the thought of the time and gradually developed ideals and purposes which make him the most remarkable of all the Pharaohs—indeed (so Breasted claims) the first *individual* in human history.

A remarkable claim, and doubtless a well-grounded one; and yet it might be urged by one not so favourably disposed towards the young king that it was just this striking originality of his, in one special sphere, that contributed most to his failure as a monarch.

On the face of it, the signs for a revolution in religion were propitious. The old gods—the names of more than two thousand are known to us, and a queer lot they are!—were still worshipped in their temples up and down the land, but it was becoming increasingly recognized that they were too limited and too obviously local to answer the religious needs of what was now become an empire. "Our gods are too small," the more thoughtful of Egyptians must have concluded; "they have their worships, each in his own city, but they cannot adjust themselves to this new state of affairs, when the bounds of Egypt are no longer within sight of the waters of the Nile but lie far beyond the desert and reach unto the most distant mountains". A super-state had come into existence: it was not unreasonable to suppose that it should be matched with a super-deity. "It can be no accident", Breasted has written, "that the notion of a practically universal god arose in Egypt at the moment when the king was receiving universal tribute from the world of that day".

Such thoughts as these had been passing through Amenhotep's mind since he first began to think for himself, and it would seem that as soon as he had the power in his own hands he resolved on giving them tangible expression. If there was one god decidedly superior to all his fellows it was Amen, or Amon, the state-god of Thebes, the Egyptian capital; and very often his name was combined with that of Ra, the sun-god whose chief centre of worship was at On (Heliopolis) in the Delta. "Amenhotep" means "Amen is content", but however it might be with the god, the king who was named after him was *not* content. He decided to abandon the style under which he had been known since he became king, and assumed instead the name of Akhnaton (or Ikhnaton, or Akhenaten). This word means "the Spirit of Aton", and Aton (or Aten) was the name given to the god whose visible symbol was the solar disc. There is not the least reason to suppose that the king thought of the sun itself as a god, but it may well be that he was deifying, as it were, the vital heat which he found accompanying all life on this earth. This view is supported by the sculptured representations of the royal family that the king caused to be placed in his palace and other buildings. In these we see Akhnaton and Nefertiti and their daughters basking in the light of rays proceeding from the solar disc—rays which terminate in hands, each one of which is grasping the symbol of life.

This outward symbol was a complete break with tradition. Up to this time the gods had been represented in human shapes or animal shapes or shapes that were half-human and half-animal. The simple-minded Egyptians never doubted for a moment that these strange creatures actually existed on earth and in heaven; and although the educated classes may have had less crude conceptions of the divine, there were few among them who were prepared for the substitution of a symbol for the gods they and their ancestors had worshipped from time immemorial. Akhnaton, however, had no patience with their scruples, and he resolved to push ahead with his religious revolution regardless of time-honoured beliefs and practices. What his heart was set upon was a complete break with the past, associated as it was with what he had come to believe was false and derogatory of the Divine Unity.

If he had been an older man he might have been a wiser, and certainly he would have had more experience in that art of governing in which compromise has so large a part. As Pharaoh his powers were unlimited, however, at least in theory, and he soon demonstrated his intention to use them to the full. He hastened to establish Aton-worship as the religion of the State. He re-named Thebes as the "City of the Brightness of Aton", and in the middle of the precincts of the Temple of Amon, the god who was to be displaced, he caused to be erected a splendid sanctuary of the new worship. The priesthood of Amon was a large and influential body, and they were supported by their colleagues throughout the land, but they seemed powerless to protect their possessions and privileges. One and all of the priesthoods were dispossessed, the official worship of the old gods ceased, and orders were given that their names should be erased from the monuments wherever they might be found. The name of Amon in particular was reprobated; and great must have been the consternation of the people when they saw workmen busily cutting away the god's name from the statues of the king's ancestors that lined the walls of the great temples at Karnak. Even the statue of the king's father was not spared, but the hated name was ruthlessly hacked out or otherwise made illegible. The word "gods" was also banned, for now the king had decreed that there were no longer gods but there was One God and only One.

When sullen resentment was intensified into bitter hate, Akhnaton determined to leave Thebes and build a new capital city on a site uncontaminated by old associations. The place chosen was midway between the Delta and Thebes, on a plain bounded on three sides by cliffs and on the other by the Nile. To this spot, in the sixth year of his reign, on the thirteenth day of the eighth month, the young Pharaoh drove in state in a two-horsed chariot; and in the presence of a crowd of officials and other notables he dedicated a large area (eight miles long from north to south and from eight to seventeen miles wide from cliff to cliff) as the site of the future holy city of Aton. The area was enclosed by fourteen boundary-marks hewn in the face of the surrounding cliffs, three on the west side of the Nile and eleven on the eastern side.

These monuments still exist, and are among the most remarkable relics of the civilization of ancient Egypt. The largest is twenty-six feet high. Each bears an inscription, sometimes as long as eighty lines, and above is a representation of Akhnaton and Nefertiti with one or more of their daughters, grouped beneath the rays emanating from the sun's disc. The site had been indicated by Aton himself, declared the king; and the name he gave to it was Akhetaton, meaning "Horizon of Aton". The modern name is Tell el-Amarna, and all about are the remains of the temples and palaces, government buildings and private residences, that were erected under the supervision of the royal architect, a man named Bek, who, we are told, was "instructed by his Majesty himself".

Akhnaton watched the city grow—that city which one of his nobles described (the description is still extant) as "Akhetaton, great in loveliness. . . . At the sight of her beauty there is rejoicing. She is lovely and beautiful, and when one sees her it is like having a glimpse of heaven". On the day when the temple was finished Akhnaton proceeded thither in his chariot, together with Nefertiti and their four daughters and a gorgeous retinue, and was received with loud shouts of "Welcome". The altar was piled with rich oblations, and we are told that in the evening ritual of "Sending the Aton to rest", Nefertiti joined with her "sweet voice" and her "beautiful hands" shook the sistrum, the jangling wire rattle used by the ancient Egyptians in their temple music.

Surely it is not unreasonable to suppose that included in the ceremonial was the recitation of one of those two Hymns to Aton that Akhnaton himself composed, and which are among the most remarkable specimens of the religious literature of the ancient world. "When thou settest in the western horizon of heaven," runs one of these noble pieces of poetry, "the earth becomes dark with the darkness of the dead. Men fall asleep in their dwellings, their heads are covered up, their nostrils are stopped and no man sees his neighbour. Everything that is theirs could be stolen from under their heads without them knowing anything about it. When it is dark all the lions come out of their dens, all creeping serpents likewise. The whole earth is silent, because He that made it and everything in it has gone to his rest. . . . But when day breaks, and Thou rejoicest and goest up on the horizon and givest light to the day . . . then the people of the Two Lands of Egypt arise, they stand up on their feet and rejoice. They wash themselves and put on their clothes, and they stretch out their hands to Thee in thanksgiving for Thy dawning."

"How manifold are Thy works!" runs another verse; "the works of the One and Only God, beside whom there is no other. It is Thou that makest the seasons, the cool of winter and the heat of summer. It is Thou who createst the man-child in woman, who makest the seed in man, who giveth life to the son in the body of his mother. To the chick within the egg-shell Thou givest breath, and when

Thou hast perfected him he breaks the shell and comes forth chirping with all his might and runs about on his two feet. . . . It was Thou who set the Nile in the Underworld, and another Nile in the sky to water the earth with rain. The lands of Syria and Nubia, the land of Egypt—Thou madest them all; Thou hast appointed each man to his own place, and provided him with everything that he needs . . ."

There's no denying that here there is evidence of something radically new. A new note has been struck, a new spirit of universalism has come into the world, and out of the dry and dusty bones of old Egypt has sprung vigorous young life. For it is no mere state-god that Akhnaton is hymning, no national deity, but One who has made the world and everyone and everything in it. "Aton, the father and the mother of all that He hath made." Seven or eight hundred years later very much the same note was struck by some of the Hebrew prophets, but there are good grounds for hailing this brilliant young Pharaoh Akhnaton as the first monotheist.

But it was after all a false dawn. The world was not ready for that sublimest of all religious conceptions, the One-ness of the Godhead. Akhnaton died, his empire on the verge of dissolution, when still little more than a youth, and his revolution died with him —or very soon after. Since he had no son he was followed on the throne by one of his sons-in-law, and he again, after a brief reign, by the husband of another of Akhnaton's daughters. His name to begin with was Tutankh*aton*, but after a time he quitted Akhetaton for Thebes and, even more significant, changed his name to Tutankh*amen*. His reign was short, but long enough to effect a complete restoration of the old worship of Amen and his fellow gods. He died, and was laid in a tomb whose magnificent treasures have been revealed in our own time. While as for Akhnaton, he was by now the "heretic Pharaoh", he was the "Criminal of Akhetaton".

MOSES

(13th Century B.C.)

MUCH OF the Old Testament—though not, perhaps, as much as it was once fashionable to think—is myth and fable, with the slenderest framework of fact.

But one of its tales, and perhaps the one best known to most of us, has been investigated so exhaustively and for so long that it is now established historical fact. Some of its details may err, but compared with much of more recent "history" it is factual indeed. Moses, as we shall see, was far from popular most of the time: no one had cause or incentive to go back, as has been done in our present century with "great leaders" in China, Russia, Germany and Italy—and elsewhere—to gloss over his faults, build up his achievement.

The words of Exodus are so familiar; the scene itself, painted on canvas, wood and stone by artists of every degree of skill for thousands of years, is so familiar, too, that the story needs little re-telling or amplification: "Moses stretched out his hand over the sea, and the Lord caused the sea to go back by a strong east wind all that night, and made the sea dry land, and the waters were divided. And the children of Israel went into the midst of the sea upon the dry ground; and the waters were a wall unto them on their right hand and on their left."

This must be Moses's most dramatic achievement. For as we know, the Egyptians galloped and thundered their way in pursuit—and were drowned to a man. The "children of Israel", the Israelites, got safely to the far side in their hundreds of thousands: years later, they reached their Promised Land, and founded their community, the state of Israel, in much the spot that it stands today.

And although we accept the fact—which, indeed, the Bible points out—that the waters were persuaded back by a freak wind and perhaps a monster tide, we cannot deny, as we follow the extraordinary adventures of these Israelite people in their search for freedom, that their ruler must have been one of the greatest in history. If we believe the Bible, he was divinely appointed: if we do not, he was humanly-, perhaps self-chosen. But until he came, the Israelites, the Jews, were in a sorry and desperate situation.

And the flight on which Moses led them was not just a dash across the border. This was the mass movement of a nation spanning no less than forty years; and while Moses was in command—as its ruler, in fact—two new generations were born, and one came to maturity. In the same extraordinary period of history the Jewish people were shaped into a pattern which has profoundly altered the shape of history since.

Before we go on to consider this man—condemned to death before his birth and on numerous occasions after it—we must take a brief, panoramic, look at the whole of Jewish history before him.

From the Persian Gulf, back "in the mists of antiquity"—or so, until fairly recently, men thought—the patriarch Abraham decided to move with his family to a more fertile, more attractive, land. His God said to him, "Get thee out of thy country, and from thy kindred, and from thy father's house, unto a land that I will show thee: and I will make of thee a great nation, and I will bless thee and make thy name great; and thou shalt be a blessing; and I will bless them that bless thee, and curse him that curseth thee; and in thee shall all families of the earth be blessed."

Abraham acted immediately on this advice: and now we know the date to have been somewhere between 2,000 and 1,700 years before Christ. He led his descendants to the coastline of Palestine, the "Canaan" or "Low Land" at the end of the Mediterranean Sea. Here they found land which was wonderfully fertile, a gentle but regular and adequate rainfall; and here the descendants of Abraham flourished and grew in numbers.

Many years later, the name "Children of Israel" was adopted by these migrants. "Israel" meant "God Fighteth", and God Himself told them, through Abraham's descendant Jacob, that he was, in effect, on their side, would always remain so: they should accordingly style themselves "Israel", or "Children of Israel". And scarcely had they done so than disaster struck: there was drought and famine in Canaan.

More advice came from above: Jacob was told to lead them to Egypt. Here, with the waters of the Nile irrigating farmland, there was little danger of drought affecting crops. The Children of Israel already knew that the finest corn crops of the known world came from Egypt; they had sent messengers and traders to obtain it. Now, once again, they girded their loins and set off.

At first the Egyptians and their ruler, their Pharaoh, welcomed them. There was room and to spare in Egypt: hard-working immigrants were just what the country needed. Joseph, Jacob's son, he of the many-coloured coat, had already found his way to Egypt, first as slave, then as a powerful man. To him Pharaoh now said: "Thy father and thy brethren are come unto thee: the land of Egypt is before thee; in the best of the land make thy father and brethren to dwell."

But soon, very soon, things changed. The Israelites settled eagerly, happily, into this new land—only to find that within a few years the Egyptians had panicked about their rate of increase. "The children of Israel", says the Old Testament, "were fruitful, and increased abundantly, and multiplied and waxed exceeding mighty; and the land was filled with them." And Pharaoh, alarmed, cried to his courtiers, "Behold, the people of the children of Israel are more and mightier than we: Come on, let us deal wisely with them; lest they multiply, and it come to pass, that when there falleth out any war, they join also unto our enemies and fight against us."

So orders were given that the Israelites be forthwith deprived of their flocks and their holdings of land: they would become prisoners of the Egyptian government, servants of the Egyptian people, building new towns, new cities. And if they faltered in the work they would be whipped to death by overseers. As afterthought, when Pharaoh realized these measures would have little effect on his real problem, orders were given that midwives would kill every male child born to an Israelite mother.

Moses entered upon the scene in the wake of this vicious edict. An Israelite woman called Jochebed gave birth to him, and bravely clung to him till he had reached the age of three months. Then, convinced that he must soon be discovered and put to death, she smuggled him to the bank of the Nile, made a little boat for him out of bulrushes and clay, and gently pushed him out into the stream. With luck—very great luck—someone might find him, perhaps not realizing that the little boy was Jewish, and save his life.

Jochebed's prayer was answered. A little further downstream, the child's tiny boat was discovered by almost the only person able to do something to save him: no less a person than Pharaoh's daughter, washing at the river bank. She lifted the child out, saw instantly that he was of Jewish birth, but gathered him gently into her arms and took him away. Before she handed him over to a wet nurse, to feed him at her breast, Pharaoh's kind-hearted daughter christened the little boy "Moses".

Somehow, though his appearance grew unmistakably Jewish and there could be no possible doubt of his origins, the young Moses was allowed to grow into manhood unmolested, even respected. Thanks to the royal favour which had been shown him, he was not made to perform manual labour like the rest of his people.

But he sorrowed greatly, watching them as they struggled to make bricks under the lash of the overseer. Day after day he was tempted to leap upon some brutish foreman and thrash him—but commonsense told him this could do no good at all to the suffering Israelites. The sight of one of their own men, mightier than themselves (for Moses had never lived on a starvation diet); mightier by far than the Egyptians (for they were a small race and Moses was by any criteria a well-built, strong-faced, man): this sight might cheer them for a moment. It might also spell their doom.

And then suddenly Moses, from the corner of an eye, saw an Egyptian foreman beating a small and helpless Jew with his cudgel. Without thinking, he flung himself upon the Egyptian, struck him a terrible blow, and killed him outright.

There was no hope of escaping detection: men had seen him perform the deed, and those who had not seen were only too anxious to incriminate this Jew, so unfairly honoured when most of the rest of his generation had been slaughtered at birth. The chase was on; and Moses fled the country.

He travelled many miles, to the land of Midian, north of the Gulf of Akaba, where he settled down to do whatever work might come his way. He became a shepherd, and being a fine-looking man, with obvious intelligence and powers of leadership, was chosen as her husband by Zipporah, daughter of a Midian chief. And it was while he tended their sheep that he had his first vision.

He was looking at a bush when suddenly it burst into flame. The fire spread till its gold had enveloped the whole plant—and yet somehow the bush was not consumed, the flame burnt on. As he watched in wonder, Moses heard a voice, then saw the figure of an angel, standing among the flames.

The angel spoke, with a message from God: "I have seen the affliction of my people which are in Egypt, and have heard their cry by reason of their taskmasters. I am come down to deliver them out of that land unto a good land, unto a land flowing with milk and honey; unto the place of the Canaanites, and the Hittites, and the Amorites, and the Perizzites, and the Hivites, and the Jebusites——"

And the angel ended with the words, "I will send thee unto Pharaoh, that thou mayest bring forth my people, the Children of Israel, out of Egypt."

Moses obeyed. He took leave of his wife, his old father-in-law, and headed for Egypt.

When he got there, things were even more difficult and unpleasant than he had imagined. Pharaoh, who had deplored the increase in Israelite numbers, now perversely objected to their removal: they were good workers, and he needed them to build his empire. Nor would he even allow Moses to take the elders out into the wilderness to perform a sacrifice. To show his anger at the suggestion, he decreed that henceforth the Children of Israel would make their daily quota of bricks, but without straw. They would have to scratch around in the stubble fields for something to bind the clay. And if they dropped by as much as one brick from their daily quota, they would be whipped to the point of death.

Moses had established himself, instantly, as the leader of his people; and a day or two later become the most unpopular member of the community. And yet, though the Israelites cursed and reviled him among themselves for being a meddlesome fool who had made their lives a million times worse, he was still their acknowledged leader.

Moses demanded explanation from his Lord—and much of what followed, seen over the gulf of years, has the ingredients of bad, "sick", comedy. Some of it, like the episode of the cudgels, is extremely funny. God told his servant Moses that he must impress Pharaoh by sorcery: he showed him how to change a stout stick, such as the Egyptian overseers carried, into a writhing serpent—and back again.

It seems that this trick was already well known in Egypt, was in fact a variant of the ancient snake-charmer's act, in which serpents are made to stand rigid, like sticks. Moses turned his "stick" into a serpent—and a moment later Pharaoh's sorcerers did the same with theirs. To make matters worse, Moses earned their undying enmity, and Pharaoh's, by being unable to stop his serpent gobbling up all the others. More restrictions, more sanctions, were piled on the protesting backs of the Children of Israel. And they made their feelings quite clear to Moses. It must have been with a feeling close to despair that he approached his God again and asked for guidance.

The Lord instructed him to threaten Pharaoh with a series of plagues if he maintained his refusal to let the Israelites leave, and Moses did so. Each threat brought a firm refusal and in its wake a sickening plague—which yet failed to move the Egyptian ruler. The waters of Egypt—after due warning—"turned to blood" and killed all the fish. Seven days of this was followed by a plague of frogs which oozed out of the blood-coloured rivers and spread, in slimy millions, over the whole of the land. Still Pharaoh refused to allow his Israelite slaves to leave. The frogs were followed by lice and flies, painful boils, hail, locusts and a total eclipse of the sun.

Pharaoh must have been the most iron-willed ruler in history. Only now, in the blackness of total eclipse, did he agree that the Israelites might leave: but not, decidedly not, with their sheep and cattle; these they must leave behind.

Moses insisted; Pharaoh was adamant.

Now came the last, most dreadful, plague of all. The Lord told Moses that "I will pass through the land of Egypt this night, and will smite all the first-born in the land of Egypt, both man and beast; and against all the gods of Egypt, I will execute judgement". If the Children of Israel wished to avoid this fate, they would have to take a certain, highly complicated, action—and from this action has descended one of the most hallowed observances of the Jewish people, the Passover. They must sacrifice lambs, mark their doors with the blood, then eat the flesh with elaborate ceremony: "It is the Lord's Passover."

And they were spared. "It came to pass that at midnight the Lord smote all the first-born in the land of Egypt, from the first-born of Pharaoh that sat on his throne unto the first-born of the captive that was in the dungeon; and all the first-born of cattle. And Pharaoh rose up in the night, he and all his servants, and all the Egyptians; and there was a great cry in Egypt——"

Moses—aided by his God—had won the day. That day was in about the year 1280 B.C.; and on it the Israelites left Egypt, the hateful land of their captivity, and headed for the land which none of them—none of those now living—had ever seen, but which was the Canaan from which their ancestors had departed, many years before, to seek better conditions in Egypt. And now there were more than half a million of them.

No sooner had they left than Pharaoh—can there have been another more impossible man to deal with, in all history, than this Rameses II?—decided to pursue them, bring back his slaves. Moses had led them via the marshy land at the north of the Red Sea and it was as they were camped here, waiting to move further north and cross on dry land, that they saw the dust of Pharaoh's chariots, as the Egyptians strove to catch them up.

The rest is history. The whole of Pharaoh's army perished with the returning waves, leaving Moses and his 600,000-or-so Israelites safe—if gasping a little for breath—on the far, eastern, side.

But there were forty years of privation and danger ahead. It was during these forty years, in which Moses became a very old man and two generations of his people died, that the Jewish people came to maturity. Time after time they raged at him, as ill luck dogged them, food and water grew short, and the wilderness hostile. But all the while God was instructing Moses in a code of thought and behaviour—a code culminating in the Ten Commandments, which were revealed to him at the summit of Mount Sinai.

There is a delightful, human, moment near the start of the forty years. Moses's old father-in-law heard that the pilgrims were coming through his land on the Gulf of Akaba, and he excitedly told his daughter, Zipporah, to make ready to meet her husband. They went out and met Moses at the head of his civilian army, and he was overjoyed at seeing them.

And this marked a turning point in the fortunes of Israel, for it took the wise old father-in-law, Jethro, no time at all to see that there was something very wrong in his son-in-law's organization of all these people. Why—the young chap was trying to do the lot himself, not *delegating*. Look, Jethro said, "the thing is too heavy for thee; thou art not able to perform it thyself alone".

And Moses, after listening carefully, took his advice, choosing able men out of the Israelite army and making them "heads over the people, rulers of thousands, rulers of hundreds, rulers of fifties, and rulers of tens——"

The years went by: the Israelites found that the present occupiers of their Promised Land were unwilling to let them enter it, and battles raged over the years. Many of the pilgrims were destined never to see it, to die in the wilderness. Children were born in that wilderness, told by their elders of the great future lying in wait.

And Moses himself was taken to the top of a mountain by the Lord, and at last given a glimpse. "This", said the Lord, "is the land."

Moses stared in wonder. This, then, was the Promised Land. After all these years, these trials——

But, the Lord went on, "Thou shalt not go over thither."

Moses died, was buried in a valley in the land of Moab. "And Moses was an hundred and twenty years old when he died; his eye was not dim, nor his natural force abated. And the children of Israel wept for Moses in the plain of Moab thirty days."

A little later, having worked a way round to the east of the land, to attack it from that quarter and cross into it over the River Jordan, they had reached their Promised Land. They were a nation, to be ruled henceforth—and literally—by the word of God. And, in God's words, they were his Chosen People.

Moses's work was done.

DAVID

(*c.* 1012–*c.* 972 B.C.)

DAVID: FEW names in history are more famous, more evocative, more fascinating. Western religion, myth, art and social history are full of its echoes. Yet the actual details of our knowledge of David are restricted to four Books of the Old Testament: I and II Samuel, I Chronicles, and the first two chapters of I Kings. The narratives contained in these are, however, most suggestive.

David's date was roughly 1000 B.C. He stands out as the first successful King of Judah and Israel, for his predecessor and strange enemy-friend, Saul, was tragically unstable. Indeed, his curious psychological relationship with David provides one of the most fascinating aspects of the younger man's character and career. All through his life David, at once warrior and musician, had an intense personality to which others reacted intensely.

This human trait has attracted all ages, and helps to compensate for certain acts of undoubted savagery. If we are apt to over-blame him for these, it is because the very name of David has become raised to a sublime level: though no plaster-saint, was he not the ancestor of Jesus Christ, his seed the vessel of Hebraeo-Christian salvation, his birthplace the equally humble birthplace of Christ? Even his unquestioned gifts as poet, musician and dancer (the three arts being then largely united) have made posterity attribute to him many of the Psalms which recent research has shown not to be his.

Surely David attracts because of his elusiveness and versatility. Which aspect is more significant, the comely shepherd lad anointed to be the future king, or that king himself in military and social splendour?; the stripling whose stone destroyed the giant Goliath, or the sweet singer and teacher of musical ecstasy?; the lover of many women, or the bosom friend of Jonathan and despairing father of Absalom?; the massacring general, the murderer of Uriah, or the gentle sparer of his foe Saul?; the historic monarch or the gipsy-like refugee from camp to camp and valley to valley? For David was all these things, in a mixture which most of posterity have found lovable.

David was born at a crucial moment in Hebrew history. The

youngest son of Jesse, a shepherd by the village of Bethlehem, his origins were humble. Yet so relatively flexible were social distinctions that this Jesse was the descendant of the well-to-do Boaz and of ancestors more impressive still. Even as a child David must have had some premonition of future greatness. When the prophet Samuel, directed by the Lord, came to Jesse's home to anoint *one* of his sons as the future chosen of the Lord, the father produced all but one of his sons in turn, and only at the prophet's insistence did he call the boy David in from his work in the fields.

Yet David seems to have had no doubt; his character already had a strange decisiveness. With typical versatility he had already slain both a lion and a bear that were attacking his sheep, and attained skill in singing and playing the harp. In fact it is in these last capacities that we next hear of him. The neurotic figure of King Saul, tragic rather than evil, now begins its extraordinary love-hate relationship with the youthful musician. The king, tormented by fears and visions, calls for a harpist to soothe his spirit. David is recommended, presents himself, and wins all hearts by his charm: Saul is delighted with him, congratulates Jesse on his son, and makes him his armour-bearer, for he had heard that the handsome lad was warrior as well as artist.

Now came a really crucial point in his career. The enormous giant Goliath, champion of the Philistines, was challenging any Hebrew to single combat. David, sent by his father with provisions for his soldiering brothers, was rebuked by them for his curiosity; but the lad amazed Saul with the proposal to fight Goliath himself, "that all the earth may know there is a God in Israel". Had he not slain a lion and a bear? Saul must indeed have been impressed, for he granted David's request. Refusing any cumbersome armour, the boy chose five smooth stones out of the brook: the first of these, thrown from his simple sling, hit Goliath on the forehead so that the giant fell. David ran up and beheaded Goliath with the victim's own sword. In panic the Philistines fled.

The delighted king took David to live with him, but his love froze into jealousy as he listened to the women dancing and singing: "Saul hath slain his thousands, and David his ten thousands." We read how "Saul was very wroth" and that he "eyed David from that day and forward". Neurotic jealousy of David's popularity, of his youth, handsomeness and skill, and an intuition that somehow this ex-shepherd boy would overpower the life and fame of Saul—all these factors led the king twice to throw a javelin at David while he was singing and playing to him. Yet David's own conduct was exemplary;

he was always to show for Saul the greatest respect. In him he found a father figure, while Saul may have found some kind of unreality and frustration in the relationship. It may well be that David's home life meant little to him; we hear little or nothing of any attempt to include his family in his good fortune, or later in his regal riches. Hence, perhaps, his eager, deep love for Saul, who at least showed some "temperament", if an unfortunate one. Throughout his life the artist in David felt bored with the ordinary. Gratitude and vanity also played their part.

For the moment he played safe, and his forbearance troubled Saul, who sent him away as a "captain over a thousand". Perhaps the upstart lad would blunder, become unpopular, or even get himself killed. He even promised him his daughter Merab in marriage, then gave her to another man, and offered David his other daughter Michal, who was already in love with him. Saul declared: "I will give him her, that she may be a snare to him, and that the hand of the Philistines may be against him." But still David observed all courtesies and was admired by all.

His greatest solace—and the most intense relationship of his life, other than his strange relationship with Saul and his love for his own son Absalom—was his close friendship with Saul's son, Jonathan. This unique bond has become a byword—more famous even than that of Achilles and Patroclus, or of Orestes and Pylades. The loyal, dashing, honest Jonathan and the genius David, prince who was once shepherd, were united on equal terms. Jonathan loved David "as his own soul", and they made a covenant of utter loyalty to each other and each other's descendants. Hence only Jonathan could act as intermediary and warn David of the king's mania to kill him. This involved much intrigue on the part of the two friends, as of the ingenious Michal also, who assisted her husband in escaping from a window, while she filled his bed with an image and a goat's-hair pillow.

When David absented himself from the royal table, Jonathan pleaded he had gone to Bethlehem on family matters and so incensed Saul that the latter threatened both his son and David with death. The final meeting between the two friends took place in a garden at night; speed was imperative; they swore eternal fidelity so emotionally that they "wept one with another".

David now embarked on some extraordinary adventures. At Nob, the priest Ahimelech gave him and his famished followers the sacred showbread to eat, as none other was available—a point raised later by the irony of Christ Himself. Fleeing to Achish, king of Gath, an hereditary enemy, he feigned madness and was successful in escaping. Next, in the cave of Adullam, he gathered a following of his own family, and of "every one that was in distress"—some four hundred men in all. Meanwhile Saul destroyed all living creatures in Nob, including Ahimelech himself. Now began a three-handed conflict between David's men, Saul's men and the Philistines. First David slaughtered the latter; then Saul pursued him. David, catching the king and his bodyguard asleep, merely cut off the skirt of Saul's robe. Such generosity moved the king and there was a brief reconciliation.

But David's cruel side soon showed itself. Because the landowner Nabal would not provision David's troops, he marched with the slaughter of Nabal's people in his mind, and was stopped only by Nabal's resourceful wife Abigail, who appeared with the required food and drink. The Lord slew Nabal and David added Abigail to his list of wives. Once more Saul harassed him; but the situation repeated itself, and David took from his sleeping enemy merely the spear and a cruse of water. Saul offered complete reconciliation, but David not unnaturally went his own way—but why to become the ally of Israel's perpetual foes, the Philistines? Here his lust for fighting and his sense of self-preservation triumphed over his patriotism and his religious feeling. As Achish's ally, his base at Ziklag, he massacred the Geshurites, the Gezrites and the Amalekites—he who had earlier slain two hundred Philistines and brought their foreskins as a marriage-gift to Michal!

The final test took place between Saul and the Philistines at Gilboa. Despite the pleas of Achish, the Philistines refused David as a treacherous ally, so he returned to Ziklag only to find it entirely destroyed by the Amalekites. Narrowly escaping stoning by his distraught people, he led them in vengeance and wiped out almost all the Amalekites. Meanwhile Saul's army was routed; he and Jonathan died. David received the news in a typical way: the news-bearer was put to death, but this was followed by one of the most exquisite and famous laments in literature. He praised and bewailed his enemy Saul and his beloved Jonathan: "Thy love to me was wonderful, passing the love of women."

David was now acclaimed King of Judah at Hebron. After long war with the house of Saul, led by Abner, David won the day, and was hailed king of a united Judah and Israel. In the event the union did not long survive his son Solomon's death; yet its spiritual impetus was enduring. The next obvious step was the conquest of Jerusalem from the Jebusites; from David's day the Holy City may date its splendour. Thither he brought the sacred Ark, and was commanded by God to build a Temple to house it. The arrival of the Ark produced wild, ecstatic dancing, in which David played a whole-hearted and graceful part—disgraceful, according to his prim queen, Michal, whose reunion with him had been a condition of his peace treaty with Saul's forces.

He now embarked on a series of aggressive wars: Philistines, Syrians and others were conquered and looted, their gold going to adorn Jerusalem's Temple, while Moab and Edom were at last annexed to the Kingdom. An account of every campaign would be wearisome; it is more heartening to think of recorded acts of royal kindness—his befriending of Jonathan's son, the lame Mephibosheth; his pardoning the shifty Shimei; and his gratitude to his aged benefactor Barzillai.

Troubles enough, however, afflicted David's reign. Some were due to his sensual temperament: by now he had collected several wives (whence nineteen sons and some daughters) and more concubines. Even so, he could not resist the sight of Bathsheba, wife of a gallant soldier, Uriah the Hittite. He made her pregnant, and then ordered Joab, his commander, to see that Uriah was killed in battle. He then married Bathsheba, but their first child died soon after birth. The prophet Nathan had sternly intervened and rebuked the king for his sin, thus creating a pattern of vital importance for the future, pointing the way towards Christian social ethics. The emotional David showed "true repentance". To compensate for the baby's death, the Lord decreed that David and Bathsheba's next son should be the wisest of all kings: Solomon.

Other offspring caused trouble. His son Amnon forced incest on his half-sister Tamar; this led to mounting feuds, in which Amnon was killed by Absalom, Tamar's full brother and David's favourite son. Absalom, an extremely handsome man, fled and soon led a revolt against his father, which won considerable support. Few pictures are richer in pathos than that of David suffering from divided emotions and the risk of a civil war. His favourite son, entangled in a tree by his long hair, was killed by Joab. Though peace was restored, the king wept and said aloud: "O my son Absalom, my son, my son Absalom! would God I had died for thee, O Absalom, my son, my son!"

There followed an unsuccessful revolt headed by the Benjamite named Sheba, and a three years' famine, appeased only by the slaughter of seven descendants of Saul, in reprisal for Saul's massacre of the Gibeonites. A subsequent victory over the Philistines (his former allies and protectors) inspired David with a magnificent hymn:

The Lord is my rock, and my fortress, and my deliverer . . .
He bowed the heavens also, and came down; and darkness was under his feet.
And he rode upon a cherub, and did fly; and he was seen upon the wings of the wind.
And he made darkness pavilions round about him, dark waters, and thick clouds of the skies.

These verses are typical of David's ecstatic style; the Psalms offer countless examples of it, as well as of softer imagery:

As the hart panteth after the water brooks, so panteth my soul after thee, O God.

Other Psalms (for instance, No. 150) call on man to celebrate God with every joy of music: "Praise him with the sound of the trumpet: praise him with the psaltery and harp." The brief lament over Saul and Jonathan is remarkably free from any mention of religion.

This humanity and artistry in David help us to sympathize with him in many seemingly monstrous misfortunes. The last chapter of II Samuel portrays an amazing "Divine Vengeance", and issues a dreadful warning. David had ordered the people to be numbered, and for the sin of taking a census he was faced by the prophet Gad with three calamities from which to choose one: seven years of famine, three months of fleeing from his enemies in hot pursuit, or three days of pestilence. Choice fell on the latter, after which David sacrificed and the Lord stayed the plague.

After forty years of reigning, David was old and physically weak. In his illness his advisers sought out a young virgin: "let her lie in thy bosom, that my lord the king may get heat." But the experiment failed, despite the beauty of Abishag the Shunammite. David's son Adonijah proposed to follow Absalom's example and usurp the kingdom. To ensure Solomon's succession, Nathan persuaded Bathsheba to plead with the ailing king for her son. David solemnly promised this, and gave Solomon a blessing and advice: "I go the way of all the earth: be thou strong therefore, and show thyself a man." His plans for the Temple and the safety of his kingdom in Solomon's keeping, David died.

The vast range of David's career, his human magnetism and versatile temperament, even some—though not all—of his faults, have endeared him across the centuries. "Son of David" was even a high title applied to Christ. Artists have found continuous inspiration in David's life and mind, two outstanding examples being Rembrandt's sombre picture of "David Playing Before Saul", in the Mauritshuis at the Hague, and Michelangelo's colossal nude statue of the shepherd-boy. Above all, David is the poetical genius of the Psalms. In one of them he enjoins us to "Praise God in the beauty of holiness". No Biblical figure has shone like David in the holiness of beauty.

SOLOMON

(Reigned *c.* 970–*c.* 932 B.C.)

SELDOM IN the history of any nation do its two most famous monarchs succeed one another as father and son; the most memorable exception is the case of David and Solomon. These two soar in importance above all other kings of Israel, of Judah or of Israel-Judah. To find a satisfying reason for this concentration of genius (though the two types of genius were widely different) is hardly possible. Why David himself chose Solomon as his successor out of his nineteen sons we cannot discover. The Bible simply tells us that the prophet Nathan foretold the birth of the future king as a divine ordinance.

Solomon's mother was Bathsheba, who had sexual relations with David while still the wife of the soldier Uriah. David arranged for this inconvenient husband to be killed in battle, and then married the widow. Their first child, however, died within a week, as a divine punishment. By compensation, the next child, Solomon, was destined to become king and excel all mankind both in wisdom and wealth. But not—so it turned out—in the purity either of his religious or sexual habits.

The career of Solomon is described in I Kings, 1-11; I Chronicles, 23 and 28-9; II Chronicles, 1-9—twenty-three chapters in all. Moreover, the account in Chronicles largely repeats that in Kings. Hence our relatively sparse information about Solomon. Even so, he stands out in his main qualities and in the chief events of his reign—the consolidation of the kingdom, the policy of peaceful neighbourliness with surrounding states, the numerous wives and concubines, most of them from these states, with the consequent influx of foreign customs and even creeds; the unprecedented luxury of his court, wisdom of his counsel, and—above all—prosperity of his people; the admiring visit of the Queen of Sheba; and the two contrasted aspects of the king's attitude to religion—his building of the splendid Temple at Jerusalem, and his later lapse into idolatry, largely under the influence of his foreign wives.

At once certain contrasts are apparent between Solomon and David. When first we read of Solomon he is the Crown Prince to whom God will grant the fulfilment of the Temple-building (denied to David as "a man of war"), whereas David appears first as a shepherd-lad. The ups and downs of David's reign may be contrasted with the security and peacefulness of Solomon's. David remains the revered ancestor of Christ and a symbol—heroic, artistic, human—for future ages. Solomon's fame is only a little less: wisdom, universal prosperity, and a luxury that did not at first deny the Lord—such are his hallmarks. This reign marked a point of rest in the long story of the tortured but imperishable Jewish people.

This "ideal" epoch was preceded by brief violence. Solomon's half-brother Adonijah had planned to seize the throne during David's last illness, gathering together a force which included Joab and the priest Abiathar; but David, informed by Bathsheba, had Solomon anointed king, and then summoned him to receive his last blessing and commands. Solomon pardoned his half-brother, but after their father's death Adonijah's tactlessness grew, and he begged Solomon (through Bathsheba) for the hand of Abishag the Shunammite. Solomon's ironic retort: "Why not ask for him the kingdom also?" showed his distrust of Adonijah; and he had him killed. Joab and Abiathar were next executed, according to David's last command; while Shimei was pardoned so long as he lived in Jerusalem. He stupidly left it in pursuit of runaway domestics, so he too perished.

The way was thus cleared for an epoch of unparalleled serenity. Splendour began with a sacrifice in the "high place" of worship at Gibeon, on whose altar the king presented a thousand burnt offerings. Then "the Lord appeared to Solomon in a dream by night: and God said, Ask what I shall give thee." Solomon, humble before the task of ruling an immense people, begged for "an understanding heart to judge thy people, that I may discern between good and bad."

Pleased that he had not requested riches, honour or long life, but wisdom, God gave him "a wise and an understanding heart; so that there was none like thee before thee, neither after thee shall any arise like unto thee", while He also awarded him what he had not asked for, "both riches and honour". In addition—"if thou wilt walk in my ways . . . then I will lengthen thy days". This is a remarkable event in the recorded story of kingship, when rulers, even when orthodox in religion, preferred the glories of battlefield and throne. Solomon awoke from his dream and came to Jerusalem; and "stood before the ark of the Lord, and offered up burnt offerings, and offered peace offerings, and made a feast to all his servants".

His wisdom was soon put to a practical test, which has become proverbial. Now the husband of the daughter of the Egyptian Pharaoh, he was appealed to by two harlots, each of whom had just given birth to a child; one of the babies had died. One of the women accused the other of substituting her own dead child and taking the living one falsely as her own. Solomon had a sword brought and proposed cutting the child in half and giving each woman one of the halves. The real mother cried out against the murder of the child, preferring that the other woman should have the living baby. Solomon decided that her concern proved her maternity, so he awarded her the child. Thus we have an early triumph of psychology over mathematics. The nation was impressed by this and similar judgments, "excelling the wisdom of Egypt". We are told—"And there came of all people to hear the wisdom of Solomon, from all kings of the earth, which had heard of his wisdom."

Three thousand proverbs and a thousand and five songs were attributed to him, though we must be wary of such figures in an age without real historians. He is also said to have "spoken" about trees, beasts and fishes; and in all this attribution there is no doubt a core of truth. He must have made a deep and forcible intellectual impression. To wisdom was added joy: "Judah and Israel were many, as the sand which is by the sea in multitude, eating and drinking and making merry." With joy went security, for we learn that "Judah and Israel dwelt safely, every man under his vine and under his fig-tree". Peace attended Solomon also in his foreign relations, while his dominions reached from the Euphrates to the Egyptian frontier.

A special friend was Hiram, king of Tyre, a great admirer of David, who congratulated the new king and readily agreed to supply him with firs and cedars for the great Temple, receiving wheat and oil in exchange. An unbroken alliance was cemented. Then, in the 480th year after the Exodus, in the fourth year of his reign, Solomon began to build the Temple. Its magnificence, described in both Kings and Chronicles, has remained legendary and even symbolic; the actual edifice was razed to the ground in A.D. 70, apparently as an example of the "Roman peace".

Built of prefabricated stone, so that no sound was heard of hammer or iron tool, the building was overlaid within with pure gold. "Cherubim, palm-trees, and open flowers" formed a main feature of gold decoration. Tyre was famous for its brass and metal-work, so Hiram again willingly used his skill in fashioning pillars, large ornaments (including "a molten sea, ten cubits, from the one brim to the other"), and sacred utensils. After seven years the Temple was complete; and thither the Ark was brought, and a solemn consecration took place. So great was "the glory of God" in the form of a cloud, that "the priests could not stand to minister". Solomon's address to the people was deep and moving, likewise his humble prayers to the Lord: "When thou hearest, forgive."

Meanwhile he was building a splendid palace for himself. After twenty years, he gave Hiram twenty cities in Galilee, though these did not please the recipient. Immense levies, largely of the subject peoples, were raised to construct cities in the outlying parts of his domain, including "cities for his chariots, cities for his horsemen". In Ezion-geber, on the shore of the Red Sea, he prepared a fleet with Hiram's help; then once in three years came his ships from Tarshish with gold, ivory, apes and peacocks. Gold was everywhere; he drank only from gold vessels, while he "made silver to be in Jerusalem as stones".

Such luxury, and more, excited the feminine and regal curiosity of the Queen of Sheba in Arabia. Loaded with precious gifts, she arrived in Jerusalem to see whether Solomon's wisdom and splendour had not been exaggerated—but no, "the half was not told me". In mutual admiration the two rulers exchanged presents (the gorgeous spices of Sheba are mentioned), and legend has added a not improbable romance—considering Solomon's liking for women—which, however, is not referred to in the Bible.

Indeed Solomon "loved many strange women"; in flat defiance of the Lord's racial and religious intolerance he chose from the surrounding pagan peoples "700 wives, princesses, and 300 concubines; and his wives turned away his heart". Gradually he began to worship his wives' gods, building "high places" for them, and practising "abominations". His father's sensuality had in Solomon blossomed into full-blooded serene enjoyment. The fury of God descended on his triple unfaithfulness: religious, racial and sexual.

For David's sake Solomon would be enabled to keep his kingdom, but after his death vengeance was promised in the shape of civil and external war. Already in Solomon's lifetime, the Lord stirred up the Edomite Hadad, ruler of Syria, whose people had been slaughtered by David, and then Solomon's own protégé Jeroboam, who planned to usurp the throne: had not the prophet Ahijah promised him the ten tribes (other than Judah and Benjamin) from the Lord? Solomon pursued Jeroboam, who fled into Egypt. After a reign of forty years, Solomon died, and war followed, with the separation of Judah and Israel, and foreign conflicts.

To Solomon were attributed certain Biblical writings—

"Proverbs", "Song of Solomon", and "Ecclesiastes". Authenticity is doubtful, as it was a habit in Biblical times to attribute works to famous names (not all the so-called "Psalms of David" are by David). Yet some connexion may well have existed.

The book of "Proverbs" has been divided by scholars into four unequal sections: (1) chapters 1-9; (2) chapters 10-22, verse 16; here are 375 proverbs, many of Solomon's own authorship. This is the oldest part of the book, and it is significant and typical of the period that the name "Solomon" has in Hebrew the numerical value of 375; (3) chapter 22, verses 17-24; these "Words of the Wise" are not by Solomon; (4) chapters 25-29.

Though to some extent these sayings are repetitive, it is difficult, in the present space, to give a full impression of their variety. Worldly wisdom, spiritual maturity, crude pseudo-realism (e.g. "Spare the rod, and spoil the child", a recurrent motive), even poetic imagery—all are in evidence. The following examples may hint at their texture and admirable epigrammatic qualities:

"*Hatred stirreth up strife: but love covereth all sins.*"
"*There is a friend that sticketh closer than a brother.*"
"*The beginning of strife is as when one letteth out water: therefore leave off contention, before it be meddled with.*"
"*Pride goeth before destruction, and a haughty spirit before a fall.*"
"*Reprove not a scorner, lest he hate thee: rebuke a wise man, and he will love thee.*"
"*In the multitude of counsellors there is safety.*"
"*Better is a neighbour that is near than a brother far off.*"
"*He that oppresseth the poor reproacheth his Maker: but he that honoureth him hath mercy on the poor.*"
"*He that hath no rule over his own spirit is like a city that is broken down, and without walls.*"
"*Where no wood is, there the fire goeth out: so where there is no talebearer, the strife ceaseth.*"
"*Where there is no vision, the people perish: but he that keepeth the law, happy is he.*"

"Proverbs" is full of contradictions, and a greater contrast still is found between that book and the next work attributed to Solomon, "The Song of Solomon" (or "Song of Songs"). Nothing less than a passionate love poem, exquisite in imagery, confronts us here. Unique in the whole Bible, it is interpreted by Jewish commentators as the union of Israel and the Sabbath, or Israel and the Torah (the "Law"), and by Christians as the union between Christ and His Church. Yet the poetry, to many modern readers, speaks for itself.

Both feminine and masculine beauty speak and hymn each other:

"*Behold, thou art fair, my love . . . thou hast doves' eyes within thy locks: thy hair is as a flock of goats, that appear from mount Gilead. Thy teeth are like a flock of sheep that are even shorn. Thy two breasts are like two young roes that are twins, which feed among the lilies.*"

Thus is pictured the maiden who calls herself "the rose of Sharon, and the lily of the valleys". Alternately ecstatic and despairing, she seeks her beloved through the night-streets; she calls on the "daughters of Jerusalem" to tell him "that I am sick of love. . . . My beloved is white and ruddy, the chiefest among ten thousand. . . . His eyes are as the eyes of doves by the rivers of waters, washed with milk. . . . His cheeks are as a bed of spices, as sweet flowers: his lips like lilies, dropping sweet smelling myrrh. . . . His legs are as pillars of marble, set upon sockets of fine gold." And she in turn has "thighs like jewels" . . . "thy navel is like a round goblet: which wanteth not liquor. . . . Make haste, my beloved, and be thou like to a roe or to a young hart upon the mountains of spices." This is a truly lyrical portrait of the Sabbath, the Torah and the Church.

The third work attributed to Solomon, "Ecclesiastes", is nearer in spirit to "Proverbs", but more solemn and continuous. Who has not heard some of these phrases?

"*Vanity of vanity . . . all is vanity. What profit hath a man of all his labour which he taketh under the sun? One generation passeth away, and another generation cometh: but the earth abideth for ever. . . .*"

"*All the rivers run into the sea; yet the sea is not full.*"

"*To every thing there is a season, and a time to every purpose under the heaven: a time to be born, and a time to die . . . a time to weep, and a time to laugh; a time to mourn, and a time to dance. . . .*"

"*Cast thy bread upon the waters: for thou shalt find it after many days.*"

As to "The Wisdom of Solomon" in the Apocrypha, impressive though it is, "Wisdom" at times becoming personified, it is a Hellenistic work, centuries later than its alleged author; and it blends Hebraic and Hellenic qualities in several moods—lyrical, historical and mystical. Also attributed to the great monarch are the later "Psalms of Solomon", a mediocre work, and the resplendent "Odes of Solomon", an early and poetic Christian composition. None the less, the very association across the ages of Solomon's name with "wisdom" cannot have been without foundation.

The name of Solomon inspired countless legends in later, particularly medieval, Jewish literature, not to mention the reverence felt for him in Islam: the Koran, for instance, states how God gave him understanding of the speech of the winds and the birds. Despite certain exaggerations, the account of Solomon's splendour and wisdom must have some basis. We can admire in him also his balance and generosity, and his freedom from racial and religious intolerance, even though he did not reach the spiritual heights of another emperor of antiquity, the Buddhist Asoka.

The theme of Solomon has continuously inspired the arts. In music, for instance, there is Handel's genially regal oratorio, "Solomon", and a work for 'cello and orchestra, "Schelomo" (the Hebrew name for Solomon), by the Jewish composer, Ernest Bloch.

ASHURBANIPAL

(Reigned 668-626 B.C.)

AMONG THE nations of the ancient world the Assyrians have a shocking reputation. For hundreds of years from their homeland somewhere in the north of Mesopotamia they dominated the Middle East, and they extended their conquests to Armenia in the north and to Egypt in the south. Throughout, their record is one of almost constant war, of battles and sieges, of cities burnt and sacked and whole peoples carried away into captivity. Page after page in the historical books of the Old Testament bear witness to their ferocious ways of making war, while the Hebrew Prophets pointed to the Assyrian monarchs as the most terrible workers of woe on those whom the Lord found it necessary to punish. In a famous line Byron wrote of the Assyrian who "came down like a wolf on the fold", and that is what he seems to have been doing most of the time.

But the bitterest critic of the Assyrians must allow that from time to time they produced kings of outstanding character, who were not only great generals but displayed very considerable gifts of statesmanship and an active interest in the arts of peace. Of these the most worthy to be remembered after the passage of more than two thousand five hundred years is Ashurbanipal, who reigned as king in his capital city of Nineveh from 668 to 626 B.C. And this for several reasons.

In the first place, he was a great conqueror, although not so great and successful as some others of his line. Secondly, he commissioned sculptors to produce pictures in stone of his achievements on the field of battle and in the chase, and in the British Museum we may see whole series of these gigantic productions, that are among the most splendid survivals of the art of the ancient world. Still this is not all. Strange as it must appear, this vainglorious conqueror, this furious hunter of men and of big game, was also a patron of science, a lover of learning, and (so it would seem) more than a bit of a bookworm!

That is indeed a strange thing to be able to say of one of the Assyrian sovereigns, and we may suspect that Ashurbanipal would have thought it hardly worth mentioning compared with what there is to say about his career in arms. Of this there is abundance: Ashurbanipal saw to that; and pretty terrible most of it is, full of vulgar boastings, gloatings over defeated enemies, and the ferociously cruel treatment that he handed out to them. Take, for instance, the series of sculptures relating his warfare with Teumann, king of Elam, a country to the south-east of Assyria in what is now Persia, or Iran. Accompanying each picture is an explanatory text inscribed on the hard stone in the cuneiform or wedge-shaped characters of the Assyrian people.

In the month of Ab (the narrative begins), which was our July, during the festival of the "Great Queen", by whom is meant the goddess Ishtar, "I was staying in Arbela, the city that is the delight of her heart, to be present at her high worship. There they brought to me news of the invasion by the Elamite, who was coming against the wish of the gods". Teumann (the report goes on) had made a solemn vow that "he would not put out another drink-offering to the gods until he should have gone and fought with Ashurbanipal and overcome him".

Continuing with his story, Ashurbanipal says that "Concerning this threat which Teumann had spoken, I prayed to the great Ishtar. I approached to her presence, I bowed myself down at her feet, I besought her divinity to save me. Thus I spoke: 'O goddess of Arbela, I am Ashurbanipal, king of Asshur, the creature of thy hands. I have sought to do thee honour, and I have gone far to worship thee, O thou Queen of Queens, Goddess of War, Lady of Battles, Queen of the Gods. . . . Behold now, Teumann, king of Elam, who has sinned against the gods, while I, Ashurbanipal, have been doing everything in my power to please them and make their hearts rejoice—he has collected his soldiers, amassed his army, and has drawn his sword with a view to invading Assyria. So now, O thou Archer of the Gods, come like a bolt from heaven and crush him in the midst of the battle!' And Ishtar heard my prayer. 'Fear not,' she replied, and she caused my heart to rejoice. 'At the lifting up of thy hands, thine eyes shall be satisfied with the judgment, I will show thee favour. . . . Thy heart's desire shall be accomplished. Thy face shall not grow pale with fear. Thy feet shall not be arrested in their march; thou shalt not even scratch thy skin in the battle. Ishtar in her benevolence—she defends thee, and before her is blown a fire which will destroy thy enemies'."

Ishtar was as good as her word, Ashurbanipal hastens to inform posterity; and in the magnificent collection of sculptures in the British Museum we have a pictorial record of the ensuing battle.

On these great slabs, the engraver's chisel has preserved each episode in realistic detail, and above each is inscribed a few lines of commentary or explanation. "Urtarku, the son-in-law of Teumann, was wounded by an arrow, but not killed. He commanded an Assyrian soldier to kill him, saying, 'Come, cut off my head and carry it into the presence of the king thy lord, in order that he may take it for a good omen and show thee mercy' "—from which it would appear that he himself had small hopes of mercy if he should fall alive into Ashurbanipal's power. Then close by we see Teumann wounded by an arrow and kneeling on the ground, while his son Tamritu tries to keep off the attackers with his bow. In the next scene, father and son have fled and taken refuge in a wood. But not for long. "With the help of Ashur"—the great god of the Assyrians —"and of Ishtar, I, Ashurbanipal, seized them, and I cut off their heads in the presence of each other." This is followed by a scene of Teumann's head "being carried quickly to Assyria as glad tidings of my victory", and in yet another slab we have the end of the story. In the garden of his palace at Nineveh the great king is shown reclining at his ease, with his queen seated before him, quaffing a cup of wine; and there on the left, behind an array of musicians and with a girl playing a harp just below, hangs from one of the trees in the garden the gory trophy of Teumann's head.

Another set of sculptures illustrates a revolt against Ashurbanipal that was instigated and led by his brother, Shamash-shum-ukin, whom he had installed as viceroy of Babylon. The prince was defeated and was burnt to death when his palace was stormed by the king's troops and set on fire. "I am Ashurbanipal, king of hosts, king of Assyria," reads the inscription, "who achieved his heart's desire by the command of the great gods. The clothing, the treasure, the royal insignia that had belonged to Shamash-shum-ukin, the brother who was a traitor, his concubines, his officers, his soldiers, his chariot and carriage of state, his pair of horses, everything of his that was desirable, men and women, both great and small—all were brought before me. . . ."

Following upon this revolt, Ashurbanipal turned his arms against Elam, which had supported his brother, and made it an object-lesson of Assyrian "frightfulness". He vaunts of the way in which he "tore off the lips which had spoken defiance, cut off the hands of those who had held the bow to fight against Assyria", and winds up his narrative with the frightful statement, "The wells of drinking water I dried up. For a journey of a month and twenty-five days the districts of Elam I laid waste; destruction, servitude, and drought I poured upon them. I burnt the trees off the fields. Wild asses, serpents, beasts of the field I caused to lie down in them in safety. . . ."

A horrible picture, and yet Ashurbanipal the big-game hunter is a not much less repulsive figure than Ashurbanipal the conqueror. The king seems to have been a patron of almost every variety of the sport. He hunted wild asses and deer, stalked them across the plains and in the foothills, netted them and lassoed them, captured them in traps and had them driven before him in a battue. But the game which he particularly affected was the king of beasts, the royal lion, and he delighted to have himself represented riding in his chariot and discharging his bow at the pursuing beasts or, more dangerously, on horseback and wielding his spear. Sometimes he even followed the chase on foot, and in one of the scenes we see him pouring out a libation over four dead lions, of which the inscription reads: "I am Ashurbanipal, king of kings, king of Assyria. In my abounding might and princely strength I seized a lion of the desert by his tail, and at the command of the gods Enurta and Nergal, who are my helpers, I smashed in his skull with the axe I held in my hands." In another relief the hunt servants are shown laying out the "bag" at the end of the day's sport, and eleven dead lions are represented and seven more that are terribly wounded. Hounds were used in the sport, and powerful brutes they were, of a mastiff-like breed; Ashurbanipal must have thought appreciatively of them, for several statuettes of dogs have been found, modelled in terra-cotta, and each bearing on its back or collar its name—"Tear-the-foe", for instance.

In the representation of these hunting scenes the Assyrian artists reached the highest level of excellence, and there is nothing in ancient art to compare with them. Two in particular have been highly praised, though the animal-lover must have other feelings—that of a lion, mortally wounded by an arrow that still sticks in his body, coughing out his life-blood on the sand, and that other, no less pathetic, of a lioness, wounded unto death, with broken back and paralysed hindquarters, rising on her front paws to hurl a last roar of defiance at her pursuers.

What a relief it is to turn from these scenes of blood and savagery to what has invested Ashurbanipal's name with the most honourable distinction! We may watch the great king now, when perhaps he has returned from an exciting day in the hunting-field—he has bathed and put on a clean robe, he has dined and perhaps called on his favourite queen in her apartments, and now he has repaired to that quarter of his palace where he keeps his books. A lamp is burning on the table, the wine-jar is conveniently placed, a cushioned seat awaits him. And going to one of the shelves that line the apartment he takes down a book—not such a book as we know, but a clay tablet, closely covered with the marks of the cuneiform script. He opens it—no, that is not the right word: how can you open a brick?—takes it to the light, seats himself, and begins to read. . . .

For the discovery of Ashurbanipal's library at Nineveh we have to thank the celebrated English archaeologist Austen Layard. He came upon it by a most fortunate accident. In 1850 he was excavating in the great mound or dust-heap at Kuyunjik, not far from Mosul, in present-day Iraq. He had already retrieved some of the splendid sculptures which we may see in the Assyrian galleries in the British Museum, and had proved beyond a doubt that the site was that of the ancient metropolis of Nineveh. But he kept on digging, and one day he penetrated into two small rooms in what must have been the palace of the Assyrian kings. They seemed to be empty, but he noticed that the floor was covered to a depth of a foot or more with what some years earlier he would have thrust aside in disdain as "strange pottery", but since then had come to realize were inscribed tablets of baked clay. They were of different sizes; the largest were flat and measured about nine inches by six and a half inches, while the smaller were slightly convex and not more than an inch or so in length. They were all covered with cuneiform writing, although on some it was so tiny that Layard had to use a magnifying-glass to see it. He gave orders that the tablets were to be collected and sent off to the British Museum, and in the course of the next few years many more tablets were unearthed by Layard's assistant Hormuzd Rassam, who was in charge of the diggings at Kuyunjik after Layard had gone back to England. Altogether some twenty-five thousand tablets reached the British Museum, but it was not for some years that the work of translating them was put in hand. Then that remarkable, largely self-taught scholar George Smith revealed to an astonished world that what Layard had discovered by a lucky fluke was nothing less than the royal library of King Ashurbanipal!

There was no doubt about it, for most of the tablets that had been recovered from the rooms at Nineveh bore the inscription, "Property of Ashurbanipal, king of hosts, king of Assyria," and many had in addition a colophon or tailpiece in some such words as these: "Palace of Ashurbanipal, king of the universe, king of Assyria, who puts his trust in the gods Ashur and Belit, to whom Nabu (the god of Wisdom) has given an open ear (clear understanding), who has acquired a bright eye, with the exquisite skill of the tablet-writer, which none of the kings my forefathers have learned—the wisdom of Nabu so far as is written therein with the stroke of the stilus, this have I written on tablets that I may read it and learn it, and have laid it up in my palace. Whoever shall take them away or deface them, or write his name in the place of my name, may the gods curse him and root out his seed from the earth."

The "books" cover a great variety of subjects. A letter of Ashurbanipal's to the mayor of the city of Sippar has been preserved, ordering him to take with him certain named officials and seek out all the tablets that were in private houses or stored in the local temple, in particular those bearing astronomical data, magical formulas, incantations and prayers, battle stories, etc., and send them all to the king at Nineveh. Warrants were dispatched to government officials throughout the empire to the same purpose: they were to be most diligent and not overlook anything. Most of the material is of interest only to the chronicler, but among the books are the great masterpieces of Babylonian and Assyrian literature, including the Epic of Gilgamesh and the story of the Creation by Tiamat the female dragon and Marduk the hero-god.

Only fourteen years after Ashurbanipal's death, Nineveh was sacked and destroyed, and the great king's library was buried in the ruins. For two thousand years and more it lay forgotten, but then it was found and restored to the knowledge of men. And how astonished would the great king be if he were to learn that his fame as a book-collector has far eclipsed all that he won with his sword!

CYRUS THE GREAT

(d. 529 B.C.)

IN ALL the Bible's many hundred pages it would be hard to find a more dramatic episode than that of the mysterious writing on the wall that presaged the imminent fall of Babylon. We may read the story in one of the earlier chapters of the book of Daniel, told with an economy of words but in such vivid phraseology that we should have no difficulty in visualizing the scene.

In the banqueting-hall of his palace Belshazzar the king is making a great feast to a thousand of his lords, and a messenger has been sent to fetch "the golden vessels that were taken out of the temple of the house of God which was in Jerusalem", in order that the king and his princes, his wives and his concubines, may drink therein. And as they are drinking their wine, and praising the gods of gold and of silver, of brass and of iron and the rest—suddenly there come forth fingers of a man's hand, writing on the wall over against the candlestick. Then the king's countenance is changed, his thoughts trouble him, and his knees smite one against the other, and he cries aloud to bring in someone who may translate what is being written. And Daniel is fetched, and the words he speaks are words of doom. . . .

"In that night was Belshazzar the king of the Chaldeans slain. And Darius the Median took the kingdom." Here the chronicler is at fault: Belshazzar was not the king, and he does not appear to have been slain, and it was not Darius who took his kingdom but Cyrus the Persian, for whom the taking of Babylon was the crowning achievement of his career of stupendous conquests.

Who Cyrus was, what was his descent and origin and place in the world before the floodlights of History caught up with him—these are questions that are likely to remain without satisfactory answer. At least four different accounts were given of his early years by writers of antiquity, and it has not proved possible to reconcile them. The most picturesquely detailed is that given by the Greek historian Herodotus, who visited Persia about seventy years after Cyrus's time. According to him, Cyrus was the son of a Persian nobleman named Cambyses and Princess Mandane, only child of King Astyages of Media, the country that lay between Persia (which was then a small territory bordering the Persian Gulf) and the Caspian Sea. Astyages had heard a rumour that his daughter's child would supplant him on the throne, and so he gave orders that the child should be killed. The savage order was not carried out, however; the boy was saved by a trick, and when he became a man he headed a revolt against his grandfather and dispossessed him and became king in his stead.

A pretty story, but probably too pretty to be true. The more sober historians of a later day have discounted practically the whole of it, with the exception that they are willing to allow that Cyrus may have been connected in some way with King Astyages. According to them, Cyrus belonged to the royal house of Anshan, a small kingdom bordering on Mesopotamia with Susa as its capital, and he succeeded his father as king of Anshan about 558 B.C. Then from a clay tablet preserved in the British Museum we learn that war broke out between Anshan and Media, and Astyages king of Media "collected his troops, and marched against Cyrus king of Anshan. His troops revolted against him, and he was seized and delivered up to Cyrus. Cyrus marched to Ecbatana, the royal city of Media. The silver, gold, goods, and substance of Ecbatana he spoiled, and to the land of Anshan he took away the goods and substance that were gotten."

In some such fashion as this, Cyrus became king of the Medes as well as of the Persians; Susa was the capital of the joint realm but Ecbatana shared its glory, and it is clear that the Medes were not at all loth to exchange Astyages for a sovereign who had already given abundant proof that he was a born leader of men. As for Astyages, Cyrus took him as a prisoner to Anshan, but (so Herodotus asserts) spared his life.

After a year or two as king of "Persia and Media and the other lands" Cyrus was moved to undertake further conquests. He invaded northern Mesopotamia, and then in 547 B.C. found his further advance checked by Lydia, the greatest power in the Western Asia of that day, and also the richest, as may be gathered from the fact that the name of its king has become proverbial for wealth.

On the face of it, King Croesus had all he could wish for. Immense treasures, a large and well-trained army, a realm which embraced the whole of Asia Minor, including the string of Greek cities along its Ionian shores. Yet he was nervous. Only the river Halys separated his dominion from that of Cyrus, and from all that he heard Cyrus was intensely ambitious and determined on a career of aggrandizement. For many years there had been good relations between Lydia and Media, and these had been cemented by family alliances, but Croesus was not at all sure that these good relations could be maintained with the new ruler of Media.

In the circumstances he thought it advisable to secure alliances with Egypt, Babylonia, and the Spartan Greeks, and he also dispatched emissaries to consult the oracles at Delphi and elsewhere, as to whether if he were to go to war with Cyrus he would be victorious? The answers returned by the oracles were ambiguous, but Croesus did not think them so. "If Croesus were to make war on the Persians," they ran, "he would destroy a mighty empire." Croesus at once jumped to the conclusion that the empire to be destroyed was that of Cyrus. But he was not quite convinced, and to make doubly sure he sent to Delphi again, putting to the oracle the question, "Shall I long enjoy my kingdom?" This time the answer was a strange one indeed. "When a mule shall become king of the Medes," it ran, "then do not waste a moment, nor blush to seem a coward, but *flee*." When his servants returned to their master with that answer it was in considerable trepidation, but Croesus was not in the least put out; on the contrary, he thought its gross improbability was a most favourable sign.

In the spring of 548 B.C. he set his armies in motion and crossed the Halys into Media, where he won an easy success against the town of Pteria, which he took and destroyed, enslaving its population. Cyrus came hurrying up but could not arrive in time to save the town, and the resulting engagement was indecisive. Then as it was getting late in the year Croesus decided to return home and go into winter quarters, thinking that Cyrus would of course do the same. But Cyrus declined to be so accommodating. He followed up Croesus's retiring forces and caught up with them outside Sardis, the Lydian capital, and inflicted on them a severe defeat. If Herodotus is to be believed, his victory was largely owing to his clever stratagem of mounting a number of his men on camels from the baggage-train and employing them as cavalry. Now, Herodotus explains, "a horse is afraid of a camel, and cannot endure either to see its form or to scent its smell". When the battle was joined, the Lydian horses no sooner sensed the camels coming towards them than they pranced and wheeled round, and in a few moments all Croesus's hopes of victory were dissipated. The Lydians hurried back to Sardis, hoping to find a safe refuge behind its walls, but Cyrus closely followed and took the place by storm.

Still following Herodotus's account, Croesus was captured and condemned to be burnt alive, but when the flames were already taking hold of the funeral pyre Cyrus was smitten with pity and ordered that he should be rescued, and he henceforth treated him with a kindly consideration. Of course the fallen monarch inquired into the prophecies that had pointed the way to his ruin. He understood clearly enough that he had misinterpreted the one about an empire that should be destroyed, but was still puzzled to understand how a mule could ever become king of Persia. The oracle was consulted again, and now it was explained that Cyrus was the mule intended, since he had been born of parents of different nations—his father a Persian and his mother a Mede. . . .

With the overthrow of the kingdom of Lydia, the dominion of Cyrus was extended over nearly the whole of Asia Minor, and soon the Greek colonies on the Ionian coasts and the adjacent islands were incorporated. In a matter of three or four years this prince of an insignificant little state had defeated two great empires and made himself master of an immense territory stretching from the Persian Gulf to the Dardanelles and Black Sea.

Still he was not satisfied. He recalled that while Babylon, no more than Egypt or Sparta, had actually assisted Croesus in his war against him, she had entered into an alliance with that end in view. They all three deserved to be taught a lesson, but Babylon was the nearest and therefore the first to be made to feel his resentment. For some years he bided his time, and no doubt completed his preparations. By 540 B.C. he was ready, and with characteristic vigour crossed the frontier and at the head of a large army marched down the Tigris and then cross country to Babylon.

Babylonia was still a great power, although not so great as she had been some twenty years earlier. In 556 B.C. Nabonidus had come to the throne of Babylonia, and he was not at all the sort of man to weather such a storm as now threatened his country. He has been described as an "amiable archaeologist", a man who delighted in digging up the foundations of ancient temples to read the inscriptions he might find there, and then adding to them a few lines of his own. He was also a keen student of comparative religion, and had formed the idea of centralizing the Babylonian religion, collecting the images of all the gods and goddesses and displaying them all together in one place in the capital. The priests were not at all taken with this idea, and (if they were to be believed) the gods and goddesses did not like it either. Thus when Cyrus drew near to the city there was something in the nature of a fifth-column at work in the place, in which, there is reason to believe, the Jews, whose fathers had been deported from Jerusalem to Babylon by Nebuchadnezzar, took a leading part.

Herodotus has some typically colourful paragraphs about what happened next. According to him the city held out quite a time, and Cyrus was greatly wrath at the delay. At length he thought out a plan. He diverted the stream of the Euphrates from where it entered the city, and then had men waiting in readiness to enter as soon as the sewer-gates were disclosed. When this happened, they rushed in, and took the Babylonians completely by surprise. Long after the outer works had been stormed, the people in the central part were still engaged in dancing and revelling, since the night was the occasion of one of their great annual feasts. It will be seen that this account is not inconsistent with the Bible narrative, although (as mentioned earlier) it was not Darius who was the attacker but Cyrus, and the king's name was Nabonidus and not Belshazzar—although Belshazzar may have been the crown prince.

Decidedly different is the account that is found on an inscribed cylinder of baked clay that is in the British Museum. The most important part of this reads: "Marduk (the chief god of Babylon) sought out a righteous prince, a man after his own heart, whom he might take in hand. . . . He beheld his good deeds with joy. He commanded him to go to Babylon, and he caused him to set out on the road to that city, and like a friend and ally he marched by his side; and his troops, with their weapons girt about them, marched with him, in countless numbers like the waters of a flood. Without battle and without fighting Marduk enabled him to enter into his city of Babylon; thus he spared Babylon tribulation, and Nabonidus, the king who feared him not, he delivered into his hand. All the people of Babylon, princes and governors, bowed down, they kissed his feet, they rejoiced in his triumph, and their countenances were bright with joy."

After the occupation of the city by his troops, Cyrus pleased his friends and went a long way towards conciliating those still opposed to him, by adopting a policy of the most complete religious toleration. He ordered that the images of the gods and goddesses should be restored to their old homes, and allowed the Jews (as we are told in the first chapter of the book of Ezra) to rebuild their Temple in Jerusalem that Nebuchadnezzar had destroyed, and he returned to them the valuable furniture and fittings that had been brought back to Babylon as spoils of war.

So ended the empire of Babylon, which had endured for fifteen hundred years. The city became one of the capitals of Cyrus's now vast empire, and there he now received tribute from "all the kings dwelling in palaces of all the quarters of the earth, from the Upper to the Lower Sea (i.e. from the Mediterranean to the Persian Gulf), and all the kings of the West Land (Arabia) who dwell in tents".

As king of Babylon Cyrus was overlord of Phoenicia and Syria down to the borders of Egypt, and Egypt was next on the list of his intended conquests. But for the present he had enough to do in organizing his huge empire. Tolerant and comparatively humane, clear-sighted and vigorous, he showed to as marked advantage as an administrator as he had done in military campaigning, and on his foundations of good government his successors were able to build for generations to come. And yet he died fighting, in a war on his eastern frontier against (according to the most generally accepted report) a tribe of savages known as the Massagetae. This was in 529 B.C., when he had reigned nearly thirty years.

Almost exactly two hundred years later another and even more famous world-conqueror visited Cyrus's tomb at Pasargadae, in the region that had been the homeland of his family. After he had read the epitaph (so Plutarch tells us), Alexander the Great ordered it to be re-cut in Greek characters. It was as follows: "O man! Whosoever thou art and whensoever thou comest (for come I know thou wilt), I am Cyrus, the Founder of the Persian Empire. Envy me not the little earth that covers my remains." The young conqueror read it, and then turned away, deeply moved.

DARIUS I

(Reigned 521–486 B.C.)

ON A rock face at Behistun, high above the caravan route that in ancient times led from Ecbatana (the modern Hamadan), where the Persian kings had their Summer Palace, down south-westwards into Babylonia, is carved a great picture in stone. For more than two thousand years it has aroused the admiration and the curiosty of passing travellers. It was so old that its origins had been lost in the mists of time. Diodorus, a contemporary of Julius Caesar, told a wonderful tale that Semiramis, Queen of Babylon, had ordered it to be carved, and that in order to reach it the sculptors had climbed the face of the mountain on a heap of pack saddles taken from her baggage train.

Others who visited Persia in later times advanced even more fanciful explanations. One towards the end of the eighteenth century was quite positive that it shows Jesus Christ and the Twelve Disciples, and in 1827 the Englishman Ker Porter was of the opinion that the figures represent the Assyrian king Shalmaneser and the Tribes of Israel whom he carried into captivity. The Persian women from the neighbouring sordid little village had their own theory. According to them it was the tombstone of a saintly man of ever so long ago, and they used to hang little strips of rag on the bushes below as some kind of offering to his spirit.

All these imaginative excursions were dispelled, however, when in 1835 a young English army officer named Henry Rawlinson succeeded in climbing up to the site and deciphering the inscriptions which surround the picture. It took him years of study, but eventually he was able to show that the sculptures represent the "Great King" Darius I of Persia, triumphing over a rival and his confederates. We know that this actually happened, since Darius himself tells us so.

To understand the happening, we must go back a few years in Persian history. When Cyrus the Great (his story is given in the previous chapter), the founder of the Persian Empire, was killed fighting the barbarian tribes in a border skirmish in 529 B.C., he was succeeded on the throne by his son Cambyses. Not content with the great realm that he had inherited from his father, the young king embarked on the conquest of Egypt. He won a surprisingly easy victory, but when he sent his armies to invade Ethiopia they suffered severe reverses, and Cambyses (so the story runs, as told by the ancient historian Herodotus—but Herodotus was a Greek, and not at all favourably disposed towards the Persians) went mad with the shock.

Then came news of a revolt back home in Persia, headed by a man who asserted that he was the king's brother Smerdis. Cambyses knew full well that this was rubbish, since he had himself given orders for his brother to be killed, and the orders had been carried out, but with the minimum of publicity. Cambyses forthwith started for the north with a portion of his army and some leading nobles, among whom was one Darius, whose father was Hystaspes, sub-king of a distant province, and who seems to have been a relative, perhaps a cousin, but certainly belonged to the royal family of the Achaemenids. On the way, somewhere in Syria, Cambyses suddenly died. The army went on, taking his body with them, and when they had returned at length to Persia they found that the pretender was in full possession of the power and glory, the treasures and the harem, of the previous monarch.

For the time being, Darius and the rest kept their own counsel and acquiesced in the new regime. Then suspicions began to be aroused among the other courtiers. The king never quitted his palace, not even to go hunting. He never gave audience to a Persian dignitary. Could it be that he was afraid of being recognized as being some other person than the real Prince Smerdis? Before long the doubts became certainty, and Darius became the centre of a small band of conspirators who were resolved to unmask the pretender and do him to death. Then came the day when Darius and six other young nobles, Persians all, made their way to where the "king" was staying, managed to obtain entrance to the palace, cut down the guards who showed resistance, and at last reached the royal sanctum and slew the pretender.

Herodotus has some particularly lively pages describing these happenings, and some of his stories are almost too good to be true. What shall we say, then, of his account of what happened next? The throne was vacant, Cambyses had left no children, and there was no heir apparent. Darius and his six associates argued the matter over and over, and at length it was agreed that one of them should offer himself as the new monarch. But which? Why, he whose horse should be the first to neigh next morning after sunrise. . . .

Now Darius had a very clever groom, and he told the man what had been decided and asked him if he could think of any way by which *his* horse should have the deciding voice. . . . The man told him not to worry: he would fix it. And this is how he did it—according to Herodotus . . . Darius's steed had a favourite mare, and after dark the groom took this mare and tied her up to a post somewhere in the suburbs. Then he brought Darius's horse to the place and walked him round and round before at last allowing them to meet. Then back to the stable. . . . Next morning the friends rode out together as they had agreed, and the wily groom saw to it that they should go very near to where the mare had been tethered the night before. Of course Darius's mount remembered—and neighed. Just at that moment, as though to clinch the election, there was a great flash of lightning, followed by a loud clap of thunder. This was taken as an indication of heavenly approval, and Darius's companions jumped down from their horses and bowed themselves in homage before the man whom they hailed as their new sovereign.

"Thus was Darius son of Hystaspes appointed king." Well, perhaps . . . But there is no doubt of the fact that he *was* appointed king, and the main outlines of the story receive striking confirmation from no less a person than Darius himself, as told in the sculptures and inscriptions on the Rock of Behistun mentioned above. We now know that the picture represents "the Great King, the King of Kings, the King of Persia, the King of the Provinces, whose name is Darius", receiving the submission of ten rebel kings or princes. Nine of the rebels are bound together by a rope passed round their necks, and their hands are tied behind their backs. The tenth is even more abjectly submissive: he is stretched on the ground before Darius, whose left foot is placed on his neck. Then in the panels surrounding the sculpture we are given the story of the revolt, told in three forms of the cuneiform, or wedge-shaped, scripts of Old Persian, Susian or Elamite, and Babylonian. Beyond the fact that the names are given differently—thus the true Smerdis is called Bardiya and the "false" Smerdis, Gaumata—the account is very much the same as what Herodotus tells us.

"When Cambyses slew Bardiya, it was not known to the people that Bardiya was slain. Afterwards Cambyses went to Egypt, and when Cambyses had departed, the people became hostile. Afterwards there was a certain man, Gaumata by name . . . he lied to the people, saying, 'I am Bardiya, the son of Cyrus and brother of Cambyses.' Then all the people rose in revolt, and from Cambyses they went over to him, both Persia and Media, and the other provinces. He seized on the kingdom. . . . There was no man, Persian or Median or of our own family, who could deprive Gaumata of the kingdom. The people feared him for his tyranny, but no one dared to say anything against Gaumata, until I came." Then, the inscription goes on, "I, with a few men, slew Gaumata. . . . I smote Gaumata. I took his kingdom from him. By the grace of Ahuramazda (the Good God of the Persian religion) I became king. Ahuramazda gave me the kingdom. The kingdom which had been taken away from my family, this I restored to its proper place."

Finally, in conclusion the king added a solemn warning to those who might come after. "Saith Darius the King: Thou who shalt read this inscription in days to come, thou who seest I have caused it to be engraved together with these figures of men—take heed that ye destroy it not nor deface it, see that thou keepest it whole. If otherwise, then may Ahuramazda slay thee, and bring thy race to naught."

For some years after his accession Darius had his hands full with revolts and dissensions of one kind or another, but as soon as he was able he devoted all his energies to the consolidation and good government of the vast empire that had fallen to his sway. His realm was indeed vast; in fact, nothing to equal it had been seen in history before, and there have been few empires to surpass it since. With its heartland in Persia, on the eastern side of the Persian Gulf, it reached to Macedonia in Europe on the one hand, and to the Indus valley in north-western India on the other. Included in the many millions of its population were peoples of very different standards of culture and civilization, ranging from Greeks in the Ionian colonies in Asia Minor to the barbarian Scythians who roamed the great plains in what is now southern Russia. Scores of different languages were spoken within its bounds, all the gods of all the religions had their worshippers in its great cities and innumerable towns and villages and the encampments of the nomad tribes. And this at a time when communications could be effected only by men on foot or on horseback.

Clearly, some form of decentralized government was imperative, and this is what Darius established. The task before him was tremendous; neither Cyrus nor Cambyses had had the time, or perhaps the capacity, to organize a system of government which would work, but Darius succeeded where they had fallen short. With the exception of Persia proper, which was considered to be deserving of special treatment as the home of the ruling race, the empire was divided into a number of provinces, or satrapies, to use the Persian term. Over the most important of these the governor or satrap was drawn from one of the great families connected with the Achaemenid dynasty, but in the case of the rest the satraps were drawn from a very wide field, the men chosen being from among the comparatively poor as well as the wealthy and high born, from the subject races as well as from the Persian stock. The satraps held office at the will of the king, and their tenure might be for life.

But however high-sounding their title, the satraps were not masters in their own house. They were almost entirely concerned with the civil administration, chiefly financial and judicial; the provincial military forces were under a commander, whose responsibility was direct to the central government. There was also in each satrapy a secretary of state, who again had direct relations with the king, and kept him informed of what was going on.

For the most part, the languages, laws, customs, and religious usages of the subject peoples were carefully respected; indeed, the Persian government showed a liberality that was in marked contrast with the attitudes adopted by other empires, contemporary and later. Darius himself, like the Persian ruling class as a whole, was a Zoroastrian in religion, holding the doctrines preached by the Prophet Zoroaster (Zarathustra) centuries before, and which are still held by the small body of religionists known as Parsees. But other religions were completely tolerated, just as the utmost liberty was granted to the Greek thinkers in the cities of Ionia to carry their speculations to the limit.

So far as the common people were concerned, it is certain that their condition was very much better under the Persians than it had been in centuries previously, or has been for most of the centuries that have elapsed since. There is no reason to believe that the rule of the satraps was oppressive. War was abolished over a very large area. The highways on land and sea were cleared of pirates and marauders, and men might move freely and safely from one end of the empire to the other. Greek travellers wandered here and there in search of knowledge or adventure or to spread the culture that was theirs. Trade was facilitated by the introduction of a coinage system that was noteworthy for its purity, and the gold "daric", named after King Darius, became the "sovereign" of the near and middle east. Of course people grumbled at the burden of taxation, but this was certain and regular, and once it had been paid they were left very much to themselves. Probably the obligation of military service was the most unpopular burden, but this affected only a small proportion of the young men, since the imperial standing army was remarkably small.

When his administration had been put on a stable footing Darius turned his attention to more magnificent if less useful projects. At Susa, the winter capital, he caused to be erected a splendid palace, but this was far eclipsed by the summer residence of the Persian kings that was built at Persepolis, "the city of the Persians", as the Greeks named it. Even in ruin this is still wondrously beautiful—ruin which was begun by Alexander the Great's mad act of arson in 330 B.C. What, then, must it have been like when the sculptures were fresh from the chisel, the coloured enamels glowed, the rich stuffs and embroidered hangings formed a fit and proper setting for the display of brave men and lovely women who were assembled at Darius's court!

For many years now the great complex has been in course of excavation, and extraordinary marvels have been restored to the light of day. Among the buildings that have been explored is that which housed the ladies of the court, but outstanding is the series of sculptured friezes—if placed end to end they would constitute a panel five or six feet high and nearly a thousand feet long—that adorn the staircase of the royal palace. Among the figures represented are men bringing tribute to the Great King, and what a magnificently varied crowd they make! Here stalk tall Sardians from Lydia, leading humped cattle and bearing shields and lances; and there are Susians from Bhuzistan, one of whom has a lioness in tow while others are carrying her cubs. These solemn-looking fellows in peaked caps are Scythians from Turkestan, these with the curled beards are Syrians, and those men in tight tunics and full trousers who are leading a camel come from what is now Afghanistan. Thus we have a most vivid picture of some of the peoples who were amongst the Great King's subjects. But even better is this splendid sculpture of Darius himself, seated on his throne, holding in one hand a sceptre and in the other a lotus, symbols of royal dominion.

Something more remains to be added, if we are to form a reasonably complete picture of the magniloquently styled monarch. Unchallengeably superior as he was as an administrator, Darius was a far from successful man of war. When he had been not long on the throne he led an expedition into Scythia, probably with the idea of securing his northern frontiers. He crossed the Dardanelles on a bridge of boats at the head of a great host of (so it is said) some 700,000 men, and reached the Volga. But then he had to turn back, and he got back home with the loss of 80,000 of his troops. Then in 498 B.C. his Greek subjects in Ionia revolted, with the aid of Athens and other Greek cities on the European mainland. The Ionians were crushed, but the Persian army which invaded Greece was defeated by the Athenians and their allies in 490 B.C. at Marathon, one of the really decisive battles of the world. Darius was preparing another and greater expeditionary force to teach the Greeks a lesson when he died, in 486 B.C. He was buried in a tomb cut in the rocks overlooking Persepolis, and still the inscription may be read: "I am Darius the Great King, King of Kings, King of countries inhabited by all kinds of people, King of this great earth, far and wide . . ."

LEONIDAS

(d. 480 B.C.)

ONE OF the most romantic figures in history is the Spartan King Leonidas. We know little of his qualities as a ruler, for these have been overshadowed by his abilities as a general, but it is reasonable to assume that a personality and example which could make men fight to the end for a lost cause would make them serve faithfully and well as subjects.

It is in fact the quality of leadership for which we remember Leonidas of Sparta. We cannot even be sure that he was a good general, for generals need more than leadership to win their battles.

And Leonidas lost his.

But it is as leader and hero that he has earned a place in every history of his period ever likely to be written.

That period is the fifth century before Christ, and the setting is ancient Greece. One of the city-states in that confederation was Sparta, set in a broad plain on the right bank of the River Eurotas, twenty miles from the sea. It was a small and warlike state, dominated by a warrior caste of less than thirty thousand men calling themselves "Spartiates" and controlling both "Helots" who had been the original Achaean inhabitants and were now slaves, and a provincial population of "Perioechi" who dealt with mundane matters of trade and industry.

Leonidas succeeded to the throne of Sparta after the deaths of his two elder brothers, in about 488 B.C., and married the sister, Gorgo, of his half-brother Cleomenes. It was a difficult time for the whole Greek peninsula, for the Persian Emperor Xerxes was bent on a war of subjection which would make them all, much as the Spartiates had made of their predecessors, slaves and bringers of tribute. There had been skirmishes and worse, but six years after Leonidas had mounted the throne of Sparta the Persian army was on the move.

Ten years before, the Greeks had thrashed these same Persians under their emperor Darius at the battle of Marathon. In the meantime, Darius, harried by rebellious elements all over his empire, had died, leaving the mounting of a huge attack which would avenge Marathon to his young son Xerxes. Xerxes lost no time in doing so. His vast empire was divided into twenty "satrapies", and each of these was now called on to provide a contingent. As Herodotus put it: "There was no nation in all Asia which Xerxes did not bring against Greece."

News of Persian plans and Persian moves travelled ahead of Persian army and navy, and the Greek city-states had already called together a Pan-Hellenic Congress to consider the threat. Xerxes had sent messengers to all of them—all but the two he planned to crush forever, Athens and Sparta—demanding a symbolic gift, by return, of earth and water, twin symbols of submission. From Athens and Sparta the gifts would not be acceptable: bloody and total defeat was Xerxes's plan for these two.

And although a few states sent tokens, the great majority resolved to fight at the side of Athens and Sparta. The question was: where to make a stand against an army and navy so vast? There were thousand upon thousand of Persians crossing the Hellespont over the mile-long bridge they had slung across at the narrowest point, using three hundred ships, and laying a wooden roadway across their decks. Another bridge would soon be completed. But this was only a part of the force Xerxes was starting to deploy. In addition to this uncounted, uncountable, army marching into Greece, there was a fleet of three thousand naval transports preparing to sail across the Aegean in a massive Combined Ops expedition which would destroy for ever the ability of all Greeks—Athenians, Spartans and the rest of them—to wage war, or resist the spread of Persia.

The Pan-Hellenic Congress decided, in some haste, to defend Greece along the line of the Isthmus of Corinth, the narrow channel that divides the large southern part of Greece, the Peloponnese, from the northern and central parts. But when the plan was considered with more care, the Greeks realized that if the Isthmus were chosen as line of defence, the Persians could mount such an attack, using the whole of north and central Greece as base, that the Peloponnese must soon fall into their hands.

This was unthinkable.

If, therefore, Greece were to be saved, she must be defended, inch by precious inch, from the north down. But as both Greek army and navy (or the contingents, aggregated, from the city-states) were inferior in numbers to those of the Persians, this could only be done in the narrow seas and the narrow passes.

They decided to precipitate, if they could, a naval battle in the cramped and narrow Euboean Channel between their east coast and the large island of Euboea—a hundred miles long—and couple this naval tactic with the defence of the narrow pass of Thermopylae. This, they felt, was the only place the Persian army, marching south from its bridge crossing, could get between the impassable mountains and the sea. A picked band of men, it was argued, could hold the pass forever—or at least long enough to goad the Persians into trying to outflank them from the sea. Once Xerxes attempted the narrow channel with his fleet, the Greeks were confident of being able to defeat it. To this end they mounted a naval force out of all proportion to the mere 5,000 men they allotted King Leonidas of Sparta, with which he was expected to hold back the might of the Persian army. Three hundred men of Leonidas's force were his own Spartans.

Soon the Persian army, as had been prophesied, arrived at the Pass of Thermopylae. Like Leonidas's men, they camped and took stock of the situation. Xerxes had agile spies on horseback, able to describe the defenders to him: according to these there were a mere three hundred men in position.

This in fact was the Spartan contingent, the remainder of the five thousand being concealed from sight, and even when he learnt that these were Spartans, the most warlike people in Greece, the Persian emperor assured himself that no body of men, however brave, however well-armed, would take on any army several thousand times its own size. He waited four days: then, in some exasperation, he sent his first cohorts to crush them.

But as Herodotus was to report of that day, "The Greeks made it plain enough to anyone, not least to the Emperor Xerxes himself, that he had many men, but few soldiers." No soldiers, that is, which could be compared to the well-armed Greek ones, under the inspiring leadership of a Spartan king. The Persians had travelled many hundreds of miles and they always travelled and fought light. But their few, simple, weapons were of little use against the well-armed, well-armoured, Greeks. And though it was soon apparent to Xerxes's generals that they had five thousand men to deal with, rather than a mere three hundred, the Persian army was still enormously, absurdly, the larger force.

At the end of the first day the Persian vanguard had made no impression on the defenders of Thermopylae, whose bravery, arms, and discipline under Leonidas were assisted by the fact that the Pass was a mere fourteen yards across: no attacking army could deploy more than a few men at a time along so small a front. Xerxes replaced his vanguard by crack troops, "The Emperor's Immortals" under the general Hydarnes, but these fared little better. Leonidas, too, could replace his front line, using the various city-state contingents, the Thebans, Thespians, Corinthians and the rest of them, in strict succession, keeping only the Phocians, the largest single group, numbering a thousand, to guard a path to their rear. Were the Persians to discover this path, which ran from near their own encampment, right round behind the Greek position, they could easily outflank and threaten the defenders. In the unlikely event of this happening, Leonidas had posted the thousand Phocians around the southern end of the path, where it entered the valley behind him.

But Leonidas was betrayed. A Greek, Ephialtes, greedy for gold, approached Xerxes along this very path, and agreed to show it him, for a reward.

The deal satisfactorily completed, Ephialtes led Hydarnes and his Persians back along the path, and this large force surprised the Phocian defenders, cut off from the direct command of Leonidas, so that they fled in confusion, then regrouped themselves on a hilltop. Hydarnes ignored them, pressed on into the valley and up against Leonidas's rear.

And now there was consternation in the ranks of the Spartan king. For had not their seer, Megistas, prophesied defeat? And had not an Oracle stated that Sparta would fall to a foreigner unless one of her kings was killed in battle?

Part of the five thousand defected immediately: there was no point, if one believed in the prophecy of Megistas, no point at all in being present at assured defeat; and there was no point fighting—if one subscribed to the Oracle's point of view—for a king whose death alone would assure victory. And Leonidas, anxious to fulfil the Oracle's prophecy with his own life, sent others away, retaining only his own Spartans, with the Thespians and the Thebans. The Thespians, we are told, would not have left him, even if ordered, and he kept the Thebans to test their allegiance to the Greek cause,

Meanwhile the might of the Persian army was assembling behind this little force, assembling at the top of the slope which ran down to the valley, the slope down which thousands of barbarians would rush, when the order was given, to destroy Greece for ever. For this was what the young Xerxes, pouring a libation to the rising sun, had promised his generals, and this is what he firmly believed would be the outcome.

At last, as the sun rose the height of distant trees, the Persians flooded down. And now the character of the fighting changed: here were a few hundred men only, facing certain death, and determined to die well; taking ten, fifty, a hundred, each of the enemy with them before they could fight no longer. And they did. Led by the three hundred Spartans and their king, the Greeks fought with amazing gallantry and—though the outcome was foredoomed—amazing success. They fought first with spears; and when these broke, with swords, then with teeth and with hands. They inflicted such shocking casualties on the Persian hordes that, in order to get these into battle, the Persian commanders were forced to drive them on with whips.

But Leonidas, as the Oracle had foretold, died, at the head of his men, and all three hundred of his Spartans fell with him. Most of the other Greeks defected to the enemy, and of those who were not killed by them the majority were branded with hot irons as everlasting proof of their defeat.

One little band of men fought to the last to save the body of Leonidas, but, when they were heaped in piles around it, the Persians were able to seize it. Xerxes, enraged and horrified by the casualties which had been inflicted on his own army, ordered that it be decapitated, then crucified. The bodies of the others were buried where they had fallen, and later three memorial columns were erected at the spot in their memory.

These three columns might well commemorate Thermopylae, the Spartans, and, above all, Leonidas; for whenever heroism is mentioned the three spring to mind. In fact, that gallant defence of a lost cause against overwhelming odds had little bearing on the rest of the war. It inspired the Greeks—though its outcome distressed them—yet at the same time it inspired Xerxes and his Persians to an all-out effort to destroy them.

But Greece went on, from losing this battle so heroically, to winning the war, and we cannot leave this description of Leonidas and his battle without taking notice of the probable outcome. For if that war had been lost, the whole of Greek civilization would have been lost with it. We might now, in Britain, as all over the continent of Europe, share an Asian culture and speak in Asian tongues.

But this was not to be. (At least, not then: though there are ominous similarities in this history of the fifth century before Christ and that of the twentieth after Him.) The Greek fleet, outflanked from the land, sailed hurriedly south.

And now Themistocles of Athens came into his own. He had always maintained, against the advice, even the frank hostility, of others, that the saving of Greece would, in the long run, depend on its fleet. To this end he had built up a large one for his own Athens, and now, summoning to him the naval contingents, small and even smaller, of the other city-states, he was able to muster a powerful sea force. He rushed this towards the Island of Salamis in the Saronic Gulf, west of Athens, the last defence of the Isthmus of Corinth. By a trick, he was able to persuade Xerxes to try and "bottle up" the Greek fleet in the narrowest part of the Gulf, and here, with their heavier, more armoured—and far fewer—ships the Greeks were able to sail into the tightly packed mass of Persian shipping and rip it to bits. Persian oars were torn off, the hulls were rammed and sunk, and those that refused to sink were boarded and destroyed.

Xerxes and the Persian empire had received a blow from which they never recovered, but it was left to the following year, 479 B.C., for the final land battle of Plataea, and the final defeat of the Persians—by Spartans avenging their king.

PERICLES

(490–429 B.C.)

THE HISTORIAN Herodotus alleges that a few days before the Athenian statesman Pericles was born his mother, Agariste, had a prophetic dream: she dreamed that she would "bear a lion", a son who would be a remarkable leader of men. In fact when this son matured he was for three decades the outstanding personality not only in Athens but in the whole Greek world.

Pericles's parents both belonged to the governing class of the City. His mother was a great-niece of Cleisthenes, the law-giver, and she had been given the name of an ancestor, the daughter of a Synconian tyrant whose wooing—after a year of fierce athletic competition—at the Olympic games had become legendary. Pericles's father, Xanthippus, had held high command in an Athenian naval unit which had defeated what remained of Xerxes's, the Persian king's, fleet.

Xanthippus took a keen interest in political affairs. Athens was then still governed by the Council of the Areopagus, a body which originated in the seventh century B.C. The members of the Areopagus, called archons, all came from the two wealthiest classes of the City. Few authenticated facts about the Areopagus have survived, but at the time of Pericles's birth many far-sighted Athenians, including his father, already believed that the Areopagus system of government was not as democratic as it should be. The reformers were led by an activist, Ephialtes, who, in public utterances, discussed the corruption and fraudulent practices of which the archons were frequently accused. Unfortunately little is known about Ephialtes's life, but historians seem to agree that he himself was an honest man.

There is no question that in Xanthippus's household Ephialtes's activities were frequently discussed in the presence of young Pericles. Though his parents were enthusiastic about reform, it is doubtful whether, despite their intelligence, they understood the dangers inherent in a sudden change of the system of government. For in common with many liberals throughout the ages they did not foresee that without an educated middle class the democracy they contemplated was not workable in the long run. During the fifth century no effort was made to establish any kind of popular education. Intellectual life and learning was confined to a few wealthy families who could give hospitality and a position to resident tutors for their sons. This lack of a more general education was a tragedy for Athens after Pericles's death, because when, under his rule, Athens had become a world power, there were not enough trained men to carry on his work and maintain his achievements.

Pericles himself enjoyed the type of education his parents' wealth and position made possible. The boy had many tutors. From his earliest youth, as was usual for the sons of upper-class Athenians, his military training was never neglected, but he was also taught to develop and use his mind, to think logically, and, above all, objectively and dispassionately. Damon, a prominent scholar of the age, who had propounded various theories of music, was one of his teachers. Another was Zeno, the Eleatic philosopher from Cyprus, who explained to Pericles that he must distrust knowledge acquired purely through the senses; that he must instead rely only on logic and reason.

Young Pericles's most influential teacher was the philosopher-scientist Anaxagoras of Clazomenae, who, in modern terms, was really the earliest atomic scientist. For he believed in the existence of what he called "tiny seeds" from which the entire universe is made up. In other words, he impressed upon Pericles that all matter consisted of some kind of atoms.

Anaxagoras was convinced that all physical phenomena are based on natural causes. By imbuing his pupil with his attitude towards nature, he helped to liberate Pericles from the religious superstitions then widely accepted in Athens. Anaxagoras's influence on Pericles was permanent and far-reaching: for in his maturity Pericles helped to emancipate Athenian culture from the domination of the priestly class and it was he who gave his City the foundations of a secular civilization.

Pericles's character and temperament responded naturally to the discipline of his education. It was his nature to react to the problems of life in a cool, rational manner. His reserve seemed impenetrable and he was always a hard man to know well. He disliked and avoided convivial drinking parties, so popular amongst his contemporaries, and he chose his friends and associates with discrimination. His sculptured head by Cresilas, a copy of which is in the British Museum, shows us the calm face of a withdrawn and determined man who seems to be gazing into space above the troublesome conflicts of the moment. When one looks at the portrait it is difficult to remember that this apparently aloof and detached statesman was one of the most eloquent orators of ancient Greece.

Pericles presented a striking contrast to Cimon, the genial and very convivial hero of the Persian War, who was the leader of the conservatives in the Areopagus during Pericles's youth. Cimon wanted to bring about an alliance between Athens and Sparta—that is to say between the governing classes of the two City States—and when the serfs, the so-called helots, rebelled in Sparta, Cimon went with an armed force to help quell this rebellion. This intervention by an Athenian force in the affairs of Sparta was not generally popular in Athens. Even some of Cimon's drinking companions disapproved of what they considered his pro-Sparta attitude which they thought unpatriotic. Ephialtes and his followers in the democratic party welcomed this opportunity to discredit Cimon further, and he was finally ostracized and forced into temporary exile.

Cimon's disappearance from the political scene left the progressive party in the ascendancy. Pericles, by this time, was acknowledged as Ephialtes's second in the command of the party. Pericles, with Ephialtes and their followers, were now determined totally to reform the government and judicial system of Athens. Their opportunity was at hand, because, without Cimon's leadership, the conservatives on the Council of the Areopagus were disorganized and indecisive.

Ephialtes, for months past, had been preparing public opinion for the revolutionary changes he was contemplating. He had cleverly instituted proceedings against various Areopagites for fraud and corruption. Finally, a year after Cimon's departure, Ephialtes and Pericles officially deprived the Areopagus of all its power with one exception: the Areopagites were allowed to continue as judges in cases of murder.

A Council of Five Hundred—an assembly—and popular law courts took over the functions heretofore carried out by the Areopagus. The members of the Council of the Five Hundred as well as the men who served as judges and magistrates were now chosen by lot from all eligible citizens of Athens. Thus the government of the City was no longer conducted only by the wealthy and prominent; by the luck of the draw every citizen had a chance to take part in public and judicial affairs. It must, however, be mentioned in this connexion that, despite Ephialtes's and Pericles's reforms, the Athenians accepted as citizens eligible for government responsibility only a small minority of the population as a whole.

Ephialtes did not live to see the fruition of his ideas. The conservatives hated him too much, and he was assassinated. Pericles escaped the wrath of his opponents and succeeded the murdered man as the leader of the progressives. During the decade following Ephialtes's death Pericles firmly established the remarkable reforms they had planned together.

Pericles soon demonstrated that he was an imaginative as well as a practical statesman. He understood, for example, that many of the citizens chosen by lot could not really afford public service—which meant giving up gainful occupations—unless they were paid. He therefore introduced a system of payment from the public treasury for services to the state, a system unheard of in ancient Greece before this time. Judges and lesser magistrates, too, were paid a salary and jurymen were given a fee. Pericles also supported measures to give financial aid to the men (and thus to their families) called up for naval and military duties.

Patriotic or ambitious Athenians, now financially free to play a part in the government or the judiciary, were eager to have the luck of the draw. It was natural that they wanted to increase their chances, and the smaller the number of eligible citizens the greater were these chances. Before the age of Pericles the legitimate son of an Athenian father—regardless of his mother's origins—became an Athenian citizen when he was eighteen years old. Now there was great pressure to alter these rules. In 451 B.C. Pericles gave way to these pressures and a law was passed confining citizenship to men who were of Athenian descent on both sides. Not all Athenians welcomed this law, for they remembered many distinguished citizens—for example Cleisthenes, the law-giver, or Themistocles, the naval commander—who were not of purely Athenian origin.

Domestic reforms were not Pericles's only preoccupation. He was equally concerned with foreign affairs and he was radically changing the course of the City's foreign policy. His predecessors, though loyal Athenians, had been more willing to consider Greece as a whole. Pericles, on the other hand, was determined to create an Athenian empire, and to expand the geographical, political and commercial domination of the City. In about 461 B.C. he began to realize his expansionist vision.

He built up a large army and a superb fleet with which to fight for the expansion of Athenian power. To protect Athens itself against attack, fortifications were erected along the route to the port of Piraeus. He secured Athens's Aegean possessions and thus, after the defeat of Corinth and Aegina, made her the greatest trading nation in Greece. Athenian merchants now did business freely with Egypt and Carthage; their goods were sold in ports all over the Mediterranean. Politically, too, under Pericles's leadership, Athens became the dominant power in the Delian League. He also increased the influence of the City by settling groups of Athenians in the various territories conquered by his armies.

For thirty years—until 431 B.C.—Pericles was able to hold his empire together and to maintain the peace. He and his contemporaries could not have understood that the power structure he had created, the battles he had won, the cities he had conquered, would be forgotten by posterity except among scholars, or schoolboys struggling to remember dates and names for an examination paper. What posterity has never forgotten, and will never forget, is that Pericles by his encouragement of the arts and sciences created a lasting empire of the mind.

The Parthenon, largely the work of Phidias, the sculptor; the work of the great dramatists—Aeschylus's *Agamemnon*; Sophocles's *Antigone*, *Electra*, or *Oedipus*; Euripides's *Medea* or *Orestes*—none of these and other marvellous works of art would have been produced without Pericles's support and encouragement of the artists. One of the reasons why, under Pericles's guidance, the cultural life of Athens showed such a consistently high standard was his concern not only with men of genius, but with more ordinary artists and performers as well. Craftsmen as well as sculptors were encouraged; a concert hall, the Odeion, was built for popular concerts by flute and zither players, or singers who never became well known.

In his cultural and political life Pericles obviously had a remarkable ability to bring out the best in people. In his private life he was apparently less successful. He had no gift for the marriage relationship. His wife, a relative, remains a shadowy figure. Not even her name is known. He divorced her in 445 B.C. and his two sons by her were undistinguished and died young. To his mistress, Aspasia of Miletus, on the other hand, he was bound by ties of lasting affection and of mutual interests. It was said by one of Sophocles's disciples that Aspasia was accepted by Pericles and his circle of friends as an intellectual equal.

Aspasia remained faithful to Pericles when, in 431 B.C., the long peace ended, the Peloponnesian War began, and the Athenian Empire was finally destroyed. For the other Greek states had begun bitterly to resent the paramount authority of Athens and, led by Sparta, they had decided to make an effort to cause the downfall of "the tyrant Athens".

At home in Athens, too, Pericles now had many enemies. He had been in power for so many years that many Athenians simply wanted a change. The conservatives, of course, had always opposed him, but by this time some progressives as well were jealous of his dominating position. His adversaries began by attacking his friends: Aspasia, accused of impiety, was successfully defended by Pericles himself, and went free. Anaxagoras, arrested for atheism, was allowed to go into exile; Phidias, unjustly accused of stealing funds from the goddess Athene's treasure, died in prison.

These were bad days for Pericles, especially as the plague was raging in Athens. In 430 B.C. he was accused of fraud and deposed. But this gross injustice appalled so many Athenians that he was reinstated shortly before his death in 429 B.C. The history of Athens after his death showed that his passing was disastrous for the City: there was no man with his vision, authority and integrity to continue his achievements.

Shortly before his death, in a famous speech honouring the dead in the Peloponnesian War—a speech recorded by Thucydides—Pericles formulated for the last time his faith in his kind of democracy; he reminded Athenians never to neglect their political duties; he insisted that, despite their obligations as citizens or soldiers, they should cultivate their minds and their taste for what was beautiful in art and literature. "We shall assuredly," he wrote prophetically, "not be without witnesses . . . there are mighty monuments of our power which will make us the wonder of this and of succeeding ages."

ALEXANDER THE GREAT

(356–323 B.C.)

TO FEW men of action, or other human beings, is the title "Great" given without hesitation: Alexander, son of King Philip of Macedon, and conqueror of Greece and the Near East, has always been one of these. His youth, his personal magnetism, the sweep of his conquests and the mere thirteen years they involved, his cosmopolitan vision and union of Western and Asian cultures, and his founding of international cities like Alexandria in Egypt—such are the reasons for his acclaim.

A fame which soon became literally legendary must in addition have enjoyed some rare personal origin of which we now possess mere hints. It is clear that he arrived at a psychological turning-point in the history both of Hellas and of the Near East. Alexander can be praised most for his vision, by which he accelerated—but did not create—a union and free flow of diverse cultures. His own marriages to Asian princesses formed a part of this policy.

But our admiration for his vision must not blind us to his many faults, let alone those of his un-visionary father, Philip. Centuries later Christianity achieved an equal cosmopolitanism without the necessity of war, as did Buddhism in India and the Far East. Alexander remains a "happy warrior", impulsive in battle and even endangering his life through his ardour.

The situation into which Alexander was born illustrates this. The year was 356 B.C. The many city-states of Greece were re-arranging the chessboard of their alliances and conflicts. To some—though not to Aristotle, himself teaching in Athens, though born at Stagira—the creative age of the city-state, the *polis* (hence our "politics", etc.), was past, and Greece needed to unite, both for her own political salvation and to propagate her culture. Further, only when united could the Greeks conquer Persia, their old foe in the "eternal war" between Asia and Europe—a fact that had never prevented one city-state from intriguing with Persia against another.

Now an apparent leader of the Greeks had arisen: curiously enough, from Macedon, a land to the north of Greece proper, inhabited by a somewhat primitive people ruled by kings of largely

Greek culture and race. Perhaps this marginal role of Macedon gave her king, Philip, a freshness of outlook and a "social-climbing" urge to conquer Hellas with her enormous prestige. Also, the relative primitiveness of his people implied strength and resolution.

Philip himself, in a stormy palace quarrel, had become king at the age of twenty-four; his son Alexander also incarnated the magic vigour of youth. By 338 B.C. Philip had subdued Thessaly, Illyria and Thrace, and had finally secured the mastery of Greece proper by his victory at Chaeronea over Thebes, Athens and their allies.

At the first pan-Hellenic congress held in Corinth, Philip proclaimed his intention to invade Persia. Yet the Greeks were not truly united behind him; their democratic traditions were against kingship, and Macedon was felt to be a semi-Greek outsider. The opposition to Philip, led by the Athenian orator Demosthenes, can thus be understood, however "inopportune historically".

His father's rash personal life provided a stormy background for the seething young Alexander. Philip dismissed the lad's mother, the fiery Epirot princess Olympias, to marry Cleopatra, niece of his general Attalus. At the wedding feast Alexander threw his drinking-cup at Attalus who had hinted that the prince was illegitimate; the sozzled Philip, sword in hand, reeled and fell. At which Alexander jeered: "Behold the man who would pass from Europe to Asia, and trips in passing from couch to couch!" Alexander fled; later Philip recalled him, but Olympias wove intrigues which culminated in Philip's murder in 336 B.C. Meanwhile Cleopatra had borne Philip a son.

Now king, Alexander was threatened on all sides: Greeks, Illyrians, his Thracian tributaries, all were restive, while Attalus in Asia supported the claim of Cleopatra's infant. Unlike his father, the impetuous Alexander acted swiftly; he had Attalus murdered (Olympias dealt with Cleopatra and the baby), subdued Thessaly, conquered the Thracian Triballi tribe on the Danube, received the alliance of some Celts, and rushed to save Macedon itself from attack by the Illyrians.

In the hour of victory he now learned that Thebes had rebelled, and that other Greek states were in ferment, intriguing with Persia. Thebes he smashed, and razed it to the ground; its people were sold into slavery. However, he left one house standing: that of the poet Pindar. This love of culture, which at Thebes stood in contrast to his general savagery, made him conciliatory to Athens. All Greece now stood under his command.

Young, magnetic, swift, beloved of the gods, Alexander was ready for the revenge *against* Asia. This must be emphasized, in view of the change his attitude underwent when once *in* Asia. It is only then that his cosmopolitanism awoke, and—in the words of the historian Eratosthenes: "As in a cup of friendship he mixed the nations." Only then could Plutarch's eulogy apply: "Virtue was by his side, and in him she engendered daring."

Philip was a bare conqueror; his son was to perceive the spiritual union and mission of Greece, and later still to extend this concept of friendship (*philia*) and "one-mindedness" (the Stoic *homonoia*) from family to city-state to Hellas up to Mankind itself. Yet can we blame the opponents of Philip and the early Alexander for not foreseeing this? Aristotle had been Alexander's tutor: from him the prince learnt Platonic philosophy ("kings shall be philosophers"); but to Aristotle's advice to be a political leader to the Greeks and treat them as friends, and to the "Barbarians" a mere enlightened despot, Alexander replies boldly.

In choosing advisers and assistants, "he did not mind whether one of them came to him with a Greek cloak and a spear or a Persian buttoned coat and a scimitar". Their "virtue or lack of virtue" was all that mattered. Yet Aristotle's instruction in the nature of the Greek city inspired Alexander to found Greek cities as far as Afghanistan (Bactria).

His career is now a blazing series of almost symbolic events. With 30,000 infantry and 5,000 cavalry he crossed to Asia Minor, vividly aware of his descent from the hero Achilles, sacrificing at places sacred in Greek tradition, commanding desolate Troy to rise again. Persians and their vassals of Asia Minor were defeated at the River Granichus, at Miletus, at Halicarnassus, all in 334 B.C. Halicarnassus suffered the same barbarous destruction as Thebes. The cities of the Ilyrian League submitted without resistance, so Alexander—like the Persians—left their constitution intact. The next year at Gordion, he cut with his sword the "Gordian knot", the cunningly tied cord of bark of a cornel tree, and so fulfilled the prophecy that he would rule Asia.

Meanwhile King Darius of Persia (who had ascended his throne in the same year as Alexander) resolved to join battle in Cilicia. A beloved monarch, he was no genius like the Macedonian. His empire was ill-organized, but he was employing 15,000 Greek mercenaries. On the plain of Issus Alexander gained a decisive victory; Darius fled in haste, leaving even his mother and wife behind. Alexander's extremely courteous treatment of these captives surprised the world and witnesses to a certain generosity in his nature.

Darius wrote a letter pleading for an alliance, but the victor's reply was haughty. Here Alexander founded the first of his cities, Alexandretta, the name clearly revealing his self-exaltation. The road being now open to Syria, he proceeded to attack the disunited Phoenician cities; Tyre capitulated after an eight-month siege (January-August, 332 B.C.), and suffered savage slaughter, while the remnants (some 30,000) were sold into slavery. The essentially compromising Darius sent Alexander an offer to the effect that he could have all the lands west of the Euphrates, and his daughter's hand. Alexander turned down the offer. Tyre was followed by Gaza, the Philistine capital, which endured slaughter on an even greater scale.

Egypt, always a restless part of the empire, was now cut off from Persia. No resistance was offered and, in the Pharaoh's capital, Alexander first showed his cosmopolitan vision by making sacrifices to Apis and other Egyptian gods, and so gaining goodwill. To deepen his rank as King of Egypt, he proceeded to the oracular sanctuary of Amen, where the priests arranged for the god to declare Alexander his son (a necessary title for all Pharaohs). Alexander never divulged his dialogue with the god. Here there may have been a genuine, if self-centred, "mystical" impulse blended with political opportunism. Cyrene submitted, and his domain adjoined that of Carthage.

Of vast historic importance was his founding of the city of Alexandria; its site was a stroke of genius. He filled it with Greeks, Asiatics, and the Jews to whom he always showed favour. Greek manners entered Africa, Greek trade prospered, and the native Egyptians to some extent suffered. None the less, Alexandria—city with the world's first lighthouse—became a beacon of multi-national culture whose effect on the future can hardly be overrated.

Returning to Asia, Alexander refused (though prudently) to "steal victory" by night, and in broad daylight put the Persians to utter rout at Gaugamela, 331 B.C. Darius fled into the mountains, his Persians with him, carrying along with them the troops already placed at the rear. Alexander hastened on to Babylon, a city as proud as Tyre, which yet received him with open arms. The satrap, Mazaeus, surrendered city and citadel, and the conqueror typically retained him in his post. As in Egypt, Alexander now appeared as the protector of the native faiths; those had been scorned and persecuted by the Zoroastrian "fire-worshippers" (though strictly they revered fire merely as a symbol of the Divine). Alexander restored the temples, notably the grandiose temple of Bel, which Xerxes had destroyed.

After resting in Susa, the luxurious summer capital, Alexander pressed on, forcing the tribes of the Uxian Pass to pay him tribute, towards the Persian Gates, a narrow defile leading to Persis. This pass seemed impregnable, and winter snow increased Alexander's dilemma, for this, the only route to Persia's royal cities, had to be crossed. Based on the clever device of dividing his forces, his nocturnal attack led to a sweeping victory. Then in ancient Persepolis he stayed four months, receiving the submission of local peoples, and—in a frenzy of Greek (and perhaps pro-Babylonian) vengeance—burning down the temple of Xerxes.

Meanwhile Bessus, satrap of Bactria, had conspired against his master Darius, who perished; but Alexander dispatched the royal corpse with all honour to the Queen-Mother and later hunted Bessus down and had him mutilated and crucified. In this, perhaps, he acted as an "Asiatic" monarch, punishing the killer of a fellow-king, like himself "divine". Alexander did not hesitate to adopt the arbitrary splendour of Eastern monarchism, despite the restiveness this caused among his democratic Greeks. He adopted Asian dress and customs, even encouraging prostration in his presence, in accordance with his general, and indeed enlightened, principle of putting Western and Eastern manners and men on an equality.

The foundation of mixed cities (usually called Alexandria in his typical mixture of vision and egotism) was part of this policy; he transplanted willing Asians to Europe and vice versa. Religions, too, were reconciled, though this was of course more natural in antiquity: at his great banquet at Opis on the Tigris, the loving-cups were shared by men of many races, and the libations chanted, by Greek seers and Persian Magi alike, to "God", not to Zeus or any Asian deity as such. He further encouraged his European associates to marry Persians, and he himself—though often judged indifferent to women—married Roxana, daughter of the Sogdian prince Oxyartes, and later added two other Asian princesses (this was not repugnant to custom, and was useful politically). In his assumption of Oriental pomp and "divinity" he naturally offended his Macedonians; yet his tremendous, cordial personality won them back—after a few executions!

The urge to conquest increased. Successfully he had manoeuvred his troops and his policies in regions scarcely known to the Greek mind. Now, emboldened, he subdued Hyrcania and Gedrosia in Afghanistan. Thus was opened the path to India across the Hindu Kush range. Bactria, Sogdia (with Samarkand) were vanquished after strenuous efforts in a rigorous climate, whose hardships

Alexander was willing to share with his humblest follower. Then, three years after the death of Darius, Alexander prepared to conquer India, thus anticipating by 2,000 years the next European conquest of those regions! The foresight, the organizational power, and the geographical intuition displayed by Alexander were enormous. He was accompanied, too, by merchants (often Phoenician), literary men, historians, craftsmen, engineers and other specialists.

India—which, to the Greeks, existed on the world's edge—lay before him. Skilfully playing one quarrelling state against another, he crossed the Indus and received the homage of the Prince of Taxila (a prized vassal) and other states. Taxila's rival, Prince Porus, defied Alexander but was routed with his elephants at the Battle of the Hydaspes (326 B.C.). Alexander then treated him with a generosity both genuine and opportunist. Next the Punjab was conquered; but at the River Hyphasis his weary troops, faced with a desert march of eleven days, struck, and Alexander yielded, thus depriving himself for ever of reaching what he *thought* to be the world's end, bounded by the ocean. Retracing their steps, his men subdued the warlike Malli. Alexander was wounded; his troops, believing him dead, indulged in a vengeful massacre. Sind was overcome with difficulty, and at last Alexander, full now of naval plans, sailed in the Indian Ocean. His friend Nearchus was detailed to discover a seaway for commerce between the West and the Far East.

Alexander himself marched through Gedrosia in the most terrible conditions of all his campaigns; then he reached Susa, Ecbatana, and proceeded to Babylon, on the way defeating the Cossaean brigands and receiving embassies from countries in three continents. At Ecbatana he suffered overwhelming grief at the death of his bosom-friend Hephaestion, and crucified the physician who had failed to save him. (Such contrasts are in character; here we can only touch on the murder of his foster-brother Clitus in a drunken brawl.)

But his next scheme was not to be fulfilled. Preparing to circumnavigate and conquer Arabia, he died of a fever at Babylon in 323 B.C., aged thirty-three. Since thirteen years produced such amazing results, who can tell what another two decades of life would have yielded? His mind, at once visionary and practical, would surely have explored new regions, discovering the true geography of India and at least making contact with China. His realm might well have extended from Libya to the Ganges, or beyond. It is this charting of ever new domains—of trade, geography, culture, as well as war, this raising of the Greek curiosity to a new dimension—which attracts us in Alexander still.

CHANDRAGUPTA MAURYA

(*c.* 321–*c.* 298 B.C.)

THERE HAVE been emperors of India right into the twentieth century, and many of them were foreigners. The "Mogul" emperors from central Asia were as little akin to their Hindu subjects in race, language or religion as was Queen Victoria.

And men may debate till the end of time whether it was Victoria or the Moguls who did the greater good—or the greater harm—to that subcontinent. There can be no real answer: yardsticks vary.

But though the achievement of the last Indian emperors may be in dispute, there is no argument about those of the first.

His name was Chandragupta Maurya.

He reigned for the quarter century between 321 and 296 B.C., founding his own family dynasty. From the rise of this Maurya dynasty, Indian history becomes suddenly clear: chronology, despair of the historian, begins to make sense. An empire has sprung into being, joining the fragments of what, till now, has been only a vast southern bulge on the map.

We know quite a lot about this period in Indian history, and for that we are indebted to three sources. The Greeks came to India with Alexander the Great and wrote of their impressions; there are lengthy stone inscriptions made by Chandragupta's grandson, Asoka; and there is a remarkable treatise written by Chandragupta's chief minister, Kautilya, which shows us clearly how the Empire was run.

Chandragupta, we learn, seized the throne of the kingdom of Magadha, in eastern India (and now part of Bihar), from the last of its kings. There is a theory that he was in fact the illegal son of that king by a low-caste woman, but in any case the seizure was effected by organizing a revolt within the kingdom. At the same time, the ambitious young Chandragupta launched an attack on the garrisons left behind by Alexander in the Indus basin. We know that Alexander died in Babylon in June, 323 B.C., and that the attack was launched against the forces of his successor. It was successful; the Macedonian garrisons were overrun; and Chandragupta now ascended the throne of an empire. He gave himself the title of emperor, and he is the first strictly historical person to hold it.

He had captured Alexander's Indian domains, but the successors to Alexander lost no time in trying to regain them. One of these, Seleukos, crossed the Indus again, but was roundly beaten. Chandragupta's terms for his surrender involved the handing over of a number of provinces: in return the new emperor magnanimously presented five hundred elephants and agreed to take a daughter of Seleukos as wife.

A treaty so concluded might well last, and we can be grateful that it did; for now Seleukos sent, as his ambassador to Chandragupta's court, a remarkable man called Magasthenes. The ambassador kept an account of what befell him in this eastern land, with a minute description of its institutions and geography. Sadly, we no longer possess that account, but so much of it was borrowed by other authors that we still retain a clear idea of the India of Chandragupta's day. We know that the emperor was a stern, even cruel, ruler, and that the Maurya dynasty he founded ruled with even greater efficiency than did the Moguls two thousand years later. The Moguls, despite their militarism (even cooks in the palace had a military rank), had difficulty in resisting European encroachment when it came, but Chandragupta had no difficulty in flinging back the might of Macedon and exacting large tribute. He had, as well as a fine army, a highly developed civil service capable, in theory at least, of controlling an empire of any size.

The capital was Pataliputra, near the site of present-day Patna, and built on a tongue of land jutting out into the River Ganges where the smaller Son River joined it. It was thus a natural defensive position, triangular in shape, with water along two of its three sides. Its ruins are almost hidden by the towns of Patna and Bankipore, and the river confluence itself has shifted, but we can still trace the old river beds, see the remains of jetties, as well as fragments of the wooden palisade which surrounded the city. There were 570 watchtowers looking over this wall, and 64 well-guarded entrances in it.

There was a magnificent wooden-and-stone palace in which Chandragupta resided and from which he conducted the affairs of his empire. The exterior columns were picked out in gold and silver, and the splendid park which surrounded it was dotted with fish-ponds, trees and ornamental shrubs. We know from Megasthenes and others that Chandragupta never appeared in public without being carried in a golden palanquin or on a gold-draped elephant. His clothes were of the finest cotton, richly embroidered, and the royal food was served from golden vessels, six feet across. He had what we today call a harem, though that word was to come later, with the arrival of the Muslims; and, rather surprisingly perhaps, his palace was guarded by a regiment of armed women, his Amazons.

The Hindu religion looks askance at hunting, but Chandragupta and his two great successors had large deer parks and game reserves set aside for their personal use, right up until the time that Asoka embraced Buddhism and gave it up.

In addition to the harem and the Amazons, there were the familiar "dancing girls" of Eastern legend, to provide almost every service a monarch could require, from actual dancing, via garland-strewing and housework, to diplomacy. Some, in the Mata Hari tradition, were active and dangerous members of the Secret Service.

Alexander's influence on India was comparatively slight and short-lived, but the fact that Chandragupta's empire in the west, in the Punjab, had lain close to the eastern limit of the Persian empire meant that many Persian customs were adopted; even, in certain situations, the worship of fire.

The emperor was absolute ruler of his domain, but in his minister's treatise on State craft, the "Arthasastra", we learn that "Sovereignty is only possible with assistance. A single wheel can never move. Hence the king shall employ ministers and hear their opinion." And this same work, by the hand of his old and trusted adviser, Kautilya, urges that the sovereign never take the advice of less than four ministers on any subject.

Sometimes Chandragupta did; often he did not. Certainly he had his way in most things, though well aware, as rulers must be, that if one antagonizes too many, one is likely to be deposed or even assassinated. So great was Chandragupta's fear of the latter fate that, according to Megasthenes, he refused to sleep in the same bed two nights running, or to rest at all in the hours of daylight.

His powerful army had four arms: infantry, cavalry, chariots and elephants. The Commander-in-Chief rode on a war elephant covered in armour, with sharp barbs on each tusk, and two soldiers to control it. Lesser officers travelled in chariots drawn by two or four horses, with infantry guarding them. Chandragupta's army at one stage numbered 600,000 infantry, 30,000 cavalry, 8,000 chariots and 9,000 elephants. It was superbly disciplined and it was paid, not feudally, but directly by the state. It had no difficulty in conquering all its enemies, from Seleukos to the rulers of bordering states. (Kautilya's treatise states flatly that "any ruler at the circumference of the empire is an enemy".)

The administration of this formidable force seems to have been on thoroughly modern lines, with a War Office divided into departments controlling Admiralty, Transport and Supplies, Infantry, Cavalry, Chariots and Elephants. The men were divided into squads of ten, companies of a hundred and battalions of a thousand.

The armament was as formidable as the organization. Each elephant carried three archers plus driver, each chariot a minimum of two fighting men plus driver, all armed with lances. The infantry carried broadsword, javelin, bow and shield; and every man and every beast was armoured.

There was an ambulance service with surgeons and female nurses.

But even with this immensely powerful apparatus at his disposal, Chandragupta preferred, whenever possible, to take the advice of Kautilya: "Intrigue, spies, winning over the enemy's people, siege and assault, are the five means to capture a fort."

The type of government is shown, perhaps, in Chandragupta's word for it. "Dandaniti" means, simply, "Punishment", and indeed any crime, however petty, was punished with great severity. Unless a suitable and rapid confession were obtained, torture was carried out to extort it.

But this cruelty was normal for the period, and India's first emperor can be counted one of her greatest. Even his death was noble. He had listened to the prophecy of a saint, Bhadrabahu, that his lands would suffer a famine for twelve years, and many men would perish: the only escape would be a wholesale migration to more fertile land in the south. But no one else would listen to the prophecy. When it seemed about to be fulfilled, Chandragupta, to point the urgency of the matter, abdicated, to the consternation of his subjects, and began to lead a party of emigrants south, exhorting others to join him. Amazed, uncomprehending, many did, and were saved, while a dreadful famine ravaged the lands they had left.

When Bhadrabahu died Chandragupta was grief-stricken. He starved himself to death.

The empire went on. The twelve lean years gave way to plenty and Chandragupta's son Bindusara took over what was, in every way, a going concern. He extended still further the bounds of his domain, so that soon it extended, literally, from coast to coast. He in turn handed it over to his own son, Asoka, who without materially increasing the size of the empire strengthened its organization. He became, late in life, the most devout of Buddhists (at which point he gave up using his game reserves) and dispatched missionaries to as many lands as he had heard of, or could reach. He was a great builder, largely of temples, and many of these stand today as his monument and that of the Maurya dynasty.

But, as Chandragupta had feared throughout his own, the life of an emperor, even of an empire, is at the mercy of the assassin's sword. The Emperor Brihadratha was killed by his own Commander-in-Chief in 185 B.C., and the Maurya dynasty ended. By this time the empire itself had begun to fall to pieces, lacking the firm hand of Chandragupta and his immediate successors. The subsequent history of India, for several hundreds of years, is confused and muddled. Then, at the start of the fourth century A.D., came a new, powerful, dynasty, that of the Guptas. This, by a confusing accident of nomenclature, was founded by another Chandragupta.

The Gupta dynasty brought a Golden Age of Hindu Culture, but it too fell, and was followed by a confusion of rulers until the tenth century A.D. Then the Muslim hordes swept down over the northern hills, bringing with them an alien religion, Islam, which owed allegiance to a "Caliph" outside India's borders. Previous to this, every invader from the north (and none, until the arrival of Europeans in the fourteenth century, came any other way) had been assimilated, his religion and his customs blending into the previous pattern. But with the coming of Islam that process ceased. Islam, to its adherents, was the one and only True Faith: any unbeliever must either be forcibly converted or put to the sword. The new invaders embarked on campaigns of punishment, but punishment unlike Chandragupta's "Dandaniti" which was designed to govern: punishment for its own sake, to show the infidel his worthlessness and grind him underfoot.

These early Muslim invaders gave place to a finer breed who shared the same faith. Believing them to be Mongols, which they were not, the inhabitants of India now styled them "Moguls" and under this alien Mogul empire the country again prospered.

India has had her share of great emperors. But perhaps the greatest was the first.

ASOKA

(Reigned *c.* 273–232 B.C.)

WAR HAVING been decided upon, the Indian army rapidly crossed the border into Kalinga and were soon carrying all before them. The troops they encountered were dispersed. Towns and villages were occupied, and those that put up any sort of resistance were stormed and burnt, and their populations put to the sword or driven into the jungle to die of hunger and exposure. The streets were piled with corpses. Tens of thousands were enslaved, and the cries of outraged women and children rendered fatherless were heard from one end of the land to the other. At length the war was won, and the victors returned home. The generals went to the palace to report to their royal master that the tasks entrusted to them had been successfully accomplished. They thought he would be pleased, as indeed almost any other monarch would have been pleased. But the man in the case was Asoka, and that made a difference.

At this time—the year was about 261 B.C.—Asoka had been king of most of northern India for some dozen years, or eight years if we date his reign's commencement from his coronation. He belonged to the Maurya dynasty that had been founded by Chandragupta Maurya in about 322 B.C., the year after the death of Alexander the Great, with whom he had had some friendly contacts when the Greek conqueror had penetrated as far as the Indus. Asoka followed his father Bindusara on the throne in 273 B.C.; he was not the eldest son, but he seems to have acted for some years as heir apparent, and no doubt he had shown signs of capacity to rule. Since his coronation or consecration was delayed for some years it has been surmised that there was some opposition to his accession, but the story that he killed ninety-eight or ninety-nine brothers in order to clear the way to the throne is a silly fable put out by the monkish chroniclers of Ceylon, who wanted to make out that he was a very wicked fellow before he became converted to their faith.

From what may be learnt from the inscriptions that he caused to be made (and there is not the slightest reason to doubt their essential truth) the young Asoka was not very different from the ordinary run of kings met with in Indian history. He lived as his predecessors had lived, surrounded by every luxury and tempted by every pleasure. He enjoyed his days in the hunting-field. He joined in the feasts and dancing and theatrical displays that helped to pass the time for his courtiers. We are told that he liked his wine and good food, being specially fond of peacock's flesh, and he spent much of his time with the ladies of his numerous harem. As a ruler he was not at all inclined to temper justice with any exceptional measure of mercy.

But the Kalinga war worked a great change in him. The Kalingas occupied the territory to the south-east of his kingdom in the coastal region of the Bay of Bengal. No doubt they had been making themselves a bit of a nuisance, and it would not be difficult to find a pretext for teaching them a lesson. So he gave the necessary orders, and his soldiers carried out their instructions. But the reports of victory gave him no pleasure; on the contrary, they filled him with anguish. He suffered a great revulsion of feeling, which found expression in an inscription for which it would be hard to find a parallel. It is one of the "Rock Edicts" that he had engraved on great slabs or faces of rock so that they might be read by all who knew how, and this is what it says:

"When the king had been consecrated eight years, Kalinga was conquered by His Sacred and Gracious Majesty. A hundred and fifty thousand persons were carried away from thence captive, a hundred thousand were there slain, and many times that number died. No sooner had the land of the Kalingas been annexed than His Sacred Majesty felt remorse for having conquered the Kalingas, because the conquest of a country that had not been conquered before involves the slaughter, death, and carrying away captive of the people. And that is a matter of the most profound sorrow and regret to His Sacred Majesty. . . ."

Thereupon (the inscription goes on) His Sacred Majesty had begun to take under his protection the Law of Piety, to show his love of that law, and to inculcate it. With the result that, "if a hundredth part, or the thousandth part, of all the people who were then slain, done to death, or carried away captive, were to suffer the same fate, it would be a matter of regret to His Sacred Majesty. Moreover, should any one in future do him wrong, that too must be borne with, as far as it possibly can be . . . For His Sacred Majesty desires that all living beings should have security, self-control, peace of mind, and joyousness."

Yes, indeed, it would be hard to find a parallel to this extraordinary document. A king whose dominions extended from what is now Afghanistan to as far down in the peninsula as Madras, had said—

what?—that he was sorry! Sorry for something that is a commonplace in the records of imperial power but which he had come to consider a crime against humanity.

Two further inscriptions, known as the Kalinga Edicts, emphasize the lesson that he had learnt and which he now wished to impress on all those who governed in his name. They are addressed to high officers in the provincial administration, and in them he asserts that "all men are my children" and warns them against displaying envy and impatience in their rule, lack of perseverance, harshness, want of application and indolence. Let them watch their behaviour in future, for they could rest assured that the king's eye was upon them and any failure in their duty would be visited with his extreme displeasure.

Up to this time Asoka had been, it would seem, an adherent of the Brahmanical form of Hinduism, but now he became a convert to the great rival faith of Buddhism, which had been first preached by Gautama the Buddha perhaps three centuries before. His instructor in his new religion, and perhaps the man responsible for his conversion, was one Upagupta, the fourth in succession from Buddha as the "patriarch" of the Buddhist Church. Together they toured the principal holy places of the Buddhist world, and at each Asoka caused to be erected a monument commemorating his visit. Perhaps it was Upagupta who persuaded him to give up hunting and the practice of eating meat, and to prohibit the slaughter of animals for the royal kitchen.

One tradition has it that the king became a Buddhist monk, and it may very well be that he did so for a time, after the fashion of Buddhists in Burma and elsewhere. What is quite certain is that he became a powerful supporter of Buddhist missions. From his inscriptions we learn that he dispatched missionaries to many parts of the Indian peninsula, to Burma, and even to the succession-states of Alexander's empire in Asia and North Africa. It is not impossible that some knowledge of the Buddhist faith may have been carried to Europe by one of the missionaries he sent out.

But the most successful of these missions was the one he sent to Ceylon, or Lanka as it was styled in those days. This was in about 250 B.C., in response to an invitation from Tissa, king of the island, who was Asoka's almost lifelong friend. A young man named Mahendra, who was Asoka's younger brother or perhaps his son, was the principal missionary, and to this day his name and fame is perpetuated by monuments and relics in various parts of the island. He was accompanied by his sister Sanghamitra, who, we are assured, was as successful in winning women to Buddhism as Mahendra was among the men. The mission was a complete success, as is evidenced by the fact that from that day to this Ceylon has been a predominantly Buddhist country.

Mention has been made of Asoka's inscriptions. There are many of these, made on rocks and pillars and on the walls of caves, and together they constitute what has been called the most remarkable set of inscriptions in the world. They are to be found scattered over the length and breadth of India, from the north-west corner of the Punjab to Mysore, on the coasts of the Arabian Sea and the Bay of Bengal. Some of them are historical, some are political, but nearly all are moral. Never before had a great sovereign taken such pains to instruct his people in the ways of good behaviour, and there have been few to follow his example. If we seek to know what Asoka's own personal code of morals was we may discover it most concisely formulated in one of the "Minor Rock Edicts", as follows:

"Thus saith His Majesty. Father and mother must be obeyed. In the same way respect for all living creatures must be enforced. Truth must be spoken. These are the duties of the Law of Duty which must be practised. The teacher must be reverenced by the pupil, and a proper courtesy must be shown to all relations. This is the ancient standard of duty, which if it is followed leads to length of days. And according to it men must act."

Time and again Asoka refers to the "Law of Duty". In what does this consist, he inquires in one of the Pillar Edicts; and goes on to answer, "many good deeds, compassion, liberality, truthfulness, and purity of life". In the Rock Edicts he states that it includes the proper treatment of slaves and servants, hearkening to what one's parents have to say, showing liberality to friends and acquaintances, relations, Brahmans, and ascetics, and refraining from killing living creatures. In another he bids men to beware of lauding their own faith too highly and of belittling the faith of others; the religions of other people are all deserving of reverence (he says), for one reason or another.

As was (and is) the custom in Oriental lands, Asoka's rule was an intensely personal matter. Deeply interesting is one of the Rock Edicts that shows him at work. "For a long time past," he says, "it has been the rule to do business only at certain times. But now I have made arrangements that at all hours and in all places—whether I am at dinner, or in the ladies' apartments, or in my private room, or in the royal mews, or in my carriage, or walking in the palace gardens—wherever I may happen to be, the officers bearing official reports should have immediate access to me on the people's business. I have given instructions that immediate report is to be made to me at any hour and in any place, because I am never altogether satisfied with the way business is despatched. All my exertions are directed to one end, that I may discharge my debt to every creature, and that while I may make some people happy in this world, they may all in the next attain to heaven."

In addition to the rock inscriptions, ten of the surviving pillars that Asoka caused to be erected on Buddhist sites are inscribed. One of these is in the Lumbini Gardens, just over the border in Nepal, marking Buddha's birthplace. Another, and the most famous, is at Sarnath, four miles north of the holy city of Benares, on the site of the Deer Park where Buddha preached his first sermon. Here there is a great stupa (domed mound) of solid brickwork, enclosing the much smaller stupa that Asoka built. Close by is the stump, still 17 feet high, of the Asokan Pillar; originally over 50 feet in height, it was cut from a solid block of stone, quarried more than twenty miles away, and dragged to this spot.

When Sir John Marshall, the pioneer of Indian archaeology, excavated the site he found lying near by the broken portions of the upper part of the shaft and a magnificent bell-shaped capital with four lions above, supporting in their midst a stone wheel, the symbol of the Buddhist Law or Dharma that Buddha first "turned" at Sarnath all those many centuries ago. Marshall was astonished by the excellent state of preservation of the sculptures. He acclaimed the bell and lions as "the finest carvings that India has yet produced, and unsurpassed, I venture to think, by anything of their kind in the ancient world". Another stupa with the remains of an Asokan pillar were located at Sanchi in Bhopal, and Sir John Marshall carefully restored the ancient monument to its original form.

After more than forty years on the throne, King Asoka died in 232 B.C. According to one version, he began to lose grip on affairs towards the end of his reign, and at length retired to a Buddhist monastery tired and disillusioned; but according to another, and, it is good to learn, better authenticated account, he continued to the end the same masterful striver after his people's welfare that he had been in his prime. His great name and example have never been forgotten, and to the founders of the Indian Republic in 1947 it seemed the most natural thing in the world that they should adopt the Sarnath capital as the device for the national seal, while in the middle of the national flag an "Asoka wheel" stands out in navy blue against the central band of white.

HANNIBAL

(247–182? B.C.)

HANNIBAL IS one of the very few great men of antiquity known to the wide public, who was neither Greek nor Roman nor Hebrew, though he was related by race to the latter. Moreover, he was an enemy of Rome: yet our tradition, in many ways Rome's successor, often admires him. His name itself, derived as it is from Baal, brings to mind the god who was Jehovah's rival in the Old Testament and whose priests were butchered by Elijah. It is interesting that a fellow-Semite, Sigmund Freud, tells—in his autobiography and elsewhere—how from boyhood he studied and admired the great anti-Roman hero.

We may further regard Hannibal as one of the line of significant North Africans, later to include great Christian thinkers like St. Augustine and Tertullian, as well as many of the creators of Moorish Spain with her tolerant international culture. Indeed such an exceptional figure as Hannibal may serve to make our historical judgments more subtle, create an awareness of the values that can exist on both sides of a conflict, and show us that our own culture and its ancestry are not unique.

Who was Hannibal? He was a Carthaginian, and Carthage was a long-standing, prosperous colony of Phoenicia. By Hannibal's time, Carthage was already mistress of a small empire, including territories in Sicily, long a source of dispute with the Greeks. Thus both a Phoenician and an African tradition were involved.

The Phoenicians, an unusual people, deserve considerable study. To them much of the pre-Hellenic culture of the Mediterranean Basin was due. Known in the Old Testament as Canaanites, they were principally a trading and maritime community; already in the middle of the second millennium B.C., their caravan routes reached, through Damascus, to the Euphrates, while in the West their commerce stretched, through Sicily, North Africa and Spain, as far as Cornwall. Pre-eminently they developed and traded in metals, fabrics and other products of a technical skill which, according to tradition, they handed on to Crete and thus Greece, and therefore the modern Western world.

To the Greeks they gave the principles of the alphabet, and the intermingling of Phoenician and Greek religious symbols (as with Aphrodite and Adonis) continued for many centuries. Trading with Babylon, they conveyed elements of its civilization to the West. Their subsequent conquests by Assyria, Babylon, Egypt, Persia and Greece (Alexander the Great) hardly concern us here; what is significant is that the Phoenicians were great colonizers, founding cities as far west as Cadiz (about 1100 B.C.), and also in Cyprus, Sicily, Malta and North Africa, and that as a result they were in perpetual contact and frequent conflict with the Greeks and their colonies.

One of the most powerful Phoenician colonies was Carthage, a few miles from modern Tunis, founded around 800 B.C. A natural site for international commerce, Carthage soon founded colonies of her own. After ousting the Greeks from the Spanish coast and most of Sicily, Carthage, the largest and richest city in the Western Mediterranean, had an empire comprising a number of coastlands—North African, Southern Spanish, Sicilian, Sardinian and Corsican. It was in Sicily that she first confronted Roman power. Carthage, like Venice later, preferred diplomacy to war, and she and Rome had made three treaties respecting "spheres of influence", before the tragic oversight of not defining such spheres in Sicily led to a conflict. This was over a third party, the Mamertines, discharged auxiliaries from Campania in Southern Italy, whose town, Messana, had been conquered by Hiero of Syracuse. A Carthaginian flotilla came to their aid, but the Mamertines then called in the Romans, as "fellow-Italians", to help oust the Carthaginians in their turn.

Through folly and obstinacy Rome and Carthage drifted into an undesired war—the First Punic (that is, Carthaginian) War, which lasted from 264 to 241 B.C. Rome built up her naval power, then invaded Africa, throwing away her victory at Ecnomus by demanding impossible terms of surrender, and goaded Carthage into an eleventh-hour rally which culminated in victory over Rome in the valley of the Bagradas, near Carthage (255 B.C.). Rome had to evacuate Africa. But the next years saw massive Roman attacks on Sicily, ending in another victory for Carthage: the exhausted Romans, who could have accepted a compromise which divided Sicily between Carthaginians, Romans and Greeks, wrecked their chances through listening to their diehard Regulus.

The tepid armistice gave time to Carthage to stage a decisive counter-blow under the young commander Hamilcar Barca, father of his country's most famous citizen, Hannibal. But eventually he had to accept peace on Rome's terms in 241 B.C. The very next year, taking advantage of Carthaginian dissensions, Rome sided with mutinous mercenaries in Sardinia and declared war on the legitimate government of Carthage, refusing arbitration. Carthage had no choice but to accept Rome's grabbing of both Sardinia and Corsica, and to pay a further 1,200 talents as indemnity. Whatever the Romans' fears of Hamilcar, through such high-handed sharp practice, they tarnished their reputation for fairness and increased their own insecurity by inciting Carthage to implacable revenge.

Hamilcar nursed his nine-year-old son, Hannibal, on hate, making him daily swear revenge on Rome by the family altar. If Rome by her greed and folly increased her own insecurity, it is equally tragic that Hamilcar, his son-in-law Hasdrubal, and Hannibal himself procured the far worse downfall of their country. At Carthage there was almost always a peace party, desiring merely the free passage of trade between Syria and the Atlantic; but the Barcas scorned this tradition. The First Punic War had been one of exhaustion: a course based on mercantile caution and the need to rely on mercenaries from the African interior. Hamilcar's dynamism and frequent imperialism changed this. Personality becomes important: Hamilcar and Hannibal possessed the genius of binding mercenaries in devotion to their own person, an art by which Caesar later reached monarchical rank in Rome. Today we think not so much of the individual Roman generals, but of Rome, while the name of Hannibal eclipses that of Carthage.

Under Hamilcar, Carthage recovered her resources through a series of conquests (obtained often by diplomacy) in the interior of Spain, rich both in mines and in military material. Rome gradually awoke to the situation, and made a treaty, protecting the Greek colony of Saguntum near Valencia, while Hasdrubal promised not to cross the River Ebro. In 221 B.C. Hasdrubal was murdered, and his severed head dramatically thrown into Hannibal's camp. The new leader—married to the daughter of one of the chiefs of Castulo—picked a quarrel with Saguntum, perhaps to forestall a second Messana incident with its resultant Roman aggression. But Rome, for once irresolute, accepted two rebuffs to her protests, while the Carthaginian peace policy of Hanno was brushed aside by the ardent Hannibal.

Hannibal's eight-month siege of Saguntum ended in victory, with the vanquished committing suicide on a pyre in their market-place (a tragedy repeated two generations later by the Carthaginians themselves). The Roman Senate, jolted into action, demanded the surrender of Hannibal. This was refused and Rome declared war in 219 B.C.

At this point Hannibal produced his master-stroke of strategy. He resolved to cut off Roman man-power at its source and cross the Alps into Italy—one of the most daring feats in military history, and one which has become proverbial. Unlike Napoleon's comparable march into Russia, Hannibal's plan met with success. Not that crossing the Alps proved easy: snow, ice and inhospitable cold combined with hostile mountain tribes to reduce Hannibal's man-power to some 26,000.

Yet he conquered Northern Italy within two months; the Roman general Cornelius Scipio, hastily recalled from Gaul, was no match for him in the preliminary skirmish by the River Ticinus; farther south, near Placentia, an enlarged Roman force suffered further defeat at the River Trebia, their 400,000 men being reduced to 10,000. On this the Romans withdrew from Northern Italy, leaving the hitherto hesitant Gauls to join Hannibal. Then Central Italy witnessed his great victory at Lake Trasimene, where he employed his usual tactics of decoying an attack on his relatively weak centre, followed by a surprise-rout of the attackers from all sides.

After Trasimene, Rome waited, adopting "Fabian" tactics, so called from the commander-dictator Fabius Maximus: the poet Ennius praised him as "the man who singly saved the state by patience". For, though theoretically Hannibal now had a clear road to Rome, no town of Central Italy threw open its gates to him, and he had no base for supplies. Preferring to ferment rebellion in Southern Italy, he received no welcome there, and was shadowed by Fabius, whose brush with him in Campania proved a failure, due to a really ingenious ruse of Hannibal: 2,000 oxen were driven by night to the Roman camp, their horns tied with lighted faggots, so frightening the Romans away. Yet Fabius's mere presence kept the allies of Rome in the south from joining Hannibal.

In 216 B.C. Roman impatience erupted and courted the disaster of Cannae: in this open Apuleian plain their 50,000 men were annihilated by Hannibal's 40,000, thanks to his usual tactics and the co-operation, in Greek style, between a containing and a striking force. Yet once again Hannibal's luck proved almost his undoing. Cannae turned out to be a lever for Roman revival; unheard-of patriotic sacrifices issued in a new effort; in the words of the Greek historian Polybius, the Romans were never as intractable as in defeat. Practically the whole of Southern Italy was won over by Hannibal (and his promise not to impose forced levies on them), while Capua, the chief industrial centre, was delighted to house and supply his army. Yet the ease and languor of that sensuous region undisciplined Hannibal's men, and the name of Capua in this sense became proverbial.

In addition, he had to face the growing increase of Roman manpower, while Central Italy's loyalty to Rome cut him off from his Gallic allies. He tried with little success to snare his enemies into fresh traps; in 212 B.C. he gained Tarentum (through treason), but the starvation of Capua into surrender in the next year outbalanced this. Rome meted out savage "peace-terms" to the Capuans. Three years later, by another act of treason, Tarentum was recovered by Rome; and Hannibal could only look for reinforcements from an external source—in fact, from Hasdrubal, who was allowed by his government to quit Spain, thus leaving it exposed to the Romans. This move helped to ensure the final Carthaginian defeat: for Hasdrubal was beaten by the Romans on the banks of the Metaurus, and he himself perished. Hannibal was allowed to retire for four years in the remote hills of Bruttium, in the Italian south. These periods of brooding seem typical, if ominous, throughout Hannibal's career.

Other factors, however, were already entering the situation. There were the kaleidoscopic relations of Rome and the varied powers of Greece, Sicily, and Asia Minor; but this was a war on many intermittent fronts. In 215 B.C. Philip V of Macedon allied himself with Hannibal, no doubt with the intention of winning an eventual foothold in Southern Italy. He was no match for the Romans, and the First Macedonian War (on Philip's territory) ended in his defeat. In Spain, after both brothers Scipio had perished with most of their forces, the younger Scipio (their son and nephew) achieved final victory there (206 B.C.).

Meanwhile Sicily was the scene of blood-letting operations; Hieronymus of Syracuse promised aid to Carthage, but was murdered before this could take effect; but his republican opponents and the pro-Carthage party united to oppose the Roman general Marcellus, who had landed on the island and massacred the inhabitants of Leontini. Marcellus defeated Syracuse through treachery, having broken his word to the Syracusans. The other Sicilian cities, terrorized by Roman atrocities, soon submitted. But Carthage was to be pierced still more vitally, on her own soil. A reluctant Senate was overruled by popular clamour, and permitted Scipio to retaliate upon Carthage the devastation of Italy.

Intrigues among African rulers increased the opportunities of both sides: the Numidian Syphax (Hasdrubal's son-in-law) fought for the Punic cause, while Scipio won over Massinissa of eastern Numidia; a to-and-fro conflict ended in the Roman victory of Cirta. The Carthaginians recalled Hannibal and Mago from Italy; Mago died on the journey; and Hannibal, deserted by his Italian allies, finally met Scipio in a fruitless personal interview. For Scipio's terms had been accepted by both sides; but their enormity (cession of Spain, reduction of the navy to twenty warships, and a huge indemnity) incited a group at Carthage to break off the armistice. The renewed conflict ended in the utter defeat of Carthage at Zama in 202 B.C. Hannibal himself, one of the few survivors, insisted sensibly on an immediate peace. Scipio doubled the previous punishment, while his further clause—that Carthage must not wage war without Rome's consent—led at length to the Third Punic War.

Carthage, by improving the cultivation of her hinterland, began to recover, and Hannibal showed himself a statesman, seeking to democratize his city's government, in both financial and other matters. But this decade of calm with Rome came to a harsh end when Hannibal's opponents accused him before the Roman Senate of collusion with Rome's enemies in the eastern Mediterranean, and even requested a Roman embassy to lay complaints against him before the council of Carthage—a sure sign of amicable relations with Rome. Hannibal fled to Tyre, and thence to Ephesus, the capital of Antiochus III.

He was coldly received and—against his advice—Antiochus, involving himself in the complex chessboard of Greco-Roman politics, answered the appeal of the Aetolians of Asia Minor and declared war against Rome. Hannibal led Antiochus's fleet and was defeated in 190 B.C. The king's military forces were destroyed in the same year at the battle of Magnesia. Rome took a deeper foothold in the Near East, and demanded Hannibal's extradition. He fled once more, this time to the court of Prusias, king of Bithynia, in North-west Asia Minor. Sensing that Prusias, who had enlisted him as a naval commander, would soon yield to Roman pressure, Hannibal took his life by poison.

His memory, and Roman dread of him, remained. Rome was so blinded by past memories that she did nothing when Carthage was invaded by Massinissa, the Numidian king, and Carthage had appealed for "permission to resist". Rome forced on a weakened Carthage the Third Punic War (149-146 B.C.), which ended in the Punic capital being razed to the ground, the survivors sold as slaves, and its site cursed solemnly into eternal desolation. Thus was fulfilled the refrain of the proverbially "honest" Cato who had concluded every speech with the words, "Carthage must be destroyed" (*delenda est Carthago*). The same year, 146 B.C., witnessed the Roman power "settle" the Greek question by razing Corinth to the ground, and selling the Corinthians as slaves. So the excuse—given by G. K. Chesterton and similar apologists—that Carthage had to be destroyed because of its primitive religion which at times included human sacrifice, is seen to be hollow.

Nor could the Rome of crucifixions and, soon, of gladiatorial massacres boast of humaneness. In any case Hannibal stands above such disputes. The calumnies of later Roman historians have been mostly disproved, and there is nothing to show—for instance—that Hannibal transgressed the usages of antique war. Still, the strength of the anti-Hannibal tradition indicates his magnetism. His long career, with its strange interludes of waiting and even of peace, his single-minded patriotism and ultimate series of defeats, mark him as a doomed, lonely figure. Of Hannibal's intensity, significance and tragic influence there can be no doubt.

JULIUS CAESAR

(102–44 B.C.)

THE GREATEST man in the Roman world—yes, there's no doubt that Julius Caesar was *that.* Some historians, and among them those of international authority, have made much greater claims for him. He was the greatest man not only of the Roman world but of antiquity; nay more, looking through the long lists of rulers, kings and emperors and the rest, they have failed to find an equal of this man who refused the style of king but whose name—Caesar—has become the synonym for commanding majesty and power. Great as a general, great as a politician, great as a far-seeing statesman, great as an orator, great as an historian and man of letters—Julius Caesar does indeed, as Shakespeare makes Cassius so grudgingly avow, "bestride the narrow world like a colossus. . . ."

Born in 102 B.C., or it may have been two or three years later, Gaius Julius Caesar, to give him his full name, was of the most ancient and aristocratic lineage. Although he himself, rationalist as he was, must have smiled sometimes at the conceit, there were some who said that he was not only of royal but divine descent, since Venus, the goddess of Love, had married a Trojan prince and so become the mother of the legendary founder of the Julian house. All the same, circumstances and perhaps personal inclinations attached him to the comparatively democratic "Popular" party. His aunt had married Marius, the leader of the *Populares*, and he himself was married as a youth of seventeen to the daughter of Cinna, another leader of the faction that was opposed to the aristocratic party under Sulla, Marius's great rival. A year or two later, when Sulla had become supreme in the state, the young man was ordered to put away his wife. He refused, and his life was saved only through the intercession of powerful friends in Rome. "You fools," Sulla is reported to have told those who pleaded for Caesar, "you little know what you are asking. That young fellow will prove much more dangerous than any number of Mariuses."

But though he had been reprieved, Caesar was far from safe, and for a time he skulked in the mountains until he managed to get across the sea to Asia Minor, where he served in the Roman army that was campaigning against Mithridates, the king of Pontus. At the siege of Mitylene in 80 B.C. he first distinguished himself as a soldier when he saved the life of a hard-pressed comrade. On the death of Sulla two years later, he hurried back to Rome, but for the while he kept himself aloof from the dangerous game of politics and made a career for himself at the bar. His political leanings were shown clearly enough, however, when he ventured to act as prosecutor of one of Sulla's principal lieutenants, who was charged with gross extortion and cruelty when he was governor of the Macedonian province.

To improve himself in rhetoric, Caesar went to Rhodes to take a course of lessons under a celebrated master of that art, and it was probably at about this time that he had his famous encounter with Mediterranean pirates. These ruffians captured the ship in which he was a passenger, and put him to ransom. While his messenger was away collecting the money, Caesar made himself quite at home with his captors. He told them amusing stories, joked with them, joined in their exercises, and, always in the highest good humour, told them what he would do with them when he got the chance. They laughed and joined in the fun. But Caesar was as good as his word. As soon as his ransom had been paid over and he had regained his liberty, he went to Miletus, hired some warships, and made straight back to the pirates' stronghold. He took the place by storm, captured the pirates, and ordered them to be crucified as he had assured them that he would. He also got back the money that had been paid as his ransom. . . .

Still on the fringe of the political arena, Caesar spent the next few years as a gay young man-about-town. His family were not rich, but there were plenty of moneylenders who were glad to accommodate him. He spent money like water, on expensive pleasures—women particularly, since he was as fascinating to them as they were to him—and on building up a body of popular support for the time when he might need it. Then in 68 B.C. he got his first official appointment under the Government, as a *quaestor*, which secured him a seat in the Senate, and in 63 B.C. he was appointed *Pontifex maximus*, a position of great dignity and importance in the religious establishment of the Roman state.

He was on the way up, and his rise was furthered by his successful administration of a province in Spain. So capable did he prove that in 60 B.C. he was chosen by Pompey, the famous general who was then the virtual head of Rome, to form with him and Crassus what is called the 1st Triumvirate. To strengthen the union between himself and Pompey, Caesar gave Pompey his daughter Julia in marriage. Then after a year as Consul, Caesar applied for, and was granted, the proconsulship of Gaul and Illyricum, the Roman dominion that extended from what is now the south of France to the Adriatic. His enemies—and he had plenty—were glad to see him leave Rome, and they no doubt thought that Gaul would prove the grave of his reputation. After all, he had up to now shown no special military gifts. But Caesar knew what he was doing. He realized that the path to power in the Roman State lay through military victory, and he believed, as firmly as he believed in anything, in his "star".

Nor was he wrong. In a series of campaigns he extended the Roman dominion to the Atlantic and what a thousand years later was to be known as the English Channel. Year after year his dispatches to the Government in Rome told of ever larger conquests, of ever greater victories. Sometimes he suffered a reverse, but not often; and when he did, he was relentless in his determination to win the last and decisive battle. His soldiers idolized him, even while they feared him. He demanded great things from them, and saw that he got what he demanded; but he showed them how to do it. He was no behind-the-lines general, ordering his men into the breach while he looked on from a distance. He was always up there, in the front line or very near it. He would march beside his legionaries on foot, and out-tire the best of them. He set the pace for his cavalry. He would seize a spade and give a hand in digging in. He ate the same food as his men did, he drank the same sour wine, he refused to sleep in a tent when his men were out in the cold and wet. He was never a specially strong man, physically: he seems to have been subject to epileptic seizures—but when campaigning he seemed as hard as nails. And of course he was brave. Many and many a time when his men were hard-pressed by the hosts of Gauls they were vastly cheered by the sight of their general hurrying up to their assistance, brandishing his weapons and shouting words of encouragement. "Cowards die many times before their deaths," are among the words that Shakespeare puts into his mouth; "the valiant taste of death but once".

If we would read the history of those years of almost constant campaigning, from 58 to 49 B.C., where better than in those *Commentaries* ("memoirs") of Caesar's own writing, that are among the masterpieces of Latin literature? Of particular interest to us are the chapters describing his two invasions of Britain. The first was in 55 B.C., when the Roman expeditionary force sailed from Boulogne and the men got ashore on the coast at Deal. This first "invasion" was nothing more than a reconnaissance, and after three weeks Caesar went back across the Channel. But in the summer of the next year he returned, and this time he penetrated as far as the valley of the Thames in Middlesex. After considerable fighting, the Britons under Cassivellaunus sued for terms, gave hostages and agreed to pay tribute. Whereupon Caesar sailed back to Gaul, where there was always a risk that the recently subdued natives might make a fresh bid for their independence.

In fact, they did rebel, and for several years Caesar found a worthy match in the young Vercingetorix. Once he was defeated, and the Roman position in Gaul was threatened as it had never been before. But Caesar managed to unite his forces, and at Alesia in 52 B.C. crushed the Gaulish armies and obtained Vercingetorix's surrender. This was the end of resistance to Roman rule: henceforth Gaul was a great and increasingly prosperous province of the Roman realm.

Caesar's victory was opportune, for affairs at Rome demanded his attention. The Triumvirate was on the verge of dissolution. Pompey was estranged, and Crassus had gone off to the east, where he met disaster and death in battle with the Parthians. Caesar's term of office in Gaul was nearing its end, and already his enemies in Rome were talking of what they would do to him when he had returned to civil life. They complained of his having overstepped his authority, of having embarked on grandiose schemes of conquest, of cruelties inflicted on poor inoffensive barbarians. . . .

All these things were reported to Caesar in his camp, and, being the man he was, it is not surprising that he resolved to get in the first blow. Although he had only one legion under his immediate command, and Pompey had been boasting that *he* had only to stamp on the ground and legions would rise up to do his bidding, he resolved to march on Rome. Early in January, 49 B.C., he took the decisive step of crossing the Rubicon, the little river that was the boundary of his command. As he watched his men plunging into the stream he walked up and down the bank, and some who were near said that he muttered the words "*Jacta alea est*", "the die is cast".

Whether he spoke the words or not, the die *was* cast; and in open defiance of Pompey's government, Caesar marched with all speed on the capital. Pompey's support disintegrated, and he was forced to flee overseas. Ceasar entered Rome in triumph.

Almost without a blow Caesar had become master of Rome, and he was forthwith granted dictatorial powers. But Pompey and his friends rallied, and for the next five years Caesar was chiefly engaged in defeating, first, Pompey at Pharsalia in Greece, soon after which

Pompey was murdered in Egypt; next, Pompey's sons in Spain; and then the army of those Roman leaders who constituted what was known as the "senatorial party", i.e., those who clung to the old, time-honoured system of republican rule through the Senate.

A strange interlude in this torrent of campaigning is the time spent by Caesar in Egypt, when he had an affair with the beautiful young Queen Cleopatra, who bore him a son. After this he proceeded to Asia Minor, where Pharnaces, the son and murderer of King Mithridates, was causing trouble. Caesar made short work of *him*. In his message to the Senate he reported: "*Veni, vidi, vici*": "I came, I saw, I conquered".

At length he returned to Rome, and was accorded yet another "triumph"—he had had four already. Vast crowds acclaimed him as he passed in his chariot through the streets on his way to the Capitol. Great hopes were centred upon him, great things were expected of him. The old system of government had broken down: a new system must soon come to birth—but what? We shall never know what vast schemes were fermenting in the brain of the man who was now hailed as *Imperator*, the first of the "emperors" to walk the stage of history, but we may perhaps get some idea of them from what he managed to accomplish in the all too short period that was left to him.

He reformed the calendar, in a way which has endured in its essentials to our own time. He planned the codification of the Roman law. He urged the establishment of public libraries. He reduced the rate of interest charged by money-lenders, and strove to lessen the burdens of taxation on the mass of ordinary citizens. He set up *municipia* in the towns, the forerunners of our local authorities. He dissolved the "clubs" by means of which the political gangsters in Rome had made a mockery of democratic forms. He cut down the issue of free corn to the lazy proletarians of the capital. He planted colonies of his veteran ex-servicemen throughout the land. He had plans drawn up for enriching Rome and the other great cities with splendid buildings, and he ordered a complete geographical survey of the immense region that had been brought within the realm of Rome. He proposed to drain the Pontine marshes, to give Ostia a bigger and better harbour, to dig a canal through the isthmus of Corinth.

These are only some of the schemes that were hatched within his teeming brain, and some of what he not only proposed but actually accomplished. But there was so much more that he wanted to do—if he had time! He was at the top of his form as an administrator, as a captain, as a statesman of outstanding grasp and capacity. And he enjoyed his position, no doubt about it. There was a marked streak of vanity in his make-up. He sanctioned the re-naming of one of the Roman months after him—the month that ever since has been July, and approved the issue of coins bearing his engraved portrait, a distinction granted to none before him. He was glad when they authorized him to wear the splendidly embroidered robe and laurel wreath that were the insignia of great and successful generals—especially perhaps the laurel wreath, since this would serve to disguise the baldness of which he was so painfully conscious. And then there was the occasion when his chief lieutenant Mark Antony offered him the crown—was he altogether sincere when he turned it down, or would he have liked to have been pressed a little harder to accept it? The greatest of men have their little infirmities of mind. . . .

But now the last act of the tremendous drama was about to be played. The "old order" had still plenty of supporters, and though some of these were politicians on the make, others were high-minded patriots who dreamed of a restoration of the ancient ways of government. There were men like Cassius who resented their "petty" condition. Now they joined together in an attempt to bring him down, and foremost among the conspirators was a young man named Brutus who had fought against Caesar and had been pardoned by him and admitted to high office. More than fifty persons were in the plot, and news of it leaked out. Many people warned Caesar of what was afoot, but he took no notice: he believed still in his "star". The day appointed for the murder was the Ides of March (15 March, 44 B.C.), and the night before Caesar's wife had a fearful dream and on waking she urged him not to attend the meeting of the Senate called for that day. Caesar hesitated, but there was important business on the agenda, and he set out for the council-chamber. On his way through the crowded streets several tried to attract his attention with warning messages; a Greek philosopher thrust into his hand a paper giving the names of the conspirators—Caesar took it, glanced at it, and he was still holding it in his hand when he took his seat in the chamber.

Then Brutus and his confederates drew near, and one of them presented a petition for the great man's consideration. Others did the same. Caesar put them on one side, whereupon one of the men gave a pull at his robe. This was the pre-arranged signal, and they all made a rush at him with their daggers.

For the most part they were young men and vigorous, and he was middle-aged and grown heavy and less active than in the days when he had soldiered with his men in Gaul. But he put up a good fight. He struggled, unarmed though he was, tried to push them away, and then struck at them with his metal stilus or pen. Then he saw Brutus was among his assailants. "What, you too, Brutus?" he said, and covering his body with his robe so that he should fall decently, suffered himself to be overborne. He fell, with twenty-three wounds in his body, at the foot of the statue of his great rival Pompey, which, with characteristic magnanimity, he had allowed to be re-erected in the Capitol.

Such was their mad fury, some of the murderers had wounded one another in their bloody work. Now they rushed from the scene, exultingly shouting that the Tyrant was no more! They called upon the people who were there to rejoice with them; but the people hung their heads, or muttered a prayer, or fled.

So Caesar died: "the noblest man", to quote from Shakespeare's immortal lines again, "that ever lived in the tide of times".

CLEOPATRA

(69–30 B.C.)

"Age cannot wither her, nor custom stale
Her infinite variety."

SUCH IS the tribute of Shakespeare in his *Antony and Cleopatra*, and it echoes the fame of centuries. More cynically precise, Pascal remarked that, had Cleopatra's nose been a little different, the history of the world would have been changed. To posterity the last queen of Egypt has indeed stood as a type of glamorous feminine beauty, luxurious in exotic cunning and colourful decadence.

Yet such a judgment does Cleopatra a real injustice. History, sparse in female rulers, has seen few to match her in political astuteness; for some thirty years she played—from her own standpoint—a wise game on the chessboard of Mediterranean politics, competing, amongst others, with the greatest statesmen and generals of Rome. That she should have made two of these—Julius Caesar and Mark Antony—her lovers shows in itself a firm political grasp, though naturally the personal element was not lacking. This is true particularly of her relationship with Antony.

Other queens and empresses have ruled, but few have surpassed Cleopatra; her end, which marked the end also of centuries of Egyptian tradition, and was due both to the childish quarrels among Roman leaders and to her meddling in their strife, was tragic. And we should think of her in tragic, or at least serious, terms, rather than frivolous.

Of course this is not to deny her personal attractiveness, of which she made conscious use as a diplomatic and political weapon. On one point the traditional attitude seems in error: Cleopatra was not specially "beautiful", as we can judge from the coins that have survived. She was rather the bewitching type, an enchantress in voice, movement, manners, mood and conversation; and it is certain that she was well educated, not only in the Egyptian tradition but still more in the Hellenistic art and thought around her. She befriended and subsidized the astronomers of her country, and lent one of them to Julius Caesar to assist in forming the new

Julian Calendar (which remained in use for many a century). Some intellectual quality must have added to her attraction for men; indeed, if she was inferior in this respect to Caesar, she was surely the cultural superior of Mark Antony.

Who, then, was Cleopatra, and how did she emerge on the turbulent international scene? One of the few queens in Egypt's history, and the only one in her own Ptolemaic dynasty, she was without Egyptian blood. A Macedonian Greek, she was descended from the first Ptolemy (Soter, "Saviour"), one of Alexander the Great's generals, who, on Alexander's death in 323 B.C. took charge of the province of Egypt. Themselves Greek in race and custom, the Ptolemies (especially the first two kings) took care to understand and respect Egypt and her traditions. They upheld the native religion and patronized the priesthood; they adopted many Egyptian customs, such as marriage between royal brother and sister; they sought the welfare of their land and brought it peace. While Egypt as a whole remained Egyptian, Alexandria and some other cities nourished a truly cosmopolitan life and culture, to which Greeks, Egyptians, Jews, Phoenicians, and many more, contributed. Alexandria's lighthouse was one of the Seven Wonders of the World, and its library unique.

To such a land, probably the most prosperous of its time, the growing might of Rome looked enviously; while Egypt in turn felt both the value of Roman friendship and an envy of Roman conquests in the Near East. Cleopatra symbolized both these tendencies: to the Romans, the magic and wealth of age-old Egypt, and, in herself, an ambivalent admiration and fear of Rome. She was born in 69 B.C.; curiously enough, the name of her mother is unknown. Cleopatra itself was a fairly common name (an instance is Cleopatra of Jerusalem, one of Herod the Great's wives). Her father was Ptolemy Auletes ("the flute-blower"); in 59 B.C., when Cleopatra was ten years old, he had been expelled by his own subjects, and had come to Rome to seek aid in his conflicts with relatives who had denied him the throne.

The triumvirate then governing Rome (Caesar, Crassus and Pompey) had long coveted Egyptian resources, and Caesar and Crassus proposed open annexation; Ptolemy's request played into Roman hands, with every influential senator intriguing for favour. Ptolemy found himself forced to pay over vast sums (to Caesar alone, 6,000 talents), underwriting huge loans from Roman bankers, who came in effect to control Egypt. Egypt accepted the suzerainty of Rome, to mark which, and to protect both Ptolemy and the usurious interest on the loan, a Roman garrison was stationed on her soil. Ptolemy also had to hand over Cyprus to the Romans.

The restored Ptolemy soon died, leaving his kingdom to his sixteen-year-old daughter Cleopatra and her ten-year-old brother Ptolemy (officially also her husband). But a faction favouring Ptolemy drove her out, and Egypt was governed by his guardian, the eunuch Pothinus, the rhetorician Theodotus, and the military leader Achillas. When Pompey and Caesar quarrelled and Pompey lost the battle of Pharsalia (48 B.C.), he fled to Egypt where Achillas feared that the Roman garrison might go over to him, their old commander. Caesar pursued him with 4,000 men and acted as conqueror.

Cleopatra now manoeuvred herself into the palace, by the ruse of being concealed in a mattress, and the notoriously sensual Caesar yielded to her bewitchment. But Caesar's bland assumption of power affronted both the Ptolemy party and the mass of the people, who, together with Achillas's army (which could be called both Egyptian and Roman), blockaded the palace, cutting off Caesar's communications with the island of Pharos and the sea. Five months of war ensued, with changes of luck on both sides. Caesar at one point had to swim for his life from a sinking ship, holding his notebook above water in his left hand. He also had the Egyptian fleet set alight; the famous library caught fire; and Caesar's men captured the lighthouse while the Egyptians were busy putting out the flames. Eventually, with the help of Mithridates of Pergamus, Caesar was victorious; the boy Ptolemy, trying to escape, was drowned, and Caesar set up Cleopatra and a still younger brother (also a Ptolemy) on the throne. At the same time Caesar married Cleopatra, affecting the religious beliefs which in Egypt linked kingship with divinity. Cleopatra bore him a son, Caesarion, her only child.

Meanwhile there was trouble elsewhere in the empire; and Caesar had just been named Dictator for the second time, and had appointed as Master of the Horse the young, ardent, magnetic Mark Antony. Clearly Caesar's presence at Rome was essential. Why did he delay another four months in Egypt? To consolidate his victory over Egypt, or over its queen? Mainly the latter, for Caesar was an enormously complex character, a fact which in itself must have charmed Cleopatra. His magnetism, his intellect both theoretical and practical, his strange "clemency" and lack of malice (well demonstrated in Bernard Shaw's *Caesar and Cleopatra*), his experience in many fields—all these surely made him a fascinating companion and influenced Cleopatra. We do him an injustice if we think of Caesar purely as an austere statesman and general: on the contrary, he was also incorrigibly sensual, and was notorious in youth for his amours.

With Cleopatra he journeyed down the Nile to Egypt's southernmost frontiers. Then he returned to his "business" elsewhere. But within two years he had invited her, with Caesarion, to Rome, seeking to make her his Roman consort. This, the pride of the Romans, still European and insular in some respects, could hardly stomach. On the model of the Pharaohs, he erected a shrine in the name of Jupiter Julius, with his own statues, and dedicated to Cleopatra, "Queen and Goddess", a temple of Venus Genetrix, the Goddess-Mother. It seemed that, in Egyptian style, he would become a God-King. Such activities increased Roman distrust and Cleopatra went home. Then, in 44 B.C., despite his many excellent reforms, Caesar was assassinated on the Ides of March. This caused an upheaval. For the moment, Rome had avoided a monarchy which would have made her interests subordinate to those of the ever-growing empire. Caesar's death led to civil war and indeed to the triumph of the monarchical principle in the person of Octavian, Caesar's great-nephew and adoptive heir. Mark Antony and Lepidus moved that Caesar's acts be recognized as law and a general amnesty granted.

Antony's arrogance and irresponsibility later provoked much hostility and he narrowly prevented some of his legions deserting to Octavian. Eventually these two forces came to blows and Antony was defeated near Mutina (43 B.C.). He escaped into Gaul, and in this venture showed his best qualities, sharing hardships with the ordinary soldiers. It was not for two more years that Cleopatra was to meet Antony in state and then in love. True, as a girl she had met him fourteen years earlier in Alexandria, and even then Antony's soul had taken fire.

Octavian sought reconciliation with Antony and Lepidus, and near Bologna the three agreed on a five years' triple authority—the "Second Triumvirate"—Antony's sphere of government being the two Gauls (France and Northern Italy), with the exception of the district round Narbonne. The three now embarked on a horrifying series of proscriptions and executions. Meanwhile Caesar's assassins, Brutus and Cassius, had manoeuvred and held the whole of the Eastern Empire. The Triumvirs made war against them, and in the two battles of Philippi were completely victorious (42 B.C.). The spoils were now re-divided: to Antony was allotted the Eastern world, to Octavian the Western, while Lepidus was given Africa.

Antony sped into Greece, there to extract cash from the miserable people of Western Asia. Establishing himself at Tarsus (later St. Paul's birthplace) in midsummer 41 B.C., he received the most momentous visit of his life. The next eleven years were his last, as they were to be Cleopatra's also, and their two lives became mingled as fire with fire. Now began one of the most famous love affairs in history. But our judgment of Cleopatra is partial if we ignore her political astuteness even in such a context.

She dreamt of expansion to the East—Syria, for instance—and she had somehow either to oppose, or to blend with, Roman expansionism. To achieve this, she needed to break the autarchy menacing her in Egypt itself: monopolies of the Royal Bank, of salt and oil, perpetual leases on state lands and so forth. All these she abolished, restoring freedom of trade and the money market. To create the necessary sound currency she reformed the finances of the Temples to the benefit of the state. This reform implied an increased military strength: surely her charms could win this from Antony!

This hard-headed voluptuary sailed up the River Cydnus to be greeted by Antony: attired as Venus, encircled by Cupids and Graces, and resplendent in a barge whose poop was burnished with gold, whose sails were purple and whose silver oars moved to the sound of music. Antony followed her to Alexandria, thus fulfilling both the erotic impulse and his yearning for the gorgeous East. Cleopatra could answer every trait in her lover's nature with superior cunning and finesse. Only his directness, his blend of nobility and coarseness which gained him the devotion of his soldiers, lay outside her competition. It was her sport to deceive Antony: her final ruse, the report of her suicide, led Antony to kill himself.

For two years they enjoyed every luxury life could afford. But Fulvia Antony's fourth wife, herself twice a widow and implacably ambitious, incited Antony's brother to make war on Octavian, furious as she was at being deserted for Cleopatra. At last Antony broke through his lethargy and left for Athens. Fulvia's death soon facilitated a reconciliation between Antony and Octavian, who gave Antony his sister Octavia in marriage. But quarrels reappeared, and after three years Antony returned to Cleopatra.

Cleopatra's influence was now complete. Antony handed her slabs of Roman territory, unfortunately including Jericho, the property of King Herod of Judaea, Antony's friend. Taking advantage of Antony's absence in Parthia, Cleopatra visited Herod, sold him back Jericho with its rich balsam-groves, and sought to seduce him. The brilliant, if cruel, Herod replied with mere courtesy. This insult she never forgave. With Mariamne, Herod's discontented wife, she kept up a correspondence of intrigue and sympathy. At one point she offered Mariamne and her mother refuge in Alexandria, but Herod foiled their plans.

Thus neither Cleopatra nor Antony shone in fidelity. Yet they complemented each other in their diversities and similarities. The latter included sudden rage, a streak of unbalance, "kingliness" and a taste for extreme luxury. If this trifling disgusted Octavian and other Romans, their anger grew into alarm when Antony celebrated a Roman-style triumph in Alexandria, when he aped the god Dionysus and adopted Greek habits, and when he posed as the god Osiris with Cleopatra as Isis, and her head appeared with his on coins. Antony's will leaked out; in it he had directed that he be buried in Cleopatra's mausoleum and that their children succeed to the Egyptian throne.

The climax came in 32 B.C., when Octavian declared war against Cleopatra—really against Antony. Antony then divorced Octavia and married Cleopatra, his sixth wife. Now Cleopatra made a fatal move: though as a woman unused to the reality of war, she still insisted on accompanying her fleet to Actium near Corinth, where Antony and Octavian faced a crucial battle. Before the decisive moment, she escaped with her fleet; and Antony followed suit, fleeing from Octavian into his wife's arms. Enraged at his desertion, his forces went over to Octavian, who soon, as Caesar Augustus, became emperor.

Shakespeare describes how Cleopatra's arts still overcame Antony's fury. For eleven months Octavian left them in nervous peace, which Cleopatra filled with abortive schemes like a flight east of Suez, where Rome's name was unknown. She then started secret negotiations with Octavian, trusting in her charms; Octavian's replies seemed encouraging and Antony locked himself up.

Eventually Octavian landed in Egypt; Antony marched against him, but retired when his fleet deserted him. Dreading his wrath, Cleopatra shut herself up in her mausoleum, and caused Antony to be told the news of her "suicide". He stabbed himself, and when almost dead learned of her last deceit; carried to her place of retreat, he begged to give her "of many thousand kisses the poor last". Heaved up by cords through the window, he was united with her shortly before his death.

Then Cleopatra consented to see Octavian; her intuition (and the words of the Roman envoy) told her that she had nothing to hope for from the emperor, whose courtesy was merely a scheme to bring her to Rome to grace his triumph. She had long been experimenting with poisons and means of death, and the bites of aspic-snakes soon soothed her, as well as her attendants, Charmian and Iras, into oblivion. There:

. . . she looks like sleep,
As she would catch another Antony
In her strong toil of grace.

Egypt's last queen has fascinated the ages. Of the numerous dramatic works based on her story may be mentioned Shakespeare's magnificent *Antony and Cleopatra*, Dryden's *All for Love* and, nearer our own time, the witty *Caesar and Cleopatra* of Bernard Shaw.

AUGUSTUS CAESAR

(63 B.C.–A.D. 14)

SOME MEN are born great, some achieve greatness and some have greatness thrust upon them. Gaius Octavius, generally known by the title bestowed on him by the Roman Senate in 27 B.C. of Augustus, is undoubtedly one of the men who achieved greatness. He was the founder of the Roman Empire. This empire was to last, at its fullest extent and with what is called the Roman Peace virtually unchallenged throughout the known world, for well over two hundred years.

During the reigns of Hadrian which began in A.D. 117 and of the two Antonine emperors who followed Hadrian, the empire was to know its most humanly civilized period. Even before the death of Marcus Aurelius in A.D. 180 the barbarians were beginning to cause alarm on the frontiers, and the third century was to be a time of decline and disorder; but at the beginning of the fourth century a new lease of life was brought temporarily by Diocletian and Constantine, the latter of whom founded the Eastern or Greek Empire. Rome as the Imperial City of the West was to disappear in the fifth century but was to leave behind a memory and an institution, the Holy Roman Empire, which was to haunt the minds of Europeans from Charlemagne to Napoleon.

The genius of Augustus moulded the Roman Empire. It was he who fixed its limits, who forebade, for instance, the Roman commanders of the legions to penetrate into the great oak forests and marshes of Germany. It was he who created its constitution—giving the emperor (Augustus never used the title himself) all ultimate power but preserving the old forms and some of the old powers of the Roman Republic. It was Augustus who made the system of administration which worked so well in Asia Minor, North Africa, Iberia, Gaul and Britain. Augustus Caesar was a patron of the arts on a grand and discerning scale and what is called the Augustan Age saw the genius flower of Vergil and Horace and of the great historians such as Livy. When, during the first two centuries of our era, men realized that they were living in peace and in a world unified by a single civilization which built roads and collected taxes from Asia Minor to the Atlantic, they recognized the work of Augustus.

The man of these great achievements lacked the lustre of many other great men. He was neither bold nor generous; he was not a great warrior and in his fight for power he won by duplicity and trickery and by making the right decisions cautiously. He was to a supreme degree a politic man, never unnecessarily making enemies, but ruthless when it paid to be. He was a cold fish in fact and as such he appears in Shakespeare's two great dramas *Julius Caesar* and *Antony and Cleopatra.* But in addition to his political gifts which are, in human terms, not altogether admirable, he had the ability to make friends, choosing them wisely and sticking to them. A slightly unfavourable view that one could have of him during his period of struggle is redeemed, in his later age, by his devotion to and ability for public affairs.

Physically he was not an imposing man, being about five-foot-seven in height and always negligent of his personal appearance. He did not enjoy good health, suffered from bladder trouble, and could not bear the cold; in winter he wore no less than four tunics with a heavy woollen gown, and beneath them a woollen chest-protector, underpants and woollen garters. He was inclined to doze a great deal in the day and not only when he was old. Sensual but not exaggeratedly so, he was frugal in eating and drinking. He entertained often but carefully and, when necessary, magnificently. Suetonius, the Roman historian who lived in the age of Hadrian but had many contacts with people who had known Augustus, described him, in spite of his physical deficiencies, as "remarkably handsome and of a very graceful gait even as an old man". His picture of Augustus in his old age is as follows:

> "*He always wore so serene an expression whether talking or in repose that a Gallic chief once confessed to his compatriots:* '*When granted an audience with the Emperor during his passage across the Alps, I would have carried out my plan of hurling him over a cliff had not the sight of that tranquil face softened my heart; so I desisted.*' *Augustus's eyes were clear and bright and he liked to believe that they shone with a sort of divine radiance: it gave him profound pleasure if anyone at whom he glanced keenly dropped his head as though dazzled by looking into the sun. In old age however his left eye had only partial vision. His teeth were small, few and decayed; his hair yellowish and rather curly; his eyebrows met above his nose; he had ears of a normal size, a Roman nose and a complexion intermediate between dark and fair.*"

Gaius Octavius was born in 63 B.C. when the Roman Republic was the Great State of the civilized world, though torn with dissensions between rival generals and strife between the Patricians and the Plebs. When Alexander the Great's empire had broken up, the Romans had conquered all Italy rather slowly, from Naples to the north of the peninsula, and built a chain of forts guarding against the warlike Gauls who, in 390 B.C., had beseiged Rome itself. By 146 B.C., Rome, after three savage wars, had destroyed Carthage, the seat of the powerful Semitic commercial empire, selling the inhabitants into slavery and ploughing the blackened ruins of the great city into the soil. Rome had also conquered the Greek cities in the south of the Italian peninsula, Sicily, Iberia and most of Asia Minor. In 65 B.C. the Romans took Jerusalem. In 89 B.C. all free-born Italians were automatically Roman citizens, for, unlike the Greek City states, Rome knew how to assimilate, and this was indeed the essential part of her genius.

The Roman Republic during this period of immense expansion which followed the victory over Carthage was very different from the unified and disciplined aristocratic State which had waged its early wars against the Etruscans and Gauls. Strife between the Senate and the rest of the Roman Plebs, led often by discontented aristocrats, was continuous. It was made inevitable perhaps by the constitution of the Roman Republic which, out of fear of the ancient monarchy which was abolished in the sixth century B.C., split the powers of government between two Consuls, elected annually, and a number of other elected officers.

The aristocratic Republic could not keep peace in its own city at times, though its armies held down the conquered provinces most efficiently. In Augustus's childhood, spent in the country at Velitri where his family came from, two very great military commanders, Pompey the leader of the conservative party, and Julius Caesar, were fighting for supreme power. Julius Caesar had conquered Rome's last and greatest prize, Gaul, defeated Pompey, stamped out all resistance to his power in Africa and Spain and in 45 B.C. had returned to Rome, bringing to the task of re-organizing the government a mind at once supple, imaginative and experienced. He was inclined towards social reform, towards admitting greater representation of the people, a programme which inspired the Gracchi in the old days. With his popularity and his military reputation Caesar could have done anything. But he could not preserve his life and, on the Ides of March in 44 B.C., he was assassinated, falling under the daggers of Brutus and Cassius and a circle of determined defenders of the old order.

Augustus's father's family did not belong to the Patrician Order, although his father, Gaius Octavianus, had been admitted to Senatorial dignity. But, through his mother, the young Octavius was a nephew of Julius Caesar. The great man liked his nephew, used him in the wars and in his will made him his heir, adopting him into the Julian family. Thus after the Roman usage Gaius Octavius became Gaius Julius Caesar Octavius. Augustus was then nineteen. He was immensely rich and he was on the threshold, with some rivals, of supreme power; young as he was, he was determined to stake his chance. Brutus and the party which had opposed Julius Caesar retired from Rome. The young Augustus made himself the leader of the conservatives who hated Mark Antony, the brilliant lieutenant of Julius Caesar who was out and out for the people. There was a period of uneasy peace and then of war between the two avengers of Julius Caesar. However, when many military commanders, including Lepidus, declared themselves for Mark Antony against the conservatives, Augustus decided to desert the conservative faction and join his two rivals. As a member of the Triumvirate Augustus led an army into Asia Minor and defeated Brutus and Cassius at the Battle of Philippi. The empire was then divided between Mark Antony and Augustus, with Lepidus, already shown up as a man of no account, being given Africa until such time as his partners were able to oust him. Augustus chose as his share, Italy, and the poorer provinces of Gaul and Iberia, leaving to Mark Antony the rich lands of the East. Augustus had a lot of fighting to do in mastering his share of the world and he suppressed a revolt in northern Italy led by a brother of Mark Antony with a severity uncommon even in those days. He had to fight intermittently in Italy for eight years.

Mark Antony fell under the sway of Cleopatra, the Queen of Egypt, who had been once a mistress of Julius Caesar. For her he abandoned if not ambition at least the hard work which ambition needs. He still did not take his young partner Octavius very seriously and he repudiated Octavius's sister whom he had married as part of the pact between them. To a letter of reproof from Augustus Mark Antony wrote:

"*What has come over you? Do you object to my sleeping with Cleopatra? But we are married; it is not even as though this is anything new—the affair started nine years ago. And what about you? Are you faithful to Livia Drusilla? My congratulations if, when this letter arrives, you have not been in bed with Tertullia or Terentilla or Rufilla or Salvia Titisenia—or all of them. Does it really matter so much where or with whom you perform the sexual act?*"

War broke out finally between Rome and Egypt and at Actium in 31 B.C. Augustus's fleet defeated that of Antony and Cleopatra. After this battle Antony sued for peace, but Augustus ordered him to commit suicide and satisfied himself that he had obeyed by inspecting the corpse. Augustus was anxious to save Cleopatra as an ornament for his triumph and he actually summoned snake charmers to suck the poison from her self-inflicted wound, supposedly the bite of an asp. Though he allowed the lovers an honourable burial in the same tomb, Augustus put to death Caesarion, the son of Cleopatra and Julius Caesar, as well as Mark Antony's son by his own sister Fulvia. But for some reason or other he spared Mark Antony's children by Cleopatra and brought them up as his own.

The age of Augustus begins after the great battle of Actium. The empire was founded in 27 B.C. when the Senate with the agreement of the Roman people conferred on Augustus the title of Princeps (Prince of the Senate) and Father of his country. Augustus never used the title of Emperor and only, towards the end of his life, allowed altars to be erected to him as a God because he thought it helped to maintain order. He could not, as it were, escape the divine honours which were thrust on him. Retaining under his command the Legions—which were, of course, the source of real power—Augustus carefully preserved the established form of Republican government. From time to time he stood for, and was of course elected, Consul; he attended the Senate's proceedings and like anyone else asked permission to speak or give evidence in a law case; he voted in elections like an ordinary man of the people. The gratitude of the Senate towards a military leader who might have abolished their privileges was founded on obligation. The Equestrian order representing the upper-middle-class, members of which represented the people, felt, in their turn, that Augustus was entirely their man. Huge sums of money were collected for Augustus on his birthdays by popular subscription. Already rich, Augustus often used this money for the beautification of Rome. He rebuilt the temples of the gods. Together with control of the army, he kept under his direct rule all the Roman provinces outside of Italy. He modernized the administration both of Italy and of the empire, introducing accounting systems and bureaucratic methods used long ago in Egypt. He chose all the governors and minor officials, excluding ignorant amateurs of noble houses or adventurers. Two of his friends were of great use to him: one was Maecenas, the rich man who was the patron of Horace and who found Augustus many servants and officials; the other, Marcus Agrippa, his companion in arms and adviser on military and political matters who married Augustus's daughter Julia.

Augustus married three times. The first marriage was of short duration. From his second wife, Scribonia, whom he divorced because she nagged him, he had a daughter Julia. His third wife, Livia, the one woman he truly loved until his death, bore him no children. He adopted the two sons of Agrippa and Julia and had them constantly with him. But both died young and Augustus had to adopt his stepson, Tiberius, as his heir. Tiberius had a dark and vicious character and he lowered the tone of Roman high society when he was emperor. But he was to prove, nevertheless, an able successor so far as the administration of the empire was concerned.

Augustus fell ill during a journey in southern Italy and on the way back to Rome stayed at his father's house at Nola where he died, some say in the very room in which he was born, on 19 August, A.D. 14. His will contained the following clause: "my estate is not large, indeed my heirs will not receive more than one million five hundred thousand gold pieces; for although my friends have bequeathed me some fourteen million in the last twenty years, nearly the whole of this sum, besides what came to me from my father, from my adopted father and others has been used to buttress the national economy." On the day before he died he frequently inquired whether the news of his illness was disturbing people. Suetonius writes: "Augustus called for a mirror, and had his hair combed and his lower jaw, which had fallen from sickness, propped up. Presently he summoned a group of friends and asked—have I played my part in the farce of life creditably enough?—adding a verse used by actors at the end of a play:

> If I have pleased you, kindly signify
> Appreciation with a warm goodbye."

The work of this great man was not only successful in materially re-organizing Rome and its dominions. He undoubtedly aroused a new spirit in the Italians and in other Roman citizens of the past empire. This spirit was a religious devotion to the greatness of Rome. It was not imperial glory or military chauvinism that Vergil expresses in his many verses about the destiny of Rome; it is rather the sense that this city, its people and citizens carry out a mission of ensuring peace and order throughout the world. In some ways this was not very different perhaps from the imperialist feeling in Britain at the end of the reign of Queen Victoria. The Romans felt that they were assuming "the White Man's Burden". Historical comparisons, however, are usually misleading. The Roman Empire was fundamentally different from that of Britain in the nineteenth and early twentieth centuries. Rome's power was based on the assimilation of *élites* and of subject peoples. Rome succeeded in imposing a unified civilization on the world, something Britain never tried to do. Augustus's great achievement, and the one which ensured that his system of government would last in spite of unworthy successors, was that the vast mass of Roman citizens from Mesopotamia to the north of Britain felt that the central power of Rome had become, in the words of H. A. L. Fisher, "consistently helpful, benign and even paternal".

HEROD THE GREAT

(Reigned 40–4 B.C.)

TWENTY CENTURIES of Judaeo-Christian tradition have not unnaturally found in Herod the Great something of an enigma. If he is "great", what then is greatness? One may answer: personality, will-power, historical, political or military importance; the moral element in greatness would seem to be lacking. And indeed Herod was all too often guilty of crime and atrocity, taking advantage of his position to commit or command brutal acts. Yet even here it is possible to exaggerate, or rather to set the whole picture in an unbalanced light; and modern research has certainly revised some of the harsher episodes: for instance, the Massacre of the Innocents, as described by Matthew (Chapter 2) and by no other evangelist, is now regarded as probably false.

As for the other qualities of greatness, there is no doubt but that the founder of the Herodian dynasty (though it lasted for only 140 years) possessed them. At one of the turning-points of the history of the West and the Near East he stands as a leading figure, in close contact with other protagonists—among others, the Roman emperors, the soldier-statesman Antony, the gifted and intriguing Cleopatra, Egypt's queen—and with all the main currents of belief and culture, Jewish, Greek, Roman, Egyptian.

Nor were these contacts, though full of manoeuvres, mere intrigues for power; he genuinely fought, for example, to protect the Jews from Roman oppression, reviving their glories while moderating their dangerous nationalism. It is a measure of his personal astuteness that Jews, in his lifetime and later, regarded him in this light, though this Semitic king was no Jew but an Edomite and an Arab. Again, by his passion for Greek culture and institutions he incarnated the generous, tolerant spirit of that cosmopolitan age; similarly, as the moving spirit behind many splendid buildings and new towns, and as a promoter of trade, he deserved well of his contemporaries. Famous, too, were his personal handsomeness and glamour, derived possibly from his Arab mother; these he bequeathed to his children and grandchildren. Yet, for political reasons, he could withstand the wiles of the almost naked Cleopatra!

In all he did one finds great independence and sense of effect; still more closely can he be compared to an Italian prince of the Renaissance, with the same force of personality, greed for power, sensitive culture and patronage of art, as well as a baffling blend of splendour, refinement, crudity and brutality. Surely such a personality deserves close study.

The origins of Herod, and thus of his whole dynasty, were indeed peculiar. It would seem almost incredible that they should lead to the jealously-guarded throne of David. Many details are obscure, but we know that Herod on his father's side was an Idumaean or Edomite from the country between Egypt and Palestine, containing the coastal town of Askalon, once of Philistine fame, in which Herod's grandfather is said to have been a servant in the temple of Apollo-Melkarth. This blend of Greek and Phoenician religions is certainly a strange background for a future Jewish king. A further tradition asserts that Herod's father was kidnapped by Edomites.

In any case his father, Antipas or Antipater (a name that recurs with some confusion among his many descendants, notably King Herod Antipas), was an outstanding man. Born a temple-cleaning slave, he quickly rose to military and diplomatic activity. With a skill his son was later to show, he manoeuvred his own advancement when Pompey captured Jerusalem in 63 B.C. Pompey made short work of the internecine conflict between the last of the Maccabaeans, and appointed Hyrcanus II ruler, though in fact Antipas wielded the power. Judaea—whose variable territory usually extended from Acre in the north to Idumaea and Egypt in the south—was made a tributary state of Rome. Antipas seized his chance in 48 B.C. to combine loyalty with ambition by aiding Caesar in his conflict with Pompey in Egypt. After Caesar's victory at Pharsalus, he made Antipas Procurator of Palestine, a post comparable to that of a modern Viceroy.

Antipas gave his son Herod the governorship of Galilee. The assassination of Antipas two years later led to Caesar appointing Herod Tetrarch (regional governor) of Judaea. Already he had begun his career of building by founding, or enlarging and adorning, towns like his Galilean capital of Sepphoris, and by erecting fortresses like those at Jotapata in the north, and Masada.

Sepphoris, where Herod lived for so much of his life, merits a short description. Its Hebrew name is Tsipori, from *tsipor* (bird), as the town stands "perched like a bird on the top of a mountain". Herod filled it with beauty: villas, gardens, palaces, a Greek amphitheatre and hippodrome. He followed this Hellenizing style also in Jericho, Samaria (rebuilt), in Caesarea (which he founded), and even in Jerusalem itself. Needless to say such building operations—Augustus mocked that Herod spent as much money on building as if he owned all Syria and Egypt!—pleased the mass of the people to whom they brought employment and prosperity, as well as the less bigoted among the educated; but the pious Jews abhorred the Greek influence which only emphasized the foreign origin, not of course Greek, of their daring *parvenu* ruler.

Herod seems to have been tortured by an ambivalent, love-hate relationship towards the Jewish religion. As a gesture he adopted the Jewish faith, but the inner and outer insecurity of his throne led him to stress his Hebraic sympathies (as in the superb rebuilding of the Temple in Jerusalem) and to defy the representatives of the tradition. Both the priestly hierarchy and the Sanhedrin, or High Council, soon were reduced to a smouldering obedience. Immediately on receiving the Tetrarchate, he daringly opposed the Sanhedrin, who protested against his illegal execution of Ezechias, a bandit leader, and gained his point.

All of which increased Jewish contempt for this descendant of the cursed Ishmael—from whom the Arabs, too, claim descent—the son of Abraham's concubine Hagar, the descendant also of the cunning and detested Esau. Many of Herod's acts of sudden cruelty may be partly explained by his guilty and terrified reaction to his origin and to his subjects' scorn on its account. For his mother Cypros—an Arab, a Nabataean, less Jewish still but less hated for her race—he felt a great devotion: he named his finest palace, at Jericho, after her. From her he probably inherited good looks, charm and generosity. Many critics would perhaps add, his arbitrary "Oriental" despotic cruelty, though of this the Arabs hardly possessed a monopoly.

From the day when, 40 B.C., Octavian (later known as the Emperor Augustus) and Antony together obtained for him the crown of Judaea, Herod's career may be divided into three periods. The first, 40-25 B.C., covers what may be called his years of development; the second, 25-13 B.C., saw the years of royal splendour; while the third, 13-4 B.C., consists largely of domestic troubles and tragedies. The characteristics of each period, however, reappear in the others. Thus in all epochs of his life he betrayed the qualities attributed to him by the Jewish historian, Josephus: "He was such a warrior as could not be withstood"; and "... a man of great barbarity towards all men equally and a slave to his passions."

Domestic tragedies indeed pervaded his entire career; his affection for his brothers Phasael (died in captivity 40 B.C.) and Pheroras (died 5 B.C.) stands out almost uniquely amid his tortuous personal relationships. As to wives, he had ten of them! The five most important were: Doris, daughter of a priest, whom he married in 42 B.C. (their son Antipater he caused to be killed thirty-eight years later, five days before his own death); then Mariamne, granddaughter of Hyrcanus II, from whom he had two sons (likewise murdered) and two daughters—Mariamne he also had slain; then he had another Mariamne, daughter of the high-priest Simon, by whom he had one son; Malthace, whose offspring included the future rulers Archelaus and Antipas; and Cleopatra of Jerusalem, mother of Herod Philippus, later Tetrarch of Ituraea, and the sole member of the line who was universally admired.

In 42 B.C. Parthian horsemen invaded Asia Minor, Syria and Palestine. Jerusalem was captured; Herod's brother Phasael committed suicide and in his memory Herod named the first of the three towers in his new palace at Jerusalem. At the same time the Maccabees, ever hostile to Rome, rose and allied themselves with the conquerors. The Maccabee Antigonus was proclaimed king and Herod fled. First he plunged into the wild rocky desert of Judah. Then he routed Antigonus's troops south-east of Bethlehem.

He now embarked on an exciting journey. His aim was Rome; but first he had to seek help in Alexandria from his friend Antony. Going by fast camel through Beersheba and the mountains, he passed through Raphim into Egypt. Here, unlike the easier-going Antony, he proved himself a match for the scheming Queen Cleopatra. He stood courteously firm against her wiles and proceeded to Rome. There, playing on his country's strategic position and Antigonus's hostility to Rome, he received the greatest prize of his life by being made king of Judaea. He was given Roman troops to suppress any rising of the "fanatical Jews".

He defeated Antigonus at the battle of Arbela. His enemies fled with their families, but Herod pursued them and killed them cruelly. Antigonus was executed at Antioch, and in the next year, 37 B.C., Herod won Jerusalem after stiff resistance. He executed all the members of the Sanhedrin except one whose eyes were put out. Then he married Mariamne, daughter of the widowed Maccabee Queen Alexandra. Beautiful and spirited, Mariamne fell for Herod's brilliance and charm, but politics and cruelty soon upset the marriage. Alexandra resented Herod and in addition had plans for her handsome fifteen-year-old son Aristobulus. Queen

Cleopatra also resented Herod's coolness towards her, and the two ladies conspired. Cleopatra, opposing Herod's expansionism with her own, aimed at possessing all Palestine. With Antony campaigning against the Parthians, she travelled to Jericho, where Herod received her with due splendour, but remained cool towards her sensual advances.

Meanwhile the stiffly pious Alexandra formed an anti-Herod league with Cleopatra. So in 35 B.C. she wrote for Cleopatra's aid in making young Aristobulus high priest. Cleopatra wrote to Antony, who sent his representative Dellius to survey the scene. Dellius schemed to bring Mariamne and Aristobulus to Alexandria, but Antony invited Aristobulus alone. Mariamne was turning against Herod by now because of his cruelty. Alexandra sought to escape with Aristobulus to Egypt, but her plot was foiled. Then Aristobulus was drowned in mysterious circumstances. Antony summoned Herod to explain the situation and Herod's charm won his old friend over. But Herod had begun to bring about his own destruction. The new high priest was a Hellenizing Sadducee, but Herod's passion for things Greek—theatres, sculpture, painting, baths, sports and hippodromes—thus offending the stricter Jews, proved dangerous.

In 31 B.C. Octavian defeated Antony off Actium, near Corinth, in one of the world's most fateful battles. Cleopatra made her escape, and the appalled Herod showed his nerve and skill by visiting Octavian at Rhodes and actually winning over the new victor, who admired his courage and confirmed him as king. But Herod's prudent fears as to his fate at Octavian's hands had made him place his family in safety. As usual, he went too far and handed Mariamne and her mother over to the "care" of two advisers, with orders for the two ladies to be killed if things went badly for Herod with Octavian. One of these advisers revealed the plot; on his triumphant return Herod had him executed.

Then, fearful for his safety, Herod bowed to suggestions that the two ladies were conspiring against his life and had them both murdered. These murders tortured Herod for the rest of his life. Never again was he to be himself. Remorse impelled him to name the finest tower in his new Jerusalem palace after Mariamne. His tormented conscience, added to a disease which provoked hallucinations, also led him to almost insane acts of criminal violence; yet with this there co-existed the keen-sighted, magnificent statesman.

He now began to build: not only fortresses to protect his own power, but he indulged in splendour and beauty for their own sake.

Thirty B.C. saw the beginning of the building of Fort Antonia in Jerusalem; 25 the creation of Caesarea both as a port and as royal residence; 23 his palace by the west gate in Jerusalem; and 20 his Jerusalem Temple, universally praised, and an object of both tourist interest and veneration. Further achievements were the building of Samaria and of Jericho (his Winter Palace, named after his mother Cypros, was excavated as late as 1951), the founding of Sepphoris, complete with Acropolis, hippodrome and Greco-Roman villas, and the building of a temple to Apollo at Rhodes and elsewhere to other pagan gods.

This building activity, perhaps his most inspired and permanent work, procured him popularity with a large number of his subjects, who saw him as the symbol of peace, order and achievement. Even so, by acts of folly he often played into the hands of the Maccabees, Pharisees and nationalists who detested him, even though they would claim him as a Jew when it suited their purposes. An instance is his nocturnal plundering of the treasures in the tombs of David and Solomon, to assist his building programme.

Sickening though it may be to record further murders (like those of two of his sons, or of Pharisees and others who had prophesied the end of his reign, or the possible Massacre of the Innocents), it can at least be noted that Herod bore with exemplary fortitude his appalling illness, a variety of the plague, beginning with a painful inflammation of the back of the head. Mental derangement and even hallucinations followed, aggravated by who knows how much remorse? Yet as a statesman he received and questioned the Three Magi on their way to Bethlehem, also convening a cowed Sanhedrin to answer learned problems.

In 4 B.C. Herod died at Jericho, having first ordered his son and daughter-in-law, Alexas and Salome, to gather all the priests and upper-class Jews to the Jericho race-course and have them massacred. Some 15,000 such persons were thus assembled after his death, but Alexas called off the massacre. Herod was buried with brilliant pomp in his own creation, the Herodian Palace nearby.

Despite his compulsive cruelties, Herod won the admiration of fellow-statesmen, who yet were not blind to his darker side. The Emperor Augustus, playing on the Greek words *hus* (pig), and *huios* (son), jested: "Better be a pig of Herod than a son". For Herod, the ambivalent persecutor of Jews and defender of their interests in the Diaspora, was still Jew enough not to eat pork. In the era of the psychiatrist Herod would have proved a fascinating and rewarding study.

BOUDICCA

(d. A.D. 62)

IN A.D. 59, King Prasutagus died.

He was a good man, proud of his East Anglian kingdom of the Iceni, and of his handsome wife, his two daughters. He admired the Romans who had entered his country, because they were wiser than he, and generous. Already they had made a large grant of money to the kingdom. On his deathbed, then, he had no doubts about making the Roman Emperor co-heir with his two daughters. This would be insurance against having Rome do harm to his kingdom or to his family—though in any case that was unthinkable—and it was a first step to having the kingdom of the Iceni incorporated peacefully within the great Roman province of Britain.

He died in peace—but his scheme failed entirely to achieve its object. No sooner was he dead than the Romans demanded back the "grant" they had made him: it had been nothing of the sort, it was a loan, and repayment had to be made immediately. Co-ownership of a kingdom which they regarded in any case as their own was not repayment. The Emperor Nero—if he ever learnt of this comic legacy—would laugh out loud.

And so, with a senseless brutality, the Romans decided to reclaim their loan in kind, by seizing the royal family, selling it into slavery. As for Prasutagus's widow, she was flogged almost to death, and her two daughters publicly raped.

But the widow, Queen of the Iceni, was no ordinary woman: she was Boudicca (or as it is sometimes spelt, with rather less accuracy, Boadicea) and in the words of the historian Dio: "She was huge of frame, terrifying of aspect and with a harsh voice. A great mass of bright red hair fell to her knees. She wore a great twisted golden necklace, and a tunic of many colours, over which was a thick mantle, fastened by a brooch."

A vivid picture of a Celtic heroine—the most vivid we have. If Boudicca was really like this, the Romans were indeed fools to molest her.

Generations of English schoolboys have waxed indignant over the indignities inflicted on Queen Boudicca. But it is reasonable to guess, knowing the way the Romans ruled their island province, that they were provoked to these atrocities. The Romans of the time were an inferior, subordinate lot in the east of England, led by the biggest Roman fool of all, Catus Decianus; but no doubt Boudicca refused to pay, and perhaps she even—considering her stature and her reputation—threatened.

At this moment in Britain's island history, the Roman governor, a fair-minded man by name Suetonius, was moving his legions westward to attack the Druids of North Wales, the mystic priesthood which had been inciting the Britons to resist. His absence with most of his army was put to good use. Inflamed by the red-haired Boudicca, the rulers of all the little British kingdoms—the Iceni, the Trinovantes, the Catuvellauni and nearly a score of others—got together under her banner. They had between them a number of grievances; and in the understanding phrase of another historian, Tacitus: "They compared grievances and inflamed each other by the constructions they put on them." The Iceni had the obvious one of an outraged royal family; the Trinovantes objected to the behaviour of Roman veterans billeted in Colchester. And so on. Each tribe had something of which it could complain. To cap it all, there was this news of a Roman advance against the cherished Druidic religion, in Anglesey.

And so, from all parts of Britain, a vast army assembled by stealth, small bands of men slipping through the forests to join the forces of vengeance massing in the land of the Iceni.

The legions under Suetonius reached the Menai Strait. Here they were held up briefly by an armed mass of bearded and dishevelled men and women, chanting, waving torches. Then the Romans crossed, by boat and horse, and methodically butchered the Druids, chopped down their sacred groves. And as they were consolidating this feeble victory, news came of revolt in their rear. The Roman town of Colchester had been sacked by Boudicca's forces.

The Roman garrison at Lincoln had sent a relief force of five thousand men taken from the IXth Legion and its auxiliaries—and this too had been ambushed and destroyed.

Suetonius, still in Wales, but preparing with all haste to return, digested the news. There was now no force in the east of England able to do battle with Boudicca, who must by now have an army of tens, perhaps hundreds, of thousands. Colchester had gone, in a sickening wave of atrocity which made the rape of Boudicca's daughters seem a triviality. And soon, for there was no time to save them, London and St. Albans must follow.

Suetonius, two hundred and fifty miles away, started his return with an advance guard of fast cavalry. By forced marches he reached the outskirts of London within a few days. The city had not yet been attacked but the situation was hopeless: the foolish, cowardly, Catus Decianus had fled overseas, taking soldiers with him, and the brash new city, still but twenty years of age, was indefensible. Suetonius had to take the painful decision of surrendering it to angry barbarians in the hope of saving the rest of Roman Britain. There was no hope of getting his main force in position: he had come ahead with cavalry alone, and the bulk of his army was still in Wales. Suetonius retraced footsteps and left the citizens of London to their fate.

Boudicca's army, much of it a rabble, was difficult to command, and even the forceful queen was delayed in her move south after the sacking of Colchester. Had she moved more swiftly, Suetonius himself would have been captured and his army made impotent. But he escaped toWales, and the Britons, thirsting for plunder, took London. There was no resistance, and every kind of foul atrocity was perpetrated. The Roman women, and those British ones friendly to the Romans, or perhaps just unlucky enough to happen to be in Londinium, "had their breasts cut off and stuffed in their mouths, so they appeared to be eating them. Then their bodies were skewered lengthwise on sharp stakes."

Verulamium—St. Albans—followed a few days later. The three chief cities of Roman Britain had been destroyed with 70,000 of their inhabitants massacred. But none of these three was a military position, and this is where the red-haired queen made her big mistake. Vengeance was all very well, but unless she prevented a Roman counter-attack she was doomed. It was possible now for Suetonius to gather strength, get reinforcements, ponder the horrors which were being relayed to him.

But whatever force Suetonius mustered would be minute, in comparison with the vast number which had rallied, were still rallying, to the banner of Boudicca.

The queen, though, had her problems. Her forces were undisciplined and even the force of her personality failed to stop the looting, the wholesale murder that was going on in the three towns and in isolated communities between. She had little sympathy with the victims, but she desperately needed speed, to pursue the Roman general and destroy him before it was too late. Her rabble made that impossible.

At last she got it assembled and set off north-westward after

Suetonius. Wives of the British warriors travelled with the long column in ox-drawn waggons, and they trundled through the Chiltern Hills, on into the Midland forests.

We do not know where Suetonius chose to meet this army, but it seems the choice was his, for he had found a fine defensive position (perhaps near Towcester). It was early autumn. The site he chose—and wherever it was, it must now have been altered out of all recognition by centuries of deforestation and agriculture—had a forest in the rear, a level plain in front, and was set in a narrow defile. The Romans occupied this densely, for it was cramped, with infantry in the centre, cavalry on the wings. The British—the largest force ever to have been assembled in the island—filled up the open plain with waggon-loads of screaming women massed together at the back.

The Romans were nervous and probably very frightened, with this savage host in front, out-numbering them so enormously, but Suetonius held them together, much as Boudicca, in her way, was doing with her own force. "Don't think of booty," he ordered the legions. "Win the battle and you will have everything. Throw your javelins first, on the order, then move in with the short sword."

The British charged.

He waited to the last moment before ordering javelins. Then, in two big volleys, the slender spears sailed high into the air and down into the advancing horde. In the resulting confusion the infantry moved in with vicious short swords, far handier than the long British ones. The British had chariots, in one of which stood Boudicca, long red hair flowing behind her as she led the charge, but almost immediately these were disorganized by a disciplined enemy, and routed by Roman cavalry.

In the end it was waggons, hundred upon hundred of them which, in Celtic tradition, had been brought, loaded with women and supplies, to park behind the warriors, which brought ruin to Boudicca's army. The chariots, forced into unexpected retreat, tangled with the waggons, and the Roman archers, gleefully killing horses and oxen, watched while infantry moved in and finished the work.

It was soon over, with casualties, if we can believe them, of eighty thousand dead on the British side against four hundred on the Roman.

Boudicca escaped, hotly pursued, and knowing there could be no hope of clemency when she was caught. There was nothing for it but to take poison and this, with her two daughters, she did—much as Cleopatra, in a similar predicament, had done a hundred years before.

With the death of Boudicca—with the defeat of her force in battle—the confederacy of Britons ended, but the rebellion continued, tribe by tribe. It had been, for Rome, a major disaster, her three finest towns laid waste, her rule flouted, her citizens massacred. Viewed from Rome, there had been something sadly wrong with Suetonius's handling of the people, and of their revolt: he would have to go. But in the meantime rule would have to be re-established, by as brutal means as necessary. Thousands of mercenaries were rushed across the Channel and the North Sea to bring the provincial forces up to strength, and over. A terrible vengeance was extracted, particularly against the Iceni. Boudicca had taken her own life, but her people would suffer for her, and they did.

Our picture of the barbarian queen is a vivid one, but there are gaps in our knowledge, fancifully sketched, about which we may never know the truth. We know her forces were skilful with the tiny, manoeuvrable, chariots: we also know no British chariot ever had the scythed wheels of legend, which have been fitted to the impossible, bronze, vehicle, in which Boudicca rides along the Thames embankment. The Victorian sculptor Thomas Thornycroft had long dreamed of a colossal work depicting this early heroine. Slowly, lovingly, he planned his vast statue, and was given every encouragement by the Prince Consort. He had completed the plaster cast when he died, and the finished work in bronze was not ready to be mounted on its pedestal until 1902, fifty years after the sculptor's work had begun. In many ways it is a handsome work, but it bears little resemblance to the real Boudicca and practically none to her chariot. The queen's bronze vehicle has been, not inaccurately, likened to "an armoured milk float", and certainly no warrior would have been able to fight from it.

But the idea of Boudicca has long gripped man's imagination. These lines from the poet Cowper (they are on the statue's base) are only a few among many:

"Regions Caesar never knew
Thy posterity shall sway,
Where his eagles never flew,
None invincible as they."

Perhaps the words of Winston Churchill, who knew as much about the British people, present and past, as anyone, may serve to sum up the rebellion by which we remember the red-haired queen in her chariot. "This is probably the most horrible episode which our Island has ever known. We see the crude and corrupt beginning of a higher civilization blotted out by the ferocious uprising of the native tribes. Still, it is the primary right of men to fight and kill for the land they love, and to punish with exceptional severity all members of their own race who have warmed their hands at the invader's hearth."*

**History of the English-Speaking World.*

TRAJAN

(A.D. 53–117)

"I NOW discharge my promise, and complete my design, of writing the history of the Decline and Fall of the Roman Empire, both in the West and the East. The whole period extends from the age of Trajan and the Antonines to the taking of Constantinople by Mohammed the Second——"

So wrote the historian Edward Gibbon in 1788, after the twelve long years he had laboured over this history; the "years of health, of leisure and of perseverance" for which he had prayed when he began. His prayer was answered: he has left us perhaps the finest historical work in the English language.

The Turk, Mohammed II, who, as Gibbon tells us, conquered Constantinople and ended the Roman Empire, was a brilliant general and a wise man, and we consider him in another article. But what can be our excuse for including, in this compendium of great rulers, a Roman Emperor who, according to the greatest authority on the subject, started off a tragic "Decline and Fall"?

The reason is simply that one can fall only from a height: in the reign of the Emperor Trajan the Roman Empire reached that height. In Gibbon's words it reached with him "its full strength and maturity".

It is Trajan's misfortune that as one of the greatest men of antiquity his name is forever linked with the collapse of history's greatest empire. It reached its greatest extent during his lifetime—and from the moment he was taken ill in the year 117, a few months before his death, it tottered to a slow, lingering and ignominious collapse.

In fact, that collapse took rather more than thirteen hundred years: Mohammed II's capture of Constantinople, the last-ditch, eastern, capital of a dying empire, was not until 1453. But the process began at the end of Trajan's life.

Marcus Ulpius Nerva Trajanus was—surprisingly perhaps—a Spaniard, though there was Italian blood in his veins. He was born near Seville in the year A.D. 53. His father was a general of some distinction in the Roman army, an army in which promotion was almost entirely based on merit, whose greatest generals might come from any Roman province between Gaul and Africa. The boy Trajan was keen to emulate him and he succeeded, working his way up from the bottom of the army pyramid to fight under his father's command in several theatres of war and get promotion as a brave and talented officer.

By A.D. 88 he was a man of thirty-five, commanding a legion in his native Spain, having already served as an officer in Germany and in Syria. His fame had spread back to Rome itself, not only to the senate and people, but to the emperor, who was keeping an eye on the career of this brilliant general. That emperor was Nerva, a mild and ineffectual little man, only too conscious that he cut a less imposing figure than his tyrannical predecessor, Domitian. Domitian had been unfortunate enough to get himself assassinated, but he was looked back upon in awe. Nerva was looked down upon —particularly by his own Praetorian Guard—and when this Guard mutinied in Rome at the end of the year 97, he hastily adopted as his successor a man who would be bound to appeal to it and to the Roman army. It was the custom, at this stage of Imperial history, for the emperor to choose his own successor, who need not—indeed, more often, should not—be a near relative: life within the family of an average Roman emperor was not likely to nurture qualities of greatness.

The obvious choice was Trajan, and the army accepted it with delight.

A few months later Nerva was dead. Trajan, good soldier that he was, did not rush to Rome to accept his honour. He had recently been appointed military governor of Upper Germany, he was on a tour of the Rhine and Danube frontier defences, and he completed it, ensuring that the empire would be able to look after itself in the troublesome areas before going to his capital to assume the purple.

His reign lasted twenty years. The empire, as we have seen, reached its greatest extent in those years, for he was above all a brilliant and ambitious general. But he was well aware of his responsibilities in other fields: the magnificent buildings, theatres, libraries, aqueducts and monuments which he ordered to be erected are as fine as any. He even ordered the digging out of the old canal between the Mediterranean and Red Seas. This had been originally made for very small craft in about 2000 B.C. and had fallen into disuse. The Persian Darius had it re-opened in the sixth century B.C., but it soon silted up, grew useless. Under Trajan it became a valuable waterway—though after his death, too, it was allowed to silt up.

Seventeen hundred years later it was reclaimed as "The Suez Canal".

But it is as a just and gallant conqueror that we remember him: his reign was the last major extension of the Roman Empire by conquest. As Gibbon puts it, "he received the education of a soldier and possessed the talents of a general. The peaceful system of his predecessors was interrupted by scenes of war and conquest; and the legions, after a long interval, beheld a military emperor at their head. The first exploits of Trajan were against the Dacians, the most warlike of men, who dwelt beyond the Danube and who, during the reign of Domitian, had insulted with impunity the majesty of Rome. To the strength and fierceness of barbarians they added a contempt for life, which was derived from a warm persuasion of the immortality and transmigration of the soul."

Dangerous indeed: such an enemy, with such a creed; and these inhabitants of what is now Rumania and part Hungary had for many years forced their more civilized neighbours to buy them off with large annual payments of gold. Trajan defeated them, made their land a Roman province. "Decebalus, the Dacian king, approved himself a rival not unworthy of Trajan: nor did he despair of his own and the public fortune till, by the confession of his enemies, he had exhausted every resource both of valour and of policy. This memorable war, with a very short suspension of hostilities, lasted five years; and as the emperor could exert, without control, the whole force of the state, it was terminated by the absolute submission of the barbarians."

Decebalus committed suicide and Trajan, annexing all his lands as a Roman Province, declared a public holiday in Rome: the celebration and feasting in honour of this great victory went on for one hundred and twenty-three days.

Almost immediately after this he moved south-east into what is now Jordan, took the capital, Petra, and the remaining country of the Nabataeans, incorporated them successfully into the Roman Empire.

Parthia is the ancient name for what is now a part of Persia, but in the time of Trajan it was the centre of the large Parthian Empire, sometimes an ally and sometimes a vassal of the Roman. There had been skirmishing on the border between the two empires and in 114 Trajan set off to annex the Parthian Empire. He wintered at Antioch and in the spring of 115 began a brilliant campaign which subjugated almost all of it. He then pressed south along the River Tigris, "in triumph", says Gibbon, "from the mountains of Armenia to the Persian Gulf. He enjoyed the honour of being the first, as he was the last, of the Roman generals who ever navigated that remote sea. His fleets ravaged the coasts of Arabia. Every day the astonished senate received the intelligence of new names and new nations that acknowledged his sway."

But while he was away on this southern conquest, a revolt broke out behind him, in Parthia. He returned to the Parthian capital, Ctesiphon, punished the ring-leaders and appointed a strong, wise man as King of Parthia.

But still: "Trajan was ambitious of fame; and as long as mankind shall continue to bestow more liberal applause on their destroyers than on their benefactors, the thirst of military glory will ever be the vice of the most exalted characters. The praises of Alexander, transmitted by a succession of poets and historians, had kindled a dangerous emulation in the mind of Trajan. Like him, the Roman Emperor undertook an expedition against the nations of the East, but he lamented with a sigh that his advanced age scarcely left him any hope of equalling that renown."

This was true: he had greatly extended the Roman Empire (extended it too far, his successor was to decide), but was in his sixty-fourth year. He fell ill in Parthia, headed back for Rome.

At Selinus in Cilicia, now part of Asiatic Turkey, he died. His body was cremated and the ashes taken to Rome where they were placed inside the tall column he had erected in the Forum Trajanum.

And so, like other great rulers, Trajan died miles from home, victim of one of his own campaigns. He left his empire far larger than it had been on his accession, and Rome a more beautiful city; left behind a well-deserved reputation for fairness, mercy and honesty in addition to that of a great soldier, so that two hundred and fifty years after his death the Roman Senate, greeting a new emperor, could hope that he would "equal the virtue of Trajan".

But by this time the empire over which Trajan had ruled was crumbling on all sides. Trajan perhaps may be blamed for some of this: he chose as his successor the young Publius Aelius Hadrianus. The Emperor Hadrian, as he thus became, on the eleventh of August, 117, was determined to make his empire more manageable, and in order to achieve this he began by abandoning Mesopotamia and Assyria to the Parthians. He adopted a policy—which would have made Trajan's ashes turn over inside his column—of appeasing dissident tribes, so that his empire dwindled further. Soon the River Euphrates was re-established as the eastern boundary.

Among the people Trajan conquered were many Christians, and Christianity has something for which to thank him. It was an age of great cruelty, great religious intolerance, particularly towards the infant religion of Christ. The Emperor Nero had set the tone of the era by massacring Christians in their thousands in the autumn of A.D. 64. There had been a great and grievous fire in Rome—for which some historians hold Nero responsible as incendiary—and the blame for this was laid on the Christians as reason for the massacre. Subsequent emperors dealt harshly with the survivors and with other Christians swallowed up in the empire, but Trajan, as one can see from his correspondence, bent over backwards to be lenient, while carrying out the laws of Rome. The younger Pliny, Roman Governor of Bithynia in Asia Minor, had written to Trajan in the year 112. Should he punish Christians, according to the law, even when no other offences were proved?

"Do like this," wrote Trajan. "Christians are on no account to be sought out. If, however, a man is actually accused and then, after careful process of law, proved to be a Christian, he must be punished. But if he *now* says that he is not a Christian any longer, he is to be pardoned, whatever he may have been in the past."

This—in such a period of history—was generosity indeed. Later emperors were less lenient and there were many mass matyrdoms, notably in the years 250 and 257 under Decius and Valerian. At last, in the fourth century, the Emperor Constantine became a Christian himself and stamped out religious persecution with his Edict of Milan.

HADRIAN

(A.D. 76–138)

FOR NINE people out of ten the vices and follies of the emperors who succeeded the great Augustus, who died in A.D. 14, remain the dominant impression about the early Roman Empire. This applies not only to those whose knowledge is largely drawn from the many popular novels written about Rome, but also to those who in their youth studied the classics and Roman history.

Tacitus, one of the most fascinating historians who have ever lived, contributes greatly to this impression. Tacitus was a stern Republican of the old school and his great and sombre history of the Roman Emperors is concerned with the misdeeds of the wielders of a power whose existence he hated. He is a powerful witness for the prosecution; but a wise judge would sum up the period rather differently. Tiberius, Caligula, Nero and Domitian were, in differing ways, sinister characters, criminally self-indulgent, and they debased Roman society. On Nero's death there was a short period of anarchy, and had this lasted the empire would have been shaken to its foundations. But the vices of the emperors did not alter the administrative machinery which governed the civilized world, nor had their extravagances affected the provinces. In the small market town of Chaeronea, Plutarch could correspond with intellectuals and politicians all over the world and compose his Lives of Greeks and Romans. Egypt knew peace and in Gaul and in far-away Britain cities were founded on the Roman model, complete with temples, baths, amphitheatres and bookshops. Great roads holding the empire together continued to be built.

In any case, the period when there was folly at the top was not a very long one. In A.D. 69 a rough practical soldier, Vespasian, became emperor and there began a period when capable, well-meaning men succeeded each other, each emperor collaborating with and adopting his successor. This period, the Golden Age of the Roman Empire, lasted for 111 years until the death of Marcus Aurelius in A.D. 180.

In the middle of this period, from A.D. 117, reigned the Emperor Hadrian, soldier, administrator, man-of-letters, intellectual; a ruler who more than any other worked to civilize his subjects and who seemed to embody Plato's ideal of the philosopher king. Hadrian indeed had a great love for the strong Greek element in Roman culture. Now like Trajan, his predecessor, the last of the conquering Roman Emperors and a great builder of cities, temples, triumphal arches and aqueducts, Hadrian was a Spaniard, a fact which shows how far the Roman Empire had ceased to be first of all Roman and then Italian and had become world-wide. Hadrian's ancestors, it is true, were Roman, but his family had lived in Spain for well over one hundred and fifty years—so that he would properly be called a Roman-Spaniard in the way that Algerians whose fathers had come from France between 1830 and 1870 were known as French-Algerians. Trajan, and even more Hadrian, felt themselves different from the Italian aristocracy in that they quite naturally thought in terms of the whole empire and considered themselves as citizens, and rulers of an empire, not as the chief men of Rome.

Publius Aelius Hadrianus was born in A.D. 76, lost his father in early youth, one of his guardians being Ulpius Trajanus, who became emperor in A.D. 98. Trajan employed his ward, who was a soldier, on various frontiers, and when Trajan died Hadrian was commanding the Roman army in Asia Minor. Though he was adopted by Trajan, Trajan's intentions never seem to have been absolutely clear as to whether Hadrian was to be his successor. It is said that he became emperor partly because Trajan's wife, Plotina, also a Spaniard, was determined that he should be. Trajan died, as he was leaving Asia Minor for Rome, in a small port of Cilicia. It is possible that Plotina forced the obstinate old man on his deathbed to declare Hadrian his successor, and there is a story that, in a darkened room, Trajan's physician counterfeited his then unconscious patient's voice and read out his last wishes.

Hadrian, in Antioch, was consumed with the anxiety of ambition which was about to be thwarted or realized. He consulted soothsayers and magicians and had brought up from one of the dungeons a prisoner awaiting crucifixion whose throat was slit in his presence by a sorcerer, in the hope that in some way or other the man's soul would reveal the future. Hadrian's army enthusiastically backed him for victory in the imperial stakes. When he was declared emperor, there was no opposition from the Senate or from the people in Rome.

Shortly after his accession, however, when he was away from the capital, four men of consular rank were put to death by the chief of Hadrian's Praetorian guard for conspiring against Hadrian's life. One of these, Lucius Questus, who had been governor of Mauritania, was an old rival of Hadrian and had tried to kill him in a contrived hunting accident. Hadrian on his return was extremely angry at this action, or pretended to be, because it was illegal to punish men of Senatorial rank without the agreement of the Senate. He promised the Senate that such a thing should never happen again. It was obviously part of his policy to build up the prestige of this body which had been severely damaged by its servility towards the unworthy emperors of the past. He strove to maintain what was by now partly a fiction—that the Roman Empire was ruled not only by the Emperor as Princeps or prince of the Senate, but also by its old Republican constitution. Hadrian may also have been alarmed by the conspiracy for, when he placated the Senate, he gave large sums of money to the people and cancelled arrears of taxation, having the evidence of such arrears publicly burnt in the great Forum built by Trajan. Thereafter, Hadrian had no fear of domestic enemies and he spent no less than twelve of the twenty years that he was to be emperor outside of Italy.

The empire over which Hadrian ruled had largely been created by the Roman Republic. On the north-west of the empire was the island of Britain which, though visited by the legions of Julius Caesar, had been largely conquered later by the Emperor Claudius. The frontier of the Roman Empire ran along the Rhine and the Danube to the Black Sea. It embraced Asia Minor west of a frontier with Armenia and along the Euphrates with Mesopotamia. The empire included Palestine and the Arabian Peninsula, Egypt, Libya and all that is now called North Africa; and then it included all the Iberian peninsula and Gaul. The Mediterranean was an entirely Roman sea. Trajan had crossed the Euphrates and had also conquered Armenia; one of Hadrian's first decisions was to give back Mesopotamia and Armenia to their former rulers and so to strengthen the Roman frontier. Trajan had also crossed the Danube and occupied what the Roman cartographers called Dacia which corresponds to modern Rumania and Transylvania. Hadrian thought of retiring from Dacia but for various reasons was unable to do so.

The first of the many journeys which took up the greater part of his reign was to Britain where he built a great rampart from the Tyne to Solway Firth, known as Hadrian's Wall. This was a part of the shrinking policy. During Trajan's reign, and particularly during his Eastern wars, Roman legions had had to be withdrawn from Britain and the IXth legion had been cut to pieces by the Picts and Scots during an uprising. In Eboracum (York) Hadrian, on a green knoll, watched the first levy of British auxiliaries march past him. This was a sign of the times for, before the end of the century, the Roman Empire was desperately enlisting native troops—kinsmen of the very Goths and German tribes who were threatening it. The Roman legions, the bodies of perfectly trained, long-service, heavily armed but quick-marching infantry with their own artillery and cavalry, were getting very thin on the ground. They were no longer able to recruit from the good country stock from which most of their soldiers had come at the beginning of the century.

Hadrian knew that the Roman Empire had not nearly enough men to defend it. He spent a whole winter in Londinium (London). The first Roman Emperor to visit the remote island for any length of time, he was also the first to give long and detailed attention to the British administration. One city had got into debt through building baths on too ambitious a scale; with problems such as this the emperor concerned himself as well as with strategy of the empire.

A great deal is known about Hadrian's character, not only through his public acts but through letters and chronicles and through the work of two near-contemporary historians, the Latin, Spartianus, and the Greek, Dio Cassius. Both of these writers had copies of an autobiography which Hadrian wrote in the latter part of his life and published under an assumed name. Unfortunately all copies of this autobiography disappeared shortly after his death. Hadrian was first of all a man of works, an administrator who, as Roman Emperor, was able to work directly on realizing his dream of unifying the empire. The administrator was concerned with re-organizing the systems of agriculture throughout the empire with increasing shipping and industrial enterprises, with increasing the numbers of professional men such as doctors, lawyers and engineers. Hadrian was a great builder of cities. He was also, and above all, an artist. An historical reconstruction of Hadrian by Marguerite Yourcenar, called *The Memoirs of Hadrian*, describes Hadrian's dominant impulse:

> "*My ideal was contained within the word 'beauty', so difficult to define despite all the evidence of our senses. I felt responsible for sustaining and increasing the beauty of the world. I wanted the new cities to be splendid, spacious and airy, their streets sprayed with clean water, their inhabitants all human beings whose bodies were neither degraded by marks of misery or servitude, nor bloated by vulgar riches; I desired that the schoolboy should recite correctly useful lessons; that the women presiding in their households should move with maternal dignity, expressing both vigour and calm; that*

gymnasiums should be used by youths not unversed in arts and sports; that the orchards should bear the finest fruits and the fields the richest harvests. I desired that the might and majesty of the Roman peace should extend to all; that the most humble traveller might wander from one country or one continent to another without vexatious formalities and without danger, assured everywhere of a minimum of legal protection and culture; that the sea should be furrowed by brave ships and the roads resounding to frequent carriages; that in a world well ordered, the philosophers should have their place and the dancers also. This ideal, modest on the whole, could easily be realized if men would devote to it one part of the energy which they spend on stupid or cruel activities; great good fortune has allowed me a partial fulfilment of my aims during the last quarter of a century."

In Athens, the city he loved most and felt most at home in, he built the temple of Olympian Zeus and restored many old buildings. As an intellectual he was passionately interested in the religions of Greece and Asia Minor and was initiated into the Eleusinian mysteries. It was in Athens that Hadrian received a long missive from the Christian bishop Quadratus. His views about Christians and Christianity are ably summed up in *The Memoirs of Hadrian.* They were those of a highly civilized, highly educated and tolerant man.

"*I read Quadratus's work and was even interested enough to have information collected about the life of the young prophet named Jewus who had founded the Sect, but who died a victim of Jewish intolerance about a hundred years ago. This young sage seems to have left behind him some teachings not unlike those of Orpheus, to whom at times his disciples compare him. I can discern through this teaching the appealing charm of the virtues of simple folk, their kindness, their ingenuousness and their devotion to each other. Within a world which remains, despite all our efforts, hard and indifferent to men's hopes and trials, these small societies for mutual aid offer the unfortunate a source of comfort and support.*"

But Hadrian was aware of what he considered dangers. Glorification of the virtues befitting children and slaves was made, he thought, at the expense of more virile and more intellectual qualities. He felt too that with all the appealing qualities of Christians there was the fierce intransigence of the sectarian in presence of forms of life and of thought which are not his own, the insolent pride which makes him value himself above other men. Hadrian believed that the Christian injunction to men to love one another was too foreign to the nature of man to be followed with sincerity by the average person who, he thought, would never love anyone but himself.

Towards the Jews Hadrian displayed great practical tolerance. He constantly met their leaders and listened to their complaints which he judged understandable but insufficient to explain their refusal to live amicably with the Greeks and Romans in Palestine. Much of Jerusalem had been destroyed by Vespasian in the previous century. Hadrian began the rebuilding of Jerusalem under the name of Aelia Capitolina. Although he favoured treating Jewish susceptibilities with respect he did not succeed in preventing a Jewish revolt in A.D. 132, and at his death relations between the authorities and the Jewish people were in confusion.

As a young man Hadrian married Trajan's niece Sabina, largely as a stepping-stone in his career. She was apparently a cold and rather formal woman. As empress she was not surprisingly annoyed by Hadrian's long absences. She held a court of her own. Hadrian mildly disapproved of certain tendencies among the intellectuals at this court. His marriage was largely a matter of convention. He had affairs with high-born women in Roman society and frequently visited the many places of debauchery in Antioch, Alexandria, Capri and elsewhere. Like many Greeks and Romans, his love was for boys rather than women. His great favourite Antinous died on a journey with Hadrian in Egypt. He had Antinous embalmed and was for long inconsolable. Hadrian founded a city in South Arabia in honour of Antinous. The city was in ruins by the end of the eighteenth century and by the middle of the nineteenth century what remained of its triumphal arches and theatres had been carried off for use in a neighbouring Arab town.

Towards the end of his life, Hadrian named a young patrician of considerable gifts, with whom he had been in love in his youth, as his heir. But Lucius Ceionius died, and Hadrian's choice finally fell on a middle-aged respectable Roman land-owner of great honesty called Arrius Antoninus, the first Antonine emperor. Hadrian insisted that Antoninus should at the same time adopt his successor and that this should be a young man, Annius Varus, who ruled later under the name of Marcus Aurelius.

Hadrian's last years were spent in Rome, where he built his great mausoleum which forms part of the Castello St. Angelo, several temples and his huge villa at Tibur. He disliked the public games, circuses and gladiatorial combats which took place so frequently at Rome, but he learnt to preside over them with equanimity and dignity. A man of the empire, he never felt quite at home in his capital. Throughout his reign he paid immense attention to the betterment of Roman and all human societies. He forbade the sale of slaves for gladiatorial and immoral purposes, and he made the enfranchisement of slaves easier. He abolished the giving of gifts either by rich or poor to the emperor. The authority to collect taxes was no longer sold as an office of profit; taxes were collected throughout the empire by State officials. A postal service was instituted throughout the empire. This soldier who preferred peace as a policy, this aesthete who was also a practical man, was above all a great civilizer, a well-wisher for mankind as a whole. He wrote a number of poems—his best-known, *Animula Vagula Blandula*, translated by Alexander Pope, treats of the human soul as it is about to meet death, a subject always much in his mind.

In his private life, Hadrian showed some of the not-unexpected defects of a man-of-letters who is also an all-powerful ruler. He liked the society of learned men, but he was inclined to be jealous of them and he frequently turned them to ridicule. His character was at times contradictory. Spartianus has described him as "grave and gay, affable and over-dignified, cruel and gentle, mean and generous, only consistent in his inconsistency". Possibly this was written of Hadrian at the time when his personal character showed itself at its most capricious, during a long and painful illness—dropsy of the heart. By the people of Rome he was more feared than loved and, according to Gibbon, the Senate doubted, after he died, whether he should be pronounced a god or a tyrant. The final honours given to his memory were largely procured through the offices of the emperor who succeeded him. This was a somewhat unkind fate for the most capable and the most well-meaning of all the Roman Emperors and the man who worked most steadfastly for the public good. Perhaps, however, the reluctance of the Senate to pronounce him a god was all the same an indirect tribute to the liberal attitude of mind which the Emperor Hadrian had always encouraged.

MARCUS AURELIUS

(121-180)

INSPIRED AND perhaps misled by Gibbon, historians have placed too much emphasis on the alleged causes of the fall of the Roman Empire. More remarkable than its fall was the fact that the Roman Empire held together for so many centuries and bestowed upon its subjects generations of peace, prosperity and security such as they had never experienced before and did not experience again for more than a thousand years.

The empire lasted for five centuries—longer than any other empire in history. For all its faults and deficiencies, it was the most successful empire ever devised by man. It was more successful than the British Empire, because the Romans practised no colour or race bar. Its very existence sets the Romans apart as one of the truly great peoples of history. They were not brilliant intellectuals like the Greeks. They were a practical people: they did not innovate, they adapted. They had a sense of law and justice which has endured through the centuries. The Roman Peace they gave to Europe and North Africa was one of the blessings of history. The fall of their empire was inevitable, part of the process of history and of the evolution of the European races.

In a famous passage in his *Decline and Fall*, Gibbon says that the age of the Antonines was "the period in the history of the world during which the condition of the human race was most happy and prosperous".

Roman civilization was at its zenith. Large, well-built cities, with amphitheatres and great aqueducts whose stately remains astonish us to this day, were connected by means of splendid roads. Their prosperity can be seen in the lavish scale of the public entertainments which had to be paid for out of public funds. Under the wise rule of such emperors as Trajan and the Antonines, the empire grew more humane and more united. Cultural and political harmony was reached, with all the provinces in the empire attaining equal status, as Julius Caesar had originally planned. The age of the Antonines has been called "one of those rare interludes when humanity seems to be given a respite from its self-inflicted sufferings". It achieved what the Middle Ages strove for in its conception of "Christendom", and what the modern world hoped for in the League of Nations and the United Nations.

Under the excellent rule of the Antonines, the empire enjoyed a standard of living not reached again in Europe for many centuries. It increased to its greatest extent under Trajan. After that it slowly declined. But what the Romans had built was so enduring that its disintegration took hundreds of years. It was not, for instance, until A.D. 410 that the Legions finally left Britain.

The beginnings of decline were seen under Marcus Aurelius, when the empire suffered its first serious invasions from the outside, and war and pestilence were brought to the heart of the Roman world.

Marcus Aurelius, the greatest of the Antonines, was born on 25 April, A.D. 121, during the reign of Hadrian, under whose enlightened autocracy the empire was vigorously strengthened. Marcus started life as Marcus Aurelius Annius Verus, after his father Annius Verus who was Prefect of Rome and three times Consul. They were a Spanish family who had received patrician rank under Vespasian. Marcus's father died when he was three months old and the child was brought up by his grandfather, Marcus Annius Verus, a distinguished Senator who was Consul three times, a singular honour.

Annius Verus senior had a splendid mansion in the fashionable Caelian district of Rome and here Marcus spent his tender years in the very best Roman society. Romans had their snobberies as other peoples, and one of them was the necessity of speaking Greek from an early age, Greece being the source of all culture. Roman parents employed Greek girls as wet nurses for their children, with the result that they grew up bi-lingual.

Marcus was a serious and solemn child from infancy, despite being brought up by his grandfather, a genial man with a taste for sports. Emperor Hadrian, who took a great interest in young Marcus, called him Verissimus on account of his academic accomplishments.

Hadrian had adopted as his successor Titus Antoninus Pius, the uncle of Marcus Aurelius, on condition that Antoninus in turn adopted both Marcus, who was then seventeen, and Lucius Verus, then seven, whose father, Aelius Caesar, had originally been intended by Hadrian to be his successor, but who had died before Hadrian.

Antoninus was an experienced administrator, a man of great personal quality and intelligence, and when he adopted Marcus he made the youth break his earlier betrothal to Ceionia Fabia in order to become betrothed to Faustina, who was the one surviving child of Antoninus.

Marcus had already come under the influence of the Stoic philosopher, Apollonius of Chalcedon. Stoicism was the most important school of philosophy at Rome just then, and Marcus was profoundly influenced by it, and was in fact its last great exponent.

The Stoic philosophy has been described as one of endurance rather than of hope, and the word stoic has passed into the English language with this meaning. Stoicism was of course a great deal more than that. For Marcus Aurelius it was a way of life, a pattern of behaviour of the highest ethical and moral kind. It was a philosophy which required an iron will and a spartan mind. It was the philosophy of the intellectual and the aristocrat and embodied all the best Roman attitudes.

A Stoic always died in the finest and most edifying manner. Seneca, forced to commit a Roman suicide, dictated eloquently to his secretary to his last breath, while the poet Lucan, dying a similar death, expired while reciting his own verses.

In the year A.D. 139 Marcus was designated Consul, in preparation for his future role, and took up residence in the House of Tiberias on the Palatine Hill. Here he pursued the simple philosophic life as well as his political duties as Consul and Quaestor to Emperor Antoninus. His consular duties required him to take a leading part in the proceedings of the Senate and the administration of affairs, and he was a member of the Imperial Council which conducted the business of the empire.

He and Faustina were married in A.D. 145. He was twenty-two and had become Consul for the second time. Coins were struck to celebrate the occasion. He also received the title Caesar.

Verus, whom Antoninus had also adopted at the behest of Hadrian, and who was destined to be co-emperor with Marcus, was a very different type of young man. He liked sports and pleasures of all kinds and revelled in the sanguinary gladiatorial spectacles of the circus, while the studious Marcus found the circus boring and always took a book to read.

Antoninus Pius died in A.D. 161 at the age of seventy-five, and his end was as tranquil as his life had been. He commended Marcus to the state as his successor, and said nothing about Verus, well knowing that that young man was not cut out for the imperial role.

However, Marcus had a genuine reluctance to assume supreme power in the empire. His *horror imperii* was partly due to a natural modesty, and he also wished to honour Hadrian's desire that he and Verus should rule jointly after Antoninus. Marcus insisted that

Verus should share the imperial power with him, despite the urging of the Senate that he should take the sole administration.

The Senate bowed to his wishes and decreed the joint imperatorship, and Marcus became Imperator Caesar Marcus Aurelius Antoninus Augustus, while Verus was designated Imperator Caesar Lucius Aurelius Verus Augustus. Marcus, at forty, was plainly the senior partner and was ten years older than his co-emperor.

Their first duty—as of all the Roman emperors—was to secure the support of the Army. They paid a large sum (20,000 sesterces) to the Praetorian Guard in return for their oath of allegiance.

Antoninus, who was deified at his death, left the bulk of his large fortune to his daughter Faustina, who in the year of her husband's accession gave birth to twins, one of whom was the ill-fated Commodus.

At the beginning of the new reign trouble broke out in the empire. The King of Parthia invaded the Roman-protected Kingdom of Armenia, and war was threatening in Britain and on the German frontiers. Neither Verus nor Marcus had any military experience, their training for the purple having been seriously neglected in this important respect.

Nevertheless, Verus, being the younger and more robust, went to take command of the Imperial Armies at the Parthian front, and with him went wise and experienced military advisers. Both the Senate and Marcus were anxious to get Verus away from Rome where his pleasures and immoralities were becoming something of a scandal. It was hoped that army life would reform him.

It did nothing of the kind, of course. Verus took his military duties lightly, and showed more interest in the fleshpots of the Eastern Mediterranean than in the dusty battlefields of distant Parthia. Command of the army was left to more competent and responsible men, which was as well. Verus naturally took the credit for the inevitable Roman victory. The troops hailed their absent commander as Imperator, and he was given the title Armeniacus. By A.D. 166 victory in the East was complete. Verus's contribution to it had been confined to riotous living at Antioch where he revelled in all the Levantine vices.

The victorious army returned home, bringing disaster with it, for it had become seriously infected with the plague in Mesopotamia. As the troops returned to their homes in the various parts of the empire, they spread the pestilence with them and the result was the most widespread plague in all antiquity which had serious economic consequences for Rome.

In A.D. 169 Verus died suddenly of a stroke. Rome was full of rumours of the wildest kind—that Verus had been murdered by Marcus, by his wife, by Marcus's wife—none of which were ever seriously believed.

Marcus Aurelius now ruled alone and was probably relieved to be no longer encumbered by Verus. Marcus, with more experience and confidence, now fully embraced his destiny in true Stoic spirit.

Although the *pax Romana* reigned over the majority of the empire, there was always fighting to be done on the frontiers. In the northern provinces the war against the barbarian intruders was going badly, and Marcus now spent several years fighting with his armies.

In A.D. 170 the Marcomanni, a German tribe, came across the Alps and invaded Italy itself—the first time an invader had been on Italian soil for hundreds of years. Barbarian armies also invaded the Balkans and overran Thrace and Macedonia with much pillage and slaughter. In A.D. 171 the Moors crossed the Straits of Gibraltar and invaded Spain. Marcus's legions took vigorous counter-measures and the invaders were no match for the Roman arms.

In all these wars, alarms and military operations, Marcus was always the fair and temperate ruler who never failed to listen to the advice and opinions of his subordinates. In addition to the mammoth task which occupied his day-to-day life, he found time not only to conduct judicial affairs, but also to write his book *Meditations*, upon which mainly rests his noble reputation as the epitome of the philosopher-king.

He was not a strong man and suffered greatly from the cold of the northern winters. He ate little and developed chest and stomach trouble—probably an ulcer—which gave him great pain. He took a drug called *theriac*, which contained opium, to alleviate the pain. He later found that he could not do without the drug, which suggests that Marcus Aurelius became an opium addict. But he used opium only to ease his constant pain and make him sleep.

His latter years were also troubled by rumours of the unfaithfulness of his wife. According to the stories, Faustina, with that wantonness which seemed not uncommon among the high-born ladies of ancient Rome, disported herself with many lovers. She was said to have had a great fancy for low-born ballet-dancers and gladiators. She had been accused of sexual intimacy with Emperor Verus and even of murdering him. But Rome had always been a hotbed of vicious slander and calumny, particularly about the Imperial family, and Marcus was satisfied that none of the charges was true.

In A.D. 175 Marcus received news that Avidius Cassius, Commander of the Roman Army in Asia, had revolted and proclaimed himself emperor. Faustina was again accused of being behind this. She was reported to be in despair about Marcus's health, and not unreasonably fearful about their son Commodus becoming emperor. But Cassius's revolt came to nothing as he was murdered within three months of his bid for power.

Marcus visited Egypt, Palestine and Syria on a successful journey of pacification, during which time Faustina died at the age of forty-six. She had borne him eleven children. He had always trusted her despite the malicious gossip about her, and he greatly mourned her death, which event was naturally enough surrounded by rumours of the most sensational nature in Rome.

The emperor had been absent from Rome for eight years, and he returned there in A.D. 176 with the object of preparing his son Commodus for the succession. Marcus was fifty-five, in ill health and knew he had not much longer to live. Establishing his son as his successor was perhaps Marcus Aurelius's only act of unwisdom. History has criticized him for sacrificing the well-being of millions to his fond partiality for his worthless son, and for choosing a successor in his own family rather than from among men who were infinitely better qualified to rule. Even if he had been ignorant of Commodus's true character, he must have been aware that the boy had not inherited his virtues and his talents.

The persecution of the Christians has also been held against him as a bitter paradox in such a pure and noble man. Marcus, however, under Roman law as it stood had little option but to take action against the Christians who ostentatiously refused to take part in emperor-worship which was part of the fabric of the Roman state. The emperor was the incarnation of government and his deification was more a political than a religious act. No one really supposes that the irreligious, free-thinking Romans regarded their deified emperors with the same emotional awe and reverence as the Christians regarded their God. The primitive Christians were fanatical and narrow and obsessed with martyrdom. The secrecy of their worship gave rise to scandalous rumours about their practices. They were dead to both the business and the pleasures of the world. Until the rise of the Papacy they contributed nothing to the practical conduct of affairs. To them the Roman Empire was an evil thing and they ardently prayed for its destruction. Persecution was inevitable.

In the last few years of his life Marcus Aurelius had no peace. In A.D. 179 he and Commodus were with the Army on the German frontier where a great victory was won. In March of the following year he was taken seriously ill at Vindobona (Vienna) and he knew his time had come.

The Army loved Marcus, and when they heard they were stricken with grief. He commended Commodus to their protection. On the evening he died a tribune came to him and asked him for the watchword.

Marcus Aurelius said: "Go to the rising son, for I am already setting."

CONSTANTINE THE GREAT

(288?-337)

IN THE summer of A.D. 306 the Roman legions in York, who had with them some troops drawn from Gaul, proclaimed Constantine, the son of their commander Constantius who had just died, as *Caesar et Imperator*. It is not clear whether the soldiers intended to make Constantine the Caesar of Britain and Gaul, or the ruler of the vast Roman Empire. Constantine himself, a prudent but determined young man then in his thirties, may not have made up his mind either. But, after nineteen years of civil war fought in Gaul and then in Italy which his troops invaded rapidly, Constantine became the Roman Emperor, with no one to dispute his absolute sway from Persia to Britain.

His reign is of immense importance for two reasons. He made Christianity the official religion of the Roman Empire and, twenty years after he had crossed from Britain, he decided to remove the seat of government from Rome to the East. He built a city on the Bosphorus on the site of two ancient cities, Chalcedon and Byzantium, which he called Constantinople. This city was to carry on, in a manner of speaking, the Roman Empire in a Greek guise after Italy, Gaul, Britain, Spain and Africa had been lost to the barbarians.

Along with the founding of Constantinople, the reign of Constantine begins a period when the empire becomes distinctly like an Asiatic empire; an all-powerful monarch was addressed as "Lord" and his subjects prostrated themselves on the ground before him. The great Augustus who founded the empire had ruled as *Princeps*' sharing power with the Senate. This principle of government was continued by Trajan and Hadrian, both of whom, and particularly the latter, respected the Republican form of government. But under Constantine this was no more the case and the Roman Empire became in form what it had long been in practice, a despotism.

The emergence of Christianity, the founding of an eastern empire and the transforming of the political institutions of the empire were all the consequences of the terrible events which fell on the Roman Empire after the Golden Age, the reigns of Nerva, Trajan,

Hadrian, Pius Antonius, and Marcus Aurelius. From then, until the arrival to power of Diocletian, a peasant soldier from Illyria who was the predecessor of Constantine, the empire had had twenty-three emperors of whom all but three were killed by their rivals. These emperors were many of them bad, but all were insecure. After the dark and gloomy Commodus, the son of the philosopher-king Marcus Aurelius, it was the legions, from their headquarters in Gaul or Dalmatia or the East, who were liable to choose the Caesar Augustus, either on account of his wealth and generosity or his popularity. One, the Emperor Phillip, in the middle of this troubled period, was alarmed by a revolt which broke out among the legionaries of Dacia shortly after his accession. A stern and courageous Senator named Decius rebuked him and said the revolt would easily collapse. The emperor sent Decius to quell the revolt. But when Decius arrived in Dacia the rebel legions proclaimed him their leader and forced him, or persuaded him, to comply with their wishes. In due course Decius defeated the Imperial Army, put Phillip and his family to death, and was compelled to accept the purple.

It was in this terrible third century that the invasions of the Goths, Visigoths, Vandals, Franks and Alemanni, which were later to overwhelm the Western Empire, began to become a major danger. Already in the reign of Marcus Aurelius the Marcomanni and the Quadri, tribes who lived in Bohemia and Moravia, had broken the Roman peace, invaded Italy and besieged some towns in the north of the peninsula. Throughout the century insecurity was as general as peace had been before; at the end of the century, one of the capable emperors, Aurelian, thought it necessary to fortify Rome itself. Writing of the middle years of this century, the historian Gibbon says:

> "*During that calamitous period, every instant of time was marked, every province of the Roman world was afflicted by barbarous invaders and military tyrants, and the ruined Empire seemed to approach the last and fatal moment of its dissolution.*"

The Roman legions and regular auxiliaries amounted to a force of no more than 650,000 men, a small number to defend so large an empire. It was, however, adequate so long as Roman training and superior Roman weapons were in the hands of tough peasants drawn, at first, from Italy and the hardy regions of Greece and then from Gaul and Spain. But it became impossible to maintain the quality of the far-flung legions or their numbers. The peasant population of Italy had decreased. The birth-rate had fallen. A terrible plague had decimated the population of Italy during the reign of Marcus Aurelius and again at the end of the third century. The instability throughout the territories of the empire meant that able men no longer came forward to serve in the municipalities of the empire. Some of the great Roman roads, the foundation of the imperial military power, fell into disuse through disrepair. Yet, strangely enough, the third century did not witness the dissolution of the Roman Empire. In the East some territory was lost to oriental princes, but substantially the *Imperium* was maintained. Along the Danube and the Rhine, the old limits set by Augustus, Rome preserved her frontiers. In Britain, Hadrian's wall was re-fortified and improved by the Emperor Severus; Constantine's father, on the eve of his death, had just repulsed an invasion of Picts and Scots.

But if the empire was largely maintained, it was necessary to adopt a policy of allowing the barbarians to settle inside the empire and, in return for helping to defend it, to enjoy their own customs, which often remained warlike. The Roman peace and the Roman civilization were becoming threadbare. Unquestionably the great structure was on the verge of collapse when in A.D. 284 the legions stationed on the north-east of Italy made Diocletian, a peasant soldier from Illyria (what is now Yugoslavia), emperor.

Diocletian was the reincarnation of a type of soldier-administrator who had made Rome great from the days of the Republic. Men such as he had recurred sufficiently frequently throughout the life of the empire to save it. Diocletian tackled the two great dangers—the insubordination of the legions, which led to constant civil wars and the instability of the imperial power, and the ever-growing pressure of the barbarians, by one ingenious master-plan. The empire should henceforward be ruled by a college of four men—two imperial rulers, the Augusti, and under them two Caesars who should be their successors in due course. At the same time he de-centralized the military command and the civil administration. Rome became simply the nominal capital of the empire.

From Treves on the Rhine, Constantius, one of the two Caesars, governed Gaul, Britain and Spain; and from Milan another Caesar looked after the provinces of Illyria, Dalmatia and the north-east. The second Augustus was in charge of Africa and Italy, whilst Diocletian himself governed the East from Nicomedia in Asia Minor. From a military point of view, the system was at first remarkably successful. Gaul, which had been particularly disorderly, was pacified. A serious revolt in North Africa was ended and Egypt was reconquered. All the Asian provinces acknowledged the

Roman sway. At the age of fifty-nine, having only once visited Rome which he disliked, and that only for a Triumph, Diocletian and his fellow Augustus, Maximian, abdicated in order to enjoy the pleasures of private life.

The political remodelling of the empire collapsed at once under the effect of rival ambitions. There were at one time no less than six rival Caesars in the field. Constantine's conquest of power was repeating what had happened in the past, and when he emerged finally victorious there was no question of ruling the empire through a college. But there was no going back on Diocletian's obviously correct view that Rome was unsuitable as the centre for the defence of the huge empire against the many pressures, from many sides, of the barbarians.

Constantine had been a protector of the Christians long before he mounted the imperial throne. Like some of the Frankish and Gothic kings of the early Middle Ages, Constantine is said to have had a vision assuring him that it was the Christian god who would give him victory. Indeed Constantine is said by a contemporary historian, Eusebius, to have seen a Flaming Cross with on it the words "By This Conquer" as he was about to cross the Alps in a surprise invasion of Italy in A.D. 312. Constantine's character makes it unlikely that his conversion to Christianity was the result of a vision of this kind or of any genuine spiritual experience similar to that of St. Paul.

In *The Decline and Fall of the Roman Empire*, the great English historian Gibbon has pointed out the curiously discordant and almost irreconcilable elements in the character of Constantine. Of Constantine's admirable qualities he writes:

"*The person, as well as the mind, of Constantine had been enriched by nature with her choicest endowments. His stature was lofty, his countenance majestic, his deportment graceful, his strength and activity were displayed in every manly exercise; from his earliest youth to a very advanced season of life, he preserved the vigour of his constitution by a strict adherence to the domestic virtues of chastity and temperance. He delighted in a social intercourse of familiar conversation, and though he might sometimes indulge his disposition to raillery with less reserve than was required by the severe dignity of his station, the courtesy and liberality of his manners gained the hearts of all who approached him.*"

But yet the man who accomplished the conquest of the empire and its re-organization, and for a while its re-vitalization, was certainly the murderer of his son Crispus, who had become too popular with the people and with the army, of at least one nephew, and of many respectable and intimate friends whom he had begun in his old age to suspect of treachery. He was also probably the murderer of his second wife, Fausta, the mother who bore the son who succeeded him. Seated securely on the throne, the great man of action became, late in life, the easy prey of rumour-mongers and the victim of sycophants. It was, no doubt, this side of Constantine's character which so ardently followed the example of Diocletian in breaking with the austere Roman political traditions and adopting its style of an oriental despot. Not only the inner nature of this great man seemed to have altered after his accession to the throne; he even changed his appearance, and this hardy soldier wore false hair of various colours and loaded himself with diadems, gems, bracelets and rings.

The idea of Constantine as a saintly Christian ruler, which was, not surprisingly, propagated by the Fathers of the Church, is somewhat damaged by the fact that Constantine did not himself become a Christian until he was on his deathbed, in A.D. 337. Constantine's policy towards Christianity must be seen rather as that of a far-sighted ruler than a believer.

So far as statistics are reliable, the Christians at the beginning of the fourth century A.D. did not comprise more than a fifth of the population of the empire and were most numerous in Asia Minor, North Africa and Gaul. The severity of the persecution of Christianity in the reigns of Nero and some emperors in the third century has been greatly exaggerated; the persecution in the reign of Diocletian was undoubtedly far more severe. But Christianity had emerged the stronger from being a persecuted and forbidden religion. The growing insecurity of the third century, the breakdown of values, had no doubt drawn many of the best and most ardent men and women towards a religion of love, which placed its chief accent on the after life. Intelligent men no longer, as in the time of Hadrian, were disposed to dismiss Christianity as a noble philosophy perhaps but one which had a debilitating affect on a virile character. Many of the Fathers of the Church appeared, even to non-Christians, as men of character and remarkable energy. It was Constantine's mind rather than his heart which made him the protector of Christianity. As H. A. L. Fisher writes:

"*The Christians had given their proofs. They had survived persecutions, they were organized. Constantine made up his mind to enlist the support, to control the activities and to appease the dissensions of this influential society . . . The barbarians, the legions, the vast proportion of the civilian population of the West were still pagan. But there was this difference between paganism and*

Christianity, that while the pagans, with polytheistic hospitality, were willing to receive the Christian god, the Christians regarded the pagan divinities as malignant demons . . . To a deserving prince a well-organized and convinced minority fortified by sacred books and a clear-cut creed, might well seem to be a better ally than a superior number of indulgent and various-minded sectaries."

Constantine's services to the Church were immense. He became a lucid mediator in the many disputes between rival Christian sects and, therefore, exerted a direct influence in the formation of Christian dogma. In A.D. 314 the sect of African puritans, known as the Donatists, were cast out of the Church. More important still was the Council of Nicaea held in A.D. 325, the first Ecumenical Council of all Christian churches, which witnessed the rejection of the Arian heresy and the drawing together of Church and State.

Constantine, like Diocletian, was an Illyrian by birth, coming from Nish. He therefore all the more readily saw that the empire could not be defended from Rome and he was determined to choose as the capital of the empire a city which would also be the best strategic defence centre. He decided on the shore of the Bosphorus as the point from which Europe and Asia Minor could best be ruled and defended, and therefore he began to build the great city of Constantinople. Constantine's idea in founding a new capital was not only defensive and military. The new Latin city (Roman senators and knights were encouraged to move to Constantinople) was also to be the first Christian capital of the world. Constantine himself, carrying a lance in his hand, led a great procession which fixed the boundaries of the new city. To those who remonstrated that he was taking in too much land, the emperor is said to have answered: "I shall still advance until He, the invisible Guide who marches before me, bids me to stop." Large as Constantine planned the city, it had to be enlarged not fifty years after his death, so great was the influx of citizens behind the fortified walls.

A description made around A.D. 430 of Constantinople stated that there were, when the city was founded, a Capitol, or school of learning, a circus, 2 theatres, 8 public and 153 private baths, 52 colonnades, 5 granaries, 8 aqueducts or reservoirs of water, 4 spacious halls for the meetings of the Senate or courts of justice, 14 churches, 14 palaces and 4,388 houses which, for their size and beauty, deserved to be distinguished from the multitude of plebeian habitations. It was undoubtedly a splendid city, but the greatest architectural glories such as the Church of Saint Sophia were to be built much later. Constantine's creation was decorated with copies of masterpieces brought from Greece and the great cities of Asia Minor. Its beauty was second-hand, for the decadent Roman Empire had none of the aesthetic vitality and dignity of Athens. It is noteworthy that skilled architects and masons were so hard to find when Constantinople was being built that apprentices had to be trained hastily in special schools set up by the emperor's orders.

Constantinople never became a Latin city and, indeed, shortly after its foundation, the Roman Empire of the West crumbled away before the renewed onslaughts of the barbarians, combined with continued civil wars between Romans. On the other hand, Constantine's child was to stand until the middle of the fifteenth century—for over a thousand years—as a bulwark of Christian and Greek civilization until in 1453 it was captured by the Turks. However much of the character of Constantine may have degenerated in his later years, there can be no doubt of the greatness of his achievements and the sureness of his vision of the future.

ATTILA

(d. 453)

MORE PERHAPS than any other nation, the Huns have a history which is that of their greatest son. We know remarkably little about them before the arrival of Attila and very soon after his death they vanish from the pages of history.

Who were they?

No one really knows. There is a pleasing and convenient theory that they were once the warlike Hsiung-Nu tribes of Asia, referred to in Chinese histories, but there are plenty of good arguments against it, and we can only submit it as a theory. At least one historian has debunked it in the grand manner: "It is a mortal step from the kingdom of the northern Zenghi to the steppes of Russia, and he who takes it is supported on the wings of fancy and not on the ground of fact."

So much for the problem of their coming. As for their going, they left their name behind them, to be applied by the Romans to every wave of savages which assailed them. And we ourselves have been known to use the word "Huns" when we wish to speak evil of our enemies.

Their greatest leader—if greatness be measured by power—was Attila, the "Scourge of God", who reigned less than twenty years and was remembered, in terror, for a thousand. A contemporary summed him up as: "Short, squat, with deep eyes, flat nose and thin beard. He is truculent and blustering, but of simple tastes. While his lieutenants dine off silver and eat luxuries, Attila eats only meat, and off a wooden plate."

Hardly an attractive fellow. But Attila, the Scourge of God, hacked out a place for himself in history, while many of the educated and the beautiful whom he slaughtered have been forgotten.

There is a legend which persists in many East European tongues that years after the Huns were (or were not) the Asian Hsiung-Nu, a large group of them settled in the Caucasus. For a brief period in history they were peaceful folk, tending their cattle and their little ponies. One day a heifer was stung by a gadfly and tore off westward, splashing into the marshy waters of the Strait of Kerch. The herdsman followed it and was surprised to find that the marsh which spread out over the horizon, and had always seemed the western limit of the world, gave way to fertile, rolling plains. He retrieved his frightened heifer, got it back to the land of the Huns, and then told his friends of the paradise he had discovered. A little later the Huns waded over to this eastern Crimea and slaughtered the Goths who lived there.

From now on Hunnish legends, and what little history exists, deal entirely with conquest and slaughter.

We know that in A.D. 395 these new barbarians launched their first big invasion of the Roman Empire, pouring westward over the River Danube. At the same time, they launched a great attack on the Romans' Eastern Empire, based on Constantinople. "Behold, the wolves, not of Arabia, but of the North, were let loose upon us last year from the far-off rocks of Caucasus, and in a little while overran great provinces. How many monasteries were captured, how many streams reddened with human blood! Antioch was besieged, and the other cities washed by the Halys, Cydnus, Orontes and Euphrates. Flocks of captives were dragged away; Arabia, Phoenicia, Palestine and Egypt were taken captive by their terror. Suddenly messengers ran to and fro and the whole East trembled, for swarms of Huns had broken forth from the far distance. They filled the whole earth with slaughter and panic alike as they flitted hither and thither on their swift horses. The Roman Army was away at the time and was detained in Italy owing to the civil wars. May Jesus avert such beasts from the Roman world in the future! They were at hand everywhere before they were expected: by their speed they outstripped rumour, and they took pity neither upon religion nor rank nor age nor wailing childhood. Those who had just begun to live were compelled to die, and in ignorance of their plight would smile amid the drawn swords of the enemy——"

So it was written at the time.

Eventually the Huns were held in the East, though they retained many of the lands they had overrun. Then, at the start of the fifth century, they took another plunge westward. This time they drove other barbarians before them: Vandals and Alans poured westward over the Rhine, fleeing in terror into the Roman province of Gaul, while the Huns at their back laid waste to Germany.

The first Hun we know is Uldis, who in A.D. 408 led another expedition against the Eastern Empire and was narrowly stopped from seizing it all. But it was Uldis who finally made the Romans see that a crash programme of defence must be put in hand immediately: and if it had not been for Uldis and his depredations, the ravages of Attila might have been still greater: there might today be a nation of Hunland.

In about A.D. 432, one Rua enters the pages of history as the leader of the Huns. He sent emissaries to the East Romans demanding tribute, and when these played for time he prepared a massive campaign against them. The empire was saved—for the time being—by Rua's death and the accession of his two nephews, Bleda and Attila. The two young men decided they stood to gain more by repeating their demand for tribute than by waging war, and they summoned Roman emissaries to their city of Margus (now Pozarevac in Yugoslavia) where they parleyed with them, on horseback. The Huns were happiest on the backs of their fleet little horses, but for Romans this was an uncomfortable, indeed undignified, position. Yet it would have been even less dignified to stand on the ground and talk up to the little men, and they remained, like their hosts, unwillingly astride.

Perhaps this accounts for the crippling terms to which they agreed. Old Rua had fixed an annual tribute of three hundred and fifty pounds of gold: Bleda and Attila, with their threat of a devastating campaign, were able to force this up to seven hundred pounds a year, at the same time imposing a number of other conditions in this "Margus Peace" of A.D. 435.

The peace lasted some six years. Then—perhaps the Romans had been dilatory in their tribute—the brothers attacked again, in 441. The Huns razed a number of East Roman cities, including Singidunum, which is now Belgrade. There was a brief truce in 442, but the attack was continued in 443, and the barbarians got to the walls of Constantinople where at last they were held, though they had completely wiped out the large Roman force in the Peninsula of Gallipoli. The Romans sued for peace and now the brothers were able to demand arrears of tribute amounting to some 6,000 pounds of gold. No one dared to question the arithmetic; the huge tribute was handed over, and the annual stipend was now trebled, to 2,100 pounds.

In 445—and the incident is brushed aside in chronicles of the period as being of small account—Attila murdered his brother Bleda and took over the running of what had now become a Confederacy of tribes, by himself. From now on he was an absolute ruler, more absolute and autocratic, perhaps, than any other in history. He planned his campaigns down to the last detail without any advice from his followers; his negotiations, though he might send others to conduct them for him, were planned in the same way, and however long he might allow them to take, Attila knew the outcome from the beginning.

Justice for all his people was in his hands and his alone. A case would be brought to him, sometimes from the farthest part of his shifting, horse-borne empire, and the parties would stand meekly outside the little man's log hut and say their piece. The leader's judgement was given instantly, without reference to anyone else, and it was never questioned. Some of this unquestioning obedience sprang from superstition, which the sharp-witted Attila was quick to use to his own advantage. A few years previously a herdsman had found a very old sword buried in the grass and brought it to the leader. Attila promptly declared that this was the long-lost sword of the War God: fate had decreed that he, Attila, was to inherit it, and from now on none of his campaigns would fail, and no nation—including his own—would be able to stand against him.

In 447 he launched another huge attack—far larger than that of 441—against the Eastern Empire. He devastated the Balkans, went on into Greece. Three years of negotiation then followed. Attila attached great importance to these negotiations: not to their outcome, which he had already planned, but to their duration. He sent as emissaries, when he did not go himself, large parties of his closest lieutenants, who would then be fêted and made much of by the terrified opposition, to return months, sometimes years, later, laden with gifts. This helped ensure the loyalty of the lieutenants, for there was little, apart from tribute gold, which the king of the nomadic Huns could give them.

But slowly, as ideas of luxury and easy-living filtered in, the character of the Hun nation was changing.

A treaty was signed after years of profitable negotiation with the Emperor Theodosius. The Romans agreed to pay still more tribute and evacuate a wide belt south of the Danube, which thus became Hun territory.

A little later Attila turned his attention westward, to Gaul. No doubt he could have overrun the country in a few weeks, but the taste for negotiation had seized him, and he now declared—much as Hitler was to do fifteen hundred years later—that he wanted only the small Visigoth kingdom within Gaul, based on Toulon. He had no more territorial demand than this: the Western Emperor, Valentinian, need have no worries on that score.

We will never know what Attila's real intention had been, for now came the notorious affair of Justa Grata Honoria.

Honoria was the Emperor Valentinian's sister. She got herself involved with a royal steward; the liaison was discovered, and the man put to death. Honoria was then engaged, against her will, to an elderly Roman senator and in her despair wrote to Attila begging him, in return for a large gift of gold, to come and marry her himself.

In fact, her motives were completely political: she had planned to make her steward emperor and become his empress; the elderly senator was a non-starter for this sort of contest; Attila might well succeed. She sent a messenger to him, bearing her ring as proof of authenticity, and he duly delivered his message. What Attila's reaction was at first we do not know, but the messenger was captured on his return and made to pour out the whole dark secret to the Emperor Valentinian before he was executed. Honoria was hastily despatched to her mother, and we hear no more of her.

But now, of course, Attila demanded Honoria as his bride, and with her half of the Western Empire as dowry.

This time he had bitten off more than he could chew. The Romans resisted him and allied themselves with the Visigoths he had already decided to conquer. A war broke out, and at first it seemed the Huns were winning. They nearly captured Orleans before the tide of battle changed dramatically, and the barbarians were flung out of Gaul, in this Attila's first and only defeat.

He recovered sufficiently from this stunning blow to his pride to attack Italy in the following year, where he sacked a number of northern cities, including Milan and Verona. Plague, though, was raging in the peninsula and he decided not to pursue the campaign across the Apennines.

Meanwhile, in August, 450, a new Eastern Emperor had taken over, a strong man who refused flatly to hand over any further annual tribute. Negotiation took place and Attila failed in this as he had failed in battle: the Romans refused to budge, even refused to hand over the usual lavish gifts to the negotiators.

Furious, Attila prepared another attack on the East, an attack so devastating that there would be no doubt left in any Roman mind that his orders were to be obeyed, and promptly.

And now another woman was his undoing, and the undoing of his kingdom.

Just before the campaign was due to begin, in 453, Attila decided to take another wife. She seems to have been German and of great beauty, and we know her name was Ildico. As usual, Attila drank enormously before, during and after the wedding ceremony and retired to the marriage bed in a coma. When he drank his nose often bled, and it had done so more than once during the evening, round a roaring fire. When he was escorted to bed the bleeding had stopped.

But the next day, the sun was high in the sky and starting to descend when Attila's servants decided to enter his room. They forced their way in and found him dead, drenched in blood and with his weeping bride beside him. There was no trace of a wound and there is little doubt that he had suffocated in his sleep during another violent attack of bleeding from the nose.

His body was laid out in a silken tent, and while this was being done the most skilled horsemen in the kingdom galloped round him, chanting war cries. Others slashed their own faces with their swords, so that "the greatest of all warriors should be mourned with no feminine lamentations and no tears, but with the blood of men".

So ended the life of the greatest ruler of the Huns, and with it the strength of the nation. The kingdom was parcelled out among his sons who, unlike Attila and his brother Bleda, chose to rule their portions separately. This, coupled with the growing taste for new luxuries, and Roman inducements for Hun warriors to enter the Imperial armies, weakened the Hun nation so that within a hundred years it had ceased to exist.

But as a name symbolizing ruthlessness, rapacity and skill at arms, it remains, with that of its greatest leader.

JUSTINIAN I

(483–565)

To those for whom history is largely based on English history, Justinian, the Byzantine monarch of the sixth century, warrior and law-giver, who for a brief moment reconquered Italy and Spain from the Barbarians, is a dim and baffling figure, belonging neither to the Ancient world nor to the Middle Ages. He reigned during a period when English history also was dim and baffling, when dates and facts are uncertain.

Constantine, the Roman general who had started his conquest of power from Britain at the beginning of the fourth century, had, for a while, revived the great Roman Empire of which the British people felt themselves to be part. But by the end of that century, Goths, Visigoths, Vandals and then, behind, the Huns had poured into Western Europe, driving before them Franks and Alemanni and the Angles and Saxons. The Roman Empire was no more, and perhaps its final date was 453 when Rome, having been captured by a Gothic chieftain in the pay of the Eastern Emperor in 410, was sacked once again by the Vandals who had settled in North Africa. It was incidentally in Romanized Britain that the invading barbarians met the fiercest resistance and, as Gibbon states in his *Decline and Fall of the Roman Empire*:

> *The continent of Europe and Africa yielded, without resistance, to the barbarians; the British island, alone and unaided, maintained a long and vigorous, although an unsuccessful, struggle against the formidable pirates who, almost at the same instant, assaulted the northern, the eastern and the southern coasts.*

Whilst the western part of the Roman Empire collapsed before the conquering hordes, no victorious Goths entered the eastern capital of Constantinople; and the Roman provinces of Greece and Asia Minor, though disturbed by invasions, still largely accepted the rule of the Eastern Emperors. For this much was due to the great land walls which protected the city on the west and to the supremacy which the Graeco-Romans, and later Greeks only, maintained on the sea. Constantinople was impregnable by land or by sea. Its Greek and oriental population, though lacking the stern civic virtues which had once been those of the Romans, were militarily far more disciplined and skilled than the invading barbarians. The policy of the Greek Empire was directed by civilized and cunning leaders who knew how to use both their military power and their wealth.

Christianity survived in the West, particularly in Italy and in Gaul, where the first Frankish king, Clovis, who united most of France, adopted the religion which had its centre in Rome. It survived because the barbarians accepted it. But Christianity played a major part in preserving the unity of the eastern part of the Roman Empire. It was the bond between Constantinople and the provinces of Asia Minor and Greece. Constantine had been supremely wise in making the second capital of the Roman Empire a new city which would, from its foundation, be a Christian city. Then, in the last half of the fifth century, when the ruin of the western part of the Roman Empire was consummated, and into the beginning of the sixth century, the Eastern Empire was ruled by three men of great ability, Leo I, Zeno and Anastasius I. They were cautious and prudent rulers, men of energy, but who never were led into rash enterprises or wars which would have drained away the resources of their city and the loyal provinces.

When the Emperor Anastasius died in A.D. 518, a violent quarrel over the succession broke out, and civil war seemed likely. But Justinus, the commander of the Imperial guard, was proclaimed Augustus by his soldiers and the Senate acquiesced. Justinus, who reigned as Justin I, was sixty-eight, a quiet unambitious man, virtually illiterate when he came to the throne. Like Diocletian and Constantine he came from Illyria (Yugoslavia today). He reigned for nine years: the only event of note during this period was that he put an end to a schism between the churches of Rome and Constantinople which had lasted for forty years—and was of course to come alive again. Justin I died in A.D. 528 and was succeeded by his nephew Justinian, who, during his uncle's reign, had been thoroughly prepared for taking over the throne.

Justinian had the virtues of a hard-working civil servant of great intellect with the peculiar stamp of what is today called Byzantinism—persistence in aim, refinement of thought and extreme deviousness and cunning. Neither he nor Zeno nor Anastasius were men who appealed to the imagination or the affection of their subjects. At the height of his power, Justinian was derided by rioters in his imperial city and perhaps only saved his throne because of the boldness of his wife, the Empress Theodora. Yet, but for a few internal crises of which these Nika riots were the most dangerous, Justinian exerted an unquestioned authority which was both that of a great military conqueror as well as a pernickety hide-bound official who poked his nose into everything. Under his rule, the economy of the empire prospered, Constantinople grew richer and more beautiful. One of Justinian's passions was building, and particularly the building of churches—the world-famous church of Saint Sophia was one of the fruits of this passion. His most indisputable achievement was the codification of Roman law, which Justinian put in hand and supervised, and which is known as the Corpus Juris Civilis.

The fundamental conception of Roman rule, whether in the time of the republic or of the empire, founded by Augustus, was the importance and indeed the sanctity of Law. The Byzantines respected the law as a written heritage from the past, regulating man's relations to other men and to society, with fervour and with even more intellectual and disputatious passion than the Roman world of Augustus or Hadrian. But by the time of Justinian the huge mass of law had become unwieldy and excessively complicated; it was additionally complicated when Christianity became the official religion of the empire in the fourth century during the reign of Constantine. Justinian's commissions of lawyers headed by the celebrated Tribonian laboured, and laboured successfully in the opinion of posterity, to simplify and co-ordinate this heritage.

About a fourth section of the great corpus of Law, the Novellae, the new laws issued by Justinian subsequent to the publication of the Code, opinions are more divided. The Novellae are far less widely known even by lawyers than the Code. Many historians consider that they show a too rigid conservatism, and amount to a somewhat depressing attempt to enforce religious orthodoxy on every department of life. Nevertheless, the Novellae constitute an attempt to unify Graeco-Roman and Christian traditions, and if they are somewhat over-didactic they are often subtle and sometimes rather curious, as witness the following extract dealing with gardens:

He had been receiving many complaints about the misdoings of gardeners in this blessed city and its suburbs. They form a union which underestimates the value of gardens when the owner is letting them out and tremendously over-estimates the value when the owner is taking them over again and paying compensation for improvements. The prefect of the city is to put an end to this abuse.

Justinian's imperial policy was a more spectacular achievement than his work as a legislator. Justinian deliberately set himself to restore the whole of the Roman Empire. In fact, he never attempted to recover Gaul or Britain. As for Britain, his map-makers and generals seemed to have been doubtful exactly where it was, some considering it an island off the coast of Spain and others confusing "Brittia" with Denmark.

However, Justinian's achievements were considerable. Having defeated Persia, the only menace in the East, in a three-years' war, Justinian sent his greatest general, the justly famed Belisarius, to the conquest of North Africa, which was in the hands of the Vandals. This was carried out successfully and the Vandals were virtually exterminated and, indeed, pass out of history. Italy was in the hands of a number of Gothic kings, many of them Christian and some of them professing respect and even paying homage to the empire. It might have been a wiser policy on the part of Justinian to have tried patiently to persuade or bribe them into a fuller obedience and then perhaps to have forced them to renounce their independence and become servants of the empire. But Justinian decided on conquest and, in A.D. 535, Belisarius landed in Sicily with a small army of some eight thousand soldiers. He captured Naples and Rome with great speed, defeating a number of Gothic armies. The Greek mailed cavalry and mounted archers and the clever use which they made of sea power was invincible at first. By A.D. 540 a Byzantine official, known as the Exarch, nominally ruled Italy from Ravenna on the north-east coast.

But the fortunes of war were to change. Fresh waves of barbarians under a new leader, Totila, poured into Italy, and for a time the Goths recovered all Italy except Ravenna and Ancona. The Byzantines enlisted Goths on their side: this may have made the fighting even more savage, giving it the character of a civil war. According to a Byzantine historian of the time, when the Goths and Burgundians recaptured Milan in A.D. 539 they slaughtered the whole male population of this city, some three hundred thousand. Belisarius, whom the emperor treated with harsh injustice and whom the empress hated, was recalled. Victory went to Justinian in the long run and the power of the Goths was broken for a long time by the generalship of a typically Byzantine figure, an aged eunuch, Narses, who united military ability with a most unscrupulous diplomacy. Italy was devastated by these wars which lasted twenty-eight years. Rome became an impoverished city of a few thousand people with its great entrepôts, granaries and aqueducts in ruins. But Justinian could write to the imperial proclamation which said:

God has permitted me to bring the Persians to conclude peace, to subdue the Vandals, the Alemannis and the Moors, to recover all Italy and Sicily and we have good hope that the Lord will grant us the rest of the Empire which the Romans formerly extended to the limits of the two oceans and which they lost through indolence.

About Justinian's personal character and abilities there is a diversity of opinion among historians. Most agree that he was a man of extraordinary industry and quickness of mind and a man with bold ambitious views. Throughout his life he was accustomed to spend whole nights in study, particularly of his dominant interest which was theology. He was able to choose able servants, though many of them were extremely corrupt, and towards the end of Justinian's reign the economy of the empire suffered from legal plundering as well as from the fact that Justinian undertook too many things at once.

He was obviously very much influenced by his wife Theodora, who was not only empress but a co-sovereign. The subtle Justinian turned to profitable use the fact that he and his wife were known to have differing views on certain subjects. If he was ungrateful and suspicious, he disliked putting people to death and had, on the whole, a reputation for clemency. He was not a morally impressive character, but he was almost certainly not the highly unpleasant individual who emerges from the contemporary account of the historian Procopius. Procopius wrote the official history of Justinian's wars and then later, and perhaps moved by resentment from insufficient favour, the celebrated *Secret History* in which Justinian appears as a monster. Inspired as it is by hatred, pure hatred at moments, Procopius's view of Justinian has to be taken into account because it is that of a contemporary with a first-hand knowledge and that of a man of considerable intelligence. Of Justinian's character Procopius writes:

He was neither particularly tall, nor stunted, but of moderate stature; not thin, however, but slightly plump. His face was round and not uncomely and even after two days fasting his complexion was ruddy. Of his character I could not possibly give a precise description; he was at the same time malevolent and gullible, the type people describe as being both fool and knave. He never spoke the truth himself, but was always crafty both in word and act, and yet always easily at the mercy of those who wish to succeed him. His character showed, indeed, an unusual blend of foolishness and maliciousness. He was full of dissimulation, treachery and affectation; he secretly nurtured resentment, was double-faced, a past-master in the art of acting a part; his tears were always ready, not in response to suffering but because he could always turn them on to help the requirements of the occasion. He was always lying, not just casually but on paper and with the most solemn oaths and that too to his own subjects. As a friend he was faithless, as a foe implacable. He had a consuming passion for murders and money. Such being Justinian's character how could anyone portray it adequately? For these vices, and many others worse than these, he displayed in a superlative degree. It seemed as though nature had taken all the wickedness of all mankind and planted it in the soul of this one man.

If one puts on one side Procopius's attribution of evil motives as the root of Justinian's nature, maybe some of the characteristics described hit off the real man.

Procopius's portrait of the Empress Theodora has been adopted by some serious historians such as Gibbon and has been the basis for many popular novels which show her as one of the most wicked and debased women in the world. In her youth there is little doubt that she was an actress and a prostitute; the two professions in Byzantium were often combined. Justinian made her acquaintance when she had returned from a number of discreditable adventures in Libya and Alexandria. He married her not without having to overcome opposition from the wife of his uncle, the emperor. His love survived his marriage.

She may have been cruel to her enemies and delighted to witness their torture in the dungeons of her palace; she may have had her illegitimate son put out of the way; she was certainly a woman of character and spirit and a faithful wife as well as a useful one to Justinian. She was small in stature with beautiful features, large eyes with a piercing glance. The stiff saintly figure of the contemporary mosaic portrait of the empress in the Apse of San Vitale in Ravenna would appear the antithesis of the monster described by Procopius. The true character lies no doubt somewhere between. Her career shows that she was at the very least an extraordinary woman, born to shine in any situation or in any country.

If, in retrospect, Justinian's great wars may be considered errors, nevertheless they undoubtedly enhanced the renown of the Byzantine Empire, and Justinian's reign as a whole certainly contributed to the astonishing survival of this Greek heir of the Roman Empire. Thanks to Byzantium, the Slavs of the Balkans and of Russia made their first and unforgettable contact with Christian civilization and thought, whilst in Asia many states imitated the institutions of a city which had shown such a high survival value. Though often defeated by the Moslem armies in the early Middle Ages, Byzantium was never conquered by the Saracens and long helped to defend the West. It lasted as a Christian citadel until 1453, when it fell to the Turks.

The greatness of Justinian does not rest on his wars. It rests as much if not more on his great buildings and on his work as a lawgiver. His character is difficult to determine accurately, but he was certainly bigoted, despotic and without many humanly attractive features. In one of his many brilliant summings up of great figures in history, H. A. L. Fisher writes of Justinian:

> *A man so jealous, vain, and irresolute, a man of whom no design was too great, no detail too small, no superstition too absurd, and no subject irrelevant or remote, cannot excite admiration. With almost infinite resources of skill and industry, he appears to have lacked the higher gifts of statesmanship, the energetic will, the true sense of proportion, the capacity for taking unpleasant decisions. Few men whose personality is so uncertain fill a greater place in history. As for a moment we tread beside him through the corridors of the past, we seem to see the shades of night battling with the blood-red sunset of imperial Rome.*

MOHAMMED

(570?–632)

ARABIA AT the close of the sixth century was a country of gross idolatry, superstition, ignorance and intemperance, a divided country where tribe warred with tribe, clan with clan. Miraculously, one man, Mohammed, by the force of his tremendous personality, completely transformed the life of this people; in the incredibly short space of twenty odd years he united them in the bonds of a lasting faith and laid the foundations of a mighty empire.

Mohammed was born in Mecca around A.D. 570. His clan was the powerful Koreish to which all the Meccan notables belonged. The Koreishites were the guardians of the Kaaba within whose walls were 360 crude stone effigies of deities. From all parts of Arabia an endless stream of pilgrims came to Mecca to worship in the holy shrine.

Mohammed, who had lost both parents (his father had died before his birth, his mother when he was six), was brought up by Abu Taleb, his uncle. Abu Taleb was a merchant, and in due course Mohammed became the leader of his caravans. It was during the long journeys across the desert that the contemplative side of his nature was formed.

Honest, truthful, reliable, Mohammed was well-liked in Mecca; although not much of a talker, he had a pleasant manner, a ready laugh and an attractive smile. He was considered an oddity, however, for his kindness to animals and his complete lack of interest in women.

At twenty-three, Mohammed entered the service of a wealthy widow, Khatija. Khatija, who was in her fortieth year but still comely, gradually lost her heart to her handsome young camel-leader, and at the end of two years offered him her hand. Surprisingly, she bore her husband six children, four daughters and two sons, both of whom died at an early age. The marriage was an extremely happy one, and during the twenty-one years that it lasted Mohammed never gave a thought to another woman.

Mohammed's tastes were simple, but while wealth meant nothing to him it gave him leisure for contemplation. Khatija's cousin, an old man named Waraka, had often accompanied him on the caravan journeys; a convert first to Judaism and then Christianity, he had taught Mohammed much about these two religions. Mohammed now had time to ponder over what he had learnt, and the more he pondered the more he doubted the ritual of the Kaaba; finally, he rejected it altogether, utterly convinced that there was only one God. There is nothing strange in the fact that he identified this Supreme Being with Allah, the Lord of the Kaaba, for Allah is a contraction of *al-ilah* which signifies *the* God. A prophet was needed to teach men that Allah alone, the source of everything in this life and the hereafter, should be worshipped, Mohammed told himself: surely, he thought, this prophet would soon appear. . . .

A great need for solitude filled Mohammed. Not far from Mecca was a towering boulder, Mount Hira, and in the small, dark cave in its rocky side he passed long hours in meditation. In A.D. 610 came the Call.

One day, when he was at home, he suddenly began to tremble violently, the sweat broke out all over his body, and he lost consciousness. When he had fully recovered from this mysterious attack, he went as usual to the cave, and at nightfall lay down, wrapped in his mantle, on the rocky floor. He had scarcely closed his eyes when a voice called: "Mohammed!" At first he dared not open his eyes, but it repeated his name so insistently that at last he looked up. There before him stood a shining Being. "Recite!" it commanded him, "Recite in the Name of the Lord who created all things, who created man from a clod; recite in the Name of the Most High who taught man the use of a pen, and taught him what he knew not." Awestruck, Mohammed obeyed, and when he was word-perfect the Being said: "Oh, Mohammed, truly thou art the messenger of Allah, and I am the angel Gabriel." With that, the angel vanished.

Overcome with this stupendous announcement, Mohammed stumbled out of the cave, hastened blindly home, woke Khatija and stammered out the revelation that had been made to him. Instantly, joyfully, she accepted him as Allah's chosen Prophet.

Mohammed had expected a second revelation almost immediately, but when none came he was assailed by doubts and fears. The story goes that in his despair he was about to fling himself from Mount Hira when Gabriel reappeared and said once more: "Truly thou art Mohammed, the Messenger of God." It was, however, through prayer and fasting that Mohammed became convinced that he had not dreamed the Call.

The most important members of Mohammed's first small band of converts were his close friend, Abu Bekr, a rich merchant (Abu Bekr was to become the first Caliph), and Ali, the young son of Abu Taleb, whom Mohammed had taken into his home.

The meetings of these early converts were held in secret, for Mohammed was fully aware of how bitterly the Koreishites would oppose him. "Recite," he would say to his listeners, and they would memorize the words Allah spoke through his mouth. These sayings were later written down, traditionally on palm-leaves, and after Mohammed's death were embodied in a single manuscript: the Koran.

The second revelation made to Mohammed was all-important. In four years he had made only forty converts; now he was commanded: "Rise and Warn."

Mohammed did not hesitate. He summoned the Koreishites to Mount Hira, and standing above them on a rock, an impressive figure in his mantle, with his flashing black eyes and flowing beard, he said solemnly: "I am commanded to warn you that you will know no profit now or hereafter if you do not acknowledge the One and Only God." The enraged Koreishites stopped to hear no more.

From now on Mohammed openly preached Allah's precepts which constituted, in effect, a whole programme of social reform. As more and more Meccans professed the Faith, Islam*, the Koreishites, thoroughly alarmed, took steps to suppress the movement. Led by Abu Sofian, commander of the Meccan army, and Abu Jahl, an important official, the persecution of Mohammed and his followers, the Moslems, began. Mohammed was beaten up and stoned, and many of his supporters were savagely tortured. Unafraid for himself, Mohammed persuaded a band of Moslems to seek safety in Abyssinia; convinced that the Prophet intended to establish an army there, Abu Sofian confined the Prophet and his adherents in a wretched quarter of the city where they remained for three years. Not long after they had been released, worn out by the hardships she had endured, Khatija died.

At fifty, Mohammed found himself a poor man once more, for Khatija's wealth had long vanished. This did not trouble him, for the sole use he had for money was to give it to the needy.

Within a few months of Khatija's death Mohammed married

*The name Islam is derived from *Salama*, meaning peace, submission to God. *Salama* is also the root of Moslem which signifies one who surrenders to Him.

again—married twice. Sawda was middle-aged and plain, the widow of a Moslem who had died for the cause—Mohammed married her to give her a home. Aisha was only seven; she was the daughter of Abu Bekr, and Mohammed probably married her to honour his friend. He did not consummate the marriage until Aisha was ten, an age at which many girls in the East are mature. Aisha was the only virgin he was to know. Mohammed subsequently took six more wives, only one of whom, Zeinab, can be said to have attracted him; he married the other five either to afford them his protection or to ally himself with an important clan. Aisha, spirited and gay, while she could not take Khatija's place in his heart, was his favourite wife. She was barren, and strangely none of the rest bore him a son.

In A.D. 620 an apparently trivial incident proved to be the turning-point in Mohammed's life. A small band of pilgrims from Medina heard him preach. Now the Medinese were vaguely monotheistic owing to the fact that one or two Jewish tribes lived close to their city; they also knew from these Jews that the Hebrew people lived in expectation of a prophet. The impression made by Mohammed on this band of pilgrims was so great that they were convinced he was the prophet in question. The following year, with a large number of their fellow-citizens, they returned to Mecca, embraced Islam, and begged Mohammed to come and dwell amongst them. Their invitation could not have come at a more opportune moment, for the persecution had grown so severe that the Moslems went in daily fear of their lives. Mohammed, therefore, made a pact with the Medinese: provided they would give refuge to his followers, he would do as they wished. The pilgrims gladly agreed.

A.D. 622 was the year of the Hegira, the Year of the Flight or Emigration. One by one, small parties of Moslems secretly left Mecca until finally only a handful remained in the city. Mohammed was making the necessary arrangements for these few to follow the rest when he himself was suddenly forced to flee.

One evening a Moslem burst into the Prophet's house with the dire news that Abu Sofian and Abu Jahl intended to kill him that very night. Ali, snatching off his uncle's cloak, told him and Abu Bekr to fly for their lives; as soon as they had gone, he bolted the door, barred the shutters, and, wrapping himself in the cloak, lay down on the bed. When the would-be assassins arrived they found that they could not get in without using force; peering through a crack in the shutters, they saw the well-known mantle and decided to wait till Mohammed came out in the morning. By the time they discovered they had been tricked, Mohammed and Abu Bekr were some miles away in the desert.

Mohammed had foreseen that if he and Abu Bekr started off for Medina by camel, the Koreishite horsemen sent to pursue them would follow their track and would swiftly overtake them. The fugitives, therefore, had set out on foot by a devious route, and when daylight came they hid in a cave. It so happened that a small band of Koreishites, finding no camel-tracks, made a detour which brought them to this cave; they dismounted, intending to search it, but when they noticed a spider's web across its mouth they decided it was a waste of time.

At last Mohammed and Abu Bekr reached an oasis near Medina where they rested and bathed and gave thanks to Allah. The news of their arrival soon reached the city, and a crowd of Moslems hastened to greet their Prophet. Mounted on an almost white camel, Mohammed rode into Medina where he was given a tumultuous welcome. The legend goes that he said he would build his mosque wherever the camel halted—that intelligent animal stopped at the perfect site! Mohammed had not been long in Medina before Ali, together with the few Moslems who had remained in Mecca, rejoined him in the city.

In spite of repeated demands by Abu Sofian and Abu Jahl, the Medinese obstinately refused to expel the Prophet. Seething with anger, Mohammed's two arch-enemies dispatched skirmishing parties to raid the outskirts of the city. These razzias were common amongst the Arabs, therefore Mohammed saw nothing wrong in ordering his followers to ambush Meccan caravans. When one Meccan was killed, Abu Sofian and Abu Jahl had the pretext they needed for taking up arms against the Moslems.

In A.D. 624, the Fourth Year of the Flight, news reached Mohammed that Abu Jahl with an army of a thousand men was marching towards Medina. Although he had denounced the shedding of blood in battle, the Prophet, as the defender of Islam, proclaimed the Jehad, the Holy War.

Mohammed could only muster some three hundred ill-trained, poorly armed men, but undaunted he led them out of the city and decided to make his stand at Jadr, a sandy plain crossed by a brook which had been dammed here and there to form reservoirs. With inspired strategy, he stationed his "army" round the reservoir nearest to the enemy, and blocked the others; he thus had command of the all-important water supply. Mohammed, watching the progress of the battle from a hill, saw that the Meccan troops, forced to fight in the blazing heat, unable to quench their thirst, were nevertheless gaining the upper hand. Scooping up a handful of sand, he flung it towards them, shouting, "Confusion on your faces!" As if by a miracle, a sudden sandstorm arose and blew straight towards them; stung by the burning grains, they began to fall back. "On, on!" yelled Abu Jahl, and galloping forward, engaged a Moslem leader who, after a furious combat, unseated him and cut off his head with a single sweep of his scimitar. With their leader dead, the Meccan forces withdrew ingloriously.

Abu Sofian swore revenge, and in the Fifth Year of the Flight he marched against the Moslems with a far larger army. This second battle took place at Mount Uhud. Mohammed, who had disposed his small force as brilliantly as at Jadr, had given his archers strict orders not to move from their position. Unfortunately, as the enemy reeled back beneath the onslaught of the Moslem swordsmen, the archers disobeyed him and rushed forward to attack, thus leaving a gap through which the Meccan soldiers poured. Mohammed, as he galloped into the thick of the mêlée to rally his men, crashed to the ground beneath a hail of spears and javelins; Abu Sofian saw him fall, and shouted aloud in triumph, but after the Moslems had been forced to retreat to Medina, he searched in vain for Mohammed's body amongst the slain. It was not until he was on his way back that he learned that, far from being killed, Mohammed had only been slightly wounded. Furious with rage, as soon as he had mustered a huge army he set out to take Medina by force.

A Persian convert, experienced in siege warfare, saved the city. He told the defenders to dig a trench too wide for a horse to leap across; thus when the Meccan troops galloped forward to attack, they found themselves separated from the walls by this moat, from behind which the Moslem archers shot their arrows with deadly accuracy. Day after day they vainly returned to the assault; night after night they shivered in their camp in the bitter winter weather. Then the rain came pelting down, and when a sudden tearing wind blew down their tents, causing their horses to stampede, they retreated in wild disorder.

After this humiliating failure to take Medina, Meccan prestige fell very low, while that of the Prophet soared. All the tribes in the vicinity of the city rallied to him and embraced Islam. He became so powerful that Abu Sofian was forced to conclude a treaty with him, which among other concessions gave him the right to lead Medinese pilgrimages to Mecca. An infringement of this treaty roused Mohammed's just anger, and in the Seventh Year of the Flight he marched on the Holy City.

As Mohammed advanced across the desert the Bedouins flocked to join him; it was with an army ten thousand strong that he reached the gates of Mecca. Abu Sofian surrendered abjectly, and the Prophet entered the city. There was no bloodshed—Mohammed even spared the life of his arch-enemy.

Once within the walls, Mohammed donned the pilgrim's white robe, and with a party of his followers similarly attired made his way to the Kaaba. One by one the stone idols were ground to powder; the moment that Mohammed had dreamed of so long had arrived at last.

Abu Sofian and all the Meccans professed Islam. From Medina, Mohammed, now virtually ruler of Arabia, dispatched ambassadors to Rome, Egypt, Persia, Abyssinia to spread the Faith.

The Tenth Year of the Flight saw what was to become known as the Farewell Pilgrimage. Forty thousand pilgrims followed Mohammed to Mount Arafat; from its summit as dawn broke, he led them in prayer and recited to them from the Koran. Then in a loud voice he cried: "Oh Lord, I have delivered my message and accomplished my work."

Not many months after his return to Medina from this pilgrimage his health began to fail. In A.D. 632, the Eleventh Year of the Flight, Mohammed died with his head in the lap of Aisha, his favourite wife.

Of all great leaders, none has been so much maligned as Mohammed. Many of his detractors have called him an arch-impostor, an accusation to which his tremendous achievement gives the lie. Only a man of burning sincerity, utter integrity, could have established a Faith which today draws more converts than any other religion.

ABD AL-RAHMAN

(d. 788)

WHEN THE Abbasides (descendants of Mohammed's uncle, Abbas) overthrew the Omayyad Caliphate in Syria in 750, two brothers fled to escape the ensuing massacre and sought refuge in a village near the Euphrates. Run to earth, they plunged desperately into the river. The elder, eighteen, managed to struggle to the far bank. Exhausted and dripping, he looked back for his thirteen-year-old brother to see that the youngster had been overtaken and hauled back; a moment later he was beheaded before the horrified watcher's eyes.

The surviving brother was Abd al-Rahman, and this grim tragedy was to mark his first step on a road that was destined from then on to be punctuated with violence and peril, but which, nevertheless, was to lead the young fugitive to great eminence and power as founder of the Moorish emirate (later caliphate) of Cordoba, in Spain.

Abd al-Rahman's belief in his destiny had been deep-rooted since a day when, as a child, a prophecy had been voiced in his hearing by his great-uncle, Maslama ben Abd el Malik, who had looked in to see his grandfather, the caliph Hisham.

The caliph had been on the point of sending his grandson away, but the great-uncle had restrained him, saying: "Let the child be, for I see in him the man of the Omayyads who will revive this dynasty after its fall."

From that moment, Abd al-Rahman observed that his distinguished grandfather seemed to display a special partiality towards him.

After his breathless escape from the Abbasides, Abd al-Rahman became a wanderer. In time he got to Palestine and then crossed Egypt into Ifrikia, following the established caravan route. He stayed for a while at Kaironan, in Tunisia, until suddenly arrested and brought before the Governor of Ifrikia, Ibn Habib. He was recognized by a former servant of his great uncle who promptly proclaimed him as "destined to conquer Spain, and no doubt Africa as well". He declared that it had been prophesied that the conqueror would have two curls upon his brow. When the Governor saw that the wanderer did indeed have two such curls his first impulse was to have him put to death as a potential rival to his authority. But the old servant intervened and vowed that destiny would never permit that.

So Abd al-Rahman was spared, though his followers were killed and had their goods seized.

Whether legend, or superstition, based upon Eastern fatalism, tipped the scale in favour of the wandering Syrian from the territory of Damascus cannot be said; but it is a fact that he went on to fulfil the prophecy.

He knew that Ibn Habib was ambitious of creating an independent realm for himself in Africa, so deemed it prudent to resume his wanderings. He made his way through Morocco and settled for a time near Ceuta, among a Berber tribe, the Nafza, to which his mother, a former African slave, had belonged. These tribesmen befriended him, and plans began to take shape in his mind. Spain, in the grip of anarchy, lay near, and there were Omayyad partisans there whom he hoped to gather round him. He sent one of his followers, Badr, to take soundings among old soldiers from Damascus, now known to be in Elvira and Jaen.

At that time a dissolute and brutal tyrant called Somail had conquered the Yemenites, aided by the governor, Yousouf, so the Yemenites welcomed Abd al-Rahman's approach, which offered a chance of revenge. Eventually, Abd al-Rahman struck, and in a battle on the banks of the Guadalquivir, between Seville and Cordoba, Somail and Yousouf were defeated. Their conqueror was hailed as Emir of Spain in 756, and it is said that on landing at Almunecar he felt "wholly possessed by his great-uncle's prediction"* made so many years before.

What kind of man was this young conqueror of twenty-five? He had already demonstrated energy, generalship and vision. Some accounts refer to him as one-eyed, but all agree that he was an impressive figure of a man; very tall, with reddish-yellow hair. The two distinctive curls upon his forehead have been referred to already. He was exceptionally virile, utterly without fear; a persuasive and eloquent talker.

Of his iron resolution in persistently following what he firmly held to be his inflexible destiny there can be very little doubt. Once he had crossed into Spain he lost no time in making himself fully independent of the Caliph of Baghdad and pursued his dream of

* *The History of Spain*. Bertrand and Petrie.

setting up a completely new Syrian-Arab dynasty. Though he made every haste to consolidate his position, he was allowed barely one year's respite from strife. Somail was much too debauched in his habits to present any real challenge; but Yousouf was sufficiently determined to venture upon rebellion once he had managed to raise 20,000 supporters.

Aided by the Governor of Seville, Abd al-Rahman met this challenge to his authority and the revolt was suppressed. The emir decided to make an example of the rebel chief and had Yousouf beheaded together with his son who had been held as a hostage throughout the rebellion. By Abd al-Rahman's command both severed heads were placed on public display on the bridge at Cordoba. As a further lesson to would-be rivals he had Somail strangled.

Though he had thus succeeded in ridding himself of his two chief rivals, his troubles were far from being over. A Yemenite rebellion, followed by a revolt in Toledo, forced the emir to stand siege in Carmona for two months. When ultimately victorious in quelling these insurrections he decided that an even more forceful gesture was called for. He had the heads of the leading rebels cut off as before; but this time he had them stuffed with salt and myrrh, packed in boxes, and sent over the long caravan route to the Caliph of Baghdad who was suspected of having stirred up the revolt. What the caliph thought of this grisly gift does not appear to be on record.

It was the Berbers who next turned upon the ambitious young emir, and they were only subdued after a series of prolonged struggles.

Then came a completely new threat in an insurrection in the north, where another of Yousouf's sons and a son-in-law had joined forces with the Governor of Barcelona. This was a formidable challenge indeed, for the trio had also invoked the powerful aid of the mighty Emperor Charlemagne, who, accompanied by his doughty nephew, Roland, marched across the Pyrenees with every intention of laying siege to Saragossa. It looked as if a tremendous clash was inevitable, but, in the event, Charlemagne and Abd al-Rahman were never destined to meet, though some historians were later to compare the character of the emir with that of the emperor. For some reason battle was never joined and the invading forces withdrew. This was the historic occasion of the epic stand made against Basque mountaineers in the Pass of Roncesvalles—the rear-guard action fought so desperately by the emperor's nephew and immortalized in "The Song of Roland".

What might have been a decidedly interesting historic clash of great leaders was avoided, Abd al-Rahman was kept feverishly engaged for most of his troubled administration in combating and crushing one conspiracy after another. He never shirked any challenge but fought tirelessly and courageously, dealing out the most savage punishments to the various enemies he brought to submission.

As the years went by, nearly everyone who could conspire against him must have done so. Even one of his brothers was among the rivals whom he had to subdue. It is small wonder, then, that his grim experiences turned him into a fearsome tyrant, obliged to rule by force. Indeed, the day was to come when the emir could move only under the staunch protection of an Imperial Guard of specially recruited Berbers; and it was always necessary for him to maintain a standing army of 40,000 European slaves (Slavonas) ever ready in the background.

The destiny he had chosen to follow so unswervingly thus turned out to be one that constantly necessitated the waging of remorseless warfare against threats of internal strife for upwards of thirty years. The wonder is that in spite of this ever-present handicap to settled rule he did succeed in establishing a centralized power and never for one moment abandoned the ideal of creating something worthwhile.

Surrounded and menaced, as he was, by every conceivable kind of barbarity, intrigue and revolt, it is probably fair to concede that a great many of the cruelties laid to his name were inevitably forced upon him by sheer weight of circumstance. Nevertheless, he was capable of showing forbearance and it has been recorded that he showed clemency towards the Christians. At least one commentator, Ibn el Athir, has described the better sides of his complex character and has credited the emir with being: "Benignant, well-informed, resolute; prompt to crush rebellion, he never remained long in repose or given over to idleness; he never entrusted the care of his affairs to anybody, and relied upon no judgment but his own."

The same commentator mentions that Abd al-Rahman was endowed with profound intelligence. And, speaking of his great courage, says that he united bravery "pushed to the point of daring" with great prudence. He also "showed himself broad-minded and generous".

When scattered scraps of information concerning Abd al-Rahman are pieced together there emerges a picture of a man of many parts. As an administrator he certainly sought vigorously to establish law and order. He organized a Council of State; reorganized the judiciary under a senior Cadi; and divided Spain into six military provinces.

His capital, probably of Carthaginian origin, and carefully colonized by the Romans, actually doubled its size under the dynasty he established.

He is credited with having started the Great Mosque at Cordoba on the site of a Roman temple and a Visigoth church, his dream being to establish a great religious centre in his chosen capital to rival those of the East. His mosque finally became the great cathedral world-famous for its beauty today.

Abd al-Rahman not only beautified his capital; he provided schools and hospitals; he also adapted and improved the old palace of Cordoba and built a country seat for himself, naming it Ruzafa to honour the memory of his grandfather, Caliph Hisham, who had built the Damascene Ruzafa.

That he was able to accomplish so much constructive work of this nature while fighting almost ceaselessly against successive threats to his realm is surely evidence enough of his boundless energy and strength of character. His capital became famous for its silversmiths, its silk embroideries and for a special kind of leather. Under his guidance it became progressive in every way.

It is obvious that the emir can have enjoyed scant leisure to devote to family life, yet he sired a family of twenty children—eleven sons and nine daughters.

One more interesting facet of his many-sided character must be mentioned. This doughty warrior, who usually dressed all in white, had great poetic yearnings, and though very little of his verse seems to have survived there are sufficient fragments to indicate the existence of a tender, deeply reflective side to his nature. Some historians have been moved to express astonishment that a ruthless man of action should have betrayed an ingrained love of beauty and refinement amounting almost to a sentimental streak. But is this so astonishing? Haven't a great many men of action revealed similar tendencies? It may even be an inevitable reaction—the assertion of a sincerely felt longing for peace and beauty to offset the turmoil and ugliness that has dogged their lives—a longing for serenity that can be captured only on paper.

The surviving verses of Abd al-Rahman undoubtedly betray a nostalgic yearning for his beloved Damascus. In one poem, inspired by the unexpected appearance of a lone palm tree in the grounds of his new Ruzafa retreat, he likens himself to this unique growth.

This palm tree, he says wistfully, "has strayed into the soil of the West, far from the land where dwell its peers. There, I say to myself, is my image. I, too, live in far-off exile".

The self-same theme is repeated with even greater feeling in another surviving fragment and suggests a veritable cry from the heart of the poet.

Traveller, You who go to my country, take with you there the salutation of half of myself to my other half.
My body, as you know, is in one place, but my heart and its affections are in another.
Marked out as it was by Destiny, the separation has had to be accomplished, but it has chased sleep from my lids.
The Divine will that ordained this divorce will perhaps decree, some day, our reunion.

That desired reunion was not to be. The self-made Emir of Spain, who had wandered so far in following what he devoutly believed to be his pre-ordained path of destiny, died in "exile" in his fifty-seventh year.

CHARLEMAGNE

(742–814)

CHARLEMAGNE REIGNED in France and over most of Western Europe from 764–814. His reign was a period of order and enlightenment at the end of what is called "the Dark Ages", but it was a brief period only and chaos came again before the civilization of the Middle Ages of the twelfth and thirteenth centuries.

Charlemagne was a contemporary of Offa, King of Mercia, the most powerful of the Anglo-Saxon kings at that time and the only monarch in Europe whom Charlemagne treated as an equal. Legends grew up about Charlemagne, and in the eleventh and twelfth centuries he was presented as a hero of chivalry. Indeed some of the troubadours and trouvères wrote about him and his knights as of another King Arthur and the Round Table. Charlemagne, however, exists as a very real and historical personage. He can be seen through the eyes of contemporaries and there is one full contemporary record, that of Einhard, a German monk, who wrote *Vita Caroli Magni*.

One must look at Charlemagne not as a knight in shining armour but rather as a recently civilized Frankish chieftain, dressed in a short tunic or linen shirt, wearing breeches cross-strapped with leather and, in the cold, a waistcoat of otter fur with a cloak. He had his legendary white beard, but certainly also the long thin moustaches of Frankish warriors. He used to carry a cane cut from an apple tree with symmetrical knots. He was probably not the gigantic figure of legend, but of moderate height (his father was called Peppin the Short), with a thick neck and a protruding stomach. He had a somewhat high voice. He was, however, a most imposing personality, choleric, tyrannical, watchful. He had much of the crude cunning of the barbarian chief, the ruler of savage men. His immense respect for learning and for wise men, which helped to make him a great ruler, had a naïvete but also a strength which a sophisticated emperor might not have had.

The atmosphere which surrounds this great monarch is not that of the Middle Ages, as we understand the term, but one much more similar to that of Anglo-Saxon England. As we shall see, in many ways England in the eighth century was more civilized than the continent. She had only so far had to face the onslaught of the Angles and Saxons and not the successive waves of barbarian conquerors which had broken over the continent as the Roman Empire had lapsed into nothingness.

In discussing the future of Europe today, the term "Charlemagne's Europe" is often used to denote a Europe based on the unity of Germany, France and Italy. Charlemagne did for a short while unite most of Western Europe, and he was crowned Holy Roman Emperor in 800 by Pope Leo III. Those of his contemporaries who could read and write, and these were mostly ecclesiastics or great nobles, saw Charlemagne literally as the restorer of the Roman Empire. The Roman Empire had officially ceased to exist in 475 when a Gothic chief, Odoacer, had deposed the last Roman Emperor and decided not to appoint another. But it had ceased to exist a long time before that when the empire had been over-run by Germanic tribes—of whom the largest were the Goths, Visigoths and Vandals. The Vandals had sacked Rome in 455 and the Goths, under Alaric, had sacked it 410. Yet the fiction of a Western Empire had been preserved.

The invaders, who kept on coming into the west all the time, settled in the empire, and Romans and Gallo-Romans (the Gauls of France who had long been Romanized) believed that the empire would completely absorb them. In 451, under a Roman general Aetius, Frankish and Alemmani tribes had defeated the Huns under Attila in a great battle near Paris in which 300,000 men had been engaged. But after the fifth century the idea that the empire would survive lived on, though as we can see today nothing really justified the belief.

A Frankish kingdom under Clovis, the first of the Merovingian kings, proved the most powerful of the kingdoms which the barbarians had hewn out of the empire: the Franks were the people who had settled in northern France and the Rhineland. After defeating a Roman general, Syragus, at Soissons, Clovis then turned on the Alemmani, a rival Germanic tribe, promising to become a Christian if he could defeat them. His wish was granted; his promise was fulfilled. Then in 507 Clovis defeated the Visigoths who possessed most of France south of the Loire and all of Spain. Clovis gave the name of France, land of the Francs, to the country which had hitherto been Gaul, the great Roman province and the land of the Celts.

The Merovingian Frankish dynasty lasted for three hundred years, longer than did the Valois or the Bourbon kings. Clovis's heirs, however, were savage despots who, as debauchery wore out their stock, lapsed into incompetent puppets. They lost many provinces which Clovis won and had little control over the rest of their kingdom. One of the last Merovingians to rule more or less effectively was Dagobert in the seventh century. But he died of old age at thirty-four, prematurely worn out, it is said, by his numerous concubines.

If Clovis's kingdom did not break up it was due to the Church, whose bishops, priests and monks supplied what existed of an administration. The Church indeed was what remained of the Roman Empire, its real heir. There were also Roman towns, in which Franks and Gauls lived like campers in a deserted palace, Roman roads, aqueducts, baths and arenas, but these were disused or ruined, except in parts of the south of France where something remained of the old civilization. The Roman Church alone worked, of all the institutions of the old empire.

At the beginning of the eighth century, the Arabs who had conquered Spain advanced into France. Officials of the Merovingian court, called the Mayors of the Palace, now took charge of the kingdom, and it was one of these, Charles Martel, who with a force of Frankish infantry defeated a Moorish army near Poitiers in 732, from which time the Arab invasion of France gradually ended and the invaders were pushed back into the Pyrenees. Charles Martel's son, Peppin the Short, was allowed by the Pope to depose the last of the Merovingian kings and, in 754, the Pope, Stephen II, came to France and crowned Peppin King of France, giving his two sons, Charles and Carloman, the title of Patricians of the Romans.

The Carolingian dynasty was now legitimate and was given a religious character or sanction which the French monarchy possessed henceforward. In return, Peppin subdued the Lombards, a Germanic tribe long settled in northern Italy (which, indeed, ruled over most of the peninsula), and handed over to the Pope territories which he took from the Lombards in central Italy. These territories had belonged to the Empire of the East, the Byzantine Empire; they became the Papal States and they were to last, as the property of the Pope, from the eighth century to 1870. The power of the Papacy increased at the same time as the power and prestige of the Frankish monarchy.

This perhaps helps to make it clear why the nobles and ecclesiastics who lived in France and Italy considered that Charlemagne, who succeeded his father Peppin the Short, had the mission to restore the secular Roman Empire, called Holy because of its indissoluble alliance with the Sovereign Pontiff. Charlemagne himself, a man of good sense, did not see himself as a Roman Emperor. He called himself "Emperor governing the Roman Empire", for he did not wish to supplant the legitimate emperor at Byzantium and, in any case, considered himself a Frankish king. But he was deeply impressed by Rome which he visited in 774; and then in 800 he had gone there to help Pope Leo III again. He was not perhaps altogether displeased when, on Christmas Day, as he was kneeling in prayer before the altar, the Pope placed the Imperial Crown on his head and a number of people present cried out: "Long life and victory to Charles Augustus the crowned of God, the great powerful Emperor of the Romans." But Charlemagne forbade his son to accept the Imperial crown.

Charlemagne was engaged in wars throughout his life. One of the first was against the Lombards, whom his father had fought; and like Peppin he fought at the behest of the Pope. But he had a personal quarrel with the King of the Lombards, Desiderius. Charlemagne had succeeded to only half the realm of his father, the northern half, his brother Carloman reigning over the rest. Carloman died three years after Peppin and Desiderius proclaimed Carloman's widow and children as rulers. Legally, this was the custom of the German tribes, who did not recognize primogeniture. Charlemagne disposed quickly of Desiderius, whom he deported to France, and crowned himself King of the Lombards.

When he went to Rome he was deeply impressed by the Christian relics, and dazzled by the splendid Church ceremonies and the beautiful Gregorian music. It was from then on that he called himself "King by the grace of God". In Rome, Charlemagne had no difficulty in legalizing his repudiation of his first wife, Desiderata, the daughter of the former Lombard king. He married a Princess Hildegarde of the Alemmani. He had already had a son from an illegal union with a Frankish noblewoman by name Himiltrude. He was to marry, later on, on Hildegarde's death, Fastrada, also a Frank, and on her death in 794 a German princess named Luitgarde. With four wives he had many mistresses, keeping them in his great palace at Aachen (Aix-la-Chapelle) which, with its baths and innumerable marble columns, was built like a Roman palace. Order reigned in the palace, which was never the scene of debauchery and drunkenness as in Merovingian times.

He brought up his family strictly and tried, unsuccessfully, to prevent his daughters marrying until he had found them the husbands he wanted. Among his pleasures in the Aachen Palace was that of swimming, and at that, even as an old man, the monarch excelled, beating young men in races.

Charlemagne fought no less than forty campaigns during his reign of forty-three years. These were, however, most of them, military expeditions which began in the late spring and ended in the summer before travelling became difficult. Some of his early wars, which were to subdue Aquitaine or Burgundy, were really more or less military promenades. So too were most of his expeditions to Italy, where he took Venice, though, later on, the Emperor of Byzantium recaptured it. The serious wars were against the Avars in Hungary and the tribes of North and East Germany, particularly the Saxons. The Saxons—the hard race which had in the past over-run Britain—wanted neither to be ruled over by Charlemagne nor to accept Christianity. They were defeated in a number of campaigns, after one of which Charlemagne had four thousand men beheaded in a single day. But this act of barbarism was exceptional. As a rule Charlemagne, when he had overcome a tribe or a group of tribes and had had homage paid to him and taken hostages for good behaviour, allowed the conquered to rule themselves according to their own laws, provided they accepted Christianity.

In some cases he brought back the population of a conquered region to Gaul and gave them land—sending Franks to colonize the conquered territory. His empire extended eastwards to the Elbe and across the Danube and to the borders of the Byzantine Empire. His success can no doubt partly be explained by the quietening of the onrush of the barbarians from the east which had already lasted four hundred years.

Charlemagne was a great man of war, but equally great as a man of peace. He organized his empire, or at least the parts of it which he could manage, such as France, the Rhineland, and Bavaria, with a new accent on justice. Like St. Louis in the thirteenth century, he employed monks and learned men as his representatives, sending them to visit all the provinces. A monk or bishop travelled with a count or military commander and they were known as the Missi Dominici—the master's envoys. One of these envoys was the Bishop of Orléans, a learned man called Theodulf, and he did not fear to over-rule local lords, to denounce bribery. In certain parts of France, Theodulf succeeded in ending certain old customs, such as trial by boiling water or red-hot irons, when there was no conclusive evidence. Instead, an accused man was made to stand upright and with his arms extended in the form of a cross: prayers were then recited by monks—and if the man made no movement at all he was judged innocent. Charlemagne himself periodically went to the less civilized centres of his realm such as Ratisbon or Paderborn to hold assemblies. He and his retinue lived in tents and so too did the chiefs and their tribesmen from distant parts who camped around the emperor waiting for their turn to consult with him.

Charlemagne summoned scholars from all over Europe to his court at Aachen. One of his aims was to set up new ecclesiastical schools in great cities such as Paris and Toulouse and to translate and restore manuscripts. One of his assistants was Alcuin, the scholar who had the celebrated monastic school at York, one of the best in Christendom. Alcuin and Theodulf busied themselves also with reforming Latin as a spoken language and re-ordering the way mass was to be said in churches and monasteries. At Aachen Alcuin presided over a sort of learned academy attended by Charlemagne, his wives and daughters and counsellors; at this school the emperor became a pupil and was known as David. Charlemagne, who could read a little but had never learnt to write, would in his old age sleep with writing tablets under his pillow so that if he was sleepless he could practise writing. Manuscripts were searched for by Charlemagne's emissaries in Italy, Greece and at the court of the great Caliph Harun-al-Rashid in Baghdad. The caliph sent Charlemagne a clock which was no less a wonder than an elephant, another gift of the caliph.

The Arab world at that time was a most civilized part of the globe and still remained skilled in war. It was against the Arabs of Spain that Charlemagne fought his only unsuccessful campaign. He invaded Spain in 778 and failed to take Saragossa, where the Moorish king defied him. Forced to retreat from Spain because of trouble in Saxony, a small rearguard of the Franks commanded by Hroudland, the Margrave of the Breton marchi, was ambushed and annihilated by the Basques in a valley of the Pyrenees called Roncesvalles. This comparatively unimportant military episode was to become a popular epic, and before the battle of Hastings in 1066 the minstrel Taillefer encouraged the Normans with a popular version of Charlemagne's deeds in Spain and the gallant Roland's great fight. Roland and Oliver and the rest of the Frankish knights were turned into typical heroes of medieval romances. The *Chanson de Roland*, one of the greatest epic poems of the world, was given its final form by monks in the twelfth century, some three hundred years after Charlemagne was dead.

No historical ruler has ever been more the subject of myth than

Charlemagne. It was said a hundred years after his death, and widely believed, that he had made a pilgrimage to Jerusalem. Charlemagne is also supposed to have had a sword called Joyeuse which contained the point of the lance with which the Roman soldier had pierced the side of Christ on the Cross. Many more extraordinary stories were told about him, which bear practically no relevance to history.

In German myths Charlemagne was said, like Frederick Barbarossa, to be awaiting a resurrection when he would win back his empire. In a Bavarian myth, Charlemagne was said to be upright in his tomb at Aachen with his white beard still growing: when his beard had three times encircled the stone table before which he was sitting the end of the world would come. His name was given in the Middle Ages to the constellation of the Great Bear which is sometimes called in English Charles's Wain (Karlswagen).

Myths apart, Charlemagne's empire was a great achievement. But the search for the unity of Christendom, which has never been successful, was more impossible in the ninth century even than in the thirteenth. Charlemagne's grandsons divided his empire into three parts. Most of Germany went to one son and France was divided into two: Lotharingia, east of the Rhône and the Saone; and Neustria, that part of France to the west of those rivers. The continent was once again in the melting pot, and in November, 885, seven hundred sailing ships full of Vikings or Norsemen were in the lower Seine, some miles from Paris. It was to be left to the Counts of Paris to create France.

HARUN-AL-RASHID

(763–809)

HARUN-AL-RASHID, caliph of the Abbasid Empire which stretched from India to North Africa, was born in 763 (though some consider it was two years later) and died in 809. His reign of twenty-three years and that of his son, the caliph Mamun, came to be regarded as a golden age for its luxury and for its renaissance in learning; it was celebrated as such by the poets, musicians and writers of the time and achieved world-wide fame through the stories of *The Arabian Nights*, in some of which the caliph Harun figured prominently.

Though the origin of many of the stories are Persian or Egyptian, they give a very good picture of the teeming life of Baghdad with its magnificent palaces and its wealthy merchant class, for the site of the city on the Tigris had been wisely chosen by Harun's grandfather, the caliph al Mansur, who had said "there is no obstacle between us and China; everything on the sea can come to us by the Tigris". Indeed, the round city of Baghdad spread in all directions and it became a centre of a world market with ships sailing up to its wharves with silks, spices and jewels from China, India, Ceylon and East Africa. Wars brought in slaves so that the market was full of Greek, Circassian and African boys and girls, the most beautiful being taken for the caliph and the nobility of Baghdad. Mr. H. St. John Philby, in his biography of Harun-al-Rashid, describes the slave market as constituting a monster chorus of beauty and talent beside which the splendours of Hollywood paled into insignificance; "sexual extravagance was the order of the day among the wealthy, while the common herd, who paid heavy taxes to support the estate and court, would seem to have been limited by economic pressure to a system of practical monogamy". The fantastic world of contrasts and uncertainties depicted in *The Arabian Nights* was not by any means all fiction; the slave in Baghdad could suddenly become powerful and the wealthy man be reduced to poverty.

The most interesting aspect of caliph Harun's reign, and the most widespread in its effect throughout the Arab world and Europe, was the renaissance in learning. The orthodox theologians of Islam, who had had great influence, knew little of the philosophy and science of ancient Greece, and anyway the whole idea of a questioning philosophy based on logic was abhorrent, for to them there was no such thing as cause and effect, but every happening was brought about directly by God; and since the Koran contained the answers given by God to everything it was impious to start asking questions about the universe.

Although Harun-al-Rashid was religiously a very devout man and did the long pilgrimage to Mecca on foot almost every other year, he was intelligent and curious, so that orders were given that the works of ancient Greece and Indian works in Sanskrit should be sought out and translated into Arabic. This saved much of the ancient wisdom from oblivion and was even more enthusiastically carried on by the caliph Mamun. It helped towards the later flowering of Averroes and Avicenna, who brought the knowledge of Aristotle and other writers to the universities of Europe. Another great advance was the introduction from China of the art of making paper, instead of having to rely on parchment and papyrus. The caliph appreciated poetry and music and there were schools of musicians under the famous Ibrahim of Mosul and Ibn Jami.

A great impetus was also given to learning by the increase at court of foreigners, especially Persians, and Magians with the learning of India; they brought with them intellectual curiosity, artistic talent and a new kind of poetry. This predominance of foreigners, who were mostly Muslims, constituted one of the main differences between Abbasid rule and that of the earlier Ummayad dynasty centred on Damascus with an Arab empire which extended to Spain in the west and to India in the east. It had been an efficiently administered empire based on the Arab aristocracy; the Arabs were given precedence over the Persians, Magians, Byzantine Greeks and others who had become Muslims, but were second-class citizens and known as *Mawali*, or "adherents". In the end the *Mawali* revolted and helped the Abbasids, who were descendants of the Prophet Mohammed's uncle Abbas, to come to power in 750; no difference was made between Arab and non-Arab and, in fact, under the caliphs Harun and Mamun the Persians had precedence in the administration, while Turks from the Oxus formed the caliph's bodyguard.

But the unity of the Arab empire was broken up into rival caliphates in Spain, North Africa and Asia. Though cruel and treacherous, the caliph Harun was an energetic ruler, sending embassies to China and to Charlemagne, who had been crowned by the Pope Emperor of the West in 800. To Charlemagne the caliph sent an elephant, a water-clock and the keys of the Holy Sepulchre at Jerusalem, but their exchanges did not lead to any closer contact; "their public correspondence was founded on vanity", wrote Edward Gibbon, "and their remote situation left no room for a competition of interests". Against the Greeks of Constantinople and revolts in the Abbasid Empire the caliph on several occasions left his life of luxury in Baghdad, or at ar-Raqqa in Syria, to lead his armies.

Harun was born soon after the great circular city of Baghdad had been founded in 762 by the second Abbasid caliph Abu Jafar, known as al Mansur, who moved from al Kufa, south of Baghdad, when his new capital was completed. Al Mansur had sent his son Mahdi, who was nominated his successor, to crush a revolt of the Governor of Tabaristan in Persia; after defeating the Governor, Mahdi had taken two Persian maidens from the Governor's household as part of the loot; one of them was Khaizaran, who bore Mahdi two boys, Hadi and Harun, at Raiy near Teheran; by the other Persian, Mahdi had a girl called Abbasa, who was to suffer a tragic end at the hands of Harun. Also at Raiy, and at the same time, Fadl was born, son of the Persian Yahya ibn Barmak, whose father, Khalid, held high office under the caliph Mansur. Harun and Fadl became foster-brothers, for the two mothers were friends and used to exchange infants at the breast.

Nothing much is known about Harun until after the death of al Mansur in 775, when the new caliph, Mahdi, sent his eighteen-year-old son Harun in command of an expedition of one hundred thousand men against the Greek Empress Irene of Constantinople. With Harun as adviser was Yahya ibn Barmak, who came of a distinguished family of Persian landlords and whose grandfather had been the *Barmak*, or guardian, of the principal Zoroastrian temple in Persia; but both Khalid and his son Yahya had become Muslims. Harun's expedition pursued the Greek army to the Bosphorus and forced the empress to sue for peace and to pay a large annual ransom. The caliph Mahdi was so pleased with his son's achievement that he nominated Harun to be Governor of the western provinces from Syria to Azerbaijan. He was also given the title of al-Rashid—the Virtuous or Orthodox—and nominated second in succession to the caliphate after his brother Hadi.

Harun's mother, Khaizaran, had been made queen by marriage with the caliph over whom she exerted a considerable influence. Her favourite son was Harun and she persuaded Mahdi to make him the next caliph instead of the elder brother Hadi; but Hadi, who was fighting a campaign in Persia, refused to be set aside, and the caliph, accompanied by Harun-al-Rashid, set out with an army from Baghdad to enforce respect. On the way the caliph ate a poisoned fruit, intended by a jealous concubine for another woman, and died at the age of forty-three. Harun-al-Rashid then showed great statesmanship; he had the army with him and he could very easily have carried out his father's wishes and assumed the caliphate, but instead he sent a message to Hadi to come at once to Baghdad to be made caliph, an act which infuriated Khaizaran. Under the new caliph she was confined to the women's quarters and not allowed to have the influence that she had had before, but among her ladies-in-waiting she planned Hadi's downfall.

The caliph Hadi made the mistake of setting aside Harun's rightful claim to the succession and nominating his own son to succeed him; when Yahya did his best to dissuade the caliph from this action, he was thrown into prison. While Hadi was at Mosul he fell ill and was smothered by his concubines, a death which had almost certainly been planned by his mother, Khaizaran, who had everything prepared for the proclamation of Harun-al-Rashid as caliph. This was done without opposition in 786 when Harun was twenty-three years of age. Harun's son, al Mamun, was born to a Persian slave-girl on the day of the caliph's accession; later another son was born to his wife Zubeida, who was granddaughter of the former Caliph al Mansur, and therefore her son took precedence in succession over al Mamun. Later, after Harun's death, the conflict between the Persian-born son and the Arab-born son was to be fought out in a civil war, leading finally to the victory of the abler al Mamun and the Persian element.

The rivalry between Arab and non-Arab Muslims continued during the reign of the caliph Harun, but the Persian element was dominant, largely because of the great power wielded by the Barmakis, as Yahya and his two sons, Fadl and Jafar, came to be called. Yahya, then forty-eight, was vizier, a fit recompense after being imprisoned for defending Harun's right of accession; Fadl was his deputy in the administration of the empire and the younger son, Jafar, was made Secretary and Controller of the Imperial Household; both sons were known as "the Little Vizier". Jafar, because of his eloquence, intelligence and charm, became the boon companion of the caliph, who suffered from sleeplessness and liked someone intelligent to talk to, or there would be carousal with drink and women late into the night and perhaps a visit to different parts of Baghdad in the early hours of the morning. In some of *The Arabian Nights*' stories the caliph is accompanied by Jafar, as well as by Abu Nawas, the poet and licensed jester, and Mesrur, the Negro executioner. The caliph's relations with the Barmak family were very close, and as they administered the empire it was natural that Persian customs should predominate, which was welcomed by the caliph.

Whereas under the Ummayad dynasty there had been some semblance of the Arab democracy brought from the deserts of Arabia, at least for Arabs, and the ruler was kept under some check, under the caliph Harun the Persian doctrine was accepted that the ruler had divine right. Any opposition to the caliph was treason and it was regarded as natural that he should be despotic and have people imprisoned, tortured and killed at his will; Harun made at times tragic use of his despotic powers. While the court presented a gay, learned and civilized aspect, there were unfortunate ex-favourites lying in prison and perhaps being tortured to obtain information on others.

The caliph was a generous spender, but the empire was efficiently administered and it is estimated that the annual income from it (after Spain and most of North Africa had been lost) amounted to about sixteen million sterling a year. That was great wealth in those days, especially when the Government did not bother about general education or the social conditions of the masses; Harun thought of the poor to the extent of giving forty pounds daily in alms. As part of his religious devotion Harun-al-Rashid maintained rest-houses along the route of the pilgrimage to Mecca. Communications within the empire were well looked after; there were, for instance, the desert route from Baghdad to Damascus and thence through Palestine to Egypt and across North Africa, and the roads north-westwards to the Byzantine frontier, but the most important route was the Persian highway eastwards with fortified caravanserais throughout its length, which helped armies to be moved quickly; there was also a remarkable postal system with post-masters acting as spies for the caliph. Most of the trouble came from Syria and Persia, and about eight years after his accession Harun moved his capital from Baghdad to ar-Raqqah in northern Syria, so that he could the better control these areas and deal with the contumely Emperor Nicephorus, who had succeeded the Empress Irene.

There are various views of the caliph Harun-al-Rashid; some refer to his energy, ability and intelligence, while others emphasize his cruelty and treachery, but all have condemned his treatment of the Barmak family. Not only had Yahya and his two sons worked hard and efficiently for the Abbasid Empire, but the family had always been very close to the caliph; Yahya, his guardian as a boy, Fadl, the caliph's foster-brother, and Jafar, his boon companion—how intimate were the relations of the caliph and Jafar has been much discussed. There is a story that the caliph was found staring across the Tigris at Yahya's large palace and exclaiming: "Yahya seems to have taken all the business in hand without reference to me. It is he who is the caliph in reality, not I."

That may have been part of the reason that made him turn against the family, but it was probably another form of jealousy, for the first to die was Harun's boon companion Jafar, executed by Mesrur while he prayed; the head was brought to Harun, who addressed his charges to a Jafar who could not answer as he used to do. The most likely reason for this murder concerns Abbasa, Harun's half-sister, for whom he had a great admiration; the caliph wanted her to be present when he and Jafar had their carousals, but this would not have been correct Islamic etiquette. He got over the problem by arranging that Jafar and Abbasa should go through a marriage ceremony, but it was made clear that this was only nominal and it would anyway have been unfitting for a commoner to marry a close relation of the caliph. Abbasa, so the story goes, fell in love with Jafar and arranged that she should take the place of a slave girl who used to be sent on Friday nights to Jafar's room. Jafar was horrified, fearing what the consequences might be, but even so they continued to meet and two sons were born who were sent away in secret to be brought up in Mecca. One story says that the caliph had Abbasa and her two sons also killed.

Yahya, now an old man, and his son Fadl were cast into prison at ar-Raqqah and orders issued that all the property belonging to any member of the Barmak family was to be confiscated. Fadl became paralysed from the shock of his brother's death and he and his father died in prison a little time before Harun himself died in 809. The caliph died of cancer in Persia at the age of forty-seven while accompanying his army on an expedition to suppress a rebellion led by Rafi ibn Leith of Samarkand. The caliph had reached a place called Tus when he knew that he was dying and he had his grave dug close by. Just before he died the rebel leader's brother was brought as a prisoner and the caliph was asked what should be done. "If I had no more breath left," said Harun the Virtuous, "but to say a single word, it would be *slay him*."

ALFRED THE GREAT

(849–99)

IN THE annals of the English nation no man merits a higher place than Alfred the Great: stainless in character, brilliant as warrior, statesman, lawgiver, scholar and champion of Christianity. He delivered his country from brutal invasion and conquest by hordes of heathen Danes, and began the task, completed by his son and grandson, of welding the whole of England into one united realm.

It had not always been that. When the Anglo-Saxons emerged, at the end of the sixth century, from the Dark Ages, during which their hordes had flooded, wave after wave, into Christian Britain, plundering, massacring, obliterating all traces of its ordered Roman civilization, they were divided up into some seven petty kingdoms, which made ruthless war upon each other. Although in the eighth century the kings of Mercia, the midland state, claimed sovereignty over England, Northumbria, Wessex and Kent still had their own kings. In 828, Egbert, King of Wessex and grandfather of Alfred, defeated the Mercians at Ellandune, and became ruler of all southern England from Kent to the Devon border.

But now internal strife was stilled by a darker menace. Near the end of the eighth century the first Viking raiders had made their appearance. Three of their long ships attacked the Wessex coast. Then they ransacked the monasteries of Lindisfarne, Iona, Ireland and North Wales, collecting rich plunder and massacring the monks or taking them to sell as slaves. Amazed at such easy success, the Danes and Norsemen set out in ever-growing numbers on these marauding expeditions, which grew from raids to invasion, conquest and land settlement. Danes subjugated East Anglia, Yorkshire and Mercia, while Norsemen penetrated Cumberland and Lancashire, and joined hands with their Danish cousins across the north of England.

Finally the Danes set about the conquest of Wessex. Advancing up the Thames valley in 871, they met the West Saxon army at Ashdown, in the Berkshire downs. The Saxons were in two forces, under King Ethelred and his younger brother, Alfred. While Ethelred prayed for victory, Alfred plunged furiously into the fray.

Presently his brother joined him and in savage fighting they routed the Danes, who fled in confusion back to Reading. It was their first defeat in pitched battle in England since their invasions in force.

The war continued fiercely, and in the first half of 871 nine battles were fought. Then Ethelred died, and his brother Alfred, who had won the enthusiastic trust of the Saxons, was elected king by the Witan—the national council.

Alfred, born at Wantage in 849, was now a young man of about twenty-two; of poor health, a cultured scholar, with an unusually wide outlook for a man of that time. His father had twice taken him as a boy to Rome, where he was confirmed by the Pope and saw something of the world beyond Britain. In 868 he had married Ealhswith, who bore him two sons and three daughters.

Shortly after his accession he suffered a severe defeat at Wilton, and saw he must gain time to re-organize his defences. He made a peace treaty with the Danes, who were themselves not unwilling to disengage their forces from Wessex. Presumably he paid them a "Danegeld" to buy the treaty. But it gave him five years of relative peace to consolidate his realm. The Danes drew back into the Midlands, where they firmly established themselves and many of them settled down to farm life.

The more mobile warriors among the Danes, however, still were resolved to conquer Wessex, and under their new chieftain, Guthrum, they planned in 877 a system of combined attacks by land and sea. They drove overland to Wareham and by sea to Poole Harbour. Alfred tried to buy them off again. They swore a peace and forthwith broke it and captured Exeter. But their sea army was smashed by a storm near Swanage, which sank 120 ships and drowned over 5,000 warriors. The Danes swore a fresh peace.

Five months later, in January, 878, came Alfred's darkest hour. As he and his army were celebrating Twelfth Night at their headquarters in Chippenham, the Danes struck. The Wessex army scattered, its survivors creeping home or flying overseas. Alfred with a few faithful followers took refuge in the Isle of Athelney, among the marshes of Sedgemoor. He had no army, no money, no visible prospect of being able to resume the offensive against the victorious Danes, who now deemed themselves masters of Wessex.

Legends have gathered round his doings during this period in hiding. Men told how, disguised as a harper, he visited Danish camps and gained information about their strength and probable movements. They recounted, for the age-long delight of youngsters, how the housewife of the cottage where he was concealed left him to watch the baking of cakes. Intent on his plans, he did not heed them, and was roundly berated by the angry woman when she returned to find them burnt.

Somerset still kept pockets of Saxon resistance here and there. A Danish force, after plundering in Wales, attacked a stronghold in Exmoor. But the Saxons made a sudden sortie and killed the Danish chief and most of his troops. Alfred saw that the time had come to strike. He had established contact with the thanes of Wiltshire and Hampshire, who were groaning under the Danish yoke, and now he summoned them to join him and the men of Somerset at a point near Selwood.

There was magic in the name of Alfred; and a large army gathered and hailed him as one risen from the dead. He led them towards the Danish headquarters at Chippenham. The Danes issued forth to meet him at Ethandune (now Edington) and the greatest battle of his career was fought with desperate fury. It ended in victory, and he pursued the Danes and beleaguered Guthrum's camp. Guthrum begged for peace, offering to give hostages and withdraw from Wessex.

Alfred had a better plan. Dane and Saxon must learn to live together in England. A lasting peace must somehow be established between them, and it would not be achieved by slaughtering the defeated enemy. So he brought Guthrum and thirty of his chief earls into his camp and induced them to accept Christianity and be baptized. He himself was Guthrum's sponsor. Then he feasted them and settled with them the Treaty of Wedmore, by the terms of which the Danes were to remain to the east of Watling Street, the Roman road running from London to Chester. Thus the east and north of England—known as the Danelaw—were for the time being left in Danish hands; but the Midlands and the South were acknowledged as Alfred's realm. In 886 he gave his eldest daughter, Ethelflida, in marriage to Ethelred, the Mercian regent, thus binding the Midlands to Wessex. In 885 he had swept the Danes from London, which he fortified and re-established as the major port it had been in Roman times.

After the Treaty of Wedmore, Alfred enjoyed for fourteen years an uneasy peace, or something as near peace as those troubled times allowed. He busily employed this respite to bring his powers of statesmanship to bear on the organization of his country for defence. He divided the "Fyrd"—the mass rally of the country's manpower—into two parts, so that if one half of the men were summoned to battle, the other half would be guarding their families and tending their fields. He fortified the country by building defensive boroughs along the Thames valley, the south coast and the western borders. To each was assigned a district which would provide its manpower and maintain its fortifications. He saw the need for sea-power to resist the pirate raids of Danish long-ships, and to this end built a fleet of bigger vessels. Thus Alfred became the founder of the British Navy.

After his capture of London, Alfred made in 886 a further treaty with Guthrum. It defined the frontier of the Danelaw as running up the Lea Valley, east of London, thence to Bedford and by the Ouse to Watling Street. To check the constant fighting between Danes and English, a tariff of compensation payments was fixed for anyone killed of either race: 200 silver shillings for a Danish or English peasant, and 8½ marks in pure gold for men of higher rank. Such money settlements reduced the danger of blood feuds.

Alfred now set to work to codify the laws of England, which had been a chaos of local rules and customs. He sought to revise and combine these with regulations borrowed from Mosaic laws and Christian principles. His Book of Dooms (laws) formed the basis for administration of justice in Courts of the Shires and Hundreds, and with additions and modifications became the ancestor of our Common Law of today. He instilled throughout the nation so great a respect for law that it was commonly said that in his day one might leave precious jewels hanging on a roadside bush, and no one would venture to take them.

Alfred was not content to make his realm strong and law-abiding. He was determined it should become educated. Though forced by circumstances to fill the role of a warrior,. he was at heart a scholar. In these more peaceful years he set himself to provide his people with literature in their own tongue. He translated from Latin into Anglo-Saxon Bede's *History of the English People* and various religious works. He translated or compiled handbooks of theology, history and geography and rendered parts of the Bible into the common tongue. He brought over scholars from the Continent and drew learned refugees from the Danelaw. He started the first "public schools" for the sons of the nobility, to teach them to read and be better fitted to undertake administrative responsibilities. He started the compilation of the Anglo-Saxon Chronicle, which from his time kept a continuous record of the nation's history.

Alfred specially concentrated upon reviving the life of the English Church. In those dark and troublous times it could become influential to educate and unify the nation, and to link it with the former heathen of the Danelaw, among whom Christianity was now rapidly making progress. The Church had been shattered by the Danish invasions, in which monasteries had been destroyed and churches robbed and burned. The quality of the priesthood had fallen so low that few of them could read, still less understand, the Latin of their missals. Alfred founded monasteries and built churches. He brought distinguished churchmen from the Continent, corresponded with leading scholars, and is even alleged to have sent a mission to India.

Alfred was that rare bird, a really all-round man, interested in all the many facets of the life of his time, and gifted more than most for dealing with them. He was a keen huntsman, who could teach verderers and falconers the skills of their callings. He fostered the manufacture of high-quality jewellery and goldsmiths' work. He was a builder, pressing on with the building or restoration of towns, and constructing fair dwellings for his own courts. His court indeed became famous abroad for its learning, piety and culture.

He was yet to face further trouble with the Danes. In 891 Guthrum died, and the rather wavering peace he had kept with Alfred was at an end. At the time a great Viking host was ravaging northern Europe, besieging Paris and devastating northern France. Meeting desperate if disorganized resistance, they grew famished in the desolate countryside; so they decided to invade England and settle there. In 892 this great heathen army disembarked on the south coast of Kent and set up camp at Appledore. Another party sailed up the Thames and landed near Sittingbourne.

Thanks to Alfred's re-organization of her defence system England could put up a far stronger resistance than fifteen years before. Alfred himself was in poor health, but he had capable deputies in his son Edward and his son-in-law, Ethelred of Mercia, to lead his armies. They set about mobilizing the Fyrd, while Alfred tried to make terms with the Viking leader, Haesten. A peace was signed, but quickly broken, not before Alfred had induced the heathen Dane to let his two sons be baptized.

Haesten made a fortified camp at Benfleet, but Edward and Ethelred brought an army from London and stormed it, killing or scattering the invaders, burning their boats and looting their stores. Haesten's wife and sons were captured. Alfred sent them back to him. People thought this generosity to a brutal foe incomprehensible. But the Christian deed had a happy sequel. Haesten never fought Alfred again.

Another Danish force, drawn from Danes of the Danelaw, came round by boat to attack Exeter and thrust inland. But Edward and Ethelred, riding to its relief, met a column of Danes near Aldershot, defeated and pursued them for twenty miles, till they swam the Thames to get away. Yet another force brought their boats up the Lea, but Alfred barred the stream below them, and they fled across country, leaving their ships behind. By 896 these fresh Danish thrusts weakened and the invaders withdrew to the Danelaw or Normandy.

Intermittent raiding and conflict went on, however, for another forty years, until the ultimate unity of the land under English rule was achieved by Edward, Alfred's son, and Athelstan, his grandson, when not only the Danelaw but Northumbria, Strathclyde and the Welsh princes accepted the supremacy of the English crown. There was one last struggle when in 937 the Scots, Danes and Northumbrians, with Vikings from Iceland and Ireland, met the English in the great battle of Brunanburgh. Alfred's grandson, Athelstan, won an overwhelming victory, and thereafter styled himself King of All Britain—*Rex totius Britanniae*.

Alfred had not lived to see this consummation of all his efforts to unite the English realm, of which he had by arms and statesmanship through thirty critical years laid so well the foundations. He died in 899 at the age of fifty-two, leaving an England which from warring tribes he had transformed into a nation, and delivered from being overrun and obliterated by hordes of heathen invaders; an England with an established system of national and local government; with good laws and just administration; with a rising standard of education, literacy and art; with a universal acceptance of the Christian faith and an increasingly powerful and active Church.

He was reverenced and loved by all his people. In the following age they told of his exploits, held by his laws, and established his fame in history as Alfred the Great.

KING WENCESLAS

(d. 929)

THE LITTLE central-European country of Czechoslovakia—considerably smaller than Britain—is one of the most ruggedly attractive in the world: its capital of Prague has often been called the most beautiful city in Europe. The city is set in the middle of the Bohemian plain, a hill-rimmed saucer, tilted so that it slopes gently from south to north. It seems peaceful and quiet—yet some of history's darkest, most bloody deeds have been perpetrated there, over the past one thousand years.

The country itself is a recent creation, hacked out of the old Austro-Hungarian Empire at the end of the first world war and embodying a number of one-time kingdoms: Bohemia, Moravia and Silesia which speak the Czech language, and others, farther east, which speak Slovak. Each of these areas has a long and vivid history: none more so than Bohemia.

Caesar and Livy both refer, with some respect, to a powerful Celtic tribe, the Boii, and it is from these first inhabitants that Bohemia derives its name. Shortly before the birth of Christ they were defeated by other invading tribes and vanished from the pages of history. Their conquerors vanished, too, in the fifth century A.D., when the warlike Czech tribe took over. A few hundred years later, Christianity was introduced into the country and adopted by the ruling dynasty of these Czechs—though not, as we shall see, by all of them.

The greatest member of this ruling (and to West European ears, unpronounceable) dynasty, the family Premyslide, has a name known to schoolboys over half the world: Good King Wenceslas. Not too many kings are remembered as "good", but every verse of that long and rollicking carol points out that Wenceslas deserved to be.

He was born in the last days of the ninth century A.D., elder son of Uratislas, the Duke of Bohemia. The Duke was a devout Christian, but his wife was a pagan. This sort of situation, with husbands or wives espousing the new religion and their wives or husbands the old, was fairly common in these early years of

European Christianity. The pagan wife Drahomira bore her husband two sons, Wenceslas and Boleslas, managing to retain a hold on the younger boy while Wenceslas, at the Duke's insistence, was sent to be brought up by his grandmother Ludmilla. The old lady was as devout a Christian as her son the Duke and she sent young Wenceslas to a Christian college a few miles outside of Prague. Here he was diligent in his studies, particularly the sciences, in which he made great progress, and in all the varied accomplishments necessary for a European nobleman of the ninth century. He was also fortified greatly in his faith and was singled out as a good and virtuous Christian. He was exceedingly kind to any man or woman in trouble or distress, and the Christmas-carol story, of his inviting the poor man into his palace to share a meal, is only one of a great many. We learn that Wenceslas from an early age had "all the virtues which compose the character of a Christian and a saint".

He was still a very young man when his father died, and his pagan mother Drahomira seized the reins of government. While her husband lived she seems to have kept her hatred of Christianity in some sort of check, but now she rapped out a whole series of laws, closed down all Bohemia's churches and prohibited the teaching of the new religion. Christians were forbidden to teach children, whether the subject be mathematics or music or Latin, and an infringement of this law was punished by death. Many Christians were massacred.

Young Wenceslas, horrified at this, managed to get most of the power out of his mother's hands and assert his new position as Duke of Bohemia. He was backed by the majority of his Czech people, who agreed when he divided the country into two spheres of influence in order to give his younger brother Boleslas a domain of his own.

Unfortunately for Wenceslas, his young brother, who had been brought up by the pagan Drahomira, was as rabidly anti-Christian as she, and the pair of them now began to plot ways of overthrowing him and his religion. No doubt it would be necessary to have him killed, and that would be messy and troublesome, but in these early days of the tenth century it would hardly be unusual.

First they would have to put the old grandmother to death.

Ludmilla soon learnt of the plot against her life, but she was calm and philosophical, making no effort to avert a fate which she believed to have been ordained for a purpose. If by her death the Christian religion could be furthered, then it would not have been in vain. She began to give away all her goods to the poor, to pray daily that she might meet her fate with dignity and without rancour.

The assassins sent by Boleslas found her kneeling at prayer in her own private chapel, and they strangled her there, with her own veil.

Wenceslas, viewed from our vantage point of a thousand years on in time, seems to have been rather too forgiving a Christian for his own good. Instead of having his brother and mother locked up or put to death for this hideous crime, he devoted himself to prayer that they might be converted from their wicked ways. They were left in freedom to continue their plotting against him. At one point it seemed to the young duke that his prayers were being answered, for Boleslas came into his chapel one day and knelt down at the altar.

(If it served to lower the Duke's defences, Boleslas cared not a whit how often he went into a church, how ostentatiously he knelt to pray.)

The Holy Roman Emperor Otto I ruled a large area of Europe which included Bohemia, and that year he called a meeting of his subordinate rulers at Worms on the Rhine. Wenceslas made haste to attend. He travelled on horseback as fast as he could, often riding by night, but still arrived late for this "Diet", having stopped to pray for a deliverance for his country. While many of the other small rulers resented this, the great Otto knew a good man when he saw him, and respected Wenceslas for it. He immediately gave him the title of King of Bohemia, with the privilege of bearing the imperial eagle on his standard.

(Wenceslas, incidentally, went on to the end of his short life styling himself simply as Duke—but over all Europe he was known as the King of Bohemia.)

Otto also handed over some precious relics of St. Vitus and St. Sigismund which the devout and grateful Wenceslas took back with him to Prague, planning to build a new church to house them.

But in his absence his mother and brother had again been imposing restrictions on Christians: their excuse was that Christians had been holding meetings, making themselves a menace to Bohemian law and order. Wenceslas duly investigated the charges, found them false and reversed the laws. He warned his mother that any further intrigue would be punished.

"My son—how could you, for one moment, think that your own mother, who carried you in her womb, would intrigue against you? How ungrateful you are!"

"Perhaps——"

"But come, let us forget these family quarrels and feast together. Your brother's wife has been safely delivered of a son, there will be music and feasting——"

And Wenceslas, who had sworn a vow of virginity, but was glad that his brother and his brother's wife were now parents of a son who would some day rule Bohemia, agreed to attend the celebrations.

It was 27 September, in the year nine hundred and twenty-nine.

A chill evening, for Bohemian winters are as icy cold as the summers are hot: there was much drinking of mulled wine. The King of Bohemia's brother and mother greeted him effusively, showed him the infant, which had been placed on a skin-padded wooden bench to be admired, and the child whooped with delight as Wenceslas picked it up.

The music began, the candles were lit as the sun dropped over the edge of the Bohemian plain, there was wild dancing and eating and drinking. The hours flew past, and almost before he knew it the time was a minute to midnight.

"Come, my brother, to this little chapel in the trees, for I know that at midnight you will pray, as you always do——"

"Yes," said Wenceslas. "I pray. And I will go to your chapel."

Boleslas left the festivities to lead him there and the king went into the chapel alone. He made his way to the altar and knelt.

But now Boleslas, exactly as he had planned, was leading six men up the street from their hiding place, leading them back to the chapel and, on tiptoe, through the door. So devout was the king that he heard not a sound as the seven men approached.

They were behind him now, an arm's length off, and they halted, listened for a moment to the muttered prayer. Then Boleslas gave the signal.

The first man's dagger plunged deep into the back of the kneeling king. He half turned, a look of horror tinged with sadness on his face, and the second man knifed him in the shoulder.

The king seemed to feel no pain as the third and fourth blows were administered; he rose slowly to his feet as Boleslas prepared for the *coup de grâce*.

"Why, my brother, oh *why*?" were the last words the king was heard to say, as the lance sank deep into his chest. Still he came on, and the assassins, shocked by what they had done, backed away.

Surely the man should be dead, with so many grievous wounds, the blood gushing over his kingly robes?

He came on, one more step. Then, hands clasped in a final silent prayer, he fell.

He lay there and the slowly widening pool of red reached the altar steps, spilt down them. It was a few minutes after midnight on 28 September.

King Wenceslas was soon avenged. The Emperor Otto heard of the crime and led a vast army, virtually a crusade, into Bohemia, laying waste in his anger a large part of it. The wicked Drahomira, evil power behind the throne, was put painfully to death, and Boleslas, though his life was spared, was at first imprisoned, then released to become a vassal king of a subject Bohemia. On the Emperor Otto's orders all banished priests were recalled, the Christian religion was restored, and Christians throughout Bohemia were given freedom to worship where and how they wished.

The martyred king was entombed in Prague and almost immediately miracles were reported. Blind men touched the tomb and their sight was restored, the sick were made whole, the dead brought back to life. No doubt much of this was fanciful but the legend of the martyred king and his miracles spread rapidly, and Boleslas, fearful that the people would now rise up against him in their anger and shame, ordered that the body be moved to another resting place, the Church of St. Vitus in Prague. He would dearly loved to have burnt it or thrown it into the Vltava, but he knew the people of Bohemia would never countenance it. Perhaps, though, a change of location might put an end to the miracles?

It did not. For many, many years people reported miraculous happenings in the Church of St. Vitus.

Boleslas died, a guilty, unloved king, tortured by his own conscience and the contempt of his people. He was succeeded by his son Boleslas II, who was a pious and good man, basing his life on that of his uncle, "Good King Wenceslas". He was in addition a good general and extended his rule into Moravia and parts of Silesia and Poland. Bohemian history at this time is noted for the alternation of good rulers with bad, and the next one, Boleslas III, was a disaster, losing all Bohemia's foreign possessions and his own throne, to be replaced by a Polish prince, Vladivoj.

There are many churches to the memory of St. Wenceslas: the first, surprisingly, being erected in Denmark, a few years after the martyr's death. He is remembered widely, even in present-day Communist Czechoslovakia, as a wise ruler and an early Christian martyr.

OTTO I (THE GREAT)

(912–973)

EMPEROR CHARLEMAGNE, King of the Franks, who had been crowned in Aix-la-Chapelle (Aachen) in 800, had consolidated his realm and had made a supreme effort to establish a permanent Western empire which included some lands beyond the River Elbe. Charlemagne's plans had, however, been frustrated after his death, for he had appointed his three sons as his heirs. Then Louis, called the Pious, who finally succeeded Charlemagne, divided the empire amongst *his* three sons, who were all weak and ineffectual men, and during their reign Charlemagne's great dominions fell apart.

It was not until one hundred and fifty years later that this empire was revived and expanded by Otto I, called the Great even while he lived. He not only strengthened the power and the prestige of the empire itself, but dramatically made Italy a part of his dominions. This inclusion of Italy brought about the creation of the Holy Roman Empire in the medieval world.

Otto was born on 23 November, 912. He was the eldest son of Henry I, called the Fowler, Duke of Saxony, who in 919 had been chosen as German king by the other German rulers. Otto, Henry's son by his second wife Matilda, had two younger brothers and three sisters. Henry, a simple straightforward man, cared more about his country than about his own aggrandizement. He went to war not to exercise and to show off his armies' prowess, but only when he thought armed conflicts inevitable.

Matilda, Otto's mother, on the other hand, relished her position of power and regal dignity. She was a domineering woman who acknowledged only God as her superior. She was pious in the extreme and finally ended her days in a convent.

Henry's and Matilda's marriage was not a peaceful relationship. Otto's childhood was disturbed by his parents' quarrels. For Matilda was quite determined that her second son—several years younger than Otto—was to succeed her husband. Henry was equally determined that Otto was to be the heir to the throne. These altercations continued until Henry's death in 936, when Otto, then twenty-four years old, did in fact succeed his father.

In his younger days Otto must have welcomed the weeks he spent away from his mother, and he gladly joined his father's troops when they were fighting recalcitrant tribes in Bavaria or Swabia. It was also a relief to Otto when, at the age of seventeen, he was married to Edith, a daughter of Edward the Elder of England, and established his own household away from his parents.

Otto's education bore no resemblance whatsoever to the modern meaning of the word. He was, of course, by his mother, given a thorough religious training. Throughout his life he was considered a deeply religious man. He rarely missed early mass. He founded a number of famous convents and appointed many new bishops. He revered the Church, but he never considered himself a servant of the Church. He was her master.

Otto had no book learning. In fact he was never taught to read or to write. As a mature man this lack of education and his dependence upon his literate courtiers irked him. His illiteracy is not, however, reflected in those of his letters which have been handed down to us, for they clearly show how well he formulated his ideas and intentions in the documents dictated to his secretaries.

Despite his own lack of learning Otto respected scholars and always welcomed them to his court. And when he was thirty-five years old he taught himself the letters of the alphabet and acquired a certain ability to read manuscripts. He learned a little French, but did not speak the language. He had no knowledge of Latin, at a time when a proficiency in Latin was the mark of a man's real culture. Otto's lack of education did not hinder the development of his keen native intelligence. He had a splendid memory and very good judgment of men.

He loved hunting and riding wild horses and was a man of great physical courage. His manner was reserved and he was usually calm and dignified. Even as a young man he was more respected than loved. For his calm demeanour could sometimes suddenly change: he had a violent temper, though he forgot his outbursts more quickly than they were forgotten by the men in his court.

Otto's physical presence encouraged the awe with which he was regarded by his followers. There are no pictorial relics of Otto—apart from blurred likenesses on great seals—but Widukind, the Saxon historian, left a vivid description of Otto's person. This historian recorded that Otto was a tall, powerfully built man who demanded and got implicit obedience. "His eyes sparkled," Widukind wrote, "and struck men at whom he was gazing like a stroke of lightning . . . the hair on his chest was so thick that it was like a lion's mane. . . ."

When Otto was crowned in Aix-la-Chapelle in 936 by Hildebert, Archbishop of Mayence, he made it quite clear that he intended to be an absolute ruler. To emphasize the subservience he demanded from all of the German nobles, Otto had the Dukes of Bavaria, Swabia, Franconia and Lorraine wait upon him at the banquet which followed the coronation ceremonies in the cathedral.

This personal service by the dukes was a most important symbolic act. Otto's father had treated the other dukes almost as his equals; during his reign Germany had been something like a confederation. Otto, on the other hand, when he was waited upon by them during the banquet, indicated that henceforth they would be his vassals and that power would be vested in his person alone.

The dukes naturally resented this decrease in their influence. Soon some of them gathered together bands of armed followers and revolted against Otto. One of his half-brothers, Thankmar, went so far as to rebel against Otto in Saxony itself. Eberhard, the Duke of Franconia, came to Thankmar's assistance, but Otto succeeded in quelling this rebellion with the help of the Duke of Swabia who—luckily for Otto—had quarrelled with Eberhard.

Soon another insurrection followed. This time the insurgents were led by Otto's brother Henry, who was still angry because—despite his mother's wishes—Otto and not he had been chosen to succeed their father. Henry was joined by Giselbert, Duke of Lorraine, and by the Duke of Franconia. Henry and his allies marched from Lorraine towards the Rhine. Otto hastened with his troops to meet the rebels, but he did not have enough boats to ferry his entire force across the river. When he met Henry's armies, therefore, he was greatly outnumbered. Nevertheless, Otto was victorious—he was a clever strategist—and his victory was attributed by his superstitious people to a "Holy Lance" he carried. With this "Holy Lance" in his hand he continued, in a number of battles, to defeat Henry and his friends. Henry finally fled and escaped to the court of King Louis IV of France.

After the routing of his enemies Otto was too clever to seek further revenge. His aim was peace and unity in Germany, and when enough time had elapsed for the revolting nobles to calm down, he tried to win their friendship. His brother Henry was forgiven, appointed Duke of Bavaria and became a loyal follower of his king and brother. Otto retained a personal overlordship of Franconia, but he pacified Hermann, Duke of Swabia, by marrying one of his sons to one of Hermann's daughters. One of Otto's loyal followers, Conrad, the Red, was created Duke of Lorraine.

When peace within Germany seemed established, Otto made known that he planned to "secure" his Eastern frontiers. In common with other German rulers and leaders since Otto's days, he wanted to conquer and hold the tribes and territories in the East. Otto's *Drang nach Osten*—which made him a popular figure during Hitler's regime—caused him, first of all, to conquer Bohemia.

Then he turned to the Slavonic tribes living beyond the rivers Elbe and Oder. This war against the Slavs was terrible, causing vast devastation, mass executions and cruelty on both sides. It could have been but little comfort to the inhabitants of these ravaged regions when, after their defeat, Otto founded several bishoprics in the district. Garo, Otto's uncompromising representative in the Slavonic territories, was named as the Bishop of Magdeburg.

While Otto's eastern lands were being "pacified", he was having trouble with France. Louis IV, who had harboured Henry after his flight, was hoping to gain sovereignty over Lorraine. Otto had strong family feelings and he was particularly displeased with Louis who had married Otto's sister. Otto was too angry to attempt negotiations with his brother-in-law. He marched his troops into France and successfully attacked Louis. Later Louis was again defeated, this time by his rival Hugh the Great, Duke of France. Hugh irritated Otto as much as Louis had done, for Hugh, too, was Otto's brother-in-law: the husband of another sister. Now Otto was tired of these family quarrels. He defeated Hugh's forces at Rheims and then insisted that Hugh and Louis settle their differences amicably. Otto appointed himself as an arbitrator and intervened whenever Hugh and Louis seemed on the verge of fresh dissent.

Otto's prestige in Europe as well as in Germany was soon very great and it was not surprising that he became involved in Italian affairs. In Italy, Berengar II, Margrave of Ivrea, a cruel and unscrupulous man, had succeeded King Lothar. Berengar was trying to seize the dowry of Adelaide, Lothar's widow. The Italian bishops, who themselves had suffered under Berengar's rule, were enraged when he imprisoned Adelaide. She was a clever and attractive woman and she had managed to escape. She was still, however, in danger and the bishops and her other friends appealed to Otto to come to their assistance. He responded to this appeal, came with an army to Lombardy, and forced Berengar to accept the subordinate position as his vassal in northern Italy. Otto then assumed the title of King of Italy. In the meantime he had fallen in love with Adelaide. Several years had now passed since the death of his first wife, Edith, and he and Adelaide were married in Pavia.

Already Otto hoped to include Italy in his empire, but before he could make plans to realize this ambition he was summoned back to Germany where his son Ludolf—fearing the rivalry of Adelaide's future sons—was conspiring with the disloyal Archbishop of Mayence and others to undermine Otto's authority. At the same time some of Otto's Magyar vassals were in revolt and had attacked Bavaria.

While Otto was quelling these insurrections in Germany the situation in Italy had become more unsettled than ever. The Duke of Lorraine—whom Otto had appointed as his representative in Lombardy—had joined Berengar in an effort to undermine Otto's position in Italy. In 961 Pope John XII—notorious for his debauched way of life—appealed to Otto to help him get rid of Berengar. Otto returned to Italy, and after Berengar's resistance had been broken Otto was generally acknowledged as King of Italy, and his sovereignty of southern as well as northern Italy was firmly established.

Otto's power was now supreme in Italy, and on 31 January, 962, in St. Peter's in Rome, he was crowned with all pomp by John XII as Holy Roman Emperor. Not only had Otto thus achieved supreme secular authority in Europe; beyond that—and this is historically of the greatest importance—he made himself the head of the Church. For he forced the Pope to swear an oath of allegiance to himself, and John XII thus became Otto's vassal. Later, when John showed signs of regretting this oath, Otto deposed him. Otto selected Pope Leo VIII as John's successor and decreed that henceforth no Pope should be elected without his consent.

The bitterness felt by most churchmen because of this decree was expressed by Benedict, a Roman monk, who wrote: "Woe to thee Rome that thou art crushed and trodden down by so many peoples; who hast been seized by a Saxon king . . . and thy strength reduced to nought."

When Otto had settled affairs in Rome he returned to Germany, but after the sudden death of Pope Leo in 965 the Roman clergy and nobles tried to elect the Pope of their choosing without Otto's consent. He hurried back to Rome and against the wishes of the Romans he appointed the Bishop of Narni as the new Pope. He was Pope John XIII. The Romans were dissatisfied, temporarily drove John XIII into exile, and Otto faced an awkward situation. However, by 966 he had imposed his will on the Romans and John XIII returned to Rome.

Then Otto left Italy for the last time and the closing years of his life were peaceful. He died on 6 May, 973, and was buried in the Cathedral of Magdeburg which he had built. He had accomplished what he set out to accomplish: he had revived Charlemagne's Holy Roman Empire, he had forcefully subdued the turbulent German tribes and instilled in the Germans the beginnings of a national pride. He had spread the teachings of Christianity—as he understood them—and at the same time had brought the Papacy under his control. He had increased Germany's *Lebensraum* in the East.

Whether or not, in the long run, Otto's expansionist policies benefited Germany and Europe as a whole only students of Germany's history after Otto's reign can judge.

BRIAN BORU

(926–1014)

"STOUT, ABLE, valiant, fierce, magnificent, hospitable, munificent, strong, lively and friendly. The most eminent of the west of Europe."

Quite a testimonial. It is for Brian, from a contemporary; and from what we are able to piece together about him, accurate, even discerning. He was all these things, and we can add to the list that he was a Christian and devout: he was slain—a very old man—as he knelt near the battlefield to pray. He had resisted all entreaty to take himself to a place of safety.

Like many great men of his period, Brian had a pedigree that was largely imaginary, an Arthurian fantasy of blood-drenched heroes stretching back through the dawn of history, through darkness and out into the magic world of mythology. But from the ninth century we can trace it with some accuracy, thanks largely to the vivid details we have been given of ceaseless, bloody war between Irishman and Dane.

The Danes came to Ireland early in the ninth century, stealing up the River Shannon in long, slender boats, leaping ashore to lay waste to the country, plunder what they could from it and move on: or, when the fancy took them, to settle.

A little later they met shattering, unexpected defeat at the hands of the tribal chief Corc and here history begins. We can follow Corc's line down through his successive descendants, Lachtna, Lorcan and Cenedid, the gallant Cenedid who died fighting the Danes, a hundred and twenty years after his great-grandfather had thought, with reason, that he had flung them into the sea forever. Cenedid—a name more memorable in its modern form of Kennedy—was killed in 951. He left two sons, Mahon and Brian, and these continued the fight: waging non-stop, guerrilla war against the Danes from the unbroken forests which, in those distant days, swept down to the edge of the Danish town of Limerick. They suffered impossible hardships, never able to stay in a spot long enough to organize supplies, always harried, pursued, by a larger, better-armed, well-fed force.

Eventually the young King Mahon, weak from wounds and starvation, seeing no end to the conflict, made peace with the Danes.

But his brother Brian refused to do so, went on attacking, his force getting gradually smaller. At last, with only fifteen able-bodied supporters left, he confronted his brother.

"Why, O King," he demanded, "have you chosen to make this wicked truce? Is not your country my country, the country of our father who was killed for it? Do we not both wish it to be free? Can you not fight for it, with me?"

"Your country," said Mahon, "is mine indeed. But look at those you have made fight for it. Where are they now? Dead, for the most part, homes and villages burnt to the ground."

"Better death than dishonour."

"A fine thought. And how many are there to share it with you? Fifteen men, it would seem, in all Ireland."

"There are more—and they will come."

"You are a brave man, my brother. And a fool. Why should the blood of Ireland be spilt in a hopeless cause? Look—my own supporters are at peace with the Danes. At peace, well-fed. And alive."

A strong argument, but Brian ignored it—and so strong was his personality, so right his cause, that he brought Mahon over to his side. The Kingdom of Munster, under its king and his younger brother, prepared for war. Inspired by the alliance, the people of Munster rallied to the flag.

When the attack, after careful preparation, was launched against Limerick, it was strikingly successful. The Danish stronghold was wrested from its commander, Ivor, thousands of Danes were killed. The capture was followed by wholesale, systematic looting, of jewellery, leather, satin, silk—and of boys and girls for slavery.

And then Mahon, King of Munster, most respected king in all Ireland, indulged in an odd form of sport. Having slaughtered almost all the male population of Limerick, he led out the women, young and old, hundred upon hundred of them, and made them get down on hands and knees in a large circle. The circle was some two furlongs round, on a stretch of open land outside the burning town. And here, within and around this circle, he and his men engaged in running races throughout the whole of one day, the border of their track marked out by the kneeling bodies of Danish women.

When night fell and the sports were over, the women still capable of getting to their feet were allowed to do so. Those not wanted by the victors trooped back to the charred remains of their city, to fossick in the ruins.

Months went by and the Danes returned with a fleet, but by now the spell of Danish power was broken and they were easily beaten off. Mahon was King of Munster in reality, with none—or so it seemed—to contest his claim. Nine good years passed.

But in 976 Mahon was butchered by a gang of conspirators, a bloody ruse of the sort that has punctuated Celtic history. Donnabhain, trusted friend of the king, paid him a visit, partook of his hospitality, overpowered him and called up the rest. One of these, Maelmuadh, butchered the king. Maelmuadh, when the news came out, was cursed by all the clergy of Munster.

A little later, he, too, was butchered on the battlefield. But by this time the Danes, invited back by the conspirators, were spreading over Munster.

Brian was now a reluctant king and he swore to avenge his brother. Gathering an army about him, he first killed Ivor the Dane; then, systematically, he cleared islands and forts of Ivor's men. Donnabhain, the Judas who had handed Mahon over to his death, now panicked and sent for Harold, the Dane who styled himself King of Munster. Harold assembled a large force and met Brian. In the battle that followed, the Danes were soundly beaten and Harold and Donnabhain killed.

By 984 Brian was truly King of Munster and supreme in the south of Ireland. He then easily subjected the titular "King of All Ireland", Maelsechlainn, who ruled in Meath. Gradually he overcame both Connaught and Ulster. And now to the man who was real King of Ireland, tribute and captives poured in. (His title of "Boru" comes from the old Irish "boroma", or "tribute".) He was all-powerful. At the same time, he was a good and wise ruler. He sent abroad for books that his people might learn wisdom, established professorships all over his kingdom and paid the incumbents lavishly. He built churches. There was lawlessness in the land and Brian of the Tribute set out to punish this with a severity which would be horrifying today, but was typical of the period: eleventh-century hands and feet were hacked off for venial offences, tongues and eyes torn out for what might merit a stiff reprimand in the twentieth. Slowly, law, order and the blessings of knowledge settled into Munster, began to spread over Ireland. There is a belief in Ireland that the first years of the eleventh century were good and peaceful, under the strong rule of Brian; but history fails to confirm this. Plots, insurrections, murders and assassination continued apace, with the ever-present Danes to complicate each issue, give each plotter and assassin hope of reward.

This idyll of peace and prosperity—and though it was largely illusory, Brian deserves great credit for his efforts to achieve it—was shattered by a new and vicious quarrel between Brian and the King of Leinster. Leinster's king, with Danish backing, had decided he, not Brian, should be acknowledged King of All Ireland. He challenged the army of Munster to dispute his claim.

And so, on 23 April, 1014, Brian crossed the Shannon to engage the armies of Leinster and the Danes. He was eighty-eight years old, still strong in mind and body, still in absolute command of his army and its strategy, and of the hearts of its men. He had no doubt that with God's guidance he would defeat the enemy, for he was fortified by the knowledge that he defended the religion of Christ against the heathen worship of Odin.

At Clontarf the two armies met. For Brian and his followers it was a Crusade, and banners with the Cross of Christ were whipping in the wind when the first steel met. The battle had begun with the premature charge of a part of Brian's force under his son, the headstrong Murchadh, which was repulsed. The two opposing forces settled down to bloody combat at close quarters.

A little apart from the fighting, but in his own small tent, pitched far in front of the Munster encampment, the aged King Brian prayed. He sang psalms, recited prayers, a Pater Noster. According to Irish sources, he did this accompanied only by one young page, completely unprotected, as the battle raged less than a mile away. Danish history agrees that the old king was in an exposed spot, but states that, apart from the young page who prayed with him, Brian was at the centre of a ring of armed men.

The boy, hearing ever-louder sounds of battle, the groans of the dying, the clash of metal, asked his king whether he would not move. The outcome of the battle was far from clear, but the danger to an old man was growing. "I pray you, Sire—move before it is too late!"

"Oh God, thou boy, retreat becomes us not. And I myself know that I shall not leave this place alive. And what would it profit me?"

"But, Sire——"

"Enough."

A moment later the boy looked out and cried, "Blue, naked, people are advancing on us". And this, to one who had not yet seen them at close quarters was exactly what the Danish soldiers looked like, in their close-fitting blue *byrnies*.

"It matters not, boy."

The tent flap was flung open, three men burst in. They ignored the page and seized the old man, still on his knees.

"The king," said one.

"It is not the king. It is one of their priests. He is praying."

The old man, ignoring them, went on praying.

"One does not slay a priest."

"But this is no priest. Look—that is a king's mantle. Kill him."

And the three Danes killed Brian of the Tribute, King of Munster and All Ireland, in his tent.

He had been, by the standards of his time, a good king, and, by any criteria, a wise and brave one. He had succeeded, not entirely for reasons of aggrandizement, in making himself ruler of an all-but-united Ireland. Had his line been spared, he and his descendants might have made that unity a real thing, made Ireland strong and great, for even in the moment of his death Brian's army was winning a resounding victory against the Danes and his Irish enemies.

But with Brian gone, and with him his son Murchadh, who had begun the Battle of Clontarf and was to survive it by only a short time, the line had ended. Ireland descended again into the pit of intrigue and petty warfare from which she took so many years to rise.

In his long life—but a moment against the span of Irish history —Brian Boru won for himself undying fame as a great and good ruler who proved his country could be united. He has been compared with King Robert Bruce of Scotland, and the Battle of Clontarf with that of Bannockburn, for both men were wise rulers and both battles inflicted shattering defeat on their enemies. But Bruce's Scotland was more stable than Brian's Ireland, and Bruce was fighting with his country behind him against a single, clear-cut enemy, not a fifth-column like that which was helping the Danes. And Bruce survived the battle, was able to consolidate his victory and bring to Scotland the peace and justice for which he had fought.

But though Brian's line was extinguished and therefore his victory not as conclusive as it might have been, he has gone deservedly into history as a wise and brave ruler, one of his country's greatest sons.

CANUTE

(995–1035)

ENGLAND'S POSITION as an island has always been considered her greatest protection against invasion. But England's immunity from invasion dates only from the Norman Conquest. Before that Saxon Britain endured centuries of invasion, and was pillaged and plundered, its inhabitants slaughtered by generations of sea-borne invaders who came mainly from Scandinavia. These bold and ruthless Vikings—the Northmen or the Danes, as the English called them—ravaged the coasts of all Europe, from the Orkneys to the Isles of Greece.

The word Viking simply means warrior. The fiercest and most successful of them came from Denmark, and they were not all uncivilized. They had settled in the valley of the Seine and formed the Dukedom of Normandy. William the Conqueror was one of their descendants.

Two Vikings who had a great effect upon English history were Sweyn Forkbeard, King of Denmark, and his son Canute.*

In 1013 Ethelred the Unready was on the throne of Wessex, the last Saxon kingdom in a Britain where the Danish influence had been spreading for a long time. Ethelred was a weak and cowardly man, quite unfit to rule. After a generation of peace from the ancient enemy in Denmark, the country was once more subjected to Viking raids. In vain the ineffectual Ethelred tried to buy the invaders off with the traditional Danegeld. He then attempted to strengthen his position by marrying Emma, sister of Duke Richard of Normandy. He gained a beautiful wife, but little more. Emma was called the Pearl of Normandy on account of her beauty.

Ethelred found that there was no way of buying off Sweyn. He was determined to add England to his dominions, and in 1013 he landed with a great army and claimed the crown. After some bitter, sporadic fighting, the country capitulated. The craven Ethelred fled to Normandy with his bride.

But Sweyn died within a few weeks of his success, and Canute, who had accompanied his father on the expedition, was proclaimed

*The true form is Cnut. Canute is the Latin name used by medieval historians.

king. He was nineteen, a brave and talented young man, to be numbered among England's greatest rulers.

However, with the death of the terrible Sweyn Forkbeard the English gained heart. The Witan, a more or less haphazard assembly of ecclesiastics, nobles, royal officials and other magnates which existed to advise Anglo-Saxon kings, then plucked up courage and invited Ethelred to return to the throne. This Ethelred eagerly did, taking full advantage of the revulsion of feeling in his favour. But his subjects found him unchanged, and as mean, cruel and faithless as ever. Fortunately for his unhappy realm he was a sick man and he died in 1016, to be succeeded by his son Edmund Ironside.

Edmund was a brave and worthy man, in direct contrast to his despicable father, but the Saxon sun was setting, and though London and other parts of the country accepted him as king, the north, which was mainly Danish, was for Canute, who was in the country with a great fleet and a strong army. During 1016 Canute and Edmund fought bitterly for the English crown. Canute tried several times to take London, without success. He eventually defeated Edmund at Assandune (now Ashington) in Essex, but there was nothing final about the victory and Canute had to agree to partition of the kingdom. The two monarchs, both men of worth, met at Olney, an island in the Severn, and decided that Canute should rule Mercia and Northumbria, while Edmund should have Wessex, London and East Anglia.

Edmund did not live long to enjoy the fruits of this patched-up peace, which on the face of it did not seem likely to last for long. Within a few months he was dead, poisoned it was said by one, Edric Streona, who during the late fighting had joined whichever side seemed to have the best chance of winning. The Witan, weary of the war, then elected Canute as king of the whole kingdom.

Canute more than justified the wisdom of their choice, even though no exercise of wisdom was involved in this particular instance. The Witan had no choice and only wished to have an end to this wretched squabble for the crown. Kings were not so important in Anglo-Saxon England as they were after the Conquest when they became hereditary. Before 1066 the monarchy was largely elective.

Canute was no Viking adventurer. The age of the Vikings was at an end, as Canute well knew. On his mother's side he had Slavonic blood in him and this tempered the fierce and reckless Viking blood. He was also something of a statesman and this showed immediately in his dealing with the two young sons of Edmund Ironside—mere children of course, but important children. Canute did not put them to death, which might have been excusable in that rough age. Instead he sent them to the court at Sweden. It might be thought that Canute set a good example—which was not followed—to the monarchs who sat upon the English throne after him, a number of whom were faced with the problem of disposing of persons dangerously near an insecure throne. The more probable explanation for Canute's apparent generosity lay in the fact that the English throne, being largely elective, the children were no threat to him.

One of the first things Canute did was to put away his Danish wife and propose marriage to Emma, widow of Ethelred. Despite the lady's legendary beauty, this was a political marriage above all else. He wished particularly to have friendly relations with Emma's brother, the powerful Duke of Normandy, who despite his own Viking ancestry could not have viewed the events in England with any great favour. Even then the Dukes of Normandy had their eyes on the desirable throne of England.

Emma, who well knew the unpleasant character of her late husband, was not averse to the match. On the contrary, she was prepared to leave the two sons she had borne Ethelred in her brother's care in Normandy, and once more ornament the English throne as consort to the young Canute. She was older than he, yet she had retained her beauty. She put but one condition to the union—one which Canute found not unflattering. It was that the succession to the English throne should go to the son which she would bear him, and that the sons by their other unions should be excluded. Canute agreed, and the beauteous Emma once more became Queen of England, and bore Canute a son who became Hardicanute, and king after his father.

One of the first of Canute's forthright measures was to put to death the perfidious Edric Streona, who was suspected of poisoning that valiant adversary Edmund Ironside. Canute had no use for men like that. Canute also sent back to Denmark the army which had enabled him to gain the throne, and he paid off the great Viking fleet which had brought the army to England and whose existence was a threat and a source of fear in the country. This wise but difficult act of demobilization was only brought about by paying £83,000 in Danegeld, an enormous sum in those days, which the country had to raise in the form of taxes. But it was a wise and statesmanlike move.

One of the most important things that Canute did for England was to reconcile the Danes and the English, and give them equal rights before the law. This had been one of the grievances of the English in Mercia and those parts dominated by the Danes.

Canute gained great favour among the monastic chroniclers by his attitude to Christianity. His father had been a pagan and Canute himself had been nurtured in the worship of Woden. Legends exist about the miraculous manner in which he was converted to the true faith. But in those days Christianity was the mark of civilization (such as it was), and Canute was anxious to shake off his Viking role and join the mainstream of history. All the Vikings who had settled in Europe became Christian, and Canute did so with great enthusiasm and gained high favour among his contemporaries by founding abbeys, making gifts to monasteries and churches, by promoting churchmen to high office and doing reverence to saints and holy places. He made laws for the rigorous payment of tithes and church dues, for the observance of the Sabbath and the suppression of heathenism. In 1026 he went on a pilgrimage to Rome and was present at the coronation of Emperor Conrad III.

Canute was one of the great law-givers of English history. He gave to free Englishmen the first charter of liberties, and his legal system survived and formed the basis of English law under the Norman monarchs. What was known as "Cnut's law" in the succeeding centuries was a system of government which recognized the ancient and approved customs.

He was the first English king to establish a strong central government in the country. He travelled around with his staff of secretaries, scribes and legal advisers, and was the first king to have this kind of permanent secretariat.

Canute was not the first foreigner to rule successfully over a people whose customs, language and manners were at first strange to him, and he was certainly not the last. But England was only part of his great kingdom. In 1018 he became King of Denmark, then much larger than it is now, and he also conquered Sweden and Norway during his busy and eventful life. No other English king before or since has ruled over so large a portion of Europe. His comparatively early death prevented the establishment of a powerful Nordic empire bridging the North Sea, the possible historical consequences of which make interesting speculation. Canute's successors looked across the English Channel rather than the North Sea, and thus paved the way for the Norman Conquest.

In 1031 Canute conquered Scotland and forced King Malcolm to recognize his overlordship. Malcolm's nephew Duncan also did homage to Canute, and also a certain Maelboethe, both of whom were immortalized by Shakespeare, the latter as Macbeth.

It is evident that Canute thought more highly of England than of any of his possessions. He sent English missionaries to convert his pagan subjects in Scandinavia to Christianity. He gave England an especial undertaking that the country would be free from Viking raids which it had suffered for so long. When he was in Rome he wrote to the English people a letter containing, besides many elevated moral sentiments, regrets for his past misdeeds and promises for the future. In it he ordered his royal officers to do justice to all men whatever their estate, and not to extort money wrongfully under the pretext of the royal necessities. "I have no need," he said magnanimously, "of money gathered by unrighteousness".

Like all monarchs, he suffered from fawning courtiers. There is the famous story of when he was at Southampton, and was addressed as "Lord and master of the sea as well as of the land". To establish the literal incorrectness of this sentiment, which is certainly not so fulsome as some which have been bestowed upon rulers, and as a lesson in Christian humility, he had a chair placed at the water's edge before the incoming tide, and he challenged the sea to wet the feet of him whose ships sailed upon it and against whose land it dashed. The tide accepted the challenge and wet Canute's feet and clothes and Canute said: "Behold how feeble is the power of kings of men, for the waves will not hear my voice. Honour the Lord only, and serve him, for to him all things give obedience."

The story may or may not be true and to many it merely illustrates Canute's rather ostentatious religious sentiments, which were natural and perhaps necessary in an age when men were being converted from the old paganism to the new religion which was to be the cornerstone of Europe in the centuries to come.

But Canute, Dane though he was, deserved well of his adopted land, to which he had given order, law, unity and good government.

Canute died in 1035 at the age of forty, which was not young in those days when men lived hard and the normal span of life was short, but it was not long enough for Canute's work to be enduring. All too quickly England slipped back into the old chaos and disorder. It had to wait for the coming of Canute's kinsfolk, the Normans, to be moulded finally into the kingdom and country we know today.

WILLIAM I (THE CONQUEROR)

(1027?–1087)

THE ONLY English ruler who is given the title "The Great" is the noble Alfred. He merits the title but he was not King of all England: it would be more fitly given to William I, Duke of Normandy, usually called "The Conqueror". Attila, Genghis Khan and Napoleon were conquerors. William was a great warrior but he was above all the man who founded England, and, being a great administrator, gave it some of those features which made England, in less than a hundred years' time, already the first modern nation.

The Norman Conquest brought the Anglo-Saxon realm out of the orbit of the Scandinavian Empire and into the evolving world of Latin Christianity and feudalism. The Norman Conquest was the final ingredient which made the England of today. The very English language was transformed as a result of the Conquest into the language of Chaucer and Shakespeare. The effect of the Norman Conquest was to drive the Anglo-Saxon language underground, to make it a tongue only spoken by the ruled, by the simple and poor. Anglo-Saxon in the mouths of such men lost its Germanic inflections and general heaviness, and when, as happened astonishingly quickly, Normans and Anglo-Saxons found they were one people, the language emerged as more simple, direct and flexible than it had been and also enriched by Norman French. So the very English language was the fruit of the Norman Conquest.

Not much more than one hundred and fifty years before 1066, Norsemen, sailing in their conquest of foreign lands, landed at the mouth of the Seine, and the first leader of these men, Rolf the Ganger, agreed to hold the lands he had won as vassal of the King of France. Very quickly these Norsemen conquered what is now all Normandy. They were a warlike and cunning people, more ferocious and ruthless than the inhabitants of the surrounding areas. But they took to Christianity and were great admirers of learning which was largely in the hands at that time of the Church. The Duchy became a very well organized unit, and the Duke had much more power over his subordinate nobles and chieftains than had the French king over his.

WILLIAM I (THE CONQUEROR)

William was born in 1027. He was the fruit of a love affair between his father, Duke Robert of Normandy, and Arletta, the daughter of a tanner of Falaise. Duke Robert had no legitimate issue and so in 1042, when he went on a crusade from which he never returned, he left his bastard as Duke. Tall and strongly built, with an air of majesty even as a young man which inspired awe, William had first to suppress various revolts which broke out against him, leading his men himself with a huge battle-axe.

The inhabitants of Alençon rebelled against him and to mock his birth they hung hides on the walls of their city with "Work for the Tanner" written across them. William cut out the eyes and cut off the hands of the prisoners he had taken and threw them into the city. He was soon undisputed master of his Duchy and when the King of France twice invaded Normandy he twice defeated the French armies.

No knight under heaven, it was said at this time, was William's equal. And no man dared say him nay. He showed, however, another side of his nature to those men of the Church, by no means all, whom he respected. From Abbot Lanfranc, afterwards to be Archbishop of Canterbury, he took advice. Once in a fit of temper he ordered the great scholar Anselm, who was also to play an important part in the history of England, out of the country. Hearing Anselm was proceeding very slowly he rode after him to hurry him on. "I'll go faster if you'll give me a better mount than this poor palfrey," said Anselm. The Duke laughed and they became friends.

William looked across the water. From nearly the beginning of the century to 1042, England had been ruled by the great Danish King Canute and by his unworthy sons. The House of Alfred was restored in Edward the Confessor who had spent his youth in Normandy at the court of William's father. Edward lived as a monk, and though married was obviously going to have no children. He loved the Church above all things and preferred the civilized Normans to his own subjects. He gave land to Norman knights on the borders of Wales and he installed Normans as bishops.

The heir to Edward the Confessor's throne by blood was a young boy, Edgar the Atheling; but though blood counted, no one could be king without the consent of the great Anglo-Saxon nobles or thanes. The monarchy in fact was partly elective. Edward had almost certainly promised William of Normandy the crown after him. The saintly king was no ruler and there was no central power of law anywhere in the land, each thane doing what he liked in his own domains. The kingdom was in fact falling to pieces, and sooner or later seemed likely to lapse back into the hands of the Scandinavians. No wonder then, when Edward the Confessor died in 1065 the English thanes decided that in spite of rivalries they would elect the strongest of their nation, Harold Godwin the Earl of Wessex, as Edward's successor. Harold, who had very carefully placated Edwin and Morcar, the lords of the North, by siding with them in a quarrel with his own brother Tostig. And so, in the words of the Anglo-Saxon chronicle, on the very day that Edward died:

Earle Harold was now consecrated King and he met little quiet in it as long as he ruled the realm.

William fell into a fury when the news was brought to him, as he had expected to be summoned to the Witan in London at least to state his claims. If Edgar the Atheling were set aside he had a certain claim in blood which, apart from his bastardy, was a better one than Harold's. Edward the Confessor was the son of a daughter of William's grandfather.

Still more was he angered because of a curious incident. Harold Godwin had either been wrecked off the coast of Normandy or, according to the Normans, sent by Edward the Confessor on a mission to William of Normandy to assure him of the throne. In any case, however it happened, William received Harold with great friendship and took him on a military expedition in Brittany—thus in fact showing that Harold served under him as a warrior and was therefore his vassal. Before Harold was allowed to return to England he had to swear fealty to William as future King of England in the presence of a large concourse of knights and barons. He took the oath, he could not in fact do otherwise; and then according to some sources, having sworn on a simple altar table, the table was shown to conceal the bodies of various holy martyrs. Harold's perjury was considered so serious that even on the eve of the Battle of Hastings some of his advisers thought he should not fight against William in person.

By Christmas of that year he was crowned king in Westminster Abbey, the great Saxon church which it had been Edward the Confessor's life work to build. Though there was bitter fighting in the north and west of England, though the Danes were to help the English rebels, the success of William's achievement was never in much doubt after the events of 1066. England was substantially conquered by an army of some twelve thousand Norman and French knights, men-at-arms and archers at the Battle of Hastings, or as it is sometimes called Senlac, fought in October. Harold was killed in the battle and with him many of the famous nobles and warriors.

Harold had been obliged in the late summer to raise an army and march north to fight a Scandinavian invasion led by Harold Hardraada, with his brother Tostig. After the victory at Stamford, he learnt that the Normans had landed in Sussex. Instead of waiting for William near London and getting the largest possible forces together, he decided to dash to Hastings to give battle. William very wisely hoped he would do this and had on purpose remained near his ships. When William had landed he had slipped on the sand and his followers, aware that they were on a rash enterprise, were alarmed. "See," said the Duke, rising to his feet, "I have firmly grasped the soil of England in my hands."

The battle was a hard-fought one. The English, dismounted, fought in a close formation protected by their huge shields. One Norman attack, uphill, was decisively beaten back. William ordered his cavalry, later, to pretend to flee from the battle. The English ranks broke up in pursuit and the Normans turned on them. Even then the English were able to reform, and it was not until late in the evening—with the Norman archers shooting up into the air so that their arrows would strike downwards, and William himself leading the furious attacks of the Norman knights—that victory came. Harold died, an arrow through his eye, and William refused him burial; and so the last Anglo-Saxon king rotted on the ground.

After Hastings, William again delayed. Edwin and Morcar, the thanes of the North, did not proclaim Edgar the Atheling as king at once. This they were to do, too late, in 1068. After this rebellion William devastated practically the whole of Yorkshire and the northern thanedoms of Burnisia, on the borders of Scotland. The truth was that though the Anglo-Saxons under local leaders such as Hereward the Wake in the fen country would fight bravely, the kingdom itself was so anarchic that it was not possible to rally men against Normans for the defence of the country. In 1067, for instance, William was already able to use the English Fyrd, the armed militia of the Anglo-Saxons, against some forces under the command of Harold's sons at Exeter and in the west.

However, William had to use all his driving force and ruthlessness to make himself really master of all England and to secure the nominal vassalage of the King of Scotland. When Edwin and

Morcar rebelled with the help of the Danish king, and the Welsh poured across the border into Cheshire to fight the Normans, the king answered with terror, devastating most of Yorkshire and County Durham. After "the harrying of the north" the great Norman castles were quickly erected on huge earth mounds piled up by Saxon serfs. The citizens of London saw the huge dungeon of the Tower dominate the city. Though the peasants pursued their ancient systems of farming as before, and though the Norman king was inclined to help the townspeople and merchants and to grant them charters, large parts of England, particularly the marches of Wales and Scotland and the Danelaw in the east, were very much under a military occupation. And the majority of the Anglo-Saxon nobles lost their lands forever.

Good came from the very thoroughness of the Conquest. King William had no intention of allowing Saxon thanes or Norman barons to challenge the power of the Crown. He refused to allow any single lord to hold large estates grouped together but scattered their lands about the country. The king, therefore, was far more powerful than any of his subjects, and accordingly his sheriffs and governors were respected. England, like Normandy, became a more modern and centralized kingdom than anywhere else in Christendom. The king, as his subjects knew, was avaricious—not personally but for his kingship. The great Doomsday Book was an extraordinary innovation for the eleventh century. The Anglo-Saxon chronicler describes it with wonder and also with the sort of scornful surprise that a king should bother so much about such things.

Then the king sent his men over all England into every shire and had them find out how many hundred hides there were in the shire, or what land or cattle the king himself had in the country or what dues he ought to have in twelve months. Also he had a record made of how much land his Archbishops had, and his Bishops and his Abbotts and his Earls—and they are related at two great lengths—what or how much everybody had who was occupying land in England, in land or cattle, and how much money it was worth. So very narrowly did he have it investigated, that there was no single hide nor yard of land, nor indeed (it is a shame to relate but it seemed no shame for him to do) one ox nor one cow nor one pig was there left out and not put down in his record: and all these records were brought to him afterwards.

From his wife Matilda, a daughter of the Count of Flanders, he had four sons: Robert Duke of Normandy; Richard, killed as a youth whilst hunting; William II and Henry I, both of whom succeeded him; and five daughters. He was a faithful husband without personal vices. In old age he was somewhat corpulent, but still muscular and agile, with short moustaches on each side of his upper lip and close-cropped hair. A monk of Caen wrote:

> *The King excelled in wisdom all the princes of his generation, and among them all he was outstanding in the largeness of his soul.*

He was great in body and strong, tall in stature but not ungainly. He was also temperate in eating and drinking. Especially was he moderate in drinking, for he abhorred drunkenness in all men and disdained it more particularly in himself and at his court. In speech he was fluent and persuasive, being skilled at all times in making clear his will. If his voice was harsh, what he said was always suited to the occasion. He followed the Christian discipline, and whenever his health permitted he regularly, and with great piety, attended Christian worship each morning and evening.

His death took place during an expedition in Normandy to punish the men of Mantes who had raided his territory. During this expedition the great king was struck with violent pains in his intestines. On Tuesday, 9 September, 1087, he woke from sleep and heard the great bell of Rouen Cathedral and saw the sun—but died soon after. As often happens when a great man died in those days, those around the bedside were filled with alarm. A monkish chronicler notes that the physicians and others who were present, who had watched the king all night, seeing him expire so suddenly and unexpectedly were much astonished and became as men who had lost their wits. The wealthiest of them mounted their horses and departed in haste to secure their property. But the inferior attendants, observing that their masters had disappeared, laid hands on the arms, the plate, the robes, the lining, and all the royal furniture and, leaving the corpse almost naked on the floor of the house, they hastened away. William was afterwards buried in great pomp in the Cathedral at Caen.

An Anglo-Saxon chronicler states:

> *This King William was a very wise man and very powerful and more worshipful and stronger than any predecessor of his had been. He was gentler to the good men who loved God, and stern beyond all measure to those people who resisted his will. Amongst the good things he did, the security he made in this country is not to be forgotten—so that any honest man could travel over his kingdom without injury with his bosom full of gold: and no one dared strike another however much wrong he had done him. And if a man had intercourse with a woman against her will, he was forthwith castrated. He ruled over England and by his cunning it was so investigated that there*

was not one hide of land he did not know. Wales was in his power, he built castles there and entirely controlled that race.

However, the Anglo-Saxon chronicler also goes on to speak of William's pride and ends:

Alas, woe, that any man so proud should go, and exalt himself and reckon himself above all men. Though Almighty God show mercy on his soul and grant unto him forgiveness for his sins.

The judgment of posterity is certainly with those who admire William's greatness of soul and mind, and rather less with those who bemoaned his pride. He can claim to be the begetter of the English realm.

FREDERICK BARBAROSSA

(1120–1190)

IN A cavern in the Kyffhäuser mountain in Thuringia there has been sitting for nearly eight hundred years an old man in royal robes with a crown on his head. He is asleep so that his eyes cannot be seen, but they are large and blue. A slight smile plays round his broad humorous mouth. His hair is silver, but his beard has touches of red in it and has grown so long that it has pushed right through the table before him. Ravens fly round the mouth of the cave and some day, when they depart, the old man will wake up, take his shield and sword and save Germany from her enemies. So runs the legend of Frederick Barbarossa (1120-1190), and it is still alive in Germany today, for the red-bearded emperor has rightly been called the greatest figure in early German history after Charlemagne.

Elected king in 1152 in succession to his uncle, Conrad III, he faced a formidable task. Germany was like a melon sliced into segments, and in the centuries following Charlemagne's division of his empire amongst his sons these segments had tended to split off. In a vast country stretching from the North Sea to Italy and from Burgundy to the boundaries of Poland, the tribal groups of Burgundians, Swabians, Bavarians, Saxons and East Franks had developed an independent life under their own rulers, held together only by an elected king whom German princes looked on not as a superior, but as the first among equals.

This loose conglomeration faced a number of threats. Danes, Northmen, Poles and Magyars pressed in from the perimeter. Rival dukes, when they were not repelling invaders, fought for power among themselves, and for many years before Frederick's accession there had been an internecine struggle between the House of Hohenstaufen (called the Waiblings) from which Frederick came and the Saxon House of Welf, which since the eleventh century had supplied three German emperors.

There was also a complicated issue of spiritual versus temporal authority within Germany. Charlemagne had been declared by the Pope to be Emperor of the Roman Empire and this established a precedent for future Popes to appoint the man of their choice as temporal ruler over Christendom. In the early Middle Ages the theory was that Christianity had both a spiritual and a temporal head—Pope and Emperor—and this was symbolized in the picture of two swords which defended the Faith. But this segregation of powers never took place. The Popes had their political ambitions and within Germany they sought to influence the whole life of the country through their legates and bishops recognizing them as the supreme head, temporal as well as spiritual, of whom the emperor was merely a kind of liegeman. This German emperors could not accept, particularly as they needed the support of churchmen in maintaining their own authority.

So under Frederick's predecessors a continual struggle for supremacy had developed between emperors and popes, made more acute in the time of Otto the Great (see earlier chapter) by his invasion of northern Italy, its reduction to a satellite kingdom and his banishment, on grounds of treachery, of the Pope who had crowned him emperor in Rome. Otto then styled himself Holy Roman Emperor, a title which was not finally dropped until 1806.

Thus was born the Imperial Idea to which much of Frederick's life and energies were dedicated and the Idea was quite new, fitting the times. Frederick gave it form. Within Germany the longstanding contest of Welf and Waiblingen would be brought to an end, not by crushing the Welfs, to whom he was related on his mother's side, but by making them yet stronger and then enlisting their support to create a new Imperial splendour. This was based on the idea of power derived directly from God, confirmed, not conferred, by the Pope. A clear division must be made once more between spiritual and temporal authority, the Pope must be relegated to his proper sphere and be deprived of the capacity to make trouble. This meant that the cities of northern Italy must be thoroughly subjugated to the Imperial rule so that they could not intrigue with the Pope and he would have the Imperial power on his door-step. The wealth of the cities would also fill Frederick's coffers, providing him with the resources which his German kingship lacked.

To realize this Idea Frederick possessed outstanding qualities: political skill, courage, perseverance, piety, a love of adventure and the ability to conciliate which went with great personal charm. After his election he hastened to make peace with his proud and powerful Welf kinsman, Duke Henry the Lion, by restoring to him Bavaria, part of his dukedom which Conrad had seized. Two years later he toured the Rhineland and the Palatinate, ruthlessly suppressing feuds between rival lords until throughout the Reich, as it was said, "it seemed better to keep quiet, as the emperor was restlessly travelling around, hanging or beheading every peace-breaker he captured". He then turned to Poland, technically held by its Dukes in fief to the Reich, where Duke Boleslav, nicknamed Curly-Hair, was building the country into a threatening and independent power. Within a month Frederick had subdued him, imposed a crippling fine and restored Boleslav to his allegiance.

Meanwhile, Frederick with a thousand knights had journeyed to Italy for his coronation in Rome by the English Pope Hadrian IV, had freed Hadrian from a Roman mob stirred up against him by the religious fanatic Arnold of Brescia, but aroused the Pope's deepest suspicions by refusing to hold his stirrup for him when he dismounted from his palfrey. Soon Hadrian was claiming that he had "conferred" the crown as though it were a benefice and Frederick was retorting, in a circular published throughout the Reich, that he had received it from God alone "through the election of the Princes" and would rather die than accept such a doctrine.

The controversy between Pope and Emperor became more acute. Faced with the possibility of Italy united under Hadrian, Frederick tried to strengthen his grip on the northern cities. In June, 1158, he appeared in Verona with an army fifty thousand strong and on the pretext that Milan was oppressing her smaller neighbours besieged the city and compelled it to capitulate. At Roncaglia, with the help of Italian lawyers, he then issued a series of laws, regulating the dues to be paid to him by the cities and appointing royal officers to administer them and prevent strife between rival factions.

This was a success, but the Italians did not willingly submit and the death of Hadrian brought Alexander III to the Papacy, a man as intelligent and resolute as Frederick himself, who deeply mistrusted him and saw his Chancellor Reinald as the arch-enemy of Christendom. Frederick secured the election of an anti-Pope, Victor IV, held his stirrup and kissed his feet; but the puppet proved of no account. Alexander excommunicated the emperor and Milan promptly revolted. This time the population was starved out and the city razed to the ground.

It was war to the knife. The Lombards rose against the harsh German administration, actively encouraged by Alexander III, who had taken refuge in France. The walls of Milan were rebuilt. Frederick kept his grip on the Italian towns with difficulty and redoubled his efforts to destroy Alexander's influence. When Victor IV died in 1164 he had another anti-Pope elected, Paschal III, and three years later stormed into Italy with a large army to capture Rome itself. The city fell. Alexander, who had meanwhile returned, fled to Sicily and Frederick procured the enthronement of Paschal. But retribution, apparently divine, then descended. In the summer heat plague suddenly struck the army, the soldiers died like flies and Frederick was forced to make an ignominious retreat with the survivors through the northern territories flaming with revolt. He crossed the Alps without arms, disguised as a servant.

He was now faced with a Lombard League sworn to wrest independence from the Germans, and in 1176, descending for the last time to reassert his authority, he was heavily defeated at Legnano and obliged to make terms which left him with a vague imperial suzerainty over cities which from now on counted as allies rather than subjects. The time had come for reconciliation with the Pope. Both Frederick and the aged Alexander saw it as their task to give "eternal peace" to a war-weary world. In October, 1176, the Emperor's emissaries prostrated themselves before the Pope at Agnani and difficult negotiations began, resulting in an arrangement which left the Pope still dependent on the emperor's temporal power and placed the northern cities under their joint supervision. Well might Frederick be prepared, in a splendid ceremony at St. Mark's in Venice, to kneel to Alexander and receive the kiss of peace.

Nine years later Frederick bequeathed a promising strategic situation to his Hohenstaufen successors by marrying his eldest son Henry to Constance, heiress presumptive of the Norman King Roger of Sicily. By that time Frederick was undisputed master of Germany and the threat of a warlike nobility from the north, coupled with a well-trained Saracen army and a powerful fleet from the south, was well calculated to soften the Papacy. But in the long result neither Popes nor emperors were the victors. The Hohenstaufen dynasty was destroyed, but the Popes became subservient to France, lost heavily in prestige and the way was opened for the Protestant Reformation. Meanwhile, in his declining years, Frederick, once "Hammer of the Godless", became the "Most Christian Son of the Church".

Within Germany his success was unqualified. Here all his fine qualities combined to consolidate the Reich, foster trade, prosperity and learning. Henry the Lion, placated in earlier years, refused to accompany the emperor on his later Italian expeditions and built up a Saxon empire within the empire stretching from North and North-west Germany to Thuringia. His aggressiveness earned him many enemies among his princely neighbours, and when they complained and he refused to obey an Imperial summons to answer their accusations, Frederick in a lightning campaign occupied Saxony and banished his rival to France. Henry's Duchy was then sagaciously divided amongst the nobility, now put on its best behaviour by the dismal fate of the Lion.

By smashing the most powerful duke in Germany Frederick set the seal on his claim to be Holy Roman Emperor in fact as well as in title. Without the support of the nobility and of the Church, which he was able to dominate owing to the weakness of the Papacy, he could not have created the conditions needed for commercial and social prosperity. During his reign fine roads were built in Swabia, establishing new trade routes for transcontinental traffic. Between 1150 and 1175 the number of German towns, all of them in Staufian territory, almost doubled, their construction heavily subsidized by Frederick. On his initiative special trading centres were set up for the European market. A unified coinage was introduced in the area of the Lower Rhine. The middle class, comprising craftsmen and merchants, was strongly encouraged and a rigid caste system was softened by permitting members of the Imperial administration to rise into the aristocracy. Thus a basis was formed for the later glories of the Hohenstaufen period when trade, security and territorial expansion went hand in hand and the refinements of medieval chivalry flowered into splendid literature.

Frederick was regarded in his time as the perfect knight and it was as a Crusader that he died. Now, nearing seventy, as the ruler of an empire comprising more than half the Christian world, he answered the call of Pope Clement III to lead the princes of Europe to Palestine where the Holy Places were again in deadly peril. The Imperial glory was laid aside. Donning simple dress, thinking himself no more than a pilgrim and a follower of the Lord, he summoned the princes of the Reich to a "court-day of Jesus Christ", leaving the throne empty in symbolic fashion. They promised their help; a large army was collected and to the admiration of Christendom the old man led it in person overland towards the Bosphorus while the English crusaders under Richard Coeur de Lion and the French under King Philip chose the sea-route.

At first everything went well. From rulers along the route and the Emperor Isaac at Constantinople promises of provisions and an unmolested passage had been obtained. But trouble started as soon as the army reached Byzantine territory. The encampment was attacked at nights, food was scarce and the population had fled from the towns, taking everything with them. An army which Isaac sent to attack the Crusaders was defeated and, despite this extreme provocation, Frederick bargained with him afresh with tolerable good humour. Agreement reached, the army arrived at the Hellespont almost a year after it had left Germany.

The advance through Asia Minor began and Frederick addressed his troops: "Brothers, be strong and full of confidence, the whole land is ours!" Isaac helped him on his way and no more trouble was met till in May the army reached the kingdom of the Seljuk Turks. Here, too, the Sultan Kilidsh Arslan had promised his support, but it was soon clear that he had no intention of keeping his word. The men marched on through mountainous country bereft of cattle and all sign of life. It was extremely cold. Swarms of hostile horsemen descended. Frederick and his army seemed to be trapped.

They plodded on with their heavy horses and massive armour, aiming for a town beyond the mountains where they hoped to find food. But a hostile army thirty thousand strong blocked the only pass. Half starved, they struggled over by a different route and pressed on towards the town—to find it foodless, deserted. There they celebrated Whitsun and after mass there was a banquet consisting of boiled horse-skins.

Thirty miles away was the Sultan's capital, the wealthy Iconium. Still harried by savage, elusive horsemen, the crusading "army", now dwindled to six hundred knights, groped towards it, clinging to this last hope, another mirage perhaps. Their wits were beginning to turn: the Bishop of Würzburg had a vision of St. George in the sky and many said they had seen miraculous white birds circling the emperor's tent.

Iconium was garrisoned and a Seljuk army was waiting outside the town. No one knows the exact size, but perhaps the German chroniclers are right when they say that Frederick with his starving few scattered a force a hundred times as strong. At any rate, they reached the Sultan's gardens, then split into two parties, one to capture the town, the other to act as rearguard under Frederick's command. When assailed again by the reformed horsemen he spoke to his knights with tears streaming down his face and his words are on record: "Why do we hesitate? Why do we tremble? Christ conquers, Christ is King, Christ is Emperor. Our death is our reward. Into battle, warriors; win the Kingdom of Heaven with your blood!"

That night the Sultan was begging for peace, offering mules, horses and food, and within a week the band of brothers, refreshed and confident, having won one of the most brilliant victories in German history, was moving, the last obstacle gone, towards the Holy Land. Ahead went Frederick, the old man of whom his chronicler wrote: "In all the world there is not his equal to be found."

Did he remember the prophecy that he would die by drowning, or that other saying that he would win the Reich like a fox, preserve it like a lion, but die like a dog? Not at this moment, surely. The spiritual goal was beckoning and he felt strong for all his years. Near Seleucia, on the coast opposite the eastern end of Cyprus, mountains had to be crossed and Frederick chose a path bordering a fast-flowing river. It was June, the heat was intense and the going very difficult. Sometimes he and his friends had to crawl on all-fours, until a ford was found and he crossed with his horse to the far side. There, resting in the burning sun, he had some food, then said he would bathe again. The other men warned; he disregarded them and went down once more into the cold water. They saw his arm suddenly rise, then he disappeared. Much later, after a difficult search, they found his body. It was Sunday, 10 June, 1190.

The chronicler closed his book. On meeting in Seleucia many of the knights who had come so far turned their horses for home and within twenty years his bones, even, at first carefully preserved in Tyre, had been lost. But legend brought them home and today, when they see the clouds surging up above the Kyffhäuser, German peasants still say with mingled fear and hope: "Kaiser Friedrich is brewing!"

SALADIN

(1138–1193)

Sir Walter Scott, in his introduction to *The Talisman*, explained that he was drawn to his subject by the "singular contrast" between Richard I, King of England, and his opponent in the Holy Land, Saladin the Sultan: "The Christian and English monarch showed all the cruelty and violence of an Eastern Sultan; and Saladin, on the other hand, displayed the deep policy and prudence of a European sovereign, whilst each contended which should excel the other in the knightly qualities of bravery and generosity."

This seemed a paradox to the novelist in 1830, for the countries of Europe had long been powerful, while Islam had lost much of its great civilization of the past; but at the time of Saladin, born in 1138 and died in 1193, the Saracens were heirs to a civilization four centuries old, and medieval Europe came to learn much from Arab literature, science, architecture and state-craft. To the Muslims the Christians were idolators, for they worshipped a Trinity of three Gods; to the Christians the Muslims were infidels to be destroyed.

Saladin stands out among Saracens as well as Christians as a great general, a just, religious and kind man, whose generosity was often so quixotic that the Crusaders were astounded and his own companions critical; he always kept his word even though the Crusaders repeatedly broke theirs, absolved by their priests on the argument that an oath to an infidel was invalid. His high qualities are described by Christian as well as Arab chroniclers at the time of the Third Crusade. In Europe Saladin is remembered for his qualities as a man, while in the Arab world he is honoured more for political reasons, because he succeeded in uniting Egypt, Syria and Mesopotamia in one empire and because he freed most of Palestine of the invaders. "Jerusalem," wrote Saladin to Richard, "is holy to us as well as to you . . . Think not that we shall go back therefrom . . . And as for the land, it was ours to begin with, and you invaded it; nor had you taken it but for the feebleness of the Muslims who then had it; and so long as this war lasts God will not permit you to set up a stone on it."

Forty years before Saladin's birth the First Crusade would

probably not have succeeded if the great Seljuk Sultan, Melik Shah, had not died in 1092, so that when the Crusaders arrived the empire was already broken up into petty kingdoms ruled often by former Mamluk slaves. One of these was Zengy, ruler of Mosul, and it was through him that Saladin's family received preferment.

When Zengy and his army suffered a defeat in Mesopotamia they wanted to avoid being massacred by retreating across the Tigris at a point controlled by the castle of Tekrit, commanded by Ayyub Nejm ed-Din, a Kurd of the Rawadiya clan, born near Dawin in Armenia. Ayyub agreed to let Zengy and his army be ferried across, although he knew that this would infuriate the Abbasid Caliph of Baghdad; indeed, he and his brother, Shirkuh, were later ordered to go. On the night they left in September, 1138, a son, Yusuf, was born to Ayyub; later he was to be given the title of Salah ed-Din, "Honour of the Faith". The family sought refuge with Zengy, and Ayyub, in recompense for saving the army, was made Governor of Baalbeck, and there Yusuf, or Joseph, spent his childhood; when he was nine years old Zengy was murdered in his tent and Ayyub had to move to Damascus, where he became commander of the army. His brother Shirkuh, known as "the mountain-lion", had taken service with Nur ed-Din, who had succeeded his father, Zengy. Nur ed-Din wished to occupy Damascus and sent Shirkuh in command of his army to negotiate with his brother, Ayyub, who treated the matter as a family affair, handed over the city and became governor.

Yusuf or Saladin seems to have led a retired life, interested in literature and discussing religion with the ulema, but at the age of twenty-six, much against his will, he was drawn into the battle for Egypt. Nur ed-Din was now King of Syria and a powerful rival to Amalric, the Crusader King of Jerusalem, so that neither wished to allow the other to increase his power by capturing Egypt; this was under the nominal rule of a young Shia caliph, el-Adid, the last of the Fatimid dynasty which had ruled for two hundred years. Amalric invaded Egypt in September, 1163, and Nur ed-Din ordered Shirkuh to take the army there with Saladin who distinguished himself as a soldier and was given his first command as governor of Alexandria; there he was besieged for seventy-five days, but peace terms were arranged on 4 August, 1167, under which it was decided to leave Egypt to the Egyptians, at any rate for a period. Saladin was a guest in Amalric's camp and made friends with a famous Crusader, Humphrey of Toron, showing great interest in the vows taken by Christian knights. It was related by the Christian chroniclers, but not by the Arab, that Saladin went through the ceremony of Christian knighthood; perhaps these stories were told to try to account for Saladin's knightly qualities which could not, they thought, be derived from Islam.

There was another expedition to Egypt, and Shirkuh, who was now Vizier, died from over-indulgence in March, 1169. The caliph chose his nephew Saladin as Vizier, largely because he seemed an unambitious and pliable young man, but the caliph was soon to regret his choice. Saladin's strong religious beliefs, which had made him a recluse, now became an inspiration to him to establish a Muslim empire which would be strong enough to drive the Crusaders out of the Holy Land. "When God gave me the land of Egypt," said Saladin later, "I was sure that he meant me to have Palestine as well." The older emirs were jealous that a man of thirty should have so coveted a post, but Saladin took up their challenge and showed great tact, wisdom and cunning in winning many to his allegiance. He overcame plots, army mutinies and Crusader invasions; when the caliph died at the age of twenty he made the chief eunuch at the palace, Kirkush, see to it that there were no more Fatimites capable of ruling Egypt. Saladin was Sultan of Egypt in all but name.

Nur ed-Din had himself become jealous of Saladin's rapid rise to power and planned to bring an army to Egypt to humble him, but he died suddenly in May, 1174, at the age of fifty-six. His loss was felt deeply, for he was a pious, just and able administrator who used the public revenues for the good of the people. The only person to benefit was Saladin. There was now bitter hostility between the house of Zengy and the house of Ayyub and it was not until April, 1175, that Saladin was in a position to declare himself King of Syria as well as King of Egypt. He could now plan his *jehad* or holy war.

King Amalric had died soon after Nur ed-Din and there was a regent for King Baldwin IV, a boy of thirteen and a leper. Saladin was back in Cairo for a year in 1176, supervising the building of colleges, the great dyke of Giza and planning his citadel. It was a life of great activity supervising the administration of two such different countries as Egypt and Syria, dispensing justice, receiving envoys, settling the jealousies of an elaborate court; most of all he enjoyed the company of poets, philosophers and religious men, putting all at ease, so that the noise of the conversation shocked those who had been accustomed to the staid levees of Sultan Nur ed-Din when each man sat rigid "as if a bird were perched on his head".

He lived piously and simply and was extraordinarily patient; he considered always that he held his high post for the good of the people. "Seek to win the hearts of your people and watch over their prosperity," said Saladin to his favourite son, ez-Zahir, when he was being sent to take over a provincial government; "for it is to secure their happiness that you are appointed by God and by me . . . I have become great as I am because I have won men's hearts by gentleness and kindness". This was true and it was a remarkable achievement, considering the size of the kingdom he controlled and the wild independence of some of the many races making up the Saracen world from Armenia and Kurdistan in the north to Tunisia in the west and the Sudan in the south. "He was," writes Sir Steven Runciman in *A History of the Crusades*, "a Kurd of no great family who commanded the obedience of the Muslim world by the force of his personality".

Saladin left Cairo for the last time on 11 May, 1182, and set up his headquarters in Damascus. There had been breaches in a truce with various emirs, but he made no move against them until the truce had expired and then he subjugated Mesopotamia and captured Aleppo. He was a great general, taking much care to reconnoitre the ground himself where he intended to give battle; he controlled his troops from his headquarters or would ride through the arrows between the battle lines accompanied only by a page with a spare horse; he would appear in all parts of the battlefield encouraging his men but he did not fight himself unless the enemy were gaining an advantage.

It was his good intelligence service and his careful choice of ground which won him the great battle of Hittin, a little west of Lake Tiberias, on 4 July, 1187, when the Crusaders had to fight after a long march in the summer heat without water. It was one of the most important battles in the history of the Middle East and the greatest reverse that the Crusaders had suffered; Jerusalem was taken in September and all Palestine was at the mercy of the Saracens. For nearly a hundred years Jerusalem had been the capital of the Latin kingdom, and when Saladin came in September to besiege it the thousands of Christians within must have been fearful lest the Muslims should take revenge for what had been done when it was first captured. Stanley Lane-Poole, in his biography *Saladin*, refers to "the savage conquest by the first crusaders in 1099 . . . when the blood of wanton massacre defiled the honour of Christendom and stained the scene where once the gospel of love and mercy had been preached", but, as he adds, "never did Saladin show himself greater than during this memorable surrender". There was no revenge or indiscriminate killing and all the people were ransomed. The Christian chronicler Ernoul, Squire to Balian of Ibelin, who had commanded the defence, wrote that the Muslim guards kept strict discipline so that there was no ill-usage of Christians, "such was the charity which Saladin did of poor people without number"; but when the refugees reached Tripoli on the coast, which was still held by the Crusaders, they were refused entrance.

The overwhelming defeat of the Crusaders at Hittin and the fall of Jerusalem had caused consternation in Europe. Archbishop William of Tyre had hurried to Sicily to get aid and then to France and England. The Pope issued an appeal to the knights of Christendom and thousands prepared themselves for the Third Crusade. Kings and princes contributed treasure, but the largest contribution came from what was known as "the Saladin tax", which was, in the words of Edward Gibbon, "the noblest monument of a conqueror's fame and the terror which he inspired"; he points out that, although it was raised for the service of the holy war, it was so lucrative that it was continued and became "the foundation of all the tithes and tenths on ecclesiastical benefices". Huge armies with their supplies, horses and siege-weapons gathered under the most powerful kings and knights of Europe—the ageing Emperor Frederick Barbarossa, King Richard I (who had succeeded Henry II to the throne of England), and King Philip of France. There were gathering of troops and plans drawn up between the kings at the hill-top Cathedral of Vezelay in Burgundy.

It took them a long time to reach the Holy Land and Saladin had plenty of time to complete the defeat of all the Crusaders in Palestine, so that the armies of the Third Crusade would have found no easy means of gaining a footing on the coast. But Saladin made the very great mistake of withdrawing from the siege of Tyre which became a rallying point for the Christians. Saladin was suffering from recurrent illness and he always had difficulty in keeping his troops together for a siege; nor did he follow up the defeat of the Crusaders in front of the great fortress of Acre in a bitter fight on 4 October, 1189. The situation changed radically with the arrival of strong forces from England, France and Germany with their huge siege-engines.

In July, 1191, the Saracen fortress of Acre was surrendered. Humiliating terms to save the lives of the garrison had to be accepted by Saladin although his large army was undefeated; but Richard, in cold-blood, ordered the beheading of two thousand seven hundred hostages. "After Saladin's almost quixotic acts of clemency and generosity, the King of England's cruelty will appear amazing," wrote Stanley Lane-Poole. Richard's extraordinary strength and courage put heart into the Crusaders and they won the battle of Arsuf, but they never reached Jerusalem. The Crusader army turned back to the coast in 1192, defeated by the cold of a Palestine winter and the fact that Saladin's army was still intact; a treaty was signed at Ramla in September; Richard left Palestine in October. Saladin held Jerusalem and all Palestine except for the coastline from Tyre to Jaffa.

Saladin agreed that Christian pilgrims should come to visit Jerusalem and he granted the request of Hubert Walter that four Latin priests might celebrate their service in the Church of the Holy Sepulchre; a similar request from the Byzantine Emperor for priests of the Orthodox Church was refused; this was the origin of that quarrel between the French and Russians over the custody of the Holy Places which nearly seven centuries later was one of the causes of the Crimean War. It was at this interview with the Bishop of Salisbury that Saladin said that he admired Richard's bravery but thought that he often incurred unnecessary danger. They had, indeed, a great respect for one another and exchanged many courtesies; when Saladin had seen Richard fighting on foot during one battle he had had a horse sent to him, but Saladin had always refused to meet him. Saladin told the bishop that he would himself rather be gifted with wealth, wisdom and moderation than "with boldness and immoderation". He thought that Richard got too involved with the fighting himself; Saladin, however, always seemed to be at the place he was most needed, either in defence or attack. When it was thought that the Crusaders under Richard would march on Jerusalem and there was considerable consternation among the Saracens, Abdel Latif, a well-known Baghdad physician, was surprised to see Saladin personally supervising the defence of the city, "even carrying stones on his own shoulders and everybody, rich and poor, followed his example".

By the age of fifty-five Saladin had worn himself out and he died leaving no personal possessions on 3 March, 1193, in Damascus where is his tomb. "Our Sultan," wrote Baha ed-Din, his secretary and biographer, "was very noble of heart, kindness shone in his face, he was very modest and exquisitely courteous".

HENRY II OF ENGLAND

(1154–1189)

THE STRONG administration of William the Conqueror served England well. William II, known as William Rufus, was a self-indulgent, reckless king, but he maintained the royal authority against the fierce ambitions of the barons. His younger brother, Henry I, the man who said, "An unlettered king is a crowned ass", married the daughter of the King of Scotland who, on her mother's side, was descended from Anglo-Saxon kings.

During Henry I's reign the towns of England were granted, many of them, charters, thus helping to deliver the merchant classes from the domination of the barons. Great prelates like Anselm and John of Salisbury encouraged learning and the Church produced a generation of clerks and lawyers who no longer thought of themselves as Norman or Anglo-Saxon but as English. The army with which Henry I firmly defeated his brother Robert Duke of Normandy and which, at the victory at Tenchebrai in Normandy, avenged the Battle of Hastings as it were, was an English army though its leaders bore Norman names. Under Henry I's strong rule England prospered.

But on Henry's death in 1135 a period of misrule began. Henry's only son, William the Atheling, had been drowned off the coast of France, and when the king learnt the news it was said he never smiled again. He had one daughter, Matilda, whom he had married first to the Holy Roman Emperor and then, when she was widowed, to Geoffrey Plantagenet, Count of Anjou. The nobles swore to accept Matilda as queen. But on Henry's death, Stephen, Count of Blois, the son of one of William the Conqueror's daughters, Adela, claimed the throne. It was indicative of the new forces of the times that though most of the nobles of the south of England held aloof from Stephen, the City of London's acceptance of Stephen was decisive. Matilda invaded England and a long period of civil war followed, a dark night for the people of England in which every baron and local chieftain did what he liked. However, and this again was significant of the new times, the influence of the Church and of the great Archbishop, Theobald of Canterbury, restored peace, though an uncertain one. It was agreed by the various factions that Stephen should reign until his death and be succeeded by Matilda's heir, Henry, Count of Anjou.

England was then to have one of the greatest of all her kings and one of the most extraordinary men called to the throne. Henry, the son of Geoffrey Plantagenet, was first of all very much a foreigner, having been born in Anjou and possessing, through his father and grandfather Henry I, other parts of northern and western France. Shortly before he became King of England he married Eleanor of Aquitaine, who owned most of south-western France and who had been the bride of Louis VII, King of France, whom she could not stomach. When she left the French king, she it was who proposed herself to Henry Plantagenet to whom she had long been attracted. Henry thus became the ruler of an empire which ran from the Cheviots to the Pyrenees, and included the highly civilized cities of the south-west of France with a small court where the troubadours flourished as well as the wild tribes of Wales and the grim fortresses of northern England.

Henry spent much of his time out of England, yet England was always his chief concern. He left his foreign fiefs to his lieutenants and then later, with unhappy results, to his sons. Although his empire rivalled that of the Holy Roman Emperor and in size eclipsed the land of the King of France, Henry was of all kings the man who loved grandeur and pomp the least. He had a contempt for the trappings of monarchy, dressed himself very carelessly in ordinary clothes and mingled as familiarly with peasants and merchants as with his courtiers. He was a scholar speaking many languages and, inspired by the civil and political ideas of the rising civilization of Italy, he was above all a man of business and progress. Nobody could have been better fitted for such a vast task as the Angevin Empire—as Henry's domains were called—for he had a passion for administration and was a man of ceaseless, restless energy. Gerald of Wales, a writer of mixed Norman and Welsh ancestry, a scholar of Paris and who, as royal chaplain, had known the king well, described him:

> *Henry II, King of England, was a man of reddish, freckled complexion with a large round head, grey eyes which glowed fiercely and grew bloodshot in anger, a fiery countenance and a harsh cracked voice. His neck was somewhat thrust forward from his shoulders, his chest was broad and square, his arms strong and powerful. His frame was stocky with a pronounced tendency to corpulence, due rather to nature than to indulgence which he tempered by exercise. For in eating and drinking he was moderate and sparing and in all things frugal in a*

degree permissible to a prince. He was addicted to the chase; at crack of dawn he was off on horse-back, traversing wastelands, penetrating forests and climbing the mountain-tops, and so he passed restless days. At evening on his return home he was rarely seen to sit down either before or after supper. He was a man of easy access, and condescending, pliant and witty, second to none in politeness, whatever thoughts he might conceal in himself.

It was no joke being attached to Henry's court, and this bow-legged, hot-tempered monarch had little concern for those who followed him as he went about England enquiring into the administration of justice, or the way taxes were collected, or why such and such a castle erected without permission during the war of Stephen's reign had not been pulled down. Professor Coulton's *Life in the Middle Ages* reproduces the complaints of a certain Peter de Blois, one of Henry's servants, who after complaining of the poor food and drink served out by the royal stewards, bemoans the king's restlessness:

If the king had promised to stay anywhere, then be sure that he will set out at daybreak, knocking all men's expectations by his sudden change of purpose. Whereby it cometh frequently to pass that such courtiers as have let themselves be bled, or have taken some purgative, must yet follow their prince forthwith without regard to their own bodies, and, setting their life on the hazard of a dice, hasten blindfold to ruin for dread of losing that which they had not nor never shall have. Or again if the prince had proclaimed his purpose for setting out for a certain place, then he will surely change his purpose; doubt not that he will allow it be until mid-day. Here wait the sumpters standing under their loads, the chariots idly silent, the out-riders asleep, the royal merchants in anxious expectation, and all men murmuring together; men flock around the court prostitutes and vintners to get tidings of the king's journey.

He speaks of the king's entourage wandering for three or four miles through unknown forests at night and fighting for huts more suitable for swine than men to sleep in. He ends by asking God to teach the king to know himself to be but a man.

Although Henry was never haughty and liked good conversation and laughter, he had a diabolical temper. His son, Richard Coeur de Lion, said that one of his father's maternal grandmothers was a demon who could not abide the secrets of the mass. Her husband, according to the story, had ordered four knights to take her to church. "When there she threw away her mantel that she was holding and left her two sons under her right side of her mantel, and with her other two sons that she had under the left side of the mantel she flew out at the window of the church in the sight of all men and was never seen after that time." Henry's hot temper led him to quarrel with his son Richard, and it was partly responsible for the act which earned him the greatest notoriety, the murder of Thomas à Becket, Archbishop of Canterbury, in 1171.

Henry was not directly responsible for this murder. At the height of his quarrel with the Archbishop Henry was in France and was reported to have said: "Will no one rid me of this turbulent priest?" Four knights took him at his word, crossed the sea and murdered Thomas à Becket in the cathedral. Henry made a public act of contrition and submitted to the Papal Legates, promising to carry out all their conditions for absolution—some of which he had not the slightest intention of performing, nor they, as a matter of fact, of enforcing. He admitted, however, before the Papal Legates that: "He had been the cause of the Archbishop's death, and that what had been done was for his sake."

Henry's relations with Thomas à Becket and the causes of their quarrel throw a great light on Henry's character and on his work. Thomas à Becket was the son of two Normans in a humble position who had settled in London. He was educated by the monks of Merton Priory, introduced as an able young man to Archbishop Theobald, was sent to Rome, came to Court, and within a month or two of Henry's accession to the throne was made Chancellor of England—an astonishingly rapid rise for a young man of no birth.

Henry found in Becket, sixteen years older than he, the qualities he most admired—conscientiousness, energy, intelligence and at the same time an agreeable manner, a love of singing and dancing and jesting which the Angevins brought into England with them. Thomas à Becket, six feet high, with a strong jaw and a slight stutter in his speech which only made more attractive his ready wit, loved luxury and dressed in scarlet furs with gold-work on his cloak. Though the king himself had no fancy for luxury, the two men were the closest of friends and Henry treated Becket as his equal.

When Henry made Becket Archbishop of Canterbury, the latter told the king that there might be trouble between them. He knew Henry's plans for the Church. Henry was determined, in the interests of good order in his kingdom, that the Church Courts, which had the right of trying and sentencing any monk or cleric, or any servant of the Church, should no longer interfere in the course of justice. It was said that in Henry's reign no less than a hundred murders had been committed by a "clerk" who had escaped with light punishment. After Thomas à Becket's appointment various test cases took place and the Archbishop clearly felt himself obliged to fight in favour of the Church. Becket was not supported by all the bishops and was forced to a half-retreat, answering the question did the bishops obey the king with the phrase: "Aye, my Lord, saving our Order." The king grew enraged with the man who had once been his closest friend. They made an attempt at a personal reconciliation, meeting on horseback in a field near Northampton; but here too after some friendly words they began to quarrel.

At the Council of Clarendon in 1164 the king summoned the bishops to sign and seal an agreement which was much wider in scope than merely the question of the Church Courts. Becket tried and failed to leave the country. The quarrel dragged on. Becket went into exile for six years, and there was a reconciliation when the two met in 1170.

Becket went back to Canterbury. Local magnates who had been given his land, and who had now to pay homage for them, were hostile, but the common people who considered that Becket was a saint waded out into the sea to meet him. The Church was still the friend of the people, a help against local tyranny and a giver of education. Becket preached a sermon on Christmas Day, 1170, in which he excommunicated some knights who had been offensive to him and spoke of his own likely martyrdom. It was after this that the four knights who were with the king in France took ship to Canterbury and committed the murder, in the Cathedral itself.

Although the people venerated Becket, Henry's work for order in the realm was securing their attachment. The greatest of King Henry's work lay in the reform of the law. He introduced trial by jury. What Henry did above all was to make the Crown, through its courts, the source of all justice, one which completely took the place of the private courts and tribunals of the barons. The whole of England was governed by the king's servants—sheriffs, judges and coroners; much of France, the King of France's domains, remained a number of separate states, each duke or count being the source of power and justice in his territory, only acknowledging the King of France as overlord.

Above all, the system of law Henry adopted was the ancient common law, enriched by Norman-French legal concepts, and not a new code of law drawn up by the king which could be changed by another king. Henry completed the work which William the Conqueror had begun, using as his instruments the new science of politics, developed in the Italian cities, and the new educated men, who came out of the middle classes, as his agents. In the Assize of Arms in 1181, Henry II encouraged his subjects to keep their own arms and armour. The yeoman archers who were to do such good service at Crécy and Poitiers were the first fruits of this policy. The king trusted his subjects, and regarded the local militias, which could take up arms at any moment, as his best assurance against any rebellion by the nobles.

This restless, energetic, unostentatious, highly intellectual monarch, who worked so well for England and for his vast domains in France, who was for a time the most powerful monarch of Europe, had to face, at the end of his life, trials which did not wreck his work but which brought him to a miserable end. He had, from the beginning, dominated his powerful wife, Eleanor of Aquitaine, and taken mistresses as he wished. Although strongly attached to his family, he behaved not only as an autocrat but with a certain meanness towards all his children, except to his youngest son, John.

He behaved as a tyrant towards his sons in that he gave them rank and lands but kept them short of money. His son Henry he had crowned King of England so that there could be no dispute about the succession. Yet this son rebelled against his father with the help of the King of France and of his fourth son, Geoffrey. The revolt was suppressed and later the young King Henry died of fever.

Eleanor encouraged Richard and Geoffrey against their father. Richard, known later as Richard Coeur de Lion, was a remarkable man endowed as was his father with restless energy and intellectual qualities, though not of such a practical disposition. The Angevins had in all of them something of the same demonic energy as Henry. They were liable to be suspicious and unforgiving. Richard, Duke of Aquitaine, made war on his father for a second time and had as his ally the new King of France, Phillipe Auguste, a powerful ruler. The youngest son John joined them, unknown to his father, Henry II was forced to retreat before his enemies at Le Mans, though vowing vengeance. He fell ill and was obliged to sue for a truce; when he met Richard and Phillipe Auguste to parley the shadow of death was on his face.

When he lay sick at his castle at Chinon, having been forced to accept the terms of his foes, he was told that John his favourite had joined his enemies. That night in high fever his bastard son, also called Geoffrey, held him in his arms and the king acknowledged that he alone had been a true son; he muttered the well-known phrase, "Shame, shame on a conquered king". He was buried at Fontevrault near Chinon and the last act of this great king was, like the first, played out in France. But his lifework had been for England. As the historian G. M. Trevelyan has written:

"Of all the holders of the island crown, no one has done such great and lasting work as Henry Plantagenet, Count of Anjou. He found England exhausted by nearly twenty years of anarchy with every cog in the Norman machine of State either broken or rusty with disuse. He left England with a judicial and administrative system and a habit of obedience to government which prevented the recurrence of anarchy in spite of the long absences of King Richard and the malignant follies of King John. After the death of Henry I, the outcome of bad government was anarchy; after the death of Henry II, the outcome of bad government was constitutional reform. And the difference is a measure of the work of the great Angevin."

RICHARD, COEUR DE LION

(1157–1199)

THE MEMORY of Coeur de Lion, the lion-hearted Plantagenet king, was for centuries dear and glorious to his English subjects. He was extremely popular in his day, despite his extravagant and rapacious demands upon England's treasury, and his almost total neglect during his absentee reign of the country's administration. He was remembered in subsequent ages as one of the great knights of chivalry, unsurpassingly brave, a man who placed valour and honour above all other qualities.

The Turks and Saracens against whom he fought remembered him in a different way. For generations his was a terrible name in the Holy Land. Syrian mothers used it as a bogy-man to silence their infants, and if a horse turned unexpectedly from its path its rider would exclaim: "Dost thou think King Richard is in that bush?"

He was born in 1157, the second son of Henry II by Eleanor of Aquitaine. His mother was a lady of great significance in English medieval history. She was a woman of remarkable beauty, character and ability, whose immense dowry included the great duchy of Aquitaine, which comprised the whole of South-west France, then the homeland of chivalry. Eleanor's marriage to Henry II brought this large new area of France under the English crown, which already ruled over Normandy and the rest of North-western France.

Eleanor had been married to King Louis VII of France, but in 1152 the marriage was annulled. She then married Henry Plantagenet*, Count of Anjou, who was technically speaking a vassal of the King of France. But when Henry succeeded unexpectedly to the throne of England as Henry II in 1154, Louis realized what a mistake he had made in divorcing Eleanor. The acquisition of Aquitaine made Henry's territories in France larger than his English realm. His vast possessions made him more powerful than France, and even than the Holy Roman Empire. Louis was mortified and thus began the long series of wars between England and France which were waged intermittently for three hundred years.

* From the family badge *planta genesta*, a sprig of broom.

Eleanor had the reputation of being something of a virago, and Henry found her extremely difficult to live with. She had of course much to complain of, for he was constantly unfaithful to her. They quarrelled bitterly and frequently. She bore him five sons and three daughters, and she supported her sons in their great rebellion against their father in 1173.

Henry instituted a machinery of government which brought about the end of the personal rule of the Norman kings. After the miserable anarchy of Stephen's reign, England readily accepted Henry's bureaucratic monarchy, the benefit of which was plainly seen in the ensuing reign—or non-reign—of Richard I.

Richard spent his youth in his mother's homeland of Aquitaine and there he acquired a passionate love of music, poetry and chivalry. When he was eleven his father made him Duke of Aquitaine. With the title also went the power to rule Aquitaine independently, and this he did for a number of years. His iron rule caused much discontent. He became so powerful that his elder brother Henry, the heir-apparent, demanded that Richard should do homage to him. Richard's scornful refusal led to a fratricidal war in which Henry invaded Aquitaine and was killed during the fighting in 1183.

Henry II's struggles with his rebellious sons brought an outstandingly successful reign to an end in bitterness and confusion. Richard's relationship with his father was of the worst. Richard had many reasons to feel personally aggrieved. He had, for instance, been betrothed to Alice, sister of Philip II of France. Henry, who had the morals of a tom-cat, took a fancy to his son's affianced and seduced her with the result that she gave birth to a son.

When Richard became heir to the thrones of England and Normandy, Henry wanted him to renounce Aquitaine in favour of Prince John, his beloved younger son. Richard flatly refused. He loved Aquitaine. It was his home. England and Normandy were foreign countries to him. Another civil war ensued, Richard sought alliance with King Philip (Philip Augustus) of France, whom he recognized publicly as the overlord of his French possessions. Henry's attempt to crush Richard's rebellion failed ignominiously, and the old king's heart was broken when he found that his youngest and favourite son John had joined Richard against him.

On 6 July, 1189, Henry died. At this time Queen Eleanor was held in "honourable captivity" at Winchester. For fifteen years she had been more or less a prisoner owing to her ardent and active support of her sons' rebellion.

Richard was the undisputed heir, even though Henry had

obstinately refused to acknowledge him as such. The first thing Richard did when he heard of his father's death was to order his mother's freedom and he made her regent until he came to claim his kingdom.

On 20 July he was acclaimed Duke of Normandy, and on 13 August he landed at Plymouth and began a royal progress which culminated in his coronation on 3 September. Though he had been born in England, he had lived all his life in Aquitaine and had returned to England only for two short visits, at Easter, 1176, and Christmas, 1184. He was therefore not only as much a foreigner as Dutch William and George I, but he was also a complete stranger to his people, though of course they knew a great deal about him by reputation.

He was thirty-one, tall, strong-limbed, splendidly handsome, with reddish-gold hair and piercing blue eyes. He caught the imagination of his people right from the start. He was a Crusader, having taken the Cross in 1187, the first prince on the north of the Alps to do so, and this, combined with his legendary valour and chivalry, made him a romantic hero in the eyes of his people.

In the age of faith the Crusader was a hallowed figure, the Champion of Christ. When Richard ascended the throne of England, people were still inflamed with the magic and the wonder of the Crusades, a movement which had the double purpose of satisfying at the same time the dictates of piety and the craving for war and plunder. So great in fact was the prestige of the Crusader that Richard retained the love and loyalty of his English subjects, even though he squeezed their treasury dry to pay for his life of wasteful warfare, and though he regarded the English with barely-disguised contempt, and spent a mere six months of his ten years' reign in England.

Richard was well aware of his brother John's treacherous character. John was vain, capricious and grasping, lacking in the administrative ability which had distinguished his father. He was also totally lacking in principles, and Richard showed little disposition to trust him, though he provided for him well enough by giving him the south-western part of England as his principality in the vain hope that it would keep him quiet and out of mischief.

Richard's magnificent coronation is the first one in English history to be described in detail by contemporary chroniclers. The feast which followed was described as being "of the greatest profusion, richness, variety and plenty".

Richard had prohibited all Jews from his coronation feast,

and the people interpreted this as royal licence to indulge in a little anti-semitism on their own account—a very popular pastime in the days of the Crusades, as at other times. The mob added to the coronation festivities by beating up and killing all the Jews they could find, and plundering their property. Many Jews barricaded themselves in their houses, which the mob then set on fire. Soon there was a full-scale riot going, and half of London, then nearly all built of wood, was ablaze.

Richard was a man of no mean temper, and when he found his coronation feast disturbed in this manner his anger knew no bounds. He had been insulted on the day of his crowning. The plunder of the Jews who were under his royal protection was an especial loss to him, for the Jews paid him well—a kind of protection money. The Jews had been brought into England by William the Conqueror. As they were the historical enemies of Christ, anti-semitism was the logical consequence of the crusading zeal which was sweeping Europe.

Though Richard ordered condign punishment for the rioters, only three of them were found and hanged. None of the others could be identified. Richard gave strict orders for the protection of the Jews in future.

As soon as he was crowned, Richard busied himself planning for the Crusade which he was to make in the company of Philip of France and Leopold of Austria. He used reckless methods of raising the money. Offices and honours were put up for auction to the highest bidder. He raised 15,000 marks by remitting to William the Lion of Scotland the rights over Scotland which Henry II had secured by the Treaty of Falaise. Having sold all he could in the way of offices and privileges, Richard departed from England in the summer of 1190 with a force of about 4,000 men-at-arms and a fleet of about 100 ships.

He left the country in the corrupt hands of William Longchamps, a Frenchman who hated and despised the English. Longchamps's oppressive rule resulted in a great struggle between him on the one side and Prince John and the barons on the other. The barons, growing in power and responsibility, enforced the submission of Longchamps without bloodshed. In previous reigns these men would unhesitatingly have plunged the country into civil war. Henry II's life-work had not been in vain. In fact it saved England from anarchy during the non-reign of his son.

It was Richard who showed the greatest irresponsibility. He was unmarried and had no heir, and he had left for the Crusade, with all its attendant personal dangers, without making any provision for the succession.

On the journey to the Holy Land he wintered in Sicily where he occupied himself in quarrelling with Philip. In the spring he interrupted the voyage to Palestine in order to conquer Cyprus, and did not join the Crusaders besieging Acre until June, but he immediately made his presence felt, Acre being finally conquered mainly owing to his energy and skill.

Though this Third Crusade has been described as the most "courtly, chivalrous and romantic" of all, the temper of its leaders could hardly be so described. They hated each other more fiercely than they did the common enemy. Richard's arrogance earned him an unpleasant reputation among the Orientals of the country in which they fought. They considered that his magnificence and military renown were depreciated by the lack of dignity he displayed in his unprincely quarrels with Leopold of Austria and Philip of France.

Philip, a better statesman than warrior, wisely decided he had sacrificed his health and interests long enough in this barren though glorious enterprise. He had likewise had enough of Richard's insults, so he sailed for home and made more effective retaliation by entering into negotiations with Prince John with the object of invading Richard's French possessions. He offered John the hand of his sister Alice into the bargain.

It cannot be imagined that John was tempted by the prospect of marrying this much-soiled royal maiden who had been the mistress of his own father, but he was unquestionably interested in filching his brother's French possessions. The fact that Philip was Richard's suzerain, or overlord, in France, gave some kind of legality to the offer. Doubtless Alice had been introduced into the bargain with the object of these Plantagenet realms being eventually reunited to the French throne.

However, Queen Eleanor got wind of what was afoot and that formidable lady had no difficulty in bringing her treasonable son to heel.

Meanwhile in the Holy Land Richard won a brilliant victory over the forces of Saladin and twice led the Crusader host within a few miles of Jerusalem. But dissensions among the warriors of the Cross made it impossible to continue, and so the Crusade ended ingloriously but not inexpediently on 2 September, 1192, with Richard making a truce with Saladin whom he seemed to like rather better than his fellow Christian warriors.

Alarmed by reports of John's intrigues in England and France, he hastened home. But owing to the hostility of Philip he could not take the obvious route through Marseilles, and Toulouse was in the hands of his enemies. He decided to return via the Adriatic and Austria. But, passing through Vienna on 20 December, 1192, in disguise, he was recognized and captured. He was held in the Castle of Durenstein by Leopold of Austria whom he had grossly insulted at the time of the fall of Acre, and who now demanded an enormous ransom for his release. But early the following year Leopold was forced to surrender his valuable prisoner to Emperor Henry V. Despite the fact that Richard, as a Crusader, was under the Church's protection, the enormous sum of 150,000 marks had to be paid for his release.

This considerably taxed the resources of England. All the same they gladly paid and gave Richard a tumultuous welcome when he returned in March, 1194, and they also insisted upon giving him another coronation, this time without the anti-semitic embellishments.

A curious relationship now existed between Richard Coeur de Lion and his English subjects. It is difficult for us to imagine the awe and adoration in which they held him—the returned Crusader whose lion-like courage and daring deeds of valour for the cause of the Holy Cross were the talk of the known world. Like Churchill, he had become a legend in his lifetime. Richard of England was the hero of half of Christendom on that day and his people were overwhelmed with pride to be his subjects.

But Richard did not return this feeling. England had disappointed him. He had come back from the Holy Land a changed man, disillusioned with crusading, embittered by the indignity of his incarceration in Austria, angry at the plotting that had been going on behind his back while he was far away fighting for the True Cross. He was lean and tanned by the Levantine sun, his face lined with illness, his frame toughened by his privations. He had never spared himself and he never asked his soldiers to encounter dangers which he was not prepared to face himself. And when he looked upon his stay-at-home subjects, his fleshly barons, and the plump, prosperous citizens of London, he was displeased. Coldly he acknowledged their ecstatic plaudits, and just as coldly he demanded more money from them.

He stayed in England merely a few weeks and then returned to France and devoted the rest of his reign to Normandy and Aquitaine, determined to avenge himself upon Philip of France who had incurred his especial anger for deserting the Crusade in order to plot against him.

Richard did not return to England again. He left its government in the competent hands of Hubert Walter and devoted the rest of his life to his favourite occupation and that at which he most excelled—war. Although he got the best of Philip in the field, he was unable to sustain the economics of war with his inferior resources, despite the exactions he made upon England.

He met his death as he would have wished, on the field of battle, being wounded in the left side by a bolt-shot from a crossbow at the siege of Châlus Castle on 26 March, 1199. At first he concealed his injury and tried to pull out the bolt himself. It broke off, leaving the iron head in the wound. Mortification set in and he died on 6 April after naming his brother John heir to the realm of England and all his other lands.

GENGHIS KHAN

(1167?–1227)

THERE HAVE been conquerors galore, throughout history, who have sprung from nothing. Napoleon, the moody little Corsican from an undistinguished family, went on to hold half Europe to ransom. Mao Tse-tung, small-time teacher, became ruler of a vast population. Hitler had his day.

But one man stands alone.

There has never been another like him. There can never be another, since that first bomb dropped on Hiroshima. If ever half the world is laid waste, it will be done impersonally, almost without human intervention. There will be a barren waste, a desert—with no one left, to loot or rape or plunder.

But, in the thirteenth century, and within the walls of a single city, Herat, in what is now Afghanistan, the Emperor Genghis Khan supervised the massacre, in one blood-filled week of vengeance, of 1,600,000 people. And before those men, women and children were dead, many had suffered torture and mutilation of a kind which is almost impossible to imagine. Arms, legs, were hacked off, and the bleeding, screaming trunks were flung into the road, to roll helplessly away and die in agony. Children, a dozen or more at a time, were skewered like shish-kebab on lances, or burnt alive in great wailing heaps, while their mothers, hideously mutilated, were forced to stand by and await their turn.

A man is product of his time, and the time was cruel. But Genghis Khan—"perfect warrior", the name meant—was the most bloodthirsty man in history. Under his example and his orders, men performed prodigies of sadism, unrepresentative of any time, even their own.

This great ruler, as historians usually point out, was born in a tent. But this is the least remarkable fact about him. Everyone, for as far as eye could see or imagination reach, was born in a tent: there was no other form of habitation in that part of Asia. It was near the shores of Lake Baikal, and he was named Temuchin by his father Yesukai, leader of a group of small Mongolian tribes who warred constantly with each other. He had just killed a rival chieftain of that name: on returning to his tent he found the new-born child with its mother, his wife, and prised open the infant's clenched fist. Inside was a red-brown clot of coagulated blood, like a stone. This, to the superstitious father, represented the body, the fortunes, of the Temuchin he had just slain, and he gave the name to his son.

Temuchin found himself on the throne at thirteen, when his father died: almost immediately a number of the small tribes which comprised the kingdom began to secede. Temuchin had no experience of dealing with such a situation, but his indomitable mother, a Mongolian Boadicea, rallied troops and brought the rebels back into the fold. The leaders were punished with great cruelty, while the young ruler watched.

Soon he was able to take over the rule of the kingdom from his mother—rule which consisted largely of subduing or trying to subdue every tribe on his borders, then ensuring that it remained well-disciplined. He soon showed qualities of generalship and an aptitude for large-scale treachery which even in those times must have evoked the admiration of his contemporaries. Before long he had made himself emperor of all the Mongol tribes, and in 1206 he summoned the most notable men within this empire and allowed them to name him Genghis (perfect warrior) Khan (king).

He was now strong enough to indulge in a private dream. He would invade distant China, the fabulous, almost mythical Cathay. There had been many Mongol attempts to penetrate her Great Wall, but all had failed. Now Genghis Khan was able to muster an enormous army of horsemen and by sheer brute numbers to burst through the Chinese defence. Burning, killing, raping, the Mongol hordes penetrated to the sea, destroying much of an ancient civilization, one of the oldest and finest in the world.

Having reduced Cathay to a smoking, stinking ruin, corpses piled high in every town and village, the Perfect Warrior retired to his capital. One of the reasons for his continued and increasing success may have been an insistence on keeping his capital at desolate Karakoram, that bleak Mongolian city, when he could have had any of the fine cities of China, or later, Persia, for the taking. His vast army was not allowed to get soft from easy living in conquered lands. It remained, between campaigns, camped outside the walls of Karakoram, mile upon mile of felt "yurts", or tents, full of warriors ready to be formed up, mounted, and sent to any part of the world.

It was not long after the Chinese campaign that Genghis,

learning of the riches to be had in the west, decided to cross the Hindu Kush, that huge mountain range which had always cut the Mongols and other plains-people off from the civilizations of western Asia.

In 1219 he set out—on one of his few peaceful missions. He had sent messengers to the large Muslim state of Khwarizm, stating that as he now had conquered China his country was "a mine of silver and a magazine of warriors", and he had little interest in fighting but much in trade. What could he get from Khwarizm in exchange for some of his own riches?

The Shah, Mohammed, was at first well-disposed to this, but the local Governor, in Otrar, was foolishly rude. Genghis had anticipated a reply by sending a small advance party of traders and these were pointlessly, callously, butchered by the Governor. Genghis, beside himself with rage, demanded the Governor be extradited and sent to him for justice.

Mohammed refused.

Thus began a campaign which, in its speed and ruthlessness, eclipsed the one into China. It began with two Mongol armies, under two of Genghis's sons, Juji and Jagatai, which swept all before them. One army, Juji's, was resisted at first by Mohammed's larger one, a force of 400,000 men, but the Mongols went through these like a knife through butter, and within hours 150,000 of the defending army were dead on the field.

Meanwhile the second army, under Jagatai, had penetrated to Otrar, the offending city, and laid siege to it. The siege lasted five months, but at the end it fell and every inhabitant was put to the sword, including the Governor, for whom a particularly public and revolting torture was provided first.

A third army leap-frogged Otrar, and a fourth, commanded by Genghis himself, headed for Bokhara. The cities of Tashkent and Nur surrendered to him as he approached—which helped them not at all, for they were both sacked—and Bokhara put up a short resistance before capitulating. As he entered it, Genghis shouted to his officers, "The hay is cut: give your horses fodder!"

This picturesque invitation to plunder was seized on by the entire army. Everything portable was taken, everything not small enough was smashed to convenient pieces. Every inhabitant was butchered, many after the most appalling tortures and mutilation; almost every building was burnt to the ground.

Within a day, one of the world's great centres of learning, the "Centre of Science", was a smoking ruin.

Genghis retired to his Court at Karakoram, leaving the "mopping up" to others, who successively laid waste to the cities of Ness, Merv and Nishapur. This last offered a determined resistance, street by street, but was at last overpowered. Apart from some four hundred skilled workers who were sent in chains to Mongolia, every soul was butchered. The city of Herat miraculously spared itself by surrender—unlike those less fortunate ones on the way—and the Mongols put a governor in charge. They continued their pursuit—first, of Mohammed, then, when they learned he had died suddenly of pleurisy, of his son Jelaleddin, whom they pursued deep into India. When he took sanctuary in Delhi, they gave up the chase, but by this time they had ravaged Lahore, Melikpur and Peshawar.

Suddenly news reached Genghis that the Governor of Herat, the one he himself had put in charge, had been deposed. He decided instantly to send a punitive expedition. When it reached there, the doomed city fought bravely and held out for six months, but at last Herat fell.

It was during the week that followed that 1,600,000 people were massacred.

From this hideous campaign of vengeance Genghis turned to the business of extending his Mongol empire. The most attractive direction now seemed due west, and his armies were ordered through Azerbaijan into Georgia. They took Astrakhan, near the Caspian Sea, pursued its fleeing defenders to the River Don.

The Russians now chose to defy him: Genghis sent them envoys whom they killed. A little later the Russian army had been destroyed and the Mongols, after ravaging Bulgaria, began their long, slow, progress home.

While all this had been going on, Genghis, from a distance, was controlling another campaign in China, and that whole land of Cathay and the regions about it had become a Mongol province. As soon as his western campaign had been cleared up, he made his way to China to take charge.

Like his father, and most Mongols, Genghis Khan was a superstitious man. Late one night during this expedition to China he saw five planets in a certain conjunction, and his courage died within him. This, to a simple man—and Genghis had never learnt to read or write—was the end. He would die, and soon.

He gave up his command of the campaign, headed home for Karakoram, and almost as soon as he began the long journey the "sickness" came over him.

The spirit had fled from the greatest conqueror of all time. He continued the homeward journey, but death grew ever nearer and he made no effort to hold back its approach.

He reached one of his "travel palaces", a large rest-house for his own use, on the banks of the River Sales in Mongolia, and there he died.

He had decreed that his son Ogotai should succeed him, but the death of the world's greatest ruler, miles from his capital, boded so evil for the empire, held such dire possibilities of treachery and *coups d'état*, that as the body was carried northward to its final resting place the guards killed everyone that passed. Only in this way could they maintain secrecy until Ogotai had been proclaimed ruler.

A few generations after Genghis Khan's death his empire had vanished. Under degenerate successors it had shrunk to nothing, leaving only the memory of a wholesale cruelty which has never been surpassed. To be fair to the man, we can remember him for one or two other things: he was, as well as a general, an imaginative ruler. There was complete religious freedom in his empire, for Genghis allowed all his varied subjects to worship in their own way, and Karakoram was full of different places of worship. He also had one of the world's best postal services, with a chain of relay stables stretching from China to the Dnieper, to let the great Khan keep in touch with every part of his domain.

In the main, we have much to remember about the great Genghis Khan—but little for which to thank him.

FREDERICK II

Roman Emperor and King of Sicily and Jerusalem

(1194-1250)

FREDERICK II, who was born in 1194 and died in 1250, was described as *Stupor Mundi*, "Wonder of the World". Between Charlemagne, who was crowned Roman Emperor by the Pope in 800, and Napoleon Bonaparte, there was no ruler to equal Frederick in genius. It was a brilliant and extraordinary life made tragic by his prolonged battle with the Papacy which prevented him from carrying out in full his great reforms for the creation of the first state in Europe.

"We, who read and ponder the annals of history, never found such an instance of intense and inexorable hatred as that which raged between the Pope and Frederick," wrote Brother Matthew Paris, monk of St. Albans, who was the fairest and most detailed chronicler of the time. He is referring especially to the battle between Frederick and Pope Gregory IX who had taken his name from that other Gregory, the VIIth, who had excommunicated the powerful Henry IV, Emperor-elect of Germany and Italy, and forbade anyone to serve him as king. It was a fearful enough sentence in those days to bring Henry to Canossa and beg on his knees that the Pope should lift the ban. Even the great Emperor Barbarossa, Frederick I of Hohenstaufen, paid homage to the Pope on his knees, after the defeat of his armies by the Lombard League, the Pope's allies.

When the Emperor Barbarossa was drowned leading a Crusade to the Holy Land he was succeeded by his son, Henry VI, in January, 1186. Henry married Constance, the daughter of Roger II of Sicily, and presumptive heir to that kingdom which consisted of the island and the south of Italy. The Pope, Celestine III, was opposed to the marriage, since the Emperor Henry intended to try to unite Germany and Sicily under one empire which would threaten the encirclement of the Papal States of central Italy, but the Pope was constrained in the spring of 1191 to crown Henry and Constance as emperor and empress. Henry then proceeded to the conquest of Sicily which had been divided up among a number of feudal barons, who had elected as their king Tancred, an illegitimate grandson of King Roger II; but three years passed before Henry won Sicily and this he did by massacring many of the Sicilian aristocracy in a terrible act of treachery. In December of that year, 1194, Constance gave birth to a son at Jesi, near Ancona, and he was christened at Assisi with the names of his two distinguished grandfathers, Frederick and Roger; Frederick, who was to become Emperor Frederick II, had already been made "King of the Romans", the title held by the emperor-elect.

The Emperor Henry VI fortunately died before he could carry out any further cruelties, which were shocking even to an age which was accustomed to refinements of torture, but his early death left his wife to deal with a gang of German soldiers of fortune who expected to take over Sicily for themselves. Constance was regent and a capable woman, determined that her infant son should be king, and she turned for help to the Pope, now Innocent III; she and her son were crowned in Palermo in the summer of 1198. She died in the autumn and Frederick became a ward of the Pope in a kingdom of confusion with rival factions fighting for control.

Frederick was ignored and would have starved if the poorer citizens of Palermo had not taken pity and looked after him in their own houses. At the age of seven he was kidnapped by men sent by the Markward of Anweiler, who was intent on obtaining the kingdom for himself. Even at that age Frederick's precocity and his consciousness of his position is revealed in a letter written to the Pope by a man in Palermo: "Nor did he forget his royal estate and, like a mouse who fears the pursuit of a ferocious animal, he threw himself upon those who were about to seize him, trying with all his force to ward off the arm of him who dared to lay hands upon the sacred body of the Lord's anointed."

Fortunately the Markward died a few months later otherwise Frederick might have been blinded and castrated as Tancred's son had been by order of Frederick's father.

After that Frederick was left free to lead his own wild life with grooms and huntsmen; this did not improve his manners, but taught him how ordinary people lived, which was an advantage when he came later to draw up his famous laws for his kingdom. He studied languages, including Arabic, and read widely; he was encouraged by the Papal Legates and by Muslims at the court who carried on the learning which had helped to make Sicily under the Norman kings the most cultivated court in Europe.

"He is never idle," wrote a contemporary of Frederick, ". . . and so that his vigour may increase, he fortifies his agile body with every kind of exercise and practice of arms. . . . To this is added a regal majesty and majestic features and mien, to which are united a kindly and gracious air, a serene brow, brilliant eyes, and expressive face, a burning spirit and a ready wit. Nevertheless his actions are sometimes odd and vulgar, though this is not due to nature but to contact with rough company."

At fourteen Frederick came of age and the Pope chose as his wife Constance of Aragon, who was widow of the King of Hungary; she was ten years older than Frederick and taught him some manners. A son, Henry, was born, and Frederick was determined to try to ensure his son's succession to the empire although Frederick himself had only a precarious hold over his kingdom of Sicily. Frederick's right to succeed his father as emperor had been ignored and Otto had been elected by the Ghibelline, or pro-papacy princes of Germany; at the age of seventeen Frederick had to prepare against an invasion of the island of Sicily after Otto had occupied all the mainland part of the kingdom. But suddenly there was a reversal of fortune; the Guelf faction in Germany, who were in favour of the Hohenstaufen family, succeeded in overcoming the Ghibelline faction. The Guelf princes deposed Otto and elected Frederick as emperor, and at the beginning of 1212, when Frederick was eighteen, the German ambassadors came to Sicily to invite him to Germany as emperor-elect.

Frederick would have been a happier man if he had remained King of Sicily, but he was conscious of what he considered to be his destiny and he accepted. The Pope insisted that he should first come to Rome to pay homage and made him promise to give up Sicily to his son, who had been made King of Sicily. Innocent III believed that by having a regent under his control he would avoid the danger of the unification of the empire with Sicily, but Frederick had other ideas which he was wise enough to keep to himself.

There were many factions hostile to Frederick in Germany, but through his diplomacy he managed to overcome them. He was crowned with various titles but he still had to be crowned by the Pope to confirm him as emperor. Frederick did not care for Germany and was longing to return to Sicily. He took two steps which would clearly antagonize the Papacy, but Innocent III had been succeeded by the gentle Honorius and Frederick believed he could overcome opposition by promising to lead a Crusade to retrieve Jerusalem.

Frederick had his wife and infant son brought to Germany and had him elected in April, 1220, as the future King of Germany, without the consent of the Pope; by this means Frederick believed he had ensured his son's succession to both Germany and Sicily. He next wrote to the Pope to say that he wished to discuss with him and obtain "the favourable issue to our demand that we may keep to ourselves the Realm of Sicily for our life". In great state he came to Rome. Frederick's decision to equip and lead a Crusade did much to mollify the Pope, for Frederick was now the most powerful ruler in Europe and was the only leader likely to succeed in the capture of Jerusalem; Frederick also agreed that the administration of the kingdom of Germany and that of Sicily should be kept entirely separate. On 22 November, 1220, the great ceremony was held in Rome and Frederick received at the hands of the Pope the imperial crown of Charlemagne. He had achieved his ambition of being anointed emperor and retaining Sicily, so that his empire could be compared to that of the Roman Caesars with lands touching the English Channel, the Baltic and the Mediterranean. He had made concessions with regard to ecclesiastical privileges within his empire, but this did not affect his power as a temporal ruler.

Frederick hurried back to his beloved Sicily and at Capua issued a series of laws based on earlier Norman laws, which had made the kingdom of Sicily the most prosperous in Europe. By excluding the Genoese and Pisans he saw to it that the rich wheat and wool trade, and the fact that Sicily was a great entrepôt for commerce between Africa and Europe, should enrich the state and not other middlemen. He encouraged the growth of new crops and improved the breed of horses and mules; mares, according to the detailed Capuan laws, were to be covered by horses and asses in alternate years. Castles built since the reign of William II, the last of the legitimate Norman kings who had died five years before Frederick's birth, were to be destroyed or become state property; a fleet and an army were built up. The first modern state of Europe was being created by Frederick, "the greatest single force in the Middle Ages", wrote H. A. L. Fisher.

There was considerable resistance from those who lost castles and lands; Frederick had no intention of setting out on the promised Crusade until his kingdom was in order; besides he needed time for Sicily to become prosperous again so that he could finance the great undertaking. He had agreed to construct a fleet of fifty transports to carry two thousand knights and ten thousand soldiers;

the ships were very ingeniously built; part of a side could be let down so that the knights disembarked mounted and ready to meet the enemy; Frederick was ahead of his time with many of his ideas. A further reason for delay was a war against the Muslim population of western Sicily; after finally defeating them he settled several hundred thousand Muslims as farmers on the plains of Apulia and formed a Saracen army garrisoned at Lucera where an entire Saracen town was created.

The gentle Honorius died in 1227 and was succeeded by Gregory IX, who was to be Frederick's formidable opponent. Frederick, after waiting seven years, was at last preparing to go on the Crusade. The fleet sailed with its great army, but after three days at sea Frederick developed an epidemic which had already killed many hundreds of Crusaders and he turned back while the others went on; he decided that he would recover in Sicily rather than die at sea. Gregory IX was furious, considering that this was just another excuse for avoiding the Crusade, and excommunicated him, issuing a violent attack on Frederick for what were considered to be his misdeeds against the Church: "We shall proceed against him as if he were a heretic; we shall absolve his subjects of their oath of allegiance, and we shall strip him of his kingdom which is our fief." The Crusade could only achieve success if the emperor were in the Holy Land, but it was more important to Gregory to discredit him. No one believed that an excommunicated man would lead a Crusade and most of the forty thousand knights and soldiers who had set off with the emperor returned from the Holy Land when they heard of the excommunication.

Historians, such as Mr. T. L. Kington, have criticized the Pope for his hasty action; Miss Georgina Masson, in her *Frederick II of Hohenstaufen*, argues that Pope Gregory was intransigent and vindictive because he had the intelligence to realize that Frederick's ability and his newly organized system of government would be a dangerous threat to the Church of Rome and, indeed, the lay state and the Reformation did ultimately reduce the powers of the Roman Catholic Church.

Frederick hit back in a circular to all the rulers of Christendom setting out his case: "The Roman Empire, the bulwark of the Faith, is being assailed by its own fathers." The kings, clergy and people of Europe watched to see whether the outcome would be another Canossa and a victory for the Pope. Frederick tried in vain to make his peace with Gregory. He had no intention, however, of being stopped from going on his Crusade. When he had fully recovered from the epidemic and set his kingdom in order, for the Pope's hostile acts had caused him many difficulties, he set out for the Holy Land, to the amazement of Europe and to the annoyance of the Pope.

It did not seem possible that the emperor could achieve anything, for the Pope was the dominant figure in all Crusades, and the knights in the Holy Land were divided in their allegiance. Jerusalem had been in the hands of the Saracens since its capture by Saladin forty years earlier, in 1187, and neither the Third Crusade with King Richard I of England and King Philip of France, nor the Fourth nor the Fifth Crusades, had succeeded in winning it back. But Frederick had for a long time had good relations with al-Kamil, Sultan of Egypt, and his ambassador Fakhr ad-Din; through diplomacy Frederick was able to gain what the armed might of Christendom had failed to achieve. In the Treaty of 1229 those parts of Jerusalem which were holy to Christians were returned to them, while the Muslims retained what was holy to them, the Dome of the Rock and the Mosque of al Aqsar. In the Church of the Holy Sepulchre Frederick crowned himself King of Jerusalem, for the Pope's Patriarch would have nothing to do with the ceremony.

Frederick returned to Sicily triumphant; the legend had begun to grow that he was *Stupor Mundi*. The Pope was chagrined and, after forcing Frederick to make many concessions, the ban of excommunication was lifted in August, 1230; but he continued to be very watchful. The Pope disliked many things in Frederick's remarkable Constitutions of Melfi, drawn up by a team of able jurists; there were, for instance, schools for training civil servants and doctors; men were taught law to dispense justice on the principle that all were equal before the law, so that prelates and nobles no longer had jurisdiction in criminal cases. Although an autocrat, Frederick was concerned about the freedom of the individual. "Nothing is more odious," he said, "than the oppression of the poor by the rich."

The Pope also hated and condemned Frederick's sophistication and curiosity, probably gained from his early association with cultivated Muslims. The emperor, said the Pope, only believed what was proved by reason or shown to exist in nature; for the Pope this was a most serious accusation. Frederick's court was full of learned men and elegant poets who wrote, as he did himself, in the Sicilian dialect; Dante was later to describe him as the father of Italian poetry, though he consigned him to hell for his unbelief. The emperor's book on the Art of Hunting with Birds (*De Arte Venandi cum avibus*) showed great observation and has remained a classic. He encouraged the well-known philosopher and astrologer, Michael Scott, to translate important works from the Arabic, such as Averroes's commentaries on Aristotle's works, and he was himself a student of Aristotle, whose works were condemned at that time by the Church. Frederick's court was an early flowering of the Renaissance, but such learning and sophistication did not show itself again in Europe for another two hundred years.

Frederick was, too, a great builder. He established castles in Apulia and the island of Sicily to maintain lines of communication for the administration of his empire, but they also expressed his love of beauty and of nature. The site and design, for instance, of the famous Castel del Monte, looking over the Apulian coastal plain, has an honoured place in the history of architecture. Some of these castles had luxuries borrowed from the East, such as bathrooms and lavatories with running water, probably unknown elsewhere in Europe at that time; indeed, the fact that the emperor believed in cleanliness and took a bath every day was regarded as a scandal. The imperial caravan when it travelled through Italy must have roused great wonder—the Saracen cavalry, an elephant, a giraffe (the first to be seen in Europe), hounds, falcons, hunting leopards and cheetahs, lions and lynxes; and on the camels, curtained in mystery, came the emperor's harem of lovely Saracen dancing girls about whom the prelates made sure that Europe should hear much. The emperor, auburn-haired and slim (he ate only one meal a day), rode in the caravan on his black charger, Dragon.

The struggle with the Papacy continued and it was inevitable since it was a dispute over temporal power. Frederick was not content to rule his kingdom of Sicily and leave Germany entirely to his son Henry, for both countries were part of the empire. In order to maintain his lines of communication between the two he needed to overcome the hostility of the states of the Lombard League which lay across his path—Milan, Brescia, Piacenza, Bologna, Faenza and Parma. The Pope, however, could not agree to see these powerful allies of his subdued, since without temporal power in those days the Pope would have had little influence. If Frederick had succeeded in vanquishing the Lombard League, Italy would have been united over six hundred years before it was achieved under the House of Savoy; whether it would have remained united is another matter.

Frederick considered that the Pope, by his support of the Lombard League, was encouraging insurrection against the empire, which was to him a sacred institution, based on the natural laws of society; people needed the empire, for they required order and it was for the empire to fulfil their need by having just laws. When Frederick found his ambitions to achieve orderly government continually opposed by Gregory he decided on a policy of trying to deprive the Papacy of all temporal power. It was a clash between two beliefs fervently held—a battle that had to come sooner or later, but it was tragically epitomized in the persons of two passionate individuals, Frederick and Gregory. It led to the destruction of Frederick and his whole family and to the shelving for several centuries of imaginative ideas and principles of government; later it led to the Pope's exile to Avignon and eventually to the stripping of all temporal power from the Papacy.

In the spring of 1239 Gregory excommunicated Frederick for the second time; it was the only way he could try to subdue the emperor who had become extremely powerful, supported as he was against the Pope by most of the kings of Christendom, who were apprehensive of the support given by the Pope to the insurgent Lombard League; the Pope, commented Matthew Paris, had tried to persuade the people "that obedience consisted in revolt, and duty in forgetting oaths". In a circular letter to the rulers of the west Frederick had written: "This matter touches you and all the kings of the earth; when your neighbour's wall is on fire, your own property is at stake."

The kings of England, France and Hungary sent forces to help the emperor against the Lombard League. In a famous encyclical Gregory IX, who was nearly a hundred years old, attacked Frederick violently for all manner of sins, many invented: "A furious beast has come out of the sea whose name all over is written *Blasphemy*; he has the feet of a bear, the jaws of a ravening lion, the mottled limbs of a panther . . ." Frederick replied by calling "this false Vicar of Christ", Anti-Christ. He decided to end the Pope's power by capturing him in Rome, for the people were calling for the emperor and many of the cardinals had deserted the ageing Gregory.

It seemed to Frederick, as he approached Rome, that he had achieved his final ambition and that he would reign in the imperial city of the Caesars with the Pope doing his bidding. Gregory himself believed that he had lost the battle; the indomitable old man led a procession through the Roman streets full of hostile crowds and flanked by a few faithful cardinals, who carried the most sacred relics of the Church, the heads of St. Peter and St. Paul. At a moment when he could make himself heard the Pope declaimed:

"These are the ancient relics of Rome for which your city is venerated. . . . It is your duty, Romans, to protect them." Taking the Papal tiara from his head he laid it on the relics exclaiming: "Do you Saints defend Rome if the men of Rome will not defend her?" In a sudden emotional fervour the Romans swung to the support of the Pope and the walls of the city were manned.

Frederick retired, for he did not intend to lay siege to Rome. Twice more Frederick advanced on Rome and retired; the first time Gregory died as Frederick's army was advancing to the city; the second time the new Pope, Cardinal Fieschi of Genoa, who became Innocent IV, escaped dressed as a soldier and helped by the Genoese; he set up his court at Lyons, where he held a Council at which he deposed Frederick in 1245. "For too long I have been the anvil," declared Frederick, "now I wish to be the hammer"; but he had only five more years to live and his position was gradually being undermined. In Germany he had had to depose his son for incompetence and for allying himself with Frederick's enemies, the Milanese; Frederick had lost much of his popularity because he had not come to the help of the Germans when they had to withstand the invasion of the Mongols who had overrun Hungary, although he sent circulars to rulers urging resistance.

He suffered a serious setback in February, 1249, when he failed to capture Parma and his main route across the Appenines was closed to him. There were various attempts on the emperor's life planned by the Pope, and Frederick became suspicious of all, including his closest companions. In 1250 he died still fighting for freedom from the Papacy, and was buried in a porphyry sarcophagus in Palermo. "Let those who shrink from my support," the Emperor had written in one of his letters to rulers, "have the shame, as well as the galling burden of slavery. Before this generation and before the generations to come, I will have the glory of resisting this tyranny."

LOUIS IX (SAINT LOUIS)

(1214-70)

The French kings who are the subjects of essays in this book represent, each of them, the spirit of an Age and not only of a reign in French history. Louis XIV is the central figure of the solemn and magnificent seventeenth century; Henry IV, with his pointed beard, his wit, his gallantry, his commonsense, is a typical Elizabethan; and the at once ridiculous and terrible Louis XI, the Spider King whom Sir Walter Scott portrayed in *Quentin Durward*, is the king who, in the early Renaissance, laboured to make a nation against the old order—like Henry VII of England.

To those who only read history occasionally, Louis IX, St. Louis, is a much vaguer and less attractive figure. This is largely because the thirteenth century seems part of a very long, dreary period known as the Middle Ages, principally concerned with the endless battles of kings and nobles from, let us say, William the Conqueror until the Tudors. We may all have been attracted by the Crusades and by the story of Crécy and Agincourt; we may, some of us, realize that in Italy life was more varied and interesting in the Middle Ages than it was in northern Europe; nevertheless, one century seems much like another, and the important men wooden and unconvincing as human beings.

Yet the thirteenth century, in France and in England, was a time of enlightenment and achievement. France had one of her greatest ages from 1180, when St. Louis's grandfather, Philip Auguste, became king, until the death of St. Louis's grandson, Philip the Fair, and the beginning of the Hundred Years' War between France and England early in the fourteenth century. The kings of the House of Capet won back their lands from England and, with the aid of the people of France, had subdued the great nobles who were, some of them, richer and more powerful than the King of France.

In Paris great masters such as St. Thomas Aquinas and Albertus Magnus taught at the Sorbonne where Roger Bacon studied. Owing to the work of monks and friars during the past two hundred years there were plenty of educated men, even of humble rank, in the towns and, thanks to relative peace, there were people of every sort. Indeed, the population of France was probably greater in the reign of St. Louis than it was at the time of the French Revolution, whilst England at the beginning of the reign of Edward III had a larger population than one hundred and fifty years later.

The towns flourished. Many of them had paved streets and in Paris there were no less than twenty-six large bath-houses, for cleanliness of body had become a passion with the new city bourgeoisie. France had grown rich, in part because it lay on the great trading routes to northern Europe along which travelled the luxuries which Europe had discovered in the Middle East during the Crusades of the eleventh and twelfth centuries. Lowlands and marshes were drained, forests were cleared. Farm animals, particularly sheep and pigs, increased enormously in numbers during the thirteenth century. All sorts of plants were first introduced from the East, such as the apricot tree, rice, maize, spinach, artichokes, shallots and many kinds of herbs. The popular literature of folk tales and fables shows the independence of mind of the time. Among the major arts which were first created in the twelfth and thirteenth centuries in France and Flanders was that of stained glass.

This brings us to the greatest aesthetic achievement of the time, the building of the Gothic cathedrals. Some were built or largely built in the twelfth century: others were completed in the fourteenth century; but the great period of construction lies in the thirteenth. Now a point about these Gothic cathedrals is that they cannot be considered like the Pyramids as the work of a society which crushed the individual and used him as a mere servant. The cathedrals are the work of planners and architects about whom we know comparatively little in the first place; but every cathedral or church of this time cries out that it is the expression of hundreds of skilled artisans in wood and stone and in iron and bronze. Individual fantasies in gargoyles, carvings of bishops' thrones, screens or misericords shows that hundreds of ordinary men took part in creating these great works of art. Nor was enthusiasm restricted to artisans and craftsmen; writers of the time record that noblemen and their ladies, shopkeepers and peasants harnessed themselves to the carts bearing the heavy stones, wood, lime or oil needed for building. Minstrels and trumpeters headed great processions of people bearing materials, and when at night such a procession arrived on the site the carts were emptied by the light of torches, hymns were sung, and it was said that blind men recovered their sight and that the paralytic walked.

Throughout the land, particularly during the reign of St. Louis, there was a feeling of security. The king reigned and dispensed justice, not as a tyrant but as the representative of God and as the head of an ordered society. How different life was to be during the next hundred years, after Philip the Fair, when, as the result of the Hundred Years' War and the Black Death, France was delivered over once again to the robbers, barons and marauding soldiers, and when men were to live in caves and eat grass. The very secret of building the Gothic cathedrals was to be forgotten.

Louis's father reigned for only a few years after the death of Philip Auguste. Louis was only twelve at his father's death and his right of succession was disputed. Twice, factions of the nobility took up arms. Louis's mother, Blanche of Castile, one of those dominating female figures such as Catherine de Medici or Anne of Austria, fought with courage and cunning for her son. The support given to the Crown by the people of the towns and by the Church was so strong that the issue was never very much in doubt. St. Louis's reign really begins in 1236, after he had been married for two years to Marguerite of Provence, who brought her lands into the royal domain. Queen Blanche did not abandon power lightly to her son, and Louis appeared extravagantly respectful to his mother. The old queen, presumably out of jealousy, wanted to keep Louis from seeing too much of his wife and so, early in their marriage, Louis and Marguerite had to meet on a small private turning stair which linked their apartments in the Palace at Pontoise, near Paris, where they lived for much of the time. But, in the long run, Louis was a much stronger character than his mother and, although until her death he put up with her caprices, he had his way in all essential matters.

His wife Marguerite bore him nine children. She too had something of her mother-in-law's determination to play a part in politics, and Louis, but with greater sternness than he had shown to his mother, kept her at arm's length. He was anything but uxorious. However, he took her with him on his first Crusade: this was that she might also reap the spiritual reward which came to those who fought for the Cross.

Louis, both as an adolescent and grown man, was of striking beauty. He was firm and smooth of face and, as all his contemporaries noted, his look was mild and kind. Many people speak of his "dove's" eyes. He was extremely tall and elegantly built, and when he was in armour with a gold crown on his helmet, Joinville writes: "Never was so fine a man under arms, for he stood alone, above all his people from the shoulders upwards." From an early age Louis fulfilled his Christian duties as man and king with a sort of fanaticism. He would leave his palace early in the morning to distribute money as anonymously as possible to the poor. He would rise from bed at midnight to hear the Mass for the dead, and regularly attended all the offices of the Church throughout the day. When he rode abroad, his chaplains accompanied him to read the appropriate services. On Fridays he avoided any kind of gaiety and on that day he never wore a hat in memory of the Crown of Thorns. Often in church he would prostrate himself on the stone floor for so long that his attendants grew impatient. When he roused himself he would sometimes not know where he was. Of course, like Henry III and most medieval monarchs, he washed the feet of the poor.

As close companion Louis kept with him a monk who was a leper, and in Palestine during his Crusade he helped bury the putrefied remains of massacred Christians. He was avid of mortification and confessed that he took on repugnant tasks not because they were necessarily the most useful but because they were the most disagreeable to him. Only after his death did men discover the many practices and torments he imposed on himself.

With all these religious extravagances, the king was careful not to overdo his Christian acts so that they might in any way undermine his authority. He liked, for instance, dressing in a monkish habit, and there is the story that his wife once reproached him for his dislike of dress and for his simple robes trimmed with rabbit or squirrel. "Madame," he answered, "if it pleases you to see me richly dressed I will be so; but since conjugal love enjoins on each spouse to please the other, then you must do me the pleasure of leaving your rich dresses and conforming to my fashion as I do to yours." No more was heard on that subject from the queen.

On occasions he appeared in all the magnificence of a monarch with a vermilion surcoat, ermine and jewelled sword. "In such a fashion one must dress that wise men will say that one does not overdo it, nor young men of the time say that you do too little," said Louis. He was of such a totally integrated character that he was never at a loss for a reply to man or woman. Once, to a fishwife who shouted out as he passed that he was more like a monk than a king, he answered gravely: "You speak the truth I am sure. I am not worthy to be a king, and if it had pleased our Lord there would have been another in my place who would have known better how to govern the kingdom."

Louis had the inner gaiety and confidence of a saint and loved jests and songs with his companions. He was a man of action, totally unlike the saintly Henry III of England, and so strong was his will that all men feared him. The worldly cautious Joinville, who was to be his chronicler as well as his friend, not only appreciated Louis's greatness but loved him dearly. Louis once asked Joinville if he would rather wash the feet of lepers or commit a mortal sin. Joinville answered that he would much rather commit a mortal sin. "That is ill said," answered the king; but it did not impair their friendship.

It was inevitable that this most Christian king should take the Cross. He went, in 1248, on a Crusade which was directed at Egypt where the power of the Saracens was centred. With eighteen ships and accompanied by his two brothers, Alphonse of Poitiers and Charles of Anjou, as well as by his wife, Louis took Damietta on the mouth of the Nile in 1249 and ought then to have advanced at once on Cairo, which he would infallibly have taken. But instead the Crusaders dallied and enjoyed the fleshpots of the Near East, whilst the king prayed. The Sultan brought up reinforcements and fifty of his officers who had abandoned Damietta were strangled. When Louis's army finally marched towards Cairo it was delayed at a river crossing near Mansourah and could not succeed in building a bridge. Fourteen hundred French knights crossed by a ford and took Mansourah; unfortunately the infantry could not cross by the ford and the knights were unable to hold their own on the opposite bank. The Egyptian Mamelukes were strengthened, the French advance-guard and the rest of the army, was beseiged on all sides. The Saracens blocked the river from Damietta so that no food could reach the French. An attempt was made to retreat but Louis's army was decimated by dysentery from which he himself suffered, and he was finally forced to surrender. In Damietta the queen and a small force held out.

The captured king was made to embark in a war-galley on the Nile. He was escorted by a large number of Egyptian boats which led him in triumph to the sound of cymbals and drums, whilst, on the bank, the Egyptian army advanced beside the ships. The prisoners followed the army with their hands bound. The Egyptians were embarrassed by the too great number of prisoners and, one night, these prisoners were led in bands of three or four hundred to the banks of the Nile where, after having their heads cut off, they were thrown into the river. Louis and those of his nobles still alive were ransomed and returned to the queen at Damietta, which, of course, was surrendered to the Egyptians. Characteristically, King Louis refused to take advantage of an error of calculation made by the Egyptians in the amount of his ransom and he insisted on the proper sum being paid.

After this disaster, Louis spent two years in Palestine where he did his best to prop up the Christian principalities. But this, too, was on the whole unsuccessful. The crusading ardour of Europe was over and Louis received little help from other Christian countries.

If this Crusade can be blamed as a folly on the part of the king it nonetheless redounded to his credit in the Christian world. After his return he won two great victories at Taillebourg and Saintes over the English who had invaded South-western France in support of some rebels against the king. To the surprise of all his subjects Louis, after these victories and the retreat of the English, gave back three provinces of France to Henry III, stating that it was fitting that between Christians and cousins there should be peace and amity. Louis, however, stipulated that the English king should pay him homage for these provinces, and also should abandon all claims to the throne of France. Louis, in this, showed a touching faith in the continuance of the feudal system—for why should he not let the English king own land in France as his vassal? He failed to foresee that already national feeling was stronger by far than feudalism. But this spectacular policy of seeking Christian friendship was in keeping with the medieval tradition of Christendom, and, had there been more men as Christian and as powerful as St. Louis, Europe might have become, by the fifteenth century, a politically united continent. His political unwisdom, however, had at least one reward in his time. Henry III and his barons submitted their quarrels later to the arbitration of St. Louis, another unprecedented act.

Much of Louis's time was devoted to the administering of justice. Joinville had this picture of the king holding his informal court in the wood of Vincennes, just outside Paris:

> *Many times it happened in the summer that the king went to sit in the wood of Vincennes after hearing Mass, and leant against an oak and made us sit round him, and all those who had affairs to attend to came to speak to him without disturbance of an usher or anyone else. And he would ask: "Is there no one who has a plea?" And those who had rose and then he said: "Keep quiet all of you and judgement will be dealt to you in turn." He then summoned lawyers to speak.*

Joinville also describes him as administering justice in Paris in the same way. "I saw him several times in the summer going to judge cases for his people in the Palace garden, dressed in a coat of coarse stuff with an outer coat of tyretaine (a stuff half wool and half cotton) without sleeves, a mantle of thick black silk fastened round his neck, his head well combed out and without a hat but with a coronet of white peacock feathers around his head. And he had a carpet spread for us to sit round him; and all the people who had matters to bring before him stood round him and he gave judgment in the way I have described before in the wood of Vincennes."

All over his kingdom Louis sent seneschals, or *baillis* as they were called, to ensure justice, choosing very often poor friars or men who knew the conditions of the humble as his agents. In his instructions to his son, Louis describes the principles on which royal justice was to be carried out. "Dear son, if it should be that you come to reign, see that you have the mark of a king, that is to say that you are just and that you will never refuse justice on any consideration. If it happens that a dispute between rich and poor comes before you, support the poor rather than the rich, and when you've heard the truth, do justice to them. And if it happened that you have a dispute with another, support the claim of the other before your council and do not show your great interest in the dispute until the truth be shown."

In the summer of 1270 Louis embarked from Aigues Mortes on his second Crusade, which was against Tunis. He believed, quite wrongly, that the Bey of Tunis was intending to become a Christian and therefore his Crusade would turn into a visit of friendship. Other people say he was persuaded to sail to Tunis by his brother, Charles of Anjou, who had become King of Sicily and wanted someone to check the pirates who used the port. Joinville strongly advised the king against the Crusade. "Those," wrote Joinville, "who recommended the Crusade to him were guilty of mortal sin; for the whole kingdom was at peace and he with all his neighbours . . . a great sin did those commit in view of King Louis's great bodily weakness. He could not bear to be carried in a vehicle or to ride on horseback. His weakness was so great that it gave him pain when I carried him in my arms from the house of the Count of Auxerre to the Franciscan monastery where I took leave of him. And even though he was so feeble, if he had remained in France he could still have lived and done much good and many good works." Louis landed at Carthage in mid-summer. The pest was raging in Tunisia, and after a victorious fight before the walls of Tunis the

French army was immobilized by sickness. On 25 August the king himself died of the plague.

As a ruler Louis was perhaps less able and successful than his grandfather and his grandson. He made mistakes—the two Crusades, the giving away of land to the English. He stood for a cause, that of a united Christendom, which was a lost cause and perhaps always an impossible one. Yet, as a ruler, he reinforced the belief of the French people in monarchy: indeed, he made the idea of monarchy beloved among the people. As a chronicler says of him: "He shunned discords, he avoided scandals and he hated disagreements. For which reason the waves of bitterness were held back on all sides and disturbances were driven away." St. Louis embodied a unique moment in history when a saint successfully ruled a great kingdom. During his reign the manuscript painters with their vivid designs and bright colours flourished. Their illustrations of some of the Book of Hours leaves behind an impression of extreme devotion, vividness, and childlike power such as no other art has attained to. Joinville, writing of St. Louis, says: "And as the writer who has finished his book illuminates it with gold and blue, so the said king illuminated his kingdom."

KUBLAI KHAN

(1215?-1294)

In Xanadu did Kubla Khan
A stately pleasure-dome decree:
Where Alph, the sacred river, ran
Through caverns measureless to man
Down to a sunless sea.

KUBLAI KHAN has haunted the imagination of man for seven centuries. Coleridge's half-glimpsed vision in his magic lines has all the strangeness of a broken dream, and the remarkable story of the Mongols, of whom Kublai Khan was the last and the greatest, is an astonishing mixture of awful nightmare and glittering splendour such as the world has not known before or since.

The Mongol saga which astonished and dazzled the world lasted for a brief century. The fierce nomadic tribes of the Mongolian plains had always fought each other until the beginning of the thirteenth century, when they were miraculously welded together into a nation under Genghis Khan, a leader of great genius and ruthless ambition. They thundered into history, invading China, India, Turkestan, Persia and Russia. They were irresistible and their number seemed limitless. They were savage and ruthless and gave no quarter as they ravaged and butchered across the whole continent of Asia and into Europe.

These terrible horsemen from the distant plains aroused such dread and committed such wanton slaughter that they made an outstanding contribution to what was called "the Martyrdom of Man". The Mongols are said to have won as much by the terror they inspired as by actual fighting. Two and a half million corpses marked their passage across the central Asian state of Khorasan. At Balkh, a great and splendid city, every single man, woman and child was massacred, and when Marco Polo passed through the place fifty years later it was still just a pile of ruins. Genghis Khan erected immense pyramids of skulls to remind the inhabitants that he had passed that way and resistance was useless.

The strange thing was that after the slaughter of these terrible invasions the Mongols proved to be wise and enlightened rulers of the vast empire they conquered. It could be said that those who survived the sword of Genghis Khan were lucky in more than one sense. Previous to the invasions most of these people lived in squalor and servility. Those who survived enjoyed a period of peace and prosperity such as had not been known before. There was complete religious toleration—something unknown in those times—and all the trade routes of Asia were open to travellers and merchants from all lands.

The empire of Genghis Khan stretched from the Black Sea to the Pacific Ocean and as far south as the Himalayas. His sons had been trained as leaders and rulers to hold down his immense conquests, but Genghis had little faith in them. He died in 1227 at Ha-lao-tu, on the banks of the River Sale in Mongolia, his sons and grandsons standing around his bed, and it was said by the Mongol chronicler Sanang Setzen that the dying man pointed to his eleven-year-old grandson and said: "One day he will rule and his will be a greater age than mine."

The boy thus picked out for greatness was Kublai, the second son of Tule, who was the youngest of four sons of Genghis by his favourite wife. Kublai had to wait for more than thirty years before he could even begin to fulfil his grandfather's prophecy. In the meanwhile family quarrels threatened to break up Genghis's vast dominions.

Kublai's brother, Mangu, became Grand Khan before him, and under his rule more conquests were made. Baghdad was captured and the last of the Abbasid Caliphs was tortured to death and three-quarters of a million of his subjects massacred. All of China was conquered and subdued at the cost of the lives of eighteen million Chinese. Mangu died fighting at Ho-Chow in 1259, and Kublai succeeded him as Grand Khan after some dispute with other members of the family, which was settled in the usual sanguinary fashion.

Kublai had very different ideas to those of his bloodthirsty and barbaric family, who loved war for its own sake and seemed to revel in the slaughter and bloodshed which had made their name synonymous with the worst kind of barbarism.

When his brother had been Khan, Kublai's preference for negotiation rather than slaughter had brought him under the displeasure of the warlike Mangu, but when Kublai succeeded he soon proved the superiority of his more pacific policies. But he was no weakling. His rule was firm. He was the first to rise above the innate barbarism which had so far characterized the Mongol rulers.

He was forty-four, of medium height, dark-eyed and, according to Marco Polo, who knew him well, had a prominent and splendid profile, a fair complexion and an impressively regal air.

His long and busy reign transformed the huge Mongol Empire and brought a peace and prosperity to Asia which it had not known before and which it did not experience again for many centuries. The prosperity was centred on China, which was then the wonder of the world and enjoyed a wealth and luxury unknown in Europe. The splendour and magnificence of Kublai Khan's empire, as told by Marco Polo, haunted the imagination of the West for centuries and inspired the great voyages which later set out from Europe to discover the fabled riches of the Indies and Cathay.

China's two leading cities, Peking and Hangchow, were its main centres of trade. To their gold and silver markets came traders from all over Asia. The streets were full of rich bazaars, and magnificent warehouses lined the waterfronts. Rivers and canals, spanned with innumerable bridges, carried a constant stream of merchandise in gaily coloured junks. The people prospered on the highly skilled industries which made cloth of silver and gold, fine silks and taffetas. Merchants travelled many thousands of miles to buy these beautifully made luxury goods of China.

All the roads and trade-routes of Asia were open to travellers at this time. An Italian handbook for merchants published in 1340 said that the road to Cathay "is perfectly safe whether by day or by night, according to what the merchants say who have used it". This could not be said for travel in Europe at that time, but during the Mongol Dynasty the whole of Asia was open. Chinese silk was brought to Europe for the first time since the days of the Roman Empire, and it was highly prized.

It was the first time in history that an Emperor of China was known by name and deed in Europe. Kublai's seals on letters sent from Tabriz to France are still preserved in Paris. Adventurers and travellers from eastern Europe, as well as the Polos from Venice, served Kublai as ministers, generals and governors.

Kublai Khan encouraged Europeans to come to China in order to solve his administrative problems. His own Mongols were not civilized enough to govern an educated and sophisticated country like China, and he dared not put Chinese in high administrative positions in case they rebelled and undermined his authority. He sought men of talent and education from all over the known world.

At his court in Peking were received ambassadors from every country on earth.

Just as Europeans took every opportunity of this unprecedented chance to get to know more about the mysterious East, Kublai Khan on his part had an inexhaustible curiosity about what took place beyond the distant limits of his immense empire. He was a man of keen intelligence and an insatiable desire for knowledge. China had exercised its age-old spell upon its conquerors and the Mongols were eager to be educated by their highly civilized subjects. They abandoned their old capital of Karakoram, and Kublai built the splendid city of Cambaluk, or Peking, the glories of which so impressed Marco Polo.

Kublai seemed to possess a good deal of natural benevolence and magnanimity. He also had a great love of splendour. The magnificence of his court was the marvel of the world. His palace at Peking was large enough to accommodate a thousand knights and was surrounded by a wall sixteen miles in circumference. His banqueting hall seated six thousand guests. It was decorated with tapestries of green and gold and ornamented with chrysoprase, silver and gold. The walls of Kublai's private apartments were lined with skins of ermine, and the audience chamber was decorated with ermine and zibelline, delicately worked in intaglio.

The gardens of the mighty Khan were nature reconstructed, as befitted the greatest emperor upon the earth. There were gardens and fountains, rivers and brooks, lakes and forests and artificial hills.

So twice five miles of fertile ground
With walls and towers were girdled round:
And there were gardens bright with sinuous rills
Where blossomed many an incense-bearing tree;
And here were forests ancient as the hills,
Enfolding sunny spots of greenery.

Coleridge was doubtless inspired by Marco Polo's rhapsodies on the subject.

Kublai Khan was treated like a god. When he ate, his attendants stuffed silk napkins in their mouths so that their breath should not contaminate his food. Silence was always observed in his presence by all ranks of his subjects. Courts at Peking were traditionally held in almost complete silence, and no noise was permitted within half a mile of where the Khan was. Everyone attending court took slippers of white leather so that the beautiful carpets, which were curiously wrought in silk and gold in a variety of colours, should not be soiled. They also took small cuspidors with them, for obviously no one could spit upon such priceless floor-coverings.

Kublai had a number of wives—at the time of Marco Polo, towards the end of his reign, there were four "of the first rank who are esteemed legitimate"—and he also had a harem of concubines on the grand scale as befitted the greatest emperor upon earth.

These girls were selected according to a well-established custom of the Mongol princes. Every two years his agents went to the Tartar province of Ungut, whose women were noted for their beauty and fairness of complexion. Several hundred maidens were assembled and their beauty judged as though they were precious stones, in carats, each feature—hair, mouth, countenance, figure—being judged separately and receiving a certain number of carats. Those estimated at twenty or twenty-one carats were taken to the Khan's court for further elimination.

After personal inspection by their prospective lord and master, thirty or forty chosen maidens were entered for the final heat as it were. Following the most intimate physical inspection, each girl was placed in the care of the wife of a noble whose duty it was to see that they had no concealed imperfections. The matrons slept with the girls to ensure that they had sweet breath at all times, that they did not snore, toss and turn in their sleep, or suffer from body odour.

The presumably fortunate girls who came through this final scrutiny then had the honour of sharing the emperor's bed. The intimacy, however, was not *à deux*, for Kublai Khan always had five girls at a time. These girls waited on his every wish, and as Marco Polo delicately puts it, "he does with them as he likes". Each party of five girls remained with him for three days and three nights, when the next five girls on the rota came on duty. He had no personal male attendants, but throughout his reign was always waited upon by relays of beautiful young females. He thus became the father of forty-seven sons, and daughters who were not numbered. In battle his army was largely officered by his own sons.

Kublai Khan was extremely interested in religion. Such was his liberal mind that all religions interested him and he made a study of each one. He had earnestly considered the religions of the Jews, the Buddhists and the Moslems. But it was Christianity which fascinated him the most.

When Nicolo and Maffeo Polo arrived at his court about 1265 they were the first Western Europeans he had met, and Kublai was particularly interested in them as they were Italians who came from the very home of the Christian Church. The Polo brothers, wise and prudent travellers, had already taken the trouble to master the Tartar language, and found themselves immediately at home in the company of the Grand Khan. Traders to their fingertips, there was nothing in the way of material things which they could sell to the Khan, who possessed everything man could wish for upon earth, so they sold him their religion.

Kublai was fascinated, particularly in the story of Jesus Christ, though the subtlety of the Crucifixion escaped his oriental mind. He could not understand why such an exalted man should have made the sacrifice of permitting himself to perish miserably on the Cross. What really interested him about Christianity was the institution of the Papacy. The Pope, with his wealth and pomp and enormous but mysterious power, was someone after his own despotic heart. This he could readily understand and this perhaps was the thing about Christianity which really appealed to this great Eastern ruler.

He told the Polo brothers that he would like them to return to the Pope at Rome as his ambassadors with the request that a hundred men of learning should be sent to instruct the Tartar people in Christianity and the liberal arts. Years later the Polos returned with Nicolo's young son Marco. The Dominican friars the Pope had sent with them had lost heart early in the journey across Asia and turned back.

They did not succeed in converting Kublai Khan to Christianity. Although he recognized its intrinsic superiority, it did not have the spectacular powers, the miracles, the black magic and the general entertainment value which protagonists of the more barbaric religions then practised in China used as methods of conversion. It was probable that Christendom's failure to provide the teachers he asked for was the real reason why Kublai Khan turned to Tibetan Buddhism as the most effective means of civilizing his countrymen. Tibetan Buddhists were given positions of great power in his empire.

Kublai Khan made several attempts to extend his realms, but generally without success. Two bids to conquer Japan failed, as did an attempt to invade Cochin China (South Vietnam) and Java. He did, however, successfully subjugate Burma.

He died in 1294 at the age of eighty-two, greatly revered by his subjects, and renowned all over the then known world.

His death was marked by one of those dark Mongol customs

which has made their name a by-word for barbarism. It was said that all of his wives were buried alive with him, and that any of his subjects who dared to look upon his bier as it was borne to its last resting place were summarily slain by his Mongol mourners with the injunction: "Your master needs you in heaven. Go and serve him there."

But he was not a barbarian and would not have approved of servants thus acquired—supposing that he found his way to heaven.

Kublai Khan was a giant figure in the tumultuous centuries of the Middle Ages, standing astride the world like a colossus, ruling more territory, more subjects, than any other monarch on the face of the earth. He bridged the two worlds of East and West, then unknown to each other, and for a brief and magic period opened the way for them to know and understand each other. His reign was a bright gleam of light and reason in the dark centuries which went before and which followed.

After his death the Mongol Empire collapsed, the darkness once more descended upon the vast spaces of mysterious Asia, and the barriers of misunderstanding and suspicion came down between East and West.

EDWARD I

(1239–1307)

SOME MONARCHS are remembered by their personalities or their capacity to stir the imagination, others by the vigour and force of their actions. King Edward I stands apart in English history, for he is best remembered by his good works—the Model Parliament of 1295 and the improvement in the laws and the legal system which he carried out. Some of his laws are still in force today.

The eldest son of Henry III, he was born in 1239. In his early years he witnessed the disastrous rule of his father, who was influenced by favourites and the French followers of his queen, Eleanor of Provence, who swarmed into England in her train and were soon filling the chief positions in the land.

In 1258 the barons, led by Simon de Montfort, compelled Henry to hand over government to them. De Montfort, a Frenchman of far-reaching intelligence and ambition, whose family had made a great fortune out of the unspeakable Albigensian Crusade, had come to England to claim the earldom of Leicester, had become one of the leading barons in the land, and had married the king's sister.

Led by de Montfort, the barons took up arms against the king and defeated him, and de Montfort became virtual dictator. He summoned what has been regarded as the first real English Parliament in 1265. He formed the great conception of Law as something above the king, and held that the king's true strength lay in Parliament. In de Montfort's 1265 Parliament an important new class of members was present—the Commons, which was destined to give it its future greatness.

Edward had originally come to an understanding with de Montfort and for a time it looked as though the two men might make common cause. This naturally brought Edward into conflict with his father. But Edward's main concern was the preservation of the Plantagenet dynasty, and he strove to persuade his father's royalist party to adopt a more liberal and national spirit. During the fighting between the king and de Montfort, Edward fought on his father's side.

The two armies met at the decisive Battle of Lewes on 14 May, 1264, an encounter which does nothing for Edward's reputation as a soldier. De Montfort and the rebel barons, whose soldiers were said to have worn the white cross of the Crusader, were joined by a large body of Londoners. Henry had the advantage of numbers and quality, though his forces were tired from long marching.

This advantage, however, was thrown away by Edward, who at the head of his knights impetuously pursued the left wing of de Montfort's army, consisting mainly of Londoners, off the field. As de Montfort's standard was in this left wing, Edward ruthlessly chased the Londoners into the swampy ground near the River Ouse, killing large numbers of them and capturing the de Montfort standard.

When Edward returned to the main battle, flushed with what he imagined was victory, he found that de Montfort had not been where his standard had flown, and during Edward's absence had won the day.

After the Battle of Lewes both Edward and his father were virtual prisoners of de Montfort and the barons. But dissension broke out between de Montfort and his followers during which Edward escaped, gathered an army and met de Montfort's forces at Evesham on 4 August, 1265. Edward had learned the lesson of Lewes and himself employed a stratagem which led de Montfort into a trap and to his final defeat on Green Hill outside Evesham, where, after a heroic resistance, de Montfort was slain among his devoted friends and followers.

Edward now showed his true statesmanship and was soon in firm control of the policies of his discredited father. He sought no vengeance on de Montfort's followers. In fact he assimilated many of the de Montfort ideals, with the result that he was acclaimed by the Londoners as de Montfort's heir and successor.

Peace now settled upon England after the civil war which was terminated by the Battle of Evesham. The moderate spirit which seems to have come to the conflicting elements in the kingdom was due to several reasons. The people had faith in the heir to the throne, and knew he would give them the kind of government they wished. England, too, was conscious of emergent nationhood after centuries of being part of an Anglo-French kingdom. Her sovereigns had lost most of their French possessions, and although the battle to retain them was to last a hundred years and more, England was now the centre of the monarch's interests and activities, whereas during the reigns of Henry II and Richard I France occupied as much if not more of the king's time as England did. Thus England came more and more to realize her nationhood and independent power.

So peaceful were the final years of Henry III's reign that Edward went on a crusade in 1270, the funds for which were willingly provided by the country, which was in the mood to expiate for its civil strife by mounting an attack upon the enemy of Christendom. Edward and his followers arrived at Acre in May, 1271, despite the fact that a truce had been concluded with the infidel. Edward refused to be party to this treason to Christendom, but neither his energy nor his valour could do much to prop up the decaying Crusading movement. News of the declining health of his father was used as an excuse to come home.

He was in Sicily when he heard of the death of Henry III on 16 November, 1272. Four days later at Henry's funeral he was recognized as King Edward I of England by the English barons. Affairs in England were so peaceful that Edward came home leisurely, and made a royal and friendly progress through Italy, France and Gascony, his own hereditary duchy. He arrived in England in August, 1274, and was that month crowned at Westminster.

He was thirty-five years old and a magnificent figure of a man, towering above his contemporaries to the then rare height of six feet two inches. Like his knightly ancestor, Richard Coeur de Lion, Edward was a romantic, but he was a practical one. Though his mind was steeped in the legends of King Arthur, his boundless energies were devoted to the establishment of a really effective administration. A man of considerable intelligence, he had a complete mastery of the law, and was an eloquent and convincing orator. Though reasonable in the council chamber, his Plantagenet temper was uncertain and was greatly feared. He was no saint, and was guilty of vindictive cruelty, in the typical Plantagenet manner, to his enemies.

But his domestic life was above reproach, and his friends and subordinates could always rely upon his loyalty and his trust, which was unusual with a medieval king. He had married Eleanor of Castile in 1254 and she bore him four sons and nine daughters, though only one son (Edward II) and five daughters survived infancy.

Thus the man who succeeded Henry III was a very different person to the cavalry leader whose impetuosity had lost the Battle of Lewes eight years previously. Edward's character had developed and hardened in the rough school of duplicity and double-dealing which characterized the politics of his age.

Edward has been described as a revolutionary conservative. Although maintaining the *status quo*, he revolutionized the English administration, and brought to an end feudalism in the country's political life. Nothing that he did was either new or original, but it was necessary to the development of the nation. He limited the amount of money which was paid to Rome, and ended the Papal overlordship of England which his grandfather King John had been forced to grant as the price of patching up his damaging quarrel with Pope Innocent III.

Apart from occupying himself with administration and legislation, Edward set about the conquest of Wales in the early part of his reign. The Welsh of the mountains had never submitted to any of the conquerors of Britain. Neither Roman, Saxon, Dane or Norman had subdued them. Strong fortresses had been built by the Anglo-Norman nobles who had been granted Welsh lands and who were engaged in constant warfare with the native clans. Edward extended this method of conquest and built many castles in Wales, some of which, including Conway, Rhuddlan, Carnarvon, Caerphilly and Harlech, can be seen today.

Prince Llewelyn (the Last) of Wales had been recognized by Henry III as Prince of Wales—the first and also the last native prince to bear that name. Edward required Llewelyn to pay homage to him as his overlord. Llewelyn, over-estimating his power, refused to do this. So in 1277 Edward invaded North Wales where Llewelyn had his stronghold and after a skilful campaign forced him to surrender. The attempt to put Wales under an English administration failed and war broke out again. Llewelyn was finally killed in a skirmish in 1282. The resistance of the Welsh was crushed and Edward divided the country into shires and hundreds, introduced English laws and issued charters to encourage commerce.

In 1284 Queen Eleanor gave birth to a son at Carnarvon Castle, and there is a legend that Edward presented the babe to the Welsh as their own prince who could speak no English. Young Prince Edward was formally created Prince of Wales in 1301.

Between the years 1285 and 1289 Edward was on the Continent. Philip III of France had died and was succeeded by Philip the Fair, to whom Edward performed an act of public homage, the French king being his overlord for Edward's possessions in France, and Edward was very punctilious about these necessary medieval formalities. His business on the Continent included attempts to improve the administration of his duchy of Gascony and a successful mediation of a quarrel between the houses of Anjou and Aragon.

While Edward was abroad the administration at home deteriorated to such an extent that the country was thrown into confusion. When he returned he found he had to dismiss most of his judges and ministers for corruption.

Persecution of the Jews had grown worse. They had been introduced into England by William the Conqueror, their legal position being that of royal chattels. The kind of religious fervour which the Crusades had inflamed led to all sorts of atrocities being perpetrated upon the Jews, who could not leave the country to escape the terror unless they obtained royal permission. In 1290 Edward expelled all these unfortunate people from England. This was not an act of terror but a merciful release. It was three hundred and fifty years before the Jews returned in any numbers to England.

Having conquered Wales, Edward then turned to Scotland, which he found a much more difficult task and one which was to occupy him for the rest of his life.

After the death of Alexander III the Scottish throne had several claimants. Edward was asked to arbitrate and he chose an Anglo-Norman named John Balliol, whom he claimed as his vassal and from whom he demanded homage. At first the new king was prepared to agree, though his subjects were not. Balliol himself soon rebelled but was defeated by Edward at Dunbar.

As a sign of the intended incorporation of the Scottish kingdom with the English, Edward took the Coronation stone from Scone and carried it to Westminster, where it remains to this day, a matter over which some Scottish nationalists are still at issue with the English Crown.

Edward's great work was the Model Parliament. He was determined to govern with the support of his own subjects. "What touches all," he declared, "should be approved of all."

In 1295 he summoned the most representative Parliament that had met in England up to that time, comprising the three estates, lords, clergy and commons. It is called the Model Parliament because all subsequent Parliaments in England have followed the same pattern. At first it sat in a single chamber and was presided over by the king sitting on his throne. Before him was his Council, headed by the Chancellor and comprising judges and justices. The chamber was flanked on one side by the bishops and clergy and on the other by the lords and barons. At the far end of the chamber was a bar, on the other side of which stood the Commons whose leader was later known as the Speaker.

When the king had put his proposals to Parliament, the various estates retired to separate chambers and discussed and voted on the proposals, then returned to the Parliament chamber with their decisions. It was not until after the death of Edward I that Parliament split into the two Houses of Lords and Commons. But Edward established the Parliamentary constitution of England and instituted the government which we have today. That was his great work, and he brought to bear upon it an intelligence unrivalled in his day, a mastery of the law, and an idealism inspired by the best virtues and philosophies of his time.

Edward, however, did not form Parliament for it to govern. His intention was that it should be a consultative body. The idea of delegating any of his royal authority or dispersing any of his powers was as foreign to him as it would have been to any Plantagenet. The decisions were taken by him in consultation with his Council. He called Parliament for a discussion and an exchange of views in the national good. Parliament was to augment the royal power by approving the decisions he had already made. Democracy was not in anyone's mind, and was in fact quite foreign to the philosophy of thirteenth-century government. But it did give Lords, Commons and Clergy a sense of responsibility and implanted the seed of government by consultation, agreement and debate in which representatives of all sections of the country took part—the seed, in fact, of democracy.

The reign of this great king ended in turmoil and frustration. Again and again Scotland rose in revolt under their leaders, William Wallace and Robert Bruce. Again and again Edward marched north and defeated them. In 1298 William Wallace, betrayed into Edward's hands, was brought to London and executed.

The century ended in bloodshed, with Robert Bruce once more raising the standard of Scottish liberty. In 1307 Edward, now old and worn, raised his finest army against Bruce, but he was detained at Carlisle by illness. He sent an advance guard ahead under the Earl of Pembroke who routed Bruce at Perth. Edward followed, carried on a litter. On 7 July he died, and with his last breath asked that his body should be borne at the head of his army until Scotland should be completely subdued.

But it was not to be. His son, Edward II, who was destitute of any great purpose in life and thus the complete opposite of his father, did not seriously pursue the campaign after Bannockburn.

ROBERT BRUCE

(1274–1329)

Bannockburn betwixt the braes,
Of horse and men so chargit was
That upon drownit horse and men
Man might pass dry atour it then.

AND INDEED the narrow stream, the Bannockburn, as this eye-witness report tells us, was stuffed—piled high—from bank to bank with dead and dying English chivalry. Knights, chargers, filled it: the water was stained dull crimson.

But the English, under Edward II, were brave and determined. The forces had met just before dusk, contact was broken off for a few hours during the semi-darkness of a northern night, and fighting began as the sun rose on the second day. Much deployment and re-deployment had taken place during the night, with the Scots under Bruce digging pits about their several positions and covering these with grass and straw, like traps for wild animals. Outnumbered, they prepared to meet their enemy in tight circles of armed infantry, and when dawn came these "schiltrons" proved all but impervious to the horsed attacks launched on them. The English knights, finding lances suddenly useless against a solid mass of mutually supporting armour, a vast tank with a hundred legs, hurled swords and maces in despair before turning to flee.

And then, with the appearance of what seemed a whole new Scottish army—in fact they were camp followers, whooping with delight, eager to join the soldiers—the English fled in shameful defeat, many of them across the Bannock Burn, running blood-stained to the Forth and the sea.

The Scots under their king Robert—Robert Bruce—had won in these two June days and a night of 1314 a resounding victory, against vast numerical odds. They had dealt England and her foolish, effeminate king (the first Prince of Wales, he had been) a blow which was to make Scotland free of English domination. Had Bruce not then behaved with rather more magnanimity than was wise, had he and his army been more prepared for their thumping victory, relations between the two countries might have stabilized at once into a lasting peace, instead of drifting unhappily on for a number of years.

But Robert Bruce, even if victory took him unawares, had achieved a great one, the greatest in Scots history. He was able to concentrate the remaining fifteen years of his life on being a king—on the wise and just rule for which he is now remembered. When he died, in 1329, in his simple house on the west coast—not for Bruce a castle or a palace, but a modest dwelling where he could watch his young son grow up a Christian, away from the sound of war—he was, to all his subjects, and many who were not, "Good King Robert".

"Good" is an epithet sparingly distributed among Scottish sovereigns—and half an hour with any book of Scots history will make the reason abundantly clear—but Robert was a profoundly good one. Kingship seems to have made him so, for there is much with which we can find fault before his accession. But as king he established, as no ruler of Scotland had or has done, a complete understanding and sympathy with his subjects.

He was—once he reached the throne—utterly just, endlessly patient, and for a brilliant leader in time of war surprisingly wise in matters of peace. He died, aged fifty-five, mourned throughout his kingdom, not yet certain that he had achieved its freedom or not, and sad that he had never fulfilled his vow to embark on a crusade. His last request was that his heart be taken from his body, embalmed and carried by a goodly knight to Jerusalem. It never got there: Sir James Douglas was killed on the way. The relic, in its silver box, was eventually deposited in the monastery of Melrose, while Bruce's body was buried in the abbey church of Dunfermline. Six days later, the Pope issued a bull permitting Robert Bruce's coronation by the Bishop of St. Andrews.

History is the study of accidents, and the thrones of England and Scotland might well have been joined by this time, with Bruce remaining a law-abiding Earl of Carrick. But this was not to be. In one of the more romantic accidents of history, the last Scots king of the Canmore line died through a whim to be bedded with the young French wife he had left on the far side of the River Forth. It was 18 March, the year was 1286, and Alexander III had been dining in Edinburgh castle, drinking the good red wine of Bordeaux, when the urge seized him. Ignoring the warnings of his nobles, he got from the table, mounted a steed and rode furiously to the ferry at Dalmeny. Here the ferry-master implored him to return to his castle, but the king brushed aside the entreaty and was rowed across two miles of icy, churning water to Inverkeithing. Once again he was urged, this time by one of the bailies of the town, to go back, or at least spend the night in Inverkeithing. A storm had got up, the wind was howling in from the North Sea, there was no moon. It is interesting to compare the man-to-man relationship between Scottish monarch and his subjects with the respectful attitude of the English to their own. "What are you doing out in such weather?" said the bailie. "Get back, get back! How many times have I told you, midnight travelling will do you no good——"

But King Alexander III refused, as bluntly, to return. It was true the weather had got worse, but the urge to visit his young Queen Yolande, the fact that he had already survived a perilous trip across the Forth, made it impossible for a man of spirit to retrace footsteps or even postpone till the morrow reunion with his wife. He set off along the coast road to his manor of Kinghorn—and was never seen alive again. Somehow in the dark he got separated from his guides and was found the next morning at the foot of the cliff, his neck broken.

Yolande, only six months wed, had been his second wife: now she was his widow. The two sons of the first marriage were already dead, and now the heir to the throne of Scotland was a sickly little girl of three, across many miles of water. This "Maid of Norway", little Margaret, was the child of Alexander's daughter, also dead, once married to the King of Norway.

At first it seemed a desirable state of affairs. England, Scotland and Norway were all in favour of a marriage between the little Maid and the heir to the English throne. But in September, 1290, after all arrangements had been made, the Maid of Norway died on her way to England. She was to have been joined with a young man she had never seen, a man who would, twenty-four years later, be thrashed at Bannockburn by another who had taken the throne of Scotland.

On her death, the bridegroom's father, Edward I, took matters into his own hand and marched into Scotland to claim the country and its castles, on the shaky grounds that he must have them to pass on to the successful contender for the Scottish throne. He followed this up by selecting, with some show of legality, a king for Scotland, John Balliol. It was the reluctance of this vassal king's subjects to stump up money and men for the English monarch's adventures in France that brought about Balliol's downfall. He was forced to renounce his allegiance to the English throne, then to abandon his own.

Edward now appointed, as he had for Wales, a "Governor" for Scotland. It was done with more show of legality, and agreed to by a fair proportion of Scottish nobles, who no doubt regarded it as a temporary expedient which would let them retain lands they had acquired in England. But among the disaffected was William Wallace, who rose, with thousands of others, in an ill-starred revolt. After years of see-saw campaigning, he was captured by Edward in 1305 and brutally executed as a traitor, his head impaled on London Bridge.

At this time the young nobleman Robert Bruce had just passed his thirty-first birthday. Already he had lived a full, not to say dramatic, life. His grandfather had been claimant to the Scottish throne when little Margaret died—the throne awarded to John Balliol—and the younger Bruce, though angry that his family's claims had been overruled, decided at first to support Edward. Confused, ambitious, he then proceeded to change sides with some frequency, fighting both for and against the English king. It was the hideous death of Wallace which finally decided him to have no further truck with England. His father had died in the previous year; Robert Bruce was now owner of vast estates in Scotland, another in England, a house in London and a manor at Tottenham: so we can discount any theories that he was a disappointed man. But he had made up his mind by the end of 1305 to win the throne of Scotland for a Scotsman, and preferably himself. His family's claims had been only marginally less valid than Balliol's, and now that Balliol ("Toom Tabard," the Scots called him, the "Empty Coat") had proved himself incompetent, Robert Bruce's mind was made up.

Soon, though, he was involved in the least savoury episode of his life. Another claimant was John, "The Red," Comyn, and in a quarrel within the sacred precincts of Greyfriars Church in Dumfries, Bruce killed him. Historians disagree as to the reason behind the deed. Some maintain Comyn was about to betray to the English king a joint plan of revolt. Others maintain it was just rivalry for the throne of Scotland. Some say Bruce did not strike the fatal blow, that it was done by his companions. Others, on the contrary, say Bruce had the dying man brought to him at the altar steps and there dispatched him. Some say Bruce wounded Comyn and that his companions made sure of his death. It seems likely, though, that the killing was unpremeditated and the climax of a sudden quarrel.

Six weeks later, knowing he had set in motion half a dozen different chains of events—the Pope had excommunicated him, Edward thirsted for his blood, every man's hand was against him—and knowing it was too late to turn back, Bruce had himself crowned King of Scotland at the traditional site in Scone, even though the Stone of Destiny had been removed to Westminster, and the crown was still with Balliol. Only four bishops and four earls, from all Scotland, were present as the Countess of Buchan placed the golden coronet, specially made for the occasion, on the new king's head.

A little later the Countess was captured by the English. For her crime, she was locked in a cage and suspended *four years* from the wall of Berwick Castle, to be gaped at by the populace. A similar fate befell Bruce's sister. Both, miraculously, survived to be released.

The history of the next years is confused. King Robert captured a number of English-held castles and extracted oaths of allegiance from a large part of the population. But he was a hunted man, with most of his family in captivity or done to death, and the English in hot pursuit. For months he and a few loyal supporters were harried through the highlands of Perthshire. A little later he had to leave Scotland and hide on the island of Rathlin: by the spring of 1307 he was an exile on the Isle of Arran. Perhaps it was now that he observed the determination of the spider, trying again and again to spin its web, finally succeeding, which has come down to us through the years as part of the Bruce story. Edward I—"Hammer of the Scots" he liked to be styled—came within an ace of capturing him on several occasions, but at last that irascible monarch died, during a last northward advance, in Cumberland. Old and ailing, he had been carried for most of the way in a litter at the head of his army. His dying words were to hand over the task of conquering Scotland—and Bruce—to his son, that Prince of Wales whose child marriage with the Maid of Norway had been frustrated. Fortunately for Bruce and for Scotland, the new Edward II was not of the same calibre as his father. Slowly the tide began to turn in Bruce's favour, as he and his ever-increasing band of followers captured, one by one, every castle held by the English till only Stirling held out.

And so we come to Bannockburn, and the summer of 1314. The English Governor of Stirling Castle, surrounded by a force led by Robert's surviving brother, Edward Bruce, agreed to capitulate if the English failed to relieve him by Midsummer Day. It was a gentlemanly sort of arrangement and Edward Bruce for his part agreed to wait.

Thus, thanks to a gesture unappreciated by the ruler of either country, the decisive battle drew near. Robert was averse to a pitched battle against the far greater numbers of an English army, and Edward II, comfortable in England, had little desire to lead one. But honour now compelled them both. It also determined the day, for 24 June would be Midsummer Day, and for Edward there was no time to lose. He rushed north with an army which may have numbered 100,000, and was in any case far larger than Bruce's.

As we have seen, the Scots won a resounding victory. Edward II reached the castle he had come to relieve, a tattered fugitive: the Governor, Sir Philip Mowbray, told him he was about to capitulate, and the unhappy English king fled to Dunbar. He was lucky. Many of his followers were struck down in their retreat—though Bruce had a kinder heart than was customary in those days—and those that were captured were used to ransom Scots prisoners, including Bruce's wife the queen and her daughter. The ransom extracted by the Scots for English prisoners brought sudden, undreamed-of wealth to the country.

Bruce's victory was not the end of the war, but it was decisive. The blood that flowed for nine more years served no purpose at all. The Scots captured Berwick in 1318 and were able to plunder northern England almost at will: the English came north again, looted the abbeys of Melrose and Holyrood and burned Dryburgh. But in 1323 Edward made a truce for thirteen years. It was broken by fighting between his young and warlike son, succeeding to the English throne in 1327, and small bands of Scottish raiders, but a year later a treaty was signed, in Northampton, which formally recognized Robert Bruce as King of Scotland. A year after that Bruce was dead.

Without doubt, he was a great king. We can largely discount his shifts of allegiance before he became one: patriotism in 1300 was a different thing to that of six hundred years later: a man had to fight for the side his family wanted, preferably the one most likely to win, or it would mean extinction. As king, he defeated his country's enemy, tried hard for and finally succeeded in a just peace, and made sure there would be no disputed succession after his death by tying up the details with strict fairness and legality. He made a lasting treaty with France at Corbeuil in 1326, re-organized the Scottish parliament to include representatives of the Burghs—a new and startling innovation in a feudal society—and left his country ordered, prosperous and proud.

Robert Bruce combines in a unique and fascinating way the qualities of brilliant general and skilful knight-at-arms—a knight who could rally an army, in the early stages of Bannockburn, by reining aside and smashing with an unbelievable blow the heavy helmet and the skull of Sir Henry de Bohun as the Englishman charged him. He was with it a schemer, probably a murderer, and the wisest, fairest ruler in Scots history.

EDWARD III

(1312–77)

THE FIFTY-YEAR reign of Edward III from 1327-77 stands as one of the most glorious in English history, in spite of miseries at its close. Edward, for a time, appeared the most powerful monarch in Europe and his court the most brilliant in Christendom.

Among the Norman and Angevin or Plantagenet kings who had ruled England since the Norman Conquest there had been weak and bad rulers such as John and Edward II, the father of Edward III, but the strong and able dominated. A powerful royal administration had been established throughout the country, and so the English, enjoying more internal peace and security than did their neighbours on the Continent, began to see themselves as one nation. The archers and men-at-arms who won the great victories of Crécy and Poitiers and the naval battle of Sluys felt themselves to be free men, subjects of the king and not of local barons.

Since the reign of Henry II they had been encouraged to use their own weapons and were organized in local militias, obedient to the Crown. England had grown rich too, not only in the export of the best wool in the world to Flanders, but also in the manufacture of woollen cloth. In one year, it is said, Edward III received the huge sum in those days of £80,000 from duties levied on wool. The towns flourished. In the reign of Edward III the total population of England, about three million, was greater than that a hundred years later. It was above all the fact that England had become a nation which gave, in the middle of the fourteenth century, a special lustre to the island kingdom, for all that its people had not the industrial ingenuity of the Flemings or the civilization of northern Italy and the south of France.

The English language was now that of nobles, yeomen, as well as of the peasants. Edward III was the first English king to speak English and not French as his natural tongue. "Let clerics indite in Latin," writes an author who translated French Romances into English at this time, "and let Frenchmen in their French also indite their quaint terms, for it is kindly to their mouths; but let us show our faculties in such words as we learnt in our mother tongue."

Geoffrey Chaucer, the first and one of the greatest of English poets, appeared in the reign of Edward III. Chaucer's verse, and above all the *Canterbury Tales*, is a monument to the English civilization of the time.

Edward III, like his great grandfather Edward I, had a troubled succession. His father, Edward II, had been a weak king. A man of fine stature, athletic, good at handicrafts, he showed himself unfit for the business of ruling. He had strong homosexual tendencies and it was his undue partiality for his favourites which caused his wife Isabel, the daughter of the King of France, to lead a rebellion against him. He was forced to abdicate in favour of his son and was imprisoned and cruelly treated until he died.

Edward III became king at the age of fifteen and was married a year later, in 1328, to Philippa of Hainault. The paramour of Queen Isabel, the Earl of Mortimer, was the real ruler of England for some time after Edward's accession. It was touch-and-go whether Edward would survive the increasing enmity of the ambitious Mortimer. But during a Council meeting at Nottingham, Edward and his supporters entered Nottingham Castle, where Isabel and Mortimer were living, by a subterranean passage at night, forced their way into Mortimer's apartments, trussed him up and sent him to the Tower of London. Mortimer was later drawn on an ox-hide to the gallows at Tyburn and hanged in public. The queen was gently treated by Edward, in spite of her complicity in his father's murder.

The handsome Edward, an accomplished knight, versed in lore of hunting and falconry, was a great performer at joust and tourney. It was inevitable that war should be his pastime. Very soon after he began to reign he resolved to avenge his father's defeat by the Scots at Bannockburn. He made war on his own brother-in-law, King David, and won a great victory at Halidon Hill over the Scots; but he wisely gave up the hopeless attempt of conquering Scotland. His eyes turned towards France for many reasons—France had helped the Scots, French interference with the cities of Flanders with whom England did so much trade, and Edward's great possessions in France—which still included most of Aquitaine in the south-west.

When Charles II, the father of Edward's mother Isabel, died, he left as direct successor to the French throne a fifteen-year-old daughter who, already a widow herself, gave birth to another daughter. The French nobles proclaimed Charles's cousin, Philip of Valois, King of France, and this was generally acknowledged by the nation. Isabel, however, claimed that her son Edward, who was a nephew of Charles VI, had a better right than Philip. However, in 1329, Edward III, in the Cathedral of Amiens, paid homage to Philip for his lands in France. This did not prevent him later from reviving his claim and proclaiming himself King of France, a title which thereafter every English sovereign bore until George III.

But the Hundred Years' War between England and France was not, in substance, a dynastic war. Some of its roots were undoubtedly in rivalry over the rich lands of Flanders that were the main causes of Anglo-French wars. But the war, never a continuous affair but rather a series of discontinuous campaigns waged by smallish invading English armies, had its origin largely in the martial ardour of the English. Like their master King Edward, the young knights and squires were burning to prove their strength and chivalry overseas. It was the parliaments composed of barons and representatives of the land-owning classes and even the rich burgesses of the towns who, at first, urged Edward to conquer France and supported him with men and money. Froissart, that great chronicler of Europe in the fourteenth century, wrote:

> *The English will never love nor honour their king unless he be victorious and a lover of arms and war against their neighbours and especially against such as are greater and richer than themselves. They take delight and solace in battles and slaughter; covetous and envious are they above measure of other men's wealth.*

This was certainly true at the beginning of Edward's reign, though the Commoners were heartily sick of war by the end.

Edward III at first tried to invade France through Flanders, and he entered into league with the German princes whom, as Pitt did against Napoleon, he supplied with money to fight the French. But this came to little except a great waste of money. In 1340, however, 150 English ships with the king in command sailed from Suffolk and engaged "a great fleet of masts"—some 190 ships of the French king—in the harbour of Sluys. The ships were manned by Normans and the men of Picardy who were good sailors. The English sailed into the harbour and used grappling irons to attach themselves to the enemy's ships and, as at Crécy, the long-bow archers caused havoc among the enemy. English nobles and men-at-arms swarmed over the enemy ships and, by sunset, the French were beaten. Edward III was wounded in the leg. This first English sea victory made Edward famous. He was offered the title of Holy Roman Emperor, which he refused. But his wars and the subsidies to Flemings and Germans had nearly bankrupted him—indeed he defaulted on his debts to the great banking houses of Florence, two of which were forced to go into liquidation.

But six years afterwards, in July, 1346, Edward set out on the great direct invasion of France, capturing Caen, in Normandy, a city larger than any English city of the time except London. Edward took his army within a dozen or so miles of Paris. But he could not take Paris. The French king was approaching with a huge army whilst Edward's had suffered heavy losses from disease as well as fighting. He had to retreat northwards for home, and he crossed the Somme near its mouth. He halted in Ponthieu, near the village and the forest of Crécy, turning at bay on his enemies much as Henry V was to do at Agincourt.

On 25 August, in a great thunderstorm, the large French army, mainly of heavily armoured and beautifully caparisoned knights and mounted cavalry with Genoese crossbowmen, caught him up. There was great confusion, for King Philip first ordered the advance columns of his army to halt and then, groups of French knights in the rear protesting, decided to begin battle at once. His Genoese crossbow archers and infantry, tired by marching, blinded by a sudden storm after the rain, fell in hundreds before the English bowmen: they flung away their weapons and started to retreat. As they fled, they were ridden down by the French knights anxious to be at the English. Edward's army was drawn up in two forward arrays of dismounted men with archers, one commanded by the Black Prince, Edward's son, then aged seventeen. King Edward commanded a centre formation slightly behind the other two: the king himself, with a white staff in his hand, mounted on his war-horse, stood by a windmill overlooking the field.

The French made fifteen separate charges on the English during that day, each time suffering terribly from the arrows of the English. At one moment a messenger was sent to Edward to say that the Black Prince was sorely pressed. "Is my son dead or hurt?" the king asked the messenger. "No, sir," answered the messenger, "but he is hardly matched, therefore he has need of your aid." "Return to him," said the king, "and say that they can send no more to me as long as my son is alive: and say to them that they suffer him this day to win his spurs; for if God be pleased I wish this day to be his, the honour thereof, and for them that be about him."

After Crécy, Edward had nothing for a while to fear from the French king's army. According to English reports, eleven princes, one thousand two hundred knights and about thirty thousand common men lay dead on the field. Few prisoners had been taken, an unusual thing for war at that time and due to the small number of the victors and their fear of taking any risks. Edward continued his march homewards, and settled down to the siege of Calais which his fleet was blockading. The siege lasted a long time and this much annoyed him. When the town at last surrendered, Edward at first intended to sack it and to murder most of its inhabitants, but then agreed not to do this provided that six of the most prominent burghers of the town appear before him with halters round their necks ready for hanging and the keys of Calais in their hands. The king received them angrily and proposed to execute them at once. He was only deterred, unwillingly, by the entreaties of his queen.

It is interesting to compare the king's surly behaviour to these commoners who had defied him and fought bravely with the way he treated some noble prisoner who, later, had attempted to recapture Calais. To their leader Froissart makes the king say: "Sir Eustace, you are the most valiant knight in Christendom. I never have yet found anyone in battle whom, body to body, has given me so much to do as you have this day. I adjudge you the prize of valour. I present you with this chaplet as being the best commander of this day, and I beg of you to wear it all this year for love of me. I know that you are a lover of damsels and noble ladies; therefore tell it wherever you go that King Edward gave this to you. You also have your liberty, free of ransom, and may go tomorrow, if you please, wherever you like."

The king returned to England in 1347, and there was a period of revelry and jousting and magnificent entertainments. The king fought the Spaniards at sea, and accepted a personal challenge to combat from a French knight. In 1356 his son, the Black Prince, won a victory even more splendid than that at Crécy. This was at Poitiers, and he won it again thanks to the valour and discipline of the English and the out-dated tactics of French chivalry. King John of France was captured. The Black Prince served his illustrious captive bare-headed as a mark of respect, and himself brought him to London. Other less successful forays into France were undertaken. Finally the Treaty of Calais gave the English the whole of Aquitaine, that is most of South-west France, free of homage, and Calais. In return Edward renounced his claim to the kingdom of France.

Before Edward's death the war in France underwent a new phase. In 1369 Charles V repudiated the Treaty of Calais and Edward III re-assumed his claim as King of France. But the French, under leaders such as Bertrand du Guesclin, fought very differently, avoiding large battles, ambushing the English forces and harrying them on their forced marches through hostile country. Most of Aquitaine was lost and the English people grew tired of the war. The Black Prince, sick of a fever which was shortly to carry him off, returned to England. When a truce was made in 1375 all that remained in English hands were the ports of Brest, Calais, Bordeaux and Bayonne. The whole Angevin empire was lost.

During the later years of the king's reign the Black Death hit England several times. It was a time of social unrest which broke out in great violence at the beginning of the reign of Richard II, the son of the Black Prince. Edward III, always much given to the lusts of the flesh, went into a sort of premature dotage in his infatuation for his last mistress Alice Perrers. The king's third son, John of Gaunt, was the real ruler of the kingdom, although his corrupt faction was opposed by the Black Prince. In 1376 the Black Prince, supported by the Commons and by many ecclesiastics, triumphed over John of Gaunt and called what was known as "the Good Parliament" in London. Alice Perrers was banished from the Court and John of Gaunt's exactions were ended. But the death of the Black Prince gave John of Gaunt the chance of returning to power and reversing the acts of Parliament. Edward's reign ended in general disappointment. He died suddenly at Sheen, near Richmond, apparently talking merrily with his courtiers a few minutes before he grew pale and his breath failed. As he expired, most of the courtiers having run away in fright, it is said that Alice Perrers pulled the rings off his fingers.

Edward III was not as strong and resolute a king as William I or Henry II, and inferior perhaps in strength of character to his grandfather Edward I. But he was a brave knight and an excellent commander of men, even if, as a general, his plans were too ambitious as a rule to be carried out. For all his warlike and amorous propensities he had an eye to the well-being of England and could claim to be the founder of the English fleet. All his life he protected the English and foreign weavers whom he had been persuaded to settle in East Anglia. If he died after his best period, it was clear there was something august and calm about this king who represented England at the time when national self-confidence was so strongly expressed. The tomb in Westminster Abbey, made from a wax portrait modelled from Edward's dead body, expresses the greatness of a king who, in the words of a chronicler of the time, was brave in war, affable and pleasant to all men.

TAMERLANE (TIMUR)

(1336–1405)

THE DEEPEST lake in the world—well over a mile, straight down, between its glassy surface and its pitch-dark, stony bottom—is in southern Siberia. It is four hundred miles from the north end to the south, and at its widest point a fisherman would have to row fifty miles to get from one bank to the other. It abounds in freshwater fish of strange and exotic variety: delicacies to the human community which lives around its shores, as well as to the colonies of seals that inhabit the rocky northern fringes.

It is called, in the language of the easy-going, peaceable Mongol people who live there, *Dalai-Nor*, or The Holy Sea. The Russians, who control this part of the world, call it Lake Baikal, the name by which it is most familiar to us, but it is as *Dalai-Nor* that it has been known for centuries. It was here that the far-from-peaceable Genghis Khan was born, in the middle of the twelfth century, here that he inherited a small Mongolian kingdom at the age of thirteen, and from here that he set out to conquer the world. His exploits are dealt with in another article, but we may stop for a moment to consider the people from which he sprang; the strange, wild land which gave them birth.

They were Mongols, short squat men with narrowed eyes, living a nomad life and sleeping in tents of matted hair and rancid butter. They lived by hunting: when they killed an animal they devoured the whole thing, raw. They were horsemen, probably the finest horsemen the world has ever known, and their staple drink was mare's milk. For festive occasions they drank it fermented, often from the skull of an enemy. (The term "Tatar", usually mis-spelt "Tartar", is variously used for all Mongols of this period, or for one tribe, or for a group, and has, for this reason, little meaning. It also has no traceable etymology; except that in medieval times the word "Tatary" was used in Europe to mean Central Asia.)

There were many of these Mongol tribes: *Kipchaks*, *Karaits*, *Naimans*, *Uighurs* and *Kirghiz* were but a few abounding in the time of Genghis Khan. Others, hundreds of years before, speaking the same language, had fought a way westward off their wide Mongolian plain, left their mark on Europe. These were *Huns, Goths, Seljuks, Vandals*: like their successors they were happier in the saddle than out of it and able to go for days without food or water. When the time came, they were ready and anxious to make up for this privation by orgies of food and drink.

They were fighters: a man was seldom without his breastplate and his spear.

Genghis Khan built up a superbly successful military machine, a machine which laid waste to much of the known world, taking what it could carry in the way of riches and slaves, dragging it back to the Mongolian plain, destroying the rest. But after the death of Genghis, the quarrelling of his descendants started to break up his empire and his army. The rot was halted for a time by the great Kublai Khan, who ruled for thirty-five years in the latter half of the thirteenth century, and was a wise man who loved art and literature. He did much to hold the empire together in peace and to encourage the arts throughout it: while he lived, the Mongol empire remained great.

But after this golden age it separated into a squabbling confederation of tribes—much as it had been at the birth of Genghis. It was in one of these tribes, the *Barlas* clan, living in the hills south of Samarkand, that the chieftain's wife gave birth to a son and named him Timur. It was 1336.

Timur, not without plotting and intrigue, succeeded his father and was crowned king, or "Khan", of the tribe, in 1369, when he was thirty-three. By this time he had conquered a number of other small Mongol clans and was lord of a considerable territory. He had also been badly wounded in the foot by an arrow so that he became, in the Mongol language, *Timur-i-leng*, or "Timur-the-Lame".

In a very few years' time, when fame, notoriety, had spread westward, the European mispronunciations "Tamerlane" and "Tamburlane" would strike terror into the hearts of men.

His army, smaller than that of his predecessor—though it would soon be as large—was better armed, better trained. It could travel fantastic distances non-stop on its little ponies. It was heavily armed with spears, lances, maces, scimitars, both long bows and short; its soldiers wore finely meshed armour and pointed helmets.

It was supported by spies who went ahead and reported on the enemy before contact was made. It had gunpowder.

It was a formidable force. And yet the most powerful Mongol

group was not Timur's but the so-called "Golden Horde", an assortment of tribes which had banded together to ravage their neighbours. So great had been their success that they travelled from battle to battle bearing huge quantities of loot, earning for themselves a name which sowed envy and panic.

Timur resolved to defeat them, take away their power, their gold.

Fortune played into his hands. There was a quarrel in their ruling house and one of the princes, Toktamish, fled to the little court of Timur and demanded asylum. This Timur gave eagerly, and when the Khan of the Golden Horde demanded his return a highly convenient war broke out, with "underground" supporters of Toktamish supporting Timur's forces. Very soon Timur had overthrown the Golden Horde and placed Toktamish as his own puppet on the throne.

He now invaded Persia, where the proud city of Isfahan resisted him. When eventually it fell, he decided to use it to terrorize the rest of his enemies, present and future. He massacred the inhabitants, piling seventy thousand of their heads into one hideous pyramid beside the city wall. From here he pushed his army down to the Persian Gulf, on to Kabul and Kandahar, laying waste the country as he went. His armies also pushed westward into Europe, with Timur organizing and supporting as many as half a dozen different campaigns at the same time. One of these was soon directed against Toktamish, the puppet king of the Golden Horde, who had managed to raise a large force against him—men who resented this usurper from the once-humble tribe of *Barlas*. But Timur managed to defeat the Golden Horde this second time, to scatter it for ever. It was probably his greatest military feat—though it sounds small in comparison with the destruction of North India or of Persia—for the forces involved were the greatest in the world. At the end of the campaign the defeated tribes which had not been dispersed beyond recall, to end their days as bitter little groups moving aimlessly over the Asian plain, rallied to Timur and became part of his swelling Mongol Empire.

And so his progress, much of it mere senseless brutality, went on, rising to a bloody crescendo in the last half-dozen years of his life. He captured Baghdad: when it rose a little later in revolt against him, he ordered that each of the ninety thousand Mongol soldiers who had helped quash the rebellion bring him one enemy head. These, too, he piled in a pyramid, before turning towards India, going down through the Khyber Pass, sacking the cities of Meerut and Multan on the way. Once on the Indian plain, he was faced, as Alexander had been, with the new weapon of war—elephants: the master tactician and strategist lured the ruler of Delhi and his elephants out into the open where the little Mongol cavalrymen could manoeuvre. The Indians were easily overcome and Timur captured their elephants, taking them back in triumph to Samarkand, bearing the spoils of India, leaving behind him utter devastation. India had been ruled for several hundred years by Muslims—followers of the same, Islamic, faith as Timur—but he destroyed this ruling house, massacring its Hindu and Muslim subjects indiscriminately, and made no effort to replace it with anything else. All he had wanted from India was loot: as a territory it was too far away, too inaccessible, to add permanently to his dominions.

(It was over a hundred years before a new ruling house established itself in India. Then, at the start of the sixteenth century, another band of Central Asian Mongols, with the blood of Timur, and of Genghis, and of Kublai Khan, flowing in their veins, set up a great Indian empire, the Mongol, or "Mogul", Empire.)

This reluctance on the part of Timur to consolidate so many of his conquests saved many kingdoms and cultures in Europe and Asia. After his victorious sweep across North India, he turned west again to attack the Turks (who as descendants of another Mongol chief, Osman, or "Ottomans", had overrun Asia Minor) and also the Egyptians. He swept across their lands, capturing the Turkish capital of Brusa, sacking Damascus, inexplicably sparing Jerusalem. In the first year of the fifteenth century, Timur was standing with one foot in South-east Europe.

He turned back again, to Samarkand, the city he loved; and Europe and Christianity were spared. By now, well over sixty years of age, he had become obsessed with beautifying Samarkand, so that it might outshine the beautiful and opulent cities with which his travels had brought him in contact. He sent for craftsmen and artists from these lands and set them to work as masons, wood-carvers, sculptors, goldsmiths in Samarkand. He had definite ideas of his own, and impressed his own sombre taste on all their work. Soon Samarkand was one of the wonders of the world, with vast palaces, handsome dwellings, innumerable monuments, all of them covered with ornate and sometimes beautiful carved work in stone, wood and precious metals.

Still the urge to conquer was with him. He began, in 1402, planning the conquest of China. This strange Eastern land had already been subjugated by Mongols: Kublai Khan had set himself up as first emperor of the "Yuan" dynasty. He had been a wise and good emperor and during his reign China became more powerful than ever before or since, extending from the Dnieper River to the Pacific Ocean, from the Arctic Ocean to the Straits of Malacca. But after Kublai's death the Mongols had been thrown out and replaced by the native "Ming" dynasty. Now Timur resolved to regain China.

As we have seen, he was capable of conducting several campaigns at the same time, and while he was laying plans for the Chinese assault he attacked and defeated Turkey.

But at last, in 1405, Timur-the-Lame set off for China. And it was during the journey that he was overtaken suddenly by a violent illness and died—much as his ancestor Genghis Khan had done—and in the course of a similar expedition.

Indeed, there are many points of resemblance between the two great Mongol conquerors. Both were helped greatly, as youths, in the early establishment of their power, by the loyalty and bravery of womenfolk, mothers and sisters who planned and intrigued for their advancement. Both men loved fighting for fighting's sake, caring less for territorial expansion than for loot and the smell of battle. Both were followers of Islam, but whereas Timur was devout, almost bigoted, Genghis Khan had been easy-going in matters of religion and encouraged absolute freedom of worship throughout his vast empire. Both combined great personal bravery with an absolute ruthlessness: between the pair of them, the numbers massacred must have exceeded the total bag of any hundred other conquerors in history.

The conquests of Timur make those of Napoleon and Caesar insignificant, for he had every attribute to which a commander can aspire: he was brave, hardy and incredibly strong; he understood the minds not only of his own men but of his enemy; he was a master tactician and strategist. In the brief intervals between campaigns he would indulge himself in long hours of chess, sometimes against relays of opponents—and he always won. Chess is not a fast game, but Timur adapted his chess moves to the field of battle and played them at speed. One of his favourite maxims was: "It is better to be on time, at the right place, with ten men, than late with ten thousand." Another, still more characteristic, perhaps, was: "Might is right."

With the death of Timur, as with that of Genghis, the Mongol Empire relapsed into warring factions. Thanks to Kublai Khan, it had recovered after Genghis; after Timur it was finished.

SIGISMUND

(1368–1437)

The death of Charles IV, Emperor of the Holy Roman Empire, King of Bohemia, on 29 November, 1387, marked the end of an epoch. Wise, clever, ruthless, Charles had brought prosperity to Bohemia and had founded the University of Prague. He has been called the last splendid embodiment of the Middle Ages.

His garish funeral at Prague was lit with touches of half-barbaric medieval chivalry—the five hundred and sixty-four black knights with huge smoking candles pounding the January dawn to the wild and doleful music, the columns of slouching monastics, the ten sombre horsemen proudly bearing the banners of the ten lands ruled over by the dead emperor, who followed upon his bier, magnificently crowned, wrapped in purple and gold, splendid rings glittering upon his white-gloved hands, his great black beard gleaming in the smoky dawn—more regal in death than he was in life, when he had not been an impressive-looking man.

Behind the splendid corse and the sea of banners walked ten-year-old Sigismund, destined to be more famous than his formidable father, though now he was second to his 26-year-old brother, Wenceslas, upon whom the purple fell after the death of his father, and who had already been elected king of the confederation of German states, which carried with it the title of emperor, with a power which was only nominal. An emperor who wished to wield the powers implicit in this ancient Roman title had to seize them and force his will upon his widely scattered empire which bridged the Alps and stretched down to Italy and the Mediterranean.

Wenceslas was not made of this stern stuff and failed to reach the high standard of his father. He had a greater passion for hunting than for statecraft, and was so fond of his hounds that he took them to his bed, and there was a story that his first wife, Johanna of Bavaria, was bitten to death by one of them. He was a perverse man. He took to drink and would roam the streets at night and break into houses and violate the wives of respectable citizens. A cook whose roast did not meet with his approval was himself roasted upon the spit by Wenceslas.

Discontent at his incompetence, perfidy and continual absence from the seat of government, lost him the empire. One by one its cities and territories turned against him, and in 1400 the Rhenish electors declared him deposed and elected Rupert III, Count Palatine of the Rhine, in his place.

It was an age of cruelty, cunning and treachery. The only rulers who survived the jungle of those medieval monarchies were those who exercised the most cunning, the most ambition and the most ruthlessness, and in the exercise of these unlovely but necessary qualities Sigismund far excelled his elder brother.

Sigismund had grown up something of a dazzling figure. Tall, slim, he had a fine face—a splendid nose, deep-set eyes and a long, forked, well-cared-for beard. He was every inch the stop-at-nothing king of medieval legend—a great hunter, a great drinker, a great womanizer, without morals but possessing a fierce religion, cultivated and cruel, charming and ambitious, greedy and faithless. A great orator, he could speak fluently in seven languages. His domestic life was something of a scandal even in those dissolute times. He had mistresses even before he was in his teens. His beautiful second wife, Barbara, Countess of Cilly, exerted an extraordinary influence over him, and was just as licentious as he was, openly seeking lovers for herself while he was womanizing.

Sigismund had become the Margrave of Brandenburg on his father's death, and had been educated at the Hungarian court which he had scandalized with deeds of amour not usually associated with schoolboys. He was crowned King of Hungary in 1387, after a series of dynastic murders over the succession, sharing the crown with his first wife Mary, who was heir to the throne and who died in 1395.

While brother Wenceslas, with his mixture of perversity and stupidity, was gambling away the imperial family inheritance, Sigismund's time was occupied in trying to hold the unstable throne of Hungary, and also in holding in check the Turks who took advantage of the state of affairs in Hungary to invade the country.

This resulted in a crusade against the infidel being proclaimed by the Pope Boniface IX, and Sigismund presented something of a shining image by leading the combined armies of Christendom against the Turk. Nobles and knights, distinguished adventurers, war-loving princelings flocked in their thousands from every part of Europe to fight under the banner of the Cross which Sigismund held aloft in Hungary. Insubordination in this motley army of individualists and quarrels with the Pope, rather than lack of generalship on Sigismund's part, was responsible for the defeat of the forces of Christendom in 1398. Sigismund then fell back upon a defensive policy for Hungary, with more success.

Sigismund now turned his attention to the more attractive proposition of succeeding his childless brother, Wenceslas, as emperor. But Wenceslas had thrown away the great family heritage while Sigismund had been fighting the Turk, and had already been deposed. Sigismund never forgave his brother. He had to wait until Rupert III, who had succeeded Wenceslas, died in 1410.

During the intervening years Sigismund was busy with war and suppression. He returned to Hungary to put down popular uprisings due to the spread of the dangerous teaching of John Huss that all men were equal. To this wicked doctrine was added the heresy that man should worship God according to the dictates of his conscience—evils which had to be stamped out with every instrument of terror and oppression. Hungary was only cleansed of these satanic delusions after great slaughter, mainly the work of the Papal Inquisition which completely depopulated large areas of the country in the process.

Meanwhile Sigismund had been elected emperor in 1411 and he then addressed himself to putting right the great and terrible scandal which existed in the Church. During the fourteenth century the Popes had been residing at Avignon where they had reigned in opulent and magnificent state. In 1377 Urban VI was elected Pope and decided to return to the historic Papal seat at Rome. The College of Cardinals, who were mostly French, were so incensed that they elected another Pope and declared the election of Urban void. But Urban refused to be deposed, and so there were two Popes, each excommunicating the other, and each having his supporters in different countries.

This state of affairs so damaged the reputation of the Church and was creating such widespread anti-clericalism that the leaders of the Church met at the Council of Pisa in 1409. But they merely made matters worse by electing a third Pope. As neither of the other Popes recognized the authority of the Council, there were now three Popes each claiming the supreme power and authority of Christ's Vicar on earth.

The most dangerous result of this state of affairs was the heresy of Protestantism (though this name was not used until the time of Luther, a hundred years later). It was not a new discovery that many of the eternal truths taught by the Church were not to be found in the Bible. The thing which aroused so many people against the Church was the wealth, immorality and corruption of the clergy, which contrasted unfavourably with the life of Christ and His Apostles. Men like Wycliffe and Huss did more than ask questions to which the lax Church of their day had no effective answer. They did not so much want to reform the Church. They questioned the whole idea of Papal authority. The Great Schism merely underlined everything Wycliffe and Huss were saying. The Papacy indeed seemed to have the death-wish in the fifteenth century and did nothing to put its house in order until it was too late.

John Huss became one of the Protestants' great martyrs and none of those responsible for his martyrdom suffered more obloquy than Sigismund.

Huss became rector of the Bethlehem Chapel in Prague in 1402 and began violently attacking the immoralities of the clergy and challenging the authority of the Papacy itself. Weakened by the Schism, the Church found it difficult to deal with him, for whichever Pope tried to tackle him had enemies supporting one or other of his rivals, who were thus able to use Huss and his heresy as ammunition for the battle which was going on in the Church.

Wenceslas, though he had lost the empire, was still King of Bohemia, which was a more realistic and substantial sovereignty and which was inherited and could not be taken away from him by the German Electors.

Wenceslas, as did all rulers, supported one or other of the rival Popes, and he stood by Huss when the Prague clergy tried to bring him to book for heresy in the name of Gregory XII of Rome. Wenceslas did this merely because he was opposed to the Bohemian Church supporting this Rome Pope. Wenceslas used Huss as a pawn in his battle with his own clergy, supporting him in the teeth of their opposition. This kind of support, though it may have delayed his going to the stake, did Huss little real good.

Sigismund in the meanwhile was setting about the great task which was his most important historical act—the re-unification of Christendom by healing the Great Schism. For this purpose he persuaded John XXIII, who had succeeded the Pope elected by the Council of Pisa, to convoke the Great Council of Constance. In calling this Council Sigismund had to use all his powers of statesmanship and persuasion in order to get together the secular as well as the religious princes of Europe. Union of the Church must be brought about at any cost, he told them, and with this everyone agreed. The scandal of the triple Papacy could no longer be tolerated.

The Council of Constance met on 5 November, 1414, and lasted until 22 April, 1418. It was one of the most famous occasions in the history of Christendom. It was a vast and tumultuous assembly of prelates, monks, doctors of law, princes and ambassadors, and it was held in an atmosphere of incomparable splendour and uninhibited immorality which was remembered for centuries in the good city of Constance.

The most important act of the Council was the deposition of the three Popes and the election of a new one, Martin V, thus bringing to an end the Great Schism.

The Council had also been set up to deal with heresy in the Church, and Huss was summoned to appear before it. Huss agreed to go to Constance after Sigismund had promised him protection and a safe return to Prague. Sigismund was not foolish enough to imagine that once the Council had got Huss into their power that they would let him return free to Prague—if they found him guilty of heresy, which was a capital crime in the eyes of the Church. Sigismund has in fact been harshly criticized for an act of bad faith which cost Huss his life.

There are two points to be made in Sigismund's favour. Firstly, as an obedient son of the Church he would have committed a mortal sin himself if, the Council having found Huss a heretic, he had enforced his promise and returned Huss to Prague. Sigismund could, and did, argue that when he gave Huss his promise he did not know he was a heretic, and no good son of the Church could protect a heretic.

The second point is perhaps more important. Granted duplicity on Sigismund's part—there was evidence that Huss was a heretic before he promised him safe conduct—the life of Huss was of less importance than the reunion of Christendom. When Huss was first arrested at Constance, Sigismund threatened to release him by force, but the cardinals came to see him and gave him to understand that in their view the extirpation of heresy was even more important than healing the Schism in the Church. It may have been a bluff, but Sigismund was not prepared to risk a breach with the Church over Huss and have the work of the Council of Constance ruined. Huss was a pawn in the game, like so many others had been. But Huss was emotional dynamite in the centuries to come, and so Sigismund's reputation in history—at least so far as Protestant countries are concerned—was ruined.

Some reports say that Huss was sentenced to death in the presence of Sigismund, others that he was absent from Constance during the martyrdom. It makes no difference. Sigismund had made it plain that he was not prepared to lift a finger to save a heretic from the flames.

In fact after the death of Huss, Sigismund sent a manifesto to his brother Wenceslas demanding vigorous action to suppress the Hussite movement in Bohemia. Huss was supported by many knights and nobles in Bohemia, who sent a letter to the Council of Constance, condemning Huss's execution in the strongest terms. Sigismund was also violently denounced for his part in Huss's death. Disturbances broke out and in the middle of them Wenceslas had a fit of apoplexy and died.

This left Sigismund the titular King of Bohemia, but it was seventeen years before his estranged subjects would acknowledge him. Meanwhile violent fighting broke out in Bohemia and the long trail of bloodshed began as Queen Sophia, the widow of Wenceslas, whom Sigismund had deputed to rule, tried to put down the Hussites, but in vain. Sigismund, reviled as the betrayer of Huss, was unable to get the support of the German princes for his war against the Bohemian heretics, and a Papal crusade against them was without success.

An important element in Sigismund's utter failure in Germany was the attitude of the German princes, who wanted to strengthen their power at the expense of his, and who were moving away from the Papal orbit, whatever sympathy they might or might not have had with Huss's teaching. In the spread of Protestantism lay the key to their independence, as they discovered in the coming century.

Whatever his failures in Germany, Sigismund succeeded in Hungary where he established good government and introduced many prudent political reforms. After the abortive crusade against the Turk, he changed his tactics and organized such excellent defences against the invaders that Hungary was able to keep them at bay for decades to come.

He became King of Lombardy in 1431, was crowned emperor by the Pope in 1433, and recognized, though only nominally in Bohemia, where he was never forgiven, in 1436. He died at Znaim in Bohemia in 1437 in his sixty-ninth year, and has gone down in history as one of the few far-sighted rulers in a century of unenlightened princes.

HENRY V (OF ENGLAND)

(1387–1422)

On Sunday, 11 August, 1415, a great armada of fifteen hundred ships put to sea from creeks and harbours facing the Isle of Wight and headed towards France. From a clear sky a hot sun poured down on brightly painted bulwarks, sails embroidered with heraldic beasts, pennons, helmets, shields and the glossy rumps of horses.

From the masthead of the king's flagship flew a banner representing the three persons of the Trinity and the arms of St. Edward, St. George and England. A crown of copper-gilt shone on the top-castle. On board the fleet were 2,000 men-at-arms and 8,000 archers, about 25,000 horses and a large number of specialists—miners, carpenters, armourers, smiths, gunners—as well as members of the king's retinue which included fifteen minstrels. The baggage was enormous. Each man-at-arms had his suit of armour and personal weapons—sword, dagger and mace or hatchet—each archer had his long-bow and forty to fifty arrows of which a reserve stock was also carried. There were tents and all their equipment for the king and his senior nobles, the royal beds, the royal cutlery of silver, crowns and boxes of jewels. In the holds were stored massive siege equipment, gunpowder for the artillery and siege-guns, some of which measured two feet across the mouth.

As the fleet manoeuvred out of the Solent, three ships caught fire. This was considered a bad omen and timid advisers urged the king not to sail with his troops. But he ignored them. He had made his will, his clergy had given a unanimous blessing on the enterprise, he was convinced that he was about to fight in God's cause and had no doubt of its justice.

The cause was to take possession of Normandy in absolute right—territory held to be the domain of English kings since William the Conqueror—and also to lay claim to the throne of France, asserting a right of succession through Henry's great-great-grandmother Isabella, wife of Edward II and daughter of King Philip IV of France. The claim had first been raised by his grandfather, Edward III, and already the English nation looked back on nearly eighty years of sporadic warfare in France which had left Edward III as sovereign over one-third of the country. But some of his gains had since been lost, lands still held in France were not conceded by the French as absolute possessions and the royal throne was as distant as ever. To Henry V, young, tested in battle against the Welsh, with his warrior's soul, his realistic, calculating mind, his ambition, his trust in heaven, this situation proved an irresistible lure. A glorious achievement, sealing his grandfather's labours, gleamed ahead. Behind, still within the memory of old men, shone the magnificent victories of Crécy and Poitiers. Afire with militant piety, the king even dreamed, once France was under his sway, of leading Western Europe in a crusade against the Infidel.

But he was not trusting only in God and his strong right arm. His hopes were based on practical realities. In France rival factions distracted the country. Since 1380, the feeble, vicious and demented Charles VI had been on the throne, but for many years the real power had been disputed between Louis of Orleans, the king's youngest brother, and John, Duke of Burgundy, his cousin. In 1407, Orleans had been murdered at the instigation of the Duke and the rivalry between their parties had flared into bitter hatred. The Orleanist cause was supported by royal dukes and their hopes centred on the Dauphin, a sickly boy whom they expected in due course to dominate as they dominated his father. Meanwhile, their power was threatened by the Duke of Burgundy who apart from the Duchy ruled wide tracts of land in northern France and, through marriage, most of what are now Belgium and Holland. With both parties Henry had negotiated, fruitlessly, as he expected and perhaps intended, with the Orleanists and more hopefully with the duke, whose hatred of the Orleanists was matched by a desire to maintain friendship with England because his Flemish weavers were dependent on English wool. Henry could count on his neutrality, if not on his active help.

Behind him Henry left a kingdom more secure than ever it had been in his father's time. Henry IV had been a usurper and spent most of his reign, until disease enfeebled him, quelling revolt at home, in Wales, in Ireland and invasion from Scotland. From the age of sixteen his son had helped him in his task, acting as the King's Lieutenant in Wales against Owen Glendower, leading the charge against Henry Hotspur at the battle of Shrewsbury and, after rebellion had been crushed, sharing in government as a member of the Royal Council, as Warden of the Cinque Ports,

Constable of Dover and Captain of Calais. He still found time, it was said, for riotous living, being "in his youth a diligent follower of idle practices, much given to instruments of music and fired with the torches of Venus herself". But responsibility brought out the iron in his temperament and his coronation banquet presented a symbolic picture: amid the revelry and feasting the twenty-five-year-old king sat remote with a serious expression, not touching the food. This set a note of intensity for the new reign. Henry felt sure of his heritage and sure of himself. His courteous but purposeful demeanour aroused admiration and loyalty. His appearance was impressive: smooth, oval face, a long, straight nose, full lips, a powerful jaw and hazel eyes, normally mild as a dove's, but blazing when in anger. Behind them men sensed an unconquerable spirit and they remembered his ancestors, Edward III and the Black Prince.

You are their heir; you sit upon their throne;
The blood and courage that renowned them
Runs in your veins; and my thrice puissant liege
Is in the very May-morn of his youth,
Ripe for exploits and mighty enterprises.

At home, in the first months of his reign he felt strong enough to release from imprisonment the young Earl of March, rightful heir of Richard II. But on the Lollards, descended from the "poor preachers" of John Wycliffe, his hand fell heavily. These men, proclaiming the supremacy of the individual conscience, became allied to political revolt and were regarded with terror by contemporaries. We should call them Christian Communists. Their offence was heightened by their attitude to articles of faith dear to the pious and it was their declared policy to plunder the Church. They seemed to threaten the very fabric of the State. They had been persecuted under Henry IV and the process was intensified by his son. Armed demonstrations were crushed and their leader, Sir John Oldcastle, a former companion in arms of the king, was executed. For a Lollard the alternatives were clear: renunciation of his heresy or the stake. These severities enabled Henry to sail for France with a reasonable assurance that the country was secure behind him.

The crossing took three days and early on 14 August the troops began to disembark at the mouth of the Seine near Harfleur. It was a professional army, not a medieval levy, indentured for service and paid at regular rates. But it was not homogeneous. Besides English, there were many Welshmen, Irishmen, Gascons and other foreigners in the ranks and to control his force the king imposed strict discipline.

Harfleur, valuable as a base from which to advance into Normandy or towards Paris, was in a naturally strong position on the north side of the Seine estuary. The only possible approach was from the south-west, but a wide moat, an alert and enterprising garrison and heavily strengthened defences made attack difficult even from this quarter. For a month the siege went on in broiling heat, while dysentery scourged the army, killing or putting out of action more than two thousand of the troops. Henry's miners tunnelled and the French countermined. Their men-at-arms made damaging sorties. English siege-guns hurled huge stones at the walls—and as fast as they crumbled the French repaired them. All this time the king worked as hard as any of his men, planning, supervising, inspecting, encouraging.

Finally, short of food and ammunition and closely beset at the south-west gate, the garrison surrendered, and Henry, clothed in royal gold, enthroned in a silken tent on a hill-top, received the keys of the town from a delegation wearing shirts of penitence with ropes round their necks. He told them they had withheld his town of Harfleur from him in defiance of God and all justice. Nevertheless he would be merciful. An English garrison was installed. The inhabitants were allowed to remain provided they took an oath of allegiance; gentlemen of wealth were required to ransom themselves, and only the infirm, the aged and the very young were turned out of the town—useless mouths, a source of weakness to the garrison. This was considered just by the standards of the time.

The troops available for further operations were now reduced to 900 men-at-arms and 5,000 archers. A march on Paris was out of the question. There remained three possible courses: to go home, to enlarge the district around Harfleur, or to march inland, regardless of resistance offered, as a demonstration of the royal claims. The last was obviously a dangerous course. The whole force might be destroyed, the king killed or captured. Nevertheless, against the strong advice of his war council, he chose it. He had already challenged the Dauphin to single combat for the throne of France and received no answer. To go meekly home now, or to sit at Harfleur would be to abandon his cause, which he believed was also God's. "Even if our enemies", he said, "enlist the greatest armies, my trust is in God, and they shall not hurt my army or myself. I will not allow them, puffed up with pride, to rejoice in misdeeds, or unjustly, against God, to possess my goods. . . . I have a mind, my brave men, to encounter all dangers. . . ."

So, on 6 October, the king with his small army, mostly on foot, set out, heading near the coast towards Calais, 160 miles away. This was not to be a pillaging expedition. The inhabitants and their property were to be respected and the troops were not to take anything beyond essential food.

Days passed almost without incident. Cannon fire from the towers of Arques, south-east of Dieppe, was met by a warning from the king that he would burn the town if resistance was offered. Twenty miles farther on, at Eu, a sortie by French men-at-arms was driven back and the troops calmly encamped for the night beyond the town. Thirteen miles ahead lay the River Somme and the ford Blanche-Taque which Edward III had crossed and Henry now looked forward to finding guarded by English troops which he had ordered to be detached from Calais.

Then, six miles from the river, came disastrous news from a solitary French prisoner, quickly confirmed by Henry's scouts. The ford was guarded on the far bank not by Englishmen but by a force of six thousand French. . . .

Incredibly, this French force had come up from nearly a hundred miles away to the south and got to the ford before the English. There was nothing for it now but to turn back to Harfleur or march east up the left bank of the Somme to find another crossing-place. The army marched east, but faced with an uncertain route and a strong enemy ahead spirits began to falter.

More disappointments were in store. Upstream at Abbeville the bridge over the Somme was guarded and French troops were in force on the far side. The little army slogged on and every crossing proved impassable, either destroyed or strongly defended. Rations were running short. The men were living on walnuts and dried meat. And every step they took was leading them farther away from Calais and safety. Now, avoiding a northward bend in the river, the king took them still farther eastwards, to a point near the headwaters of the Somme. The archers were marching with the increased burden of stakes, sharpened at both ends, which the king had ordered to be cut down and used, planted in the ground, against cavalry attacks. At last, two unguarded fords were found and the army, with its horses and baggage, was able to cross entire. That night the men went to sleep in good spirits. No major obstacle, they believed, now lay between them and Calais.

But at that moment, six miles away to the north, a French army of 24,000 men was entering the town of Péronne. This huge force had come from two directions: a part from Blanche-Taque and another north-east from Rouen, where King Charles VI and his Dauphin had sped its departure. United, the royal dukes, the flower of French chivalry, had only one aim: to bring the English to battle and destroy them. Heralds were sent to King Henry to inform him of this and inquire his route. He replied without anger or fear: "Straight to Calais".

21 October. It was raining heavily as the English resumed their march, north-west, towards the coast. The French army was no longer in Péronne, but a mile outside a cross-roads churned by thousands of feet showed that it had moved east to advance parallel to the English. They gazed on these "strangely trodden" tracks with awe and the chaplains prayed earnestly that God would turn away the power of the French.

Three days later, fifty miles farther on, a scout descended at full gallop from a hill-top and reported: in the valley beyond, the French like "an innumerable host of locusts" were streaming inwards towards the Calais road to cut off the advance.

The king remained calm, committed himself and his army to God and deployed his men on a ridge facing the enemy. It was there that, in his hearing, a knight expressed longing for 10,000 more archers and the king rebuked him. He would not, if he could, increase his number by one. "For those whom I have are the people of God, whom He thinks me worthy to have at this time. Dost thou not believe that the Almighty, with these His humble few, is able to conquer the haughty opposition of the French?"

But there was no battle that day. The light would soon fade and fighting in the dark was no part of medieval tactics. The French had formed into line of battle, but now they moved off in columns again until, like an unwieldy centipede, they came to rest athwart the Calais road and encamped for the night near a place called Agincourt.

Half a mile away, Henry billeted his men in a village. But many had to sleep in the open, exhausted and hungry under almost continual rain. Next day, the Feast of St. Crispin and Crispinian, they expected to die. Earlier, the camp had been noisy, until under dire penalty the king enjoined silence. All the greater seemed the clamour of the French as it drifted across the fields. Their fires burned brightly. Knights sat dicing and drinking on bundles of straw. Servants bustled, shouting, to and fro. At the back of their camp it is said that there was a brightly painted cart in which they intended to parade the captured English king through Paris.

Henry certainly would not be captured alive, but, outnumbered by over four to one, he doubted despite his brave words that victory was possible. Negotiators were sent to the French seeking a free road to Calais in return for the surrender of Harfleur, but the bargain was rejected. So the night wore on, the only sounds in the English camp the clanging of armourers' hammers, the murmuring of priests as they gave the men absolution. The king, too, must surely have moved amongst them, as he had done earlier in the day, "animating them with his intrepid demeanour and consoling expressions".

25 October, 1415. With the daylight both armies slowly moved into position, one thousand yards apart. At the north end of a field sown with young corn and flanked by woods the French formed three lines of battle, each five or six men deep, the first two lines consisting of dismounted men-at-arms and the third line of horsemen. On each flank a body of six hundred cavalry was stationed. Crossbowmen and gunners completed the array. To the south, the English had troops only for a single line of men-at-arms, four men deep, divided into three divisions interspersed with wedge-shaped clumps of bowmen with more archers on the wings. The centre was commanded by the king, resplendent in a suit of shining armour and a surcoat embroidered with the arms of England and France.

Priests were brought to the fore and told to pray continually. Henry received the Sacrament, then put on his gold-plated helmet surmounted by a gold crown studded with jewels. He addressed his troops, reminding them of former victories, of the justice of his cause and that at home in England wives, children and parents awaited their return covered with glory. "Sir," they replied, "we pray God give you a good life, and the victory over your enemies."

For four hours the armies faced one another, the French well knowing that the English would have to attack that day or else perish from cold and hunger. So at eleven o'clock Henry gave the order to advance and the whole line moved forward to within bowshot range, which at extreme distance was three hundred yards. A hail of arrows descended on the French and stung their cavalry into a charge.

The English long-bow now came into its own. Not until the American Civil War were there weapons of equal range and accuracy. At two hundred and fifty yards a skilled archer could lodge his shaft in the eye-slit of a knight's helmet and he could fire an arrow every ten seconds. As the heavy cavalry rolled forward, riders and horses were shot down pell-mell. Many that reached the archers were impaled on the stakes which had been planted slant-wise in the ground and the whole attack broke up in confusion, riderless horses plunging back into the front line of French men-at-arms now lumbering slowly forward in full armour towards their English opponents.

A situation disastrous to the French now developed. A knight required space in which to wield his weapons, but the French started their advance too closely packed and to protect themselves, as they thought, against the archers they formed into columns yet more dense. The arrows took a murderous toll. Outside ranks pressed in towards the centre and when the French reached the English men-at-arms many found themselves barely able to lift an arm. Their impetus dented the front, but then those pressing from behind knocked them over and, unable to get up, they were clubbed to death where they lay. The English rallied and soon corpses in their hundreds were piling up before the line. Then the archers from the flanks, a shrilling, tattered throng, dropped their bows and picking up abandoned weapons started hacking nimbly in the unwieldy mass. The heaps of killed, suffocated and wounded grew higher and higher. The French second line came forward, suffered the same fate and an hour after the battle began the fighting had ceased and the English were sorting out the prisoners.

Some time later, while the English were still busy with their prisoners, a party of marauders broke into the baggage train at the rear and a dangerous situation arose. The French third line of cavalry had so far not moved and was watching the scene from afar. If it attacked now the English scattered over the field might be caught in front and rear and some of those French knights still lying on the ground might be helped to their feet and start slaughtering their captors. To avoid this possibility, which might turn victory into disaster, Henry ordered all prisoners to be killed. This has since been described as a "cruel butchery", but contemporary writers were not so severe.

But the French horsemen withdrew from the field and, after this alarm, the search for plunder filled the rest of the day. Evening saw King Henry at table in the nearby village, modestly ascribing the victory to God, and next day, having killed eight thousand of the enemy in battle to their own loss of a few hundreds, his troops marched forward, booty-laden and escorting fifteen hundred prisoners, all of them nobles, on the road to Calais.

The glittering victory of Agincourt marks the high-point of Henry's career. It made him, says Sir Winston Churchill, "the supreme figure in Europe". Thereafter, in further campaigns, he subdued all of Normandy and his position was consolidated by Charles VI who, in 1420, recognized him as heir to the Kingdom of France and regent during his life. To seal the compact, he married Charles's daughter, Catherine, and it seemed possible that all of Western Europe might become united under his sway in a Crusade against the Heathen.

But in 1422 Henry died in France, probably of dysentery, while his nominal regency was still far from established in fact and thereafter, until the Hundred Years' War came to an end in 1453, English military fortunes fluctuated in France until the intolerable scourge of war created a national spirit and the Maid of Orleans brought about a turning of the tide.

Harfleur was finally lost in 1449, Rouen in the same year, Normandy in 1450, and at last the English were driven off the Continent and left with only one possession—Calais. Two years later, England plunged into civil war yet more murderous, more destructive of life than the long and fruitless campaigns in France.

So perished the vision of Henry V. But there is left a picture of a true Englishman inspiring to all generations, a brilliant soldier, an able organizer, a sound diplomatist, in the words of the historian Stubbs: "Splendid, merciful, truthful and honourable; discreet in word, provident in counsel, prudent in judgement, modest in look, magnanimous in act." No king in English history has been so dearly loved.

LOUIS XI

(1423–83)

TRAVELLING IN the French kingdom became safe again around 1447, for the first time since over a hundred years, when the English invasions and other disorders had destroyed the king's peace. Charles the Bold, Duke of Burgundy, the last and greatest enemy of the French kings, died in that year, leaving no male heir. His Duchy reverted to the French crown.

Many travellers on the roads of that time were liable to meet a cortège consisting of a few mounted Swiss archers, a few men-at-arms bringing up the rear and, in the middle, riding on a mule, a little man with very thin legs and a long crooked nose. He would be dressed in a coarse cloth, with a large fur-lined hat from which was suspended a number of little medallions of saints. With him would be four or five companions also soberly dressed. The unknowing traveller would have stared curiously at what might have been a well-protected party of merchants. But if the traveller had known it was King Louis XI of France he would have trembled.

The king was not majestic but he was terrible. Everyone had heard of "the King's Orchard" at Plessis-les-Tours, near Amboise, where the bodies of the king's enemies swung to and fro from the branches of trees, of the château itself with its powerful fortifications and look-out points, its packs of dogs and its iron cages in which other enemies of the king were shut up to waste away slowly. Unless the king was in a great hurry, the traveller might well be summoned to speak with him and he would meet someone who was like a man of business, easy and jocular in discourse, who would ask a number of practical questions—if he thought the traveller had any useful knowledge about the state of farming, the kind of industries and crafts of the neighbourhood, the best kinds of wines and food.

For King Louis XI went about his country informing himself ceaselessly. No king cared less for ceremony or appearance: when he reached a town, he often entered it by a back street, to the confusion of the mayor and the notables of the district waiting for him. At Tours once when a great mystery play had been prepared for his entertainment, and the painter Nichols Fouquet had designed a special backcloth, the king refused to attend and said he took no pleasure in such things.

His court was very boring no doubt for the nobility, and though on occasions the king gave a great fête, this was rare. The king himself was liable to be found on a Sunday after mass eating in a tavern. He took pleasure in drinking with some of his advisers and counsellors who were drawn from the middle classes, and with these, seated between their flattered wives, drinking and exchanging coarse jokes, the king seemed at his happiest. At his house in Paris—he never lived in the royal palace of the Louvre—and at Plessis-les-Tours men of all sorts were summoned to meet him. Many of these were paid agents or royal spies; and the king kept a huge number of dossiers concerning the lives and habits of his important subjects. He admitted to boundless curiosity. To a friend he wrote: "I have a woman's nature; when someone tells me something in obscure terms, then I must know, at once, what it means."

In the hundred years from the middle of the fourteenth century to the middle of the fifteenth, French civilization had all but been destroyed. The wars with England which began in 1340, with Edward III's naval victory at Sluys and his first invasion of France, war had indeed only been intermittent; but the armies had brought disorder and devastation and, when the armies were gone, the countryside and towns were terrorized by bandits, demobilized companies of men-at-arms, French and English, commanded by pirate captains. Anarchy affected a very large part of the kingdom—Normandy and Brittany, the whole south-west as far east as Rodez and Montpelier, all the north of France, the Paris region and the country around Orléans. In those parts of France which had been so prosperous and peaceful in the reign of St. Louis there were large regions where people lived in caverns, ate grass and roots and sometimes took to cannibalism. In the less affected parts, where agriculture continued in some fashion, bullocks, cows and even sheep learned by instinct to run for shelter behind the village walls when the church bell tolled the coming of marauders.

The first part of the war saw the great English victories of Crécy and Poitiers where the French nobility with out-of-date tactics were defeated by the smaller but more modern army with its long-bow archers. At Poitiers, the French king, John, was captured and spent the rest of his life in London. But by 1380, forty years after the war had begun, the English had been swept out of the country and lost all the rich provinces they had held before the war began. France in 1364 had had an able king in Charles V, who chose his advisers from men of ability. The French troops were led by Bertrand du Guesclin, who avoided pitched battles and used guerilla tactics against the English. The English ships were chased from the sea.

But thirty years later Henry V once more invaded France and once more the French nobility, who had learnt nothing, were completely defeated by the English at Agincourt. Ten thousand men fell in this battle, one of the bloodiest in the Middle Ages. When, two years later, Henry V invaded France from Normandy, the French king Charles VI was already mad and France was torn by a civil war between the king's brothers, the Dukes of Orléans and Burgundy. The latter, John the Fearless, sided with the English. When, in 1442, Charles VI and Henry V both died within three months of each other, the young child Henry VI, in Windsor, was proclaimed King of France. The Dauphin, "the King of Bourges", as he was called in mockery, gradually won back his crown, with the help of Joan of Arc. By 1450 the English were once more driven out of France, out of all but Calais, which Edward III had captured and peopled with Englishmen. They even lost the great port of Bordeaux.

Although a sense of patriotism had been born in these terrible wars and the Burgundians were now considered traitors, French unity based on the king in alliance with the Church and people, a king powerful enough to withstand the great nobles, was still to be restored. The great nobles indeed, and with them scores of lesser barons and knights, had been accustomed to doing as they wished during the hundred years of anarchy. Many of the great nobles claimed to be sovereign owners of their lands. Some such as the Duke of Brittany and the King of Provence were richer than the King of France. Above all the Duke of Burgundy, prince of the Blood Royal, was an independent sovereign of far greater power than his nominal overlord. His province of Burgundy had been relatively untouched by wars; and he owned also the more prosperous and civilized Low Countries to the north of France, with a capital at Brussels.

Nor was the King of France in the fifteenth century assured, as had been the old monarchs of France of the House of Capet, of the loyalty of the Church and the towns. After the first phase of the war with England, when King John had been captured, Paris and other cities had set up what had amounted to short-lived republics and there had been peasant risings in northern France. The Church, which in the twelfth and thirteenth centuries produced so many great philosophers and men of action, had lost her mission of scholarship and good works. There were two, and at one moment three, Popes in the fourteenth century. Religious feeling, though still ardent, had become superstitious in the extreme. It was the age of witch-hunting, when the civilized world listened to a German friar Sprenger with his violent admonitions against women and his capacity to arouse the crudest superstitious feelings.

The arts flourished in Italy and in Germany, but in France around 1450, when it was desired to repair the great bridge across the Loire at Orléans, not even a master mason could be found capable of such work. The art of building the great Gothic cathedrals was no longer found in the country which the Germans across the Rhine had, in the thirteenth century, thought of as God's country—"*Gott im Frankreich*".

1461 saw the English expelled from France and engaged in their own civil war—the Wars of the Roses. The Dauphin, whom Joan of Arc had succoured—the lazy, trifling, timorous Dauphin of whom it was said that when young he had the soul of an old man—reigned at last in peace. His spirit seemed to be reborn as a result of a liaison with a beautiful woman called Agnes Sorel. Charles VI, known as the Well Served, surrounded himself with wise and able counsellors, including the great merchant of Bourges, Jaques Coeur, and good soldiers such as Dunois and Richemont, who had fought side by side with Joan of Arc. He did much to restore the kingdom. Nevertheless, he was unable to tackle the major task of re-asserting the monarchy against the great nobles, and when the Duke of Burgundy refused to come to Paris to pay him homage he was obliged, out of prudence, to allow the duke to abstain from doing so. He had to fight a rebellion of other vassals and to see his own son, the Dauphin Louis, join the rebels. He had few illusions about Louis's loyalty, but he had some idea of his abilities. When Louis, after the rebellion, took refuge with the Duke of Burgundy, Charles said: "The Duke is harbouring a fox who one day will eat all his hens."

Charles suspected Louis of having poisoned Agnes Sorel. He also suspected that he himself in 1461 was the victim of his son when he died of a constriction of the throat and probably of a cerebral haemorrhage. He had never attempted to disinherit his son, a sign perhaps that the prescience of a king was stronger than the rancour of a man. King Charles's doctor was Louis's agent and had kept him informed about his father's health which, since 1457 when the king had suffered from a thrombosis of the leg, had been precarious. Louis had a mania for spying and plotting. He made no pretence about being anxious to succeed to the throne. But men everywhere in those days all too readily saw poisoning as parricide: Louis can almost certainly be acquitted.

Louis was thirty-eight on his father's demise. Still in exile, he dashed to Paris at once. His coronation was celebrated with great splendour, and his uncle, the Duke of Burgundy, attended it and even put the crown on the new king's head. The duke gave many sumptuous entertainments to citizens of Paris—where, since the beginning of the century, the Dukes of Burgundy had been popular. Yet, strangely enough, when the duke measured himself against his puny and undignified nephew he didn't succeed in getting his way. The men he proposed for important posts in the kingdom were politely set on one side. Someone asked Duke John, as he was leaving Paris, how he had enjoyed his stay. "I do not know," said the duke, "but it has pleased me so much that I am glad to be gone".

At the beginning of his reign King Louis XI threw down a challenge to all his powerful enemies. In the north he bribed the towns in Belgium which were claimed by Burgundy to declare for France. He deliberately offended the Duke of Normandy, the King of Provence and other powerful vassals by attempting to impose the royal authority. There was soon a League of the Public Good, as it was called, formed against him and, after a short, undecisive war, Louis was forced to promise his enemies all they asked. But he had, as it were, unmasked them. He learnt their secrets and weaknesses in the negotiations. The King of France suffered by being forced to make concessions; but the great nobles were exposed to the whole nation as self-seekers, enemies of unity. The king gained.

Louis never minded humbling himself for the moment. Fearing that the English, who were then at peace under Edward IV, might invade France in alliance with the Duke of Burgundy, Louis paid an annual tribute to the King of England and bribed some of his Ministers. He allowed Edward IV to call himself King of France without protest and even signed his letters to him as Prince Louis.

John the Fearless, Duke of Burgundy, died and was succeeded by Charles the Bold, a more bitter enemy of Louis than his father, proud, unbending, but, fortunately for Louis, devoid of a sense of the possible. Charles was grand and rash. In his long struggle with him, Louis made one mistake. Having bribed the duke to accept a temporary truce, he went to visit him at Peronne with a safe conduct. Alas for the king. Whilst he was the duke's guest the news came that Liège had revolted against Burgundy and that the revolt had been encouraged by Louis's agents. For a few days the king was caught in a trap. But he agreed he would go with Charles to suppress the rebels, and he had the humiliating experience of seeing the citizens of Liège crying "Vive le roi" just before they were butchered by Burgundian men-at-arms. Cardinal Balue, who had led the king into the trap at Peronne, was shut up in an iron cage at Plessis where he stayed for many years.

From all his misfortunes Louis learnt something which he put to account. Gradually, what with natural deaths, assassinations and seizures of lands, he broke the powers of the individual dukedoms and his rule bit by bit became unquestioned from the Pyrenees to the Low Countries, except for the great wound of Burgundy in the east. Charles the Bold was encouraged by Louis to go to war in Italy and with the Swiss. After two defeats at the hands of the Swiss, Charles the Bold met his death when he was trying to capture Nancy in eastern France, which he wished to make the capital of Lotharingia, a new kingdom embracing Burgundy and the Low Countries. By Salic law his only child, a daughter, could not inherit the royal duchy, though she kept Flanders, which was a private possession. Burgundy reverted to Louis. On the news of Charles's death it is said the king could not contain himself with joy. He took possession of Burgundy at once, bribing the duke's followers, executing those who made difficulties. Louis was called "the universal spider", and the largest and fattest fly had at last entangled himself in his web.

Louis devoted himself to the prosperity of his kingdom. To carry out his tasks he enlisted the more able administrators he could find abroad, including Englishmen and Scots, into his personal service. He invented the first postal system, carrying letters by fast post-chaises between the principal towns. He encouraged the nobility to enter trade. He started to reduce the customs barriers which existed between one province and another and often one town and another. He brought Italian artisans to settle in France and introduced the great silk industry to Lyons. He made it compulsory to develop minerals. He was no friend of the poor or needy and it was the rich merchants and bourgeoisie who profited from his reign. But what a tragedy it would have been for France if a more virtuous, but less able and unscrupulous, king had come to the throne in this bitter period when recovery was beginning and still unsure. The true value of his reign was not perceived until long after it had ensured for France a period of solidity and prosperity.

Louis did for France very much what Henry VII did for England.

Both were men of similar characteristics. But Louis's task was harder than that of the Tudor king, as it required a character which was so extreme as to be a sort of horror and a sort of wonder. Louis was extremely religious, but it was the religion of the base merchant not of the prince, and a matter of superstition rather than faith. He thought that God, the Holy Virgin and the saints could be bought to help him in his affairs as well as to guarantee him salvation. He even believed in bribing the saints of his enemies, and professed particular devotion to St. Claude, who was the patron saint of the Duke of Burgundy.

Like many great men Louis was an odd mixture of contrasts. With all his cunning he was extremely talkative and apparently indiscreet. Commines, a statesman and historian whom Louis seduced from the service of the Duke of Burgundy, records that Louis once said: "What harm my tongue has done me." He had few affections and treated his family badly. He had mistresses but none had any influence on him. He could never bear to be still, a characteristic reinforced by a skin disease he contracted in old age which he exacerbated by too much wine drinking. He was in appearance and manners anything but master of himself, yet master of his kingdom he certainly was. His energy was extraordinary—his skill at embroiling his adversaries remarkable as was his resolution. He was without conscience or pity.

For many years Louis had paid his doctor a large sum each month to look after his health, yet he also surrounded himself with quacks and astrologers. When he died at Plessis-les-Tours in 1483, probably of dropsy which was followed by two attacks of paralysis, he remained to the end master of himself—speaking, as Commines noted, "driely as though never ill and incessantly saying things which made good sense". Politics and prayer alternated. On his own orders he was buried, not in St. Denis, but very simply in a small church at Clery. Fifteen years after his death it was said of him that he was the most terrifying king France had ever had. He had certainly put all his diabolical qualities to good use.

MOHAMMED II (THE CONQUEROR)

(1429–1481)

THE TURKEY of today is a proud country—but it is in size a mere fraction of the great empire of years gone by. At one stage this "Ottoman Empire" embraced the whole Balkan peninsula, including most of what are now Greece, Bulgaria, Rumania, Hungary, Albania and Yugoslavia. Now only a small part of what remains Turkish is in Europe: less than 10,000 square miles out of 296,000.

The rise of this Central Asian people is one of the most fascinating tales in history. Unlike the Mongols who had come from the same area, led by Genghis Khan and Tamerlane, men who entered Europe and Asia Minor only to kill and plunder, the Turks stayed behind to build. They were eager to learn from the more cultured people they overran, and they consolidated their new empire, made it strong. They were, on the whole, good to those they conquered.

It was in the year A.D. 1000 that these nomads from the Asian plain crossed the River Oxus under their leader Seljuk and swept on down to the Anatolian peninsula between the Black Sea and the Mediterranean. Their move had been forced upon them by other tribes at their back; and soon, in their flight, they found themselves up against the eastern boundary of the Byzantine Empire. They were resisted and they fought the Emperor Romanus and his forces, defeating him in 1071, advancing deep into Anatolia.

This, they decided, was where they would stay. They treated the local Christians with respect, settled themselves around the town of Konia, which became their capital.

They spent the remainder of the eleventh century consolidating their position, dividing Anatolia into provinces, appointing a ruler for each. While they were doing this they eagerly absorbed what they could of the Greek and Persian cultures which had preceded them. They began to build fine houses, adapting the styles of these two civilizations to their own tastes and needs, began to encourage all manner of art. They had arrived in Anatolia as nature-worshippers, animists, but now they embraced Islam, the religion of Allah and his Prophet Mohammed.

Like other empires, the Turkish one under Seljuk and his successors was destined to fade away: the Turks grew soft in their new environment and at the same time found themselves with too small a population to fill the administrative posts which were required to run an empire. The Seljuk empire withered.

But another branch of the same, Turkish, people, led by a man called Osman and variously called "Osmanlis" and "Ottomans", came to take their place. They, too, had been fleeing from Mongol tribes in Central Asia, and they settled with delight into the fertile Anatolian plain.

They remained, peaceably at first, under the control of the decayed Seljuk empire, but when one of its rulers, Ala-ed-Din, chose to select an Ottoman to be governor of the north-west of his territory, the newcomers began their process of assimilation. They grew rapidly in numbers and in strength, and by virtue of being hard-working and intelligent soon had numbers of the people around them working for them, as servants, artisans, farm managers. Like the Seljuks, the Ottomans had arrived in the area as pagans, and went on to embrace Islam, in the early fourteenth century. At the same time, they were prepared to tolerate Christianity as practised by the Greeks, and very soon they had absorbed many people from that older civilization. Ottoman mosques began to be built like Byzantine churches. The Greeks were allowed to worship in their own churches, but many of them, fed up with the controversies of medieval Christianity, embraced Islam.

The Greek city of Brusa was surrendered by its commander to the Ottoman Turks and this became their first capital. By now their eyes were turned firmly towards Europe and a policy began of conquest alternating with peaceful infiltration. Gradually the Turks spilt over into Europe, settling among the people, intermarrying, following the example of their rulers who married European princesses.

Many of the people overrun in this way welcomed the Turks: the Bulgars greeted them with delight as a protection against their cruel Christian neighbours.

Within a few years the only part that remained outside the Turkish dominions—or, to be more accurate, inside it, but not subject to Turkish rule—was the city of Constantinople on the Bosphorus. There was no sign of its people, however feeble and decadent, handing over this capital of a once-great Roman Empire.

The Turks decided to take it.

But in 1402 their plans were rudely shaken. The Mongol Timur, or "Tamerlane", swept down into Anatolia: in July of that year a big battle was fought at Ankara, and the Turks were utterly defeated.

But—as we can see in the article on Tamerlane—the great Mongol's conquests were usually in the form of paralysing raids. He laid waste, took as much loot as his army could carry and made his way back to Samarkand. This is what he did in 1402, and the Turks were able to regroup and recover. It is interesting to note that the Greek and Slav prisoners who had been incorporated into the Turkish army made no attempt to desert or mutiny when that army was crushed by the Mongols. One of these contingents was the so-called "Corps of Janissaries", composed of conquered Christians. This had become one of the finest units in the Turkish army and would remain so for hundreds of years, until its disbandment.

There were other, smaller, Turkish communities in Asia Minor—for the Seljuks and the Ottomans had not been the only groups to flee from Asia. These little "Emirates" were peacefully absorbed, often by straightforward purchase, into the rapidly expanding Ottoman empire.

When the Sultan Mohammed II became ruler in 1451 he sat on the throne of a powerful empire extending to east and west of the city of Constantinople. Half a century before, his people had prepared to take it by force: Mohammed made plans to do so now. During the half-century the Turks had been content to leave this foreign outpost in their territory, much as the Chinese are prepared, for the moment, to tolerate Hong Kong, but with the accession of Mohammed II all that changed. He was a man of boundless ambition, soon to be known as "Al Fatih", or The Conqueror; he prepared to make this the first, the greatest, conquest of his reign.

He made sure of his flanks by diplomatically paying a visit to nearer Asia to sign a treaty with a rebellious Emir, and to Europe to do the same. Then he built a powerful fortress covering both sides of the Bosphorus. When the Emperor Constantine XI protested, Mohammed simply declared war.

Constantine was a brave man and with only eight thousand soldiers he refused to surrender against Mohammed's quarter of a million. The city was surrounded by water to north, east and south, projecting as it does from Europe into the Bosphorus. That on the north was a narrow inlet from the Bosphorus, the "Golden Horn". Landward defences were extremely strong, as were those covering the Bosphorus, and Mohammed, failing to breach any of these, tried to force his Turkish fleet into the Golden Horn. This was thwarted by a boom placed across the entrance by Constantinople's defenders.

Mohammed now performed the first of the military miracles for which he is famous. He decided to move his fleet *overland* from the Bosphorus into the Golden Horn.

His commanders assured him this was impossible. He brushed aside their objections.

A few days later a road was built, under his personal direction. It was rather more than a mile long and surfaced with wooden planks. It ran from a point on the Bosphorus north of the impregnable entrance to the Golden Horn and climbed a hill of almost three hundred feet to descend again to the narrows of the Golden Horn.

Regiments of men were put to work greasing it with animal fat.

A day later the defenders of Constantinople were appalled to see a Turkish fleet bear down on them from the north, overland. Each ship had sails spread and two men on board, at bow and stern, while other men drew it at the end of long ropes. Eighty large vessels had made their way overland in the course of a night, and now, as dawn broke, the last ones slipped silently into the narrow waters of the Golden Horn, a few hundred yards from the north wall of Constantinople.

The ships opened fire, and simultaneously the soldiers attacking overland, from the west, doubled the ferocity of their attack.

Despite this the defenders hung on gallantly, almost incredibly, for another seven weeks.

Mohammed's Christian Janissaries were his crack troops and these he kept in reserve until the very end. Then, at the head of them himself and shouting, "Advance, the city is ours!", he made his charge. Constantine, last of the Roman emperors, died gallantly commanding his defenders: Mohammed entered the town over his dead body.

It was 29 May, 1453.

The siege had been long with heavy casualties on both sides, and much of the city destroyed. But Mohammed, when the fighting had ended, did everything possible to ensure that what was worthwhile in the Byzantine Empire would be retained. A few institutions were altered and laws changed, but Greek names were kept and—by the standards of the day—respect was shown for the conquered. As against the plunder of Constantinople two centuries previously by the Christian Crusaders, hardly any looting took place—though, of course, Constantinople was by this time an impoverished city, with little to loot. Slaves were taken, but the Christian communities that remained were given full equality: the Greek patriarch was even crowned by Mohammed himself.

But despite this show of magnanimity, many of the learned men and scholars of Constantinople began to make their way westward, into Europe. It was Turkey's loss, but for Europe as a whole a tremendous gain, for these men re-lit the flame of scholarship which had been snuffed out by the coming of the barbarians, and carried it over a dark and decadent Europe.

Gradually everything worthwhile left Constantinople—the culture, the art, the learning—only the vice and corruption of an old and cynical city remaining.

Mohammed could see the process happening before his eyes, and he was saddened by it. He remembered the fate of the Seljuk Turks who had lacked capable administrators, and he implored the conquered Greeks and other nationalities to stay and help him run what he hoped would be the greatest, the wisest, empire in history.

As far as Constantinople was concerned, he had no success. But his consolidation of the rest of his empire was sound and he went on to make further conquests. The fleet which had so dramatically surprised Constantinople was doubled, trebled, in size and went on to become the "Scourge of South Europe". Greece was taken over in the five years between 1456 and 1460, and a few years later Mohammed The Conqueror entered Italy.

The Turkish, or Ottoman, Empire reached its greatest extent after the death of Mohammed, but he had shown the way. And to our present time there are men who talk of The Day the Ships Came Sailing Overland.

IVAN III (THE GREAT)

(1440-1505)

IT WAS once said that Russia occupies a greater place on the map than it does in history. This may not be true today, but it certainly was in the Middle Ages.

The peoples who originally settled in the vast lands of Russia were made up of many tribes—Slav, Norse, Hun, Balt, Turk and others. The Russian peoples adopted the Greek form of Christianity in the tenth century. They knew little of Europe to the west of them, but had frequent intercourse with Constantinople. This might have led to a rapid advance in civilization and culture—for Constantinople had guarded the learning which was then lost to Western Europe—but for a great historical catastrophe which set Russia back for centuries.

Lying squarely in the path of the Mongol hordes who swept in from the vast spaces of the east in the thirteenth century, Russia took the full force of this terrible human onslaught. Huge armies of savage horsemen under Batu Khan, one of the successors of Genghis Khan, invaded Russia about 1237, and ravaged the country with fearful slaughter and destruction.

Many of these Mongols settled in Russia and were known as Tartars (or Tatars). Among them was Batu himself. He pitched his magnificent, so-called golden, tent on the banks of the Volga and became the first Tartar Khan. His Tartars and their descendants were known as the Golden Horde.

The Russian princes were for a long time dependants of the Great Khan in China and had to make humiliating pilgrimages to his distant court, some three thousand miles away, and prostrate themselves before him. Both their crowns and their heads were frequently disposed of by this oriental despot and his successors.

The great Mongol Empire crumbled, but the Tartar occupation left its mark and the Tartars remained in Russia. The princes of Moscow imitated the khans rather than the western rulers of Europe, of whom they knew nothing. In their crude and barbarous court they adopted an Asiatic ceremonial and etiquette. Their manners, customs, dress and accoutrements of war were Chinese.

The name Czar, adopted by Ivan the Terrible in 1547, is Asiatic in origin, and is not, as many think, derived from Caesar. Russia did not become Europeanized until the time of Peter the Great.

Moscow emerged as the dominant Russian principality during the years 1240 to 1480 when Russia was under the yoke of the Golden Horde. Each prince of Moscow had to make a shameful journey to the Khan of the Golden Horde at the Tartar capital of Saray, near the mouth of the Volga, to receive investiture from the Tartar overlord. The khans regarded the Muscovite dukedom as the most important in Russia which led to the rise of Moscow. The Muscovite princes gradually extended their boundaries and became more and more powerful as the Tartars of the Golden Horde gradually declined, so that by the middle of the fifteenth century the Tartars were no longer capable of imposing their will on Moscow.

The Prince of Moscow who finally put an end to the Golden Horde and united all of Russia under his own rule was Ivan III, known as Ivan the Great. A hard-headed man of single purpose, he devoted his whole life to the goal of an all-Russia union to replace the existing confederation of princes which was both anarchic and inefficient.

The son of Vasily II, he was born in 1440, and was co-regent during the last few years of the reign of his father, who was blind. Vasily lost his sight in a manner typical of the times. In the early years of his reign he had to fight for his throne with his cousin Kosoy, who was seized and blinded at Vasily's orders. Ten years later Vasily fell into the hands of Kosoy's brother, who put his eyes out in revenge.

Ivan came to the throne on his father's death in 1462. He inherited a wild and backward state, whose progress had been stunted by the devastations of the Mongol invasions.

No country in Europe had suffered so much from these Asiatic hordes whose effect was to stultify every aspect of national growth. While the rest of Europe was progressing towards some kind of civilization and order, the principalities of Russia were under the yoke of an Asiatic oligarchy, which professed no religion at a time when religion was vital to man's progress,* whose past glory lay in senseless slaughter and destruction, and whose sole genius lay in war. Unlike other European intruders, they never assimilated with those they conquered, and were thus going against the stream of history.

*The Tartars later became Moslems.

Ivan went about the uniting of all Russia under his rule in a way which showed that he had a cool, strategic plan. His main military operation was to be against the Grand Principality of Lithuania, which in those days occupied roughly what is now the western part of the U.S.S.R.—Belo-Russia and the Ukraine.

Lithuania had largely escaped the Mongol invasions of the thirteenth century. The Lithuanians were a virile and powerful people who had peacefully infiltrated into the West Russian lands about the time of the terror of the thirteenth century, in a way which considerably benefited the inhabitants.

Before he undertook the task of annexing Lithuania, Ivan secured his other three fronts. The Golden Horde to the south was troublesome, though by now greatly enfeebled. To the east was the Khanate of Kazan, another Tartar horde, in the middle reaches of the Volga, independent of the Golden Horde in the south, more powerful and more dangerous to Moscow. To the north was the Republic of Novgorod, a large territory centring upon the prosperous trading city of Novgorod on Lake Ilmen. The city enjoyed a restricted kind of democracy, and its population was said to be in the region of 400,000 in the fourteenth century. It escaped the Mongol invasions, the hordes of cavalry being unable to cross the marshes which protected the city.

Ivan first turned his attention to Kazan. After preliminary incursions he began a full-scale invasion in 1469, but the campaign was only partially successful. After some indecisive fighting, Ivan's brother, Prince Yury, laid siege to the city of Kazan, which capitulated upon honourable terms when he cut the water supply. Ivan did not conquer Kazan, but at least neutralized it while he turned his attention to Novgorod and Lithuania.

Novgorod had many ties as well as differences with Moscow. Vasily II had died in the middle of one of these quarrels, and during the first eight years of Ivan III's reign relations worsened and tension mounted. Ivan's representatives were insulted at Novgorod. He had plenty of pretext for war.

Novgorod sought a military alliance with Casimir IV, King of Poland and Grand Prince of Lithuania, but Casimir did not respond, although Lithuania had always been on friendly terms with Novgorod. Casimir had no desire for war with Moscow, though he was willing enough to plot against Ivan.

Ivan invaded Novgorod in 1470 and obtained a speedy victory. He did not at first claim total sovereignty over the conquered Novgorodians but made them abandon their alliance with Poland

and Lithuania and cede to him a large part of their northern colonies.

With oriental patience Ivan then awaited a pretext to strip Novgorod completely of its independence. This occurred in 1477 over the apparently trivial matter of the Novgorodian ambassadors addressing him as "Sovereign" instead of "Sir". As there was a strong pro-Muscovite faction at Novgorod this was perhaps not significant. But when Novgorod repudiated its ambassadors' use of the title Sovereign, Ivan's troops once more set out for the obstinate city. Novgorod surrendered again and was forced to recognize Ivan as sovereign. Ivan then stripped it of every pretence of independence, and crushed a further show of resistance by removing one thousand of the most influential and wealthy families to Moscow and replacing them by powerful families from Moscow.

Thus Novgorod lost its proud independence, its wealth and its trade with Europe. It was forced to cut all its ties with the West and with the Hanseatic League. Several other minor principalities were also absorbed into Ivan's territories, either by conquest, annexation or marriage.

Ivan now turned his attention to his southern flank where he was faced with two Tartar khanates—that of the Golden Horde, or the Khanate of Astrakhan, whose ruler was named Ahmed; and the Khanate of Crimea, which included a large part of southern Russia as well as the peninsula of Crimea itself and which was ruled by Mengli Girey.

Fortunately for Ivan's plans, there was bitter rivalry between these two khanates. Ivan sought an alliance with Mengli, while King Casimir, no doubt divining Ivan's intentions upon his own territories in Lithuania, urged Ahmed to attack Moscow, promising that he would invade from the west.

The princes of Moscow had for centuries paid tribute to the khans of the Horde whose ancestors had conquered them. In 1476 Ivan flatly refused to do so, and curtly rejected Ahmed's claim of overlordship. In 1480 Ahmed's armies invaded the territories of his rebellious vassal, in the expectation that Casimir would support him by attacking Ivan's western flank. But Casimir had internal troubles of his own, and failed to fulfil his part of the bargain. His troubles were added to by the marauding attacks upon his provinces of Podolia (now South-west Ukraine) by the forces of Mengli Girey at the instigation of Ivan.

Ahmed lost his nerve. The two armed hosts glowered threateningly at each other across the River Ugra, and after a few skirmishes

Ahmed retired to the Volga where his practically undefended camp was attacked by the forces of an obscure Tartar chieftain from Siberia. Ahmed was killed and the whole operation against Moscow collapsed. The Golden Horde disintegrated. Ivan's hand was no doubt behind the raid on Ahmed's camp, and the act marked the end of Russia's two hundred and fifty years of subservience to the descendants of the conquering Mongols.

The year 1480 is a milestone in Russian history. It was the date when she emerged as a nation. Never again was a Prince of Moscow summoned before the once-dreaded ruler of the Golden Horde. Ivan III accomplished this historic victory mainly by diplomacy and with a minimum of military effort. He had plenty of trouble with the Tartars afterwards, but their yoke had been thrown off for ever.

For the next two decades Ivan occupied himself with the subjugation of Lithuania. King Casimir died in 1492, and his son, the Grand Prince Alexander, became the ruler of Lithuania.

Though fighting began in the 1490s in the form of border affrays instigated by the Muscovites, Ivan was busy in the diplomatic field before he sent his main armies in.

Alexander did not want war. He put out peace feelers, and suggested a marriage with Ivan's daughter Elena. He was left in no doubt that Ivan wanted back the Lithuanian territories which had originally been Russian. The marriage nevertheless took place at the Lithuanian capital of Vilna in February, 1485; after much haggling and argument between the contending parties, Elena, who had no say in the matter of course, obediently going to her fate to marry a man she had never seen. Her fate could have been worse, for Alexander was a dashing and handsome young man.

Ivan's hopes that the marriage would enable him to infiltrate into the Lithuanian court came to nothing. Alexander did not want Elena's crude and rough-mannered retinue in his more civilized Western court, and sent them back to Moscow, to Ivan's intense annoyance. Ivan intended his daughter to be a spy for him in the enemy's court, and instructed her to influence her husband politically in favour of Moscow's interests.

In this respect the marriage was a total failure. Though it was not a failure from the conventional point of view, Elena seems to have fallen in love with her good-looking and gifted young husband. He treated her well and her loyalties soon changed to his. It is likely, too, that she found the more civilized court of Alexander an agreeable contrast to the crudities of the Kremlin.

But she would not change her faith. Her husband was a Roman Catholic and she was Greek Orthodox, and despite great pressure she refused to join the Roman Church. In 1500 Ivan used this as a *casus belli* for starting the Lithuanian war. Alexander had pledged that he would not use pressure to make Elena change her faith. This undertaking apparently was not kept. Great pressure was put upon her by members of the Lithuanian Catholic Church, who were urged on by no less a person than the Pope himself (Alexander VI, the Borgia Pope). Members of the Greek Orthodox Church in Lithuania were also subject to persecution. Ivan, who always liked to have a pretext, then officially declared war on Lithuania.

The Russian and Lithuanian armies met at Vedrosha, where the Lithuanians were routed after a long and bloody battle. Alexander lost the greater part of his army and the Russian casualties were heavy, too. Vedrosha gave Ivan large territories of eastern Lithuania which he desired to add to his domains. But the war dragged on until 1503 when Alexander was forced to sue for peace. Elena also pleaded with her father to cease the war, denying she was persecuted for her faith and saying that in Alexander she had found the perfect husband, who was tolerant and generous and had shown her great kindness.

A truce, rather than a peace, was agreed by which Ivan kept all the Lithuanian territory he had conquered. Some idea of where Ivan's conquest had led him may be gained from the fact that the boundary still fell short of Smolensk and Kiev, which remained in Lithuania.

Thus at the end of his turbulent reign Ivan the Great realized his dream of ruling all Russia and shaking off the hated Mongol yoke. Russia became a single country, and systematic foreign relations were for the first time started.

We have very little knowledge about Ivan himself and his private life. He was an autocrat who rode rough-shod over all opposition and he dealt firmly with his often rebellious relations. His personal appearance, we are told, was remarkable. Tall, thin, slightly stooping, there was something about his face, it was said, which inspired such awe that women fainted at the sight of him. His only known vice was gluttony.

An interesting figure in his life was his second wife, the mother of Elena. This was Zoe, niece of the last Byzantine emperor, who is thought by some to have introduced Byzantine etiquette and ceremony into Ivan's somewhat crude court. After marrying Zoe—whom the Russians called Sofia—Ivan adopted the Byzantine

Imperial double-headed eagle in his emblem. Following the fall of Constantinople and the Eastern Empire in 1453, many people regarded the Grand Dukes of Moscow as the successors of the Byzantine emperors.

Nineteenth-century historians have portrayed Sofia as a haughty Byzantine princess who urged her husband to rid himself of the shameful Tartar yoke in 1480 and inspired him to the unification of all-Russia under his rule. Modern scholarship, however, does not bear out this romantic view of Sofia. Ivan needed no such inspiration for his life's work. His marriage with this last princess of Byzantium is certainly significant, and doubtless she brought some of her rich cultural background with her, but there is no evidence that she influenced his policies. She bore him seven children.

Ivan the Great died on 27 October, 1505, at the age of 66, after a reign of 43 years. He died apparently unmourned and unloved, yet Russia owed him much, for he made her into a nation. He deserved the appellation "the Great" as much as Peter I and Catherine II.

RICHARD III

(1452-1485)

THE BRIEF and sombre reign of Richard III, battle-filled, stained with treachery and murder, centres on a short, slight, tight-lipped figure whom historians, from Tudor times to the present day, have defended or attacked with equal zeal. Many contemporaries looked on him as the Devil Incarnate and twenty years after his death Sir Thomas More in his history started the legend that Richard was deformed in body as well as soul. Shakespeare sees him as the greatest monster in English history and puts into his mouth the line: "I am determined to prove a villain." That he was a villain, despite efforts to prove the contrary, seems clear.

He was born, sickly and undersized, in October, 1452, as the twelfth of the thirteen children of Richard, Duke of York, and Cecily, known as "Proud Cis", the daughter of the first Duke of Westmorland. On his father's side he was descended from Edmund, the fifth son of Edward III, and on his mother's from Lionel, Duke of Clarence, the second son. Thus the House of York had prior claim to the throne after the murder of the childless Richard II, himself the son of Edward III's heir, the Black Prince. But the House of Lancaster, descended from Edward III's third son, John of Gaunt, also had a claim, and though it was inferior it had forcibly been made good in 1399 by Henry Bolingbroke who had invaded England, seized Richard II and established himself on the throne as Henry IV.

The Wars of the Roses between York and Lancaster broke out in 1455, when Henry IV's grandson was on the throne, and as a toddler of three young Richard saw his father return from the victory of St. Albans, the first blood-letting in the thirty years' struggle, where the Duke had gained possession of Henry VI and soon after forced the feeble-minded monarch to grant him the succession to the throne.

The violent shifts of the dynastic struggle filled Richard's childhood. His father's pact with Henry VI disinherited the king's son, Edward, Prince of Wales, and Queen Margaret of Anjou, one of the most determined and resolute women in history, took up arms in his defence. Gathering a Lancastrian army, she defeated a Yorkist force at Ludlow, the Duke of York fled to Ireland and at the age of seven his son Richard became a temporary prisoner of war. Released after a Yorkist victory, he moved with his mother to London, where, early in 1461, they received tidings of disaster. The Duke had been killed and now his head with a paper crown was rotting on Mickle Bar, the highest gate of York city. His grieving widow, in terror for her son, dispatched him to Holland.

Another change of fortune brought him back. His admired and handsome brother Edward, despite defeat by the Lancastrians, found the road to London open, entered it with his army, was greeted with enthusiasm by the citizens and declared himself king. As he grew up Richard became an ardent supporter and Edward soon needed his subtle brain. As a redoubtable soldier he could deal with Lancastrian revolt, whether centred on Henry VI who was carted round like a piece of luggage from battle to battle, or on the still indefatigable Margaret of Anjou who clung through amazing vicissitudes to her son, the Lancastrian heir. Edward triumphed over them all and in 1464 the unprotesting person of King Henry was seized in Lancashire, conveyed to London and after a mock procession through the streets with a straw hat on his head conveyed to the Tower. But then the Earl of Warwick, who claimed a large share in these successes, turned against his master, allied himself to the Lancastrian cause and succeeded in restoring Henry to the throne. Edward, with his brother Richard, fled to the Court of Burgundy.

At this point Richard emerges into the full light of history. In Burgundy he planned with Edward an armed descent upon England and, an essential prelude to its success, the weakening of Warwick's power by winning back to his Yorkist allegiance their brother George, Duke of Clarence. Clarence, aged twenty-one, had been won over by the king-maker in the hope of obtaining the succession and had contributed handsomely to his success. But now Clarence was beginning to wonder: would the throne ever be his so long as the son of Margaret of Anjou was alive, that handsome heir of Henry VI? Richard sent emissaries, played on his doubts, and Clarence, already once foresworn, prepared to play traitor again.

Under the management of his dynamic brother, Edward landed at Ravenspur in Yorkshire. York would not open its gates until, on Richard's advice, he pretended that he had only come to reclaim his personal estates. But then, refreshed, he marched southward, managed to slip past Warwick's forces coming to meet him and placed himself between his enemy and London. At Banbury, Clarence, marching from the west ostensibly to attack him, embraced him instead and their two armies joined forces. It was a triumph for Richard, made complete soon after at Barnet where Warwick was killed and his army routed. Richard's own company had dealt him the death-blow.

Edward was now king again. Henry VI, mild and unprotesting, was taken back to the Tower. But his wife Margaret, newly landed with a force from France, offered Edward a new threat. Again the diplomat Richard got to work and persuaded one of her captains to change sides. The battle was fought at Tewkesbury, the nineteen-year-old Richard, his slim, wiry form encased in white German armour, commanding the van of four thousand men. It was a disaster for the Lancastrians. Margaret was taken prisoner and her son, the Prince of Wales, slain.

With the last hope of the Lancastrians dead and the White Rose triumphant there remained only one possible rallying point for Edward's enemies, Henry VI, devout, uncomprehending, eking out his days in the Tower. After Tewkesbury, Richard hastened to London on his brother's orders and spent the night of 21 May, 1471, in the Tower. On that night Henry died, of "sheer melancholy", it was claimed.

For the next twelve years Edward reigned unchallenged, much occupied with sensual pleasures and bored by the task of government. Richard built up a solid reputation in the north as a zealous and fair-minded administrator. With his wife, Anne Neville, daughter of Warwick the king-maker and former wife of Edward Prince of Wales who was killed at Tewkesbury, he lived a quiet life, but his mind revolved an interesting question: when Edward died who would succeed him? He had two sons, born in 1470 and 1473, but Richard knew that before marrying their mother, Elizabeth Woodville, Edward had been "troth-plighted" to a Lady Eleanor Talbot. The union had been consummated, but no marriage had taken place. Could not this fact be used to illegitimize Edward's children? In that case, only one barrier stood between Richard and the throne: his elder brother Clarence, and in 1478 Clarence was convicted of high treason, sent to the Tower and seen no more—drowned, it was said, in a butt of Malmsey wine. So Richard watched and waited, grave, competent, impeccably loyal.

The king died suddenly from his excesses in 1483, having appointed Richard in his will to act as regent for his son. At York, very correct, he dressed himself and his gentlemen all in black, attended a Requiem Mass and took the oath to Edward the Fifth. But he did not forget the troth-plight and, when he came to think of it, he could remember rumours that his own deceased brother had not been sired by his father, but by some person unknown. Such rumours were damaging to Proud Cis, but they could be used. And there was another circumstance of the greatest importance. Secretly, much to the fury of the higher nobility, Edward IV had married a lady of low quality. Elizabeth Woodville was a daughter of Sir Richard Woodville, one-time steward to the Duke of Bedford. This was bad, but worse was the reckless way in which the king had showered favours on his wife's brothers and sisters, of which she had twelve. Rancour against him had simmered for years and now, after his death, Richard knew that he could rely on a large body of the nobility for their support.

Methodically Richard made a plan. The first step was to gain possession of the boy-king who was at Ludlow on the Welsh border. This was easily done. The king, with a heavy escort commanded by his maternal uncle Lord Rivers, was intercepted on his way to London by Richard in Northamptonshire. Rivers and other officers were arrested, the escort was embodied in Richard's forces and the proud regent, with deep obeisance, led the way to the capital—ostensibly for his sovereign's coronation. Rivers and his friends were executed within a month.

In London Richard also acted swiftly. On the feeble pretext that it would be safer and more dignified for him there, the twelve-year-old king was lodged in the Tower. Meanwhile the Council of Regency was empowered to issue writs in his name and ordered to prepare the Coronation. The moment had almost arrived for the *coup d'état*, the accusation which would give Richard the throne. One last rival had first to be disposed of—Richard, the king's nine-year-old brother—and incredibly his mother surrendered him to the smiling Protector from sanctuary at Westminster and he, too, vanished into the Tower. Now the stage was set.

The Coronation was fixed for 22 June. Three days before, the Bishop of Bath and Wells was prodded into publicly proclaiming Edward IV's troth-plight with Lady Eleanor Talbot, the consequent illegality of his marriage with Elizabeth Woodville and the bastardy of all his children. Richard professed to be much surprised. The Coronation could not, of course, take place, and on the day itself, instead of the boy-king enthroned in splendour, London saw one Doctor Shaw, a firebrand preacher, repeat the accusation at St. Paul's Cross on the text "Bastard slips shall not take root" and call on his audience to acclaim Richard, who conveniently happened to be present, as their rightful king and true son of his father. Even Edward IV's legitimacy was impugned. The appeal fell flat, likewise another public harangue delivered by Richard's friend, the Duke of Buckingham, in the following week.

But this did not prevent a dutiful and packed Parliament proclaiming the deposition of Edward the Fifth and, soon after, with much show of reluctance, Richard, besought by Buckingham, accepted the throne. He was crowned with impressive ceremonial on 6 July, 1483. Perhaps he felt joy and satisfaction on that day, but he was to feel little thereafter.

He went on a progress through the Midlands, righted wrongs, bestowed favours and courted popularity. But the people were suspicious and, in the south, where resentment at his usurpation was particularly strong, the demand was raised that the princes should be released from the Tower.

So we come to Richard's principal crime. In the same month of his coronation he resolved that the princes must die. Sir James Tyrell, devoted and ruthless, was sent to London with an order to the Constable of the Tower to deliver him the keys for one night. His groom, Dighton by name, and one of the gaolers did the deed, suffocating the boys while they slept and burying the bodies under a mass of rubble by a staircase leading to the chapel in the White Tower, where the bones were found during alterations in the reign of Charles II. From this time, as the story goes, Richard knew no peace, but saw enemies everywhere, was forever fingering his dagger and at night pacing, ghost-haunted, in his chamber.

Troubles soon descended. Buckingham, the former bosom friend, rose in rebellion, concerting his plans with Henry Tudor, Lancastrian heir to the throne. At the same time there were risings in the south, provoked by rumours that the princes had been murdered. Richard crushed all with ruthless hand. Henry returned to Brittany whence he had come; Buckingham was captured and immediately beheaded.

Richard was granted a strife-free interlude in which he showed himself an enlightened reformer, but his crime clung to him, and when, in April, 1484, his young heir, now Prince of Wales, died the question of succession was reopened and many Yorkists as well as Lancastrians flocked to the banner of Henry Tudor in Brittany. A marriage was projected between him and Elizabeth, daughter of Edward IV, and Englishmen saw in this prospect of uniting the Roses a means of ending the sickening bloodshed.

Early in 1485 news came that Henry meant to land in the spring. Richard acted with resolution, setting up his headquarters at Nottingham, arranging for relays of horses to bring early news of an invasion, collecting money and troops. In June he issued a proclamation. It was meant to be a rallying cry against "Henry Tydder, descended of bastard blood" and his band of "murderers, adulterers and extortioners", but it had little effect and troops were slow in coming in.

Two months passed. Richard went hunting in Sherwood Forest, in the summer-decked glades pondering the innocence of nature, the treachery of his enemies. Then, on 7 August, 1485, Henry Tudor's expedition landed at Milford Haven and, though with only two thousand men, he at once proclaimed Richard a usurper. With his force enlarged by three thousand Welshmen, delighted to welcome a descendent of Owen Tudor, he marched eastwards, gathering more recruits as he went. But when the rival armies finally met at Market Bosworth, the king had managed to muster twelve thousand men, while Henry had only half the number. All depended on the Stanleys of Cheshire. They marched with the king, but would they fight for him?

On the night before the battle it is reported that Richard had fearful dreams. But next morning he harangued his captains in splendid style. "Dismiss all fear . . . Everyone give but one sure stroke and the day is ours. What prevaileth a handful of men to a whole realm? As for me, I assure you this day I will triumph by glorious victory or suffer death for immortal fame."

No Mass was said. The king took no food. Fasting, he entered battle at eight o'clock in a suit of polished steel, wearing his crown. The country was undulating, with dales and hills. On one of these, Ambien Hill, Richard's forces were arrayed with the Stanleys on lesser hills to either side. Henry attacked from the south, facing a steep slope topped by cannon brought from the Tower of London. The fighting with axe, mace, lance and arrow was confused and bloody. Henry's men were halfway up the slope when Richard called on Lord Stanley to attack them in the flank. Instead, Stanley marched his soldiers to Henry's succour. Crying "Treason!" and seeing that all was lost, Richard galloped down with about a hundred knights into the thick of the fight—his aim to slaughter the Welshman. Sir William Stanley from the other flank could have helped him at this moment, but stood his ground. Hand-to-hand, Richard slew Henry's standard-bearer and Sir John Cheyney, his Cavalry Master, then Stanley with his horsemen surged into the struggle—for Henry, not for Richard. A mace crashed on his helmet. He was borne down, axed, stabbed and trampled. His crown was retrieved from a bush and placed on Henry's head and the mangled corpse of the last of the Plantagenets, with the long hair hanging down, was tied naked on a horse and carried into Leicester as a show for the people.

So Henry Tudor reigned and, marrying Elizabeth, daughter of Edward IV, brought the long and murderous Wars of the Roses to an end. In the thirty years' struggle it is calculated that 100,000 men had died, died for a reconciliation which now, at last, placed a new dynasty on the throne. All Englishmen believed that a new age had dawned.

FERDINAND V (THE CATHOLIC)

(1452–1516)

and

ISABELLA I

(1451–1504)

THE STORY of Ferdinand and Isabella is the story of the birth of Spain as a nation. Their marriage enabled Spain to become a united country after seven centuries of war and anarchy. They laid the foundations for the vast Spanish Empire in the newly-discovered Americas, and put Spain upon the road to greatness.

In this joint enterprise in kingship, Isabella was unquestionably the senior partner. Not only was she more gifted than her husband, she greatly excelled him in integrity and moral qualities. She had a talent for statesmanship, while his talents were more for warfare. They made a remarkably effective partnership.

Isabella was born on 22 April, 1451, daughter of John II, King of Castile, and was a descendant of John of Gaunt, third son of Edward III of England. Isabella's father was an amiable, indolent intellectual who neglected his kingdom for his literary pursuits and left the affairs of state to his favourites with disastrous results. This accomplished but incompetent king had two wives and three children—by his first wife a son who succeeded him as Henry IV, and by his second wife a son and daughter, Alfonso and Isabella.

Ferdinand's father was King of Aragon, also called John II. Ferdinand was born on 10 March, 1452, and at the age of ten became heir to the throne upon the death of his brother. From that date Ferdinand was taken away from his studies and spent his life on the battlefield and in the saddle by the side of his father, whose long and turbulent life was spent in conquest, violence and civil war, typical of fifteenth-century kingship.

The two kingdoms of Castile and Aragon then made up the Spain as we know it today. Aragon comprised the north-eastern part from the Pyrenees to just below Alicante, and Castile the rest of the country. Castile was much larger, more important and powerful.

Isabella was four when her father died and her brother Henry IV became King of Castile. He was known as Henry the Impotent, and impotent he was in every meaning of the word. Extravagant and debauched, he possessed none of the cultivated tastes which were his father's redeeming feature. In 1462 his beautiful and unvirtuous queen, Joanna of Portugal, gave birth to a female child, also called Joanna, which though accepted by the impotent Henry was widely believed to be illegitimate.

Upon her father's death Isabella was sent with her mother to live in seclusion in the little town of Aravalo. Here under her mother's guidance, and far from the corrupting atmosphere of her brother's immoral court, she was trained and brought up with care and wisdom, and well instructed in the practical pieties of the age. She was naturally of a pious disposition and her mother implanted in her serious mind such strong religious principles that nothing in after-life could shake them.

The disputed child of Queen Joanna brought the question of the succession into violent dispute, and Henry summoned Isabella and her brother Alfonso to his court to keep an eye on them, well knowing that his rebellious nobles would try to use them. He was right. In 1465 young Alfonso, then eleven, was set up as King of Castile in opposition to Henry, and the country was riven by strife.

Isabella was then sixteen—a tall, demure, attractive girl, with a clear, fresh complexion, light-blue eyes and auburn hair. Her portraits depict her as having well-nigh faultless features upon which sat an engaging expression which was a mixture of intelligence and feminine sweetness. It has been said that Isabella's Spanish admirers were so smitten by her moral perfections that they tended to exaggerate her physical beauty.

She was, of course, a very marriageable commodity. Not only was she exceedingly personable, but much more important was the fact that on the death of her brother Alfonso in 1468 she was declared heiress to the throne of Castile, the claims of Queen Joanna's child being set aside.

The princes of Europe contended with each other for her hand, but Isabella, who had reserved the right to pick her own husband, showed an unerring judgment and faith in her destiny by choosing her cousin Ferdinand of Aragon, with the conscious object of uniting Spain into one kingdom. Ferdinand was no stranger to her. They spoke the same language and enjoyed the same customs and institutions.

Ferdinand was eighteen, and a well-built, muscular young man, a great horseman, who excelled in all the field sports of his day and who was already experienced in battle. Even in his youth his receding hairline gave him an almost bald appearance. He had a sharp-voiced eloquence by which he had no difficulty in asserting his considerable authority. But his rather cold and suspicious nature alienated him from many of his future subjects.

The marriage articles signed on 7 January, 1469, firmly established Ferdinand as the junior partner in this historic dynastic union. In vain Henry IV opposed the marriage, which took place on 19 October, 1469, in his absence. Henry's profligate and unheroic reign continued in uninterrupted anarchy and corruption until his unlamented death in 1474, when Isabella ascended the throne of Castile amid general rejoicing.

Ferdinand immediately showed the less pleasant side of his character as well as demonstrating a typical essay in fifteenth-century kingsmanship. Rushing to Isabella's side, he claimed the crown of Castile for himself on the ground that a female was excluded from the succession and that the sovereignty devolved upon him as the nearest male in line. Spain's highest ecclesiastical court decided that a female could sit upon the throne of Castile, though not upon the throne of Aragon. Ferdinand would not at first accept their judgement, but Isabella smoothed his ruffled pride with true feminine tact and guile. He was forced to capitulate anyway, for his attempt to grab the throne for himself had no support in Castile, where it would not have been tolerated. The Castilians wanted Isabella, well aware of her great qualities which were not shared by Ferdinand. In 1479 Ferdinand's father died and Ferdinand ascended the throne of Aragon, and the two kingdoms were united.

Administratively Isabella made a splendid start, converting the dismal anarchy of the previous reign into a state of order such as Spain had not known before. She reformed justice, re-codified the laws, regulated trade, agriculture and the currency, and re-established the royal authority which had fallen into contempt during the lawless reign of her brother. She brought the rebellious nobles of Castile to heel. With the firm re-establishment of royal authority, the Spanish grandee acquired dignity and responsibility, as well as a splendour which was to dazzle and astonish the world. Isabella herself carried out these reforms, sometimes enforcing her mandate personally, fearless of her own safety.

The courage, intelligence and integrity of their young queen, as well as her beauty and dignity, created a great impression upon her subjects. The court circles were cleansed of the immoral and wanton atmosphere of the previous reign. Although Isabella raised court life to a high standard of virtue and dignity, it lacked nothing in splendour. Its fêtes and tournaments were magnificent and attended by all the trappings of chivalry. To it were invited artists, poets, musicians and men of letters which gave the Spanish court a true intellectual atmosphere.

Isabella's independence of Rome, her restriction of the secular power and influence of the Church in Spain, and the setting up of her own Inquisition independent of the Papacy are among the distinguishing features of this strong Catholic monarchy.

Not all of her enactments were constructive or enlightened. Medieval Spain differed from other European countries by the large numbers of Moors and Jews within its borders, among whom there was undoubtedly a lot of the kind of heresy which the Inquisition had been created to deal with. The Jews were the historical enemies of Christianity and had been persecuted for centuries. In 1478 Isabella set up the Spanish Inquisition to deal particularly with the Jews.

Why the virtuous, upright and intelligent Isabella allowed the establishment of this cruel and shameful institution of religious barbarity in her fair and smiling realm of Castile is not so surprising as has been made out. Isabella—for all her admirable qualities—was a woman of her age. It was a superstitious, bigoted and cruel age. Criminals were dealt with harshly. Torture and cruel death were not considered incompatible with the workings of justice. Isabella's pious upbringing had brought her very much under the influence of priests and monks, some of whom nourished ambitions of power when they knew their young charge was destined to become queen. None was more ambitious than a certain Dominican monk, Thomas de Torquemada, who became her confessor and who extorted from her a promise that when she came to the throne she would devote herself to the extirpation of heresy. The time arrived when Torquemada demanded that she should keep this ominous promise.

She was reluctant, perhaps for obvious reasons of humanity. Under tremendous priestly pressure, she decided finally to demand of the Pope a bull authorizing an Inquisition which would be answerable to her, not to the Papacy. Her desire to have control over this terrible instrument of religious persuasion was doubtless prompted by the best possible motives. Sixtus VI did not like the idea at all, but was unable to resist the powerful monarchy which was bringing order and prosperity to the Spanish peninsula.

Thus the Spanish Inquisition was established and it became a powerful and sinister institution, which in the hands of the Spanish crown was used to further the power of Spain rather than that of the Church. Isabella and Ferdinand were in fact determined to control the Church in the same way as they had controlled their nobles, their cities and their economy.

The Spanish Inquisition was established in Castile in 1480 and Torquemada became Inquisitor General in 1483. Soon the Inquisition was operating over all the dominions of Ferdinand and Isabella. Their first victims were the converted Jews and Mohammedans. In twenty-five years nearly 350,000 suspected heretics were dealt with, of which 28,000 were condemned to death, and 12,000 actually burnt at the stake. Most of these victims of the Holy Office were tortured unspeakably, and those not condemned to die were fatally injured or maimed for life.

So great was the terror which fell upon the Jews, who were the principal sufferers, that many fled to France, Germany and Italy, where the accounts of their treatment added to the accumulating scandal on the condition of the Mother Church. The scandal was so great that Sixtus himself was moved to rebuke the intemperate zeal of the Spanish Inquisitors, though the Holy Father soon digested his conscience; for in 1483 he was encouraging Isabella—who seemed to have a twinge of conscience herself at the time—to further efforts in seeking out heresy.

In 1494 the Pope conferred upon Ferdinand and Isabella the title of "the Catholic Monarchs", on account of their virtues, their zeal for the faith, the subjugation of Granada, and "the purification of their dominions from the Jewish heresy".

The conquest of Granada—the last remaining bastion of Mohammedanism in the Spanish peninsula—was successfully undertaken between the years 1481 and 1492. The brilliant Moorish civilization had flourished in Spain while the rest of Europe was sunk in barbarism. Although its great days were long over, it had contributed much to Spain. The Moors' beautiful and desolate ruins even now haunt the landscape of the fair country they made their own for seven centuries.

The conquest of this last Moorish stronghold by the Catholic monarchs was prosecuted with fanatical zeal and with all the barbaric usages of the time. Though not to be compared with the horrors of modern warfare, it was rich in both atrocity and chivalry, and was concluded with an ungenerous peace which leaves yet another stain upon the memory of Ferdinand and Isabella.

In 1492 Ferdinand and Isabella issued a decree expelling all Jews from Spain. The odium for this action is not entirely theirs. The high priests of the Inquisition had been long urging it. Torquemada in particular had great power over Isabella's mind. She felt bound to surrender her own judgement in matters of conscience to her religious guardians. But Isabella cannot be held entirely blameless for this great crime against the Jews, for she, too, suffered from the deep moral depravity of the medieval Catholic Church. She did not have the spiritual courage to ask the terrible questions which were being asked in Germany at that time.

Between 160,000 and 180,000 Jews were driven out of Spain by the edict of 1492. Their departure brought great economic distress to Spain, for in turning out their most talented and industrious citizens Spain became speedily and permanently crippled economically. But even their more enlightened contemporaries did not regard it as incredible that monarchs of such political sagacity should do such an act. The expulsion of the Jews was regarded as a sublime sacrifice of temporal interests for a religious principle.

Christopher Columbus came to Spain in 1484 after having unsuccessfully tried to interest various other monarchs in his plan to sail westwards around the world to China and the Indies. Ferdinand and Isabella were in the middle of the war with Granada, and little notice was taken of Columbus. It was another of Isabella's confessors, Juan Perez, who inspired her to give Columbus her royal ear. But there was more scepticism than enthusiasm for the expedition, despite Isabella's legendary exclamation that she was ready to pawn the crown jewels of Castile if there wasn't enough money in the treasury.

Actually the expedition was very cheaply financed. It cost no more than 17,000 florins, and never did so modest a sum reap so golden a harvest. On Columbus's return in 1493 the Pope, Alexander VI, made Spain the magnificent presentation of all the lands a hundred leagues west of the Azores which had been discovered and which were to be discovered.

The exploration of Central and South America quickly followed. Conquest and conversion to Christianity soon firmly entrenched Spain in the golden lands of America, enabling her to draw rich treasure as well as to spread the true faith under the velvet terror of the Spanish Inquisition. But these fabulous riches from the El Dorado beyond the sunset did not benefit the Spanish people. It was all used to build up the glory of Spanish arms and to finance innumerable wars in Europe. Spain entered into her period of colonial greatness fatally weakened economically by the anti-semitic and anti-Moorish policies of Ferdinand and Isabella.

Two of Isabella's children made marriages which had important political and dynastic effects in Europe. The Infanta Dona Catalina, known in English history as Catherine of Aragon, became the wife of Henry VIII, whom he divorced in order to marry Anne Boleyn. The Infanta Joanna was married to Archduke Philip of Habsburg. This brought the Habsburg dynasty to Spain, which was something of a disaster. Joanna's son was the great Emperor Charles V. In 1503 Joanna became insane.

Having acquired and built up an important kingdom in Europe and an empire in the new world which promised to pour into her lap all the fabled treasures of the Indies, Isabella, in the noontide of her success, was taken ill and died at the age of fifty-four, on 26 November, 1504.

Upon her death mad Joanna was declared queen, with Philip of Habsburg her consort. Ferdinand, in accordance with Isabella's will, had to give up the crown of Castile, but claimed regency in the name of his insane daughter.

The absence of Isabella's firm hand upon the helm of national affairs was immediately felt. Philip claimed the throne, and Ferdinand's authority was undermined by unrest and rebellion and he was not able to re-assert himself until Philip's early death at the age of twenty-eight in 1506.

With a mad queen on the throne, the Castilians were only too glad to have Ferdinand back as their king, if only to prevent conditions slipping back to the bad old days of Charles IV, for Ferdinand was not popular. Ferdinand shut Joanna away in a palace, where she survived for forty-seven years. Once more firmly on the throne he ruled Spain until his death in 1516, when his grandson, Charles V, inherited the throne, after whose reign the golden visions of Ferdinand and Isabella were all dissipated in the sterile religious wars which ruined and exhausted Spain during the next two centuries.

HENRY VII, KING OF ENGLAND

(1457–1509)

On 22 August, 1485, some 20,000 men fought a battle near Bosworth in Leicestershire, some 13,000 or so under the banner of the King of England, Richard III, and the rest, the rebel army, following a Welsh gentleman, Henry Tudor, Earl of Richmond, who claimed the English throne.

Henry Tudor had landed on 9 August, at Milford Haven in Pembrokeshire, with perhaps a couple of thousand French and Breton mercenaries and a following of English exiles. He had gathered the rest of his troops in warlike Wales and marched across England, hoping for a general rising in his favour. He hoped in vain. On the other hand, Henry was assured that his brother-in-law, Sir William Stanley, Earl of Derby, who commanded one-third of Richard's hastily got-together army, would not fight against him. His confidence in this treachery was not misplaced.

Like most of the battles of the Wars of the Roses, the comparatively small armies of knights and feudal retainers came quickly to hand-to-hand combat, mostly fighting on foot. Neither side as a rule had many archers; but both had enough to forgo the ordeal of charging on horseback against a storm of arrows. The issue of the battle was doubtful until Stanley's troops, who had refused to advance against the rebels, attacked the king's army. Richard, one of the bravest warriors of his time, dashed into the centre of the enemy, seeking Richmond himself. He was finally killed, his crown falling from his helmet under a bush where it was lost until found by Stanley and placed on Henry Tudor's head. The body of King Richard was stripped naked, tossed over a horse and, after the face had been battered against the parapet of a bridge, was irreverently buried in the church of Grey Friars in Leicester, a church since destroyed. "The majesty that doth hedge a king" had been destroyed long before this battle, and of this Henry Tudor, Henry VII, was well aware.

Since the death of Edward III in 1377, the heirs of the great Plantagenet had been fighting over the Crown. Richard II, the son of the Black Prince, was deposed by Henry of Lancaster,

Earl of Hereford, known as Bolingbroke, who was a son of John of Gaunt, a brother of the Black Prince. Bolingbroke became Henry IV. Henry V had no serious challenger but fighting broke out again in 1455 during the reign of his young son Henry VI, between Lancastrians and Yorkists. By force of arms, Richard, Duke of York, son of the third son of Edward III, Edmund Langley, Duke of York, won his claim to be recognized as Henry VI's heir. He, however, was killed by the Lancastrians. His son, Edward, won the crown at Towton in 1461, to lose it again when the great Earl of Warwick changed sides, backed the Lancastrians and restored Henry VI.

Edward returned from exile, and in 1471 defeated Warwick at Barnet. He finally defeated the Lancastrians at Tewkesbury, murdering Henry VI's young son and later, in the Tower, the ineffectual Henry VI himself. As Edward IV he now reigned in peace until 1483 when he died. These major battles had been accompanied by lesser ones all over England between the nobles who supported one side or the other.

The Wars of the Roses had not affected the daily life of the people as much as might have been expected; but they had ruined the national unity created by England's earlier kings and caused a break-down in public morality and public order. But in spite of the general acceptance of murder and bloodshed, the murder by Richard, Duke of Gloucester, the brother of Edward IV, of the two Princes in the Tower, the sons of Edward IV, may well have shocked the nation and perhaps have accounted for the comparatively small army which Richard III had at Bosworth. Against this supposition must be set the fact that Richard III was extremely popular in the north of England and that, during his two years as king, he had summoned Parliament, redressed grievances and ended abuses of the previous reign and generally shown himself an enlightened monarch.

The murderer of his brother's children he probably was; but so many men's hands had been stained with blood of kin that Richard's defeat cannot, with total certainty, be put down to a moral revulsion from him. His own recklessness and contempt for Richmond may have made him fight too hastily. His character had been blackened by the great genius of Shakespeare in the play *Richard III*, which is one of Shakespeare's finest works, in spite of being propaganda for the Tudors as well.

Fortunately for England the victor of Bosworth was very different from the open-hearted, virtuous young warrior who briefly appears in Shakespeare's *Richard III* as Richmond. Had Henry VII been another Henry V, or a pleasure-loving Edward IV, it is very doubtful if he would have kept his throne. Bosworth then would merely have been another inconclusive and bloody battle of the Wars of the Roses. Henry's claim to the throne was extremely slender, so slender indeed as to be almost non-existent. From his mother, Margaret Beaufort, he could claim to be a descendant of John of Gaunt; but it was descent through an illegitimate union, subsequently legalized by King Richard II, but with the express stipulation that this line should have no claim to royal blood. His father, Owen Tudor, a Welsh gentleman from Anglesey, had married Catherine, daughter of the King of France and the widow of Henry V.

As a result of the great slaughter of princes and nobles during the Wars of the Roses, Henry Tudor was considered the head of the House of Lancaster by Henry VI; but this scarcely made him an heir of the Plantagenet throne. There were still alive those who could claim direct descent from the last Plantagenet king through Edmund, Duke of York. There was, first of all, the daughter of Edward IV, Elizabeth; there was the young Earl of Warwick, directly descended from Edward IV's brother, the Duke of Clarence; and two sons from a sister of Edward IV, the Earl of Lincoln and Edmund, Earl of Suffolk.

In 1483, from his exile in France, Henry Tudor, when he first staked his claims to the throne, announced his intention of marrying Elizabeth if he came to the throne and thus re-uniting the two Houses of York and Lancaster. This promise he carried out, and he married Elizabeth in January, 1486, securing the ten-year-old Earl of Warwick in the Tower.

Before Henry married he summoned Parliament and secured from it what is called an Act of Recognition. This act did not in fact make him king by the will of Parliament; it merely acknowledged that he was already king, as a result of the battle of Bosworth. Precarious claim, precarious victory. Yet from the accession of Henry VII, the king with the least reputable title to succeed to the throne, England was never again to be afflicted with a dynastic struggle. There was to be a civil war during the seventeenth century, a struggle between king and parliament, but no one doubted that Charles Stuart was the rightful King of England. James II, was to be driven from his throne in 1688; but it was by the will of the overwhelming majority of the nation, and William and Mary's claim came through Mary, who was a Stuart.

The placing of the monarchy in an unassailable position was the work of Henry Tudor and of the two great Tudor rulers who followed him—Henry VIII and Elizabeth I. When Elizabeth died without issue in 1603 her successor was James VI of Scotland, the great-grandson of Margaret, daughter of Henry VII, whom he married to James IV, King of Scotland. No Tudor monarch allowed his children to marry with their subjects as had been the custom frequently in the past. The firm establishing of his rule and that of his dynasty was the greatest of Henry's achievements. He had no easy task.

The Earl of Lincoln, with the support of his aunt, Margaret, Duchess of Burgundy, who ruled the Netherlands, raised a mercenary army in that country, and disguising his own claims under that of the Earl of Warwick, whom he alleged had escaped from the Tower, had an impersonator of Warwick, a young man called Lambert Simnel, crowned king as Edward VI in Christchurch Cathedral, Dublin. The Anglo-Irish nobility were Yorkists to a man, just as the Welsh were Lancastrians. At Stoke in 1487 the rebels were defeated, the Earl of Lincoln was killed in battle, and Lambert Simnel, after exposure to the people of London, was employed as a kitchen boy in Henry's palace. Later in life he was promoted to falconer.

The second serious rebellion, backed also by the Duchess Margaret and the Yorkists, was that of Perkin Warbeck, who impersonated the younger of the princes in the Tower, Richard, Duke of York, pretending that he had escaped when his brother was smothered in his bed by Richard III's agents. Warbeck, who also received support from Ireland and from James IV for a while, finally landed in Cornwall in 1492, but ignominiously stole away from his small army to surrender to the king on the promise that his life would be spared. He was later imprisoned in the Tower with the Earl of Warwick and, unfortunately for both, he persuaded Warwick to try a joint escape. They were easily captured. Henry's policy was to avoid executions if possible; they stank of the old order. But he nonetheless executed Perkin Warbeck and the Earl of Warwick after this. Later Henry was to execute other Yorkist claimants to the throne.

The Crown had not been merely a prize to be fought over by the nobles who claimed Plantagenet blood, but it had during the Wars of the Roses become a totally valueless bauble, pledged and indebted at home and abroad. Henry's task of breaking his rivals was accompanied by measures against the power of the great feudal families, including heavy taxes on castles and on the maintenance of retainers. When the Earl of Oxford received Henry in great state, he was flabbergasted to be fined £10,000 for unlawful display. The subjection of the nobility to Henry and the exactions of the Star Chamber which carried out the punitive measures was easier because the nobility had been weakened by the civil wars. Nevertheless, only a very bold man could have acted with the speed and rigour of Henry. By 1509, when he died, he was the richest king in Christendom. The power of the king was greater than it had ever been. The country prospered under Henry's uneventful and undramatic rule; in 1497 a Venetian diplomat thought that London had become as rich as Florence or Paris, and he noted that in the Strand which leads to the City there were more goldsmiths and silversmiths than in any city he had ever visited.

Fortunes were being made as in the reign of Edward III from wool and cloth, and Englishmen, merchant-adventurers, were beginning their travels to the New World. Schools and colleges were being founded; the new rich, so prominent in the reign of the next king, were building magnificent houses.

Henry was no constitutional innovator and in fact used Parliament less and less during the latter half of his reign, particularly when he had been able to collect the money he needed from the administration of the Crown lands and the efficient collection of established duties and taxes. When Henry made war on France in 1492, Parliament voted him money. Of fighting there was virtually none except for a token siege of Boulogne; but Henry managed to get himself bought off by the French king and so collected money from this quarter too. He ruled England as an intelligent despot, giving the country an uneventful period of efficient government.

In 1501, Henry's eldest son Arthur was betrothed to Catherine of Aragon, who brought a huge dowry. Arthur died a few months after the arrival of his fiancée in London and, in 1503, the young girl was betrothed, willy-nilly, to Henry, Prince of Wales, afterwards Henry VIII. In fact, the pair did not marry until 1509, since Henry and Ferdinand first pretended to have scruples about the legitimacy of such a match and then after-thoughts about the marriage for political reasons.

At one time it was thought that Henry VII, after he had lost his wife, intended to marry Catherine's sister, Juana of Castile, the greatest heiress of Europe, who, however, was well known to be mad. He gave up this project. After his wife's death he certainly thought of marrying the young widowed queen of Naples, and among the few human things that are known about this monarch is a report in the Memorials of Henry VII of instructions sent to certain British official visitors to the Court of Naples. The king wanted to know in great detail about the queen's appearance—the colour of her hair and eyes, the shape of her nose, her lips, and how much she owed to cosmetics and how much to high heels. The observers were to mark "whether there appeared any hair about her lips or not" and "to approach as near her mouth as they may to the intent they may feel the condition of her breath, whether it be sweet or not". Henry was, of course, primarily marrying her for her fortune and of this he already had a precise knowledge.

Yet Henry VII was not a miser. He spent largely on music and books and organized magnificent State ceremonies. He began the construction of the great Henry VII Chapel at Westminster Abbey, and he largely helped, from his own purse, the completion of King's College Chapel at Cambridge. He was rather a man who, having spent his early youth in danger and exile and who had once successfully dared fate, was determined never to be caught again in a weak position and he knew that money was power. He remained, for all his cynicism, strongly religious and respectful towards the Church. Towards the end of his life he even thought of going on a crusade against the Turks—but he added a proviso that two other monarchs should come with him.

The best-known and the best portrait of Henry VII is by an unknown French painter. It shows a stern, long-mouthed, thin-lipped face beneath black velvet cap worn at the time. The eyes are slightly hooded, the hands hold a small Tudor rose. The upper part of the dress shown in the portrait is that of a banker or merchant rather than a king, and indeed the whole face is that of a man of business, cautious, politic, unostentatious and determined. Francis Bacon called him "a wonder for wise men". Known by no nick-names, even to his contemporaries, Henry revealed little or nothing of himself to any friend or mistress or adviser. He was feared rather than loved. He has been called the cleverest king who ever sat on the throne of England. His reign was certainly one of the most beneficial to the English nation.

MONTEZUMA

(1480?–1520)

HE WAS the most bloodthirsty ruler in history. He was a cannibal and a murderer.

And yet, even those who were appalled—and frightened—by his barbarities, men of an alien, Christian, culture like the Spanish conquistador Bernal, could write, as he did years later, of Montezuma's death:

"When we least expected, they came to say he was dead. Cortes wept for him as did all of us captains and soldiers. There was not one of those of us who had known him intimately that did not lament him as if he were our father. And that was no wonder, considering how good he was."

And so, on 29 June, 1520, ended the life of one of the world's most absolute, most powerful rulers, certainly one of the richest and, in a macabre way, one of the most lovable. He was a murderer on an absolutely vast scale: he ate the limbs of those he murdered. And incredibly, he managed to instil a deep love in the breasts of those who knew him.

To understand him we must take a look at the civilization into which he was born. The Mexicans had moved slowly down the length of the North American continent, having crossed, like all the other "Indians" of the New World, from North-east Asia, via the Bering Strait to what is now Alaska. Others had preceded them, but these, when the Mexicans reached the spot they cared to settle in, were defeated and destroyed. They chose as their capital an island situated many miles inland of what we now call the Gulf of Mexico, at an altitude of seven thousand feet—an island in a vast inland lake. On this they began to build their Mexico City, in 1324. Within a few years they were the most powerful community in Central America, a tough race, and intelligent—save for one blind spot—and living in the greatest luxury, on wealth they gathered annually in taxes from nearly four hundred subject towns.

But these people, with all their fantastic stores of gold and jewellery, their beautiful cottons, their chocolate, fine rubber and tobacco, so much of it denied as yet to the people of Europe, were a frightened people, organized permanently for war. They had little need to fight their neighbours; their control was absolute, their capital impregnable: they could have sat back to enjoy their wealth. But religion, their own fantastic brand of it, taught them otherwise. They knew, with every bit as much conviction as the Christian knows his God, that they were at the mercy of all their own gods, that none was merciful, that all must be placated, constantly, unceasingly, with gifts of food.

And the only food these gods would eat was a human heart, plucked beating from a human breast and placed on the altar. It was to gather victims for this ritual sacrifice that the Mexican army was always at war with one or other of Mexico's neighbours—a war fought solely for bringing home captives, to be kept to await their fate. On the appointed day, a group of prisoners would be taken from the cages, marched to the stone altar. There, each horrified victim watched the struggles of his predecessor, watched him held down on his back by four priests, one at each limb, while a fifth forced the head back to expose the throat. The sixth, the executioner—who was often the Emperor Montezuma himself—slit it, split open the chest and reached down inside to withdraw the still-beating heart. Then the limbs were cooked and eaten.

And unless this sacrifice was carried out daily—with enormous orgies of murder on certain astrologically fixed days—the sun would fail to rise, the rain to fall, maize to grow; the enemies of Mexico, both super-natural and human, would rise and conquer.

Life, for all its daily ritual of sacrifice, its aura of fear, was pleasant enough. Mexican sculpture and engineering was of a high order, the country abounded in fine roads, aqueducts, causeways. There was a legal system, an accurate calendar and a refined picture writing. Clothes and furnishings were both luxurious and beautiful, food of all sorts abounded: fruit, vegetables, succulent turkeys, and the little hairless *chihuahua* dogs bred for the table (though cattle—and horses—were unknown). Accurate and lethal weapons were made of wood, stone and bronze.

The government was headed by an elected monarch—elected by a council from among the preceding monarch's family, rather as if, on the death of Queen Victoria, the British Cabinet had settled down to decide whether the throne should go to the Prince of Wales or to some other royal relative. Once elected, the new monarch, though he had to study the appetites of the gods, was treated as one himself, a god who ruled the twin powers of army and church, had absolute power over his subjects.

It was to this throne that Montezuma—"Courageous Lord" in the Mexican language—was elected, at the age of thirty-five, on the death of his uncle. Already a warrior and legislator, he was devout and became more so, anxiously studying the Mexican scriptures. One in particular worried him: it told of the great battle between the War God and his rival, Quetzalcoatl, which ended in the latter's exile. He had sailed away on a magic raft, sailed away to the sunrise, with a final threat: "I will return in a One-Reed Year and re-establish my rule. It will be a time of great tribulation for my people."

One-Reed Years, like our own Leap Years, were based on astronomy, though they recurred at irregular intervals. The year of Montezuma's birth, 1480, had been one—and no Quetzalcoatl had come. The next One-Reed Year was 1519. Whether the god came or not, the Mexican priesthood knew from their scriptures just what he would look like, how he would behave. He would have white skin and a black beard—unknown in that part of the world—and he would, immediately on landing from his magic vessel, announce his intention of stamping out the wholesale human sacrifice offered to his rival, the War God. Not only that, but he would demand all sacrifice be stopped, forthwith, even to himself. This had been his quarrel with the War God, all those years in the past.

What did one do? To resist him, a god, was unthinkable—yet to allow him to return would arouse the ire of the War God, for whom they would have to gather yet more human hearts. Who could tell which god would be victorious, which to support? It was a terrible dilemma: and now, few doubted that Quetzalcoatl was coming. The One-Reed Year had dawned, there had been strange portents in the sky, voices wailing in the night, the eruption of a long-dead volcano. The Sun God's temple had caught fire. Superstition and astrology pointed not only to an arrival but to an exact date: 22 April, 1519.

On that date—it was Good Friday in the Christian calendar—the pale-skinned, black-bearded Spanish soldier of fortune, Hernan Cortes, landed on the Central American coast, 350 miles east of Mexico City, Montezuma's capital.

The emperor soon learnt of the invasion—and his heart sank. He was desperately worried: it would be disastrous to allow the god to return, for he and all his subjects had been bowing down to gods which were Quetzalcoatl's sworn enemies—and yet it would be still more disastrous to resist. All he could do was send messengers to the coast with gifts, urging Quetzalcoatl not to come farther. The road was dangerous—had the great god forgotten?—and very tiring: if the great god would return to whence he had come, Montezuma would give him all the riches god or man could covet.

But Cortes, after he had built his coastal base—it became the first Spanish town in Mexico, Vera Cruz—started to move inland, on 15 August, 1519. Montezuma learnt each day of their progress, how the small, white-skinned party was defeating armies from other tribes on the way, including a huge force of the savage Tlaxcalans. He sent another message to Cortes, asking how much he would demand as annual tribute—any amount of gold, silver, precious stones, slaves—not to visit Mexico City. With the messengers he sent priceless gifts, a foretaste of what would be coming.

But on and on came Cortes, replying courteously, thanking the sender for each load of gifts as it came. Eventually, in November, his Spanish force reached the lake in which the magnificent City of Mexico stood, on its island, with causeways running, some of them miles long, to the shore. (The lake today is almost dry: the city has spread over much of the lake bed.) Guided by Montezuma's emissaries—for the emperor no longer believed it possible to stop the Spanish progress—they marched along one of the causeways, as curious Mexicans paddled about them in long canoes and bejewelled lords came down to greet them.

And then, as they passed the fortress of Xoloc on this seemingly endless causeway, mile upon mile of it, they came face to face with Montezuma.

He got down from the litter in which he had been carried from his palace, and advanced on foot towards them, under a canopy of feathers and rich embroidery. Mexican nobles held the canopy, others unrolled a carpet before him so the golden sandals would not touch common dirt.

"As we approached each other, I dismounted and was about to embrace him," wrote Cortes, "but the two lords in attendance prevented me with their hands, so that I might not touch him."

There was complete silence. Then Montezuma, standing straight and tall, his feathered headdress swaying above them, addressed the returning god. He spoke with courtesy, without servility, thanked the god for the trouble he had taken in getting back to Mexico, the hardships he had undergone, and his words were translated by the beautiful and nobly-born "Doña Marina", the Mexican girl who had been handed over to Cortes, on the coast, as a gift. "Welcome to this land. Rest now, you are tired——"

Perhaps Montezuma was hinting that his visitor, when he had taken this rest, might be content to leave, to return to that eastern land, taking gifts.

But the Conquistadores never left. With their greed, their incomprehension of the people, their beliefs and their feelings—above all, their fears—they succeeded in destroying Mexican civilization almost completely within two and a half years of Cortes's arrival in Vera Cruz. With the single, foul, exception of human sacrifice made by a frightened people, much of it was fine and worthwhile, and we are the poorer by its disappearance.

The Spaniards, made welcome by the emperor, given a sumptuous palace for their own use and all the food, drink and gifts they could—for the moment—desire, still distrusted their hosts. At last, after months of misunderstanding, culminating in a skirmish between Cortes's base party at Vera Cruz and a nearby Mexican garrison, for which Montezuma was wrongly held to blame, the emperor was removed from his own palace and taken—with the greatest courtesy—to the Spaniards' one, as prisoner.

This was Cortes's greatest, fatal, mistake. His most potent supporter in Central America was Montezuma: the emperor believed him to be Quetzalcoatl and, as many of his subjects and ministers did not, that Quetzalcoatl would defeat all other gods. Had Cortes supported Montezuma to the hilt, all might have been well—but he did nothing of the sort. By June of 1520 the emperor was doubly discredited in the eyes of his people: not only was he prisoner, but he had misled them about the intentions of the god. Time and again he had told them to be calm, that Quetzalcoatl would leave: he had revisited his kingdom, been well pleased, and was going, taking his white-skinned followers with him. He had given his word. And each time, Cortes, thirsting for yet more wealth, had broken that word.

And so, at the other end of the city, the Mexicans were electing a new emperor. Goaded to fury by the installation of a statue of the Virgin in one of their temples, urged on by another god, Smoking Mirror, who demanded Cortes's death, and, finally, enraged by the killing of some uniformed dancers in the street by one of the Spanish captains who thought they were coming to attack the garrison, they prepared to rise against the invader.

Cortes had been back at the coast, at Vera Cruz, defeating—and winning over to his side—a large Spanish force dispatched by the Governor of Cuba, Velasquez, who had learned he was being cut out of any honours or profit gained from the Mexican sortie. (It had set sail from Cuba, been largely financed by Velasquez—and Cortes was now dealing direct with the King of Spain.) On hearing rumours of a Mexican rising, Cortes rushed back, with his now greatly enlarged force, and entered a sullen, hostile city.

The Mexicans struck on 25 June. They removed bridges from the causeways, making retreat impossible, and attacked the Spaniards' palace.

The battle raged; the sun burnt down into the huge courtyard, there were shrieks and the steady thud of rocks crashing against the walls, the occasional whine of a spear. Then all would be still as attackers and attacked took stock. Finally, Cortes decided to promise, yet again, that he would leave Mexico City with his men, for ever. After all, he still had his firm base of Vera Cruz: later, if he wished, and he probably would, he could come back, retake the capital.

But to tell the besiegers this in the midst of what had become a major battle (several Spaniards had been captured already and sacrificed, hearts torn from the living body, at the top of the War God's pyramid in full view of their horrified comrades-in-arms) he would need Montezuma.

At first the emperor refused. Then, though he agreed, he said it would be useless: "I cannot get them to stop fighting against you, for they have elected another sovereign and are resolved you shall not leave the city alive." He put on his ceremonial dress, the bejewelled golden crown, with the long plume, the silken shawl, the gold sandals. About his neck was a golden chain; there were turquoise ornaments through the lobe of each ear, a piece of jade through his nostrils. His face was painted with coloured stripes—green, orange, white.

He mounted the ramparts and the Mexicans, when they saw him, lowered their weapons.

He spoke, shouted, into the sudden silence. "My people—fight no more, for it is useless and unnecessary. This time I promise you, as the great god Quetzalcoatl has promised me, that he and all his lords will go."

Some in the crowd began to weep, and the Spanish soldiers who had accompanied the emperor—the ex-emperor, for he had already been superseded, by election—lowered their shields for a moment and left him unprotected.

There was a sudden, hysterical volley from the street below and a stone struck Montezuma on the side of the head. He stood erect, hand raised, for a moment longer, then fell.

Sadly, the Spaniards carried him back through the palace to his apartments. Tenderly, they cared for him—but the will to live was gone. The Great Montezuma, as they always called him, with love and respect, grew weaker every day. On 29 June, 1520, he died.

The Conquistadores, badly cut up, many of their number sacrificed, escaped. A few months later they came back and laid siege to the city themselves. On 15 August, 1521, it fell, and was totally destroyed.

Gradually it was rebuilt, and Christian churches erected on the sites of the old temples. The Mexicans had little trouble adopting Christianity because, though they had fought him, they still believed Cortes had been their returning god Quetzalcoatl: the new religion was thus guaranteed by a survivor of the old. And to this day, in parts of Christian Mexico, there are peasants who worship, in addition to the Trinity, the twin figures of Quetzalcoatl and Montezuma.

The reign of Montezuma was a splendid and glittering one—and unbelievably cruel. Some historians have put the annual number of human sacrifices in his capital as high as 20,000.

But—perhaps—one may feel remorse that it should all, good as well as bad, have been totally destroyed by an invader—masquerading as a god.

HENRY VIII
(1491–1547)

THAT UNPRETENTIOUS and somewhat drab figure, Henry VII, had not laboured in vain to establish his succession. No king began his reign more assured of the loyalty of his subjects than did Henry's son, Henry VIII—bluff King Hal, as he was later to be called.

As a young man Henry VIII charmed not only the people and the courtiers but wise and learned men such as Sir Thomas More, Erasmus, the great Archbishop Warham of Canterbury. Just as Edward III had been the image of the chivalrous medieval king, so Henry was that of the great monarch of the Renaissance. He was hearty, dashing, affable, open-handed, a lover of sports and of music, in both of which activities he was no mean performer himself. He is the author of *Greensleeves*.

He liked popularity and he knew how to make himself popular. He was extremely handsome and fond of clothes and magnificence. An Italian diplomat wrote that he was "the handsomest potentate I have ever seen—above the usual height, with an already fine calf to his leg, his complexion very fair and light, with auburn hair and a round face so beautiful it would become a pretty woman". Then Henry was also intelligent, a great linguist, a patron of learning and the arts, and, with all that, he had an orthodox cast of mind. There was no truer son of the Catholic church than the young monarch who called himself the Defender of the Faith.

He married Catherine of Aragon in 1509; she had been kept in England for many years after her engagement to Henry's elder brother Arthur, who had died whilst her father Ferdinand and Henry VII tried to make up their minds about her future. The still-young queen, in spite of her Spanish-ness and a certain stiffness of character, was also popular and remained so during her subsequent misfortunes.

Right at the beginning of his reign Henry executed two ministers of his father, Empson and Dudley, who had been responsible for some of the more severe exactions during the late reign and who were generally, perhaps inevitably, and almost certainly unjustly, hated. They went to the scaffold on a trumped-up charge of treason.

Although this move threw a sinister light on the nature of the new king, it was widely popular, betokening an end to the rather stern period of rule from which the country had benefited but of which it was tired.

Unlike his father, Henry VIII embarked early in his reign on an ambitious foreign policy, the main aim of which was to recover English possessions in France. As the son-in-law of Ferdinand, King of Spain, and as a zealous Catholic, Henry joined Spain and the Holy Roman Empire and the Papacy in alliance against Louis XII of France. The English people seemed to welcome this new attempt to aggrandize England, and Parliament, in 1512, voted money for the war on the Continent and also for the inevitable war with Scotland likely to follow as a result of the Franco-Scottish alliance.

The king's successes on the continent were more showy and costly than real, although an English victory at the Battle of the Spurs, near Boulogne, won Henry some renown. But France was no longer the weak and divided power that she was in the fourteenth century, and England, for all the wealth that the last king had gained, was unable to keep an army on the Continent for more than a few months at a time at the most. After 1520, when Henry VIII and Francis I of France met at the Field of the Cloth of Gold at which both the French and English courtiers tried to outdo each other in splendour of appearance, Henry's policy was to hold a balance between France and the immensely powerful Emperor Charles V, whose Habsburg dominions now included Spain as well as the Netherlands. But no great success came of Henry's policy, and when, in 1521, France and the empire made peace at the Treaty of Cambrai, England's interests were not satisfied.

The only great victory won during this early part of the king's reign was against the Scots in a battle at which Henry was not present. At Flodden, in 1513, the aged Earl of Surrey won a decisive victory against James IV of Scotland, who, together with some 10,000 Scots, was killed on the field of battle. For the rest of Henry's reign English influence in Scotland remained powerful.

Whilst the king, apparently, played, England was administered by the great Cardinal Wolsey. Wolsey's career and relationship with the king had some similarity to those of Thomas à Becket with Henry II. Like Becket, Wolsey was of humble birth, the son of an Ipswich butcher. He commended himself to Henry VIII by his wit, intelligence and great efficiency and, like Becket, he loved magnificence. Wolsey took a degree at Oxford when he was fifteen, entered the Church, became Chaplain to Henry VII in 1507, a member of the King's Council when Henry VIII came to the throne; he swiftly became Bishop of Lincoln, and from 1514 Archbishop of York, and then Chancellor, and therefore the first of Henry VIII's Ministers. He obtained a Cardinal's hat and became the Papal Legate and, at one time, he even hoped to become Pope. There was no limit to his ambitions.

There seemed no limit to his power either, but for all the great offices he held, and for all his papal and ecclesiastical titles, he was never anything more than a general manager of Henry VIII's estates. Wolsey had been the main organizer of the king's military expeditions, just as it was his diplomacy which bound Henry, on the whole, to the Pope and the emperor. When Henry VIII tired of his attempts to make England a great continental power and, when he began to see the importance of the Protestant German Princes and of France, he began to criticize Wolsey and to listen to the many people who hated Wolsey for his arrogance.

Wolsey's fall came when he failed to get the Pope to annul Henry's marriage to Queen Catherine; and when it came it was sudden. Forced to resign the Chancellorship, he was allowed to attend to his duties as Archbishop of York, something he had scarcely done before, after he had given the king his magnificent palace at Hampton Court. But Henry had second thoughts. Wolsey was summoned to London on an accusation of high treason. He died on the way, at Leicester, and it is recorded that he said: "Had I but served my God with half the zeal I served my King, he would not have given me over in my grey hairs." The great Cardinal had none of Becket's spiritual power and resolution and before the king's displeasure he split like a rotten bough.

Among Wolsey's enemies had been a dark-haired maid of honour to the queen, Anne Boleyn, of whom Henry was strongly enamoured and to whom he wrote some celebrated love-letters and a beautiful poem in which he compares his love to the evergreen holly. Henry's passion for Anne Boleyn was real and he meant it when he wrote the following lines:

Now unto my lady,
promise to her I make,
from all other only,
to her I me betake.

Yet it may be that this passion perhaps only lent enchantment to Henry's decision to divorce Catherine.

It was difficult then, and it is impossible now, to assess how much infatuation and how much policy played in Henry's decision; but probably policy counted for more than passion, for though Henry was an amorous man he was even more a deeply ambitious king. Catherine had borne him seven children but none of them had survived for more than a few months, except a female child, Mary, born in 1516. The king was determined to have a son. The king's anger with Wolsey for failing to get the marriage annulled, the breach with Rome which led to the Act of Supremacy in 1534, were above all, it would seem, the consequence of the Tudor itch for a male heir and for a settled succession.

Henry had some reason to be vexed with Papal authority. His sister Margaret had obtained a divorce from her second husband, the Earl of Angus, and there had been many other cases of annulled marriages of princes. The difficulties, as Henry understood them, were simply that Catherine was the niece of the emperor, and Pope Clement VII was the emperor's prisoner. The emperor's armies had sacked Rome in 1527. Henry was determined that his marriage to Anne Boleyn should be legitimate, thinking again of an heir to the throne.

During the divorce proceedings, Sir Thomas More, Chancellor after Wolsey's fall, lost his head for refusing to accept the Act of Supremacy, as did Bishop Fisher, another former friend of Henry's. Sir Thomas More was the man whom Henry as a young king would frequently visit, putting his arm round his neck as they walked in More's beautiful garden in Chelsea. More, in those early days, had expressed surprise that the young royal theologian should so adamantly defend the power of the Pope as to say to him: "For we received from the Holy See our Crown Imperial." This was a doctrine which More, the staunchest of Catholics, had never heard advanced before.

Henry's matrimonial affairs continued, to the end of his life, to be greatly concerned with this desire for male heirs. He was unlucky in the business of begetting. Anne, after a daughter who was to become Queen Elizabeth I, had borne a still-born male child. Anne Boleyn, accused of infidelities which were probably real, went to the block for failure to help the English Crown effectively. Her marriage was annulled by Archbishop Cranmer on the grounds that marriage with a former mistress was void in the eyes of the Church. Fortunately this counterfeit argument did not make Elizabeth illegitimate.

From his third wife, Jane Seymour, Henry obtained a son, Edward VI, Henry's successor indeed, but a sickly intellectual boy who was to die young of consumption. Jane Seymour herself died in childbirth. In 1540 Henry made a political marriage with Anne of Cleves, English policy then seeking a Protestant alliance against the Pope and emperor. The marriage was annulled by mutual consent and by an Act of Parliament. Anne's ugliness lost Henry's minister, Thomas Cromwell, who had planned the marriage, his head. Cromwell was hated by conservative aristocracy of whom the Duke of Norfolk was the leader.

Henry had his eye on the Duke of Norfolk's niece, Catherine Howard, and she became his fifth queen. In November, 1542, however, Parliament passed an Act of Attainder against her, and she was executed on the grounds of unchastity before her marriage and of culpable indiscretion after it. Henry's last wife, Catherine Parr, was a widow, thirty years of age, who looked after him in his last years and who survived him.

In 1529 Henry summoned a Parliament. He was now to preside over the great social and ideological revolution, the effect of which was to establish Crown and Parliament together as the bulwarks of the new England. To ensure divorce from Catherine, he had to make himself Head of the Church in England and for this he needed Parliament.

The Parliament which assembled in 1529 and which sat for seven years was the first English Parliament which represented not merely the feudal nobility but the new England of rich merchants, the new landowning classes, the rich merchants and important citizens of the towns. This Parliament expressed a new mood in the country and it was a mood which suited the king. It was bent on carrying Henry VII's administrative reforms a stage further and its principal target was the Church, which owned between one-fifth and one-third of the total land of the country. Whilst the bishops' lands formed part of the taxable wealth of the country, the extensive domains of the monasteries and convents were the property of the Pope. The dissolution of the monasteries in England was an inevitable step and no modern nation, Catholic or Protestant, could come into being when such a concentration of wealth and influence remained outside the jurisdiction of the State.

The dissolution was carried out harshly and unjustly in many places and the suppression of centres of education and of good works was bitterly resented in many parts of England. But most of the monasteries no longer performed the functions which they had done in medieval England. If the moral laxity of certain monastic houses was exaggerated by Thomas Cromwell, who was responsible for their break-up, many of the 560 houses with their great properties were occupied by some score or even less of monks or nuns, and hence were inevitably parasitic organizations.

The dissolution brought immense wealth to Henry VIII, who created from the people who bought the monastic lands from the Crown a new class of landed men. These new land-owners, unlike the remnants of the feudal aristocracy, felt themselves and their future to be intimately bound up with both the king and Parliament. The ecclesiastical legislation of Henry's reign was therefore of the first importance in carrying on and consolidating the silent social revolution begun by the first of the Tudors. When, in 1543, Henry VIII confirmed the members of the House of Commons in their freedom from arrest he said:

> *We be informed by our judges that we at no time stand so high in our estate royal as in the time of Parliament, when we as head and you as members are conjoined and knit together in one body politic.*

It was by refusal to accept this basic idea of the inter-relation between king and Parliament that James I lost the esteem of his subjects and his son, Charles I, his head.

Henry's revolution in church affairs was not, in his mind, nor in that of the majority of his subjects, a break with the Catholic Church. It was simply an affirmation that the Church could not stand outside the law and the economic needs of England. Essentially it was the same in motivation as the various Acts of Henry II in the thirteenth and Edward III in the fourteenth century to assert Royal over Papal supremacy. Henry's revolution was anti-clerical but not anti-Catholic. The doctrine of Henry's Church was virtually unchanged after the Act of Supremacy. But, of course, a stronger movement was working in English minds at the time. The setting up of the Bible in English, which took place in Henry's reign, was of major importance for the growth of English Protestantism. But the effect of Henry's character and views was that of moderating the violence of religious reformism and, but for the Act of Supremacy, of maintaining the Church of England as part of the ancient body of European Christianity.

The end of Henry's reign saw renewed costly and also ineffective wars with France and Scotland and an extension, remarkably successfully carried out, of English administration in Wales. Henry's work for the British Navy was of great importance and it was thanks to it that towards the end of the century England could face war with Spain and defeat the Armada. Towards the end of his life Henry grew more and more tyrannical. Some years before his death an ulcerated leg gave him continued pain and prevented him taking exercise. He grew immensely fat and had to have a cage with a pulley to carry him upstairs. His face was swollen, his eyes hidden. A writer of the time describes him as having "a body and a half, very abdominous and unwieldy with fat. And it was death to him to be dieted, so great his appetite, and death not to be dieted, so great his corpulence". He died in April, 1547, holding the hand of Archbishop Cranmer, the main author of the Book of Common Prayer which remains one of the abiding glories of Henry's reign.

Over and over again Henry, to men and women, showed himself a capricious, heartless and bloodthirsty tyrant. "He spared no man in his rage and no woman in his lust," it was said of him. Hundreds of Catholics were massacred for resisting his orders, hundreds of Protestants were burnt for refusing to accept the Six Articles of the Church of England. A man was hanged for eating flesh on a Friday. His great victims to perish on the headsman's block included two queens, three ministers of the Crown, Sir Thomas More and Bishop Fisher, the Earl of Surrey, the Abbots of Fountains and Jervaulx, the Marquis of Exeter and the Countess of Salisbury—descendants of the Plantagenet kings.

Yet this toll of blood did not shake the Crown. Henry was a despot, but the satisfaction of his desires and the alleviation of his fears seemed to the majority of his subjects to be carried out in the public interest. It was for the sake of getting rid of Catherine, his first queen, that Henry embarked on the breach with Rome which led to the Act of Supremacy. But this, together with the dissolution of the monasteries, was in accordance with English thinking. The Reformation, which came, in its true form, in the next reign, divided the country. But it was because King Henry had taken the country with him in the first steps that England was spared the wars of religion which so long harassed France and devastated Germany. Henry gave England a Parliament with an importance and a representative quality which no other similar body on the Continent was to possess until after the French Revolution.

If Henry had died in 1529 his hands would not have been stained with so much blood, but he would have left the memory of a playboy king. As it is, Henry stands out among the greatest of English kings. He showed a remarkable insight into the feelings of his subjects. Self-indulgent as he was, he was industrious and worked hard and consistently for the greatness of England. Perhaps this was why to the very last, even when he was blotched and bloated, he remained a popular monarch.

CHARLES V (Emperor)

(1500–1558)

GREAT MONARCHS nearly always have some uncommon qualities of intellect and personality. Charles V, who was certainly the greatest European monarch of his time, is a remarkable exception. An ordinary, commonplace, unprepossessing man, son of a mentally defective mother, he dominated Europe and eclipsed monarchs far more gifted than himself.

Charles was born at Ghent on 20 February, 1500, to a great heritage. He belonged to that unique European family the Habsburgs, who have married their way to power throughout the centuries.* His grandfather, Emperor Maximilian I, brought about the most gainful marriages of any Habsburg. To the Habsburg inheritance of Austria he acquired the Netherlands by marrying Mary of Burgundy. His crowning triumph of matrimonial statecraft was marrying his son Philip to Joanna, the daughter of Ferdinand and Isabella of Spain (*q.v.*). This brought a splendid inheritance to the Habsburgs which included not only Spain, but half of Italy, Sardinia and the vast and rich empire of Spain in the New World which Columbus had discovered for Isabella and Ferdinand. It was a golden windfall for the Habsburgs, but a disaster for Spain, which had just been united in nationhood by Ferdinand and Isabella and had a glorious future before it. That this future was not realized was mainly due to the intrusion into their history of the Habsburgs, none of whom—not even Charles V—had any talent for statesmanship.

Philip died and Queen Joanna went mad. Their son was Charles, who at the age of eleven inherited the kingdom of the Netherlands from Philip. His grandfather Maximilian appointed his daughter Margaret, Charles's aunt, to act as Regent for him, a job which this talented woman performed with great success.

In Spain, Ferdinand, husband of the late Queen Isabella, became king again, as his daughter Joanna, Charles's mother, was unfit to rule. Ferdinand died in 1516 and Charles inherited Spain and its great empire.

*The Habsburgs gave rise to the proverb: *Bella gerunt alii, tu, felix Austria, nube.* (While others wage war, you, happy Austria, marry.)

This youth, who was the greatest of the Habsburgs and represented them at the summit of their power, and upon whom fell a kind of illusory greatness, had a thin pale face and a projecting lower jaw which made both talking and eating difficult. He was very conscious of his impediment. He spoke little and was shy and awkward at court, where he made the worst possible impression upon foreign ambassadors who described him as a weakling, without character, and practically half-witted. At this time Henry VIII, handsome, brilliant, talented, was on the English throne, and Francis I, courtly, gallant, full of easy charm, was King of France. It was an age of young rulers, and Charles, the most powerful, looked the most unpromising.

How wrong was the contemporary assessment of this fledgling emperor is a matter of history. When it came to shaping European history, the glamorous monarchs of England and France did a great deal less than Charles who, despite his modest talent and ability, possessed a strength of will and determination which did not show in his youth. The fact that the task of ruling his vast dominions was beyond him does not detract from the fact that the tremendous and devoted effort he made was enormously to his credit and showed him to be a man of character and integrity.

He became King of Spain in January, 1516, but did not visit his Spanish dominions until the autumn of the following year, for many preparations were necessary before the royal fleet especially fitted out for Charles and his eight hundred attendants was ready to sail. Charles embarked on 8 September, dressed in a high-collared crimson satin tunic, a sleeveless cape fastened with a jewelled brooch, high leggings over scarlet stockings and a crimson cap. With the gaily attired young monarch went his sister Eleanor, and the voyage was a happy and exciting adventure for these exalted youngsters, in the springtime not only of their lives, but of this fabulous century.

Their first duty was to see their poor mad mother. Charles had not seen her for many years, so it cannot be thought that it was a particularly distressing meeting. Queen Joanna did not recognize them, as her disturbed mind could not admit to the fact that her children could have grown up.

Charles was received badly in Spain. He could not speak a word of Spanish and he was surrounded by Flemish attendants who were distasteful to the haughty Spaniards who did not like foreigners. Spain bitterly resented the Habsburg marriage which had brought them a foreign monarch. If they were to have a Habsburg at all they would have preferred Charles's younger brother, Ferdinand, who at least had been brought up in Castile. The kingdoms of Castile and Aragon had lately been united to form Spain, which just then required wise and firm government. This the inexperienced Charles was quite unable to provide and he began his reign with some disastrous mistakes. When he took the oath before the Cortes of Castile he affronted the Castilians by appointing Flemish ministers over them. At Saragossa, the capital of Aragon, he was badly received, the Aragonese making it plain that they would rather have Ferdinand. His reception at Barcelona, Valencia and Valladolid was no better.

In 1519 he heard news of the death of his grandfather, Emperor Maximilian, and he left Spain in a hurry, appointing Bishop Adrian of Utrecht—another hated foreigner—to be regent in his place, to the grievous annoyance of his Spanish subjects who were in a state of open revolt within a few weeks of his departure. The rebels believed that Charles's mother was not really mad, but had been imprisoned in the Castle of Tordesillas so that Charles should have the throne. They could not seriously have believed this, for it was notorious that Joanna had been insane for many years. Their act of capturing the mad queen and discovering the sad truth about her condition is eloquent of their desperation to have a Spaniard on their throne. The revolt then collapsed.

The death of Maximilian, said to be the vainest of the Habsburgs, left open the question of the Imperial crown of the Holy Roman Empire, which consisted mainly of the patchwork of Germanic states. Maximilian naturally wanted to keep this in the family, but the emperors were elected by the Germanic princelings. It was not a hereditary crown. Charles, conscious, as all Habsburgs, of his destiny, thought the purple should fall to him.

But he had two rivals—Henry VIII of England and Francis I of France. Of the two Francis was more serious, and was his enemy as well as his rival. Francis and Charles were at war with each other during most of their reigns.

On his way from Spain to Germany in 1519 Charles, hearing that Francis had arranged a meeting with the King of England, forestalled him by going to see Henry first. He reckoned he had some claim on Henry who was married to his aunt, Catherine of Aragon. Cardinal Wolsey met Charles at Dover and greeted him with a long speech in Latin of which the unlettered Charles couldn't understand a word.

The following day Henry accompanied Charles to Canterbury to visit Catherine, and was impressed by his intelligent conversation and pleasant manner. The astute Henry knew he had more to gain from Charles than from Francis. When Henry attended the splendid but inconsequential Field of the Cloth of Gold given in his honour by Francis, he placed more importance on a quiet meeting he had in France with Charles who didn't have to erect pavilions of gold cloth in order to gain Henry's ear.

Francis was genuinely afraid that if Charles became emperor too much power would be concentrated in his hands, and his fears were shared by Pope Leo X, who supported Francis's candidature for the Imperial Crown. Perhaps the Pope's support of Francis was the kiss of death, for some of the electors were Protestants, or at least shared the anticlericalism which was rampant in Germany at that time. In any event they chose Charles and he was crowned emperor at Aix-la-Chapelle on 20 October, 1520.

He was twenty. He had never been to Germany before, and he could not speak the language of his imperial subjects any more than he could speak the language of his Spanish subjects.

Germany of those days consisted of a hundred or so states, each with its own method of government and taxation, its own army and foreign policy—with the emperor as its overlord. To combine these states into a united nation like France was one of Charles's ambitions. Another great problem faced him as a faithful Catholic. All over Germany voices were being raised in angry protest against the Church—its wealth, its abuses, its corruption, its immoralities. The Reformation movement led by Martin Luther was growing rapidly. Lutherans believed that obedience to the teaching of the Bible was all that was necessary to a Christian and denied the infallibility of the Pope. The Church was alarmed at this spread of heresy and demanded the destruction of Lutheranism.

Charles's election as emperor had been greeted with elation in Germany, for the reformers expected that he would be on their side. But they misjudged Charles. He believed that the Church should be reformed, but he was against any change in its doctrines. For his part he failed utterly to grasp the significance of the Reformation and could not see that the points of view of the Protestants and the Catholics were quite irreconcilable.

But Charles refused to condemn Luther unheard, despite the urging of Pope Leo, and he summoned him to the assembly at Worms, where Luther refused to recant, saying he would not act against his conscience. There was nothing more that Charles could do and Luther was outlawed. A month later the famous Edict of Worms forbade the preaching of the new doctrines.

Charles had two other big problems to deal with—the continuous war with Francis and the invasion of the infidel Turks into Hungary and against the eastern frontier of his empire.

In fact Charles was probably one of the most harried monarchs who ever lived. He spent his whole reign travelling the length and breadth of his vast dominions to meet first one enemy then another. Not only was he dedicated and conscientious in the pursuit of his impossible task. He was also brave, for he led his armies personally in the field. But he was beset with so many problems, he never had time to solve any of them. He never learned how to govern, he had so many burdens on his shoulders. All through his reign he was haunted by his early mistakes, particularly those he made in Spain. Nevertheless he did not fail. He kept his scattered empire together. He made a brave attempt to bring the Lutherans back into the fold of the Mother Church, and he held up the advance of the Turks. He did this by dogged determination and hard work.

The continual enmity of Francis involved Charles in a protracted series of wars. One of the causes of this enmity was the feeling Francis had of being hemmed in between Charles's widespread territories. Both Charles and Francis claimed Burgundy and Milan, and the fight for these and other possessions went on between France and the overgrown power of the Habsburgs long after Charles and Francis were dead.

Most of the fighting took place in northern Italy, where neither Francis nor Charles distinguished themselves on the field of battle. Charles's greatest success was at the battle of Pavia, where his army, desperate, half-starved, turned on an apparently victorious French army which was attacking Pavia, and in a spectacular reversal of fortune destroyed it. Francis was wounded and taken prisoner and had to sign the Treaty of Madrid on 13 January, 1526, in order to get his freedom.

During that year Charles married Isabella, the Infanta of Portugal. In the true Habsburg tradition, he married for her rich dowry, though he fell in love with her after marriage. He had been engaged some ten times before and had an illegitimate daughter, Margaret, but he remained true to his wife while she lived. He never had a mistress or a court favourite as was usual in that immoral age. The only women who exercised any influence over him apart from his wife were his Aunt Margaret and his sister Mary, who both took over from him the burden of government in the Netherlands. In the same way his brother Ferdinand ruled in Austria and Germany during Charles's long absences.

After Pavia Charles ran short of money, despite the golden resources of his empire in the Americas, and was unable to pay his troops, who lived by plundering. They attacked and pillaged Rome, while the Pope fled in terror to the Castle of St. Angelo. This act aroused the conscience of the world, and Charles was held responsible, for while the sacred city was being sacked and despoiled by the Spanish and German ruffians of his army he was in Spain celebrating the birth of his son Philip with tournaments and festivities.

At this time both the Pope and Henry VIII, playing the Machiavellian game, had gone over to the side of France in order to prevent Charles becoming too powerful. The Pope in particular was afraid of Charles calling a General Council of Christendom in order to settle the Lutheran controversy. This was certainly in Charles's mind, but the Papacy were firmly against it, afraid it would damage the prestige of the Church.

With both England and France now allied against him, Charles lost all his gains in Italy except Naples and Milan. He was unable to assist his armies there, for the Spanish Cortes declined to grant monies which could be used for war against the Pope. But a sudden reversal of fortune occurred when Francis caused Genoa to revolt by putting a French Governor and garrison over them. The Genoese fleet thereupon went over to Charles and the French were forced out of Genoa. With the tide turned Charles was supreme in Italy once more, and came to terms with Pope Clement, who crowned him with great pomp at Bologna in 1530. He was the last emperor to be crowned by the Pope.

In the nine years in which Charles had been absent from Germany, Lutheranism had become firmly established. In 1535 there had been a peasant revolt in which the princes had been vicious in their alarmed retaliation. Luther, horrified at the dreadful result of his teachings, changed his policy in order to re-establish the authority of the princes. In 1526 the Diet of Speyer gave the rulers the right to determine the religion of their subjects.

Charles was engaged at the far eastern boundaries of his great empire where the Turks were at the gates of Vienna. Charles, with his usual dogged energy, assembled a fine army of Spaniards, Italians, Germans and Flemings. Suleiman the Magnificent, the Turks' famous Sultan, wisely withdrew in the face of Charles's imposing host.

Charles hastened to Spain, for there was no rest for him, to face the Turks on the Mediterranean front. Leading his troops in person, he conquered Tunis and freed hundreds of Christian slaves. Acclaimed as a hero, he returned to Italy to have another war with Francis in the late 1530s which ended with yet another inconclusive truce.

For the next sixteen years Charles continued to wrestle with his three great tasks—each one of which would have taxed the energies and abilities of any ruler. From fighting the Turks in Hungary or the Mediterranean, he went to wrestle with the Lutherans' consciences, and there was always Francis harrying him in Italy and elsewhere with constant warfare. He had no hope of solving the intractable problem of the split in the Church and a bitter civil war broke out in Germany. He defeated the army of the Protestant princes' Schmalkaldic League at Mühlberg, even though he was in wretched health and suffered continuously from gout.

In 1547 Francis died, to Charles's great relief. The tired, overtaxed emperor then made great efforts to effect peace where there was no peace. By 1552 all of Germany was once more aflame with war. Surrounded by his foes, Charles left Augsburg for Innsbruck, from whence he had to make an ignominious flight in a snowstorm at midnight across the Brenner Pass, carried on a litter and with only six attendants. Weary and disillusioned, he was already considering unshouldering his enormous burden.

The bitter civil war in Germany was finally pacified by the Peace of Augsburg in 1555, which laid it down that in future any prince might be allowed to choose his own religion, and his subjects must accept his choice or go into exile.

In that same year Charles solemnly abdicated at Brussels before the assembled deputies of the Netherlands. He gave his empire and his German lands to his brother Ferdinand, and Spain, the Burgundian lands and Italy to his son Philip.

He retired to a small house attached to the monastery at Yuste in Spain. Then came the happiest time of his life, for he was by no means a recluse. He took with him his favourite books and pictures, his fine clothing and jewels, and he kept in constant touch with his friends and relations. His son Philip often came seeking his advice. He enjoyed gardening and watching Torriani at his bench making clocks and mechanical toys.

But his health was bad. He still suffered from gout and his insatiable gastronomic indulgence considerably shortened his life. He enjoyed his retirement for only two years, and a little before his death he held a rehearsal of his own funeral. The last of the great Holy Roman Emperors died on 30 September, 1558, clasping his wife's crucifix in his hands.

CATHERINE DE' MEDICI

(1519–89)

CATHERINE DE' MEDICI of France rivals Mary I of England as Europe's most vilified queen. It was fortunate for her that John Foxe's *Book of Martyrs* was published before the Massacre of St. Bartholomew, or she would have been mercilessly pilloried in that famous work of Protestant martyrology. Catherine cannot escape responsibility for that terrible event. Her name is for ever besmirched with it. But she was not the only ruthless and cynical person in Paris at that time. Religious fanaticism belonged to the people. Their rulers took political advantage of it.

The name of Medici, too, was no recommendation. As a family, they were alleged to be steeped in crime and vice and to be adept at poisoning their political rivals. Catherine de' Medici was accused of introducing this toxic form of politics into France in order to gain power. No doubt much of this was exaggerated, but in the final count Catherine does not escape blameless, even if the excuse is made for her that she was after all only a creature of her age.

Legend has it that the Medici family was founded by Perseus, and that Benvenuto Cellini's famous bronze of Perseus holding on high the head of Medusa was executed at Florence to symbolize the victory of the Medici over the republic. The Medici name is an illustrious one in the chronicles of Florence, and they were princes of the state as well as of commerce. Lorenzo the Magnificent was one of the greatest figures of the Renaissance. Two Medicis became Popes and two queens of France. They were one of the great families of Europe.

Catherine was born in 1519 at Florence, the daughter of Lorenzo II, the Duke of Urbino, and Princess Madeleine de la Tour d'Auvergne. Both her parents died when she was a child, and she was adopted by her uncle, Pope Clement VII, and educated at a convent. Clement was the Pope who refused Henry VIII his divorce from Catherine of Aragon.

Clement arranged an excellent marriage for his orphaned niece with Prince Henry of Valois, the second son of King Francis I of France. The marriage took place at Marseilles in 1533. Both bride and bridegroom were fourteen, and as was not unusual in royal marriages saw each other for the first time when they met at the altar.

Catherine went to the Court of her father-in-law and at first showed no sign of the dominant personality she later became. Straight from the convent she had much to learn, and she learnt her lesson well in the brilliant and sophisticated Court of Francis I.

When the Dauphin died in 1536, Henry unexpectedly became heir to the throne and Catherine the future Queen of France. All the same she was not liked, and malicious tongues wagged about her, saying that she had employed one of the Medici family poisoners to do away with the Dauphin.

But the greatest threat to Catherine's influence was Diane de Poitiers, a middle-aged adventuress, who completely captivated the young Prince Henry, and inflamed him with a passion which lasted until the day of his death. Diane de Poitiers was a clever and ambitious woman who successfully set out to dominate the future king. It was said that she had also been the mistress of his father, Francis I, though this story has little foundation. Francis died in 1547, and though Catherine de' Medici became Queen of France in name Diane de Poitiers was virtual queen. She set about the task of enriching herself and her family. Henry II gave her the Duchy of Valentinois as well as many of the crown jewels.

During this time Catherine de' Medici waited patiently in obscurity. For the first ten years of the marriage she bore Henry no child. Her enemies accused her of lesbianism, and there was talk of divorce even before the old king died. But Henry was fond of Catherine in a brotherly kind of way, and with his accession to the throne the necessity of having children was taken more seriously, and then Catherine bore him sons and daughters in rapid succession.

The Reformation which had been demanded in vain from the Papacy in the fifteenth century was now being brought about in the Church without the assistance of the Popes, to the accompaniment of much strife, persecution and bitterness. In France Protestantism evolved into a political party called the Huguenots, the leader of which was Gaspard Coligny, Admiral of France.

Henry II was a bigoted Catholic, and ruthlessly opposed Protestantism, using his royal authority with great severity against all opposition. His death on 10 July, 1559, following a head wound received while tilting with the Count de Montgomery at a royal tournament was no cause for universal sorrow, even though his heir was a sickly, nervous boy of fifteen, Francis II.

The first thing Catherine de' Medici did was to banish Diane de Poitiers from the Court and force her to give up the crown jewels Henry had given her, as well as many valuable lands and possessions. Diane retired to her château at Anet, where she died in 1566.

The boy king during his brief reign was completely dominated by his mother and his wife. Francis was married to Mary Queen of Scots, who, at the age of seventeen, and in the full bloom of her legendary beauty, became Queen of France. Mary was related to the powerful Guise family, who were the leaders of the Catholic faction in France. Through her, Francis Duke of Guise gained control of the army, and his brother, Cardinal of Lorraine, held a high position in the councils of State.

The youthful king suffered from a hereditary disease which made him impotent. All the same, he and his young and glamorous queen were said to be devoted to each other. Mary, at this stage in her famous career, had little interest in politics, and was content to be completely under the influence of her uncles, the two powerful Guises.

The Guises came from Lorraine and were considered by many to be no more French than the Italian Queen Mother. Their rivals were the Bourbon branch of the royal family led by the King of Navarre and the Prince of Condé, who were Protestants. In this battle for power in France Catherine de' Medici held a key position, and she now began to play a skilful game which showed that she had learned much during the years of her husband's reign when she had waited patiently in the background, living a passive but observant life. But those days were over, as France very soon discovered.

The Guises did not like her, and she was determined to break their power. She was equally determined not to throw in her lot with the Protestants. By habit and tradition a Catholic, she did not intend that the Protestants should gain the upper hand. She did not want them crushed either, as they were too valuable a counterbalance to the powerful Guises. She eventually proved a match for them all.

By the end of 1560 the sickly Francis II was in his grave and the predominance of the Guises was seriously undermined. Naturally enough they accused the Queen Mother of poisoning her son—after all she was a Medici. Catherine's second son, Charles, now came to the throne at the age of ten, as Charles IX. As was to be expected, he was completely dominated by his formidable mother, now forty-one, shrewd, vigorous, with a taste for power, and who immediately had herself made regent.

Up until that moment she had appeared to be little more than the retiring and self-sacrificing widow of Henry II. Suddenly she was supreme in France, unexpectedly imperious, and both the Bourbons and the Guises were forced to bow to her. They underrated her only at their peril, for she had a fine and subtle political sense and an Italian adroitness at intrigue. Behind her she had powerful men like Montmorency, Constable of France, Michel de l'Hôpital, who was Chancellor and her spokesman in the States General. For many years she now ruled France.

The impassioned religious battle of the Reformation, which stirred all Christendom as it had never been stirred before, left Catherine de' Medici cold. Like many people of today, she wondered what all the fuss was about. Trifles like images and vestments and whether the Mass should be said in Latin or French were certainly not worth fighting over in her opinion, and should be settled at a conference table. She shared none of the violence and intolerance of the Catholics and Calvinists, and believed that their differences could only be solved through the middle path of toleration.

She was, of course, entirely right in this, and hers was the only sane voice in France, if not Europe, at that time. But all her efforts at compromise came to nothing on account of the rage, suspicion and hatred which the division of Christianity had created in men's minds. Frenchmen found it impossible to worship God in their own particular way without fighting each other.

Her curiously modern approach to a subject which her age found quite intractable culminated in a meeting she summoned in August, 1561, of the leaders of both religious sides, at which she tried to get them to agree to some common ground. But the men of God only came to blows. Catherine then granted the Huguenots restricted rights of worship. The result was civil war.

The Wars of Religion, as they were called, began with the Massacre of Vassy on 1 March, 1562, and continued for the rest of Catherine's life. The fanaticism of both sides made the struggle more ferocious and brutal than an ordinary war. Terrible cruelties were committed, and the country was devastated. The Catholics were actively supported by Philip II of Spain, the Pope and the Italian states, while Elizabeth of England, the Lutherans and Calvinists of Germany and the Low Countries supported the Protestants.

During the first war, which lasted a year, both sides lost their leaders, including the powerful Duke of Guise, who was killed while attacking Orléans in February, 1563. The Peace of Amboise followed a month later, after which Protestants and Catholics united to drive out the English who had invaded France.

Catherine still wanted to settle the burning religious issue peacefully. She tried to persuade Philip II to form a Catholic Holy Alliance which would combat heresy without the use of force. But the time for reason and moderation was not yet, and the war broke out again. Neither side could gain a decision.

By 1570 Catherine, weary of the conflict and unable to crush the Protestant rebellion, once more tried negotiation. This time she proposed two diplomatic marriages, one between her son, Henry, and Elizabeth of England, and the other between her daughter, Margaret de Valois, and Henry of Navarre. Only the latter union was agreed, and Catherine thus became reconciled with the Protestants.

The Huguenot leader Coligny was allowed to return to Court and was admitted once more to the Council of State. It was a move Catherine quickly repented. Charles IX, now twenty, married to Elizabeth of Austria, dreamed of cutting a figure in the world. He was getting tired of being tied to the political apron-strings of his formidable mother. He received the celebrated Coligny with open arms, and the two became great friends.

Coligny, determined to emancipate the young king from the powerful influence of Catherine, put forward a proposition for ending the ruinous civil war which was tearing France apart and which threatened to break out again. He proposed a great national war against Spain. In this way the people of France would combine, regardless of their religious differences, and attack the Spanish Netherlands, with Charles at the head of the Army.

The idea appealed immensely to Charles who very much wanted to distinguish himself on the field of battle, but it greatly alarmed both the Queen Mother and the staunchly Catholic Guises. Their attempts to prevent it resulted in one of the most appalling massacres of European history.

Originally the intention was to get the dangerous Coligny out of the way by having him assassinated. This, in theory, was no difficult operation in the circumstances existing in France, and was nothing that Catherine de' Medici would have on her conscience, murder being part of the working of politics as she conceived it. The murder was arranged with Henry of Guise.

Just at this time there took place in Paris the marriage of Henry of Navarre—the heir to the French throne, should the sons of Catherine de' Medici die childless, which seemed probable—and

Margaret of Valois, Catherine's daughter. Henry of Navarre was France's man of destiny, who was to become the first of the Bourbon kings. The marriage was greatly favoured by Charles IX, though as a "mixed marriage" it scandalized the Catholics.

Three days after the marriage an attempt was made to murder Coligny as he left a Council of State meeting in the Louvre. The attempt failed and Coligny was only superficially wounded by shots.

The king was furious, and in order to prevent his discovery of her part in the attempted murder Catherine invented a story of a great Huguenot conspiracy led by Coligny. Charles took a lot of persuading, but his mother knew how to handle him and finally convinced him that what she said was true. Then the unstable Charles gave the fatal order to kill all the Huguenots in Paris.

The Huguenots had gathered in great numbers in Paris for the wedding between Protestant Henry of Navarre and the king's sister, and on the eve of St. Bartholomew's Day, 23 August, 1572, the signal was given and the massacre of the Huguenots began. Among the first to be killed was Coligny. In two days it was estimated that 10,000 Protestants had been killed. Once the slaughter had begun, it was impossible to restrain the fanatical populace, and the massacre continued in Paris until 17 September. It spread to the provinces, where it continued until 3 October. It was estimated that the number killed throughout France was 50,000.

The blame for this atrocity rests heavily upon Catherine de' Medici, who, unlike the populace, did not even have the excuse of fanaticism. She was not, however, universally blamed. Far from it. She received the congratulations of all the Catholic powers, and Pope Gregory XIII ordered that bonfires should be lighted and that this example of French loyalty to the Church should be signalized by a medal of commendation.

This shocking event did nothing to check Catherine's supremacy in France. Charles IX died two years later, haunted, fever-stricken, melancholic, and was succeeded by his brother, Henry III, another impotent weakling whom Catherine was easily able to dominate. The war and bloodshed between Protestants and Catholics continued until her death in January, 1589. Within a few months Henry III was murdered, and the religious fratricide in France was not stopped until Henry of Navarre ascended the throne as Henry IV.

He became a Catholic and under the Edict of Nantes granted toleration of worship to the Protestants. "Paris is worth a mass," he said, an attitude which Catherine of Medici would have thoroughly approved.

PHILIP II

King of Spain, Naples and Sicily

(1527–98)

THE RISE of Spain in the sixteenth century to a position of world power is one of the most dramatic events in world history. Whilst in the Middle Ages England and France, in different ways, were becoming powerful nation states, the Iberian peninsula was split up into a large number of Christian and Moorish principalities. At the end of the fourteenth century the Christian kings had conquered the Moors, all but the rich and highly civilized kingdom of Granada in the south-east. There was, however, no unity in the peninsula and it was not until the second half of the fifteenth century, when Castile and Aragon were united under Isabella and Ferdinand, that Granada fell and, with the exception of the western kingdom of Portugal, the rest of Spain acknowledged the sway of the monarchs of the two most powerful kingdoms.

Spain was born slowly and late but destined to become almost at once a world power such as had never been seen before. For a short while Spain ruled over an enormously larger part of the world than Rome had ever done. As events showed, it was an ephemeral empire constantly at war, and Spain had not the strength to sustain it nor sufficient economic foresight to use the immense wealth which she won from the New World to keep the homeland of this empire strong. But throughout the sixteenth century—from Henry VII to Queen Elizabeth—when Englishmen looked abroad they saw Spain as by far the most powerful nation of the world. Spain was a dominant power in Italy, the most civilized part of Europe, and owned the Netherlands which comprised Holland and Belgium and a large part of northern France; indeed French frontiers at that time began on the Somme. Spanish infantry were the best in Europe, and Spain's power at sea, though increasingly challenged by the English and Dutch pirates, was considered invincible until very late in the sixteenth century.

Marriage turned Spain into a European power at the same time that the Conquistadores who followed Columbus gave her a colonial empire. The daughter of Ferdinand and Isabella, Juana, married Philip, the son of the Habsburg Archduke of Austria, Maximilian I, who was also the Holy Roman Emperor, overlord, that is to say, of most of the kingdoms of Germany.

Maximilian by marriage had obtained Burgundy (which he afterwards lost to France) and the Netherlands. By another marriage he became lord of the Duchy of Milan, one of the richest parts of Italy. Now Maximilian's grandson by the marriage of Philip and Juana inherited Spain and her immense empire and also the Italian possessions of Spain—which included Sardinia, the kingdom of Naples and of Sicily. So this young Habsburg ruled over between a third and a half of Europe—excluding the large part of eastern Europe in the hands of the Ottoman Turks. This grandson, duly elected Holy Roman Emperor, was Charles V, whose aunt, Catherine of Aragon, married Henry VIII of England. The huge domains and the great ambition of Charles V led him into the wild dream, which was rather more than two hundred years old, of trying to unite Christendom. His European policy failed. Charles could, however, very fairly claim that he was a "European".

He was distinctly more an Austrian than a Spaniard in character and mind, but more than either he was a man of the Low Countries. He was most at home in Brussels, and when he came to Spain, as he did at infrequent intervals, he brought with him Flemings as advisers and friends. Towards the end of his life he grew rather more Spanish and married the daughter of the King of Portugal. After her death, he married his young son Philip to another Portuguese princess who died two years later in childbirth, bringing Philip a son, Don Carlos, who was later to cause him much misfortune.

In 1554 Charles V, still bent on his dynastic policies, married his dutiful, serious-minded son, for a second time, to a woman of thirty-six, Mary Tudor, Queen of England, the daughter of Catherine of Aragon. In 1556 the now aged Charles V summoned his son Philip from England, where he was expecting a son from his new wife, to Brussels, where he announced his abdication and his retirement to a monastery in southern Spain. But now the House of Austria limited its ambitions. The Holy Roman Empire and the lands of Austria went to Charles's brother. Philip, now Philip II of Spain, received by far the major part—Spain and its empire, the Low Countries, Milan and the old Spanish possessions in Italy.

In July, 1554, Philip landed in Southampton with the Duke of

Alba and a number of grandees and their wives and the next day he rode to Winchester, through pouring rain, where the queen was waiting for him. It poured with rain and the king was soaked to the skin. He was taken to her apartments in the bishop's palace through a number of narrow gardens between high walls and up a winding staircase to a back door into the great hall. One of Philip's biographers, Mr. William Thomas Walsh, has described the scene:

> *It was Philip's first glimpse of his second wife; she was walking up and down as he entered, a short slender woman in a black velvet gown with a petticoat of frosted silver and a jewelled girdle and collar. Her complexion was red and white, her hair reddish, her face round, her nose rather low and wide, the whole expression indicating great kindness and clemency; and, adds the Venetian ambassador, to whom we are indebted for the description of Mary, were not her age on the decline, she might be called handsome rather than the contrary.*

Philip on his father's instructions did everything he could to please the English, including the drinking of beer, a beverage which, according to Froude, made him shudder. He became popular with the English, though the very Protestant burghers of London distrusted him. He was a good horseman, and with his white skin, flaxen hair and beard he might have been an Englishman. The marriage was not unpopular either, and it will be remembered that Mary's mother, Catherine of Aragon, had been very much liked by the English people.

The marriage was to the advantage of England, for among its terms was that England should not be drawn into Spanish wars. Charles V, anxious about his Europe rather than his Spain, wanted to see the long-standing, close relationship between England and the Netherlands strengthened so that these countries should for ever stand as a barrier against France. When it was announced that Mary was pregnant there was much public rejoicing except among the extreme Protestant section of the population. The pregnancy turned out to be an illusion. By that time the Marian persecutions of Protestants had begun and the queen was fast losing her popularity.

Historians disagree over Philip's role in this, but most authorities consider that ever mindful of what his brief had been from his father, he advised against the persecutions and other acts liable to inflame English opinion. Philip was not against the persecution of heretics in general, but he was above all politic. He reconciled Princess Elizabeth, the daughter of Anne Boleyn, with her half-sister the queen, and after he had left England for Spain, and when it was clear that Mary would never bear him a son, he supported, by every means in his power, the accession of Elizabeth to the throne, even though she was suspect of leaning towards the Protestants. He preferred a heretic Queen of England with whom he was on good terms to the Catholic Mary Stuart who was closely bound up with France and was another pretender.

In 1559 Philip returned to Spain which he was never afterwards to leave. Not liked in the Low Countries or in Germany, he became the most Spanish of kings, and by temperament and character admirably suited to rule the Spaniards. He governed Spain as autocrat, keeping power in his own hands over everything, making his decisions slowly and after a great deal of thought. From the Escorial, the monastery-palace which he built near Madrid, the king's written orders made their way across the Atlantic and all over Europe, precise, carefully worded and no doubt by the time they reached his viceroys or commanders in Brussels or Mexico City, often infuriatingly out-of-date.

Philip believed in slowness and method. He was not an absolute monarch in the sense that Louis XIV was. Every Spanish province had its Cortes or its Junta with carefully preserved traditions and prejudices. Philip had to go before all these bodies before he received a penny in taxes or could be sure of enforcing his laws. He completed the unity of Spain, balancing the needs of sovereignty and the rights and susceptibilities of the Spanish provinces in a system of government which combined absolutism and enlightened evolution. As a recent historian has said: "Whatever else he did for the Spaniards, he knew how to govern them."

The reign of Philip II is notable for the revival of the Inquisition in Spain which had flourished in the reign of Ferdinand and Isabella. The Inquisition has incurred abroad, and particularly in Protestant countries, a hatred which it only partly deserves. In the Netherlands, where increasingly it was used not to convert heretics so much as to enforce Spanish domination, it was no doubt a detestable institution. In Spain too the burning of heretics cannot commend itself to the general conscience of mankind. But the fact is that the Inquisition was popular with the nation as a whole, and the small extremist sects of Protestants who had grown up in Barcelona or Seville were feared and disliked as allies of Spain's enemies. The people also feared, and were jealous of, the numerous converted Moors and Jews whose reliability as Christians and Spaniards was examined by the Inquisition. Heresy was strangled at birth; if the means employed were sometimes atrocious the executions and expulsions fortified the weak plant of Spanish unity and saved Spain from the religious civil wars which brought France to the brink of ruin.

From the start of his reign until its end, Philip was committed to waging wars on several fronts. The unavoidable struggle was against the Turks, a war to which he was committed as the head of the most powerful Christian kingdom of Europe, a Mediterranean power directly threatened by the Turkish fleet and the ally of Austria most threatened by the Turkish armies. In the reign of Charles V, Suleiman the Magnificent's forces defeated and killed the King of Hungary at the battle of Mohacs in 1526 and three years later nearly took Vienna. Although Charles V managed to check the Turkish advance into Europe, he suffered severe reverses on sea and in North Africa.

Philip was more successful than his father by waging war in the Mediterranean more prudently. He relieved Malta rather at the last moment. He refrained from offensive operations, concentrating on protecting Italy and the coast of Spain. In 1571, in alliance with the Pope and the Republic of Venice, the Spanish fleet commanded by John of Austria, Philip's illegitimate half-brother, inflicted a crushing defeat on the Turks at Lepanto. All the sovereigns of Europe, including Queen Elizabeth, sent messages of congratulation to Philip. Lepanto did not end the Turkish menace, but, after Lepanto, though the Turks drove Spain from parts of Tunisia, Turkish sea-power slowly declined.

In Charles V's reign Spain and France had constantly fought each other in Italy and the Low Countries, with the Pope, Venice and England now on one side, now on the other. In 1559 there supervened a period of peace between Spain and France. Philip married Henry II's daughter, Elizabeth of Valois, after Mary's death, his third diplomatic marriage. But, soon after, the wars of religion in France saw Spanish armies fighting in France on the side of the Catholic League, sometimes against the King of France. Philip considered himself the defender of the Catholic faith everywhere; but it was because a France which tolerated religious freedom would inevitably be drawn to support the revolt of the Netherlands that Philip intervened so persistently.

The Netherlands were economically of vital importance to Spain, a market for her wool and her raw materials from America and the source of her textiles, her metallurgical needs and a great deal of her munitions of war. Antwerp, Bruges, and Ghent were great banking and entrepôt centres which rendered vital services to Spain. These close economic ties made the Spanish connexion not irksome to the nobility and merchants of the Netherlands and, under Charles V, their country was part of a European empire and ruled by a prince who understood them.

Philip, however, was a Spanish king. Further, he was determined to check the rapid spread of heresy—Lutheran, Calvinist and Anabaptist—in the Netherlands, and so, little by little, the revolt against Spain became general. Spanish troops by 1557 were concentrated massively in the Low Countries under the Duke of Alba to break revolts which were gradually winning over the Flemish nobles such as Egmont and the Prince of Orange. For a time Alba and his seasoned troops succeeded in repressing revolts, and at the Battle of Gembloux in 1578 the Spanish victory decided the maintenance of the southern provinces in their Spanish allegiance. The northern provinces, which are now Holland, defied Spain on land and sea with their pirate ships.

Open war with England did not begin until 1585. Of course, England and Englishmen sympathized with the Protestants in France and with the rebels in the Netherlands. But Philip had been careful never to support, in any incriminating or decisive manner, the Catholic fifth-column in England, and Elizabeth had pursued a middle-of-the-road policy in religious matters.

The cause of the open clash between Spain and England was the activities of the English mariners who were determined to break down the Spanish ban on trade with the New World, first in the Caribbean and then in the Pacific. Piracy was a sign of England's weakness and inability to challenge Spain's empire in a serious manner. It amounted to "singeing the King of Spain's beard", in Drake's celebrated phrase. The Spanish treasure-fleets, and Spanish trade, were comparatively little affected. The exploits of Drake aroused tremendous patriotic enthusiasm in England. The feeling of insecurity which Spanish merchants and traders began to have was more important than their actual losses; nevertheless, men hesitated a little before investing in trade ventures and a great cry arose in Spain for punishing England. Philip, prudent as ever, began to see, as the exploits of British seamen grew more daring, that Elizabeth was waging an undeclared war against him at sea, and, what counted for more, in the Netherlands.

Philip's fortunes seemed to reach a new height. The Turks had been defeated; the affairs of the Catholic League in France were going well; the Pope, so often opposed to Spain, was friendly. In 1583 Philip became King of Portugal and at one stroke acquired

Portugal's vast possessions in Africa and in India. With Lisbon in his hands a vigorous emphasis on Atlantic policy was inevitable. He began to build up the Great Armada to conquer England. The defeat of this Armada in 1588 was the greatest blow Philip had ever sustained. It was a triumph for English seamanship, even if it was the winds which finally blew the huge fleet of Medina Sidonia around the inhospitable coasts of Scotland and Ireland. But the defeat of the Armada did not shatter Spain's maritime power. Yet Spain waging war now with England, Holland and France was much weaker ten years after the Armada's defeat, and the great outburst of Spanish energy which had begun a hundred years before with the conquest of Granada and the voyage of Columbus was beginning to ebb away.

Philip knew a period of great happiness from his marriage with Elizabeth of Valois, whom he sincerely loved and who bore him two daughters. To them Philip was strongly attached, and in his letters to them at various ages one gets a glimpse of the man behind the cold formal exterior. The period of domestic happiness was spoilt by the terrible affair of Don Carlos, Philip's son, with his over-large head, his stammer, recurrent fevers and violent temper. Don Carlos did not appear likely to make a suitable heir to the throne. He had absurd ambitions, among them that of being sent as Viceroy to the Netherlands. He immersed himself in intrigues which, though childish, were dangerous since he was the heir to the throne. His private behaviour grew more eccentric. He would seize women in the streets, kissing them exuberantly and, at the same time, insulting them. He was impertinent to ladies of the Court and only reverenced the queen, whom he appeared to love almost as though he would be his father's rival.

As a matter of duty, the king felt obliged to act after many provocations. In January, 1568, he kept Don Carlos in the strictest seclusion in the Alcazar Palace. Philip wrote to the Pope and to his ambassadors abroad giving his reason for this painful decision. He could not bring himself to speak of Don Carlos as insane, nor did he accuse him of sedition, but he stated that it would be dangerous for Spain and the world as a whole if Don Carlos were to be allowed to succeed him.

Then in July, 1568, Don Carlos died in prison in circumstances which are unknown. There is no evidence that he died of strangulation or beheading or poison; nor either that he died as a result of his own excesses in prison. The death of Don Carlos was followed by a bitter blow in October of the same year in the death of Elizabeth of Valois. Philip married a fourth time; his wife, Anne of Austria, gave him a son, Philip III. All who knew the King realized that his great affection for his two daughters by Elizabeth was a sign of his attachment to the only family happiness he had known.

A balance-sheet of Philip's achievements would be read somewhat as follows. Against him it can be said that he did not disengage Spain from any of the many-sided struggles against the Turks, in Italy and France, in the Low Countries and in England, which exhausted her vitality. He bears the responsibility for this because he deliberately decided everything himself. He failed to have a sufficiently practical view of economics and social affairs and he allowed the Spanish countryside to be depopulated and industries to decay, relying on the silver brought to him from the New World in his galleons. Whilst not normally a man of blood, he believed in repression and supported the Spanish Inquisition and the Roman Inquisition in the Netherlands. If his enemies accused him of frequent villainies and of the murder of Don Carlos, the latter is certainly unproven, and his general behaviour towards his enemies, or half-enemies, was no worse than that of other sixteenth-century sovereigns.

There is much to be said in his favour. He governed Spain well, completed Spanish unity and did much to favour science and the arts. Spain had conquered Mexico and Peru, and the worst excesses of the Conquistadores had taken place before he reigned. It was during his reign that Spain sent to the Americas its best bishops and monks and professors and that the great work of civilizing the colonies took place. Indian students attended the great University of Mexico, founded in his time. Latin America under Philip grew a thousand firm roots in Latin and Christian culture. By his policies, Spain preserved the Catholic faith in the southern provinces of the Netherlands and shielded her own people from religious conflict.

Finally, it must be said of Philip as a ruler that, except for the Protestant provinces of the Netherlands—those which make up Holland—he lost nothing and added Portugal to the Spanish Crown. Spain at his death was exhausted, but still for a long while preserved her hegemony in Europe. Many historians consider that Philip's father, Charles V, was a far greater man. He may have been a more attractive character in some respects. But his great dynastic designs failed, his defence of the Church was ineffective and he left the Spanish Treasury bankrupt. Philip II, on the other hand, succeeded in what he set himself to do. His device could well be that of one of Spain's enemies, the Prince of Orange: "I will maintain."

ATAHUALPA

(*d.* 1533)

OF ALL the Europeans who went to the New World in the wake of Columbus, the Spaniards made the worst colonists. While others sought trade, they sought only gold and silver, and they succeeded in turning the natives' happiness and prosperity into misery and death, and wrecking their own economy in Spain in the process. The only civilizing agency which the Spaniards took to the New World was that of their Church, which finally had to restrain the scandalous rapacity of the Castilian adventurers.

But at first there was no restraint. Cortes destroyed the Aztec civilization in Mexico in 1520 by the use of every means of guile, treachery and cruelty. Loot was the main consideration of these conquering Spaniards, and when they heard stories of the fabulous Kingdom of Gold to the south they turned their eyes to Peru where the young Inca Emperor Atahualpa had just ascended the throne in Cuzco, the ancient Andean capital.

This civilization had flourished for two and a half thousand years and had been developed by various peoples, the last of whom were the Incas, who incidentally claimed for themselves a disproportionate amount of the credit for it. While the Incas did not have the same skills as the Aztecs, they excelled at engineering, constructing great roads, tunnels and bridges, and built spectacular monuments and fortifications.

In their cities among the cloud-capped mountains dwelt extraordinary ant-like communities where every person was moulded rigidly into an unalterable caste system. It was a strict totalitarian society in which everyone had his place, had to do prescribed work, and dress in a certain manner. Commoners were allowed to wear only simple clothes. Nobles were richly attired. At the top the emperor, in the finest clothes of all, was supreme and divine. He married within his family, usually his sister, in order to keep the blood-line pure. But he enjoyed a large selection of concubines and propagated numbers of natural children. Polygamy was permitted to the nobles, but not to the commoners, who were allowed only one wife. Obedience to the law was everywhere enforced with stern severity. The Incas worshipped the sun, of which their emperor—known as the Inca—was the deification on earth. The Incas' form of state socialism involved the suppression of personality and enterprise, though it provided the people with a certain security.

Inca agriculture was probably in advance of anything in Europe at that time. They had developed spinning, weaving and pottery-making to a great art. The country was rich in gold and silver mines, which were the personal property of the emperor, as were the large flocks of llama and alpaca which provided food, wool and transport. The horse was unknown in America until the Spaniards came. Yet, despite their civilization, the Incas had not discovered the art of writing, nor how to make a wheel.

Atahualpa's father was Huayna Capac, who was one of the great Incas. Atahualpa was not his true heir, as his mother was the daughter of the King of Quito, which Huayna Capac conquered. It is not likely that this princess was Huayna's lawful wife, for according to Inca custom that could only be his sister. By his sister Huayna had a son, Huascar, who by rights should have been his heir.

But the Inca developed a great love for his son by the Quito princess, and saw in him more promising qualities than in Huascar, so he resolved to break from tradition and divide his empire between his two sons. It was not surprising therefore that after the Inca's death in 1525 the brothers fell out and went to war with each other. Atahualpa won and at his moment of triumph the Spaniards invaded.

Though a brave, ambitious and clever young man, Atahualpa did not have his father's foresight or vision. But he was bold, high-minded, and, within his lights, liberal. A talented and valorous commander, he was accused of being cruel in his wars. He was said to be handsome, though there was a fierce expression to his face, emphasized by bloodshot eyes.

Francisco Pizarro, the man whose cupidity was most aroused by the legendary wealth of the Inca empire, was a Spanish adventurer of illegitimate birth who had been with Balboa at the historic moment of the first discovery of the Pacific. Ruthless, greedy, treacherous and possessed of great courage, Pizarro had the vices, but not the virtues, of Cortes. He had got himself commissioned by Charles V to undertake an expedition of exploration and conquest down the west coast of South America, then completely unknown territory. In 1529 he was made Governor and Captain General of the Spanish colony of New Castile—as Peru was then called. His commission was to go and conquer it. He was required to take a specified number of priests with him to convert the conquered Incas.

In 1532 Pizarro arrived in the dominions of Atahualpa, then totally unaware of the fact that his ancient empire had already been annexed by a monarch he had never heard of. The Spaniards were fired by tales of the incredible wealth awaiting them in the splendid land of the Incas, where the streets of the cities were said to be paved with gold.

Pizarro cautiously penetrated into Peru. His tiny, well-equipped army consisted of a mere 180 men and 27 horses for use as cavalry. When a captured Peruvian told him that the Inca awaited him with an army of more than 50,000, Pizarro paused and decided to proceed by guile. As he approached Caxamalca, where Atahualpa had his headquarters, he sent emissaries ahead proposing a meeting.

Atahualpa sent one of his nobles to meet Pizarro. The encounter took place in a pass in the Cordilleras. The Peruvian, while extolling the military might of his master, expressed the Inca's desire to extend hospitality to the strangers. Pizarro was less diplomatic, reminding the Peruvian of the inferiority of the Inca to the great and powerful monarch who ruled over the white men, and pointing out the ease with which a few Spaniards had overrun this great continent. But he came in a friendly spirit, declared Pizarro magnanimously. He had been led to visit Peru by the fame of the Inca, and to offer him his services in his wars, and he trusted his friendly spirit would be reciprocated.

We are not told how Atahualpa received this hardly gratuitous offer of a military assistance he did not require. The Inca was not deceived by the overtures from these mysterious strangers from an unknown world who fearlessly entered his realms after a march which would have daunted the boldest spirit in Peru. Atahualpa was credited with the intention of luring them deep into his land and then destroying those he did not wish to capture.

He did not dream that Pizarro's plan was to capture him. Indeed, the audacious and inspired plan of this unprincipled Spanish adventurer must commend itself to anyone who admires desperate daring. Pizarro's dealing with the last of the Incas is reckoned to be the blackest page of Spain's shameful colonial history. But it was the only way in which he, with a mere 180 men at his command, could conquer a nation which had a large army in the field. Pizarro decided to strike right at the heart, knowing that the Incas, without their leader, would collapse.

Pizarro with his little army entered Caxamalca on 15 November, 1532, and sent an invitation to the Inca to visit him for a conference. Atahualpa agreed and came into Caxamalca the following evening. He arrived in state, carried on a magnificent litter, accompanied by unarmed attendants.

There is no doubt that Atahualpa made this visit in good faith, though he probably distrusted the Spaniards' sincerity. In accepting their hospitality, he intended to impress them with his royal state. It never occurred to him that any attempt would be made upon him—here in the middle of his own empire, where he was absolute, where his word meant life and death, and where his armies were but a few miles away. The Spaniards, despite their frightening weapons, were absurdly few in number. He plainly did not understand the sort of men he was dealing with.

The Inca was first of all approached by Vicente de Valverde, Pizarro's chaplain, a Bible in one hand, crucifix in the other. The priest, through an interpreter, stated baldly and dogmatically the tenets of the Christian faith as seen through Roman Catholic eyes. He told him that the Pope had authorized the Emperor Charles V to conquer and convert the country of the Incas. Therefore Atahualpa must abandon the errors of his own faith, become a Christian and acknowledge Charles V as his master.

Atahualpa had difficulty in grasping the chain of argument by which the priest connected Pizarro with St. Peter. But the demand that he should abdicate his monarchy in favour of another was plain. He indignantly refused to recognize Charles V. "As for the Pope of whom you speak, he must be crazy to talk of giving away countries which do not belong to him." By what authority did Valverde speak? The priest replied the Bible and handed it to Atahualpa, who looked at it and threw it contemptuously on the ground.

"Tell your comrades that they shall give me an account of their doings in my land," he exclaimed. "I will not go from here until they have made me full satisfaction for all the wrongs they have committed."

The indignant Valverde, outraged at the Inca's insult to the holy book, hastened to Pizarro and recounted what had happened. "Set on them at once," the priest said. "I absolve you." Pizarro then gave the signal and his men fell upon the unarmed Peruvians from all sides and butchered them in hundreds. The bloodthirsty Spaniards wanted to kill the Inca as well, but Pizarro rescued him with his own hands, receiving in the process a minor cut—the only wound inflicted on a Spaniard that day. The unhappy monarch, strongly secured, was removed to a building nearby under heavy guard.

Upon the news of the capture of Atahualpa, the regimented and ant-like society of the Incas was immediately paralysed. The country was so dependent upon the monarch's orders that when he was captured by the invaders Peru was helpless. Pizarro's gamble came off brilliantly.

The Spaniards kept Atahualpa prisoner for many months. He impressed them by his dignity, good humour and fortitude. He was allowed to carry on his government while in the Spanish hands, and his captors marvelled at the utter servility the Peruvians displayed to him.

The Spaniards allowed him the consolation of his wives and concubines. At the same time they were busy propagating the true faith among the heathen Incas, and they converted one of the Caxamalcan temples into a church.

Atahualpa himself was not long in discovering that amidst all this show of religious zeal the passion which burnt most fiercely in the hearts of his conquerors was the lust for gold. He therefore offered Pizarro a room full of gold and silver in exchange for his freedom. Pizarro avidly accepted, though he had no intention of keeping the bargain. Atahualpa sent his emissaries to collect the treasure and assemble it in Caxamalca.

Having ensured, as he thought, his freedom, Atahualpa became acutely conscious of the existence of his brother Huascar, whom he had dethroned and imprisoned, and who as the son of his father's sister-wife was the true heir and the true Inca. Atahualpa had everything to fear from Huascar now, so he gave secret orders for his death, which his slavish minions immediately executed. Huascar was drowned in the Andamarca River, declaring, it is said, with his dying breath that the white men would avenge his murder and his brother would not long survive him.

Pizarro was angry at the news, for Huascar was an amiable and more pliant man whom he could have bent to his will more easily than the strong-minded, independent and determined Atahualpa.

Atahualpa kept his word about the ransom and soon a vast quantity of gold and silver, worth something like three million pounds, was placed before the greedy, gloating eyes of Pizarro. The Spaniards revelled in their rich treasure and even shod their horses with silver.

Meanwhile Atahualpa's demands for the freedom he had so dearly bought fell upon deaf ears. Pizarro had heard rumours of a rising among the Peruvians and he used that as an excuse for not honouring his bargain. Atahualpa heard the rumours—which were not true—with incredulity, as he knew that not one of his subjects would dare to go to arms without his authority, in which fact lay the key to the Spaniards' success.

Things now moved rapidly towards the inevitable climax of this dismal triumph of civilization over barbarism. More Spaniards arrived from Panama. There were rumours of a large invasion from Quito, and once more Pizarro accused Atahualpa of raising the country against the Spaniards. Pizarro was now under tremendous pressure from some of his compatriots to execute the Inca. But Pizarro was answerable to his emperor in Europe, and dare not in the circumstances do this without a trial.

Atahualpa was then brought before a farcical tribunal and accused of usurping the Inca crown, assassinating his brother Huascar, misusing the public revenues of his country, idolatry, adultery, polygamy and inciting insurrection against the Spaniards. The Spaniards, of course, had no jurisdiction in any of these matters. Nevertheless, they found him guilty and sentenced him to death by being burnt alive at the stake.

This scandalous injustice was even too much for some of Pizarro's gang of bandits and criminals. Indignant voices were raised, but in vain, at this outrageous treatment of a prince who had received nothing but wrong at their hands. They had no authority to sit in judgment on a sovereign in the heart of his own dominions. This wholly reasonable, even Christian, view was not shared by Father Valverde, who gave it as his opinion that the Inca deserved death.

On 29 August, 1533, Atahualpa was led out into the great square of Caxamalca, chained hand and foot, attended by Father Valverde striving to persuade him to embrace the faith of his conquerors before he died. Valverde had made many previous attempts to convert him to Christianity, but had never been able to convince Atahualpa.

However, with the doomed Inca bound to the stake, the Spanish priest was able to give him the most convincing argument that Atahualpa had heard so far. If he became a Christian, he would be strangled quickly instead of enduring the painful death of the fire.

Upon receiving this ultimatum, the unhappy Atahualpa, looking bitterly into the face of this contemptible priest, agreed and embraced the alien God of these cruel strangers who had come to loot and ravage his country. The shameful ceremony was performed by Father Valverde, who baptized the new convert Juan de Atahualpa.

Thus the last of the Incas was garrotted at the stake like a common criminal. He was about thirty years old. With him died the Peruvian empire which swiftly fell into the hands of the Spanish invaders and became part of the far-flung territories of Charles V, Emperor of the Holy Roman Empire.

The treatment of Atahualpa was widely condemned at the time, even in Spain. Pizarro and his lieutenants all came to violent and miserable ends and did not live to enjoy the treasure they took from the Incas.

WILLIAM THE SILENT

(1533–84)

FEW MEN have won fame because of their silence, and fewer still have been passionately admired for it. William, Prince of Nassau-Orange, Stadtholder (or Governor) of the Netherlands, and chosen leader in their revolt against Spanish tyranny—a revolt whose success he did not live to witness—was indeed a wise, strong and silent man. Strength and wisdom were the salient qualities which gained him fame. His celebrated "silence" was, in a sense, a by-product of these higher qualities.

To see this more clearly we should try to view William against his turbulently varied background. In the mid-sixteenth century, the seventeen States of the Spanish Netherlands comprising what are now Holland and Belgium, owing allegiance to the Habsburg emperor Charles V in Madrid, were naturally restive; but the inevitable conflict was in itself related to *three* conflicts, which proved by no means parallel in every change of circumstance.

First, there was the national consciousness gradually rising against foreign domination; secondly, often contradicting this, was the religious conflict between Catholics and several Protestant sects, themselves by no means united, but split into Calvinists, Lutherans, Anabaptists and so on; and thirdly we find the tension, if not always actual conflict, between the northern Germanic majority (including roughly the whole of modern Holland and Flemish Belgium) and the southern Walloon minority (equivalent to the modern Belgian south). The intertwining of these three conflicts produced an incredible maze of attitudes and often apparent paradoxes; to manoeuvre a course through them to find national unity and a freedom both political and religious was the aim of every Netherlands statesman.

But few succeeded in maintaining the precarious balance, while at the same time appearing honest and selfless; and none succeeded in such a task as well as William. His "silence", epitomizing his calm temperament, cautious yet alert, stood in contrast to the more ebullient nature of more "glamorous" figures like the noble but somewhat hasty Count Egmont, a half-Walloon, who later was treacherously executed by the Spaniards. William stands for solidity as well as alert, rational action, a typical combination of Dutch qualities, which to many may seem characteristic also of the British nature in time of trial.

Hence his countrymen's enduring love for William, who was in fact the founder of the present royal house of Holland. He remains the symbol of their rise to freedom and of the prelude to the epoch when the Dutch nation shone most prominently on the European stage. It must be admitted, certainly, that William has not inspired writers or dramatists of other nations, while Egmont is the subject of Goethe's famous drama (for which Beethoven wrote incidental music), though the English historian, Motley, won international renown with his book, *The Rise of the Dutch Republic*, a passionate defence of the Netherlanders' struggle against Spain, in which William the Silent is the undoubted hero.

William was born on 25 April, 1533, the son of the Count of Nassau, at Dillenburg in Germany. In those days estates were often held in different lands, and territorial frontiers themselves tended to be loose (the so-called Holy Roman Empire still occupied large areas of many quite diverse countries); so it was not surprising when, at the age of eleven, William inherited also the title and estates of Prince of Orange.

These possessions were in the Netherlands: their centre was at Breda in Brabant, with further land in the provinces of Holland and Zealand, where later William was to become Stadtholder. His parents reserved the Countship of Nassau for his younger brother John (himself to become a stormy petrel, now helping, now hindering the more far-sighted William), while William was sent to Brussels to be educated as a Catholic at the court of the Emperor Charles V. Here he doubtless gained both personal contacts and experience of statesmanship. In 1555 it was on his young shoulders that the prematurely old Charles leant as he told the assembled States of his seventeen Netherlands provinces that he was resigning the crown to his son, Philip II, later to marry England's Queen Mary.

At this scene of abdication both Charles and his audience wept, and it is important to stress the attachment to the dynasty felt by these provinces despite many provocations. The attitude was, in fact, ambivalent; a real love of freedom lay in the Netherlandish nature, whether that of Friesland fishermen, of the burghers and merchants of the city-states, or of the landed aristocrats. Doubtless William at first shared in this; and his gradual appearance as the leader of anti-Spanish revolt shines all the more tellingly for his prudence and lack of fanaticism. The same qualities were revealed in his religious policy; a firm but unbigoted Catholic, he strove for religious freedom and Protestant rights, even alienating many of his Catholic friends.

The liberation of the Netherlands from Spain ranks as a major event in Western European history; with Switzerland, the Netherlands produced a true democracy, in the sense of orderly freedom, government by the people, liberty of thought and conscience, and tolerance towards minorities and refugees. This liberation took a hundred years and was criss-crossed by innumerable paradoxes and complications. If one man can be said to be its architect, William the Silent is that man. Yet he was assassinated in 1584, at Delft, by a Catholic fanatic, eighty-one years before the final retreat of the Spaniards. Had he lived he might or might not have accepted a constitutional crown. His office of Stadtholder was one held by a member of one of three great families, though in 1555, before Charles's abdication, Philip had caused indignation by refusing the appointment to either William or Count Egmont, and installing a protegé of his own, the energetic Cardinal Granvelle. His reforms—partly concerned with altering the Church authority so as to strengthen that of the king—produced a torrent of indignation. Orange, Egmont and Hoorn, three of the main lords, withdrew from the Council of State until Philip should recall Granvelle. This he did angrily, and his natural sister, Margaret of Parma, was declared Regent.

Meanwhile religious persecution under the Counter-Reformation had reached such heights that Egmont, a fervent Catholic himself, rushed desperately to Madrid to plead with Philip. Flattering promises from Philip raised his hopes, soon to be dashed by the Edict of Segovia, reinforcing persecution. This was the signal for general unrest. William estimated a total of 50,000 victims as having suffered by 1566, and both Protestants and humane, patriotic Catholics felt the need for a national movement. The great nobles resigned in protest; the coolest-headed among them, William, bided his time. But a league of nobility was formed, including William's Calvinist brother, Louis of Nassau, and many members of the "lower nobility" who were less connected with the Government. The Assembly, or "Compromise", of nobles found recruits quickly.

A petition was drawn up, demanding the end of persecution and the Inquisition; and William—unlike Egmont—was for open support of the league when its four hundred nobles solemnly approached the regent in Brussels. Never had the unity of the Netherlands been so clearly expressed. All classes felt this; ballads and other revolutionary literature circulated, and the regent was frightened into caution. Her advisers prepared a scheme of "Moderation", mildly tempering the Edicts, but the people scorned it. Conceiving it to imply toleration, Protestant refugees returned, and a fierce enthusiasm prevailed, especially among the Calvinists. This led to further restrictive measures and, in turn, a mad outburst of sacrilege, image-breaking and the plundering of churches. This produced general disorder; and the Government, playing one faith against another, regained some support from the moderates. However, the people's temper made a trial of strength inevitable.

William was for armed resistance, if only Egmont and Hoorn would co-operate. Philip had threatened even more savage measures, but the co-operation did not materialize. Only the Calvinists stiffened themselves into determined resistance amid the hesitant confusion. William did all he could to assist their freedom of worship, as Stadtholder in the north and as Burgrave of Antwerp, often against the will of Catholic officials. Yet he could not openly identify himself with their cause, partly because most of his own troops came from a Catholic or Lutheran Germany.

Still in the "wondrous year" 1566 the Calvinist forces suffered sharp defeats. William, unlike Egmont, refused to take the fresh oath of allegiance demanded; but, residing at Antwerp, he also declined to admit the rebel forces marching against it. He was resolved on his own chosen "middle path"; at peril of his life he kept the city barred, while Government troops cut down the rebels outside. In this he had the backing of most of the population of Antwerp, though he was largely denounced elsewhere as a traitor. With mixed feelings he saw the revolt everywhere fade out. His position had become such that, in common with many other nobles, he left the country.

This was indeed the hush before the storm, the step backward to prepare a victorious advance. Resolved to recruit an army in Germany, he retired to his ancestral castle at Dillenburg in 1567. Well can we imagine his reflections, feelings and decisions on policy designed to further the great purpose to which he felt irresistibly called. He was to personify the united Netherlands, above all clash of race, interest and religious denomination. The ground had been well sown by the forces of that league who had presented the petition at Brussels. They joyously called themselves "the Beggars", a title that arose in humorous and accidental fashion.

As the soldiers of the league marched along, the die-hard duke, Berlaymont, scoffed at them as "that pack of beggars" in the French phrase: "*Ce n'est qu'un tas de gueux*", French being still the Court language. The nation "Dutched" "*gueux*" into "Geus", and the cry of "*Vive le Geus!*" symbolized the national unity.

Events moved swiftly. Philip, furious at Margaret's so-called "moderation", sent the Duke of Alba, a noted commander and a bigot also, to supersede her. On his arrival the country was in exhausted, almost contrite, mood. But Alba swept aside this chance of conciliation; he cut through existing interests, made arbitrary arrests, and governed by means of his well-named Council of Blood. Egmont and Hoorn were imprisoned. And then, in Motley's words: "Upon the 16th of February, 1568, a sentence of the Holy Office condemned all the inhabitants to death as heretics." Alba's terrorism increased.

William, who had himself been summoned in January before the ominous Council of Blood, protested in the face of all Europe, and set about recruiting troops, largely from the German mercenaries whom the recent peace after the French civil war had left without a job. William's first sallies were failures, but in April Louis scored a success at Groningen. Alba was quick in revenge; amongst the heads that fell were those of Hoorn and Egmont (whose fate the Beggars' song attributed to his "inconstancy"). William's lack of funds and his unpreparedness prevented him from striking at once into Brabant, the heart of the nation. Near Trier he collected a too vast horde of rapacious mercenaries, as well as genuine patriots. He could hardly afford to pay them all. Attacks followed, often petering out owing to the indifference of the population itself; William had to retreat, his starving army running amok, while he escaped into France, still pestered for arrears of pay. This was perhaps his lowest ebb. Yet, as he sings in the Beggars' song, the "Wilhelmus", which the Dutch still treat as a national anthem: "My heart hath remained constant in adversity."

He soon was able to return to Dillenburg, but meanwhile had cemented his most valuable alliance: that with the French Huguenots. In the Netherlands, revolt had burst out at Alba's "Tax of the Tenth Penny", by which the state was to receive a tenth of the price of every article sold. Alba's folly united Netherlanders of every class and religion. But all William's scheming for support in the country itself ended in hesitation and indifference. Only gradually was real popular support to be won. A useful addition to the cause were the curious semi-piratical "Sea Beggars", centred on Emden, whose pro-Orange activities were soon regularized by the far-seeing William.

Since the peace of 1570 in France, the Huguenot leader, Coligny, wielded influence over the young king, Charles IX; from the Huguenot port of La Rochelle, Louis of Nassau came to discuss a common war against France's old enemies, the Habsburgs. In 1572 came the decisive beginning. A premature attack by the Sea Beggars captured The Brill and Flushing in William's name; soon most towns in Holland and Zealand acknowledged his authority, as did many in Friesland and the north; and the Huguenots captured Mons in the Walloon South. Yet William, who on 23 July took Roermond on the Maas, was delayed by the usual financial problem until on 27 August he crossed the river, only to learn that three days earlier the French king had betrayed the Huguenots, and ordered the Massacre of St. Bartholomew. All hopes of French help, moral, financial and military, crashed. The Spaniards struck again, and William had to retreat, disbanding his forces, and travelling to the province of Holland.

Four heroic years followed, in which (while the other provinces looked on) Holland and Zealand stood alone against the Spanish armies. After the prolonged siege of Haarlem in 1572, which fell to the Spaniards, William recruited another army of German mercenaries, annihilated near Mook in 1574. Alba had been replaced by Requesens. In 1575 William cleverly showed his hand by causing the peace negotiations at Breda (for the Spaniards were alarmed) to break down. Soon Requesens died and Philip declared himself bankrupt! The new Governor, Don John, was impatient and arrogant; and in 1577 war flared once again.

January, 1579, saw the formation of the Union of Utrecht, by which the Northern Provinces leagued together in a separate entity; with utmost reluctance, seeing its Calvinistic intolerance, William also signed. This had the natural consequence of reconciling the Walloons to the king. General confusion ensued; one group of exiles returned, a fresh one left and the towns which had supported the Beggars drove them out. But now the geographical factor, the country's configuration, especially the great strategic rivers, was to bring ultimate success to the Revolt and unity to the land.

The new Governor, the brilliant general Alexander of Parma, was more tactful than his predecessor. William invited the Duke of Anjou, brother of the French king and a Catholic, to be sovereign. His rule was unsuccessful, yet William—urged to become sovereign himself—still felt that only French help could deliver the nation. Then Anjou died on 10 June, 1584. A month later, on 10 July, a Catholic fanatic killed William himself. The enemy gloated, but the revolt showed that it had its own life. William's death proved this, as did his own refusal of absolute power; his tactful negotiations with States' assemblies and his gifts of persuasion were not to be forgotten.

Under the excellent leadership of William's son, Maurice of Nassau, and hastened by events like the collapse of the Spanish Armada, the whole territory of the Netherlands was regained from Spain by 1600, though its sovereign nationality was not recognized officially until the Treaty of Westphalia in 1648, which ended the Thirty Years' War of Central Europe. But had William the Silent never lived, the Netherlanders' fight for freedom might have ended less happily.

AKBAR

(1542–1605)

A SCREAMING mob beat down the bronze gates, burst into the great mausoleum, opened the tomb. Then, "dragging out the bones of Akbar, they threw them into the fire and burnt them. Thus does the world treat those from whom it expects no good and fears no evil. That was the end of the life and reign of King Akbar."

To the Jesuit historian who wrote those words this final act of sacrilege was the end of Akbar. But a part at least of the good and evil men do lives after them, and the name of the great Mogul emperor is unlikely to be forgotten. He was, if not the founder, at least the organizer, of that empire which at its height, during his lifetime, covered all but the bottom bit of the Indian sub-continent, and territories beyond it. He could neither read nor write —even his own name—but his knowledge and his understanding were vast. His memory enabled him to fill his mind with more facts, ideas and dreams than any dozen normal men. And though he wrote nothing, he inspired others to write about him. From these we learn, for example, that Akbar's eyes were "vibrant like the sea in sunshine"; his manners were perfect, so that he could be "great with the great and lowly with the lowly"; that he never slept for more than three hours at a stretch; that he was an epileptic.

On a less personal note we know that he brought almost the whole of India under his subjugation, and invented a new religion.

A man, in short, of many facets. Before we look at a few, let us consider the world into which he was born.

It was a changing world, even then. The age-old Hindu domination of the sub-continent had yielded to a foreign, Muslim, force, and that too had succumbed to another, also Muslim, but more powerful still, sweeping all before it. But to put these new "Mogul" invaders in perspective we must glance at those who preceded them.

It was about the year 2000 B.C. that the Indian sub-continent, that vast and fertile land to the south of the Himalaya mountains, was entered from the north-west, by light-skinned, straight-haired, invaders. These lived for some time on the southern slopes of the Himalaya before deciding to advance farther. Then, moving east and south, they pushed the aboriginal "Dravida", the dark-skinned, curly-haired people, ahead of them, and these Dravidians, as we now call them, were forced down the peninsula towards its narrow southern tip. Many were killed, many taken prisoner by the invaders.

The invaders, who brought with them a strange, "Aryan" language, an involved Hindu religion and a developed art and architecture, founded great cities, some of which, like Benares, remain to the present day. They introduced a "caste" system, dividing people into four main groups of Priests, Nobles, Men and Serfs (Brahmins, Kshatriyas, Vaisyas and Sudras), and as the last group were almost entirely from the conquered, darker-skinned folk it was reasonable that they should choose their own word for Colour to describe it.

They introduced, in fact, a Colour Bar, four thousand years ago: an unfortunate development which is neither new nor confined to the so-called "White" races.

Hindu domination became virtually complete. Other religions, like Jainism and Buddhism, sprang up, but though Buddhism spread over much of the East, neither religion succeeded in winning over a large proportion of India's inhabitants. In the fourth century before Christ, Alexander the Great burst on the scene, but his influence, by Indian time-scales, was short-lived. Hindu dynasties continued to follow each other, and at certain periods there were many of them, ruling over different parts of the peninsula. There were still invasions from the north, but those who invaded either withdrew or were absorbed, submerged in a sea of humanity, and an age-old culture and religion.

But in about the year A.D. 1000 a new type swept down from the north, invaders with a fierce proud faith they called "Islam". These "Muslims"—followers of Islam—believed in a single God and a One True Faith, and they were determined to wipe out all infidels. This Islam was not their own private religion, it was a faith shared by a large part of the world beyond India's borders, and the new invaders were pledged to be its spearhead. They would take the word of their religious leader, their caliph, to all the world, and at the same time keep in touch—forever—with that caliphate, in Baghdad: much as the settlers of Israel were to do in modern times, they would bring in others of the same fierce faith to help them settle their new territories.

From this time on India was split in two.

The Muslim invaders chose as their capital a strategic spot in the north. Here, in and around Delhi, they fought a series of major battles with the defending Hindus: by A.D. 1200 they were in complete control of a large part of India.

But a little later these Muslim rulers, the Sultanate of Delhi, were defeated by other Muslims, infinitely more warlike, more ferocious, more bigoted, than they. They swept down, from the north as before, but less with the intention of acquiring territory or riches than with a fanatical zeal to punish the earlier invaders. For these were neglecting the True Faith. In 1398 the vicious Timur swept in from Samarkand with his army of fanatics, and butchered Hindu and Muslim alike before returning whence he had come.

Timur's dubious achievement is to have destroyed the Muslim power that preceded him and to have left nothing in its place.

The stage was set for the Moguls.

They came, at the start of the sixteenth century, and though the blood of many warriors, including that of Timur, flowed through the veins of their royal house, they brought a new, gentler approach to the business of invasion. The first of them was Babur, who overthrew the Sultan of the day and had himself proclaimed, a trifle prematurely, "Emperor of All India". He was a good man, a Muslim, but open-minded, a man who loved flowers and poetry and music. He was also a fine general and soon he had indeed conquered most of India. He died, and his weak and foolish son, Humayun, an opium addict, lost a large part of that empire within a few years, as parts of it rebelled and set up autonomous states. His son Akbar was born in 1542 while Humayun was in temporary exile in Sind. Then, when Humayun had managed to fight his way back to Delhi, he slipped, fell down the long staircase of his library, and killed himself.

Akbar, aged fourteen, was Emperor of India. His reign would coincide, very nearly, with that of Queen Elizabeth in England.

At first, affairs of state were entrusted to a regent, Bahram Khan, but within a year Akbar had decided the older man was cruel and intolerant in the way he maintained order among the various sections of the Empire, which had rebelled. The young emperor took over the Government himself.

His long, eventful reign is one of the most important periods in the history of India. Like his grandfather, he was far from a fanatical Muslim, and he convinced himself that the perfect religion must be an amalgam of many. The first invaders to come by sea, the Portuguese, had settled peaceably on the coast, and Akbar now sent ambassadors to them, asking that Jesuit missionaries come to Delhi and instruct him in their faith. He would probably not adopt it, but he wished to study it. And to the adherents of Brahminism, Jainism, Buddhism, to the Parsis and others, he sent messages, asking that they come and instruct him in their thinking and their rituals.

From his detailed studies Akbar devised a new religion, and did his best, without coercion, to spread it. In this he was hardly successful: many men, anxious to win royal favour, embraced it, but few understood it, or believed. Akbar's new faith was a short-lived affair. But he has gone into history as a ruler who established and insisted on complete religious toleration. He had been, at first, a strict Muslim, but he made good friends of his Hindu subjects, in particular the warlike Rajputs, from whom he appointed many of his best generals, and who served him faithfully and well. He married several Rajput princesses who were nominally expected to embrace Islam on joining the royal household, but most of whom, as we know, did nothing of the sort. They were not punished for the omission.

With his Rajput generals Akbar introduced the modern system of an army owing allegiance to the state and being paid directly by it, not feudally by hosts of minor nobles, who might tend to appropriate the funds for other purposes and neglect its strength.

The influence of Islam, since the first Muslim invasion, had always been a strong one, dragging men's minds and hearts back to that distant caliphate, but now Akbar tried hard to emancipate minds from that influence. From now on, if his subjects refused to adopt his new religion, preferred to regard themselves as Muslims, they must have their caliph within the empire: he, Akbar, was caliph to his Muslims.

With as much zeal as earlier Muslims had enforced their faith, Akbar now set himself to enforcing toleration. He forbade the building of mosques, and pilgrimages to Mecca, refused to tolerate even the ancient Fast of Ramadan. It had always been a Muslim joy to show the superiority of the True Faith over idolatrous, cattle-worshipping Hindus, by slaughtering cattle in public. Now this, too, was forbidden. The meat of oxen could be eaten, but the slaughter would be a private, hidden, affair.

Akbar's toleration extended to all things. He built new schools all over his vast domain, and encouraged the study of literature, and art, and language, from all over the known world. He was, as we have seen, illiterate, but he had half the world's great literature off by heart, and he dictated beautiful poems of his own composition, many of which we have to this day. He urged that Muslim painters and architects should study and profit by the earlier work of Hindu craftsmen; the new art which resulted is among the world's treasures.

And—perhaps because he could not do so himself—he encouraged the writing of history. From the thousands of years of Hindu domination we have remarkably little in the way of written history, aside from a few great epic poems: most of what we know of those early days has been learnt from paintings and the ruins of their ancient cities. But the Mogul period of Indian history is well documented.

Akbar's intentions were noble: to isolate Indian Muslims from their co-religionists outside and make them more Indian, so that the empire he ruled would one day become a united whole. But in this he failed. The majority of his Muslim subjects resented this attempt to interfere with their beliefs, and though Akbar repressed a number of efforts at rebellion he was unable to put out the flame of Islam. Much as Christianity has consolidated in times of religious oppression, so a newer, more orthodox, stricter, Islam was growing in India, determined to resist any heretical influence, whether it came from outside or the emperor himself. When, in 1582, Akbar formally renounced Islam and promulgated his own new faith—without, however, forcing it upon his subjects—rebellion began to take shape.

In September, 1605, after years of stamping out that rebellion, Akbar became ill. He grew worse, with vomiting and terrible stomach pains, then appeared to get better. Court physicians diagnosed it as dysentery; then, when the symptoms suddenly recurred, agreed that it could not be.

It was almost, one of them pointed out, as if the emperor were being deliberately, carefully and slowly poisoned.

In October Akbar died.

At his death, though successors made haste to bring back orthodoxy, the Mogul Empire tottered. Bit by bit, pieces were taken or retaken, beginning with the great fortress of Kandahar, which became a province of Persia.

By the death of Akbar's descendant, Aurangzeb, a hundred years later, the Empire had almost ceased to exist.

We can remember Akbar for having been a great general and a wise and cultured man. Above all, he was a man who by devotion to the idea of toleration made his mark not only on Indian history, but on India's thinking and India's philosophy.

HENRY IV (OF FRANCE)

(1553–1610)

HENRY IV, the first of the Bourbon line who came to the throne in 1589, the year after the Spanish Armada, is the most popular of all French kings. He is also one of the most widely admired of French monarchs outside France, particularly in England, a country which was his ally. England was his friend, and Spain, England's enemy, was also his. Many British schoolboys have heard of his "white plume" which he told his soldiers to follow at the battle of Ivry, a gesture which endeared him to his people. Two of Henry's sayings are long remembered: "I want every man to have a chicken in his pot"; and "Paris is worth a mass". This latest illustrates not cynicism but Henry's tolerant mind, so exceptional in an age of violence and bigotry.

England was fortunate in that the strong Tudor monarchy saved her from the Wars of Religion, the struggle between Protestants and Catholics which was to deluge France with blood in the second half of the sixteenth century and which was to cause the terrible Thirty Years War in Germany at the beginning of the seventeenth. When the New Learning and ideas of reforming the Church became current in France at the beginning of the sixteenth century, the French king, Francis I, his sister Marguerite, Queen of Navarre, and many of the French nobility favoured them, as did Henry VIII in England. But there was no question of the French monarch becoming head of a new Church which would be acceptable to the majority of the nation. The large majority of Frenchmen were staunch Catholics; they were faced by a small but fanatical Protestant minority, strong and indeed itself a majority in certain parts of France, such as the south-west and Normandy.

The Duke of Rohan, Princes of the Blood such as Antoine de Bourbon, King of Navarre, the Prince of Condé and the great family of Châtillon were Protestants. These nobles were, however, not, for the most part, religious fanatics themselves; they were driven to extreme positions by the violence of the Catholic reaction against Protestantism. This was headed by the Duke of Guise, a soldier who had distinguished himself in the wars in Italy, and his brother the Cardinal of Lorraine. With the Guises went the City of Paris with its great University, which was, from the beginning, a dynamo of the Catholic cause. The example of Paris was followed by many other cities of the east and north. The task of the monarchy was clearly to decide a middle way not only between Catholic and Protestant intransigence but between two powerful aristocratic factions.

Unfortunately, the last Valois king capable of governing France, Henry II, died in 1559, after an accident at a tournament, a lance penetrating his eye. The three kings who were to reign from then until 1589 were all young children at their father's death: the sickly Frances II, the incapable Charles IX and the less incapable but degenerate Henry III. The House of Valois had not the art of providing the right king at the right moment. The Queen Mother, the wife of Henry II, Catherine de' Medici, attempted a vain policy of making the monarchy strong against both factions. Religious passion and blood spoke louder than reason. The first of a long series of civil wars began in 1562. Small-scale but extremely ferocious fighting took place throughout the kingdom. There were truces, arranged by the monarchy. Francis, Duke of Guise was assassinated, to be succeeded by his even more violent brother Henry, known as Scarface. Catholics were aided by Philip II of Spain, Protestants by Elizabeth of England, and both sides employed numbers of mercenary troops from Germany and Switzerland.

In 1570 the monarch, Charles IX, appeared to lean towards the more moderate Protestant leaders and to be able to enforce, with their help, a permanent truce of peace based on toleration. A marriage was arranged between the king's sister Marguerite de Valois and Henry the new King of Navarre, who had succeeded his father, Antoine de Bourbon, who had been killed in the wars. In 1572, however, the queen decided the balance of power must be restored by more drastic means. The king's consent was obtained to a massacre, on the eve of St. Bartholomew, in August, of Protestant leaders assembled in Paris for the marriage. The massacre lasted over three days and was followed by massacres in other cities. The English Court went into mourning, whilst Philip II of Spain rejoiced, saying this was one of the greatest days of his life. The massacre settled nothing, for the Protestants found new leaders and remained under arms.

By order of the king the two Protestant princes of the Blood Royal escaped the massacre in Paris. One was the Prince of Condé and the other Henry, King of Navarre. They were picked up by guards at the tennis court of the Louvre early in the morning when the massacre started and, as they were taken to the king's apartments for safety, they heard the cries of their pages and valets who were being dragged out of their rooms and slaughtered. Both chose to abjure the Protestant faith and to live. A few months later on a cold and frosty night Henry escaped from Paris and returned to his kingdom of Navarre. He was now the Head of the Protestant cause.

When the effeminate Henry III became king, and after his brother, the Duke of Anjou, died, Henry of Navarre became the legitimate successor to the throne. The House of Valois was extinguished. The Bourbons were directly descended from the sixth son of St. Louis, and though their claim was not the only one to the throne, and it was a distant one, it was far better than any other.

Henry III tried to continue the sensible policy of moderation and of refusal to be the tool of either faction. But he was opposed not only now by the Catholic nobles but by the Holy League which the anti-monarchical, almost Republican, but fervently Catholic townsmen of Paris and other cities had formed, not only for the defence of their faith but of their privileges. They were encouraged by the luxury and immorality of the Valois Court, by the hated "Italian Woman" who ruled the kingdom and brought in the English troops, forgetting that the Guises had called in the Spaniards. In 1585 Henry was forced to make peace with the League and to outlaw the Protestants.

War was not long in breaking out again. King Henry had the Duke of Guise assassinated in his palace at Blois by a group of young noblemen known as Les Mignons. Paris rose against "M. Henry de Valois". Henry III now called on the King of Navarre to support him and the two Henrys besieged Paris. On 1 August, 1589, a Dominican monk managed to worm his way into the king's presence in the camp outside Paris and stabbed him to death, the revenge for the murder of the Duke of Guise. Henry of Navarre was now King of France—but a king with a capital in arms against him and indeed with an aged Bourbon cousin proclaimed King Charles X by the League. Never came a king into his heritage under worse conditions.

In the year of his crowning, Henry IV made public the Edict of Nantes. This ensured liberty of religion to Protestants in certain parts of France, with freedom to organize a Protestant clergy. The Edict gave them 150 strongholds, mainly in the south-west, where they could organize a local militia to defend themselves.

After two victories won by Henry IV at Arques and Ivry, the League was discouraged and Paris was again besieged by the royal forces. The king had been urged by Henry III to declare himself a Catholic and so to unite the nation behind him. But Henry knew that he could not afford to discourage his Protestant supporters for the sake of Paris. He delayed his conversion for four years, determined that first of all he should be seen as the legitimate king and not owe his crown to weakness. Meanwhile he conducted the war with clemency and moderation. He allowed foodstuffs to enter Paris during the siege, saying, "I do not wish to rule over a cemetery". Nothing could have been more admirable than Henry's sense of timing and his patience. These are not often found in conjunction with the dashing military genius and panache which he also displayed.

Paris yielded at last and gradually fighting ceased throughout the kingdom. Henry was now confronted with the problem of restoring France. "Whoever would have slept these last forty years," it was said, "would have awoken to see not France but a corpse." Perhaps France was not quite as desolate as around 1450 after the Hundred Years War. But the loss of life during the Wars of Religion had been huge; sieges, skirmishes, pillaging, sackings and burnings had created ruin everywhere; there were thousands of deserted villages, millions of acres unploughed, a shortage of draught animals—men and women commonly had to hitch themselves to the plough; roads were useless, bridges destroyed, and on the sea not a ship of the king's navy. "France and I have need of a great breath," said Henry. And the king's remark that he wanted to see every man with a chicken in his pot, and the saying of Henry's great Minister Sully that "plough and pasture are the breasts of France", are the reflection of this terrible time.

France recovered with astonishing speed, as she had done before and was to do again in her history. The king was successful because in face of political or economic problems he used commonsense and persuasion rather than acting dogmatically and violently. France, he knew, had need of an all-powerful monarchy and this he successfully constructed. He was a believer in the Divine Right of Kings, as he wrote to his friend, the new King of England and Scotland, James I. But Henry was a believer in this doctrine with many a nuance and much scepticism. To his Minister Sully, a Protestant, who kept pictures of Calvin and Luther in his antechamber, he said: "When you cease to contradict me I know you will have ceased to love me." Sully laboured to reform the administration and above all to restore the real wealth of France which lay in its land.

Henry IV had his marriage with Marguerite de Valois annulled and he married in 1660 Marie de' Medici, a fat and not very intelligent queen who gave him a son. The risk of a Protestant succeeding to the throne was thus ended. Marguerite de Valois bore him no malice and indeed she herself carried the gown of the new queen at her wedding. Marguerite herself had had many lovers and Henry had had even more mistresses. This hard-working, clever and patient monarch showed another side of his character in his love affairs. So frequent were these that Henry was known as *Le vert galant*—the ever-fresh lover. His escapades at first pleased the nation, although in his latter years there was some criticism, particularly when he fell in love with a girl of fifteen, the wife of the Prince of Condé, who had to take refuge in Brussels, from which city Henry threatened to take her by force of arms. This side of his character, however, together with his other good qualities, helped to get the love of his subjects. M. Jean Duché, the author of a rather droll *History of France as told to Juliette*, writes aptly of Henry IV:

> *After the decadent depravities of the Valois, do you know what was really the marvel of marvels? It was the fundamental healthiness of the man. In Henry IV every Frenchman recognized all that was best and truest in the essence of his race.*

About to embark on a war with the Habsburgs of Austria, Henry left the Louvre Palace on 14 May, 1610, in the afternoon, to transact some business with Sully. As so often happens, his wife and his entourage had had a vague presentiment of disaster and begged him to stop at home. In the narrow Rue de la Ferronerie, a young ardent Catholic, François Ravaillac, living on charity and crippled with debts, stabbed Henry twice near the heart as he leant over the side of his carriage reading a letter. His motive was hatred of the king as the protector of Protestants—a motive which had been common to Frenchmen some twenty years before, but which later had become detestable. The ghosts of the monk who had killed Henry III, and of the Protestant de Méré who had stabbed the first Duke of Guise, lived again in this senseless act of murder. Catholics and Protestants alike mourned Henry: "You cannot be a Frenchman," said the Duke of Rohan, "without regretting the loss to her well-being which France had suffered." Of how many kings could this have been sincerely said?

QUEEN ELIZABETH I

(1558–1603)

When Mary Tudor died in November, 1558, all but devout Romanists in England heaved a sigh of relief. Her savage persecution of the Protestants had introduced an alien virulence into English religious life, and the ultimate result, the conversion of the English to Protestantism, was exactly the opposite of that intended by the fanatical queen. Her marriage to King Philip II of Spain had dragged England in the wake of Spanish ambitions, led to war with France and the loss of Calais, the last English possession on the Continent.

All this sprang from a strange mixture of religious and personal motives: to restore the Catholic Faith and Papal Supremacy, earn a heavenly blessing on her marriage and so in due course produce a male child who would also be her Catholic heir. These aims had nothing to do with the destiny of England and they were all frustrated. When Mary's half-sister Elizabeth ascended the throne at the age of twenty-five, England was torn by misgovernment, the treasury was empty, heavy foreign debts had been incurred, the people were dispirited and independence itself was threatened by France, which had one foot in Calais and the other in Scotland owing to the marriage of Mary, the Queen of Scots, to the French Dauphin, soon to be King Francis II.

As for Elizabeth, called to rule strife-torn England with its four million inhabitants, its languishing trade and its military weakness, it must have seemed unlikely to contemporaries that this tall young woman, with her auburn hair, dark eyes, sleek olive complexion and winsome manner, would do more than scratch at the surface of national problems. Her sex told heavily against her, she had never before appeared in public life, her abilities were unknown.

But Elizabeth possessed many remarkable gifts, chief among them a strong and flexible intellect. In a letter to her brother, written when she was thirteen, she was already conscious of mental powers which "nor time with her swift wings shall overtake, nor the misty clouds with their lowerings may darken, nor chance with her slippery foot may overthrow".

But Elizabeth's brilliant mind might have been a disadvantage to her as queen without corresponding emotional gifts, and these also she possessed: high courage in times of crisis, endurance and resilience. These qualities had been tempered by adversity in her youth, once when adolescent love for Admiral Seymour, brother of the Lord Protector under Edward VI, had seemed to involve her in a plot to oust the Protector, and again, during her sister's reign, when she was falsely accused of complicity in attempted rebellion. In peril of her life, Elizabeth had learnt the value of dissemblance and prevarication. The instinct of self-preservation had taught her to walk a tight-rope amid manifold dangers and she emerged from these years as a woman in full control of herself, a thorough realist, purposeful but cautious, beneath a blithe, often ribald, exterior as tough as steel. One quality topped all others: patriotism. Against heavy odds she herself had survived. From now on, emotionally identified with the land she governed, she would work for the welfare of England.

Elizabeth was proud of being "the most English woman of the kingdom", and not surprisingly she wanted her people's affection. To rule with their "loves" was the recurrent theme of her speeches, the aim underlying her principle never to command what voluntary co-operation would achieve. The theme, an affair of the heart between the queen and Englishmen, was struck at the start when, on the eve of her coronation, she toured the City of London, arousing impassioned loyalty by a display of dignity allied to human feeling.

But undivided loyalty came only from Protestants and only from those who were not extremists. Elizabeth faced a delicate situation. On the one hand were the Romanists, fearing a restoration of heresy in the country, established in positions of power, a pool of potential treason which might be stirred from Scotland, France or Spain. On the other, exiles from Mary's persecution were flooding back, bringing with them the teachings of Calvin and insisting on their right to organize their Church and to worship in their own way. This demand, if granted, could be extended to politics, undermining the constitution and disrupting the balance of the state. To steer a middle path and establish a Church which would attract reasonable men from both sides, so forming a nucleus round which the majority of the nation could eventually rally, was an urgent necessity and its achievement one of Elizabeth's great contributions to the peace of England.

Elizabeth herself was in no way a fanatic and her inclination was to judge religious issues from a practical point of view. The disloyal Romanist bishops were deposed and replaced by moderate Protestants. England was made Protestant by law, the queen became Supreme Governor of the Church and subjects were obliged to take an oath of spiritual allegiance. A new liturgy was introduced combining, as evidence of conciliation, Protestant doctrine with Catholic ritual and its observance was imposed by Act of Parliament. All this offered Englishmen a means of reconciling their religious convictions with their patriotic instincts and, though strife continued, Elizabeth's Church grew and prospered.

Meanwhile her throne was threatened from Scotland, where French troops were fighting to gain control of the country for Mary Stuart's mother, Mary of Guise, against the Puritan Scottish nobles. The Queen of Scots was a direct descendant of Henry VII, the nearest claimant to the English throne, and if the French prevailed her claim might be made good. For close on thirty years, indeed, she was a thorn in Elizabeth's flesh. Temporarily the danger was averted by the triumph of the Scottish Protestants, discreetly assisted from England. Then Francis II of France died, Mary Stuart returned to Scotland and became a focus for Catholic supporters on both sides of the border.

Soon the problem was complicated by Mary's marriage to the feckless Lord Darnley and the birth of a son, supplying a successor to the English throne which her Privy Council, headed by the meticulous and trustworthy William Cecil, had been vainly urging Elizabeth to provide. She had consistently refused marriage for reasons of state—to keep foreign suitors in doubt and to refuse English ones was to frustrate concerted opposition to England abroad and avert the hostility of rivals at home. But when Mary gave birth to her son James, the woman in Elizabeth lamented: "The Queen of Scots is delivered of a fair son and I am but a barren stock."

Mary's connivance in the murder of Darnley and her marriage to her fellow-conspirator, Lord Bothwell, resulted in her deposition by the infuriated Scots and flight to England, where, by no means reluctant to exchange a more powerful throne for the one she had lost, she became, abetted from Spain, a centre of Catholic intrigue against Elizabeth's life. There was no easy solution to the problem she posed. Half a prisoner, she was allowed to move from one residence to another, and Elizabeth waited on events until a Catholic rebellion in northern England obliged her to confine her rival more closely. The Pope retaliated by excommunicating the English queen; there was a danger of Catholic Europe—the forces of the Counter-Reformation—combining against her, and she strove, from now on, to weaken Catholic power in France by supporting the Huguenots and Spanish power in the Netherlands by aiding Dutch resisters against the tyranny of their Spanish overlords.

This policy was moderately successful, but at home the excommunication of Elizabeth had turned her Catholic subjects into potential if not actual traitors and the danger grew from plots centring on Mary Stuart. English priests trained in France came back to fan Catholic feeling and in later years fanatical Jesuits arrived to work for the restoration of Catholicism in England. The essential issue became a simple one: Elizabeth's removal, which was only too possible, would place the Catholic Mary on the throne. Mary's removal would safeguard Elizabeth and ensure a Protestant succession in the shape of James who had been crowned king by the Calvinists in Scotland.

A series of plots, one of them revealing plans for an attack on England by all the Catholic powers and the murder by a Spanish agent of William the Silent, leader of the Dutch Protestant revolt, convinced the Privy Council that delay might be fatal and Mary must die. But Elizabeth would not sanction extreme measures until, in 1586, there was clear evidence of Mary's complicity in a fresh plot to murder her, and after Mary's trial and conviction Elizabeth at last set her hand to the death warrant, though she attempted later to shift responsibility for the execution on to her advisers.

Meanwhile in Spain King Philip's plans matured for a crusade against heretic England and the menace of invasion loomed closer during these years. From her accession Elizabeth had pursued a tortuous foreign policy aimed at preventing a foreign combination against her, weakening the Catholic forces abroad and at the same time, if possible, remaining on good terms with France or Spain. A prime concern had been to prevent the Netherlands, the Channel ports and Brittany being used as bases for invasion. It was a policy of wait-and-see, entailing shifts, strategems and apparent vacillation. To support it Elizabeth had only limited resources. But it was typically English in its defiance of rigid principle, feminine also in its flexibility and adherence to practical ends. As a result, France and then Spain had been cajoled into friendship, until King Philip acquired the throne, the empire, the resources of Portugal and the conquest of England seemed to him a practical possibility. The execution of Mary Stuart made war certain.

Spain had overwhelming power, but English seamen were confident. For many years they had harried Spanish possessions in South America, raided Spanish harbours, captured Spanish treasure fleets. In 1587 Francis Drake "singed the King of Spain's beard" by destroying ships and stores in Cadiz. The sailing of the Armada was postponed for a year and the queen waited calmly in London to hear of its fate as it moved up-Channel. The Spanish plan was to link up at Dunkirk with a force of veteran soldiers from the Netherlands under the Duke of Parma and transport them to the Essex coast. The Armada was pursued as far as Calais by the English, badly mauled there by fire-ships and next day failed even to sight the invasion barges it was supposed to meet. A sea-fight followed in which the Spaniards suffered further loss and then the surviving ships set off on the perilous voyage, round Britain and Ireland, towards home.

But Parma and his veterans still threatened and it was now that Elizabeth, riding a white horse, "attired like an Angel bright" with crown and breastplate, addressed her army of 20,000 men at Tilbury. She was not afraid, she said, to commit herself to them. She trusted their loyalty. "And therefore I am come amongst you, as you see, resolved in the midst and heat of the battle to live or die amongst you all, to lay down for my God and for my kingdom, and for my people, my honour and my blood, even in the dust. I know I have the body of a weak and feeble woman, but I have the heart and stomach of a king, and of a king of England too and I think foul scorn that Parma or Spain or any prince of Europe should dare to invade the borders of my realm. . . ."

But Parma did not come and in November, 1588, thanks were offered in St. Paul's for the Great Deliverance. One of the medals struck at this time bore in Latin the words: "God blew and they were scattered", and the Armada portrait of Elizabeth shows her seated in regal splendour, with one hand on the globe, while on a panel behind her the Armada founders in a providential tempest. All Englishmen now firmly believed that God watched over their destinies through his chosen instrument Elizabeth and, sensibly, she did nothing to disabuse them. The result was an upsurge of national morale.

Enterprise was already the hall-mark of the Age. Drake's voyage round the world in 1577, Martin Frobisher's attempt to find the North-west Passage, Humphrey Gilbert's acquisition of Newfoundland, the founding of Virginia, raids on Spanish possessions on both sides of the Atlantic, the expeditions of Walter Raleigh and the establishment of the East India Company reflected the national mood. In imaginative and speculative thought the Elizabethans were brilliant, too. Besides Shakespeare, Spenser, Bacon and Marlowe, many other writers in prose and in verse contributed to the greatest of all periods in English literature. Directly or indirectly the queen presided over all this creative enterprise, investing personally in the voyages of her seamen and attracting learned men to her Court.

Elizabeth never risked all on the single throw of the dice and after the defeat of the Armada she did not try to deliver a mortal blow at the Spanish Empire and the possibility of renewed invasion remained. But her diplomacy and the proven power of her navy kept England safe and troops could be spared for the last great achievement of her reign, the pacification of Ireland. After an attempt to anglicize the country had failed, inter-tribal anarchy was suppressed at heavy cost and by 1603 the reconquest of Ireland had been completed and the whole country was subjugated for the first time in its history.

Peace in England, peace, though under the sword, in Ireland, the establishment of a Protestant country over against the Catholic monarchies of the Continent, the frustration of foreign enemies—these were the gifts which Elizabeth conferred. With truth in 1591 she could say: "It is clear as daylight that God's blessing rests upon us, upon our people and realm, with all the plainest signs of prosperity, peace, obedience, riches, power and increase of our subjects."

Yet the image of Queen Elizabeth which we still cherish does not rest only on these achievements. We think of her political self: hard-working, imperious, courageous, enduring, seeking always a practical compromise in problems which admitted of no final solution, never a tyrant, yet not afraid to command, "no horse-leech for blood", as she said, at a time when torture and execution were the acknowledged accompaniments of rule. We see her in the gay and vigorous life of her Court with its bull-baiting, bear-baiting dramas, chess, cards and dancing in which she partook with uninhibited relish, familiar with the opposite sex, fishing, as it was said, for men's souls, free with pungent oaths and ribald jokes. A woman of glittering personality, accepted, then as now, as the presiding genius in an age of rampant individualism. "Queen Elizabeth of famous memory", as Oliver Cromwell called her, the "Gloriana" of Spenser's *Faery Queen*, Good Queen Bess, summing up two years before she died the theme of her reign in a speech to her Commons: "Though God hath raised me high, yet this I account the glory of my crown, that I have reigned with your loves."

GUSTAVUS ADOLPHUS

(1594–1632)

FOR DECADES seers and astrologers in the war-torn principalities of sixteenth- and seventeenth-century Germany had been prophesying the advent of the Lion of the North, a kind of militant Messiah who would bring salvation from afar. In 1621 the long-expected Lion of the North came from across the Baltic and blazed a trail of hope and victory throughout Germany where Protestantism was fighting for its life.

He was Gustavus Adolphus, King of Sweden, a brilliant and attractive figure in a none-too-attractive age, who became a myth and legend in his own time. His great enemy, Wallenstein, said of him that the German people awaited him as the Jews awaited their Messiah.

The sufferings of the German principalities resulted from the endeavours of the Roman Catholic world to check the growth of Protestantism which spread with alarming rapidity in northern Europe during the sixteenth century. The emperor Charles V (q.v.) was the first Catholic ruler to make a serious challenge to the Reformation, and his armies ranged throughout his vast empire trying to stamp out the conflagration lit by Martin Luther. He considered it his Catholic duty and he wore himself out trying to suppress the unsuppressible. The princes of northern Germany had too much to gain enriching themselves by seizing Church property and acquiring popular esteem thereby. The Papacy itself, enjoying the material fruits of the Renaissance, was in decline and was not prepared to go to very great lengths to re-establish its authority among those who had strayed from the true faith.

The Peace of Augsburg (1555), which gave to the Germanic rulers the freedom to break away from the Roman Church, was not really an act of religious toleration, as it only recognized the Lutheran type of Protestantism, and provided only for the religious consciences of the German princes, not of their subjects. The "religious conscience" of the princes was frequently guided by the material gain involved in going Protestant.

After a period of uneasy peace the Catholic powers, alarmed at the continuing spread of Protestantism, particularly in Bavaria and Bohemia, once more went on to the offensive. The religious aspect of the Thirty Years War which followed (1618-48) was blurred by the political and dynastic ambitions of the contestants. Ferdinand II became the Holy Roman Emperor in 1619. A Habsburg as much as a Catholic, his enthusiasm for the Thirty Years War was more political than religious. He wanted to crush Protestantism in order to enforce the Habsburg rule over his rebellious empire.

Ferdinand enlisted the services of the notorious Albrecht Wenzel Eusebius von Wallenstein (or properly Waldstein) to lead the armies of the Catholic League against the Protestants. Wallenstein, a Catholic in name only, was as ambitious as his Habsburg master, and used the war, as Ferdinand did, to extend his personal power. His armies were drawn from the dregs of European society, were unpaid and lived off the countries in which they were fighting. As a consequence the war was savage and callous even by modern standards. The people of the German countryside suffered decades of looting, violence and rapine, for which history is hard put to find a parallel. Their suffering is impossible to describe. Many were driven to cannibalism. Whole areas became depopulated.

It was in this wretched century, when men were being told that their sufferings were divine punishment for abandoning the true Church, that they turned their eyes, not south to the ancient and decadent Papacy across the Alps, but north whence their saviour, according to the prophecy, would come.

Their great champion, who did indeed come in 1621, was the most illustrious member of the royal house of Vasa, which in the previous century made Sweden into an independent kingdom.

The Scandinavian kingdoms of Norway, Sweden and Denmark came into being at the time of Charlemagne and were established by the Germanic peoples. In 1397 the three kingdoms were united under the Union of Calmar. During the sixteenth century, at about the time of the Reformation, this Scandinavian Union was broken by Gustavus Vasa, a Swede, who led Sweden to independence and was elected king by an assembly at Strangas in 1523. In that year Protestantism came to Sweden. Vasa confiscated Church property, subdued the aristocracy and set Sweden on the way to national greatness. The Swedish kings started on an era of conquest until their kingdom extended to the eastern shores of the Baltic, which is now Finland, and into Russia, which they cut off from the sea. They cast their eyes southward to Poland and Germany, for their dream was to make the Baltic a Swedish lake.

Gustavus Adolphus was born on 9 December, 1594, eldest son of Charles IX. Charles was one of those restless warrior kings, familiar in European history, whose activities were a mixture of good and bad. A fierce and despotic champion of Protestantism and oppressor of Catholicism, he carefully nurtured Gustavus Adolphus to be a doughty defender of Protestantism. He also gave the boy an excellent education. He appointed as his tutor Johan Schroderus, a learned, widely-travelled man, who was a great linguist. By the time he was twelve young Gustavus was fluent in Swedish, German, Italian, Dutch and Latin, then an international language spoken by all educated men. Later he learned to speak Spanish, Russian and Polish as well.

His father carefully trained him in statecraft, and even gave him a share in the administration. The wise old warrior's faith in his son was not misplaced, for when Gustavus Adolphus came to the throne on Charles's death in 1611 he was a prudent, accomplished young man, brilliant alike in the arts of war and statesmanship.

He was seventeen. The first thing he did was to end the somewhat fratricidal wars his father had been waging against Denmark and Russia, and he immediately created a considerable impression by the way he handled these difficult negotiations with the Danes and the Muscovites. The young Gustavus in fact lost no time in acquiring ascendancy and authority in his own country. He had a powerful and attractive personality, and a generous spirit.

He was greatly interested in reform. In 1614 he set up the Swedish Court of Appeal, which had the effect of by-passing much clumsy medieval judicial procedure. He also instituted many industrial and agricultural reforms which had a beneficial effect upon the Swedish economy.

In 1599 Spain had adopted a copper currency. Sweden had rich copper deposits, and these were developed by Gustavus, and the greatly increased exports of copper brought prosperity and economic power. Sweden thus was able to reach a position of great strength during the reign of Gustavus Adolphus, a remarkable feat for a country whose population was less than one million.

Gustavus was formally crowned in 1617 when he was twenty-three. At this time he was engaged in re-organizing his army. In contrast to most other European armies it contained few foreign mercenaries, but was exclusively Swedish. For a country with such a comparatively small population this was a great strain and a heavy burden for the people to bear. In 1620 there were local uprisings in protest against conscription. Despite these difficulties,

Sweden raised an army of exceptional quality which accomplished great feats of arms.

Gustavus Adolphus had not forgotten his training to be the champion of Protestantism. The Thirty Years War had already broken out, and he was genuinely afflicted by the misfortunes of his Protestant brethren and anxious to assist them. But all the same he was not going to devote his energies and waste the precious treasure and the manhood of Sweden purely on a religious crusade. Gustavus was probably more altruistic than his Catholic opponents, but he had a grand political aim too—the turning of the Baltic into a Swedish lake. When he crossed into Livonia (now the Russian province of Latvia) in 1621 he was hoping to extend his domains as well as to free the Protestants from the oppression of Emperor Ferdinand II and Wallenstein's armies of the Catholic League.

Although Riga capitulated to Gustavus after a month's siege, and he obtained an important foothold on Polish soil, including the vital seaway at the entrance of the River Dvina, these successes had been obtained at the cost of enormous losses, mainly due to sickness. Gustavus was forced to negotiate a truce with the Poles, and so crippling were his initial losses that it was two years before his army was refurbished and he was in a position to continue the struggle. During this time of consolidation he reinforced his army by no fewer than 10,000 men, mainly of Swedish peasant stock. It was not until 1626 that his new army was in a position to move once more. It was without doubt the best trained and most disciplined in the field at that time. It was no rabble of itinerant mercenaries, soldiers of fortune and foot-loose criminals and cut-throats, such as comprised the forces of the Catholic League. Gustavus did his best to reduce the attendant horrors of battle which the warring soldiery have throughout history inflicted upon the hapless inhabitants of the country where the fighting takes place.

In January, 1626, he attacked once more, and annihilated the Polish army at Wallhof, the Swedish troops overwhelming the Polish cavalry which previously they had always feared. A fifth of the Polish army was killed in this battle. After this great victory, Gustavus immediately consolidated his hold on Poland and advanced westward; by the end of the year he had a large Swedish fleet with 14,000 men on board anchored in the Bay of Danzig, Konigsberg had surrendered; Pillau, the only Baltic port capable of taking naval ships, was in his hands, and Danzig was blockaded. Gustavus returned to Sweden for more reinforcements—only his own personality and peculiar brand of persuasion could persuade the Swedes to give up their peaceful and profitable pursuits to join in the deathly struggle on the other side of the Baltic. In May, 1627, he returned with a further 7,000 men. After some inconclusive encounters with the formidable Polish commander, Stanislaus Koniecpolski, Gustavus directed his attack against Prussia, and particularly the Prussian ports, in order to establish a powerful base for taking the war into Germany.

Despite the ancient prophecy about the Lion of the North, Gustavus was at first regarded with suspicion by the Protestant princes of Germany, who feared that he came as a conqueror rather than a deliverer. They were better off as rulers under the loose conglomeration of the empire than they would be as part of the kingdom of this formidable King of Sweden. Despite Gustavus's pretension of being the divinely appointed deliverer of the Protestants, there was no doubt that his policy of expanding the territories of Sweden was every bit as important to him. The Protestant leaders of northern Germany therefore regarded his offers of help with some uneasiness. They well knew that everyone was in this war for what they could get out of it.

They were, however, engaged in a terrible and merciless struggle with the callous armies of the Catholic League under the formidable Wallenstein, whose arrogance and dangerous personal ambitions made him a host of enemies on his own side. In 1630 Emperor Ferdinand, under heavy pressure, dismissed Wallenstein from command and appointed Johann Tzerclaes, Count Tilly, in his place.

The minds of the Protestant princes were completely changed in 1631 by the siege and sack of Magdeburg, which was accompanied by scenes of horror, rapine and destruction reminiscent of the days of Genghis Khan. Twenty thousand of its inhabitants were wantonly butchered. It was Tilly's first success, and he tried in vain to restrain the destructive lust of the sadistic soldiers of the Catholic League. Gustavus was at this time negotiating with the Protestant princes, and was blamed on all sides for not going to the aid of the slaughtered Magdeburgers.

An army such as that of Gustavus Adolphus had not been seen in Europe since the days of the Romans. It was highly disciplined, intensively trained, well paid, and recruited from "good yeomen and stout soldiers of fortune". There were Scottish and German troops among them. Led by a general of Gustavus's brilliance, it was more than a match for Tilly's considerably larger army.

Gustavus at last reached agreement with the princes, and in

particular with the Elector of Brandenburg, who allowed him to advance across his territory. The high standard of discipline and good behaviour of the Swedish army made a remarkable impression in a country accustomed to the worst kind of behaviour from passing armies.

Gustavus met Tilly at the battle of Breitenfeld, north of Leipzig, on 7 September, 1631, and by using methods of warfare he had devised overwhelmingly defeated him. Gustavus's secret was iron discipline. His troops stood unmoved like a wall against the assaults of the enemy. The veteran armies of the League fled in disorder, leaving 6,000 dead on the field. Tilly himself, badly wounded, barely escaped with his life.

Gustavus Adolphus was now acclaimed by all Protestant Germany as the great liberator—the fabled Lion of the North. He followed Tilly south, defeated him again in Bavaria, Tilly this time being killed in the battle. The alarmed emperor hastily recalled Wallenstein, who took the League's army into Saxony, plundering and burning as he went. Gustavus met him at the battle of Lutzen on 16 November, 1632, at which Wallenstein was driven from the field after tremendous losses on both sides.

But no loss was greater than that suffered by the Swedish army. It was a wild and confused battle, fought in a thick mist. Gustavus, always in the forefront of battle, led his own cavalry in a countercharge, and was killed. It is not known exactly how, though it is believed he was lying wounded on the ground when he was dispatched by one of Wallenstein's horsemen.

It was an overwhelming blow to Sweden. With the king's death the empire melted away, despite the efforts of the regent, Count Oxenstierna, to continue the fight in Germany. With the rigid discipline imposed by Gustavus gone, the Swedish armies soon began to behave like all other armies of the period.

The Thirty Years War dragged on until 1648 when both sides were exhausted and settled their differences in the Treaty of Westphalia. This established many political changes in Europe which were to last until the Napoleonic Wars, and marked the failure of the Austro-Spanish attempt to restore Roman Catholicism in Central Europe. It took Germany a century to recover from the destruction and atrocities of this brutal war.

Gustavus Adolphus died too young to accomplish very much of what he set out to do. He was a monarch of great promise. It was a tragedy for Sweden that his brilliant but unstable daughter, Queen Christina, did not inherit his true quality of kingship.

OLIVER CROMWELL

(1599–1658)

THERE ARE historians who would not accept it as a mark of Cromwell's greatness that he was esteemed by the founder of psycho-analysis. Freud wrote in his *Interpretation of Dreams* that Cromwell had "powerfully attracted" him in his boyhood. His juvenile hero-worship was spun out to what may have been a psychologically interesting extent, for in due time he named his second son Oliver, after Cromwell.

Not for the Freudians only, Cromwell's character affords a richer vein for probing than that of any other English ruler. He was both introvert and extrovert, temperate and ruthless, conservative and destructive, freedom-loving and authoritarian, hag-ridden and flexible, contemplative in thought, impatient in action. Dedicated to the parliamentary system, he was in this degree one of its most resounding failures. He could order the obliteration of garrisons, and yet, by his steward's testimony, "did exceed in tenderness". In him contradictions abounded, often to the point of paradox.

As a Puritan, that is, an extreme Protestant, he believed that his life was being lived for him as part of the Divine Will. Yet, in the role of God's puppet, he displayed a defiant individualism, and occasionally an omniscience, that was at variance with the deep humility of his religious professions. That he was the battle-ground of desperate mental conflicts cannot be doubted. After great agonizing, spiritual conversion came when he was twenty-eight, a married man with five children. He suffered through the first half of his life from a blood infection that constantly erupted in boils and carbuncles. Cromwell on the couch would have yielded an overflowing casebook.

Estimates of his character vary as widely as those of the sum of his final achievements. The Royalists, unable to write him off, said that he was "a brave, bad man", a verdict that largely dominated discussions of his place in history for two hundred years. His reputation hung in tatters from the gibbet of time long after his bones had been dispersed.

The Scottish philosopher, Hume, conceded him "superior

genius", coupled with a propensity to "fraud and violence", the means by which he had "rendered himself first in the State". A later and not less remarkable Scottish thinker, Thomas Carlyle, came to see "that Cromwell was one of the greatest souls ever born of English kin".

Many supplementary views can be dismissed, if not ignored, such as that of John Forster, the biographer, who held it to be "indisputably true" that Cromwell was a traitorous hypocrite. One of the great students of seventeenth-century England, S. R. Gardiner, formed the opinion that what Shakespeare was in the world of the imagination, so Cromwell was in the world of action—"the greatest because the most typical Englishman of all time". To John Morley he was "a rare and noble type of leader".

Seen from abroad, he presented an equally striking if confusing spectacle. An Italian near-contemporary, Leti, arraigned him as a bloodthirsty ruler of men, "devoid of scruples and taste". An ambassador from Tuscany wrote of him in 1651 that "there cannot be discerned in him any ambition save for the public service". Guizot, the French statesman turned historian, showed towards him the sympathetic insight of one who himself had seen a revolution in the making, assigning Cromwell to a place in the company of "these great men, who have laid the foundations of their greatness amidst disorder and revolution". The renowned German historian, Ranke, treated him with objective respect. A later German generation, as of Italians, hailed him as a prototype of the leadership which, in the 1930s, inspired them to vociferously tragic response.

In his largely uncritical biography of Cromwell, Theodore Roosevelt, sometime President of the United States, declared him to have been the leader of "a movement that produced the English-speaking world as we know it at present". In general, American historical scholarship, infused though much of it has been by the Puritan tradition, has not countenanced admiration for Cromwell as man or leader of men. Dean Inge believed that Cromwell would have delighted in the *Battle Hymn of the Republic*.

John Buchan's biography of Cromwell endorsed Carlyle's long-pondered findings, while underlining the proposition that Cromwell left no enduring mark on the national life. In the eyes of G. M. Trevelyan, the social historian, he saved England from autocracy, Presbyterian tyranny, and final disruption. In John Drinkwater's play about him, cited here not for its historical value but for its popularity in the theatre of two continents, Cromwell was projected as one "who cared above all for the well-being of England, which for him meant the individual liberty and enlightenment of the English people". Hilaire Belloc summed him up as "Jehovah's own dragoon", valorous, chaste, and staunch, riding roughshod in the vanguard of a conspiracy designed to overthrow the Church of Rome.

What manner of man, then, was this who, after three centuries, continues to provoke, as Meredith phrased it, writing to Morley about Cromwell, "the raging of distempered advocates"? He was born at Huntingdon on 25 April, 1599, the son of a Protestant line enriched by lands acquired at the Reformation. The paternal ancestor four generations removed was a Welshman named Morgan A. Williams, who migrated to London as one of the followers of Henry VII. He settled down in Putney, then a thriving Thames-side port, as a functionary of the Crown responsible for the manor of Wimbledon. His son, likewise named Morgan, carried on the office and combined a brewery connexion with it. He married the daughter of another local brewer, Walter Cromwell, a Norfolk man who was the father of Thomas Cromwell, Henry VIII's minister charged with the dissolution of the monasteries. Richard, the son of Morgan Williams and Katherine Cromwell, moved into his uncle Thomas's household and duly assumed the Cromwell surname. He was looked on with approval by the king, became a highly favoured courtier, and a knight.

His son, Sir Henry, was Sheriff of Huntingdonshire and Bedfordshire, and the builder of the fine mansion of Hinchingbrooke, near Huntingdon, where he entertained Queen Elizabeth. The next in the succession, Sir Oliver, entering upon his inheritance in 1603, considerably depleted it by his lavish and possibly slavish hospitality to James I. He was compelled to sell Hinchingbrooke and retire to a modest property at Ramsey, near-by.

Sir Oliver's brother, Robert, lived in High Street, Huntingdon, on income from family property that brought him £300 a year, plus whatever was to be made from farming in a gentlemanly way; he owned grazing land just outside the town. He had been to Cambridge, read law, and sat in the House of Commons as the member for Huntingdon. His wife, a widow when they married, was a Norfolk woman named Steward, a corruption of Stewart. She was said to have been of the royal line. They were the parents of Oliver Cromwell, who had seven sisters and two brothers. He was educated at the Free Grammar School, Huntingdon, and at Sidney Sussex College, Cambridge.

A Debrett of his day would have shown that Oliver Cromwell

was connected, directly and by marriage, with a network of influential families holding sway in East Anglia and farther afield. At one time at least twenty of his relatives were sitting in Parliament, one of them his rich cousin John Hampden. The Cromwells were a parliamentary family whose generations had acquired almost an hereditary claim to stand for Parliament and to be elected to it.

In his turn Oliver Cromwell entered the House of Commons in 1628, when he was twenty-nine, as the member for Huntingdon. He had married Elizabeth Bourchier, the daughter of a well-to-do City knight whose main business interest was in the fur trade. His standing then was that of a squire with £500 a year, derived from the wills of two of his uncles. His wife had some money of her own. While not prosperous, they were comfortably off. Cromwell was free to give his time and energy to politics, while keeping a watchful eye on local land values. In 1631 he sold off some of his Huntingdon land and re-invested in pastures new at St. Ives. In 1640 he was returned to Parliament for Cambridge town. It was a turning-point in more than one man's life. The political despotism which the Tudors had bequeathed to the Stuarts was about to be challenged.

We have a word-sketch of him by a contemporary courtier, Sir Philip Warwick, who saw him at Westminster at about that time. "I came into the House one morning, well clad, and perceived a gentleman speaking whom I knew not, very ordinarily apparelled, for it was a plain cloth suit, which seemed to have been made by an ill country tailor. His linen was plain, and not very clean; and I remember a speck or two of blood upon his little band, which was not much larger than his collar. His hat was without a hat-band. His stature was of a good size; his sword close to his side; his countenance swoln and reddish; his voice sharp and untuneable, and his eloquence full of fervour."

Cromwell was then a back-bencher, earnest for his constituents, a dutiful observer of Parliamentary procedures, a speaker who neither emptied the House nor filled it. At home a regular churchgoer, the topic that excited him to his most compelling flights as a speaker was the Church itself. Much of his parliamentary ardour was centred in religion. He was moved by a crusading urge to rid the Church of England of what he conceived to be poisonous influences and practices; genuflections, vestments, graven images, Popish symbols. To him and his fellow Puritans the Bible was the key to the spiritual life. It was to be elevated to the first place in public worship, taking precedence over the Prayer Book. Preachers were to be given more authority than priests.

In Cromwell's personal life politics and religion were fused into a force that made his will a formidable instrument of power when the opportunity came for him to use it. The Bible was always at his hand, the resources of prayer constant in his life. He was on his knees every day, often many times a day. He was capable of self-discipline to the point of mortification.

He supported a movement that endowed speakers to deliver religious "lectures" on village greens and at market crosses as a way of stressing the Church's want of fervour in preaching the Word. From it came a branch of religious nonconformity in England that is still healthy and vigorous. His antipathy to the bishops, in particular, declared itself in a speech in which he complained that Papist sympathizers within the Church were being given preferment over honest men of other opinions. The speech made him the authoritative spokesman of the Puritans of eastern England, whence had lately gone the Pilgrim Fathers on their famous quest.

Both Church and State roused in Cromwell feelings of dissidence that drove him forward along his revolutionary course. Their encroachment of power, it seemed to him, would inevitably lead to the suppression of freedom of conscience. That liberty, even when, paradoxically, he appeared to be its worst enemy, was the theme and inspiration of his life.

The Puritans were a faction, by no means the nation. As one of their stalwarts, Cromwell himself took on national stature in 1641 by his prominent advocacy of the Grand Remonstrance, demanding Church reform and the modification of the king's power. He held those provisos to be of such importance for the future of the realm that, he declared, their rejection would have obliged him to sell all that he had "and see England no more". Amid intense excitement in the House, the Grand Remonstrance was passed by 159 votes to 148. From then on Cromwell was in the grip of destiny. For him there could be no going back to the squire's life. What he and others had signed with the pen they would have to defend with the sword.

On 4 January, 1642, Charles I marched with an imposing bodyguard to the House of Commons to seize for impeachment five popular members: Hampden, Pym, Holles, Haselrig, and Strode. They were tipped off in time to absent themselves from the precincts. When the king called out their names and waited imperiously, an uncomfortable silence fell on the assembled members. His demand to the Speaker for information brought that worthy to his knees with the plea that he was "but the servant of this House". Head high, eyes blazing, Charles walked out of the Chamber. As he did so there was an ominous murmuring from all sides. "Privilege! Privilege!" It was one of the great moments in English history. The bodyguard escorted the king back to Whitehall in silence. It was the five members who received the cheers.

Assuming that the king would seek to avenge his rebuff by force of arms, the Puritan party deemed it necessary that Parliament should henceforth have control of the militia. When representations to that effect were formally put to the king, he answered: "Not for an hour!" Parliament thereupon seized control, over-riding Charles's protest that no ordinance was valid without his assent and signature.

Although Cromwell was not one of the members denounced by the king, if their number had been ten, or fewer, instead of five, his name would almost certainly have been on the list for arrest. He was made a member of a committee charged with inquiring into the king's sources of advice in refusing to give up control of the militia.

By then the country was considered to be in a state of emergency. The king's obduracy had cast the shadow of civil war across the land. At Cromwell's prompting, a Committee of Safety was formed. It precipitated a cleavage that ranged the people's party on the one side, presently known as the Roundheads, and the Cavaliers, whose swords were drawn in the service of the king, on the other. The outcome was a fratricidal tragedy. Families were riven, brother set against brother. Old friendships were torn apart, loyalties wiped out. Against that sombre background, Oliver Cromwell, the cavalry captain who may never have told his men, "Trust in God, and keep your powder dry", developed the leadership that was to bear him upward to a place in the pantheon of the great rulers.

The first battle of the Civil War, fought at Edgehill, near Warwick, on 23 October, 1642, proved little except that, after an initial bloody encounter, caution was largely the mood on both sides. There was some wavering among the Parliamentary foot-troops, a situation saved by the cavalry. Four months later Cromwell was raised to the rank of colonel and given a regiment. The men in it became known as Cromwell's Ironsides. Many among them were Puritan fanatics.

From the beginning Cromwell was activated by the belief that this was a religious war, and he sought to draw into his ranks only "honest and godly men". The requirement of honesty figured in almost every letter he wrote on the subject of recruiting.

By strenuous exertions, and by taking advice from professional men of arms, he made himself the Parliamentary army's best cavalry leader. It meant, in the circumstances of the time, that he was the army's best soldier, since the cavalry was the dominant arm. His bold decision, in ordering his men suddenly to rein-in and turn on the unguarded Royalist infantry, gained the victory at Marston Moor, near York, in 1644. That success weakened the king's hold on the North, particularly in Yorkshire.

That year Cromwell became a member of a sort of inner war council, styled The Committee of Both Kingdoms. One of the first recommendations brought before it was the Self-denying Ordinance, which decreed that members of both Houses of Parliament should resign their commissions in the army in favour of professional soldiers. It also considered a plan for a new national army of 10 cavalry regiments, 12 infantry regiments, and 1 regiment of dragoons. They were to be known as the New Model Army. Sir Thomas Fairfax was appointed its commander-in-chief. Cromwell was given command of the cavalry.

Discipline in the new army was ruthlessly strict. Its officers were chosen not only for their military experience but for their ardour in the cause of defeating the king's tyranny. Remoulded, the army became a unique, single-minded, dedicated military force. Its fighting efficiency owed not a little to Cromwell's inspiration and presence; and now he was preparing to comply with the Self-denying Ordinance and hand over his command.

On 4 June, 1646, the House of Commons heard a petition from the City of London for his retention as a serving officer. A similar request came from Fairfax, who was keen to put his New Model Army to the test of battle. The House of Commons concurred and, without waiting for confirmation from the other House, Fairfax sent a message to Cromwell bidding him report to the main army headquarters at Kislingbury, near Daventry.

His arrival there, at the head of six hundred mounted men, their jingling harness brasses making fine music in his ears as he rode through the fresh green Northamptonshire lanes that June, was a personal triumph. "He was with the greatest joy received by the General and the whole army. Instantly orders were given for drums to beat, trumpets to sound to horse, and all our army to draw to rendezvous." He became the New Model Army's lieutenant-general.

As at Marston Moor, he played a decisive part in the misnamed battle of Naseby, on 14 June, 1646. The discipline of his cavalry was the best in the army. Now, once again, it proved invincible. The battle was a shattering blow to the king, revealing to him the futility and the folly of his cause. He surrendered to the Scots, who handed him over to Parliament.

Under Cromwell's direction the army took the king into custody and put him under surveillance at Hampton Court Palace. Discovering that certain members of Parliament were in secret touch with him, the Puritan leaders sent an officer named Colonel Pride to the House of Commons to arrest them as they entered. "Pride's Purge" was an unconstitutional act. It meant that the New Model Army had become a political entity.

Cromwell, with Ireton, his son-in-law, evolved a plan of pacification which they hoped would receive the approval of both sides. It was rejected by the king. Cromwell had a number of consultations with him, finally to the detriment of his own repute, for he was suspected of private connivance with Charles. Already there were muttered demands that the king's life should be forfeit. Cromwell turned a deaf ear to them. His patience was exemplary. If there was a way of peacefully and satisfactorily resolving the dilemma, he wished with all his heart to find it. In his efforts to do so he frequently retired from the public scene for long sessions of prayer.

The king broke his parole and sought refuge in the Isle of Wight. It was a fatal mistake, a signal to the headsman to begin sharpening his axe. Cromwell had genuinely wished for a clear and conscientious understanding with the king, subject to the latter's readiness to acknowledge the primacy of Parliament. Charles prevaricated, twisted, intrigued, floundered in evasions, provoking the House of Commons to pass the resolution "that by the fundamental laws of this kingdom, it is treason for the King of England to levy war against the Parliament and Kingdom of England".

The trial of Charles I was thus set in motion. There was no constitutional warranty for it and Cromwell listened impatiently to those lawyers who argued otherwise. The king refused to acknowledge the authority of the Court and to defend himself before it. Shrinking then, as on other occasions, from frightful decision and taking it only when it appeared to him imperatively necessary, Cromwell tried to avoid putting his name to the document that sent Charles to his death on the scaffold in Whitehall on 30 January, 1649. Afterwards he spoke of it as an act of justice, a word that for him always had a higher and holier sanction than that of any human court. Long ago he had declared himself opposed to the death penalty except for murder and treason.

A Council of State was formed, with Cromwell as the dominant figure among its 41 members. The monarchy, the House of Peers, and their associative symbols and influences, were swept away. Virtually, it meant creating a new State, with the squire from Huntingdon at its head. Before him lay nearly a decade of supreme authority.

What he did with it vexes historical judgement today as keenly as it did nearer his time. His life and work have been the subject of a score or more biographies, numerous treatises, endlessly recurring arguments. His name is still execrated in Ireland, where he met violence with violence, on the ground that Irish Catholics had instituted massacres of English Protestants living lawfully among them. Faced with the Duke of Hamilton's southward invasion from Scotland in 1648, he reacted with equally crushing effect.

He was the honoured champion of liberty, the hated wrecker of free institutions, a defender and an oppressor: in the eyes of his critics, all those things. As the historian Gardiner has said: "All the incongruities of human nature are to be traced somewhere or other in Cromwell's career." The same authority takes care to point out that "this union of apparently contradictory forces" is characteristic of the English people, "making England what she is today".

In 1657 Parliament, recognizing in him the representative Englishman, offered Cromwell the Crown as a means of securing a return to constitutional government and the ordered society. Prayer, intense self-communion, earnest consultation, finally evoked from him the reply: "I cannot undertake this Government with that title of king; and that is my answer to this great and weighty business." Instead, he agreed to be known as the Protector, the guarantor of liberty of conscience for all. There had never been in England a ruler whose fame shone out with such brilliance as Cromwell's in the last years of his life.

He died on 3 September, 1658. Overnight, a great storm that ripped off housetops and blew down mighty oaks betokened the end, also, of Puritanism as a political power.

CHARLES I

King of England, Scotland and Ireland

(1600–49)

NO ENGLISH monarch has cast a longer shadow than Charles I. His fate still stirs prejudice and engages sympathy, though the rights and wrongs of his case have been before the world for over three hundred years. The red roses that continue to appear annually at the foot of his statue at the junction of Whitehall and Charing Cross are an emblem of more than a martyr's blood. They commemorate the crux of a great constitutional struggle, in which the execution of the king was a sombre incident rather than a shattering event. The axeman who held up the severed head to the crowd round the scaffold in 1649 was the servant of forces more imponderable than political or doctrinal discords.

Those forces had been working in society from Tudor times. Their course was run only when at last the kingly role was reformed and modified by the demolition of Divine Right. That concept, stubbornly held by Charles I, ignored shifts of social and economic emphasis that were historically more decisive than his follies or the bigotries of his Civil War enemies. A new influence had been rising in the land, that of the propertied class, the gentry, who resented subjection to the exclusive authoritarian patronage of the Court and the old nobility. It was Charles's tragedy that he was too rigidly moulded by his birth and training to be sensitive to a social change with effects as potent as those of the French Revolution or that later enacted in Russia.

He became Charles I because fate ordained that his elder brother should not come to the Throne as Henry IX. The second son of James I, Charles was made Prince of Wales when Henry died at eighteen in 1612. As a child, born in the sign of Scorpio towards the end of November, 1600, Charles was a poor human specimen, extremely weak on his legs and incapable, it seemed, of more than spasmodic speech. His chances of survival, not to say of his developing normally, were thought slender, a doubt that was resolved by the devotion of his governess, Lady Carey, who cossetted him out of his protracted invalidism into an adolescence that saw him taking his place as a fearless horseman and an agile tennis player. His equestrian skill owed not a little to his small stature; he fancied that his horsemanship offset it. None the less, the physical transformation was remarkable.

Mentally, he remained a slow thinker who relied on silence to conceal the truth about himself. He was never a man of easy speech. His habit of reserve hid self-distrust and kept suitable advisers at a distance. The loneliness of his early years was accentuated by his lack of sympathy and humour. Yet by many he was thought "a creditable prince", whose personal life was in favourable contrast to that of the loose-living Court of his father. For his time and station, his code of conduct was a strict one, though dedicated more explicitly to the improvement of his physical prowess than to the refinement of his moral qualities. He had a known contempt for drunkenness, for example, and the grosser forms of debauchery evoked his disgust. The people saw virtue in him, and their cheers at his few public appearances in those years made music in the ears of one whose self-assurance was always in need of support.

His father, James I, had cherished the prospect of an alliance between England and Spain, to be clinched by the marriage of his son Henry to one of the Infantas. Five years after Henry's death, negotiations were reopened with Charles taking his brother's place in the rôle of suitor. There were frustrations and delays due to papal demands and to the king's tardiness in guaranteeing liberty of worship to Roman Catholics in England. Parliament urged a different course, petitioning the king to see to it that Charles married a Protestant princess. James told the Commons in effect to mind their business, which did not include interference with royal marriages. He caused the petition to be expunged from the official records and dissolved Parliament.

In the early spring of 1623 a small party of horsemen trotted sedately out of London towards Gravesend. Two of their number rode ahead, apparently in close companionship. They were heavily bearded and muffled in the folds of long riding cloaks. The beards of the two foremost men roused the suspicion of the mayor of Gravesend, who sent a messenger to trail the party down the Dover Road. His inquisitiveness was followed by abject silence when he learned that he was shadowing the heir to the Throne, travelling in elaborate incognito to Spain. His companion in disguise was the newly ennobled George Villiers, Marquess of Buckingham, "Steenie" to the king and Prince Charles. Buckingham, who had the king's highest favour, opened new doors on the world to Charles, initiating him into a wider experience of life, while being careful not to involve him in the private vices in which Buckingham notoriously indulged.

Arriving in Paris as John and Thomas Smith, the two young men secured admission to the Court and attended a masque at which the queen was present. She was a sister of the young Infanta whom Charles hoped to meet in Madrid. The queen's charms and graces spurred his eagerness to reach the Spanish capital; and during his five days in Paris he had no more than fleeting glances for the queen's vivacious, dark-eyed sister-in-law, Henriette Maria. It was afterwards reported that the princess had remarked that there was no need for the Prince of Wales to go so far as Madrid to look for a wife.

The news of Charles's mission to Spain was communicated to the people of England by bell ringing and bonfires lighted by royal command. Not all the citizens danced for joy. The Archbishop of Canterbury protested in the name of religion. Parliamentarians were angry because they had not been consulted in the name of the people. They gave the prince a great welcome when in the autumn of 1623 he returned to England, "not so much because he had come back", explained Gardiner, the learned historian, "as because he had not brought the Infanta with him". Archbishop Laud wrote in his diary that Charles was received with "the great expression of joy of all sorts of people that ever I saw".

The abortive match, which was politically rather than sentimentally inspired, was repugnant to Englishmen who remembered the Armada thirty-five years before. The collapse of the betrothal to a Catholic princess also gratified those who could not forget the more recent Gunpowder Plot.

The news-writers observed that the Spanish adventure had improved Charles's style as a public figure. He had become "a fine gentleman", they wrote. A new stateliness marked his deportment, perhaps in conscious or unconscious imitation of his recent hosts. He remained a singularly unimaginative young man, who was as capable of offending his friends as readily as those who were not his friends. "He has not the art to please", was a clerical comment on his often morose temperament.

Having been unmistakably apprised of the people's attitude to the marriage question, he proceeded with negotiations for his engagement to the young Henriette Maria of France. The House of Commons was upset again and exacted from him an oath, solemnly affirmed at St. John's College, Cambridge, that his marriage to a Catholic princess would mean "no advantage to the recusants at home".

The worth of the oath was limited if not nullified by an understanding secretly connived at by King James, Charles, and a Secretary of State, promising Roman Catholics in England a larger measure of liberty than they had previously enjoyed. James, in particular, was concerned to save those priests who were awaiting the utmost rigour of the law for privately administering Catholic rites to their flocks. Secret modifications of publicly enacted agreements were a common feature of the diplomacy of that age. In this instance the effects reverberated far. A dynamic mistrust developed between Charles and Parliament, leading to the English Revolution.

James I died on 27 March, 1625, making a pious and affecting end, partly brought about by excessive fruit eating, the physicians said. In the afternoon of that day Charles was proclaimed king. "Universal joy" greeted the event, according to Clarendon. The new monarch was hailed as a paragon of several virtues—sobriety, chastity, piety, dignity. He disliked flattery, was impervious to sycophancy, and his private life was without blame; he was seen to blush at immodest talk. He had a good appreciation of the arts, especially painting.

A portrait of him as a young man, painted by Daniel Mytens and believed to have been in the Royal collection, showed that, for all his lack of inches—he was a little over five feet—he was well proportioned, lithe, and of good bearing. Three days after his father's death he ratified, as king, the marriage treaty to which he had already put his name as prince.

The marriage took place on 1 May, 1625, Charles being represented by proxy at a ceremony conducted on a dais erected before the great door of Notre-Dame in Paris. A week's festivities followed before the young Queen Henriette (who in England soon became Henrietta) left for London and wifehood with Charles. He, meanwhile, had been chief mourner, garbed in a black cloak that hung to his ankles, at the funeral of his father in Westminster Abbey. There was criticism of the funeral sermon preached by the Bishop of Lincoln, who insisted that "no man ever got great power without eloquence". It was thought to be too pointed a reminder, in view of Charles's unreadiness of speech.

Having borne himself with approved gravity at those majestic obsequies, the new king rode to Canterbury to await the arrival of his French bride. She had been seen by an admiring Dover mariner disporting herself on the seashore at Boulogne. He informed the mayor and burgesses in a letter that she was a healthy and merry young thing who ventured "so near the sea it was bold to kiss her feet". History is cluttered with irrelevancies. Queen Henrietta's wet shoes have remained firmly imprinted in the sands of time.

On the evening of Trinity Sunday, 12 June, 1625, a Court messenger named Tyrwhit galloped the fifteen miles from Dover to Canterbury in thirty-six minutes to inform the king that his young queen, with her retinue of ladies-in-waiting and priestly advisers, was on English soil. By ten o'clock the next morning, Charles was at Dover to greet her. She was at breakfast in Dover Castle. When she knelt to do obeisance, "he wrapt her up in his arms with many kisses". Weeping, she disengaged from his embrace, apparently overcome by being among strangers. The contract of marriage was renewed in St. Augustine's Hall, Canterbury, without benefit of clergy. Public sensitiveness precluded the king from receiving the rites from a Roman Catholic, and the queen from an Anglican.

There being a plague in London (not to be confused with the later and more horrific visitation that is in all the history books), it was deemed wise to keep the royal couple away from the streets. Escorted by a mass of small craft filled with sightseers, they were rowed up the Thames in State barges to Whitehall. While bonfires blazed and cannon boomed, the dead-carts clattered over the cobbles with their loads for unmarked graves. Mingled with the thanksgiving in the churches were prayers for relief from the pestilence.

Charles was crowned in Westminster Abbey on 2 February, 1625, "a very bright, sun-shining day" (Archbishop Laud's diary). His young consort was not by his side. The Capuchin priests who had come over with her from France saw to that. She was proclaimed, but not crowned, queen later that year. As a Catholic, she could not accept the offices of the Church of England. In any event, as man and wife, differences were soon evident between them. A particular cause was Charles's growing regard for Buckingham, by then a duke. The little French queen detested him.

Charles had inherited a Throne with sharp thorns in the cushion: enormous debts, virtually war with Spain, and an intractable belief in the sovereign's right of personal rule. The last was a source of mounting strife between him and a House of Commons group resolved to stand fast for the privileges of Parliament and the liberties of the people. Opposition to Charles was coming also from another quarter, the Puritan party, animated by the theology of Calvin and a hatred of Rome.

Those dissidents in the House of Commons forced Charles to lay before Parliament a precise statement of his personal finances, complicated, as they were, by additional debts incurred since his father's death. They required to know the cost of maintaining the Navy, and demanded an estimate of the amount likely to be involved in a war with Spain.

Behind these requirements was deepening hostility to the king's closest adviser, Buckingham, who had too much power and was considered reckless in his use of it. One of his foremost critics in the House of Commons, Sir John Eliot, from Cornwall, later denounced him as the chief author of the nation's misfortunes, and the only begetter of the disaster that befell the naval expedition to Cadiz. As a climax of the agitation, Buckingham was impeached for having imperilled the national safety and honour.

The King reacted by sending Eliot to the Tower of London. In return, the House of Commons refused to transact any business until he was released. Charles then dissolved Parliament, an act designed as much to save his friend Buckingham as to preserve the sanctity of the "royal word". From that time on the people had to choose between the ultimate authority of king or Parliament. The prisons began to fill with men for whom the still small voice had become a loud imperative command.

By the end of the third year of his reign Charles was in dire trouble, with an empty exchequer, the prospect of having to make a humiliating peace with his enemies abroad, and his prerogative being attacked in Parliament by hitherto law-abiding gentlemen. The assassination of Buckingham by an Army lieutenant at Portsmouth in 1628 was a crowning personal disaster for Charles. It was said that he never threw off the effects of it in the twenty years that were left to him. So loyal was he to his friend's memory that the great historian Clarendon declared: "From that time almost to the time of his own death the king admitted very few into any degree of trust against whom Buckingham had ever manifested a notable prejudice."

One change in Charles's personal relationships at that time was remarked. The queen was pregnant again and his concern was such that at Court it was said that he had at last fallen in love with her. Unfortunately, their sudden access of felicity proved to be of ominous import for the nation. In his determination to avenge the death of his friend, the king showed himself too ready to surrender to the influence of his wife, who was even more rigidly attached than he to the Divine Right concept.

Thenceforward Charles relied on personal rule as the sole instrument of government. For the next eight years, until 1637, England had no Parliament. The king could count those years as the happiest and most settled of his life. They gave him an opportunity of practising his patronage of the arts, and of enjoying the company of Van Dyck and other painters. He added weightily to his collection of what an irate pamphleteer reviled as "old rotten pictures and broken-nosed marbles". The Italian sculptor, Bernini, commissioned to make a bust of the king, studied Van Dyck's portraits of him and announced that he had never seen "a countenance so unfortunate".

As always, Charles had not the wit to see the reality behind events, even when the surface was comparatively unruffled. They were being more observantly watched by an as yet hardly known Fenland squire, Oliver Cromwell, who, believing that he had attained to grace and salvation, also believed that he was called to high service in the land. Others of his kind, in protest against misguided kingship, joined in the Puritan emigration that was to lay the foundations of a great new overseas nation.

A new personality had arrived on the stage in Thomas Wentworth, to be ennobled presently as the Earl of Strafford. He was a Yorkshire baronet associated with Eliot, Hampden and others of their class who had assisted the fall of Buckingham. Endowed with a keen political sense and ambitious for a chance to exercise it in office, he identified himself with the king's party and was rewarded with titular distinctions and high authority in Ireland. That he was politically talented could not be denied; unluckily for him, he too obviously rejoiced in his gifts. "Of all his passions," Clarendon wrote, "pride was most prominent", and the historian's comment was justified by Wentworth's self-aggrandizement. Soon it was to be said of him that he was an even greater servant of the king than Buckingham had been. Yet the probability was that neither had a deep regard for the other. As for the queen, she at first disliked Wentworth as heartily as she had Buckingham, fearing his influence over her husband.

Events in Scotland, where Charles's attempt to force a new Book of Common Prayer on the Church of Scotland met fierce opposition, brought the two countries into conflict. On Wentworth's advice, the king summoned what was to be known as the Short

Parliament in the spring of 1640 and, also on his advice, dissolved it in three weeks for its refusal to grant him the means to equip and pay for an army to march against the Scots.

Another burning issue was ship money, levied on port authorities for protection from pirates who harried the coastal communities. So long as the funds thus raised were used for national purposes no one seriously objected. When the tax was extended inland the Buckinghamshire squire, John Hampden, refused to pay it. His action represented widespread resentment of the king's forced loans, of which ship money was by no means a solitary example. The smouldering fires of discontent were being blown into a fierce consuming flame. Hampden's proud resistance stirred the nation.

With shame and wrath in his heart, Charles gave way over a number of vital issues of the time, after vainly trying either to evade doing so or refusing his assent. Finally, summoning against his will what became the Long Parliament (1640), he found himself facing the people's champions, Hampden, Pym and presently Cromwell, across the dividing lines of power. By his side was the apostate Strafford (Wentworth), whose death-warrant he was soon unwillingly to sign. One of the effects of the resolute stand of those men was to halt the Puritan emigration. "The change", wrote an historian, "made all men to stay in England in expectation of a new world". It was a dream to be realized only through the blood and grief of the Civil War, with its horrible climax in Whitehall that cold afternoon of 30 January, 1649.

The inquest verdict has yet to be finally given. "If he were not the best king," Clarendon wrote in his great history, "if he were without some parts and qualities which have made some kings great and happy, no other prince was ever unhappy who was possessed of half his virtues and endowments, and so much without any kind of vice". Against the exemplariness of his private life is set the arbitrary temper he too often showed in the public domain. Some would say that Charles I was his own executioner.

CHARLES II

King of England, Scotland and Ireland

(1630–85)

YOUNG KING CHARLES II of England laughed as he smeared his face with soot in the chimney corner at Whiteladies during his flight from Cromwell's vengeful forces after the battle of Worcester, 1651. He was at risk of discovery and capture. Weariness was heavy upon him. Yet still he could laugh. His good humour, though it reflected a careless mind, was his title to the regard not only of those around him but of posterity. The simple absence of vanity from his nature perpetuated him in folk-memory, and the history books, as surely as his gallantries and the general jauntiness of his performance in the kingly role. He had no taste for tyranny, and he was too intelligent to be susceptible to the divine right theory that bedevilled his forebears on the throne.

If he was the most frivolous of England's monarchs, his wretched later upbringing could be held largely to account for it. An idyllic childhood in pleasant places, Hampton Court, Windsor, Greenwich, was all too soon shadowed by violence, tragedy, and grief. As a boy he heard the howling of the mob, and was touched by the desolation of his father's grim fate. At fifteen he was with the Royalists in the last phase of the Civil War, and saw the shambles that followed defeat in the West Country. At eighteen, he became a king with nowhere to lay his head.

Then there came the forlorn descent on England from Scotland, and, after it, shame and degradation, and the poverty of exile in France and Germany. Within a year he was eating his meals in taverns, too hard up to provide a table of his own. "I am sure the king owes for all he had had since April," wrote Edward Hyde, the Chancellor of his virtually non-existent Exchequer, in June, 1653. Beset by debt, and the indignities inseparable from it, Charles maintained an extraordinary hold over his sometimes despairing and often fractious Court by his gaiety of heart and the unquenchable good-humour that enabled him to laugh when disappointment clouded every prospect and idleness ate like gall into his soul.

He was kept going through the nine frustrating years that severed him from England by a zest for the ordinary simple satisfactions that was never subdued by his worst excesses. He loved to show off the few bits of finery that he had left; delighted in old wines and new tunes, and eagerly took lessons to improve his dancing and his knowledge of French and Italian. His buoyancy in one of the stormiest periods of English history may not have been admirable. Many must have envied it.

That he emerged from those early experiences as a sauntering cynic was unfortunate but hardly to be wondered at. He was always good company, and he could laugh at himself, which does not redeem the charge that he was a worthless character but takes some of the sting out of it. Although the adventurer in him found its commonest expression in dalliance, he had not a little of the temper of a rebel, including the courage. He was a fine horseman, who did not flinch from mounting the least trustworthy beast in the stable. He was unafraid of the sea in any of its moods. He could outwalk the sturdiest of his companions, and could hold his liquor beyond the capacity of most of them. He was a womanizer from the age of sixteen. Even Pepys blushed at his prowess in the sexual arena. Pretty or plain, well-born or quite otherwise, women contributed to Charles's life of indulgence its chiefest pleasures. His profound selfishness was not much mitigated by the courtesy and grace with which he was wont to invest his amorous escapades.

His small resources of sincerity were lavished on his sweet little sister "Minette", Princess Henrietta of England, who became Duchess of Orleans. He was her only hero. "She is truly and passionately concerned for the king, her brother," one of the courtiers wrote. She admired him above all other men. In return, he wrote loving letters to her, dutifully catching the mail each week, and telling her how impatient he was "till I have the happiness to see *ma chère Minette* again". It was his deepest and most genuine affection.

Those who cared most for his future feared that the years of exile tended to confirm him in his lack of responsibility and to weaken his moral fibre yet further. Hyde passed word to him to that effect that had come in letters from London. His advisers were even more worried because he made "no distinction of persons", but seemed content to choose his company where he found it. His privations were real enough to make their mark on his personal appearance. He was even unable to pay for the candles that lighted him to bed. Belts were tightened, cloaks closely drawn, against a winter that froze the birds' feet to the bough.

Unexpectedly, Charles's world was rocked by the news of Cromwell's death. He was in Holland, taking the country air and playing tennis when he heard it. Suddenly uplifted, and believing himself enamoured of the youngest daughter of the Dowager Princess of the Netherlands, he offered his hand in marriage. In spite of his brightened prospects, the Dowager Princess did not fancy him as a son-in-law. She soon made it known that there was no match.

By the spring of 1659 the Protectorate was consigned to the tablets of history, and the members of the new Council of State that succeeded it were making their meals off venison from the royal parks. Cromwell's monument in Westminster Abbey was tumbled down. Plots and plans were thick in the air, chief among them a projected rising of Presbyterians and Cavaliers that would descend on the capital from every shire and county, bearing Charles back to his rightful place. The secret date was 1 August, 1659. Treachery rose up to confuse the scene. It was disclosed that Charles, standing by to embark for Deal, was to be seized and done away with as soon as he landed.

Affairs in Kent went wrong; in Cheshire even more so. The great plot had misfired. Charles rode off to Rouen, where there might be a boat to take him to a West Country port. Briskly cheerful as ever, he wrote to Hyde that, though he was "not altogether so plump", he felt sanguine in his guise of "Mr. Skinner", and added the reflection that "sure people never went so cheerfully to venture their necks as we do".

Receiving no sign of success afoot in his favour in England, he set off on a jaunt to the Pyrenees, *en route* for Fuentarrabia, where the envoys of France and Spain were meeting to conclude a treaty. Charles proposed to impress them with all the charm that he could muster, hoping that they would respond with help, as much for him personally as for his cause. The journey was made enjoyable by "many happy accidents", of the nature of which we are left to guess, and by meals the like of which had been too long denied him. "God keep you", he wrote to Hyde, "and send you to eat as good mutton as we have". It was about the limit of his piety.

He was well received. Due honours were done. He was so gratified by his personal success that he offered marriage to Cardinal Mazarin's niece, Hortense Mancini. He was put off, politely, by the Cardinal, as virtual ruler of France. Unabashed, Charles bestrode his horse and, with only his valet, Toby Rustat, for company, rode back across France to see his sister Minette, awaiting him at Colombes. At first he did not recognize her, she had grown so much, and he kissed another, allegedly by mistake. He then rode on to Brussels over slushy roads after frosts. The capital was in the gloom of yet another hard winter, his loyal followers, awaiting him, utterly cast down. A new civil war threatened in England.

General Monk, commander-in-chief in Scotland, who was the first of the military caste to bow the head to the civil power, paraded his army and announced his intention to march down over the Border to assert "the freedom and rights of the three kingdoms". With snow in the sky and frost covering the ground, he set forth with seven thousand men. "I do not remember that we ever trod upon plain earth from Edinburgh to London," Monk's chaplain recorded. If the snow did not melt, resistance did. All Yorkshire came out to speed Monk's men on their way.

Ahead of them went rumour, excitement, doubts, fears. Rising from his bed on 30 January, young Sam Pepys remembered that "this was the fatal day, now ten years since, his Majesty died". Despite the melancholy memory, a song came to his lips. In his favourite wine-vaults he secretly raised his glass to the king whose crowning might now be a little nearer.

In Flanders, Edward Hyde, blowing on his cold fingers, wrote to a friend in London: "We all have some envy towards you that are in a place where you can want no fire, which we all do. When it will change, we yet know not." The hardships continued. Personal possessions, including the king's, were at the pawnbrokers. Charles was busy writing letters to England, a hundred and more on official business, and pouring out his tenderness for his sister in others. "You show me so much affection that the only quarrel we are ever likely to have will be as to which of us two loves the other best."

Monk's army passed into London on 3 February, 1660, heralded by trumpeters in scarlet and silver. When the City aldermen declined to pay taxes until a free Parliament was called, Monk marched in to demonstrate the authority of what remained of Cromwell's administration, the Rump, as it was derisively known. A week later, the general demanded writs for the return of the excluded members of Parliament, to be followed, he insisted, by a dissolution and a new and freely elected House of Commons.

When on 11 February Monk told the burgesses of the City what he had done, and was requiring to be done, long-pent emotions exploded in a great outburst of popular feeling. The expression on men's faces changed as if at the wave of an enchanter's wand. The English spirit was free again and the rejoicing was immense. Every street had its bonfires that night; in one more than thirty were counted. Butchers' knives flashed as carcases were roasted, while the people made bawdy jokes about "the Rump". Dancing, shouting, singing, "the common joy was everywhere to be seen". The same chronicler wrote that "it was past imagination, both the greatness and the suddenness of it". Within two days the entire nation knew what was afoot, and there were prayers for a fair wind from Flanders.

On the afternoon of 15 March a workman with a ladder on his shoulder and a pot of paint in his free hand arrived at that place in the City, close by the Royal Exchange, where the statue of Charles I had formerly stood. After his execution an inscription had been put on the wall above the site: *Exit Tyrannus, Regum Ultimus*—"The tyrant is gone, the last of the kings". The workman proceeded to paint out the inscription. Having done it, he threw his cap into the air and called out, as if he had an official mandate to do so: "God bless King Charles the Second!" His cry was instantly taken up by a thunderous shout within the Exchange. The next day the Long Parliament was voted at an end. General Monk saw Sir John Grenville and sent him off as an emissary to the king in Brussels.

Charles mounted his horse and left at once for Holland. At Breda, in counsel with Hyde, soon to become the first earl of Clarendon, he drafted a declaration ensuring a bloodless revolution and guaranteeing his subservience to a free Parliament. On 28 April the Speaker read the declaration aloud to the House, every member standing and bareheaded; one of the great House of Commons scenes. Acclamation followed. There was not a dissentient voice. The House voted Charles £50,000 and endorsed a prayer for his return. The sky that night was red with the glow of bonfires again. Bells rang from every steeple and tower and, it seemed, more wildly than before. Men were seen drinking the king's health on their knees in the streets. The miller of Charlton burnt down his old mill for joy. In the ports the pennants flew, the guns roared, sailors lined the yards to cheer. "Believe me, I know not whether I am in England or no, or whether I dream," and the Cavalier's wonderment was echoed by Lady Derby, who wrote that "the change is so great, I can hardly believe it. It is beyond our understanding".

Charles, who knew what it was to count the hours of his long absence, now had hardly a moment to himself. Delegations, applications, petitions, crowded in on him, so that he had to sit up till after midnight writing letters, public and private. Fourteen citizens of London, bringing with them a chest full of gold to the value of £10,000, were most warmly welcomed.

He went aboard the re-named flagship, the *Royal Charles*, on 22 May, 1660. To see him off there were his brothers, his sister, and his aunt, the Queen of Bohemia, she for whom *The Tempest* was written half a century before. His sister wept and clung to him, until the weighing of the anchor parted them.

He was rowed ashore at Dover in the admiral's barge on 25 May. The beach under the grey cliffs was crowded down to the waterline. Guns flamed and boomed from the escort ships and coastal forts. Stepping on to the shingle, Charles knelt as if giving devout thanks, a gesture that was pleasing to the people if not to the Almighty to whom presumably it was addressed. When he rose up it was to receive Monk's sword and the general's salutation: "God save the King!" It was echoed with a roar all along the beach and up in the town. The formalities over, Charles left by coach for London. When he was well clear of the boundaries, and the last running sightseer had been left behind, he called for his horse and, mounting it, cantered across Barham Downs to Canterbury, his first sight of England in May for what was nearly half his lifetime. "My head is so dreadfully stunned with the acclamations of the people", he wrote hurriedly to tell his sister, "and the vast amount of business, that I know not whether I am writing sense or nonsense".

It was his thirtieth birthday on 29 May; for a multitude of Englishmen, as for him, an unforgettable day. Most of them had got up with the sun, like the Lord Mayor of London, who rumbled off thus early in his coach to Blackheath, where he was to greet the king. A hundred and twenty thousand citizens assembled there, the waiting hours whiled away by observing the arrival and forming up of several regiments, and by the antics of morris dancers.

When at last the king came into view, slim and tall, with a hint of the hidalgo in his looks and style, bowing gravely to right and left and yet with no condescension in his manner, the people shouted a welcome that drowned even the church bells. At the head of "a triumph of above twenty thousand horse and foot, brandishing their swords and shouting with inexpressible joy; the ways strewn with flowers, the bells ringing, the streets hung with tapestry, fountains running with wine", Charles advanced into the capital over London Bridge and along the Strand to Whitehall, where, at last dismounted, he was "so weary as to be scarce able to speak". He was too tired to attend a service of thanksgiving in the Abbey that evening. From under his heavy-lidded eyes he smiled as he jested that he ought to have come home sooner, for everyone was telling him now that the whole nation had been longing for it.

May 29, 1660, was remarkable above many other days of great rejoicing, for it was as if overnight the past had been expunged and a new era begun. Much that was traditional, ingrained, customary, seemed suddenly deprived of force. Historical perspectives were changed. The Middle Ages, the Reformation, seemed to be set still farther back in time, their hold on the minds of men diminished. New currents moved the tide of English history, which from that time broadened out to become a great formative influence of the modern world.

Casting out the works of the Puritans, their preachments, their sobriety, their desecrations, their censorship, their oppressive godliness, the new regime rid the nation of elements of restraint and discipline that were to cost it dear in times to come, including perhaps our own. The mark of the gentleman was re-defined. He had to be adept at duelling and seduction. Excess and frivolity set the tone, amplified into licentiousness by the new race of dramatists. Privately, Charles complained of "the want of good breeding" in England. He had a preference for Paris manners.

The people at large, immunized by more than distance from the sins of Court and capital, clung to the old social order and went obediently to church again, as in former times. But a spirit of inquiry was abroad and active in distinguished minds. A new temper was manifesting itself in religion and politics. Isaac Newton had just gone up to Cambridge, in itself an event of history. Charles shared the new enthusiasms, science and philosophy, while remaining the slave of his inclinations. He became the patron of the newly founded Royal Society, signing his name with a flourish on the first page of its treasured register. He had a little laboratory of his own in the palace at Whitehall and retreated to it with unconcealed satisfaction when business became wearisome. He enjoyed distilling cordials.

The time of coronation had come. On 22 April, Charles left Whitehall at dawn by barge to make a State entry from the Tower of London to the Palace of Westminster. Once again the bells rang out while the king passed down river, smiling his pleasure in the new assurances of his popularity. He was crowned on St. George's Day. The shout that was heard at the Archbishop's bidding, "Lift up your hearts", echoed far beyond the rooftops of Whitehall. Three times Garter King-of-Arms flung the challenge to all hearers: "If anyone has cause to show why Charles Stuart should not be King of England, let him speak!" No answer came. That night a canopy of dancing light hung over London from the uncounted bonfires in the streets.

Next there was the matter of his marriage; for Charles was sure that his Commons, as he told them, would not desire him to live "to be an old bachelor". The Spanish were interested, scheming to find a way of attaching the English Crown to their purposes. They proposed several choices to him, with offers of liberal endowments, which he mistrusted. He had another prospect in view. The Queen Regent of Portugal had made it known through England's ambassador at Lisbon that if Charles would take her daughter's hand he would find that it held more than the promise of domestic felicity—keys to a chest containing half a million in gold and silver, to the gates of Tangier, and to free trade with Brazil and the East Indies. It was indeed a fabulous offer. Charles responded to it as gracefully as his more limited means permitted. When the Portuguese ambassador arrived in London Charles bestowed on him the favour of a private key to the royal garden.

It was reported in Whitehall that Catherine of Braganza was short, pretty, black-eyed, and charming. Charles wrote her letters to show that he too had charm. They were married in May, 1662, and spent their honeymoon at Hampton Court. The people were pleased with their young queen, finding her only fault to be her slightly protruding teeth.

Connubial bliss was not destined to last long. In June a son was born to Barbara Palmer, Lady Castlemaine, who christened him Charles after the king, his father. Other famous mistresses followed, the vivacious orange-seller Nell Gwynne and his beautiful French fancy Louise de Querouaille amongst them. Charles was never one to deny his own and these families were adorned with the ermine of nobility and their descendants are great names with seats in the House of Lords today.

Too indolent to be ambitious, he was often clear-seeing and could rise above the more puerile preoccupations of his temperament. Thus when the new Parliament showed an unforgiving spirit towards old antagonists, he told the members: "Let us look forward and not backward, and never think of what is past. God hath wrought a wonderful miracle in settling us as He hath done. I pray let us all do what we can to get reputation at home and abroad of being well settled." Aware of the racial discords between the two countries, he deliberately risked ill-will by sanctioning the withdrawal of English troops from beyond the Border. He was no friend of bigotry.

His moral blindness made him at times contemptible. He had a natural kindness, perhaps more accurately described as the spontaneous generosity of an essentially selfish man. He was admirably free from superstition in an age that was rampant with it. He was not utterly without religion, but he had few discernible ideals.

His attraction for the insular people whom he ruled for twenty-five years seems to have resided in his being something of a foreigner. He was the grandson of Henry of Navarre, from whom he inherited a certain courtly grace, and a good constitution, though little of the energy of that admired monarch. Politically he was also an alien, for he could understand French and Spanish motives better than those of his own country. His attachment to France was a liability that bore heavily on England.

As a king he had better talents than many who occupied the throne, and better opportunities than some of demonstrating them for his people's good. His undoubted courage lay largely dormant throughout his life, just as his cool insight into the hearts of men was rarely exercised. Only his good humour remained, and that, by the perversity of things, sufficed to give him undeserved renown.

LOUIS XIV

(1638–1715)

LOUIS XIV, the grandson of France's most popular king, Henry IV, was born in 1638, came to the throne in 1642 and died in 1715. If his reign is dated only from 1661, from the death of Cardinal Mazarin who had ruled France during Louis's minority, it outlasts those of Charles II, James II, William and Mary and Queen Anne. He was known in France and throughout Europe as "The Great Monarch", and certainly during his reign France dominated Europe, taking the place of Spain in the sixteenth century.

Louis did not invent the idea of Absolute Monarchy. His grandfather, Henry IV, took care to see that the king's power was unchallengeable and so, in England, did the Tudors. But Louis XIV gave a striking and dogmatic form to the Absolute Monarchy. He ruled France from his new and immense palace at Versailles, which became not only the centre of government but also of social power. Louis's system of despotism became a pattern for the small princes and dukes of Germany and Italy during the eighteenth century. Scores of palaces modelled on Versailles sprang up from Brandenburg to Calabria, and there were scores of Absolute Princes by divine right, some lords of only a few towns and some thousands of acres.

England decisively refused to accept the claims of the first two Stuart kings to Absolutism, and by 1688 the power of the English Parliament was affirmed, never to be seriously questioned. Holland and the Swiss Cantons also rejected this Absolute form of government. But no country rejected the pre-eminence of French civilization during the seventeenth century. French literature, philosophy, building, furniture, cloths and manners were copied by all Europe during Louis's long reign. "We conquered France," wrote Pope, referring to Marlborough's victories over Louis XIV at the beginning of the eighteenth century,

> *"But felt our captive's charms,*
> *her arts victorious triumphed o'er our arms."*

The glory of French achievements during Louis's long reign

became a part of his personal legend. Was Louis himself a very great man or did his pomp hide a rather narrow-minded, small man? "The greatest man ever born on the steps of a throne," the liberal historian Lord Acton wrote of him at the end of the nineteenth century; or was Louis nothing more than a glorified Postmaster-General, as a more recent French historian, Seignobos, has called him?

In 1682, twenty years after his personal reign had begun, few would have doubted about the answer; it would have been that this short, physically strong, dark-faced, full-cheeked man with his large Bourbon nose was the most successful of French kings. He had fought two victorious wars against Spain and Holland, mainly in the Low Countries. He had acquired Lille and many other towns which are parts of northern France. At the Treaty of Nimwegen, which ended the second war, French had, for the first time in history, taken the place of Latin as the language of the Treaty and of diplomacy. The French armies were the best organized in Europe, the work of a great civil servant, Louvois; a great military engineer, Vauban, constructed the most efficient fortresses to protect French conquests. Now it can be said that France's strength came in part from the exhaustion of the House of Austria and its adherents in Germany as a result of the Thirty Years War; it was the result, in fact, of the policy of the great Cardinal Richelieu, Louis XIII's minister. It could be said that the young French king had only to reap benefits won by Henry IV and Richelieu, and by Mazarin's finally successful war against Spain during Louis's minority.

But, undeniably, Louis XIV had conducted his negotiations and his wars with efficiency. England under Charles II had been, in the main, his ally and so had many of the Protestant German princes of Sweden. And there was another side of the picture which told in Louis's favour. France was inherently strong economically when Louis came to the throne, but a number of civil wars known as Les Frondes had taken place between 1649 and 1653. The nobility and the regional Parliaments, in constantly changing alliances, had fought against the regent, Anne of Austria, and against Cardinal Mazarin. As a boy Louis had been forced to submit to a deputation of rebellious Paris citizens being admitted to his bed-chamber whilst he pretended to sleep; he and his mother had had to fly secretly from the royal palace; he had seen his aunt, the daughter of the Duke of Orléans, turn the cannon of the Bastille on his royal army as it tried in vain to enter Paris. These civil wars had greatly damaged France's economy and, as during the Wars of Religion in the sixteenth century, Spanish troops had fought all over France in alliance with the rebels. Though the queen and Cardinal Mazarin had won in the end, the royal authority was shaky.

The young King Louis was popular and a gallant figure as he rode his Spanish steed at great ceremonies, his plumed hat in his hand, saluting the spectators with easy grace. Even when young he was majestic, with an air of grace and dignity—which owed much to his skill at dancing, which was very great. Before his coronation and his marriage to the Infanta of Spain, Maria Theresa, he had had many love affairs and particularly one which had been painful for him to break off with Marie Mancini, the beautiful Italian niece of Mazarin. Very few people, however, knew that this amiable incarnation of Royal Grace was also a man of much sterner qualities. The indignities the royal power had suffered affected him very strongly. He was determined he would rule as a king and not, as his father had done, as a king ruling through a great Minister. When Mazarin died, Louis, who always behaved gratefully to his friend and master, as he called him, said in private: "I do not know what I would have done if he had lived longer".

Within a year of Mazarin's death the king had imprisoned for life the man who seemed destined to step in Mazarin's shoes, Nicolas Fouquet, the all-powerful Superintendent of Finances who was much richer than the king, was allied by marriage to half the great nobility and who even had a number of private warships off the coast of Brittany. It was clear that the new reign was going to be quite different; the king was absolute master and whoever was going to rebel against the administration of France was going, henceforward, to rebel against the king himself. *L'Etat c'est Moi* (I am the State) was no idle word, although Louis never actually said this.

The king's private estate became increasingly richer once Louis had direct control of the finances of the kingdom. Louis chose as his principal agent Colbert; but he was careful to see that this great man who worked so wisely was never tempted to see himself as a powerful political personage. Louis worked eight hours a day regularly, always giving work precedence over pleasure. He was in every sense a professional king, writing: "The business of being a king is great, noble and delicious." He had, as a young man, confided to a friend that when he read in history about ineffective kings he had always felt uncomfortable. After a few years of direct rule, the king remitted a substantial part of the taxes paid by the poor. New industries were founded, old ones revived, overseas colonies, notably in Canada, were created and a large navy was built. No wonder the young king was popular—and he was victorious abroad, as we have seen.

It was in 1682 that Louis transferred his court to Versailles, a palace with innumerable fountains and avenues of tall poplars and oaks, constructed out of the barren bog where there had been neither running water nor a full-grown tree. Here, in a few months time, the court became permanently installed, housing 5,000 nobles in the palace itself with another 5,000 or so in the neighbourhood. Versailles had a political purpose; it was to make the nobles totally dependent on the king. The privileged inmates of Versailles had to leave their lands and chateaux to the management of bailiffs or younger sons. They had to pay dearly, in cash, for their lodgings at Court, and increasingly forfeited their financial independence. "He is a man I do not see at court" was a sentence which, coming from the king, doomed the greatest noble to obscurity and to no part in social life.

The descendants of the rebellious nobility of the fifteenth and sixteenth centuries now intrigued for the right to hold the king's shirt or to be included in this or that special reception. An extreme formality was the rule, for, by this, the king could give importance to the slightest favour or dispensation. The nobles as a rule were not given work in the administration—the king preferred men of humbler birth who had practical experience. They were used in war and, particularly in the latter years of the reign, many of Louis's prisoners in the gilded cage of Versailles paid for their lives of solemn frivolity with their blood.

Until towards the end of the century when the king was ageing, and when France's fortunes were turning sour, Versailles was undoubtedly a gay and stimulating place. The king had many beautiful mistresses—particularly Louise de la Vallière, who died in an odour of sanctity, and Madame de Montespan, who was accused of poisoning her rivals. Louis's numerous amours were due to his innately strong sensual nature, but also to the fact that the beauties of the day, whether married or single, offered themselves freely to the king, thinking, among other things, that gratifying his whims or passions was their duty. Yet his mistresses exerted no undue influence, nor did his love affairs prevent his treating his naïve Spanish wife, who never learnt to speak good French, with anything but respect and affection. She, too, and her children were seated on a throne of splendour above the brilliant mob of the great. Plays, books, music and painting were encouraged by this extraordinary gathering in one place of the most intelligent and rich people of the kingdom.

The king himself had good taste in the arts and both Racine and Molière owed much to his personal perception. Yet if Versailles had a valid purpose—that of making the king all-powerful and unchallengeable—it was also an exaggeration. Louis loved pomp and magnificence excessively, and so, when the gaiety seemed to go, the pomp and magnificence themselves became excessive, and finally somewhat stale. So utterly to divorce the nobility from the business of running the country created a class which became increasingly parasitic. Was there no middle way between the old disorder which had so often characterized France—and Versailles?

By the time Louis died life at Versailles was considered, even by most of the courtiers, as oppressive. The last of Louis's mistresses, Madame de Maintenon, whom, after the queen's death, he married morganatically, complained of its dullness. "Oh that I could tell you of my trials, that I could reveal to you the boredom which attends the Great and the difficulty they have in passing their time", Madame de Maintenon once wrote. She also once complained to her brother of the monotony of her life with Louis, saying she could not endure it any longer and she wished she were dead. Her brother's reply to her is reported to be: "I suppose you have been promised the Almighty as a husband."

The last twenty years of Louis's reign were clouded with misfortunes. The accountancy went wrong, faster with the death of Colbert in 1682 than it might have done. In 1681, when Europe was at peace, Louis sent French troops suddenly to occupy Strasbourg, a great free city, belonging to the Holy Roman Emperor, the Austrian Habsburg. Slowly all the powers of Europe decided that France must at all costs be checked. Holland had long been preparing for revenge. Many German princes turned against France as did the still militarily powerful Sweden. In 1688 William of Orange, the implacable enemy of Louis XIV, became king of England and Louis saw his once useful ally now firmly in the camp of his enemies.

In 1689 began the War of the League of Augsburg, which Louis started by occupying the whole of the left bank of the Rhine and devastating the Palatinate, an act which, for many years after, caused Germans to hate Frenchmen. The devastation had the purpose of creating a large area of "scorched earth" between France and her northern German enemies. During eight years of war France, on land, was victorious against all her enemies—Austria,

Spain, Holland, Savoy, England and many German princes. But the peace of Ryswick was a peace of exhaustion. Worst of all for Louis, the French fleet, which early in the war had transported French soldiers to Ireland to help James II, had been destroyed by the British at La Hougue. Louis kept Strasbourg though he had to make territorial restitutions which angered many of his generals. Ah, if Ryswick could have been the end of Louis's wars!

In 1701 Louis was forced, this time, into his largest, longest and most deadly conflict, the War of the Spanish Succession. The king of Spain, Louis's brother-in-law, died without a son, and the choice for Spain lay between an Austrian or a French nephew. Louis tried to find a solution by splitting up the Spanish heritage, with its great colonial empire, in a way which would be agreeable to all parties, without notably increasing the power of Austria. He failed. And so, in the last resort, he had to fight for his nephew, the Duke of Anjou, whom the Spaniards preferred as king. The war lasted until 1713 and this time it was the generals of the coalition, above all Marlborough and Prince Eugene of Savoy, who won the great victories.

At Blenheim, Marlborough with British, Dutch and Austrian troops shattered a daring attempt by the French to seize Vienna. In 1706 the Allies defeated the French at Ramillies and drove them out of Brussels and Antwerp, occupied at the beginning of the war. The third blow was at Oudenarde in 1708 and, the next year, 1709, another defeat for the French at the bloody battle of Malplaquet, near Lille. Some brilliant successes in Germany and Spain could not compensate for defeat in this vital sector. Louis sued for peace. The Allies came nearer and nearer to Paris. The winter of 1709 was a ferocious one. There were food riots all over France, particularly in Paris, and Louis and his court had to eat black bread. Much of his gold and silver plate had to be sold for the expenses of the war.

But Louis was to avoid the humiliation of military defeat after all. In England Queen Anne dismissed the war party and the Duke of Marlborough; and the Tories returned to power, anxious to consolidate their possessions overseas, including Gibraltar, which they had taken from Spain. The Emperor of Austria had died and his successor was the Austrian nephew, the Archduke Charles, the claimant to the Spanish throne. It was not considered wise to reconstitute the Spanish-Austrian Empire which had enabled Charles V to dominate Europe in the sixteenth century. There was a Franco-British armistice. Then the French, under Marshal Villars, won the great victory at Denain in 1712, a reversal of fortune which resembled the battle of the Marne in 1914. The French chased the Dutch and Austrians out of France, recovering what France had held in the Low Countries when the war began. At the Treaty of Utrecht in 1713 the Duke of Anjou was recognized as King of Spain, but no Spanish Bourbon was to be allowed to sit on the French throne. The Pyrenees were to remain the great divider. France lost Nice and Savoy, and had to destroy the fortifications of Dunkirk. She still remained the strongest power in Europe; but the victorious Absolute Monarchy had been defeated, and largely by Parliamentary and maritime England.

We poets oft begin our lives in gladness,
but thereof comes in the end poverty, despair and madness.

One can apply these lines of Wordsworth to the Great Monarch. He did not go mad. But he was overwhelmed with public and private troubles. His people had turned against him. At the beginning of his reign the French peasant was relatively prosperous and content; at the end, La Bruyère's celebrated description must be recalled:

> *Dotted about the countryside, one sees a number of wild animals, male and female, black livid and scorched by the sun, bent close to the ground, which they scratch and dig within implacable obstinacy. They appear to possess articulate speech, and, when they stand upright, they are seen to have human faces; and in truth, they are human beings.*

Louis the man is difficult to sum up. He was not particularly well educated or particularly intelligent, but he had a great deal of common sense, so much that it amounted almost to genius. He had good taste, the sort which goes with a magnificent figure, with ability to dress with the greatest elegance and to charm women. He took his profession of a king so seriously that he lacked the spontaneity and charm of his grandfather, Henry IV. He came to welcome flattery. But much of his formality was for the sake of his job. He kept a sense of proportion and of self-control and was never impolite to man or woman. John Green's summing up of Louis as a vain heartless bigot, is manifestly unfair. This judgement is the fruit of a wilful ignorance of the real man. Louis had resolution and a sense of mission. Was he heartless and something of a self-important bore? This is a question that cannot be answered. What is certain is that he was a deeply serious character.

Of his reign much can be said for and against. He established the *ancien régime* which gave an internal order and peace to France and retained its power until 1789. Was this a long or short time? 1660–1789 is a long time for internal stability to last in France. But it was a deceptive regime, not merely because it did not provide for human liberty, but because it did not go far enough in breaking down the internal barriers to commerce in France, let alone the barriers in human society. A black mark against Louis was the persecution of Protestants. In 1685 he revoked the Edict of Nantes which protected them. Hundreds of thousands of France's most industrious citizens were forced to flee abroad, to the great loss of the country. Yet this was an action which Louis XIV took against his better judgement and because the majority of his subjects wished it to be taken. They disliked the existence of a Protestant state within the state.

For many historians Louis's reign was barren of real achievements. He failed to secure France's frontiers on the Rhine; he would have been more successful perhaps if his policy had been more conciliatory, less arrogant—it is said. Voltaire said that Louis would have been the greatest of French kings if he had not built Versailles. Voltaire, an admirer of the English constitution, thought that Louis had brought clarity and order into the government of France and that this had helped to make possible the great achievements of the French spirit in what he called the Century of Louis XIV. It is a charitable judgement coming from the sarcastic critic of authority, whether royal or religious.

Voltaire may well be sounder than those who denigrate Louis XIV. With the death of Louis there began a new age, that of the eighteenth century, an intelligent, frivolous age which questioned all values. Men heaved a deep sigh of relief when Louis died. But the French seventeenth century, in the eyes of today, was a far greater age than the eighteenth century, at once more profound, more ordered, more magnificent. Louis XIV was not responsible for the genius of Pascal, of La Rochefoucauld, of Molière or Racine; but he is, in an intangible way, the necessary central political figure in a period whose achievements, particularly in literature and the arts, bear comparison with any of the very great ages in human history.

PETER I (THE GREAT)

(1672–1725)

FEW RULERS can have possessed such zest for living as Peter the Great. From his earliest days to the end of a crowded, active life he was impelled by an over-mastering urge from one activity to another, ever increasing his store of knowledge and improving his various skills in all manner of arts and crafts.

He could be described as a man ready-made for legend. Six feet eight inches in height, gaunt, tough, possessed of immense physical strength, it is said that he could snap a horseshoe in his bare hands—hands that early became calloused through the persistent vigour with which he tackled the hardest manual tasks, as an engineer, boat-builder, carpenter, waterman, cabinet maker, armourer, ironsmith, and a hundred things besides.

With his love of hard labour and skilled craftsmanship went a lively, searching mind which never ceased to quest for knowledge. He sought out the people who knew, whatever their nationality. Coming across an astrolabe, of which he could make nothing, he combed the foreign quarter of Moscow for someone who could instruct him in its uses. He introduced the first telescope to Russia; opened the first hospital; tried his deft hands on occasion as dentist and surgeon; encouraged the sciences.

This man of many parts had no liking for pomp or ceremony. He chose to dress simply; enjoyed simple food; disliked formal banquets; chose a seat near the door so that he could slip away at will, though he posted sentries to make sure that others didn't follow his example. He scorned comfort; cultivated endurance.

He disliked flattery and showed his feelings by deploring the practice among his subjects of kneeling or prostrating themselves in his presence. "I don't want people to dirty their clothes in the mud for me!" he declared.

Piety, instilled by his mother, remained with him throughout his life. He believed in God; celebrated his victories with a Te Deum; closed his letters with the phrase "God's will be done". He never spared himself. After toiling to the point of exhaustion he would take himself "to rest like Noah, and then to work again".

His capacity for working others to a standstill was matched by the gusto with which he threw himself into a night of carousal. Yet, after the wildest debauch, when his companions required two or three days in which to recover, Peter would be up and pursuing one or another of his multiple projects.

One more trait must be named. Many stories of savagery and cruelty have been told against him. He was often moved to sudden acts of violence, as when he encountered a soldier making off with a piece of copper dislodged by lightning from St. Peter's Church, Riga. Peter struck the looter so savagely that the fellow died instantly.

Without entering any plea on Peter's behalf, it must be remembered that he lived in a barbaric country in a barbaric age; and though he may have possessed one of the finest minds, it is not surprising that one so lavishly endowed with lusty appetites and great physique should be correspondingly a prey to violent passions and fits of unbridled temper.

From the foregoing summary of Peter's remarkable characteristics we may turn to consider some highlights in his momentous life. He was born in 1672, the only son of Czar Alexis. When he was acclaimed czar there was a revolt of the guards and Peter's step-sister, Sophia, had her invalid brother, Ivan, proclaimed as joint-czar, an arrangement which lasted until 1696, though Sophia was deposed in 1689 and Peter's mother was regent thereafter.

Peter spent his boyhood and early youth in the country near Moscow, evincing a great interest in military matters and forming "play regiments" with all his young friends. Records show that he made frequent demands for guns and other weapons and general equipment, for he took his military pastime very seriously indeed.

When he was only twenty-three he tasted the real thing, for he led two expeditions against the Turks and captured the fortress of Azov at the mouth of the Don, to secure access to the Black Sea.

He was already deeply interested in naval matters, and in his twenty-fourth year he set out to learn more about the outside world in general and naval construction in particular. He visited Holland and England in turn, and in both countries his principal concern was to work in the shipyards and to study navigation.

England, especially, captured his affection, and he was to say: "The English Island is the best, most beautiful, and happiest that there is in the whole world."

He crossed from Holland with a suite of sixteen aboard the *Yorke*, flagship of Vice-Admiral Sir David Mitchell. Near the mouth of the Thames he transhipped to the yacht *Mary* and, accompanied by the Admiral, sailed up-river to the Tower of London.

A modest house in Norfolk Street, Strand, was his first lodging, and he plunged straight into a great round of activity. He visited William III at Kensington Palace, and was persuaded by the king to sit for a portrait by Sir Godfrey Kneller. His days were crowded with visits to works and factories and scientific institutions. He studied watch-making closely, and wherever he went he collected drawings and models and specifications.

He soon went to study shipbuilding in the royal yards at Deptford, where, it is said, he worked with his hands as hard as anyone there. At this period he and his suite were lodged at Sayes Court, the country home of John Evelyn, the diarist. This adjoined the royal docks, to which Peter enjoyed access through a private door in Evelyn's garden. During their stay the Russians incurred a bill for damages to furniture and draperies amounting to £350 9s.—a formidable sum in those times. From itemized descriptions of the damage caused it may be guessed that plenty of revelry was indulged in by the distinguished visitors.

But with Peter, as always, such things were incidental, and he was constantly occupied with manifold interests. When not toiling in the shipyards he would be earnestly conferring with every expert he could contrive to meet. He visited Parliament, Greenwich Observatory, Woolwich Arsenal, Hampton Court, the Tower of London and the Royal Mint. The latter captivated him and he returned again and again.

He visited numerous churches, attended Quaker meetings and had discussions with William Penn and the Astronomer Royal. He watched naval manoeuvres at Portsmouth, where a 21-gun salute was fired in his honour.

When the time came for his departure he had arranged for selected experts to go to Russia. He engaged about sixty specialists in all, including ship designers, a master shipwright under whom he had worked at Deptford, an hydraulics engineer and similar key workers he knew would be needed to implement his great dream of building a modern Russian fleet. With the help of a scholar from Oxford, the first School of Mathematical Sciences and Navigation was formed in Moscow in 1701, another piece of foresight that was to pay big dividends later on.

The Baltic at that time was under Swedish domination and

Russia was locked in a struggle that was to be long and exacting. To give himself "a window on to Europe", Peter founded St. Petersburg in 1703. He entered his newly created port aboard his frigate *Standard* as part of the inauguration ceremony, accompanied by six merchant vessels. When, a little later, a Dutch vessel arrived with valuable cargo, Peter rewarded the captain and crew specially to mark this first arrival.

There were early set-backs in the struggle with Sweden, but Peter's army finally prevailed at the battle of Poltavia in 1709, and Russia gained control over Karelia, Ingermanland and Livonia.

Among the prisoners taken in this battle was Catherine Skavronskaya, the daughter of a Livonian peasant, who became Peter's mistress. Later, when he had divorced the wife who had been chosen for him by his mother when he was only seventeen, Peter was to marry Catherine and she was destined to become a great influence for good in his life. She developed into a woman of strong character, and her understanding support did much to sustain the czar in his difficult reign. It was said that Catherine alone was capable of restraining him in his more tempestuous moods; that she had only to nurse his fevered head in her lap and stroke his brow to induce in him a wonderful sense of calm and well-being.

Yet Catherine was equally tough and a vital companion to Peter in many ways. She sometimes accompanied her tireless husband on his strenuous campaigns, showing the most astonishing powers of endurance, behaving resolutely when under fire and sharing the army's hardships with the greatest fortitude.

Once a campaign ended, however, all Catherine's femininity would return and she would settle down to domestic routine. She bore Peter twelve children, and though he was suspected of occasional infidelities they were fleeting incidents and he invariably returned to Catherine, and their close bond of understanding endured. He founded the Order of St. Catherine in her honour.

By 1713 St. Petersburg had virtually replaced Moscow as capital, and Peter did all he could to encourage the use of his new port by merchants from overseas. He also started to build a Baltic Fleet. In 1715 he had the School of Mathematical Sciences and Navigation transferred to St. Petersburg and re-christened it as the Naval Academy.

In the meantime, various campaigns had gone awry. Peter's armies had suffered some reverses in Turkey, had sustained heavy defeat at Pruth, and had been forced to give back the fortress at Azov. In these desperate moments Catherine stood staunchly at the czar's side, showing the greatest courage in action, and thereby winning a regard which Peter publicly acknowledged in an official ukase that he issued in 1723.

In this document he told graphically how: "Putting aside womanly weakness, of her own will she has been present with us and has helped in every way possible, and especially in the Pruth battle with the Turks, when our troops were 22,000 in number and the Turks had 270,000 men, and it was a desperate time for us, she acted as a man, not as a woman, which is known to our whole army, and through it without doubt to the whole nation; and so for these labours of our Spouse we have decided that by virtue of the supreme power given us by God she shall be crowned which, God willing, is to take place formally in Moscow in the present winter. . . ."

Towards the close of his reign Peter had attempted to gain control of the Caspian Sea, and a struggle with Persia did, in fact, give him a foothold at Baku and elsewhere.

But throughout all his active campaigning he never once ceased to advance progressive ideas of all kinds. In his many travels, which embraced Germany, France, Denmark, Austria and Poland, he always followed his practice of cultivating the acquaintance of foreign experts. Not for him the isolation of an "Iron Curtain"; rather he clung to his own inspired conception of "a window on to Europe". He liked to know what progressive people were doing in other parts of the world, and he had the good sense to profit by such knowledge in every way he could. One typical example of such foresight was his constant engagement of foreign craftsmen and technicians. He even brought in experts for the task of seeking for minerals and other natural resources in the vast lands of Russia—things which he knew to be absolutely essential for the development of all the great industries and works that figured in his ambitious dreams for the betterment of his country.

Despite his active recruitment of the best brains and best skills he could find abroad, he must often have fretted and fumed and longed for the company and advice of people he could trust. Among his close supporters he counted Colonel Patrick Gordon, a Scot who acted as military adviser, and François Lefort, a former Swiss guard, whose special flair was the organization of official functions and ceremonies. For a time, too, in his earlier years, Peter was under the sway of a German mistress, Anna Mons, on whom he lavished many gifts until he discovered that she had played him false.

In his zest for transforming Russia into a powerful and enlightened nation Peter founded schools and colleges and saw to it that promising young Russians were given the opportunity of travelling widely and studying in other lands. Busy with the general plans for a hundred laudable projects, he yet found time to supervise the provision of various educational text-books. He also introduced a reformed alphabet and simplified form of printing, besides founding and personally editing the first Russian newspaper.

He devised extensive plans for special colleges in St. Petersburg, each designed as a watertight department concerned solely with its own particular branch of Government business. He brought in enlightened tax reforms; sponsored a variety of bold and progressive social and economic plans. Right up to the time of his death from strangury, in 1725, at the age of fifty-three, he was grappling with schemes for creating an Academy of Sciences.

Peter the Great has been justly described as "the first modern Russian". Perhaps he was too modern—too far advanced for his untutored masses whose future he strove so vigorously, and so selflessly, to fashion.

CHARLES XII

(1682–1718)

FOR THE most part Sweden has lain outside the main theatre of European history. Only now and again has this land of mountain and lake, mist and arctic cold, produced a figure who has stormed his way across the stage and driven his audience into a frenzy of admiration, of awe-struck wonder. Most impressive of these rare performers was Charles XII. The "Hero King", he has been called, and with excellent reason. But a better name for him is "the Swedish Meteor", since he flared across the sky like a meteor, and, like a meteor, disappeared into the blackness of the night from which he had so suddenly emerged.

When he succeeded his father, Charles XI, as king of Sweden in 1697 he was a youth of not quite fifteen. At that time Sweden was one of the Great Powers of Europe. The Baltic was practically a Swedish lake. The whole of Finland was Swedish, and the Swedish territories extended round the Gulf of Finland from where St. Petersburg was before long to stand, to the great port of Riga. There were also Swedish outposts in Pomerania, on the mainland immediately south of Sweden, and on the farther side of Denmark in Bremen and its neighbourhood. But Sweden was "great" not only in territory. She had an army of well-drilled veterans who had become deservedly renowned as masters of the art of war.

Young as he was, the boy-king had already shown signs of exceptional capacity, and the States-General at Stockholm lost no time in proclaiming him to be of age and investing him with full regal power. Sweden's enemies—she had plenty—were not so discerning, however; they thought the times might be propitious for an attempt at humbling the Swedish giant and restoring the balance of power in the Baltic. A good deal of plotting went on in the chancelleries of Europe, and then in 1700 Charles was called upon to meet a formidable alliance of foes. In the west, the King of Denmark and Norway sent his troops into Holstein, a duchy ruled over by a duke who had married Charles's sister, and in the east, Czar Peter—who was eventually to be styled "the Great", although there was little sign of that as yet—was set upon seizing the continental provinces of the Swedish monarchy. Nor was this all. Included in the hostile confederacy were Poland and Saxony, then united under King Augustus II.

Then it was, and so early, that Charles showed himself to be a man of commanding stature and consummate genius. Statecraft was something that he never mastered, but war—that was an art in which he had received no lessons, and needed none. Covered by an Anglo-Dutch squadron under Admiral Rooke—for by a fortunate chance Sweden and Britain were then allied—the young king led an army of five thousand Swedes across the narrow channel into the heart of Danish territory. They landed on the coast of Zealand, and Charles was among the first to leap from the transports into the water, and, sword in hand, encouraged his troops by his example. The Danes, inferior in numbers, retreated before him. Copenhagen was bombarded by the British ships, and, rather than see his capital ruined and taken by storm, the Danish king sued for terms. The war was over almost before it had begun, and Charles was left free to turn his arms against Russia and Poland.

So ended Charles's first campaign, and already he was well on the way to becoming a legend. He was still no more than eighteen, but he had proved himself a man among men. The follies of youth he left behind him, not that they had ever been much in evidence. He was not interested in women; and wine, even in moderation, was never much to his taste. Soft living did not appeal to him in the slightest. When campaigning he often disdained the use of a tent but spread his cloak on the ground and slept with his men beneath the stars. The French ambassador, used to the luxurious effeminacy of Louis XIV's court, was astounded at the plainness of the Swedish king's apparel: "no ornaments," he told his master, "and shoes with low heels!" Charles's customary dress was indeed plain, and its very plainness singled him out as we may be sure he intended.

He boasted that he had only one suit, one of blue cloth with big copper buttons, buff waistcoat, and riding breeches. On his head a coarse felt hat; round his neck a black scarf; and on his feet high boots with massive steel spurs. All external marks of rank he despised. After his first experience in the field he absolutely refused to wear a wig, and was never seen except with his hair cropped short and brushed up above his forehead. He was a soldier among soldiers, and his men adored him, even when he led them into the most impossible situations and they died in droves. He was brave to the pitch of reckless folly, he was resolute to the point of obstinacy;

he had a body that seemed to be made of iron and a mind of tempered steel. A writer of his own race has described him as "a lonely, mist-shrouded figure". Others have referred to him as a hero who might have stepped straight out of one of the ancient sagas of Scandinavia.

Leaving Sweden to be governed by his ministers—he never saw Stockholm, his capital, again—Charles crossed the sea to Livonia (Latvia) with an army of 20,000 men, and marched to meet the Russians under Czar Peter, who were besieging Narva. The Russians numbered (so it is said) 50,000 men, but they were undisciplined peasants for the most part, while Charles had with him 10,000 of the justly celebrated Swedish infantry. It was all over in a quarter of an hour. The Russian hordes fled; while as for the czar, he was already on the road back to Moscow. Such was the battle of Narva, fought on 30 November, 1700.

Now it was Poland's turn to encounter the furious Swede. Campaigning went on for three years, and ended in Charles's complete triumph. Augustus was dethroned, and a puppet prince was raised to the throne in his stead. Saxony and Poland were occupied by the Swedish armies, and Charles stood forth among European potentates as a man to be feared, and courted. Among those who visited him in his hour of triumph was the Duke of Marlborough, who, with Blenheim and Ramillies behind him, could yet manage sufficient grace to express the wish that "I could serve some campaign under so great a general as your Majesty, that I might learn what I yet do not know about the art of war".

Only Russia remained to be dealt with, and there was reason to believe that the czar would be glad to come to some arrangement. But Charles would be content with nothing less than complete victory; and as though to demonstrate his contempt for anything that Peter might do, he arrested the Russian ambassador at Dresden, a man named Patkul, and—since he had been born in Livonia and might be considered, therefore, as a renegade Swede—caused him to be put to death in the most cruel fashion. This action has left an indelible stain on Charles's memory.

Meanwhile Peter had not been idle. Twice he invaded the Swedish provinces adjoining Russia, and on each occasion had to retreat before the Swedes. But he was still a very present menace, and in 1708 Charles got together a large army and marched against the Russians. To begin with all went in his favour. At Grodno he took the czar by surprise and was within an ace of capturing him. He forced the line of the Beresina and won a battle at Smolensk. The way to Moscow seemed to lie open, the way that Napoleon was to take rather more than a century later. But now he suddenly turned southward into the Ukraine, where he apparently expected to be joined by an army of 30,000 Cossacks under their *hetman* Mazeppa (the romantic subject of Byron's famous poem), who had decided to throw over his allegiance to the czar and seek to establish an independent principality. The plot came to the ears of Peter, however, and Mazeppa brought Charles only a handful of followers. To add to Charles's worries and disappointments, a large body of Swedish reinforcements was overtaken by the czar and cut to pieces. Finally, the winter of 1708-9 was an exceptionally hard one, and Charles and his army suffered horribly from the cold and lack of supplies, deep in the heart of enemy country.

Still Charles would not abandon the idea of reaching Moscow, and although his army had now been reduced to only some 23,000 men, he insisted on continuing with the campaign. Audacious as ever, and with his customary indomitable spirit, he laid siege to the Russian stronghold of Pultowa (Pultava), north of Kiev. The defenders put up a strong resistance, long enough for the czar to bring up a large army to their assistance. The decisive battle was fought on 8 July, 1709. The Russians numbered 80,000 men, which meant that the Swedes were outnumbered by four to one. To make matters worse, Charles, who up to then had seemed to lead a charmed life, was wounded in the foot the day before, and had to be carried into battle in a litter.

At dawn the Swedish infantry were launched against the Russian field batteries, and Charles was there to give them an encouraging start. They fought as bravely as ever, but suffered horrible losses; conflicting orders were given, and they looked round in vain for their king to sort them out and give them confidence; muddle and confusion were succeeded by bewilderment and desperation, and at length the attack petered out. Most of the Swedish infantry, the pride of Charles's army, were left on the field, dead or wounded, and the rest were soon prisoners. Charles attempted to rally the remainder of his men. He had his wound dressed and ordered his bearers to take him into the thick of the struggle. The bearers were killed by a cannon-ball, and the king was mounted on a horse, his foot resting on the horse's neck. The enemy were closing in, and his capture or death seemed imminent. His horse was brought down by a Russian bullet, and he fell with it. A wounded officer proffered him his mount, which he took; and having been lifted into the saddle, he suffered himself to be led away from the scene of action. Only a couple of thousand men who had not been engaged in the battle were left to him, and further resistance was out of the question. Taking advantage of the mood of intense depression into which he had been cast, his staff urged him to lose no time in taking the only way of escape left open to him. Accompanied by a handful of troops, he crossed the frontier into Turkey, where he was hospitably received at Bender, on the Dniester.

For the next three years Charles was an honoured guest rather than a prisoner of state. During that time all his expenses, and those of his numerous household, were paid by the Turkish Government, and gifts and honours were heaped upon him with oriental profusion. But from the day of his arrival at Bender his one thought was to involve Turkey and Russia in war. In this he was at length successful, and in an action on the banks of the Pruth, Peter was surrounded by Turkish soldiers and escaped barely with his life. An armistice was arranged, on terms which Charles must have thought were far too lenient. He continued his intrigues, and to render himself more secure established himself in a fortified house a short distance from Bender, surrounded by a strong guard of devoted Poles and Swedes. The Porte—the Turkish Government—which up to now had treated him with a most singular generosity, took alarm, suspecting that whatever the king had in mind was likely to do them no good. Charles was asked to explain his actions, and when his answers proved unsatisfactory it was resolved to bring him to heel. A force of several thousand Janissaries (foot-guards) surprised his little camp and took his two hundred guards prisoners. They then attacked the house, which Charles and forty of his suite defended desperately. Charles fought like a madman, killing many of his assailants. Only when the roof was burning over his head and his very eyebrows were singed and his clothes burnt did he at length give the signal for surrender.

For a while he was kept in captivity—still an honourable one; until in November, 1714, he found the way of escape open. Sending a respectful message of farewell to the Porte at Constantinople, he set off on horseback across the continent, and the Turks must have been highly relieved to see him go.

With only two attendants, travelling by day and night, he reached Stralsund—almost the only Swedish possession left on the mainland—late at night on 21 November, 1714, after a journey of sixteen days. The Governor was in bed, but on hearing that an officer had arrived from Bender with important dispatches he gave orders that he should be admitted, and at once recognized him by his voice. The town was illuminated when the king's arrival became known, but in fact the people had small cause to rejoice. Charles's enemies at once took the field against him, and after a siege of about a year Stralsund was compelled to surrender and Charles sailed away to Sweden.

Still he was filled with those irrepressible hankerings after military glory and conquest. Everything that he had accomplished in Europe in his earlier years had been reversed, and his loss had proved Czar Peter's gain. Now, however, in an evil hour he listened to the promptings of his chief adviser, Baron von Görtz, a German officer who had been with him in Bender. Let him make peace with the czar, and then—what might he not achieve? After all, he was not much in the thirties! Fantastic dreams passed through Charles's brain; he would invade and conquer Norway, and then he would lead an army across the sea into Scotland and put the Jacobite Pretender on the throne of his fathers!

Early in 1716 he attacked Norway, having come to terms with the czar by agreeing to cede all his Baltic provinces, and for a time things went well with him. Towards the end of 1718 he was besieging the Norwegian fortified town of Frederikshald. On the afternoon of 11 December he was visiting the trenches with several members of his staff and some French officers, to see how things were going. It got dusk, but still he stayed there, leaning against the parapet, and staring across at the enemy walls. His companions urged him not to expose himself in so foolhardy a fashion, but he turned their protests aside with contempt. Suddenly his head sank down on to the folds of his cloak, his left arm dropped . . . "The king is shot!" was the cry. Death in fact must have been instantaneous.

So sudden was his end that there were some who whispered that he had been the victim of assassination. The rumours persisted, so that in 1746 his tomb in the Riddarholm church in Stockholm was opened and his corpse was given a very unscientific examination. The result was inconclusive, but a further examination in 1859 put the matter to rest. It was proved then that a musket-ball had gone through his head, and that it had been fired from above and in front.

And what was the end of it all? What was there to show for the years of warfare, the marchings, the campaignings, the days of victory and the longer days of defeat? A country brought to the edge of ruin, an empire dissipated, tens of thousands of the bravest of his race left to rot on foreign fields. Something remained, however—his legend, and as long as men hold bravery, however misdirected and fruitless, in high honour, Charles XII's name will live on. "Were Socrates and Charles the Twelfth of Sweden both present in any company," Boswell reports Dr. Johnson as asserting, "and Socrates were to say, 'Follow me and hear a lecture on philosophy'; and Charles, laying his hand on his sword, to say, 'Follow me, and dethrone the Czar'; a man would be ashamed to follow Socrates". That would have been the Doctor's own reaction, we may be pretty sure, for years before Johnson had put Charles into his poem *The Vanity of Human Wishes* as the supreme illustration of the mutability of military glory. The poem is a worthy one, the best thing in verse that Johnson ever wrote; and the concluding passage is as well known—deservedly so—as almost anything in the books of quotations:

His fall was destin'd to a barren strand,
A petty fortress, and a dubious hand.
He left the name, at which the world grew pale,
To point a moral, or adorn a tale.

FREDERICK II (THE GREAT)

(1712–86)

THE EXECUTION was fixed for 7 a.m. Only two hours before, when the massive fortress of Küstrin in East Prussia was still shrouded in November darkness, the eighteen-year-old Crown Prince Frederick was informed that his fellow-prisoner and best friend, Lieutenant von Katte, would be beheaded by the sword below the windows of his cell and that his father's orders were that he should be a witness. Their offence? Frederick had tried to escape King Frederick William's tyranny by fleeing abroad and his friend had helped him. The attempt had failed. Mad with rage and thirsting for blood, the king had clapped both young men in jail, had condemned von Katte to death, waiving preliminary torture only because he was a noble, and was now bent on teaching his son an object lesson before deciding his fate. He was brooding on the thought of death for him, too.

In those two hours Frederick was delirious with remorse and terror. He pleaded for his friend's life, offered to die in his stead, or be imprisoned for life, or renounce the throne. In vain. When the time was up he was led to the window of his cell. Katte passed below and they exchanged a last affectionate farewell. The sword severed the head at the first stroke and Frederick collapsed unconscious in the arms of his jailers.

This was Frederick William's culminating act of savagery towards his son. It had been preceded by ten years of sadistic ill-treatment which had driven the highly intelligent, sensitive and imaginative boy to despair. He had been humiliated in public, dragged by the hair, thrashed, insulted and threatened—all because his brutal father failed to see in him the makings of a soldier, thought him effeminate because he played the flute and was enraged by his refusal to surrender will and personality in return for approval. After his friend's execution Frederick's life was spared, but the shock closed his heart to love for ever and in its place grew acrid cynicism, ruthlessness and a burning urge, born of parental derision, to prove that he was not a milksop, but capable of leading the fine army which Frederick William created but never used to deeds of heroism which would win for him the respect of mankind.

So, in 1740, when his father died, two Fredericks ascended the throne of Prussia: a cultivated young man, devoted to music, literature, versifying, a tranquil life among congenial friends; and a snarling, rejected son, full of rage and thirsting for action. The rulers of Europe knew nothing of this second Frederick and expected him to leave the government to his ministers while he devoted himself to the arts. There would be no fireworks, they felt sure, from Frederick. But they were soon disillusioned.

Prussia at that time consisted of two widely separated territories, the March of Brandenburg and the former Polish fief of East Prussia, and otherwise of small, scattered areas in the west of Germany in which the ruler of Prussia was not even entitled to call himself king. The population totalled 2,200,000, ranking about thirteenth in size among the states of Europe, and partly because he did not wish to risk his splendid army (including giant grenadiers whom he collected all over the Continent), Frederick William had pursued a pacific policy which, in an age of rapacious monarchs, had not enhanced his country's prestige. His son inherited a semi-feudal social structure, a sound administration, a submissive people—and the magnificently trained army, as large as Austria's, of 80,000 men, half mercenaries, half Prussians. At once young Frederick's eye lighted on this formidable machine and within four months of his accession he launched his troops on their first war-like operation: object, to bully an aged bishop into paying a huge indemnity in return for the undisputed ownership of a small village in Western Germany. Though a minor incident, it had been cynically provoked and aroused widespread condemnation. Europe was now much concerned with the personality of this new king. From Berlin diplomats reported that he was soft-spoken, but his courtesy could not conceal a mocking, contemptuous trait. He spoke a great deal without listening to others, gesturing forcefully with white hands overloaded with rings. When provoked he could flare into uncontrollable rage . . .

Before the year was out Frederick delivered his second blow, the invasion of Silesia, one of Austria's richest provinces, at a moment when the disputed accession of the 24-year-old Maria Theresa promised weak opposition. The king, as he wrote to a friend, was frankly an opportunist, athirst for glory and bored with a sedentary life. A large army, a well-filled treasury and a lively temperament did the rest. So, with a flimsy legal claim to only part of the territory, he marched, purloined the whole of the province and then awaited reactions. The Austrians promptly took up arms, were defeated in Silesia and four years of sporadic warfare followed from which Frederick emerged as a great military commander and diplomatist, unscrupulous even by the standards of that age. Three times he had allied himself with France and then backed out of hostilities when the French seemed to become too strong. Three times he made peace with Maria Theresa, only to take up arms again when Silesia was threatened or the prospect of further booty proved too alluring. Finally, after melting his palace plate to help finance the war and risking enemy occupation of his whole country, he retained Silesia, thus increasing his territories by a third. His fellow-monarchs were now heartily afraid of Frederick, his prowess in the field, his tenacity, his cunning. Because more successful than the other sharks, he was condemned as an unscrupulous knave.

But in the long interlude of peace opening in 1745 the king showed himself in a different light, as a despotic but in many ways surprisingly enlightened and humanitarian ruler. His day usually began with flute playing and ended with a concert or recitations from his own verses, but his working hours were filled with unremitting toil for his people and he demanded the same from them. In return he gave them a revised legal system providing cheap, swift and impartial justice for all. He abolished the use of torture except for high treason. He introduced complete religious toleration so that everyone could find his own path to heaven. The peasants were given adequate security against maltreatment by their overlords. Frederick set his nobles an example by declaring himself to be the first servant of the state and demanded of them a life of dedicated service, mostly in the army. Sale of office was abolished throughout Prussia and peculation kept down by repeated surprise checks on funds.

Frederick held the purse strings, he became his own minister of trade, he supervised the whole agriculture and industry of the country by regular tours of inspection each spring and every subject could have access to the king, at least in writing, to air a grievance or make a request. He was thus a benevolent despot, or almost, but like his father he never saw beyond the duties and obligations of his subjects and was not interested in their contentment except in so far as it affected their performance as efficient Prussians. "Tired of ruling over slaves," he recorded towards the end of his life, but he never did anything to set them free.

It was after a victory over the Saxons in 1745 that Voltaire called Frederick "the Great", but it was his heroism in the Seven Years' War which really earned him the title. The diplomatic manoeuvres which preceded its outbreak in August, 1756, confronted him with a coalition bent on his destruction between France, Austria and Russia—countries with populations totalling fifty times his own. That this hostile confederacy came about at all was largely his own fault. His retention of Silesia spelt the undying enmity of Maria Theresa and the certainty that if she could find allies she would make a bid to recover it. Frederick alienated the Empress Elizabeth of Russia by mocking her admittedly erratic private life and, wrongly convinced that both countries lacked the cash to make war, allowed a defensive alliance to come about between Russia and Austria. This was his first mistake. His second was even more serious. Behind the back of his ally France he signed a Convention with England with whom she was at war in the New World, and in 1756 the age-old enemies France and Austria formed a defensive alliance which soon ripened into an agreement to partition Prussia. Early in the same year Maria Theresa and the Empress Elizabeth also agreed to banish once for all the odious Frederick from the world. So, in that summer, he faced almost certain destruction unless he anticipated the onslaught and drew the sword first.

Seven long years of bitter struggle followed. Saxony was on the brink of joining the coalition. Frederick invaded, defeated the Saxon army and an Austrian force coming to its assistance. But the main fighting was yet to come and he had no illusions. His Ministers in Berlin were told that if he were taken prisoner they should pay no attention to anything he wrote from captivity, offer no ransom and prosecute the war "as though I had never existed in the world".

The new year saw another victory over the Austrians at Prague and then a bloody defeat. In an attempt to avert disaster the king himself had led his troops into the cannons' mouth and had only turned back when an adjutant called to him: "Sire, do you mean to take the battery single-handed?" He now faced armies totalling 340,000 men against his own 90,000. "Things are beginning to look vile," he wrote to one of his generals, and then sent his sister long screeds full of rhetorical indignation. East Prussia fell to the Russians. The Swedes, who had joined the fray, were walking through defenceless Pomerania, while a Croat force stormed into Berlin and exacted a heavy fine from the inhabitants before withdrawing at the approach of Prussian troops. But Frederick's resolve never flagged. A brilliant victory, when outnumbered by two to one, over the French at Rossbach, made him the hero of all German patriots, and at Leuthen in Silesia he scattered a superior force of Austrians in a battle which Napoleon later declared was enough to make him immortal and place him among the world's greatest generals.

But the year 1758 was spent in inconclusive fighting, the king hurrying with dwindling troops to East Prussia, to Silesia, to Saxony in a vain effort to deal one of the allies such a blow that they would withdraw from the coalition. By Christmas he was calling himself a limping skeleton. The treasury was empty and the troops scraped together by his recruiting officers were of such poor quality that he hardly dared show them to the enemy.

But for five more years he fought on, through heavy defeats and hard-won victories, resolved in every fibre of his being to die rather than capitulate, deep at the back of his mind the lowering figure of his father to whom he had to prove himself a man. By the end of 1761 only Brandenburg and a small part of Silesia were still in his hands, and for the following year he hardly knew how he was to recruit an army, pay it and feed it. He carried a box of poison with him wherever he went. Then fortune suddenly smiled. The Empress of Russia died, to be succeeded by Peter III, an ardent admirer of Frederick, who at once concluded peace. Soon after the French were defeated by a combined English and German force and Frederick gained further successes against the Austrians. By 1763 the allies had had enough and the peace treaty left him with his country intact and still in possession of Silesia. He had shown himself a master of war, had defied the great powers of Europe and established the core of the future German nation. Yet when peace was signed he said that the happiest day of his life would be the last.

With equal energy he then turned to the reconstruction of his country, supervising everything from agriculture to the tax on coffee, and was so successful that at his death Prussia was more prosperous than at the start of the Seven Years' War, with a well-filled treasury, a growing population and a rate of taxation only slightly higher than at his accession. During his reign the territory had been increased by the seizure of Silesia and, under the partition of Poland in 1772 by the acquisition of Polish West Prussia, joining East Prussia to Pomerania.

In the closing years of his life—he died in 1786—Frederick showed himself to be a sound-hearted, brave old man. "Life", he wrote to a friend, "is a mean affair when one gets old. But there is a way of being happy and that is to rejuvenate oneself in imagination, disregard the body and to the end of the play preserve an inner cheerfulness, so strewing the last few steps of the path with flowers." More than any other man, he had provided a hero-figure round which, in the struggle with Napoleon and later, German nationalist feelings could concentrate. By establishing the power and military prowess of his country and by excluding Austria from the leadership of Germany he had made Prussia the centre of future national unity. And by his own example and that of his people he had raised hard work, discipline and tenacity to the status of Prussian if not German virtues.

But Frederick could see nothing of all this and probably did not care very much what happened to his country when he had gone. He did his duty to the end, rising at four every day, kept as close an eye as ever on the training of his army and studied meticulously the reports of his officials. At meals he talked extremely well on a wide range of subjects and was full of charm and courtesy to his guests, even if occasionally the old bitter cynicism would break through.

But he died like a Stoic, cheerful to the last though in great pain —and at once a great sigh of relief went up from his people. They were tired of being slave-driven, tired of great deeds. But outside Prussia contemporaries called him the hero of the century. Standing beside his grave in 1806, Napoleon said: "If he were still alive we would not be here", and to this day Germans revere the memory of old Fritz, the embodiment of will-power and tenacity of purpose, as brilliant and hard as a diamond, the warrior who in seven years of war showed a heroism in confronting fate unequalled since the days of Ancient Rome.

MARIA THERESA

(1717–80)

Maria Theresa, the mother of sixteen children, the mother of her people, noble fighter against a continent in arms, wise reformer of Austrian institutions, compelling as a figure-head and enchanting as an individual, was great both as a woman and as a ruler. We see her portrayed in middle age, seated massively in a rich embroidered gown, her strong arms resting on her lap, shelving bosom tightly encased, double chin, broad smiling mouth, high forehead, beautiful complexion, fair, silken hair, and we are reminded of the Eternal Woman who, as psychologists say, dwells in the heart of every man. It was she who was the founder of the modern Austrian State, she who personified the age-old Austrian virtues of open-mindedness, spontaneity and warmth and she who brought the hitherto remote Habsburg rule close to the people's hearts.

Born in 1717, second child of the Emperor Charles VI and of his Guelph wife, Elizabeth Christine of Brunswick-Wolfenbüttel, Maria Theresa spent a happy childhood as an ordinary princess not destined to ascend the throne. Indeed, the accession of a female was barred by law. The eldest child, a boy, had died in infancy, but Charles still hoped for a male heir and meanwhile his daughter romped in the Hofburg in an atmosphere of tolerant affection. Then, as the years passed and no boy was born, Charles prepared for the future by drawing up a document called the Pragmatic Sanction. In wars against France and Turkey this foolish man had already lost Naples, Sicily, Serbia and Wallachia from his dominions. Now, in return for signatures to his piece of paper promising European support for his daughter's eventual accession, he bartered away yet further territories and rights. It was all in vain.

When in 1740 Maria Theresa came to the throne on her father's death she faced a perilous situation. An unknown quantity, untutored in affairs of State, married to a weak husband, the Grand Duke Francis of Lorraine, she was watched in ambiguous fashion by France, Spain, Bavaria and Saxony, late signatories to the Sanction recognizing her right and guaranteeing her territories.

Apart from Austria, the Habsburg Empire included Hungary, Bohemia and Moravia, Silesia, the Southern Netherlands, Lombardy and Tuscany, far-flung dominions, some with the weakest ties of allegiance, which invited aggression. A sign of weakness on Maria Theresa's part, a warlike move by one of her neighbours and the whole pack of alleged friends might descend on her.

Apart from this, the internal situation was forlorn. She found a bankrupt treasury, an army ill-equipped, ill-disciplined and dislocated by defeat. Three field-marshals were languishing in prison for their failure on the battlefield. Her advisers, headed by the seventy-year-old Chancellor Bartenstein, were all old men, "too prejudiced", as she later recorded, "to give useful advice, but too respectable and meritorious to be dismissed". Each thought first of how the matter under consideration would affect himself.

Within eight weeks of her accession she found herself at war. On a trumped-up pretext, athirst for glory and fame, the young Frederick of Prussia invaded Silesia, at the same time sending an envoy to Vienna to suggest the cession of the province in return for his military support of Austria. Maria Theresa indignantly refused, a force was scratched together to cut off Frederick's supplies and the two armies met at Mollwitz, where the Austrians were decisively defeated. Another month, and France, Spain, Bavaria and Saxony were agreeing to partition the Habsburg Monarchy. A French army marched through Germany to help the Elector of Bavaria seize Vienna, the Saxons moved towards Moravia, Spain started to mobilize for a campaign in Italy. Maria Theresa had no army to oppose any of these advances and in no time the Bavarian Karl Albert was within thirty miles of the capital. The government fled to Hungary and Maria Theresa followed it, to plead in an impassioned and memorable scene with the Hungarian nobility for military support. Her youth, beauty and extreme distress moved the hearts of her chivalrous subjects and as she held up her baby Prince Joseph to them they burst into shouts of joy and consecrated their lives and blood to her cause.

But the Hungarian troops were no more than a rabble and Vienna was only temporarily saved by the indecision of the Bavarians. Soon they and the French were capturing Prague, watched ineffectually by the Grand Duke Francis in command of the army fetched from Silesia, and Frederick was marching into Moravia. Austria seemed doomed and Maria Theresa's palsied advisers could only think of sacrificing territory in order to buy off the wolves. At this moment she showed her splendid courage.

To one of her ministers she wrote: "What I have I intend to hold, and all my armies, including the Hungarian, shall be destroyed before I will abdicate anything. What you cannot get voluntarily you must drag from the people by force. You will say I am cruel; I am. But I know that one day I can make good a hundredfold all the suffering I must now inflict in order to save my country."

From Italy she summoned her last remaining troops, sending their commander a stirring letter accompanied by a portrait of herself and Joseph which he showed to his men, and a few weeks later he had thrown the Franco-Bavarian army out of the country, advanced into Bavaria and occupied Munich. After a single victory at Chotusitz Frederick cautiously made peace, and the Austrians soon after forced Saxony to follow suit and recovered all the places they had lost.

Despite the dangers one must not think of Maria Theresa as obsessed by her problems. Not at all. She bore two children during this time and when she could pursued the gay life she loved, dancing, skating and riding—astride, much to the horror of elderly courtiers. She supervised the education of her growing family, watched over the morals of her ladies-in-waiting and, only too glad to be advised by men of knowledge and experience, sifted in her mind the need for internal reforms.

But major reforms had to wait, for meanwhile, in 1744, Frederick became alarmed for the safety of his purloined province of Silesia and, deciding that attack was his best course, invaded Bohemia. An Austrian army followed him and to give it the best chance of success Maria Theresa managed by dint of tears and tempers—"which made both of us quite ill"—to dissuade her husband from taking command. Her feeling about his military prowess was entirely right, but wrong about his brother's, Charles of Lorraine, whom she appointed in his stead, and the result, in the summer of 1745, was a victory for Frederick, repeated a few months later when Charles risked battle again. To Maria Theresa, Frederick by now had become a monster of supernatural proportions, but his success was bringing welcome allies for her into the field, the Russians and the Saxons.

So the future was not entirely bleak when in September she attended the coronation in Frankfurt of her benign and ineffectual husband as emperor of the "Holy Roman Empire"—in inverted commas because it was no longer a living reality. But Frederick defeated the Saxons before the Russians could move, and by the Treaty of Dresden (December, 1745) peace was patched up between him and Maria Theresa. In the next three years, until the Peace of Aix la Chapelle, Austria was at war with Spain in Italy and with France in the Netherlands. As for Frederick, he knew there could be no real agreement with Maria Theresa so long as he retained Silesia and his motto was: "On Guard."

By the Peace the terms of the Pragmatic Sanction were confirmed by all Powers (excepting, of course, that the Habsburg dominions no longer included Silesia) and after 1748 there was at least a breathing space when Maria Theresa could grapple with internal problems. The diverse provinces of her domain suffered from widely differing conditions of local rule, mostly carried out by nobles who felt a law to themselves and were exempt from taxation.

The prime necessity was to establish the supremacy of the State, the power to direct local government for the general good, and this Maria Theresa sought to achieve by various means. At the same time, justice and taxation were centralized. In the economic sphere, the nobles' privilege was abolished, a uniform system of indirect taxation was introduced, barriers to local trade were broken down. Education, too, received a powerful stimulus under Maria Theresa with the object of training useful citizens able to make their contribution to the welfare of the State.

But all these reforms were dependent on the security of the realm and army re-organization was a necessity. The success achieved enabled the Austrian armies to survive the Seven Years' War.

Meanwhile Maria Theresa had borne ten children and was to produce six more between 1750 and 1756. In this task she was, as she said, "insatiable", and it was thought extraordinary that she could appear at the opera a few hours before the birth of a child and be driving through the streets a few hours afterwards. But her health and vitality were superabundant and her whole rhythm of life, her hours of sleep, work and enjoyment reflected the fact.

She needed all her strength for the trials that lay ahead. Immediately after Aix la Chapelle the empress's new foreign minister Kaunitz had recommended to her a complete reversal of the age-old hostility to France. He was sent to Paris to woo the French, but to no effect until early in 1756 when Frederick, still treaty-bound to them, signed a Convention with their enemy England to exclude the entry of foreign troops into Germany. This, seeing that Frederick had already three times deserted his French ally, turned the scales in Kaunitz's favour and in May France and Austria signed a "defensive" treaty. So Frederick faced two enemies and soon there was a third, Russia, where the Empress

Elizabeth had been relying on English help against him and now turned to Austria instead.

Soon France, Russia and Austria, where Maria Theresa had never weakened in her resolve to regain Silesia, were preparing for offensive war and Saxony promised to join them later. Frederick saw clearly his mortal peril and decided to strike first by invading Saxony. So began the Seven Years' War, ending, after his triumphant defiance of countries with a total population fifty times his own, in Frederick's retention of Silesia and the acknowledgement of Prussia's and Austria's frontiers exactly as they had been in 1756.

Throughout the struggle, with its endless marches and counter-marches and battles, Maria Theresa urged on her generals, often with detailed advice, and must often have regretted not being a commander herself. They were too slow for her, too dilatory, though no doubt the implacable empress, scribbling memoranda to them in the field, did nothing to whet their initiative. But towards the end of the war she began to see that ultimate victory was impossible and tended to become apathetic.

Peace found her aged but determined as ever to give her people good government. Devoted mother though she was, if need be she would sacrifice herself and her children to the State, and at a tender age some of the girls were married in a purely dynastic interest, Marie Antoinette, for instance, to the Dauphin of France. Long screeds of advice followed them, Maria Theresa making the mistake of believing that a mature woman's paper wisdom sent half across Europe could counterbalance the effect of fresh experience on young hearts.

Her scattered family caused anxiety, but there was a greater one at home: Joseph, her problematical heir. Joseph was a Rationalist, a free-thinker, a Spartan and a firm believer that, if only the ingredients are right, happiness can be forced upon people like a pill. He was utterly sincere, but was sadly lacking in knowledge of human nature. Above all, he wished to go ahead too fast, and given the immense resistances Maria Theresa had encountered in setting up a bureaucratic State she foresaw danger here for the future. So the closing years of her life saw them working together, he as co-regent, devoted to one another but perpetually at odds, and this added greatly to her burdens.

In 1765 her husband died and she was plunged in the bitterest grief. But the trials of the ruler did not cease. Catherine of Russia had succeeded by devious means in making Poland virtually a Russian province. Then she fought a war against the Turks, won a victory and made startling claims in the Balkans. Both Frederick and Maria Theresa felt themselves threatened and the spectre of another continental war loomed, until Joseph, acting better than he knew, sent Austrian troops to occupy a small area of Poland which had formerly been German. Catherine then switched her claims and suggested the partition of Poland between Austria, Prussia and herself, and in 1772 it came about. The hearty meal banished the fear of war, but Maria Theresa had been pushed into the venture by her son and never forgave herself.

There was one more service she could render her country. In December, 1777, Joseph was able to buy Lower Bavaria from an indigent Elector in return for immediate cash, also the reversionary title to the Upper Palatinate. He thought the ageing Frederick would not react, but he did, threatening war, as Maria Theresa had foreseen. Negotiations were started, but not pursued by Joseph, with the result that in July, 1778, the King of Prussia marched into Bohemia at the head of 100,000 men. For the empress this was altogether too much and without consulting her son she wrote to the hated Frederick the first letter she had ever addressed to him in her life, asking to resume the discussions. This did not prevent war, but it shortened its length, and at the peace, with his mother's hearty concurrence, Joseph agreed to disgorge Bavaria.

And now her work was done. She could not restrain him for ever. Her health was failing and soon, for better or worse, the eager, unwise Joseph would have to tread his path alone. She had borne many children, endured long years of war, infused her easy-going people with her own sense of purpose. But she was beginning to feel a stranger in a changing world and was not sorry to see the end. It came on the evening of 29 November, 1780, after a chill caught on a long drive in a rain-storm. She was imperturbably calm, would not sleep because she wanted to see death approaching, blessed her children and then, seeing that they were overwrought, told them to leave the room. At nine o'clock the great empress died, but in the minds of Austrians she lives on as the architect of her empire's survival and as, in her own words, "the general and chief mother of my country".

CATHERINE II (THE GREAT)

(1729–96)

CATHERINE II, Empress of Russia, universally known as Catherine the Great, shares—with the English Elizabeth I and Victoria, and the Austrian Maria Theresa (Catherine's contemporary)—a fame afforded by history to but few women rulers. Catherine's almost immediate predecessor was the able, though less significant, Empress Elizabeth. Among Russian rulers since the turbulent sixteenth-seventeenth century chaos following Ivan the Terrible and Boris Godonov, only Peter the Great is Catherine's superior in importance (though not necessarily in all his policies), while among her successors in the Romanov dynasty which lasted until the Revolution of 1917 only Alexander II is comparable to her in vision, yet her inferior in personality and will-power.

The late eighteenth century was the "Age of Enlightened Despots", and to this number—stressing the noun rather than the adjective—Catherine belonged, like Frederick II of Prussia. "Enlightened" is perhaps an ambiguous term, yet in any sense of the word many of Catherine's aims and actions can be so characterized. Less obviously enlightened, though it enlightens us as to her character, was her mode of attaining the throne.

A fatal aspect of Russian monarchy—inherited perhaps from the early rivalry of princes in the Kiev period, the cradle of Russian nationhood—was the loose theory of succession. As in the later Roman Empire, havoc was wrought through uncertainty and intrigue; the eldest son by no means always succeeded to his father. Put brutally, Catherine ascended the throne through at least connivance in the murder of her husband, Czar Peter III, orphaned grandson of Peter the Great but his antithesis in character, an irresponsible "monkey" (so he was called) with almost an "arrested development".

It is ironic that both he and Catherine should have been, in different senses, outsiders: he, brought up in Sweden as a Lutheran, not speaking Russian, and even more concerned with Scandinavian and German interests; and she, not even a Russian by birth, but a princess of Anhalt-Zerbst, yet ardent for her adopted country, a student of its customs and needs, and in character not unlike previous Romanov czars. Her husband was widely unpopular, and Catherine's accession, whatever the means employed, was applauded, and her reign of thirty-four years lasted until her death.

During Catherine's reign she fostered and developed Russian institutions and reforms, conducted highly-skilled diplomatic intrigues and several wars in the "Russian interest", while conducting in a more civilized fashion Peter the Great's "opening of a door on to Europe" for a Russia still backward by general European standards. Peter imported soldiers and technicians from the West; Catherine diffused the newest French culture (hence the term "enlightened"); and it is likely that her foreign origin predisposed her to do this. She also showed a somewhat un-Russian continuity and balance in her perseverance, as distinct from the arbitrary energy of most Russian rulers, as witness the great Peter, who founded St. Petersburg (now Leningrad) on a supposedly impossible marshy site, and helped in the work literally with his own hands.

"Her brilliance was like a fountain showering down in sparks" was the way in which the French encyclopaedist Grimm described Catherine; after talking to her he would pace his own room for hours, too excited to sleep. And next day Catherine would more than likely spend some hours—she could work fifteen hours a day—in cameo-making, or engraving, or even in painting and sculpture, or in literary work, largely satirical, though none of it first-class. Still, it shows something that an autocratic sovereign should introduce satire into her country, as well as patronizing poets like Derzhavin, one of the earliest Russians still read. Catherine, as a writer, lives only in her letters; here we find her native genius for administration, especially in its diplomatic facets. Correspondence between monarchs was common in her time, but her exchanges with Joseph II, Frederick the Great and others have a unique interest. Her exchanges with Voltaire, Falconnet, Grimm, D'Alembert and other French writers and scholars helped to initiate that ascendancy of French language and culture in Russia which lasted until 1917.

Catherine admired and promoted men for their ability (and sexual charm), and showed herself generally pragmatic and opportunistic. Her diplomacy was certainly opportunist; her finesse in playing off Prussia and Austria against each other, while seemingly the friend of each, is an example. Her curiosity was both feminine and immense. History records her also as a great, frequent and changeable lover. The long roll of her partners consists roughly of two types: younger men like Mamonov or Lanskoy, treated as pets or children; and ministers and officials of exceptional quality, like Potemkin and Orlov. Potemkin was, for her, "bold mind, bold spirit, bold heart", and "cleverer than I"; and after his death, with their real intimacy long past, she felt utterly cut off. Catherine sought courageous and forceful men, and to such her letters often appear like those of one male friend to another. She liked a comradeship in which—to use her own words—"one of the two friends was a very attractive woman". Even before her rise to the throne she played seducer and seduced. She was not on the best of terms with the vigorous, sensual, and politically irresponsible Empress Elizabeth (daughter of Peter the Great). During Elizabeth's reign, when there were really two Courts—that of the empress and that of Peter (her nephew) with Catherine—a double scandal spread: while Peter was scorned as apparently both impotent and profligate, Catherine's morals caused alarm, so that Elizabeth appointed a duenna to watch over her—but Catherine responded by falling in love with the duenna's husband!

Suspicious of the cut-and-dried, Catherine yet was capable of the hardest, most concentrated work, sometimes working in great Russian bouts and sometimes in steadier German style. Employing four secretaries, she often worked a fifteen-hour day. Her non-fiction reading ran from Buffon's *Natural History* to Blackstone's *Commentaries* on law; in mastering the latter, she presaged her own studious compilation of the new humanitarian legal code, the *Instruction* (or *Nakaz*) based largely on Montesquieu, on which she worked for eighteen months.

Indeed the impression left by Catherine remains one of blended order and caprice, of idealism and opportunism. Ideas attracted her strongly; travel excited her creative thought (the Volga, she remarked, had given her ideas to last ten years). Yet in sober fact she had little right to the throne at all. "God and the choice of my subjects" was her bland reply, but some of these very subjects continued to rebel or plot against her for over thirty years. If not in league with her husband's murderers, she did reward them, without at the same time showing any disfavour towards his followers, whether through lack of malice or diplomatic guile. Even when Pugachev, leader of the greatest of the revolts, was captured, Catherine vetoed the use of torture; and she was considerate towards her servants, which was hardly a regal virtue in that Absolutist age.

Catherine was born in Germany in 1729, married the seventeen-year-old Peter III at the age of sixteen, became empress-consort with Peter as emperor in 1762—on Elizabeth's death—and seized the throne as sole ruler after six months. At her marriage she accepted the Greek Orthodox faith and was renamed Catherina Alexéivna, although like Peter she had been brought up as a Lutheran. She treated her new religion as seriously as her affinity with thinkers like Voltaire would permit, though this did not later prevent her from exiling many of the heretical "Old Believers" into the Siberian wilds, an action dictated by political diplomacy.

Her accession brought acclaim from the most important regiments, and also an open revolt of some 200,000 peasants against their squires; artillery subdued them. Her usurpation did not go unchallenged; her son Paul (who succeeded at her death) became the unwilling aim of many intrigues to place him, the legal heir, on the throne. Others favoured a youth, Ivan VI, who at the age of *one year* had reigned for a short time. Other pretenders abounded, like the adventuress called Princess Tarakanova, who claimed to be the illegitimate daughter of the late Empress Elizabeth, and who died in jail.

The Church, too, protested in the imposing figure of Arseny Matseyevich, Archbishop of Rostov, who anathematized Catherine when she confirmed Peter II's appropriation of Church estates, now called the "economic lands" of the State. Unfrocked and twice jailed, he denounced her right to the throne and died forbidden to speak to any human being. Catherine had already dubbed him "Andrew the Babbler". Other voices sang the same tune, and the merchant Smolin—for instance—wrote to the empress denouncing her "unjust government".

Still vaster hurricanes were soon in progress: notably the revolt of Pugachev in May, 1773. Catherine's first years as ruler displayed a glaring contrast between genuine progressive efforts and complacency towards appalling social conditions. Hers was indeed the age of the "gentry" (*dvoryanstvo*), a mixed class of aristocrats and servicemen, whose power over the mass of the serfs was almost unlimited. In 1771 the great plague of Moscow killed 100,000 persons, and cannon was used to suppress rioting. The Pugachev rebellion summed up a burning discontent.

A Cossack soldier and adventurer, Emilian Pugachev, after many escapes, gathered followers and even formed his own bogus court, parading as emperor and naming two of his forts Moscow and St. Petersburg! He swore he would confine Catherine in a nunnery, and slaughtered the gentry, being now in command of a vast motley force composed of Cossacks from the Don and the Dnieper, all the Tartar and Finnish groups still smarting under Russian rule, and exiles and convicts who had escaped from their guards *en route* for Siberia. Soon he had the sympathy of the people as a whole: Bibikov, sent by Catherine to stem the tide, reported: "It is not Pugachev that matters, but the general indignation." Even when Pugachev—a price of 28,000 roubles on his head—approached Moscow, Catherine (who had at first laughed at the revolt as a farce) still urged moderation. At last—aided by a famine on the Volga—the tide turned and Pugachev was executed in January, 1775, before the delighted gentry.

As a result the lot of the peasants became still more degraded. In an edict against a ruthless serf-owner, Catherine wrote: "Be so good as to call your peasants cattle." Yet her irony was wasted. In fact, serfdom increased during her—in many ways enlightened—reign. Apparently without realizing the consequences, she made enormous grants of land to her favourites, which in fact made new serfs out of the still partly-free crown peasants. Further, she extended serfdom to the vast area of the Ukraine through a "fiscal" decree, based on the equalization and centralizing of conditions throughout the country. Her son, Paul, was to extend this system. In 1773 auction-sales of serfs were allowed. The power of master over serf knew few limits: a typical punishment would be five hundred strokes of the rod for failure to attend Holy Communion.

Yet there is another side to the picture. Catherine did help in forwarding progressive ideas. Her *Instruction* (or *Nakaz*) has clauses about equality before the law; the injustice and gradual abolition of serfdom; that education is better than punishment, and that capital punishment should be limited and torture abolished; that the peasant must have food, clothing, and even peasant judges and a jury system, and be able to buy his freedom; agriculture implies property—and so forth. To debate how these principles should be implemented, Catherine, in 1766, summoned a Great Commission, elected from all classes (even the peasants) and nationalities in the empire, consisting of 564 members. It sat for a year and a half. Catherine listened, but the final upshot was disappointing.

Still, she managed to introduce certain reforms: peasants' petitions, forbidden by law, reached the sovereign; the prize essay of her Free Economic Society decided in favour of peasant proprietorship; finance, economics, justice and public health also made some advances. Local government, public welfare, roads and canals, trade with Asia, all benefited to some degree; while hospitals, schools and the St. Petersburg Public Library were founded. The

College of Medicine, founded in 1763, was followed in 1768 by Catherine's own example of inoculation against smallpox. Yet the construction of the city of Ekaterinoslav ("Glory of Catherine") stopped early through lack of funds.

It is time now to outline Catherine's foreign policy. She corresponded with foreign monarchs (180 letters to Frederick the Great alone), and induced them to visit her. How cleverly her letters cajole, and twist each point to her own advantage! In the main her interests lay in Russia's neighbours and potential foes: Sweden (then so powerful), Poland (soon to be partitioned three times), and Turkey. Early she perceived the value of a non-committal attitude towards Prussia and Austria, and it was largely through her that these states made peace in 1763. She took the most cynical advantage of the confusions of the Polish situation; bribery, invasion of the Polish Duchy of Kurland (Latvia) and then of Poland proper, enabled her and Frederick to place on the Polish throne their favourite and her former lover, Stanislaus Poniatowski, because—as she wrote—he had the least claim, and thus would always feel dependent on Russia.

She revelled in the "happy (Polish) anarchy which we can work at will". It is true that the Polish Sejm, or Diet, continued persecuting the Russian Dissidents (Greek Orthodox) in Poland. Under the famous general Suvorov, Russia seized the chance to invade; but Turkey in 1762 promised to help the Poles. Near the Turkish frontier Poles and Jews were massacred, and reprisals led to Cossacks ravaging Turkey, and the invasion of Russia by the Crimean Tartars (1768). Catherine looked forward to this war and built on it great hopes. She was greatly responsible for its success, through her naval policy which resulted in the Russian victories of Navarino and Chesme Bay. These alarmed both Austria and Prussia.

Unscrupulous intrigues then led to the first of the three partitions of Poland among the three powers. They took over a quarter of Poland's territory, with five-twelfths of her population. The war with Turkey was renewed, with Russia finally obtaining access to the Black Sea; the Crimea was declared independent, and Christians in Turkey and Moldavia (Rumania) were "protected". Shameless bargaining with Joseph II of Austria ended in a temporary stalemate, which Catherine used to annex the Crimea (1783), to which she made a triumphal visit with Joseph II, passing like a fairy queen through southern Russia with extravagant luxuries, gaiety and welcoming deputations.

There was further trouble with Turkey, but Russia was triumphant in December, 1791. Meanwhile Poland made internal and constitutional advances. Russia invaded again and a Second Partition took place, this time without Austria. The terms provoked the revolt of Kosciusko at Cracow in March, 1794, but Suvorov's forces crushed all resistance near Warsaw in November. Catherine now took the biggest share in the Third and final Polish Partition in which the whole country was swallowed up.

As the French Revolution of 1789 expanded into terror and foreign warfare Catherine was disgusted. The reactionary in her came to dominate the enlightened humanitarian: the pro-peasant writer, Radishchev, was imprisoned. In his defence he remarked that a few years earlier Catherine would have rewarded him for his sentiments.

In November, 1796, the year of Napoleon's first victories in Italy, Catherine died and her son, Paul, became czar. A magnetic and intellectual, but also capricious and somewhat unscrupulous woman, Catherine did much for Russia to ensure her place in history as Catherine the Great.

GEORGE WASHINGTON

(1732–99)

HE WAS a great ruler and a great man—and seldom in history has a great man been laden with such a dead weight of mythology, such a worthless heap of halos, crammed one on the other like a market-porter's baskets. Only—and paradoxically—in Communist China, and for much the same reason. Each state weathered a revolution, threw off the shackles of the past, buried its former idols: and new idols had to be erected in their place. Hence Comrade Mao, the god who makes the grass grow green, the rice to shoot. And hence George Washington, The-Father-of-His-Country.

"O Washington! How I do love thy name! How have I often adored and blessed thy God, for creating and forming thee the great ornament of human kind! Thy fame is of sweeter perfume than Arabian spices. Listening angels shall catch the odour, waft it to heaven, and perfume the universe!" This, in a sermon by his contemporary, Ezra Styles of Yale. And a little later, all those anecdotes, in the biography by Parson Weems, most of them, as far as we can tell, quite untrue. The cherry tree, for example. (" 'I can't tell a lie, Pa, you know I can't tell a lie. I did it with my hatchet.'—'Run to my arms, dearest boy,' cried his father in transports.")

And later still, in the *Pictorial Life of Washington*, compiled half a century after the great man's death by Horatio Weld: "The first word of infancy should be mother, the second, father, the third, WASHINGTON."

It is proof of Washington's greatness that his reputation has survived all this. And worse.

He was descended from British stock and was in many ways the epitome of an English country gentleman, fond of open-air pursuits, moderately well educated, distant with his subordinates, but scrupulously fair. The United States of America can be grateful to the bigotry and intolerance of Oliver Cromwell's adherents, in the middle of the seventeenth century, for it was they who succeeded in having the Reverend Lawrence Washington removed from his Northamptonshire living. Soon after, the vicar died in poverty, and at this two of his sons decided to sever connexion with an unkind country and try their luck in an unknown one, across the sea.

They emigrated to the Colony of Virginia, and straightway made a success of it. From one of these two brothers, John, was descended George Washington, born, in Virginia, the 11th day of February, 1732. (Twenty years later the calendar was revised, adding eleven days to the date, so the correct anniversary of Washington's birth, as any American schoolboy can tell us, is 22 February). His education, by European standards, was sketchy, and not to be compared with that of some Virginian contemporaries like Thomas Jefferson: throughout his life he regretted this, and in particular his inability to speak French. When he became President, he refused to visit that country, rather than be humiliated by an interpreter. But George Washington, of a rich planting family (tobacco and wheat), was an intelligent young man who preferred the out-of-doors. He was a good shot with a rifle, a fine horseman. From childhood he was interested in a military career, an interest which had begun when his older half-brother, Lawrence, went off in the brand-new "American Regiment" to the West Indies. The expedition against the Spanish was commanded by Admiral Vernon and failed, but Lawrence so admired his commander that he re-christened his plantation Mount Vernon.

When George reached the age of sixteen he was invited to move in with this gay and gallant half-brother, and his sociable young wife, and it was with this couple that the future President of the United States got his first taste of social life, learning to dance, play cards, make conversation: though he still preferred the open air, life was gay and enjoyable. After dinner in the evenings there was animated discussion of the lands farther in, west of the Blue Ridge Mountains and the Alleghanies, and the chances of settling them. All this Washington listened to, for he was an ambitious young man. He desired not only to acquit himself well as an army officer—when opportunity arose, and he knew it would, even though impediments were put in the way of advancement for "Colonials"—but to acquire land. The most sensible way, it seemed, of getting involved in any westward settlement was to train as surveyor, and this he now did. He showed remarkable aptitude which, coupled with his family's importance, resulted in his being Surveyor of Culpeper County by the time he was eighteen. He even managed to claim, for himself, some 1,500 acres in the fertile Shenandoah Valley.

Two years later Lawrence died of TB, leaving Mount Vernon to his widow for as long as she lived; then—if none of his own children survived, and none did—to George.

And now came military opportunity. George had inherited from his half-brother not only Mount Vernon but the largely honorary job of Militia Adjutant—and for the keen young surveyor it would be as much a working job as he could make it. He persuaded Lieutenant-Governor Dinwiddie of Virginia to let him be the bearer of a written ultimatum to the French, who had started to build forts on the Ohio River.

It was not the most glorious start to a military career, but it brought him to public notice as a stubborn, fearless young man. He did the round trip to the Ohio in two and a half months, suffering great privation, being nearly killed on more than one occasion, and bringing back a polite rebuff from the French commander, in which, as Washington carefully explained to Dinwiddie, "It was their absolute design to take possession of the Ohio, and by God they would do it". He was commended on his conduct of the expedition and promoted to lieutenant-colonel.

A little later he was back in the Ohio country, successfully holding back a further French incursion and in the process capturing many prisoners. Promotion now took him to the rank of full colonel—though this was only a commission in the Colonial forces: the more important "King's Commission" was still denied him, and Washington, understandably, resented this. Commanding a mixed bag of militia and friendly Indians, he went on to encounter a vastly superior French force—at which point his Indians deserted. He was forced to retire with his remaining troops into a stockade (which he christened "Fort Necessity") and eventually to surrender. A bitter blow for a keen officer, even though the French released him immediately, with honour. They then made great propaganda from his chatty, sporting, diary which they had retained and which showed —or so they tried to point out—that the British, i.e., Washington, had been the aggressors, hounding the peace-loving French. For a while there was such a fuss that he resigned his commission.

But the call to glory was still great—doubly so after his defeat. A year later he arranged to join General Braddock's force in the same area, as unpaid A.D.C.—a gesture which could only be made by a brave, ambitious—and very rich—man.

This was total disaster, though Washington came out of it better than his general. Two horses were shot out from under him and he was noted as a very gallant soldier and an inspired commander. He was persuaded to take up his commission again, and now, at the age of twenty-three, he became not only a colonel, but Commander-in-Chief of the Virginia Army.

Soon afterwards illness struck, and he retired to Mount Vernon. His sister-in-law had moved elsewhere and was renting the property to him, and in their combined absence the plantations had suffered. He was also a poorer man, thanks largely to his quixotic military adventures, and he worked desperately hard, as soon as his health permitted, at making Mount Vernon, its slaves, its tobacco and its wheat, into a profitable investment.

By now, as a mature and much-respected Virginian of twenty-six, he was about to enter the fields of politics and matrimony. He announced his intention of severing his connexion with the militia, and it is here that we have a first indication of how valued he had been as commander and loved as a man. His officers implored him to stay. They wrote, "Our unhappy country will receive a loss, not less irreparable, than ourselves. Where will it meet a man so experienced in military affairs? One so renowned for patriotism, courage and conduct? In you we place the most implicit confidence. Your presence only will cause a steady firmness and vigour to actuate in every breast, despising the greatest dangers, and thinking light of toils and hardships, while led on by the man we know and love."

An odd bit of rhetoric—and there is no doubt of its sincerity.

But Washington said goodbye—or so he thought—to soldiering, and in January, 1759, married the prosperous young widow to whom he had long been engaged, Martha Dandridge Custis. She had two children by her first marriage (there would be no issue of this one) and George settled cheerfully down to being a good stepfather and—with the addition of Martha's considerable property—a very large landowner. He was richer than he had ever been and he and Martha began to entertain lavishly—for no better reason than that they both enjoyed doing so. Soon they had come in contact with most of the notable men from the English colonies in America.

We can picture him, sitting red-faced and smiling (despite the evidence of the lamentable, scowling, portraits that were done of him), at the head of a table gleaming in candlelight, listening with patience to a long anecdote by a distinguished guest. The guest would be working hard at his role—for it was an honour to be invited to a meal at Mount Vernon. The staid and genial host, hero of four campaigns, retired Commander-in-Chief, lacked but a fortnight to his twenty-seventh birthday.

And yet, sixteen years after this retirement, George Washington was General Washington, military leader of all thirteen American colonies. Slowly, inexorably, while he managed his estates, the tide of resentment against British control had been mounting in every colony. The process had been helped by the British defeat of the French in 1763, which drove France from North America and removed any need for British protection, but it was the result, in the main, of taxation which, though not heavy, was unexplained, and a generally heavy-handed treatment from London which made the colonists feel they were not part of Britain but some outlandish possession to be exploited.

The Stamp Act was passed, but repealed, and Washington himself was to write to England that those responsible for its repeal were "entitled to the thanks of every British subject and have mine cordially". But there was more taxation to come. All of it, in response to further outcry, was removed, save for that on tea, resulting in the famous Boston Tea Party, at which colonists dressed themselves up as Indians (nobody quite knew why) in order to throw a newly-arrived cargo of tea into the harbour, rather than pay tax on it. Tempers rose steadily, and on 15 June, 1775, the Continental Congress, meeting in Philadelphia, picked Washington to be General Commanding "all the continental forces raised for the defence of American liberty". There were many excellent reasons for the choice: he was a proved and brilliant soldier, a rich and cultivated man ("so that he may rather communicate lustre to his dignities than receive it"), and he was a Virginian. With the conflict between mother country and colonies so far confined to New England, a commander from outside New England was essential if all thirteen colonies were to be brought in.

Washington accepted, on the condition that he drew no salary, only his expenses. He was forty-three.

His first discovery was that his army was short—desperately short—of uniforms, food, blankets and ammunition, and that scoundrels all over the thirteen colonies were growing fat through holding back these supplies. His first months were spent combating graft and even treachery, making an army out of a largely rebellious (against its officers as much as against the English oppressor) rabble.

His first success came in March of the following year when he captured Boston from what were still known as "Ministerial" troops. But soon men's minds were made up: on the fourth of July the famous Declaration of Independence was signed.

Washington now suffered a series of reverses. Enemy reinforcements began to pour in from England, he was up against treachery of all sorts, from that of subordinate officers like the notorious Benedict Arnold to quarrelling factions in Congress. He handled the latter skilfully, keeping that jealous and mutually suspicious assembly briefed about his every move. He was badly defeated at the Battle of Brooklyn Heights, but went on to thrash his enemy at Trenton and again at Princeton. Two more defeats, at Brandywine and Germantown, and he took his army into winter quarters at Valley Forge, near Philadelphia. It was during this bitter winter of 1777-78, while his forces suffered horribly from exposure and a shortage of every sort of clothing and equipment, that he learnt the French were entering the war on his side.

From now on, though there was much hard fighting ahead, the outcome was clear. Yet it was not until 1781 that the British under General Cornwallis surrendered at Yorktown, their retreat cut off by the French fleet, under Admiral De Grasse.

The war over, a new republic in being, Washington resigned his post as Commander-in-Chief and went back to his plantations. He had been a superb soldier if not a perfect general. As a Virginia gentleman, a slave-owner (though a reasonably enlightened one, who made provision for them all to be freed on his wife's death), he was to most of his subordinates a stern, almost a forbidding, creature—and this has been caught in most of the surviving portraits. It is the face of a man who refuses to suffer fools gladly which glares at us from the five-cent stamp. But in 1781 Washington was a tired man, anxious to be allowed to stay on his property and try to recoup his failing fortunes. He achieved a few years of this, got his plantations working profitably once more, and then was elected, in February, 1789, first President of the United States of America. His sense of duty made him accept, and at the end of April he was inaugurated, in New York.

He did not enjoy his first four years in office. The members of his Government, though they respected him, were a quarrelsome lot, with widely differing ideas about what was best for the country and for their own individual states. He was reluctant to run for office a second time, but was persuaded to do so, was elected and this time inaugurated in Philadelphia. A few months later he laid the cornerstone of the Capitol building in the city of Washington.

He died 14 December, 1799, a fortnight before the end of the eighteenth century. Two years later his widow Martha died and the slaves were released.

No doubt there were others in the American colonies who would have made good Presidents—perhaps better. But somehow it was fitting that the tough, dignified, Virginia planter, who had proved himself in battle, should lead his country into peace.

LOUIS XVI

(1754–93)

Louis XVI was so overshadowed by the Revolution which destroyed him and his regime that his importance as a monarch has been perhaps overlooked. Even in the veneration accorded to royal martyrs, he is eclipsed by the tragedy of his glamorous consort, Marie Antoinette.

Louis XVI's true importance lies in the fact that the moderates, who, rather than the Jacobins, were the real makers of the French Revolution, wanted to build the new France around him. They wanted to isolate him from the courtiers of Versailles and make him into a constitutional monarch in the English style. Although the Revolution destroyed Louis, he was at first the centre of it, and he was not unsympathetic to its reasonable demands for elementary justice.

Though execrated by the Commune, Louis XVI was not in any way responsible for the conditions which led to the Revolution. The blame lies fairly and squarely with his two predecessors—Louis XIV, whose royal dictatorship undermined the ancient liberties and economic stability of his kingdom, and Louis XV, whose indolence and sloth took France to the edge of the abyss. Of the two, Louis XV—"the well-beloved"—is the most deserving of history's contempt.

Louis XVI was Louis XV's grandson. His father was the Dauphin of France and his mother was Marie Joseph of Saxony. He was born at Versailles on 23 August, 1754. When he was eleven his father died and he became heir to the throne.

Little preparation was made to fit him for his destiny. He received a sketchy education, and all knowledge of state affairs was withheld from him by his insensate grandfather. In 1770 he married Marie Antoinette, daughter of Marie Theresa, Empress of Austria.

As dauphin, Louis cut a poor figure amidst the brilliant cavaliers of his grandfather's glittering court. He was shy, reserved and harsh of voice. He lacked the excessive courtesy and exquisite manners which ever since Louis XIV the French aristocracy had cherished as something which distinguished them from the common people.

Louis XVI possessed not a shadow of the kingly dignity and regal air of his grandfather, who in consequence despised him. He was pious and lived a simple life, his one pleasure being his devotion to the chase. When he took up the blacksmith's art as a hobby, it was the cause of much hilarity at court; it greatly annoyed Marie Antoinette and was the case of many stormy scenes between them. But while a king who could use his hands at a skilled artisan's trade did not commend itself to the fastidious court of Louis XV, it did not come amiss in the spirit which was arising in France just then.

Louis XV was well aware of the storm which was brewing, but firmly believed that the existing state of affairs would last his lifetime, and that the storm was destined to burst upon the head of his successor. He therefore was safe. Indolence and ease, and the enjoyment of the passing hour alone concerned him. "*Mais après nous le déluge*", he had long been accustomed to say. In his later years he would sometimes add with a cynical smile: "I would love to know how Berry will manage to weather the coming storm."

Berry was the contemptuous name he reserved for the graceless youth who was to succeed him. Louis XV never gave him the title of dauphin.

On 10 May, 1774, Louis XV's ignoble career was terminated by a virulent attack of smallpox. Already the lick-spittle courtiers were fawning over the young king and his consort as they received the news of the end of Louis Quinze in an apartment as remote as possible from the "well-beloved's" contaminated death-room.

When the courtly sycophants saluted them as king and queen, the boy of twenty and the girl of nineteen fell upon their knees and said, "Guide us, protect us, O God. We are too young to reign." The most immoral and sophisticated court in the world knew that a very different regime had begun at Versailles.

Two hours later everyone had fled from Versailles and the infected palace was a desert. Left behind were only two or three underservants and some priests of the "inferior clergy" whose lives were sacrificed to the fatal duty assigned them of remaining to pray by the contagious body of their late lord and master and convey it with all speed and the utmost secrecy to the Abbey of St. Denis.

The new king and his consort and the younger members of the royal family retired to La Muette and with the exception of Marie Antoinette were immediately inoculated for the smallpox by the surgeon Jouberthou. Vaccination had not then been introduced generally, though its value had been long recognized by French and German physicians.

Louis XVI during his lifetime was described by those who knew him as being the most upright man in his kingdom. His chief defect was lack of firmness. He was diffident of his own powers and conscious of his lack of proper education. He allowed himself to be influenced too much by Marie Antoinette, who was strong-minded as well as frivolous.

Louis ascended the throne at a momentous crisis in the life of the nation. There was widespread disgust at the wasted and licentious reign of Louis XV. The administration groaned beneath a mountain of debts. Trade was ruined. The nobility and clergy clung tenaciously to their age-old exemptions from taxation. The time had arrived when the abuses of the ancient regime could no longer be tolerated, and sweeping reforms were demanded.

France was aflame with new ideas. Men like Voltaire, Rousseau and Montesquieu had questioned the political institutions and created the discontent in all classes of the community which led to the Revolution.

In all this Louis XVI was out of his depth. Though he was among the first to wish to repair the damage to the nation's fabric caused by the two previous Louis, he misjudged the magnitude of the problem and the temper of his people. He had no political sagacity.

Despite his shortcomings, Louis XVI was virtuous, well-intentioned and at times liberal-minded. In other circumstances he might well have been a successful and progressive king, for all his weakness and vacillations. At all times his thoughts were for his people. This was a new departure for the Bourbons, who had always been distinguished by their selfishness and egotism.

The first thing Louis did was to summon Turgot, the economist, and one of the few honest statesmen of his day, and make him Comptroller-General. Turgot demanded the most stringent economies, particularly in the royal household, and wanted to reform the whole system of taxation.

There was no sign of economy at Louis's lavish and splendid coronation in Rheims Cathedral in June, 1775. A new crown was made costing nearly a million pounds. A luxurious new state coach was built. The impoverished treasury was recklessly plundered to provide for these and other extravagant items of expenditure.

Turgot's demands encountered the most bitter opposition from those closest to the king. Enormous sums were spent to maintain the luxuries at Versailles. The king's relatives, though they had all been well endowed by Louis XV, who had left a fortune of thirty-five million francs, were dissatisfied with their annuities and were demanding more money from the state to gratify their extravagances. Queen Marie Antoinette spent money like water.

Reforming the taxation system would have meant the privileged classes paying taxes—an unheard of thing. Turgot had no chance of putting such a revolutionary reform through against the pressures which were put upon Louis by those around him who wished to keep things as they were. Turgot's suggestions were too radical and he was dismissed in 1776.

He was succeeded by Necker, who valiantly grappled with the impossible task of keeping the leaky vessel of the old French monarchy afloat. Already France, as the ally of the United States, was involved in war against England and had sent troops to America. Not only had vast sums to be borrowed to prosecute the war, but the troops returned to France infected with the heady spirit of republicanism which was sweeping the United States. Turgot had warned Louis against this danger, in vain.

The American war helped to produce the financial crisis which was the immediate cause of the Revolution. Necker was popular at first at Versailles, for he did not discourage public expenditure. In 1781, however, he lost his popularity in that quarter when he published his famous *Compte rendu* in which he drew up a balance sheet of France, showing for the first time how much the *taille* (the heaviest tax from which the privileged classes were exempt) and the hated salt tax actually took from the people, and also how much the king spent on himself and his favourites. After that Necker was dismissed at the insistence of Marie Antoinette.

In 1789 the monarchy, and indeed the country, was bankrupt. Ministers had not enough funds to meet the regular expenses of the government. Louis then called the States-General, a national assembly of clergy, nobility and commons whose function was to advise the king, and which had not met since 1614.

Louis presided at the first meeting of this ancient body on 5 May and received a warm reception. He made a brief, formal speech. But when the assembly heard that the Third Estate, the commons, was to have no say in the conduct of the nation's affairs, its mood changed.

This marked the beginning of the Revolution. The Third Estate, finding themselves excluded from the assembly, held their own meeting in a building called the Tennis Court, and took the famous Tennis Court oath not to dissolve themselves until a new constitution had been made. Refusing to disperse, it called itself the French National Assembly. Louis, not so much alarmed as influenced by his courtiers and Marie Antoinette, brought two regiments to Versailles.

Stirred up by the Tennis Court oath and the king's counter-move, and urged on by orators and agitators, the Paris mob stormed the Bastille on 14 July, 1789. "Is this a revolt then?" asked Louis when he received the news at Versailles. "No, sire," replied the duc de Liancourt. "It is a revolution."

But Louis did not agree, and saw no cause for alarm. Other members of the privileged classes took a different view. It was then that the apprehensive aristocrats started to leave France. In the next two months twenty thousand passports were issued. They were under no illusion that the days of privilege were numbered, though none guessed the violence and intensity of the upheaval which was to come.

After the fall of the Bastille, Louis's advisers urged that the royal family should go to Metz or some other frontier fortress, escorted by a strong body of troops. Marie Antoinette was strongly in favour of this, but Louis for once would not be influenced by her. He flatly refused to leave Versailles.

Louis could not be convinced that his people would do him harm, and he was not really deluded in this. He was in fact extremely popular with the people, and he knew it. The deputies of the National Assembly, who included such statesmen as Mirabeau and Necker, wanted to build the new France around him. There was no question of a republic in the minds of responsible men in 1789.

At this moment Louis had a great opportunity to make himself a constitutional monarch, and to his credit he strove his best, within the limits of his restricted intellectual powers and the handicap of his unfortunate Bourbon background. Even without vision, but with just a little more will-power, with better advisers and a different wife, Louis XVI might have done what he desperately wanted to do—save France from bankruptcy and ruin. In order to do this he was quite prepared to become a constitutional monarch on the English style. It did not cross his mind then that the monarchy itself was in danger.

Mirabeau was pleading for a strong executive backed by a limited monarchy, and if Louis had been a man of decision this might have come about. But Louis was easy-going and good-natured. His weakness was misinterpreted as duplicity. This, combined with Mirabeau's untimely death in 1791, resulted in the destruction of the French monarchy, the Reign of Terror and the subsequent Napoleonic wars.

While the National Assembly drew up the new constitution

which abolished the *ancien régime* and issued its famous Declaration of the Rights of Man, France slipped deeper into economic distress and semi-anarchy.

Louis's hesitations and indiscretions began to try the patience of his people. He hesitated to ratify the Declaration of the Rights of Man, and the story of a dinner given by the Guardes du Corps to the Flanders Regiment at Versailles greatly angered the leaders of the National Assembly. Both Louis and Marie Antoinette were at this famous dinner, during which impassioned royalist toasts were drunk by the alcoholic grenadiers. The tricolour was trodden underfoot and the song of Blondel when seeking his captive king, Coeur de Lion, was sung. They vowed to die for Louis if he were in danger.

This highly inflammatory banquet caused great offence in Paris, though its true significance was probably exaggerated. It was rumoured that under the influence of his courtiers Louis was calling together troops loyal to him in an attempt to put an end to the Revolution.

On 5 October, 1789, the Paris mob marched to Versailles and compelled the king and the royal family to return with them to Paris. There was no antagonism shown to them. Louis was in fact at this time at the height of his popularity. The people believed that if he was in Paris away from the malign influence of the Versailles court all would be well. Louis took up residence at the Palace of the Tuileries, practically a prisoner, as it turned out.

The National Assembly, which had been holding its meetings at Versailles, followed the king to Paris, and it was the first great misfortune of the Revolution, for it placed both the king and the government at the mercy of the disorderly elements in Paris. But, although radicalism was running high in the Paris clubs, there was widespread loyalty to the king.

On 14 July, 1790, at the Festival of the Federation, Louis swore to maintain the constitution. But the high hopes and emotions of the festival did not last long. It was obvious even to Louis now that the clouds were dark in the sky. The voice of the Jacobins was being heard more insistently in the Assembly. It was in the September of 1790 that he began to think of the fate of Charles I of England, and to entertain fears that he himself might meet a similar end.

The aristocrats and nobles were fleeing in droves from France in the wake of the king's unpopular brother, the Comte d'Artois. The flight of his relatives and friends naturally reflected ill upon the king. Louis had long been urged to escape himself, but had always refused.

The flight to Varennes on 21 June, 1793, was one of his worst blunders. He may have decided to make it because the death of Mirabeau in April robbed France of the greatest statesman of the Revolution, the one man who could have reconciled the new France with the ancient monarchy. Mirabeau's death was a grievous blow to both Louis and France. The royal family's flight was too conspicuous an event to escape the notice of the countryside, and Louis ensured being recognized by continually poking the best-known head in France out of the carriage window.

Nevertheless the flight did not entirely turn the nation against him. Arrested at Varennes, he was maintained as a constitutional king after the melancholy return to Paris.

Louis's flight seems to have frightened, rather than angered, his people. Their grief at the thought of losing such an indifferent ruler clearly shows that France was still profoundly royalist. The National Assembly indeed held that he had not fled, but been carried off.

But republicanism was now a force to be reckoned with. The extremists' demand to do away with the monarchy was insistent. Many openly blamed Louis. "If this country ceases to be a monarchy," wrote Lord Gower, British Ambassador in Paris, "it will be entirely the fault of Louis XVI. Blunder upon blunder, inconsequence upon inconsequence, a total want of energy of mind, accompanied with personal cowardice, have been the destruction of his reign". Gower was hard on Louis, who was in a terrible situation after the death of Mirabeau and stood quite alone. Whatever might be said of his incompetence, he was certainly not guilty of personal cowardice, as he amply proved in 1793.

The National Assembly used the pro-Bourbon plottings in Austria as an excuse to go to war with that country in April, 1792. Louis was against the war and the unpopularity of his Austrian wife rubbed off on to him. In June a mob invaded the Tuileries and would have killed Louis if he had not consented to don the "cap of liberty", the badge of the "citizen patriots".

Louis knew now that the end was not far off. The extremists of the Commune had dominated the Assembly, which became the Convention. Its first act was to abolish the monarchy and proclaim France a republic. This was on 21 September.

The fate of the royal family was now in little doubt. A large party in the Convention held that Louis was guilty of treason in secretly encouraging foreign powers to come to his aid. They brought him to trial in January, 1793, and by a small majority condemned him to death. Already the royal family were imprisoned in the Temple in circumstances of increasing privation.

On the bitterly cold morning of 21 January, 1793, Louis went to his death on the scaffold. They drove him to the guillotine in a carriage, unlike the hated Marie Antoinette, who went in the common tumbril on 16 October of that same year. The troops were out in force—National Guards and brigades of field-pieces as well as a strong military escort for the condemned monarch's carriage.

Louis was accompanied by an Irish priest, the Abbé Edgeworth, and at the guillotine he disconcerted the executioners by his proud bearing and fearlessness. On the scaffold he cried out in a loud voice: "I die innocent of all the crimes with which I am charged. I forgive those who are guilty of my death, and I pray God that the blood which you are about to shed may never be required of France."

The knife fell and the cries of thousands of voices rent the air as the king died. People dipped their fingers into the royal blood, and one tasted it, saying, "It is vilely salty". There was no mourning in Paris that day. The theatres were full and much wine was drunk. The body was taken to the cemetery of the Madeleine and covered with quicklime.

Ten days later France declared war on England, which a century and a half before had set them the example by cutting off the head of Charles I.

NAPOLEON I

(1769–1821)

BY THE beginning of October, 1795 (*Vendémiaire* in the calendar of the French Revolution), some forty thousand armed National Guards, men of the middle classes and most of them Royalists, were confident of being able to overthrow the Convention and the weak, moderate government which, in 1794, had ended the Terror and sent the great Robespierre to the guillotine. The government was in a panic. The most resolute member of the Directorate, by name Barras, was doubtful about his generals, some of whom were unreliable, others incompetent. On the night of 4 October Barras appointed a soldier, then aged thirty-six, to take command of the forces defending the government. This was a Corsican, Napoleon Bonaparte, a brigadier thanks to some services at Toulon to the Republic, but out of employment and indeed having been obliged, recently, to sell his books and his watch to live. Generals at that time were two-a-penny.

At midnight, General Bonaparte had a large quantity of cannon dragged at the gallop into the centre of Paris. When, early in the morning of 5 October, the National Guards and a great mob marched down the Rue de Rivoli and adjoining streets in the centre of Paris, they were met with unexpected, sustained, well-directed fire from muskets and cannon. Three hundred were killed in a few minutes, numbers of dead and wounded lying sprawled on the steps of the Church of San Rocque in the Rue St. Honoré, the headquarters of the revolt. The "whiff of grape shot" had killed the Royalist reaction once and for all. It had shown that cannons speak louder than words and, in not very short a time, it had also killed the First Republic. Napoleon was made a full general, and shortly afterwards Commander-in-Chief of the army in Italy. He was set firmly on the road which was to make him Emperor in 1804, the master of Europe after Austerlitz and Jena, and finally to lead him to Waterloo in 1815 at the age of forty-six.

Napoleon's family, of Italian descent, had taken the side of France when Louis XVI had annexed Corsica in 1768, the year before Napoleon was born. Napoleon, the second son of Charles de

Bonaparte and Letizia Ramalino, a woman of exceptionally firm character, was educated at a French military school. In 1789, when the Revolution began, he was a second lieutenant in the royal army. He took the oath to the Republic in 1792, and was sent to Corsica, where he unsuccessfully tried to capture Sardinia. He remained in Corsica rather longer than he was entitled to, trying to overcome the resistance of the largest faction of the Corsicans to the Terror and the Revolution.

It is interesting that at this time Napoleon showed much greater interest in the affairs of his native island than in the battles the French Revolution was fighting throughout Europe. Rather accidentally, this young man had taken part, and a very prominent part, in the recapture of Toulon from the Royalists who were supported by English and Spanish warships. Napoleon then served in Italy where he somewhat annoyed his superiors by his self-confidence. From his exploits at Toulon he had won the esteem of Robespierre's brother, a political commissar, and of other Jacobin politicians. Consequently he was not in good odour with the now ruling moderate party.

His family had been forced to flee from Corsica which had risen against the Revolution and they were living in poverty in Marseilles, his mother and sisters obliged, at some period, to take in washing. Napoleon supported them as best he could. But in Paris, out of work himself, he could not do much. His clothes were threadbare. He looked a down-at-heels adventurer in the post-Robespierrian society which was rapidly becoming elegant. Nevertheless there was something about this short young man with his Roman profile and his burning glance and his ability to argue briefly and logically which impressed both men and women. He worked sometimes in the map department of the Ministry of War, and just before the event of *Vendémiare* he was about to take service with the Sultan of Turkey.

Shortly before he left to take his command in Italy, Napoleon married a beautiful *créole*, Josephine de Beauharnais, the widow of a general who had, since her husband's death, been forced to live on her charms. Napoleon was sincerely in love and he considered too that marriage to a woman who, even if doubtfully, belonged to the upper crust of society, advanced his fortunes.

In his Italian campaign Napoleon became the most popular of French generals and Josephine was called by the Parisiennes "Our Lady of Victories". Napoleon not only won victories, such as that of Arcole and Lodi, but he also won the hearts of most of the north-Italian population for the cause of the French Republic; he also sent a great deal of money and other spoils back to the Directory.

Realizing that, with the defeat of Austria, England was now the most serious enemy, Napoleon persuaded the Directory to mount an expedition against Egypt and the Near East to strike against England's trade and her hold on India. His fleet was destroyed at Aboukir Bay by Nelson and this expedition was largely a failure, in spite of some brilliant achievements. Napoleon abandoned his army in Palestine and returned to Paris. But this failure added to his glory, for the French imagination was excited by the spectacle of a French general reading the Bible to his officers in Nazareth, riding through the streets of Jerusalem, and standing gazing at the Pyramids of Gizeh. What did he think of the Sphinx? he was asked. "It is sad, like all greatness," Napoleon replied.

During Napoleon's absence in Egypt, the Austrians and Russians had won back northern Italy. The politicians had no hold on the imagination of the people, this young general realized, and, in November, 1799, by a *coup d'état* in which he was greatly aided by his brother Lucien, Napoleon became First Consul. The Revolution continued but under a Roman guise. Later, after a plebiscite, he became First Consul for life. He recovered Italy at the important but rather lucky victory at Marengo in 1800, whilst his generals were successful in Germany. The Austrians were completely defeated and forced to sign a humiliating treaty. Napoleon now sought peace. Britain was unbeatable on the sea, and in 1801 Nelson had destroyed the Danish fleet at Copenhagen in case it should fall into French hands. But France was everywhere victorious on land and surrounded by client republics in the Low Countries, Switzerland and Italy.

By 1804 Napoleon was determined to establish his rule on a permanent hereditary basis. On 2 December, 1804, he had himself crowned Emperor of the French, taking the Crown from the hands of Pope Pius VII who had been cajoled into coming to Paris, and placing it on his own head. He swore an oath to protect liberty, equality, the rights of property and the integrity of the Republic's territory. Beethoven, who had dedicated the Eroica Symphony to Napoleon, Hero of the French Revolution, annulled the dedication when he heard that Napoleon had been crowned.

Napoleon, after a fashion, conserved the Revolution, taking away from it some of its aspirations together with its incoherence. The French people, he said, were not interested in liberty, only in equality. He took care to dissociate himself from any suspicion of attempting a restoration of the *ancien régime*, and his abduction and murder of the Duc d'Enghien, a Royalist Pretender, was intended to show that Napoleon meant to figure in history as the heir of the Revolution.

Napoleon's fame is lasting not only because of his military genius. During the comparatively few years of the First Consulate he left his mark on France as an administrative genius. One of the first tasks he carried out was to reconcile France with the Church. Napoleon had no prejudices in favour of religion and many of his generals and closest supporters were partisans of an anti-religious State. So were many French intellectuals. When the great astronomer Laplace was explaining to Napoleon his work, the latter said: "But Monsieur, I see no place for God in your work on the cosmos"; "Sire," was the reply, "I had no need of that hypothesis." The reply pleased Napoleon. But he knew that, for the vast mass of the French peasantry, God and the Church were powerful forces.

Napoleon wanted French unity. It was during the First Consulate that was established the division of France into Departments, each of which was governed by a Prefect, the system in use today. It is essentially an authoritarian method of administration, but one which, given the instability which French political life was to experience, has undoubtedly served France well. The Council of State, Napoleon's invention, was charged with the drawing up and codifying of French Law, which codes together are known as the *Code Napoléon.* As the English historian H. A. L. Fisher has pointed out, it was the greatest of his achievements in his greatest period—before, as emperor, he became involved in perpetual war. Fisher writes:

> *The merit of the civil code is not that it is exhaustive, or that it has prevented the growth of case law, or that it is flawless in form and substance; but that in firm intelligible outline, it fixes the structure of a civilized lay society, based on social equality and religious toleration, on private property and coherent family life. The moment was opportune. A few years earlier, the Code would have glittered with revolutionary extravagances, a few years later it might have been darkened by the shades of despotism.*

It was during the Empire that Napoleon completed the great reorganization of French education, from the University to the Lycée, which has also survived until today, and founded the great post-graduate schools such as the Ecole Normale. Napoleon, mainly during the First Consulate, bequeathed to France and to the rest of the world what Professor Cobban (*A Modern History of France*, Vol. II) has described as the most effective system of bureaucratic control that the Western world has known since the Roman Empire.

> *It was not a framework for the kind of society that the idealistic liberals of* 1789 *had imagined themselves to be inaugurating, nor should we treat the Napoleonic system as the mere logical sequel to the* ancien régime *and*

the Revolution and Napoleon simply as the heir of Louis XIV and the Committee of Public Safety. This is to underestimate the scope of his achievement. The GreatMonarch did not leave an imprint on French institutions that could be compared with the heritage of the Emperor. His immediate successors might repudiate his work, they could not undo it; and the Napoleonic State was long to outlive its author and the ends to which he had directed it.

"A throne is merely a plank covered in velvet," said Napoleon, and to his intimates he explained that he conferred titles on his supporters and held a court because one can ensure loyalty through absurdities more surely than through reason. If Napoleon was obviously not a true child of the Revolution, he was not a reactionary either. He was in truth an adventurer and his outlook belonged to the eighteenth century rather than to the nineteenth. His hero was Frederick the Great of Prussia. Unlike idealists who often neglect their families for their cause, Napoleon's triumph was that of his family in the largest sense of the word, almost, in fact, of his clan which included many of his generals. He was to make his brothers and sisters kings, queens, princes or princesses, a dynastic family in fact. They were, all of them, to cause the emperor some headaches, particularly the youngest sister Pauline with her love affairs, who was the most emotionally attached to him. He bore with them with remarkable patience. He thought his family was exceptionally gifted, all of them.

Until 1804 Napoleon can be seen to have carved his way to power by the exercise of will and his great gifts. After 1804, when war began again with England, and then with the rest of Europe, he was to win his greatest, most astounding victories, but he was also to be the victim not only of his own ambition but even more of the expansionist tendencies which had found expression in the French Revolution.

In this short essay it is impossible to do more than outline the career of Napoleon after war began in 1804. He decided to invade England, but when his admirals failed to get command of the Channel, he broke up his great camp at Boulogne. Austria had, with British subsidies and encouraged by the new Czar Alexander of Russia, begun war again. In 1805 he defeated the Austrians at Ulm, then the Austrians and Russians together at the greatest of all his victories in December at Austerlitz. He annihilated the Prussians at Jena and defeated the Russians again in 1807 at Friedland and Eylau. In 1808 Napoleon and Alexander met on a raft at Tilsit and divided up Europe. A German kingdom was made for Napoleon's brother Jerome; another brother, Louis, became King of Holland.

On the day he won the battle of Ulm, Napoleon had learnt that Nelson had destroyed the French and Spanish fleets at Trafalgar. It was to bring England to her knees that Napoleon started his continental blockade, closing the ports of Europe from the Mediterranean to Archangel to British commerce. To enforce the blockade he had to be master of all Europe, and, for this, war, constant war, was to be his lot. He made his brother Joseph King of Spain, switching him from his kingdom of Naples, where Marshal Murat, the husband of one of Napoleon's sisters, took his place.

The French never mastered Spain completely and, gradually, Sir Arthur Wellesley, later Duke of Wellington, and an English army transformed the sore place made by the Spanish guerrillas into an open wound. These ignorant Spaniards had not heard of Napoleon's great victories. Austria went to war again in 1809 and was defeated with some difficulty at Wagram in July, 1809. Marriage—Josephine was repudiated—to the Emperor of Austria's daughter did not admit Napoleon to the circle of respectable monarchs. Marie-Louise bore him an heir, the King of Rome, and this was some consolation. But now the Dutch insisted on trading with England and King Louis had to be removed and Holland made into a part of France. Finally, smouldering differences with Czar Alexander could not be settled, Russia began to open her ports to British ships. In 1812 Napoleon invaded Russia, won the battle of Borodino, took Moscow, which the Russians set fire to. The *Grande Armée* had to retreat from Moscow. After some successful fighting against the Austrians in Germany and after unwisely rejecting a chance of peace, Napoleon was defeated at Leipzig by an army three times the size of his. In 1813-14 he was fighting in France, his armies depleted in men and munitions. Yet though he defeated the Prussians and Austrians, his great skill was of no avail against the big battalions. Marie-Louise deserted him and fled to Vienna. He abdicated.

He was treated with leniency and given the Principality of Elba, a small island off the coast of Italy. Then, in March, 1815, Napoleon with a few hundred men landed in France. By 20 March he was sleeping in the Tuileries, the Bourbons having fled to Belgium. It would be untrue to say that the French nation fervently welcomed him back. But his return was welcomed by those in whom the spirit of the Revolution lived, mainly the common people, and by the army which could only respond to his call and throw away the lilies of the Monarchy for the Tricolor, the emblem of victory.

Napoleon decided, after trying to make peace with the Allies, to take the offensive against the British and Prussian armies concentrated in and around Brussels. On 18 June, 1815, was fought the battle of Waterloo. Napoleon was exiled to St. Helena in the charge of his principal foe, Britain, to whom he had deliberately surrendered. He was shabbily treated in many ways.

Until his coronation in 1804 and the beginning of the last great struggle which was to rumble in 1815, Napoleon had made no mistakes. He was that rare thing—an adventurer who remained constantly a realist. As a young man, at odds with fortune, he was never carried away by romantic or idealistic notions. He observed, studied, asked questions and then acted. All men were, as men of action, his inferiors. He observed things—the fortifications of a town, the geography of a battlefield, the defects and virtues of an administrative system—with complete concentration, mastering every detail with exceptional speed and complete accuracy. He studied men in the same way.

He was devoid neither of imagination nor of human feelings, though both were somewhat limited—the imagination a little too military, the human feelings limited too, tender sometimes, but also coarse and cynical. Of humanity in the Christian sense he had not much. But he in no way resembled many dictators in their contempt for human life, even though he did once say that he could afford to spend a hundred thousand Frenchmen a year. His career, after the empire, witnessed his most astounding victories, his masterpieces on the human stage. But, at this period, circumstances dictated to him. He was obliged to follow the path which his ambition, but not his reason, dictated and to aspire to the domination of Europe.

He is rightly called the Man of Destiny and destiny meant the retreat from Moscow and finally Waterloo. But unlike other dictators who have tried in vain to impose their wills on the world, his crimes never made him into a figure the world grew to hate. His career for all the suffering it caused was unsullied by the cruelty and by the fanaticism of other aspirants to world rule. His overweening ambition can be seen as in large part the consequence of the explosive force of the French Revolution. So Napoleon is remembered as a man in whom were united to a superlative degree all the qualities which make up a great man of action. He is remembered as a second Alexander the Great rather than as a descendant of Attila or as an ancestor of Hitler.

ABRAHAM LINCOLN

(1809–65)

UNTIL 1937 American Presidents-elect, chosen in November, had to wait four weary, nerve-racking months for their Inauguration, for the day in March when they actually took office from their predecessors. Since 1937, when Franklin Roosevelt's inauguration for a second term was brought forward by two months, they have been more mercifully treated, take office in January.

But for Abraham Lincoln the months from November, 1860, to March of the following year were agonizing. Slowly the stage was being set for civil war: he had to stand by, impotently watching while President Buchanan's administration grew daily more futile, as the slave-owning states of the South toyed with, then decided on, a "Confederacy", prepared to secede from the Union. There was madness in the air, with the United States split into two camps moving inexorably to war; misunderstanding and pig-headed obstinacy on both sides—and no one to give an intelligent lead to public opinion.

Lincoln could have. Lincoln might have averted the most cruel war in American history. But Lincoln was a President-elect—and nothing in the American political hierarchy is lower, feebler, more ignored. Lincoln was forced to stand by while President Buchanan, pompous, desperately unsure of himself, did nothing. Right after the Presidential election, South Carolina decided to secede; within little more than a month she had been joined by Texas, Louisiana, Georgia, Alabama, Florida and Mississippi. By February of 1861, with four weeks to run before Lincoln could take office, they had formed the "Confederate States of America", named Jefferson Davis as their President.

What were the issues which brought this tragedy about?

Slavery, and its impact on men's minds. But to say that Lincoln led the North in a war to abolish slavery is a wild over-simplification. He abhorred the institution—but what mattered to Lincoln, above all else, was the preservation of the Union. That in order to preserve it he abolished slavery is from our vantage point of a hundred years' wisdom after the event, almost irrelevant. Slavery had been waning over the years; if the United States itself had not suddenly begun to double and redouble itself in size, the problem would never have reached major proportions. That wise statesman Henry Clay, the Whig on whom Lincoln in so many ways modelled himself, had forced a compromise bill through the House of Representatives in 1820 (when Lincoln was a backwoods boy of eleven) which sought to solve the problem. His bill stated that no new slave states would be allowed north of latitude 36° 30′—or north of the southern boundary of Missouri—and had the United States remained the size it had been when he tabled that bill all would have been well. There was little agitation to introduce slavery in the new states to the north and west of Missouri: those to the south and west were welcome to the institution if they preferred it. In time, Clay knew, it would die, within these confines.

But the rush westward continued, and twenty-five years after the "Missouri Compromise" there were states hundreds of miles farther west than Clay had envisaged: states like Texas clamouring to join the Union—and with slavery. And there were plenty of supporters of their cause in the existing slave states. Complicated bills, amendments, provisos, were thought out in Washington, in an effort to restrict the spread of slavery and at the same time satisfy the sentiments of the South. Tempers, over the years, rose higher. The South believed—absolutely—that slaves were better treated, better fed, housed and guarded from sin, than many of the so-called free men of the North. The North believed, with every bit as much conviction, that slavery was a sin. Voices grew louder, hatred mounted, fear spread. Men in the South began to feel they had actually been invaded, that they were already at war: those in the North convinced themselves the South was—to quote even the level-headed Emerson—"a barbarous community". Both sides expected bloodshed.

This was the scene when Lincoln was elected for his first term. Extremist politicians in the South had warned voters that a victory by his—Republican—Party would mean the plundering of their land for Yankee benefit, and the end of slavery. The South had grown angry, restless, hysterical. It was not the question of economic loss if slaves were freed—after all, not many white people owned them: it was the spectre of black savages claiming equal rights with white men, ousting them from their jobs, outvoting them. Slavery gave the poorest white a status: the black man was always below him.

In his Inaugural Address—when at last the moment came to give it, in March, 1861—Lincon spoke to the South: "In your hands, my dissatisfied fellow-countrymen, is the momentous issue of civil war. The government will not assail you. You can have no conflict without being yourselves the aggressors. . . ."

But on 12 April Confederate batteries opened fire on Fort Sumter, in Charleston Harbour, and two days later its garrison surrendered. Lincoln now had no choice. He called for 75,000 volunteers—while Jefferson Davis, President of the Confederacy, demanded 100,000 to oppose them.

The war grew, went stubbornly on. A few weeks after his mobilization of the 75,000, Lincoln called up another 65,000 soldiers and 18,000 seamen and began a blockade of southern ports. His determination, now his hand had been forced, was to make the hateful war "short, sharp and decisive". As Commander-in-Chief of the Union forces he had to make many military decisions, to goad his generals to the utmost. Only one of these, Ulysses S. Grant, seemed to have any ability—and when it was objected that Grant was a heavy whisky drinker, Lincoln retorted that he wished he could give some of the same beverage to his other generals and make them fight. But there were other, perhaps more important, decisions for a President to make, and all of these Lincoln made with wisdom, understanding and, above all, compassion.

It has been shown, more than once, that the United States gets the man it deserves, at the moment he is needed, and Lincoln is the supreme example. At the same time as he was prosecuting the war he was pushing a bill through Congress offering pecuniary aid from the Government to persuade states to adopt gradual abolition of slavery. He was also overruling the edicts of commanders in the field who "abolished slavery" off their own bat, in the areas they over-ran: such hot-headed, hasty action would only prolong the war. He disapproved of slavery, he knew that in God's good time it would go, and good riddance, but, as he put it: "My paramount object is to save the Union, and not either to save or destroy slavery. If I could save the Union without freeing any slave, I would do it; if I could save it by freeing all the slaves, I would do it; and if I could do it by freeing some and leaving others alone, I would also do that." By pronouncements like this he was holding back violent and impractical reformers with one hand, gently urging forward conservatives with the other. At the same time he dealt with vexed problems of foreign policy, keeping the friendship of the Mexican people while not getting involved in hostilities against the French who "protected" that country; avoiding conflict with a Britain which, because of interdependence between Lancashire cotton mills and American plantations, tended to side with the Confederacy.

The war grew enormous. By 1863 the Union armies numbered almost a million men, a size they retained to the end—an end which came after four years of appalling bloodshed, on 9 April, 1865. The Confederate General Robert E. Lee surrendered his whole army on that date, immediately after evacuating the town of Richmond, Virginia. Lincoln, a regular visitor to his armies, had been with Sherman and entered Richmond the day after its surrender. He returned immediately to Washington and there, on 11 April, made his last public speech, urging the swift rebuilding of loyal governments in the conquered states.

It was Good Friday, 14 April, the sixth day of peace, that Lincoln, an exhausted man, conscious, as many of his cheering fellow-citizens were not, that there was much to be done before a worth-while peace was achieved, went with his wife and two young guests to the theatre. The sun had set, the clear bright evening had given way disappointingly to fog, and a chill had set in, as the Lincoln coach drew up outside Ford's Theatre, where Laura Keen was performing in *Our American Cousin*. It was half-past eight. They were late, but it had been understood they would be, there had been so much Presidential business to get through, so many people to see. The play stopped, the audience cheered, as the party entered the theatre and were led to their flag-draped box. Major Rathbone and Miss Harris, the two guests, were given front seats; Mrs. Lincoln sat a little behind them, and the President, exhausted, just able to smile, to wave at his ovation, slumped into a rocking chair at the back.

By the third act he had begun to enjoy the play: he was rested now, relaxed. He leant forward to see better.

A man entered the little corridor leading to the box, barred the door behind him, moved in behind the Presidential party.

A shot was heard, there was a scuffle in the box. The play stopped. Then a wild-eyed man, waving a huge knife (with which he had wounded Major Rathbone, who tried to stop him), leapt from the parapet of the box and crashed to the stage. People screamed. The man had damaged his ankle, he stood there for a moment rubbing it. Then he waved his fist, shouted something, and was gone.

The President had been shot, at point-blank range, through the back of the head; the bullet had penetrated the brain. There was little bleeding, and he was still alive. Tenderly, they carried him out of the theatre, across the road to the home of a small tailor, where he was laid on a bed. Doctors had been summoned, and they were soon there, giving stimulants, consulting each other, examining and adjusting the dressing on the wound—but everyone knew it was useless. Mrs. Lincoln sat in a front room, weeping, and members of the Cabinet came in, shook their heads in horror, and left.

At a few minutes after seven in the morning of 15 April, 1865, Abraham Lincoln died.

John Wilkes Booth, the half-demented actor who had selected himself to "avenge the Confederacy" in this way, a crank, starved of the success he was sure his looks, his voice, his athletic ability deserved, was run to earth and shot, twelve days later, in the barn where he was hiding.

Abraham Lincoln, whose life was snuffed out just six weeks after he had begun a second four-year term as President (elected by a huge majority: 212 electoral college votes against 21 for his Democratic opponent) and three weeks after his fifty-sixth birthday, had been born in Kentucky, of very poor parents, on 12 February, 1809. After several moves within the state they crossed the Ohio River to Indiana. The boy's father, Thomas, was shiftless and unsuccessful, working as the fancy took him, at carpentry and at farming, doing neither well, and all the family's clothes were made by Nancy Lincoln, his wife, from the skins of animals he shot—squirrels, racoons, deer, wolves. Wild turkeys abounded—as did enormous, vicious mosquitoes.

They lived for months in a "half-faced camp", a shelter of logs, enclosed on only three of its sides, with a fire constantly burning on the fourth, to keep warmth inside, animals out. For their first winter in their Indiana home the Lincoln family lived entirely on game, but they were gradually hacking out a clearing. At last Thomas laid claim, at the nearest government office, to some 100 acres, and paid the first instalment of 80 dollars, a quarter of the purchase price.

The following year disease struck both cattle and humans, and Mrs. Lincoln died. Young Abraham had loved her, but when Thomas went back to Kentucky in the winter of 1819, got himself another wife, the widow, Sarah Johnson, with three young children of her own, he and his sister fell yet more in love with her. She brought order out of the chaos and dirt of the Lincoln home, took the motherless children to her heart, saw to it that all five went to school.

The boy grew tall—to six feet four—and immensely strong. The community had grown with other settlers, and he was soon famous in it as an athlete and a clown, who could mimic preachers and the itinerant politicians of the state with a terrifying accuracy. At the same time he was a voracious reader.

When he was seventeen he got a job working a ferry across the Ohio; two years later, fascinated by the strange vessels he saw going up and down that mighty river, he left his job and contracted to take a cargo to New Orleans. It was a river journey on Ohio and Mississippi rivers of over a thousand miles. Here he made his first acquaintance with slavery, watching tired, patient, black men, loading and unloading cargoes of cotton, tobacco, sugar.

Shortly after his return the family moved again, to Illinois, where he got a job as store-keeper, then got involved in local politics. By 1832 he had decided to enter it properly, was canvassing the neighbourhood as candidate for the Illinois state legislature. He was heavily defeated. He took up law after having studied it in his spare time, but as both he and his partner were more interested in politics than the law that partnership failed. But in 1843, a year after the start of his not entirely happy marriage with the aristocratic Mary Todd, he entered into a successful legal partnership with William H. Herndon which lasted until his death.

In 1846 Mary, anxious to get out of Springfield, Illinois, drove him on to stand for election as Congressman, in Washington. He was elected—but unhappy with the chicanery and double-dealing of national politics, and when he was not re-elected he returned cheerfully to his Springfield law business. He became a familiar sight, dressed in black, wearing the high hat in which he crammed his legal documents—and famous as a brilliant speaker and an absolutely incorruptible man. He forgot about politics.

But in 1860 the new Republican Party nominated him, while he continued his law work in Springfield, as their "dark horse" candidate for the Presidency—a man not yet well-known enough, nationally, to have many enemies. He was—at last—persuaded to grow a beard and "get dignified", though he objected strongly to this bit of affectation. On 6 November, 1860, he was elected, and four months later he took over the thankless task of President.

When, a little over four years later, he was assassinated, the whole nation, North and South, mourned his death. Now that he had gone, men realized the greatness of this figure unique in American history. Without any formal education, he had made himself one of the finest orators of his time and perhaps its greatest statesman.

Ironically enough, his death healed many wounds, brought North and South nearer.

VICTORIA

(1819–1901)

ALEXANDRINA VICTORIA was born in 1819, four years after the battle of Waterloo. George III was still on the throne and Victoria's father, the Duke of Kent, was only the king's fourth son. But the children of Victoria's uncles all died and so, after the death of George IV and then of his brother, the Duke of Clarence, who succeeded him as William IV, Victoria succeeded to the throne.

Her father had died some time before and she had been brought up very strictly by her mother, a German princess of Saxe-Coburg-Gotha. Neither George IV nor his brothers were popular in England; they were either dissolute or lazy or stupid, and some were all three. They were disliked on the whole by the aristocracy and by the middle classes. The working classes, both the industrial workers and the insecure country labourers, were in a state of seething discontent. There was talk of bloody revolution. The coming to the throne of a young girl who, everyone knew, had been brought up by a mother who did not like the habits of the royal family, seemed to promise a new age. She was an attractive girl with her long fair hair, slightly protruding eyes and good figure.

The character of the new queen showed itself at once. Her first act was to remove herself from her mother's bedroom where she had always been obliged to sleep. Though a fond daughter, she saw to it that the now elderly and over-insistent Queen Mother was kept at a proper distance from the sovereign. During the Coronation Service in Westminster Abbey, a severe test of stamina for a fully-grown male monarch, the Bishop of Bath and Wells turned over two pages of the prayer book by mistake and brought the service to an end too soon. Informed of this by the sub-dean of Westminster, Victoria ordered the service to go back to where it had begun to go wrong. The procession before and after the Coronation was the finest ever staged in London. It was witnessed by thousands of foreigners as well as by the Londoners. The Turkish Ambassador was so amazed by the splendour of the display that he could scarcely walk to his place in the Abbey and kept murmuring: "All this for a woman."

Victoria, though she had a will of her own, was every inch a woman. This showed itself in the strong personal relations which, throughout her life, she was to make with some of her Ministers. From the first of these, Lord Melbourne, an intelligent rather cynical Whig, as the Liberals were then called, Victoria learned much about politics and life generally. She made her only political mistake in those early days by refusing to part with Lord Melbourne although the Tories had a majority in the House of Commons and Sir Robert Peel ought to have been Prime Minister. Not surprisingly the queen became unpopular in certain political quarters and was once hissed at Ascot and called "Mrs. Melbourne". There was not the slightest impropriety in this relationship. Lord Melbourne, who was devoted to the queen, invariably remained standing during the long sessions in which he informed his royal mistress about state affairs. Later, Queen Victoria transformed some part of her esteem and affection to Melbourne's successor, the Tory, Sir Robert Peel. Much later, her attachment to her Scottish servant John Brown, after the death of the Prince Consort, and the romantic relationship with Benjamin Disraeli, showed that throughout her life she was to remain very much a woman of feeling.

Two years after she came to the throne her betrothal to her German cousin, Prince Albert, with whom she had fallen in love almost at first sight before she was queen, was announced. At the time she first met Albert she wrote: "Albert's beauty is most striking and he is so amiable and unaffected—in short very fascinating." Whilst, with Lord Melbourne's aid and advice, she sought to ensure that her husband secured precedence in foreign countries, he was only given the title of Prince Consort in 1857. Victoria intended to reign as queen and not as the wife of a sovereign. Nor did she intend to be ordered about and, in spite of the prince's rather puritanical attitude to life, she continued to love balls which lasted after midnight and other jollities. But the prince's serious nature, his intelligent interest in politics, his practical cast of mind and organizing ability—combined with his good looks—quickly made him the real master. It was Albert who now explained state business to the queen, and though it was the queen who said yes or no, the decisions were really those of Albert.

Prince Albert worked very hard at being the power behind the throne. He concerned himself with the development of industry and with the encouragement of science and he was largely the creator of the international Great Exhibition in 1851, held in Hyde Park. His advice on political affairs, both internal and external, had to be listened to; often the prince's views had a positive affect on policy so great was the attention which he gave to the matters under discussion, so skilfully and with so much compelling and detailed argument were his memoranda drawn up. He worked himself so hard that his health suffered; he never relaxed and he grew bald rather early and constantly looked sallow and tired. In November, 1861, he caught what was wrongly diagnosed by the Royal Physician as influenza; it was in fact typhoid fever, and of this, combined with inflammation of the lungs, he died in December.

The marriage had been a great success for both, and for the queen a perfect fulfilment. Her love for Albert increased with her respect for him and then with her submission to his views and wishes. She lived with him the life she wished, homely and yet regal. They had nine children. They brought up their children to observe strictly all the middle-class virtues. They spent long holidays at Osborne, in the Isle of Wight, and at Balmoral in a medieval castle designed by Albert. The queen thrived. She grew stout, but with the plumpness of a vigorous matron full of vitality.

Albert's death was a terrible blow to her. She built the great mausoleum at Frogmore for him and, because it was so intimately connected with her life with him, she never again lived in Buckingham Palace for any length of time. Her true affection was accompanied by a sort of fetishism and, for the next forty years, Albert's clothes were laid out on a bed in what had been his suite at Windsor Castle, and each evening fresh water was poured into the wash basin. It was in deep mourning, two years later, that she witnessed the marriage of the Prince of Wales, later Edward VII, from a private pew at the St. George's Chapel at Windsor.

After Albert's death the queen, though attending as ever to state matters with regularity, withdrew from public life. "The Widow of Windsor" became unpopular and, since she spent little on public functions, the Civil List was attacked for being too large. But, gradually, her natural zest for living returned. Her friendship with Disraeli, who became Prime Minister first in 1868, was born of the latter's tributes to the Prince Consort's memory. Disraeli was a great flatterer; but he was also a genuine admirer of monarchy and also of this small vital woman with her strong emotions and strong prejudices. "Yours affly Victoria Regina et Imperatix," she signed her letters to him. Yet Disraeli treated his sovereign with the greatest deference at all times.

With Disraeli's great rival, Gladstone, Victoria did not get on so well. She used to complain that he would insist on addressing her as though she were a public meeting. She strongly disapproved of some of Gladstone's measures—in particular of the bill disestablishing the Church in Ireland—and made no secret of her opposition. But when the bill had passed through the House of Commons, the queen herself saw fit to write to the main opponent of the bill in the House of Lords, the Archbishop of Canterbury, urging him to accept it with certain concessions and not to delay its passage into law.

When in 1887 her reign of fifty years was celebrated by a Jubilee, she made many public appearances which included a review of the fleet at Spithead. She attended public performances of music and travelled abroad. In her later life she became the centre of a large international group, that of the related royal families of Europe. This, too, put her in the public eye and the public liked it. In 1897, when her Diamond Jubilee celebrated a reign of sixty years, the government of the day, of which Mr. Joseph Chamberlain was Secretary of the Colonies, made it a demonstration of the might of empire. Bonfires were lit on the hilltops throughout England, Wales and Scotland, and a huge procession, which included representatives from every territory in the empire—Dyaks from Borneo, Hausas from Nigeria, as well as Australians and Canadians—wound its way through the streets of London. The queen, whose age was seventy-eight, sat in her carriage for four hours and appeared none the worse for it.

The empire was indeed a fit theme for a great act of homage to the queen. When Queen Victoria came to the throne the empire was already far-flung; but it consisted mainly of a series of trading posts or small coastal settlements scattered throughout the world. The East India Company administered only a third of the Indian sub-continent, and Australia was still largely unexplored—was used as a place for sending convicts to. By the end of Victoria's reign she was Empress of India. New Zealand had been added to the Crown and so had South Africa and much of Central Africa, whilst Egypt and the Sudan were also coloured red on the maps. There had never been a larger empire in the history of the world. It was defended by the largest battle-fleet in the world which ensured the *Pax Britannica*, whilst British merchant ships carried by far the largest part of the world's commerce.

The changes in the United Kingdom were equally striking. England had been the workshop of the world even before Queen Victoria was born, and it was this which had enabled Britain almost alone to stand up to Napoleon. But it was still governed by the land-owning classes who took little or no account of the workers in the great dismal towns which were making England rich. The average life of an industrial worker in those days was twenty-five, whilst that of a middle-class person was fifty. The workers were mainly voteless, and trade-unions were prohibited. By the end of the reign the condition of the working classes still left much to be desired, but there was a universal male franchise, a really representative Parliament, and votes for women were only some twenty years away. A growing Labour Party existed. The public conscience about exploitation and the direst forms of poverty had been aroused. "We are all Liberals nowadays," said a Conservative Peer. There was throughout the nation a feeling that the spread of education, coupled with scientific progress, was leading to a Golden Age. A touching illusion perhaps, but widely felt and not altogether unnatural in a country in which science and industry had done so much and worked so fast.

Britain was immensely wealthy. Through this long reign the country had been involved in many wars, but they were mostly minor ones and mainly colonial wars. There had been no major upheaval and relatively the country had been at peace since 1815. When Queen Victoria died in 1901, at the end of the Boer War, the British felt that they were a race apart, the happy breed of Englishmen.

When it is said that Queen Victoria was a "great queen" the adjective "great" means something different from what it means when applied to Queen Elizabeth I or to Henry II or to William the Conqueror. As a ruler Queen Victoria had comparatively little to do with the creation of the British Empire or with the other main achievements of the Victorian era. She was intellectually a very ordinary person and largely unaware of the great Victorian achievements in literature and scholarship. Her taste in the arts was deplorable; her personal influence was exerted in favour of what would be considered today prudery and hypocrisy in public manners. Yet these very limitations gave her a representative character, and undoubtedly the Victorian public wanted the queen to embody an ideal of perfect domestic behaviour to which they were themselves striving. Victoria's domestic life, for example, was precisely what the new middle-classes wanted. As Lytton Strachey has written:

> "*They liked a love-match; they liked too a household which combined the advantages of royalty and virtue, and in which they seemed to see reflected, as in some resplendent looking-glass, the ideal image of the lives they lived themselves. Their own existences, less exhalted, but so soothingly similar,*

acquired an added excellence, an added succulence, from the early hours, the regularity, the plain tuckers, the round games, the roast beef and yorkshire pudding of Osborne. It was indeed a model court. Not only with its central personages the patterns of propriety, but no breath of scandal, no shadow of indecorum, might approach its utmost boundaries."

It was because Queen Victoria was such a representative figure that she had and kept the admiration and respect of her subjects. She had other qualities as well. She was utterly candid, truthful and natural, and this was one of the reasons why the nation loved her. Her natural vigour and imperiousness meant that her role as queen would never be that of a do-nothing, a creature who signs documents and sighs away her hours of work. She gave advice to her ministers on most subjects in which she had some competence. She hoped this advice would be followed; but her strong commonsense always—except in the early days of Lord Melbourne—avoided a clash in which the Crown would have been opposed to Parliament.

Although it was not the work of Victoria which caused the government of England gradually to adapt itself to the new circumstances of the nineteenth century, a less perceptive monarch would have proved an obstacle to progress. Victoria never allowed her prejudices to get the better of her. The fact that the Crown rested on one head, and that that head was hers, for so long a time meant that the British monarchy which was much disliked in the early years of the century, and might well not have survived, ended up much stronger at the end of the century. It was a period when, in other countries, monarchy had disappeared or was to disappear shortly.

VICTOR EMMANUEL II

(1820–78)

IT WAS a definite, chilling, order to stop, call a halt. Garibaldi, the great guerrilla leader who had torn the island of Sicily from Bourbon grasp, liberated its inhabitants, must *not* go on from there. He would *not* cross the Straits of Messina to the mainland of South Italy.

Kings have no need to explain themselves, and King Victor Emmanuel II of Piedmont-Sardinia did not do so. But his reasons were obvious: he was nominally at peace with the Bourbon tyrants who were enslaving their "Kingdom of the Two Sicilies"—and so was France. Mighty France had been threatening the direst consequences if this insurrection went on; and these threats were too real to be ignored.

The letter which King Victor handed his trusted messenger, Count Litta Modignani, which the count now stuffed into a pocket, dealt with none of these consequences: it was an order, pure and simple.

But as the count bowed and prepared to take his leave, the king handed him another. "This," he said, "should neutralize the first".

He showed the handwritten missive to his messenger:

"To the Dictator General Garibaldi.

"Now, having written as King, Victor Emmanuel suggests to you to reply in this sense, which I know is what you feel. Reply that you are full of devotion and reverence for your King, that you would like to obey his counsels, but that your duty to Italy forbids you to promise not to help the Neapolitans, when they appeal to you to free them from a Government which true men and good Italians cannot trust: that you cannot therefore obey the wishes of the King, but must reserve full freedom of action."

Strange goings on. But Italy a hundred years ago was a strange place. Indeed, she did not exist, except as a loose geographical expression like "Polynesia", "Iberia", "South-east Asia" or "The Balkans": she was a cluster of independent states. Each state was ruled by a petty monarch who might well have no "Italian" blood in his veins, but who owed his position to the far greater rulers of lands outside the Italian peninsula, who periodically came and fought wars among themselves on Italian soil. At the end of each campaign the country was carved up, re-shuffled, and left with its little states under puppet rulers.

Yet this had not always been so. In the great days of the Roman Empire the country had been one. Then, in the fifth century A.D., everything had changed: the once-great empire began to be ruled from Byzantium, in the east; soon after, northerners like the Lombards swept down to occupy different parts of the peninsula. Soon only the cities and the island of Sicily remained part of the Eastern Empire.

Boundaries, and the balance of power, shifted; little rulers and bigger ones came, saw, conquered and vanished: Italy remained a collection of little kingdoms until the arrival of Napoleon at the end of the eighteenth century. His republican armies swept in during 1796, full of a zeal for reform, a detestation of monarchy; and by the time the majority of them had left again for home, a large part of Italy had been reluctantly united into tidier, larger, groups under awesome titles like "The Parthenopian Republic", and "The Cisalpine Republic". This latter territory was soon styled "The Italian Republic" and in 1805 Napoleon crowned himself "King of Italy" at Milan.

A decade later Napoleon had gone, exiled not only from Milan, but from all Europe. The short-lived "Kingdom of Italy" collapsed as suddenly as its king and within months the country had been distributed among the allies who had overthrown him. Petty princes were restored, former laws reinstated, reforms abolished.

For the French, during their brief ascendancy south of the Alps, had introduced a great deal in the way of social reform. Now, as the re-seated rulers of each little kingdom began to abolish these reforms, feeling rose strongly against them. The time was ripe for revolution, all the way from the toe of Italy to the Alps: revolution against petty tyrants and also against Austria which controlled so large a part of the north.

Secret societies sprang up, as they do in oppressed lands. The most powerful of these was the *Carbonari*, the Charcoal Burners. These were particularly active in the Austrian-controlled northern state of Lombardy, and in the 1820s they actually rebelled several times, but were always crushed. Somehow, though *Carbonari* membership was large, the organization had failed to enlist the sympathy of the man in the street. Better the devil one knew—even though he be an Austrian.

Under the wise guidance of Giuseppe Mazzini a new and far more effective group sprang into being. This styled itself *Giovane*

Italia, Young Italy. As the name proclaimed, it set out to enlist the zeal and patriotism of youth; the movement grew at such speed that within two years of its inception there were over fifty thousand members. One of the most vital tasks for Young Italy was the informing of all Italy of the aims of the society, and to this end literature was printed, or smuggled in from France. Mazzini himself was exiled and took over the task of sending huge quantities of revolutionary material from Marseilles.

Mazzini fanned the flame of revolution, kept it alive, and to him must go a large part of the credit for ultimately unifying and freeing Italy. But his attempts at insurrection were failures. He had one brief success when his followers rose in Rome and took over that state. He had returned from exile and for a short time was President of this new "Republic". Then the French and Austrian armies defeated the insurrection, punished the impertinence: Mazzini was forced to flee his country again.

While all this was going on a young man watched and waited his turn.

He was the new king of a small but respected state, Piedmont-Sardinia, which embraced not only Piedmont—"The Foot of the Mountain"—but the island of Sardinia. His father had been defeated in a battle against the Austrians and had abdicated, leaving his twenty-eight-year-old son as King Victor Emmanuel II.

The young king watched and listened, as risings sparked off by Mazzini burst into flame all over the peninsula and on Sicily. He admired the great patriot—but King Victor could not be expected to share Mazzini's hatred of monarchy.

Nearer at home was another great Italian patriot, a man with as deep a fervour as Mazzini's, but wiser, shrewder. Count Cavour had begun life as a soldier, gone on to take over the management of his father's great estates, then entered politics. From Minister of Agriculture in the Piedmont government he went on to become King Victor's Prime Minister, in 1852. He founded his newspaper, the *Risorgimento*, and copies of this, urging a free and united Italy, setting out methods of achieving it, were soon being handed on from man to man throughout the length and breadth of the peninsula. All Italy began to look north, to Piedmont, for leadership: leadership in first throwing out the hated Austrians, then in supplanting or at least reforming despotic rulers—who included the foreign Bourbon family at the foot of Italy and the Pope himself in the centre.

When the Crimean War broke out between Britain and France

on the one hand, Russia on the other, Cavour advised his monarch to join these two western allies. By rightly forecasting the outcome of the war and anticipating a feeling of gratitude on the part of the victorious French and British towards a tiny state which had helped them, he got Piedmont a seat at the Peace Conference which met in Paris in 1856.

Here at last Piedmont was able to present a case—a case for all Italy—to the great powers. These listened sympathetically as Cavour outlined the injustices of Austrian rule—and at the end of the Conference it was agreed that the French under Napoleon III would rush to the support of Piedmont if that small state should somehow find herself at war against Austria.

It remained only to provoke Austria into declaring war. This Cavour and his king were easily able to do.

The result, at first, was success. The Austrians were defeated by the new Franco-Piedmontese alliance at Montebello, Palestro, Magenta, Solferino. Provisional governments were set up in Modena and in Florence; revolutions broke out in the Papal states and against the Bourbons.

Then, to Italian dismay and shock, the French made peace with Austria.

It is at this point that Victor Emmanuel makes his first real entrance on the stage of history. His Prime Minister was understandably beside himself with rage at this French perfidy, and demanded that the Piedmontese go on fighting against Austria. King Victor refused, and though the argument was long and bitter and quite unlike the normal converse between king and subject he had his way. And there can be little doubt that Cavour's hot-headed patriotism on this occasion would have ended in disaster and postponed the freedom of Italy for many more years.

Victor Emmanuel understood the French point of view, even though he deplored it. Napoleon III was afraid of Prussia and at the same time unwilling to have a powerful new Italian state come into being on his frontier. If little Piedmont tried France too hard, she might well find herself at war against both France and Austria.

Garibaldi now comes into prominence. Like Mazzini—and many others—he had been exiled for his "Young Italy" work, years before. He had returned after an adventurous life in South America and begun to raise a force of "Red Shirts" in Piedmont to sail south and liberate Sicily—for a start—from Bourbon oppressors. No doubt Victor Emmanuel had mixed feelings about this fiery republican, but the king was, above all, an Italian patriot; if Garibaldi could liberate Italy from oppression, he would get King Victor's support.

The king gave his blessing to the expedition Garibaldi now raised —Garibaldi's Thousand—and the troopships sailed out of Genoa on 5 May, 1860.

A week later the Thousand landed, unmolested, in Sicily. By happy chance, two English ships had been in Marsala Harbour and, by mooring next to these, Garibaldi prevented the Bourbon fleet from opening fire. It was far too big a risk, sinking a neutral ship.

The campaign went well. Soon the whole of Sicily had been liberated.

It was at this point that Victor Emmanuel sent his two letters to the Red Shirt leader. Garibaldi studied them and gave orders for crossing the Straits of Messina.

He crossed with his force, began marching north, up the boot of Italy. His king prepared to meet him halfway.

This decision of Victor Emmanel's took considerable courage. He might easily have returned, months later, to his capital to find the Austrians or French in residence. He might easily have been molested, assassinated, by rabid republicans. He might have been disowned by the Guerrilla General himself when they met face to face, for there was little doubt that Garibaldi now had overwhelming support, not only in Italy, but outside, especially in England. Had he chosen to oppose the royal Piedmont army he could probably have defeated it, and though he had once professed loyalty to his king there was no reason to count on that loyalty remaining.

Yet King Victor set off, at the head of his force, and headed south. The stakes were high: if he stayed at home he risked having all Italy flock to the standard of a man whom he admired but could not trust, and being deposed himself; if he went south to take a part in the liberation he risked the same thing happening, with greater violence: he risked death, as well as republicanism.

He also risked excommunication by his Pope, for the citizens of the Papal states, as he passed through, demanded to be incorporated in his kingdom, and he could but agree. The excommunication was a stunning blow to a good Catholic, but King Victor took it and pressed on south.

Just north of Naples the two forces met. What would happen? Would Garibaldi, flushed with success, deny his king—or would he hand over his conquests to the royal house? There was doubt on both sides, on that early morning near the end of October, 1860, as the armies approached.

The Red Shirts heard the sound of a military band. It was playing "The Royal March". They fingered their weapons, for only Garibaldi knew what was in Garibaldi's mind. They watched him mount his horse, set out to meet the royal army.

The king came in sight, at the head of it, and men from both sides watched anxiously as the two approached each other.

Then suddenly Garibaldi, the bearded revolutionary, swept off his hat from his kerchiefed head and shouted, at the top of his lungs, "*Saluto il primo Re d'Italia!*"

The king advanced, held out his hand. "*Come state, caro Garibaldi*?"

"*Bene, Maesta, e lei*?"

"*Benone.*"

It needs little knowledge of Italian to establish that the meeting was friendly; that the Dictator acknowledged King Victor Emmanuel II as the first King of Italy.

And now, at this dramatic moment in history, almost the whole of the Italian peninsula had been annexed to the Kingdom of Piedmont. Only Rome and Venice remained outside.

On 18 February, 1861, King Victor was proclaimed King of United Italy.

There was much still to be done. He began making urgent plans for the liberation of Venice. Soon he had allied his new Italy with Prussia: by getting into war against Austria, had succeeded in adding Venice to the kingdom.

Rome still remained. And this looked like being the toughest nut of all. For the French, while prepared to help Piedmont against Austria, were not prepared to assist her in taking over the Pope's See of Rome.

But after much skilful bargaining, led by Victor Emmanuel, French troops were removed from Rome, and his own marched in. On 2 July, 1871, the Eternal City became capital of Italy.

The Pope, Pius IX, was of course unmolested, but he refused to have anything to do with the king. In fact, the two men lived in the city for the rest of their lives and never met. The Vatican became extra-territorial.

The new king, though this grieved him, had plenty of other things to worry him. He flung himself into foreign affairs, for he knew that a new and united Italy must become a voice in world affairs.

It is largely owing to her first king that she did.

But though Italy was united, and the union confirmed by plebiscite, it would be many years before she was consolidated, made into a homogeneous whole. In fact, owing to the great social differences between north and south this has not yet been fully achieved. It has been argued that some looser form of federation between north and south, with their widely divergent backgrounds, would have been preferable; that the plebiscite which married the two gave a false impression of Neapolitan eagerness to wed the north. The polling was open, and anyone who dared vote "No" risked the disapproval and worse of others.

The king worked hard to bring about a real union, though his chief interest lay in foreign affairs, in making his country great and respected in the world.

He died, his work unfinished, in 1878, at the age of fifty-eight.

He was a good man—and they called him The Honest King: *Re Galantuomo*. This honesty, this apparent simplicity (though there is nothing simple about the pair of letters to Garibaldi), has tended to make observers write him off as a political lightweight, a man who just happened to be on the spot when Italy became united. Yet nothing could be farther from the truth: he had the greatest ability as a diplomat.

To this ability we may perhaps ascribe the fact that, as Kipling might have said (but did not), he kept his throne when all around were losing theirs. Not only did he keep it, but he transformed a tiny kingdom, a sort of Mediterranean East Anglia, or Fife, or Puerto Rico, into a great and respected monarchy.

FRANCIS JOSEPH

(1830–1916)

Emperor Francis Joseph began his long and remarkable reign over the Austro-Hungarian Empire in the significant year 1848. It was the year of the revolutions, and it was no coincidence that the young emperor mounted the ancient Habsburg throne just then.

The fires of freedom which the people had lit in the French Revolution were only damped down by the Napoleonic era and the restoration of the Bourbons. The popular rising in Paris of 1848 ended the efforts of the émigrés to turn back the clock, and touched off similar revolutions all over Europe where the peoples were struggling to shake off the absolutism of the old monarchies and gain the elementary freedoms of speech and franchise.

Since 1815 Europe had been dominated by Austria and Russia, or rather by the reactionary monarchies which governed those two countries, the peoples of which had no say in the conduct of their affairs. The Romanoffs and the Habsburgs were deadly enemies of the democracy and nationalism which was stirring in the patchwork of nationalities which comprised their empires. The vast Habsburg dominions of Austro-Hungary reached from the borders of Saxony to beyond Venice in the south and to the Carpathians in the east. It was a disorderly jumble of an empire with no natural cohesion, in which Czechs, Hungarians, Slavs, Italians, Austrians, Poles and Croats were ruled by a German minority at Vienna. These subject peoples, most of whom were living in a state of semi-feudalism and extreme poverty, were only kept down by forcible repression.

The Habsburgs were the deadly enemies of progress and change. They saw in the modernity which was dawning in Europe a conspiracy to overthrow everything they stood for. Their motto was: Rule and change nothing. Their blind policy of blocking all social progress and all movements towards freedom and nationalism in their ramshackle empire provoked the 1848 revolution in Vienna.

The emperor was Ferdinand I, who was weak-minded and suffered from bouts of insanity. The empire was ruled by the Chancellor, Prince Metternich, and other members of the ruling family, whose weak and witless administration fanned the flames of revolt. When the Vienna mob rose in 1848 Metternich fled. The rumours that Ferdinand intended to turn the guns of the army on Vienna provoked even more violence. Ferdinand capitulated, granted freedom of speech and promised a constitutional monarchy.

This was too much for the other members of the ruling family, who believed in giving nothing to the hated revolutionaries. The most powerful opposition to the weak Ferdinand came from Archduchess Sophia, Francis Joseph's mother, one of those remarkable Habsburg women who so often eclipsed their men in talent and determination. She dominated the Vienna court of the forties and fifties with her intelligence and strong personality. As reactionary as any despot of her age, she believed that the revolutionary movement in Europe was a thing of evil to be stamped out. When Ferdinand cringed before the revolutionaries, she planned a counter-revolution, the main object of which was to induce Ferdinand to abdicate in favour of her seventeen-year-old son, Francis Joseph, who was Ferdinand's nephew.

It was a shrewd move and it came off. She realized that the youthful emperor would appeal to the spirit of the new age. Her intention was to rule as the power behind the throne, in which ambition she was only partially successful.

Francis Joseph was a remarkably handsome youth, slim, well made, beautifully mannered and with a "faultless bearing". He had a limited intellect and cared nothing for literature and art. He was matter-of-fact, quick-witted and supremely confident of his own judgement of people, even when young. He was unsympathetic to all but the simple and natural realities of life. His military upbringing made him place exaggerated importance upon the martial virtues. His chief defect was a complete lack of imagination. He inherited his mother's ideas and was extremely hostile to any change.

Ferdinand's abdication was forced upon him by court circles led by Sophia, more on account of his alarming concessions to the revolutionaries than his weak-mindedness. Being weak of intellect, or even insane, is not usually considered a bar to sitting on a throne. Many crowns have reposed upon heads containing sluggish, ill-working brains. The Habsburgs wanted Ferdinand off the throne in order to crush the revolution, and perpetuate the rule of their house, which was more important to them than the interests of their peoples.

They accomplished this by a deliberate deception in promising that the youthful and romantically handsome emperor would become a constitutional monarch. This promise neither they nor, what was more to the point, Francis Joseph himself had any intention of keeping. He thus began his long reign with a lie on his lips.

At first he was largely under the influence of Prince Schwarzenberg, a reactionary member of the ruling clique, who encouraged and developed the young man's inherent despotism. The early years of the reign were marked by the suppression of liberty in Germany, Italy and Hungary, where the Magyars were ruthlessly crushed with the help of Russian forces.

In 1851 Francis Joseph revoked the constitution he had promised to the Austrian people, and at Schwarzenberg's death in 1852 he refused to appoint a successor and ruled in person. He did not believe in constitutional methods of government. He was divinely ordained to rule and for his authority to be challenged by his people was to him something like blasphemy. To maintain this out-of-date conception of kingship, his authority had to be reinforced with an oppressive system of political espionage and secret police.

Francis Joseph was no idle or feckless monarch. He worked inexhaustibly at the business of kingship and was diligent and conscientious in everything he did. He once said that the term "irresponsible sovereignty" had no meaning for him. In the early part of his reign his rule was purely personal, and for all the ruthless repression of liberty he did enact some not unwise reforms. An absolute monarch at the age of twenty-two, he displayed a remarkable self-confidence.

Bismarck, who met him at that time, wrote of him: "The youthful ruler of this country makes a very agreeable impression on me—the fire of the twenties, coupled with the dignity and foresight of riper years, a fine eye, especially when animated, and a winning openness of expression, especially when he laughs. The Hungarians are enthusiastic about his national pronunciation of their language and the elegance of his riding."

The young emperor's foreign policy at this time can hardly be judged a success. Just before the Crimean War he was on terms of close personal friendship with the Czar, but he antagonized the Russian autocrat by vacillating between one side and then the other, and he succeeded in pleasing neither. He caused severe internal economic difficulties by piling up huge armaments for use in a possible war.

The fifties were a decade of reverses for Francis Joseph. He not only lost the friendship of Russia, and gained the resentment of England and France, but the Italian part of his empire began to slip from his grasp, and by 1859 he had lost Lombardy.

In Austria he was very unpopular. His love of uniforms and military display alienated him particularly from the Viennese who had no love for the army which had so ruthlessly put down the 1848 rising. The emperor was not forgiven for going back on his solemn promise to become a constitutional monarch. The Austrians treated him with scorn and indifference, and the more he tried to become a just but severe ruler, the more his undevoted people turned against him, for they could not forgive his bad faith. They had a passionate desire for the constitutionalism he denied them.

Francis Joseph's obstinate refusal to come into the nineteenth century caused large numbers of his subjects to emigrate to the New World, among them the leaders of the 1848 revolution, and this caused the revolutionary spirit to die down into a kind of sullen apathy. Not even the attempt on Francis Joseph's life by a Hungarian named Janos Libényi reconciled him to his people, though the deed aroused much natural sympathy for him, for he sustained a deep wound and showed great courage.

Francis Joseph's marriage to Elizabeth of Wittlesbach, daughter of Duke Max of Bavaria, whose wife was the Archduchess Sophia's sister, was one of those rare royal unions which was a true love match. Elizabeth was sixteen, the most beautiful princess in Europe and indeed one of the most beautiful women of her century. Clever, brave, a little eccentric, a dreamer, a lover of literature and art, this legendary creature, who so exquisitely ornamented the imperial throne, was everything that the Habsburgs were not. The young emperor was fascinated, for she was a great enchantress. The deep differences between their two natures, which were to develop so tragically later, were not obvious to either at first.

Sophia was against the marriage. She wanted her son to marry Elizabeth's elder sister, but Francis Joseph, though greatly under the influence of his mother, would not be dictated to in affairs of the heart.

A general amnesty following the wedding on 12 April, 1854, brought great popularity to the fairy-tale princess, and some of this popularity rubbed off on to Francis Joseph, for the prisoners who were released were mainly political offenders, victims of his grim secret police.

But the happiness of the marriage was short-lived. Elizabeth could not endure the dreary rigours of Habsburg court life, or the interference of the emperor's tiresome and domineering mother. Elizabeth had been brought up in a cultured background of complete freedom, living the simple life of outdoor pursuits, and she was a fish out of water among the half-educated Habsburgs and their court of aristocratic illiterates. She constantly fled from the stifling atmosphere and spent long months abroad. Francis Joseph frequently followed her to snatch a few days out of his busy life in her treasured company. The truth was that being an empress bored her.

She was a magnificent rider who would storm bareback across the hills and follow the most strenuous hunts. She went to great lengths to preserve her famous slender figure, and would run for hours in the mountains, with her luckless lady-in-waiting panting beside her, followed by a footman whose duty it was to pick up various articles of attire the empress discarded as she quickened her furious pace.

In order to show her wonderful figure at its best on horseback, she always had her riding habit sewn on to her by her tailor before mounting. She was intensely proud of her long and beautiful hair which reached well below her waist, and the washing of which was almost an affair of state, for which twenty bottles of the best French brandy and the yolks of a dozen eggs were used.

The only son of Francis Joseph and Elizabeth, Crown Prince Rudolph, was an unusually talented young man, who inherited the artistic qualities of his mother rather than the more dynastic urges of the Habsburgs. He was everything his father was not—a liberal, an intellectual, a free-thinker.

His death at his hunting lodge of Mayerling near Vienna on the night of 30 January, 1889, is one of the many tragedies which befell Francis Joseph's family, and still remains something of a mystery. Rudolph and his mistress, Baroness Marie Vetsera, were both found dead and it was officially announced that they had both perished by Rudolph's hand. This tragedy gave rise to the wildest rumours. Everyone connected with the affair was sworn to secrecy, and the official dossier was not found when the state archives were open to inspection after the revolution which finally terminated the Habsburg rule.

There were stories that the Crown Prince's skull was smashed in and pieces of bottle glass found embedded in it, and that Marie Vetsera's body had been found nude and riddled with bullets; that the killing had been done by her jealous husband, or by Jesuitical intriguers in order to prevent a liberal emperor coming to the throne, or by Hungarian nobles with whom Rudolph had become compromised. Nevertheless, the official explanation of a suicide pact is generally accepted by historians.

The loss of their son was a terrible blow to the emperor and empress. Elizabeth never fully recovered from it. Her health had already failed and she fled from spa to spa in her attempts to escape from the Habsburgs and reality.

But there was no escape for the conscientious, plodding Francis Joseph, whose unenlightened spirit grappled manfully with the imponderable problems of the advancing century, which brought with it an ever-insistent demand for a more liberal administration. Reluctantly, and step by step, he was forced into the path of constitutionalism, though he was still a long way from permitting the people to govern. Austria lost her great influence in Europe by being defeated by Prussia in the war of 1866.

His life was clouded with personal tragedies. His brother Maximilian, who had become Emperor of Mexico at the foolish whim of Empress Eugénie, consort of Napoleon III, was shot by a firing squad of Mexico's leader, Benito Juarez. His heir, Francis Ferdinand, was assassinated at Sarajevo in 1914. His sister-in-law, the Duchess of Alençon, had been burnt alive, and then there was the Mayerling tragedy.

But the greatest blow he had to endure was the murder of the Empress Elizabeth by an Italian anarchist on 10 September, 1898, when she was boarding a steamer at Geneva. He stabbed her to the heart with an iron file, and this remarkable woman, no longer young but still beautiful, rather than lose her royal dignity, managed by a superhuman effort of will to walk nearly a hundred yards with a firm step before she collapsed and died.

"The world does not know how much we loved each other," Francis Joseph said in a voice choked with sobs when he heard the news. And this was the plain truth. The years of tragedy, misunderstanding and olympian loneliness had forged a deep bond between these two.

Francis Joseph had eighteen years yet to rule the great Habsburg empire he still held together. He became mellowed and his foreign policy increasingly pacific. His subjects now revered him. Very few of them could remember a time when the grizzled old emperor was not on the throne.

During the latter part of his life he had a close and long friendship with Katharina Schratt, a Viennese actress, a relationship which had been encouraged by the empress herself. It was almost certainly platonic.

By 1914 he had allowed the conduct of affairs to slip from his hands owing to advancing age, and he would probably have avoided declaring war on Serbia, which led to the First World War.

In his old age he was a kindly, likeable old man, adored by his modest court and his servants, who wept unrestrained at his death on 21 November, 1916, at the age of eighty-six.

Francis Joseph's importance lies not only in the fact that his long reign spanned two entirely different worlds. He was a supreme ruler in Central Europe at a time when its peoples were struggling to gain the elementary freedoms which we in Britain have long taken for granted.

His death signalled the final end of the Habsburg monarchy. His grand-nephew, Charles, entered upon an imperial destiny as brief as Francis Joseph's had been long. In 1918 the Austro-Hungarian Empire disintegrated, Austria was declared a republic and the Habsburgs were told that their presence was no longer welcome in the country. Their wealth and property were confiscated and used for the benefit of the victims of the Great War.

CETEWAYO

(*c.* 1836–84)

CETEWAYO, WHO ruled over 250,000 Zulus, was a nephew of the redoubtable Chaka. Incredible family strife marked Cetewayo's rise to power. He was the son of Mpande (or Panda) who, with his brother, Dingaan, had conspired in Chaka's assassination. Then the assassins had turned on each other and Mpande defeated Dingaan in battle, as, in a repetition of history in 1856, Cetewayo was to defeat his own brother, Umbulazi.

It was at his father's Mlambongwenya kraal, near Eshowe, that Cetewayo was born in 1826. Like all Zulu boys he was sent out to herd sheep and goats. In 1833 Mpande moved his kraal to Mangweni, on the Amatikulu River, in the shelter of the Ngoye Hills. During his struggles with his brother Dingaan, many of the latter's warriors came over to his side, and when Mpande ultimately proved victorious the Boers declared him to be King of the Zulus.

When Dingaan was later killed in battle with the Swazis, hereditary enemies of the Zulus, Cetewayo was about fifteen years old. But he was accorded no favours as crown prince. He had to undergo the same harsh military training prescribed for all young Zulus. He was required to prove himself and was sent to the Tulwana Regiment. He grew into a first-class warrior, but he was also carefully schooled in all tribal laws and customs.

In 1843, when the Boers were aggressively grabbing land from the Zulu people, they staged a commando raid, made off with a lot of cattle, and took seventeen boys and girls with them into virtual slavery. Sir George Napier, Governor of Cape Colony at the time, sent a small infantry force and, in a subsequent clash, the Boers offered little resistance. The British annexed Natal in 1844, and their Zulu neighbours to the north-east occupied an area of some 10,000 square miles.

In 1853-54 Cetewayo had full opportunity for proving himself as a warrior in an attack upon the Swazis. He joined battle with a party of the enemy, slew many in single combat and put the rest to flight. Thus his reputation grew. He displayed some of his uncle Chaka's characteristics as a leader.

Soon Cetewayo set up his own kraal at Ondini, on the south side of the Umhlatuzi River. He gathered more and more followers, especially when more trouble simmered up with the Boers and Mpande betrayed indifference. Cetewayo's younger brother, Mbuyazi, jealous of being out of things, appealed, without success, for British aid. A clash was pending between the brothers, and a young hunter-adventurer named John Dunn offered his services as mediator. He could not prevent the clash, however, and in the ensuing battle of Ndondakusuka, the army of Mbuyazi was routed and he himself was slain. So fearful was the carnage that the site became known thereafter as Mtambo—the Stream of Bones*. Among the 23,000 slain were many helpless women and children.

This holocaust moved Sir Theophilus Shepstone, then Secretary of Native Affairs in Natal, to report: "I fear that Cetewayo's successes will make him a troublesome neighbour."

The fear was to become mutual, for one result was the construction of a chain of British forts on the Natal side of the Tugela River.

In the hope of enlisting a useful ally Cetewayo invited John Dunn, who had escaped the carnage, to settle in Zululand as his personal adviser. Dunn merely made hay for himself by bartering out-of-date arms—receiving ten head of fine cattle for a musket worth about 10s. 6d. He cashed in further by setting himself up as a kind of chief over various natives he gathered into a new tribe.

Cetewayo was, to all intents, already ruler of Zululand. His nomination as Mpande's successor was clinched when Shepstone paid a visit to the royal kraal, calmly facing some angry warriors, unarmed, thereby winning their respect and that of Cetewayo himself. Mpande died in 1872, and when, in the following year, Cetewayo's coronation was officially staged, he invited Shepstone to participate in the ceremonies.

The Governor of Natal, Sir Benjamin Pine, sent a Volunteer escort consisting of 110 officers and men, with two field guns. This expedition, with a major in command, and including about 300 natives, duly reached Zululand, but Shepstone was a little put out on finding that Cetewayo had "jumped the gun" and that part of the coronation ceremony had already been completed. However, the British visitors did their best to make the final function as impressive as possible and to give it political significance as well.

A great many presents were put on display in a big marquee, specially erected for the occasion, and Shepstone's party also provided a ceremonial "crown", devised by one of the military tailors

* *The Last Zulu King*, C. T. Binns.

and modelled on a Zulu chief's head-dress. On the appointed day a glittering cavalcade marched to the royal kraal, providing a spectacle which doubtless impressed the 10,000 Zulu warriors who flocked round for the ceremony.

The occasion was seized upon by the British to proclaim new laws. Henceforth, the indiscriminate shedding of blood was to cease; no Zulu was to be condemned without open trial, and there was to be right of appeal to the king; no Zulu's life should be taken without previous knowledge and consent of the king; there should be no death penalty for minor crimes.

The coronation ceremony concluded with a seventeen-gun salute.

Before leaving Zululand Shepstone met Cetewayo with members of the King's Great Council and discussed such vexed problems as the antagonism with the Boers and difficulties with Christian missionaries over the Zulu practice of polygamy. To Cetewayo is attributed the assertion that a Christian Zulu was a Zulu spoiled. Against this it was argued that often the riff-raff among the Zulus attached themselves to the missions for easy pickings. Bishop Schroeder, anyway, made no bones about describing Cetewayo as "an able man, but for cold, selfish pride, cruelty and untruthfulness worse than any of his predecessors".

Be that as it may, it was certainly not long before trouble became manifest. The king had his fine, highly-trained Impis chafing at prolonged inaction, and though, to his credit, he organized large-scale hunting sorties to provide his full-blooded warriors with some kind of safety-valve for release of their pent-up energies, it was quite evident that he could not hope to restrain them indefinitely. Besides, from what they had already seen of land-grabbing propensities of white strangers the king and his people were naturally apprehensive.

British authorities were no less on edge, and it is not surprising that even minor frontier incidents magnified the tension. There was a case where some outraged Zulu husbands crossed into Natal to bring back a party of runaway wives; and a second incident occurred when two British surveyors were hustled by Zulu scouts who feared that the intruders were planning sites for possible gun-emplacements on sandbanks in the Tugela River.

Tension was at its height when Sir Henry Bartle Frere was appointed Governor-General of Cape Colony and High Commissioner of Natal in 1877. Sir Theophilus Shepstone, who had understood Cetewayo so well, had been succeeded as Secretary for Native Affairs by his brother, J. W. Shepstone. Sir Bartle Frere never, in fact, met Cetewayo, and had to rely on second-hand reports of frontier troubles and complaints of Zulu savagery from missionaries of different nationalities.

He was genuinely alarmed by the presence across the border of the powerful Zulu impis, and one of his first acts was to call for reinforcements. But the Government wanted to avoid a major clash and the request was refused.

Frere sent an ultimatum to Cetewayo which included, among other things, an impossible demand that the Zulu army be disbanded. Cetewayo asked for time; Frere thought this "arrogance". Troops under Lord Chelmsford were moved to the border.

Cetewayo mobilized, but gave implicit orders that his impis must not cross the frontier. He remained in his kraal. At fifty-two, fat and lazy, he had no mind for a major clash either. But he refused to be intimidated. His plea for time was rejected. In January, 1879, British forces advanced into Zululand in three main columns. Sir Henry Bartle Frere stated that the intention was merely to enforce compliance with undertakings made at Cetewayo's coronation, and added that the British Government had no quarrel with the Zulu people.

Cetewayo addressed his 25,000 warriors personally. "You are to go against the column at Rorke's Drift," he told them, "and drive it back into Natal. You will attack by daylight as there are enough of you to eat it up, and you will march slowly so as not to tire yourselves"*.

The first clash came in the battle of Isandhlwana, when the Umcityu impi, four-thousand strong, followed by others, hurled themselves upon the British column. Undeterred by heavy fire and severe losses the Zulus closed in for desperate hand-to-hand fighting in which assagais and short stabbing spears were pitted against sword and bayonet. The Zulus had been sighted at 8 a.m. By 2 p.m. the impis were victorious and in hot pursuit of survivors seeking to escape.

Then came the battle of Rorke's Drift, where a Swedish mission station had been turned by British forces into a base hospital and store depot. On the day of the Zulu assault the post was under the command of a young subaltern with 100 men and 28 patients. The story of the epic stand of this small garrison against the full fury of a Zulu impi has been told many times, and here it must suffice to record that, outnumbered by 20 to 1, the defenders repulsed repeated attacks; that 11 Victoria Crosses were won that day, and that the stubborn stand probably saved Natal from invasion.

* *Natal Witness*, 20 February, 1879.

But the disaster at Isandhlwana had driven the central British column back into Natal. Cetewayo did not send his troops after the invaders.

Pressure from London led to the removal of Sir Bartle Frere, while General Sir Garnet Wolseley replaced him as High Commissioner for Natal and the Transvaal and also superseded Lord Chelmsford as Special Commissioner and Commander-in-Chief.

For a time the Zulus inflicted humiliating defeats on the invaders until a clash at Kambula, where Zulu losses amounted to 2,000 against British casualties of under 100. This, again, was due largely to neglect to heed the king's advice about avoiding attacks on entrenched positions.

By this stage British forces were being reinforced and three columns were slowly approaching Ulundi. Messengers from the king asked that hostilities should end. Certain provisos were suggested, but ignored. The advance continued to within a day's march of the royal kraal.

At 5.30 a.m. on the morning of 4 July the distance was narrowed to 700 yards. The British forces, about 4,000 strong, with 1,000 native supporters, then waited for the Zulus to attack. This they did in force, showing their usual valour in the face of devastating fire from field guns and Gatling guns. As advancing waves were mown down, others came on, the Umcityu impi breaking through to within yards of the British ranks, only to be met by a surprise cavalry charge. By 9.30 a.m. the Zulus were in flight, having lost 1,500 men against the British losses of 12 killed and 88 wounded.

Cetewayo, watching from a ridge, also took flight.

Cavalry patrols scoured the country for him, and though a price was placed on his head, no one betrayed him. For a time he sought sanctuary in the kraal of his chief induna, Umnyamana, from whence he issued orders that peace should be made with the conquerors. Later he fled to his brother's kraal, forty miles from Ulundi; and then into the depths of the great Ngome Forest, finally reaching a kraal at Kwa Dwasa. Then, on 27 August, cornered by a detachment of dragoons, he was escorted back to Cape Town. For a time he was held a prisoner, but in the following year he was conducted to England, where his future and that of his country were candidly discussed. Terms for his restoration were finally hammered out, Cetewayo conducting himself with the greatest dignity. Queen Victoria granted him a fifteen-minute audience at Osborne, and later ordered a court artist, Carl Sohn, to paint his portrait*.

* Now in Durban.

On his restoration, in 1883, Cetewayo soon found himself in conflict with rival factions; and, in the following year, he died suddenly in circumstances which suggested that he had been poisoned. The precise truth of his sudden end could not be discovered, for his followers flatly refused to permit the king's person to be subjected to the indignity of a post-mortem. He lies buried in a remote part of Zululand—the last of the Zulu kings.

It is impossible to read the story of Cetewayo without feeling more than a little sympathy for this resolute monarch who, when forces of destiny seemed to be closing in so relentlessly upon him, was moved to protest that he had not attacked the British in Natal; they had attacked him in his own country. He had tried to defend it and had failed.

Though Cetewayo grew up in a savage country where the law was kill or be killed; and though he proved himself as a fearless warrior in youth, he developed great depth of character. In all tribulations he carried himself with dignity and restraint, and it is impossible to escape the reflection that had he been handled with more understanding a different solution to the Zulu problem might have been found, and the needless sacrifice of brave men on both sides could have been avoided.

It is ironical indeed that those who confirmed his accession and even went to the trouble of concocting a "crown" for his ceremonial coronation should so soon afterwards have destroyed him. And there is double irony in the fact that the field-pieces that fired the seventeen-gun salute in his honour may conceivably have been used to blast his valiant warriors into eternity.

Let Sir Theophilus Shepstone, who saw the Zulu monarch's rise and fall, add yet one more touch of irony and speak his epitaph:

He was a man of considerable ability, much force of character, and dignified. In all my conversations with him he was remarkably frank and straightforward, and he ranks in every respect far above any Native Chief I have ever had to do with.

EDWARD VII

(1841–1910)

EDWARD VII, portly, bearded, beautifully dressed, with his big cigar and hat tilted at a rakish angle, gazes at us with royal dignity from contemporary photographs as though from another planet. Edwardianism, in the spacious, care-free sense which the king epitomized, has gone for ever and lies on the far side of that great divide when the lights went out over Europe and were never rekindled.

They were times when seven thousand people owned four-fifths of the land in England, income tax was trifling and death-duties were non-existent. There were extremes of wealth and poverty, and though an ancient, hierarchical society was still respected and preserved it was being undermined by the new popular press, the development of working-class political activity and the spread of startling, iconoclastic ideas by writers like Bernard Shaw. But meanwhile, wealthy, industrialized England was still the hub of the greatest empire the world had ever seen and every Englishman had his place in one of the social strata, watching with more pride than envy the glittering cavalcade of high society headed by the king who as time passed became increasingly the living symbol of English manliness, sportsmanship, good nature and optimism.

The king was an ardent race-goer, liked travel and excitement, ate rich food with a Gargantuan appetite, gambled at baccarat and was a connoisseur of beautiful women. To most of his subjects these tastes were their own, writ large. They brought him down to popular level. They made him human, and it is as a human being, the first king to popularize the monarchy, that he comes down to us, with all his zest, charm, weaknesses and courage.

King Edward supplied the answer to a problem which beset his parents: how to maintain the prestige of the monarchy in an age when the sovereign reigned, but no longer ruled. What was Queen Victoria's function in a constitutional democracy where she could neither prescribe the policies of governments, nor dismiss them, nor appoint ones of her own choosing? The prince consort's answer was to make himself more expert than the experts in many departments of state and, through the queen's right to be consulted, to become a kind of permanent, unofficial cabinet minister. This solution worked well as long as he lived, but it derived from the personal talents of himself and the queen and could not be repeated. King Edward, who was not an intellectual, enjoyed the full glare of publicity on the race course, at the opera and theatre, on tours of inspection in provincial cities and as the centre-piece of the London season. From paper-work and private consultation he drew out the monarchy into public life, and gave it a democratic flavour which it has never since lost. "Good old Teddy!" shouted touts, louts and even policemen when he won the Derby for the third time—and in that cry lies an echo of his achievement.

The feat was doubly notable in that, true to their own idea of royal functions, his parents paid no attention whatever to his true personality, but tried to turn the boy Edward into a paragon of learning, industry and virtue—with the result that his performance finally proved less than average in all three. He was born on 9 November, 1841, and in December, two days before he was created Prince of Wales, his mother wrote to King Leopold of the Belgians: "I hope and pray he may be like his dearest Papa. . . . You will understand how fervent are my prayers to see him resemble his father in every respect, both in body and mind."

These prayers coincided with Albert's wish, and in consultation with his own former tutor, Baron Stockmar, he devised a stringent educational plan typical of an age which believed that education was a process of moulding, not of developing. Edward was to be treated as an empty vessel waiting to be filled and then labelled: "Fit for kingship." Taught English, French and German before he was seven-and-a-half, he was then segregated from other children, placed under a band of conscientious tutors and put to work for long hours on six days of the week, imbibing a dozen or more subjects ranging from religion to chemistry. Holidays were short and few, the pressure was intense, the luckless boy felt himself to be the constant focus of critical attention. At times, from sheer exhaustion, he sulked or burst into uncontrollable rage.

A visit to Paris, which dazzled and delighted him, showed, too, that he resented his parents' severity. "I would like to be your son," he is said to have told the Emperor Napoleon III, and he begged the Empress Eugénie to let him stay on for a few days when his parents went home.

But gradually, with great caution, the monastic seclusion was relaxed and Edward, aged fifteen and actually allowed to choose his own neckties, was sent with an adult escort on a walking tour of Dorset, to the Lake District and, for the purposes of study, to Königswinter on the Rhine. There for the first time he kissed a pretty girl, was suitably admonished and provoked the long-range ire of Mr. Gladstone, who, on hearing of the incident, called it "this squalid little debauch" and expressed the fear that the prince was being educated to wantonness.

Queen Victoria, too, was fearful for his future. He was "idle" and "weak" and his only safety, as she wrote to her daughter in Germany, lay "in his implicit reliance in everything on dearest Papa". In a few years he would come of age. Meanwhile, before freedom ruined him for ever, Papa's image must be pumped into his soul and persuaded somehow to stay there. A heavy dose of Walter Scott and French classics were considered helpful and, bored to distraction, the prince asked in vain for a military career.

All this time his true self was largely obscured for want of outlet. But his father had already noted his "remarkable social talent", and this burst into the open on a visit to Berlin when he charmed his brother-in-law, the future Emperor Frederick III, and convinced his sister Victoria that he was far from being a "very dull companion", as their mother described him. He discovered an enormous zest, sharpened by deprivation, for the colourful side of life, and that this zest had survived intact despite early training was a tribute to the vigour of his personality.

Studies at Oxford, where he did moderately well, were punctuated by visits to Canada and the United States, where his social flair was first put seriously to the test. In the States particularly he achieved a personal triumph with his tact, good humour and youthful charm, and when the queen heard of this her heart was softened. She had often rebuked him. Now she felt that he deserved the highest praise.

In September, 1861, the Prince of Wales met for the first time the beautiful young lady whom his parents had selected for him as a possible bride, Princess Alexandra, daughter of the heir to the Danish throne. Soon after, a terrible rumour reached the Prince Consort. When training at the Curragh military camp near Dublin in the summer, his son, it appeared, had had an affair with an actress. The rumour was true. Edward confessed, adding that the liaison was now over. But his father was greatly distressed and within a few weeks was dead. The cause of death was typhoid, but in the abyss of grief Queen Victoria ascribed it to her son and he was shortly dispatched on a tour of the Near East because she could hardly bear to set eyes on him.

Marriage to Alexandra, whom the queen likened to an angel from heaven, helped to reconcile mother and son, though they drew further apart in their lives, Victoria immured in black at Windsor and Osborne, while the prince, with a vast and colourful wardrobe, slipped with effortless ease into the role of social sovereign which was to last for nearly fifty years. The queen professed to see great danger to the country's stability in the frivolous existence led by the Upper Ten Thousand and deplored that her son caroused with such people. But in fact they were only part of his acquaintance, he was far too gregarious to confine his friendships to the idle rich, and as time went on he cultivated successful men in all walks of life, so widening the appeal of the monarchy at a time when the whole social fabric was undergoing a kaleidoscopic change.

Would he turn into another George IV? The queen feared that he might—and *that* the country never would stand. But she overlooked his innate moderation and good sense and also forgot that the pursuit of pleasure was almost the only activity she had left open to him. She would not allow him to represent her in public; for ten years after his father's death he was not initiated into the affairs of state and a quarter of a century passed before he was allowed a key to the red boxes containing Cabinet papers. Meanwhile the social round, the opera, the theatre, gambling, yachting, racing, shooting, country house-parties, visits to foreign relatives and trips to Paris *en garçon* filled in his time. His popularity, normally high, was temporarily damaged when he was involved in a divorce case and a gaming scandal, but it rose again when he nearly died of typhoid and soared to dizzy heights when he won the Derby for the first time in 1896.

Though condemned to the fringes of state business, he was still able as Prince of Wales to be of use in the field of semi-official diplomacy, and here his personal qualities made him supreme. A visit to India shortly before the queen became empress was a tremendous success. In Paris, friendship with men in public life allayed suspicions of England, and in Russia he won the affectionate confidence of the weak young czar, Nicholas II. Only in Berlin, where from 1888 ruled the flashy, erratic and conceited William II, was he eyed with mistrust, and relations between uncle and nephew never rose above the level of guarded hostility. To the warped view of a German observer, Edward talking to William reminded him of "a fat, malicious tom-cat playing with a shrewmouse".

Edward was sixty when he became king in January, 1901. His conciliatory temper, his patience, modesty and shrewd judgement of men had been partially obscured in the long years of idleness and there were some fears whether he was fitted to occupy the throne. But from the start of his reign, when he revealed a remarkable gift for impromptu speech-making, his personality, the innovations he made and the routine he set himself were seen as welcome contrasts to the Widow of Windsor and her semi-anonymous rule. He enhanced the ceremonial aspect of monarchy, his court became the most colourful since Charles II's, he dined out at the homes of his subjects and for at least half the year—four months of the remainder being spent abroad—he was on show to his subjects in London or the provinces.

But he was not merely a figure-head. He took an active part in speeding up final victory in the Boer War. His interest in the Navy prompted him to give unswerving support to Admiral Sir John Fisher, who put through, against the strongest service opposition, a series of much needed naval reforms, and he followed closely, with alternate encouragement and criticism, the creation of a new model army and the reorganization of the War Office carried through by Lord Haldane.

His most notable achievement was the creation in France of a more friendly attitude to England. His interest in foreign affairs was always intense and in 1901 he had done all he could to foster negotiations for an Anglo-German alliance. The project had foundered on the rock of mutual distrust and the British Government then began to consider a *rapprochement* with France. Progress was made in settling spheres of interest in Central Africa and a wider agreement was desired on both sides. But the stumbling-block was public opinion. France was suspicious of British good faith: Britons had no confidence in French strength or stability. It was at this point that King Edward was invited, on his way home from a European tour, to lunch privately with President Loubet at the Elysée. On his initiative the visit was turned into a state occasion and contrary to widespread fears proved a triumphant success.

The crowds were undemonstrative as he drove along the Champs-Elysées to the British Embassy and when he went with his host to the theatre that night his reception was icy. But his unruffled good humour, his acknowledged love for Paris and France, quickly made critics feel churlish and thawed public opinion. Within two days Paris performed a *volte-face* and milling, enthusiastic crowds were yelling at him in the street: "*Vive Edouard! Notre bon Edouard!*" The same scenes were repeated when he left. There had been cheers for the Boers on his arrival; now there were cheers for what street-hawkers called "the Czar of all the Englands". The British Ambassador reported home on a "success more complete than the most sanguine optimist could have foreseen", and before long similar enthusiasm greeted the French President in England. A year later, a far-reaching Anglo-French Agreement was signed which would certainly have been impossible but for the cordial feeling between the two countries aroused, in the first instance, by King Edward.

The king was not much interested in the colonies and was bored by home affairs, where his efforts were confined to political conciliation and protecting the royal prerogatives. From his youth he inherited a dislike of desk work, a dread of being alone and a need for constant stimulus, variety and entertainment. While the skies slowly darkened towards Armageddon he was happy, as the living symbol of British goodwill and solidity, to speed across Europe, to Paris, Berlin, Rome, St. Petersburg, in the cause of friendship and peace—equally happy to take the waters at Marienbad, cruise in the *Victoria and Albert*, or attend the Doncaster Races, and happier still perhaps in the company of his son George, heir to the throne since the death of his elder brother, to whom he was devoted. His taste for pomp and pageantry suited the mood of his people, and most of his qualities, which combined to put the monarchy in the shop window for the first time in history, helped to enhance its popularity in an age of transition. Edward was the first truly democratic monarch and the last of the play-boy kings. His optimism and broad enjoyment of life reflected times, now gone for ever, when men still believed that reason could solve all human problems and Britannia was eternally destined to rule the waves.

On the day before he died, in May, 1910, the king, with bronchitis and failing heart, gave formal audiences all day. Next morning he put on a frock-coat (he was always punctilious about dress) and lit a large cigar. In the afternoon he collapsed, and a series of heart attacks followed. But he would not go to bed and sat hunched in a chair, receiving friends who came to say goodbye. Later, he was told that one of his horses had won at Kempton Park. "I am glad," he said, then lapsed into a coma. His last words were: "I will go on. . . . I will go on. . . ."

Shane Leslie said of him: "He lived like an Epicurean and died like a Stoic", and a year later Lord Fisher wrote his epitaph in a letter to a friend: "How *human* he was! He could sin, 'as it were with a cart-rope', and yet could be loved the more for it! What a splendour he was in the world!"

MEIJI MUTSUHITO

(1852–1912)

In July, 1912, a funeral took place in Tokyo—at night, under the glare of lamps. The huge procession which followed the coffin on its ox-drawn cart included a detachment of British Royal Marines.

At the very instant the cortege started from the Imperial Palace, General Nogi and his wife, sitting in the spacious front room of their house, committed *hara-kiri*.

A little later, when the body was interred, the effigies of four warriors in full armour were buried with it.

These two happenings, so dissimilar, were in fact very closely linked—for it was by the ancient custom of *junshi* that the nobles closest to a Japanese emperor killed themselves on his death and were buried with him, in order that they might accompany him to the next world. The custom had happily fallen into disuse—partly because there had been few noteworthy emperors for hundreds of years—and now only earthenware effigies of warriors were buried. But General Nogi, in a sudden, horrifying, and probably unpremeditated gesture, showed the world that the custom was not dead. Though he had left it too late to be buried in the royal grave, he would go to the next world with his emperor.

The being who had occasioned this gesture was the one-hundred-and-twenty-second Emperor of Japan, Mutsuhito. He had succeeded to the throne while still in his teens, some forty-five years previous, and like all emperors before, or since, he was descendant of the first one, Jimmu Tenno. Jimmu, according to Japanese history, founded the empire in 660 B.C. (The date rests on no historical fact, but it is an important one, and on the 2,600th anniversary in 1940 there were great celebrations.) But Mutsuhito was the first *real* emperor to rule Japan for nearly seven hundred years.

The chain of events which brought about this virtual "restoration" of a line of emperors came about independently of young Mutsuhito—but, fortunately for Japan, he was to grow into a great and wise ruler, the most highly esteemed emperor in Japanese history. The day in July, 1912, when he was buried is known, in Japan, as The End of the Grand Era.

To put Mutsuhito—or the Emperor Meiji, to give him his official title of "Enlightened Government"—into perspective we must go back in years. Not quite to that dubious date of 660 B.C., but to the twelfth century A.D. Up to this time the emperor, though his power had dwindled, was still ruler of Japan, even though the great families were taking over much of the business of government. The Fujiwara family had been in a position of great importance for years, by the simple expedient of marrying off its young heiresses to young emperors, then persuading the emperor to abdicate the moment a male child was born and allow a Fujiwara elder to be regent. Why bother with the cares of government?—this had been the Fujiwara advice—when you can live in pomp and luxury as the husband of an heiress. The family wielded great power during the hundred years up to the time of the battle of Hastings, when a deep internal struggle in the house of Fujiwara weakened and destroyed it. (There is, of course, no connexion between the two events: the Fujiwara had never heard of England, far less Hastings: the Conqueror can hardly have heard of Japan.)

And now, with violent struggle among the Fujiwara, power fell into the hands of yet another family, the Taira. This family took over much of the remaining power of the Imperial Court, until it, too, was overthrown in a bloody campaign ending in the great sea battle of 1185. The victors were the Minamoto family, and with their coming the last vestiges of royal power vanished. Even the capital was moved—in order to get away from the "enfeebling atmosphere" of a royal court—from Kyoto to the town of Kamakura.

And yet, despite this, the emperor was still sacrosanct. Even if he did wrong—though he was getting less and less chance to do anything—he was not to blame.

From now—until the accession of Meiji—Japanese life became strongly militaristic: the *samurai*, those armoured knights, made their appearance; so did the disembowelling process of *hara-kiri*. Government was taken from the feeble hands of the court and put under a *bakufu*, or "camp office". The head of such a government was given the highest *samurai* rank of *shogun* ("Grand General for Conquering the Tribes"), and from this first, Minamoto, *shogun*, until Meiji's accession in 1876, Japanese emperors were completely impotent, constitutional monarchs.

What, then, brought about the change?

Contact with a thrusting, greedy, outside world. At first this contact, with the arrival of Portuguese Christian missionaries, was friendly, so that Francis Xavier writing home to Portugal was able to say, "It seems to me we shall never find among heathens another race to equal the Japanese". But soon, with the arrival of Spaniards, Dutch and English, who quarrelled disgracefully among themselves and denied each other's religions, Japanese enthusiasm died. The government decided to banish the lot—this would be the simplest, indeed the only, method of getting rid of these fanatical foreign creeds. So during the seventeenth century almost every foreigner was banished and Japan retired into her shell: if this was the outside world, she wanted no part of it.

But two hundred years later, in 1853, the United States, resentful at this policy of isolation and at the callous way shipwrecked American sailors had been treated, sent Commodore Perry with four warships. All four were far vaster, better armed, than anything the Japanese had seen, and, wonder of wonders, two of them were driven by steam. Perry patiently, but firmly, set out his government's demands: the opening of at least one port to American trade, the provision of coaling stations in Japan, better treatment for shipwrecked sailors. He then showed them a model railway and a model telegraph, before sailing away. He would be back in a month or so, when they had thought it out.

The Japanese, shocked by what they had learnt of the west, furious with their own rulers for having kept them so utterly in the dark about western progress, set themselves frantically to building up an army and a navy and copying, as best they could, western ocean-going vessels.

Soon after Perry's departure a Russian vessel arrived, on the same errand. The Japanese knew they stood no chance against a combination of such forces, and agreed hastily to all of Perry's demands.

But the decision was by no means unanimous: many thought the hated foreigners should be repulsed by force. The shogun, who had "so meekly acquiesced", became overnight a hated figure.

In fact this particular shogun was a wise man and he was right in his summing up of the foreign opposition. For the time being Japan *must* agree to all demands.

Opposition to the shogun and his advisers mounted at terrifying speed, so much so that even the emperor, Meiji's predecessor, overruled his instructions and gave his own order for foreign ships to be bombarded. This was done, and resulted in a terrifying return bombardment of the port of Shimonoseki, in 1864, by the fleets of Britain, France, Holland and the U.S.A. Unrest in the country rose toward civil war, and with it the influence of the shogunate declined: all criticism of the way things were being handled, had always been handled, was now directed against the shogun. In particular there was a powerful rising of clans in the west of the country, clans like the Hizen and Tosa, bent on getting rid of the shogunate.

At this point a far-seeing Englishman, Sir Harry Parkes, came on the scene. He was an experienced man, had been captured and tortured by the Chinese, and he now decided, in his capacity of British Minister, that he would back these western clans, and let it be known that the British Government favoured their claims against *bakufu*, "camp office" rule, which had gone on for too long. The emperor, Parkes announced, should come back. Being a wise and statesmanlike man, he was able to convince the western clans that this must be the end-product of their policy.

At the height of this unrest the young shogun died and was reluctantly succeeded by an elderly guardian. A year later the Emperor Komei died and was succeeded by his fifteen-year-old son, Mutsuhito—and soon after that the shogunate handed over all powers to the imperial throne. Confused fighting was to follow, but in 1869 peace came and the young emperor was able to get on with the unfamiliar job of ruling his country.

He set about it with a will, and with the ardent support of his countrymen, even those who, on the face of it, seemed most likely to suffer with the abolition of feudalism. The four western lords who had been instrumental in returning the emperor to real power now addressed a remarkable document to him: "There is no soil within the empire that does not belong to the emperor, and no inhabitant who is not a subject of the emperor, though in the Middle Ages the Imperial power declined and the military classes rose, taking possession of the land and dividing it among themselves as the prize of their bow and spear. But now that the Imperial power is restored, how can we retain possession of land that belongs to the emperor and govern people who are his subjects? We therefore reverently offer up all our feudal possessions so that a uniform rule may prevail throughout the empire."

And the statement went on: "Thus the country will be able to rank equally with other nations of the world."

The young emperor rose to the challenge of this last sentence. Soon, great numbers of Japanese, delegations from every craft, every city in the land, were touring London, Paris, New York and other world centres, behaving with the impeccable good manners so little in evidence in foreigners who had visited Japan. One delegation went with the single intention of getting revision of the treaties imposed by Commodore Perry and other western exploiters, who had given themselves extra-territorial jurisdiction and the advantage of low tariffs. The delegation failed, and on receipt of the news the emperor redoubled efforts to modernize and strengthen the country: in future Japan would stand on her own feet, resist all encroachment.

Railways began to slide their tentacles from town to town; elaborate dockyards sprang up to service a new deep-water fleet; printing presses, telegraph offices, banks—everything the visiting Japanese had seen or read of—were introduced into Japan, with the emperor urging, encouraging, all the way. Party politics was introduced. A newly-restored emperor might well have felt this a usurpation of his new power, but Meiji was convinced that this western-style method of government was best for his country. He introduced a cabinet system under a prime minister in 1885, and presented that prime minister, in 1889, with a written Constitution. But Meiji had no intention of backing off the stage: the Constitution made it abundantly clear that he, the emperor, had graciously presented it to his people and had not been forced to do so. It stated that the country would be "reigned over and governed by a line of emperors unbroken for ages eternal", and this was gladly accepted by the people. In fact, Meiji's power was great—far greater than that of any other constitutional monarch—and he was able to initiate legislation by himself. This legislation was to be laid before the Imperial Diet at its "next session", and the Diet could—which was unlikely in the extreme—invalidate it.

And now the Japanese industrial revolution began to speed, during this second half of the Emperor Meiji's long reign. Factories sprang up like mushrooms, and the ships which had so shocked and impressed the Japanese in 1853 and which they subsequently ordered, one by one, from the western world, began to be made, even faster, in Japanese yards. The foreign monopoly of the crowded and important steamship trade between Japan and China was broken by a thrusting, new, government-sponsored "Japan Mail Line". A western-style army and navy began to grow.

But despite this tremendous material achievement (or perhaps because of it) the people themselves felt ever more strongly about the extra-territorial rights of foreigners, for these suggested Japan was not regarded as a civilized fellow-nation. The foreigners showed no sign of being prepared to relinquish their concessions—until a sudden war between Japan and China over Korea. Then, with Japan winning a rapid and rather surprising victory, opinion changed. An agreement was signed in 1894 between Japan and Britain, and this was followed by agreements with other countries, giving up extraterritorial status.

But the aftermath of the China war brought sudden bitterness against the West. In the hateful "Triple Intervention", France, Russia and Germany refused to allow Japan to occupy the mainland territory she had acquired as a result of the treaty (though she could retain her new acquisition of Formosa). There were angry threats in the Japanese Diet and in the press: Japan had conquered China, she must go on, conquer the world, for her rights.

It was the Emperor Meiji who calmed this agitation. He knew, from his close study of western affairs, that Japan, if she were foolish enough to engage any western power now, would lose all she had so painstakingly built up.

He was, of course, right. And nine years later, in 1904, when Russian encroachment had grown too much to bear, the far stronger Japanese nation attacked Russia and won a decisive and startling victory. As at Pearl Harbour many years later, she struck before war was declared, though negotiations had obviously broken down. But there was little indignation in 1904. As the London *Times* put it: "The Japanese Navy has opened the war with an act of daring which is destined to take a place of honour in naval annals."

Japan was at last established as the equal of any nation—but there was no resting on laurels. The visits of beaming, polite, little men all over Europe and the United States, absorbing silently and with absolute accuracy everything they saw and heard, went on, encouraged as before by the emperor. Meiji journeyed widely himself, setting a novel precedent and coming back regularly to his domains with plans for still more improvement, expansion in education, science, industry.

This, to many, was the Grand Era, the Golden Age of Japan. And when, in 1912, the Emperor Meiji died, though it caused no check in the accelerating process of advancement which he had begun, the grief all over Japan was great. The divinity who had passed on into a new and finer world had taken over his country as a squabbling oriental state: he had left it, forty-five years later, one of the world's most respected nations.

CHULALONGKORN

Rama V of Siam

(1853–1910)

"'I HAVE sixty-seven children,' said His Majesty. 'You shall educate them and as many of my wives, likewise, as may wish to learn English. And I have much correspondence in which you must assist me. And moreover, I have much difficulty for reading and translating French letters: for French are fond of using gloomily deceiving terms. You must undertake and you shall make all their murky sentences and gloomy deceiving propositions clear to me. And furthermore I have by every mail foreign letters whose writing is not easily read by me. You shall copy on round hand, for my readily perusal thereof'."

Anna Leonowens, as play- and film-goers will know, went to Siam in the middle of the nineteenth century. The king of that country had sent for an English lady to undertake the education of his children and Major Leonowens's young widow (he had just died of heat-stroke in Malaya) accepted the post.

The account of what befell her in that kingdom provides a basis for the smash-hit musical production, *The King and I*. But for a less fanciful version of what really happened we must turn to Anna's own story, *The English Governess at the Siamese Court*, first published in 1870. The passage above gives us some idea of the Asian monarch who employed her. His name was Maha Mongkut, but he figures, in Siamese history, as Rama IV.

His son Chulalongkorn, who was to gather knowledge, ideas and a radical point of view from Mrs. Leonowens—a point of view which would greatly affect his country during a long and illustrious reign—became King Rama V. We remember him better as Chulalongkorn.

Siam, or Thailand, is a proud and independent kingdom of the Indo-Chinese peninsula. Our knowledge of the area before the fourteenth century A.D. is fairly limited. We do know that Siam, in ancient times, was inhabited by primitive aboriginal people and that gradually more sophisticated colonists moved in from neighbouring Cambodia, bringing customs and religion from India. Immigration and movement continued and a Thai race evolved.

From the fourteenth century history is clearer. There is a history compiled between the fourteenth and eighteenth centuries, *The Annals of Ayuthia*, which provides a great deal of information, and from the seventeenth century there were European missionaries who reported at length on what they found. The people were proud, handsome and with a sense of humour, possessed of an astonishingly beautiful and fertile land, and ruled by absolute monarchs of ancient lineage. Though Siamese kings today are only constitutional rulers, the basic facts are unchanged: the people are gay and kind and beautiful and almost everything grows for them, in a pleasing and varied climate. Their chief crop, for home consumption as for export, is rice, but Siamese teak is as fine as any in the world, and she produces more of it than any other country. The majority of the people are Thais, but successive migrations have settled Laos, Chinese, Malays, Cambodians and Burmese within her boundaries.

And Siam owes much to the wisdom and humanity of some of her rulers, and in particular to Chulalongkorn—King Rama V.

His father, who employed Anna Leonowens, was a devoted ruler. He did much to improve the condition of his country, planning canals, making roads, building ships and introducing the art of printing. He was the first Siamese ruler to turn his back on warfare and devote himself to the arts of peace: in Rama V's reign campaigns were no longer launched against Burma or Cambodia. His Majesty, in fact, looked far beyond these lands, to the stars, for his favourite science of astronomy became an obsession, and finally killed him: he caught a chill during an expedition in 1868 to observe an eclipse. A little later he was dead, and Chulalongkorn, aged fifteen, was King Rama V.

So deeply was the tradition of education implanted in the royal house that the country remained under a regency for five years, while the young king completed the course of study begun for him by Anna by going to observe, at first hand, the forms of government in India and the Dutch East Indies. He was the first Siamese ruler to travel outside his own domains.

But thanks to Anna Leonowens we know a good deal about his youthful upbringing. As this is not only important to our assessment of the man, but delightful in itself, we can spend a moment considering it.

He was born in 1853, eldest son of the Queen Consort, and was thus the heir-apparent when Anna came to take charge of him. He was nine, and, we are told, "a handsome lad of stature neither noticeably tall nor short; figure symmetrical and compact; with dark complexion. He was, moreover, modest and affectionate, eager to learn and easy to influence". He was familiar with slavery—and later, as a man, was to abolish it—but slavery of a kind far less degrading and unpleasant than has been usual in history. A best friend was a slave, playing games with him in the royal palace, treated as a member of the family. He studied hard, mastering the fluent idiomatic English which had eluded his father, familiarizing himself with the literature, the thought and the history of the English people. As he grew towards manhood, he began to have doubts. He would rather be poor and have to earn his living, he told his governess, than be a king. "'Tis true, a poor man must work hard for his daily bread, but then he is free. And his food is all he has to lose or win. He can possess all things in possessing Him who pervades all things—earth, and sky, and stars, and flowers and children. I can understand that I am great in that I am a part of the Infinite, and in that alone; and that all I see is mine, and I am in it and of it. How much of content and happiness should I not gain if I could but be a poor boy!"

He was ten years old.

But there was little question of Chulalongkorn being a poor boy. Only, and for a few months, when he was admitted in sackcloth to the royal monastery, "chanting", as Anna noted, "those weird hymns".

He remained there, as Siamese princes do, for half a year. When he emerged he was deemed too old to study with his brothers and sisters. He was a man now, with his own private residence, "Rose-planting House", and here he took his lessons, alone with Anna. During the last months of book-study he remained a lovable, thoughtful young man, and she was to note, years later, that "even from this distant time and place, I look back with comfort to those hours".

And as she looked, the young king was completing the education she had begun, by touring, pencil and paper in hand, the capitals of Asia.

In 1873, at the age of twenty, he took up the reins of government.

Immediately—and he must have considered it again and again as he grew up—he introduced a startling series of reforms. He abolished slavery, set up efficient and incorruptible courts of law, made important changes in the methods of gathering revenue, built huge numbers of schools. Where his father had toyed with canals, young Chulalongkorn went and laid out railways.

But, of course, his path, like those of all good men, was beset with obstruction. The rich, who had grown richer through official corruption, not unnaturally resented attempts to abolish it. At the same time, the French, empire-building in that peninsula, caused him much worry, and took up valuable time which could have been devoted to improving the lot of his people. He bitterly begrudged this. The tension mounted to bloodshed and with typical nineteenth-century diplomacy the French put in gunboats and exacted a humiliating and unfair treaty, under which they were to occupy a part of South-east Siam for many years. It was not until 1896 that Britain intervened, suddenly fearful of French designs on her own empire. A treaty was signed between Britain and France, guaranteeing the autonomy of Siam.

And now, with external affairs in order, he was able to embark on an unprecedented seven-months' tour of that outside world with which he had been forced to quarrel. He visited much of Europe and was warmly welcomed in Paris. During the tour he soaked up, like a sponge, the innovations which might help his country, while carefully considering and rejecting those that would not.

On his return he built better schools, better hospitals. But he was in little doubt of his country's real position in the world, and with particular reference to the French who had greeted him so fervently in Paris, and in Asia were eyeing him quite differently. He built up, at speed, a modern army and navy.

And by this proof of a determination to resist any further encroachment, coupled with astute diplomacy, he made of his erstwhile enemy a good and loyal friend.

He replaced a complicated system of coinage, varying from district to district, by a standard one. Then he furthered the work of unification by introducing a modern apparatus of Posts and Telegraphs and personally seeing that it worked.

And, modestly aware that he owed much of the thinking behind his reforms to western civilization, he sent several of his sons to be educated in England.

The list of reforms and improvements made by Chulalongkorn during his long reign as King Rama V of Siam is almost endless. Sadly, it makes very dull reading. Sanitation and sewage farms fail to seize the imagination: even the spread of electric lighting scarcely speeds the pulse. But all these things were needed and urgently. With Chulalongkorn, Siam got them.

He died in 1910, deeply mourned, and not only in Siam. It was the same year as brought the death of Britain's Edward VII, but

Chulalongkorn's was after a far longer reign, of forty-two years. He was only fifty-seven when he died, and it was generally agreed that his unceasing work for his people had hastened the end.

He was succeeded by his son Vajiravudh, who became, in the same tradition, King Rama VI, and reigned for fifteen years before being succeeded, on his own death, by his brother Prajadhipok. A bloodless *coup d'état* in June of 1932 turned the benevolent but absolute monarchy of the country into a constitutional one, much like England's.

A long friendship between Siam and Britain, fostered by Chulalongkorn, was broken during the Second World War. There had been a non-aggression pact between the two countries, ratified in July, 1940, but when Japan invaded Malaya at the close of the following year, Siam, surrounded by Japanese forces, was compelled to declare war on Britain and the United States, which she did on 25 January, 1942, thereby leaving the way clear for Japan to invade Burma.

During the war Bangkok, the capital, was bombed by allied air forces. But with the coming of peace, Britain and India supported Siam's entry into the United Nations.

The present king, who was born in 1928, succeeded as a minor, and shortly afterwards the council of regency was overthrown by Siam's "strong man", Pibul Songgram, who became prime minister. Yet another *coup*, in 1951, served only to strengthen Songgram's position, leaving the king as an honoured but virtually powerless constitutional monarch.

From time immemorial Thailand has leant towards the West, and this tendency was much strengthened by Chulalongkorn at the close of the nineteenth century and the beginning of our own. The West has good reason to be thankful for this inclination—though the West has not always deserved it.

We can be grateful to Chulalongkorn, and, like his own people, grateful for the statesmanship and genius of a man who brought his country from slavery and ignorance and gave it a degree of political, social and scientific advance unique in South-east Asia.

WILLIAM II

German Emperor and King of Prussia

(1859–1941)

WHEN IN 1888 the twenty-nine-year-old William II ascended the imperial throne of Germany the country had been united for only seventeen years, since, after the defeat of France, Bismarck had made William's grandfather, the King of Prussia, the first modern German Emperor. The old man had been much revered, but he was out of keeping with the spirit of a youthful nation, and his son Frederick, William's father, had succeeded him as an invalid with cancer of the throat and had died after a reign of only ninety days. Now, at last, Germans believed they had been given the figurehead they needed, and their gushing vitality, their sense of movement towards a mighty future, seemed to be matched by the young and enterprising monarch.

William certainly had intelligence and a love of display which well suited his people's mood. How were they to foresee that his reign would coincide with a period of mounting tension in world affairs, calling for infinitely more caution and sagacity than he could muster, or that it would end in world war, defeat for Germany and his ignominious abdication and flight to Holland? "Hail, Kaiser, to thee!" they shouted as, with his bristling moustache, with his own monogram planted on his face, he processed in scarlet cloak from his palace in Berlin to open the Reichstag in person, the first German Emperor ever to do so.

Inwardly William himself was far from feeling so confident. By nature he was subject to alternate moods of elation and gloom. An accident at birth had left him with a withered left arm six inches shorter than the right. This had undermined his self-assurance, and a harsh childhood discipline, designed to overcome the disability, had fanned aggressive instincts. They had been further aggravated by a supine father and an autocratic, strong-willed mother, Victoria, Queen Victoria's eldest child. William had grown into an arrogant, vain and touchy youth, at loggerheads with his mother and eager to imbibe from outsiders the flattery he never found at home. The Kaiser's inner weaknesses were obscured, however, by his frenzied activity during the first years of his reign. On the affairs of the

Fatherland or for pleasure he was perpetually on the move, until his breathless people called him the *Reisekaiser*, the travelling emperor.

With youthful idealism William conceived, soon after his accession, an ambitious programme of social legislation. This brought him into conflict with Bismarck who, as the undisputed master of Germany for fourteen years, resented the young monarch's interference and also considered that sops to the workers were dangerous at a time of industrial unrest. So, in 1890, Bismarck resigned, never to return to office, and William was left with mingled feelings of triumph and fear, mouthing phrases about "full steam ahead" for the Ship of State and wondering where he could find a new Chancellor. On one thing, however, he was determined: from now on he would have a major voice in foreign affairs.

Almost at once, under Bismarck's successor Caprivi, an error was committed by the abandonment of a Reinsurance Treaty with Russia which Bismarck had engineered. As a result, France and Russia drew closer together and Germany was confronted with a set of pincers whose jaws were forever ready to close. Other factors made caution necessary. The Turkish Empire seemed on the point of collapse, thus threatening a power-vacuum in the Balkans which would attract the conflicting ambitions of Austria-Hungary and Russia. Austria herself, Germany's only firm ally, was weakened by hostile nationalities within her own borders, while in Africa and the Far East the scramble for colonies and spheres of influence promised to keep international rivalry at fever-pitch. But, convinced that he enjoyed God's special protection and eager as ever to shine, the Kaiser threw caution to the winds and embarked on an aggressive policy, a "world policy" for the first time in German history.

Soon the world awoke to the fact that Germany was demanding her "place in the sun". After the Sino-Japanese war Kiau-Chau was leased from the defeated Chinese and further acquisitions in the Far East followed. When the Jameson Raid was defeated by the Boers, William at first thought of demanding a German protectorate over the Traansvaal, but was persuaded to send a congratulatory telegram to President Kruger instead—the only result being to infuriate Britain and compromise in advance the possibility of a firm Anglo-German understanding. Right up to the outbreak of the world war this was made yet more difficult by William's obsession with his dream-child, a large German battle-fleet, which came into being under the direction of Admiral Tirpitz. For these and other reasons an understanding with Britain was never reached and this calamity was in a large part directly due to the Kaiser.

William's megalomania, his vanity, his provocative speeches, his unreliability, his moodiness, his verbal aggression, his lack of realism and inability to learn from experience—these characteristics fairly burst the seams of contemporary memoirs and it was a tragedy that in perilous times he should have wielded such power. World suspicion of Germany grew as the Kaiser's opportunistic strokes became known: an attempt, for instance, to frighten Russia into the German orbit by pretending that an alliance was imminent with Britain, a visit to Turkey involving noisy efforts to spread German influence in the Near East. . . . Worst of all, dismissing an understanding between Britain, France and Russia as an impossibility, he failed to grasp Britain's proffered hand of friendship. So, while Germany sat on the fence, these nations came closer together and the "encirclement" of Germany came about, creating the climate for her reckless encouragement of Austria-Hungary in 1914, without which world war might at least have been postponed.

Meanwhile the zig-zag course of German foreign policy in the early 1900s was largely due to the Kaiser, the pursuit of small colonial advantages at disproportionate risk and a game of see-saw between the European powers in the erroneous belief that they would all have to pay court to Germany in the end. And when his instinct at last warned him of danger, as in the Morocco crisis of 1905, he proved unable to influence events. By that time Britain, France, Russia and Italy were all drawing together and the ring seemed to be closing round Germany. A German attempt to break it, even at the risk of war, by humiliating France on the question of French influence in Morocco, ended in disastrous failure entailing Anglo-French military conversations, and the Kaiser was left plaintively protesting to his advisers: "I told you so."

Fundamentally William was both bellicose and timorous. He possessed an aggressive spirit, but lacked a warrior's soul. He allied himself with the tradition of Frederick the Great, even of Napoleon, but never in his life seriously wanted war, at least world war. He contributed no doubt to its coming, but blindly, as one unable to conceive policy as a whole or visualize the probable results of his actions, and as the clouds gathered over Europe he watched helplessly the approaching storm, the victim of past mistakes, the victim of his excitable and erratic temperament, the victim, like all other rulers, of a chain of cause and effect which no one man could break.

As early as 1908 the European situation gave cause for alarm. The nations were aligned in two camps: Austria and Germany faced the recently formed Triple Entente comprising Britain, France and

Russia. In the Balkans, Slav nationalism was a deadly menace to Austria, on the other hand Russia hoped to profit from it when the Turkish Empire collapsed. There was a prospect, therefore, of conflict between Austria and Russia and so between the two groups of powers into which Europe was divided, and this danger was increased by Austrian intentions of crushing Serbia, the focal point of Slav agitation, when the time was ripe.

But if the local conflict led to world war, Austria would be heavily dependent on her German ally. This meant that Germany might prevent drastic Austrian action against Serbia by refusing support or threatening to refuse it. The key to the whole situation therefore lay in Berlin: if the Kaiser had made it clear to Austria that he, as the senior partner in the alliance, must call the tune, world war might have been postponed, if not averted altogether. But this, it seems, was never realized until too late and the reason was simple: to restrain Austria would have required clear-sightedness and courage. Neither William nor his Chancellors—Bülow followed by Bethmann-Hollweg—possessed these qualities, and so in 1908, in a situation closely resembling that of 1914, Austria was supported to the hilt in a rash annexation of Bosnia and Herzegovina, the Kaiser stood by his ally "in shining armour" and Russia began to prepare for a war which she now held to be one day inevitable.

From now on Germany's actions, dictated by William and his squabbling advisers, tended to increase rather than ease international tension. The illusion persisted that Germany could afford a tough policy regardless of her neighbours' feelings. Unrealistic political demands were made in return for a naval agreement which Britain requested. A renewed attempt was made to humiliate France over Morocco; as the price of her goodwill Germany demanded an exchange of colonial territories and, humiliated indeed, France drew yet closer to Britain. From this the Kaiser falsely concluded that a yet stronger fleet was necessary in order to force Britain into the German camp. This view was put to the test in 1912 when the British again tried to reach an agreement on outstanding points of contention, political, colonial and naval. It foundered on William's perverse refusal to sacrifice a single gunboat from his building programme in return for a friendship which he believed he could ultimately obtain at the pistol-point.

But truculence, always uppermost in his dealings with Britain, was succeeded by fear when in 1912 the Balkan countries drove out their Turkish overlords. Once again Germany supported Austria, this time in protests against an increase in Serbian territory. Once again Russia was incensed, to the point of mobilization. But once again world war was avoided. With horrid clarity the Kaiser saw that Germany had become a satellite of Austria and he longed to disentangle his country from complications involving the danger of war. But this mood did not last. Fear swung to the opposite pole and he began to feel that the survival of his ally depended on her dealing with the Serbian problem. Safety called for solidarity. Bethmann-Hollweg agreed with him, and when, in June, 1914, the Archduke Francis Ferdinand, heir to the Austrian throne, was murdered by an Austro-Hungarian citizen of Serb nationality, William was convinced that a reckoning was due and gave a blank cheque to the aged Emperor Francis Joseph to act as he chose against the Serbs.

Between the issue of the Austrian ultimatum and the invasion of Serbia William tried to draw back several times, but, unlike him, his Chancellor was ready to risk a world war and he actually frustrated last-minute attempts by William to act as mediator between Austria and Russia. Soon, in any case, it was too late for mediation. When Russia mobilized, for Germany faced with a war on two fronts the time-factor became all-important, and two days later William himself ordered mobilization. When he had signed the document he looked round at his Chancellor, at his Chief of General Staff and told them: "Gentlemen, you will live to rue the day when you made me do this. . . ." The approach of war filled him with black foreboding. At heart he was not an optimist, and when Britain ranged herself beside threatened France he was amazed, indignant and deeply disturbed. He railed against Edward VII, whom he had always detested and suspected of wishing to encircle Germany. Now he claimed that his uncle was stronger in death than he was in life. Then his thoughts turned to his adored grandmother, Queen Victoria. "If she had been alive," he told his friends, "*she* would never have allowed this!"

Throughout hostilities, though officially the War Lord, William never directed or even saw a battle, except from a safe distance. The protracted struggle exhausted and unnerved him, and though the fiction was maintained to the end that he held the reins of government in his hands, in the later stages he frequently escaped his responsibilities by retiring to the depths of the country, away from his advisers and from harassing decisions, such as the question of unrestricted U-boat warfare. In peacetime he had held the limelight, but in war he effaced himself so that, until Hindenburg became supreme commander, the Germans had no father-figure to look up to and listened in vain for encouragement from their Kaiser. William, in fact, was a broken reed, an actor who felt deeply humiliated that, in the grim reality of war, there was no place for his pageantry or his game of make-believe. Strong men in drab field-grey uniform ruled the country and he, as he complained, had nothing to do but saw wood and drink tea. His popularity survived so long as victories were being won, but rapidly waned as the prospect of final victory receded.

The final act in the imperial drama was written in October and November, 1918, when defeat faced Germany in the field and at home mutiny and red revolution were brewing. The Allies refused to negotiate with a monarchical government and wide sections of the German population were demanding William's abdication. He refused to go until finally, to avoid bloodshed in Berlin, the Chancellor, Max von Baden, announced his abdication—in fact, deposed him. Meanwhile a physical threat to the Kaiser was developing at Spa, where his own mutinous troops were approaching his headquarters, and it was to avert his capture, or worse, and the near certainty of civil war that Hindenburg advised flight to Holland. There was, indeed, no alternative. At last the Kaiser realized it. And so, at 5 a.m. on the morning of 10 November, in rain and total darkness, the last of the Hohenzollerns, who had been rulers in Brandenburg for over five hundred years, left Germany never to return.

Allied attempts to obtain his extradition from Holland for trial as a war criminal failed, and he died, still in Dutch exile, in June, 1941, an old man with white beard and moustaches who for many years had been almost happy in his seclusion and glad to avoid the limelight, the world of harsh reality which had dealt him such bitter blows. In the midst of the Second World War his passing went almost unnoticed and it is only today that historians are taking up the question again: to what extent was it fate and to what extent the Kaiser's own actions which led to the destruction of Imperial Germany?

GEORGE V

(1865–1936)

"If the dear child grows up good and wise, I shall not mind what his name is." Queen Victoria, benignly matriarchal, was writing to her son, the future Edward VII, about the choice of names for the latest addition to his family, the future George V. She had hoped for "some fine old name", and preferred Frederick to George, which last name, she reminded the Prince of Wales, "only came in with the Hanoverian family". She assumed that the name *Albert* (her italics) would be added: "As you know, we settled *long ago* that all dearest Papa's *male* descendants should bear *that* name, to mark *our line*, just as I wish all the girls to have Victoria after theirs." She stressed the point. "It is done in a great many families."

The "dear child" in question, born at Marlborough House, London, on 3 June, 1865, was baptized George Frederick Ernest Albert, and the verdict of posterity will no doubt be that he fulfilled his tremendous grandmother's hopes in both her stated particulars. He was good in the sense that there was no guile in him, and wise in his realization of what counts for virtue in a modern king of England. The result may well be that history will accord him a stature to which he never consciously aspired but which his character deserved.

That destiny had marked him for kingship was not apparent until he was nearing the third decade of his life. As the second son of the Prince of Wales, he was drilled from his earliest years to accept the notion that his future was with the Royal Navy, and that, subject to the demands of his place in the social order, he should look on it as his vocation. He and his elder brother Eddy (later Duke of Clarence) became cadets in H.M.S. *Britannia* at Dartmouth, where he showed up well in mathematics and still better in cutter sailing. The life contrasted sharply, at times painfully so, with what he had known before. "It never did me any good to be a Prince, I can tell you," he recalled, speaking to a member of the Household in later years, "and many a time I wish I hadn't been. It was a pretty tough place . . . the other boys made a point of taking it out of us on the grounds that they'd never be able to do it later on". When he got into a fight and came out of it with a bloody nose, he saw afterwards that it was "the best thing that could have happened—the doctor forbade me fighting any more". He passed out of *Britannia* when he was fourteen, having done "quite well" in the examinations.

His next three years were spent in H.M.S. *Bacchante*, a training vessel, in which he made three separate cruises, the last being the longest in that it took all but two years and made him acquainted with South America, South Africa, Australia, Japan, China, Singapore, and Egypt. He returned home as a midshipman in 1882, taller, heavier, and dismayed because he was quite unable to master the seasickness to which he was prone. When the *Bacchante* suffered damage in a fearful storm, he acquitted himself as well as any. Though in later years the public liked to picture him as the typical naval officer, his knock-knees and wine-bottle shoulders tended to discount that popular image.

For "Georgie", as his family called him, his naval years provided training in more than seamanship. The pattern of his future development as a man, if not as a king, was firmly drawn in those fifteen years at sea. The habits of thought, the outlook, the tastes and prejudices, the loyalties, that he formed then remained a constant of his life. He was not exposed to the doubts and re-assessments of more subtly endowed men. He had no intellectual pretensions. His values were simple, his opinions frank, his purposes honest.

Attained to man's estate, and being given command of a torpedo-boat as a lieutenant, R.N., he took part in his first State occasion by accompanying his father on an official visit to Berlin. Young Prince George was invested by the Kaiser with the Order of the Black Eagle and given honorary rank in a Prussian regiment. His mother, the Danish-born Princess of Wales, disliked the Germans, including their young emperor, Wilhelm. "So Georgie boy," she wrote to that young son of hers, "has become a real live filthy blue-coated Picklehaube German soldier! ! ! Well, I never thought to have lived to see *that*! Better that, though," she added with more exclamation marks, "than Papa being made a German admiral—that I could not have survived".

The bias implanted by his mother obviously influenced his sentiments when there arose the question of a bride being found for his elder brother, the heir but one to the throne. Prince George had read an article about it in *Vanity Fair*, which urged that the Duke of Clarence should marry an English girl. "It struck me as so sensible," George wrote to his mother. "I am afraid that both Grandmamma and dear Papa wish him to marry a German." Although the family's variegated connexions encouraged the cosmopolitanism which Edward VII practised so thoroughly, it had no attraction at all for the future George V. His ideal was the life of the squire, not the boulevardier.

The question of his elder brother's marriage was satisfactorily settled when in December, 1891, an engagement was announced between H.R.H. the Duke of Clarence and Princess Mary of Teck, maternally descended from George III. Six weeks later the bridegroom-to-be died at Sandringham, a victim of the great influenza plague of that year. The brothers had been closer in sympathies than they knew, and the younger was overwhelmed by a grief from which he took many months to recover. "Alas! it is only now that I have found out how deeply I did love him." To his distress of mind was added the apprehension of immense unsought responsibilities piling up before him like cumulus clouds over a suddenly shadowed landscape.

He was created Duke of York to give him a seat in the House of Lords. "I am glad you like the title. I am afraid I do not," his grandmother wrote to say. The name for her had "not very agreeable associations", a reference to her Hanoverian connexions. His mother wrote cheerfully: "Fancy, my Georgie boy now being a grand old Duke of York!" for once restrained in her use of exclamation marks. He was given a wing of St. James's Palace that was subsequently named York House, and provided with his own personal staff. From there he attended House of Commons debates, by way of acquainting himself with the personalities and opinions of the leading political figures, and of learning something of the intricacies of parliamentary procedure. Gladstone, at eighty-three, impressed him greatly. "He made a beautiful speech and spoke for two and a quarter hours," introducing his second Home Rule Bill. Making a speech himself on receiving the freedom of the Merchant Taylors Company, "I was horribly nervous, but got through fairly well".

His grandmother, the ageing queen, was "in a terrible fuss" about his marrying, so his father informed him. Her "most cherished desire" was that he should become engaged to his late brother's fiancée, Princess Mary of Teck, known in the family as May. To what extent his affections were committed, whether or not he married for love, or whether he saw his betrothal as a duty, what his inclinations really were is not a matter of history. What unmistakably did emerge from such doubts as there may have been was a successful union, one of the most felicitous in the annals of the monarchy. The marriage took place in the Chapel Royal, St. James's, on 6 July, 1893. The honeymoon was at Sandringham, "the place I love better than anywhere in the world," he would write in after years, when he had seen more of the habitable globe than most men.

Through the now legendary 'nineties, George Duke of York was comparatively little in the public eye. Mostly he lived the life of a prematurely retired naval officer who is fond of country things. He was frequently at Sandringham, relaxed and happy in his freedom from the distractions of court life in London. His few official tasks included a visit to Ireland, from which he returned with a permanent liking for that country and the belief that the political animosities of its people were not directed against the Crown. So strong was his conviction that he begged his grandmother to consider setting up a royal establishment in or near Dublin. The cabinet approved, the queen did not.

At her behest the young duke was privately tutored during and after 1894 in constitutional history by a Cambridge don, J. R. Tanner, of St. John's College. Indispensable to his study of the subject was Walter Bagehot's *English Constitution*. The school exercise book in which he summarized his reading of that work is preserved in the Royal Library at Windsor. He noted, for example, that "where a monarchy of the English type already exists, it offers . . . a splendid career to an able monarch; he is independent of parties and therefore impartial, his position ensures that his advice would be received with respect and he is the only statesman in the country whose political experience is continuous". Inferentially, it was an important precept. It governed and perhaps inspired his conduct in the regnant years that were to come.

The South African War gave him an alarming glimpse of the risks to which persons of his station in life were exposed when human passions outran reason. His parents were fired at by an anti-British fanatic while they were waiting in their train at the Gare du Nord, Brussels. Soon afterwards he was invited to Berlin by the Kaiser for the crown prince's coming-of-age celebrations.

"It is certainly very disagreeable to me," George wrote to his mother, "having to go to Berlin just now and in fact anywhere abroad as they apparently all hate us like poison". His entourage was booed by pro-Boer sympathizers in Berlin. That was all; but life for him could never be quite the same again. "Goodbye Nineteenth Century," he wrote, not necessarily with relief, in his diary for the last day of 1900.

Three weeks later Queen Victoria died, and he was being prayed for in the churches as George, Duke of Cornwall and York. Before the year was out his father, the new king, conferred on him the title of Prince of Wales. The delay much annoyed his private secretary, Sir Arthur Bigge (later Lord Stamfordham). He was the direct heir to the throne for the next nine years, an apprenticeship in which Bigge was one of his wisest and principal mentors. Speaking of that faithful servitor in the fullness of time, he declared: "He taught me how to be a king."

George V's accession, in consequence of the sudden fatal illness of Edward VII in the first week of May, 1910, was to make him not only head of the oldest dynasty in Europe but monarch of all that he surveyed in the very real sense that he was the first head of the British Empire who had personal knowledge of the dominions and colonial possessions comprising it. He could look back not only on his circumnavigations as a naval officer, but on the still more comprehensive voyage that he made with his wife in 1901, when they journeyed 33,000 miles in the *Ophir* and a further 12,000 miles overland, visiting Australia, New Zealand, South Africa, and Canada, and when, between them, they shook hands with 24,855 persons. (The statistics of the eight months' travelling were formidable, recorded in a no less intimidating volume of 488 pages.) George's sense of responsibility was immeasurably deepened by his overseas experiences. Yet it was his insularity that finally commended him to the hearts of his people.

Between his accession in 1910 and the outbreak of the First World War in 1914 he witnessed the diplomatic embroilments, the political struggles, the industrial strife, the social upheavals, of an age that was heading for convulsion as by a natural law. As part of those troubled times, the new king had to deal with a matter that impinged unpleasantly on his personal life. For many years there had been whispered rumours of his alleged association with an admiral's daughter whom he was supposed to have secretly married in Malta during his navy time. In 1911 new currency was given to them in print. A paper called *The Liberator*, published in Paris, purported to give factual information about the affair. A charge of criminal libel was laid against the journalist concerned. The case came before the Lord Chief Justice and a special jury. The evidence conclusively disproved the story, which the king characterized in his diary as "a damnable lie that has been in existence now for twenty years". His hope was that "this will settle it once and for all".

Against advice, he had insisted on the case going forward, a decision that aroused greater interest than the cause of it. The king himself could not be called into court. After sentence had been passed the Attorney-General read out, "by his Majesty's command", a firm denial of the rumours. That he showed moral courage, rather than mere obtuseness, was generally agreed. It was a matter of conscience to him that he should stand before his people as one who was to be trusted as fully in his private life as in his public role. His mother, Queen Alexandra, was prompt with her sympathy. "To *us* all it was a ridiculous story yr having been married before . . . ! ! Too silly for words. My poor Georgie—really it was too bad and must have worried you. It only shows how unfair the world is & how the wicked love to slander the upright and good & try to drag them down on their own level."

The coronation and a wonderful summer made 1911 a brilliantly memorable year, its climax for the king and queen the great Delhi durbar held in November. That event, the first of its kind to be recorded by news-reel cameras, was given its touch of anxiety when the Gaekwar of Baroda, making his obeisance, appeared to disdain the necessity of doing so. The newspapers gave the incident the prominence of an event. Official comment brushed it aside as having "lent itself to misrepresentation". For George V it cannot but have been an awkward episode, one more reminder of the unease of the imperial burden.

Foreign affairs engaged his attention more imperatively in those years before the storm. His personal relations with his cousin, the Kaiser, blended amicability with protocol. That monarch, and the policies of his government, increasingly exercised the king's thinking on current problems. He was in constant touch with Sir Edward Grey, the Foreign Secretary, and through him encouraged the British ambassadors in Europe to communicate direct with the private secretary, Lord Stamfordham, amplifying or explaining their official reports. He was seeing at the same time the foreign ambassadors in London, inviting them for week-ends at Windsor or Balmoral. The overriding theme of the conversations was the growing menace of Germany, particularly in terms of naval supremacy. As a sailor, King George often tested the patience of Paul Cambon, of France, and Count Benckendorff, of Russia, by dwelling on that topic to the exclusion of others of equal interest. Both were impressed by his grasp of affairs, by his great store of knowledge of what was going on in the world, by his close identity with the attitudes prevailing in Downing Street, and by his robust temper.

While he was making his mark in the private councils and

colloquies, the king was by no means unreservedly esteemed by the masses. To them he was still a remote personage who, dutifully doing what was required of him, engaged their homage but rarely their sympathies. That perspective was only momentarily foreshortened by the wave of emotion that passed through the crowd clamouring for his appearance on the balcony of Buckingham Palace when war broke out. As soon as the glass doors closed behind him he receded again in the public mind to his symbolic sceptre-bearing status as head of the Commonwealth and Empire.

Then, in October, 1915, he had a riding accident while inspecting men of the Royal Flying Corps at the Front. His mount, lent to him by General Sir Douglas Haig, took fright at a burst of cheering and fell backwards, the king still in the saddle. He was more seriously hurt than was at first disclosed; in fact, "he was never quite the same man again", by the testimony of his biographer, Sir Harold Nicolson. The news evoked a spontaneous concern that was felt rather than expressed, though the bulletins were given front-page priority. Identified thus dramatically with the casualty lists, the king was seen to be a partaker of the common human lot, no more immune from misfortune than the next man. From then on he could count on affection as well as respect. The extraordinary extent to which science would enlarge and consolidate his popularity was not then within the realm of feasible conjecture.

That he came out of the ordeal of the war with enhanced personal prestige was not questioned. His exemplary behaviour over the drink question, when it was postulated by the Prime Minister, Lloyd George, as a menace to production in the war factories, was noted in responsible sections of the community, while his contempt for reprisals against prisoners of war, of whatever side, also showed his wisdom. His part in smoothing out the frictions between political and military leaders was frequently effective, though unacknowledged at the time.

His conciliatory services were sought again when in the first post-war decade Labour thrust its way to power for the first time. He established cordial relations in particular with the railwaymen's leader, J. H. Thomas, M.P., who in due course became Colonial Secretary. During the General Strike in 1926 the king's moderating counsel was successfully proffered on more than one outstanding issue. He warned the government of the danger of introducing provocative orders and bills, and expressed his keen dislike of an intention to prohibit banks from paying out funds to the strikers' unions. When Winston Churchill made it known through the government's emergency newspaper, the *British Gazette*, which he edited, that the armed forces of the crown would receive full support in any action they might deem necessary for the security of essential services, the king communicated his displeasure to the War Office. "His Majesty cannot help thinking," wrote the private secretary, "that this is an unfortunate announcement."

The grave illness that struck the king down in the last weeks of 1929 moved the nation to depths of feeling unmatched by any similar crisis that was remembered. At a meeting of the Privy Council called to prepare a warrant for the appointment of a Council of State, his hand had to be guided by his physician, Lord Dawson of Penn, in signing the requisite document. Churches were open day and night for prayers of intercession. He was an invalid for more than three months, as a sequel to a severe lung draining operation. Shortly after the service of thanksgiving at St. Paul's for his recovery he sent for J. H. Thomas, the trade-unionist with whom he was on the friendliest terms. One of Thomas's anecdotes set him laughing so much that he had a relapse, and had to submit to a second operation, in which a rib was removed. Those around him believed that the illness had permanently weakened his constitution. It made him look older than his sixty-four years.

The world economic crisis, with its dramatic repercussions in England in 1931, was for the king a source of additional strain, not easily borne. While those closest to him saw and in some instances suffered the effects of it in his increasing querulousness and sharpness of temper, to the millions who heard his first Christmas broadcast, in 1932, he was the benign father of his people who personified the virtues of sincerity, honesty, and love of home and family. It was all there in his voice, which proclaimed him to be free of affectation and cant, a patriarchal voice rich with the overtones of experience, wisdom, and authority. It made as deep an impression in the wider world as at home. "Oh, if only he were our king too!" a German woman wrote to a London newspaper from out of the mounting anguish of life under her country's dynamically vengeful new leadership.

Jubilee year, 1935, is still remembered for the extraordinary fervour at the heart of the celebrations. "A never-to-be-forgotten day" it was, too, for the king himself, as he wrote in his diary for 6 May, after returning from the service in St. Paul's. There were flood-lit balcony appearances before vast crowds outside Buckingham Palace every night that week. When the pageantry was over, he and the queen drove through the meaner streets of the metropolis; first,

Battersea, Kennington, and Lambeth; then Whitechapel, Shoreditch, and dockland; and finally the teeming northern suburbs of King's Cross and Camden Town. His nurse, Sister Catherine Black, of London Hospital, recalled his pleasure in the welcome he had everywhere been given. "I'd no idea," he said, "they felt like that about me. I'm beginning to think they must really like me for myself." It was the naïve satisfaction of an unconceited man, who always liked appreciation and to have letters of gratitude even from obscure persons who received honours or other favours at his hands.

Broadcasting at the end of Jubilee day, he asked his myriad listeners at home and throughout the Commonwealth: "How can I express what is in my heart? I dedicate myself anew to your service for all the years that may still be given to me." The plural was poignantly redundant. His health declined after his autumn stay at Balmoral. The death of his favourite sister, Princess Victoria, was a shock. "No one ever had a sister like her," he wrote in the diary that he had kept faithfully every day for more than fifty years. His enfeeblement grew so marked that in January, 1936, a Council of State had to be convened again to act in his place. And once again Dawson of Penn was obliged to guide his hand, kneeling by the bedside. The king objected to merely making his mark, as was suggested, and struggled hard to write his usual signature. "Gentlemen," he said to the Privy Councillors as he lay back wearily on his pillow, "I am sorry to keep you all waiting like this—I am unable to concentrate."

The last diary entry was made by Queen Mary, his tower of strength throughout his reign. "My dearest husband, King George V, was much distressed at the bad writing above & begged me to write his diary for him next day. He passed away on January 20th at 5 minutes before midnight."

His great achievement was to prove to the world, through some of its most testing decades, that a constitutional monarchy is one of its soundest institutions provided that the monarch is equal to its demands and sensible always of his duties and obligations. "A king of England who is willing to be a man of his people," a Belgian diplomat had written long before, "is the greatest king in the world. But if he wishes to be more, by heaven, then he is nothing at all". George V was in all respects the man of his people, reflecting their qualities and ideals, private and public, with a sureness of touch that was akin to genius. So it is that he stands before history as one of the most respected kings of modern times.

SUN YAT-SEN

(1866–1925)

CHINA IN the second half of the twentieth century is one of the world's most powerful nations, with the enormous potential of a vast and energetic population. But this was not always the case: half a century ago it seemed unlikely that China would ever awake from what, to outsiders, seemed a complacent slumber. It was true —there had been a time, centuries before, when she was reckoned great, but now China was no more than a limping anachronism, gleefully bested by any nation which cared to come and impose "trade" upon her, a trade which was simply exploitation. The gulf between China and the world seemed to widen every day.

The man destined to lead China across that gulf was born in November, 1866. Whatever changes have taken place since his day, may yet take place, nothing will ever equal the dramatic change that came over Chinese thinking, Chinese behaviour, during the comparatively brief working life of Sun Yat-sen.

He was born in a village in the south of the country, not far from the Portuguese island settlement of Macao. He started his education in the village school and, like nearly everyone in that village and in tens of thousands of other villages throughout China, he and his family were poor. They were kept that way by high rents they were forced to pay for their land and by the depredations made upon them and their crops by imperial soldiers. For this was the day of the Manchu dynasty, the last emperors (did they but know it) of a China which had been an absolute monarchy for thousands of years. The Manchus in fact were pigtail-wearing foreigners and comparative newcomers, who had swept down over the Great Wall as recently as the seventeenth century and seized this huge and fertile country. They had forced the population to adopt this pigtail, the long, plaited queue of hair. This is often associated with ancient China—but it was a hated and compulsory innovation. During Sun Yat-sen's time one of the least important, but most emotionally-charged, manifestations of the fight for freedom was the cutting off of this hated symbol of Manchu oppression.

But this was all in the future. Young Sun, in his village, thought himself fortunate in being able to leave China at the age of fourteen and go to work for one of his two elder brothers, an enterprising fellow who had settled in Honolulu and ran a successful shop. He liked Honolulu, for the work was pleasant and left him with time to attend a Christian school. It was here that he became finally converted to that Christian faith which he had viewed with interest but without conviction from his village.

But so rapidly did Sun assimilate not only Christianity but the English language and western ways, with all manner of strange ideas about "democracy", that his alarmed older brother packed him off home to China.

And now it seemed as if the young man's link with family and village had been severed for ever. In no time he had managed to enrage the elders of the village by speaking disparagingly of idols in the local shrine: he was promptly banished from the village and sent, at the age of eighteen, to Hong Kong.

He settled well into this strange, cosmopolitan, town, for he was thirsty for new ideas, thirsty for a new philosophy which would make not only his own life more worthwhile, but that of all China. He found friends who thought as he did, and they sat up late, night after night, when studies were over, discussing the future of the world and the impact on parts of it of the exciting new, western, "Socialism". He was summoned back to his village, to be married, as was the custom, to a girl he had never met, and he went obediently. He married the girl, then left her at home with his mother while he went back to Hong Kong to finish his studies. He had just finished with one school, was going on to another; he had become firm friends with an American missionary who welcomed his help with the Chinese language and was about to baptize him in the Christian faith: a young, un-asked-for, wife had no part to play in this new awakening. He would send for her, of course, but in the meantime Sun Yat-sen was too busy for matrimony. China and her future obsessed him. Not only was he actively considering becoming either a missionary or a revolutionary—perhaps both—but he was about to embark on a medical career. One concrete, useful thing he could do for his people was to become a doctor and minister to their ills.

So, at the age of twenty-one, he entered the new Alice Memorial Hospital in Hong Kong, just started by Dr. James Cantlie. He was immediately drawn to Cantlie, they became close friends and remained so for many years.

Sun was a good student, and he graduated with honours five

years later, one of the first graduates of the hospital. But though the obvious move on graduation was to find a post as doctor, young Sun's mind was teeming with ideas of revolution. He had joined a group sworn to overthrow the Manchu dynasty, replace it with a form of Socialism, and he had been busy writing for them—writing brilliant, provocative, tracts. Now, in China where these tracts were circulating, urging overthrow of the Manchus, it was hardly surprising that a price was on his head. If he wished to look after the sick of his own people he would have to practise medicine, either in Hong Kong, which was British territory, or Macao, which was Portuguese.

How little factors—luck, the spin of a coin—affect our lives! He chose Macao, and suddenly a ban on all doctors in the territory without Portuguese qualifications ended his professional career. From now on, Dr. Sun Yat-sen would devote his energies to bringing about a new era for the Chinese people.

First, with no money and a price on his head, he would have to travel in other lands, preach the urgency of revolution in China, and beg for funds.

He went back to Honolulu, was successful in his mission and then unexpectedly met his good friend Dr. Cantlie. If Dr. Sun wanted to interest people in his exciting new ideas for a different China he should go to England.

Sun sailed, via the United States, for London.

The visit, as Cantlie had prophesied, was a success: he raised both money and moral support. But it was in the greyness of London, thousands of miles from his beloved China, that Sun Yat-sen realized the determination of the Manchu government to get rid of him and his ideas. He was lured into the Chinese Legation, overpowered and taken prisoner. He would almost certainly have been smuggled back to China and a painful death if he had not managed to get a message out to his friend Cantlie—who, like some personal deity, had returned to England, and was able to help him a third time. Cantlie was now Sir James, and a man of considerable importance in Britain. When he objected loudly about the incarceration of his friend in the Chinese Legation, no less a figure than the Foreign Secretary, Lord Salisbury, was forced to intervene. Reluctantly, angrily, the Legation handed over its prisoner.

And, a little later, revolution began in China. It was not revolution as Sun had envisaged it, and it urgently needed guidance, but it indicated at least that there were people in China dissatisfied with things as they were. The so-called "Boxers" (so styled by a European journalist who had heard they regarded themselves as "Heavenly Fists", destined to destroy all foreigners) had taken the law into their own hands, behaving much like a greatly less inhibited Ku Klux Klan, and were butchering foreigners and Chinese converts to Christianity. The Manchus, under the wily, brilliant and vicious old dowager empress, T'zu Hsi, were busily encouraging them while publicly holding up hands in horror at this "outbreak of lawlessness".

Whichever way things turned out, China was no longer asleep. Sun disapproved strongly of the action being taken against Christians, and he did what he could to arrest it, but his main work must be the consolidation of a strong revolutionary party, sworn to take over when the suitable moment arrived. He had formed his "Chinese Revolutionary League" with branches in Europe and Japan, and he had raised a great deal of money. This was being employed, for the time being, in disseminating literature which Sun wrote and which was published by a rich Chinese supporter, the American-educated Charlie Soong. Soong's firm masqueraded as a publisher of religious tracts, but in reality it devoted most of its time to printing far more explosive ones written by Sun.

(Years later Sun was to divorce the wife he had wed unseen and marry Chingling, one of Charlie Soong's three beautiful and highly educated daughters, who would be a source of strength and inspiration to him during what was left of his life. The other two Soong girls would also make interesting matches: one would become the wife of the wealthy banker, H. H. Kung—the other, Madame Chiang Kai-shek.)

The death of the dowager empress in 1908, a day after the young emperor whom she had kept virtual prisoner for many years, accelerated the process of revolution. Sun's teachings were now known all over that vast country: even his physical presence was known by many, for although much of his life had been spent outside China he was completely without fear and paid a number of visits deep into the country, despite the price on his head.

In 1911 the revolution came at last, with a rising in Hankow and the revolt of its royal garrison. Sun at the time was in America raising funds, but the revolt was acknowledged as his brainchild and he was immediately nominated first President of the new "Republic of China". He read the fact in a newspaper, halfway across the United States, and prepared to make his way back.

In January of the following year he was sworn in to the new office. He had, over the years, planned down to the last detail a

Republican government, his "Kuomintang", or "National Republican Party", and though he had little hankering for power himself he had hopes that stable government would follow the coup.

He was to be disappointed—so much so that the only way he was able to ensure stable government was by handing over, almost immediately, to the sort of President he thought the new Republic needed: a strong and ruthless man, not a behind-the-scenes idealist and reformer who had spent most of his time abroad. He urged, and it was agreed, that General Yuan Shih-kai be appointed—a doughty, if not altogether trustworthy, fighter who had wielded great influence in the Manchu court and had actually persuaded the regent, who followed T'zu Hsi, to abdicate.

But Yuan, to Sun's great disillusionment and distress, soon showed that he wanted to be dictator of this new China and had no interest at all in democracy or socialism or any of the other ideals for which Sun had been fighting. He declared himself "Emperor of China" and managed to keep himself in this anachronistic position, despite Sun's every attempt to make him see reason, right until his death, which fortunately perhaps came within a year.

A little later there came a landmark in Chinese history: the Fourth of May Incident. It was May of 1919 that the Chinese, still struggling to put their new house in order, learnt that the Treaty of Versailles, ending the First World War, had ignored them. The extra-territorial rights by which foreigners held sizeable parts of Chinese territory would be retained. The military encroachment already made by Japan would be legalized.

Angry, incredulous—for had there not been noisy praise throughout the western world for China's step into the twentieth century? Peking students marched on the foreign legation quarter to protest.

They were not allowed in. Legation quarters were extra-territorial.

And now the disillusioned Sun and his followers turned to the Soviet Union. If the West refused to help China, perhaps the U.S.S.R. would.

The U.S.S.R. did, with gifts of arms and money. And from that emotion-filled fourth of May in 1919 sprang the infant Chinese Communist party, born of gratitude to Russia. Sun, though never becoming a Communist himself, took steps to reorganize his Kuomintang party more efficiently, into Soviet shape. The Communists, for the time being, remained a small group, broadly sympathetic to Sun's aims.

Others were not. China was still divided, north from south, with the Kuomintang nominally in charge in the south and a pack of mutually antagonistic war-lords in the north. Even in the south, Sun found it again necessary, for the good of his people, to resign. He remained behind the scenes until 1921, when he was called in. A year later he was driven out by the disaffected General Chen Chiung-Ming and made a dramatic escape to Shanghai.

His loyal supporter General Chiang Kai-shek now rallied to him and General Chen was defeated. Sun Yat-sen ruled, nominally at least, over southern China.

He never succeeded, in his lifetime, in uniting the country: the war-lords were in effective control of the north when he died on 12 March, 1925. The mantle of Kuomintang leader fell on Chiang Kai-shek, who now, to raise himself above the herd of squabbling generals, styled himself "Generalissimo".

From Sun's death the Kuomintang under Chiang's conservative leadership (he believed firmly in a landlord-and-peasant economy) drew further away from the ideals of the new Communist party. Unco-ordinated civil war gave way to a clear-cut struggle between Chiang and the Communist leader Mao Tse-tung, culminating in 1949 with Communist victory and the exile of the Kuomintang to Formosa.

Had Sun Yat-sen lived longer—he was only fifty-nine when he died—it is possible this split need never have happened. But in any case, present-day Communist China, with its flexing muscles, owes its biggest debt to one man—the little Christian doctor whose energy and strange ability to make men follow in search of an ideal brought China out of the middle ages and made it a nation.

PILSUDSKI

(1867–1935)

MARSHAL JOSEPH PILSUDSKI of Poland was one of the great war figures of his time. All his life he fought for the regeneration of his unhappy country. Between 1905 and 1914 he built the disorganized Polish army into an efficient force which he commanded during the First World War; but his greatest achievements came after the Armistice. In 1920 he saved Poland from Bolshevik invasion, thereby earning the gratitude of the whole of Europe. In 1926 he emerged from retirement and ruthlessly reconstituted the entire system of Polish government, afterwards introducing a firm foreign policy which brought a sense of security to a people who, because of their geographical position, had been subjected to constant interference by their more powerful neighbours for over two hundred years.

Pilsudski was born at Zulova, a big estate forty miles north-east of Wilno (Vilna) in Lithuania, on 5 December, 1867, and was the fourth child of well-born parents whose ancestors had rendered signal services to the state. His father was a restless man full of strange enthusiasms, one of these being the yeast factory he ran at Zulova; his mother, a frail woman who burned with a patriotic ardour which she passed on to her twelve children.

Little Joseph (or Ziuk, the Polish equivalent of Joe) was a bright, alert child who loved exploring the countryside with his elder brother Bronislas. From his father he inherited a venturesome spirit; from his mother, whom he adored, he learned how Poland had been a great kingdom before her greedy neighbours the Swedes, Austrians, Germans and Russians had snatched parts of her territory. Catherine the Great had been the arch-enemy, since she had annexed the rich black lands of the Ukraine, the Grand Duchy of Lithuania and the province of Courland, thus turning a shrunken Poland into the Vistula provinces of Russia. The Congress of Vienna had promised amends, but nothing had been done until, in January, 1861, the Poles themselves had staged a hasty and ill-organized rebellion which was quickly squashed by the Czar's troops.

Joseph was seven when the family moved to a large flat in Wilno following a fire which destroyed their home and factory at Zulova, and young as he was he soon found ample proof of his mother's teachings. The Pilsudskis were devout Catholics, yet the children had to receive religious instruction from Orthodox priests, while in their schools lessons were given in Russian and use of the Polish language forbidden. Joseph and Bronislas became adept in dodging the frequent Russian ceremonies and stayed mute when told to chant "One Czar, one faith, one language!" They offended so often that though they were good scholars they were continually in trouble.

At that time Lithuania was dominated by Governor Muraviev, known as "The Hangman", a sadistic man who delighted in humiliating the Poles, Jews and Letts who formed the bulk of the population. His methods so angered Joseph that at the age of twelve he wrote and circulated among his friends a paper called *The Zulova Pigeon*, which called on all young Poles to rescue their motherland from durance vile. This was so popular that Joseph and Bronislas formed a secret "League", members of which read and discussed forbidden books and papers on Socialism that had been smuggled into the country. Their mother was delighted by their enterprise but was already suffering from an incurable disease. When Joseph was sixteen she died, leaving a void in his life which was never filled. While still dedicated to her romantic ideal, he felt he should explore the socialistic societies being formed by young Russians and went to the Ukrainian University of Kharkov to study medicine. There he found many other Polish students, but their apathetic attitude towards their own country and the triumph of czardom over the Russian movement known as the "People's Will" so angered him that after a year he returned to Wilno, where he and Bronislas revived and expanded their secret "League".

Wilno was not very far from St. Petersburg where the students, infuriated by the constant surveillance of the police, were forming terrorist bands, one of which began to devise an elaborate plan to assassinate Czar Alexander III. Bombs were to be thrown at him when he attended a memorial service for his murdered father early in 1887, and in order to ensure success they proposed to add poison to the explosives. They appealed to the Wilno League for chemicals, revolvers and funds and these were smuggled to the capital. The plot was discovered and some conspirators, including Lenin's brother, were executed, Bronislas was sent to Siberia for eight years, and Joseph, whose part had been small, for three.

With a score of others Joseph began the interminable journey to Irkutsk, where they were thrown into gaol until the Lena river froze and they could travel down it by sled. Conditions were so appalling that they revolted and were beaten unconscious by the guards. When they came to their senses they found three of their number missing, so they staged a hunger strike which proved effective but led to six months' imprisonment for Joseph and other ringleaders when they finally reached Kirensk, seven hundred miles down-river. He was put to work as a clerk in the hospital, a job which gave him an opportunity of getting to know the Russian patients and, more important, the bureaucracy which oppressed them. Memories of his ill-treatment by the Irkutsk guards smouldered within him and his determination to free Poland from the Russian yoke deepened. Through his friendship with an aged Polish exile who had been a mighty rebel in his day, he learnt many subtleties of technique and he also studied books on military strategy.

A boy had gone to Siberia: a man of single purpose returned to Wilno. Polish Socialists had now split into two groups, the P.P.S. (Polish Socialist Party) and the National Socialists. Pilsudski joined the P.P.S. but found to his dismay that they talked too much and did too little. Their leaders, working secretly from London, felt that this fiery young man with his cry of "Romantic plans, practical execution!" was too extreme altogether, but the rank and file loved him and before long he dominated the movement. His task was complex to a degree. In the Vistula provinces the Poles feared the Russians, in Galicia the Austrians, in the western districts the Germans. They had been browbeaten by foreign masters so long that they had lost all desire for a free Poland. Undaunted, Pilsudski set about rekindling the flame of patriotism in their breasts.

He scorned the safety of exile and worked inside Poland. He married a doctor's widow, also an ardent revolutionary, and they lived in the industrial town of Lodz, where Pilsudski and his friend Wojciekowski wrote and printed a paper called the *Workman*, which they smuggled to different centres in suitcases. Over the years the circulation reached over 100,000 copies and many socialist publications from outside were also distributed, and in addition to his printing and journalistic activities Pilsudski was constantly on the move, striving to bring Poles in various parts of their disrupted country into one united party. Inevitably there were periods when he had to go into voluntary exile for a time, and in 1900 the Russian police seized his printing press and imprisoned him in the Tenth Pavilion in Warsaw Citadel, from which escape was impossible. Here he feigned madness so convincingly that he was transferred to the St. Nicholas asylum in St. Petersburg, from whence a Polish doctor helped him escape.

Pilsudski and his wife then fled to London, but privation had given him arthritis and produced a tendency to tuberculosis, so they returned secretly to the mountains south of Cracow where he slowly regained strength. The outbreak of the Russo-Japanese war gave him fresh hope, and though discovery meant a life sentence Pilsudski boldly entered Russian territory to rally his supporters, while later he journeyed to Tokyo in an abortive attempt to induce the Japanese to finance a Polish rising. Finally, since the P.P.S. was desperately short of funds, he relaxed his rule of non-violence and organized several raids, the most notable of which was the Bezdany train robbery in September, 1908, which brought the Party some £33,000.

Since he was convinced that the Russians would soon rise against czardom, Pilsudski turned his energies to the training of a brigade of Polish riflemen. The weapons and ammunition were begged from sympathizers all over Europe, others were borrowed and not a few were stolen. The Poles were good fighters and there was no shortage of recruits. They had to train hard, submit to rigid discipline and live under spartan conditions, but by superhuman effort Pilsudski managed to turn them into a small but remarkably efficient force before the outbreak of war in 1914.

More than ever now was Poland the nut in the nut-cracker with the Russians massing in the east, the Germans in the west and the Austro-Hungarians in the south. Pilsudski, having made some successful forays against the Russians, boldly approached the Austrian High Command and offered the services of his new-styled Polish Legion (whose standard bore a white eagle) if they and the Germans would recognize Poland as an independent state. The answer was a grudging affirmative, for if Poland were given true freedom then the Hungarians would also demand it, while Italy's position might be swayed by any decisive announcement. Until 1916 Polish status remained undefined, though the Poles continued to fight gallantly for the Axis powers. In the December President Wilson declared that a free Poland was essential, and in the spring of 1917, when the tide was turning against them, the Germans and Austrians agreed to the creation of a free Polish state. Various pointers showed Pilsudski that this freedom was purely nominal, and in June, when every Polish soldier had to swear to obey the orders of Kaiser William II's High Command, he tendered his resignation to von Beseler, the German Governor in Warsaw. In their final interview at the Belvedere Palace von Beseler assured him that his army would be given the latest equipment, while he would receive fame and many honours. "Does your Excellency believe," replied Pilsudski, "that the hand which throttles Poland will throttle her the less if it has on every finger a ring which bears an eagle?"

The Polish Legion was disbanded, and on 22 July, Pilsudski and his Chief-of Staff, Sosnkowski, were arrested and driven to Germany. Over the next fifteen months Pilsudski experienced solitary confinement in four different fortresses, Posen, Danzig, Spandau and Magdeburg. News was kept from him, but he accepted everything philosophically, busying himself with writing accounts of the Legion's battles and long expositions on the state of his unhappy country. Suddenly, at the beginning of November, 1918, revolutionary groups surged through Magdeburg streets and Pilsudski was hurriedly conveyed to Berlin. On 9 November the Kaiser abdicated, and as he was being driven to the station Pilsudski saw the Imperial car, smothered in red flags, being paraded down the Unter den Linden. The following morning—the day before the Armistice—he arrived in Warsaw and as he feasted his eyes on that proud city rising from the Vistula he knew that all he had fought for was at last about to come true.

The task before him made all previous ones pale into insignificance. The so-called Regency Council was riven by political schisms, the garrison was German manned, the Polish Legionaries were scattered to the four winds, the country had no economy, the Polish National Socialist Committee based in Paris had names, like Paderewski, far more illustrious than his own. It is a measure of Pilsudski's greatness that, under his dictatorship, order took the place of chaos within a year and that the signatories to the Treaty of Versailles, well aware of Poland's strategic position between Bolshevik Russia and defeated Germany, restored her territories and gave her full and legal independence.

Then came Pilsudski's major error. The War of Intervention made him determined to win back the rich Ukraine and his troops advanced to Kiev, from which they were driven back with heavy losses by Marshal Budenny's Red cavalry. They were still licking their wounds when news came that Red forces under Tukhachevsky, a brilliant ex-czarist officer, had reached the Vistula and were about to storm Warsaw. A grim Pilsudski rallied his men and succeeded not only in saving the capital but in pushing Tukhachevsky's army back to Brest-Litovsk. He then began the laborious task of re-stabilizing the Polish Government and in 1924 he retired to live quietly near Warsaw with his second wife and two tiny daughters.

In 1926 some of his old enemies in the Polish Senate and Seym

(House of Commons) spread about the most scurrilous rumours asserting that Pilsudski had worked solely for personal gain and had even appropriated the Polish crown jewels from the Belvedere. Poland was still full of warring factions, many of whom believed the scandalous tales, and to quell the rumours once and for all Pilsudski marched on Warsaw at the head of three loyal regiments. Needless to say he routed his enemies and, although he refused to resume the Presidency, appointing his trusted friend Ignatius Moscicki in his stead, he continued to be virtual ruler of Poland until the end of his life.

By 1934 his public appearances had become few and those who met him reported he was mortally sick. In truth he was suffering from cancer and on Sunday, 12 May, 1935, he died. Political rancour was forgotten as all Poland mourned the country's greatest son. His bones were encased in a solid silver sarcophagus, but, at his special request, his heart was placed at his mother's feet in her grave at Wilno.

LENIN

(1870–1924)

The Russian Revolution of 7 November, 1917 (25 October in the Julian Calendar), was the greatest upheaval of its kind the world had ever known and it was engineered and led with complete efficacy and ruthlessness by one man, V. I. Lenin. Who was he, this man who changed the whole concept of life for some 170,000,000 inhabitants of one-sixth of the earth's land surface and profoundly influenced the minds of men and women in many different countries?

Lenin's real name was Vladimir Ilich Ulyanov and he was born in 1870 at Simbirsk, a Volga town later renamed Ulyanovsk in his honour. His father was of Tartar stock, a man of substance who was Inspector of Schools for the region: his mother was a German doctor's daughter and a devout Lutheran. Vladimir and his elder brother Alexei attended a good school where, strangely enough, one of their teachers was the father of Alexei Kerensky, leader of the 1917 Provisional Government. Both brothers were good scholars, wore neat dark suits with Eton collars, were devoted to the dogs, cats and birds they kept as pets and shared a favourite book, *Tom Sawyer*. Alexei was the more venturesome and made many school friends: Vladimir was a reserved child who liked nothing better than to creep into his father's study each evening and listen to intellectual discussions between Ulyanov and his friends.

From these debates the boy learnt much, and he supplemented this knowledge by voracious reading. Among Russian writers Turgenev especially appealed to him, and through the sufferings of the tragic Bazarov in *Fathers and Sons* he grew intensely interested in nihilism, reading everything he could find on the subject. Next he studied the doctrines of Engels and Hegel, and finally he discovered Karl Marx, the man who became his god; and *Das Kapital*, the book which became his bible. (The Russian authorities had allowed a translation to be issued because they thought it too incomprehensible, too dull, "to do anybody harm!") The adolescent Vladimir read and re-read the book until his head seethed with revolutionary ideas and, naturally, he confided these to Alexei, who received them enthusiastically. Night after night the brothers talked into the small hours about the plight of Russia and how she could be freed from the crushing tyranny of the czar, the civil service and the secret police. The impetuous Alexei was all for instant action and, despite his more cautious brother's repeated warnings, set off to begin his studies at St. Petersburg University confident that there he would find many young men who shared his views.

Shortly afterwards Vladimir entered the University of Kazan to study law. Shy and aloof, with a high domed forehead, a jutting chin and the oblique-set eyes of his Tartar forebears, he won the approval of his mentors by his diligence, though his contemporaries thought him over-serious. A few months later came the dire news that Alexei had been involved in a terrorist plot to assassinate Czar Alexander III. The plot had failed, but though his part in it had been a very minor one he was arrested and thrown into the fortress of Peter and Paul on Neva river. Madame Ulyanov was beside herself with anxiety, so Vladimir escorted her to the capital where she made hysterical pleas for her son's release. Her efforts proved useless: Alexei was executed and the broken-hearted mother returned to Simbirsk.

His brother's death had a profound influence on Vladimir. It crystallized all his ideas, transforming them into a burning desire to follow the long dangerous road that led to national revolution. Hard-headed, without illusions, he looked coldly upon the various nihilist groups which had sprung up all over the country, and even more coldly upon the followers of Plekhanov, Herzen and Bakunin, the leading Russian exponents of Marxism, for none of them had any constructive policy; they talked too much and did too little. He knew that it was impossible to overthrow the existing regime in a matter of months or even years: it had to be undermined slowly, stealthily, and a complete governmental system must be ready to put in its place when the final collapse came. Vladimir established the first Bolshevik "cell" in Russia, a move which resulted in his expulsion from Kazan University. Undaunted, he continued his studies in St. Petersburg and, after graduating, returned to practise law in the Volga town of Samara (now Kuibyshev).

His outward image was that of a rising young barrister, but underneath this façade he burrowed like a mole to make the tunnels linking an ever-growing number of cells. He had become, and was to remain, a fanatical visionary inspired by the belief that he was destined to "liquidate" the czarist regime and establish a dictatorship of the proletariat, and he possessed qualities of leadership which drew followers like a magnet. He had ferocious energy, a brilliant penetrating mind, a gift for succinct speech rare in a Russian and an unparalleled capacity for humiliating any disciple who had the temerity to argue with him.

In the early 1890s the Secret Police began to watch Vladimir's every movement. There was something suspect about this young man of good family whose brother had been executed and who had himself been expelled from Kazan. Quick to sense their surveillance, he moved back to St. Petersburg where he was less likely to attract attention, and pursued his underground work with such thoroughness that by 1895 he had a veritable honeycomb of cells under his control. He had a certain amount of money which he used to further his schemes, living frugally in cheap lodgings, frowning upon the creature comforts with which some of his followers surrounded themselves. He refused to have an easy chair in his room or a soft pillow on his bed, detested cut flowers and—a peculiar fetish—always insisted on his watch being fifteen minutes slow. According to Maxim Gorki he read a newspaper as if his eyes "were burning holes in it" and possessed a mind which had "the cold glitter of steel shavings". This last quality exerted such a magnetic influence that in one interview he could secure a man's life-long allegiance. As a rule he shunned feminine society, saying jestingly that no woman was capable of understanding chess, a railway time-table, or dialectical materialism, but he made an exception in the case of Nadezhda K. Krupskaya, a young woman of noble birth who shared his worship of Marx and was later to become his wife.

Vladimir imposed rigid rules of secrecy on his followers, but it was inevitable that some young hothead should extol his leader in public, and in 1897 such an event led to his arrest. He was sentenced to three years of exile in eastern Siberia and took the long nightmare journey to a place near Yakutsk on the Lena river. As a political prisoner he was not forced to labour in the Yakut goldmines and he quite enjoyed his Siberian sojourn since it gave him time to write the first few of the fifty-five books which expound his theories. Nor did he neglect the Social Democratic Labour Party of which he was founder and leader. Despite transport difficulties a steady stream of instructions reached the network of cells all over vast Russia. In these, for the first time, he signed himself "V. I. Lenin", though nobody seems sure if he took this name from the River Lena or just invented it. Ever cautious, he never used the terms Communism or Bolshevism in his communiqués—the time for that was not ripe, a fact he impressed on Nadezhda Krupskaya, whom he had married during his exile.

The Lenin who returned to St. Petersburg in 1900 was a far more mature, more powerful figure than the Vladimir Ulyanov who had gone to Yakut; so powerful that the authorities were about to exile him permanently when, of his own volition, he left Russia for Switzerland, leaving behind him a band of dedicated men to carry out the orders he sent. From shabby lodgings in Geneva Lenin published the Party newspaper *Iskra* (the spark), a smudgy ill-printed sheet which achieved an ever-growing circulation and, by its incandescent fervour, gained fresh adherents with every issue. One of these was Yosif Stalin, the shambling Georgian on whom Lenin relied more and more as his early co-adjutors Trotsky, Zinoviev and Kamenev suffered recurrent terms of imprisonment or exile. Stalin shared Lenin's quality of ruthlessness, carried out a big bank robbery to gain funds for the Party and possessed a Houdini-like gift for escaping from czarist gaols.

In 1902 Lenin and Krupskaya moved to London, where they remained for several years. Occasional meetings of the Party executive were held in London, Tammerfors and Poznan, while Lenin made two or three brief secret visits to Russia; but for the most part he remained in obscurity, pulling a multiplicity of strings with superb accuracy. Always he dreamed of the day when every Russian family should have a home of its own and electric light, but his humanitarianism was on so vast a scale that it ignored individual suffering. He welcomed Russia's frequent famines because hunger enraged the peasants against the czar, and wars because conflict between capitalist nations was bound to lead to the more terrible civil war between classes through which alone Communist peace could be established. Communism for Russia first and for the rest of the world afterwards was his programme, and not all the wild agitators among his followers could budge him. His obstinacy on this point, coupled with his denunciation of the 1905 Revolution as a rash error deserving of failure, led to a Party split which resulted in Lenin's assuming control of the Bolsheviks, while the few who urged an instant attempt at World Revolution called themselves Mensheviks and formed an opposition Party.

On the outbreak of the First World War Lenin was living in Galicia, but the Austrians kept an uneasy eye on their unwanted guest and finally deported him as an undesirable alien. He went back to Switzerland and was still there on 8 March, 1917, when rioting broke out in St. Petersburg. The army refused to quell the rioters, the Duma ignored an Imperial decree for its dissolution; on 15 March Czar Nicholas II was forced to abdicate and Kerensky formed his Provisional Government. This Revolution was not Bolshevik inspired; it was a revolt of the people against the gross incompetence of the Russian High Command and the utter collapse of the domestic economy. For the Germans the war was going badly and in Lenin they saw the instrument which would remove the Russian forces from the field, so they sent him and his companions by sealed train to St. Petersburg, where they received a tumultuous welcome on 16 April.

The Kerensky Government immediately set a huge price on Lenin's head, but he eluded capture by disappearing as suddenly as he had arrived and went to ground in Vyborg, then in southern Finland, where he spent a fruitful summer planning every least move in the coming struggle while watching the Provisional Government limping to disaster. Despite his manifold responsibilities he also found time to write *The State and Revolution*, one of his best-known books.

By the autumn the time was ripe. On 7 November Lenin's Bolsheviks struck and with a total loss of only a few hundred lives the greatest revolution in history was accomplished.

Lenin had triumphed, but power did not go to his head. Behind the slogans of "Peace! Land! Bread!" and "All Power to the Soviets" boomed the solemn warnings "He who does not work, neither shall he eat", and "From each according to his abilities, to each according to his needs". With remarkable speed he withdrew the Russian troops from the First World War, nationalized banks, industries and land, appointed the sadistic Felix Dzerzhinsky as head of the Cheka (Secret Police) and Trotsky as Commander of the Red Army. He also ensured that no leader, himself included, drew more than a living wage.

The mass of the peasants were behind him to a man; he had saved them from a war which had sapped their strength and rescued them from centuries of oppression. The Cossacks, however, who had long received gifts of land as reward for guarding Russia's frontiers, rose in revolt and civil war broke out. Foreign powers—Britain, France, Poland, Czechoslovakia and Japan—started the War of Intervention to help the White Russians to defeat the Red rabble. The Royal Navy blockaded the Gulf of Finland, Admiral Kolchak forged ahead in Siberia and in the south General Denikin fought grimly to hold the lower Volga while the Poles marched into Kiev. With hindsight we can see how intervention proved a help, not a hindrance, to the Bolsheviks. All Russians have a passionate love for Mother Russia, and the mere sight of foreigners fighting over her soil roused them to fury, and many czarist officers joined the Red Army. Trotsky chased the Poles out of Kiev and defeated Kolchak in Siberia, while Voroshilov and Stalin held Tsaritsin (Stalingrad) on the Volga, thus preventing Denikin from seizing the grain barges. The naval blockade caused terrible hardship in the northern provinces, and all over Russia incalculable damage was done, but in the end the Red Army proved victorious.

Meanwhile, in August, 1918, Lenin was shot and seriously wounded by a wild young anarchist named Fanny Kaplan, but on recovery drove himself as relentlessly as before, pressing ahead with urgent plans for universal education since 90 per cent of the population were illiterate. In 1921, however, two things forced him to beat a "strategic retreat": famine struck the Volga regions and the sailors mutinied at Kronstadt naval base. Communism was proving too heady a draught, so Lenin instituted the New Economic Policy, under which banking and agricultural systems were modified and some private trading allowed. This form of state capitalism worked (though it would have horrified Marx) and things were at last going well when, in 1922, Lenin suffered the first in a series of severe strokes. His brain was as alert as ever but he lost the power of speech and he had to sit immobile at Politburo meetings watching the bitter quarrels between Stalin and Trotsky, who hated each other. He agreed to Stalin becoming General Secretary, then appalled by his error scrawled on a pad: "He is too rough . . . this cook will make too peppery a stew. . . . I propose the Comrades find a way to remove . . ." The effort was too much. He had yet another stroke and died on 21 January, 1924.

Three-quarters of a million Russians queued up in the Arctic cold of 30 below zero to pass through the hall where he lay in state. They worshipped him. He was the man who had miraculously led them out of their medieval darkness into the light of the twentieth century. Since his death more than eight thousand large editions of his works have been published, and even today, forty-seven years later, the long queues wait patiently each day in the Red Square to enter the mausoleum where the embalmed body of their dead leader lies in its glass case, its left hand clenched in the Communist salute. To the Russians Lenin is more than a man: he is a religion.

ALBERT I

King of the Belgians
(1875–1934)

THE COUNT OF FLANDERS, brother of Leopold II, King of the Belgians, had two sons, Baudouin, born in 1869, and Albert, born in 1875. When Leopold lost his only son, a child of ten, Baudouin became the heir-presumptive.

As was only natural, the Count and Countess of Flanders, an irreproachable couple highly esteemed by the Belgians, devoted most of their time to Baudouin, and while Albert was neither unloved nor neglected he was more or less given over to the care of his two tutors. Unfortunately for him, both were mediocrities from whom he learnt almost nothing.

Shortly before his sixteenth birthday Albert was sent to the Military Academy. Suddenly flung, after the semi-seclusion of his home life, into the midst of a crowd of boisterous cadets, he felt like the proverbial fish out of water. Shyness made him awkward, and he rarely brought himself to join in the conversation of his class-mates. The sense of his own inadequacy manifested itself in sudden bursts of nervous laughter and equally sudden fits of reasonless rage which caused his fellow-cadets to think that he must have a screw loose. "My parents should never have sent me there," Albert told his biographer, Charles D'Ydewalle, "I had had no preparation for that kind of life. The study, the atmosphere, and the talk were entirely strange to me."

Luckily for Albert, he found a release for his pent-up feelings in outdoor sport. Too short-sighted to play a good game of tennis or golf, he loved riding, swimming, skating, climbing, particularly climbing.

Albert had been less than a year at the academy when Baudouin went down with pneumonia while in camp with his regiment—within three weeks he was dead.

The realization that he would one day be king must have seemed like a nightmare to Albert. It was fortunate indeed that two men of outstanding ability, Major Jungbluth and Major de Grunne, were appointed to act as his advisers. Thanks to them he gradually became filled with a new spirit of confidence.

Albert completed the course at the academy and was gazetted a second lieutenant in the Grenadier Guards. During the next few years he went on a series of travels abroad accompanied by Major Jungbluth.

Leopold duly drew up a list of eligible brides for his nephew, a list that did not include the girl of Albert's choice, Elisabeth, daughter of Duke Charles-Theodore of Bavaria. "Uncle Leo", however, could not raise any objection to the match, for the Duke had illustrious relations, none less than the great Wittelsbachs. Elisabeth, who had fallen as deeply in love with Albert as he with her, was gay and intelligent, and as fond of outdoor sports as he was—she was to be a lasting source of happiness to him, his good angel. They made a fairy-tale couple at their wedding in 1900—she so slight and tiny, he towering protectively above her.

Albert and Elisabeth settled down in Brussels in a house in the Rue de la Science, and here their three children, Leopold, Marie-José and Charles, were born.

During these peaceful years Albert set himself to fill in the great gaps in his education. He borrowed text-books and notes from his secretaries who had taken university courses in economics and politics, and pored over them as if he had been some needy student. Reading he loved and his literary tastes ranged from Paul Valéry's poems to Darwin's essays.

In 1909, Albert as king-to-be went on a state visit to the Congo, Belgium's recently acquired colony.* Nothing could have pleased him more for he had always longed to see Africa. From Johannesburg, accompanied only by an aide and a colonial official, he made an epic journey to the heart of the dark continent, covering the five thousand miles on horseback, on foot, by bicycle. In the colony he asked innumerable questions about the administration, the economy, and made notes of all the answers. This was the time when angry voices in Britain were denouncing the Belgian atrocities; naturally Albert saw nothing of this ugly side of the picture, but he was to outline a wide programme of social reform for the Congo in his first speech from the throne. This speech was not long delayed; four months after his return to Brussels, Leopold II died.

The Belgians shed no tears for the old king who had disgusted and shocked them by his behaviour to his family. Albert was the antithesis of his uncle, a devoted husband and father, and they gave the new royal family a warm welcome.

* The Belgian Congo began as an independent state, the Congo Free State, ruled by Leopold II who had financed Stanley's expeditions in this region. In 1908 he reluctantly handed it over to his country.

Albert soon showed that, unlike Leopold II, he was deeply interested in the welfare of his people. He became a familiar figure in the poorer quarters, and his humble subjects took him to their hearts. The members of the aristocracy were somewhat disenchanted, probably because they were seldom invited to the Palace of Laeken. (The truth was that Albert and Elisabeth found them a dull lot, and preferred to surround themselves with men and women who had something to contribute to the world: writers, artists, musicians, scientists, and so forth.) The conventional Belgians deplored Albert's ill-fitting suits, his hair worn carelessly long (Albert hated wasting time with his tailor and barber), and while they said patronizingly: "He's quite a good sort", they invariably added: "But what a bourgeois!" Albert, because of his shyness, was apt to be awkward at official functions, and this caused fools to remark: "What a mediocrity—he'll never hit the head-lines. . . ."

In 1913 Albert went to Germany to review the Luneberg Dragoons, of which regiment he was honorary colonel. During his short visit to Potsdam the Emperor William II burst into a violent anti-French tirade, and reminded him with a wink of complicity that he, William, had promised Leopold II to enlarge the frontiers of Belgium provided that, in the event of a war against France, he would allow the German armies free passage. He wound up by pointing to Von Kluck and remarking loudly: "That's the general who'll lead the offensive on Paris." Used as he was to the Kaiser's rantings, Albert was seriously alarmed, so alarmed in fact that he took the unprecedented step of warning the French ambassador, Jules Cambon. On his return to Brussels he confided his fears to his premier, who became equally apprehensive. The strength of the standing army was raised, and its complete reorganization begun. It was a race against time, a race that was lost: on 26 June, 1914, the Archduke Francis Ferdinand was assassinated at Sarajevo.

The events that followed need no re-chronicling. Let us move straight on to that fateful first week in August when the German ultimatum was delivered to Belgium. Either Belgium would allow free passage to her armies or she would take the consequences. . . .

White-faced, filled with icy rage, Albert strode up and down, up and down in the Palace grounds. On 3 August he mounted his horse and rode to Parliament.

The atmosphere in the crowded Chamber was tense with anxiety as the king entered in military dress, his sword at his side, and quietly took his place in the centre. It was a new Albert the spectators saw, or rather the true Albert—the born soldier, the born leader, the born king. There was no trace of awkwardness now, he was completely sure of himself. Slowly, simply, he began to speak, and when he reached the words: "I ask you, gentlemen, have you irrevocably decided to preserve inviolate the sacred land of our forebears?" all present sprang to their feet, cheering wildly. When silence fell at last he said what little more he had to say, and ended with the moving credo: "I have faith in our destiny. God will be with us in our righteous cause. Our country will not perish."

On 4 August the first enemy shell exploded on Belgian territory, killing a Belgian trooper.

From Staff headquarters at Louvain the king immediately gave the order to Liège and Namur to resist to the last. Two of the army's six divisions were sent to these fortified cities, the remaining four were dispatched to the Gette. Liège and Namur held out for far longer than the forty-eight hours that Ludendorff had predicted, but inevitably they fell. All might yet have been saved if Joffre, through a gross miscalculation of the enemy forces, had not left the divisions on the Gette to bear the entire weight of the massive German attack. It was impossible for them to contain the grey hordes who continued to advance wave after wave. In this grave hour Albert did not flinch; he possessed that almost supernatural courage which enables a man to look disaster squarely in the face and never so much as dream of the word surrender.

Antwerp had become the "national refuge". Elisabeth had taken her sons to England (Marie-José was safe in Italy) and had returned to her husband. The first stories of German atrocities began to trickle through, and new lines of care furrowed Albert's stern face. He had known that the war would be long and bloody, but never had he envisaged a campaign of terror directed against harmless civilians. Only Elisabeth gauged the depths of his anguish for his martyred people. Thanks to the king, the population of Brussels were spared the horrors that the inhabitants of the towns and villages engulfed by the war had suffered; after frantic efforts, he managed to get through to the capital and ordered the authorities to declare it an open city.

The news worsened day by day. Albert alone sustained his people's courage. As a French officer, General Agan, wrote: "The Star-spangled Banner is the national flag of the United States, but Belgium has a more vital, a more glorious standard: the king . . ."

In the first week of October the ring round Antwerp was pierced. The Government went to Le Havre; the evacuation of the city began, and Albert and Elisabeth shared in the confusion and misery of the retreat along roads jammed with refugees and ambulances carrying the wounded.

The Belgian Army, or, rather, what was left of it, had at last linked up with the British and French forces who had established a line on the Yser. Albert went to Nieuport, and stopped at the Villa Crombez to draw up the order of the day. "Oh God, what will become of us?" burst out the daughter of the house. Exhausted as he was, he managed to smile at her and say reassuringly: "All will be well—your king is with you."

From the Villa Crombez the king went to the trenches to hearten and encourage his army. Here is part of his proclamation:

> *Soldiers: Up till now you have been alone in this immense conflict. You are now fighting side by side with the gallant French and British armies. It behoves you with that courage of which you have given so many proofs, to uphold the reputation of our army. Our national reputation is at stake . . . face the future undaunted, fight on bravely. In the position in which I have placed you, may you look straight ahead, and call him a traitor who thinks of yielding. . . .*

The Belgian Army lived up to these high words; during the battle of the Yser which began four days later, it displayed the utmost gallantry. From his nearby headquarters the king, unmoved by the rain of shells, watched the course of the battle. On 25 October the Germans concentrated the full force of their attack on the sector of the line held by the Belgians, and in spite of their heroic resistance it became plain that they could not contain the enemy. On 27 October, to save the threatened French flank, the king was forced to give the order for his army to fall back to the railway embankment and for the sluices to be opened. The Germans were flooded out, their ammunition was washed away and the pressure on the French was thus relieved, but the king looked at the swirling waters with a heavy heart: every Belgian soldier had been thrown into the battle-line, he had no more reserves—for him the Battle of the Yser was the end of his active participation in the war.

Albert joined Elisabeth at La Panne, and now began the strange half-life that was to endure for months. Through the secret network radiating from Brussels he was kept informed of what was happening in Occupied Belgium—it was by means of this network that he learnt of the execution of Edith Cavell. Driven almost to breaking-point by his enforced inactivity, Albert would mount his horse and gallop madly across the dunes. Visitors came and went, amongst them the Prince of Wales; Albert, had he wished, might have gone with Elisabeth to England, but he would not leave La Panne, sustained by the knowledge that, even though there was nothing he could do, his people, so long as he remained on Belgian soil, would not give up hope. The only highlights in those grey, monotonous days were the sea-going expeditions in search of enemy submarines that he made aboard the destroyer commanded by Sir Roger Keyes.

At last, in 1918, the tide of war turned. By autumn the Germans were on the run in Belgium and the bells began to ring out. They rang for the Joyous Entry of Albert and Elisabeth into Ghent; for their Joyous Entry into Bruges; and they rang out a delirium of welcome when, a few days after the Armistice had been signed, the king and queen made the Joyous Entry into Brussels, their capital.

Now wherever he went Albert was greeted with a storm of acclaim. He had become a living legend: the Warrior King. There were to be few monarchs left in post-war Europe; at Versailles, Clemenceau was busy sweeping them away. Albert rightly foresaw that in going too far and too fast Clemenceau was endangering the peace, and told the Tiger so outright. The Tiger replied with a left-handed compliment. "Oh, kings!" he said. "Hardly two of them in a century are worth a thought. . . ."

The closing years of Albert's reign were the happiest, and towards the end there was only one cloud on the horizon: his fear of old age. To decline in strength, to be ill, infirm—this was what he dreaded most of all. It was not to be. . . .

Albert was fifty-nine. On Saturday, 17 February, 1934, he had got through the usual routine by midday. He was to preside that evening at a cycling rally, and he felt a great need to relax in the open air. He would go climbing near Namur, he decided, and, radiating health and fitness, kissed Elisabeth goodbye—for the last time.

At 2 a.m. in the morning, the party of searchers summoned by Van Dyck, his faithful valet, when his royal master had failed to return at the hour he had appointed, found the body of the king on the rocky ledge where he had fallen to his death.

In the war the king had been the standard of his people. Did any of them think as the funeral cortège wound its slow way through the streets they silently lined that the flag which symbolized Belgium's story also symbolized that of their greatest king? Black, red, yellow: these were the colours that epitomized his life: Out of Darkness, Through Fire, Into Light.

KEMAL ATATURK

(1881–1938)

As the nineteenth century progressed the Turks became increasingly a problem to themselves and to the rest of the world. They held large Christian possessions in Europe, and owing to its geographical position the Ottoman Empire blocked Slav ambitions in the Balkans or, if it collapsed, would provide a power-vacuum making all too probable a clash between Austria-Hungary backed by Germany and the Slavs supported by Russia.

So the European powers eyed Turkey with intense misgiving, made more acute by the volcano of nationalism in South-east Europe. In 1875 revolt against Turkish misrule had broken out in Bosnia and Herzegovina. Its savage suppression brought Russia into the field against Turkey. The triumph of the Russians lopped large territories from the Ottoman Empire at the ensuing Congress of Berlin: the provinces were put under Austrian administration, an independent Bulgaria and Eastern Rumelia were created, Cyprus was ceded to Britain. The Turk, the "Sick Man of Europe" as he was called, had long since lost Greece. The seizure of Algeria by France was to follow, the occupation of Egypt by Britain and the capture of Crete by the Greeks. One by one the Turkish tree was losing its branches—and the roots were rotten.

Alone among the great powers Turkey had not advanced for centuries. With Muslim fatalism the people groaned under a corrupt government headed by the cruel and despotic Sultan Abdul Hamid. The country was bankrupt, taxation oppressive, justice an inextricable tangle of religious prescript. The Turk was by nature brave, but he had long since stagnated in a land ruled by outworn custom, lethargy and brutality. The people were almost all illiterate. Britain pressed for reforms, but they were impossible so long as the Sultan, "the doom of his race" as Lord Salisbury called him, retained his prerogatives and exercised arbitrary power. So before the First World War Turkey faced a triple menace: internal decay, control from outside, or dismemberment of the remaining empire by some of the Christian powers who waited eager as jackals for it to die. A crisis was at hand—but so was the man who would master it.

In 1881 in the Turkish quarter of Salonica a son had been born to a minor government clerk named Ali Riza and his illiterate peasant wife Zubeida. On the early death of his father the penniless family moved to an uncle's farm where the boy, Mustafa, helped to clean the stables, feed the cattle and tend the sheep. A short period of schooling followed, but Mustafa ran away after a teacher had thrashed him and a place was found for him in the State-subsidized military cadet school in Salonica. He was an apt pupil, and soon the blue-eyed, sandy-haired youth found himself under the special protection of a Captain Mustafa who, to distinguish him from himself, gave him the second name of Kemal, "Perfect".

At seventeen he passed out well from the cadet school and was sent to the Senior Military School at Monastir, which was still part of the Ottoman Empire. Greece had just seized Crete and the normally dull provincial town was seething with seditious talk. Mustafa had rebellion in his blood, but to him freedom meant root-and-branch reform, not independence from Turkish rule. He studied Voltaire, Rousseau, Hobbes, John Stuart Mill, learnt French, harangued his fellow-cadets and was promoted at the age of twenty to the General Staff College in Constantinople with the report: "a brilliant, difficult youth with whom it is impossible to be intimate."

True, he never sought real human intimacy. But the danger of conspiracy was a powerful lure. At the college he joined a revolutionary society, the Vatan, dedicated to the total reform of Turkish life, and after passing a General Staff course and promotion to captain became its leader. One night, alerted by spies, the police raided a meeting and arrested all the conspirators. After weeks of solitary confinement Mustafa was released because of his military prospects and sent to Syria where his regiment was skirmishing with the Druses.

In Damascus he organized another branch of the Vatan, but a revolt starting from Syria was impossible, and hearing that the Balkans were still seething with discontent he got friends to smuggle him to Salonica. Chased by the Sultan's spies he soon had to return to Syria and then took refuge in Gaza until, there being no positive evidence against him, he was able in 1907 to persuade the War Office to post him back to Salonica, to the staff of the Third Army.

He tried to expand the Vatan, but learnt that there was another and more powerful organization, "Union and Progress", with links with the Young Turk Movement and Italian Free Masonry. Mustafa joined the committee and found its members a polyglot crowd with international ambitions far from his taste. Its leader, Enver, was a young man of humble origins, cloaking strong ambition behind dazzling charm and social grace. Mustafa, the angular misfit, hated him from the start. Dimly in his mind was dawning a vision of a modernized Turkey, but Enver and his friends thought merely of grafting new on old: the retention of the Sultanate, but the enforcement of a Constitution drafted in 1876 and never put into effect. Mustafa poured scorn on them; they excluded him from their councils, and when revolution suddenly broke out in July, 1908, supported by most of the army, it was Enver who took a leading part and reaped the applause.

At the pistol-point Abdul Hamid accepted the Constitution and a progressive government took office. Then, fanned by reactionaries, counter-revolution broke out in Constantinople and the Committee sent forces from Macedonia with Mustafa Kemal as Chief-of-Staff to a division. The insurrection was crushed, the Sultan was deposed and replaced by his feeble cousin Mehmet V. Mustafa went back to soldiering in Salonica, dissatisfied, but biding his time.

Enver and his friends were now the rulers, and Mustafa, climbing the ladder from Commandant of the Officers' School in Salonica to the General Staff, eyed them with critical disgust. To all who would listen he preached efficiency, modernization and Turkey for the Turks, until his voice reached Constantinople and in a panic Enver had him transferred to the War Office, where he could be watched.

The Italian invasion of Tripoli in 1911 sent him back to real soldiering with intense relief. But at the scene of action he was again overshadowed by Enver till Mustafa was beside himself with rage and jealousy.

A year later a mortal threat developed. All the Christian Balkan States combined to attack Turkey. Peace was quickly made with Italy. Mustafa hurried back to Constantinople and was ordered to defend the neck of the Gallipoli Peninsula against the Bulgarians, a key position guarding the Dardanelles. Meanwhile Enver made a clean sweep of his doddering colleagues in the government. But the Christians were triumphant. Macedonia had to be surrendered and it was only in the following year that Adrianople and eastern Thrace could be recovered and the threat to the homeland averted.

Enver now called on the Germans to help reorganize the army. Mustafa protested vociferously against this "national insult" and was sent, for his pains, to cool off as Military Attaché in Sofia. He was still there in October, 1914, when to his horror Turkey entered the world war on Germany's side.

Months later, while Enver was away ineffectually fighting the Russians, he was appointed to command an infantry division as yet only existing on paper to defend the Gallipoli peninsula. An English attack was known to be impending and when it came in the following April Mustafa was ready with his men fully trained. His superior, the German General von Sanders, expected the onslaught at the neck of the peninsula, but it fell on the area held by his division. The chance to act independently, without waiting for orders, brought out all that was best in him. For weeks with great courage and resolution he fought back the Australians from the key heights of Chonuk Bair, which dominated the whole of the peninsula, and by July there was stalemate. Then came the surprise landing at Suvla Bay and Mustafa Kemal was given command of scratch troops collected to meet the new threat. Again there were battles for the heights, the Turks were nearly outflanked and would have panicked but for his example. At last he sent the British reeling down the slope and with tireless energy kept the invaders at bay for three more months. When the British withdrew in December the nation looked on him as the saviour of Turkey.

But in the capital he aggravated Enver by clamouring against the Germans and, posted to command an army in Syria in the spring of 1917, he soon quarrelled with General Falkenhayn and his plans to stem the advancing British. With a lesser reputation he would have been court-martialled, but Enver allowed him to resign his command and return to Constantinople, dispatching him shortly with the Crown Prince Vaheddin on a State visit to Germany.

On his return he fell seriously ill with kidney disease, and in 1918 he was barely fit for active service when in August he was sent back to Syria to command the 7th Army, or what was left of it. The British attacked and smashed the Turkish line. With the few survivors he could collect he retreated to Damascus and, already outflanked again, from there to Aleppo—and with new vigour was fighting off his pursuers when in October an armistice was signed.

Vaheddin was now Sultan. Enver and his friends had bolted abroad and been replaced by a weak government amenable to the victors. The Ottoman Empire had been smashed. Turkey was in the grip of her enemies, and when Mustafa Kemal, the only successful general in Turkey, got back to Constantinople, Allied officers were supervising the police, the port, the dismantling of forts and the demobilization of the army.

Without success Mustafa schemed for the fall of the government and the installation of strong men. But his chance came when against strong British advice the Sultan sent him to Anatolia to quell nationalist risings and forcibly disband the last six intact divisions of the army. Kemal, it was felt, was a trustworthy soldier who would carry out his orders to the letter. He asked for and was given the widest powers—then set off, not to crush but to organize resistance under himself.

From the Black Sea coast he contacted former army commanders, the leaders of guerilla bands, local governors—all who could help to form a new army and rouse the people against the foreigners and their tool, the central government. It was agreed to call a Congress at Sivas with delegates from all over Turkey to discuss the formation of a National Assembly. On hearing of this the Sultan dismissed Mustafa from his command and he resigned his commission.

At Sivas he swept all before him. A provisional government headed by himself was formed, a "National Pact" drafted setting out the only acceptable peace terms and the delegates voted solidly for resistance to the foreigner.

This fighting spirit spread quickly throughout the country and soon the Sultan was calling on the people to fight a holy war against the Nationalists. Mustafa and his friends were outlawed and whoever killed them was promised reward in this world and the next.

For a time the hideous struggle of civil war went against the Nationalists and Mustafa was in serious danger. But he fought back relentlessly and by the autumn of 1920 popular support had turned finally in his favour. To this two events had contributed: the first session of the Grand National Assembly ending in a proud claim to be sole representative of the nation, and the Treaty of Sèvres, signed by the Sultan with the Allies, which spelt the enslavement of Turkey. Clear at last where their allegiance lay, the people closed their ranks and fell in behind Mustafa Kemal.

His troops advanced on Constantinople. The Allies were too weak to face him and in Paris the late victors, Wilson, Lloyd George and Clemenceau, looked round for help. Venizelos, the Greek Premier, had a fine army massed in Smyrna. In exchange for Turkish territory in Europe and Asia he offered to destroy the Nationalists and enforce the peace treaty—an offer gladly accepted.

For eighteen months the Greeks were irresistible. They threw a cordon to protect the quaking Sultan and his government. They drove back the Nationalists into the interior and sowed dismay among Mustafa's supporters. He rallied them with dauntless energy: "You are Turks! Will you crawl to these Greeks who yesterday were your subjects and slaves! I cannot believe it. Combine, prepare and victory is ours." He fought to maintain morale, harangued, organized, browbeat the quarrelling Nationalists and at last welded an efficient army. But the Greeks struck again in the summer of 1921. The Turks were forced to withdraw to the Sakkaria River, covering Ankara, and there for three weeks fought their hereditary enemies in a last-ditch stand. Then the Greeks fell back, burning and slaughtering as they went.

Mustafa Kemal, now called *Gazi*, the Destroyer of Christians, strengthened his army for the final reckoning. He made careful preparations and in August, 1922, launched a surprise attack, proclaiming to his troops: "Soldiers, forward! Your goal is the Mediterranean." This time nothing could stop them. The war-weary Greeks fled in utter confusion and the remnant of their army escaped by sea. Soon it was reported to be reforming in Thrace and Kemal hurried north with his tattered veterans to deliver the death-blow. Blocking his path on the eastern shore of the Bosphorus he found the small British occupation force. Taking a great risk, he marched his men through the enemy lines with arms reversed and no shot was fired. The British, their bluff called, then accepted him and his government, and a peace treaty, recognizing Turkey's full sovereignty within her own frontiers, was signed at Lausanne in the following year.

To make Turkey a strong, independent, modernized country was now the goal. Through the National Assembly he bulldozed a unanimous vote abolishing the Sultanate, and Vaheddin, with bags of jewels and the gold Imperial coffee cups, escaped to an English battleship. In his place as caliph, or spiritual ruler only, was elected his nephew, Abdul Mejid. Turkey was made into a republic and Mustafa Kemal was elected the first President. But dictatorial powers were necessary. He created a People's Party and declared it to be the only party in the State. Religion he saw as the great enemy to progress, and as long as there was a caliph he himself was not supreme and could not free the people from superstition. In March, 1924, Abdul Mejid was sent packing and the State was secularized.

There was great and growing opposition. But Kemal was utterly ruthless. Gradually he established himself as absolute dictator. With paternal rigour he then gave his people what he thought they needed. The fez, the symbol of the Ottoman past, was abolished and its wearing made a crime. Monasteries were closed, their inmates turned out to work or starve. Commercial, penal and civil codes were imported from abroad and antiquated Moslem laws were swept aside. The metric system was introduced and the Gregorian calendar. Polygamy was abolished and women were given equal rights with men. Down to the smallest detail of social life, time-honoured habits were hacked away and in the clearing made the Turk was set on his feet and told to behave like a modern man.

But only two or three per cent of the people were literate and this was partly due to the inadequacy of Arabic characters for writing Turkish. In 1928 Kemal substituted the Latin alphabet and toured the country teaching the new signs. Two years later he believed that the country was ready for a political opposition and allowed two new parties to be formed. But the experiment was a fiasco and never repeated during his lifetime. His last reform was to make compulsory the use of surnames. Hitherto men had been known by a first name followed by their trade—Ali the Ploughman, for instance. On himself the nation conferred the name Ataturk (Father Turk).

In his last years he almost withdrew from public life. Behind the father-figure was, as everyone knew, a drunken debauchee whose health had been ruined by excess. But Turks cared not a jot for his vices. The country in those years was beginning to prosper and take its place alongside the great nations of the West. The decadent past had been surmounted. There was a new spirit of enterprise. Modernization was going ahead.

All this was ascribed to Ataturk, and when he died on 10 November, 1938, the nation mourned as never before in its history. Many of his qualities were dangerous or destructive: ruthlessness, cynicism, inordinate lust for power. He was amoral and irreligious. But when he came on the scene Turkey needed a strong man and there was a corner of his heart aflame with patriotism and in love with civilization. Independence, strength, civilization were the watchwords which he left to his country. During the Second World War they guided Turkish policy and today they are as valid as ever.

FRANKLIN D. ROOSEVELT

(1882–1945)

IT WAS 1910: the Democratic Party in the State of New York had found themselves in an embarrassing difficulty. State elections were being held, for the State Senate in Albany, and for the first time in history no candidate was forthcoming. The reason can hardly have been far to seek—no Democrat had won this particular seat for twenty-eight years—but it was still a blow to Party officials that no one was prepared to contest it: however lost the cause, the candidature had always appealed to someone. Surely there was such a man still available—young and sufficiently resilient not to mind losing?

Someone suggested Franklin Roosevelt, the junior partner in a firm of lawyers, a young man from a rich and respected family. After a hurried consultation, he was approached.

Roosevelt asked for twenty-four hours to think it over. At the end of that time he had decided that, though he would certainly lose, a campaign like this would be valuable experience for a fledgling lawyer. He agreed to stand—or, to use the more vital American phraseology, to "run".

As with everything he had done, all his life, he put heart and soul into it. On 8 November, 1910, a very surprised Franklin Roosevelt was elected to the New York State Senate. He embarked on his political career, not knowing whether it would be a life's work or a few years' experience, with a light heart.

Twenty-two years later, when he was elected President of the United States, he faced a different situation with a heavier heart—but with courage and quiet optimism. The four months that elapsed between election and inauguration made the situation more ominous. By Inauguration Day—in March, 1933—a crisis of terrifying magnitude had built up. All over the country a rising flood of panic-stricken men and women was stampeding to the bank counters, demanding to withdraw savings, put them back under the mattress, in the jam-jar, up the chimney, anything rather than have them lost in a strange "depression", which had become a whirlpool.

As he stood there, at the front of the platform outside the Capitol, hand on bible to take the oath of office, there were a hundred thousand men and women in front, who had swarmed into Washington to see him do so, millions more listening at home to his words. Could this new President, returned by the biggest majority ever, justify his country's faith in him? There was silence as he ended the oath, "—so help me God," then turned from the Chief Justice, Charles Evans Hughes, to give his Inaugural Message.

It was a moving speech, interrupted many times by wild cheering, the cheering of men and women who, rightly or wrongly, felt their salvation was at hand, and the words that lingered in each mind when it had ended were: "The only thing we have to fear is fear itself——"

There was hysterical cheering when he had finished. But among men and women listening to radios all over the United States there were those who doubted his ability to deal with a superhuman problem: millions of unemployed, farms and businesses bankrupt, queues of starving people in the streets. Surely, they must have asked themselves, is *this* a time to cheer?

It was. Almost as soon as the ceremony was over, Roosevelt went into action. Bankers from all over the country had been summoned to Washington, and with them Governors of the forty-eight States. He had believed, and now he proved, that there was an old law, the "Trading-With-the-Enemy Act" of 1917, which could be used to give him emergency powers over the country's money. He rushed it into effect and soon his decisions were announced to a waiting world: from 6 March all banks would suspend operations, with the exception of making change and allowing depositors access to safe-deposit boxes, thereby getting hoarded money back into circulation; there would be, instantly, a five-hundred-million dollar cut in Federal expenditure.

Retrenchment was followed, within weeks, by the imaginative Industrial Recovery Act providing for a three-thousand-three-hundred-million dollar public-works programme, giving employment to no less than *seven million* workers. Action—drastic, controversial action—was taken over railways, house mortgages, disarmament, agriculture, the currency, reforestation, prohibition. And when the special session he had called of the 73rd Congress was over, only one of the many major bills passed had originated outside of the White House.

Never, in time of peace, had an American president, democratically elected, so dictated to his people—or had them so firmly behind him in each decision he took. (Though, when the crisis eased, panic was over, there was criticism, some of it vociferous, and the Supreme Court adjudged some of his legislation unconstitutional and therefore invalid. But by this time its work had been done.)

This crisis of March, 1933, was the second in Franklin Roosevelt's life, the second of three that tested him and which he overcame. The first was poliomyelitis: it crippled him from the waist down at the age of thirty-nine and seemed to everyone but himself, his wife and his devoted helper Louis McHenry Howe to put a complete and final stop to a political career.

The third was the Second World War, which he helped so greatly to win, and whose victory he never lived to see. He died on 12 April, 1945, a few weeks before the end of war in Europe, at the age of sixty-three.

He had been born, 30 January, 1882, at Hyde Park, the family estate on the Hudson River outside New York, with the proverbial silver spoon in his mouth, and Dutch, French and English blood in his veins. His ancestor, Claes van Roosenvelt, had come to "New Amsterdam" from Zeeland in 1644, at much the same time as his maternal ancestor, Philippe de la Noye, later Delano, arrived in Massachusetts from Leyden. Twenty years later New Amsterdam fell to the English, became New York. The Roosenvelt family made one small concession to this forcible anglicization and changed —but not immediately—the name to Roosevelt. From this pioneer family were descended both Franklin and his fifth cousin Theodore, President before him, from 1901 to 1908, and whose niece Eleanor became his wife.

Despite the boy's great passion for the navy, for ships of all sizes and sorts, he was sent to Groton School and to Harvard, not to the Naval College at Annapolis. Reluctant at first, he decided to become a lawyer, went on to do post-graduate work at the Columbia Law School in New York. By this time a dormant interest in politics had been awakened by the assassination of President McKinley at the Pan-American Exposition in Buffalo. This had brought Theodore Roosevelt, as Vice-President, to the supreme office on 6 September, 1901. He was a Republican, a member of the Party to which so many Roosevelts, originally Democrats to a man, had switched at the time of the Civil War, when the South was Democrat. Franklin Roosevelt's branch had remained true to the original party, but though he and his now illustrious cousin differed in political belief, the mere fact of having him in the White House aroused in the younger man a curiosity in the affairs of government—if only to question the more conservative views of the President.

He was married in 1905 to the shy cousin who had been his constant feminine companion. The date, 17 March, was chosen by the fact that Theodore would be coming to New York to inspect the annual St. Patrick's Day parade and wanted to give the bride away. After a wedding reception (where the young couple were completely overshadowed by their distinguished guest) they set up house and Franklin went back to his law studies. Two years later he was admitted to the bar and joined a New York law firm.

It was three years after this that the Democratic Party called on him to run for State Senator—and as we have seen, he confounded the experts by winning.

By the Presidential election of 1912 he knew a great deal more about politics, and had developed a deep respect for the quiet, idealistic Governor of New Jersey, Woodrow Wilson. Wilson had been persuaded to run for nomination as Democratic candidate for the Presidency, and Roosevelt was among those who went to the Party convention in Baltimore to support him. Here he had a first experience of the rough and tumble of American politics—and found he could be as tough as the next man. He learnt that the supporters of one of Wilson's opponents, "Champ" Clark, were proposing to storm the convention and sway the vote with a hundred men wearing Clark badges and shouting, "We want Clark!" To do this they had bribed the doormen to let in anyone with a Clark badge. Roosevelt quickly rounded up two hundred supporters of Wilson, gave them each a Clark badge, told them to show it to the doormen and be let inside.

To the astonishment of the assembled delegates, the sound of men wearing Clark badges and shouting "Clark, Clark—we want Clark!" was completely drowned by twice that number of men—also wearing the Clark badge—roaring "We want Wilson".

Whether or not this influenced the nomination we cannot say—but Wilson became the Democratic candidate and, a few months later, President of the United States. By the hallowed "spoils" system of American electioneering, Franklin Roosevelt, who had worked so hard to achieve this result, was offered a post in the new government. He refused—but then Josephus Daniels, Secretary of the Navy, asked if he would care to be his Assistant.

This was too much for a small boy who had been forbidden to join the navy. Now, aged thirty-one, he accepted with excitement and gratitude and moved his wife and family to Washington.

Here, much as his contemporary, Winston Churchill, was doing across the Atlantic, he threw himself into the business of making a modern navy out of a neglected one. He scrapped old ships, built new ones, converted the age-old "navy yards" to major industrial plants, each specializing in the manufacture of certain equipment.

And one of the first things the new Assistant Secretary did was teach his navy to swim. A large proportion of it came from the interior of the United States, miles from the sea, and a considerable number of land-reared sailors was being drowned each year. Roosevelt issued an order that each recruit be able to swim before being posted to a ship, then donated a cup to be awarded annually to the ship with the best swimmers.

War ended—a war in which his new, modernized navy played a large part—and he was nominated, in 1920, to stand as Vice-Presidential candidate with the Democratic Presidential nominee, Governor Cox of Ohio. But so unpopular had the unfortunate Wilson become, with his misunderstood, unwanted, League of Nations, his "involvement" with Europe and the world, that the Democrats were soundly beaten. The Republican Harding became President, with Coolidge, not Roosevelt, as Vice-. Having resigned his Assistant Secretaryship in order to campaign, Roosevelt found himself, for the first time in ten years, entirely out of politics. He had few regrets.

And now—disaster struck. Or, what at first seemed certain, final disaster, but what many believe spurred him on to greatness. In August, 1921, on holiday with Eleanor and the five children on his favourite island of Campobello, off the coast of Maine, he was struck down with poliomyelitis.

And it was now that he was helped enormously by a little man whose effect on American—indeed, world—affairs has yet to be determined. Louis Howe was a newspaperman from Albany, in up-state New York, older, more experienced in both politics and public relations than the "F.D.R." he met and admired. Here, Howe felt, was a wise, gifted and incorruptible man, with every additional advantage from extreme good looks to the doubtful one of wealth. At the outset, Howe decided: if Roosevelt would have him, he would become his adviser. He did so.

With the 1920 elections over, and F.D.R. back at his chosen career as lawyer, Howe headed for Campobello to say farewell. He had his own newspaper work—and a New York lawyer had no need for a chain-smoking little journalist hardened by the ways of politicians. But by the time Howe reached Roosevelt the blow had fallen. Once again the little man set aside his own work, resolved to get his protégé back into action. . . . But Roosevelt had already made up his mind to do just that, and his wife was backing him to the hilt. He went back to the office on crutches. A little later, when his old friend "Al" Smith, Governor of New York State, asked him to be Campaign Manager when he stood for Democratic Presidential nomination, Roosevelt agreed. Despite a brilliant, wildly applauded nomination speech from a Campaign Manager on crutches, Smith just failed to get the nomination—but by now it was obvious to all that physical handicap would not keep Franklin Roosevelt out of politics.

Soon after this, he learnt from another good friend (can any man have had more friends than F.D.R.?) of a small place in Georgia called Warm Springs. The waters were believed to help paralyzed people. He took a few days off from work, went there, and found to his delight that swimming in them, using his powerful arms to keep himself afloat, made his legs stronger. His visit was soon over, but he came back, again and again—to the last day of his life—to get that little added strength. In 1927, in order to share the secret with others, he started his "Warm Springs Foundation" for the relief of polio, endowed it with his own money. Only when he was absolutely convinced of the value of Warm Springs as a treatment did he enlist the aid of the general public. Money poured in—a million dollars and more—and the future of the Foundation was assured.

By 1928 he was as well as he ever would be, able to drive his own car, no longer using crutches, only a pair of canes. In that year he was elected Governor of New York State, and his four years in the office covered the 1929 stock-market crash and its immediate aftermath. His handling of the crisis within the state, his championing of the "forgotten man at the bottom of the economic pyramid", resulted in his being nominated in 1932 as Democratic candidate for the Presidency, and later in the year being elected as President by a landslide.

Within his first hundred days of office he had got a despairing country moving as it had never moved before. He made enemies, seemed even to enjoy making them, and was never afraid of making mistakes—or of putting them right. In 1936 he was returned for a second term by another huge majority. By this time he was trying, steadily and with some success, to drag the U.S. from its policy of isolation. "If war comes," he declared in 1937, "let no one imagine the United States will escape."

In September, 1939, it came. In November, against great opposition, Roosevelt recast the Neutrality Act so that Britain and France could buy arms on a "cash and carry" basis. This was followed by a series of moves to help a suddenly-isolated Britain (moves without which Britain could not possibly have survived) and which brought down storms of abuse on his head from large isolationist and pro-German forces in his country. Despite this, he was elected for a third term—the first President ever to embark on a ninth year in the White House. He pushed through the Lend-Lease Act, and the trickle of food and munitions across the Atlantic became a flood.

By the second half of 1941 Britain and the United States were allies in all but name: it took the Japanese attack on Pearl Harbour in December of that year to rationalize the situation. Now he took the sweeping and not unquestioned decision to finish off Germany first, before turning his country's might on the Japanese.

The tide of war turned slowly in the Allies' favour: in June, 1944, they invaded France from north and west. He agreed to stand for yet a fourth term, and was elected in November.

His brief Inaugural Message—his fourth—on 20 January, 1945, was the first wartime one since Abraham Lincoln's, eighty years before. He was a sick man now, with the strain of thirteen crisis-packed years in office showing only too obviously when he went for a final war-time conference to Yalta on the Black Sea, with Churchill and Stalin. A month after that the Rhine was crossed and the end was near. He never lived to see it. He had gone to his beloved Warm Springs for a few days desperately needed rest and there, on 12 April, 1945, he died of a cerebral haemorrhage.

As with Lincoln, who died in the moment of victory (but had six days in which to see it), his task was complete. He had taken charge of his country in its darkest hour, had pulled it to prosperity, self-respect, and—ultimately—military victory.

A grateful Britain passed the Roosevelt Memorial Act, empowering the Government to erect and maintain in perpetuity a statue of Franklin Roosevelt in London. He stands there still, leaning on the two thin canes he taught himself to use, amid the bustle of Grosvenor Square.

CHARLES DE GAULLE

(1890–)

EXCEPT FOR four years during the Second World War, when the Vichy Government, which called itself the *Etat Français*, was in existence, France has been a Republic since 1876. If General de Gaulle is the only French president to be discussed in this book, it is not because he is considered the most remarkable or the greatest of French presidents—though many people would consider he is—but because he is the first president to govern France, to influence all government policy to a great extent and particularly to determine foreign policy.

The French presidents of the past, very soon after the republican constitution was in being, were men who performed only representative functions. Some of them had a great influence on politics, but they exerted this indirectly and as a result of their aptitudes rather than their constitutional function. The Deputies of the National Assembly were extremely jealous in case a French President should tend to abuse the prestige his function as Head of State gave him. It often seemed that the Deputies and the Senators who, with the Mayors and other notabilities of national and local government, elected the president, preferred not to see a powerful or a popular individual as Head of the State. They feared that he might subvert republican institutions.

After the 1914 war a nonenity was chosen in place of Clemenceau, who had been so largely responsible for final victory. After the Second World War, France had, for the first seven years, a very influential and popular President in M. Vincent Auriol. But he was not as popular in parliamentary circles at the end of his term of office as at the beginning. It was felt he had done rather too much. General de Gaulle, who succeeded M. René Coty, who was M. Auriol's successor, has been in every sense of the term a ruler. Indeed he has been responsible for French policy in much the same way as an American president, constitutionally the supreme executive, governs the United States.

How were the French led to accept the immense power wielded by General de Gaulle? The answer lies in two things: the first, the immense prestige of de Gaulle, won by his actions during the Second World War; and the second the failure of the French political system after the war and the consequent discredit of the political parties and politicians. One should note *en passant* that de Gaulle has never been a dictator. He has governed according to the constitution of the Fifth Republic, accepted by 80 per cent of the nation. He may have stretched his powers somewhat, but when he was elected for a second term in 1965 and there had been two polls, he remarked aptly: "People say I am a dictator—but whoever heard of a dictator who had to go for a second ballot?"

Born in 1890 of an upper-middle-class family with a strong Catholic, intellectual and military background, Charles André Joseph-Marie de Gaulle chose the army as a career, served in the 1914 war with gallantry, being mentioned three times in Army Orders. With the help of Marshal Pétain, the commander of the first regiment in which he had served, Charles de Gaulle had a successful career, becoming in 1932 Secretary to the National Defence Council which advised governments on military policy. In the thirties he annoyed some of his superior officers by advocating a French armoured force to meet the challenge of the Panzer divisions which Hitler was preparing. With Paul Reynaud, a very able conservative politician later to be Prime Minister, as a partner he engaged in public controversy, a thing the army authorities did not like. Nevertheless, he had no thoughts of being anything but a soldier, and it was not until the Battle of France, after he had led the only two French offensives during the battle, that, at the age of fifty, in 1940, he as it were left the ranks and stepped on to the stage of history. "Gaullist" became part of the international vocabulary—at the same time as "Quisling".

The originality of his achievement during the war was that, from the very beginning, in June and July, 1940, de Gaulle insisted that his, at first, small movement, Free France, which had more reverses than successes, was the legitimate custodian of France's rights, which the Vichy Government could never be since it had betrayed France's honour. He had many quarrels with Churchill—bitter quarrels of temperament and circumstance; with Roosevelt there was a fundamental dislike. Roosevelt refused to accept de Gaulle and considered him a narrow-minded French bigot. Churchill, during the many quarrels between the Anglo-Americans and the French National Committee, tended to side with Roosevelt, though, in the last resort, he refused to abandon de Gaulle. In a well-known passage in his Memoirs he wrote of de Gaulle at that time:

I had continuous difficulties and many sharp antagonisms with him. There was, however, a dominant element in our relationship . . . I always recognized in him the spirit and conception which across the pages of history the word France would ever proclaim. I understood and admired while I resented his arrogant demeanour. Always even when he was behaving worst, he seemed to express the personality of France, a great nation with all its pride, authority and ambition.

General de Gaulle and the French National Committee emerged triumphant in the end and, from 1944 until January, 1946, de Gaulle conducted French government with vigour and restored confidence that France was not down and out. When he failed to convince other French political leaders to give greater authority to the President of the French Republic and to the government, as opposed to the legislature, in the new constitution of the Fourth Republic which was being drawn up, he abruptly left power. This was in January, 1946. An unsuccessful attempt to make a strong national party which could reform the constitution did not alter his prestige. He remained in exile at Colombey les deux Eglises and, from 1952, only making speeches on great occasions. He became a hope both for men of the Left and of the Right: the former saw him an enlightened soldier who might have to be called on to save the republic; the latter, a man who believed in a strong State and in French greatness.

The great writer François Mauriac, who was not at that time a Gaullist, when he interviewed General de Gaulle, for a French newspaper in 1954 at a time when the Laniel government was in power and French prestige at its lowest, saw him as follows:

His words are like a cold wind, coming from very far and very high, from the past when France was a great nation. He persuaded us of this at the darkest and most shameful moment of our history and there are still millions of Frenchmen who have not forgotten it. I did not ask him: "Do you agree with the Laniel government?", because, by his very presence, General de Gaulle makes the dictatorship of Lilliput invisible to the naked eye.

At this period de Gaulle may have believed that his career was over and he said to Mauriac:

I sometimes wondered—perhaps it is my mission to represent in the history of our country its last upsurge towards the lofty heights. Perhaps it is my lot to have written the last pages in the book of our greatness.

France was on the verge of civil war in May, 1958, and, indeed, had been so for some six months before, when President Coty summoned "the most illustrious Frenchmen" to form a government.

The basic reason was that in the Assembly there was no majority for any consistent policy towards the Algerian nationalist revolt which had begun in November, 1954. A majority of the Deputies knew that France could not hold Algeria down and that a purely military policy would be useless. France had already given Morocco and Tunisia their freedom. A majority of the active part of public opinion was of the same view. But there were in Parliament, and in the nation generally, and above all among the French in Algeria, a strong contrary feeling that Algeria must be kept French at all costs. And the French army in Algeria, a large part of which had fought for years after the war in Indo-China, had also become determined not to give Algeria to the Algerian rebels.

Now, since the general election of 1956 there had been a majority in the Assembly in 1956 for a policy of negotiations after a cease-fire with the F.L.N., the principal organ of the rebellion. But in fact the hold of this majority on Parliament was so unsure, and the majority itself so divided, that M. Guy Mollet, the Socialist Prime Minister from January, 1956, to July, 1957, had been obliged to do almost the opposite of what he had been elected for the purpose of doing. In *100 Great Events that Changed the World* the author has described in some detail how the clash between the army and a weak government led to the return of General de Gaulle to power. What should be noted in this essay, which is concerned with de Gaulle as a ruler, is that the breakdown of the French system of government caused by Algeria followed a long series of failures by Parliament during the Fourth Republic to decide firmly and at the right time on vital policies. A similar weakness had affected the Third Republic and many Frenchmen had felt acutely the harm which the constant instability of governments had done to the country in the thirties when there were fourteen governments in less than seven years.

When Hitler went into the Rhineland in 1936, only a caretaker government was in being. France's defeat in 1940 had, in large part, sprung from the failure of the government of the time to summon the energies of the nation to fight. The French, in fact, had begun to realize that an all-powerful National Assembly, which was itself composed of a large number of undisciplined parties and groups, might be, in theory, a perfect form of democracy but that it did not work in time of stress. Governments were not really responsive to public opinion as they were in Britain or Scandinavia or in the United States and they consequently lacked vitality. The need for a stronger State and also for a stronger executive had been one of the principal aims not only of General de Gaulle and his Free France but also of the much more Left-wing Resistance movement inside occupied and unoccupied France during the Second World War. Now at the moment of truth in May, 1958, the politicians and public opinion in France turned towards General de Gaulle.

The socialist leader, M. Mollet, and the conservative, M. Pinay, and the President of the Republic, M. Coty, turned to de Gaulle, in fact, because he was the only man whom the army in Algeria would obey and who could save the Republic from a military dictatorship or civil war. Many politicians thought that General de Gaulle could end the Algerian civil war. Having done this, they counted on his impatience with politics and with what they quite wrongly thought his incapacity to deal with everyday affairs to make him resign. He was already in 1958 only two years off seventy. Politicians guessed too that he was unlikely to try to become a dictator however great his popularity might be. He could have ruled France against the political parties in 1946, and indeed he had said this when, dramatically, one Sunday morning in January of that year, he had announced that he was abandoning his office of Prime Minister:

> *The exclusive régime of parties has re-appeared. I disapprove of it. But apart from establishing by force a dictatorship which I do not desire and which would inevitably end badly, I have no means of preventing this experiment. I must therefore withdraw.*

The drama which had marked de Gaulle's career did not end with his apotheosis as President of the Republic. It took him nearly four years to end the Algerian war and he had to overcome the implacable determination of many of the generals and colonels and junior officers of the French Army, as well as the fighting despair of the French-Algerians, before the Evian Agreements of 1962 were signed with the Algerian nationalists. There was a serious wavering of discipline in the army in 1960 and the General put on his uniform and on several occasions faced crowds of Europeans and Muslims in Algeria alone and unguarded. In 1961 a fresh revolt of the army in Algeria led by four generals was only overcome by de Gaulle's calm hold on the people. Four attempts were made to assassinate him.

After 1962 the drama of his career was associated rather with his policies, which aroused great controversy, than with his personal acts. In 1963 he virtually vetoed Britain's attempt to enter the Common Market whilst negotiations were going on in Brussels between Britain and the Six—an act which angered not only the

British but France's partners in the European Economic Community. He recognized Red China. He took France out of N.A.T.O. in 1966 and in that same year he paid a twelve-day State visit to Russia in which, an unparalleled concession on the part of the Soviet rulers, he was allowed to address huge crowds in the principal cities. Like his State visit to Britain in 1960 and that to West Germany in 1962 this old man aroused a reaction rarely given to other contemporary statesmen.

Late in 1966 he went to Ethiopia, Cambodia and the Pacific, his presence invariably arousing a sort of political excitement and anticipation not usual with State visits. He once said to Mr. Duff Cooper in Algiers in 1943: "Every day I spend five minutes thinking how what I am going to do today will appear in history." Certainly wherever he went, stopped and made speeches, often very repetitive ones, whether it was in Latin America or in the less-populated departments of France which no previous French president had ever visited, he managed to convey the feeling that an historic event was taking place.

One of his more judicious French critics has called de Gaulle "A man of Yesterday and a man of Tomorrow"; it is in the light of that phrase that one can perhaps make some judgement, a very tentative judgement, of his policies. He has constantly shown himself a man of tomorrow—that is to say, a man gifted with foresight. Early in his life there was the question of the need for armoured divisions, and in 1940 he correctly judged that Britain was "down" after the Battle of France but not "out". He correctly saw that the multi-party system combined with an Assembly which was all-powerful and in which governments were weak could not adequately govern France in times of stress. He realized with clarity that the age of holding colonial peoples in subjection was over. A long time before he returned to power in 1958 he saw correctly that Europe must have a greater degree of independence of American policy and that, to achieve this, there must be economic and political co-operation between the countries of Europe. Now over the question of tanks, and over his judgement of the world situation in 1940, he can claim to have been one of the very few Frenchmen to judge correctly. In his other judgements, and this adds to rather than detracts from their importance, he was rather the vehicle by which a widespread view became effective. De Gaulle triumphed in Algeria and freed French Africa south of the Sahara at the stroke of a pen as it were, because the majority of the French nation agreed with him even if they had found no way of expressing their opinion before.

In striving constantly to increase France's independence, General de Gaulle got rid of the humiliations and frustrations which the French had experienced after the defeat of France in 1940, a defeat followed by a series of weak governments which were alternatively cajoled and bullied by the Americans and the British. The French as a whole were glad to see that France is once again listened to by the non-aligned nations of the world, in Latin America and the Far East. De Gaulle's visit to the Soviet Union was widely approved of since it was a sign that France was capable of steering her own way in international politics. Many Frenchmen thought that by leaving N.A.T.O., the military part of the Atlantic Alliance, France had diminished the risk of world war or, if it should begin, of France's involvement.

One of the achievements of the Fourth Republic had been, first, the reconciliation with Germany begun soon after the war by Robert Schuman and Dr. Adenauer, and then the creation of common economic institutions among the Six of Europe. By 1957 the Treaty of Rome brought into being the European Economic Community with its main organism the Common Market. There was no question in General de Gaulle's mind in 1958 of France backing out of the E.E.C. He made this clear, and among the first measures which his government took was the stabilization of the franc to make it possible to accept the challenge of the Common Market. Nor did he reverse the process of Franco-German reconciliation; on the contrary, through his personal friendship with Dr. Adenauer, he brought the two countries closer than ever together. The Franco-German Treaty of 1963 provided for routine consultations between French and German ministers and, at regular intervals, between the Heads of State. Though the Germans have not in fact followed French policy towards the Atlantic Alliance, and clearly have reservations about Franco-German political co-operation, the Treaty remains a considerable achievement.

So in policies of continuing and strengthening France's membership to the Common Market and of asserting France's independence, General de Gaulle has been expressing a common purpose of the French. This accounted for the difficulty of political opposition in France; many agreed that personal rule was deplorable, but only the convinced "Europeans" who believed in the European super-State were prepared to go in for out-and-out criticism of Gaullist foreign policy, while, on economic matters, the conservative and centre parties did not agree with the Socialists and Communists.

The "Man of Yesterday" can be seen probably in de Gaulle's

excessive attachment to the idea of the Nation-State and in his suspicion of international co-operation. He may have been right that men will only die for their country and not for ideals or ideologies. But he did not point the way to a world free from national rivalries; on the contrary, he poured scorn on those who believe even in a United States of Europe.

Whether the man of yesterday predominates over his counterpart or not, it is certainly the conjunction of the two which make up de Gaulle, and one cannot help thinking that the old-fashioned nationalist, through whom speak many generations, supplies the tenacity and force of will which has enabled the man of tomorrow to act inflexibly and boldly in the present. De Gaulle is a rare combination of military man and thinker, an imaginative, cunning operator trained to command and so to know when to strike, yet also a man of far-reaching views, without either class or racial prejudices. Shortly after the First World War, de Gaulle married, in 1921, Yvonne Vendroux, the daughter of a family of industrialists in northern France. Madame de Gaulle, who with her children came to England in 1940, has fully accepted the many challenges of her husband's career. De Gaulle is a writer of great ability and, if he had remained a simple soldier, his talent as an author would probably have given him some renown. As it is, his life has been dominated by one of the highest forms of ambition, the desire to serve his country. No one has better expressed his feelings for that supernatural being *La France*, in whose existence all Frenchmen, whether of Right or Left, tend to believe, than has de Gaulle in the opening pages of his war memoirs.

> *All my life I have kept alive in myself a certain idea of France. Feeling has inspired it as well as reason, and I early came to believe that France, like the princess in a fairy tale or the Madonna of the frescoes, had an eminent and exceptional destiny. Instinctively, I imagined that Providence had created her for outstanding successes, or misfortunes which are to be a warning to the world. When it happens that mediocrity marks her acts or her attitude, I have a feeling of an absurd anomaly, imputable to the defects of the French but not to the genius of the nation. And the positive side of my mind convinces me that France is only really herself when she is in the front rank; that only great enterprises can compensate for the disrupting ferment which her people carry in themselves; that our country as she is, among the others, such as they are, must, under pain of mortal danger, aim high and stand upright. In brief France in my view cannot be France without greatness.*

MAO TSE-TUNG

(1893–)

AN ARMY of children, marching past the reviewing stand like wooden puppets on a million strings. There are thousand upon thousand of them, stretching down the long and dusty street; thousands of feet padding along in unison, thousands of voices raised in a hoarse yet high-pitched yell. It might be a cheer, or a cry of defiance.

Thousands of left hands raised: it is this which gives the appearance of a puppet army, apart from the fact that so many of the soldiers are very small and very young. And in each hand a small red book, like a passport, a driving licence. A prayer-book.

And each book, every single one of the thousands brandished in the air, has the picture of a round-faced person who might—if one did not know the face so well—be either man or woman. A pleasant, effeminate, hairless face, under a squashed brown cap. Ageless, too: the face might be thirty, sixty, ninety years old.

What better face for a god? For Mao Tse-tung is God Incarnate to millions more people than worship or even acknowledge a Christian deity. A god is a remote being, and though we each may have a private picture in our minds, some image of our god, it would be a presumptuous soul who gave his god an age, or even a sex.

And though these "Red Guards" marching down the Peking street are mostly very young and shrieking for the obliteration of a past they have never known, there are millions of grown men and women who sincerely do believe in the divinity of Chairman Mao Tse-tung, ruler of all China.

Before we consider how this very human, very fallible Chinese schoolmaster has been elevated to a position over the hearts and minds of men never achieved in the whole of history, let us see who he is and what he has done.

He was born in Hunan Province, in the southern half of the great land mass which is China—on Boxing Day, the day after Christmas, in 1893. Not that Christmas is likely to have had an effect on him, for he was a grown man before he had even heard of it. We are told that his parents were poor, but not as poor as many, for they farmed several acres near the village of Shao Shan. The Province of Hunan has soil as fertile as any in China, and the tough, resourceful men and women who farm it deserve their reputation, in the old, old saying: "China will be conquered when the last man in Hunan is dead."

For three hundred years China had been ruled by a cruel and largely corrupt dynasty, the Manchus. Mao as a young man was inspired with determination to join with others in attempting its overthrow. A very great Chinese, to whom present-day China owes a debt even greater than that owed to Mao, had published some remarkable writings on the subject. Dr. Sun Yat-sen, a southerner who had lived years in Hawaii and gone on to practise medicine in Hong Kong, was giving up his practice to devote himself to saving his country from the Manchus. All over China men were meeting in secret to discuss Dr. Sun's writings, consider how they could be put into effect.

Opportunity knocked—with the explosion of a bomb in Hankow. The Manchu dynasty took the opportunity of arresting some supporters of Sun Yat-sen for their alleged part in the "plot" and executing them out of hand. The army revolted, and Mao Tse-tung and others rushed to join it. Within a few days the Manchu governors had been driven from a number of Chinese cities and the revolution seemed well on the way to success. Mao, who had never considered a military career, became almost overnight a superb soldier with a grasp of guerrilla tactics which half the world now acknowledges, for he soon put his views on tactics into writing. He wrote other things, too: reports on conditions in Hunan, on the chances of final success for the revolution in that province; and wall-newspapers, a peculiarly Chinese institution, with headlines like "Out with the Manchus" and "Set China Free", which he stuck on the walls of buildings.

And the revolution *did* progress, at a startling rate. Within a few months Nanking had fallen to Sun Yat-sen's forces: a little later an infant "Chinese Republic" was declared. Sun Yat-sen, who had been driven from the country with threats on his life—indeed a sentence of death—now came back as its first, provisional, president.

Mao, the brilliant guerrilla fighter, resigned from the army: he had no intention of remaining a soldier; he would be, as he had always intended, a schoolmaster. In this role he could mould the minds of young men and women, make them acknowledge the rightness of Sun Yat-sen.

He spent the years 1912 to 1918—aged nineteen to twenty-five—at the Changsha Normal School in Hunan, studying to be a teacher. It was not until he went there that he saw, for the first time, a map of the world—and he was astonished. No wonder China, which had once been so certain it was the centre of the world, was not viewed in that light outside its own borders. China not only didn't occupy most of the world's surface: it was not even the largest nation.

But it would—and this fact, central to all Mao's thinking ever since, impressed itself on him at that moment—it would always have the largest population.

The supporters of Dr. Sun Yat-sen now formed themselves into a party, the National People's Party, or Kuomintang. Sun had made the old Imperial General Yuan the first president of the new Chinese republic when he himself stepped down from the "provisional" presidency. Yuan was not a man to be trusted, but he commanded some allegiance in the country and at first this seemed a wise and diplomatic move, now that he had foresworn allegiance to the Manchu emperor.

To Sun Yat-sen's dismay the old man plotted a Manchu revival, with himself as emperor. He even succeeded in outlawing the Kuomintang and producing, if not a new Manchu dynasty, at least utter chaos.

Mercifully, General Yuan died less than three months later. By this time hundreds of petty "war lords", self-styled generals, were fighting among themselves to grab as much of the territory of China as they could before order was restored. Once again Sun Yat-sen found himself in danger of his life, and he escaped, in the nick of time, to Japan.

From here he appealed, fervently, for Western help. Without outside assistance China would dissolve in total anarchy. Was it not worth while for the rest of the world, having a strong, friendly, China?

Apparently it was not: no help was offered.

Then, as world war ground to a bloody close in late 1918, hopes rose. The American president, Woodrow Wilson—and he, like Mao, was a teacher—had produced his Fourteen Points which, if implemented, would do much to help China. For a start the hateful "extra-territorial rights" which Western powers had enjoyed in Chinese cities would end.

But in May of 1919 came terrible news: the powers meeting at Versailles had no intention of supporting a new regime in China;

even less of abandoning their own extra-territorial rights within her.

The youth of China, outraged, prepared to storm foreign legations. On 4 May five thousand of them marched on the legation quarter in Peking to demand that American and European diplomats intercede with their own governments. Rioting broke out.

Much of Communist history is dotted with dates and slogans, and this "May the Fourth Incident", which sparked off riots all over China, is the most seminal of all. Probably it did, as claimed, set off the second stage in the Chinese Revolution; for the Chinese turned to Russia for help.

Quite possibly the whole course of world history was altered in May, 1919. If that be so, the Western powers are entirely to blame.

The Russians responded lavishly and fast: money, arms, advisers, all poured in—and with them, a half-understood creed called Communism.

Young Mao Tse-tung, not yet twenty-six, was an eager convert. He joined the new Communist party, sworn to dispossess big landlords, as in Russia, and make the fruits of man's endeavour equally available to all. The party grew rapidly, was acknowledged and accepted by the only slightly more senior Kuomintang: friendship reigned between the two.

And now, tragically for China—in the opinion of many observers—Sun Yat-sen died. His place as ruler of the infant republic was taken by the greatest of the war lords, Chiang Kai-shek. To raise himself above the proliferation of petty "generals" in the country, he now styled himself, as he does today, "Generalissimo".

The new, self-appointed, Generalissimo viewed Communist aims with straightforward hostility. For Chiang Kai-shek the age-old system of big landlord, little peasant, was the only feasible one for China.

Chiang's final resolve to wipe out the new Communist Party came as a result of a report, one of the many treatises which young Mao Tse-tung had produced. It called itself "Report on an investigation into the Peasant Movement in Hunan", and it was no less than a blunt suggestion for overthrowing landlords and dividing their land among peasants.

In this Mao was ahead of his party, which preferred to wait for such a development. But Chiang, who had seen Mao's Report, decided not to wait a moment longer: the infant Communist movement must be strangled, and strangled now.

There were sudden, bloody massacres by Kuomintang troops. Many people totally unconnected with the Communist movement

—plus of course thousands who were deeply involved—were killed. By 1927 the Party had gone underground. In August of that year, another history-book slogan—"The Autumn Crop Uprising"—took place and failed to achieve anything. Its instigator, Mao Tse-tung, was arrested and sentenced to death.

Dramatically, just before he was about to be beheaded, Mao escaped. Within weeks he was hidden away in the hills between Hunan and Kiangsi—and a fanatical army with him.

Chiang Kai-shek sent Kuomintang troops against them: these were wiped out, all their arms being captured for use against the next Kuomintang attack. This duly came, was similarly repulsed, and the Communist armoury swelled to an impressive size. Schoolteacher Mao Tse-tung set up a First Red Army, with himself in command.

And now, from all over China, recruits flooded in. Mao's friend Chuh Teh arrived with a complete army of his own, and joined the force. Between 1930 and 1931 this Communist force repelled four major assaults by the armies of Generalissimo Chiang Kai-shek—and then came the fifth and biggest of all.

Chiang had imported, at considerable cost, arms and advisers from Germany. He had mobilized a million men.

The Kuomintang force headed into the Kiangsi mountains. There followed some of the bloodiest fighting ever to take place in Asia. At one point it seemed as if the Generalissimo had been repulsed for a fifth time: the next day it seemed Communism in China had been wiped out.

The stage was set for the greatest historical landmark in Chinese Communist history. Mao's forces had been badly cut up and forced to split in little groups. If these were ever to coalesce, they would have to make a way, licking their wounds, to another part of China, free of Kuomintang armies. Mao decided to lead them on an almost incredible march, to the north-west provinces of Kansu and Shensi. From here, backs literally against the Great Wall of China, they would be able to resist any Kuomintang attack. For there was another threat now, which to Mao was as serious as that of the Kuomintang: the Japanese had invaded, were slowly occupying more and more of China. The Communist armies, regrouped and reorganized, would deal with that threat, a threat which was being overlooked by the Kuomintang.

Mao Tse-tung's march—and it is, above all, his—was one of six thousand miles. Six thousand miles on foot against every enemy, human and otherwise, that imagination could dream up.

It began in October, 1934, and lasted a year, during which time the Communist forces were attacked by bitter cold, burning heat, the countless armies of private war lords—and the Kuomintang itself. This "Long March" is and will remain the greatest incident in Chinese history—at least for so long as a Communist government is in power.

The march was not only an exodus: it was a hugely successful recruiting campaign and propaganda stunt. Mao organized the various parties into self-sufficient groups containing among other things a theatrical company. At every stop, however hard the day's march, the company would give a performance. During the performance orators would explain to the audience the need for a Communist China.

The march passed through eleven provinces, with a total population of two hundred million people. These were shown that "only the road of the Red Army leads to liberation". Ideas would be seeded among these two hundred million that would "sprout, grow leaves, blossom into flowers, bear fruit and yield a harvest in the future".

They did, and the power of the party grew. From its new H.Q. in the north-west it continued recruiting and by the end of 1937 Mao was the absolute ruler of ten million people. He began to worry about the fact that he had never travelled outside China, and made plans to rectify this: he never had the time.

A few months before this his forces had dramatically captured Chiang Kai-shek and the Generalissimo's life had been spared by Mao himself. A promise was extracted that Kuomintang forces would stop harrying Communists and help get rid of the Japanese.

The war against Japan was won—thanks to that country's disastrous miscalculation over Pearl Harbour—and by 1945 the Chinese Civil War was raging again. By 1949 it had been won by the Communists, and Chiang Kai-shek's discredited forces had retired to Formosa as "Republic of China" in exile.

Meanwhile Mao rushed ahead with the building of party power in the country he had just inherited. With his advisers he set to work to set himself up as a god and ensure that he remained one. The image of godliness must be constantly kept up to date: only in this way could he ensure the unswerving loyalty of the Chinese people.

We cannot even guess. But, whatever happens, history must record that without Mao China would be still a feeble, helpless giant—not one of the greatest nations in the world.

GEORGE VI

(1895–1952)

IN HIS selfless devotion to duty, his unaffected warm friendliness to all his people of every rank and class, his frank honesty of spirit and the ability with which he carried out the responsibilities of his charge, King George VI stands pre-eminent among the constitutional monarchs of Britain. It was his lot to guide the nation and Commonwealth through the dark years of the deadliest war in her history and into a new era of peace and social justice. They learned to know him not alone as their king, but as a man whom they loved.

He had neither expected nor desired the Crown. He was unprepared for its tasks and handicapped by uncertain health and a stammering speech. But when the monarchy had been shaken to its foundations by the events leading to his brother's abdication, he took up with quiet heroism the burden thrust upon him, and ascended the tottering throne.

Prince Albert Edward Arthur George, the second son of the Duke of York (later King George V), was born on 14 December, 1895, at Sandringham. His childhood had its grim aspects, for his navy-trained father was a rigid disciplinarian with fixed conventional notions. He thought left-handedness a shameful deformity; and Albert proved to be left-handed. His father's efforts to rectify this caused Albert to develop a stammer which plagued him all his life.

Like his elder brother, Edward, he was educated at home by tutors, thus losing the early training of human contacts, competitive games and studies, which a preparatory school could have given him. At the age of thirteen he was entered at Osborne Royal Naval College where, shy, nervous and hampered by his stammer in answering questions, he lingered near the bottom of his form. Two years later, in January, 1911, he moved on to Dartmouth. Here his qualities began to show themselves. He was an unyielding long-distance runner, a capable left-handed tennis player, a good horseman, good shot, gay and mischievous, warm-hearted, quietly helpful and friendly. On 18 April, 1912, he was confirmed and, in his preparation for this, experienced a spiritual awakening which persisted all through his life.

His father designed him for a naval career, and on 17 January, 1913, Prince Albert joined the cruiser *Cumberland* as a cadet for a cruise to the Caribbean and Canada. In September he was made a midshipman, and appointed to the battleship *Collingwood*. In those days life as a "snotty" was tough, but he neither received nor asked for any privileges.

He was at sea when on 4 August, 1914, the First World War broke out. But his career in the Navy was doomed to be gravely interrupted and ultimately broken off by his poor health. A month after the declaration of war he was hurriedly brought ashore for an operation for appendicitis. Still suffering internal trouble, he struggled back to his ship in February, 1915, and served in *Collingwood* in May, 1916, at the Battle of Jutland, getting a mention in dispatches for his cool courage. But his health repeatedly failed. In November, 1917, a duodenal ulcer was diagnosed and he underwent an operation. Medical opinion forbade his return to the Navy, so he transferred to the Royal Naval Air Service, and in January, 1918, was appointed to their station at Cranwell. Three months later the Service and the Royal Flying Corps were amalgamated as the Royal Air Force, and on 1 August Prince Albert joined an R.A.F. Cadet Force at St. Leonards-on-Sea, where he soon took charge of a squadron. In July, 1919, he gained his wings as a pilot. In October he went with his brother Edward to spend two terms at Trinity, Cambridge, reading history, civics and economics. On 3 June, 1920, the king created him Duke of York.

His experiences with the Royal Navy and the Air Service contributed to the development of his character, and brought to the fore those qualities which were in future years to shape his career. In the Navy he learned the great lesson of complete and unselfish devotion to duty and unremitting attention to the details of a task. He also began that keen interest in machinery which later made him a very knowledgeable visitor of works and factories.

His time among the young recruits to the flying services did a great deal to bring out Albert's gifts as a leader. He drilled them, counselled them, lived among them as their friend, and reached a sympathetic understanding of them. This inspired his scheme for setting up the Duke of York's Summer Camps, which he started in 1921. Two hundred youths from industrial establishments and two hundred senior boys from public schools met for a week's camp at the seaside, and mixed, joined in games and athletic sports and came to know and like one another. The duke himself came down for one day each year, mixing with the campers as one of them, joining in their games and entertainments and in singing the Camp Song, "Under the spreading Chestnut Tree". These camps did much to dissolve class barriers and prejudices, and to develop among the young fellows a warm friendliness for the duke and the monarchy. They continued until 1939.

At a small dance in 1920 Prince Albert met Lady Elizabeth Bowes-Lyon, youngest daughter of the Earl of Strathmore, and in the autumn he visited her home of Glamis Castle with his sister Mary. The Countess was unwell, and Elizabeth entertained her guests. Albert was greatly attracted by his young hostess, and in the next two years set about doggedly pressing his suit. Elizabeth was reluctant to exchange the happy freedom of her home for the official duties and tiresome protocol hedging the royal circle, but Albert's persistence triumphed, and on 13 January, 1923, he wired his success to Queen Mary. They were married in Westminster Abbey on 26 April.

The importance of their union for Albert's career and his life's happiness was beyond all estimation. The nation at once took to its heart this handsome and devoted couple, and for the rest of Albert's life his wife was his indispensable support and comfort, encouraging him to overcome his shyness and diffidence and to face with quiet confidence the duties thrust upon him. Their happy home life and complete mutual loyalty gave him a solid foundation on which to rest.

During the next dozen years Albert was busily engaged in those many public functions at which the presence of royalty is traditionally expected: receiving as the king's deputy various distinguished visitors to this country, and touring distant parts of the Commonwealth. In 1924–25 he went with "The Little Duchess", as Elizabeth was affectionately called, to visit Kenya, Uganda and the Sudan. In 1927 they made an extensive tour of New Zealand and Australia. Here he officially opened the new Parliament House at Canberra. At home, the duke presided in 1925 over the Wembley Exhibition; and in 1929 acted as Lord High Commissioner at the Act of Union of the Church of Scotland and the United Free Church.

He carried out such tasks with charm, efficiency and full success. The king, his father, came more and more to rely on him as his representative. Though the Duke of York lacked the gay magic of his elder brother, the Prince of Wales, he was sympathetic, responsive, cheerful and brotherly. But few realized what an ordeal these functions were for him, or how fine a courage he drew on to face them. The stammer which from childhood had afflicted him, making him tongue-tied, shy and retiring, was a heavy handicap when he was called on to make speech after public speech. Fortunately in 1926 he came upon a speech specialist from Australia, Mr. Logue, who helped him to master this defect, and ultimately he achieved a workable fluency. The matter in his addresses was always first-class.

His private life with his family was unalloyed gold. He and Elizabeth maintained an ideally happy home. In 1926 their first daughter, Princess Elizabeth—now Queen Elizabeth II—was born, and in 1930 their second, Princess Margaret. In September, 1931, they settled into the Royal Lodge in Windsor Great Park, where the duke became a great authority on shrubs, especially rhododendrons. He was an excellent shot, a keen horseman and tennis player. With sharp regret he sold his racing stud in the financial crisis of 1931 to help the nation's finances. So far as official engagements permitted, he enjoyed wholeheartedly the life of an English country gentleman.

In 1936 this peace was rudely shattered. On 20 January King George V died, to be succeeded by the Prince of Wales as King Edward VIII. He had unhappily been for some time in love with an American woman who, after divorcing her first husband, had married an Englishman, Mr. Simpson. King Edward spent much time in her company, and when, in October, 1936, her second marriage to her husband was dissolved, he made known his intention of marrying her. That this would make his abdication inevitable was borne in on him by the leaders of Church and State, and the Duke of York strove passionately to dissuade him: but in vain.

For the duke, the prospect thus opened was appalling. He was next in succession, but had never imagined he might have to ascend the throne. He had received no training in the tasks and duties of the British monarchy, and considered himself, with his faltering tongue and rather uncertain health, by no means competent for that uniquely responsible role. For a time he held out against the urging of the Prime Minister and the Primate. But his life-long dedication to the call of duty prevailed. The Throne, the central pivot of the nation and Commonwealth, was in peril, and with a supreme act of quiet courage he consented to take up the post his brother was vacating. The relief and joy of the nation and Commonwealth were unbounded.

He could not foresee how grim and heavy his new task was during the next ten years to prove. But though without any advance training in its complexities—he had never previously been shown a State Paper—he was equipped with the discipline of a naval training, with a human sympathy, a store of common sense, and a humble trust in the guidance of Almighty God. The wisdom of the simple-hearted can often yield wiser solutions than the ingenious schemings of the would-be clever.

Shadows were already beginning to gather over the world scene. Hitler had begun his aggressive moves in Europe with his re-militarization of the Rhineland, and Mussolini had snatched Abyssinia in defiance of the League of Nations, while Japan had overrun Manchuria. The system of collective security was a vanished dream. The one bright gleam came from the increasing friendship of Britain and the U.S.A., which was immensely strengthened by a State Visit which King George and Queen Elizabeth in May and June, 1939, paid to Canada and the United States. It was the first time in history that a reigning British sovereign had entered the U.S.A., where the people were amazed and delighted to find them not stiff figures but friendly, informal and charming. They won the hearts of all, especially of President Roosevelt, and the resulting good-will was to prove a priceless asset in the years of world war which loomed so closely ahead.

On 1 September, 1939, Hitler invaded Poland, and even the reluctant Chamberlain was compelled two days later to declare war. King George VI found himself at the head of a nation drawn into the most devastating conflict in modern history, against the most powerful, unscrupulous and dangerous foes that had ever combined for world-wide aggression.

The British people will ever remember with pride how nobly their king and queen bore themselves through the horrors of that struggle, where the battlefields were not only on land and sea but in the air all over the island. They refused to withdraw to some remote safety, but usually stayed on in the heart of London at Buckingham Palace, which was repeatedly bombed before their eyes. Whenever any town or city was badly blitzed the royal couple might be found next morning inspecting the damage and cheering and consoling the sufferers. They visited aircraft factories, munition works, coal mines, encouraging the war workers in their tasks. With his engineering experience, King George was no mere distinguished visitor, but an understanding and sympathetic friend of the men and women on the shop floor.

Repeatedly the king travelled to the battle-fronts to move about among the troops. In October, 1939, he spent two days with the Fleet at Invergordon, and in December visited the British Expeditionary Force in France. In June, 1943, he spent some days with the British forces in North Africa, and paid a surprise visit to Malta, where he was greeted by the beleagured islanders with wild enthusiasm. Ten days after D-day he crossed to the Normandy beaches to witness the progress of the Allied troops.

While as a constitutional monarch he left the final decisions on the multitudinous political and military issues to his Ministers, King George's advice and suggestions about them were of crucial value, and provided the best answers to a number of difficult problems. By untiring application and shrewd good sense he had made himself a master of statecraft.

The national welfare benefited richly from this when, at the end of the war, a Labour government for the first time took office with a sweeping parliamentary majority, and initiated a far-reaching programme of changes in domestic and imperial affairs. The king's conduct in face of the critical issues that arose was constitutionally faultless, and his brotherly goodwill and sound sense led the Labour leaders to a new high esteem for the value of the British monarchy.

In 1947 the king took his family with him on a visit to South Africa, where for the time the racial and political discords with Britain were submerged beneath an outburst of loyal affection. Soon after their return he gave his consent to the betrothal of Princess Elizabeth to Lieutenant Philip Mountbatten, formerly a prince of the Greek Royal House. It was an ideal love match, and the nation welcomed it enthusiastically. The day before their wedding on 20 November, the king created Philip a Royal Highness and Duke of Edinburgh. Britain has deep cause for thankfulness that its future queen gained so splendid a Consort—manly, valiant, clear-thinking, energetic, high-principled. But for King George joy was tinged with sadness at parting from his beloved daughter.

On 26 April, 1948, King George and Queen Elizabeth celebrated their Silver Wedding, and faced a great and spontaneous demonstration of their people's love and loyalty. Through those past twenty-five years they had knit Crown and Nation together by their unsparing public service and warm-hearted leadership and example. They had become a symbol of unfaltering fidelity to duty, warm devotion to their people's welfare, and the kindly relations of family life.

But by November the king's health began to fail. He had to undergo an operation on his legs in the following March. Then in 1951 cancer of the lung was diagnosed, and a major operation became necessary. Medical opinion recognized that the end could not be far away. Yet he had a cheerful Christmas with his family at Sandringham, and at the end of January, 1952, he saw Princess Elizabeth and her husband off at the airport for a visit to East Africa. Returning to a pleasant gathering of friends at Sandringham, he had a good day's shooting there on 5 February. Peacefully he retired at night to rest. His waking was to a dawn that does not fade.

History will record him as a monarch universally and deservedly beloved, who reached the highest pinnacle of honour, not by brilliance of his gifts, but by courage, kindliness, humility and utter loyalty to the call of duty.

JOHN F. KENNEDY

(1917–1963)

THREATS TO one's life are not taken very seriously if one is president of the United States: John Kennedy had received no less than eight hundred and sixty during his first year in the White House. There were renewed threats when, after thirty-four months as President, he decided to visit Dallas, Texas—but by now the total of threatening letters and telephone calls had become uncountable. Kennedy had been pressing hard for a Civil Rights Bill which would guarantee equal status with whites for the American negro, and in the process had alienated much of the south, which from time immemorial had always voted for his Party, the Democrats, but now showed some sign of changing its affiliation.

Courage was never lacking in Kennedy's make-up, and it required political courage to push a bill which many regarded as political suicide: it also needed physical and moral courage to set out on a tour of the hostile south at this moment. But in November, 1963, John Kennedy and his young wife did so.

There were awkward incidents, but on the whole the tour had been a success, when on the 22nd they flew into Dallas airport. Here, as in other centres, were the cheering crowds and a band—even if the crowd were not as big as others that had greeted them. A quick review of a detachment of soldiers at the edge of the tarmac and the president and his wife got into an open car with Governor and Mrs. Connally to drive into the Dallas city centre.

There were twelve cars in the procession, with theirs in the lead, all of them keeping to a strict twenty-five miles an hour, as they came into town. Here the crowd was denser.

Suddenly there was a shot. Then two more in rapid succession. A woman screamed, the scream was taken up, and the first car in the "motorcade", the presidential car, accelerated in an instant to forty, fifty, seventy miles an hour and tore off alone.

It was minutes before anyone knew what had happened; to this day there is doubt. But somehow John Kennedy had been shot and was dying, his head cradled in his wife's lap, as the big car roared through the centre of Dallas to hospital.

It was too late: the president was dead when they reached it. An hour later Lyndon B. Johnson, the vice-president, and a Texan himself, who had been travelling two cars behind in the procession, was sworn in as 36th president of the United States. John Kennedy, the youngest elected president in American history, was dead. (Theodore Roosevelt had been younger on taking office—but he, like Johnson, took over at a moment of tragedy, with the assassination of McKinley.) Where, asked the world, do we go from here?

He had been born in Brookline, Massachusetts, a suburb of Boston, on 29 May, 1917. His grandfather was an immigrant who had left Ireland in the grip of potato famine and made a fortune in his new country, which he passed on to John Kennedy's father, Joseph, and which was enormously increased by that shrewd businessman's handling of it. Joseph arranged a trust fund for each of his nine children, to give each of them one million dollars at the age of twenty-one. At the same time he set out to organize his children's future in other ways: he had dealt with the little matter of finance, none of them was likely to feel the need of money or what it could buy; all that remained was to see that each boy and girl used what talents the Good Lord had given and grew up a credit to God and to old Joe.

For a start, young Joe—Joseph P. Kennedy, Jr.—would be President of the United States.

This has always been the American dream, but few parents can have taken it as seriously as Joe Kennedy—or had more right to do so. For as one of the richest men in the United States, a lavish contributor to Democratic Party funds who would become, in the late nineteen-thirties, American Ambassador to the Court of St. James, on first-name terms with the great of both countries, Kennedy Senior had every reason to believe his intelligent—and dutiful—eldest son capable of getting to the White House. He asked him to take up politics: the boy agreed.

But fate played tricks and Joe Junior was killed fighting for his country in a war Joe Senior had made every effort to keep away from, even to the extent of letting Britain, its Court of St. James and the rest of it, sink quietly into the sea. Fortunately for Britain and the world, this ambassadorial advice was rejected by President Roosevelt.

With the death of young Joseph Kennedy the plan had to be thought out again, and it became the turn of his younger brother John to become a politician—a prospect which appealed very little. He had distinguished himself in the navy, being wounded yet getting the crew of his sunk torpedo-boat to safety, towing another wounded man through many miles of shark-filled Pacific by a lifebelt strap gripped between his teeth, and after a long spell in hospital he took up journalism. While his father was ambassador he had studied under the famous Professor Laski at the London School of Economics, and had written, during the first months of the war, a thesis about Britain's unpreparedness. It was a remarkable, well-argued document and it was later published as a book, under the title *Why England Slept* (of which Joe Senior gave copies to both Winston Churchill and King George VI).

But before long parental pressure and his own fascination by the game decided him on a political career. He was elected Congressman for Massachusetts in 1946, at the age of twenty-nine. With his father's enthusiastic support, financial as well as moral, he went on to become a United States Senator, from Massachusetts, at the age of thirty-five. But we must not fall into the trap of believing great wealth responsible for his successes. In many ways his inherited wealth, his father's well-known ambitions, and in particular the family's Catholic faith, were a great disadvantage: John Kennedy, with a clear, incisive mind of his own, made his own way.

In 1956 he ran for the vice-presidency of the United States, and though he failed to achieve it, he had made a name for himself in national politics. The Democratic Party began to consider him as an outside possibility for the Presidential election of 1960. The possibility grew when he was returned to the Senate in 1958 with a record-breaking majority: when 1960 came round he was nominated Democratic Presidential candidate, with the Texan, Lyndon B. Johnson, as candidate for Vice-President—a junior role which the older man at first refused.

The campaign and the election, between Kennedy and Richard Nixon, President Eisenhower's Vice-President, was hard-fought and bitter. For the first time there were televised debates between the two candidates, seen and studied all over the United States, from Kennedy's east coast state to Nixon's California. The Junior Senator from Massachusetts did well in these debates, showed a calm mastery of his facts and of his temper which impressed viewers—while at the same time his very presence on ten million television screens served to make this almost unknown young man as familiar a public figure as the Vice-President of the United States.

But Kennedy was a Roman Catholic, and this political disability, which had effectively blocked the much-loved "Al" Smith's progress to the White House a generation before, did much to hinder him.

On 8 November he was elected—by a very small margin indeed. Later, research showed that his faith cost him a million-and-a-half votes, so we can take it that his majority was a very adequate one, on the real issues involved.

Much like his great democratic predecessor, Franklin Roosevelt, Kennedy made major government appointments largely from the ranks of "intellectuals", men who had distinguished themselves academically, or in the highest echelons of industry. These included Adlai Stevenson as Ambassador to the United Nations, and Dean Rusk as Secretary of State. He chose his younger brother Robert as United States Attorney-General, an appointment which—naturally—brought forth cries of "nepotism" and "a royal family", but which to the surprise even of some of John Kennedy's greatest supporters and believers was a considerable success.

He had married, when he was a junior member of the Senate, and she a junior reporter detailed to interview him, the dark-eyed, attractive Jacqueline Bouvier, and she now made an instant hit as "First Lady". Like her husband she had definite ideas on most things, including interior decoration. Her extensive changes to the inside of the White House made her hit on the happy idea of doing a televised "tour" of the building, followed from room to room by a camera, while she described to the people of the United States the interior of a great home most of them would never see. Even in a more cynical Britain the programme was a marked success.

The two Kennedy children, too, in a world which has its doubts about American children, caught the imagination of millions.

But all this is incidental: why was John Kennedy great? Pretty wives, well-behaved children, wartime bravery, great wealth, vast charm—none of these, together or separately, is a passport to Valhalla.

Let us cast our minds back to October, 1962. For some of us, in Britain as in other parts of the world, this may be acutely embarrassing. For when Kennedy was taking the decision which was, if not to save western civilization and life itself, at least to postpone its destruction, almost all the British press—and much of it among America's other allies—was vociferously shouting him down. Only one major British paper came out whole-heartedly in his support; the editor of one of the greatest even telephoned New York and suggested to radio commentator Alistair Cooke that Kennedy's action was based on a monstrous American fraud: that the pictures Adlai Stevenson was showing to the United Nations of Russian missile bases in Cuba were ingenious snapshots of papier-mâché.

But despite this—and one wonders whether some of the same thoughts passed through John Kennedy's mind in 1962 as had passed through his father's, in 1940—the President of the United States held firm. The world, which for the first time in history had stood on the actual brink of nuclear war, came back from the edge.

The crisis had been brewing for months. As early as July, American intelligence knew that the Soviet Union was increasing its aid to Cuba. When pressed, the Russians had assured the U.S. that this build-up, so close to American shores, was all part of Cuba's defence.

But near the end of October a reconnaissance aircraft brought back a picture which told a different story. Missile bases of a type which could only be offensive were now facing deep into the North American continent; more were being finished. Experts studied the prints far into the night, but there was no question about it.

Kennedy took the firm decision not to allow the bases. A mere promise by the Russians not to use them, to stop sending any more weapons to Cuba, would be quite insufficient—though this was the absolute maximum most of the world wanted him to demand. The island of Cuba would be blockaded by the United States Navy, ceaselessly observed from the air, until bases and weapons were removed.

The world—aghast—held its breath. Would the Russians back down, or would one or other of the antagonists fire the first and fatal shot?

The blockade was imposed, despite Russian threats of instant, devastating, retaliation. Then Mr. Krushchev backed down, agreed to remove his bases, and Kennedy wisely resisted any temptation to gloat. He imposed no time limit for the removal of the weapons, demanded only assurances that they were, in fact, going to be removed, assurances which he would then verify by aerial reconnaissance.

In four weeks they had been dismantled, the Soviet troops and technicians were on their way home. For the first time, a part of the western world had stood up to the Soviet Union and, paradoxically, Soviet-United States relations were better immediately after this crisis than at any time since the end of the war.

A year later John Kennedy was dead. He had made his mark in the world and at home and no doubt he would have offered himself for re-election in 1964 and served a total of eight years, for his record was outstanding in many fields. Apart from his battle of nerves with Mr. Krushchev in 1962, he had been forced to handle, within three months of his inauguration in the previous year, the fiasco of a disastrous "rising" in Cuba—a deplorably planned insurrection which was to be aided by an invasion of Cuban exiles. Kennedy, who inherited the plan from his predecessor and had no chance to alter it, was abused from all sides, for its inception and its failure, but he took the abuse calmly—though it stung—and went on with plans for a meeting with the Russians, for the huge increase in space research which he instigated and, above all, for his Civil Rights Bill —which was passed, with hardly a word of dissent, after his death. Like Lincoln, whose death from an assassin's bullet did much to smooth the way to peace at the close of the Civil War, Kennedy's did a great deal to ensure the passage of one of the most important and controversial pieces of legislation in American history.

He was dead, the world mourned, and its great flew to Washington to walk behind his coffin. As for his assassin, Lee Harvey Oswald—who recently bought a rifle similar to the one found in the Dallas building from which the shots had come, and who had been seen leaving it—was arrested and almost immediately shot dead by another man who announced, to shocked and astonished bystanders, "I did it for Jackie Kennedy".

A Commission was set up to investigate the assassination: its report, "The Warren Report", stated that Oswald was without doubt the assassin. Many people, particularly outside the United States, found, as they sifted through the pages of printed evidence for themselves, that they could not agree. In the hearts and minds of many, the case, the tragedy, is still unsolved.

But in those same hearts and minds, as in millions of others, the name Kennedy will remain: reminder of a great man who fought for his country and his principles—and died for them.

INDEX

38212004290760
Main Adult
923.1 C225
Canning, John, 1920-
100 great kings, queens,
and rulers of the world.

RODMAN PUBLIC LIBRARY
215 East Broadway
Alliance, OH 44601

THE McGRAW-HILL COLLEGE HANDBOOK

W9-BIJ-951

FREE COPY FREE COPY FREE COPY

FREE COPY

McGRAW-HILL, INC.

New York St. Louis San Francisco Auckland Bogotá
Caracas Lisbon London Madrid Mexico City Milan
Montreal New Delhi San Juan
Singapore Sydney Tokyo
Toronto

CHECKLISTS

THE McGRAW-HILL COLLEGE HANDBOOK

FOURTH EDITION

Richard Marius
Harvard University

Harvey S. Wiener
Adelphi University

FREE COPY

THE McGRAW-HILL COLLEGE HANDBOOK

This book was developed by
STEVEN PENSINGER, INC.

Copyright © 1994, 1991, 1988, 1985 by McGraw-Hill, Inc. All rights reserved. Printed in the United States of America. Except as permitted under the United States Copyright Act of 1976, no part of this publication may be reproduced or distributed in any form or by any means, or stored in a data base or retrieval system, without the prior written permission of the publisher.

This book is printed on acid-free paper.

Acknowledgments appear on pages 696–698, and on this page by reference.

1 2 3 4 5 6 7 8 9 0 DOC DOC 9 0 9 8 7 6 5 4 3

ISBN 0-07-040481-X

This book was set in New Baskerville by Ruttle, Shaw & Wetherill, Inc.

The editors were Steve Pensinger, Jeannine Ciliotta, and David A. Damstra;

the designer was Jo Jones;

the production supervisor was Kathryn Porzio.

The cover was designed by Joseph Gillians.

R. R. Donnelley & Sons Company was printer and binder.

Library of Congress Cataloging-in-Publication Data

Marius, Richard.
The McGraw-Hill college handbook / Richard Marius, Harvey S. Wiener. — 4th ed.
p. cm.
Includes index.
ISBN 0-07-040481-X
1. English language—Grammar—Handbooks, manuals, etc. 2. English language—Rhetoric—Handbooks, manuals, etc. I. Wiener, Harvey S. II. Title.
PE1112.M33 1994
808'.042—dc20 93-29714

INTERNATIONAL EDITION

Copyright 1994. Exclusive rights by McGraw-Hill, Inc. for manufacture and export. This book cannot be re-exported from the country to which it is consigned by McGraw-Hill. The International Edition is not available in North America.

When ordering this title, use ISBN 0-07-113482-4.

FREE COPY

ABOUT THE AUTHORS

Richard Marius has been the Director of Expository Writing at Harvard since 1978, in charge of a course that all Harvard students must take. His program includes a large writing center and interdisciplinary work in writing across the undergraduate curriculum. He teaches a popular advanced writing course, and in 1990 the student government at Harvard gave him the Levenson Award for outstanding teaching by a member of the senior faculty. In 1993 he was awarded the Harvard Foundation Medal for furthering good race relations in the Harvard community.

He was born on a farm in Tennessee and worked on a small county newspaper for five years while he finished high school and then took a degree in journalism at the University of Tennessee, Knoxville. Later he took the M.A. and the Ph.D. at Yale. He is the author of two biographies, *Luther* in 1974 and *Thomas More* in 1984. *Thomas More* was a finalist in the nonfiction category for the National Book Award. He has published three novels, *The Coming of Rain* in 1969, *Bound for the Promised Land* in 1976, and *After the War* in 1993. He writes a regular book review column for *Harvard Magazine,* and his articles have appeared in publications as diverse as *Esquire* and the medieval journal *Traditio.*

He has published many articles about the teaching of writing, and he has written or coauthored three writing textbooks. Since 1986 he has directed a two-week Governor's Academy for Writing each July for Tennessee teachers from kindergarten through twelfth grade to help them teach writing more effectively. By 1994 over 1500 teachers had attended the Academy, and Tennessee's governor has made him a Tennessee Colonel for his efforts in their behalf. In 1992 then Governor Bill Clinton of Arkansas made him an Arkansas Traveler for his work with schools and teachers in that state.

FREE COPY

Harvey S. Wiener is Vice Provost for Academic Affairs at Adelphi University. He is the author of many books on reading and writing for college students and their teachers, including *The Writing Room* (Oxford, 1981). His book for parents, *Any Child Can Write,* was a Book-of-the-Month-Club alternate. A revised edition appeared in 1990. He has written two other books for parents, *Talk with Your Child* (1988) and *Any Child Can Read Better* (1990). He has written for network television and was trained in the Columbia Broadcasting System's daytime television Writer Development Project. He was founding president of the Council of Writing Program Administrators (CWPA) and chaired the Teaching of Writing Division of the Modern Language Association (1987).

Born in Brooklyn, he has worked in education for more than thirty years. He has taught writing and literature at every level from elementary school to graduate school. A Phi Beta Kappa graduate from Brooklyn College, he holds a Ph.D. in Renaissance literature from Fordham University. He has won grants from the National Endowment for the Humanities, the Fund for Improvement of Postsecondary Education, the Exxon Education Foundation, and the Ford Foundation.

FREE COPY FREE COPY

CONTENTS IN BRIEF

FREE COPY

FREE COPY

FREE COPY

FREE COPY

CONTENTS

BOOK TWO USAGE RULES AND OPTIONS 209

PREFACE

The fourth edition of the *McGraw-Hill Handbook* is a sign of the solid place it has gained in the teaching of English composition in colleges and universities in the United States. We are proud of its acceptance by the women and men who teach this most demanding of disciplines and the steady dialogue in person, by mail, and increasingly by E-mail that we have had with teachers who use the book in the classroom. We have incorporated a great many suggestions from these conversations in this edition.

We are also gratified by the recognition of our efforts to present a handbook that does not condescend to students or to teachers. Like all living languages, English changes as the people who use it change. Our language is not a dead butterfly in a glass case; rather, English flutters brightly in the sun of human experience and at times does things that no one quite understands. Why does "ain't" have such a bad reputation? Why do words like "shrewd" dramatically change meaning from one century to another? Where do new words come from? Unlike some handbooks, ours admits the puzzles when we find them. We believe that good writing is a matter of principles rather than rules, and we try to be honest when we find the principles fuzzy.

English does have some rules, but we make a distinction between those that can be broken now and then and those that cannot. We do not scream in agony at the sight of a split infinitive, but we do think tacking a plural verb onto a singular subject confuses readers. We think some sentences can end with a preposition, but we don't think good writers can use double negatives. We try to hold to principles, to state them clearly, and to illustrate them by the work of good contemporary authors.

We are proud that our handbook has been widely recognized as treating women and minorities with respect, and gratified by Professor Deborah Kennedy's special commendation of *The McGraw-Hill College Handbook* for its attention to gender and inclusive language in her article "Inclusive Language" in the spring 1992 issue of *Women and Language* (p. 46). We have presumed throughout that women and minorities should be treated with the same dignity and respect accorded to white males, and we have examined every line of the fourth edition to make sure that we maintain our own high standards.

Our handbook offers no easy route to glory: *The McGraw-Hill College Handbook* assumes that students must write regularly and revise continually if they are to become good writers.

We have practiced our own philosophy in preparing the fourth edition. In the previous three editions, we worked hard at providing clear explanations of both the process and the product of writing. How do writers write? What can they do to make their work clear, logical, and (we hope the word is not out of date) elegant? We considered these issues always with students in mind, always with the desire to convey the results of our study in a way that was friendly without being condescending, clear without being shallow, and accurate without being pedantic. The testimony of the hundreds of teachers and thousands of students who have used this book throughout the United States and Canada has been that we succeeded.

Once again in this edition, we focus as much on process as we do on product. Too often handbooks concentrate on showing students correct written products without telling them how to produce one. In our writing process chapters we have given a realistic account of how writers write. We have provided drafts of a typical first-year student's paper and showed the changes on the way to a final draft. Students who follow our trail through this process will arrive at a piece of work that will make them proud of their effort and their accomplishment.

Note that we have not forgotten product in our interest in process. To provide process without giving some idea of a goal is a bit like constructing an elaborate rocket to be fired off into space without a target. We try to help students write essays that will be coherent expositions of their own thoughts about evidence, however the evidence is defined. We show students how to revise and how to think about their writing so that they become their own best critics.

We expect this book to be used in composition classes for first-year students and in other courses in writing offered by English departments. We value literature, and we draw many examples from it. But we also think that students should write well in courses across the entire curriculum. We assume throughout that students can be helped by our book in whatever courses they take. In a new chapter and throughout the text, we provide examples from writing about history, psychology, economics, physics, biology, business, engineering, sports, and other fields to illustrate our conviction that good writing is necessary to any discipline.

Above all, we want students to learn to write by writing. If we taught kids to play baseball in the way that we have traditionally tried to teach them to write, baseball would not be our national sport. Just imagine saying, "Now in first grade, we are going to study the *Baseball Rulebook.* We are going to study that rulebook every year for twelve years. And if you memorize the rulebook, we may let you finally play a game." We teach baseball by letting kids play, by telling them a step at a time that three strikes make an out, three outs make a half inning, a caught fly ball is an out, and so on. We should teach writing the same way. Let writers write; help them with the conventions as they go along. We all learn to write by discovering that we all have something to say if we try hard enough. We want to help students make that great discovery.

In This Edition

We worked hard to shorten the third edition and keep it comprehensive. In this fourth edition we have done some further tightening, eliminated some examples and added others, and reworked the entire text to make it even more readable. We have added many more Checklists. We have revised and rewritten exercises, and added some in a continuing effort to make the book serviceable to the first-year student. We have added an ESL appendix for students who want more help with some of the more difficult problems of idiomatic usage. We have also worked on the design, to make it more attractive and functional.

We have returned to our earlier practice of providing two research papers, one in literature and one in science, to buttress the interdisciplinary character of the book. Once again we show both the APA and the MLA reference styles, with examples and in detail.

Reviewers and users of the three previous editions of *The McGraw-Hill College Handbook* have continually commented warmly on its stylistic excellence. We have worked hard in this revision to hold to the standard we have set for ourselves. We have been told that we have written a handbook that can be read with pleasure and used with profit. We think we have written a handbook for these times, and yet a book that respects and uses the strengths of tradition.

Supplements

We have provided a package of aids that teachers will find helpful throughout the course, and supplements that students will find useful in enhancing their work.

For teachers, the aids consist of:

An **Instructor's Manual** that contains teaching tips, answers to exercises, and additional testing materials for the classroom teacher; and the McGraw-Hill **Computerized Diagnostic Tests.** For these we thank Santi Buscemi of Middlesex County College.

For students, the supplements include:

The **McGraw-Hill Workbook,** which includes exercises that may be assigned by the teacher, prepared by Mark Connelly of Milwaukee Area Technical College, for which an **Answer Key** is available. The **McGraw-Hill On-Line Handbook** is a computer disk that can be stored in memory and accessed to answer questions about grammar and usage. The **McGraw-Hill Practice Program** is an interactive software tutorial with exercises. **Writer's Tools** is a HyperCard stack with two sets of tools to help with writing.

Acknowledgments

We are grateful to the many people who have helped us with this book in all four of its editions. Teaching English composition is probably the most difficult job in any university—and often the least rewarded. Perhaps the very difficulty of our profession makes its members feel so strongly the mutual obligations and respect that bind us all together. We have been the beneficiaries of helpful opinions from many teachers in the field who have reviewed this book in its various stages, and we could not have done our work without their searching commentaries, their occasional sharp criticism, and their generous and steadfast encouragement.

Because so much of the structure and personality of the three previous editions persists in this revision, we want once again to thank and acknowledge all those who helped with their reviews of this and the many drafts of the previous editions: Jay Balderson, Western Illinois University; Raymond Brebach, Drexel University; Richard H. Bulloch, Northeastern University; Santi Buscemi, Middlesex County College; David Chapman, Texas Tech University; John Chard, Gloucester County College; Joseph J. Comprone, Michigan Technological University; Virgil Cook, Virginia Polytechnic Institute; Harry H. Crosby, Boston University; Janet Eber, County College of Morris; Robert M. Esch, University of Texas at El Paso; Peter Farley, Adelphi University; James A. Freeman, University of Massachusetts at Amherst; Dennis R. Gabriel, Cuyahoga Community College; Pablo Gonzales, Los Medanos College; Frank Hubbard, Marquette University; Maurice Hunt, Baylor University; Lee A. Jacobus, University of Connecticut, Storrs; Ben Jennings, Virginia Highlands Community College; Larry Kelly, Widener University; Russ Larson, Eastern Michigan University; Peter D. Lindblom, Miami-Dade Community College; Joe Lostracco, Austin Community College; William MacPherson, Essex County College; Sheila J. McDonald, C. W. Post Center, LIU; Donald A. McQuade, University of California, Berkeley; Robert Meeker, Bloomsburg University; Doris Miller, U.S. Air Force Academy; Pat Murray, DePaul University; Sharon Niederman, Metropolitan State, Denver; Rosemary O'Donoghue, Western New England College; Jack B. Oruch, University of Kansas, Lawrence; Margaret Panos, Southeastern Massachusetts University; Compton Rees, University of Connecticut; Karen Reid, Midwestern State University; Kathleen W. Ritch, Santa Fe Community College, Gainesville; Annette T. Rottenberg, University of Massachusetts at Amherst; Donald C. Stewart, Kansas State University, Manhattan; John Stratton, University of Arkanas, Little Rock; Margaret A. Strom, Eastern Maine Technical Institute; Sebastian J. Vasta, Camden Community College; Bryant Wyatt, Virginia State University.

John C. Bean, Seattle University; Kathleen Bell, Old Dominion University; Mark Coleman, Potsdam College; Larry Corse, Clayton State College; Joe Glaser, Western Kentucky University; Rosalie Hewitt, Northern Illinois University; Pat C. Hoy II, New York University; Beverly Huttinger, Broward Community College; Larry P. Kent, William Rainey Harper College; Patricia Maida, University of DC; David A. Martin, University of Wisconsin, Milwaukee; Joseph McLaren, Mercy College; Albert H. Nicolai, Jr., Middlesex County College; Della H. Paul, Valencia Community College; Dorothy U. Seyler, Northern Virginia Community College; Donnetta Heitschmidt Suchon, Daytona Beach Community College; Carroll L. Wilson, Somerset County College; and members of the English faculty at the United States Military Academy, West Point.

We want to say again how much we have enjoyed working on this book. We have had the pleasure of thinking through our long experience as deeply engaged teachers of writing and the greater satisfaction of thinking through our glorious English language in its rich and lively American version. We have worked far into the night more times than we can possibly count in producing the four editions of this book. We have never been content to study other textbooks and to rephrase their advice; we have gone directly to the English prose that we both love to see how it works and to express our finding in the spirit of discovery and excitement that stands behind all true scholarship.

We have picked up many debts through the years. Dozens of people at McGraw-Hill have helped, sometimes giving us excellent technical advice, sometimes making evenings ring with laughter over the dinner table after long, long hours of difficult work.

For this edition we are especially grateful to C. Steven Pensinger, who cheerfully and energetically took this project under his general editorial wing for the third edition and remains steadfastly with us in this one. Jeannine Ciliotta has served as the developmental editor for the last two editions, spending hours with us on the telephone, working out an infinity of details. Developmental editors should have a special place in heaven, reserved for those patient and responsible shepherds who keep their sheep from running off in twelve different directions at once. David Damstra has been steadily on the mark in seeing that the text we wrote is the one that gets bound and printed. His friendly voice, booming through the telephone, has kept us on schedule during the long production of this book.

Both our families have put up with our silences at our computers while we labor to prune back old prose and to write something fresh and new. Our wives receive our loving gratitude not only for their support, but for the enthusiasm they have always managed to muster when we felt compelled to read to them something we had written that we thought deserved to be memorized by schoolchildren. They managed to like our words, and after a great many years, they seem to like us, too.

Perhaps most remarkable, we have worked closely with each other now for fifteen years through four editions with a mutual respect and affection that endure.

Richard Marius
Harvey S. Wiener

TO THE STUDENT

The best way to use this book is to keep it handy as a reference. Pick it up every day and browse through it at random. When your teacher assigns a section, read it carefully and do the exercises to fix its principles in your mind. By all means read Chapters 1 through 3 before you begin to write your first paper.

The index and the contents will help you locate information that deals with your special problems and interests. For easy reference, the correction symbols appear inside both front and back covers. The checklists, which you can use to review or as handy summaries of important points, are listed inside the front cover. Topics covered in the ESL appendix are listed inside the back cover. The appendix itself, which offers additional help (guidelines, examples) with special problems in English, is keyed into the text by a tree logo and a table number in the margin at the appropriate point.

The ability to write well can give you both pleasure and power. You owe it to yourself to discover the joy of writing, the excitement of expressing your ideas, your feelings, your thoughts, your discoveries, your opinions about everything from daily events to the demands of a promising future. As you learn to write well, you will also discover that people are more likely to respect and accept your opinions because you express them in writing that engages and persuades your readers.

Some textbooks seem to promise that they can make writing easy. They are wrong. Good writing always takes hard work, and all writers are sometimes discouraged. Effective writers go back to work after their discouragement and try again. We hope that *The McGraw-Hill College Handbook* can make writing less difficult and can give you guidance and pleasure along the way.

Richard Marius
Harvey S. Wiener

THE McGRAW-HILL COLLEGE HANDBOOK

PART ONE
WRITING ESSAYS AND PARAGRAPHS

PART TWO
WRITING CLEAR AND EFFECTIVE SENTENCES

PART THREE
USING WORDS EFFECTIVELY

BOOK
ONE

THE WRITING PROCESS

PART

ONE

WRITING ESSAYS AND PARAGRAPHS

CHAPTER

1

PLANNING A PAPER

In your composition course—and all the way through college—you will be writing papers. The first two chapters of this handbook describe the steps you take from choosing a subject to completing the final copy. These steps are the **writing process.** It begins when you start thinking about a topic, continues through your first efforts at shaping it, passes through several revisions, and concludes with the final copy you turn in to your instructor. The writing process may include taking notes, making lists, sketching outlines, and experimenting with sample sentences and paragraphs. It involves writing drafts of the whole paper and changing them dramatically as you develop a clearer sense of what you want to say.

Writers develop their topics in many ways, so don't think of the writing process as a sequence of activities that are the same for everyone or that, even for the same writer, are the same for every writing project. Nor do the activities always proceed in the same sequence. Some take place almost simultaneously. But from the time they consider writing something until they produce the final copy, most writers take similar steps. Sometimes you can skip one step or another, but most often you will do them all, and you might even have to do one several times. Few writers can dash off a sensible essay; most have to work long and hard. It will help you to think ahead of time about the different activities involved in the writing process so that you can organize yourself to work efficiently and well (see Checklist 1.1). The first step in preparation is called **prewriting.**

1a Using Prewriting Techniques

Prewriting includes a number of steps that prepare you to begin your essay. They help you think about your topic and define it. Here are some steps to help you work out ideas for writing.

Thinking: Let Ideas Float

Good writing begins with clear thinking, but most of our thinking begins in a muddle. Many different ideas crowd into our heads, some of them useful, some useless, some contradictory. Some are so vague that we don't know at first whether they're useful or not. Thinking about your subject is a process of sorting out good ideas from bad ones, the relevant from the irrelevant, the shallow from the creative.

Remember, too, that all your thinking does not go on at your desk. You may get good ideas when you are walking, riding a bike, taking a shower, or talking with friends. Keep your writing task on your mind. Think about it whenever you can. Bring it up in conversations. Ask yourself how you can use material you learn in other courses to enrich a paper you write in composition.

✓ CHECKLIST 1.1: PREWRITING STEPS

- Practice prewriting: thinking, listing, reading, talking, questioning, freewriting, clustering.
- Limit the topic.
- Plan your approach.
- Consider your audience.
- Choose supporting evidence.
- Draft a thesis statement.
- Organize your ideas.
- Create a rough outline.
- Review the rough outline.

Listing: Jot Down Ideas

Sometimes the best way to think about your subject is to jot down some ideas in a notebook—disconnected sentences that may provoke other ideas. Moving a hand across a page seems to move the brain. One idea generates another. The more you write, the more inspiration you get. Carry the list around with you. Let it grow over several days as your thoughts develop and become more specific—one or two sentences or phrases scribbled in the morning, another few dashed off as you return from class, perhaps something jotted down in class itself. Ideas come at unexpected times. Keep a notebook ready to catch them.

Here's a sample prewriting list. It develops an example we'll follow throughout Part One. The composition instructor has assigned her students to write "a personal reaction to something you have read recently."

1a plan

John Williams, a student in her class, thinks he'll write about Stephen King's novel *The Shining*, which he read over the summer. He jots down some ideas.

Stephen King and horror

Why do people like Stephen King?

He writes horror stories—but so do lots of people.

but all my friends read Stephen King, so do I—why?

He writes about familiar things but gives them a twist—families, fathers and sons.

That's the real horror of The Shining—a father turns against his son.

happens in real life, children are abused.

Danny Torrance loves his father, and I think the father loves him.

the horror comes from something familiar turning ugly, murderous.

Science fiction never did grab me; it's unreal, but Stephen King writes about things we know—or think we know.

like a big house, a hotel, up in the mountains of Colorado, a family goes up there to be caretakers for the winter.

house is haunted.

hotel has been used by criminals, owned by the mob and all sorts of criminal types.

The evil hangs in the building, and it infects Jack Torrance, Danny's father, and Jack tries to kill his family.

Danny is rescued by a black man who has the same mysterious power Danny has—to communicate as though by radio from mind to mind over miles and miles.

We all want a loyal friend like that, somebody who rescues us when the time comes.

What does it all mean?

King writes with lots of suspense, but that's not the only reason people read him.

more to The Shining than just a suspense story.

This list records many fragmentary ideas about Stephen King's *The Shining* and how one student set about writing about it. John has an idea but does not yet have a topic. He knows only that he has been strongly affected by the book, and he wants to write something about it. He goes on thinking about the book and making notes. He comes to recognize that what fascinates him about *The Shining* is King's talent for portraying horror. Then John makes another list.

Subject: Stephen King's Secret of Horror

the feeling of feeling threatened.

For a child the world is mysterious and sometimes frightening.

Parents are bigger than we are.

Most of the time they love us.

We love them, too.

But sometimes they get mad at us.

We know they can hurt us.

Some parents do hurt children.

Stephen King takes this natural love/fear relationship and turns it into a great story.

Jack Torrance, a man down on his luck, becomes caretaker to an old hotel in Colorado during the winter when the hotel is closed.

He takes his wife and son back there with him.

The boy Danny has a strange power.

The hotel has been owned by criminals.

As the months pass, the ghosts in the hotel take over Jack Torrance's soul.

He tries to kill his son, but the son is rescued by a black man named Dick Hallorann who also has the power, the shining, that allows him to communicate with Danny.

Many things in the world can hurt us, things very near and dear to us.

The Shining teaches us to keep on doing what we can, even when everything turns against us, even parents and friends.

That conclusion seems weak.

How do I think about horror and make it worthwhile?

Why do we read horror stories?

With the second list, John has explored ideas of horror in *The Shining*. He has defined a topic. Successive revisions of the list will eliminate some points, expand others, and add some that are not now on it. Writing a list of ideas prepares you to write the paper itself.

You can use the same process in planning a paper based on a written text instead of a personal experience or personal reaction. If your assignment is to analyze a short story, an essay, or some other text, read it through quickly. Then read it again and jot down ideas about it. Make connections. Let your mind rove freely. As you jot down your thoughts, your mind will generate other ideas, and you can write them down too.

Save *everything*: all your lists, your scribbled notes, your practice sentences. You may want to come back to them as you develop your topic. Only when your assignment has been completed and graded should you consider throwing anything away.

Reading: Learn About Your Topic

Good writing flows from knowledge. You must know something about a topic to write about it well. A paper that merely asserts uninformed opinions will rarely interest anybody—not even the person who writes it. We read to learn, and mere opinion is not interesting unless the person with the opinion is a widely recognized authority or famous. Otherwise we want to know the facts that made the writer form the opinions he or she has. Only then can we decide whether the opinions are worthwhile. Facts come from study: lots of study.

Of course, many interesting papers do not depend on research. Writing about a personal experience or a personal reaction may not require you to work in the library. But seeing how others have written about similar experiences or reactions may help you focus your ideas, and most topics will be much better if you do some general reading about them. Often reference books and magazine articles will suggest ideas you have not thought of. Several hours of browsing in the library and taking notes give many writers just the materials they need to develop a topic with confidence. You may also wish to interview people who know about your subject.

For example, if you decide to write about a novel by Stephen King, you will find abundant materials in the library: articles about King, interviews with him, reviews of his books, biographical blurbs. Your reference librarian will assist you in finding these articles, and they may help you shape your ideas. Be sure to keep track of your sources so you can give credit to these articles if you use them in any way.

Reading about and around your topic broadens your understanding and will give you facts you can draw on later.

Talking: Listen to What You and Others Have to Say

Talk to everyone you can about the topic. Talking about a subject is not just a good way to know what you are thinking and express it better; talking can actually be a process of discovery. Sometimes ideas and connections come out in conversation that you didn't know were there.

Talking is also a good way to uncover areas where you don't have enough information and to narrow your topic to something manageable. Your instructor may divide your composition class into small groups so that you can talk to others about the topic you're considering and hear about their topics.

Talk about your topic with your roommates, with friends over lunch, with the friends you jog with or with some of the people you work with. "I'm writing a paper on Stephen King's novel *The Shining*. Have you read it? I think he really understands some of the fears children have. What do you think?"

Of course the purpose of discussing your topic with others isn't simply to hear yourself talk. Listen to what your friends and colleagues have to say. Their questions will let you know where you haven't explained your ideas clearly, and their opinions will suggest new angles, fresh approaches, and reasonable cautions that can help you shape your topic.

Questioning: Ask the Journalist's Questions

To stimulate ideas, writers frequently ask themselves questions about a subject. One good way to organize questions is to think of the five *W*s of journalism. In writing a news story, reporters are taught to ask, and answer, *who, what, where, when,* and *why*.

To use the journalist's questions, identify your subject at the top of the page. Then, with ample space for your answers, write *who, what, where, when,* and *why*. Here are John's questions.

Subject: Stephen King's Secret of Horror

Who are the main characters?

Who exactly is the father, Jack Torrance?

Who exactly is Danny?

Who are the most important minor characters?

What happened in the hotel when Danny and his father and mother went there?

What are the supernatural elements in the story?

What happened to Jack Torrance?

What had Danny's father done before the story opens that lets us know he's a dangerous man?

Where does the story take place?

Where is Dick Hallorann when he gets Danny's call for help?

Where does the end of the story take place?

When does the story take place?

When did the criminal things in the hotel happen?

When does Danny recognize he had the power of "the shining"?

Why does the story scare us so much?

Why does Stephen King write about children so much?

Why does the evil in the hotel take possession of Danny's father?

Why does Danny say at the last that the man trying to kill him is not really his father?

If you ask as many versions as possible of the five *W*s, you begin to see how much you have to write about. You will not want to answer all the questions you ask. Not all of them will contribute to your essay as you develop your thesis. But as you ask questions, you will open mental doorways that will help you think of things to write.

Freewriting: Write Nonstop for Ten Minutes

Some writers discover that they can overcome writer's block if they make themselves sit down at a table—or a computer—and write without stopping for ten or fifteen minutes. If you suffer anxiety when you get ready to write a paper, try this technique, which is called **freewriting.**

Sit down and write anything that comes into your head about your subject. Write without trying to control the direction or the organization of your prose. Don't worry about spelling, grammar, or punctuation. Just write. Here is John Williams's freewriting:

King. Stephen King. I don't know what to write. What am I going to write about? Well, when I read Stephen King's stories, I feel a thrill of terror down my spine, and somehow I love it, but I don't think it's just an excuse to take an emotional bath. My English teachers don't always think that King is a serius writer, not like Hemingway or Falkner or Morison or Austin or all those people we read in the litrature textbooks and the anthologies. I like Stephen King, and my friends like him, and we read him when we don't read anything else sometimes, and ever once in a while I find out that one of my English teachers in schools reads Stephen King on the sly and likes him, too. Now why do we like to be scared out of our wits? And why does he scare us so much? When you think about it, there have been a lot of good writers who scared the wits out of the people at the time--Edger Allen Poe for one and even Nathaniel Hawthorn for another with his story about the man who had a garden of poisoned plants, and when the daughter raised in that garden tried to kiss somebody or get out of the garden, she was likely to die. And maybe there have been a lot more writers who tried to scare us and couldn't pull it off, which is what happens in a bad mystery or a bad horror story or some of the horror flicks that get so stupid that you laugh where you are supposed to scream. I think King scares us because he talks about the things that make little children afraid, and he remembers that when we grow up, we are still little children inside, and we still have our fears only now they are translated into a lot of fears that surround us in life that are a lot more real than the fears we had as kids. I'm afraid of failing this course or of not graduating from college or of not getting a job or of not being able to afford my car payment. Maybe all these things will turn out all right, but I don't know that now, and I'm scared. It's almost a happy thought to remember when I was afraid of the dark or thought that there might be a monster under my bed at night or in the closet or somewhere out there in the dark trying to get in the window. I've grown up, and I don't think much about those fears in my childhood anymore, but when I read Stephen King, they all come back, and I remember them, and it's almost like saying, Hey, you got through all those fears and made it to being an adult more or less, and so you are going to get over all these fears, too, and they are going to go the same way that those old fears of yours did. Still, Stephen King remembers that we don't get rid of all our fears, and we shouldn't because there are a lot of things in life to be afraid of even when we grow up, and he says I think that we ought to remember what it is to be afraid when we are children because life is scarry. But if we keep on and face our fears and make friends and try to be loyal to them, we will get through most of the things that scare us.

These sentences are a long way from being a finished essay. But ideas are beginning to flow. The writer is beginning to get thoughts in order.

Clustering: Draw a Subject Tree

As your ideas begin to take shape, begin **clustering** them—tying related ideas together. As you put ideas together you begin to expand them, to complicate them and make them more interesting, and to see connections that help you organize your paper.

You might cluster thoughts by listing or even outlining, but if it helps you to visualize connections, try drawing a subject tree like the one shown here for John Williams's ideas for a paper on Stephen King. The subject tree allows you to jot down ideas in a rough organization, with your general subject as the trunk from which more specific ideas branch out. As you can see, a subject tree produces a number of ideas that can be developed into a paper. Drawing a tree helps you identify possible topics in relation to a general subject. The subject tree breaks knowledge down into manageable chunks, and you can then put those chunks together. Many writers find that drawing a subject tree is a good way to tie related ideas together.

Subject Tree

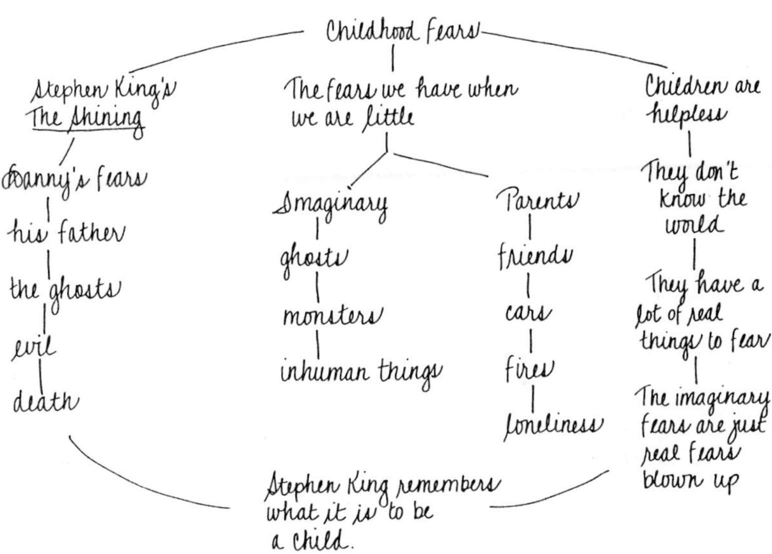

■ **Exercise 1.1** Use some of the prewriting techniques explained on the previous pages to explore three of these general subjects.

1. a book or article you have read recently
2. AIDS and morality
3. violence in the movies
4. gun control
5. attitudes toward the homeless
6. advertising of alcohol and tobacco
7. the work ethic during a recession
8. gender roles for children
9. feminism and multiculturalism

10. the pressures on college and professional athletes
11. sexual harassment on campus or in the workplace
12. free speech vs. politically correct speech
13. the responsibilities of citizenship in a democracy
14. religion and politics

1b
Limiting the Subject

The subjects of some papers you write in college will be assigned. In other cases you may be free to select your own subject. Sometimes you will know immediately what you want to write about. But more often writers find their topics by a slow, uneven process. Perhaps you may want to write about feminism and multiculturalism—how to reconcile a feminist viewpoint with an appreciation of the many different cultures that coexist in the United States and throughout the world. Hundreds of books and articles related to this general topic have appeared in the last five years alone. Where do you begin? You can't treat the topic in its entirety, and generalizations by themselves aren't interesting or convincing. Pick a specific place or time or incident, and start there.

The Persian Gulf War, for example, focused a great deal of attention on the Muslim view of women in their place in society. An interview with a thoughtful woman in a National Guard unit called to service during the war could focus the problem—an independent American woman in Saudi Arabia, where women are not allowed to drive cars—and be the basis of an excellent paper. Further reading might help you address more broadly the conflict between a feminist perspective and traditional societies. You might not be able to solve the problem, but you could explore the implications of the tension between respect for self and respect for others.

Limiting your subject not only makes it manageable; it sharpens your focus and makes it interesting as well. Checklist 1.2 suggests a series of steps that will help you trim and focus your subject. Even topics in the "still less broad" column my be further narrowed. Only you can decide how much to limit your subject. Your decision will depend, in part, on the sheer physical demands of the task: How many pages do you have to write? How long will that take you? How much time do you have? Also consider the limits the subject itself may impose: How much has been written about the subject already? What do I have to do to say that is new or different or mine alone? Can I learn enough about the subject to write about it well before my deadline?

✓ CHECKLIST 1.2: LIMITING A TOPIC

Too broad	gender roles for children	*The Shining*
	children depicted in movies	horror in *The Shining*
Still too broad	bravery on the part of little girls and boys in the movies	horror in *The Shining* comes from the familiar turned ugly
Less broad	Dorothy in *The Wizard of Oz* vs. Kevin McCallister in *Home Alone*. How are they alike? How are they different? Have gender roles for children changed in the past half century?	the natural love/fear between parent and child is universal and is the basis of the horror in *The Shining*
Still less broad		

As you limit your subject, you bring it more and more under control. Your mind will start generating ideas about it. As your focus becomes more specific, it will also get more penetrating. Record ideas as they come to you, and add them to your prewriting materials.

■ **Exercise 1.2** Using Checklist 1.2 as a model, limit, in a series of steps, two of the subjects you selected in Exercise 1.1.

1c Planning Your Approach

How will you present your topic to your reader? Writers use four long-established **modes** of writing and speaking: description, narration, exposition, and argument.

- *Description* tells how something looks or sounds or tastes or feels or smells.
- *Narration* tells a story, usually in chronological sequence.
- *Exposition* explains.
- *Argument* usually maintains a point of view against some opposition.

Most writing involves combinations of these modes. You rarely find a description that does not involve narration, a narration that does not have some description in it, or an exposition or argument that does not include the other two. Many essays use all four modes. It helps to know the modes so you can plan how you'll approach your subject.

Much college writing is expository because college papers usually explain texts, statistics, events, or observations. The line between an expository paper and an argumentative paper may be thin. You may explain your interpretation of a short story, for example, to prove that someone else's interpretation is incorrect. Then your exposition becomes an argument.

Checklist 1.3 shows how John Williams might plan his approach to his subject along four distinct lines. You can see how easy it is to move from one mode to another. You can also see that the final purpose of your paper will lead you to emphasize one of these modes above the others. A news story for your college paper may tell of the dean's decision to close the library on Friday night without telling how the dean looks when she makes the announcement and without arguing that the decision is right or wrong. But it may explain why the dean has made her decision, and it may tell the story of student reactions. If you write an editorial arguing that the library should remain open on Fridays, you may not use description or narrative at all, but you will probably use some exposition to set up your argument.

✓ CHECKLIST 1.3: APPROACHING THE TOPIC

Mode	Purpose
■ Description	To describe what I imagine the Overlook Hotel looks like- not Stephen King's word-for-word description, but the picture in my mind that he has created.
■ Narration	To tell the story of what happened to the Torrance family during that winter.
■ Exposition	To explain how an isolated house that looks like a dream-come-true turns into a nightmare.
■ Argument	To argue that Stephen King understands that the worst fears for children and adults are those threats that no one can understand.

■ **Exercise 1.3** Using Checklist 1.3 as a model, select one of the topics you used in Exercise 1.2 and jot down some thoughts about how you would approach it using each of the four models. If you would find it helpful, devote a short paragraph to each of these questions:

What do I want to describe?
What stories do I want to tell?
What do I need to explain?
What do I want to argue?

1d Considering the Audience

Who will read your writing? Don't think of your audience as only the teacher who will grade your paper. Write to interest others—your friends, other members of the class, relatives, other people you know. Try to write a paper for people you admire.

For some writing assignments, the audience is "built in." If you are preparing a résumé, for example, and writing a letter of application, your audience is a potential employer in your field. Keep that reader in mind as you write. You will want to sound polite, convincing, self-confident without being boastful. If, on the other hand, your assignment is to review a school play or a local production for submission to the school or local newspaper, you will want to sound knowledgeable and enthusiastic without being bubbly or discerning without being snobby.

For all types of assignment, you will need to consider the **discourse community**—people who share certain interests, knowledge, and expectations and who also share some customary ways of communicating with each other. Each of us belongs to several discourse communities. Baseball fans make up a discourse community. They talk and write about the game in familiar ways, and they understand each other, even if people outside the community don't know what the fans are talking about. Consider this sentence:

> Mickey Mantle switch-hit for the Yankees for eighteen seasons, compiling a .298 lifetime batting average and a phenomenal slugging average of .557.
>
> —Dick Curry

Every baseball fan would understand this sentence, but for someone outside the fans' discourse community, the sentence is gibberish. Now consider this statement from the discourse community that includes biologists:

> Endocytosis of liposomes occurs in a limited class of cells; those that are phagocytic, or able to ingest foreign particles. When phagocytic cells take up liposomes, the cells move the spheres into subcellular organelles known as lysomes, where the liposomal membranes are thought to be degraded.
>
> —MARC J. OSTRO

To a biologist, these sentences are clear; to people outside the discourse community of biology, they are gibberish—just like the baseball fan's language to the nonfan. Historians, specialists in literature, economics, philosophers, astronomers, model-railroad enthusiasts, pilots, engineers, surgeons, lovers of fishing, and thousands of other groups have their own discourse communities. In each of these communities, certain expectations about language control the way members communicate with each other. Think about your audience when you write. What do you have to explain to your readers? What do they know? You don't have to define *switch-hitter* to a baseball fan; you don't have to define *liposomes* to a biologist. But you should probably define both terms to someone outside those discourse communities.

In a college composition class, you usually assume that your audience includes the other members of the class and the instructor. What do they know about your subject? How much do you have to tell them? If you are working on a paper about *Hamlet* and everybody in the class has read the play or seen it, you waste time and space by summarizing the plot. But if you write about a novel or short story you know others have not read, a short plot summary might be in order. It might help to keep the journalist's questions in mind. When you introduce a new character, identify the person: "Margaret Fuller, the nineteenth-century New England writer"; "Richard Wright, author of *Native Son* and other books." As your essay unfolds, keep your readers informed about *who* is acting, *what* is happening, *where* the action is going on, *when,* and, if possible, *why.*

Think of your readers as good people whom you deeply respect, and you will get just that kind of reader for your work.

In some ways, you create your audience as you write. If you write sensibly, interestingly, clearly, and with occasional flashes of wit, you will win the audience that does most of the reading in America. If you try to be cute or show off or fill your pages with slang and private jokes, you aren't taking your readers seriously, and they won't take what you have to say seriously either—including your opinions. If you write with passionate emotion and uncompromising anger, your audience will be a small group of people whose passions rule the way they look at the world. If you write in a dull, plodding effort to fill pages and to avoid taking risks, you probably will not get any audience at all—except your instructor, who is paid to read your writing no matter how dull it is.

■ **Exercise 1.4** Explain in a brief paragraph how each audience listed below might influence the content, style, and language of John Williams's essay on Stephen King.

1. people your age who share a liking for Stephen King
2. people your age who do not share your opinion
3. a class of eighth graders
4. older people who dismiss horror stories as having no intellectual content at all
5. older people who argue that violence depicted in fiction and in the movies generates violence in real life

1e Choosing Supporting Evidence

Generalizations are boring. Assertions are convincing. When you make them, you must give evidence to back them up. You may have strong opinions, but unless you're a well-known authority no one will accept them just because they're yours. And even if you are an authority, you won't get away for very long with telling people what they ought to think without giving them the reasons why.

Explain yourself. Provide evidence. If your instructor writes "Be specific" in the margin of a paper, she is probably asking you to give some details to support the generalization you have made. If you say "Using a computer has made writing easier for me," you have not explained anything. But if you say this, you are using details to support your generalization:

```
My computer has made writing easier for me because it has reduced the
physical strain of writing. I can insert and delete without having to type
the whole essay over again. I can move sentences and paragraphs around in
my work so that it all fits together better. I can revise on the screen,
and I can correct my errors. The computer also has a spell checker so that
I can avoid misspellings. And the automatic formatting means that I do not
have to be careful about margins; the computer does all that for me, and my
work comes out looking clean and neat and authoritative. I can also keep
copies of all the versions of my work.
```

If you say, "The comic strip 'Calvin and Hobbes' is interesting," you have not persuaded anybody to read it. But if you explain how the strip shows a little boy's imagination working with a stuffed animal that comes to life when no one else is present, you may interest your reader enough to open the newspaper to the comics and read the strip.

Kinds of Evidence

There are several kinds of evidence you can use to support your generalizations and assertions:

- *Personal observation and experience:* These include details that appeal to the senses—actions, colors, sights, sounds, smells, tastes—and stories from your own life. These help readers bring their memories to you and give credibility to your beliefs.
- *Authorities:* These include quotations, paraphrases, summaries, and descriptions from books, magazines, radio, television, films, or interviews. They support your arguments by presenting the opinions of experts.
- *Statistics and cases:* These include information not easily challenged. They lend weight to your assertions.

These kinds of evidence do not exclude one another. A paper that uses statistics or quotes authorities may also use images to call forth concrete sensory responses. A recent newspaper article explaining that the U.S. debt was approaching $1 trillion included these graphic details: $1 trillion is enough dollar bills to give one to every ant in the United States or, placed end to end, to reach the star Alpha Centuri, more than five light-years from earth. By converting numbers into something we can see or imagine, we make the meaning of the numbers more vivid.

When you consider your subject and your audience, think about the evidence that will best suit your purpose. Ask yourself how you will gather the evidence you need. For most papers, questions like those in Checklist 1.4 will be helpful.

✓ CHECKLIST 1.4: FINDING EVIDENCE

- What experiences in my own life will help me make this topic interesting?
- What have I read recently—or what can I read before I write—that will help me develop or support my topic?
- What have I heard on the radio or seen on television or in the movies that will help me develop or support my topic?
- What have I learned in recent conversations with friends, parents, relatives, teachers, and others that will help me develop or support my topic?

- What reference materials are likely to include the facts I need?
- What do people in my audience know about my topic? What will interest them? What will bore them? What may even surprise them?

■ **Exercise 1.5** Go back to the topic you used in Exercise 1.3. Write a paragraph describing your intended audience and suggesting some types and sources of evidence you might use.

1f
Writing a Thesis Statement

Define your main idea, or **thesis**—the essential thing you want to say about your subject—before you sit down to write your paper. You do not have to put a thesis statement in every paper. It would be awkward to write, "The thesis of this paper is that the threat that Jack Torrance is to his son is much like the threat that many parents are to their children." But you should be able to write out a thesis statement that summarizes the point you want to make in your paper.

As you write and revise, you may change your mind about your thesis. Writers often start a paper and discover that their original thesis is not exactly what they want to say. Listen to the proddings of your mind, and when they become insistent, change your thesis. Revision and refinement are essential to the writing process.

All the same, you will save yourself much time, and you will write much more to the point, if you formulate a main idea before you begin your first draft. You may change it slightly or transform it into something altogether different later on. But you may very well keep the same main idea from first draft to final copy. Having a thesis focuses the mind and helps you control the sentences and paragraphs that make up your composition.

Once you have narrowed the focus of your topic, construct a **thesis statement**—one sentence or more that tells your readers what they will be reading. The thesis statement also establishes the tone of the essay and tells readers why they should read your work. It lets them know what to expect and helps them decide whether to read on. It may show your position on the subject as well. The following limited topics at the left led writers to produce the thesis statements at the right.

Limited topic	Possible thesis statement
Surprise endings in fiction	The good surprise ending, as in William Faulkner's short story, "A Rose for Emily," makes us feel that we should have expected it, for in subtle ways the writer prepares us for it throughout the story.
The morals of lyrics in video and rock music—reality and fantasy	The lyrics in rock music, including the music that we see on videos, are often filled with references to sex that may seem vulgar and obscene, but they also often express a longing for enduring love and loyalty in a world where young people know that most love affairs and half the marriages do not last very long.
Special effects in movies and what they do to our feelings about reality	Special effects in movies do such a good job of making us believe the unbelievable for a couple of hours that our whole conception of reality has changed, so that we expect special effects in everything—including the classroom.
The fears of childhood in Stephen King's *The Shining*	Stephen King's novel *The Shining* is a modern parable of the fears of childhood and the fantasies that children manufacture to get over those fears—which are often real.

■ **Exercise 1.6** Return again to the topic you used in Exercise 1.3. Write a broad phrase that covers the subject, then write a thesis statement.

1g Organizing Ideas

With your thesis statement before you as your controlling idea, begin organizing your supporting ideas. As you write your thesis statement, you will probably think of more ideas related to your topic and ways to expand ideas you have already recorded. Don't hesitate to add these new ideas to your prewriting notes. At this time, review all those notes. Select the ideas that are relevant, and cluster them. Think of how to fit your thoughts into a coherent essay. What do you have to put first so that readers can understand what comes later on? Which ideas belong together? If you cluster ideas before you write, you improve the chances of producing a clear essay that moves confidently from point to point from beginning to end.

You can do this clustering in many ways—by cutting and pasting, by drawing lines and arrows from one point to a related one, or by identifying ideas that belong together with a letter or a symbol in the margin. Some writers look at the lists or jottings produced in prewriting and recopy them into groups of connected thoughts. Some writers draw another subject tree. This time, however, the ideas need to be put in some sequence or hierarchy. If you do this cutting and pasting on a computer, make a backup copy before you start. You may change your mind and want to return to your first arrangement.

Arranging Information

Different topics and different purposes call for different kinds of organization. You can present your ideas in several different ways. Here are some common principles of organization:

- A *chronological arrangement* relates events as they happened in time. The first event is the first one you treat in your essay, and the last event comes at the end of your paper. Accounts of personal experiences and overviews of historical events are often arranged chronologically.
- A *spatial arrangement* presents ideas in the order of their physical relationship to one another. Choose a logical starting point and move through space systematically. A description of a painting in a university museum or in a local art gallery might begin with the central focus and then move outward to the edges of the canvas, up, down, right, and left.
- A *deductive arrangement* moves from the general to the specific. An essay examining surprise endings in fiction might begin with the generalization that such endings are best when they sneak up on us and go on to cite examples of stories in which, on reflection, we find that the endings were inevitable but we were kept from being able to predict them by the skill of their authors (see also 35c).
- An *inductive arrangement* moves from the specific to the general. John Williams's essay on childhood fears in *The Shining* might begin by citing examples of Danny's fears, move to similar examples from John's own childhood, and conclude that King has written a modern fable of childhood fears and fantasies (see also 35b).
- An arrangement by *order of importance* assigns a hierarchy to ideas. An argument for term limits for members of Congress might present five reasons, moving from the trivial to the profound. Most

deductive and inductive essays also present ideas in descending or ascending order of importance, respectively. An essay on the morals of rock music might begin by quoting some lyrics and acknowledging that many are raw and sexual and imply a lack of commitment, then quote other lyrics to show a fear of loneliness and a desire for love that lasts longer than a night, and finally conclude that the lyrics of rock music express the desire for love that many young people do not see in their parents. To make a cumulative argument like this, you must decide which ideas are more important than others and choose the order that fits your subject and your thesis.

Creating a Rough Outline

When you arrange your ideas, when you put them in sequence, you have created a rough outline. This outline is an informal list, a private convenience for you. It does not need to follow a prescribed form but should be detailed enough to help you see the shape and direction of your paper. It will also help you decide what you have to say and how to say it. It will raise helpful questions about limitations. Checklist 1.5 shows the elements that should be included in your outline.

From prewriting notes, John Williams prepared this rough outline:

Thesis statement: Stephen King's The Shining illustrates the frightening fantasies many children have in a world where they are helpless and the fantasies that help them get through their fears.

Introduction: Start with my fears at sleeping alone in the upstairs back bedroom of our house when I was a little child and my fantasies of having Spider Man as a big brother to protect me.

1. Summarize briefly Stephen King's novel The Shining. How pleasant the prospect of a winter with a mother and father in an old hotel in Colorado, all alone, all they could eat, a great old house to roam through.
2. How King's child character Danny has fantasies about an imaginary friend Tony, but how he also has psychic powers, and in the end a sort of big brother character comes to rescue him from the evil that has overwhelmed the hotel.
3. The story makes most people remember childhood fantasies--helplessness before a world that children do not know very well and cannot control, a world that seems mysterious. Fantasies of having a

friend who will help even against your parents when they become threatening.

4. In a lot of ways, Stephen King's novel is like the comic strip "Calvin and Hobbes," where the mean little kid Calvin has a stuffed tiger named Hobbes who becomes a real tiger when nobody else is around. The tiger is the older friend who takes care of a little boy.
5. When we grow up, we still live in a world that can be a scary place. But we don't have imaginary friends to take care of us. We make up other things to imagine--organizations, sports, fame, whatever. And we expect these things to take care of us.
6. Life may not be a mystery of the sort that Stephen King gives us in The Shining, but it is a mystery of its own kind, and a lot of times we feel helpless when we face parts of it. I wish I had a big brother or sister right now to give me advice about this paper.

Conclusion: Stephen King is a serious writer who uses a different kind of story to say serious things.

✔ CHECKLIST 1.5: MAKING A ROUGH OUTLINE

A rough outline should include

- thesis statement
- introduction or opening
- ideas or main points, in numbered sequence
- conclusion

You might prefer to write up a fully developed, formal outline (discussed in 34b). But a rough outline, a list of points you want to cover, is usually enough. As you write the first draft of your paper, you may change your rough outline around and include some new ideas. But even if you don't follow your original plan exactly, the outline is a first stab at unity and coherence. A paper has *unity* if all the ideas support the thesis. A paper has *coherence* if each thought flows logically into the next, allowing readers to see the connections.

Reviewing the Rough Outline

Reviewing his rough outline, John recognized that he was not going to be able to tell a simple story in chronological order. He had several points to make within the framework of an essay that takes Stephen King's novel *The Shining* very seriously, and somehow he must wrap these points around his thesis—that King is writing about life in such a way that most of us can recognize our own fears and fantasies in his work.

John can see several difficulties. He does not want to be preachy, and he does not want to make anyone think that the main reason we read a novel is to take lessons from it. He has read *The Shining* and enjoyed it, and he sees some serious ideas in it. Approaching those ideas will take some hard thinking about organization and tone.

You will find reviewing your rough outline similarly profitable. It will save you time later on. Sometimes you may write several drafts of the rough outline—just as you may write several drafts of the paper itself. Each outline and each draft allows you not only to think more about your sentences and your style, your audience and your evidence, but also to think more about the subject and to reconsider your earlier ideas about it. As you work through drafts, your mind becomes a lens that takes a sharper and sharper focus on what it is seeing so that finally you are clear about what you are writing and where you want your paper to go.

■ **Exercise 1.7** Make a rough outline for an essay on the subject you selected for Exercise 1.6. Repeat the thesis statement, then write a series of statements that support your thesis. Exchange outlines with someone in your class. When you have read each other's outlines, discuss them using Checklist 1.6 to guide your comments.

✓ CHECKLIST 1.6: GETTING READY TO WRITE

- Is the thesis clear enough and limited enough to make for a good paper?
- Does every entry in the outline relate to or support the thesis statement?
- Is the introduction interesting enough to make you want to read on?
- Is the conclusion satisfying, and does it follow logically from the points that have been made?

CHAPTER

2

WRITING AND REVISING A PAPER

This chapter will take you through the steps involved in producing successive drafts of a paper and the final copy. Follow the steps carefully. John Williams's essay on *The Shining* is again used as an example to help you understand what you are doing in drafting your own composition.

2a Preparing the First Draft

With the benefits of your prewriting and your rough (or formal) outline at hand, you can start writing. Don't try to make your first draft perfect. Don't worry about errors of facts, questionable spellings, or awkward constructions. Write your first draft as fast as you can. Concentrate on producing a flow of ideas. Once you have written a draft, you can correct your errors, smooth out the rough places, and shape the whole into a pleasing design.

Don't worry about a title now. If you think of one, fine. If not, come up with your title later on. Don't even labor over your opening at this point. Just get started. A good way to start your essay may occur to you as you write. Here is the first draft of John Williams's essay. The comments in the margins were written in peer review by another student in the class.

When I was a little boy, I slept in an upstairs room with my older brother Fred. Our house was on the edge of the town where we lived, beyond our house were fields ^ woods, and at night it was quiet as the grave. Fred was ten years older than I was. He worked six hours a day in the local Burger-King and

and

went to night school at the community college near our house. My parents made me go to bed before he came home.

So I went to bed with the lights out. Alone in a room upstairs that seemed huge. I listened to the house creak and pop like old wooden houses do in the night when it gets cool, and I was afraid. There's this scene in the comic strip "Calvin and Hobbes" where Calvin imagines the monsters coming out from under his bed, and I can understand it because I could imagine gangstters under my bed hiding from the police and having guns, and when I turned the light out, I thought they would come out and kill me. Our house was a hundred years old. I don't know how many people owned it before we bought it. Especially I thought about the guy who built the house, you know, the person who owned it first a hundred years ago and thought that since he had designed it and built it or had it built, it was his forever. You know what the three bears said about Goldilocks. "Whose been sleeping in my bed?" And I thought of ghosts really mad at me and saying, "Who's been sleeping in my room."

So I used to lie up there and turn up another fantasy, that Spider Man was my friend, maybe even my older brother, and he was standing guard over me in the dark and that when gangsters came out from under the bed or out of the closet, Spider Man would wrap them all upin his web stuff that he carries around with him all the time, and they would be absolutely helpless, and the police would haul them off to jail, and I would definitely be a hero.

I thought of all that in reading The Shining by Stephen King. It's a story about a father named Jack, a mother named Wendy, and a boy named Danny. Jack is a writer, a former drunk, out of a job. At some point in the past he has abused Danny. Probably when he was drunk, and he has lost his teaching job because he has a terrible temper. Anyway, he gets a job looking after a big old hotel in Colorado through the winter when the place would be snowed in and just needs somebody there to take care of it. The whole family would be cut off from the rest of the world when the first big snow comes.

sentence fragment?

Is there just one scene? Do you need this?

spelling?

I like all this. But I'm not sure what you are writing about? When are you going to get to the point?

Now I see what you are doing. Why not put the Stephen King part first so we will have your thesis right away?

sentence fragment?

In one way, the story looks like the American dream, a family with everything they want, bound together for months when they have to depend on each other. They have to eat all their meals together and talk to each other, and you'd think it'd be just great.

This is good.

But the old hotel is filled with ghosts of the evil deeds that have gone on there in the past when it was owned by criminals and used for all sorts of evil purposes, including murder. Danny has a kind of power called the "shining", and he can see things other people can't. He sees the ghosts. And then jack begins to see them, too. All the evil ghosts living in the house, haunting it, and they try to possess both Danny and Jack. In the end Jack goes crazy--or else he is possessed by the ghosts. But Danny resists because he is innocent, and Jack comes after him and tries to kill him.

Comma should go inside quotation marks.

Danny uses the shining to send a call for help through space to a friend. A cook he has met at the beginning of the book named Dick Hallorann who also has the shining. Hallorann throws down everything to come across the country to rescue Danny and saves Wendy, but Jack dies, and the hotel burns up.

sentence fragment?

Stephen King has taken these childhood fantasies and made a really good story about them. Only in his book these fantasies are real, and the house truely is haunted. Danny has his own superhero, Dick Hallorann, to help him, a kind of big brother the way I made Spider Man my big brother when I was a child and afraid. But of course we know the book is <u>not</u> real. It is a story, a novel. We know Stephen King has made it all up.

spelling?

But we also know he is making it all up from something we know--fantasies. We meet ourselves and our fears in <u>The Shining</u>. And yes, most of us when we are children both love our parents and fear them at the same time. Stephen King has picked up that idea, too. What happens to us if the people who are supposed to protect us, suddenly start trying to kill us. In real life, children really do suffer abuse from their parents sometimes. Sometimes parents even kill them.

I would put the Stephen King part first, and I would expand this part.

Stephen King is dealing with all these ideas. It is a very powerful story, and Stephen King is a serious novelist.

Your conclusion seems to fall off. I would expand it.

You probably noticed lots of errors in this first draft: many ideas are rambling and unclear, and some sentences are shaky. Remember that John concentrated on recording his thoughts and did not worry about being correct. He got his ideas down on paper and can fix his errors later.

■ **Exercise 2.1** Revise John's paper. You may not have read *The Shining,* but by now you know enough about it to follow John's argument. Correct any errors you see, smoothing out sentences, eliminating unnecessary words and phrases, and perhaps adding thoughts of your own.

2b
Revising the Draft

After you complete the first draft of a paper, take a long break. Put some time and distance between you and your essay, and clear your mind. Your mind has a powerful ability to work when you don't realize it's working. When you're incubating an idea, your mind is working whether you realize it or not.

You will also find it helpful to do what John has done with his first draft. He has given it to someone else for **peer review,** a reading for comments and suggestions for revision by friends or classmates. John, likewise, has read and commented on the first draft of the person who read his paper. Your instructor may divide your class into writing groups for this purpose. If you aren't in a class-assigned writing group, consider starting one with a few friends. You'll find their serious attention to your writing extremely helpful.

In your writing group, ask for comments and corrections of the kind your instructor would make. Keep your criticism constructive and to the point. Don't simply ask, "What do you think of my paper?" Your reader will almost always say, "I like it." Ask, rather, "What do you think I'm trying to say?" As your reader tells you what he or she reads in your text, you may discover that you have not made your purposes clear. Once you and a friendly reader have agreed that the most important issue is what you want to say, you can talk about the paper in such a way that you learn from the discussion. Talking is an excellent way to think. Checklist 2.1 will help guide peer comments and discussion.

✓ CHECKLIST 2.1: PEER REVIEW GUIDELINES

- Put comments as they occur to you in the margins.
- List three things you really like about the essay—what are its strengths?
- List three things in the essay that need improvement—say what's wrong *and* suggest how the problem might be fixed.

When you return to your draft, reread it carefully several times. Study the comments made by others during peer review. Be prepared to change the content, the words, the sentence structure, the organization, and even the thesis of your essay. After talking your paper over with your writing group, you may have decided to go off in an entirely different direction. As you revise, you'll cut some things out and add others. You'll change some words, and substitute more precise language for generalities and clichés. You may want to shift sentences from one place to another or shorten or combine them. If you have a title already, look at it carefully to be sure it fits your topic and the readers you want for your essay. At this point, work on your opening and introduction to make sure they, too, engage your readers and point them in the right direction.

Revised drafts can get messy. Whenever your draft gets too messy to read easily, prepare a new draft. If you use a computer, you can mark up your printed copy, make the changes in your computer file, and print out a new copy—which you may mark up again. Most writers need to write at least two drafts of anything they compose. Professional writers and good student writers nearly always do more. In revising, be as clear as you can. Be sure every sentence makes a clear statement. Some sentences, hastily written in a first draft, will require radical surgery. Try to anticipate the clarifications your readers will need and clarify before they have to ask. Finally, check your draft for errors in spelling, punctuation, and grammar. Make sure each sentence ends with a period or a question mark. (Don't overuse the exclamation point! It can become tedious!) Look for troublesome forms of verbs, vague pronoun references, misplaced modification, or any other kind of error that may distract a reader from what you have to say. Checklist 2.2 outlines things to consider as you revise. When you have produced a readable draft, show it again to a friend or your writing group. Now read your draft aloud to yourself. As you hear what you've written, awkward sentence structures and even errors in grammar will jump out at you, and often improvements simply flow.

✓ CHECKLIST 2.2: REVISING DRAFTS

Revising ideas

- Is the thesis clear? (1f)
- Does the paper speak consistently to an audience? (1d)
- Are there enough details, enough facts, to support your major points? (1e)
- Does the paper show unity? Does it stay on track? Do all the ideas relate clearly to each other? (1g)
- Is the paper coherent? Are the internal transitions from point to point clear? (1g)
- Is the language of the paper precise? (3c, 9c, Chapter 13) Should any general words be made more specific?

Revising organization and structure

- Do the opening and the introduction capture and hold the reader's interest?
- Does the conclusion complete the ideas established and supported in the paper? (3d)
- Do the first and the last paragraphs in the paper somehow reflect one another? Are some words or ideas mentioned in the introduction mentioned again in the conclusion?
- Does the title engage the reader's attention?

Revising sentences and words

- Are periods and other end marks used to set off sentences?
- Have run-on sentences been separated by end marks or combined with connecting words and suitable punctuation? (Chapter 13)
- Have sentence fragments been connected to other sentences by adding subjects, verbs, or both? (14a)
- Are parallel ideas expressed in parallel forms? (Chapter 6)
- Have needless shifts in tone or point of view been corrected? (Chapter 20)
- Do modifiers stand near enough to the words they describe to avoid ambiguity?
- Do subordinate sections relate correctly to main clauses? (6b)
- Does each sentence state its information clearly?
- Is there variety in sentence structure?
- When read aloud, does every sentence sound right?

Verbs and other words

- Do subjects and verbs agree? (Chapter 15)
- Are verb tenses correctly formed and consistent? (16a–b)
- Have unnecessary shifts in tense, mood, voice, number, or emphasis been corrected? (Chapter 20)
- Are the pronoun references clear? (Chapter 17)
- Have all unnecessary words been eliminated?

Punctuation and mechanics

- Are punctuation marks used correctly to make meaning clear?
- Are apostrophes placed to show possession or contraction? (Chapter 24)
- Are quotation marks used in pairs to set off someone's exact words? (25a)
- Do italics, numbers, and symbols follow conventional uses? (Chapters 29, 30)
- Do capital letters follow the conventions of American English? (Chapter 28) Is the title correctly capitalized and punctuated?
- Have troublesome words been checked in a dictionary or with your computer's spell checker for accurate spelling? (Chapter 27)

John reconsidered his first draft (pages 27–29) carefully. His peer reviewers helped him find errors in grammar and spelling and some confused diction. But he realized that correcting these errors was not the major task he faced. He had to reshape the thoughts in his first draft into a coherent essay. That took some careful revising.

He also had to think about his audience. Who would read this paper? How could he make the paper appeal to people who did not know him and who did not think that horror stories were worth writing about or reading? What was his thesis?

He went back to his rough outline and studied it, then went back even further to his freewriting. This retracing of his steps showed him how far he had come and gave him confidence to continue. It also gave him a better sense of what he wanted to say and how he needed to shape his essay. The comments made by a fellow student during a peer review helped focus John's attention on some essential issues.

John worked through his first draft carefully, willing to make drastic revisions. Here's his readable revision. This is the second draft, which his instructor said she would read and comment on. The comments in the margin are hers.

2b
dev

Stephen King in <u>The Shining</u> has written a novel about childhood fears that may seem fantastic but that have a reality in the modern world that we all know, either personally or by reading the newspapers and seeing the television news. This is not a novel to be dismissed as a horror story filled with cheap thrills. This is a novel to make us think about life as it is in the world.

Opening sentence includes essential information but is awkward, wordy

A lot about the novel seems fantastic. Because it deals with the supernatural. Jack Torrance is a bad-tempered writer, not very successful, who has lost his teaching job because he got into trouble. Now he gets a chance to be the guardian of an old resort hotel in the mountains of Colorado, the Overlook, for a winter when the place is shut in by snow.

sentence fragment

Rewrite this sentence to make it smoother

Torrance takes with him his wife Wendy and his little son Danny. Earlier, during a drunken rage, he broke Danny's arm. But that was a while ago. Now the three of them are going to be alone in the hotel all winter long.

In some ways it looks like the American dream--a big house, all the food they can eat, lots of room and lots of time to do whatever they want, time to be together and enjoy each other, and time for Jack to finish writing a play he is working on. But the American dream exists in fiction to be torn apart.

transition

Danny has a supernatural gift, a kind of second sight, that allows him to read minds. When he and his parents arrive at the Overlook as the hotel is getting ready to close down for the winter. He meets a black cook named Dick Hallorann who also has this gift. Hallorann is on his way to Florida to spend the winter, but he will become essential to the story.

fragment

Ok, I see-- do you want to give this away at this point in your essay?

Part of the story is, of course, that the hotel is haunted, it has been owned by criminals, and it has been the scene of every kind of evil from sexual orgies to murders. As the snows come, and Wendy, Danny, and Jack are shut away from the world, the ghosts try to posess both Danny and Jack. Jack, with his weak character, falls victim to them, but Danny in his inocence does not. In one of the most scarriest scenes in the book, Jack is tracking Danny through the hotel to kill him.

spelling

tense shift

spelling spelling

Danny, however, sends a mental message to Dick Hallorann, begging for help. And Hallorann comes all the way across country, rents a snowmobile, gets to the Overlook just in time to save Danny. The hotel burns. Jack dies. Wendy and Danny escape.

I recognize a lot of my own childhood fantasies here. I suppose other readers do the same. When I was a little boy I had to go to bed in an upstairs room of our big house all alone. I used to imagine monsters under the bed or murderers in the closet waiting until I turned out the light before they did something terrible to me.

It was scarry, but I fought the fear by pretending that Spider Man was my big brother and that he was there in the room with me and that he would protect me from anything. I would whisper, "Goodnight Spider Man," and I would go to sleep, leaving him to protect me.

spelling

Dick Hallorann is to Danny like Spider Man was to me or like Hobbes is to Calvin--a big brother who will do anything for Danny, who loves him, protects him, and talks to him. Stephen King has taken our fantasies and made them work for him and for us in the novel.

Children live amid lots of fears. When we are very small, we even fear our parents. They are a lot bigger than we are. They know a lot more than we do. Sometimes they get mad at us. And we know they can hurt us. Yet they love us, and we love them.

Most children, I hope, grow up to realize that the love is much more important than the fear, and when we are grown, we think back on the good things our parents have done for us rather than linger over the bad. A lot of the bad turns out to be fantasy, we imagined some evil there when our parents were trying to do us good.

sense?

But wait a minute! It isn't all fantasy. Some parents abuse their children and even kill them. And in countries at war, children may be killed by bombs and guns. Even in many of our big cities, innocent children get caught in the crossfire of gang wars and are shot down dead just because they happened to be in the wrong place at the wrong time.

Where is this detail going?

2b dev

You can even say that some of these children are killed by ghosts from the past. A father may abuse his children because he was abused by his own father when he was a child. That's what seemed to happen to Jack Torrance in the novel. He carries the ghost of memory in his head and in his impulses.

good conclusion - makes connections

So when you think about Stephen King's The Shining, and when you read it and feel scared, you may be reading a parable about human life and history. That's why I think Stephen King is so powerful. And that's why I think he can be so scarry. He thinks up stories that, when we think about them, go right down to the heart of the way human beings are. It looks like fantasy when we read it, but it holds onto us because we know deep inside that he is writing about truth.

spelling; avoid repeating word think.

This is a nice essay on Stephen King that makes me take him seriously as a novelist. You have done a good job relating the book to life. I think you may spend a little too much time on plot summary. See if you can reduce this section.

I've marked some sentences that you might rewrite to make more clear, and I've marked some places where you repeat words unnecessarily. You make several comma faults in this paper. This is an error that you can easily correct. See 14a in the McGraw-Hill Handbook.

■ **Exercise 2.2** Study the second draft of John's paper and 2e. Compare your revision of his first draft (Exercise 2.1). List three ways his second draft is better than yours. List three ways yours is better.

■ **Exercise 2.3** Divide your class into small groups and compare John's second draft with his first draft. Where has he revised sentences? Where has he changed paragraphs around? Where has he expanded information? What has he cut out? Why do you think he made each of the changes he made? Do you approve of all the changes? Why?

2c
Proofreading

Both before and after you prepare your final copy, comb your essay for mechanical mistakes and correct them. This step is called **proofreading.** Proofreading requires careful examination of each line of text. Proofread your first draft before you rewrite it into your second draft, proofread the second draft, and proofread the final copy before you submit it. Hold a ruler or a blank sheet of paper beneath the line you are studying. Examine each sentence for missing words and punctuation. Check each word for missing or incorrect letters. Proofreading a paper by reading backward from the last sentence to the first is another good technique. It makes you see each letter and each word and each punctuation mark independently of the context. Some writers touch the point of a pencil to each syllable to help them read more slowly. Again, it is always a good idea to read your work slowly aloud to yourself.

2d
Preparing the Final Copy

Remember that your instructor must grade many papers, and remain alert and careful through them all. Messy papers make life hard for the busy instructor—just as a poorly printed article, filled with typographical errors, makes life hard for any reader. Sometimes you will find a mistake in a paper just as you are ready to hand it in. Always correct the mistake, but do so as neatly as you can. If you proofread carefully before you are ready to hand in your finished draft, you can avoid messing up your paper with lots of handwritten corrections, especially if you write with a computer. See Checklist 2.3 for some general guidelines.

✔ CHECKLIST 2.3: STANDARD ESSAY PRESENTATION

Format

- Use one side of each page.
- Number pages consecutively, starting with page 2 of your composition. The first page is not numbered but is considered page 1 nonetheless. (Do not count the cover page or, if you submit one, the outline page.)
- Use arabic numbers in the upper right-hand corner or centered at the top of each page. Be consistent in whatever form of pagination you use.

- Leave margins of $1\frac{1}{4}$ or $1\frac{1}{2}$ inches at the top, sides, and bottom of each page. On typewriters, a left margin at 10 and a right margin set at 70 are usually acceptable. On word processors, turn justification off for a "ragged right" margin and better word spacing.

Title

- Center the title on the first page, $1\frac{1}{2}$ inches below the top margin, or on the first line for handwritten copies.
- Leave one line of space below the title.
- Capitalize the first letter of all major words (nouns, pronouns, verbs, adjectives, adverbs) in the title, including the first and last words, no matter what part of speech they are, e.g.:

```
Choosing the Right Running Shoes
```

- Capitalize the first letter of prepositions of five or more letters, e.g.:

```
Going Against the Current: Life on a Houseboat
```

- Do not place a period at the end of the title or underline the title or enclose it in quotation marks. (The title of a book, an article, or a poem that appears within your title does need correct punctuation. See 28c and 33a.)
- If you use a cover page, repeat the title at the top of the first text page of your essay.

Cover page

- The cover page usually includes your name, your course name and number, the submission date, and the instructor's name. But your instructor may have different requirements.

Typed and word-processed papers

- Use $8\frac{1}{2} \times 11$ unlined white bond paper, not onionskin and not paper treated to allow corrections with pencil erasers, which smudges easily and often becomes unreadable. If you use a computer printer with tractor-fed continuous-form paper, tear off the perforated strip on each side of the paper and separate each page.
- Use *only* black ribbon; if the type looks faded, change the ribbon. Instructors have a hard time reading an almost illegible paper typed with an exhausted ribbon. Be kind to your instructor.
- Double-space between lines; indent paragraphs five spaces.
- After periods, question marks, exclamation points, and colons, use two spaces; after commas and semicolons, use one space.
- Do not use a space before or after a hyphen. To type a dash, use two consecutive hyphens (--) without any spacing between the dash and the words on each side.

```
Dashes--as in this example--set off thoughts for emphasis.
```

- If you use a typewriter, make corrections with a typewriter eraser, a correcting tape on the typewriter, or a correction fluid. Do not strike over incorrect letters. For errors discovered after you have removed your pages from your typewriter or printer, make corrections in pen with blue or black ink, or do the pages over.
- If you use a computer, be sure you have not left in words you intended to delete or deleted words you meant to leave in.
- If you use a typewriter, be sure the type is clean and the letters clear.
- If you use a computer and a dot matrix printer, try to use a printer or typeface that has true descenders. That is, the tails on the letters *g, j, p, g,* and *y* should come down below the baseline for the rest of the type. (See Appendix B.)

Handwritten papers

- Use $8\frac{1}{2} \times 11$ paper with lines spaced about $\frac{3}{8}$ inch apart. For a clear layout, skip every other line.
- Use blue or black ink; write on one side only.
- Indent the first line of every paragraph about one inch.
- Make occasional corrections with an ink eraser or correction fluid, or draw a neat line through words you want to delete. Write in the new words above the deletions, using skipped lines and marginal space for additions. If there are more than a few corrections, write the page over again.
- Make your handwriting readable. Like it or not, willingly or not, your instructor will be profoundly influenced by your handwriting. Don't let good thoughts be condemned for bad script. Use a firm, clear period at the end of each sentence, and leave space before the next sentence. Dot *i*s and *t*s directly above the letter. Avoid loops and curlicues, especially when you make capital letters. Make sure readers can distinguish between the *r* and the *n*, the *v* and the *u*, the *u* and the *n*, the *o* and the *a*, the *l* and the *t*, and the *e* and the *i*. Be careful to round off the *h* so it does not look like an *l* followed by an *i*. Be sure to make the letters *m* and *n* so that they do not look like the letter *u* standing alone or combined with another letter.

■ **Exercise 2.4** Write an essay describing a personal experience or a personal reaction to something you have read recently. As you go through all the steps involved in writing, save the materials listed below. Put them in a large envelope and submit them to your instructor with the final copy.

1. prewriting notes
2. a limited topic for the paper
3. a description of the audience for your paper
4. a list of your supporting evidence

5. a thesis statement
6. an outline, if your instructor requires it (See 36b)
7. a first draft
8. a second draft and any subsequent drafts
9. a final copy

2e
Making Further Revisions and Corrections

When your instructor returns your paper, read it carefully. Study the summary remarks that describe the strengths and weaknesses of your work. Examine the marginal notations, and be prepared to make revisions on the basis of the commentary you find there. You can learn to prevent errors next time around by correcting your mistakes and by responding to suggestions about style, organization, and content.

Revision toward perfection is the essence of the writing process. Some instructors build stages for revision into their course structures. They may, for example, make it a practice to read and comment on second drafts of student essays, grading only the third and final copy. Other instructors require students to revise essays after they've been graded and to submit them a second time. The point is that you learn from doing—from actually revising—rather than simply reading the instructor's comments. Even if your instructor does not require revisions, revise and correct your papers on your own. You'll be amazed at what you learn in the process, and you probably won't make the same mistakes again. See Checklist 2.4 for guidance.

✓ CHECKLIST 2.4: CORRECTING EVALUATED PAPERS

- Follow your instructor's guidelines for revisions. Some instructors read drafts and make comments *before* the paper goes into final form. Others encourage full rewriting based on comments written on final drafts. Be sure to correct errors before you do complete revisions of graded papers.
- Learn the symbol and comment system your instructor uses.
- Make all corrections in pencil or a different color ink so that you and your instructor can see what you have done.
- As you make corrections, draw a line through the marginal symbol to help yourself keep track of what you have finished.
- Write short corrections clearly, directly above the error noted by your instructor.

- Rewrite any weak sentences in the margin (if there is room) or on the reverse side of the page. If you rewrite on the reverse side of the page, put an arrow in the margin to signal your instructor to turn the page over to see your revision.
- Keep a record of your mistakes. All writers tend to fall into patterns of error. If you keep a record of your errors, you can discover your own patterns and so be on the lookout for the errors you are most likely to make.

Your instructor may evaluate your paper with comments, questions, and marking symbols. An alphabetical list of common correction symbols keyed to this handbook appears on the inside front cover. If you see || in the margin of your paper, for example, the list on the inside cover tells you that || is a shorthand notation for faulty parallelism and that Chapter 6 explains the problem and how to correct it. If your instructor uses chapter and section numbers to indicate corrections needed, check the inside back covers of this handbook for a quick guide. If you don't understand a comment or a symbol, make an appointment to discuss the paper with your instructor. Or you may want to visit your campus writing center and go over your paper with a tutor.

■ **Exercise 2.5** Following the instructor's comments on John Williams's second draft of his essay on *The Shining* (pp. 34–36), make revisions and corrections. Rewrite sentences or entire paragraphs.

■ **Exercise 2.6** Revise and correct the composition you prepared for Exercise 2.4 according to your instructor's comments.

CHAPTER

3

WRITING STRONG PARAGRAPHS

Paragraphs are the building blocks of essays, and it's fair to say that an essay's structure is only as strong as it's paragraphs. This chapter examines the structure within paragraphs and focuses on opening and closing paragraphs in particular.

3a
Understanding Paragraphs

Paragraphs help writers organize their work in steps, and they help readers follow the writer's thought through a text.

Paragraphs also relieve the eye. Few sights are as forbidding as a long block of printed text with no indentations. The indentation assures us that a text is manageable, that it can be broken down into parts which the mind can absorb one at a time. Without the white space of the indentations, a text looks like some monstrous thing we must swallow whole.

Paragraphs do not stand alone. They are not essays in themselves, although some textbooks pretend they are. Once in a while you may write a single paragraph—a caption for a photograph, for example, or a brief memo in an office. Otherwise paragraphs are part of the flow of a larger text. They have meaning only as they are joined to the whole.

How long should a paragraph be? There are no absolute rules. The decision is partially visual. Newspaper editors favor short paragraphs, sometimes only one or two sentences long. Newspaper readers often skim rather than study, and newspaper columns are thin; a long paragraph might run down an entire page. Magazines and books have longer paragraphs, largely because type columns are wider. As you read the paragraphs in this book, you'll see much variety in length. In your college writing, it is usually good to have at least one or two indentations on an $8\frac{1}{2} \times 11$ inch sheet of paper.

A new paragraph usually signals a slight change in emphasis in the paper, a step from one subtopic to another within the body of the text. This paragraph, the one you are reading right now, deals with the purpose of paragraphs in general. The previous paragraph considered how paragraphs look. When we, as authors, sensed our topic changing from the appearance of paragraphs to their purpose, we made a new paragraph by indenting.

The first sentence in a paragraph shows the direction of the sentences that follow it. The writer decides to change emphasis, indents, and then writes a sentence that indicates the shift. The next sentence must develop in some way the thought announced by the first sentence. Here is an example in a story from *Sports Illustrated* about the 1992 winter Olympics.

> American women finished higher than American men in every sport in which both fielded teams, except cross-country and biathlon, in which the two sexes were equally inept, neither one cracking the top 10. In every other discipline, on snow and on ice, in traditional sports and in first-time Olympic sports, the dynamic and surprising U.S. women outdid their brethren. Composing just 34% of the U.S. team—55 of 161 athletes—the ladies wearing stars and stripes took home 82% of the medals.
>
> —E. M. SWIFT

The first sentence in this paragraph announces that American women did far better than American men in the winter games. The following sentences build on the first, adding details that support the generalization.

Always be sure in your paragraphs that every sentence has a clear relation to the first sentence. When you change the emphasis slightly, indent and start a new paragraph. Here is the next paragraph from the article in *Sports Illustrated.*

> This imbalance is a new phenomenon. Taken as a whole, in the previous two Winter Olymics, the American medals have been split—eight for men, eight for women. So why, in 1992, is there suddenly a gulf? What has enabled American women to succeed in Winter Olympic sports at a rate U.S. men can't match?
>
> —E. M. SWIFT

E. M. Swift, the writer of this report for *Sports Illustrated,* changed emphasis from the first paragraph to the next. The first sentence of the second paragraph announces, "This imbalance is a new phenomenon." Every other sentence in this paragraph relates directly to the first sentence, proving first that the imbalance is new and then asking for an explanation.

Smith's paragraphs thus move through the article in blocks of factual information carefully organized to amplify the first sentence in each paragraph.

3b
Building Unified Paragraphs

Now that we have seen the importance of the first sentence in the structure of the paragraph, we can talk about the *controlling idea* of the paragraph. We expect a paragraph to have some single purpose, some point that all the sentences of the paragraph work together to make. A paragraph achieves unity if it supports a controlling idea.

Giving Each Paragraph a Controlling Idea

To speak of the controlling idea of the paragraph is another way of saying that every sentence in the paragraph must be related to a topic introduced by the first sentence. Sometimes the controlling idea is expressed as a generalization, usually in the first sentence. Both paragraphs from *Sports Illustrated* quoted above illustrate this kind of generalization. The generalization in the first paragraph is this: American women finished higher than American men in almost every sport in which both fielded teams. The generalization in the second paragraph is this: This imbalance is new. Every sentence in each paragraph supports the generalization made in its first sentence.

Traditionally, textbooks have called such a general sentence the **topic sentence.** Nearly always, the generalization that makes a topic sentence comes first in the paragraph. But sometimes the generalization will occur later on. In the paragraph below, the generalization comes in the second sentence.

> The steam locomotive evokes nostalgia among many people. **The nostalgia is better than the experience of the steam locomotive ever was.** The steam locomotive was a dirty, dangerous, and generally disagreeable companion to American life for well over a century. It spread filthy, black smoke over large areas of every city it served, and it usually left a thick film of oily grime on the face of every passenger in the cars behind it. It started fires along the sides of the tracks in woods and fields. It was so heavy that it pounded rails until they broke, and when it crashed and turned over—as it frequently did—it poured flames, steam, and boiling water onto the fireman and the engineer in the cab. It had so many moving parts under high stress that it often

> broke down, stranding passengers for hours. And it was absurdly inefficient and costly to operate.
>
> —DICK CURRY

Notice that although the second sentence is the generalization that unites all the facts in the paragraph, the first sentence does a necessary job of introduction. The first sentence announces the subject, and the rest of the paragraph develops its controlling idea by building on some thought expressed in the first sentence.

Many paragraphs do not contain a generalization, a sentence that can be called a *topic sentence* in the old meaning of that term. A paragraph that describes something or that tells a little story will seldom have a general sentence. Here's a paragraph from an article about chili peppers.

> In her kitchen, where a *ristra*—a bouquet of deep-red peppers—hangs, Zamora serves me some green chiles she has just pulled from the freezer and cut up. The mesquite imparts a wonderful smoky flavor. For Christmas, she tells me, the feast at her house will feed 50 people, and will include homemade tortillas, tamales, and *carne adovada,* a dish with garlic, pork, and red chiles that cooks all night in the oven. "I don't know what it is," she says, "If I don't eat chiles on a regular basis, I get weird." She's not the only one. Zubin Mehta, former music director of the New York Philharmonic, who now lives in Los Angeles, grows hot peppers in his garden. He carries them in a jeweled silver case so that when he goes to a restaurant he can supply the chef with his favorite ingredient.
>
> —JIM ROBBINS

This paragraph does not have a generalization, but we know from the setting established in the first sentence that the subject is chili peppers. Sentence by sentence, the writer details the love some people have for this blindingly hot spice.

Some paragraphs begin with a broad statement that is then limited by a second sentence. The rest of the paragraph builds on the second sentence. Some writers call this a "funnel" paragraph. In the following example, the paragraph begins with a general statement, but the rest of the paragraph is built on the second sentence.

> Much modern technology for the home focuses on the kitchen, seeking to combine energy efficiency with convenience. The microwave oven does both, but does it cook food as well as the gas or electric models? Yes, if you are baking potatoes or cooking bacon or warming up a TV dinner or thawing out a package of frozen spinach.

> Microwaves are great for cooking fish. But if you want to brown a steak or boil an egg or bake a pie, your microwave will not do the job.

Many paragraphs begin with a statement that the rest of the paragraph contradicts. This is the way the Rev. Martin Luther King, Jr., began the following paragraph on the actions of police in Birmingham who arrested black Americans for protesting racial segregation in 1963.

> It is true that they [the Birmingham police] have been rather disciplined in their public handling of the demonstrators. In this they have been rather publicly "nonviolent." But for what purpose? To preserve the evil system of segregation. Over the last few years I have consistently preached that nonviolence demands that the means we use must be as pure as the ends we seek. So I have tried to make it clear that it is wrong to use immoral means to attain moral ends. But now I must affirm that it is just as wrong, or even more so, to use moral means to preserve immoral ends. Maybe Mr. Connor and his policemen have been rather publicly nonviolent as Chief Prichett was in Albany, Georgia, but they have used the moral means of nonviolence to maintain the immoral end of flagrant racial injustice. T. S. Eliot has said that there is no greater treason than to do the right thing for the wrong reason.
>
> —MARTIN LUTHER KING, JR.

Some paragraphs introduce the topic with a direct quotation that intrigues the reader about the information to come. In this example, the controlling idea comes in the second sentence.

> "I thought it would be a quick in-and-out job," John Hohmann told me as we stood on the rim of a basalt cliff and looked at the ancient ruins below. In the summer of 1990, the 37-year-old archaeologist had come to east-central Arizona to investigate this prehistoric village. Known to white settlers for more than a century as Casa Malpais (Spanish for "house of the Badlands"), it had been surveyed by previous archaeologists but never excavated.
>
> —DAVID ROBERTS

Some paragraphs introduce the topic by posing a question at the outset. The rest of the paragraph offers some kind of response. The response may be the writer's answer, or it may suggest or report an answer that someone else has given, or it may be a comment on why the question has been asked. In the following paragraph, an economic writer for *Time* ponders the effect of a slowdown in the Japanese economy.

> But will the stall in Japan spell trouble for the fragile American economy? Last year American companies shipped $48.1 billion worth of goods to Japan, making it the second largest U.S. export market. A recession in Japan could hurt the recovery by slowing demand for American products. In addition, Japanese business could try to bolster sagging domestic profits by aggressively selling more products overseas, an action that would surely worsen trade tensions. Finally, since Japan helps finance the U.S. budget deficit, some fear that a significant curtailment of Japanese investments in the U.S. could drive interest rates higher.
>
> —*Time*

As these examples demonstrate, not all paragraphs are structured in the same way. Moreover, the position of a paragraph in an essay may make special demands. The paragraphs that open and close essays have a relationship to the essay as a whole that alters their form. The opening paragraph of an essay must present not only its own controlling idea but the controlling idea of the essay as well. Or an opening paragraph may set the scene, with its final sentence summing up the scene and explaining its importance. Or that explanation may not come until the second paragraph. Scene-setting first paragraphs often open articles in popular magazines because they make readers want to know what will happen next. Although the first sentence in such a paragraph is not, strictly speaking, a topic sentence, it sets the direction for what comes next. The following opening paragraph is another example of a funnel paragraph.

> The bands are marching, the tailgates swinging open for the ritual of picnics and parties. The beverages are heady, the boosterism infectious, the old school colors vivid and bright. This is college football, as the television slogan goes, a great way to spend an autumn afternoon.
>
> —*Newsweek*

Often an introductory paragraph simply tells a story. The first sentence begins with a striking detail, and the following sentences build on it. A later paragraph introduces the topic illustrated by the opening story. The role of the first sentence in such an opening paragraph is to catch the interest of readers and to make them keep on reading.

> Some five hundred years ago, just about the time of Columbus's voyages to the New World, a massive springtime mud slide, set off possibly by a small earthquake, swept out of a canyon during the night, burying a large part of the village of Ozette in the territory of the

Makah Indians on the northern Pacific coast of present-day Washington State's Olympic Peninsula. In a few frightful minutes, humans and their buildings, canoes, utensils, and other possessions were covered under many feet of silt and sand.

For centuries they lay hidden in silence. Then, beginning in the 1960s and continuing for eleven years, archaeologists excavated this remarkable miniature New World Pompeii, revealing—in a completeness almost unparalleled in American archaeology—the details of Native American life as it existed in this part of the continent about 1492. Because of subsurface drainage, the silt and clay deposits above the village had remained moist throughout the years, preserving in excellent condition the lower walls of the structures and a stunning variety of the contents of the houses. Although animal tissue, hair, and feathers had not survived as well, objects made of wood and other vegetable fibers were found in almost the exact condition they were in at the time when the spirits turned against the people.

—RICHARD D. DAUGHERTY

The standard topic sentence is most valuable when you write paragraphs about ideas, when you explain something, or when you make an argument. Such paragraphs help an essay develop its thesis step by step. Topic sentences define these steps clearly and help both writer and reader know where they are going. In narratives and descriptions, you may write paragraphs that do not have a topic sentence. But in all paragraphs, the first sentence should introduce words or ideas that are developed in the following sentences. Follow your first sentence in a paragraph with a second sentence that expands on some thought or idea. Follow that sentence with a further development of thoughts you have expanded on in the second sentence—and so on until the end of the paragraph.

■ **Exercise 3.1** Write a couple of pages about something you have recently witnessed—an episode on the street, an athletic contest, a program you saw on television, some trouble you had with a car. Don't labor over your writing. Get your ideas on paper quickly.

Now study your writing and see how the first sentence in each paragraph introduces the subject you explore in the rest of the paragraph. You will usually discover that when you tell a story of something you have seen or experienced quickly, the paragraphs develop naturally from the first sentence.

Now write a couple of pages on something you have been thinking about lately—a political campaign, the ideas expressed in a difficult course, some problem you have seen reported on television or in the newspapers. Examine your paragraphs to see if they develop naturally from the first sentence in each one. How many of your paragraphs include a standard topic sentence, a generalization that summarizes the rest of the paragraph?

■ **Exercise 3.2** Develop each of the following sentences into a topic sentence, and write a paragraph about it.

1. Some people say that football is popular because it is a violent game.
2. Owning an automobile creates personal independence but damages community life.
3. Attending college while one has young children at home is an ordeal.
4. The long hours I spend on my job make it hard for me to study sometimes.
5. The person who comes back to school after years in the so-called real world brings a lot of experience that is helpful in learning.

■ **Exercise 3.3** State the topic of each of the following paragraphs in your own words. Then say whether the writer states that topic in a topic sentence. That is, does the writer's first sentence merely provide the first thought in a series of thoughts about a general topic? Or does the writer summarize the paragraph in a general sentence? Explain how some words in the first sentence of each paragraph are developed in succeeding sentences.

> The Africans who were to become Americans came from a region of West Africa that fanned from its westernmost tip, around the Senegal River, south and east, along the Bight of Benin, and south again below the Congo River to include a region we now call Angola. Hardly a people living within this vast region, stretching inland for two to three hundred miles, was unrepresented in the creation of the Afro-American people. Bambara, Fulani, Mandinka, and Wolof from the Senegambia, the collection of peoples from Dahomey called Whydahs, the Ashanti, Coromantees, Fanti, Ga, Hausa, Ibo, Yoruba, Angola—they all came, like migrants from Europe and later from Asia, to mix their seed and substance in the making of the American.
>
> It was a treacherous and awful journey from whatever point they started, down the coast, through the unimaginably inhuman Atlantic crossing, into American slavery. Nor was that journey vast and torturous merely in physical distance and bodily pain. Those who were forced to make it traversed worlds of mind and spirit, leaving what they were and becoming the forebears of a people yet to be. Each

man, woman, and child made that internal journey alone; but collectively, their odyssey is one of the great epics of modern times.

Some who started out did not make it. Disease, frailty, brutality, and suicide took a heavy toll. But those whose way was stopped short for whatever reason will not hold us long, for ours is the story of those who have endured, whether due to strength or chance or will to survive or abject surrender. These were the people who would become Afro-Americans.

NATHAN IRVIN HUGGINS

Making All Sentences in a Paragraph Support the Main Idea

Every paragraph needs a logical structure based on a main point. The succession of sentences and the flow of ideas help create that structure. Any sentence that distracts readers from the main idea violates the architecture of the paragraph. In the following paragraph, several sentences wander away from the main idea.

> After strenuous exercise, the body enters a dangerous period that cooling off can help prevent. When you are swimming or running, a large blood supply from the heart brings your arms and legs the oxygen required for muscle activity. The human heart works like a pump. When the right upper chamber of the heart (the *auricle*) fills with blood, blood rushes down into the right lower chamber (the *ventricle*). When this chamber fills, the strong muscles in its wall pump tired blood into an artery that speeds the blood to the lungs. As you exercise, the muscles squeeze, and blood going back to the heart gets an added push as long as you move your limbs. But if you stop suddenly, all this extra blood stays there; your arm and leg muscles are no longer helping your heart pump the blood around. Blood that remains in the arms and legs is blood kept away from vital organs like the brain. But if you *cool off,* that is, slow down your activity gradually, you'll help bring your pulse rate and your body temperature down slowly, helping your muscles rid themselves of metabolic waste, and, most important, you'll keep the blood flowing normally through your body.
>
> —DICK CURRY

The controlling idea of this paragraph may be stated like this: If you stop doing vigorous exercise suddenly, you can cause a strain on the heart and other body organs. But a gradual cooling off after vigorous activity prevents this strain.

Now look at sentences three and four. These details about how the heart operates are interesting, but they distract from the controlling idea of the paragraph. These sentences have no place here, although they might work well in another part of the paper. The paragraph is clearer and reads more smoothly with the distracting sentences removed.

In revising your essays and paragraphs, check each sentence in a paragraph carefully against its main idea, and remove sentences that do not support that idea.

■ **Exercise 3.4** The following paragraphs contain sentences that distract from the controlling idea. Locate those sentences, and rewrite the paragraph without them.

> School textbooks can make some children feel excluded from American life. Only a few years ago first graders learned to read out of books about Dick and Jane and their dog Spot. Children in the first grade are very impressionable. We know that television commercials can create materialism in them and that all sorts of subtle influences shape their view of the world. Dick and Jane were white. They lived in a nice single-family house in a suburb with sidewalks and friendly policemen and postmen, and their dog Spot never bit anybody. The textbooks were on slick paper and had cloth bindings. Daddy wore a suit to work and carried a briefcase. Mother stayed home and kept house and cooked a lot. Mother and Daddy never got a divorce, and Dick and Jane never played with any black or Hispanic children because such children were not to be found in the suburb—or in the textbooks. No father in the neighborhood was unemployed, and nobody ever went without a meal, and there were no homeless people anywhere. Even Spot looked well fed. Children whose parents were divorced, or children who were not white and middle-class, or children who lived in housing projects where there was violence and other kinds of crime could hardly find anything familiar in Dick and Jane.
>
> —DICK CURRY

■ **Exercise 3.5** Write out the controlling idea for each of the following paragraphs. Explain how each sentence in each paragraph supports that controlling idea.

Lunch-Hour Courage

In grade school, she and I were in the same class—even though she was two years my senior—called "E.S.L.," short for English as a Second Language, where a hodgepodge of non-English-speaking children sat in varying degrees of shameful ignorance. It was a strange class made up of youngsters from extremes of culture and maturity, from an 8-year-old girl just arrived from China to a 15-year-old Cuban boy with dyslexia who had been left back four times.

Our teacher tried, in vain, to bring some sanity to the impossible task that she had been charged with, and here, in this atmosphere of chaotic uncertainty tinged with the shame of not belonging, Sukhee, a proud sixth-grader, and I, her diffident younger sister, first learned our ABC's.

Our classroom, although chaotic, was a haven of sorts from the outside throughout most of the day, but lunch period robbed us of this shield, and we were subject to all the belittling remarks and stares of other children. In actuality, these were nothing—a snicker or two, a mimicry of our accents—but they bothered my timid mind sufficiently to make the lunch hour the most dreaded one of my day.

At these times, Sukhee seemed to me an incredible pillar of strength. She would adopt none of the cowed stance that I couldn't help from adopting, and would look back, if anyone mimicked her appearance or accent, with as much blaze in her eyes as the other person dared to match. Others were never able to insult her because she never let herself become degraded in her own eyes.

On one occasion when she spoke rather loudly in Korean in the cafeteria, I, worried of the foreign inflections of our language becoming the butt of their joke, begged her to speak quietly as to be inaudible. I will never forget her reply as she answered me with a quiet puzzlement in her eyes. "Would you then have me speak in a language that neither I nor you understand? Until I become proficient enough in English to speak comfortably, the only language I know is my own, and I will not have your fear of some bully stop me from making use of my voice as loudly as I like."

It has been some six years since our E.S.L. experience, and Sukhee and I have managed to learn enough English to communicate without discomfort. We have also grown; we have changed. Sukhee, however, remains the one person of my acquaintance who possesses true integrity of character. She has an intimate sense of the woman that she is. She does not compromise her person for easy conveniences, nor does she make apologies for her being. She doesn't need to because she has pride springing from a hard-gained knowledge of what she can and cannot do.

Her self-respect, real and as essential a part of her as her eyes or brain, frees her from petty preoccupations concerning self and allows her to contemplate the scheme of things beyond her own individual will or desire. For this I think humans are said to be above animals and for this I will always envy and admire her unreservedly.

—YOUNGJU RYU

3c Building Coherent Paragraphs

In coherent paragraphs, thoughts follow one after the other, with connections easy for readers to see and understand. Readers don't like to feel that something has been left out, that a new term has been introduced without adequate preparation, or that a person is mentioned as though they should know who it is when in fact the writer has not mentioned the person before.

Coherence is achieved through the arrangement of information. In revising your essays and paragraphs, look carefully at the first sentence in each paragraph to see what ideas in it you will develop in the next sentence and so on through all the sentences in the paragraph.

Linking Sentences and Ideas

Several techniques can help you achieve coherence. Repeating important words or phrases is one, and using parallel structures is another. Transitional words and expressions such as *therefore, since, moreover, for example,* and *in the first place* (see below and 13e) are an excellent way to bridge sentences and even paragraphs. Combine these techniques to write paragraphs that hold together around a central topic.

Repetition

In the following paragraphs, boldface print highlights repetition that creates coherence. Study the paragraphs carefully to see how ideas are developed, how words tie previous information to new information being introduced, and how various thoughts are explained. You can draw circles around the words in boldface and connect the circles to see how the patterns of repetition hold the essay together. But notice that each re-

3c
¶ coh

peated word or phrase appears in a sentence in which new information is being introduced.

> When Thurgood **Marshall** stepped down from the Supreme Court, it marked the passing of a **generation** of **black civil-rights lawyers** who, in the words of one observer, "linked the passion of Frederick Douglass demanding **black freedom** and of William Du Bois demanding **black equality** to the undelivered promises of the **Constitution** of the United States." **Marshall** was perhaps the most visible member of that **generation,** but it's key figure—a **lawyer** who in many ways pioneered the idea of using the **Constitution** to promote **racial justice**—was a man named Charles Hamilton Houston, who is today largely unknown.
>
> The grandson of slaves, Houston was born in Washington, D.C., in 1895, attended **segregated** schools there, and then went off to Amherst College, in Massachusetts, from which he graduated, magna cum laude and Phi Beta Kappa, in 1915. After serving as a lieutenant in the Army during the First World War, Houston attended Harvard Law School, became the first black member of the law review, and earned his LL.B. in 1922 and a doctorate in 1923. Over the next dozen years, first as a teacher at Howard University Law School and later as its dean, he became one of America's preeminent legal educators, and he transformed an unaccredited night program into an accredited full-time institution with a national reputation for training **black civil-rights lawyers.** "A **lawyer's** either a **social** engineer or a parasite on society," he used to tell his Howard students.
>
> No armchair academic, Houston was himself a brilliant **trial lawyer** and **social engineer.** When he started practice, in 1924, federal and state laws imposed **racial segregation** throughout American life. Eleven years later, he became special counsel to the Nationl Association for the Advancement of Colored People, and in that post he devised the long-range legal strategy that ultimately led the Supreme Court, in **Brown** v. Board of Education, to declare such laws contrary to the **Constitution. Thurgood Marshall,** one of Houston's star pupils, briefed and argued the **Brown** decision, and credited Houston with being "the **engineer** of all of it."
>
> —*New Yorker*

Observe the careful development of these paragraphs by examining the patterns of repetition that the words and phrases in boldface show. The tribute opens with a reference to Thurgood Marshall's retirement from the Supreme Court. The paragraph gradually narrows, funnel fashion, to the main subject, Charles Hamilton Houston. In this paragraph and those that follow, repetitions of words and ideas, such as *generation, black, civil rights lawyer, constitution,* and *engineer,* provide coherence. These repetitions keep us tracking the thought of the writer. The conclusion, with its reference back to Marshall, neatly ties the entire tribute together.

Every sentence after the first sentence in a coherent essay looks both backward and forward. The writer brings up a word or a related idea he or she has used before, repeats it, and adds to it. This pattern of repetition and addition is essential to any good piece of writing.

Sometimes the repetition of a single word or phrase is so insistent that it sounds like a drumbeat. This deliberate repetition can be effective in an occasional paragraph. Be sure, if you use such a form, that you include some new information along with the repetition. The information should develop some thought important to your essay.

> We do not chose to be born. We do not chose our parents. We do not chose our historical epoch, or the country of our birth, or the immediate circumstances of our upbringing. We do not, most of the time, chose to die; nor do we chose the time or condition of death. But within all this realm of choicelessness, we do chose how we shall live, courageously or in cowardice, honorably or dishonorably, with purpose or in drift.
>
> —JOSEPH EPSTEIN

Parallel structure

Repeating the forms of clauses, phrases, or sentences can also tie thought units together in paragraphs. In the paragraph below, parallelism (discussed in Chapter 6) dramatically links criticisms of Britain's King Charles I (1600–1649), the only English king to be judged a criminal by his people and executed by beheading.

> We charge him with having broken his coronation oath; and we are told that he kept his wedding vow! We accuse him of having given up his people to the merciless inflictions of the most hot-headed and hard-hearted of prelates; and the defense is, that he took his little son on his knee and kissed him! We censure him for having violated the articles of Petition of Right, after having, for good and valuable consideration, promised to observe them; and we are informed that he was accustomed to hear prayers at six o'clock in the morning! It is to such considerations as these, together with his Van Dyck dress, his handsome face, and his peaked beard, that he owes, we verily believe, most of his popularity with the present generation.
>
> —THOMAS BABINGTON MACCAULAY

3c
¶ coh

Transitional expressions

Transitional expressions are words or phrases that tell a reader something like this: "I now lead you carefully from the point that I have just made to another that I want to make. Stay with me." The most obvious transitional expressions are words such as *moreover, furthermore, nevertheless, however, but, or,* and *and.* These expressions, in boldface in the paragraph below, look back to the thought just expressed and announce that readers will now move to a related but slightly different point.

> Asian students may have trouble with English because most Asian languages lack the articles *the* and *a.* Verb tenses may **also** create difficulties, **for** in Asian languages the past and the present tenses are often expressed not by verbs but by adverbs. **For example,** to form the future tense, Chinese speakers may say, "Tomorrow I go to Beijing." **Or** to make the past tense they say, "Last week, I go to Shanghai." **However,** difficulties in the use of English articles may be overcome with practice.

Transitional expressions are useful, but don't overdo them. Most well-constructed paragraphs hold together without obvious transitional words and phrases. Punctuation often links ideas, as in this example. (The dash is discussed in 26a.)

> Many things we take for granted today would have seemed like magic to people even twenty years ago—the desk-top computer, for example.

Two sentences in succession may sometimes imply cause and effect.

> My parents quarreled incessantly. They were divorced when I was seven.

To make your writing efficient, you may end up deleting unnecessary transitional expressions as you revise. The rule comes down to this: don't use traditional expressions unless you *must* use them to be clear. A steady repetition of *moreover, furthermore, nevertheless, but,* and so on can easily bore your readers.

■ **Exercise 3.6** Rewrite the following paragraph, putting in transitional devices where they are needed and taking them out when they are not necessary. Be prepared to explain why you have removed a transitional device, why you have put one in, or why you have left one in the original paragraph.

> Writing is difficult for almost everybody, even professional writers. Specifically, writing requires hours of concentrated work. Further-

more, writers must usually withdraw from others while they write. In addition, writing exposes many writers to a constant sense of failure because they do not think they are doing well. For example, Thomas Hardy became disillusioned with his fiction. He therefore stopped and turned to poetry after he had produced some of the greatest novels in the English language. In the same way, Virginia Woolf fell into such despair about her work that she eventually committed suicide. Accordingly, we can see that both teachers and students are perhaps pursuing a false hope if they think writing can be made easy. In other words, a writing course may make your writing better. But it may not make it easier.

Linking One Paragraph to the Next

In an essay, the transitions between paragraphs are as important as coherence within paragraphs. Transitional expressions can help readers follow the direction of your thought as you move from one paragraph to the next. But coherence is complex, and merely patching over gaps between ideas with transitional expressions won't help you achieve it.

TRANSITIONAL EXPRESSIONS

To show relations in space

above, adjacent to, against, alongside, around, at a distance from, at the, below, beside, beyond, encircling, far off, forward, from the, in front of, in the rear, inside, near the back, near the end, nearby, next to, on, over, surrounding, there, through the, to the left, to the right, up front

To show relations in time

afterward, at last, before, earlier, first, former, formerly, further, furthermore, immediately, in the first place, in the interval, in the meantime, in the next place, in the last, later on, latter, meanwhile, next, now, often, once, previously, second, simultaneously, sometime later, subsequently, suddenly, then, therefore, third, today, tomorrow, until now, when, years ago, yesterday

To show something added to what has come before

again, also, and, and then, besides, further, furthermore, in addition, last, likewise, moreover, next, nor, too

To give examples or to intensify points

after all, as an example, certainly, for example, for instance, indeed, in fact, in truth, it is true, of course, specifically, that is

To show similarities

alike, in the same way, like, likewise, resembling, similarly

To show contrasts

after all, although, but, conversely, differ(s) from, difference, different, dissimilar, even though, granted, however, in contrast, in spite of, nevertheless, notwithstanding, on the contrary, on the other hand, otherwise, still, though, unlike, while this may be true, yet

To indicate cause and effect

accordingly, as a result, because, consequently, hence, since, then, therefore, thus

To conclude or summarize

finally, in brief, in conclusion, in other words, in short, in summary, that is, to summarize

---

The opening sentence of a paragraph in the body of an essay usually looks back to information in the previous paragraph and forward to information about to be disclosed. Boldface print in the excerpts below shows how that first sentence in a paragraph looks both backward and forward.

> When Africans first got to New York, or New Amsterdam as the Dutch called it, they lived in the farthest downtown portion of the city, near what is now called The Bowery. Later, they shifted, and were shifted, as their numbers grew, to the section known as Greenwich Village. The Civil War Draft Riots in 1863 accounted for the next move by New York's growing Negro population.
>
> **After this violence** (a few million dollars' worth of property was destroyed, and a Negro orphanage was burned to the ground) a great many Negroes moved across the river into Brooklyn.
>
> —LEROI JONES

> Among those who now take a dim view of marijuana are Dr. Sidney Cohen, a drug expert at the University of California at Los Angeles, who once described marijuana as "a trivial weed," and Dr. Robert I. DuPont, former director of the National Institute on Drug Abuse, who had lobbied for marijuana's legalization.
>
> **According to these and other experts,** it is no longer possible to say that marijuana is an innocuous drug with few if any health effects aside from intoxication.
>
> —JANE E. BRODY

Sometimes the sentence that looks both backward and forward is the last sentence in a paragraph.

> Why is marking up a book indispensable to reading it? First, it keeps you awake. (And I don't mean merely conscious; I mean wide awake.) In the second place, reading, if it is active, is thinking, and thinking tends to express itself in words, spoken or written. The marked book is usually the thought-through book. Finally, writing helps you remember the thoughts you had, or the thoughts the author expressed. Let me develop these three points.
>
> If reading is to accomplish anything more than passing time, it must be active. . . .
>
> —MORTIMER J. ADLER

Sometimes you may want to write a bridge paragraph, one that calls attention to your sense that you are carrying your readers from one part of your essay to another that is somewhat different.

> I have, I hope, cleared the ground for a dispassionate comparison of certain aspects of Shakespeare's technique in the Henry VI plays with his technique in the "romance" histories. Now, perhaps, some general remarks about the structure of the trilogy will be helpful.
>
> —PAUL DEAN

■ **Exercise 3.7** Discuss the various devices used to build coherence within and between paragraphs in the following selection from an essay in *Sports Illustrated* on the revelation by the media that former tennis star Arthur Ashe had the AIDS virus.

Discuss these questions: What theme joins all these paragraphs? What words carry the theme from one paragraph to the next? How do the last sentences in each paragraph look forward to the next paragraph? How do the first sentences in each paragraph look back to the last paragraph?

> The first telephone call came to my office in early September. Another call came two months later, just days after Magic Johnson had stood at a podium in Los Angeles and delivered the shocking news that he was infected with the AIDS virus. Both callers were credible members of the tennis community, and both had the same message: "You know about Arthur Ashe. He's got AIDS." Maybe I should have reacted to this disturbing information strictly as a journalist. After all, I'll wave the First Amendment flag until my arm falls off. And I'll defend until my last breath the public's right to know practically everything about anyone who falls into the category of "public figure."
>
> But now my journalistic instincts were overcome by compassion and concern. I had been well acquainted with Ashe personally and professionally for more than a decade. Long before that, I had ad-

mired his athletic skill—and more important, his dignity. My admiration for him had grown even stronger in recent years as I watched him fight racism, apartheid, and inequities in college athletics, and as he shared with me some of the insights and convictions that made him a respected champion of human rights throughout the world.

So that's why I said nothing. Not to the managing editor of this magazine. Not to my friends. Not even to Arthur. I could have picked up the telephone and asked him. But I didn't. I could have broached the subject during one of the many conversations we had since I received the first tip about him. But I didn't. In November, soon after Magic's announcement, Arthur and I spoke on the phone about AIDS and the backlash that Magic would surely face because of his promiscuous life-style. The questions were on the tip of my tongue. Were my sources right? And, if so, did Arthur feel any compulsion to join Magic as a spokesman in the fight against AIDS? But I didn't ask. I couldn't.

Last month Ashe was my guest at the United Negro College Fund's annual dinner in New York. Magic was one of the honorees. At one point the discussion at our table turned to Johnson's efforts to promote AIDS education and awareness, but by then I had just about put the calls about Arthur out of my mind. I had decided that if he wanted me to know about his condition, he would tell me. Otherwise, it wasn't my business. I had placed his privacy ahead of any desire to break the story in SI—and it wasn't a tough decision.

—Roy S. Johnson

Arranging Paragraph Ideas According to a Coherent Plan

How you organize information in any one paragraph is similar to how you arrange information to support the point you want to make in the paper as a whole (3d).

Chronological arrangement

Perhaps the most familiar way to present information in a paragraph is chronologically—telling events in the order in which they happened, one after another. We tell most stories chronologically.

The sun rose slowly out of the hazy sea as we hiked through the great olive grove at the foot of Mount Iouktos on the Greek island of Crete. By seven o'clock, we had started our slow climb up the mountain, following a trail that twisted back and forth as it snaked its way towards the summit. We left the olive trees behind quickly and entered a rocky world where a few poplars cast an occasional weak shade. By ten o'clock, the sun had burned the haze off the sea, and its heat bore down on us. We became thirsty, but we had brought no water. By eleven, our clothes were soaked with sweat, and the heat made everything shimmer so that the tumbled rocks seemed to dance crazily amid heat waves. By now we could see for miles down the island, and to the west the huge bulk of Mount Ida rose into the hot blue sky. By noon, nearly crazy with heat, thirst, and fatigue, we got to the top. A little whitewashed chapel with a tile roof stood there, and beside it was a cistern with a bucket attached to a long rope. We dropped the bucket down into the darkness of the cistern and heard a great, reassuring splash. Quickly we pulled the bucket to the top and drank greedily. Then we sat in the shade of the church and looked out over one of the most beautiful landscapes I had ever seen.

—Dick Curry

Spatial arrangement

You might also decide to present information spatially, by locating yourself and your readers somewhere in a scene and then moving through space—from back to front, from top to bottom, from left to right, or in some other logical way. In describing landscapes, paintings, buildings, streets, and all geographical areas, you can move through space, taking your readers with you.

Practice writing paragraphs such as the one below by standing in front of the scene you are to describe and mentally blocking it off in sections. If you carry a notebook, jot down some things you see in each section of your imaginary frame.

I walked out on the bridge and looked down at the lock. The canal flowed into the lock through a sprung wooden gate just under the bridge. It ran between two narrowly confining walls for about a hundred feet. Then, with a sudden boil and bubble, it broke against another gate, spilled through, and resumed its sluggish course. The walls of the lock were faced with big blocks of rust-red sandstone. Some of the stones were so huge that they could have been hoisted into place only with a block and tackle. It was beautiful stone, and it had been beautifully finished and fitted. Time had merely softened it. Here and there along the courses I could even make out the remains of a mason's mark. One device was quite distinct—a double-headed arrow. Another appeared to be two overlapping equilateral triangles. I went on across the bridge to the house. The windows were shuttered and boarded up, and the door was locked. No matter. It was enough just to stand and look at it. It was a lovely house, as beautifully made as the lock, and as firmly designed for function. It gave me a pang to think that there had once been a time when even a lock tender could have so handsome a house. A phoebe called from a sweet-gum tree in the dooryard. Far away, somewhere down by the river, a mourning dove gave an answering sigh. I looked at my watch. It was ten minutes after ten. I started up the towpath.

—BERTON ROUECHÉ

Chronological and spatial arrangements often work together, as you can see in both previous paragraphs.

Deductive arrangement

Paragraphs may also be arranged for a balance of generalization and specific details. In a deductive arrangement, the generalization comes first, and the details that support it follow.

> We tell stories in order to affirm our being and our place in the scheme of things. When the Kiowas entered upon the Great Plains they had to tell new stories of themselves, stories that would enable them to appropriate an unknown and intimidating landscape to their experience. They were peculiarly vulnerable in that landscape, and they told a story of dissension, finally of a schism in the tribe, brought about by a quarrel between two great chiefs. They encountered awesome forces and features in nature, and they explained them in story too. And so they told the story of Man-Ka-Ih, the storm spirit, which speaks the Kiowa language and does the Kiowas no harm, and they told of the tree that bore the seven sisters into the sky, where they became the stars of the Big Dipper. In so doing they not only accounted for the great monolith that is Devils Tower, Wyoming (in Kiowa, Tsoai, "rock tree"), but related themselves to the stars in the process. When they came upon the Plains they were befriended by the Crows, who gave them the sun-dance fetish Tai-Me, which was from that time on their most powerful medicine, and they told a story of the coming of Tai-Me in their hour of need. Language was their element. Words, spoken words, were the manifestations of their deepest belief, of their deepest feelings, of their deepest life. When Europeans first came to America, having had writing for hundreds of years and lately the printed press, they could not conceive of the spoken word as sacred, could not understand the American Indian's profound belief in the efficacy of language.
>
> —N. SCOTT MOMADAY

Inductive arrangement

An inductive arrangement builds through pieces of information to support a generalization that comes at the end of a paragraph. The writer presents details one after another and draws a conclusion from them. In the following paragraph, historian Nell Irvin Painter tells how the late nineteenth-century United States conquest of Hawaii, the Philippines, and Puerto Rico, with their populations of nonwhite natives, made some white Americans think of depriving black Americans of the vote.

> The white supremacist solution to the "Negro problem" was the repeal of the Fifteenth Amendment to the U.S. Constitution, which gave blacks the vote after the Civil War. White supremacists had wanted to reverse the amendment for years, but northern Republicans had objected. By 1900 the notion no longer seemed so farfetched to the northerners. The realities of empire enlightened northern Republicans who had previously championed universal manhood suffrage for the South. "The mind of the country North and South, especially since the acquisition of Hawaii, Puerto Rico and the Philippines," noted the new mayor of Wilmington, North Carolina, "is in a more favorable condition to consider such a proposition than ever before." The Fifteenth Amendment stood, but in name only. Before the twentieth century had advanced very far, all the sizable nonwhite populations under American control enjoyed only limited civil rights, whether as noncitizen Native Americans or Chinese, subjects in the islands, or disenfranchised black citizens in the South.
>
> —NELL IRVIN PAINTER

Arrangement by order of importance

You may also decide to arrange the elements by order of importance, starting with the least significant or least dramatic information and building to a climax with the most significant or most dramatic.

> Shakespeare came to London at a fortunate time. If he had been born twenty years earlier, he would have arrived in London when underpaid hacks were turning out childish dramas about brown-paper dragons. If he had been born twenty years later, he would have arrived when drama had begun to lose its hold on ordinary people and was succumbing to a kind of self-conscious cleverness. But his arrival in London coincided with a great wave of excitement and achievement in the theatre, and he rode with it to its crest. William Shakespeare brought great gifts to London, but the city was waiting with gifts of its

own to offer him. The root of his genius was Shakespeare's own, but it was London that supplied him with the favoring weather.

—MARCHETTE CHUTE

■ **Exercise 3.8** Explain the arrangement of the following paragraphs—whether the main idea comes first and then is supported by details or whether the details come first and the main idea comes last. Decide whether the paragraph primarily tells a story or argues a point.

Last week, as President Bush was preparing a major televised appearance to mark the unmet deadine for congressional passage of his economic program, a recently published collection of President Franklin D. Roosevelt's radio addresses known as "fireside chats" arrived in the mail from the University of Oklahoma Press, and we began reading. The historians Russell D. Buhite and David W. Levy, who edited the book, point out in their introduction that the Great Depression was a domestic crisis like no other, and they don't suggest that the fireside chats might offer any guidance for the nineteen-nineties. Yet it is hard to read them and not think that among Roosevelt's ideas there is at least one that a great many Americans would be ready to see revived in the near future: the notion of a Presidential address as a way of actually talking to people about something.

—*New Yorker*

The preacher preached a wonderful rhythmical sermon, all moans and shouts and lonely cries and dire pictures of hell, and then he sang a song about the ninety and nine safe in the fold, but one little lamb was left out in the cold. Then he said, "Won't you come? Won't you come to Jesus? Young lambs, won't you come?" And he held out his arms to all us young sinners there on the mourners' bench. And the little girls cried. And some of them jumped up and went to Jesus right away. But most of us just sat there.

—LANGSTON HUGHES

Once in a long while, four times so far for me, my mother brings out the metal tube that holds her medical diploma. On the tube are gold circles crossed with seven red lines each—"joy" ideographs in abstract. There are also little flowers that look like gears for a gold machine. According to the scraps of labels with Chinese and American addresses, stamps, and postmarks, the family airmailed the can from Hong Kong in 1950. It got crushed in the middle, and whoever tried to peel the labels off stopped because the red and gold paint came off too, leaving silver scratches that rust. Somebody tried to pry the end off before discovering that the tube pulls apart. When I open it, the smell of China flies out, a thousand-year-old bat flying heavy-headed out of the Chinese caverns where bats are as white as dust, a smell that comes from long ago, far back in the brain. Crates from Canton, Hong Kong, Singapore, and Taiwan have that smell too, only stronger because they are more recently come from the Chinese.

—MAXINE HONG KINGSTON

Linking Ideas with Pronouns

By replacing nouns, **pronouns** help achieve coherence, joining one part of a paragraph to another. Pronouns with clear antecedents refer readers to a previously identified noun and help the writer connect ideas in a paragraph without having to mention the nouns again and again.

When you use pronouns, pay attention to the antecedents. Be sure they are clear. When used well, pronouns fix attention on ideas that hold a paragraph together. Look how confusing this paragraph is because of the pronouns:

> Crowds came to look at the rare books and manuscripts in the exhibit to mark the fiftieth anniversary of the college library. They were from all over the world, representing many different languages and races and customs. The president and the dean circulated among them with great satisfaction, because with so many different people interested in them, and crowding around them and exclaiming over them, they were sure to collect more money to help the librarians do their job better in the future.

Are the books and manuscripts from all over the world, or is it the crowds that come from many different languages, races, and customs? Are the president and the dean circulating among the books and manuscripts or among the crowds? Are so many people interested in the president and the dean or in the books and manuscripts? Are the librarians going to help do their own jobs better in the future or will they help the president and the dean do *their* jobs better?

To eliminate these confusions, the entire paragraph has to be revised:

> Crowds poured into the library to see the exhibit of rare books and manuscripts, an exhibit celebrating the library's fiftieth anniversary. The exhibits represented languages, races, and cultures from all over the world. The president and the dean circulated among the crowds, pleased with the excitement visible everywhere and knowing

that it would now be easier to solicit donations that would help the work of the librarians.

Using Supporting Details

Coherence is also achieved through a balance of generalization and detail. Paragraphs that contain details only are flat. Paragraphs that contain nothing but general statements are weak. Strong paragraphs display a balance of the general and the specific. This subordination of some ideas to others also helps tie the paragraph together.

Read the following paragraph carefully. What's wrong with it?

> The parking problem here at school is really terrible. Everybody complains about it. It sometimes takes hours and hours to find a space. Students are late to class because they can't park their cars. Why can't the administration do something about it? With all the money the university is spending on football, you would think they could put a little into student parking. It's really hard on commuter students who have to come from jobs to classes with little time to spare. The situation is a disgrace.

Now compare that paragraph, which consists of nothing but assertions, with the one below, which includes substantiating details. Notice, too, the way the details build in intensity and the concluding sentence of this paragraph anticipates the next.

> On Friday of last week I drove to school from my night job at a hotel and arrived at 9:45 for a ten o'clock class. A parking sticker that cost me $250 for the year tells me that I have the right to park in any student parking lot. But on Friday I drove around parking lot A, and parking lot B, and parking lot C without finding a space. Finally, in desperation, I drove up to parking lot M a mile away from my class. There I found plenty of parking, but by the time I raced to the Mahan Building, where my accounting class was in progress, it was 10:20, and Professor Lewis stopped his lecture as I came in and said, "Well, we are certainly happy that Mr. Jenkins has decided to join us this morning. I hope you didn't disturb your sleep just to be with us this morning, Mr. Jenkins." I felt my face turn hot, and I knew I was blushing from anger and embarrassment. What can we do about parking? I have ten suggestions to make to the administration.

As the effects of these two paragraphs demonstrate, generalizations are always more powerful if buttressed with specific examples. Readers want to know why you think what you think. Giving them details and evidence makes them see the steps that led to your conclusions and makes your paragraphs convincing and coherent.

Of course not every point you make in a paragraph can or should be supported by specific details. In a long essay, a paragraph may present several generalizations or abstractions without supporting data. But effective writing uses details of the kinds elaborated below. Without them, readers would remain vague about what the writer is trying to say, and if they do understand, they may not be convinced.

Sensory details

Sensory details help readers bring their own memories to your prose. When you write, use nouns that tell us of sights, smells, sounds, tastes, and feelings. Don't overdo it, but try for some sensory effects. The writer of the following paragraph could have said something prosaic like this: "After 1821, traffic along the Santa Fe Trail became heavy." Instead, he chose to make the scene more vivid:

> They sailed the Great Plains like naval flotillas, four columns abreast, each column counting as many as 25 high-wheeled wagons, stowed with trade goods and canopied by billowing canvas, pulled by plodding 12-ox teams, churning long wakes of dust on winds that rippled the prairie grasses. They were headed for Santa Fe.
>
> —Rowe Findley

✓ CHECKLIST 3.1: FINDING AUTHORITIES TO QUOTE IN A PAPER

- Who has studied this topic and written about it?
- Who has been an eyewitness to some of the events I am writing about?
- Who has been affected by the subject of my paper?
- Is there any scientific evidence that I can quote in support of my position?
- Is there any statistical evidence on this topic?
- Has an important person made a statement about this topic?
- Do I have any experience that will help persuade my audience?

Statistics and cases

Statistics and cases are the language of facts and figures. You can often use them effectively to support a topic (see Checklist 3.1). *Statistics* are numerical data; *cases* are specific instances involving people and events.

Statistics give authority to your statements. Notice how the numbers in the first paragraph below help the writer make his point that although many American Indian children leave the reservation to attend public schools, some tribes feel a strong need to preserve their traditional schools on their reservations.

> In 1969 there were 178,476 Indian students, ages five to eighteen, enrolled in public, Federal, private and mission schools. Approximately 12,000 children of this age group were not in school. Of the total in school, 119,000 were in public schools, 36,263 in boarding schools operated by the Bureau of Indian Affairs, 16,100 in Bureau day schools, 108 in Bureau hospital schools, and 4,089 in dormitories maintained by the Bureau for children attending public schools. The Bureau operated 77 boarding schools, 144 day schools, 2 hospital schools, and 18 dormitories. The number of Indian children being educated in public schools has steadily increased, aided by the financial assistance provided local school districts under the Johnson-O'Malley Act of 1934 (which provided financial support, in cooperation with the Department of Health, Education, and Welfare, to aid federally affected areas). The closer relationship between state school systems and the Indian system has been welcomed by many Indian groups. Sixty-one tribes have established compulsory education regulations that conform with those of the states where they live.
>
> On the other hand, some more traditional Indian groups have rebelled at efforts to close down reservation schools. The attempt of the Bureau of Indian Affairs to close down, on July 1, 1968, a small grade-school at Tama, Iowa, created an instant reaction. Forty-five Mesquakie Indian children were attending school there on the reservation purchased by their ancestors, a separate body of the Sac tribe which, with the Fox, had a hundred years earlier been pushed out of Iowa into Kansas. The Mesquakie Indians, who had not been consulted about the closing of the school, promptly sought judicial relief. They got it in September 1968, in the Federal District Court at Cedar Rapids, when United States District Court Judge Edward J. McManus ordered the school reopened in the fall. The Mesquakie were able to call upon a number of influential white friends in their attempt to retain their Indian school. The validity of integration into a white school system that is often both distant from and cold toward Indian values can be questioned, as the Mesquakie questioned it.
>
> —WILCOMB F. WASHBURN

■ **Exercise 3.9** Here are several opening sentences. Choose one, and finish the paragraph, using supporting details to make your writing vivid.

1. When I came to this country, my first attempts to speak English became adventures.
2. Why don't we judge human nature by the many people who do good things rather than by the few who do bad things?
3. The comic strip "Calvin and Hobbes" tells us of a little boy and his imagination.
4. Students can use computers for many purposes.

3d Using Appropriate Paragraph Forms

The purpose of a paragraph also affects its structure. Telling a story almost always means a chronological arrangement, for example, while analyzing cause and effect may shape a paragraph into two parts. Likewise, a paragraph that serves to open or conclude an essay must be structured to meet the special demands of placement.

Shaping Paragraphs to Function

The purpose of a paragraph—sometimes the same as its controlling idea—often imposes a certain structure on it. The following examples of paragraph forms are offered for your study and imitation: narration, process analysis, comparison and contrast, classification, cause-and-effect analysis, and definition. In the next few weeks, as you read to complete course assignments or simply for pleasure, stop and look at the paragraphs before you. Try to figure out what they're doing and how they work. Do they tell a story, explain something, analyze an event, describe a place or a person? As you construct your own essays, use the examples here to help build the kinds of paragraphs you need to develop your topic.

Narration

Use narrative paragraphs to tell a story. Such paragraphs usually proceed in chronological order.

> Banyan Street was the route Lucille Miller took home from the twenty-four-hour Mayfair Market on the night of October 7, 1964, a night when the moon was dark and the wind was blowing and she was out of milk, and Banyan Street was where, at about 12:20 A.M., her 1964 Volkswagen came to a sudden stop, caught fire, and began to burn. For an hour and fifteen minutes, Lucille Miller ran up and down Banyan Street calling for help, but no cars passed and no help

> came. At three o'clock that morning, when the fire had been put out and the California Highway Patrol officers were completing their report, Lucille Miller was still sobbing and incoherent, for her husband had been asleep in the Volkswagen. "What will I tell the children, when there's nothing left, nothing left in the casket," she cried to the friend who called to comfort her. "How can I tell them there's nothing left?"
>
> —JOAN DIDION

Process analysis

Use process analysis in paragraphs to explain how to do something or how to make something. These paragraphs also generally proceed by chronology. Here is a paragraph on how to check the inflation on your bike tires if you don't have an air pressure gauge with you.

> There's a great *curb-edge test* you can do to make sure your tires are inflated just right. Rest the wheel on the edge of a curb or stair, so the bike sticks out into the street or path, perpendicular to the curb or stair edge. Get the wheel so you can push down on it at about a 45 degree angle from above the bike. Push hard on the handlebars or seat, depending on which wheel you're testing. The curb should flare the tire a bit but shouldn't push right through the tire and clunk against the rim. You want the tire to have a little give when you ride over chuckholes and rocks, in other words, but you don't want it so soft that you bottom out. If you are a hot-shot who wants tires so hard that they don't have any give, you'll have to stick to riding on clean-swept Velodrome tracks, or watch very carefully for little sharp objects on the road. Or you'll have to get used to that sudden riding-on-the-rim feeling that follows the blowout of an overblown tire.
>
> —TOM CUTHBERTSON

Comparison and contrast

Organize paragraphs by comparison and a contrast if you want to highlight similarities or differences or both.

You may make comparisons between conditions existing at two or more times or between people, places, or things existing at the same time. But be sure that your comparisons are sensible and teach something. You can compare any two things with each other—a computer train with a short story, for example. Both have a beginning, a middle, and an end. Both are designed to carry people along. But meaningless and trivial comparisons like these annoy most readers. Annoyed readers usually stop reading.

The following paragraph compares a 1992 Buick with a 1952 model.

> The 1952 *Buick* measured an inch shorter and two inches wider than the 1992 model. Inside, the old car has five inches less shoulder room in front, seven-plus inches in back. Yet we found the old car's seating much more comfortable, even with three abreast. Not even modern ergonomics can compete with the old-fashioned extravagance of a high roof, high bench seats, and flat floor. The back seat felt like a limousine's, with wide-open spaces to stretch one's legs.
>
> —*Consumer Reports*

Classification

Use classification to divide a large group into several smaller parts so that readers can see different elements in a group that, at first glance, may seem to be without variation. Like comparison, classification helps to organize complicated information. Here is a paragraph that classifies maple syrups.

> When syrups are graded, it's primarily according to color and flavor, with Grade A assigned to the more delicately flavored syrups. Grade A syrup usually comes in one of three colors: light amber (called Fancy in Vermont), medium amber, or dark amber. The darker the color, the stronger the caramelized sugar taste. Stronger-tasting than dark amber, and darker still, is Grade B syrup, used mostly in cooking.
>
> —*Consumer Reports*

Causal analysis

Organize paragraphs around an explanation of cause and effect when you want to explain why something happened or to report on the results of a happening. Here are two paragraphs that give the cause and effect of the plague that ravaged Europe in the late Middle Ages. Note that the analysis of cause and effect is given partly in the form of a narrative—an *analytical* narrative that explains as it tells a story.

> In October 1347, a fleet of Genoese merchant ships from the Orient arrived at the harbor of Messina in northeast Sicily. All aboard the ships were dead or dying of a ghastly disease. The harbor masters tried to quarantine the fleet, but the source of the pestilence was borne by rats, not men, and these were quick to scurry ashore. Within six months, half of the population of the region around Messina had fled their homes or succumbed to the disease, Four years later, between one-quarter and one-half of the population of Europe was dead.

The Black Death, or plague, that devastated Europe in the 14th century was caused by bacteria that live in the digestive tract of fleas, and in particular the fleas of rats. But at that time, the disease seemed arbitrary and capricious, and to strike from nowhere. One commentator wrote: "Father abandoned child, wife husband, one brother another, for the plague seemed to strike through breath and sight." The pestilence was widely held to be a scourge sent by God to chasten a sinful people.

—CHET RAYMO

Definition

Use paragraphs to define objects, concepts, ideas, terms, political movements, and anything else that may be important to your essay. A useful definition first identifies something as a member of a class of similar things; then it states how it differs from everything else in its class. Simple, concrete objects may be identified in a single sentence.

> A feast is a meal that is rich and abundant and that usually includes many guests.

Here a feast is first classified as a meal. What distinguishes it from a picnic, a breakfast, a lunch, a dinner, or a snack is that it is rich and abundant and usually includes many guests.

Always define the essential terms in any essay you write. Definitions of abstract terms may require an entire paragraph or several paragraphs. A defining paragraph usually comes near the beginning of an essay so readers will be sure to understand the term as the writer uses it throughout.

We have a roster of diseases which medicine calls "idiopathic," meaning that we do not know what causes them. The list is much shorter than it used to be; a century ago, common infections like typhus fever and tuberculous meningitis were classed as idiopathic illnesses. Originally, when it first came into the language of medicine, the term had a different, highly theoretical meaning. It was assumed that most human diseases were intrinsic, due to inbuilt failures of one sort or another, things gone wrong with various internal humors. The word "idiopathic" was intended to mean, literally, a disease having its own origin, a primary disease without any external cause. The list of such disorders has become progressively shorter as medical science has advanced, especially within this century, and the meaning of the term has lost its doctrinal flavor; we use "idiopathic" now to indicate simply that the cause of a particular disease is unknown. Very likely, before we are finished with medical science, and with luck, we will have found that all varieties of disease are the result of one or another sort of meddling, and there will be no more idiopathic illness.

—LEWIS THOMAS

■ **Exercise 3.10** Here is an excerpt from an essay on *JFK,* a film directed by Oliver Stone purporting to prove that President John F. Kennedy's assassination in 1963 was the result of an elaborate conspiracy that included agencies of the United States government. Discuss the various paragraph forms the author uses to make his point—narration, process analysis, comparison and contrast, classification, causal analysis, and definition.

There is no single way to do history on film. The traditional division into the dramatic work and the documentary is increasingly irrelevant as recent films (*JFK* included) often blur the distinction between the two. My own research has suggested that history on film comes in a number of different forms. *JFK,* despite the many documentary elements it contains, belongs to what is certainly the most popular type of film, the Hollywood—or mainstream—drama. This sort of film is marked, as cinema scholars have shown, by a number of characteristics, the chief being its desire to make us believe that what we see in the theater is true. To this end, the mainstream film utilizes a specific film language, a self-effacing, seamless language of shot, editing, and sound designed to make the screen seem no more than a window onto unmediated "reality."

Along with "realism," four other elements are crucial to understanding the mainstream historical film:

Hollywood history is delivered in a story with beginning, middle, end—a story with a moral message and one usually embodied in a progressive view of history.

The story is closed, completed, and, ultimately, simple. Alternative versions of the past are not shown. . . .

History is a story of individuals—usually, heroic individuals who do unusual things for the good of others, if not all humankind (ultimately, the audience).

Historical issues are personalized, emotionalized, and dramatized—for film appeals to our feelings as a way of adding to our knowledge or affecting our beliefs.

Such elements go a long way towards explaining the shape of *JFK.* The story is not that of President Kennedy but of Jim Garrison, the heroic, embattled, incorruptible investigator who wishes to make sense of Kennedy's assassination and its apparent cover-up, not just for himself but for his country and its traditions—that is, for the audience, for us. More than almost any other historical film, this one swamps us with information. Some of it, in the black-and-white flashbacks that illustrate the stages of the investigation, is tentative or contradictory. (So much is thrown at us that, on a single viewing, the viewer has difficulty absorbing all the details of events discussed and shown.) Yet, even if contradictions do exist, the main line of the story is closed and completed, and the moral message is clear: the assassination was the result of a conspiracy that involved agencies and officials of the U.S. government, the aim of the assassination was to get rid of a president who wished to curb the military and end the Cold War, and the "fascist" groups responsible for the assassination and subsequent cover-up are a clear and continuing threat to what little is left of American democracy.

—ROBERT A. ROSENSTONE

■ **Exercise 3.11** Write a short paragraph on two of the following topics, and discuss with the class the technique of development you have used in each.

1. the difference between intelligence and education
2. different types of eaters
3. how to repair a bruised ego
4. different types of roommates
5. movies you hate

■ **Exercise 3.12** For each paragraph form, select one topic and write a practice paragraph.

1. *Narration:* (*a*) what you and some friends did on a Saturday night recently, (*b*) a visit to a doctor, (*c*) your decision to buy a new or used different car
2. *Process analysis:* (*a*) cooking a simple recipe, (*b*) how to study for an exam, (*c*) learning a foreign language, (*d*) adjusting to a new town when you move
3. *Comparison and contrast:* (*a*) a novel and a film based on the novel, (*b*) two movies featuring the same actor or actress, (*c*) the writing courses you had in high school and this writing course, (*d*) downhill skiing and cross-country skiing, (*e*) writing with a pencil and writing on a computer
4. *Classification:* (*a*) supermarket shoppers, (*b*) clothing styles for different activities, (*c*) television programs, (*d*) trees in your neighborhood

5. *Causal analysis:* (*a*) effects of nuclear war, (*b*) why some people write well and others do not, (*c*) why some people like to read and some do not, (*d*) why people smoke cigarettes
6. *Definition:* (*a*) racism, (*b*) an examination, (*c*) a triathlon, (*d*) argument, (*e*) religion, (*f*) jazz, (*g*) rock music, (*h*) heavy metal music, (*i*) folk music.

Constructing Opening and Closing Paragraphs

Opening and closing paragraphs are extremely important to your essay. Your opening paragraph makes readers decide to keep reading or to lay your work aside. Your closing paragraph wraps up your essay and gives your readers some final thought to remember.

Your opening paragraph should announce the general topic of your essay and be interesting enough to make people read on. The opening paragraph usually implies a promise you make to readers to do something in your essay. Your concluding paragraph should end with the promise kept. Often the concluding paragraph repeats the thoughts and words of the opening paragraph to give readers the sense of having come around to the goal the first paragraph set for them.

A few audiences may expect your opening paragraphs to outline everything you intend to do in your essay. Descriptions of scientific experiments almost always start with such an outline, called an *abstract* in the scientific discourse community. But if you are writing about some personal topic or about something you wish to explain or report, your first paragraphs usually give only an inviting glimpse of what lies in store for the reader.

Note how the opening paragraphs that follow introduce a subject and set the tone.

> Nearly 70 percent of Americans are worried about the quality of their drinking water, according to a recent survey. Much of their concern centers on how water looks, tastes, or smells. Unfortunately water that is hazardous to your health usually looks, tastes, and smells just fine.
>
> —*Consumer Reports*

> Juliette Sauget set out for Paris at the age of seventeen in the company of an elder, married sister who resided there. Born in 1886 into an impoverished woodcutter's family, Juliette left home as a gesture of solidarity with another sister, whom her father had struck in anger. In Paris, her married sister advised her to work as a domestic servant, because Juliette needed lodgings as well as a job. In her first position, she complained one night at supper that the seventeen-year-

old son of the family had come to her room with the intention of having sexual relations with her. The family laughed in reply, so she felt she had to leave. This incident marked the beginning of a series of jobs: first in Paris, then in Amiens—the capital of her home province, where other of her siblings resided—then back in Paris. Eventually, she developed a social life at the public, outdoor dances in Paris. At age twenty-four, she became pregnant.

—RACHEL G. FUCHS AND LESLIE PAGE MOCH

Television has all but swallowed American politics and sport. Now it is closing in on the nation's moral dilemmas. Debates of the toughest questions (abortion, the death penalty, for example) look like wrestling or professional football. When Robert Harris was executed in California last week, the event had a strange gaudy quality, somehow commercial and electronic. Perhaps one day prisoners will go to the gas chamber with product-endorsement logos on their prison pajamas.

—LANCE MORROW

Introductory paragraphs which summarize the paper that follows are standard format for scientific writing. They assume a previous interest by specialists, who can quickly see if the topic of the paper fits their specialty.

In this paper I shall consider several educational issues growing out of A. R. Jensen's paper, "How Much Can We Boost IQ and Scholastic Achievement?" (Jensen, 1969). The first deals with the question of how education should adjust to the incontestable fact that approximately half the children in our schools are and always will be below average in IQ. Following this, I take up some of the more moot points of the "Jensen controversy"—what does heritability tell us about teachability? What are the prospects for reducing the spread of individual differences in intelligence? And what are the educational implications of possible hereditary differences in intelligence associated with social class and race?—ending with some implications that these issues have for educational research.

—CARL BEREITER

Most professional writers never end an article or an essay with a summary. A good concluding paragraph completes the paper logically and clearly, perhaps drawing a conclusion that expresses some meaning to be found in the information presented in the essay. The following paragraphs, from two of the essays whose opening paragraphs appear above, express the general meaning of the essays they conclude.

Single pregnant migrants were integral to the process of urbanization and geographic mobility. Pregnancy motivated some migrations and was the result of others. These women's experience enriches our understanding of migration, urbanization and life in the metropolis. Likewise, the complex patterns analyzed here echo in other cities and in other times.

—RACHEL G. FUCHS AND LESLIE PAGE MOCH

The answer is all of the above. Emphasis on the entertainment. People pay millions to watch terminators and terminations. They have a taste for it. The distinction between actual death and special effects get blurry in this culture. It thins to vanishing. Reality and unreality become ugly, interchangeable kicks. Perhaps if Harris had been spared, he might, like Audie Murphy, have been hired to play himself in the docudrama.

—LANCE MORROW

■ **Exercise 3.13** Look at all the articles in a popular magazine that you enjoy reading, and carefully compare the first and last paragraphs of each article. What relation do you see between the two paragraphs even before you read the article? Describe to others the connections between each first and last paragraph that you study.

■ **Exercise 3.14** Take one of your own essays and compare the first and last paragraphs. What similarities do you note between them?

3e Revising Paragraphs

As you revise the rough draft of your essay, focus on each individual paragraph. Make sure each one is unified, coherent, and well developed (see Checklist 3.2).

Because the controlling idea of your paragraph should guide any changes you make, start by rereading your paragraph carefully to determine the controling idea you want to express. You may want to add elements, eliminate elements, or subordinate one element to another. A paragraph such as the one that follows requires revision.

✓ CHECKLIST 3.2: REVISING PARAGRAPHS

- Is the paragraph an appropriate length? Does a new paragraph begin where there is a change in emphasis?
- Does the paragraph have a controlling idea? Does each sentence in the paragraph support the controlling idea?
- Does the paragraph demonstrate coherence? Does each sentence flow into the next, expanding a thought or idea already introduced?
- Does the paragraph use repetition to advantage? Does it display parallel structure? Are transitional expressions appropriate?
- Does the paragraph look back to the one before it and forward to the one after it?
- Are the ideas in the paragraph arranged to suit the purpose?
- Are supporting details used effectively?
- Are generalizations and specifics balanced?
- Does the opening paragraph interest the reader and announce the topic?
- Does the concluding paragraph pick up on words and ideas announced in the opening paragraph and demonstrate to the reader that the essay has done what it promised?

> Wood-burning stoves are helping many Americans beat the cost of fossil fuels and save money. Wood is still plentiful in the United States. Many states set off parts of their state forests where residents can cut designated trees at no charge. Some wood stoves give off emissions that may cause cancer, and people in big cities find wood more expensive than other sources of heat. But the technology of wood stoves has improved so that they can be very safe as well as efficient. The federal government now has standards that wood stove manufacturers must meet. Unfortunately, wood stoves are sometimes bulky and ugly and take up too much space in small rooms. Sometimes they make rooms too hot. Many homeowners who have gone to wood stoves for heat report savings of hundreds of dollars each year over the former price of heating their houses with oil. And many of them enjoy the exercise of cutting wood.

Here the paragraph has been revised:

> Wood-burning stoves are helping many Americns beat the high costs of fossil fuels. In recent years, the prices of oil and gas have come down, but these are limited fuels, and the prices are bound to rise again. So the availability of cheap fuel is still worth considering—

and wood is cheap in some parts of the United States. A cord of wood, a stack measuring 4 × 4 × 8 feet, costs just over a hundred dollars in a typical heating season. Many states like Massachusetts and Montana set off parts of their state forests where residents can cut designated trees at no charge. On a warm summer morning, one may see dozens of families sawing trees and loading vans or pickup trucks with logs for use as a winter fuel. Not only can wood be obtained cheaply, but also the technology of wood stoves has improved; the new models are far more efficient than the old ones. Now a family can heat a house with a wood stove with a minimum of waste or expense. A good airtight wood stove heats a room far more efficiently than does a conventional fireplace or a Franklin stove. Many homeowners who have turned to wood stoves for heat report savings of hundreds of dollars each year over the price of heating their houses with oil.

■ **Exercise 3.15** Revise the following paragraph for unity, coherence, and development.

The blizzard began early on the morning of February 6. The snow began falling before dawn. The flakes were small and hard. The snow itself was very thick. By nine o'clock, six inches of white covered the streets. Commuting traffic was reduced to a crawl. None of this affected me, since the schools were closed, and I stayed home, warm and cozy by the fire. I read the morning newspaper, which had arrived before the snow was very deep, and I kept refilling the coffee mug that sat beside me on a glass-topped table. By ten-thirty, the streets were impassable, and motorists were abandoning their cars. By noon, the offices in the city that had opened despite the storm were closing and sending workers home. At three o'clock, the mayor declared a state of emergency and asked schools, churches, and synagogues to give shelter to people stranded by the storm. Seeing all those people gathered together in houses of worship gave you a nice feeling about human nature, which some writers have claimed is evil. By six o'clock, the city was locked in the enchantment of a profound silence. Two feet of snow lay in the streets, and more was falling.

PART

TWO

WRITING CLEAR AND EFFECTIVE SENTENCES

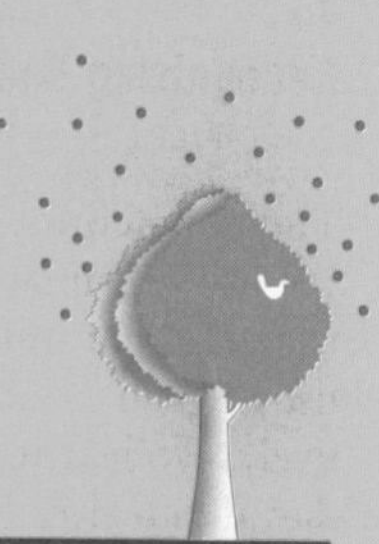

CHAPTER

CHAPTER

4

BASIC SENTENCE GRAMMAR

To write well and to understand how you can revise your writing to make it better, you must know how to use the elements of the English sentence—elements traditionally called grammar. **Grammar** is two things:

1. A collection of forms that make sense in sentences
2. The language we use to talk about such forms

4a
Recognizing Basic Sentence Forms

The first definition of grammar is much more important than the second. We use grammar all the time as a set of forms that make sense. Most of us use grammar well enough to make people understand what we mean. We use English grammar and the forms of the English sentence almost instinctively. We learned them when we learned to talk, and we use them every day all our lives.

The word *forms* is essential to understanding grammar. We react to sentences as forms, familiar patterns that we recognize because they are so common. We have heard them since we first heard language, and we have used them since we first began using words in sentences. We cannot change them on whim because everyone else who uses English knows them and uses them by habit.

We probably started by giving something a name that got results. "Milk!" we shouted, and somebody gave us milk. A little later we said, "Give me milk." Still later we said, "Will you please give me some milk?" or "I prefer milk, please."

As we grow older, we learn to work many kinds of thoughts into the basic sentence forms. If you hear somebody say, "I picked up the telephone," you know what the speaker means. But if somebody says, "Picked

I the telephone up,'' you run the statement through your mind again. What is this person saying? The form is not right. People don't say, ''Drove I the car this morning to work'' or ''Stood bravely he the last until.''

The sense of sentence form is so strong in us that we can frequently understand a sentence even when we don't know what every word means. If somebody says, ''Give me the phlumpis on the table,'' we hear the form or pattern, recognize it as a request or a command, and look on the table to see what the ''phlumpis'' is. The form tells us to do something with something called a ''phlumpis,'' and we do it. The sentence form is grammar in action.

In English, there are only a few basic sentence forms, although as you will see, you can make some changes in the basic form of any sentence.

The most common sentence form tells us that someone or something does something to something or someone else.

The man next door kills ants by spraying them with window cleaner.

This is a simple pattern. The man next door does something to the ants. It may seem odd to kill them with window cleaner. Even so, the sentence tells you he does it, and you can imagine him pumping away with a little spray bottle aimed at the ants. Using this common pattern, you can substitute nonsense words and still have an idea of what the sentence means.

The aardcam next door grinks ants by cooming them with dab.

You know that something called an ''aardcam'' is the actor in the sentence. You know that ''grinks'' expresses the main act and that ''cooming'' expresses a helping act to the main act. ''Dab'' is some kind of tool, some instrument, something used in the action. You know that something is doing something to the ants because you recognize a basic pattern of the English sentence.

Another sentence form tells us that something acts but nothing receives the action.

The telephone is ringing.

The thermometer exploded.

The lilacs bloomed.

Another sentence form describes a state or condition of being. The actor in the sentence exists in a certain way. The sentence expresses no action; it is simply a statement that something *is* (or was or will be), or that it exists with a certain quality.

The telephone is black.

The man was old and feeble but still witty and interesting.

Another sentence form tells us that something is acted upon. In such a sentence the recipient of the action is the most important thing in the sentence.

Amy Huang was honored by the Rotary Club today.

The striking airline workers were ordered back to work.

These basic forms help sentences make sense. That is what the word **sentence** means—a group of words that make sense. They make sense because they communicate through patterns that we recognize and expect. We can easily understand the sense of the following statements.

It rained last night.

The dust on the book made me sneeze.

Junior soccer leagues are becoming popular in suburban communities.

The Toronto Blue Jays won the 1992 World Series.

She fixed five flat tires in an hour.

Some word groups look like sentences at first glance. They begin with a capital letter and end with a period. But we cannot make sense of them because they don't follow a familiar pattern that communicates.

Shafts of light into the valley.

Driving through the rain.

The most frequently abused drugs.

None of these groups of words has a recognizable sentence form. In each case, we must add words to make a pattern that communicates a sensible statement.

The rising sun threw shafts of light into the valley.

Driving through the rain, Bill shuddered at the cold.

The most frequently abused drugs are alcohol and tobacco.

As all these examples prove, you do not have to know or use grammatical terms to recognize sentence patterns. But if you do know the terms, you can talk more precisely about grammar and you can understand better what your instructor says to you in class and in comments on your papers. The rest of this chapter reviews basic grammatical terms.

4b
Reviewing Basic Sentence Structure

The part of the sentence that names what the sentence is about is called the **subject.** The part of the sentence that makes a statement or asks a question about the subject is called the **predicate.** The boundaries of the sentence are clearly marked off by a capital letter at the beginning and a period, a question mark, or an exclamation point at the end. Within these boundaries, every sentence contains at least one subject and one predicate that fit together to make a statement, ask a question, or give a command.

Here are some examples of basic English sentences.

Desert winds blow fiercely.

The sun is rising over the Caribbean.

Your computer blew up yesterday.

The Soviet Union no longer exists.

Sarah repairs automobiles.

Is Carlos allergic to cigarette smoke?

Does Aida own her own business?

[You] Bring me the report.

[You] Pass the spaghetti.

The Subject

ESL 1*

The subject and the words that describe it are often called the **complete subject.** Within the complete subject, the word (or words) that serve as the focus of the sentence may be called the **simple subject.**

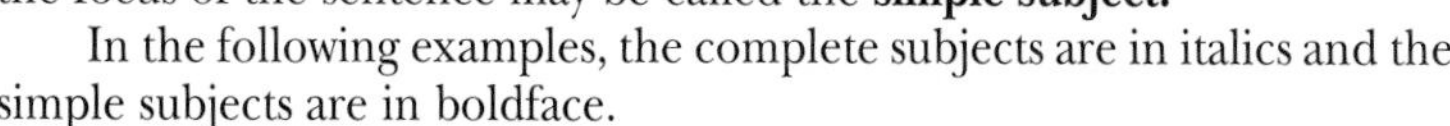

In the following examples, the complete subjects are in italics and the simple subjects are in boldface.

The quick brown ***fox*** jumps over the lazy dog.

Shing-Wen Lee won the game with a triple in the ninth.

The huge black ***clouds*** *in the west* predicted a violent storm.

*Each ESL appendix box is referenced at the appropriate point in the text by a marginal icon (the tree) and the box number.

A **compound subject** consists of two or more subjects joined by a connecting word such as *and* or *but* (discussed in 4c).

> *Original* ***thinking*** *and bold* ***design*** have distinguished her architectural career.

The Predicate

4b gram

The predicate asserts something about the subject. The predicate, together with all the words that help it make a statement about the subject, is often called the **complete predicate.** Within the complete predicate, the word (or words) that reports or states conditions, with all describing words removed, is called the **simple predicate** or the **verb.** A verb expresses action or a state of being.

In the following sentences, the complete predicates are in italics and the simple predicates (the *verbs*) are in boldface.

> The quick brown fox ***jumps*** *over the lazy dog.*
>
> Shing-Wen Lee ***won*** *the game with a triple in the ninth.*
>
> The huge black clouds in the west ***predicted*** *a violent storm.*
>
> Original thinking and bold design ***have distinguished*** *her architectural career.*

Like subjects, predicates may also be compound. In a **compound predicate,** two or more verbs are joined by a connecting word.

> The huge black clouds in the west ***predicted*** *a violent storm and* ***ended*** *our picnic.*

Sometimes one verb combines with another to form a verb of more than one word, called a **verb phrase.** The verb phrases are in boldface in the sentences that follow.

> Gold **was discovered** in California in 1848.
>
> He **might have seen** that film before.
>
> Original thinking and bold design **have distinguished** her architectural career and **have made** her rich.
>
> The oldest building on campus **would have been demolished** if she **had** not **made** a generous donation to save it.

Another way to locate verbs is to memorize the verbs that serve as **auxiliaries**—that is, helpers to other verbs. These auxiliaries are always verbs and never anything else. The most common helping verbs are *am,* *is, are, was, were, shall, will, could, would, have, has, had, do, does, did, be, been, might, can, may,* and *must.* (Verbs are discussed further in Chapters 15 and 16.)

Recognizing Subjects and Predicates

One way to find the subject and the predicate components is to look at what the sentence says and to ask two questions about its meaning.

1. Who or what is the sentence about? *(subject)*
2. What statement is the sentence making about the subject? *(predicate)*

Perhaps the best way to find basic sentence components is to first look for the verb (the *simple predicate*). Remember that verbs express action or state of being.

> Churchill **spoke** to England.
>
> The hippopotamus **was** beautiful.

It is even easier to find verbs if you remember that they change their form in accordance with the way they are used in a sentence. Because verbs change their forms to show time, or *tense* (discussed in 4c), you can locate verbs easily by forcing such a change in a sentence. If you use a word like *yesterday, today,* or *tomorrow* at the start of a sentence whose verb you are trying to identify, the only word that changes will be the verb.

> I eat green vegetables.
>
> *Yesterday,* I **ate** green vegetables.

> Mr. Smith goes to Washington.
>
> *Tomorrow,* Mr. Smith **will go** to Washington.

✔ CHECKLIST 4.1: TESTING FOR VERBS

- Change a sentence by using *yesterday, today,* and *tomorrow* at the beginning. The word that changes is a verb.

  He played shortstop.
  Tomorrow he **will play** shortstop.
  Today he **plays** shortstop.

- Learn the most familiar helping verbs: am, *is, are, was, were, shall, will, could, would, have, has, do, does, did, be, been, might, can, may, must*

- Use *I, he, she, it, you, we,* or *they* before the word you think is a verb.

If you make sense with this combination, the word you are testing is a verb.

Word	**Test**	**Verb?**
try	I try she tries	yes
olive	I olive (?) they olive (?)	no
laugh	they laugh	yes
laughing	I laughing they laughing	no

Once you find the verb, you can find the subject easily. Just put the verb in a question asking who or what does the action of a verb. Say the word *who* or *what;* then say the verb. The answer to your question will be the subject of the sentence. Generally, subjects of verbs are **nouns** or **pronouns,** words that name persons, places, things, ideas, or objects (discussed in 4c). But other words may sometimes be subjects.

We **have been working** all night. (*Who* has been working all night? **We.**)

Trout fishing **is** a popular sport in northern New England. (*What* is a popular sport in northern New England? **Trout fishing.**)

Lee **invaded** the North twice during the Civil War. (*Who* invaded the North twice during the Civil War? **Lee.**)

■ **Exercise 4.1** Draw a vertical line dividing the complete subject and the complete predicate in each sentence below. Then draw one line under the simple subject and two lines under the simple predicate, as in the following example.

My writing assignments in school/have always caused me much difficulty.

1. After many years, Ottawa finally has accepted a land of self-rule for Canada's Eskimos.
2. Twenty percent of the country will be carved out from the Northwest Territory.
3. More than 17,500 Eskimos will live in Nunauut, which means *our land* in Inuktituk, the Eskimos' language.

4. The vast region unfamiliar to most Canadians begins at the sixtieth degree of latitude and stretches more than fifteen hundred miles to Alert, the last settlement before the North Pole.
5. Human traces have been identified more than four thousand years back.
6. Norsemen explored the region during the eleventh century A.D.
7. Maritime explorers, missionaries, and adventurers followed.
8. Ottawa, Canada's capital city, was required to assume responsibility for Eskimos by a 1939 court order.
9. Eskimos, or Inuit, no longer hunt seals, whales, and polar bears as nomads.
10. Government centers with typical problems of urban life now form the core of many Eskimo communities.

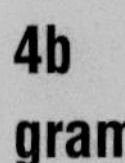

■ **Exercise 4.2** Write five original sentences. Draw a slash between the complete subject and the complete predicate. Then draw one line under the simple subject and two lines under the simple predicate.

Other Predicate Parts

In addition to verbs, complete predicates may also include sentence elements that modify, or help describe other elements.

Direct objects

The **direct object** tells who or what receives the action done by the subject and expressed by the verb. Not every sentence has a direct object, but many verbs require one to complete their meaning. Such verbs are called transitive verbs, from the Latin *trans,* meaning "across." A **transitive verb** carries action from the subject across to the direct object. In the examples below, direct objects are in boldface.

Catholic missionaries established the **school.**

Snopes burned **barns** all over the country.

Louis Gosset, Jr., lost thirty-five **pounds** for his role in *Diggstown.*

I have read that **story.**

We heard the distant **voice.**

In these examples, the verbs are transitive. They report actions done by the subject to the direct object.

A verb that does not carry action to a direct object is an intransitive verb. An **intransitive verb** reports action done by a subject, but it is not action done to anything. The following verbs are intransitive.

The ship **sank** within three hours after the collision.

Our dog **vanished** in the summer.

She **jogs** to keep fit.

4b gram

✔ **CHECKLIST 4.2: TESTING FOR DIRECT OBJECTS**

In looking for direct objects in sentences, ask the question *what* or *whom* after the verb. The answer will be the direct object.

- The children crossed the street.
  The children crossed *what?* the street. *Street* is the direct object.
- The Jets beat the Colts again.
  The Jets beat *whom?* the Colts. *Colts* is the direct object.

Direct objects, like subjects, are generally nouns or pronouns (discussed in 5c) or are word groups that act like nouns or pronouns.

Indirect objects

ESL 9

Sometimes, in addition to a direct object, a predicate also includes a noun or pronoun specifying to whom or for whom the action is done. This is the **indirect object.** It appears after the verb and before the direct object. Indirect objects occur fairly infrequently and are usually used with verbs such as *give, ask, tell, sing,* and *write.*

The tenants gave the **manager** their complaints.

Tell the **teacher** your idea.

Jack asked **George** an embarrassing question.

✔ **CHECKLIST 4.3: TESTING FOR INDIRECT OBJECTS**

If you ask the question *to whom* (or *for whom*) or *to what* (or *for what*), the answer will be the indirect object.

- He sang me a song.
  He sang to whom (or for whom)? me. *Me* is an indirect object.

- My father gave the television set a furious kick.
  My father gave to what? the television set. *The television set* is an indirect object.
- Bettina told the children a story from West Africa.
  Bettina told to whom? the children. *Children* is an indirect object.

■ **Exercise 4.3** In each sentence below, write *DO* over the direct object of the verb and *IO* over the indirect object.

1. Poverty-stricken laborers often suffer malnourishment from birth.
2. In Brazil's Northeast a poor diet of manioc flour, rice, and beans has given many workers minimal chances for normal lives.
3. Malnourishment produces retarded mental development, and some Brazilian laborers have brain capacities that are 40 percent less than average.
4. Diets drastically low in protein give adults far less than average heights as recorded by the World Health Organization.
5. Pediatric experts have told the Ministry of Health the grim news that more than 40 percent of the children in Northeast Brazil are born malnourished.

Complements

Complements complete descriptions of subjects and objects.

A **subject complement** is located on the other side of the verb from the subject and adds information about the subject. The verb that joins a subject and its complement is called a linking verb. A **linking verb** joins a subject to some further description of itself not included in the subject.

The most common linking verbs are the "to be" verbs—*is, are, was,* and *were.* But many other verbs also link a subject to a descriptive word. Observe the subject complements after the linking verbs in the following sentences.

My father is **a welder.**

America looked **good** to me after my long absence.

The poodle smelled **fresh** after his bath.

An **object complement** comes immediately after a direct object and helps complete the description of the direct object by the verb.

She called me **a bonehead.**

She said I drove her **crazy.**

My aunt dyed her hair **blue.**

I liked my eggs **scrambled.**

Like subject complements, object complements add to the description of the object. Complements may be nouns, pronouns, or adjectives (discussed in 4c).

■ **Exercise 4.4** Complete the following sentences in any appropriate manner, and indicate whether you have supplied a subject complement or an object complement by writing *SC* or *OC* after each sentence.

1. The university was ________.
2. The breeze felt ________.
3. He got the answers ________.
4. I was often ________.
5. My professors were ________.
6. I shut the door ________.
7. The patient grew ________.
8. You look ________.
9. I'll give you ________.
10. He took his coffee ________.

✓ CHECKLIST 4.4: TYPICAL SENTENCE PATTERNS

You have already seen how important sentence patterns are in English. Here are the most typical sentence patterns.

Pattern 1 **subject + verb**

We	laughed.
The flowers	bloomed.
The house	was destroyed.

Pattern 2 **subject + verb + direct object**

Ann	used	the jackhammer.
Dickens	wrote	*David Copperfield.*
She	told	the story.

Pattern 3 **subject + verb + subject complement**

Our house	was	large and cold.
He	looked	good.
The crowd	became	noisy.
The contract	seemed	fair.

Pattern 4 **subject + verb + direct object + object complement**

They	called	Lindbergh	a fool.
He	named	his son	John.

Pattern 5 **subject + verb + indirect object + direct object**

Lee	gave	Longstreet	the orders.
Smoke	gives	me	a headache.

The basic patterns can be rearranged in a variety of ways.

subject complement + verb + subject

Fair lie the fields of England.

direct object + subject + verb

These bones he removed.

4c Reviewing the Eight Parts of Speech

Sentence elements consist primarily of a subject and predicate. Each is made up of one or more words that themselves can be classified as **parts of speech.** The eight parts of speech are verbs, nouns, pronouns, adjectives, adverbs, conjunctions, prepositions, and interjections. We classify words as one or another part of speech according to the role they play in a sentence.

Verbs

Verbs report action, condition, or state of being. Verbs are the controlling words in predicates, but verbs themselves are controlled by subjects.

Number and person

The **number** of the subject determines the number of its verb. If a subject is only one thing, we say that it is *singular.* If it is more than one, we say that it is *plural: dog* is singular; the plural form is *dogs.* Verbs reflect these differences in subjects by taking a singular or a plural form.

In the **first-person singular,** I speak of myself. In the **first-person plural,** we speak or write of ourselves. In the **second-person singular and plural** (the forms are the same), you are addressed. In the **third-person singular,** someone speaks or writes about somebody or something who is not being addressed. In the **third-person plural,** someone speaks or writes about more than one person or about more than one object.

Verbs also show whether the action of the sentence is taking place now, took place in the past, or will take place in the future. Study the following examples.

4c gram

	Singular	**Plural**
First person	I read.	We read.
Second person	You read.	You read.
Third person	She reads.	They read.
First person	I loosen.	We loosen.
Second person	You loosen.	You loosen.
Third person	It loosens.	They loosen.
First person	I build.	We build.
Second person	You build.	You build.
Third person	He builds.	They build.

All these verbs are in the present tense. Notice that the only change that takes place is in the third person singular; a final *-s* is added to the common form of the verb. Most—but not all—verbs will add this *-s* in the third person singular.

Verbs must agree with the person of the subject. In the present tense (explained in more detail below), an *-s* is usually added to the verb in the third-person singular. Other tenses are shown by a change in the helping verb.

I **run.**	He **runs.**	They **run.**
I **am running.**	He **is running.**	They **are running.**

Helping verbs and verb phrases

ESL 4

Helping (or **auxiliary**) **verbs** help a single verb express a meaning that it could not express by itself. A **verb phrase** is the helping verb plus the main verb. The final word in a verb phrase, the **main verb,** carries the primary meaning of the verb phrase. Sometimes more than one helping verb accompanies the main verb. In the following sentences, the verb phrases are in boldface; HV appears over each helping verb, and MV appears over each main verb.

HV MV HV MV

The plane **will have left** before we **can get** to the airport.

HV MV HV MV

He **had been walking** for hours before he **was found.**

HV MV

He **is biking** to Vermont from Boston.

HV MV

They **will arrive** in time for the game.

HV MV

Contrary to his opinion, he **does** not **have** any imagination.

HV HV MV

Cy Young **has** always **been considered** one of the best pitchers in baseball history.

Notice that sometimes words not part of the verb phrase come between the helping verb and the main verb.

Here are some typical helping verbs.

be	do	can
being	did	shall
been	does	will
is	has	might
am	have	could
are	had	would
was	must	should
were	may	

Sometimes particles are added to verbs. **Particles** are short words that never change their form no matter how the main verb changes. They sometimes look like other parts of speech, but they always go with the verb to add a meaning that the verb does not have by itself.

Harry made **up** with Gloria.

He made **off** with my pen.

She filled **out** her application.

Tenses

English has three simple **tenses** (or times): present, past, and future.

Present: She **works** every day.

Past: She **worked** yesterday.

Future: She **will work** tomorrow.

The simple past tense of most verbs is formed by adding a final *-ed* to the common form of the present, or a simple *-d* if the common form of the present ends in *-e*.

Present: I **save** a little money every month.
The dogs in our neighborhood **bark** at night.

Past: I **saved** a thousand dollars last year.
The dog next door **barked** all night long.

But many verbs in English are irregular. **Irregular verbs** form the simple past tense by changing a part of the verb other than the ending.

Present: We **grow** tomatoes every year on our kitchen window shelf.
I **run** four miles every day.
I **go** to the grocery store every Saturday morning.

Past: We **grew** corn back in Iowa.
Coe **ran** the mile in three minutes and forty-six seconds in August 1981.
I **went** to the grocery store last Saturday.

The future tense of verbs is always formed by the addition of **shall** or **will** to the common form of the present.

Present: I often **read** in bed.

Future: I **shall read** you a story before bedtime.
She **will read** you the ending tomorrow morning.

Chapters 15 and 16 provide a detailed discussion of verbs.

■ **Exercise 4.5** Underline the verb phrases in the following sentences. Include particles as part of the verb phrase. Write HV over the helping verbs and MV over the main verbs.

1. Firebombs had forced the closing of the London subway system for almost four hours.

2. Has she rebuilt the Jeep engine?

3. The Cleveland Indians have not won a World Series since Harry Truman's administration.

4. She ought to be here any minute.

5. We send out for pizza every Saturday night.

6. Our friend Miguel Borinquen has spent Thanksgiving with us for years.

7. They should never have used up all the bok choy in the stir-fry.

8. He was regularly falling off the water skis.

9. People are moving to California every day.

10. They made out their route to northern Burma.

Nouns

ESL 10

Nouns are the names we use for people, places, animals, things, ideas, actions, states of existence, colors, and so forth. In sentences, nouns serve as subjects, objects, and complements. (Nouns may also be appositives; see the entry for *appositive* in the Glossary.)

Common nouns name ordinary things. Common nouns include the following words and thousands more.

ability	democracy	justice	rope
baseball	desks	library	showcases
beauty	geometry	man	smell
car	glory	music	students
cattle	glove	philosophy	synagogue
color	horses	profession	tension
defeat	house	proficiency	woman

Proper nouns are the names given to persons, places, and things to set them off from others in a group. Proper nouns always are capitalized. Proper nouns include the following—and thousands more.

Amtrak	Germany	New York
Donald A. Stone	Greek Orthodox	Omaha
Frenchman	Helen	State Department
General Dynamics	Ms. Howard	

4c gram

Compound nouns consist of two or more words that function as a unit. They include such common nouns as *heartache, mother-in-law, father-in-law, great-grandmother,* and *world view.* Compound nouns also may be proper nouns—*International Business Machines, Federal Bureau of Investigation, Suez Canal,* and *Belmont, Tennessee.*

How do you recognize nouns? Sometimes nouns reveal themselves by their endings. Words that end in *-ty, -tion, -sion, -or, -ism, -ist, -ment, -ness, -ship, -ture, -ance,* and *-ence* are usually nouns.

But be careful. Some words with these endings may also be verbs, such as *mention.*

Jackson made **mention** of you in his letter. (noun)

I hope you will **mention** my request to him. (verb)

ESL 12

Articles

Often nouns appear accompanied by **articles,** which limit or specify their function (see below). Articles are *a, an,* and *the.* One of the best ways to test whether a word in a sentence is a noun is to see if you can put an article in front of the word and still make sense of your sentence.

Number

Nouns can be singular or plural. You usually form the plural by adding the *-s* or *-es.* You form irregular plurals by other endings or by internal changes. (Regular and irregular plural forms are discussed in Chapter 27.)

Singular	Plural
nest	nests
dog	dogs
humanist	humanists
bush	bushes
church	churches
child	children
woman	women

Possessive form

Some nouns show ownership or a special relation to another noun in the sentence. The possessive form of nouns is formed by adding *-'s* or a simple apostrophe ('). Possessives can be either singular or plural.

Singular	**Possessive**	**Plural**	**Possessive**
girl	girl's notebook	guests	guests' invitations
insect	insect's sting	neighbors	neighbors' car

These qualities of plurality and possession can help you identify nouns in sentences. If you can make a word plural or make it show possession, it is a noun.

✓ CHECKLIST 4.5: TESTING FOR NOUNS

- Use *a, an,* or *the* before the word.

Word	**Test**	**Noun?**
razor	a razor, the razor	yes
book	the book	yes
raining	a raining, the raining	no
laughingly	a laughingly, the laughingly	no

- Make the word plural.

Word	**Test**	**Noun?**
egg	eggs	yes
soon	soons	no

- Make the word show possession.

Word	**Test**	**Noun?**
child	the child's blanket	yes
criticize	the criticize's thing	no

■ **Exercise 4.6** Write a short paragraph about something you did yesterday. Underline all the nouns.

4c gram

Pronouns

Like nouns, pronouns serve as subjects, objects, and complements in sentences. A **pronoun** is a word used in place of a noun. As pronouns stand in for nouns, you must always make clear to readers what nouns the pronouns stand for. A pronoun that lacks a clear antecedent causes great confusion. (Pronouns are discussed more fully in Chapter 17.)

There are many kinds of pronouns, and we use them for different purposes.

Personal pronouns refer to one or more persons: *I, you, he, she, it, we, they.*

Indefinite pronouns make statements about a member of a group when we are unable to name which one we mean: *all, any, anyone, each, everybody, everyone, few, nobody, one, someone.*

Reflexive pronouns refer to the noun or pronoun that is the subject of the sentence; they always end in *-self: myself, himself, herself, yourself, ourselves.*

She allowed **herself** no rest.

He loved **himself** more than he loved anyone else.

ESL 1

Intensive pronouns have the same form as reflexive pronouns; they add special emphasis to nouns and other pronouns.

I **myself** have often made that mistake.

President Harding **himself** played poker and drank whiskey in the White House during Prohibition.

Demonstrative pronouns point out nouns or other pronouns that come after them: *this, that, these, those.*

That is the book I want.

Are **those** the books you bought?

Relative pronouns join word groups containing a subject and verb to nouns or pronouns that the word groups describe: *who, whom, that, which.*

Dravot in Kipling's story was the man **who** would be king.

The tools **that** I lost in the lake cost me a fortune to replace.

The doctor **whom** you recommended has been suspended for malpractice.

Possessive pronouns show possession or special relations: *my, his, her, your, our, their, its.* Unlike possessive nouns, possessive pronouns have no apostrophes.

She was **my** aunt.

Their cat sets off **my** allergies.

The fault was **ours,** and the worst mistake was **mine.**

Interrogative pronouns introduce questions: *who, which, what.*

What courses are you taking?

Who kept score?

Which of the glasses is mine?

Like nouns, pronouns can be singular or plural, depending on the noun they replace.

KINDS OF PRONOUNS

Personal pronouns	Indefinite pronouns		Reflexive pronouns	Intensive pronouns
I	all	no one	myself	myself
you	any	one	yourself	yourself
she	anybody	ones	herself	herself
he	anyone	somebody	himself	himself
it	anything	someone	itself	itself
we	each	whichever	oneself	oneself
they	everybody	whoever	ourselves	ourselves
me	everyone	whomever	yourselves	yourselves
her	few		themselves	themselves
him	many			
them	nobody			

Demonstrative pronouns	**Relative pronouns**	**Possessive pronouns**	**Interrogative pronouns**
this	that	my	what
that	which	mine	who
these	what	your	which
those	who	yours	
	whom	her	
	whoever	hers	
	whomever	his	
	whose	its	
		our	
		ours	
		their	
		theirs	

■ **Exercise 4.7** Fill in the blanks with any pronouns that make sense. See how many different pronouns you can use in each blank.

1. ________ always wanted to put a small motor on ________ hang glider.
2. ________ house is on the street next to ________ school.
3. ________ who can square dance is welcome to ________ party.
4. The president ________ said he would be at the party.
5. ________ is in charge of ________ goat?
6. ________ must we do to pay ________ mechanic?
7. ________ of the parts must be replaced?
8. The snake was ________, but I kept quiet when ________ was found on the couch of the adjoining apartment.
9. "The most important principle in dancing," ________ told ________, "is to think of the music and not ________ feet."
10. When ________ drove the car through ________ kitchen window, the impact ruined ________ cake ________ happened to be in the oven at the time.

Adjectives, Articles, Adverbs

Adjectives and adverbs describe other words more fully or more definitely. Adjectives and adverbs modify other words; that is, they change, expand, limit, or otherwise help describe the words to which they relate.

Adjectives

Adjectives modify nouns and pronouns. That is, they help describe nouns and pronouns in a sentence by answering questions such as *which one, what kind, how many, what size, what color, what condition, whose.* Adjectives appear in boldface in the sentences below.

The **pale** sun shone through the **gloomy** clouds.

Six camels trudged across a **vast white** desert.

Harry's little blue Volkswagen died **one icy winter** morning.

4c gram

Adjectives come immediately before or immediately after the words they modify, although they usually come before.

The **tired, thirsty,** and **impatient** horse threw its rider and went back to the barn.

The horse, **tired, thirsty,** and **impatient,** threw its rider and went back to the barn.

ESL 13

Subject complements

An adjective modifying the subject of a sentence sometimes appears on the opposite side of a linking verb from the subject.

The horse looked **tired, thirsty,** and **impatient.**

My friend was **ill,** and I was **worried.**

In these examples, the adjectives are subject complements.

✔ CHECKLIST 4.6: TESTING FOR ADJECTIVES

Ask questions such as:

- Which one? **That** man was the murderer.
- What kind? The **dead** leaves clung to the old tree.
- How many? The train had **six** cars.
- What size? The **tall** building is Holyoke Center.
- What color? The **brown** grass showed that we needed rain.
- What condition? **Sick** people often have no energy.
- Whose? **My** coat is the one with the hole in the sleeve.

Articles

An **article** is a word used with a noun to limit or specify its application. The articles *a, an,* and *the* function as adjectives. The articles *a* and *an* are indefinite and singular; they call attention to any one of several things.

> He sent me **a** card.
>
> Richard III cried, "**A** horse, **a** horse, my kingdom for **a** horse!"

4c gram

The article *a* appears before words that begin with a consonant sound; *an* appears before words that begin with a vowel sound.

> a dish, a rose, a year, an apple, an entreaty, a European, an hour, a historian, an ideal, an enemy, a friend, an umbrella, a union, an understanding

ESL 12

The word *Europe* begins with the vowels *eu,* which in this case are sounded as *yu.* So we speak of "*a* Europe at peace" or "*a* European in America." A few English words that begin with the consonant *h* have a vowel sound and are preceded by *an.*

> an hour, an honest man, an honor, an honorable schoolboy

The article *the* is used with both singular and plural nouns. It always means "this and not any other." Often the difference between using *a* or *an* and using *the* depends on the writer's idea of how specific the following noun is.

> **Definite:** He came down off **the** mountain and found **the** road. (No other mountain and no other road will do.)
>
> **Indefinite:** He came down off **a** mountain and found **a** road. (The writer does not know or care what mountain the man descended or what road he found. Maybe the man himself didn't know.)

Degree

In comparisons, adjectives show degree or intensity by the addition of an *-er* or *-est* ending or by the use of *more* or *most* or *less* or *least.* In the **positive**

degree, no comparison is intended. The **comparative degree** singles out one object in a set of two. The **superlative degree** singles out one object among three or more.

Adjective: **large**

Positive degree: She owned a **large** hat.

Comparative degree: Her hat was **larger** than mine.

Superlative degree: She owned the **largest** hat in the theater.

Adjective: **sophisticated**

Positive degree: Joan's analysis of *Moby Dick* was **sophisticated.**

Comparative degree: Joan's analysis of *Moby Dick* was **more sophisticated** than Emily's.

Superlative degree: Joan's analysis of *Moby Dick* was the **most sophisticated** in her class.

Adverbs

Adverbs modify words or sentence elements that cannot be modified by adjectives. Since adjectives can modify only nouns and pronouns, adverbs are left to modify everything else. They usually modify verbs, adjectives, and other adverbs, but they sometimes modify prepositions, phrases, clauses, and even whole sentences. (Adverbs are discussed more fully in 19c.)

Adverbs answer several questions, such as *how, how often, to what degree (how much), where,* and *when.*

Wearily he drifted **away.**

She did **not** speak **much today.**

Adverbs may modify by affirmation or negation. *Not* is always an adverb.

He **surely** will call home before he leaves.

They shall **not** pass.

We **never** will see anyone like her again.

Many adverbs end in *-ly,* and you can make adverbs of most adjectives simply by adding *-ly* to the adjective form.

Adjective	**Adverb**
large	largely
crude	crudely
beautiful	beautifully

4c
gram

✔ CHECKLIST 4.7: TESTING FOR ADVERBS

Ask questions such as:

- How? He **cheerfully** gave up the money.
- How often? **Sometimes** I wonder what she means.
- To what degree? I **intensely** dislike having to look for a parking place.
- Where? Odysseus, following the defeat of Troy, turned **homeward.**
- When? **Yesterday** I took my last exam.

ESL 14

A great many adverbs do not end in *-ly.*

> often, sometimes, then, when, anywhere, anyplace, somewhere, somehow, somewhat, yesterday, Sunday, before, behind, ahead, seldom

And many adjectives end in *-ly.*

> costly, stately, lowly, homely, measly, manly, womanly

Conjunctive adverbs

Some adverbs can serve to connect ideas between clauses. These are **conjunctive adverbs,** such words and phrases as *accordingly, consequently, hence, however, indeed, meanwhile, moreover, nevertheless, on the other hand,* and *therefore* (see 13e).

> Descartes said, "I think; **therefore** I am."
>
> He opposed her before she won the primary election; **however,** he supported her afterward in her campaign.

Swimming is an excellent exercise for the heart and for the muscles; **on the other hand,** swimming does not control weight as well as jogging and biking do.

Unlike *coordinating conjunctions* (discussed below) or *transitional expressions* (discussed in 3c), conjunctive adverbs cannot bind clauses together. If you use one of the conjunctive adverbs between clauses, you also must use a semicolon or a period. This rule makes it easy to tell a conjunctive adverb from a coordinating conjunction. Conjunctive adverbs may shift positions within a clause.

Coordinating conjunction: Swimming is an excellent exercise for the heart and for the muscles, **but** swimming does not control weight as well as jogging and biking do.

Conjunctive adverb: Swimming is an excellent exercise for the heart and for the muscles; **on the other hand,** swimming does not control weight as well as jogging and biking do.

The best test for an adverb is to find what it modifies and then to ask yourself the appropriate adverb questions. If a modifier does not help describe a noun, a pronoun, or some other noun substitute, it has to be an adverb. If it does modify a noun, a pronoun, or some other noun substitute, it cannot be an adverb.

Degree

Adverbs, like adjectives, show degrees by the addition of an *-er* or *-est* ending or by the use of *more* or *most* or *less* or *least.* Whether modifying an adjective or another adverb, the words *more, most, less,* and *least* are themselves adverbs.

Adverb: *fast*

Positive degree: Olga ran **fast.**

Comparative degree: Olga ran **faster** than Jack.

Superlative degree: Olga ran **fastest** of all her playmates.

Adverb: *sadly*

Positive degree: My visitors said goodbye **sadly.**

Comparative degree: They spoke **more sadly** than I did.

Superlative degree: I spoke **most sadly** when they told me that they had decided not to leave.

POSITIVE, COMPARATIVE, AND SUPERLATIVE DEGREES

Positive (one object is)	**Comparative (of two objects, one is)**	**Superlative (of three objects, one is)**
Adjective:		
swift	*swifter*	*swiftest*
She was **swift.**	She was **swifter** than Tom.	She was the **swiftest** runner in the fifth grade.
Adverb:		
swiftly	*more swiftly*	*most swiftly*
She ran **swiftly.**	She ran **more swiftly** than she ever had.	Among all the fifth graders, she ran **most swiftly.**

■ **Exercise 4.8** In the following sentences, underline the adverbs and draw a circle around the adjectives.

1. Later he drifted silently across the warm, moonlit street.
2. Clearly solar heat offers many advantages, but both the equipment and its installation have high costs.
3. Japanese planes roared swiftly over the motionless battleships at Pearl Harbor early on Sunday, December 7, 1941.
4. Many state education departments now enthusiastically support the use of hand-held calculators on various mathematics and science tests in elementary and secondary school classrooms.
5. I learned to appreciate Hebrew by hearing our cantor sing during the Friday-night Sabbath services, but I never understood exactly what the songs meant because I did not know the language well enough.

Conjunctions

Conjunctions join elements within a sentence. These elements may be words, or they may be groups of words like clauses or phrases (see 4d, 4e).

Coordinating conjunctions (or, simply, **coordinators**) join elements of equal weight or function. The common coordinating conjunctions are *and, but, or, for,* and *nor.* Some writers now include *yet* and *so.*

She was tired **and** happy.

The town was small **but** pretty.

They must be tired, **for** they have climbed all day long.

You may take the green **or** the red.

He would not leave the table, **nor** would he stop insulting his host.

Correlative conjunctions are conjunctions used in pairs. They also connect sentence elements of equal value. The familiar correlatives are *both . . . and, either . . . or, neither . . . nor,* and *not only . . . but also.*

Neither the doctor **nor** the the police believed his story.

The year 1927 was **not only** the year Lindbergh flew solo nonstop across the Atlantic **but also** the year Babe Ruth hit sixty home runs.

Subordinating conjunctions (or **subordinators**) join dependent or subordinate sections of a sentence to independent sections or to other dependent sections (see 4e). The common subordinating conjunctions are *after, although, as, because, if, rather than, since, that, unless, until, when, whenever, where, wherever,* and *while.*

The stylus will not track records **if** there is not enough weight on it.

Although the desert may look barren and dead, a vigorous life goes on there.

He always wore a hat **when** he went out in the sun.

Stories about divorce are common on television and in the movies **because** so many Americans have been divorced.

The use of conjunctions to improve your writing is discussed in Chapter 6.

Prepositions

ESL 15

Prepositions are short words that work with nouns or pronouns as modifiers, often specifying place or time. The noun or pronoun is the **object** of the preposition. In the following sentence the prepositions are in boldface and their objects are in italics.

Suburban yards now provide homes **for** *wildlife* that once lived only **in** the *country.*

The preposition, its noun, and any modifiers attached to the noun make up a **prepositional phrase.** Prepositional phrases act as adjectives and adverbs. The main function of prepositions is to allow the nouns or pronouns that follow them to modify other words in the sentence. Here are common prepositions.

about
above
across
after
against
along
amid
among
as
at
before
behind
below
beneath
beside
between
beyond
by
despite
down
during
except
excluding
following
from
in
including
inside
into
like
near
of
on
over
since
through
to
toward
under
underneath
until
up
upon
via
with
within
without

Some prepositions consist of more than one word.

according to
along with
apart from
as to
because of
by means of
by way of
except for
in addition to
in case of
in front of
in place of
in regard to
in spite of
instead of
on account of
up to
with respect to
with reference to

Prepositions usually come before their objects. But sometimes, especially in questions, they do not. Grammarians debate whether prepositions should end a sentence. Most writers favoring an informal style will now and then use a preposition to end a sentence.

Which college do you go **to?**

Which lake does she live **by?**

For more formal choices, you could restate these questions.

To which college do you go?

By which lake does she live?

Many words used as prepositions serve as other parts of speech as well. They often serve as adverbs or as subordinating conjunctions.

He arrived **after** midnight. (*preposition*)

Jill came tumbling **after.** (*adverb*)

After Jack broke his crown, Jill fell down, too. (*subordinating conjunction*)

Interjections

Interjections are forceful expressions, usually written with an exclamation point, though mild ones may be set off with commas.

They are not used often in formal writing except in quotations of dialogue.

Hooray! Ouch!
Oh, no! Wow!

"Wow!" Davis said. "Are you telling me that there's a former presidential adviser who hasn't written a book?"

How Words Act as Different Parts of Speech

A word that acts as one part of speech in a sentence may act as other parts of speech in other sentences or in other parts of the same sentence. The way the word is used will determine what part of speech it is.

The **light** glowed at the end of the pier. (*noun*)
As you **light** the candle, say a prayer. (*verb*)
The **light** drizzle foretold heavy rain. (*adjective*)

The cobra glided **outside.** (*adverb*)
The child played on the **outside.** (*noun*)
The mongoose waited **outside** the house. (*preposition*)
The famous **outside** linebacker was terrified by this scene. (*adjective*)

When will he come home? (*adverb*)
He will come **when** he is ready. (*conjunction*)
They decided the where and **when** immediately. (*noun*)

■ **Exercise 4.9** Fill in the blanks in the following sentences with any words that make sense. The word in parentheses at the end of each sentence tells you the part of speech that will go in the blank. But don't worry about that. Look at the names of the parts of speech, and use your intuition to fill in the blanks. The exercise will prove that you have a feeling for the parts of speech even if you don't readily come up with the names. You will build confidence as you study the other sentences.

1. The dinosaurs ________ extinct millions of years ago. (verb)
2. Emma bought ________ a hamburger for lunch. (pronoun or noun)
3. The ________ swerved and hit the guardrail. (noun)
4. The leaves on the maple tree in the yard ________ red. (verb)
5. "________!" he cried. "That hurt." (interjection)
6. The English troops retreated ________ from Lexington. (adverb)
7. Collecting hand-painted tin soldiers was ________ hobby. (pronoun)
8. I had to buy textbooks ________ supplies on the first day of the semester. (conjunction)
9. Alcohol is one of the ________ dangerous common drugs. (adverb)
10. Our arrival was delayed ________ we had a flat tire. (conjunction)
11. She welded the ________ to the bicycle. (noun)
12. Come ________ my house for the party. (preposition)
13. It rained all ________ the game. (preposition)
14. France ________ California produce some of the finest wines on earth. (conjunction)
15. Radios ________ from cars in cities by the thousands every year. (verb)
16. The ________ problem was how to buy a motorcycle without going into debt. (adjective)
17. The ________ bicycle is much more complicated than its ancestors. (adjective)
18. We painted the bedposts ________. (adjective)
19. The trip turned into a ________. (noun)
20. The New York Mets began playing baseball ________ 1962. (preposition)

4c
gram

■ **Exercise 4.10** Write original sentences in which you use each word below according to the directions. Use a dictionary when you need help. Dictionary entries identify the various ways words are used and may give examples that will help you create sentences of your own.

1. Use *leap* as a noun, a verb, and an adjective.
2. Use *beyond* as an adverb, a preposition, and a noun.
3. Use *after* as an adverb, a preposition, and a conjunction.
4. Use *rain* as a noun, a verb, and an adjective.
5. Use *lapse* as a noun and a verb.

4d
Identifying Phrases and Clauses

A **phrase** is a group of related words without a subject and a predicate.

They **were watching** the game.

The child ran **into the lake.**

Grinning happily, she made a three-point shot.

To succeed in writing, you must be willing to revise again and again.

Diving for treasure is sometimes dangerous.

A **clause** is a group of grammatically related words containing both a subject and a predicate. An **independent clause** can usually stand by itself as a complete sentence. A **dependent,** or **subordinate, clause** often cannot stand by itself because it is introduced by a subordinating conjunction or a relative pronoun and therefore the clause alone does not make sense. In the sentences below, the independent clauses are in boldface, the dependent clauses in italics.

She ran in the marathon *because she wanted to test herself.*

She said *that she felt exhausted after fifteen miles.*

They took *what they could find.*

When we had done everything possible, **we left the wounded to the enemy.**

See also 4f.

4e
Reviewing Types of Phrases and Their Uses

English sentences contain three basic types of phrases: prepositional phrases, verb phrases, and absolute phrases.

Prepositional Phrases

ESL 2

Prepositional phrases always begin with a preposition and always end with a noun or pronoun that serves as the object of the preposition. The noun or pronoun in the phrase can then help to describe something else in the sentence. A prepositional phrase generally serves as an adjective or an adverb in the sentence in which it occurs.

Adjective prepositional phrase: The tree **in the yard** is an oak.

Adverb prepositional phrase: He arrived **before breakfast.**

To identify an adjective prepositional phrase or an adverb prepositional phrase, use the same tests you used for simple adjectives and adverbs (see 4c). In the sentence below, the adjective prepositional phrase (in italics) answers the question *which book;* the adverb prepositional phrase (in boldface) answers the question *why.*

4e gram

Ditmars's book *about North American snakes* sold well **because of its outstanding photographs.**

Verb Phrases

ESL 4

Verb phrases are combinations of verbs including a main verb and one or more auxiliary verbs (see 4b, 4c). But verb phrases, or **verbals,** also include words formed from verbs that do not function as verbs in sentences. Verbals can stand alone as parts of speech, or they can be part of words attached to them to make a verb phrase. There are three kinds of verbals: infinitives, participials, and gerunds.

Infinitives and infinitive phrases

The infinitive of any verb except the verb *to be* is formed when the infinitive marker *to* is placed before the common form of the verb in the first-person present tense.

Verb	Infinitive
go	to go
make	to make

Infinitives and infinitive phrases function as nouns, adjectives, and adverbs. Here, too, the tests for adjectives and adverbs come in handy. In the sentences below, examine the various ways the infinitive phrase *to finish his novel* can function.

To finish his novel was his greatest ambition. (noun, the subject of the sentence)

He made many efforts **to finish his novel.** (adjective modifying the noun *efforts*)

He rushed **to finish his novel.** (adverb modifying the verb *rushed*)

ESL 16

Participles and participial phrases

Participles are made from verbs. **Present participles** suggest some continuing action. **Past participles** suggest completed action. The present participle of verbs is formed when *-ing* is added to the common present form of the verb. (The present participle *being* is formed from the infinitive *to be.*) The past participle is usually made by the addition of *-ed* to the common present form of the verb, but past participles are frequently irregular. That is, some past participles are formed not by an added *-ed,* but by an added *-en* or by a change in the root of the verb.

> I have **biked** five hundred miles in two weeks.
>
> I have **driven** five hundred miles in a morning.
>
> I have **fought** to change speed limits on two-lane roads.

Because they do represent action, participles can be used in a wide variety of ways. In the sentences above, the participle is part of a verb phrase. But participles also can act as adjectives. In the sentences below, the participial phrases modify the subjects.

> **Creeping through heavy traffic,** the messenger on the bike yelled angrily at pedestrians.
>
> **Insulted by the joke,** the team stormed out of the banquet.

Gerunds and gerund phrases

A **gerund** is the present participle used as a noun. A **gerund phrase** includes any words and phrases attached to the gerund so that the whole serves as a noun.

> **Walking** is one of life's great pleasures. (subject)
>
> **Walking swiftly an hour a day** will keep you fit. (subject)
>
> She praised his **typing.** (object)
>
> He worked hard at **typing the paper.** (object)

Absolute Phrases

An **absolute phrase** consists of a noun or pronoun attached to a participle without a helping verb. It modifies the whole sentence in which it appears. Remember: the inclusion of a helping verb would make the participle part of a verb phrase.

> **Her body falling nearly a hundred miles an hour,** she pulled the rip cord, and the parachute opened with a heavy jerk.

Falling nearly a hundred miles an hour, she pulled the rip cord, and the parachute opened with a heavy jerk.

The storm came suddenly, **the clouds boiling across the sky.**

■ **Exercise 4.11** Write sentences using the following phrases.

1. was dreaming (verb phrase)
2. beside the river (prepositional phrase)
3. the train having arrived (absolute phrase)
4. to use a computer (infinitive phrase)
5. sleeping in the woods (participial phrase)

■ **Exercise 4.12** Identify the phrases in **boldface** in the following sentences. Tell what kind of phrase each one is and how it is used in the sentence.

1. The sheriff strode into the bar, **his hands hovering over his pistols.**
2. "Where is that cat?" he shouted, **his eyes darting around the room.**
3. **Whispered softly and urgently,** the question rippled down the bar.
4. **Opening the door softly,** the cat slinked into the room.
5. **Over the barroom** a great hush fell as the sheriff and the cat stared at each other.
6. The sheriff wiped his eyes **to see better.**
7. "Time's up for you, cat," the sheriff shouted **in the great, expectant silence.**
8. **Licking his fur indifferently and sitting down,** the cat seemed to nod behind the sheriff.
9. **Frightened and dismayed,** the sheriff looked behind him.
10. A thousand cats were softly padding **through the open door.**

4f Recognizing Clauses

Clauses have subjects and predicates and may be independent or dependent. Sometimes we call independent clauses *main clauses* and dependent clauses *subordinate clauses.*

An **independent clause** usually can stand on its own as a complete sentence. A **dependent clause** cannot. It serves another clause as an adjective, an adverb, or a noun. In the sentences below, the independent clause is in boldface, the dependent clause in italics.

> **He swam across the lake** *after the sun set.*
>
> **He claimed** *that he swam across the lake after the sun set.*

4f
gram

An easy test for dependent clauses is to see if they are introduced by a subordinating word or group of words (see 4c and 6b). The subordinator tells you that the clause to follow is to serve another clause. In the following sentence, the subordinate clause (in boldface) serves as an adverb answering the question *why*.

ESL 17

> I am going to bed **because I am tired.**

Here are some subordinating conjunctions: *after, although, as, because, before, if, once, since, that, though, till, unless, until, when, whenever, where, wherever, while, as if, as soon as, as though, even after, even if, even though, even when, for as much as, in order that, in that, rather than, so that, sooner than*

Some subordinators are relative pronouns: *what, which, who, whom, whose, that.* The subordinators *that* and *which* are sometimes left out of sentences before dependent clauses. In the following sentences, the dependent clauses are in boldface, and the subordinator has been omitted.

> Many poor people in Latin America believe **they can gain dignity only by revolution.**
>
> She said **she would enroll in evening school and work during the day.**
>
> We thought **Miami might win the Orange Bowl this year.**

English sentences contain three basic types of clauses: noun clauses, adjective clauses, and adverb clauses.

Noun Clauses

A **noun clause** is a clause that acts as a subject, object, or complement.

> **Subject:** **That English is a flexible language** is both glory and pain.
>
> **Object:** He told me **that English is a flexible language.**
>
> **Complement:** His response was **that no response was necessary.**

ESL 18

ESL 19

4f gram

Adjective Clauses

An **adjective** (or **adjectival**) **clause** modifies a noun or pronoun. A relative pronoun is used to connect it to the word it modifies.

The contestant **whom he most wanted to beat** was his father. (adjective clause modifies the noun *contestant;* relative pronoun *whom,* which stands for its antecedent *contestant,* serves as the direct object of the infinitive *to beat*)

The computer **that I wanted** cost too much money. (adjective clause modifies the noun *computer;* relative pronoun *that* serves as the direct object of *wanted*)

The journey of Odysseus, **which can be traced today on a map of Greece and the Aegean Sea,** made an age of giants and miracles seem close to the ancient Greeks. (adjective clause modifies *journey;* relative pronoun *which* serves as the subject of *can be traced*)

Adverb Clauses

An **adverb** (or **adverbial**) **clause** serves as an adverb, frequently (but not always) modifying the verb in another clause. Adverb clauses are often introduced by the subordinators *after, when, before, because, although, if, though, whenever, where,* and *wherever,* as well as by many others.

After we had talked for an hour, he began to look at his watch. (adverb clause modifies the verb *began*)

He reacted as swiftly **as he could**. (adverb clause modifies the adverb *swiftly*)

The desert was more yellow **than he remembered**. (adverb clause modifies the adjective *yellow*)

■ **Exercise 4.13** Identify the clauses in each of the following sentences. Draw one line under any dependent clause and two lines under the independent clause.

Example:
When he was a pilot on the Mississippi River in his youth, Samuel Clemens learned the lore of the people along its banks.

1. Before she set out on the Appalachian Trail, she had to buy a good backpack.
2. A retrospective of Georges Seurat's life was presented to the American public on the centenary of the artist's death.

3. Although Hollywood remains the film capital, New York City's Upper East Side and Greenwich Village have provided memorable settings for several important movies.
4. When knighthood was in flower, life was bloody and short.
5. Women now do many things that society prevented them from doing not long ago.
6. In college football, the running game is more important than it is in professional football.
7. A joyous feature of modern American music is New Orleans polyphony, which is the blare and howl of a marching band's horns along with vibrant drum rhythms.
8. The state of Texas has decided that high school athletes must pass all their academic work if they are to play sports.
9. George Armstrong Custer and the Seventh Cavalry perished because they attacked a village where thousands of Indians were ready to fight.
10. Medical evidence has been building up for years to prove that cigarette smoking causes lung cancer and heart disease.

■ **Exercise 4.14** Write sentences using the following dependent clauses. Tell whether you make each an adjective, an adverb, or a noun.

1. because we awoke late
2. when she spotted the fox
3. as soon as she could
4. after she had won the state lottery
5. although he erased the answers
6. where the dinosaur bones were found
7. whenever he stirred the sauce
8. before the fire started
9. though the night had long since fallen
10. if she would fix the muffler on her car

4g Identifying Types of Sentences

We can classify sentences by numbers of clauses and how the clauses are joined. The basic sentence types in English are simple, compound, complex, or compound-complex. We also classify sentences by purpose: declarative, interrogative, imperative, and exclamatory.

Simple Sentences

4g gram

A **simple sentence** contains only one clause, and that clause is independent, able to stand alone grammatically. A simple sentence may have several phrases. It may have a compound subject or a compound verb. It may even have both a compound subject and a compound verb. But it can have only one *clause*—one subject and one verb that combine to make a clear statement. The following are simple sentences. Some are quite complicated, but they are *all* simple sentences, each with one independent clause.

> Large land reptiles have been unable to evolve in the presence of large land mammals.
>
> The bloodhound is the oldest known breed of dog.
>
> He staked out a plot of high ground in the mountains, cut down the trees, and built his own house with a fine view of the valley below.
>
> Historians, novelists, short-story writers, and playwrights write about characters, design plots, and usually seek the dramatic resolution of a problem.
>
> Singing, brawling, shouting, laughing, crying, and clapping every moment, the fans turned out every night hungry for a pennant.

Compound Sentences

A **compound sentence** contains two or more independent clauses, usually joined by a comma and a coordinating conjunction such as *and, but, nor, or, for, yet,* or *so.* A compound sentence does not contain a dependent clause. Sometimes the independent clauses are joined by a semicolon, a dash, or a colon.

> The sun blasted the earth, and the plants withered and died.
>
> He asked directions at the end of every street—but he never listened to them.

A compound sentence also may consist of a series of independent clauses joined by commas or semicolons, usually but not always with a conjunction before the last clause.

> They searched the want ads, she visited real estate agents, he drove through neighborhoods looking for for-sale signs, and they finally located a house big enough for them and their pet rattlesnakes.

> The trees on the ridge behind our house change in September: the oaks start to redden; the maples pass from green to orange; the pines grow more dark.

Complex Sentences

A **complex sentence** contains one independent clause and one or more dependent clauses. In the following sentences, the dependent clause is in boldface type.

> He consulted the dictionary **because he did not know how to pronounce the word.**
>
> She asked people **if they approved of what the speaker said.**
>
> **Although football players are reputed to be the most powerful athletes in team sports,** the winners of the World Series beat the winners of the Super Bowl in a celebrity tug-of-war on network television one year.

Compound-Complex Sentences

A **compound-complex sentence** contains two or more independent clauses and at least one dependent clause. In the following sentences, boldface type indicates dependent clauses.

> She discovered a new world in international finance, but she worked so hard investing other people's money **that she had no time to invest any of her own.**
>
> **Although Carrie Nation was an extremist in the temperance movement,** her belief **that God had called her to break up saloons with her hatchet** was widely applauded in her time.
>
> **After Abraham Lincoln was killed,** the government could not determine **how many conspirators there were,** and **since John Wilkes Booth, the assassin, was himself soon killed,** he could not clarify the mystery, **which remains to this day.**

Classification by Purpose

We also classify sentences by the kind of information they convey—by whether they are statements, questions, commands, or exclamations. End punctuation helps identify the purpose of the sentence.

Sentence type	Meaning	Example	End punctuation
Declarative	Makes a statement	He stopped watching *Gilligan's Island* reruns.	Period
Interrogative	Asks a question	Did he stop watching *Gilligan's Island* reruns?	Question mark
Imperative	Gives a command, makes a request	Please stop watching *Gilligan's Island* reruns.	Period
Exclamatory	Expresses strong emotion	I'll smash the TV if you don't stop watching *Gilligan's Island* reruns!	Exclamation point

■ **Exercise 4.15** Classify the following sentences as simple, compound, complex, or compound-complex.

1. The winter of 1542 was marked by tempestuous weather throughout the British Isles: in the north, on the borders of Scotland and England, there were heavy snowfalls in December and frost so savage that by January the ships were frozen into the harbor at Newcastle.

   —ANTONIA FRASER

2. Prints, with woodblocks as the oldest form, began life humbly, not as works of art but as substitutes for drawings or paintings when multiples of a single image were needed, probably as long ago as the fifth century A.D. in China.

   —JOHN CANADAY

3. Using her own surreal version of the stream of consciousness monologue, Tatyana Tolstaya depicts the missed connections and lost opportunities that define her characters' lives with uncommon compassion and humor.

   —MICHIKO KAKUTANI

4. True to his species, the white-tailed buck moved in ghostlike silence over a deep carpet of leaves lying faded, dry and crisp as cornflakes on the Ozark ridge.

   —MICHAEL PEARCE

5. Until recently the main preoccupation of Cuban dissidents was monitoring human rights violations.

—ANNA HUSARSKA

6. Although America has some fine native cherries, some of the very best wild cherries to be found came originally from seedlings of cultivated varieties, and the birds have been the chief agents of scattering the seeds.

—EUELL GIBBONS

7. The notion of the painter as a sort of boon companion to the hangman is carried on by Leonardo, who was fond of attending executions, perhaps to study the muscular contortions of the hanged.

—MARY MCCARTHY

8. When he had eaten seven bananas, Mr. Biswas was sick, whereupon Soanie, silently crying, carried him to the back verandah.

—V. S. NAIPAUL

9. The people who developed the English language were more interested in making distinctions between boats than they were in the differences between colors and feelings, not to speak of tastes and smells.

—WALTER KAUFMANN

10. Inside the tough-talking, hard-jogging man of 40 who is identified largely by his work, there is a boy trying not to cry, "Time is running out."

—GAIL SHEEHY

■ **Exercise 4.16** Combine the following groups of sentences into compound, complex, or compound-complex sentences. You will often have to add conjunctions or relative pronouns. Sometimes you will want to delete some words. See how many combinations you can work out from each group.

1. A pitcher can throw a baseball faster than ninety miles an hour. Batters may be severely injured if they are hit. Every batter must wear a helmet at the plate.

2. Singapore banned the sale, production or import of chewing gum. The ban started early in the New Year. It is another in a series of restrictive measures for the island. These measures have given Singapore the reputation of an overly regulated, highly antiseptic community.
3. Orson Welles terrified the United States with his radio presentation of *War of the Worlds* in 1938. Hitler was pushing Europe into war. News bulletins regularly interrupted broadcasts. Welles made the program sound like a news broadcast. He made people think that Earth was being invaded from Mars.
4. The Mississippi Delta has some of the richest farmland in the world. It grows more cotton than any comparable area on earth. It was not thickly settled until after the Civil War. Mosquitoes gave people in the Delta yellow fever.
5. Almost a million accountants now work in the United States. The profession is still growing. Positions will increase by 30 percent over the next ten years. These figures have been reported by the Bureau of Labor Statistics.

CHAPTER
5

SENTENCE LOGIC

Every sentence should make a clear statement that readers can understand. Often sentences answer some or all of the journalist's questions, the questions we want answered when we read a report of an event: *who, what, when, where, why,* and sometimes *how.*

Short, simple sentences like these offer little difficulty.

The world came to life at dawn.

The Soviet Union crumbled in 1991.

The snow fell softly all night long.

Even when your sentences are long and complicated, you can simplify your thinking by asking which of the six questions they answer. In writing, you need to strive for clarity and logic. To write clear and logical sentences and paragraphs you can use five strategies that most writers know: (1) Prune irrelevant details that can derail your readers. (2) Give proper emphasis to the most important parts of your sentence. (3) Clearly establish cause-and-effect relations. (4) Limit your generalizations. (5) Use concrete terms when you define a word.

5a Pruning Irrelevant Details

Unnecessary information may confuse your readers by blurring the central thought of your sentence. Everything in a sentence must support the central statement. If ideas are not related to the central statement, prune them.

In a first draft, you may include irrelevant details as you try to put down everything you know about a topic. When you revise, cut out these details so that everything in each of your sentences will contribute to the major statement you wish to make.

Draft: *The Adventures of Huckleberry Finn,* by Mark Twain, who lectured widely in the United States and Great Britain, received only one review when it was published in 1884.

Revised: *The Adventures of Huckleberry Finn,* by Mark Twain, received only one review when it was published in 1884.

Often you can revise a sentence so that all the details in your first draft can be made to support the major purpose of the sentence.

Revised: Although Mark Twain lectured widely in the United States and Great Britain and was well known to the public, *The Adventures of Huckleberry Finn* received only one review when it was published in 1884.

But you should never cram too many ideas in a sentence. As a general rule, aim at stating one central idea in every sentence. When you have several important ideas to communicate, put them in separate sentences.

Draft: World War I began on July 28, 1914, when the Austrians, whose army was huge but badly commanded and badly supplied and was also made up of many rival nationalities, attacked the city of Belgrade, in what was then called Serbia, though recently part of the nation of Yugoslavia, a country once again in turmoil after the Soviet Union loosened its grip on Communist Europe and rival nationalities began fighting.

This sentence contains too much information. What is its purpose? Is it to tell us when the war began? Or is it to tell us why the Austrian army was much weaker than it appeared? Or is it to tell us where Belgrade is? Or is it to describe rival nationalities in the Balkans?

Revised: World War I began on July 28, 1914, when the Austrians attacked the city of Belgrade, in what was then called Serbia. The Austrian army was huge, badly commanded, and badly supplied, but the Serbians were no match for it by themselves, and so they had to call on the Russians for help. The Austrians thereupon called upon the Germans for help against the Russians. The German war plan called for defeating the French before turning against Russia, thereby avoiding war on two fronts. The Germans attacked France through Belgium, compelling Britain to come to the aid of its Belgian ally. Suddenly all Europe was in conflict.

■ **Exercise 5.1** Rewrite the following sentences to clarify the main statement in each of them. You may choose to revise to make two sentences with related thoughts if you want to express two distinct statements. You may want to leave out some of the information given in the sentences so that the statements you preserve will be clear.

1. My mother, who always hated to wash windows or clean house but preferred to work in her flower garden, worked on newspapers for twenty years in places as diverse as Beaumont, Texas, and Montgomery, Alabama.
2. Notoriously hard to spell and difficult grammatically, the English language has spread all over the world largely because of the power and influence of the United States and the British Empire and Commonwealth.
3. Scurvy, a disease once common among sailors who spent many weeks at sea, can be prevented by eating citrus fruits, which grow in warm climates and can be preserved at sea because of their thick skins.
4. If Lincoln had not sent ships to supply the federal garrison at Fort Sumter in Charleston Harbor, the British might have recognized the Confederacy as an independent nation so that they might ensure a steady supply of southern cotton to British textile mills, which by 1861 were using steam engines.
5. Terrorism is one of the frightening symbols of modern society because it is violent, bloody, and merciless and often completely anonymous, since the terrorists sometimes do not know and do not care who their victims are, but they know that a bomb exploding in an airport or a bullet tearing through the body of a police officer will get publicity, which they think will make them look important in the eyes of the world, and they think that if they are important, they may be able to get their way.

5b
Deciding on Proper Emphasis

The most emphatic places in a sentence are the beginning and the end. Most sentences begin with the subject. The person, place, or thing that the sentence is going to be about comes first, so that readers will have it in their minds for the rest of the sentence.

In your first draft, you may be concerned only to get ideas on paper. When you revise, think about what element in each sentence you want to stress. Then make sure to arrange your sentence to provide the intended emphasis. Eliminate statements that don't contribute to that emphasis. For more information on emphasis, see Chapters 6 and 7.

Draft: When you are looking for a good book, try *Moby-Dick,* which you will find to be a great one.

Revised: *Moby-Dick* is one of the greatest books in American literature.

5c Expressing Cause and Effect

Simply by being close to one another, elements within a sentence may imply a causal relation. If you do intend to suggest cause and effect, make sure the link is clear. Be logical when you attribute an effect to a cause, and avoid statements that imply causality you do not intend.

In your first draft, you may put elements together in a sentence. When you revise, ask yourself if they belong together and, if they do, if the link between them is apparent or requires expansion.

Confusing: In 1950 the most popular song in America was "Tennessee Waltz," and the United States went to war in Korea.

Was the popularity of "Tennessee Waltz" the cause of the Korean War? The thought needs filling out to clarify the writer's point: that two contradictory things were happening at the same time.

Revised: In 1950, when the most popular song in America was the slow, dreamy "Tennessee Waltz," the United States went to war in Korea, and a peaceful dream ended for thousands of young men.

Confusion may also result from joining a dependent clause to an independent clause in such a way that a cause-and-effect relation seems to be implied.

Confusing: When he saw the movie *Casablanca,* my friend Bert had a heart attack.

Did the movie *Casablanca* cause Bert to have a heart attack? Probably not. But a rapid reader might think that it did. Again, a solution is to expand the thought so that readers will not think you are implying cause and effect.

Revised: While he was watching the movie *Casablanca* last week, my friend Bert had a heart attack. He seemed to be in perfect health, and he was enjoying himself, but suddenly he was doubled over with a near-fatal seizure.

Some conjunctive adverbs and coordinating conjunctions establish negative relations. Words such as *but, although,* and *however* alert the reader to a contrast or qualification. Use them only when you intend such a contrast. Again, you may have to fill out the negative link you are implying. Confusion results if you use one of these words to join two statements that are unrelated to each other.

Confusing: **Although** I like to read, television is exciting.

Revised: **Although** I like to read, it is easier for me to watch an exciting television show in the evening when I am too tired to concentrate on the printed page.

■ **Exercise 5.2** Rewrite the following sentences to eliminate faulty patterns of cause and effect. Add information when it is necessary to clarify sentence logic.

1. Personal computers were unknown thirty-five years ago, and Elvis Presley was in his prime.
2. Anabolic steroids have been shown to produce a host of illnesses including cancer while they are helping build huge, muscular bodies for weight lifters and football players, and athletes often use them.
3. Because the thief was finally captured, some politicians do not believe in light sentences for chronic criminals.
4. If you see a Woody Allen movie, he captures the humor and suffering of middle-class urban men and women today.
5. When you go to college, many teachers love to write and talk to students about research and writing.

5d Limiting Generalizations

Statements that assert too much on too little evidence have little credibility. They reveal that the writer has not studied the material enough to be aware of the exceptions serious observers know about. Be especially careful of sentences that assert *all, always,* and *never.*

In your first draft, you may want to do little more than express your opinion or main point. When you revise, examine your generalizations to make sure that they are valid, and limit them if they are not.

Misleading: Students nowadays lack dedication and seriousness, and they seldom read anything but the sports pages and the comics.

Revised: Some students I have known lack dedication and seriousness, and they seldom read anything but the sports pages and the comics.

Misleading: There never has been another play as good as *Macbeth.*

Revised: *Macbeth* is an excellent play because Macbeth's flaws are the flaws of all of us.

Misleading: Everyone is agreed that Faulkner's story "A Rose for Emily" is not one of his better works because it is too melodramatic.

Revised: Some critics believe that Faulkner's story "A Rose for Emily" is not one of his better works because, they say, it is too melodramatic.

■ **Exercise 5.3** Rewrite the following sentences to qualify sweeping generalizations. Don't hesitate to change words if the changes improve the sentences.

1. On the expressway the other day, the driver of one car shot another driver who dented his fender. This kind of thing happens because people in big cities are stressed beyond limits and prone to violence.
2. My cousin Charles was furious because he could not get anybody to speak English when he asked directions in Paris no matter how much he shouted at them. His experience proves that the French all hate the Americans except when France needs American help in time of war.
3. Members of the crime syndicate are always photographed smoking cigars, and the cigar has long been regarded as a symbol of success by everyone who thinks about such things.
4. The photographs of the ship *Titanic* lying on the bottom of the Atlantic Ocean since it sank in 1912 prove that travel by ship was much more dangerous than travel by airplane is today.
5. Colstrop's necktie was found at the scene of the murder along with his wristwatch, his notebook, and a pair of his trousers. So he was the killer, and the courts will convict him.

✔ CHECKLIST 5.1: MAKING SENTENCES MAKE SENSE

As you revise your sentences, consider internal sentence logic. Ask yourself these questions.

- Is all the information related to the central statement?
- Does the sentence emphasize the central statement by appropriate arrangement of elements?
- Does the presentation of information clarify the relation between cause and effect?
- Are generalizations reasonable and supported?
- Are intended definitions clear and not reliant on cognates?

5e
Defining Terms

Defining a word by repeating it or by using one of its cognates is not helpful. **Cognates** are words that come from the same root. *Grammar* and *grammatical* are cognates. So are *describe* and *description, narrate* and *narration, compute* and *computer,* and *nostalgic* and *nostalgia.*

In your first draft, in order to get your point across, you may use words that you yourself understand. When you revise, however, think about your words from your reader's point of view, and define or explain those that need explaining.

> **Poor:** A grammar book teaches you grammar.
>
> **Revised:** A grammar book explains the system of rules about word endings and word order that allows a language to communicate.

> **Poor:** A community is a group with communal interests.
>
> **Revised:** A community is a group that shares similar ceremonies, goals, habits, and patterns of work.

In defining, avoid using the words *is when.*

> **Awkward:** Fascism is when a military dictator rules with the help of secret police and won't allow freedom of the press or assembly.
>
> **Revised:** Fascism is a political system ruled by a military dictator with the help of secret police and characterized by terror and strict censorship of the press to limit popular assemblies and suppress freedom of speech.

■ **Exercise 5.4** Rewrite the following sentences to give proper definitions. Use a dictionary when necessary (see 12b).

1. An accident is when you have something happen accidentally that is unexpected and usually harmful, although accidents can be lucky, too.
2. A traffic jam is when traffic is jammed up on the streets.
3. A computer is a machine used for computing.
4. A quarterback is a back on a football team.
5. A poet is a man or a woman who writes poetry.

CHAPTER

6

COORDINATION, SUBORDINATION, PARALLELISM

To develop sentences effectively, distinguish between main ideas and subordinate ideas and bind related thoughts together with parallel construction. Your readers should be able to follow your train of ideas from the beginning of a sentence through to the end. Improper coordination or subordination can interrupt the flow and make your readers struggle to understand the main points you are trying to make. A lack of parallelism disrupts the relation between the parts of a sentence and weakens its force.

6a Expressing Equal Ideas: Coordination

Establish equal emphasis between parts of a sentence by using coordinating conjunctions or suitable punctuation or both.

Coordinating Words, Phrases, or Clauses

The conjunction *and* always calls for equal emphasis on the elements that it joins.

> The bear **and** her cubs ate the food in camp.
>
> The bear **and** her cubs ate the food in camp **and** destroyed our tent.
>
> At the end of our climb we were hot **and** tired.
>
> He drank only coffee, tea, **and** milk for a week.

A comma can sometimes replace the *and* in a series.

He zigzagged, fell, rolled, ran into my waiting hand.

—E. B. WHITE

Wistfully, admiringly, the old voice added, "It's snug in here, upon my word!"

—KATHERINE MANSFIELD

The conjunction *or* also joins equal sentence elements.

He could go by bus **or** by train.

They knew that they must work out their differences over money **or** get a divorce.

Coordinating Clauses

Coordination can establish clear relations among equal thoughts or ideas by joining clauses or short consecutive sentences.

They hesitate, and they regret, and sometimes they petition; but they do nothing in earnest and with effect.

—HENRY DAVID THOREAU

When you use *and, but, or, for, nor, yet,* or *so* to connect independent clauses and thus coordinate related statements of equal importance, use a comma.

To act is to be committed, and to be committed is to be in danger.

—JAMES BALDWIN

I buried my head under the quilts, but my aunt heard me.

—LANGSTON HUGHES

You can also use a semicolon to connect related statements that are equally important.

We walked, and he talked; the musical irresistible voice seemed to set the pace of our march.

—EMLYN WILLIAMS

Sometimes both a semicolon and a coordinating conjunction introduce an independent clause (discussed in 23a).

> The hands of the man who sawed the wood left red marks on the billets; and the forehead of the woman who nursed the baby was stained with the stain of the old rag she wound around her head again.
>
> —CHARLES DICKENS

■ **Exercise 6.1** Rewrite the following sentences to provide proper coordination. You may want to write more than a sentence for some of the examples.

1. He loved to shave in the morning because he liked the softness of shaving cream, the clean feel of the razor on his cheek, the smell of his after-shave, and he enjoyed taking a shower, too.
2. We drove to Baltimore last month, and to Wilmington the month before that, and next month we hope to drive to Providence.
3. Police officers in old movies often seem hard, cynical, and yet they are honest.
4. Truck drivers in this country complained bitterly about unreasonable speed limits, the high price of diesel fuel, and many of them refused to slow down.
5. Our friends would eat out on Saturday night, go to a movie, visit with each other, or they would do something else to have a relaxing good time.

6b Expressing Unequal Ideas: Subordination

In some sentences, one idea depends on another. For example, one condition or event may cause another; one event may come before another; one observation may explain another. **Subordination** establishes the dependence of one idea on another by shifting emphasis away from supporting elements so that major statements emerge clearly.

Clauses, phrases, and single words can all be subordinate units in a sentence. The subordinate element usually enlarges on some element in the main part of the sentence. As you write and revise, keep clearly in mind the main thoughts you want to communicate. Then subordinate other elements to those main thoughts.

Subordination Within Sentences

In the following paragraph, readers would have trouble finding the statements that carry the writer's major line of thought. Each sentence in this paragraph is clear, but together the sentences create confusion because they do not show proper subordination.

6b
subord

Draft: Columbus discovered the New World in 1492. He made his voyage in three tiny ships. No educated person at that time believed that the world was flat. Columbus was well educated. The Greeks had taught that the world was round. They had taught that two thousand years before Columbus. On a round world, a sailor might head west to lands others had found by sailing east. Columbus wanted to find a new route to China and to other lands in Asia. Others had reached those lands. They had sailed around the southern tip of Africa to get there. Columbus thought the world was much smaller than it is. He thought he could get to Asia in about a month. Suppose America had not been in the way. He would have had a voyage of three or four months. He did not find the East Indies or China or Japan. America was in the way. It is a good thing America was in the way. Columbus might have sailed his three ships into an enormous ocean. His sailors might have starved to death. The ocean would have been far larger than anything Columbus could have imagined.

Revised: With tiny ships, Christpher Columbus discovered the New World in 1492, although he never understood just what he had done. Neither he nor any other educated person in his time believed that the world was flat. From the time of the ancient Greeks, two thousand years earlier, educated people had believed that the world was round, and that a ship might reach Asia by sailing west, around the tip of Africa. Because Columbus thought the world was much smaller than it is, he expected to find the East Indies, China, or Japan. Instead he found America. Had this continent not been in the way, he might have sailed his crews to starvation in an enormous ocean far larger than any sea he had imagined.

ESL 17

Subordinating conjunctions, often called **subordinators** (see p. 109), help to build subordinate clauses. Some examples are *after, because, since,* and *when.* Commas may also set off subordinate sections from a part they modify, especially when a subordinated element opens the sentence (discussed in 22b).

Where the road forks, you will find the graveyard.

Unless you object, I will plug my ears at the rock concert.

Because great horned owls are so big, they can sometimes kill and eat cats.

Until you remove the engine head, you cannot see the pistons.

He taught me **how to throw a curve.**

Although she looked tiny, she was a superb police officer.

The position of a subordinator in relation to the clause it introduces affects the meaning of a sentence.

She did not eat **because she was angry.**
She was angry **because she did not eat.**

When the police arrived, the burglars ran away.
When the burglars ran away, the police arrived.

After he had completed a fifty-yard pass, we cheered him.
After we cheered him, he completed a fifty-yard pass.

Relative pronouns—*who, whom, that, which, what, whoever, whomever, whose*—also signal subordinate elements in a sentence (discussed on p. 100).

The plane rose into the sky **that had turned fierce and gray.**

Uncle Kwong, **whom no one liked anyway,** refused our invitation.

Notice how the use of subordinators speeds up the pace of the following sentences.

Without subordinators: My cousin does my taxes every year. He is an accountant. He helps me with many suggestions. These suggestions allow me to take several deductions. These deductions reduce my tax bill considerably.

With subordinators: Because my cousin is an accountant, he does my taxes every year, suggesting several deductions that reduce my tax bill considerably.

Embedding

As you've already observed, short sentences are easy to understand, but several of them in a row may be monotonous even if they are clear and correct. Look at this example.

She was sad. She did not look back. She mounted the seawall. She was bowed by her burden of failure, sorrow, and self-contempt.

Now consider this example. With the same ideas and words several sentences have been reduced to modifiers. This technique is called **embedding.**

> Sadly, without looking back, she mounted the seawall, bowed by her burden of failure, sorrow, and self-contempt.
>
> —CONSTANCE HOLME

Embedding compresses a great deal of information into a few words by establishing subordination. Consider these additional examples.

> We can turn poetry toward biology. We can suggest a closer relationship between them. This creation of a relationship would follow a long line of similar suggestions. Other disciplines have made these suggestions.
>
> To turn poetry toward biology and to suggest a closer relationship between them is only to follow in a long line of similar suggestions made by other disciplines.
>
> —ELIZABETH SEWELL

> The White Star liner *Titanic* was the largest ship the world had ever known. The *Titanic* sailed from Southampton on her maiden voyage to New York on April 10, 1912.
>
> The White Star liner *Titanic,* largest ship the world had ever known, sailed from Southampton on her maiden voyage to New York on April 10, 1912.
>
> —HANSON W. BALDWIN

> She was falling asleep. Her head was bowed over the child. She was still aware of a strange, wakeful happiness.
>
> Even as she was falling asleep, head bowed over the child, she was still aware of a strange, wakeful happiness.
>
> —KATHERINE ANNE PORTER

Using this technique, you can embed several enriching thoughts within one base sentence and transform a whole group of ideas into a statement in which unstressed elements modify main ideas precisely. By using coordination along with subordination, you can expand your options for embedding and transforming sentences. Look at these examples.

The fissions generate heat, and in a power reactor this heat produces steam, which drives electric turbines.

—JEREMY BERNSTEIN

Equality with whites will not solve the problems of either whites or Negroes if it means equality in a world society stricken by poverty and in a universe doomed to extinction by war.

—MARTIN LUTHER KING, JR.

■ **Exercise 6.2** Using the subordination techniques illustrated in 6b, revise the following sets of sentences. Make any necessary changes to create logical, correct sentences. You may want to see how many different combinations you can make of each example.

1. Bilingual education is expanding in many schools. It is designed for children. The native language of these children is not English. It may be Spanish. It may be Chinese. It may be Vietnamese. It may be Korean. It may be some other language.
2. This auditorium was huge. The acoustics were terrible. The tenor nearly screamed at us. But no one could hear him beyond the ninth row. The soprano looked as if she was trying. But her voice sounded like a whisper in the balcony. The singers walked off the stage. They had played only two-thirds of the first act. The baritone was in tears.
3. *JFK* was released in 1991. It was directed by Oliver Stone. Stone's film reopened the controversy over President John Fitzgerald Kennedy's death. The conspiracy theory is alive again. Many people fault Stone for giving the American public a false view of history.
4. A uniform can symbolize a worker's status. Status means power. People see authority in some uniforms. A person in a police uniform shows by dress that he or she has authority to make people stop. A person in a nurse's uniform shows by dress that he or she can dispense medications. Sometimes uniforms are not prescribed. But people try to wear clothing that makes them look as if they belong. Male college professors used to wear tweed jackets. Their tweed jackets were a kind of uniform.
5. I read the same want ads over and over. I was looking for a job for the summer. The recession clearly had affected the job market. Few jobs were available for college students. I would have done anything reasonable. I would have worked nights or days. All I found was a job shining shoes. This was at the airport thirty miles away. I quit after two days.

Avoiding Too Many Subordinate Structures

Too much subordination may distract readers and confuse your main statement. Be sure not to overload your sentences.

Overloaded: He was a stamp collector of considerable zeal who bought stamps at the post office on the day they were issued and fixed them with loving care in large books which had leather bindings, treasuring them not merely for themselves but for the enormous profit that he hoped to gain from them in the passage of years when they had increased in value.

Revised: A stamp collector of considerable zeal, he bought stamps at the post office on the day they were issued and fixed them carefully in large, leather-bound books. He prized them not only for themselves but for the enormous profit he hoped to gain from them when, after many years, they had increased in value.

Overloaded: Jackson Bingle, leader of the rock group called the Howlers, who had been known for his ability to scream over the sound of drums, a primal shriek that had amazed critics and delighted audiences while dismaying parents, learned during his annual physical, administered by T. J. Summers, head of Whooping Crane Hospital, that he had lost seven-eighths of his hearing, so he told reporters this morning.

Revised: Jackson Bingle told reporters this morning that he had lost seven-eighths of his hearing. Bingle, leader of the rock group called the Howlers, had been known for his ability to scream over the sound of the drums. His was a primal shriek that had amazed critics and delighted audiences. It also dismayed parents. Bingle said he learned of his hearing loss during his annual physical administered by Dr. T. J. Summers, head physician of Whooping Crane Hospital.

■ **Exercise 6.3** Revise the following sentences to eliminate excessive subordination. You will have to write at least two sentences for each one that appears below.

1. Big city mayors, who are supported by public funds, should weigh carefully using taxpayers' money for personal needs, such as home furnishings and decorations, especially when municipal budget shortfalls have caused extensive job layoffs, angering city workers and the general public.
2. The new sun creams, which contain various sun-blocking chemicals, help protect against skin cancer, long a hazard to people who spend too much time in the sun, and against aging, which seems

to be at least partly a consequence of the ultraviolet rays of the sun, and they have also been shown to retard the graying of hair.

3. Literacy should mean not only the ability to read and write, which is an essential skill in our culture, but also the ability, which is very much appreciated by academics, businesspeople, and professionals, to talk about many topics with intelligence—which may be another way of saying that true literacy embraces curiosity and the love of learning.

6c
Writing Balanced Constructions: Parallelism

Some sentences repeat the same form for balance or emphasis. This repetition of form is **parallelism.** The elements in a parallel construction are equal or nearly equal in grammatical structures and importance. Parallel constructions may help you make lists, join similar ideas, or build emphasis. The coordinating conjunctions *and, but, or, nor,* and *yet* always join parallel structures.

The simple parallel structure is the series with two or more elements in it.

She loved to read **magazines** and **newspapers.**

She loved to read **books, magazines,** and **newspapers.**

At Gettysburg in 1863, Abraham Lincoln said that the Civil War was being fought to make sure that government **of the people, by the people,** and **for the people** might not perish from the earth.

He **did the dishes, ran the vacuum, put out the garbage,** and **swept the walk.**

He **runs marathons** and **she runs sprints,** but **they train** together.

Many performers live **to hear** the roar of the crowd, **to feel** the love of their fans, and **to enjoy** the attention of reporters.

Making Comparisons and Contrasts

Parallelism helps make comparisons and contrasts more emphatic.

Weak: She preferred **to buy** a house rather than **renting** one.

Parallel: She preferred **to buy** a house rather than **to rent** one.

Better: She preferred **buying** a house to **renting** one.

Weak: The new library was larger than the old one, more beautiful than any other building on campus, and **it cost too much money.**

Parallel: The new library was **larger** than the old one, **more beautiful** than any other building on campus, and more **expensive** to build than anyone had imagined.

6c
parallel

Coordinating Elements

Some word pairs help coordinate elements in parallel forms. Examples are *both . . . and, either . . . or, neither . . . nor, not only . . . but also,* and *whether . . . or.* Such pairs, often called **correlatives,** always indicate a choice or a balance between equal elements. If you use these pairs to join unequal elements, you disrupt the relation between those elements and lose the grammatical sense of the sentence.

Faulty: Most soldiers in the Civil War were **neither heroic nor were they cowardly.**

Parallel: Most soldiers in the Civil War were **neither heroic nor cowardly.**

Faulty: The parking lot for commuters was **both small and it was crowded.**

Parallel: The parking lot for commuters was **both small and crowded.**

When you use a single coordinating element, such as *and* or *or,* be sure that you join equal elements.

Faulty: His favorite pastimes were reading, walking, **and he liked to skate on frozen ponds in winter.**

In this sentence, the words *reading* and *walking* prepare us to find a similar word after *and*—a gerund, such as *skating* or *thinking.* Instead we find not another gerund but an independent clause, and we feel that something has been left out. You can amend the sentence in this way.

Parallel: His favorite pastimes were reading, walking, **and skating.**

Confusion can arise with a breakdown in parallelism when *or* joins unequal elements.

Faulty: They could see a movie, a play, **or** talk all night.

Something is missing in such a sentence; the breakdown in parallelism makes it seem that they could "see talk" all night. The writer must mean this instead.

Parallel: They could see a movie or a play, **or** they could talk all night.

Making Lists and Outlines

In lists and outlines the meaning is clear only when the items are parallel.

Faulty:

Americans now rely on the automobile because:

1. cities are sprawling; public transport poor
2. habit
3. the cheapness of gasoline for so long
4. parking lots provided for employees and students by businesses and schools.

Parallel:

Americans now rely on the automobile because:

1. cities are sprawling and public transport is poor
2. they have formed the habit of driving cars everywhere
3. gasoline was cheap for a long time
4. businesses and schools provide parking lots for employees and students, encouraging them to drive.

Repeating Words

Repetition helps achieve parallelism and adds a certain rhythm or emphasis to your sentences. You do not always have to make that choice, but from time to time, repetition will strengthen your style.

Note that the sentences *without* repeated elements in the following examples are correct and parallel. They are simply not as strong.

They thought it was better **to** agree than quarrel.

Parallel: They thought it was better **to** agree than **to** quarrel.

They searched for the lost keys **in** the house, yard, and street.

Parallel: They searched for the lost keys **in** the house, **in** the yard, and **in** the street.

For the handicapped, getting an education is often **a** tribulation, necessity, and victory.

Parallel: For the handicapped, getting an education is often **a** tribulation, **a** necessity, and **a** victory.

I decided to leave when I realized **that** I had offended him, he was angry, and my apology would do no good.

Parallel: I decided to leave when I realized **that** I had offended him, **that** he was angry, and **that** my apology would do no good.

■ **Exercise 6.4** Rewrite the following sentences to create parallel forms.

1. Harrison Ford was a hot-rod driver in *American Graffiti,* a rocketship pilot in *Star Wars,* and he played Indiana Jones, the archaeologist in *Raiders of the Lost Ark,* and was an injured lawyer in *Regarding Henry.*
2. Orson Welles starred on radio, he directed and appeared in movies, and toward the end of his life advertised wine on television.
3. We biked around the reservoir, over the hills, enjoyed the country roads, and we ended at the ice cream store.
4. In the summer I like to visit Lake Louise, race along the shoreline by bike, or enjoy fishing from my uncle's rickety boat.
5. Many people in America are unhappy because of jobs not leading anywhere, with their families, and they don't like where they live either.

■ **Exercise 6.5** Revise the following sentences to repeat introductory words before parallel forms to make the parallelism more striking.

1. The new ultralight aircraft can land on a sandbar, back lot, or open field.
2. She enjoyed buying antique cars, refinishing them, and to drive a shining vehicle down Main Street every Sunday afternoon.
3. They piled their books on the sofa, tables, and beds.
4. She made three promises—that she would try the machine out, write up a report about it, and tell her friends if she liked it.
5. The railroad tracks passed through a tunnel and then over a river and highway.

Parallel Clauses

To make clauses parallel, introduce them in the same way. If you begin a clause with *and which, and that, and who,* or *and whom,* be sure that it follows a clause that begins with *which, that, who,* or *whom.*

The peach tree, **with** its sugary fruit and **which** was not known in the Middle Ages, seems to have developed from the almond.

Parallel: The peach tree, **which** has a sugary fruit and **which** was not known in the Middle Ages, seems to have developed from the almond.

Walt Whitman, **influenced by Emerson** and **whom multitudes loved,** was the first great American poet to praise cities in his verse.

Parallel: Walt Whitman, **whom Emerson influenced** and **whom multitudes loved,** was the first great American poet to praise cities in his verse.

Walt Whitman, **whom Emerson influenced and multitudes loved,** was the first great American poet to praise cities in his verse.

✔ CHECKLIST 6.1: ARRANGING SENTENCE ELEMENTS TO CLARIFY MEANING

As you revise your sentences, consider the relation of sentence structure to meaning. Ask yourself these questions.

- Are ideas of equal importance presented with coordination?
- Are ideas of equal importance presented through parallel structures?
- Are ideas of unequal importance presented through subordination?

■ Exercise 6.6 Revise the following sentences to make good parallel constructions.

1. The movie *Gone with the Wind,* filmed in Technicolor and which cost millions of dollars to make, was the first talking movie about the Civil War to be a success at the box office.
2. Television, the great rival to the movies and which movie people hated at first, was not allowed to show the Academy Awards until 1952.
3. Many Japanese Americans, treated badly in this country during the war and who were sent to internment camps, shared their thoughts and feelings at the recent Pearl Harbor memorial services.

4. She hoped to win her first marathon, the one she entered at Boston and which led over a hilly course.
5. He brought home a new computer, very compact, expanded memory, expensive, and which he could not afford.

CHAPTER

7

EMPHASIS AND VARIETY

Two ways to gain and keep readers' attention are to provide proper emphasis and to supply variety. When you arrange information carefully in a sentence, you can emphasize important ideas and put less emphasis on less important ideas. When sentences vary in pattern and length, your ideas will engage your readers' attention more readily and the monotonous repetition of the same forms will not distract your readers.

7a Using Periodic Sentences

A **periodic sentence** has a strong word or phrase at the end, just before the period. The complete meaning is apparent only when you come to the end and have read the last few words.

> If asked to name the central quality in Faulkner's work, one is likely to give the quick answer "Imagination."
>
> —MALCOLM COWLEY

Sometimes a periodic sentence ends with a striking thought rather than with a striking word.

> The original Hopalong Cassidy was created by Clarence E. Mulford, a Brooklyn marriage-license clerk who at the time had never even seen the West.
>
> —JAMES HORWITZ

When you have several facts to convey in a sentence, it is nearly always a good idea to put the more important ones toward the end to give a sense of building toward a climax. The most important fact in the following sentence is the part played by John Muir in establishing Yosemite National Park, not the fact of his wearing a beard:

> **Wrong emphasis:** John Muir, the naturalist who was more responsible than any other single person for establishing Yosemite National Park, took long, solitary walks and let his beard grow long and tangled.
>
> **Revised:** John Muir, a naturalist who took long, solitary walks and let his beard grow long and tangled, was more responsible than any other person for establishing Yosemite National Park.

7b
Avoiding Weak Endings

A weak ending lets readers down because it leaves them with a sense of unfinished business or a sense that they've been taken in—that the writer has no real goal in mind.

> **Weak:** Young people in 1946 and 1947 turned from the horrors of World War II to a love affair with the jukebox, however.
>
> **Better:** Young people in 1946 and 1947, however, turned from the horrors of World War II to a love affair with the jukebox.
>
> **Weak:** The huge demonstrations in Washington against the Vietnamese war in the 1960s may not have been supported by a majority of the American people, nevertheless.
>
> **Better:** Nevertheless, the huge demonstrations in Washington against the Vietnamese war in the 1960s may not have been supported by a majority of the American people.

■ **Exercise 7.1** Rewrite the sentences below to make periodic sentences. If necessary, delete some words and phrases or invent others that capture the central idea.

1. Adlai Stevenson, laboring against the awesome power of Dwight Eisenhower's smile, lost the presidential elections of 1952 and 1956, as everyone knows.
2. Fiction writers do not often talk very well to interviewers about how they write, so Malcolm Cowley says.
3. The inspector found the body in the kitchen. When she had arrived on the scene, the house was locked and silent. She had the officers break down the door.

7c
Using Free Modifiers and Absolutes

In a **cumulative sentence,** several free modifiers or absolutes are appended to the predicate, thus giving new layers of meaning to the basic assertion of the clause.

A **free modifier** is a participle or participial phrase that occurs at the end of a clause and modifies the subject. The free modifiers in the following sentences are in boldface type.

> The motorcycle spun out of control, **leaving the highway, plunging down the ravine, crashing through a fence, coming to rest at last on its side.**

> The ocean beat against the shore in long swells, **roaring above the sound of the wind, threatening the tiny houses, slamming against the great rocks on the beach.**

An **absolute** (discussed on p. 115) consists of a noun and a participle. At the end of the clause it modifies, an absolute adds meaning to the whole. The absolutes in the following sentences are in boldface.

> He crossed the finish line in record time, **his lungs nearly bursting with his effort.**

> The barn burned, **the flames rising two hundred feet into the night sky.**

A cumulative sentence may use absolutes or free modifiers or both. A noncumulative sentence completes its thought with a subject complement, a direct object, or an adverb with an adverbial phrase. The sentence below concludes its thought with an adverbial phrase.

> The house stood silently **on the hill.**

But the sentence can be revised so that it completes its thought with absolutes and free modifiers.

> The house stood silently on the hill, baking in the hot sunshine, its broken windows gaping open to the ragged fields, its roof collapsing, its rotting doors hanging open, its glory departed.

Study the following cumulative sentences, and see how elements added to the end of the predicate help them accumulate force.

He emptied them thoroughly, **unhurried, his face completely cold, masklike almost.**

—WILLIAM FAULKNER

Another characteristic was that once a Veragua had caught and gored a man or a horse he would not leave him but would attack again and again, **seeming to want to destroy his victim entirely.**

—ERNEST HEMINGWAY

■ **Exercise 7.2** Combine the following sentences to make cumulative sentences.

Example:
He sat at the typewriter. His teacup was at his left. The wind was blowing outside. The clock was ticking over the fireplace.

He sat at the typewriter, his teacup at his left, the clock ticking over the fireplace, the wind blowing outside.

1. She studied the map of the block. She was thinking of the fine old buildings that would have to be torn down. She was thinking of her own creation that would take their place. Her ideas were rushing in her head like a flood.
2. He got down from the train and looked around. He saw the courthouse. He saw the city square. It was vacant at this hour of the morning.
3. She saw him. He was working in the field. He was holding a long black hoe. His father gave it to him many years ago.

■ **Exercise 7.3** Look around the room where you are sitting and write three cumulative sentences that describe some of the things you see.

7d
Using the Active Voice

In general, use the active rather than the passive voice. The subject of a sentence in the active voice performs the action of the verb; the subject of a sentence in the passive voice is acted upon. (The active and passive voices of verbs are discussed on p. 257.) Look at the difference:

Weak: His decision not to run for reelection to the presidency in 1968 was announced on television on March 31 of that year by Lyndon Johnson.

Revised: On March 31, 1968, President Lyndon Johnson announced on television that he would not run for reelection in the fall.

As a rule, use the passive voice only when the actor or agent in the sentence is much less important to your statement than the recipient of the action.

Estes Kefauver **was elected** to the Senate in 1948.

She **was taken** to the hospital last night.

Passive voice constructions have a way of creeping into our writing, and it pays to look at your revisions with an eye to using the active voice. A good rule of thumb is that whenever you use the passive voice, explain to yourself why you chose it over the active voice.

7e
Emphasizing with Repetition

Add emphasis by repeating key words or phrases in consecutive clauses or sentences.

Let every nation know, whether it wishes us well or ill, that we shall pay *any* price, bear *any* burden, meet *any* hardship, support *any* friend, oppose *any* foe to assure the survival and the success of liberty.

—JOHN F. KENNEDY

7f
Varying Sentence Length

Give special emphasis to ideas by writing a very short sentence to follow several long ones.

The real objection to capital punishment doesn't lie against the actual extermination of the condemned, but against our brutal American habit of putting it off so long. After all, every one of us must die soon or late, and a murderer, it must be assumed, is one who makes that sad fact the cornerstone of his metaphysic. But it is one thing to die, and quite another thing to lie for long months and even years under the shadow of death. *No sane man would choose such a finish.*

—H. L. MENCKEN

■ **Exercise 7.4** Rewrite the following sentences to emphasize the elements you think are most important or most dramatic. You may change or delete words and phrases as long as you keep the central idea. Try to find several ways of dealing with each sentence.

1. The college library was locked up by the head librarian, G. W. Cranshaw, who said he got tired of seeing all those careless and sweaty students handling the books.
2. How strongly we believe in something, especially when it is something we think we ought to believe and maybe don't but won't admit it, and somebody comes and asks us if we believe it, is not measured well by statistics.
3. Now swimmers can buy little floats with bright colors on the top and clamps on the bottom under the water, and they can swim out to sea and take off their bathing suits and clamp them with the clamps and go skinny dipping if they want to.

7g
Varying Sentence Type

Sentence variety is the spice of lively writing, and you should strive to write sentences varied enough to hold your readers' attention throughout your paper.

Vary the patterns and the lengths of sentences to keep readers alert and involved. If you repeat any sentence pattern too often, you will bore your readers. It is a good idea to learn and practice variations in the basic writing pattern. The basic pattern in modern English writing is *subject + predicate* (discussed on pp. 85-92). In this example, the subject is in bold and the predicate is in regular type.

> **My father and my stepmother** left on the noon plane to Atlanta.

The most common variation on this pattern is to begin with some kind of adverbial opener.

By the late afternoon, they will be at home.

Because they live so far away, we see them only once or twice a year.

Tomorrow they will telephone.

Another variation is to begin with a participle or a participial phrase that serves as an adjective.

Smiling, he walked confidently into the room.

Stunned by the stock market crash, many brokers committed suicide.

Sentences also can open with an infinitive phrase or a coordinating conjunction.

To protect my mother, I'd made up stories of a secret marriage that for some strange reason never got known.

—SHERWOOD ANDERSON

But, say you, it is a question of interest, and if you make it your interest, you have the right to enslave another. Very well. *And* if he can make it his interest, he has the right to enslave you.

—ABRAHAM LINCOLN

In the first passage below, the sentences all begin with the subject; they are all about the same length; and they are all short. They are clear and understandable, but notice the improvement in the second passage, where the combined and embedded elements create a pleasing variety in both length and sentence structure.

He dived quickly into the sea. He peered through his mask. The watery world turned darker. A school of fish went by. The distant light glittered on their bodies. He stopped swimming. He waited. He thought the fish might be chased by a shark. He satisfied himself that there was no shark. He continued down. He heard only one sound. That was his breathing apparatus. It made a bubbling noise in operation.

He dived quickly into the sea, peering through his mask at a watery world that turned darker as he went down. A school of fish went by, the distant light glittering on their bodies, and he stopped swimming and waited a moment to see if the fish might be chased by a shark. Satisfying himself that there was no shark, he continued down. The only sound he heard was the bubbling noise of his breathing apparatus.

The improved version combines thoughts, reduces the number of sentences, and cuts down the repetition of the pronoun *he.* The sentence patterns now are more varied and interesting.

7h
Using Rhetorical Questions

Asking a question will require your reader to participate more actively. Questions that require no answer or for which the answer is demonstrably obvious are called **rhetorical questions.**

> Is not marriage an open question, when it is alleged, from the beginning of the world, that such as are in the institution wish to get out; and such as are out wish to get in?
>
> —RALPH WALDO EMERSON

Rhetorical questions that allow the writer to supply the answer can sometimes be effective transitional devices.

> The movie is called *Rock 'n Roll High School,* and for anyone not into punk, it has only one conceivable point of interest: Can Van Patten act as well as he hits a tennis ball? The answer is no, which is not to say that he isn't a promising young actor. It's just that as a tennis player he is a good deal more than fine.
>
> —*Sports Illustrated*

But avoid beginning an essay with broad rhetorical questions that might better be phrased as sharp thesis statements. "Why should we study *Huckleberry Finn*?" "How did the Peace Corps begin?" "Was Rodney King guilty as charged?" Such openings may lead readers to suspect that the writer did not take the trouble to think of something better. Save your rhetorical questions for an occasional paragraph that comes in the body of a paper after you introduce your subject in some other way.

7i
Using Exclamations

Occasionally an exclamation helps vary a series of declarative sentences, but use this sentence type only on rare occasions and for special effects.

Clearly, even if there were a limit on the length of sentences to twenty words, it would not be possible to characterize any individual knowledge of English by claiming that he carried around a list of all its sentences in his head! But there is in fact no limit to the length of a sentence. A sentence twenty-one words in length can be made longer by adding another modifier or a subordinate of some kind—and so on.

—HELEN S. CAIRNS AND CHARLES E. CAIRNS

✓ CHECKLIST 7.1: STRENGTHENING SENTENCE EMPHASIS AND VARIETY

As you revise your sentences, consider reworking sentence patterns for proper emphasis and pleasing variety.

Emphasis

Analyze one sentence at a time. For appropriate emphasis, consider these options.

- Promote rhythm or cadence through deliberate repetition.
- Strengthen the sentence ending by making the sentence periodic.
- Strengthen the sentence ending by making the sentence cumulative.
- Strengthen the sentence action by making the voice active.

Variety

Analyze one paragraph at a time. If the sentences are monotonous, consider these options.

- Vary sentence length.
- Vary sentence openings with adverbs.
- Vary sentence openings with participles or participial phrases.
- Vary sentence openings with infinitive phrases.
- Vary sentence openings with coordinating conjunctions.
- Invert subject and verb.
- Use a rhetorical question.
- Use an exclamation.

7j
Inverting Subject and Verb

For variety, you can put the verb before the subject. This is another device to use only rarely:

> Beyond is another country.
>
> —Robert M. Pirsig

> From high above in the swirl of raging wind and snow came a frightening, wonderful, mysterious sound.
>
> —Mark Helprin

■ **Exercise 7.5** Revise the following set of simple sentences to form two coherent paragraphs made up of sentences that are varied in style and in length. You may change or add words but not facts. Look for places where you can subordinate one idea to another, both to reduce the number of words and to create a pleasing style. Experiment. Try the techniques of sentence revision described in Chapters 5–7. Compare your version with the work of others in your class.

1. Bluegrass music was popular in the rural south before World War II.
2. It features hand-held instruments.
3. These include the banjo, the guitar, the fiddle, the mandolin, and sometimes the dulcimer and the bass fiddle.
4. Bluegrass songs are in the tradition of the mountain ballad and the Protestant hymn.
5. It began as the music of poor southern American mountaineers.
6. Bluegrass songs are about love affairs gone wrong.
7. Sometimes they speak about the fear of hell.
8. Sometimes they describe conversion experiences.
9. Sometimes they express the yearning of the soul for heaven.
10. Bluegrass bands never use electrified instruments.

PART
THREE

USING WORDS EFFECTIVELY

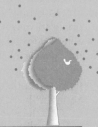

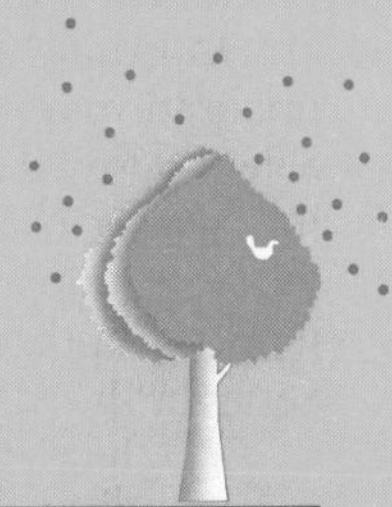

CHAPTER

8

CHOOSING TONE AND DICTION

The language you choose conveys more than the meaning of individual words. It says something about you—the writer—as well as something about what you think of your audience. Careful writers control their language so that their writing conveys what they mean on all levels. In revising drafts of paragraphs and sentences, be sure to pay attention to tone and diction. **Tone** is the style and manner of your expression—formal or informal, highly technical or broadly appealing. **Diction** is the specific word choice that achieves clarity, accuracy, and effectiveness.

In writing and revising, your goal should be to use language appropriate to your subject. Choose the tone and diction that fit your topic. Select words that state your meaning exactly. Avoid a style that is too informal or chatty, but don't be stiff and pompous. A breezy, informal tone is not appropriate for a paper on cancer treatments, nor is a sober tone appropriate for an essay on hang gliding. Don't write about the World Series or the Super Bowl as if they were as important as war or disease.

The best way to gain a sense of language is to read as much as you can. Whether you are preparing to write about literature or natural science or history, take some time to read what writers in the field have written. Try to use their tone and diction as models for your own style.

8a Checking Diction

When you revise, examine your word choice to be sure it is appropriate for your subject and purpose. Slang, dialect, jargon, and foreign terms have a place in communication, but they may create barriers and wrong impressions.

Using Slang

Slang words are emotional but inexact; they are also only briefly in use. Use slang only when it is appropriate to the subject and tone of your essay. Consider the following pairs of sentences.

> **Inappropriate:** In *Heart of Darkness,* we hear a lot about a dude named Kurtz, but we don't see the guy much.
>
> **Revised:** In *Heart of Darkness,* Marlow, the narrator, talks almost continually about Kurtz, but we see Kurtz himself only at the end.

> **Inappropriate:** When Thomas More saw how Henry VIII was going, he might have run off to France to save his hide, but he stayed on and got his head chopped off for his trouble.
>
> **Revised:** When he saw the direction of Henry's mind, Thomas More might have fled to France to save himself, but he stayed on until he was imprisoned and put to death.

Some slang terms are always entering the mainstream of the language, and many American journalists adopt a breezy, informal tone. But even these journalists do not fill their prose with slang. Instead, they use slang to fit a special mood that they are trying to convey.

> But Boston is also a city that historically has pricked the social conscience of many well-heeled undergraduates.
>
> —HOWARD HUSOCK

> Minutes before the camera's ruby light flashed on, cable TV's garrulous impresario was already well into his inaugural address before a gathering of Atlanta VIPs.
>
> —*Time*

Even when an informal tone is appropriate, be cautious. Slang can spoil good writing and make careful readers scorn your work. Never try to be cute when you write.

You must use slang, however, if it is part of a direct quotation. There the prose is not yours but that of your source, and you must quote that source exactly if you are using quotation marks.

> "He whopped me good," Turner said of the tackle that made him fumble.

Using Dialect

Some inexperienced writers use dialect to show the ethnic or regional origins of people, but dialect is very difficult to do correctly. Inexperienced writers frequently get it wrong and may appear to be making fun of the people they are writing about.

> **Dialect:** "Ah'm a-goin' raght over thar," she said, "an if'n you'd go along, hit'ud be a big hep, and Ah'd be much obleeged."

> **Revised:** "I'm going right over there," she said with a strong Appalachian accent, "and if you'd go along, it'd be a big help, and I'd be much obliged."

Avoiding Jargon and Technical Terms

8a
diction

Jargon is the language of specialists. It includes unfamiliar words, new compounds, and ordinary English words used in ways that are unfamiliar to most people. For example, people who use computers speak of "booting a disk," making "hard copies," and "accessing the program."

Jargon has a place when specialists talk to each other, but if you want to be sure your readers understand you, avoid jargon. It not only makes simple thoughts seem complicated, but it puts people off, making them feel like outsiders. Experienced readers rarely take jargon seriously. Consider this paragraph written by an academic author.

> **Jargon:** Romantic love is characterized by a preoccupation with a deliberately restricted set of perceived characteristics in the love object which are viewed as a means to some ideal ends. In the process of selecting the set of perceived characteristics and the process of determining the ideal ends, there is also a systematic failure to assess the accuracy of the perceived characteristics and the feasibility of achieving the ideal ends given the selected set of means and other pre-existing ends.

The paragraph means something like the following.

> **Revised:** People in love see only what they want to see in the beloved. They want to believe in an ideal, so they do not question the accuracy of what they see or ask themselves if the ideal they imagine can be attained.

Here is another example. Notice how pompous the unrevised writing sounds.

Pretentious: Baxter felt a pang of existential anxiety when he contemplated his English exam.

Revised: Baxter worried about his English exam when he thought about it.

Jargon and technical terms from one field are always inappropriate in another.

Jargon: The interface of the Honors Committee and the dean's office impacted student access to rare books.

Revised: Relations between the Honors Committee and the dean's office affected student access to rare books.

When you think you may be using unnecessary jargon, ask yourself what you are really trying to say. Put that meaning in the simplest sentence you can write. Don't use words most people do not understand unless they are necessary to say exactly what you want to say.

Avoiding Obsolete and Foreign Terms

Obsolete or archaic words and expressions can confuse your reader or misstate your meaning; they may also distract your reader from your subject into wondering about you.

Archaic: It was clear ere she left that the problems had not been resolved.

Revised: It was clear before she left that the problems had not been resolved.

Use foreign words only when they are necessary. It is pretentious to use foreign expressions when English will do.

Pretentious: Her collection of exotic clamshells was her only *raison d'être.*

Better: Her collection of exotic clamshells was her only reason for living.

Pretentious: Sarah's *Weltanschauung* extended no further than her daily whims.

Better: Sarah's view of the world extended no further than her daily whims.

■ **Exercise 8.1** Rewrite the following sentences to change language that might be inappropriate in a formal paper. Try to keep the meaning of each sentence intact.

1. When the ump called nine consecutive strikes on three batters, Manager Sparky Anderson got his back up.
2. When the Germans were presented with the Treaty of Versailles in 1919, they really got sore.
3. Maybe the concert of the Boston Symphony Orchestra will be so wicked that the audience will fork over megabucks to go with the flow.
4. Ross Perot was a shrewd old geezer who made a pile of money and decided to go for broke in 1992 by running for President.

■ **Exercise 8.2** Rewrite the following sentences to eliminate foreign words or stilted expressions. You may need to look up words in your desk dictionary. Don't try to translate the foreign words literally; try to put their meaning into fresh, idiomatic English.

1. The freshmen thought that the *summum bonum* of college life was to own a convertible.
2. Max said that if his roommate kept on smoking cigars in bed at night, it would be a *casus belli.*
3. A common multidimensional learning problem for students of the typewriter and the violin is the dexterity factor, for in both cases erroneous application of the fingers has the end result of a negative production response.
4. A sophomore is a kind of *tertium quid* between freshman and upper-class students.

8b Using Idioms Correctly

Idioms are habitual ways of saying things, and they usually cannot be translated from one language to another. Sometimes they cannot be transferred from one region to another within a country. If you say in French to a Frenchman, "I'm going to eat a hot dog with mustard," he will hide his pet poodle. If you ask a mountain southerner in the United States for a poke, he will hand you a paper bag; if you ask a New Yorker, he may hit you in the mouth.

Idioms involve more than regional speech. They are customary forms of expression that are not always logical. Often they involve selection of the right preposition. We are not angry *against,* but angry *with;* we do not go *with* the car but *in* the car or, simply, *by* car. The same point can be made about the phrase *different than.* We say "Fred is *different from* his older brother," not "Fred is *different than* his older brother."

Some verbs may take particles (see p. 95) to clarify their meaning. Particles look like prepositions, but they are really a part of the verb form, and they can make a big difference.

Harry made **up** with Gloria.

Harry made **off** with Gloria.

Harry made **out** with Gloria.

Selecting the right particle involves knowing idiomatic English. Sometimes particles aren't needed, and they should be eliminated when they don't add or detract meaning.

Draft: We will meet **up** with him in Denver.

Revised: We will meet him in Denver.

Idiom is difficult because it is a reflection of customary speech patterns, and custom often refuses to obey logical rules. Inexperienced writers often have trouble with idioms when they use unfamiliar words or expressions and do not know how to put them together the way experienced writers use them.

■ **Exercise 8.3** Rewrite the following sentences to correct mistakes in idiom.

1. We celebrate Labor Day at the first Monday after the first Sunday in September.
2. Lyndon Johnson became president on November 1963.
3. My mother introduced me with her friend.
4. Previous to the meeting, we agreed to talk only an hour before adjourning.
5. Newton's general principle states that all bodies have a force of gravity proportionate with their mass.
6. Jazz music has been traditionally centered around the experience of black musicians playing in small groups.
7. He deaned the faculty for ten years and then returned to teaching because he wanted to make something of himself.
8. The sun arose that morning at six o'clock.

9. Shiela's dress needs ironed.
10. Where's it at?
11. Computers promise to us much more efficiency than typewriters could ever give.
12. Tom used a strip of masking tape to get the fur of cat off the seat.

✔ CHECKLIST 8.1: CHECKING TONE AND DICTION

As you revise paragraphs and sentences, think about tone and diction—the tone you want your writing to set and the impression you want it to convey. Examine your choice of words. Ask yourself these questions.

- Is the tone appropriate for the subject?
- Is the tone appropriate for the audience?
- Are slang words, dialect, jargon, obsolete and foreign terms, if they appear at all, used deliberately and with full awareness of their meaning and the impression they convey?
- Are idioms correct?
- Are connotations correct?

8c
Undertanding Denotations and Connotations

Words have both primary meanings, called **denotations,** and secondary meanings, called **connotations.** Connotations allow some **synonyms**—words with the same meaning—to work in some contexts and not in others. You can say that your friend Murdock *evaded* the requirement that everyone learn how to swim before graduation, or you can say that he *flouted* it, or you can say that he *escaped* it. Each way we know that Murdock did not learn how to swim and that he did not obey the rule. But if he *evaded* the rule, he slipped away from it slyly. If he *flouted* the requirement, he may have announced publicly and arrogantly that he did not intend to observe the requirement. If he *escaped* the requirement, something may have happened to make the college forget to enforce the rule for him.

Here are some words with similar denotations but different connotations.

requested, demanded
ignored, neglected
unsympathetic, intolerant
confused, dazed

Beginning writers often have trouble with connotations. The best remedies are to note how experienced writers use different words and to study the dictionary for various connotations. Beware of using a thesaurus, as it lists synonyms only. If you're not sure of a synonym's connotation, consult a dictionary.

■ **Exercise 8.4** Write sentences that use the following words correctly. You may use several of the words in one sentence if you can do so gracefully.

1. ambitious, greedy
2. successful, enterprising
3. proud, arrogant, haughty
4. hit, smash, collide
5. drink, guzzle, sip
6. eat, gobble, pick at

CHAPTER

9

USING IMAGERY AND FIGURATIVE LANGUAGE

Lively writing creates word pictures for the reader. With concrete nouns and verbs that appeal to the senses, you can change an abstract idea into something vivid and specific. If you write, "The trees were affected by the bad weather," you do not give your readers much to picture in their minds. But if you write, "The small pines shook in the wind," the concrete nouns and the verb create an image.

Figurative language helps you build images. A **figure** states or implies a comparison between your subject and something else. If you write, "The small pines shook in the wind," you are being literal. If you write, "The small pines trembled with fear like children scolded by the wind," you are being figurative. The figure compares the trees to frightened children and the wind to a person scolding them. The English language is rich in figures because they help express ideas clearly and succinctly.

9a
Using Concrete Nouns and Verbs

Nouns and verbs that are specific rather than general create an image and have an impact. Generic, unspecified nouns (*tree,* instead of *pine*) and verbs (*were affected,* instead of *shook*) merely report that something happened, but not what. Examine this paragraph.

> Often the positions people take on energy are an index to how they stand on other issues. Conservatives, liberals, and radicals tend to congregate in causes, and if you tell me where you think we ought to get our energy, I can probably tell you what you think about what we ought to eat and how we ought to spend our time. But nearly

everybody on every side of every current issue agrees that we should use solar energy.

This paragraph contains no errors in grammar, and it is fairly clear. But its prose style does not engage our attention, and when we finish reading it, we have a hard time remembering it.

Now study this version (italics added).

> Every source of energy seems to have become a political issue. Tell me whether you think the path to a happy future lies with *solar heating* or with *nuclear furnaces,* tell me how you feel about *oil shale* and *coal* and *corn-fed gasohol,* and I'll tell you where you stand on *welfare reform, environmental policy, vegetarianism, busing, back-packing,* and *abortion.* But there is one kind of energy that attracts a diverse following: *photovoltaics,* the art of converting *sunlight* into *electricity.*
>
> —TRACY KIDDER

Notice how the italicized words—all concrete nouns—create a strong impression.

■ **Exercise 9.1** Read the following paragraph and pick out the concrete details.

> In the smallest of these huts lived old Berl, a man in his eighties, and his wife, who was called Berlcha (wife of Berl). Old Berl was one of the Jews who had been driven from their villages in Russia and had settled in Poland. In Lentshin, they mocked the mistakes he made while praying aloud. He spoke with a sharp "r." He was short, broad-shouldered, and he had a small white beard, and summer and winter he wore a sheepskin hat, a padded cotton jacket, and stout boots. He walked slowly, shuffling his feet. He had a half acre of field, a cow, a goat, and chickens.
>
> —ISAAC BASHEVIS SINGER

9b Using Metaphors and Similes

Comparisons can make your prose more vivid, but be sure they are appropriate to your subject, your tone, and your audience.

A **simile** is a comparison that uses the word *like* or *as.*

My love is **like** a red, red rose.

—ROBERT BURNS

Tom Birch is as brisk **as** a bee in conversation.

—SAMUEL JOHNSON

Mortality weighs heavily upon me **like** an unwilling sleep.

—JOHN KEATS

A **metaphor,** or implied comparison, speaks of things or of actions as if they were something other than what they are. Because of its compression, a metaphor may have stronger force than a simile.

The dice are the gods of the backgammon wars.

—E. J. KAHN, JR.

Marcel Duchamp once referred to dealers as "lice on the backs of artists"—useful and necessary lice, he added, but lice all the same.

—*New Yorker*

At least half of all writers, major or minor, have suffered from writing blocks—from inner resistance to dragging oneself, hour after hour, to the bar of self-judgment, and forcing oneself, before it, to confront that most intimidating of objects to any writer: the blank page waiting to be filled.

—WALTER JACKSON BATE

■ **Exercise 9.2** Complete the simile that will describe each of the following actions or objects. Try to avoid any similes that you have heard before. Add as many words as you need.

1. My mother was as angry as ________.
2. The biscuits were as light and fluffy as ________.
3. The coin gleamed in his hand like ________.
4. My flower garden was as wild as ________.
5. Our football team was as inept as a group of ________.

■ **Exercise 9.3** Write a descriptive paragraph on two of the following subjects, using a simile and a metaphor in each.

1. the first time you voted in a national election
2. a child learning that her parents will be divorced

3. the announcement that your father has won a beauty contest
4. deciding to buy a new car
5. recognizing that a friend is an alcoholic

✔ CHECKLIST 9.1: BUILDING WORD PICTURES

As you revise, look for ways to make your language strong and lively. Reflect on how you express yourself. Can you make your expressions more memorable? Can you recast them to build word pictures? Ask yourself these questions.

- Are there generic, unspecified nouns that can be replaced with concrete nouns?
- Can static verbs or passive voice constructions be replaced with strong, action-oriented verbs?
- Can a simile be introduced?
- Can an action or impression be recast as a metaphor?
- Are cliché's making the prose seem tired (and the reader, too)?

9c
Avoiding Clichés

A **cliché** is an overworked expression. The moment we read the first word or two of a cliché, we know how it will end. If someone says, "She was as mad as a ________," we expect the sentence to be completed by the words *wet hen* or *hornet.* If someone says, "My biscuits were as light as ________," we expect the sentence to be completed by *a feather.* If someone says, "His prose is as heavy as ________," we expect the sentence to end with *lead.*

We have heard these expressions so often that our minds are dead to them even when we understand what they mean, and they no longer create vivid pictures in our imaginations. The table on the next page lists some common clichés to avoid. You can probably think of others.

Usually it's best to rephrase a cliché as simply as you can in plain language.

> **Cliché:** When John turned his papers in three weeks late, he had to *face the music.*

Better: When John turned his papers in three weeks late, he had to take the consequences.

Cliché: Harvey *kept his nose to the grindstone.*

Better: Harvey gave close and unceasing attention to his work.

■ **Exercise 9.4** Rewrite the following sentences to eliminate the clichés. Be adventurous. Try to think up some similes or metaphors that convey the meaning of a cliché without repeating its tired words.

1. Although he had worked like a dog all week long, the conductor seemed as cool as a cucumber and as fresh as a daisy when he mounted the podium and raised his baton to his orchestra.
2. The letter announcing the prize came to her like a bolt from the blue, making her friends green with envy, while she herself felt worth her weight in gold.
3. Bollinger believed that he had a right to be president of the university, since he had paid his dues as a lower functionary for years, sometimes feeling in the depths of despair over the way people treated him like a dog, believing often that he was doomed to disappointment in life, but determined to put his shoulder to the wheel.

COMMON CLICHÉS

abreast of the times
acid test
add insult to injury
agony of suspense
beat a hasty retreat
better half
beyond the shadow of a doubt
blind as a bat
blue as the sky
bolt from the blue
bottom line
brave as a lion
brown as a nut
brutal murder
bustling cities
calm, cool, and collected
cold, hard facts
come to grips with
cool as a cucumber
crazy as a loon
dead as a doornail
deaf as a post
deep, dark secret
depths of despair
diabolical skill
distaff side
doomed to disappointment
drunk as a lord
every dog has his day
face the music
fair sex
few and far between
fire-engine red
flat as a pancake
gild the lily
green with envy
heave a sigh of relief
heavy as lead
hit the nail on the head
in this day and age
ladder of success

last but not least
little lady
live from hand to mouth
livid with rage
nose to the grindstone
nutty as a fruitcake
110 percent
the other side of the coin
paint the town red
pale as a ghost
pass the buck
pick and choose
poor but honest
poor but proud

pretty as a picture
primrose path
proud possessor
quick as a flash
quiet as a churchmouse
reigns supreme
right as rain
rise and shine
rise to the occasion
sadder but wiser
sharp as a tack
shoulder to the wheel
sink or swim
smart as a whip

sneaking suspicion
sober as a judge
straight and narrow
tempest in a teapot
tired but happy
tried and true
ugly as sin
undercurrent of excitement
untimely death
walk the line
wax eloquent
white as a ghost
white as a sheet
worth its weight in gold

CHAPTER

10

MAKING EVERY WORD COUNT

One key to good writing is making sure you have all the words you need to make your meaning clear—and no more. Extra words are something to avoid.

10a
Including Necessary Words

Include all the words that are necessary to make sentences clear and complete.

Completing Verbs

Many verb forms include several words. Helping verbs and particles are needed to make tense or meaning clear. Be sure to include all necessary verb parts.

> He **is writing** about the beehives.
>
> I **have seen** what he **has done.**
>
> She **has taken** a minute to rest.
>
> The plum pudding **was scorched** around the edges.
>
> Josie and Phil **felt** like **dressing up.**

Do not leave out part of a compound verb when the tense of one part of the verb varies from the tense of the other part.

> **Incomplete:** Caldwell **has** long and always **will be** sympathetic to those who think jogging is boring.

Revised: Caldwell **has** long **been** and always **will be** sympathetic to those who think jogging is boring.

Using the Subordinator *That*

In **indirect discourse**—statements rephrasing the statements of others without directly quoting—the subordinator *that* introduces the subordinate clause. Sometimes it is necessary.

He sent the message **that** canoes were unable to navigate the Platte River.

But sometimes it is not. Omit *that* only if the subordinate clause is so simple that its meaning is instantly clear.

Loretta Lynn sang songs women love.

■ **Exercise 10.1** Check the following sentences for missing words. Add words where they are needed. If a sentence is clear and grammatical as it stands, put a check by the number.

1. He told the staff men and women deserve equal pensions.
2. He taken the car to a junkyard and found many people in business suits now go to junkyards to get parts for old cars they want to keep running a few more years.
3. I been here now for thirty years and never seen so little rain.
4. Air travel getting so expensive only the rich and people on business able to afford it now.
5. She told her daughter driving across the country and staying in motels were much more expensive than flying.
6. I will have been sick for two weeks on Monday and tomorrow see a doctor.

Using Articles, Prepositions, and Pronouns

ESL 12

Include the articles, prepositions, and pronouns that are necessary for idiomatic expressions.

All **the** people in the room had quit smoking.

A dog that bites should be kept on **a** leash.

He gave me **the** books he liked best.

This kind **of** dog is noted for its affection.

He did not like taking **from** or giving **to** the fund.

You do not have to repeat a preposition before every word in a series, but if you do repeat it before any of those words, you must repeat it before all the words.

Draft: He loved her for her intelligence, her beauty, and **for** her money.

Revised: He loved her **for** her intelligence, **for** her beauty, and **for** her money

Making Comparisons Clear

10a clar

Include a possessive form when you are comparing possessions or attributes.

Wordy: Plato's philosophy is easier to read than **that of** Aristotle.

Revised: Plato's philosophy is easier to read than **Aristotle's.**

Use *other* and *else* to show that people or things belong to a group with which they are being compared.

Gone with the Wind won more awards than any **other** film in Hollywood history.

Professor Koonig wrote more books than anyone **else** in the department.

Use the word *as* twice when you use it to compare people or things.

His temper was **as** mild **as** milk.

Avoid the vague comparison implied in the word *that* used as a weak synonym for *very*.

Weak: Professor Koonig was not **that** dull.

Revised: Professor Koonig was not **very** dull.

When you are tempted to use *that* as a vague comparative, think of something concrete and lively, and use the comparative form *as . . . as* instead of *that.* Or use *so . . . that* and a clause.

Professor Koonig was not **as** dull **as** some cows I have known.

Professor Koonig was **so** dull **that** he could make flowers wither.

Be sure your comparisons are always complete. If you have just said, "Professor Koonig is dull," you can say immediately afterward, "Professor Donovan is more interesting." But you cannot say in isolation, "Professor Donovan is more interesting." You need to name who or what forms the rest of the comparison. You may say, "Professor Donovan is more interesting than Professor Koonig."

■ **Exercise 10.2** Add words as they are needed in the following sentences. If a sentence is correct as it stands, put a check by the number.

1. She was happy as I have ever seen anyone when she graduated from West Point.
2. He took the car in to have the transmission replaced, the body painted, and seats covered.
3. This type grass seed does not do that well in shade.
4. The car I drove to the beach was worse than any car I have ever driven.
5. Pete Rose was not that fast, but he always played hard as a boy even when he was forty years old.

10b Avoiding Wordiness

If you eliminate words that do not contribute to your meaning, you make every word count. Avoiding wordiness does not mean that you must write in short, choppy sentences or that you must reduce your prose to its bare bones. It does mean that every word should be necessary to your thought, because words that add nothing will obscure your meaning and bore your readers.

Eliminating Unnecessary Words

The following paragraph, a response to an assignment requiring an explanation of **expository writing,** is a good first draft, but it is entirely too wordy. The writer put down thoughts as fast as they came to mind, without pausing to edit. Then she revised the draft to eliminate wordiness and to make her points more effectively.

Draft: Briefly, expository writing is the kind of writing that develops an idea. It is not quite the same as narration, which tells a story, though you and I both know that narratives may contain many ideas. But that is not their main purpose. If I tell you that last night I was eating in a restaurant and found a pearl in my oyster, that is narration. And expository writing is not the kind of writing that describes something, though descriptions may include several of the most important ideas that a writer considers significant. If I describe how the campus looks under a deep, thick white snow and describe the way people wade through the snow and leave tracks on its pure and immaculate surface, then that is description. But if I go to the theater and see a play and come home and write down an interpretation of it, then I am doing expository writing even if part of the exposition is to describe the action of the play itself. And if I go on and talk about the aforesaid snow that I have talked about falling on the campus and if I tell the story about how the history department got out in it and started aggressively and energetically throwing snowballs at the dean, and if I then go on and try to explain why historians on this campus are at this point in time and always have been bellicose, then I am combining description, narration, and expository writing. But the main thing I want you to be conscious of is how you should classify the kinds of writing that are likely to go on in a single piece of writing and you've simply got to remember that it is not an example of expository writing unless it is writing about expounding an idea.

Revised: Expository writing develops ideas; narration tells stories; descriptions tell how things look. If I tell you that last night in a restaurant I found a pearl in an oyster, I am narrating. If I write of a deep snow on campus and how people wade through it and leave tracks, I am describing. But if I interpret a play, I am writing exposition, even if part of my essay describes the action of the play itself. And if I describe snow, and tell how the history department threw snowballs at the dean, and try to explain why historians at this university are bellicose, I am combining description, narration, and exposition. Remember that all three kinds of writing may appear in a single piece, but only expository writing interprets an idea.

The writer has recast the entire paragraph as well as several of its sentences. She has found ways to shorten sentences. She has presented her definitions at the beginning, as quickly as possible, and she has combined sentences to save words. (Helpful discussions are found in Chapters 5 and 6.)

Eliminating Redundant Constructions

As you revise for wordiness, look out for redundant words and phrases, the unnecessary repetitions that slip easily into first drafts. Conscious, deliberate repetition can help you emphasize ideas (see p. 151); meaningless repetition only makes for flabby sentences. Avoid redundant constructions.

> The candidate repeated the answer again.
>
> He expressed a number of clever expressions much to the audience's delight.
>
> Her dress was blue in color.

■ **Exercise 10.3** Edit the following paragraphs to make them more concise.

> I am going to tell you how much fun and profit there is in it for you to build your own house. If you have the time and a little energy and common sense, then you can build your very own house, save a ton of money, and have lots and lots of fun as you build your house. When it's all done and your house is standing there, built by you and maybe some members of your family, you will be proud of it, really proud. And think of all the fun you've had!
>
> Most of us, including probably you and me, usually think there is some kind of strange, secret mystery to the occult art of carpentry, but building things with wood is not a mystery at all. It takes lots and lots of care and lots and lots of hard work, but just about anybody can do it. You can do it too. The enjoyment you'll experience as well as all the money you'll save will make you enjoy this experience.

■ **Exercise 10.4** Underline the redundancies in the following examples.

1. at three A.M. in the morning
2. in modern times in the twentieth century today
3. return to the old neighborhood again
4. in my opinion, I think
5. the autobiography of her life
6. resultant effect of the report
7. quite tiny in size
8. the surrounding environment
9. unemployed workers now out of work
10. rectangular in shape

Eliminating Fillers and "Waiting Words"

When we speak, we often use phrases that serve as "waiting words"—they let us keep talking while we think of something more to say. These waiting words often creep into writing, where they take up valuable room without doing any work. Common waiting words include *like, you know, sort of, kind of, what I mean is, so to speak, in other words,* and *in the final analysis.*

Other common phrases are cumbersome, roundabout, habitual ways of saying something when we need only a word or two. And some of them are junk—words we can get rid of altogether without losing any real meaning.

Study the checklist and the recommended substitutions.

10b clar

✓ CHECKLIST 10.1: ELIMINATING FILLERS

When you see	Substitute
■ at the present time ■ in the present circumstances ■ at this point in time ■ at this moment ■ in this day and age	now, today, nowadays
■ at that point in time ■ in those days ■ in that period	then
■ in many cases	often
■ in some cases	sometimes
■ in exceptional cases	rarely
■ in most cases	usually
■ consider as, consider as being	consider
■ prior to	before
■ subsequent to	after
■ despite the fact that ■ regardless of the fact that	although
■ due to the fact that ■ for the purpose of ■ by virtue of the fact that ■ the reason is because	because
■ in a position to, in order to	can
■ in the area of	near, in
■ in the event that ■ in the event of ■ in case of	if (*with a verb*): If fire breaks out . . .

■ in terms of The new curriculum was designed in terms of student needs and faculty ability.	*Usually recast sentence to eliminate:* The new curriculum considers both student needs and faculty ability. The new curriculum was designed to match faculty ability with student needs.
■ in the final analysis	finally, *or drop entirely*
■ in no uncertain terms	firmly, clearly, *or eliminate*
■ in the nature of	like
■ refer back	refer

■ Exercise 10.5 Edit the following sentences to eliminate redundancies and fillers.

1. He is of a complex character.
2. She is of a generous nature.
3. The car was of a green color.
4. The weather conditions are bad.
5. Traffic conditions are congested.
6. Ted's leg injury was a serious crisis for the soccer team.
7. LaToya gave the officer her personal opinion.
8. Wesley looked at the referee in a suspicious manner.
9. Through repeated practice Elise was able to master the free throw.
10. The old post office was razed to the ground to make way for the new shopping mall.

■ Exercise 10.6 Edit the following paragraph to eliminate unnecessary words and phrases. You may find some words and phrases that are not in the checklist. Think hard about each sentence to see if you can eliminate padding and wordiness.

Due to the fact that at this point in time we have an energy crisis of a severe nature, we need to devote ourselves to a good rethinking of the academic calendar. At the present time, schools in the area of the United States begin in September and end in May or June. The reason is because schools once upon a time used to begin right after the harvest in societies of an agricultural character. But by virtue of the fact that buildings must be heated in the wintertime, schools in the cold regions of the earth are now paying out millions of dollars for fuel bills—money that might do much more good if it were put into faculty salaries, student scholarships, the library fund, the athletic program, or things of these kinds and of that nature. A solution to the problem may be of a simple nature: make the academic calendar according to the weather conditions prevailing in the different areas where the schools happen to be located.

Avoiding Word Inflation

Do not inflate simple thoughts with overblown language (see p. 175).

Inflated: Owning a gun for protection could be a consequence of several other factors. It could be the logical extension of a general home defense orientation. One mode of behavior for individuals who are vulnerable to crime is to increase their personal security, which leads them to a general home defense orientation and the acquisition of a gun.

Better: Some people buy guns to defend their homes, especially when they feel threatened by crime.

Inflated: Lucinda Childs's early development as a choreographer in the 1960s paralleled the rise of minimalist art. And while her work is extremely complex in its patterning and ordering, this complexity is grounded in the permutations of simplicity expressed in a few steps and their repetition.

Better: Lucinda Childs' early choreography in the 1960s developed alongside the work of the minimalist painters. Although she creates complex patterns and sequences, she uses only a few simple steps repeated with slight changes.

✓ CHECKLIST 10.2: MAKING EVERY WORD COUNT

As you revise, check to see that all necessary words are in place. Examine each sentence. Ask yourself these questions.

- For multiple verbs, are all verb parts present?
- Is the subordinator *that* used when necessary?
- Is use of articles, prepositions, and pronouns idiomatic?
- Are comparisons complete?

Then look for words you can trim.

- Can any words be eliminated without sacrificing meaning?
- Have all redundancies been eliminated?
- Have fillers been eliminated or replaced?
- Has word inflation been successfully avoided?

■ **Exercise 10.7** Edit the following sentences to make them more concise and clear. You may want to make two sentences where the writers have written one. Use the dictionary when you must.

1. A total site signage program is being studied, and if the study analysis dictates to relocate the stop sign, it will be done as a part of the total signage program and not as a result of your suggestion.
2. Dissatisfaction over the lack of responsiveness and accountability of decision makers is itself a primary source of the recent precipitous decline in confidence and trust that citizens hold for the national government.
3. We had no primary intention at that point in time to micromanage the news from the Persian Gulf war, but we did want to implement directives to keep people from knowing more than was good for them.

CHAPTER 11

AVOIDING BIAS

Words can wound. No moral writer should ever wish to wound anyone by using words that injure others. Our language reflects the sad tendency of some human beings to identify groups as "the other," as people who are different and who are therefore to be scorned, mocked, humiliated, and even despised. Avoid **biased writing**—writing that continues stereotypes or that demeans, ignores, or patronizes people on the basis of gender, race, religion, country of origin, physical abilities or disabilities, sexual preference, or any other human condition. As this chapter makes clear, avoiding bias is a lot more complicated than simply not using derogatory words and slurs.

11a Avoiding Sexism in Writing

Men and women should be treated as individuals, not primarily as members of opposite sexes. Neither sex should be stereotyped or arbitrarily assigned to a leading or secondary role.

Even those who are committed to the principle of equality have to guard against bias in writing. Our language is full of concepts, conventions, labels, and clichés that can slip into writing, perpetuating stereotypes and inequality even when we honestly do not mean to do so. Make sure your written expressions match your principles and intentions.

Avoiding Sexist Labels and Clichés

Many labels and clichés imply that women are not as able or as mature as men. Consider the meaning of words and phrases such as *lady, the weaker sex, the fair sex, the little woman, girl, gal, broad, dame, my better half, working mother, housewife, poetess,* and *coed.*

All these terms imply that women have only one proper role in society. *Ladylike,* for example, is often intended as a compliment but may in fact disparage women. A "ladylike" woman is polite and cooperative. She does not assert herself as successful men are expected to assert themselves, and she is not taken quite so seriously as men are. Behavior that in men is admired as *assertive* is often criticized in women as *abrasive* or *aggressive.*

Here are some clichés and labels to watch out for.

Women as appendages

Traditional titles such as *Mrs.* and *Miss,* identifying women either by their relationship to husbands or as without husbands, are an example of the way in which the conventions of the English language perpetuate inequality. Do not refer to women as *Mrs.* or *Miss* unless you are also referring to men as *Mr.,* and be certain when you use *Mrs.* or *Miss* that it is the woman's preference. If you are uncertain, use *Ms.,* a title introduced in the early 1970s to parallel *Mr.,* which identifies an individual by sex but does not specify marital status. If a woman has another title, such as *Dr., Rev., Prof.,* or *Lt.,* use it in the same contexts in which you would use such titles for a man.

Biased: Albert Einstein and Mrs. Mead
Einstein and Mrs. Mead

Revised: Dr. Einstein and Dr. Mead
or
Albert Einstein and Margaret Mead
Einstein and Mead

Here is another example.

Biased: Jane Austen, Mrs. Gaskell, and George Eliot described life in the provinces; Dickens described life in the city.

Revised: Austen, Gaskell, and Eliot described life in the provinces; Dickens described life in the city.

Another way to revise the sentence would be to use first names for all authors—Jane Austen, Elizabeth Gaskell, George Eliot, and Charles Dickens. This solution prevents any confusion between George Eliot and T. S. Eliot.

Avoid unnecessary reference to or emphasis on a woman's marital status. Refer to a woman by the name she prefers, whether that name is her birth name or her name by marriage. Do not describe women as if they were appendages to men.

Biased: Elizabeth Wallingford, wife of car salesman John T. Wallingford, has been appointed chief justice of the State Supreme Court by Governor Emily Katz.

Revised: Elizabeth Wallingford, dean of the Law School at Sourmash State University, has been appointed chief justice of the State Supreme Court by Governor Emily Katz.

Also avoid identifying women by reference to their children if the children have nothing to do with the subject you are discussing.

Biased: Molly Burdine, mother of six, will represent Sourmash State University at the national meeting of the American Association of University Professors in Washington.

Revised: Molly Burdine, professor of government, will represent Sourmash State University at the national meeting of the American Association of University Professors in Washington.

Women described in terms of appearance

Don't write as if the most important quality a woman has is her appearance.

Biased: Major is a remarkably talented automobile mechanic, and his wife Estelle is pretty enough to have been a Miss America when she was young.

Revised: Major is a remarkably talented automobile mechanic, often employed by his wife, Estelle, who designed some of the cars he works on.

Women described as unusual in the workplace

Don't describe women's jobs as though special attention must be called to the fact that a woman holds such a position. Such language indicates that a writer is surprised a woman has accomplished such things and implies that most women are incapable of such feats. Don't refer to some jobs as if only women can hold them.

Biased: Judge Wallingford has been a poetess as well as a lady lawyer and judge.

Revised: Judge Wallingford is a much-published poet, and she has managed to keep writing poetry while she has worked first as a lawyer and then as a judge.

Biased: Emily Katz decided early in life that she would be a career woman.

Revised: Governor Emily Katz decided early in her life to go into politics.

Biased: I thought the waitress was very pretty, so I left her a big tip.

Revised: The server did a very good job. She refused to give my friend Clarence another drink when she saw he was having too much, and I gave her a large tip as a mark of my gratitude.

Biased: We advertised for a new secretary because we thought we needed another girl in the office.

Revised: We advertised for a new staff assistant because we had too much work for the staff on hand.

Biased: Although Monique was a woman, she refused to be satisfied with being a receptionist in the hospital.

Revised: Monique worked as a receptionist at Mt. Auburn Hospital one summer while she was in college. There she became so interested in the sick and their problems that she went on to medical school and became a psychiatrist and now counsels the terminally ill and their families at the same hospital where she once had a summer job.

Women described as not equal with men

Don't refer to women as inferiors who should be protected from situations that might be acceptable to men. Don't describe them as weak, hysterical, or helpless, nor their concerns as trivial, humorous, or unimportant.

Biased: It was not the sort of story that should have been told with ladies present.

Revised: It was the sort of story that could only have been told by a man who had been deluded since he was six years old by the idea that using vulgar words for natural functions made him seem grown-up.

Biased: After much negotiation Queen Isabella, with a woman's intuition, gave Columbus his chance.

Revised: After much negotiation, Queen Isabella decided to support the venture Columbus proposed.

Don't write as if men were the only people who counted in certain situations or as if women are or were invisible. When you use the word *man,* be sure you are referring to an adult male and no one else. Avoid the use of *man* and *mankind* to stand for all members of the human race.

Biased: Man has spread all over the world from his origins, probably in Africa.

Revised: Human beings have spread all over the world from their origins, probably in Africa.

Biased: We needed people to man the telephones during the fund drive.

Revised: We needed people to answer the telephones during the fund drive.

Biased: Politicians try to guess what the man in the street thinks about the issues.

Revised: Politicians try to guess what typical citizens think about the issues.

Biased: The pioneers moved west, taking with them their women and their children.

Revised: The pioneers moved west, men, women, and children enduring the hardships of the long journey.

Avoiding Bias Against Men

Most of the recommendations and examples given so far in this chapter relate to bias against women. It is equally important to avoid stereotyping men, especially in the context of home and family life. Do not assume that men are dependent on women for advice on what to wear or eat. Nor should men be characterized as inept in household maintenance or child care. Avoid using expressions such as *henpecked husband* and *boys' night out.*

Biased: Ryan was a house husband, taking care of Beth when she wasn't in preschool.

Revised: Ryan took care of Beth when she wasn't in preschool.

11b Recasting to Avoid Sexism

Writing bias-free prose requires careful thinking. Here are some specific techniques to help you recognize and check bias. A careful and accurate choice of words often provides a ready solution.

Parallel Language

Use parallel language for men and women.

Biased: men and ladies
man and wife

Revised: men and women *or* gentlemen and ladies
husband and wife *or* man and woman

Genderless Nouns and Verbs

Many English words assume that the doers are men. Examples are given below. Replace gender-specific words with genderless words whenever you can.

not policeman *but* police officer

not stewardess *but* flight attendant

not cameraman *but* photographer

not businessman *or* businesswoman *but* businessperson, business executive, store owner, manager, proprietor, merchant

not clergyman *but* minister, priest, rabbi *or* member of the clergy

not forefathers *but* ancestors

not spokesman *but* spokesperson

not chairman *but* chair *or* presider

not congressman *or* congresswoman *but* representative *or* member of Congress

not man-made *but* artificial, synthetic, manufactured, constructed, *or* of human origin

If there is not a simple substitute for a gender-specific word, revise the expression in another way.

Biased: There are only six crews available to **man** the trucks.

Revised: There are only six crews available to **operate** the trucks.

Biased: The sob sister's account was less than truthful.

Revised: The account in the newspaper was so sentimental that it wasn't truthful.

Avoiding Masculine Pronouns and Nouns

Whenever possible avoid using the pronouns *he, him, his,* and *himself* as indefinite pronouns. One satisfactory way to avoid masculine pronouns is to use the plural forms.

> **Biased:** Every student who wrote his name on the class list had to pay a copying fee in advance and to pledge himself to attend every session.
>
> **Revised:** Students who wrote their names on the class list had to pay a copying fee in advance and to pledge themselves to attend every session.

Often you can avoid the maculine pronouns by revising the sentence to eliminate the pronouns altogether.

11b bias

> **Another revision:** Every student who signed up for the class had to pay a copying fee in advance and pledge to attend every session.

In many instances you can say *he or she, his or her, her or him.* We seem to accept such constructions readily nowadays.

> If anyone finds a rock in the soup, **he or she** should be careful not to break a tooth.
>
> Anyone who reads Shakespeare eventually finds **his or her** life reflected in some of the characters.
>
> Once the winner of the lottery is known, we will send **him or her** to Ptomaine Ptolemy's Turkey Tavern for a free meal.

Avoid cumbersome constructions such as *his/her* and *s/he.* As yet these constructions are not acceptable English. Also try to avoid cumbersome repetitions.

> **Awkward:** Each student in the psychology class was to pick up a different book according to his or her interests, to read the book overnight and to do without his or her normal sleep, to write a short summary of what he or she had read, and then to see if he or she dreamed about the book the following night.

Such sentences must be entirely rewritten.

Revised: Every student was to choose a book, read it overnight, do without sleep, write a short summary of the book the next morning, and then see if he or she dreamed about the book the following night.

Some writers alternate *he* and *she, him,* and *her,* using one gender in one paragraph and another in the next. This alternating may be effective, especially when combined with plural forms and with sentences requiring no personal pronouns referring back to indefinite pronouns. But switching back and forth can also be distracting.

Many speakers and some writers use a plural pronoun to refer to an impersonal singular antecedent: "The person who left *their* suitcase on the bus can call for it at the office." But writers and editors often consider such usage nonstandard. You can revise the sentence to avoid the pronoun: "The person who left a suitcase on the bus can call for it at the office."

Using the neuter impersonal pronoun *one* can help you avoid the masculine pronouns.

> The American creed holds that if one works hard, one will succeed in life.

But again, probably the best way to handle such a problem is to rewrite the sentence.

> The American creed holds that those who are willing to work hard will succeed in life.

In the past, some writers have used the feminine personal pronoun *she* for references to ships and countries. This usage is no longer recommended. Use the pronoun *it* for such references. Keep in mind that *it* is not genderless; it's gender is neuter.

■ **Exercise 11.1** Rewrite the following sentences to eliminate biased writing.

1. A sports writer must try to be fair to his own favorite teams and to their opponents.
2. When the dishwasher breaks down, we grit our teeth and call the repairman, knowing that he will charge us too much money and that we may have to call him again soon.

3. Any country musician worth his guitar knows that true bluegrass music does not use drums. He would also refuse to use an electric guitar.
4. Working women often have to come home from the office or the shop and fix supper for their families and do the laundry.
5. Deborah Townsend, the chairman of the city council, used her cellular telephone to summon policemen after the councilmen got into a fight over where to have their annual picnic.
6. An old wives' tale holds that if you see a black cat run across a graveyard at night, you can listen very carefully and hear the dead talking with their wives and children.
7. Although she was the mother of three children, Professor Helen Burns of the Sourmash University's History Department wrote three books on Egyptian religion in two years and led a tour of faculty members and their wives to the Nile Valley.
8. The ladies worked in the kitchen to prepare the meal while the men sat around the television set watching football.

■ **Exercise 11.2** All of the following words and expressions display bias. Suggest at least one alternative for each. If a word or phrase should probably be avoided altogether, put a check beside it. If a word or phrase cannot be avoided, explain why.

1. manpower
2. seamstress
3. manslaughter
4. lady doctor
5. tomboy
6. early man
7. widower
8. actress
9. landlord
10. housewife
11. busboy
12. middleman
13. fellow worker
14. career girl
15. cleaning lady
16. ombudsman
17. heroine
18. right-hand man
19. manhole
20. Jewess
21. yes-man
22. divorcee
23. workmanship
24. journeyman
25. suffragette
26. freshman
27. one-upmanship
28. bachelor's degree
29. sissy
30. longshoreman
31. majorette
32. fish wife
33. handyman
34. workman's compensation
35. gal Friday

11c
Avoiding Other Kinds of Bias

Women are not the only people to be humiliated by stereotypes. Ethnic and religious groups, the handicapped, gays and lesbians, and some occupations are often degraded by the way some people talk and write about them. Analyze your prose to avoid biased assumptions and implications.

Avoiding Assumptions About Groups

All stereotyping is unfair. Making generalizations about people ignores individual differences and potentials. Ascribing qualities to people based on their religious, racial, or ethnic backgrounds reveals the writer's limitations while also doing an injustice to the groups described.

Ethnic and religious groups

When writing on topics in history and the social sciences, inexperienced writers need to take special care not to use their own cultures as the standard for comparison. The term *culturally deprived,* for example, implies that one group has culture and another does not. The American Psychological Association recommends this test: substitute your own group for the group you are discussing, and if you are offended by the resulting statement, revise your comments to eliminate bias.

Study the examples of bias below to detect unwarranted assumptions about people and language that can insult and humiliate.

> The Bonfiglio family seems to have become wealthy without help from the Mafia.

The assumption is surprise that a wealthy Italian family is not connected to a criminal organization.

> Blacks may not make a lot of money, but they know how to have fun.

The assumption is that all blacks are poor and somehow care more about having fun than working.

> I offered him the apples for five dollars a bushel, but he tried to jew me down to three dollars.

Using *jew* as a verb implies that Jews are always seeking bargains and that the rest of us are not.

> Some of my best friends are Jews, but you have to watch them in a business deal.

This sentence is a crude way of excusing oneself for prejudice but then affirming the prejudice just the same.

> Greeks and Chinese don't know how to do anything but open restaurants.

This sentence ignores all the contributions of Greek and Chinese people to culture, politics, business, and good order in American history.

> Although the Browns are Catholic, there are only three children in the family.

This sentence implies that Catholics have lots and lots of children because of their religion.

> I was surprised to learn that although she is a Baptist, she has a Ph.D. in nuclear physics from Cal Tech.

This sentence implies that Baptists are usually ignorant.

Other groups

No group should be the victim of careless generalizations or stereotyping. Study the examples below to detect unwarranted assumptions about people on the basis of their abilities, disabilities, occupations, or sexual orientations.

> Although Conrad is confined to a wheelchair, he is a good receptionist.
>
> Football players are not known for their great intelligence; be sure you give him an easy question.
>
> Gays and lesbians in the military services would be dangerous companions in combat. The rest of us would be trying to save our lives, but all they would think about under fire would be sex.

Several terms in the past have been used to refer to individuals with disabilities, and groups representing their interests have at times promoted one or another. *Special education* is now widely used to describe programs for students with physical, mental, or emotional disabilities. Federal regulations implementing the Americans with Disabilities Act (1991) point out that the term *handicapped,* used in earlier federal legislation, is today objected to by individuals with disabilities and organizations representing them. The regulations recommend the term *disability,* recognizing that "the terminology applied to individuals with disabilities is a very significant and sensitive issue. As with racial and ethnic terms, the choice of words to describe a person with a disability is overlaid with stereotypes, patronizing attitudes, and other emotional connotations."

References to Black and Other Americans

Language has been cruel to American blacks. They have been the victim of a great many terrible words. And in some respects they have been the victim of efforts not to discriminate against them. The word *Negro,* capitalized, was the polite word of choice for two centuries. It was derived from the Latin word for *black,* and in the 1960s the Rev. Martin Luther King, Jr., used it regularly, as did the celebrated black writer from Tennessee, Alex Haley, author of *Roots.*

Black leaders such as Malcolm X objected to *Negro* because it seemed to put black Americans into a special and inferior category. The word *Negroid* had a vaguely pejorative sense; "Negroid" features were not considered attractive. The slogan "black is beautiful" challenged the Hollywood notion that the only beautiful people were blond white women. Blacks also resented *Negro* because it allowed many prejudiced people to imagine they were not prejudiced because they used it instead of an ugly word. Many whites could use the word and still refuse to admit black people to the country club or the fraternity or even the public schools. To many, *Negro* became a symbol of hypocrisy.

In the 1970s, *black* became the word of choice, a neutral description parallel to *white.* Almost overnight the word *Negro* dropped out of use. Careful writers never use it now unless they are quoting from speeches and documents from the past.

A few years ago the black leader Jesse Jackson suggested yet another change. Instead of *black,* he advocated the term *African-American.* Despite polls that show that about 70 percent of black Americans don't like the term and prefer to be called *blacks,* it is used more and more frequently. If the term is generally adopted, it runs counter to the general trend of language to shorten and simplify frequently used terms.

No one can ever predict how language will be used in the future. For now, hardly anyone considers *black* a prejudiced word. Attentive writers will consider carefully the changing connotations of words and will always strive to use words that are both common and untainted with bias. Obviously pejorative names used for any ethnic group are to be avoided at all costs.

In recent years the terms *people of color* or *colored people* seem to be coming back into general use. These terms were considered derogatory in the early years of the civil rights movement, though the leaders of the National Association for the Advancement of Colored People, founded in 1910, never felt compelled to change the organization's name. Of course the term *people of color* also includes Asians and American Indians.

The term *Native Americans* has been increasingly used for the peoples who occupied the American continents at the time of Columbus. Because Columbus and others assumed he had sailed to India, he called these people *Indians,* and all European languages quickly adopted the name. But it was clearly off the mark, and in recent years many people have objected to it.

Still, American Indians resolutely call themselves *Indians* and *American Indians.* The American Indian Movement has been one of the most active civil rights groups among the various tribes without feeling any compulsion to change its name. Currently it seems that both terms—*Native American* and *American Indian*—are acceptable. Unacceptable are terms that assume American Indians are more savage and bloodthirsty than the general run of human beings or that label them by a supposed skin color. "Redskin" is the most common of these terms, and attentive writers will not use it. "Wild Indian" is another such term. Terms like "Indian giver" for those who give a gift and then demand it back are equally unfair and should be avoided.

Writers and others should not assume that all Indian tribes were alike, that they all wore Sioux war bonnets, or that they all hunted buffalo or that they said "How" when they greeted each other. If anything, Indians in the Americas were far more diverse than Western Europeans have been for centuries, and the various tribes maintain many differences. Nor should Indian cultures be depicted as frozen in time, forever like those whites described at the time of contact. Like all human cultures, Indian cultures develop and adapt.

The term *Hispanic* has been used to designate anyone from Latin America, but it is coming under increasing attack by many who find it overgeneral. A Mexican is not identical to someone from Argentina; a Panamanian has a different culture from that of a Cuban or a Bolivian. It would seem wise to identify such people by their country of origin instead of by some assumed general identity in the word *Hispanic.* (The same cautions apply to words such as *Latino, Anglo,* and *Chicano,* all of which may carry pejorative meanings.) For many of the same reasons, persons from Asia often object to the label *Oriental,* a word that also embodies a European perspective on the world. Again, it would seem wise and fair to identify a person by country of origin instead of by some assumed general identity.

The best rule is always good faith and sympathy. Imagine how it would feel to be insulted for some quality over which you have no control. Imagine how it would feel to be assumed ignorant or incapable because of some physical attribute you possess, when you know yourself to be educated and able.

■ **Exercise 11.3** Look up the etymology of the following words in a dictionary. If you don't know what *etymology* means or how to use a dictionary, consult Chapter 12. When you have learned the word origins, decide whether or how you will use these words. Discuss them with your classmates.

1. paddy wagon
2. gyp
3. Indian giver
4. Near East
5. German measles
6. Mohammedan
7. dumb
8. nonwhite
9. Scotch
10. mulatto
11. Mongoloid
12. Eskimo
13. jerry-built
14. flesh (color)
15. maiden name
16. gringo
17. sinister
18. Caucasian
19. hunk
20. Dutch treat

✔ CHECKLIST 11.1: AVOIDING BIAS

Habits of thinking and conventions of speech sometimes work against your honest and unbiased intentions. As you revise, look carefully at your prose to make sure it is saying what you want it to say. Ask yourself these questions.

- Are titles, clichés, or labels presenting a limited view of women?
- Are women referred to as appendages of men—as daughters or wives or mothers, instead of as individuals in their own right?
- Are women described in terms of their appearance when appearance isn't relevant?
- Are women's accomplishments, particularly in the workplace, treated as curious or exceptional?
- Are assumptions made about the roles and abilities of either sex?
- Are gender-specific words used when they refer to individuals of both sexes?
- Do pronouns assume that individuals are of a particular sex when, in truth, they are not?

- Are assumptions or implications made about ethnic or religious groups?
- Are certain qualities ascribed to individuals or groups on the basis of background or physical features?
- Are the terms selected for reference to any group pejorative or not the term that most members of the group prefer?
- Are any word choices or underlying assumptions potentially hurtful?

If the answer to any of these questions is "yes," rethink your intentions and revise your prose.

CHAPTER

12

USING A DICTIONARY AND THESAURUS

A good dictionary is an essential tool for every writer. You should consult your dictionary every time you have the slightest doubt about the spelling, meaning, proper use, pronunciation, or syllabication of a word.

12a Choosing Useful Dictionaries

The most useful dictionaries for college writers are desk dictionaries—books of a convenient size to keep on the desk, handy to consult as the need arises. Words and usages that do not appear in the standard desk dictionaries may be found in an unabridged dictionary or in an appropriate specialized dictionary. Any good library has many excellent dictionaries in its reference room.

Selecting Desk Dictionaries

A standard desk dictionary contains 140,000 to 180,000 entries. It may include drawings as well. Illustrations are useful because they can show something that otherwise cannot be defined easily in words.

Many dictionaries are called ''Webster's.'' The name means only that they follow the general methodology of Noah Webster's two-volume *American Dictionary of the English Language,* published in 1828.

The following desk dictionaries are all useful to college students:

- *Random House Webster's College Dictionary*. McGraw-Hill Edition. New York: Random House, 1991. With 180,000 entries, this is one of the largest desk dictionaries. When it was published, it created a great deal of controversy because it includes many new coinages related to feminist and multicultural issues. It also offers "usage notes" that give advice on the connotations of words. Here, for example, is a note on the word *lady:*

> Uses that are commonly disliked include LADY in compounds or phrases referring to occupation or position (*cleaning lady; forelady; saleslady*) and as a modifier (*lady artist; lady doctor*). Increasingly, sex-neutral terms replace LADY (*cleaner; supervisor; salesperson* or *salesclerk*). When it is relevant to specify the sex of the performer or practitioner, *woman* rather than LADY is used, the parallel term being *man: Men doctors outnumber women doctors on the hospital staff by three to one.*

This dictionary lists definitions in order of common usage, beginning with the most commonly used meaning of the word and proceeding through less common meanings.

- *Webster's New World Dictionary.* Third College Edition. Cleveland, Ohio: New-World Dictionaries, 1988. The prefatory materials in this dictionary do not tell us how many entries it includes, but it is large and readable. Like the *Random House Webster's College Dictionary,* the biographical and geographical entries are in the main body of the work and not confined appendixes at the rear. The editors of the dictionary especially pride themselves in their listings of Americanisms—those many words that have one meaning or connotation in American English and another or none in the British isles.
- *Webster's Ninth New Collegiate Dictionary.* Springfield, Mass.: Merriam-Webster, 1983. This dictionary is based on *Webster's Third New International Dictionary,* generally regarded as the standard one-volume unabridged dictionary in English. Biographical and geographical entries appear in appendixes. The dictionary has about 160,000 entries, many from the sciences. It lists the meanings of words in the order in which they came into use. Exemplary sentences from works of well-known writers illustrate usage, and an occasional usage note offers guidance in the different connotations of synonyms.

Consulting Unabridged Dictionaries

In theory, an unabridged dictionary should include every word in the language. In practice, such inclusiveness is impossible. Yet a couple of unabridged dictionaries come close to the ideal, and college writers should learn about them and continue to use them long after college.

- *Webster's Third New International Dictionary of the English Language.* Springfield, Mass.: G. & C. Merriam, 1961 and later enlarged editions. This enormous unabridged dictionary occupies a prominent place in the reference room of any respectable library. When it first appeared, purists greeted it with howls of outrage, and a few people burned it in protest. Because it is descriptive rather than prescriptive, many people thought that it symbolized the decay of the English language. It takes a relaxed attitude about usage; if a large number of people define a word in a certain way, the dictionary includes the definition in its list of definitions. The dictionary includes *ain't* and other words not regarded as standard English, and in the editions after 1967, profane and obscene words are also included. Although the *Third* is now generally recognized by publishers as the authoritative dictionary for American English, many also concede that it can lead inexperienced writers astray because it does not warn them that certain usages are unacceptably casual, confusing, or avoided by careful writers.

- *The American Heritage Dictionary of the English Language.* Third Edition. Boston: Houghton Mifflin, 1992. The long-awaited third edition of the *American Heritage Dictionary* is much larger than the second edition and in size now occupies a place somewhat between the standard desk dictionary and the so-called unabridged dictionaries that usually have a special stand in the reference rooms of libraries. It is renowned for its panel of writers and editors who, during the preparation of each edition, vote on the usage of controversial words. Their votes are included in usage notes, but the dictionary's editors are not reluctant to dispute their own panel, as they do in the usage note to *hopefully* used as an adverb meaning "It is hoped." A great majority of the usage panel voted against this usage, but, say the editors, "It is not easy to explain why critics dislike this use of *hopefully.*" This dictionary is great fun and carries enormous prestige. But it is heavy enough to need a handle if you carry it from room to room.

- *The Oxford English Dictionary.* Second Edition. Prepared by J. A. Simson and E. S. C. Weiner. 20 volumes. Oxford: Clarendon Press, 1989. This is the premier dictionary of the English language, the indispensable tool for any serious scholar of English literature. The project conceived in Britain in 1857 and was published in parts (the first covered *A* to *ant*) between 1884 and 1921. It was ultimately ten volumes. Supplements immediately followed, and the second edition is twenty volumes. The *OED,* as it is known, lists every word the editors have been able to find in English manuscripts and books, provides variant spellings (American spellings are variants), and identifies the most common spellings in each century. It provides definitions of words and illustrates all the definitions by brief quotations. It is now available on compact disk (CD-ROM), allowing for computer searches that speed up the use of the dictionary considerably. A new and much expanded edition is promised shortly. It, too, will appear on compact disk. A two-volume edition of the older *OED* is in print—with type so small that most people must use a magnifying glass to read it.

Using Specialized Dictionaries

Many highly specialized dictionaries may be found in the reference room of any good library—biographical and geographical dictionaries; foreign language dictionaries; medical dictionaries of legal terms; dictionaries of philosophy, sociology, engineering, and other disciplines; dictionaries of slang, word origins, famous quotations, first lines of poems. These dictionaries may help you write an essay or simply enlarge your background knowledge necessary to comprehend and explain various subjects. Browse through them when you are deciding on a topic for an essay. Your reference librarian can help you locate the dictionaries that may be helpful to you in the general field of interest you choose to write upon.

12b
Reading Entries in a Standard Desk Dictionary

All dictionaries contain guides to their use. In these guides, usually located in the front of the dictionary, you will find the meanings of the abbreviations used in the entries, and you will also find a list of the special cautions dictionaries use for words that the editors consider *slang, vulgar, informal, nonstandard,* or something else worthy of notation. When you use a dictionary for the first time, study these instructions carefully. They usually contain sample entries that will help you get the most from the time you spend consulting the dictionary.

An entry in the *Random House Webster's College Dictionary* is shown on the facing page.

Spelling, Syllabication, and Pronunciation

Entries in a dictionary are listed in alphabetical order according to standard spelling. In the *Random House Webster's College Dictionary,* the verb *compare* is entered as **com·pare.** The dot divides the word into two syllables. If you divide the word *compare* at the end of a line, the hyphen goes where you find the dot in this example. Phonetic symbols in parentheses show the correct pronunciation; explanations of these symbols appear on the bottom right column of each right-hand page in the dictionary. The second syllable of *compare* receives the greater stress when you pronounce the

Word division | Pronunciation | Part of speech | Past tense and past participle

com•pare (kəm pâr′), *v.*, **-pared, -par•ing,** *n.* —*v.t.* **1.** to examine (two or more objects, ideas, people, etc.) in order to note similarities and differences: *to compare two restaurants.* **2.** to consider or describe as similar; liken: *"Shall I compare thee to a summer's day?"* **3.** to form or display the degrees of comparison of (an adjective or adverb). —*v.i.* **4.** to be worthy of comparison: *Whose plays can compare with Shakespeare's?* **5.** to be in similar standing; be alike: *This recital compares with the one he gave last year.* **6.** to appear in quality, progress, etc., as specified: *Their development compares poorly with that of neighbor nations.* **7.** to make comparisons. —*n.* **8.** comparison: *a beauty beyond compare.* —***Idiom.*** **9. compare notes,** to exchange views, ideas, or impressions. [1375–1425; late ME < OF *comperer* < L *comparāre* to place together, match, v. der. of *compar* alike, matching (see COM-, PAR)] —**com•par′er,** *n.* —**Usage.** The traditional rule states that COMPARE should be followed by *to* when it points out likenesses between unlike persons or things: *She compared his handwriting to knotted string.* It should be followed by *with,* the rule says, when it examines two entities of the same general class for similarities or differences: *She compared his handwriting with mine.* This rule is by no means always followed, even in formal speech and writing. Common practice is to use *to* for likeness between members of different classes: *to compare a language to a living organism.* Between members of the same category, both *to* and *with* are used: *Compare the Chicago of today with* (or *to*) *the Chicago of the 1890s.* After the past participle COMPARED, either *to* or *with* is used regardless of the type of comparison.

Definitions | Idiom | Etymology | Usage

12b dict

word correctly. You say "comPARE." In this dictionary, the syllable that receives the primary stress is given an accent mark at the end (′). Down the column from *compare,* you find the word *compartmentalization.* It is pronounced with the heaviest stress on the syllable *za,* but it has a secondary stress on the syllable *men.* The syllable with the heavier stress has the darkest accent mark (′); the syllable with the secondary stress has a lighter accent mark (′).

Plurals of nouns are usually not given special notice if they are formed by the addition of *-s.* Irregular plurals such as *children* for *child* are noted.

Parts of Speech and Various Forms

The abbreviation *v.* immediately after the pronunciation tells you that *compare* is most frequently used as a verb. The *-pared* shows the simple past and the past participle forms. If the past participle differed from the simple past, both forms would be included. (Look at the verb *drink* in your dictionary; you will see the forms *drank* and *drunk.*) The *-paring* gives you the present participle form and shows that you drop the final *e* in *compare* before you add the *-ing.*

The *-n.* indicates that on occasion *compare* can be used as a noun.

The next abbreviation—*v.t.*—stands for *verb transitive,* indicating that the definitions that follow show the verb used in a transitive sense, that is, with a direct object. A little farther down in the entry *v.i.* (verb intransitive) introduces definitions showing the verb used in an intransitive sense, without a direct object. Still later, after the abbreviation *n.* is a definition and an example of *compare* used as a noun, as in the phrase *beyond compare.*

In this entry the word *Idiom* signals a special meaning not necessarily included in the simple definition (see p. 162). To *compare notes* is an idiom meaning *to exchange views, ideas, or impressions. Comparing notes* does not necessarily mean that two people sit down with notes they have made on a subject and compare them. In English, you *compare notes* even when there are no notes, just ideas in your mind that you want to talk about with someone who has similar ideas.

Definitions

As we have seen, the several meanings of the word are arranged according to the parts of speech that the word plays in various contexts. For *compare,* the definitions begin with its meanings as a transitive verb. If appropriate the editors note in italics whether word or a defintion of a word is *non-standard, informal, slang, vulgar, rare, poetic, archaic, regional,* or *foreign.*

12b dict

Word Origins

At the end of most entries in this dictionary is an **etymology**—a brief history of the word—set off in brackets. There we see the date of the first known use of the word in English together with the earlier words from which it is derived. We see that *compare* came into English between 1375 and 1425 and that it comes from late Middle English, derived from the Old French word *comperer,* which came from the Latin verb *comparāre,* which meant "to place together" or "to match." This word in turn came from the Latin *compar,* meaning simply "alike" or "matching." Just a few lines can reveal a great deal about the history of a word and its related meanings—information that can sometimes be a very great help to a writer seeking a precise meaning for his or her thoughts.

Usage

Finally, a usage note follows some main entries in the *Random House Webster's College Dictionary.* For *compare,* the traditional rule for using *to* or *with* is given, together with examples and some comments on common practice.

Finding Other Information

Other entries and other dictionaries give additional information, including abbreviations, synonyms, and antonyms. Sometimes cross-references send you to words with similar denotations but different connotations. Some dictionaries list alternate spellings, always giving preferred spellings first or placing the full entry under the preferred spelling only.

■ **Exercise 12.1** Which of the following words can be used as verbs? What cautions does your desk dictionary offer about using them? Indicate with a *T* or an *I* whether a verb is transitive or intransitive. Put *TI* before verbs that can be both.

1. total
2. outside
3. fritter
4. issue
5. freak
6. victory
7. hipster
8. interface
9. grunt
10. postulate
11. access
12. occasion
13. impact
14. envelop
15. effect
16. hype
17. keyboard
18. input
19. workout
20. estimate

■ **Exercise 12.2** Write out your own short definition for each of the following words, noting the part or parts of speech that you think each word may serve. Then check your definitions with those in a standard desk dictionary. If you don't know a word, try to guess what it means before you look it up.

1. effete
2. jejune
3. jangle
4. parameter
5. pestilent
6. nomenclature
7. manufacture
8. relationship
9. mucus
10. mule

■ **Exercise 12.3** Look up the etymologies of the following words in your desk dictionary. Do the origins of a word help you understand its modern meaning?

1. gynecologist
2. gymnasium
3. geology
4. infringe
5. muck
6. eugenics
7. democracy
8. gender
9. conceit
10. otter

■ **Exercise 12.4** If you haven't done Exercise 11.3, do it now. It is a lesson in using a dictionary as well as in avoiding bias.

■ **Exercise 12.5** Dictionaries differ. Look up the following words in at least two different dictionaries to find variations in spellings and preferred spellings. Compare your answers with your classmates. How do you account for the differences?

1. underway
2. mustache
3. idiosyncrasy
4. indispensable
5. adviser
6. combating
7. theater
8. insure
9. defence
10. glamour
11. traveler
12. catalog
13. archaeology
14. tranquillity
15. sizeable
16. threshold
17. idyll
18. esthetic
19. specter
20. acknowledgment
21. life style
22. decision maker
23. policymaker
24. socio-economic
25. childrearing

The size of a standard desk dictionary limits the information that each entry can include. But either alphabetized with other words or in appendixes you can find the correct spellings of important place names, the official names of countries with their areas and populations, and the names of capital cities. Biographical entries give the birth and death years and enough information about the person to explain his or her importance to society.

Many dictionaries also include lists of abbreviations and symbols, names and locations of colleges and universities, titles and correct forms of address, conversion tables for weights and measures, and even guides to punctuation, capitalization, and the use of italics.

✓ CHECKLIST 12.1: USING A DICTIONARY

- Use the *guide words.* At the top of each dictionary page, *guide words* (usually in boldface) tell you the first word and the last word on the page. Since all entries are in alphabetical order, you can locate the word you are seeking rapidly by looking for guide words that would include your word somewhere between the two of them.
- Use the *pronunciation key.* The letters and symbols used to indicate pronunciation are explained in a separate section at the front or the back of a dictionary and often summarized at the bottom of each

right-hand page of entries. Always pronounce new words carefully aloud to help you remember them and to integrate them in your spoken vocabulary.

- In checking definitions, pay attention to the *part of speech.* The same word serving as different parts of speech can have different meanings. Thus you can turn on a *light* (noun), but a butterfly that *lights* (verb) on a leaf. You will find both meanings (among many others) in a dictionary, and you will have to choose the meaning appropriate for your use. Parts of speech are often abbreviated (*n.,* noun; *v.,* verb; *adj.,* adjective; *adv.,* adverb). The abbreviations the dictionary uses are usually identified in prefatory material.
- Always test the meaning you find. To check whether you have selected the correct meaning, substitute the meaning for the word in the sentence you are writing or reading.
- Try alternate spellings if you cannot find the spelling for the word you are looking up. Don't give up if you can't find a word on a first try. Use alternate phonetic spellings. For example, if you tried to look up a word you thought was spelled *troff,* you wouldn't find it. You should try *trouf, truff,* and *trough.* (*Trough* is correct.) Many spell checkers on word-processing programs for computers will do this searching for you. But *be sure* to check the meaning of the word in a good dictionary. Spell checkers can't tell you if you've used *their* or *there* correctly, only that such a word does exist in English. And they can't always help you find the word you're looking for any more than a dictionary can. The spelling *troff* makes a computer fix on the *tro,* and from this spelling you might get the alternatives *troll, trout, troop,* or *trots*—none the word you are seeking.

12c Using a Thesaurus

A **thesaurus** (the word means "treasury" or "collection" in Latin) is a dictionary of synonyms, sometimes without definitions. Several kinds of thesauruses are available. Many are called "Roget's" after Peter Mark Roget (pronounced Ro·zháy) who in 1852 published the first *Thesaurus of English Words and Phrases.* The guide went through twenty-eight editions before he died in 1869, demonstrating the attraction a handy reference to synonyms may be to writers and speakers and others interested in language. The synonyms are not limited to words but include phrases and expressions.

- *Roget's II: The New Thesaurus.* Boston: Houghton Mifflin, 1988. In this dictionary of synonyms, each synonym is given a short definition. The word *distinction,* for example, is given four definitions. One is "Readily seen, perceived, or understood." The thesaurus gives as a synonym for this meaning the word *apparent.* On looking up *apparent,* you find the definition, "Readily seen, perceived, or understood," and next to it the synonyms "clear, clear-cut, crystal-clear, distinct, evident, manifest, noticeable, obvious, patent, plain visible." This is an excellent thesaurus to use when you feel a little unsure of the precise meanings of some synonyms.
- *Roget's International Thesaurus.* Fifth Edition. Edited by Robert L. Chapman. New York: HarperCollins, 1992. This thesaurus holds to Roget's original method, classifying words into various categories that he thought embraced nearly all human concepts. To each general category he assigned a number, and by means of these numbers he made cross-references so that you can readily pass from one category to another in the search of a synonym that will produce just the right meaning. In the fifth edition, words set in boldface are listed in alphabetical order in the index. The user still has to first look up a word in the index in the back of the book, then turn to the number in the front of the book.

  This is by far the most popular thesaurus, but it does not define the words it lists. It is therefore most useful for the experienced writer who already knows the definitions of words and merely wants to be reminded of synonyms that may add color, variety, or precision to a piece of prose.

Most writers find a thesaurus a great pleasure to use. But be cautious. Be sure you understand the full meaning of the words you use. Be sure they are not inappropriate for your purposes. And don't use fancy words when simple words will do.

✓ CHECKLIST 12.2: USING A THESAURUS

- Know how the words are arranged. In many thesauruses, the words are arranged in simple alphabetical order. In *Roget's International Thesaurus,* the words are listed in numbered categories. You need to use the index to find the word whose synonyms you seek. In other kinds of thesauruses, the words are listed alphabetically, and you use the thesaurus much as you would a dictionary.
- Never use an unfamiliar synonym that you pick up from a thesaurus without looking it up in the dictionary first. Otherwise you may write something ridiculous, impolite, or incomprehensible.

- Test the replacement word carefully in your sentence. Watch particularly for appropriate connotations as well as denotations.
- Reject high-sounding or multisyllabic words simply for the impression you think they might create. Use a thesaurus to find a more precise word, not a fancier one. Inexperienced writers can be seduced by "fine" or unusual language inconsistent with their writing style and often misleading or ridiculous.

■ **Exercise 12.6** Find five synonyms for the word *excitement* in a thesaurus. Write a sentence for each of the synonyms, using the words correctly. Use a desk dictionary if you need to check on the connotations of a word.

PART FOUR
UNDERSTANDING GRAMMAR AND WRITING CORRECT SENTENCES

PART FIVE
UNDERSTANDING PUNCTUATION

PART SIX
UNDERSTANDING MECHANICS

BOOK TWO

USAGE RULES AND OPTIONS

PART FOUR

UNDERSTANDING GRAMMAR AND WRITING CORRECT SENTENCES

CHAPTER

CHAPTER

13

CORRECTING RUN-ONS AND COMMA SPLICES

Appropriate punctuation and conjunctions can correct two common sentence errors: run-ons and comma splices. A **run-on error** occurs when two independent clauses run together. A **comma splice** occurs when two independent clauses are linked by a comma. You can see both errors in the example below. *A* is a comma splice; *B* is a run-on.

> Fuel emissions at Yosemite National Park can disrupt the delicate ecological balance, [*A*] authorities have acted firmly against pollution [*B*] they have banned the automobile in Yosemite Valley.

Independent clauses may be joined or separated correctly in several ways: by using end marks, by using a comma and a coordinating conjunction, by using a semicolon, and by using subordination.

13a Using End Marks

A period at the end of an independent clause, followed by a capital letter at the beginning of the next word, will give you two correct sentences.

> Fuel emissions at Yosemite National Park can disrupt the delicate ecological balance. Authorities have acted firmly against pollution. They have banned the automobile in Yosemite Valley.

Sometimes you can use a question mark or an exclamation point to separate the clauses.

Run-on: Are liberal arts graduates desirable employees in business many corporations report their strong interest in women and men with humanities backgrounds.

Corrected: Are liberal arts graduates desirable employees in business? Many corporations report their strong interest in women and men with humanities backgrounds.

Comma splice: I made it, I passed the bar exam, I can be a lawyer!

Corrected: I made it! I passed the bar exam! I can be a lawyer!

■ **Exercise 13.1** The items below contain one or more run-on errors or comma splices. Correct them by creating complete sentences separated by appropriate end punctuation and, where necessary, appropriate capitalization.

1. The economy withered in 1991 corporate bankruptcies rose 40 percent over 1990.
2. Despite the rise in fares, short ocean voyages continue to draw vacationers for all over America now "cruises to nowhere" have grown in popularity.
3. Regular cleaning of the Lincoln Memorial in Washington has eroded the marble, the National Park Service will have to repair it.
4. How can noise ordinances protect city dwellers against loud portable radios cradled like babies in the arms of strolling adolescents the police seem reluctant to arrest young offenders, since a loud radio is not a violent crime.
5. When my mother first got a job, I had to make some sudden adjustments, I had to deal with an unexpected feeling of abandonment the first time I came home from grade school to an empty house and realized that Mom was not there to greet me and that everything seemed still and dead.

13b
Using a Comma and a Coordinating Conjunction

A comma alone is not strong enough to mark off one independent clause from another (see p. 113). A coordinating conjunction is also required. **Coordinating conjunctions** join equal elements. The most common coordinators are *and, but, or, for, nor, yet,* and *so.*

Notice how a coordinator is used correctly in the following example.

Fuel emissions at Yosemite National Park can disrupt the delicate ecological balance, **so** authorities have acted firmly against pollution.

The comma and the conjunction *so* coordinate the independent clause in a compound sentence.

Comma splice: Cortez first introduced chocolate to Europe, the Spaniards later added sugar for sweetening.

Corrected: Cortez first introduced chocolate to Europe, and the Spaniards later added sugar for sweetening.

13c Using a Semicolon

13c run-on

When the ideas in two independent clauses are closely related, a semicolon stresses the relation. The first word after a semicolon begins with a lowercase letter unless the word is a proper noun. When a conjunctive adverb such as *also, however,* or *therefore* or a transitional expression such as *for example* or *on the contrary* (see 13e) appears between two independent clauses, you can separate them with a semicolon. Remember, however, that the period is a more usual mark of separation than a semicolon. When you use a period, you of course have two sentences; if you use the semicolon, you have one sentence.

Federal authorities in Yosemite National Park have acted firmly against pollution; they have banned the automobile in Yosemite Valley.

By connecting the independent clauses, the semicolon stresses the point that the second clause is a consequence of the first.

Comma splice: A good researcher may not know all the facts however, she should know where to find them.

Corrected: A good researcher may not know all the facts; however, she should know where to find them.

Occasionally a writer will use both a semicolon and a conjunction to mark off independent clauses (see 23a).

> Nothing could be more racy, straightforward, and alive than the prose of Shakespeare; but it must be remembered that this was dialogue written to be spoken.
>
> —W. SOMERSET MAUGHAM

When independent clauses are short and closely related in structure and meaning, some writers occasionally join them with a comma to achieve a special effect.

> You fly in with the goods, you fly out with the lucky.
>
> —JOHN LE CARRÉ

■ **Exercise 13.2** Correct run-on errors and comma splices in the following sentences. Use either a coordinating conjunction and a comma or a semicolon, but be sure that your corrections yield logical sentences. Mark sentences that require no correction with a check.

1. The snow started falling at five o'clock then the wind began to blow hard from the north.
2. The best way to keep warm in icy weather is to wear layers of clothing moreover wool is much warmer than cotton.
3. In their own countries Soviet scientists are no longer needed for nuclear arms development, however, other countries actively seek their skills.
4. Fewer jobs are open for teachers every year, yet many college students major in education to obtain teaching certificates.
5. The heavy black clouds meant rain, they came on swiftly with thunder and lightning.

13d Using Subordination

Finally, subordination correctly joins independent clauses into a single sentence. **Subordination** establishes the dependence of one idea upon another through use of a subordinator such as *when* or *because* and a comma at the end of the clause.

Comma splice: Fuel emissions at Yosemite National Park can disrupt the delicate ecological balance of the region, authorities there have acted firmly against automobiles.

Corrected: Because fuel emissions at Yosemite National Park can disrupt the delicate ecological balance of the region, authorities there have acted firmly against automobiles.

Run-on: Authorities have acted firmly against pollution—they have banned the automobile in Yosemite Valley.

Corrected: Authorities who have banned the automobile in Yosemite Valley have acted firmly against pollution.

Also corrected: Acting firmly against pollution, authorities have banned the automobile in Yosemite Valley.

■ **Exercise 13.3** Use subordination to correct run-on errors and comma splices in the sentences below. Mark correct sentences with a check.

1. Learning to read lips is not easy young children can adapt to this preferred method of teaching language to the deaf more easily than older people can.
2. *Europa Europa,* a brilliant film, was not nominated by Germany for an Academy Award, some people believe that it embarrassed Germans about the treatment of Jews during World War II.
3. Play, which allows a child's free expression, has an important role in early childhood education. However, children must keep some real control over the situation if play is to encourage real learning.
4. The Mediterranean fruit fly larva can leap distances of five inches, it has no legs.
5. The Super Bowl in January has now become an unofficial national holiday, people who hardly follow professional football during the regular season gather at parties before huge color television sets, eating and drinking and enjoying good fellowship and sometimes watching the game.

■ **Exercise 13.4** Correct the run-on errors and comma splices in Exercise 13.1, this time by joining complete thoughts either through coordination or subordination (13b and 13d).

13e
Recognizing Sources of Run-ons and Comma Splices

Certain conjunctive adverbs (p. 106), transitional expressions (p. 57), and subject pronouns (p. 100) at the beginning of a sentence can mislead you into producing these errors. Quoting the work of other writers in your text also requires special attention.

Recognizing Conjunctive Adverbs

Conjunctive adverbs connect ideas between clauses. Examples include *accordingly, also, anyway, as a result, besides, consequently, finally, furthermore, hence, however, incidentally, indeed, instead, likewise, meanwhile, moreover, nevertheless, nonetheless, now, otherwise, still, suddenly, then, therefore,* and *thus.* If you use one of the conjunctive adverbs between clauses, you must use a semicolon or a period. Remember that a comma belongs right after a conjunctive adverb.

> **Comma splice:** The price of gold varies greatly every year, nevertheless, speculators purchase precious metals in large quantities and hope always for a price rise.
>
> **Corrected:** The price of gold varies greatly every year; nevertheless, speculators purchase precious metals in large quantities and hope always for a price rise.
>
> **Run-on sentence:** Salt air corrodes metal easily—therefore, automobiles in coastal regions require frequent washing even in cold weather.
>
> **Corrected:** Salt air corrodes metal easily. Therefore, automobiles in coastal regions require frequent washing even in cold weather.

Recognizing Transitional Expressions

Transitional expressions such as *after all, after a while, as a result, at any rate, at the same time, for example, for instance, in addition, in fact, in other words, in particular, in the first place, on the contrary,* and *on the other hand* also require the use of a semicolon or period. Again, commas belong right after these words.

> **Comma splice:** Richard Rodgers's music continues to delight audiences everywhere, in fact, revivals of *Oklahoma!, Carousel,* and *The King and I* pack theaters every year.

Corrected: Richard Rodgers's music continues to delight audiences everywhere. In fact, revivals of *Oklahoma!, Carousel,* and *The King and I* pack theaters every year.

Run-on sentence: Americans continue their love affair with the automobile at the same time they are more successful than ever before in restricting its use.

Corrected: Americans continue their love affair with the automobile; at the same time, they are more successful than ever before in restricting its use.

Recognizing Subject Pronouns

The subject pronouns that may lead to comma splices and run-on sentences are *I, you, he, she, it, we, they,* and *who.*

Comma splice: Disneyland is fun for everyone, I think I enjoyed it as much as my ten-year-old niece did.

Corrected: Disneyland is fun for everyone; I think I enjoyed it as much as my ten-year-old niece did.

Run-on sentence: The weather disappointed Vermont vacationers—they wanted snow in January, not warm, sunny skies.

Corrected: The weather disappointed Vermont vacationers because they wanted snow in January, not warm, sunny skies.

Divided Quotations

In divided quotations or in consecutive sentences within a quotation, be sure to punctuate complete sentences correctly.

In a dialogue, commas are not sufficient to set off independent clauses.

Comma splice: "Speak up, amigo," Juanita said, "I can't hear you."

Corrected: "Speak up, amigo," Juanita said. "I can't hear you."

✓ CHECKLIST 13.1: CORRECTING RUN-ON ERRORS AND COMMA SPLICES

- Use a period, a question mark, or an exclamation point.
- Use *and, but, or, nor, for, yet,* or *so,* preceded by a comma.

- Use a semicolon to coordinate closely related ideas in consecutive independent clauses.
- Use subordination to relate some ideas that might otherwise be expressed in independent clauses.

Exercise 13.5 Use the words in brackets correctly in the sentences that follow. Correct the punctuation and capitalization where necessary.

1. [they] Federal investigators cleared the Senator _______ found no evidence that he had bribed a Treasury agent.
2. [however] The new regulations restricting study abroad have many loopholes _______, the Chinese government is not enforcing the rules too precisely.
3. [however] He said _______ that the car would never run again.
4. [it] The dulcimer has a soft, sweet tone _______ was long ago replaced by the guitar in bluegrass music.
5. [I] "Not I," she replied with a scowl "_______ never liked him."

✓ CHECKLIST 13.2: REVISING TO CORRECT SENTENCE ERRORS

13e run-on

Examine drafts of your papers carefully for run-on errors and comma splices. If you have trouble with these errors, spend extra time trying to locate and correct them. Try these techniques.

- Read your papers aloud slowly. When you read aloud slowly, your ear probably will pick out the independent clauses. They will sound like complete sentences, and you are likely to pause for breath at the end of each one. When your voice clearly stops and drops, look for a period or a semicolon at that point.
- Before you write your final draft, count your sentences. Number your sentences all the way through the draft of your paper. Then see if you have separated them with the right punctuation and capitalization. If the number of sentences seems small in relation to the length of the draft, you may have committed some run-on errors.
- Read your papers backward from the last sentence to the first. When you use this technique, you can consider each sentence as a separate unit of meaning apart from the surrounding sentences. Each sentence appears as a complete statement on its own, and implied connections, such as those made through transitional expressions, adverbs, and pronouns, cannot trap you into making errors. You

must read very carefully, being sure that each group of words you read aloud forms a complete sentence or a complete independent clause.

- Watch for the words and phrases that often cause run-on errors or comma splices at sentence junctures (see 13e). Subject pronouns, transitional expressions, and conjunctive adverbs frequently appear at sentence junctures. Words and phrases in these groups can trap you into writing run-on errors and comma splices. If you look for those words and phrases when you read over your drafts, you can often locate and correct your mistakes.

■ **Exercise 13.6** In each item below, underline the sentence element that gave rise to the run-on error or the comma splice. Correct the errors by using any of the methods explained in this chapter.

1. Mounting financial problems have forced many colleges to take dramatic steps, for example one college sold its two hundred acre campus and moved to smaller quarters.
2. A hush fell over the crowd then a small man with an empty sleeve on his coat and a hideously scarred face got out of his seat and hobbled to the platform.
3. Public transportation is quick and safe on the other hand it does not offer the flexibility and privacy of travel by car.
4. Sidesaddles allowed women to ride horseback modestly in an age of long, thick skirts, however, such saddles were extremely dangerous because they did not allow women to grip the horse with their legs.
5. A two-cycle gasoline engine is excellent for lawn mowers and for boats equipped with an outboard motor it is not good for larger machines because its lubrication is uneven at the higher temperatures larger machines generate.

■ **Exercise 13.7** Numbers in parentheses at the end of the sentences indicate the number of run-ons and comma splices each sentence contains. Revise any incorrect sentences using any of the methods explained in this chapter.

1. Raccoons once won people's hearts as furry creatures with black masks now as rabies is sweeping many metropolitan regions raccoons are feared and hated, they have lost their attractiveness as adorable cuddly animals. (3)

2. In the past police would receive occasional complaints about raccoons, they overturn garbage cans or bite their way through trash bags, however, last year police in some regions received three or four raccoon complaint calls a week. (3)
3. In December police shot and killed four raccoons, one was rabid, in fact raccoons are identified as major carriers of rabies it is a sometimes fatal disease. (4)
4. Many see as essential the need to protect people from rabies nevertheless they are unhappy with the usual way of dealing with the problem—shooting the raccoons. (2)
5. The slaughter may not be necessary apparently only one in six raccoons has rabies, unfortunately people respond to early reports of rabies by trying to destroy every raccoon they encounter, a more humane response might be to innoculate raccoons, there are procedures available to accomplish this goal, the costs are high. (6)

CHAPTER

14

CORRECTING SENTENCE FRAGMENTS

End marks—periods, question marks, and exclamation points—separate grammatical units that are complete sentences. To be complete grammatically, a sentence needs both a subject and a predicate. A grammatically incomplete unit starting with a capital letter and closing with an end mark is called a **sentence fragment.**

In the following sentence fragments, the writer makes an incomplete word group look like a sentence by using a capital letter for the first word and placing a period after the last.

> And tried the hot tamales.
>
> Watching the ducks on the lake.

You can easily spot sentence fragments when they appear in isolation. But when a fragment is buried in surrounding sentences, you may have trouble seeing it and correcting it.

> We enjoyed our stroll through the park. **Watching the ducks on the lake.** The leaves were changing color.
>
> We visited a new Mexican restaurant downtown. **And tried the hot tamales.** They burned my mouth for a week.

Each of these fragments can be added to the preceding sentence to form one complete sentence.

> We enjoyed our stroll through the park, watching ducks on the lake.
>
> We visited a new Mexican restaurant downtown and tried the hot tamales.

■ **Exercise 14.1** Identify the fragments below. Put a check by any complete sentences you find.

1. Without any funds from the federal government or from foundations.
2. Who ate twelve tacos.
3. Surrounded by rich farmland and dense forests.
4. Driving through the California desert with the temperature at 114 degrees.
5. Johnny Cash sings many songs about prisons and prisoners, their loneliness and their hardships.
6. Since she stopped drinking milk.
7. That woman holds two jobs.
8. Country music wailing with pain and loss.
9. A woman who holds two jobs.
10. Country music wails with pain and loss.

■ **Exercise 14.2** Identify the complete sentences and the fragment or fragments in each selection below.

1. Alcohol can damage heart muscle tissue in a condition called *alcoholic cardiomyopathy*. Which can be fatal. Especially to people who cannot leave alcohol alone.
2. The Federal Communications Commission proposes opening a swath of radio frequencies. Hoping to expand new mobile communications. To reallocate frequencies not used by utilities, railroads and police departments.
3. New studies have revealed important information about dyslexia. A reading problem that affects about 10 percent of children. Not necessarily permanently, the studies show.
4. Human beings develop intellectually in leaps from one stage to another, say some important theorists in psychology. Such as Erik Erikson and Jean Piaget.
5. Working for the government sometimes requires great personal sacrifice, but the rewards of public service are great. By hard work and careful attention to detail, a government worker can do much good for the society at large.

14a Making Fragments into Complete Sentences

No handbook can give a complete set of rules for converting fragments into sentences, but the following examples show some typical problems and ways to remedy them.

- Join the fragment to the sentence that comes before it.

  Fragment: Television brings current events to life. **Through interviews and dramatic images.**
  Corrected: Television brings current events to life through interviews and dramatic images.

  Fragment: Jean Rhys's *Good Morning, Midnight* is a novel about Sasha Jansen. **A lonely woman in Paris.** She searches desperately for escape from a dismal past.
  Corrected: Jean Rhys's *Good Morning, Midnight* is a novel about Sasha Jansen, a lonely woman in Paris.

- Add the fragment to the beginning of the sentence that follows or precedes it. Your intended meaning determines whether you connect a fragment to the sentence before or to the sentence after it. Sometimes neither option will produce a sentence that makes sense and pleases stylistically.

  Fragment: **Watching ducks glide across the lake.** Men and women sit everywhere beneath the flowering dogwoods and talk softly in the afternoon sun.
  Corrected: Watching ducks glide across the lake, men and women sit everywhere beneath the flowering dogwoods and talk softly in the afternoon sun.

- Add or remove words to convert a fragment into a complete sentence, or change the wording of the fragment itself.

  Fragment: On Sundays in May at the seashore everyone can relax. **Watching the lobster boats come in.**
  Corrected: On Sundays in May at the seashore everyone can relax. Children enjoy watching lobster boats come in.
  or
  On Sundays in May at the seashore everyone can relax. Children watch lobster boats come in.

14a frag

■ **Exercise 14.3** Return to Exercise 14.1. Correct each fragment by using the techniques explained in 14a. Be sure that your new sentences make sense. Read them aloud.

✓ CHECKLIST 14.1: CORRECTING SENTENCE FRAGMENTS

Correct sentence fragments according to sentence logic and your own stylistic tastes. Take one of the following steps.

- Connect the fragment to the sentence before or after it.
- Add a new subject, a new verb, or both, and add any other necessary words.
- Remove any words that keep the fragment from being a complete sentence.
- Make a present or past participle into a verb by adding a helping verb such as *am, is, are, was,* or *were* before the participle or by changing the participle into a correct verb form.
- When necessary, add a subject to the fragment to convert it into a complete sentence.
- Change an infinitive to a verb by removing *to* and using the correct form of the verb. Or you can sometimes use *like, likes, want, wants, plan, plans, try, tries, am, is,* or *are* before the infinitive. Sometimes you will have to add a subject to fragments that contain an infinitive.
- Make any necessary changes in the wording of the fragment to convert it into a complete sentence.

■ **Exercise 14.4** Find the thirteen fragments in the following selection. Correct each one by adding it to an adjacent sentence, by adding words to it, or by removing words from it. Be sure that each sentence has a subject and a predicate.

The yellow ribbons, symbols of support for our armed forces fighting in the Persian Gulf, now torn and pale. Still wrapped around the oak trees near the army air field in Savannah, Georgia. Where crowds once cheered and waved American flags. To welcome home the men and women. Who fought in Operation Desert Storm. Coming back from the war in the Persian Gulf.

As in other places. The war is a faded memory. Something from our past. All over America people talk of other issues. The failing economy. The increase of crime in our cities.

The Gulf War is a war few of us think of any more. As we worry about domestic problems. But the war is not a forgotten dream. For those who fought there. And their families.

14b
Recognizing Words and Phrases That May Cause Fragments

When you begin sentences with present and past participles, infinitives, and certain adverbs and subordinators, you may trap yourself into producing an incomplete sentence. If, when you revise your drafts, you check carefully for words in these groups at the beginnings of your sentences, you may spot unwanted fragments.

Recognizing Incomplete Verb Forms

Some verb forms cannot serve as sentence predicates. They look like verbs, but, as they serve other functions in their sentences, they can be misleading.

Present participles are verb forms ending in *-ing,* such as *singing, running, speaking, trying, shouting, working,* and *flying* (see p. 115, 16a). They are not verbs, but modifiers, and they cannot stand alone in an independent clause.

Fragment: **Running wildly in the hills.** The stallion looked untamed and beautiful and somehow ghostly.

Corrected: Running wildly in the hills, the stallion looked untamed and beautiful and somehow ghostly.

Past participles are verb forms ending in *-ed, t,* or *-n,* such as *dressed, faded, hurt,* and *driven* (see 16a). Like present participles, they function as modifiers and cannot stand alone.

Fragment: The toast popped up. **Burned black as coal.** It looked like a piece of volcanic rock.

Corrected: The toast popped up, burned black as coal.

Infinitives are verb forms introduced by the word *to,* which is called the **infinitive marker** (see p. 114). Infinitives include such forms as *to play, to scream, to study,* and *to eat.* Like participles and participial phrases, they express action vividly and sometimes seem so strong that writers may think them capable of standing alone as sentences.

Fragment: The mayor spoke forcefully. **To convince her audience of the need for tax reform.**

Corrected: The mayor spoke forcefully to convince her audience of the need for tax reform.

Recognizing Adverbs, Subordinators, and Connectives

Adverbs, subordinators, and connecting words and phrases that often begin fragments include *also, as well as, especially, for example, for instance, just like, mainly,* and *such as.* In speaking we often use fragments along with adverbs and connecting words, but when we write, we must be sure that adverbs and connecting words or phrases lead into complete sentences.

> **Fragment:** An individual spectrum exists for each element. **For example, hydrogen.** It has a red, a blue-green, and a green line.
>
> **Corrected:** An individual spectrum exists for each element. For example, hydrogen has a red, a blue-green, and a green line.

Subordinators that may lead writers into making sentence fragments include conjunctions, such as *as long as, after, although, as, as if, as soon as, because, before, wherever, once, while, how, provided, if, since, so that, though, unless, until, when, where,* and *whether,* and relative pronouns, such as *what, which, who, whoever, whose, whom, whomever, whatever,* and *that* (p. 109).

> **Fragment:** The University Government Association gives students a voice in making policy. **Because they, too, should influence the university administration in matters of academic, social, and cultural welfare.**
>
> **Corrected:** The University Government Association gives students a voice in making policy because they, too, should influence the university administration in matters of academic, social, and cultural welfare.

14b frag

✔ CHECKLIST 14.2: CHECKING FOR INCOMPLETE SENTENCES

To avoid sentence fragments, you must first be able to recognize them.

- Read your sentences aloud, or get a friend to read them aloud to you. Distinguish between the pause that a speaker may make for emphasis and the grammatical pause marked off by a period, a question mark, an exclamation point, a semicolon, or a colon.
- Read your paper from the last sentence to the first, or have a friend read the paper aloud in that way to you. Stop after you read each sentence and ask: Is it complete? Does it make a complete statement or ask a complete question?
- Check for subjects and predicates. Every complete sentence must have at least one subject and one predicate.
- Look at sentences that begin with present and past participles, connective words and phrases, and subordinators.

14c
Using Fragments for Special Effects

Although most formal writing requires complete sentences, sentence fragments can occasionally achieve special effects. Writers of fiction use fragments to record dialogue, since when we speak, we often use incomplete sentences. However, the context always makes the meaning of the fragment clear.

Although they can be effective and acceptable in the hands of skilled writers, fragments are still rare in the expository writing you will do in college. Use them carefully. In writing for your courses, when you write a fragment, you may even want to mark it as such with an asterisk and a note at the bottom of the page. Your teacher will then know that you have made a deliberate choice, not a mistake.

> Jean leaned back, her hands clasped round a knee, looking at the water below them. "I came to a decision last night, Dan." It was unexpected, and he glanced at her. **"Yes?"** She shrugged. **"Nothing momentous.** But I think I'll definitely try for a teacher training course when I get home. **If I can find a place."**
>
> —John Fowles

> I had a sudden mad impulse to pack my bags and get away from both of them. Maybe it wasn't a question of choosing between them but just of escaping both entirely. **Released in my own custody. Stop this nonsense of running from one man to the next. Stand on my own two feet for once.**
>
> —Erica Jong

Fragments may also appear in nonfiction, especially when the writer is striving for an informal, conversational effect.

> But such was Autry's impact that even the action-all-the-way Cowboys had to have somebody in their films who could sing a few cowboy songs while the hero stood around listening and tapping his foot. Charles Starrett was good enough not to need any yodeler's slowing up his action. But you couldn't buck the fashion. Anyway, Dick Weston did not exactly stop the show. **And never would if he went on calling himself Dick Weston.** The name was definitely not a bell ringer. **No matter how many times you said it.**
>
> —James Horwitz

Questions and exclamations often have impact when written as fragments. To call attention to an idea, writers can use fragments effectively.

> **American culture?** Wealth is visible, and so, now, is poverty. Both have become intimidating clichés. **But the rest?**
>
> —PETER SCHRAG

> Whatever economic sanctions can achieve will be duly tested. A semblance of Western resolve has been temporarily achieved. **At a considerable price.**
>
> —*New York Times*

■ **Exercise 14.5** In each selection, correct each fragment by adding it to the sentence that comes before or after or by changing it into an independent sentence. Put a check by any selection that is correct as it stands.

1. In 1980, the Supreme Court ruled that scientists could patent bacteria made in laboratories. An important decision that has made profitable genetic engineering possible.
2. In and around Boston, the sixty-eight institutions of higher learning draw both full-time and part-time students, numbering more than 150,000. Of these over 60 percent come from states other than Massachusetts.
3. When I approached him after school for extra help with my algebra. He replied that he had already given me enough time. That I should try to find a tutor. Who could explain things slowly and carefully.
4. A University of Manchester astronomer, who thrilled sky watchers when he reported discovery of a planet around a neutron star. Retracted his announcement.
5. Abigail Adams championed women's rights. Writing about new legislation to her husband John early in the history of the United States. She said, "I desire you would remember the ladies and be more generous and favorable to them than your ancestors." A strong remark, considering the times.

■ **Exercise 14.6** Return to Exercise 14.2. Correct each fragment. Do not change correct sentences.

■ **Exercise 14.7** Using the following fragments, construct complete sentences. You may add anything you want to make the sentences complete.

1. Slipping across a patch of ice.
2. The coiled snake under my bed.
3. A woman of enormous strength and speed.
4. When I had discovered myself walking in my sleep.
5. When you open the refrigerator door and find the milk spoiled and the bread hard and stale.

■ **Exercise 14.8** Identify the fragment in the following passages. Then explain why you think each writer used a fragment instead of a complete sentence. If you wanted to avoid the fragment, what would you do?

1. Mr. Fitzgerald and his wife, Kathy Fitzgerald, realized that if their hopes for filming the script were to be realized, they would need more help. Which they got in the form of Tom Shaw, a well known production manager and old friend of John Huston, who left a big-budget Barbra Streisand picture to take charge of *Wise Blood.*

   —LINDA CHARLTON

2. And so whenever we go to Detroit we always go to visit this friend of our girlhood. Who knows how we looked before our teeth were straightened. Who knows how we talked before our voice got unBrooklyned. Who knows what we ate before we learned about artichokes. And who, by her presence, puts us in touch with an earlier part of ourself, a part of ourself it's important never to lose.

   —JUDITH VIORST

3. But how many women can name marriage itself as a source of our turbulence? More often than not, we were the ones who most wanted to get married. Besides, if not marriage, what *do* we want? Divorce? That is too fearsome.

   —NANCY FRIDAY

4. Milan is quite an attractive little city. A nice cathedral, *The Last Supper,* a very glamorous train station built by Mussolini, La Scala, and many other enjoyable sights.

   —FRAN LEBOWITZ

CHAPTER

15

MAKING SUBJECT AND VERB AGREE

When a verb is singular, its subject must be singular; when a verb is plural, its subject must be plural. When a subject is in the first, second, or third person, the verb must match it (as we saw on pp. 93–94). This matching in number and person of subjects and verbs is called **agreement.**

In the present tense, the presence of the *-s* suffix at the end of a subject or verb usually indicates a plural subject or a singular verb.

Our *dog* **sleeps** in the basement.

Our *dogs* **sleep** in the basement.

The suffix *-s* (or *-es*) on a noun subject generally means that the subject is *plural.* The suffix *-s* (or *-es*) on a present-tense verb usually tells you that the verb is *singular.* Singular noun subjects, which usually do not end in *-s,* accompany singular verbs, which usually do end in *-s.*

Agreement: singular noun subject; singular verb, third person, present tense

An *orchid* **costs** too much.

The *house* **needs** paint.

The *day* **goes** by quickly.

Plural noun subjects, which usually do end in *-s* (or *-es*), accompany plural verbs, which usually do not end in *-s.*

Agreement: plural noun subject; plural verb, third person, present tense

Orchids **cost** too much.

The *houses* **need** paint.

The *days* **go** by quickly.

15a
Making Noun Subjects and Verbs Agree

Using Singular Noun Subjects Ending in *-s*

The letter *-s* at the end of a word is not always a suffix denoting the plural form. Some singular nouns end in *-s*, and they, too, must match singular verb forms.

Glass **breaks.**

Moss **grows.**

Fungus **spreads.**

Using Plural Noun Subjects Not Ending in *-s*

Some nouns do not use the suffix *-s* for the plural form (see pp. 366–367). But no matter what the form is, a plural subject requires a plural verb.

Children **giggle.**

Men **guffaw.**

Alumni **contribute.**

15b
Making Pronoun Subjects and Verbs Agree

Using Singular Pronoun Subjects

The third person singular pronouns *he, she,* and *it,* like the nouns they replace, require singular verbs.

She **raises** tomatoes.

He **keeps** the cat away.

It **eats** all the seedlings.

Using the Pronouns *I* and *You*

Even though the pronoun *I* is singular, it always takes the present tense verb without a singular *-s* ending.

I applaud. **I write.**

I dream. **I cry.**

The pronoun *you* functions as both a singular and a plural, but it always takes a plural verb—that is, a verb without the *-s* suffix.

You **live.**	I **am.**
You **laugh.**	You **are.**
You **love.**	She **is.**

Using Plural Pronoun Subjects

They **applaud.**

We **love** trains.

■ **Exercise 15.1** In the sentences below, subjects are in italics and verbs are in boldface. If subjects and verbs are singular, make them plural; if they are plural, make them singular. You may need to change other words as well. Follow the example.

Example:
A *field mouse* **takes** cover in the house when the *temperature* **drops.**

Field mice **take** cover in the house when *temperatures* **drop.**

1. The *horses* **gallop** swiftly over the plains.
2. A *city* **provides** many interesting things for people to do.
3. A *flu epidemic* **affects** old people severely.
4. *I* **drive** her to class on Mondays, but on Thursdays *she* **insists** on taking the bus.
5. *Terror* **stalks** some neighborhoods; *people* **face** the possibility of violence every day.

15c Using Plural Verbs with Subjects Joined by *and*

Sometimes a plural subject consists of two singular nouns joined by *and.* These are considered plural subjects and require a plural verb.

Pepper and garlic **flavor** the soup.

Greed and arrogance **disgust** most people.

Queenie and Clarence **work** on cars.

When subjects joined by *and* suggest a single idea, they may take a singular verb, but such uses are rare.

The *tenor and star* of the show **is** out with the flu.

The words *each* and *every* preceding singular subjects that are joined by *and* require a singular verb for the whole subject, even though the subject may sound plural.

In the Nittany Mountains, *each dawn and dusk* **fills** the sky with soft, pink light.

When *every window and every door* **shuts** out drafts, your furnace will burn less oil.

In the rare instances when *each* follows subjects joined by *and,* you may choose either a singular or a plural verb, whichever sounds better to you.

In the Nittany Mountains, dawn and dusk each **fill** (or **fills**) the sky with soft, pink light.

AGREEMENT OF SUBJECT AND VERB

Singular subject	**Singular verb**
I	love
He	loves
The compact disc	was spinning
Our class	laughs
He	sings
The dog	barks
You	are
She	is
Anybody	can
Every one of them	is
Each of us	was
Either Burriss or Ted	is
Neither Dorothy nor John	is
Everyone	is
The friend who	was coming
The committee	is meeting
Mathematics	is

AGREEMENT OF SUBJECT AND VERB *(Continued)*

Plural subject	Plural verb
Dogs, walruses, and seals	bark
They	are barking
He and I	sing
All of them	are
All of us	were
Both Burriss and Ted	are sitting
The three friends who	were coming
The committee members	are meeting

15d
Learning a Special Case: The Verb *To Be*

With the verb *to be,* observe the rules of agreement in both the present and past tense (see p. 248). In the present tense, the various forms of *to be* are irregular and require selective use with subjects.

am: When *I* **am** tired, I cannot think.

is: The *door* **is rattling.**
Martha **is** late again.
He **is serving** tables.
It **is** dawn, and still *she* **is studying.**

are: The *waves* **are racing** to the shore.
They **are gardening;** *we* **are resting.**
When *you* **are finished,** you can go.

In the simple past tense both singular and plural verbs use the same form for all subjects—except for the verb *to be,* which has two past tense forms, *was* (singular) and *were* (plural).

was: The *ball* **was** high.
He **was** merely pink, but *I* **was** lobster-red.

were: As *you* **were reading,** the *children* **were planning** their little surprise.
The *refugees* **were standing** patiently in line.

The rules of agreement also apply to the present perfect tense (see 16a). In the present perfect tense, the helping verb *has* is singular and the helping verb *have* may be either singular or plural.

I **have biked** across the country twice.

He **has** often **complained** about his back.

They **have been** out all night.

TO BE

	Singular	Plural
Present:	I am you are she is	we are you are they are
Past:	I was you were it was	we were you were they were

15e Watching Out for Intervening Words

15e agree

Make your verbs and subjects agree when misleading words or phrases come between them.

Large *sums* of money **go** to national defense.

One *error* in a column of figures **throws** computations off by thousands.

Words such as *in addition to, as well as, along with, plus, including,* and *together with* do not affect the number of the subject. They usually serve as prepositions introducing the object of a preposition, which can never be the subject of a verb (as we saw on p. 109).

The price, including the tip and taxes, **was** $45.

Although such a sentence may be grammatically correct, it may still be awkward. Revise awkward sentences whether they are grammatically correct or not.

One of my happiest childhood memories **is** of a baseball game between the Philadelphia Athletics and the St. Louis Browns. I can still see the bright colors of the grass and the uniforms, and I can still feel the excitement of the crowd.

The *Marx brothers,* including Groucho, still **make** audiences laugh in *A Night at the Opera,* filmed half a century ago.

The plural subject *Marx brothers* requires a plural verb, **make:** the phrase *including Groucho* does not influence the number of the verb.

15f Making Subject and Verb Agree: *Or, Either-Or, Neither-Nor*

And connects subjects to make them compound and plural. *Or* has a different effect. It says, literally, take one or the other, not both. Subjects connected by *or* are therefore singular and take singular verbs. So do subjects connected by *either . . . or* and *neither . . . nor.*

A simple fungus *infection or a rash* between the toes **is** often extremely painful.

Either running or swimming **improves** the heart's performance significantly.

When a subject with *or* or *nor* contains both a singular and a plural part, the verb agrees with the nearest part of the subject.

Either fine art or old coins **make** a good hedge against inflation.

Either old coins or fine art **makes** a good hedge against inflation.

Neither Jack Miller nor his friends the Stanleys **like** beer.

Neither the Stanleys nor their friend Jack Miller **likes** beer.

15f/g agree

Combined singular and plural subjects often sound awkward. Consider revising them to make compound subjects that may be expressed easily by a plural verb.

Old coins and fine art **make** a good hedge against inflation.

Both the Stanleys and their friend Jack Miller **dislike** beer.

15g Keeping Agreement in Special Cases

Making Indefinite Pronouns Agree

Singular indefinite pronouns, such as *anybody, anyone, anything, each, either, everybody, everyone, neither, nobody, no one,* and *one,* require singular verbs.

Use singular verbs with singular indefinite pronouns even when a prepositional phrase with a plural noun comes between the pronoun subject and the verb.

Everyone **is** on strike.

Nobody **likes** a losing team.

Everyone in all the departments **is** on strike.

Nobody among ardent fans **likes** a losing team.

With the more ambiguous indefinite pronouns *all, any, more, most,* and *some,* use singular or plural verbs, depending on whether their meaning is singular or plural in a particular sentence.

She listens carefuly to the children because *some* of them **have** mature ideas.

He made a cake last night; *some* of it **is** still on the table.

The pronoun *none* has been a subject of much debate. Strict grammarians point out that *none* means "no one" and therefore should always take a singular verb. But many writers make the same distinction with *none* that they make with *any*. When *none* refers to a plural noun, some writers use a plural verb. When *none* refers to a singular noun, these writers use a singular verb.

None of my students **are** here yet.

I read his *novel* and discovered that *none* of it **was** any good.

None of these ancient peoples **were** horse nomads.

Using Relative Pronouns as Subjects

When the relative pronouns *who, that,* and *which* appear as subjects, use a verb that agrees with the antecedent of the pronoun.

Readers learn about new products from advertisements *that* sometimes **mislead** by making fantastic claims.

Chow Leung is one of those physicians *who* **work** compulsively.

Be sure you identify the antecedent correctly. In the sentence above, the antecedent is *physicians,* but in the sentences below, it is *one.*

Chow Leung is the only one of those physicians *who* **works** compulsively.

The Glass Menagerie is one of Tennessee Williams's plays *that* **experiments** with slide photography.

Watching Agreement in Inverted Sentences

When you invert the normal sentence order you have to look carefully for the subject. Don't be tricked by the first noun you see.

Below the waves **lurks** a great white *shark.*

Beside the brook **grow** *tulips* in a profusion of color.

Beginning a Sentence with *There* or *Here*

When a verb follows *there* or *here* at the beginning of a sentence, make sure the subject that follows the verb agrees with it.

Here **lie** the *ruins* of a once-thriving civilization.

There **are** five broken *pencils* on the desk.

There **is** a heavy glass *door* at the end of the corridor.

Making Linking Verbs Agree

Linking verbs must agree with their subjects, not with complements of the subjects.

Scholarship and study **are** her passion.

Her *passion* **is** scholarship and study.

If such sentences sound awkward, revise them to make them smoother.

Her *passions* **are** scholarship and study.

She **loves** scholarship and study.

Making Collective Nouns Agree

Collective nouns stand for or suggest a unit. They are singular in form, even though they have plural meanings. *Army, audience, class, committee, majority, minority, team,* and *group* are examples. When collective nouns stand for a single body acting as a unit, they take singular verbs.

ESL 11

This *class* **meets** too early.

An *army* **needs** good leadership and a good cause.

The parking *committee* **issues** permits to students.

The football *team* **travels** to East Lansing tomorrow.

When collective nouns refer to individuals or factions, however, and not to a group acting in concert, they take a plural verb.

The *majority* of the people **were** in favor of reform.

One-third of the team **have** forgotten their jerseys.

Sometimes neither plural nor singular sounds correct.

The graduating *class* **was** already going its separate ways.

The graduating *class* **were** already going their separate ways.

The *couple* **was** arguing with each other.

The *couple* **were** arguing with each other.

These sentences should be revised to make them sound less awkward.

The *members* of the graduating class **were** already going their separate ways.

The *two* **were** arguing with each other.

15g agree

When plural nouns specifying quantities suggest a single unit, they take a singular verb.

Ten minutes **is** not enough time to see the Acropolis.

Two hundred *dollars* **is** not much to pay for a bike these days.

Two-thirds of the pie **was eaten.**

Using Singular Nouns That Look Plural

In contrast to collective nouns, some nouns appear plural in form but are singular in meaning. *Mathematics, politics, athletics, ethics, kudos,* and *pediatrics* are examples. A book or other work that has a plural title is also singular. All these nouns take singular verbs.

Gulliver's Travels **is** both a fantastic narrative and a serious satire on the human condition.

Politics **is** both a science and an art.

Mathematics **is** difficult for many people.

■ **Exercise 15.2** Change the infinitives shown in brackets into the correct forms of the *present tense* verb. Make sure the subjects and verbs agree.

[to be]	**1.** The two books about health care for the senior citizen ______ not providing enough data.
[to choose]	**2.** Neither she nor I ______ horror movies.
[to want]	**3.** Each of the children ______ to do some of the gardening.
[to win]	**4.** The battery-powered car regularly ______ praise fron environmentalists.
[to require]	**5.** Economics ______ careful study both for governments and for people planning to buy a new house or car.
[to give]	**6.** She is the only one of the trustees who ______ any consideration to what faculty members and students want.
[to be]	**7.** A desk with several drawers ______ all you need.
[to recommend]	**8.** Our group unanimously ______ an end to parking fees.
[to need]	**9.** Each man and woman on the boat ______ a life jacket.
[to stand]	**10.** Beyond the elms ______ a small cabin.
[to be]	**11.** Connie, as well as both her aunts, ______ looking forward to seeing the movie again.
[to have]	**12.** Either Theo or his brothers ______ the key.
[to be]	**13.** Three-quarters of the game ______ over.
[to be]	**14.** Neither the jewelry nor the silverware ______ missing.
[to be]	**15.** There ______ considerable politics involved in the appointment of Supreme Court justices.
[to be]	**16.** She wonders which of the students ______ telling the truth.
[to make]	**17.** An extra fifteen pounds ______ a big difference in how your clothes fit.
[to be]	**18.** Peanut butter and jelly ______ her favorite sandwich.
[to be]	**19.** "Live and let live" ______ the moral of the story.
[to get]	**20.** Everybody ______ seasick in gale winds.

✔ CHECKLIST 15.1: ANALYZING SUBJECTS TO MAKE VERBS AGREE

When checking sentences to make sure that subject and verb agree, first determine whether the subject is singular or plural. Here are some questions to ask.

- Is the subject singular? Then the verb must be singular.
- Is the subject plural? Then the verb must be plural.
- Is the subject the pronoun *I* or *you?* Then the verb must take the appropriate form, which may look plural but will be correct for these pronouns.
- Is the verb a form of *to be* or another irregular verb? These verbs have many variants, especially in the present tense. You may need to consult a dictionary or a style guide if you don't know the appropriate form.
- Is the subject a compound joined by *and?* Then the verb must be plural, unless the two nouns constitute the same thing (e.g., "first and best"). Analyze the subject carefully.
- Is the subject a compound joined by *or?* Then the verb must be singular, unless both elements or the element nearest the verb is plural.
- Are there intervening words between the subject and verb? Don't let them throw you off.
- Is the subject a singular indefinite pronoun? (Remember that *everybody* and *everyone* are singular.) Then the verb must be singular.
- Is the subject *none?* Then the verb can be singular or plural, depending on *none*'s meaning.
- Is the subject a relative pronoun? Then the verb can be singular or plural, depending on whether the pronoun's antecedent is singular or plural.
- Does the sentence begin with *There* or *Here?* Then look for the subject to follow the verb.
- Is the subject a collective noun? Then the verb will likely be singular, unless the noun expresses the idea of individuals or factions operating independently.

CHAPTER

16

USING VERB FORMS CORRECTLY

Verbs can take a variety of forms, depending on how you use them. This chapter teaches you how to make the various verb forms work for you.

16a
Reviewing the Principal Parts of Verbs and Verb Tenses

Tense means "time." Verb tenses show the time of the action described by the verb. To form tenses correctly, you must know the **principal parts** of the verb. The principal parts are the *present* form, the *past* form, and the *past participle.*

The *present* form (the *infinitive* form without the infinitive marker *to*) is listed alphabetically in the dictionary; it is often called the **dictionary form.**

Dictionary forms: sing, dance, delight, slice

Infinitive forms: to sing, to dance, to delight, to slice

To make the *past* form of most verbs, add the suffix *-d* or *-ed* to the dictionary form.

I ask**ed,** you play**ed,** he danc**ed,** she slic**ed,** we calculat**ed,** they open**ed**

Recognizing Participles and Helping Verbs

The **past participle** also is usually formed by the addition of *-d* or *-ed* to the dictionary form of the verb. But unlike the past form, the past participle always requires a helping verb to complete the phrase. (The past participle form is sometimes used as a verbal; see p. 115.)

Helping (or **auxiliary**) **verbs** help form tenses. The common helping verbs are *have, has, had, am, is, are, was, were, be, being, been, do, does, did, shall, will, should, would, can, may, might, must,* and *could.* Helpers may also be groups of words such as *have to, ought to, used to, is going to,* and *is about to.*

I **should have predicted** that result.

We **were finished** by noon.

He **had planted** his garden before he left for work.

ESL 16 The important helping verb *do* in its various forms helps other verbs to make emphatic statements, to ask questions, or to make negations.

I **do** work!

Do I work?

I **do** not work.

The **present participle** is formed by the addition of *-ing* to the dictionary form. (Spelling changes that occur when *-ing* is added to some verbs are discussed on pp. 362–363.) Although the present participle is an essential verb form, it is not usually listed among the principal parts. Remember that the **gerund** has the same form as the present participle, but gerunds are always treated as nouns (see p. 115). Here are some present participles.

singing, dancing, delighting, slicing

Understanding the Three Simple Tenses

There are three basic tenses in English—present, past, and future.

Simple present

The *simple present* of most verbs is the *dictionary form,* which is also called the **present stem.** To form the third-person singular from the simple present, you usually add *-s* or *-es* to the present stem.

I run	we run	I go	we go
you run	you run	you go	you go
he run**s**	they run	she go**es**	they go
I join	we join		
you join	you join		
it join**s**	they join		

Simple past

To form the simple past of regular verbs, *-d* or *-ed* is added to the present stem. The simple past does not change form.

I escaped	we escaped
you escaped	you escaped
he escaped	they escaped

Sometimes the simple past is irregular. Irregular verbs form the simple past tense not with *-d* or *-ed* but by some other change, often a change in an internal vowel.

I ran	we ran
you ran	you ran
she ran	they ran

Simple future

The simple future is made with the helping verbs *shall* and *will.*

I shall go	we shall go
you will go	you will go
she will go	they will go

Traditional grammar holds that *shall* should be used for the first person, *will* for the second and third persons. In practice, this distinction is often ignored; most people write, "I will be twenty-five years old on my next birthday."

Understanding the Uses of the Simple Present

The *simple present* has several uses. It makes an unemphatic statement about something happening or a condition existing right now.

The earth **revolves** around the sun.

The car **passes** in the street.

It expresses habitual or continuous or characteristic action.

Porters **carry** things.

Dentists **fill** teeth and sometimes **pull** them.

Rocky McKnuckle **fights** with everybody.

> The organization of his government always **seems** more important to an incoming president than the organization of his White House.
>
> —THEODORE H. WHITE

It expresses a command indirectly, as a statement of fact.

> Periodicals **are** not to be taken out of the room.

It reports the content of literature, documents, movies, musical compositions, works of art, or anything else that supposedly comes alive in the present each time it is experienced by an audience.

> Macbeth **is driven** by ambition, and he **is haunted** by ghosts.
>
> The Parthenon in Athens **embodies** grace, beauty, and calm.

Some writers use the present tense to describe historical action on the theory that history happens to us again each time we read about it. This *historical present* is awkward to sustain in English; in general, you should avoid it. A wise rule is to write about the past in the past tense.

> **Historical present:** When Tom Paine **calls** for America's independence, he **is speaking** as an English radical.
>
> **Past:** When Tom Paine **called** for America's independence, he **was speaking** as an English radical.

16a
verb

Understanding the Three Perfect Tenses

In addition to the simple present, past, and future, English verbs have three perfect tenses—the *present perfect,* the *past perfect,* and the *future perfect.* The **perfect** tense expresses an act that will be completed before an act reported by another verb takes place. For that reason, a verb in the *perfect tense* should always be thought of as paired with another verb, either expressed or understood.

Present perfect

In the *present perfect* tense, the action of the verb started in the past. The present perfect is formed by the helping verb *has* or *have* plus the past participle.

> I **have worked** hard for this diploma.

The work you began in the past has just ended. This compound sentence is implied: "I have worked hard for this diploma, but now my work is ended."

She **has loved** architecture for many years, and now she *takes* architecture courses in night school.

The interest in architecture began in the past and continues into the present.

Past perfect

The *past perfect* tense reports an action completed before another action took place. The past perfect is also formed with the past participle, but it uses the helping verb *had.*

I **had worked** twenty years before I saved any money.

The act of working twenty years has been completed before the act of saving took place.

They thought they **had considered** all the dangers when they decided on the attack.

The act of considering all the dangers had been completed before the act of deciding took place.

The past perfect, like the present perfect, implies another act that is not stated in the sentence.

He **had told** me that he would quit if I yelled at him. I yelled at him, and he quit.

Future perfect

The *future perfect* tense reports an act that will be completed by some specific time in the future. It is formed by the helping verb *shall* or *will* added to *have* or *has* and the past participle.

I **shall have worked** fifty years when I retire.

He **will have lived** with me ten years next March.

Understanding the Progressive Form

ESL 5

The **progressive** form is used with all tenses to show that an action continues during the time that the sentence describes, whether that time is past, present, or future. It is made with the present participle and a helping verb that is a form of *to be.*

Present progressive: I am working.

Past progressive: I was working.

Future progressive: They will be working.

Present perfect progressive: She has been been working.

Past perfect progressive: We had been working.

Future perfect progressive: They will have been working.

Here are some more examples of progressive forms:

I **am working** on a new book.

I **was working** in the kitchen when the house caught fire.

They **will be working** in the garage tomorrow afternoon.

Understanding the Principal Parts of the Most Common Irregular Verbs

Although the principal parts of most verbs are formed quite regularly, many of the most frequently used verbs are **irregular:** their past tense and their past participle are not formed simply by an added *-ed.* The only way to master them is to memorize them.

If you are unsure of the principal parts of a verb, always look in a dictionary. If the verb is regular, a dictionary will list only the present form, and you will know that you should form both the past and the past participle by adding *-d* or *-ed.* If the verb is irregular, a dictionary will give the forms of the principal parts.

The most important irregular verb is *to be,* often used as a helping verb. It is the only English verb that does not use the infinitive as the basic form for the present tense. Study the following forms.

TO BE

	Singular	Plural
Present:	I am you are she is	we are you are they are
Past:	I was you were it was	we were you were they were
Past perfect:	I had been you had been he had been	we had been you had been they had been

The following is a list of the principal parts of the most common irregular verbs. (Some verbs in this list are not irregular but are included because they confuse many people.) Notice that the past or the past participles of some irregular verbs have more than one form.

COMMON IRREGULAR VERBS

Present stem	Past stem	Past participle
awake	awoke	awoke/awakened
become	became	become
begin	began	begun
blow	blew	blown
break	broke	broken
bring	brought	brought
burst	burst	burst
choose	chose	chosen
cling	clung	clung
come	came	come
dive	dove/dived	dived
do	did	done
draw	drew	drawn
drink	drank	drunk
drive	drove	driven
eat	ate	eaten
fall	fell	fallen
fly	flew	flown
forget	forgot	forgotten/forgot
forgive	forgave	forgiven
freeze	froze	frozen
get	got	gotten/got
give	gave	given
go	went	gone
grow	grew	grown
hang (things)	hung	hung
hang (people)	hanged	hanged
know	knew	known
lay (to put)	laid	laid
lie (to recline)	lay	lain
lose	lost	lost
pay	paid	paid
ride	rode	ridden
ring	rang	rung
rise	rose	risen
say	said	said
see	saw	seen
set	set	set
shake	shook	shaken
shine	shone/shined	shone/shined

COMMON IRREGULAR VERBS (*Continued*)

Present stem	Past stem	Past participle
show	showed	shown
sing	sang	sung
sink	sank	sunk
sit	sat	sat
speak	spoke	spoken
spin	spun	spun
spit	spat/spit	spat/spit
steal	stole	stolen
strive	strove/strived	striven/strived
swear	swore	sworn
swim	swam	swum
swing	swung	swung
take	took	taken
tear	tore	torn
tread	trod	trod/trodden
wake	woke	waked/woke/wakened
wear	wore	worn
weave	wove	woven
wring	wrung	wrung
write	wrote	written

■ **Exercise 16.1** In the following sentences, supply the correct form of the verb that appears in parentheses at the end of the sentence.

Example:
The book had **been published** before he knew anything about it. (publish)

1. The plane ________ before we can get to the airport. (go)
2. He will ________ the house by the time we get back from our vacation. (clean)
3. He ________ while we were singing in the living room. (cry)
4. They had often ________ together in the same place where the shark attacked. (swim)
5. On the western frontier, horse thieves were sometimes ________ without a trial. (hang)
6. The balloons had ________ before the children arrived for the party. (burst)
7. Macbeth was ________ from a great victory when he met the three witches. (return)
8. She ________ for you at this very moment. (search)

9. Johnson, whom you see over there on the ballfield, has _______ that bat for an hour and a half. (swing)
10. He _______ to escape from his job whenever he can. (like)

16b
Observing Correct Sequence of Tenses

If you use more than one verb in a sentence, be sure that the time of the verbs flows logically from one to the next. This means that past, present, and future actions must appear in sequences in a logical order.

While I **am writing,** I **like** to listen to the radio.

In the example above, two actions take place at the same time—the present. Both are reported in verbs using the present tense.

He **says** that Hamlet **felt** only self-pity.

In this example, the action of *saying* appears in the present; it is a comment on something that happened in the past.

Dickens **was** already famous when he **made** his first trip to America.

In the example, the two verbs both report past action; both are in the simple past.

The child **was crossing** the street when I **saw** the car bearing down on her.

In the example, the past progressive is used with the simple past, the action *crossing* continuing to the definite point when I *saw.*

He **had been** in Vietnam for a year when he **began** to write his book.

In the example above, the past perfect *had been* indicates an action in the past that continued before the action expressed in the simple past tense *began.*

When I **get up,** he **will have been gone** for hours.

In this example, a future time is indicated by the adverb *when* and the present *get up*. The future perfect *will have been gone* indicates an action that will be completed before the action of getting up takes place.

Ordinarily, a past tense in the first clause of a sentence cannot be followed by the simple present, the present perfect, or a future tense.

> **Incorrect:** Sir Walter Scott **wrote** many novels because he **is** always in debt and **needs** to make money.
>
> **Revised:** Sir Walter Scott **wrote** many novels because he **was** always in debt and **needed** to make money.

However, you may use the present tense or the future tense in the second clause if it expresses a general truth always in force and follows a first clause containing a verb such as *say, tell, report, agree,* or *promise.*

> They **agreed** that friendships between the sexes **are** not so difficult now.
>
> He **says** that he **will pay** the bill next month.
>
> He **says** that he **has paid** the bill already.
>
> He **says** that he **paid** the bill last month.

For more on the correct sequence of tenses, see 20a.

■ **Exercise 16.2** Fill in each blank with any verb that makes sense. Use the tense given in parentheses.

Example:
After John **had been dancing** for three hours, he realized that the band had stopped playing. (past perfect progressive)

1. He ________ white water rafting five times and plans to go again. (present perfect)
2. Tomorrow ________ the first day of the rest of my life. (future)
3. Ralph ________ in the bank when the robbery took place. (past perfect)
4. Hitchcock always ________ in his own movies. (present)
5. Canada geese ________ continually while they fly. (present)

■ **Exercise 16.3** Fill in each blank with a logical tense of the verb given in parentheses.

1. They were going out the back door when she ________ the bell. (ring)

2. You ________ home by the time you get this letter. (arrive)
3. They ________ for about an hour when the fire broke out in the boat. (sail)
4. Winter ________ by the time you come home from the army. (go)
5. They ________ the split pea soup now. (eat)

16c Using Mood Accurately

The **mood** of a verb expresses the attitude of the writer. Verbs have several moods—the *indicative,* the *subjunctive,* the *imperative,* and the *conditional.*

Understanding the Indicative Mood

The **indicative** is used for simple statements of fact or for asking questions about the fact. It is by far the most common mood of verbs in English.

The tide **came** in at six o'clock and **swept** almost to the foundation of our house.

Can he **be** serious?

Understanding the Subjunctive Mood

The **subjunctive** conveys a wish, a desire, or a demand in the first or third person, or it makes a statement contrary to fact.

I wish I **were** a bird.

Helen wishes she **were** home.

Would that I **were** home!

He demanded that his son **use** the money to go to college.

He asked that she never **forget** him.

If only I **were** in Paris tonight!

If I **were** you, I'd read the short story one more time before the test on Tuesday.

The subjunctive form for most verbs differs from the indicative only in the first- and third-person singular. Note that the present subjunctive of the verb *to be* is *were* for the first, second, and third persons, singular and plural.

Were she my daughter, I would not permit her to date a member of a motorcycle gang.

If we **were** born with wings, we could learn to fly.

Even if you **were** to promise that each of you would have the assignment completed, I would not postpone the test.

If they **were** self-confident, they would not have turned down the invitation.

When the subjunctive is used with the verb *to be* to express commands or wishes in the third-person singular or the future tense in the first or third person, the verb form is *be.*

If I **be** proved wrong, I shall eat my hat.

Let there **be** light.

Grammar **be** hanged!

If this **be** treason, make the most of it!

The subjunctive is used in clauses beginning with *that* after verbs that give orders or advice or express wishes or requests.

He wishes that she **were** happier.

She asked that he **draw** up a marriage contract before the wedding.

In these examples, a request is embodied in a *that* clause. Since no one can tell whether a request will be honored or not, the verb clause is in the subjunctive.

Should and *had* may also express the subjunctive.

Should he step on a rattlesnake, his boots will protect him.

Should you find yourself unhappy in your new job, don't hesitate to ask to be reinstated here.

Had he taken my advice, he would not have bought stock in a dance hall.

Take care not to confuse the conditional with the past subjunctive. Do not say "I wish we *would have* won the tournament." Say "I wish we *had* won the tournament."

Understanding the Imperative Mood

The **imperative** expresses a command or entreaty in the second-person singular or plural, and the form of the verb is the same as the indicative.

In the imperative sentence, the *subject* of the verb is always *you,* but the *you* is usually understood, not written out.

> **Pass** the bread.
>
> **Drive** me to the airport, please.
>
> **Leave** the room!
>
> **Watch** your step!

Sometimes *you* is included for extra emphasis.

> You **give** me my letter this instant!

■ **Exercise 16.4** Identify the moods of the verbs in italics in the following sentences. Over each italicized verb, write *I* for indicative, *S* for subjunctive, or *IM* for imperative.

1. If she *was* awake, she must have heard the noise.
2. Soldiers in their last year of service *count* the days until their release.
3. He said that Japan *has* one of the lowest crime rates in the world.
4. If Brian Wilson *were* still *writing* surfing songs, the Beach Boys might not be numbered among rock and roll's great singing groups.
5. *Had* you *been* here, we might not have quarreled.
6. *Don't burn* the toast.
7. If horses *were* smarter, they would never put up with bridles and saddles.
8. You better not *go* in.
9. She demanded that he *eat* the whole banana.
10. If I *had helped* him study, he might have passed the test.

Understanding the Conditional Mood

ESL 8

The **conditional** makes statements that depend on one another; one is true on condition of the other's being true. A conditional sentence contains a clause that states the condition and another that states the consequence of the condition. Most conditional statements are introduced with *if.*

> **If** communist governments had been able to produce enough food for their people, they would not have collapsed in 1989.
>
> **If** you will be home tonight, I'll come over.
>
> Even **if** the strike is settled, they will still be angry.

Like the indicative, the conditional requires no changes in ordinary verb forms. The difficulty comes in distinguishing the conditional from the subjunctive. Remember that the subjunctive is used for conditions clearly contrary to fact.

If he **were** here right now, we would be happy.

The example above, in the subjunctive mood, means that he is not here, we know that he is not here, and we are not happy. The following example is conditional.

If he **is** there, we will be happy.

We do not know whether he is there or not. We make a simple statement of fact. If we discover he is there, we will be happy.

If the circumstances are in the past, use the subjunctive for conditions that were clearly not factual and the indicative for conditions that may have been true. The verb *would* or *could* is used as a helping verb for statements that give the supposed consequences of conditions that were not factual.

If he **were** there that night, he **would have had** no excuse.

He was not there; the *if* clause uses the subjunctive, and the clause stating the consequences uses *would.*

If he **was** there, he **had** no excuse.

He may have been there; we do not know. If he was indeed there, he had no excuse. The indicative mood is used in both clauses as a simple statement of fact.

The past perfect is used in past conditional statements when the condition states something that was not true.

If Hitler **had stopped** in 1938, World War II **would not have come** as it did.

Avoid using the conditional in both clauses.

Incorrect: If she **would have gone** to Paris, she **would have had** a good time.

Correct: If she **had gone** to Paris, she **would have had** a good time.

Take care not to confuse the conditional with the past subjunctive.

Incorrect: I wish we **would have won** the tournament.

Correct: I wish we **had won** the tournament.

16d
Using the Active and Passive Voice

Learn the difference between the active voice and the passive voice. Use verbs in the active voice in most sentences; use verbs in the passive voice sparingly and only for good reason.

The voice of a transitive verb tells us whether the subject is the actor in the sentence or is acted upon. (A transitive verb carries action from an agent to an object. A transitive verb can take a direct object; an intransitive verb does not take a direct object. See 4b.)

When transitive verbs are in the **active voice,** the subject does the acting. When transitive verbs are in the **passive voice,** the subject is acted upon by an agent that is implied or expressed in a prepositional phrase. (Intransitive verbs cannot be passive. You can say "My brother *brooded* too much," but you cannot say "My brother *was brooded*.") In the passive voice, the transitive verb phrase includes some form of the verb *to be.*

Active: She **mailed** the letter.
John **washed** the dishes.

Passive: The letter **was mailed** by her.
The dishes **were washed** by John.

Readers usually want to know the agent of an action; that is, they want to know *who* or *what* does the acting. Since the passive often fails to identify the agent of an action, it may be a means of evading responsibility.

Active: The senator **misplaced** the memo.
The Mustangs lost because Al Tennyson **missed** a tackle on the punt return.

Passive: The memo **was misplaced.**
The Mustangs lost because a tackle **was missed** on the punt return.

Use the passive when the recipient of the action in the sentence is much more important to your statement than the doer of the action.

✔ CHECKLIST 16.1: AVOIDING COMMON ERRORS IN VERBS

Verbs present many possibilities for error. Here are a few to watch for.

ESL 6

	Faulty	Correct
Irregular verbs		
■ Avoid confusing simple past with past participle.	I **seen** her last night. He **done** it himself.	I **saw** her last night. He **did** it himself. He **had done** it himself.
■ Don't try to make irregular verbs regular.	She **drawed** my picture. We **payed** for everything.	She **drew** my picture. We **paid** for everything.
Transitive and intransitive verbs		
■ Don't confuse *lay* (trans.) with *lie* (intrans.).	I **lay** awake every night. I **lay** my books on the desk when I come in. I **laid** down for an hour.	I **lie** awake every night. I **laid** my books on the desk when I came in. I **lay** down for an hour.
■ Don't confuse *set* (trans.) with *sit* (intrans.).	He pointed to a chair, so I **set** down. She **sat** the vase on the table.	He pointed to a chair, so I **sat** down. She **set** the vase on the table.
Tense		
■ Don't shift tenses illogically.	The car **bounced** over the curb and **comes** crashing through the window. I **asked** him not to do it, but he **does** it anyhow.	The car **bounced** over the curb and **came** crashing through the window. I **asked** him not to do it, but he **did** it anyhow.
Mood		
■ Don't confuse conditional with past subjunctive.	I wish he **would have come** sooner. I would have been here if you **would have told** me you were coming.	I wish he **had come** sooner. I would have been here if you **had told** me you were coming.

16d verb

My car **was stolen** last night.

Who stole your car is not known. The important thing is that your car was stolen.

After her heart attack, she **was taken** to the hospital in an ambulance.

Who took her to the hospital is unimportant; the important fact is that she was taken.

Scientific researchers generally use the passive voice throughout reports on experiments to keep the focus on the experiment rather than on the experimenters.

When the bacteria **were isolated,** they were treated carefully with nicotine and **were observed** to stop reproducing.

■ **Exercise 16.5** Rewrite the following sentences to put the passive verbs in the active voice.

1. The paintings on the wall of my kitchen were done by my daughter.
2. At a hundred years of age, Hal Roach was presented with the Smithsonian's highest award for his pioneering film comedies.
3. The movie *Citizen Kane* was made by Orson Welles, was the recipient of many awards, but was not viewed by Welles himself for years afterward.
4. In the 1950s, color was used by filmmakers to compete with television where all the programs were still being shown in black and white.
5. A redistricting plan was revealed yesterday in the state capitol by a joint legislative committee.

■ **Exercise 16.6** The following sentences were all written by professional writers. Analyze each verb to see whether it is in the active or the passive voice. Tell why the passive is used when you do find it.

1. Some birds can be identified by color alone.

—Roger Tory Peterson

2. The radio was silenced, and all that could be heard was the echo of the Mayor's voice.

—Mark Helprin

3. His purpose on this earth, I was convinced, was to corrupt life. While other kids were plied with fairy tales and ghost stories, he burdened our minds with Tolstoy and Shakespeare and the Bible.

—LINDSAY PATTERSON

4. At this point, a doctor was summoned; a formal pronouncement of death was made; and Big Jim's carcass was dragged, feet first, and for the last time, through the front door of his saloon.

—JOE MCGINNISS

5. Many statesmen feel that weapons are in themselves evil, and that they should be eliminated, as you would crush a snake.

—E. B. WHITE

16e Using the Infinitive

The **infinitive** is the present tense of a verb with the marker *to.* Grammatically, the infinitive can complete the sense of other verbs, serve as a noun, and form the basis of some phrases.

The *present infinitive,* which uses the infinitive marker *to* along with the verb, describes action that takes place at the same time as the action in the verb the infinitive completes.

to go:

He wants **to go.**

He wanted **to go.**

He will want **to go.**

ESL 7

The *present perfect infinitive,* which uses the infinitive marker *to,* the verb *have,* and a past participle, describes action prior to the action of the verb whose sense is completed by the infinitive. The present perfect infinitive often follows verb phrases that include *should* or *would.*

to have seen:

I would like **to have seen** her face when she found the duck in her bathtub.

An **infinitive phrase** includes the infinitive and the words that complete its meaning.

Her attempt **to bicycle through a New York subway tunnel** was frustrated by an express train.

To take such an immense journey required courage and money.

To dance was his whole reason for living.

Her only aim was **to dodge his flying feet.**

He studied **to improve his voice.**

Sometimes the infinitive marker is omitted before the verb, especially after such verbs as *hear, help, let, see,* and *watch.*

She heard him **come** in.

They watched the ship **sail** out to sea.

She made him **treat** her with respect.

In general, avoid split infinitives. A **split infinitive** has one or more words awkwardly placed between the infinitive marker *to* and the verb form. The rule against split infinitives is not absolute: some writers split infinitives and others do not. But the words used to split infinitives can usually go outside the infinitive, or they can be omitted altogether.

Split infinitive: He told me **to** really **try** to do better.

Better: He told me **to try** to do better.

Some writers believe that split infinitives are acceptable.

The government was little altered as Mr. Bush touched down at Andrews Air Force Base at 6:30 P.M. **to** gracefully **assume** the duties but not the powers of the Presidency.

—*Time*

Exercise 16.7 Rewrite the following sentences to eliminate split infinitives.

1. Enrique wanted to completely forget his painful romance.
2. They intended to speedily complete the job.
3. The pilot wanted to safely and happily complete the trip.
4. The United States Football League vowed to strictly refuse to sign college football players before they had played in their senior year.

5. Her invitation seemed to really be genuine, but I suspected her intentions.

■ **Exercise 16.8** Correct the errors in the following sentences. If a sentence is correct as it stands, place a check beside the number.

1. He come home last night and find the dog sick.
2. They take the kickoff and get to work and have a touchdown in five minutes of the first quarter.
3. She worked hard and done a good job.
4. After a long day, it's always good to lay down.
5. He lay his pants over the back of the chair last night and go right to sleep and don't wake up until this morning at ten o'clock.
6. The turtle swum after the goldfish.
7. They hung him by the neck until he were dead.
8. Suzanne Yip drunk three beers and then had passed out on the front steps just as I rung the bell.
9. She shown me the right path but I seen a snake and ran.
10. A blue jay had flew into the storm window and had broke the glass into thousands of pieces.

CHAPTER

17

USING PRONOUNS CORRECTLY

Pronouns take the places of nouns in sentences. If we had to repeat the noun *house* every time we wrote about the ideal *house* in the sentence below, we would have awkward and unwieldy prose.

> The house stood on a shady street, and the house looked large and comfortable, as if the house were perfectly suited for a large family and for two sets of grandparents visiting the house for long periods.

We use pronouns to avoid awkwardness, to simplify style, and to express certain ideas clearly. (See p. 100 on identifying pronouns.)

We could not express some ideas without pronouns. Many sentences require first-person pronouns (*I, we, our,* and *ours*) or second-person pronouns (*you, your,* and *yours*), and no other words can serve in their place.

17a
Coordinating Pronouns and Antecedents

By themselves, pronouns are indefinite words, therefore, most pronouns require an antecedent to give them content and meaning. The **antecedent** is the word the pronoun substitutes for. The antecedent usually appears earlier in the same sentence or in the same passage. In the following example, the antecedent for the pronoun *it* is *snow.*

> The *snow* fell all day long, and by nightfall **it** was three feet deep.

Some pronouns are **indefinite,** taking their meaning not from an antecedent but from the sentences in which they are located.

Anybody who wants to see the concert should get a ticket two months in advance.

Some pronouns are **intensive.** They end in *-self,* and they add emphasis to the noun or pronoun they follow.

John **himself** admitted his error.

The legal battle about who owned the field went on for years while the field **itself** grew like a jungle.

No matter how you may judge my actions, you **yourself** would have done the same thing in my situation.

When these pronouns ending in *-self* are used as direct objects or objects of prepositions, they are **reflexive.**

I hurt **myself.**

Alice went to the game by **herself.**

Making Pronouns Refer Clearly to Antecedents

Pronouns that do not refer clearly to their antecedents or that are widely separated from them may confuse your readers. Often the only way to remedy such confusion is to rewrite the sentence.

17a pron

Confusing: Albert was with Beauregard when **he** got the news that **his** rare books had arrived.

Who got the news? Did the rare books belong to Beauregard, or did they belong to Albert?

Improved: When Albert got the news that **his** rare books had arrived, **he** was with Beauregard.

Now the sentence is clear. The rare books belong to Albert, and he got the news of their arrival while he was with Beauregard.

Generally, personal pronouns refer to the nearest previous noun, but don't count on your readers to understand that or figure it out. Revise the sentence whenever the pronoun antecedent is potentially unclear.

Making Pronouns Agree with Their Antecedents

Pronouns must agree with their antecedents in number and gender.

Singular antecedents require singular pronouns. Plural antecedents require plural pronouns.

The *house* was dark and gloomy, and **it** sat in a grove of tall cedars that made **it** seem darker still.

The *cars* swept by on the highway, all of **them** doing more than fifty-five miles per hour.

Roosevelt and *Churchill* found radio a perfect medium for **their** speaking talents.

Use a singular pronoun when all the parts of a compound antecedent are singular and the parts are joined by *or* or *nor.* Notice how the pronouns in the following examples also agree with their antecedents in **gender,** or sexual reference in grammar.

Either *Ted* or *John* will take **his** car.

Neither *Judy* nor *Linda* will lend you **her** horn.

But if Ted and John own one car in partnership, you should write, "Either Ted or John will take *their* car." And if Judy and Linda own only one horn between them, you should write, "Neither Judy nor Linda will lend you *their* horn."

Sometimes you must revise a sentence because a single pronoun will not do.

Incorrect: Neither *Patricia* nor *John* would let me borrow **his** lawn mower.

Revised: Neither Patricia nor John would let me borrow a lawn mower. Patricia would not lend me her lawn mower, and John would not lend me **his.**

Another revision: Patricia would not lend me **her** lawn mower, nor would John lend me **his.**

Referring to Antecedents of Unknown Gender

Books on writing used to recommend the masculine singular pronoun to refer to a noun or pronoun of unknown gender.

Any *teacher* must sometimes despair at the indifference of **his** students.

Everybody can have what **he** wants to eat.

Such language, though grammatically correct, is now viewed as sexist. Writers who are sensitive to the implications of the words they use avoid sexist language. The problem apparent in these sentences is not difficult to fix.

Any teacher must sometimes despair at the indifference of students.

Teachers must sometimes despair at the indifference of their students.

You can all have what you want to eat.

Everybody, order anything you want!

We can all have what we want to eat.

All participants can have what they want to eat.

Chapter 11 explores biased language and describes various remedies for it.

When referring to the whole, collective nouns—*team, family, audience, majority, minority, committee, group, government, flock, herd,* and many others—use single pronouns.

The *team* won **its** victory gratefully.

In elections, the *majority* has **its** way.

The *committee* disbanded when **it** finished **its** business.

However, if the members of the group indicated by a collective noun are being considered as individuals, a plural pronoun is appropriate.

The hard-rock *band* broke up and began fighting among **themselves** when **their** leader was converted to Mozart.

17a
pron

In British English, collective nouns usually take plural pronouns and plural verbs.

The cricket *team* quit playing when **they** discovered that **their** spectators had fallen into a profound sleep.

The *government* have refused to elaborate on **their** earlier brief announcement.

■ **Exercise 17.1** Rewrite the following sentences to correct errors in pronoun antecedents. If you find no error in a sentence, put a check by it. You may rewrite a sentence to keep some pronouns, or you may eliminate the pronouns altogether.

1. The ship sailed under the Golden Gate Bridge as it put out to sea.
2. The painter complained to her model that she was too pale.
3. Everyone on the men's swim team should bring their goggles to tomorrow's practice.

4. It says on the menu that the special is fried eggplant.
5. The traveler bought a melon from the peasant as he stood in the shade on the road below Lamia, the city on the hill.
6. The passengers boarded the buses after they sat idly for several hours.
7. Neither Lewis nor Alfred brought their toothbrush.
8. If anyone wears polyester shirts, they will be much hotter in summer and much colder in winter than with cotton shirts, but they can enjoy them for years.
9. Sara phoned Luz when she was rushing out to take the children to a Cub Scout meeting.
10. Neither Ellen nor Mike rode her bicycle to school that day, although they usually rode in together every morning.

ESL 1

Avoiding Pronouns Without References

Some writers use such pronouns as *this, that, they, it, which,* and *such* to refer not to a specific antecedent, but to the general idea expressed by a whole clause or sentence. Using pronouns in this way is imprecise and often misleading.

> Andy Warhol once made a movie of a man sleeping for a whole night, **which** was a tiresome experience.

Was the movie tiresome to watch? Or was making the movie the tiresome experience?

> **Revised:**
>
> Andy Warhol once made a tiresome movie of a man sleeping for a whole night.
>
> Andy Warhol once went through the tiresome experience of making a movie of a man sleeping for a whole night.

Differentiating Between the Expletive *It* and the Pronoun *It*

The pronoun *it* always has an antecedent; the **expletive** *it* serves as a grammatical subject when the real subject is placed after the verb or is understood.

> **Pronoun *It*:** In rural America when a barn burns, **it** often takes with **it** a year's hard work for a farm family.

Expletive *It:* In rural America, when a barn burns, **it** is difficult for a farm family to recover from the loss.

The expletive *it* serves as the grammatical subject of the independent clause that it begins. The sentence could read, "When a barn burns, to recover from the loss is difficult for a farm family." But such a sentence, although correct grammatically, sounds awkward in comparison with the sentence that uses the expletive *it.*

Try to avoid using the expletive *it* and the pronoun *it* one after the other.

Weak: What will happen to the kite? If **it** is windy, **it** will fly.

Improved: What will happen to the kite? It will fly if the wind blows.

The expletive *it* is correctly used without an antecedent. But other pronouns used without antecedents are both awkward and unclear.

Vague

They say that the heat wave will break tomorrow.

They say Philip dyes his hair.

They say we can expect a higher rate of inflation next year.

They haven't plowed the back roads yet.

17b
pron

Who is *they*? Sometimes *they* can be identified. If so, be specific; if not, recast the sentence to avoid vagueness.

Better

The heat wave is supposed to break tomorrow.

Philip's former wife says he dyes his hair.

The front-page article in today's paper says we can expect a higher rate of inflation next year.

The road crew has not plowed the back roads yet.

17b
Addressing Your Readers

In the first example below the writer announces that he will talk with the reader throughout as though in a discussion. The tone is informal and the pronoun *you* appropriate. In the second example, the writer chooses a more formal tone. The pronoun *one* does the service that *you* might perform in a less formal piece.

> The book's no good to you now. Neither is scientific reason. You don't need any scientific experiments to find out what's wrong.
>
> —ROBERT M. PIRSIG

> One notices, as one rarely does when dining in company, the lengthiness and noisiness of one's chewing, the slight awkwardness with which one handles one's cutlery, one's ineptitude with lettuce.
>
> —JOSEPH EPSTEIN

Let the tone and intention of your essay determine whether you will use the pronouns *I, my, me,* and *mine.* Many teachers tell students to avoid using first person singular pronouns to prevent student writers from calling attention to themselves and getting in the way of the subject they should be writing about.

Intrusive

> I think Carew is a handsome man, but I don't mean that in the conventional sense. I think that the most arresting features on his face are a tiny turned-up nose and a mouth that in my opinion is a mile wide, and I believe it can exaggerate the mildest emotion. When he smiles, I believe the light can be seen as far away as Newport Beach. When he's downcast, I'd say there's an eclipse of the sun.

Nonintrusive

> Carew is a handsome man, but not in the conventional sense. The most arresting features on his face are a tiny turned-up nose and a mile-wide mouth that can exaggerate the mildest emotion. When he smiles, the light can be seen as far away as Newport Beach. When he's downcast, there's an eclipse of the sun.
>
> —RON FIMRITE

The first person singular pronouns are appropriate when you are writing about some personal experience that is the center of your prose.

> From all available evidence no black man had ever set foot in this tiny Swiss village before I came. I was told before arriving that I would probably be a "sight" for the village; I took this to mean that people of my complexion were rarely seen in Switzerland, and also that city people are always something of a "sight" outside of the city. It did

> not occur to me—possibly because I am an American—that there could be people anywhere who had never seen a Negro.
>
> —James Baldwin

First-person singular pronouns are also acceptable when you are weighing two contradictory opinions and want to let readers know which side you are on.

> Many scientists believe that all matter in the universe will fall back to a central mass, which will eventually explode again in a "big bang" like the one that created the universe. Others believe that the universe will end in the solitary deaths of all those stars scattered at an infinite distance from one another in space. I am inclined to accept the second view.

Avoiding the first person can help you avoid wordiness, but when you believe you must use it, you may do so with a good conscience. No rule of written English or good taste holds that you should always avoid saying *I, me, my,* and *mine.*

17c pron

17c Avoiding the Unnecessary Pronoun After a Noun

In the following sentences the pronouns in boldface are redundant and should be omitted.

> George Bush **he** liked to fish.
>
> My mother **she** graduated from college when I graduated from high school.
>
> The newspapers **they** admitted that advertising sometimes influences their editorial policy.

■ **Exercise 17.2** Rewrite the following sentences to eliminate pronoun errors. If a sentence is correct, put a check beside it.

1. He liked to read in the bathtub in the summer and to regulate the water temperature with his toes and to keep the door shut and locked, which was inconvenient for others in the family, since the house had only one bathroom.

2. The movie *Apocalypse Now* was based partly on a novel by Joseph Conrad. It is likely that it suffered because Marlon Brando was so fat in it that it was hard to take him seriously. It looked as if he himself had not taken the movie seriously, and despite the money spent on promoting it, it is clear that it failed to meet expectations about it.
3. As a sequel to *Gone with the Wind* the novel *Scarlet* it was a smash commercial hit but reviewers they attacked it for being dull and inconsequential.
4. The house it was small and cramped for a family of four, and my mother and father, they loved each other, and they made the house seem as big as all creation.
5. The readers of this page will forgive this writer perhaps if he indulges himself in a personal recollection of hearing Hank Williams sing at the Grand Ole Opry in Nashvile.

17d
Recognizing the Proper Cases of Pronouns

Pronouns often change their form according to their use in a sentence. The **case** of a pronoun is a form that shows the pronoun's grammatical relation to other words in the sentence. English has only three cases—the *subjective* (sometimes called the *nominative*), the *possessive* (sometimes called the *genitive*), and the *objective* (sometimes called the *accusative*).

Indefinite pronouns (*anybody, everybody;* see p. 100), the pronoun *it,* and the pronoun *you* change form only for the *possessive* case. We speak of *anybody's* guess, *its* color, and *your* writing. The pronouns *I, we, he, she, they,* and *who* change form in each of the three cases.

PERSONS AND CASES OF PRONOUNS

Personal pronouns	**Singular**	**Plural**
Subjective		
First person	I	we
Second person	you	you
Third person	he, she, it	they

PERSONS AND CASES OF PRONOUNS (*Continued*)

Personal pronouns	**Singular**	**Plural**
Possessive		
First person	my, mine	our, ours
Second person	your, yours	your, yours
Third person	his, her/hers, its	their, theirs
Objective		
First person	me	us
Second person	you	you
Third person	him, her, it	them
Relative pronouns		
Subjective	who	who
Possessive	whose	whose
Objective	whom	whom

Using the Subjective Case

Pronouns that act as subjects or as subject complements are in the *subjective case.*

He and **I** read books all summer long.

She was the candidate **who** I thought deserved the victory.

17d pron

It could have been **anyone.**

Mark's best friends were **she** and **I.**

Leave the message for **whoever** comes into the house first.

Notice that the subject of a dependent clause is always in the subjective case, even when the dependent clause serves as the object of another clause. *Who* and *whom, whoever* and *whomever,* are likely to give you the most trouble. When in doubt, find the verb of the dependent clause. Its subject will be *who,* even if *who* in the independent clause is the recipient of the action or the object of a preposition.

Using the Possessive Case

Pronouns that show ownership or a special relation are in the *possessive case.*

Their cat climbed up on **his** roof and ate **our** bird.

Her critics were louder than **her** admirers.

My uncle was **my** only relative **whose** tastes were like **mine.**

The decision was **theirs** to make after we had made **ours.**

Notice that personal pronouns in the possessive case have two forms—*my* and *mine,* for example. The first form is an adjective—**my** books. The second form actually means *my ones* and stands alone as a subject complement. *Mine,* in the first-person singular, is the only subject complement that does not end in *-s.*

Those books are **mine.**

The towels are **theirs.**

His is the only pronoun that is the same as both adjective and complement.

These are **his** books.

The books are **his.**

Notice also that, unlike nouns, pronouns in the possessive case do not add *-'s. It's* is not the possessive of *it;* it is a contraction for *it is. Who's* is a contraction for *who is.*

Using the Objective Case

Pronouns that are indirect objects, direct objects, or objects of prepositions are in the *objective case.*

The company gave **her** a contract to design the building.

The team chose **me.**

Just between **you** and **me,** I thought the play was terrible.

They believed **him** to be better qualified.

She asked **him** to call **her** that evening.

She wondered to **whom** she should give the spices.

17e Using Pronouns Correctly

The checklist below provides useful hints for correct pronoun use in places that sometimes give writers trouble.

✓ CHECKLIST 17.1: SOME USEFUL PRONOUN RULES

ESL 1

- The subject of a dependent clause is always in the subjective case, even when the dependent clause serves as the object for another clause.

  Dr. Hiromichi promised the prize to **whoever** made the best grades.

  She was the writer **who** I thought deserved to win the Pulitzer Prize.

ESL 3

  Leave the message for **whoever** comes into the house first.

  The child **who** we believed had fallen from the bridge in fact had jumped to retrieve her ball.

- Objects of prepositions, direct objects, and indirect objects always take the objective case.

  She called **him** and **me** fools.

  It was a secret between **you** and **me.**

  A package arrived for Beverly and **him.**

  The old man pushed Rocco and **her** aside and then hobbled down the stairs.

  She glared at Pei Ching and **me.**

  She gave the driver and **me** quite a lecture on road safety and courtesy.

  Who's kicking **whom?**

17e pron

- When a noun follows a pronoun in an appositive construction, use the case for the pronoun that you would use if the noun were not present. Note that in these examples the presence of the noun does not change the case of the pronoun.

  He gave the test to **us** students.

  Freedom of speech is very important to **us** lawyers.

  We students said that the test was too hard.

  We lawyers must protect freedom of speech.

- *Than* and *as* often serve as conjunctions introducing implied clauses. In these constructions, we understand the idea that follows a pronoun at the end of a sentence. The case of the pronoun depends on how the pronoun is used in the clause we would write if we expressed the thought. (Implied clauses are sometimes called elliptical clauses.)

  Throughout elementary school, Elizabeth was taller than **he.**

  I always thought I was smarter than **she.**

  The Sanchezes are much richer and more miserable than **they.**

- Differences in case can cause differences in meaning. In the first sentence below, *Odetta* likes *Jorge* more than *I* like Jorge. In the second sentence, *Odetta* likes *Jorge* more than *she* likes *me.*

✓ CHECKLIST 17.1: SOME USEFUL PRONOUN RULES *(Continued)*

Notice how the difference in case changes the meanings of these two sentences.

Odetta likes *Jorge* more than **I.**

Odetta likes *Jorge* more than **me.**

- Pronouns that are the subjects or the objects of infinitives take the objective case.

They thought **her** to be an excellent choice for department head.

I believe **them** to be tedious and ordinary.

Lincoln decided to consult Johnson and **him.**

The conference leaders wanted to choose Martinez and **her.**

- Use the possessive case before gerunds. Use the subjective or objective case with present participles used as adjectives.

Gerund (an *-ing* verb form used as a noun; see p. 115)

His returning the punt ninety-six yards for a touchdown spoiled the bets made by the gamblers.

Her hanging a light above the painting softened the reds and darkened the blues.

Present participle

They remembered **him** laughing as he said goodbye.

Through the wall they heard **him** sighing with pain.

- Pronouns agree in case with with the nouns or pronouns with which they are paired.

Compound

He and Juan Sebastian del Cano sailed around the world.

She and Carla ran a design studio.

Appositive

The captain chose two crew members, **her** and **me,** to attempt the rescue.

The state honored two women, Carla and **her,** for their contribution to the project.

The last two crew members on board, **he** and **I,** drew the first watch.

Two teachers in the audience, my mother and **I,** whistled through our fingers.

■ **Exercise 17.3** Circle the correct pronoun within the parentheses in the following sentences.

1. He wrote the book for Nini, for (she, her) of the quick quip.
2. Of all the English kings, Henry VIII was the one (who, whom) I think was most cruel.
3. Between her and (I, me) arguments never occurred.
4. I had no objection to (she, her) walking across the country.
5. The candidates seemed to most Americans, including (I, me), to represent a choice between foolishness and stupidity.
6. They were both scheduled to speak—Brian and (he, him).
7. Jackson is the sculptor (who, whom) I believe to be worthy of the Sting Memorial Award.
8. Clark Gable played the same role again and again for (whoever, whomever) directed him.
9. (Whoever, Whomever) wins the Student Council election is unimportant to you or (I, me).
10. Eisenhower was the president for (who, whom) the college was named.
11. Elizabeth got better grades in algebra than (I, me).
12. (We, Us) students had bought a block of tickets to the hockey game.
13. Henry, Jason, and (I, myself) were selected to review the honors policy.
14. Leroy expected the culprit to be (I, me).
15. Beth watched (she, her) struggle to hold back tears.
16. Professor Wu wasn't as strict with Martha and (I, me) as (we, us) feared.
17. Everyone but Justin and (I, me) made it back to the bus on time.
18. Donald wouldn't think of letting (we, us) women help clear the table.
19. The young boy (who, whom) had stolen the parking place walked swiftly.
20. My father disapproved of (me, my) voting for a Democrat.

CHAPTER 18

ADJECTIVE AND ADVERB MODIFIERS

Adjectives and adverbs are describing words. Because they qualify the meanings of other words, we say that they *modify* other parts of speech.

Adjectives tell us what kind or how many. Adverbs tell us where, when, why, and how. Adjectives modify nouns and pronouns; they do not modify anything else. Adverbs modify verbs (including verb phrases), adjectives, other adverbs, and sometimes whole sentences.

18a
Modifying Nouns and Pronouns with Adjectives

You can identify adjectives by locating words that answer one or more of these questions about nouns or pronouns: Which one? How many? What color? What size? What kind?

The adjectives in the following sentences are in boldface.

The road was **long, hard,** and **twisting.**

She was a **brilliant** architect and a **good** tennis player.

The **red** Buick belonged to my aunt.

The **six large** men were brothers.

Writing is always **difficult.**

You may use adjectives before or after the noun or pronoun they modify.

The building, **ugly** and **tall,** burned down last night.

The **tall, ugly** building burned down last night.

The **old** car, **battered** and **rusty,** finally died.

Present and past participles of verbs often serve as adjectives:

Running hard, the bank robber fired back over his shoulder at the police.

The trip was both **exhausting** and **rewarding.**

The **gathering** night was filled with stars.

Buried alive for days, he survived to tell about the earthquake.

Tired and **discouraged,** she dropped out of the marathon.

A noun can be used as an adjective.

Cigarette smoking harms your lungs.

People who drive six miles for a six-pack do not help the **energy** crisis.

The **Marshall** Plan helped rebuild Europe after World War II.

Adjectives can also serve as nouns. All the words in boldface in the sentence below are normally adjectives, but here they clearly modify a noun that is implicit though not stated: *people* or *persons.* The words therefore assume the function of the implicit noun and become nouns themselves.

The **unemployed** are not always the **lazy** and the **inept.**

Using Adjectives After Linking Verbs

A linking verb, usually a form of *to be,* always links a subject with an adjective or a noun that adds to the description of the subject.

Charles was **fast** and **reliable.**

The road became **difficult.**

Avoiding Jargon

Bureaucratic jargon teems with nouns used as adjectives when perfectly good adjectives are available or when the sentence is better recast in standard English. Be careful when you use nouns as adjectives: it's easy to pile them up.

Jargon: An **opposition education** theory holds that children learn Latin best under strict **discipline** conditions.

Revised: An alternative theory of education holds that children learn Latin best when strict discipline is enforced.

In the hands of a seasoned bureaucrat, a multitude of nouns used as adjectives can serve much the same function as the passive voice (see 16d): it can obscure facts that the writer prefers not to make clear.

Pursuant to the environmental protection regulations enforcement policy of the Bureau of Natural Resources, special management area land use permit issuance procedures have been instituted.

We may surmise that the bureau is issuing permits for use of lands designated as "special management areas." But what are "special management areas"? They are ecologically fragile lands that the government had decided to protect against development. In other words, the bureau is inviting firms that want to develop those lands to go ahead and do so now. They need only secure a permit, which the bureau is prepared to issue to them. The bureau's "policy" is to ignore regulations established to protect the environment. The bureaucrat who wrote the statement knows that the developers' lawyers will understand it and that the public will not.

■ Exercise 18.1

1. Write a sentence in which the adjective *powerful* appears before a noun subject and the adjectives *frightening* and *fierce* appear as subject complements.
2. Write a sentence in which the adjective *cheerful* is used in a phrase immediately after the noun or pronoun that it modifies.
3. Write a sentence in which the adjective *reckless* is used as a noun.
4. Write a sentence in which the adjective *dreamy* is used to modify the subject.
5. Write a sentence in which the noun *flower* is used as an adjective.

18b Using Adverbs to Modify Verbs, Adjectives, and Other Adverbs

Adverbs modify verbs, adjectives, and other adverbs. They answer the questions When? Where? How? How often? How much? To what degree? Why?

The child ran **quickly** into the house.

The game was **hotly** contested.

The water was **brilliant** blue and **icy** cold.

He spoke **more** slowly at the end than at the beginning.

Yesterday she was in Chicago.

The lamp is right **there.**

ESL 14

He came **painfully** to the door.

She **seldom** comes to visit anymore.

We were **greatly** relieved to receive your letter.

She was **completely** surprised at the results.

Dickens mixed humor and pathos **better** than any other English writer after Shakespeare; **consequently** he is still read by millions.

Most adverbs are formed by the addition of *-ly* to the adjective form, but adverbs may also end in *-wise, -where,* or *-ward.* And many adverbs have no special ending. Among them are *anew, soon, never, ever, almost, already, well, very, often, rather, yesterday,* and *tomorrow.*

The surest way to recognize adverbs is by understanding how they work in a sentence.

18c adj/adv

■ **Exercise 18.2** Fill in the blanks in the following sentences with adverbs that make sense.

1. She waited ________ at the airport for the team to make its way ________ home.
2. Lincoln was ________ witty, but he was also ________ sad.
3. ________ the sun was shining when I got up, and a great blue heron flew ________ over the waters of the lake.
4. Doctors have ________ accused boxing of being responsible for serious brain injuries among fighters.
5. Gina moved ________ slowly into the room.

18c
Using Adjectives and Adverbs Appropriately

As modifiers, adjectives and adverbs have related but distinct functions. To avoid potential problems, pay attention to these special cases.

Avoiding Adjectives When Adverbs Are Called For

In common speech we sometimes use adjectival forms in an adverbial way; in writing, this colloquial usage should be avoided.

Nonstandard: He hit that one **real good,** Howard.
Both *real* and *good* are adjectives, but they are used here as adverbs, *real* modifying *good* and *good* modifying the verb *hit.*

Revised: He hit that one to the warning track, Howard.

Nonstandard: She **sure** made me work hard for my grade.
The adjective *sure* here tries to do the work of an adverb modifying the verb *made.*

Revised: She certainly made me work hard for my grade.

Using Adverbs and Adjectives with Verbs of Sense

Verbs of sense (*smell, taste, feel,* and so on) can be linking or nonlinking. You must decide whether the modifier after a verb of sense serves the verb (adverb) or the subject (adjective). Study the following examples:

Adverb: The dog smelled **badly.**

Here the sentence means that the dog had lost its sense of smell and could not track anything.

18c adj/adv

Adjective: The dog smelled **bad.**

Here the sentence says that the dog needed a bath.

Adverb: I felt **badly.**

The speaker is saying that her sense of touch was bad, perhaps because her fingers were numb.

Adjective: I felt **bad** because she heard me say that her baby looked like a baboon.

The speaker is saying, "I felt that I was bad because she heard me make such a terrible remark." A similar expression would be this: "I felt *guilty* because she heard me make that remark." You would not say "I felt *guiltily* because I hurt her feelings."

Distinguishing Adjectives and Adverbs Spelled Alike

Some words have the same spelling in adjective and adverb forms. Not every adverb is an adjective with *-ly* tacked to the end of it. In standard English, many adverbs do not require the *-ly,* and some words have the same form whether they are used as adjectives or as adverbs. When you are in doubt, consult your dictionary (see p. 200).

WORDS THAT ARE BOTH ADJECTIVES AND ADVERBS

Adjective	**Adverb**
fast	fast
hard	hard
only	only
right	right or rightly
straight	straight

■ **Exercise 18.3** In each of the following sentences, locate the words misused as adjectives and put the proper adverbs in their place or vice versa. You may simplify the sentence by eliminating the misused adjective or adverb.

18c adj/adv

1. I felt really badly because he took my advice about seeing the film and hated every minute of it.
2. He did terrific on the exam, and I was real unhappy about his success.
3. John sure felt good because he ran so fast in the race.
4. McDonald looked greedy at the fried chicken on his neighbor's plate and decided he would go to Kentucky real fast.
5. She sat still while the poisonous snake twined silent in the arbor just over her head, but she was right scared.

■ **Exercise 18.4** Fill in the blanks in the sentences below with any adverb that makes sense. Avoid the easy choices of *very, well,* and *badly.*

1. As the rains grew heavier, the houses were ________ damaged by the flood.
2. The procession wound ________ through the narrow streets and across the square, where the police had ________ blocked off traffic.

3. One by one the graduates paraded _______ across the stage, shook hands _______ with the college president, received their diplomas, and stood _______ for a moment while relatives snapped their pictures.
4. Despite their _______ competitive spirit the skaters made friends _______ with other contestants for the pairs final title.
5. Jokes are _______ funny because we do not expect the punch line.

18d
Using the Comparative and Superlative Degrees of Adjectives and Adverbs

Adjectives and adverbs are often used to compare. Usually an *-er* or an *-est* ending on the word or the use of *more* or *most* along with the word indicates the degree, amount or quality.

The simplest form of the adjective or the adverb is the **positive** degree, the form used when no comparison is involved. This is the form you find in the dictionary.

Adverb: The dog ran **quickly** out of the house. (*adverb*)

Adjective: The dog was **quick.** (*adjective*)

18d adj/adv

The **comparative** degree is used when two things are being compared. You can form the comparative degree of many adjectives by adding the suffix *-er,* or by using the adverb *more* or *less* with the positive form. The adverb *more* or *less* is also used to form the comparative of most adverbs.

Adverb: The dog was **quicker** than the rabbit.

Adverb: The dog was **more quick** than the rabbit.

Adjective: The dog ran **more quickly** than the rabbit.

Adjective: The rabbit ran **less quickly** than the dog.

Use the **superlative** degree of both adjectives and adverbs when you compare more than two things. You can form the superlative of an adjective by adding the suffix *-est* to the positive form, or by using the adverb *most* or *least* with the positive form. The adverb *most* or *least* is used to form the superlative degree of an adverb.

Adjective: She was the **happiest** of the three women.

Adjective: George was the **most gloomy** person I ever knew.

Adverb: They sang **most happily** when they had eaten well.

Some adjectives and adverbs are irregular. They change form to show degree.

FORMS OF IRREGULAR ADJECTIVES AND ADVERBS

Positive	Comparative	Superlative
bad	worse	worst
good	better	best
little	less	least
many/much	more	most
far	farther	farthest

Some Rules for Using Degrees

18d adj/adv

- Do not use the superlative for only two things or units.

  Not: Of the two brothers, John was **quickest.**

  But: Of the two brothers, John was **quicker.**
- Do not use the comparative and superlative degrees with absolute adjectives. **Absolutes** are words that in themselves mean something complete or ideal, such as *unique, infinite, impossible, perfect, round, square, destroyed,* and *demolished.* If something is *unique,* it is the only one of its kind. We cannot say, "Her dresses were *more unique* than his neckties." Either something is unique or it is not. "The answer to your question is *more impossible* than you think," is also wrong. Something is either possible or impossible; it cannot be *more* or *less* impossible.
- Avoid using the superlative when you are not making a comparison.

  Dracula is the **scariest** movie!

  The scariest movie ever filmed? The scariest movie you have ever seen? The scariest movie ever shown in town? In common speech, we frequently use expressions such as *scariest movie* or *silliest thing* when we are not in fact comparing the movie or the thing with anything else. In writing, such expressions lack the vocal emphasis we can give them when we speak. They become merely wordy and imprecise, taking up space without conveying any meaning.

- Avoid adding an unnecessary adverb to the superlative degree of adjectives.

  Not: She was the **very** brightest person in the room.

  But: She was the brightest person in the room.

  Not: The interstate was the **most** shortest way to Nashville.

  But: The interstate was the shortest way to Nashville.

- Avoid making illogical comparisons with adjectives and adverbs. Illogical comparisons occur when writers leave out some necessary words.

  Illogical: The story of the *Titanic* is more interesting than the story of any disaster at sea.

  This comparison makes it seem that the story of the *Titanic* is one thing and that the story of any disaster at sea is something different. In fact, the story of the *Titanic* is about a disaster at sea. Is the story of the *Titanic* more interesting than itself?

  Illogical: Building houses with brick is harder than lumber.

  What is being compared here? Is the *act* of building harder than the *thing* we call lumber? The comparison is illogical because acts are different from things and so cannot be compared with them.

  Illogical: Mr. Lincoln's speech was shorter than Mr. Everett.

  In this sentence, one might suppose that Mr. Everett was six feet tall but that Mr. Lincoln's speech was only five feet.

18e
Avoiding the Overuse of Adjectives and Adverbs

Too many adjectives or adverbs can weaken the force of a statement. Strong writers put an adjective before a noun or pronoun only when the adjective is truly needed. They rarely put more than one adjective before a noun unless they need to create some special effect or unless one of the adjectives is a number or part of a compound noun, such as *high school* or *living room.*

Weak

The **sleek-looking high-speed jet** airplane has radically altered the **slow** and **unsteady** rate at which our **current Western** technology and today's **apparent** culture have spread.

The **clean** and brightly **lit** dining car left a **cold** and **snowy** Moscow well stocked with **large** and **sweet fresh red** apples, **many** oranges, **long green** cucumbers, **delicious chocolate** candy, and **countless** other **well-loved** delicacies.

Improved

The jet has radically altered the rate at which **Western** technology and culture have spread.

—JAMES BURKE

The dining car left Moscow well stocked with **fresh** apples, oranges, cucumbers, **chocolate** candy and **other little** delicacies.

—HEDRICK SMITH

Adverbs should be used in the same careful way. Instead of piling them up, use strong verbs that carry the meaning.

Weak: The train **went very swiftly** along the tracks.

Improved: The train **sped** along the tracks.

■ **Exercise 18.5** In the following sentences, use any adjectives you choose to fill in the blanks. But whatever adjective you write in must be in the proper degree—positive, comparative, or superlative. Be adventurous. Avoid common adjectives such as *good* and *bad*.

1. On the court Magic Johnson was a ______ dribbler than many other players in the NBA.
2. Alaska is the ______ of all the states.
3. Lassie is a ______ actor than John Travolta.
4. Station wagons are ______.
5. Percy owned the ______ leather vest in his motorcycle gang.
6. Country music recordings now are generally the ______ among a range of musical offerings.
7. Rain is generally ______ than snow or ice.
8. The president of the university is ______ than the faculty.
9. The sea is ______ than the desert.
10. Dick Tracy was ______ than Batman.

18e
adj/adv

■ **Exercise 18.6** Revise the sentences below to correct inappropriate use of adjectives and/or adverbs.

1. She felt badly that her mother was more prettier than she was.
2. Hopefully, I can find a real good job when I graduate.
3. Her long, thin, red-nailed fingers quickly raced silently over the polished white ivory keyboard.
4. Run to town real quick and find Dr. Clemson.

5. The most happiest days of my life were spent when I was a tiny tough troublemaking child on the large, wide-open ranch owned by my uncle Huey.

■ **Exercise 18.7** Eliminate as many adjectives as you can in the following paragraph:

The old, bent, wrinkled man stood still and thoughtful on the crowded edge of the crowded, busy, narrow street and looked down to the tall, lighted, brick building which loomed up in the thick, damp, gray mist of the early, chill, autumn, overcast, threatening night. He felt in the deep, warm, dark pocket of his new wool black tweed overcoat for the hard, blue, loaded automatic pistol and checked the tiny metal safety catch on the lethal, heavy, criminal weapon. The important, threatening, dangerous gun was there, ready, waiting, eager to be fired.

CHAPTER

19

AVOIDING MISPLACED MODIFIERS

In English, clarity depends on the word order within sentences. We expect most adjectives and adjectival clauses and phrases to stand as close as possible to the words they modify. But other words often separate adverbs and adverbial phrases from the words or phrases they modify. We say, "They began their job yesterday," not "They began yesterday their job." And we also write sentences such as "When she was young, she played softball every Saturday," in which the adverbial clause and the simple adverb are separated from the verb by other words.

We have to know when we can separate modifiers from the words or phrases they modify and when we cannot. And in general we can separate adverbs and adverbial phrases from the words they modify more easily than we can separate adjectives from the words they modify.

Yet even adverbs and adverbial phrases can be misplaced. An adverbial phrase ordinarily modifies the nearest verb. It may be separated from that verb by other words, but English idiom joins adverbs and adverbials to the nearest possible verb. When another verb gets in the way, our writing gets into trouble, as in the following sentences from a humorous squib in The *New Yorker.*

> Wednesday morning, Lee's oldest son Mike signed a national letter of intent with Indiana University to play football for the Hoosiers in the family kitchen at 3838 Ashland Drive in West Lafayette.

The writer intended to make the adverbial prepositional phrase *in the family kitchen* modify the verb *signed.* But since it is nearer to the infinitive phrase *to play football,* it seems to modify that phrase, giving the impression that Mike is going to be running for touchdowns over the kitchen sink.

During the lecture, Johanson will describe the discovery of a band of the new species of hominids who appeared to have been killed simultaneously by some disaster with color slides.

The writer has intended to make the prepositional phrase *with color slides* modify the verb phrase *will describe.* But it is nearer to and appears to describe the noun *disaster* and seems to be an adjectival phrase.

These errors should remind you to keep the related parts of a sentence as close to each other as you can. Otherwise you may confuse your readers.

19a
Avoiding Dangling Participles

Introductory participles and participial phrases must modify the grammatical subject of the sentence. Participles that do not modify the grammatical subject are called **dangling** or **misplaced participles.** A dangling participle lacks a noun to modify. Study these examples.

Incorrect

Having studied small-engine repair in night school, fixing the lawn mower was easy.

Driving along Route 10, the sun shone in Carmela's face.

Using elaborate charts and graphs, the audience understood the plan.

Running down the street, the fallen lamppost stopped her suddenly.

Having thought for a long time, the idea of a community patrol group emerged.

The work was hard, sweating over hot machinery, bending in cramped spaces, sometimes mashing his fingers, skinning his knees, twisting heavy wrenches, and getting home late and exhausted every night.

Revised

Having studied small-engine repair at night school, Jane found that fixing the lawn mower was easy.
or
After Jane studied small-engine repair in high school, fixing the lawn mower was easy.

Driving along Route 10, Carmela found the sun shining in her face.
or

As Carmela drove along Route 10, the sun shone in her face.

Using elaborate charts and graphs, the mayor explained the plan to the audience.

or

Because the mayor used elaborate charts and graphs, the audience understood the plan.

Running down the street, she saw the fallen lamppost, which stopped her suddenly.

or

As she ran down the street, the lamppost stopped her suddenly.

Having thought for a long time, the committee finally developed the idea of a community patrol group.

or

After the committee thought for a long time, the idea of a community patrol group emerged.

He worked hard, sweating over hot machinery, bending in cramped spaces, sometimes mashing his fingers, skinning his knees, twisting heavy wrenches, and getting home late and exhausted every night.

Usage Note

Informal usage frequently accepts the following forms, which combine an introductory participle as a modifier of the expletive *it* (see 17a), especially when the participle expresses habitual or general action.

Walking in the country at dawn, it is easy to see many species of birds.

The statement is general, expressing something that might be done by anyone. Many writers and editors would prefer this revision: "Walking in the country at dawn is an easy way to see many species of birds."

When beginning a new exercise program, it is good to have a complete physical examination by a doctor.

The statement is general, and to many writers it seems preferable to an even more informal statement like this one: "When you begin a new exercise program, you should have a complete physical examination by a doctor." But many other writers—perhaps a majority—would revise the sentence to avoid the dangling modifier: "Anyone who begins a new exercise program should have a complete physical examination by a doctor."

■ **Exercise 19.1** Rewrite any of the following sentences that have dangling participles. If a sentence is correct, put a check beside it.

1. Daydreaming about his new job, the doorbell startled him.
2. Working hard through the night, I finished the job by daybreak.
3. Looking up, the long V-shaped flock of geese could be seen by everyone in the valley.
4. Racing through the hall, my nose suddenly detected the acrid smell of smoke.
5. Backed into a corner and hurt, the bell barely saved him.
6. Walking along the street, the city seemed calm.
7. Using a word processor, he was able to revise his paper in a couple of hours and turn in the finished product the next day.
8. Having played hard, the loss was bitter.
9. Taking the child by the hand, the hot dog stand was just a short distance away.
10. Having been aged in an oak barrel for twelve years, he discovered that the wine was exactly to his taste.

19b Avoiding Misplaced Phrases and Clauses

Place phrases and clauses used as modifiers as near as possible to the words they modify.

Prepositional Phrases

Prepositional phrases used as adjectives seldom give trouble. We use them commonly in speech, and these speech habits transfer readily to writing:

> The book **on the table** belongs to me.
>
> We lived in a house **near the school.**

Prepositional phrases used as adverbs are harder to place in sentences, and sometimes writers lead readers astray by misplacing adverbial phrases.

> He saw the first dive bombers approaching **from the bridge of the battleship.**
>
> The multipurpose knife was introduced to Americans **on television.**
>
> He ran the ten-kilometer race from the shopping mall through the center of town to the finish line by the monument **in his bare feet.**

Revised

From the bridge of the battleship, he saw the first dive bombers approaching.

The multipurpose knife was introduced on television to Americans.

In his bare feet he ran the ten-kilometer race from the shopping mall through the center of town to the finish line by the monument.
or
From the shopping mall through the center of town to the finish line by the monument he ran the ten-kilometer race in his bare feet.

Clauses

A misplaced clause is one that modifies the wrong element of the sentence.

Confusing

Professor Peebles taught the course on the English novel that most students dropped after three weeks.

For five years Dixon worked all day as an accountant to support her family and after supper went to night school to study law, which was hard, but finally she got her degree.

Revised

Professor Peebles taught the course on the English novel, a course that most students dropped after three weeks.

For five years Dixon worked all day as an accountant to support her family and after supper went to night school to study law. It was a hard schedule, but she finally got her degree.

■ **Exercise 19.2** Rewrite the following sentences to correct errors in modification.

1. Marco Polo traveled overland to China with his father and his uncle to visit the Mongol Empire, which was very dangerous.
2. He stood in the middle of the room and shouted at everyone in his pajamas.
3. He apologized to his teacher for his paper over the telephone which was smeared with ink and covered with egg and coffee stains.
4. She wrote the outline of her book on the wall in the kitchen with a black crayon.
5. When she was a little girl, she used to lie awake at night wishing that she had a horse in her bedroom.

19c
Placing Adverbs Correctly

ESL 14

Adverbs can modify what precedes or what follows them. Avoid the confusing adverb or adverbial phrase that seems to modify both the element that comes immediately before it and the element that comes immediately after it, as in these examples.

To read a good book **completely** satisfies her.

Changing gears **continually** gives mental exercise to people who ride bicycles.

To speak in public **often** makes her uncomfortable.

Revised

She is completely satisfied when she reads a good book.
or
She is satisfied when she reads a good book completely.

Continually changing gears gives mental exercise to people who ride bicycles.
or
Changing gears gives continual mental exercise to people who ride bicycles.

When she speaks in public often, she feels uncomfortable.
or
Often she feels uncomfortable when she speaks in public.

Be cautious when you use adverbs to modify whole sentences. Here are two examples.

Unfortunately, *The Quiz Kids* lost its popularity as an afternoon game show.

Presumably, the climber was killed in an avalanche three years ago, although his body was never found.

Some authorities maintain that these adverbs modify the entire sentence; others insist that the adverbs modify only the verbs in the clauses where they appear. In either case, the meanings of these sentences are clear. But other adverbs are much more ambiguous when they modify full sentences.

Hopefully he will change his job before this one gives him an ulcer.

Who is doing the hoping? Is it the person who speaks the sentence or the person who is the subject of the sentence?

Revised: We hope he will change his job before this one gives him an ulcer.

Similar confusions occur when other adverbs modify whole sentences:

Briefly, Tom was the source of the trouble.

Does the writer wish to say briefly that Tom was the source of the trouble? Or was Tom briefly the source of the trouble but he then mended his ways?

Revised: To put it briefly, I think Tom was the source of the trouble.

The following sentence does not mean what it says:

Happily, the mad dog fell dead before it could bite anybody.

The grammar of this sentence indicates that the mad dog fell dead very happily before it could bite anybody. The writer doubtless means that people on the street were happy that the mad dog fell dead before it could bite one of them. Why not write that?

19d
mod

■ **Exercise 19.3** Rewrite the following sentences to eliminate the confusion caused by the placement of adverbs. If a sentence is correct, place a *C* beside it.

1. The car starting easily made this the best day of my trip.
2. Hopefully, she will be able to buy another red coat like the one she lost on the train.
3. A scholar who studies often goes to sleep over her books.
4. People who love to criticize books sometimes do not write books themselves.
5. Happily the child ran to the father she had never seen before.
6. His mother only could forgive him.

19d Putting Limiting Modifiers in Logical Places

In speaking we sometimes put modifiers in illogical places, but the sense of what we say is clear from tone of voice, gesture, or general context. In writing, the lack of logic that results from misplacement of modifiers can cause confusion. Limiting modifiers, words such as *merely, completely, fully, perfectly, hardly, nearly, almost, even, just simply, scarcely, only,* must be placed directly before the words or phrases they modify.

Confusing

The **almost** exhausted man finished the marathon.

The restored antique cars paraded proudly through the **completely** admiring town.

Revised

The exhausted man **almost** finished the marathon.

The **completely** restored antique cars paraded proudly through the admiring town.

Confusing

He **only** had one bad habit, but it **just** was enough to keep him in trouble.

They were all **nearly** about to graduate, but they wouldn't **even** send one invitation because all of them decided **almost** that the commencement speaker would insult the intelligence of the audience.

Revised

He had **only** one bad habit, but it was **just enough** to keep him in trouble.

They were **nearly** all about to graduate, but they wouldn't send **even** one invitation because all of them decided that the commencement speaker would insult the intelligence of the audience.

■ **Exercise 19.4** Explain the meaning conveyed by the placement of the adverb in each of the following sentences. Make any revisions necessary to clear up the confusion.

1. The lawyer spoke to her *only* client after he quieted down.
2. The lawyer *only* spoke to her client after he quieted down.
3. The lawyer spoke *only* to her client after he quieted down.
4. *Only* the lawyer spoke to her client after he quieted down.
5. The lawyer spoke to her client *only* after he quieted down.

✔ CHECKLIST 19.1: CHECKING THE PLACEMENT OF MODIFIERS

English depends on word order for clarity. Adjectives and adverbs are best placed next to the words they modify. When you revise sentences, check adjectives and adverbs. If they are awkwardly placed or possibly confusing, move them. Ask yourself these questions.

- Does an introductory participial phrase modify the subject of the sentence?
- Are prepositional phrases placed next to or near the words that they modify?
- Are clauses placed next to the words that they modify?
- Do limiting adverbs appear directly *before* the words or phrases that they modify?
- Do adverbs appearing in the middle of sentences clearly modify only one sentence element?
- If an adverb modifies an entire sentence, is the meaning unmistakably clear?

CHAPTER

20

AVOIDING CONFUSING SHIFTS

To keep your sentences clear and harmonious, you must be consistent in your use of verbs and nouns. Avoid jarring shifts in point of view and sudden outbursts of emotion—what is sometimes called purple prose.

20a Being Consistent in Verb Tenses

Watch out for shifts from one tense to another within paragraphs or within sentences. Some shifts are acceptable; others are not. When you write about the content of any piece of literature, you usually use the present tense. Be careful not to shift out of the present tense when you have decided to use it for such a purpose. Make sure your tenses are consistent not only within sentences, but from one sentence to another. Be especially careful when you quote a passage that is in the past tense. Do not shift your description of the passage into the past tense if you have been using the present. Here is an example:

> David Copperfield **observes** other people with a fine and sympathetic eye. He **describes** villains such as Mr. Murdstone and improbable heroes such as Mr. Micawber with unforgettable sharpness of detail. But David Copperfield **was** not himself an especially interesting person.

Being Consistent in Narrative

Avoid the temptation to lapse into inconsistent tenses when you are telling a story. Sometimes the events you are relating become so vivid to you as you speak or write that you slip into the present tense. The inconsistency may be acceptable in conversation, but it confuses readers.

Inconsistent: The wind **was howling** and **blowing** a hundred miles an hour when suddenly there **is** a big crash, and a tree **falls** into Rocky's living room.

Consistent: The wind **was howling** and **blowing** a hundred miles an hour when suddenly there **was** a big crash, and a tree **fell** into Rocky's living room.

Inconsistent: Every day the parking lot **fills up** by eight in the morning, and commuting students arriving after that **could not find** parking paces.

Consistent: The parking lot **fills up** by eight in the morning, and commuting students arriving after that **cannot find** parking places.

Being Consistent in Successive Clauses

Inconsistency may creep into your writing when you combine present perfect and past perfect tenses with present and past tenses of verbs.

Inconsistent: She **has admired** many strange buildings at the university, but she **thought** that the Science Center **looked** completely out of place.

Consistent: She **has admired** many strange buildings at the university, but she **thinks** that the Science Center **looks** completely out of place.

In writing successive clauses, you must be sure that you take into account the continuing action of the first clause. The thought expressed in the consistent sentence is like this: *She has admired and still admires many strange buildings at the university, but she thinks now that the Science Center looks completely out of place.* Verbs in successive clauses do not have to be in the same tense, but they should follow each other in tenses that make good grammatical sense.

✓ CHECKLIST 20.1: SOME RULES FOR SUCCESSIVE TENSES

- The present tense may be followed by another present tense:

  Dogs **bark** to show that they **are** interested in something, or to show that they **are afraid,** or to announce that someone—perhaps another dog—**is invading** their territory.

- The present tense may be followed by a past tense:

  Michaelson **says** that transistors **made** stereo systems cheaper but **reduced** the fidelity of sound created by vacuum tubes.
- The present can be used with the present perfect.

  Quality control in the American automobile industry **is** a long-standing problem that **has made** millions of Americans **think** that Japanese cars **are** better.
- The present can be used with the future tense:

  We **predict** that word processors **will replace** electric typewriters in most offices by the end of this decade.

✓ CHECKLIST 20.2: TIPS FOR TENSE CONSISTENCY

- Do not use the present tense with the past perfect tense unless a suitable tense follows the past perfect.

  Inconsistent: She swears that she **had registered** her car properly.

  Consistent: She swears that she **had registered** her car properly before she **received** a ticket for having an improper license plate.
- If you are not going to follow the past perfect with a clause that contains a verb in the past tense, change the past perfect tense to a more suitable form.

  She **swears** that she **registered** her car properly.
- The simple past can be followed by another simple past:

  College football **was** so violent early in this century that President Theodore Roosevelt **threatened** to abolish it.
- The simple past can be used with the imperfect:

  Everyone **was** eager to know if she **was going** to enter the fifty-mile road race.
- The simple past can be used with the future:

  They **told** me that the tire shipment **will arrive** next week.
- The simple past should not be used with the present perfect, although in informal speech we sometimes do use the two tenses together.

  She **reports** that she **runs** nine miles every morning.

  She **reported** that she **had been running** nine miles every morning.

■ **Exercise 20.1** Examine the verbs in boldface in the sentences below and make any necessary corrections for consistency in verb tense.

1. Researchers who **experiment** with dolphins **had found** that these creatures **are** as sophisticated and devious as humans, especially in courtship.
2. Bottlenose male dolphins **have formed** social units that **recruited** another group of males, which **helped** wage battle on a third group.
3. These actions **were occurring** as the males **look** for fertile females and **could steal** them from competing bands of dolphins.
4. Scientists at the University of Michigan **have observed** male dolphins surrounding females and **determined** that the males' leaping and somersaulting **are** ways to keep females in line.
5. Oceanographic researchers **have reported** their findings to the National Academy of Sciences and **presented** dramatic evidence to support their assertions.

20b
Being Consistent in Mood

20b shifts

The mood of a verb is a distinguishing form that indicates whether or not an assertion is intended as a statement of fact (see pp. 253–257). The indicative mood makes simple statements or asks simple questions. The conditional mood makes statements that would be true if something else were true. The subjunctive mood conveys a wish, desire, or demand, or makes a statement contrary to fact. It is now used rarely in English. (If I *were* in Rome on Easter morning, I would hear thousands of church bells. I am not in Rome on Easter morning, and I may not be there when Easter comes; so I use the subjunctive mood in the clause *if I were*.)

Avoid inconsistent shifts from the indicative to the conditional or from the conditional to the indicative.

Inconsistent

He **will go** to night school and **would take** a course in hotel management.

ESL 8

If he **goes** to night school, he **would take** a course in hotel management.

If he **were** absent, he **will fail** the course.

Consistent

If he **could go** to night school, he **would take** a course in hotel management.

He **would go** to night school, and he **would take** a course in hotel management, if he **could get** out of jail.

He **will go** to night school and **will take** a course in hotel management if he **gets out** of jail.

If he **is** absent, he **will fail** the course.

If he **were** absent, he **would fail** the course.

■ **Exercise 20.2** Correct the confusing shifts in the following sentences. If a sentence is correct as it stands, put a check by the number.

1. Archeologists have been surveying the earth with satellites, and they found many remnants of a lost city buried in Arabian sands.
2. Mercutio has to die in *Romeo and Juliet,* or else he would have carried the play off from the two young lovers, who are not nearly as interesting as he was.
3. The band hit a sour note, and the drum major gets sore at the tuba section.
4. Children who often are noisy at a concert annoyed their parents.
5. King James I, who died in 1625, had never taken a bath in his adult life, and those who prepared him for burial have to scour his underwear off his body.

20c
Being Consistent in Voice

The voice of a transitive verb is either active or passive. In clauses in the active voice, the subject does the acting; in clauses in the passive voice, the subject is acted upon (see p. 257). Inconsistency in voice sometimes arises from a writer's desire for variety in sentence forms. But when the actor remains the same, do not change voice.

Inconsistent

The Impressionist painters **hated** black. Violet, green, blue, pink, and red **were favored** by them.

The bulldozer **clanked** into the woods and **bit** into the ground. The trees and the earth **were ripped up.**

In each pair of sentences above, the writer uses first active voice then passive voice. The shift is jarring.

Consistent

The Impressionist painters **hated** black. They **favored** violet, green, blue, pink, and red.

The bulldozer **clanked** into the woods, **bit** into the ground, and **ripped up** the trees and the earth.

Note that you can go easily from a linking verb of simple description in the active voice to a verb in the passive voice in the next clause, thereby keeping the focus on the subject of greatest interest.

Today the majority of American Indians **are** poor, uneducated, and unhealthy. They **have been isolated** from the rest of the country, deprived of the benefits of the land that **was taken** away from them by force, and **forgotten** by the people who robbed them.

McNabb **rode** his motorcycle through the plate glass window and **was taken** to the hospital as soon as the ambulance could get there.

The best advice about the passive voice is to use it infrequently and only with good reason.

20d
shifts

20d Being Consistent in Person and Number of Nouns and Pronouns

In speaking and writing in an informal tone, we often use the pronoun *you* instead of the more formal pronoun *one* (see pp. 268–270). Using *you*—addressing the reader in the second person—is perfectly legitimate. What is not legitimate is shifting between *you* and *one* in the same sentence.

Consistent: If **you** smoke cigarettes, **you** run a high risk of getting lung cancer.

Inconsistent: If **one** smokes cigarettes, **you** run a high risk of getting lung cancer.

Here are some other consistent alternatives:

If **one** smokes cigarettes, **one** runs a high risk of getting lung cancer.
or

Anyone who smokes cigarettes runs a high risk of getting lung cancer.
or
People who smoke cigarettes run a high risk of getting lung cancer.

If you address your reader directly as *you,* you may write in the third person from time to time. But you cannot shift from the third person to the second person or from the second person to the third person in the same sentence.

Consistent: **You** will always find good writing to be hard work. **Good writers** never think that their craft is easy.

Inconsistent: **People** flying across the country nowadays discover that **you** can get many different fares to the same destination.

Make pronouns agree with antecedents, but avoid sexist language (see Chapters 11 and 17).

Awkward: **Anyone** who **rides** a bicycle every day will discover that he or she develops some muscles not developed by jogging.

You can substitute consistent plural forms:

People who ride bicycles every day will discover that **they** develop some muscles not developed by jogging.

Or you can avoid the need for a pronoun:

Anyone who rides a bicycle every day will discover that some muscles that are little used in jogging are being developed.

Anyone who rides a bicycle every day will discover that the exercise develops some muscles that are not developed by jogging.

You can make a much more sweeping revision:

Bike riders do not exercise some of the muscles used in jogging and usually discover that they get sore quickly when they try to run around the neighborhood at night.

Or a simpler one:

Daily bicycle riding develops some muscles not used in jogging.

20e
Being Consistent in Point of View

Maintain a consistent point of view in your writing. **Point of view** is the position from which you present information. Note the example of inconsistency here:

> He sat idly in his seat and looked down at the land pouring beneath the low-flying plane like some immense sea whose waters reached to the sky. The green of the forest enchanted him. Everything was primitive and nearly unspoiled. Here and there a house stood in a solitary clearing that, from above, looked like a raft afloat on the great ocean of green. He saw it for a moment, and then it was whisked away behind him. In the houses, people were sitting down to supper, unfolding napkins, looking expectantly at the head of the table where the father gravely bowed his head to say grace.

The point of view is of someone in an airplane looking down on the land passing underneath. But in the last sentence we shift to a scene that such a traveler cannot see. The writer should revise the last sentence to match the point of view of the rest of the passage.

> **He could imagine that** in the houses people were sitting down to supper, unfolding napkins, looking expectantly at the head of the table where the father gravely bowed his head to say grace.

■ **Exercise 20.3** Rewrite the following sentences to eliminate confusing shifts. If a sentence is correct as it stands, put a check beside it.

1. American landscape painters of the nineteenth century viewed the American wilderness as the handiwork of God; signs of God's work were seen by them in lakes, mountains, and prairies.
2. Government paperwork costs forty billion dollars a year, and government accountants are working to trim those costs—and making more paperwork as they do so; you can see the problem.
3. When anyone rides the Green River rapids with your glasses on one can have them knocked off, and you won't see the magnificent rock formations.
4. People who take pictures sometimes find that they get tired carrying a camera, and they often stop taking pictures all at once, the way some people stop smoking.
5. Anyone who writes a long letter of complaint is frustrated when they get a form letter in return.

■ **Exercise 20.4** Rewrite the following paragraph to correct the confusing shifts.

> In Thomas More's book *Utopia*, which is the name he gave to an island supposedly located off the coast of the New World, the people of his commonwealth wear unbleached wool, eat together in great halls, punish adultery with death when one is convicted twice of the offense, and allow husbands and wives to inspect each other naked before they are married so one will not be deceived by the other. The Utopians have no individuality. They tried as hard as they could to eliminate passion. More had made no mention of any artists among them.

20f
Avoiding Excessive Emotionalism

You may have strong feelings about a subject, and having discussed some of the issues in an essay, you may be tempted to conclude with a highly charged ending so readers will know where you stand. Emotionalism in writing is almost always a mistake. Readers tend to dismiss the opinions of ranters and to laugh at their "purple prose." You may embarrass even those people who agree with you if you present your opinions in an irrational way. Readers want to like the person who has written the prose they read; otherwise they will not enjoy spending time in the writer's company. Few readers like to spend time with an angry or overwrought or sarcastic person.

Consider the excessive emotionalism in this paragraph:

> Lord Crenshaw strode mightily into the room, his bushy eyebrows looking like forests waving in the mightiest of all God's storms, his cold blue eyes flashing like bolts of lightning as he looked around at the assembled guests. Philippa felt her heart go bang in her chest with a wild emotion, wilder than anything she had ever felt before, wild as the incandescent lava that bursts from a volcano and pours down the mountainside, burning up all the reserve and all the hesitation that she might have felt. This was the famous Lord Crenshaw, dauntless leader of Wellington's right at Waterloo, the bold, brave man who flung his great arms skyward and shouted at his troops to hold fast while all around his gallant head the bullets whizzed and whirled, the thunderhead of a hero whose voice sounded like ten thousand organs booming through ten thousand cathedrals. People nodded gravely to him, knowing his reputation for sudden anger, for

the outburst that could lead to the duel at sunrise that had more than once snuffed out the tender flower of a young life before it could grow and flourish and become a mighty tree. As he entered the room, a silence like that of Judgment Day itself fell over everyone, and it seemed that the world held its breath while he walked to the buffet and thundered a command to the trembling waiter here. "Give me a ham sandwich," he said. "And hold the pickles."

■ **Exercise 20.5** Rewrite the passage about Lord Crenshaw.

✔ CHECKLIST 20.3: ENSURING CONSISTENCY

Lack of consistency in the use of verbs and pronouns and sudden shifts in point of view can distract your reader from what you are saying to how you are saying it. To help ensure consistency, ask yourself these questions as you revise.

Tense

- Are tenses consistent, following one another within sentences in correct and logical sequence?
- Is the mood of each sentence consistent in itself?
- Does the voice used from one sentence to the next serve to keep the emphasis on the subject you want to emphasize?

20f shifts

Pronouns

- Are pronouns consistently formal or informal, with occasional shifts between sentences but no shifts within sentences?

Point of view

- In narratives, is perspective or point of view consistent?
- Has "purple prose" been eliminated?

PART FIVE

UNDERSTANDING PUNCTUATION

CHAPTER

21

SELECTING END MARKS

In English, as in most other languages, the system of **end marks** gives writers a means to separate sentences and signal their purpose. There are three end marks—periods, question marks, and exclamation points.

21a Using the Period

Use a period after a sentence that makes a statement, that gives a mild command or makes a mild request, or that asks a question indirectly. Commands showing strong emotion require exclamation points, discussed in 21c. Direct questions require question marks, discussed in 21b. The use of ellipses is discussed in 26f.

Making Statements

Simple statements end with a period. Most English sentences are simple statements.

Soap melts in the bathtub.

Every year Americans buy more bicycles than cars.

The building burned down last night.

Making Mild Commands

Nonemphatic requests that do not ask a question also end in a period.

Please go with me to the lecture.

Consider your opponent's views carefully when you are making an argument.

Lend me the car, and I'll do the shopping.

Using Indirect Questions

Statements about questions end in a period. In the following examples, the words *why, where, who,* and *how* ask questions indirectly.

People wonder why they have to pay such high taxes.

She asked me where I had gone to college.

They demanded to know who was responsible for the killings.

He wanted to know how I had come to that conclusion.

21b
Using the Question Mark

Use a question mark after a direct question, but not after an indirect question.

Who wrote *One of Ours?*

She wanted to know who wrote *One of Ours.*

If a question ends with a quoted question, one question mark serves for both the question in the main clause and the question that is quoted.

What did Juliet mean when she cried, "O Romeo, Romeo! Wherefore art thou Romeo?"

If a question is quoted before the end of a sentence that makes a statement, place a question mark before the last quotation mark and put a period at the end of the sentence.

"What was Henry Ford's greatest contribution to the industrial revolution in America?" he asked.

"What did the president know and when did he know it?" became the great question of the Watergate hearings.

Occasionally a question mark changes a statement into a question.

You expect me to believe a story like that?

He drove my car into your living room?

To emphasize parts of a series of questions, you can use question marks to separate them into fragments.

And what will we leave behind us when we are long dead? Temples? Amphora? Sunken treasure?

—MARYA MANNES

To express uncertainty about a word or a date, you may use a question mark. In such usage the question mark means that no one can be sure if the date or word is correct. You should never use such question marks merely to show that you have not bothered to look up the information.

Napoleon Bonaparte's brother-in-law, Joachim Murat (1767?–1815), was king of Naples for seven years.

21c Using the Exclamation Point

Use exclamation points (!) sparingly to convey surprise, shock, or some other strong emotion.

The land of the free! This is the land of the free! Why, if I say anything that displeases them, the free mob will lynch me, and that's my freedom.

—D. H. LAWRENCE

Moon, rise! Wind, hit the trees, blow up the leaves! Up, now, run! Tricks! Treats! Gangway!

—RAY BRADBURY

Commands showing strong emotion also use exclamation points.

Stay away from the stove!

Help!

Avoid using too many exclamation marks because readers will not respond with the excitement that an exclamation mark is supposed to call up. For a mild statement, use a comma or a period.

"Ah, what a beautiful morning," she said, throwing the windows open onto the new day.

Socrates said, "Know thyself."

■ **Exercise 21.1** Use periods, question marks, and exclamation points where they are required in the sentences below.

1. He asked if Mr. Kuhns worked for UNESCO or for the FBI
2. "Was it you," she asked, "who painted that wall purple"
3. What did he mean when he asked me, "Is your car an antique"
4. Stolen The money was stolen Right before our eyes, somebody snatched my purse and ran off with it
5. "Help me" he said "I want to learn how to dance"
6. "Isn't the true folk instrument the dulcimer" she asked
7. You expect me to wear a clown costume and ride that unicycle to the mall
8. Pick up the papers Don't you think it's fair for each of us to try to keep this room clean
9. She asked if Sara changed the tire herself or waited for the tow truck to arrive
10. "Where will it end" he asked

■ **Exercise 21.2** Compare the effects of different punctuation marks on the sentences in each pair below. Imagine situations in which you might have used each version of each sentence.

1. **a.** You don't have to tell me.
   b. You don't have to tell me!
   c. You don't have to tell me?
2. **a.** You called the police.
   b. You called the police?
   c. You called the police!
3. **a.** What will you contribute—your time, your talent, or your money?
   b. What will you contribute? Your time? Your talent? Your money?

CHAPTER
22

USING COMMAS

When you speak, you pause to emphasize elements of a sentence and to catch your breath. Commas show these pauses within written sentences. Commas also set off sentence elements, clarify the relations of some sentence elements to others, and serve in standard ways in dates, addresses, and other conventional forms.

22a
Setting Off Independent Clauses

Use commas to set off independent clauses joined by the common coordinating conjunctions *and, but, or, nor, so, yet, for.*

Her computer broke down, and she had to write with a pencil.

He won the Heisman Trophy, but no pro team drafted him.

The art majors could paint portraits, or they could paint houses.

Many Americans did not at first understand jazz, nor did they enjoy listening to it.

He strained to hear her, for she spoke barely above a whisper.

Many people don't understand punctuation, yet they use it correctly anyway.

Printing has made language much less flexible than it once was, so the rules of English grammar will probably not change much from now on.

Some writers do not separate short independent clauses with a comma.

He stayed at home and she went to work.

22b
Setting Off Long Introductory Phrases and Clauses

Use commas after long introductory phrases and clauses. A long introductory phrase or clause is easier to read and understand when a comma separates it from the rest of the sentence.

> After he had sat in the hot tub for three hours, the fire department had to revive him.
>
> If you plan to lose fifty or more pounds, you should take the advice of a doctor.
>
> After standing as a symbol of oppression and fear for twenty-six years, the Berlin Wall at last was broken down.
>
> Hounded by the media after charges and countercharges in their child custody suit, Woody Allen and Mia Farrow have lost the cherished privacy of their personal lives.

Short opening phrases do not have to be set off by commas.

> After the game I drifted along with the happy crowd.
>
> Before the wedding they discussed household duties.
>
> In their coffeehouses eighteenth-century Englishmen conducted many of their business affairs.

Always put a comma after an introductory subordinate clause (as explained on p. 136).

> When we came out, we were not on the busiest Chinatown street but on a side street across from the park.
>
> —MAXINE HONG KINGSTON

> Although the struggle and competition for national or international power may not be explained wholly and simply as analogous to the power drive in personal relations, the personal may provide significant insight into the political.
>
> —KENNETH B. CLARK

Commas also set off introductory interjections, transitional expressions, and names in direct address.

Yes, a fight broke out after the game.

Nevertheless, we should look on the bright side.

To be sure, no one was killed.

Consequently, we will play again next year.

I'll say this, Soon Lee. You understood him first.

Golda, come here right away.

Pablo, why are you doing this?

22c
Setting Off Clauses and Phrases That Modify

Setting Off Absolutes

Any absolute—a phrase that combines a noun with a present or past participle and that serves to modify the entire sentence (as discussed on p. 115)—must be set off from the rest of the sentence by a comma.

The bridge now built, the British set out to destroy it.

The snake slithered through the tall grass, **the sunlight shining now and then on its green skin.**

Setting Off Participial Modifiers

Use commas to set off participial modifiers at the beginning or end of a sentence.

Having learned that she failed the test, Marie had a sleepless night.

Resolving to study harder, the next morning she went directly to the library.

They toiled all night on the engine, grinding and adjusting the valves, polishing the cylinders, cleaning the pistons, replacing the rings, installing a new fuel pump, and putting in new spark plugs and points.

She rushed down the corridor, holding the report in her hand.

We climbed the mountain, feeling the spring sunshine and intoxicated by the view.

■ **Exercise 22.1** Put commas where they are needed in the following sentences.

1. Many graduates seek jobs in media and entertainment fields but opportunities for beginners are limited.

2. Having missed the plane we had to take the bus to New York.
3. Although you need to know grammar exercises in grammar cannot help you write well unless you read a lot.
4. Adrienne was to be sure a steady performer.
5. Nevertheless Greek wine has become popular in America and is often sold in restaurants that he said do not specialize in Greek food.
6. He fired to second his throw beating Henderson to the bag by a step.
7. Pay something if you can but if you cannot go in and enjoy the exhibit anyway.
8. After he had watched television all night long his eyes turned to egg white and his brain became glue.
9. With student populations increasing people with the Ph.D. degree can get jobs again.
10. Acknowledging dramatic increases in world temperature scholars are growing more and more alarmed about global warming.

Setting Off Nonrestrictive Clauses and Phrases

Use commas to set off nonrestrictive clauses and phrases. **Nonrestrictive clauses and phrases** can be lifted out of sentences without any resultant change in the primary meaning of the sentences. The paired commas that set off a nonrestrictive clause or phrase announce that these words provide additional information.

> My dog Lady, who treed a cat last week, treed the mailman this morning.
>
> In the middle of the forest, hidden from the rest of the world, stood a small cabin.

Setting off a phrase or a clause with commas can often change the meaning of a sentence. In the first sentence below, the commas make the clauses nonrestrictive. There was only one commencement speaker, and that speaker happened to be a sleep therapist. In the second sentence, the absence of commas makes us suppose there must have been several speakers. The clause is **restrictive:** it defines the noun and is essential to its meaning. The writer must single out the one who spoke for three hours. By calling the speaker a sleep therapist, the writer says that although there were several speakers, there was only one who was a sleep therapist, and that person was the one who spoke for three hours.

The commencement speaker, who was a sleep therapist, spoke for three hours.

The commencement speaker who was a sleep therapist spoke for three hours.

■ **Exercise 22.2** Use commas to set off clauses and phrases in the following sentences. In some you have a choice. You can make the clause or phrase restrictive by not setting it off with commas, or you can make it nonrestrictive by using commas. In such cases, explain the changes in meaning so that you may be clear as to what they are and why they occur. At times simple common sense will tell you whether to make the clause restrictive or nonrestrictive.

1. The chain saw which had a two-cycle engine gave him a sense of immense power as he took it in his hand and walked into the woods filled with oaks and maples.
2. Fly fishing a difficult and sometimes dangerous sport requires much more skill than fishing with worms from a boat on a still lake.
3. The McCormick reaper which was invented by Cyrus Hall McCormick vastly increased wheat production in the nineteenth century.
4. Farmers who are by profession often isolated and independent have never been drawn in large groups to communism, but they have been attracted by fraternal organizations which have helped them meet together to satisfy social and economic needs.
5. Bats flying mammals found all over the world probably seem odious to many people because they look like rats that fly.

22d
Separating Elements of a Sentence

22d ,

Use commas to separate elements of a sentence to avoid confusion.

Confusing

Every time John raced small boys could leave him behind.

No matter how fast he ran the course was too hard for him.

To John Smith seemed odd.

Revised

Every time John raced, small boys could leave him behind.

No matter how fast he ran, the course was too hard for him.

To John, Smith seemed odd.

22e
Separating Items in a Series

Use commas to separate items in a series. A **series** is a set of nouns, pronouns, adjectives, adverbs, phrases, or clauses joined by commas and—usually—a final coordinating conjunction. Note that American writers put a comma before the coordinating conjunction at the end of a series.

Nouns

Winston Churchill told the English people that he had nothing to offer them but blood, toil, sweat, and tears.

Carrots, sweet potatoes, and other yellow vegetables help prevent cancer.

Pronouns

You, we, and they all have some things in common.

We saw you, him, and her walking on the beach.

Adjectives

My teacher's notes were old, yellow, and worn.

She was a helpful, surprising, and amusing person.

Adverbs

The three outlaws walked slowly, silently, and cautiously into the Sunday school.

She played steadily, intently, and cautiously.

Phrases

The college raised fees, reduced maintenance, fired assistant professors, turned down the heat, but went bankrupt anyway.

Lincoln's great address commended government of the people, by the people, and for the people.

Clauses

The traffic was heavy, the parking lot was full, rain drenched the city, and I was late.

She combed the dog's hair, he started the car, Jack brought down the ribbon, and we were all ready for the show.

22f
Separating Two or More Adjectives

Use commas to separate two or more adjectives before a noun or a pronoun if you can use the conjunction *and* in place of the commas.

Lyndon Johnson flew a short, dangerous combat mission in the Pacific during World War II.
(Lyndon Johnson flew a short **and** dangerous combat mission in the Pacific during World War II.)

Computers are expensive, necessary, and complicated.
(Computers are expensive **and** necessary and complicated.)

If you cannot make an *and* fit easily between the adjectives, omit the comma.

A devastating civil war erupted following the government's collapse.

Six thin green pines stood against the evening sky.

Four old red coats lay piled in a corner.

Adjectives preceding the noun they modify do not require a dividing comma when they mention color, size, age, location, or number. But if you mention several colors or sizes or numbers before nouns, separate the adjectives with commas:

The auto industry first painted its cars a universal black, but now assembly lines turn out thousands of green, silver, gold, blue, crimson, tan, gray, and brown cars.

22g
Setting Off Direct Quotations

Use a comma with quotation marks to set off a direct quotation from the clause that names the source of the quotation.

When the source comes first, the comma goes before the quotation marks. When the quotation comes first, the comma goes before the last quotation mark.

> She said, "I'm sorry, but all sections are full."
>
> "But I have to have the course to graduate," he said.
>
> "A rule is a rule," she said sweetly, "and you will just have to postpone your graduation."

No comma is used if the quotation ends in a question mark or an exclamation point.

> "Do you believe in grades?" he asked.
>
> "Believe in them!" she cried. "I've had them."

In some cases, a colon can be used before a quotation (26a).

■ **Exercise 22.3** Place commas where they belong in the following sentences.

1. The old gray mare is not the superb creature she used to be says the old song.
2. Three happy little children came to the door shouting "Trick or treat!"
3. The hospital smelled of floor wax linen and iodine.
4. She righted the boat ran up the sail grabbed the rudder and flew before the wind.
5. The storm broke suddenly and furiously the lightning crashed from a black sky and the cattle ran off into the dark.
6. "North Dakota is sky prairie wheat and hospitality" she said. "You must go there Charles. You will never see colors so pure land so vast or cities so clean."
7. The poor the speaker said commit far more violent crimes than do members of the middle class and the saddest thing he thought is that poor people are most likely to kill or maim members of their own families.
8. To be sure the recession is not limited to America.
9. Nevertheless Elton John's music still thrills audiences of preteenage adolescents young working professionals and the mothers and fathers of people in both those groups.
10. Consuelo you must speak energetically sadly and eloquently.

22h
Using Commas for Special Effect

Sometimes commas help achieve special effects, and sometimes their use is optional.

Substituting for Words

Use a comma to take the place of a word omitted from a sentence. A comma frequently takes the place of the conjunction *and,* and in some constructions it can take the place of other words as well.

> Power staggers forward, then falls facedown in the dust.
>
> —PHILIP CAPUTO

The comma can also take the place of *and* in a series.

> The joke was stale, flat, vulgar.

In sentences that express a contrast, the comma can stand for several words.

> Lombard the actress was funny, not sophisticated.
>
> She said her cat was big, bright, and fast, not economical.

Providing Emphasis

Use commas to give special emphasis to words and phrases, even when commas are not grammatically necessary. Here commas create the pauses that would occur if you were speaking the sentences aloud.

> It seems impossible to get a saint, or a philosopher, or a scientist, to stick to this simple truth.
>
> —D. H. LAWRENCE

> He found hamlets of three decaying houses with the corrugated iron of their roofs grinding and clanking in a hot wind, and not a tree for miles.
>
> —WILLIAM GOLDING

Setting Off Parenthetical Elements

Use paired commas to set off parenthetical elements. **Parenthetical elements** are words, phrases, or clauses set within sentences which add further description to the main statement the sentence makes. Always set such elements off by paired commas—a comma at the beginning of the element and another at the end.

> Brian Wilson, however, was unable to cope with the pressures of touring with the Beach Boys.
>
> Senator Cadwallader, responding to his campaign contributions from the coal industry, introduced a bill to begin strip mining operations in Yellowstone Park.
>
> Our Latin teacher, Mr. Harrison, was devoted to making us love the language.
>
> Jeannine is, we agree, a great editor.

22i
Using Commas with Numbers, Names, and Dates

Commas play a special role in clarifying numbers, place names, and dates.

Separating Parts of Place Names and Addresses

Use a pair of commas to separate parts of place names and addresses.

> At Cleveland, Ohio, the river sometimes catches fire.

The comma separates the city, Cleveland, from its state, Ohio. Another comma comes after Ohio to set off the state from the rest of the sentence.

Commas set off pairs of an address in sentences and in addresses on letters and envelopes.

> He lived at 1400 Crabgrass Lane, Suburbia, New York.
>
> My address is:
> 63 Oceanside Drive, Apartment 3
> Knoxville, TN 37916

Separating Parts of Dates

Use paired commas in dates when the month, day, and year are included.

On June 6, 1993, my parents reaffirmed their marriage vows in St. Patrick's cathedral.

On October 17, 1989, the largest earthquake in America since 1906 shook San Francisco.

No comma is necessary when the day of the month is omitted.

Germany invaded Poland in September 1939.

British and European writers use a form of the complete date that requires no comma at all.

She graduated from college on 5 June 1980.

Separating Digits in Numbers

Commas separate digits by hundreds except for years and references to page numbers.

Jackson received 647,276 votes in the 1828 presidential election.

The entry for Tennessee is on page 2304.

✔ CHECKLIST 22.1: AVOIDING UNNECESSARY COMMAS

- Do not separate subject, verb, object. A comma should not separate a subject from its verb or a verb from its object or complement unless a nonrestrictive clause or phrase intervenes.

  Faulty

  With trembing hand, the child grasped the spoon.
  The tulips that I planted last year, suddenly died.

  Correct

  With trembling hand the child grasped the spoon.
  The tulips that I planted last year, which seemed to be doing well, suddenly died.

- Do not separate prepositional phrases from what they modify. A prepositional phrase that serves as an adjective is not set off by commas from the noun or pronoun that it modifies.

  Faulty: The best part, of the meal, is coffee.

  A prepositional phrase that serves as an adverb is not set off from the rest of the sentence by commas.

  Faulty: He swam, with the current, rather than against it.

- Do not divide a compound verb with a comma.

  Faulty: He ran, and walked twenty miles.

  But if the parts of a compound verb form a series, set off the parts of the verb with commas.

  He ran, walked, and crawled twenty miles.

- Do not use a comma after the last item in a series unless the series concludes a cause or phrase set off by commas.

  He loved books, flowers, and people and spent much of his time with all of them.

  Three "scourges of modern life," as Roberts calls the automobile, the telephone, and the polyester shirt, were unknown little more than a century ago.

- Avoid commas that create false parentheses.

  Faulty: A song called, "Faded Love," made Bob Wills famous.

- Do not use a comma to set off a dependent adverbial clause at the end of a sentence. In practice this rule means that you should not use a comma before words such as *because, when, since, while, as, neither,* and *either.*

  Faulty: He looked forward every year to June, because he always made a long bike trip as soon as school was out.

  But if the clause beginning with *because* begins the sentence, follow the rule on p. 313.

  Because he always made a long bike trip as soon as school was out, he looked forward every year to June.

Exercise 22.4 Use commas correctly in the sentences below.

1. The speaker was rude pompous tiresome.
2. She purchased eggs rolls and butter from a small corner store in Cincinnati Ohio on June 7 1993 just before her son's birthday.
3. I shall be thirty on April 7 1994 when I shall be in London England
4. Dugan takes the Ford Martha the Toyota.
5. Water flows over the rocks for a mile then plunges fifty feet into a lake.

Exercise 22.5 Eliminate the unnecessary commas in the following sentences. Be careful! Some of the commas belong where they are. If a sentence is correct as it is written, put a check by it.

1. According to Hedrick Smith of the *New York Times,* life for the average Russian, has been one long round, of corruption, lines, and alcoholism.

2. Events, in Yugoslavia, in the winter and spring, of 1992, made many people wonder if the cold war, was over.
3. A controversial issue, in 1992, was the recession, and whether the country was recovering or falling deeper into a very, unpleasant, economic situation.
4. A story in the Sunday, *New York Times,* of November 26, 1989, held that crack dealers on the street, did not make much money, and were terrorized, by their overlords, in the illegal, drug trade.
5. The Oakland, Athletics, swept the San Francisco, Giants, in the 1989, World Series, despite the disruption, of the earthquake.
6. John Grisham's, *The Firm,* and *A Time to Kill,* were two of the big, paperback best-sellers, of 1992.
7. It is sometimes not easy to tell, when you have drunk, too much beer to drive safely.
8. Since divorce has become common, in America, many children are growing up in homes with only, one parent.
9. With the lessening of restrictions, on travel between East, and West in the 1990s, many people hoped that the East, German athletes would compete, in more athletic contests, in the West.
10. Laptop computers became, much, much smaller than ever, some of them weighing less than three, or four, pounds.

CHAPTER

23

USING SEMICOLONS

The semicolon is a stronger mark of punctuation than the comma, and it can be used to join sentence elements that cannot be joined by a comma alone. Semicolons can join certain independent clauses and set off elements within a series when commas are used within the elements.

23a Joining Independent Clauses

Use a semicolon to join independent clauses, either with or without the help of a coordinating conjunction or a conjunctive adverb.

> Silence is deep as eternity; speech is shallow as time.
>
> —THOMAS CARLYLE

> Before 8000 B.C. wheat was not the luxuriant plant it is today; it was merely one of many wild grasses that spread throughout the Middle East.
>
> —JACOB BRONOWSKI

In each example, two clauses are closely related—one of the reasons for using the semicolon. The writers could have separated the clauses with a period, but they chose semicolons to stress the relation of ideas in the clauses.

In the example below, the semicolon is not necessary, as the independent clauses are joined by the coordinating conjunction *but;* but by reinforcing the pause between clauses, the semicolon adds emphasis to the second one.

> In the first draft I had Bigger going smack to the electric chair; but I felt that two murders were enough for one novel.
>
> —RICHARD WRIGHT

In this example, a semicolon used by itself between two clauses implies a contrast between them.

> Lucy had completed the assignment; Philip had not.

Often we express such contrasts in **elliptical constructions,** in which commas substitute for words left out that are clearly understood.

> In America, traffic problems are caused by cars; in China, by bicycles.
>
> In the Middle Ages, many children were abandoned by their parents; by the nineteenth century, comparatively few.

Use a semicolon to join independent clauses separated by a conjunctive adverb. Conjunctive adverbs such as *however, nevertheless, moreover, then,* and *consequently* connect ideas between clauses, but they cannot work without the right punctuation. For these sentences, place a semicolon before the conjunctive adverb, and a comma after it.

> He had biked a hundred miles in ten hours; nevertheless, he now had to do a marathon.
>
> Sheila had to wait at home until the plumber arrived to fix the water heater; consequently, she was late for the exam.

■ **Exercise 23.1** Review the following sentences for the proper use of semicolons. Supply semicolons where they are needed. Eliminate semicolons that are incorrectly used. If a sentence is correct as it stands, place a check beside it.

1. She was unable to keep the appointment; since she was delayed in traffic; because of the wreck.
2. The sun is our most potent source of energy, nevertheless, research in harnessing solar power has gone slowly.
3. The United States and Canada have relatively few varieties of poisonous snakes; but the climate is warm enough to allow many such snakes to flourish should they be accidentally introduced.
4. Western movies once showed hostile Indians attacking covered wagons drawn up in circles on the plains; although no such attack ever occurred in fact.
5. Videocassette recorders allow many people to rent movies on tape and to play them at home through their television sets moreover, the rental fee for the tape is much less than it woud cost a family to see a movie in a theater.

6. Nuclear war is a horror that no one wants to imagine; yet imagining it may help us prevent it.
7. November is a month that is much abused and often unfairly so; true, the leaves fall, and cold weather begins; but November gives us three holidays—Election Day, Veterans Day, and Thanksgiving.
8. I like Brian De Palma's films, however, they sometimes scare me.

■ **Exercise 23.2** Punctuate the following sentences correctly.

1. Some were satisfied others disgruntled.
2. He needed seven hours of sleep a night she only five.
3. Cancer is more feared heart disease more fatal.
4. In her room there were three pictures in mine one in his none.

23b
Separating Elements in a Series

Use a semicolon to separate elements in a series when some of those elements contain commas. These elements can be a set of nouns, pronouns, adjectives, adverbs, phrases, or clauses.

> They are aware of sunrise, noon and sunset; of the full moon and the new; of equinox and solstice; of spring and summer, autumn and winter.
>
> —ALDOUS HUXLEY

23b ;

> The committee included Dr. Curtis Youngblood, the county medical examiner; Roberta Collingwood, the director of the bureau's criminal division; and Darcy Coolidge, the chief of police.

Use semicolons to separate elements that contain other marks of punctuation.

> The assignment will be to read Leviticus 21:1–20; Joshua 5:3–6; and Isaiah 55:1–10.

■ **Exercise 23.3** For each set below, write a single sentence using semicolons correctly. Make reference to all the people and identify them by their jobs.

1. Dr. Mary A. Carter is a professor of history. Mr. Glenn G. Swenson is a football coach. Dean Sylvia Paoli was the moderator of the discussion. Dr. Carter and Mr. Swenson debated the place of intercollegiate athletics in education.
2. Ronald Martin designs computers. Elizabeth Ingersoll is an architect. Joseph Greenberg is a science teacher in Bradford High School in Fulton, Maine. The three of them led a discussion on the future of home computers in business and education.

■ **Exercise 23.4** Explain the use of the semicolon in each sentence below.

1. George Bush was elected president in 1988; Bill Clinton, in 1992.
2. The company had branches in Cleveland, Ohio; Paris, Tennessee; Del Rio, Texas; and Reno, Nevada.
3. Our guests included John Fox, the administrative dean of the Graduate School; Bill Dean, a good friend; and Tom Fox, John's son.
4. She had appeared in summer stock in *Mary, Mary; The Prisoner of Second Avenue;* and *Come Back, Little Sheba.*
5. He visited us at Thanksgiving 1992 with his sister; afterward we never saw him again.
6. We cooked a large meal together; then we sat down together and ate.
7. Elizabeth claimed to despise Darcy; nevertheless, in the end she married him.
8. Alcohol is the most dangerous drug; nicotine kills almost as many.
9. A little exercise each day can lengthen your life; it can be as little as a walk around the block.
10. He asked me what I wanted; I could not tell him.

CHAPTER

24

USING APOSTROPHES

Apostrophes show possession and indicate omitted letters in words written as contractions. They are used in such a wide variety of ways that they can be confusing. Contractions offer little difficulty, but be sure to learn the difference between the possessive case and the plural form of nouns. The apostrophe is used to form the possessive case of all nouns and of many pronouns. It is not used to form a plural.

24a Showing Possession

Writers can choose among several forms to indicate ownership or possession. In special cases, these forms can also show that an entity has a particular attribute, quality, value, or feature.

Children's toys could mean:
toys *of children*
toys *for children*
toys *belonging to children*
toys *owned by children*
toys *that children own*

Everybody's dreams could mean:
dreams *of everybody*
dreams *for everybody*
dreams *everybody has*
dreams *belonging to everybody*

Most writers would use the first form above without spelling out one of the full phrases. Without such words as *of, for, belonging to,* and *owned by,* only the apostrophe plus *s* (-*'s*) conveys the intended sense of possession. Writers often use possessive forms even when the concept of possession seems uncertain. In the examples above, *everybody* does not possess *dreams* in the same way that *children* possess *toys.* Accepted usage also requires apostrophes with concepts of duration and of monetary value.

an **hour's** wait	two **minutes'** work
a **dime's** worth	five **dollars'** worth

Two elements are usually required to show possession correctly with an apostrophe. Someone or something is the possessor, and someone or something is possessed. The word for the possessor takes an apostrophe, either along with an *-s* or alone if the word already ends in *-s*. The word for person or entity being possessed usually appears just after the word with the apostrophe, as in *Jane's tools*.

THE POSSESSOR AND THE POSSESSED

	Possessor	**Thing, attribute, quality, value, or feature possessed**
the woman'**s** shovel	woman'**s**	shovel
a child'**s** bright smile	child'**s**	bright smile
Juanita'**s** son	Juanita'**s**	son
the robber**s'** clever plan	robber**s'**	clever plan
five dollar**s'** worth	dollar**s'**	worth
everyone'**s** plans	everyone'**s**	plans
babie**s'** books	babie**s'**	books

Sometimes the thing possessed precedes the possessor. Sometimes the sentence may not name the thing possessed, but its identity is clearly understood by the reader. Sometimes we indicate possession by using both the *of* form and an apostrophe plus *s* or a personal possessive pronoun.

The motorcycle is the student**'s.**

Is the tractor Jan Stewart**'s?**

24b

I saw your cousin at Nicki**'s.**

He was a friend of Rocco**'s.**

This dress of Mother**'s** is out of style.

That child of **his** rakes our leaves every fall.

24b Distinguishing Between Plurals and Possessives

Most nouns require *-s* endings to show the plural form: boy/boy*s*; girl/girl*s*; teacher/teacher*s*; song/song*s*. Possessive forms require the apostrophe plus *s* ('s) ending: boy/boy*'s*; girl/girl*'s*; teacher/teacher*'s*. The possessive form and the plural form are not interchangeable.

Incorrect: The teacher's asked the girl's and boy's for attention.

Correct: The teachers asked the girls and boys for attention.

An apostrophe plus *s* at the end of a word makes that word the possessor of something.

■ **Exercise 24.1** Identify each word in the following list as plural or possessive; then use each word correctly in a sentence.

1. a. women	**b.** women's	**c.** woman's
2. a. man's	**b.** men's	**c.** men
3. a. child's	**b.** children	**c.** children's
4. a. cats	**b.** cat's	**c.** cats'
5. a. professor's	**b.** professors	**c.** professors'

■ **Exercise 24.2** In each of the following sentences, underline the word that shows possession and put a check above the word that names the entity possessed. (The entity possessed may be understood but not named.)

1. Plucking feathers on turkeys is not everyone's idea of a good job.
2. If the responsibility is the mayor's, then our citizens' group should push her to act.
3. At Mario's, the waiters serve with elegance; the diner's pleasure is the staff's only concern.
4. She brought me six dollars' worth of flour.
5. They went on a week's vacation together.
6. Gloria's smile welcomes students to the Writing Center.

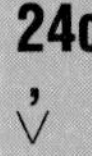

24c Forming Possessives

To form a possessive, add an apostrophe plus *s* to a noun or pronoun, whether it is singular or plural, unless the plural already ends in *s*; then add an apostrophe only.

Noun/pronoun		As a possessive
baby	singular	a baby's smile
men	plural	the men's club

Noun/pronoun		**As a possessive**
Wanda	singular	Wanda's sundae
hour	singular	an hour's time
anyone	singular	anyone's idea
children	plural	the children's papers
Keats	singular	Keats's books
babies	plural	the babies' smiles
companies	plural	the companies' employees

Most writers add both an apostrophe and a final *s* to one-syllable singular nouns already ending in *-s* and to nouns of any number of syllables if the final *-s* is hard (as in *hiss*).

James'**s** adventure, Ross'**s** flag, Elvis'**s** songs

Proper names of geographical locations and some organizations do not take apostrophes.

Kings Point, St. Marks Place, Harpers Ferry, Department of Veterans Affairs

For hyphenated words and compound words and word groups, add an apostrophe plus *s* to the last word only.

my father-in-law'**s** job

the editor-in-chief'**s** responsibilities

the union leader'**s** supporters

To express joint ownership by two or more people, use the possessive form for the last name only; to express individual ownership, use the possessive form for each name.

Felicia and Elias'**s** house

McGraw-Hill'**s** catalog

Felicia'**s** and Elias'**s** houses

the city'**s** and the state'**s** finances

■ **Exercise 24.3** Change each word in parentheses into the correct possessive form by adding an apostrophe alone or an apostrophe plus *s*. A word may require a plural form before you change it to a possessive.

Example:
The two (woman) **women's** cars blocked the driveway.

1. (Mr. Cass) ________ contribution to the primaries brought praise from the (governor) ________ reelection committee.
2. The (assistant editor) ________ idea was to run three (student) ________ biographies in each issue.
3. The (Lady) ________ Auxiliary League drew hundreds to its Fourth of July picnic; (everyone) ________ praise meant that the tradition would continue next year.
4. In (Dickens) ________ novel *Great Expectations,* (Pip) ________ adventures hold every (reader) ________ attention.

■ **Exercise 24.4** Change the structures that show ownership to possessive forms that use apostrophes.

Example:
The announcement of the secretary of state
The secretary of state's announcement

1. the cars of Kim and Thai
2. a patent belonging to my sister-in-law
3. the book written by Julio Garcia and John Youngblood
4. the smile of Doris
5. the value of fifty cents

24d
Showing Omission

Use an apostrophe to indicate letters or numbers left out of contractions or letters omitted from words to show regional pronunciation. In a **contraction**—a shortened word or group of words formed when some letters or sounds are omitted—the apostrophe serves as a substitute for omitted letters.

it's	(for *it is* or *it has*)
weren't	(for *were not*)
here's	(for *here is*)
comin'	(for *coming*)

Apostrophes can also substitute for omitted numbers. "The '50s were a decade of relative calm; the '60s were much more turbulent." But it is usually better to spell out the decades. "Many people claim that the fifties were much more turbulent than we remember and that the sixties only continued trends begun a decade earlier."

✔ CHECKLIST 24.1: AVOIDING INCORRECT APOSTROPHES

A common error is placing apostrophes where they don't belong. As you revise, check your apostrophes.

- Don't use an apostrophe plus *s* ('s) to show the plural of a letter, number, or word used as a word rather than as a symbol of the meaning it conveys. Underline such elements (to indicate that they would be set in italics if your story or essay were set in type) and add -s, without an underline.

  Committee has two *m*s, two *t*s, and two *e*s.

  There are twelve *no*s in the first paragraph.
  He makes his *2*s look like *5*s.

- To show possession with personal and relative pronouns and the pronoun *it,* use the special possessive forms, which never require apostrophes (my/mine, your/yours, his, her/hers, our/ours, their/theirs; whose, and its).

  His cooking won a prize.

  Its fur was shedding.

  They knew **our** secret.

  Is he a friend of **yours?**

  The rake is **hers.**

- When an apostrophe appears with an *s* in a pronoun, the apostrophe probably marks omissions in a contraction.

  It's too hot. (It + is)

  Who's there? (Who + is)

  If **you're** awake, please call. (you + are)

■ **Exercise 24.5** Correct any words in boldface either by removing incorrectly used apostrophes or by adding apostrophes where they belong. Some words are correct and require no change. Place a check above them.

1. **Iris** cat lost **its** way, but one **neighbors** boy helped her find it.
2. There **wasnt** enough attention placed on writing **skills'** in college English curricula in the **60s.**
3. In the word **occurrence,** the two ***c*s** and two ***r*s** confuse even college **students'.**
4. If the **ideas'** are **hers', it's** wise to give her credit for them.
5. Many **childrens parents'** bought these **dolls** before the **companies** recalled them at the **governments** request.

CHAPTER 25

USING QUOTATION MARKS

Quotation marks ("...") always work in pairs. They are used to enclose words, phrases, and sentences that are quoted directly. Titles of short works such as poems, articles, songs, and short stories also require quotation marks, as do some words and phrases that you wish to use in a special sense.

25a Enclosing Direct Quotations

A **direct quotation** repeats the exact words of a speaker or of a text. Direct quotations from written material may include whole sentences or only a few words or phrases.

> James Baldwin wrote of his experience during his childhood, "The only white people who came to our house were welfare workers and bill collectors."
>
> James Baldwin wrote that the only white visitors he saw in his home as a child were "welfare workers and bill collectors."

The examples in the table on page 336 will help you see how direct quotations are used and punctuated in sentences.

In writing dialogue, use quotation marks to enclose everything a speaker says. When one person continues speaking, use quotation marks again if the quoted sentence is interrupted.

> "I don't know what you're talking about," he said. "I did listen to everything you told me."

Sentence: Quoted words first

Sentence: Quoted words last

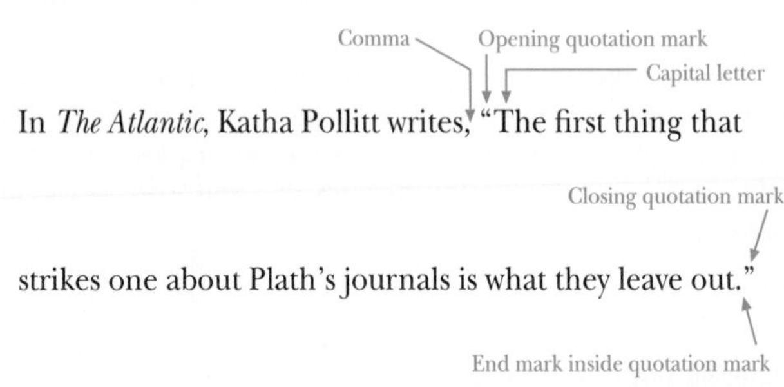

Comma
Opening quotation mark
Capital letter
In *The Atlantic,* Katha Pollitt writes, “The first thing that
Closing quotation mark
strikes one about Plath’s journals is what they leave out.”
End mark inside quotation mark

Sentence: Quoted words interrupted

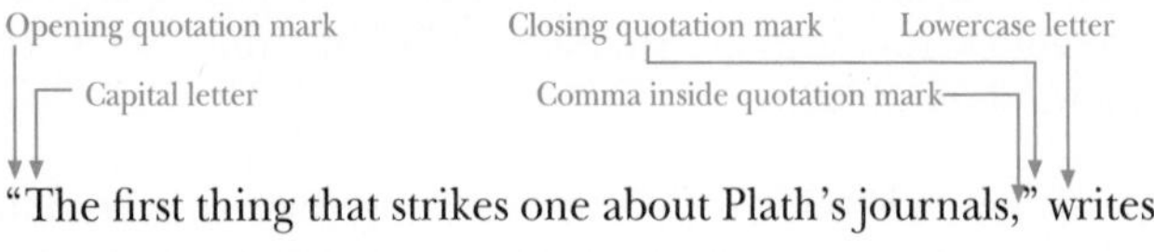

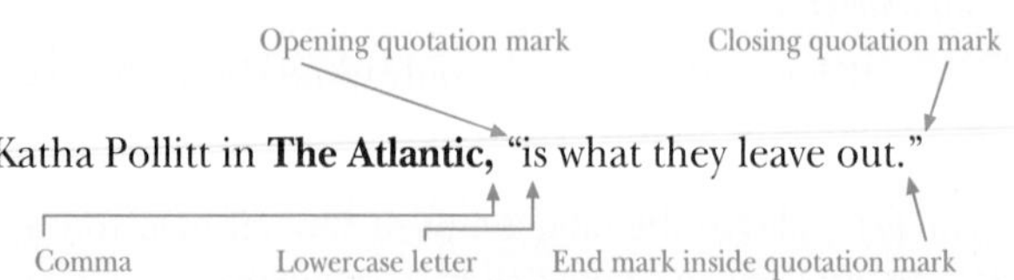

Note that no comma precedes the quotation when it completes the meaning of the sentence and that the existing initial capital letter in the quotation is made into a lowercase letter:

James Baldwin wrote of his childhood experiences that "the only white people who came to our house were welfare workers and bill collectors."

An **indirect quotation** is a **paraphrase.** That is, you express in your own words the meaning of someone else's words. Quotation marks are not used with an indirect quotation.

Casey confessed that he enjoyed blowing the whistle more than anything else he did as a locomotive engineer.

Odette asked if she could borrow my chain saw.

When you quote more than four typed lines, set them off from the text. Start a new line for the quotation, type it double-spaced, and set every line off by a ten-space indentation from the left margin. Double-space above and below the quotation. *Be sure that you indent every line in a block quotation.*

Usually introduced by a colon, a block quotation is *not* set off by quotation marks. If the block includes a direct quotation, however, use quotation marks as they are found in the text. The example that follows shows you how to do this.

Some of the most interesting pages in Schorske's book describe how Sigmund Freud arrived at psychoanalysis and the interpretation of dreams and so made a revolution in our understanding of how the mind works. But as Schorske points out, the young Freud's first passion was not the working of the mind but classical archeology:

> He consumed with avidity Jakob Burckhardt's newly published *History of Greek Culture,* so rich in materials on primitive myth and religion. He read with envy the biography of Heinrich Schliemann, who fulfilled a childhood wish by his discovery of Troy. Freud began the famous collection of ancient artifacts which were soon to grace his office in the Berggasse. And he cultivated a new friendship in the Viennese professional elite—especially rare in those days of withdrawal—with Emanuel Loewy, a professor of archeology. "He keeps me up till three o'clock in the morning," Freud wrote appreciatively to Fliess. "He tells me about Rome."
>
> —CARL SCHORSKE

25a "/"

Use block quotations sparingly because they cut down on readability. Try instead to paraphrase the material and include it in the text, giving proper credit to your sources (see 33b, c, and d).

Two or three lines of poetry may be run into your text, much like any other short quotation. Line breaks are shown with a slash.

> In the nineteenth century Wordsworth wrote of the weary acquisitiveness of our modern age: "The world is too much with us; late and soon, / Getting and spending, we lay waste our powers: / Little we see in Nature that is ours."

Longer verse quotations are indented block-style, like long prose quotations. If you cannot get an entire line of poetry on a single line of your typescript, you may indent the turned line four spaces to the right of the line above it.

> Ah, what can ever be more stately and admirable to me
> than mast-hemm'd Manhattan?
> River and sunset and scallop-edg'd waves of flood-tide?
> The sea-gulls oscillating their bodies, the hay-boat in the twilight,
> and the belated lighter?
> What gods can exceed these that clasp me by the hand, and with
> voices
> I love call me promptly and loudly by my nighest name as I
> approach?
>
> —WALT WHITMAN

A pair of single quotation marks (made with the apostrophe on the typewriter) is used to set off quotations within quotations.

> What happened when the faculty demanded an investigation of dishonest recruiting practices in the athletic department? The president of the university said, "I know you're saying to me, 'We want an honest football team.' But I'm telling you this: 'I want a winning football team.' "

25b
"/"

25b
Using Other Punctuation with Quotation Marks

A comma or period at the end of a quotation is always set before the last quotation mark. A question mark is set before the last quotation mark if the quotation itself asks a question. Punctuation marks that come before the quoted material are not included within quotation marks.

"The worst movie I've ever seen is *Jaws*," he said.

"How can you say that?" she asked. "I loved *Jaws*.

"How can I say that?" he said. "I'll tell you how I can say that; I can say that because I saw it eight times!"

She said, "I think *Jaws II* is even better." Then she asked, "Have you seen it?"

"Yes," he replied. "I have. I saw it four times."

"Then," she countered, "do you still say, 'The worst movie I've ever seen is *Jaws*'?"

Standard practice is to place the period before the final quotation mark even when the quotation is only one or two words long. A question mark or an exclamation point is placed after the last quotation mark if the quoted material is not itself a question or an exclamation.

He had what he called his "special reasons."

Why did he name his car "Buck"?

"Because," she said, "people pass it all the time."

Standard practice is to put colons and semicolons after the final quotation mark.

"I think the jokes in this book are terrible"; she made the remark at the top of her voice, and since I wrote the book, I was hurt.

Dean Wilcox cited the items he called his "daily delights": a free parking place for his scooter at the faculty club, a special table in the club itself, and friends to laugh with after a day's work.

25b
"/"

■ **Exercise 25.1** Punctuate correctly the following sentences. Some sentences require no additional punctuation.

1. I want you to write a book Ted told me one night.
2. He said Give me a manuscript, and I'll get it published.
3. She told me that she would rather play tennis than eat.
4. He said to his friend I bought the car on credit.
5. The wind is rising she shouted Make the boats secure The hurricane is coming.

25c
Enclosing Titles

Use quotation marks to set off a variety of titles, such as essays, book chapters or sections, short poems, short stories, songs, articles in periodicals, radio or television program episodes, and for all unpublished works. Use italics, or underlining, for all other titles (see p. 396).

> "How to Die: The Example of Samuel Johnson" is the title of a recent article in the *Sewanee Review.*
>
> The chapter was called "Another Question of Location."

Note that the titles of songs and short poems are usually put in quotation marks. Often the distinction is based on whether the work was published separately or included in a larger work. Works published separately appear in italics. Titles of long poems are put in italics. In manuscripts and typescripts prepared with printers that do not have an italic font, underline to show what would be italicized in print (see 30a).

> Robert Herrick wrote the poem "Upon Julia's Clothes."
>
> George Noel Gordon, Lord Byron, wrote *Childe Harold's Pilgrimage.*
>
> John Milton wrote "On Shakespeare" in 1630, thirty-seven years before *Paradise Lost,* his major poetic work.

QUOTATION MARKS TO ENCLOSE TITLES

Essays

"A Hanging"
"Once More to the Lake"

Book chapters or sections

"The Girl in Conflict" (Chapter 11 of *Coming of Age in Samoa*)
"Science and Technology" (Part IV of *The Universal Almanac*)

Short poems

"Daffodils"
"Love Song"

Short stories

"A Wagner Matinee"
"The Tell Tale Heart"

Songs

"My Way"
"Friends in Low Places"

Articles in periodicals

"Post-Soviet Baltic Republic: Still Stunted and Struggling" (in the *New York Times*)
"Scotland Yard of the Wild" (in *American Way*)

Radio and television program episodes

"I Can't Remember" (on *48 Hours*)
"Voyage of the Hokule' a" (on *Best of National Geographic*)
"The Final Problem" (on *Sherlock Holmes Mysteries*)

25d Indicating Special Use

Use quotation marks to show that someone else has used a word or phrase in a special way that you or the general public may not use or agree with completely.

> The "worker's paradise" of Stalinist Russia turned out to be a combination of slums, shortages, secret police, and slave-labor camps.
>
> George had the "privilege" of working his way through school by cleaning bathrooms.
>
> For them, getting "saved" is clearly only the first step.
>
> —FRANCES FITZGERALD

Sometimes inexperienced writers use quotation marks to apologize for the informality of certain expressions. They want to indicate their awareness that such expressions are not usually found in serious writing. They think the quotation marks show readers that they know better.

Apologetic

People in California are "laid back."

You can accomplish great things only if you "keep your nose to the grindstone."

I thought he was "cute."

In fact, quotation marks used in this way only mark the writer as inexperienced. Experienced writers simply avoid using slang, clichés, and expressions that call for an apology. When you are tempted to use apologetic quotation marks, take time to think of a better way of expressing yourself.

Revised

People in California pride themselves on living for pleasure without taking anything too seriously.

You can accomplish great things only if you pay attention to what you are doing.

I thought he was attractive.

But if you have a good reason for using a cliché or a slang expression and are sure you can justify its use, use it—without quotation marks.

■ **Exercise 25.2** In some of the following sentences, quotation marks are incorrectly used. Correct any incorrect usages, and put a check by those instances in which quotation marks are used in the right way.

1. "Traditional Principles of Rhetoric" is the title of a chapter in Kenneth Burke's book "A Rhetoric of Motives."
2. "Gee whiz," he said, "I could rap with you all night long."
3. When I waited to do my term paper until the night before it was due, I was really "up the creek without a paddle."
4. "And the Thunder Rolls" is a song Garth Brooks sings.
5. I wanted to know if I could bring my "kids" to the party.
6. She was "put off" by my reaction to her paper.
7. "To His Coy Mistress" is a celebrated poem by Andrew Marvell.
8. Most "utopian" communities emphasize rigid conformity, hard work, and puritanical ethics.
9. "Lochinvar" is a rousing poem by Sir Walter Scott.
10. Hitler's "triumph" was Germany's "tragedy."

✔ CHECKLIST 25.1: PLACING PUNCTUATION WITH QUOTATION MARKS

Convention calls for the placement of other marks of punctuation inside closing quotation marks. Some cases do require other punctuation outside quotation marks. And you often have to take into account the meaning of the sentence in relation to the material in quotation marks. As you revise, look for closing quotation marks and these marks of punctuation. Make sure that you place them in the right order.

- Periods always belong inside quotation marks.
- Commas always belong inside quotation marks.
- Semicolons always belong outside quotation marks.
- Colons always belong outside quotation marks.
- Exclamation points belong inside quotation marks if they are part of the statement or title quoted but outside quotation marks if they are end marks for the entire sentence.
- Question marks belong inside quotation marks if they are part of the question or title quoted but outside quotation marks if they are end marks for the entire sentence.

CHAPTER

26

OTHER MARKS OF PUNCTUATION

End marks, commas, semicolons, apostrophes, and quotation marks are the most common marks of punctuation in English. Additional marks give more subtle meaning to your written expression. These include dashes, colons, parentheses, brackets, slashes, ellipses, and hyphens.

26a Using Dashes

The dash (—) sets off words, phrases, and sometimes whole sentences so that they receive special emphasis. Think of the dash as a very strong pause intended to give special emphasis to what follows—and sometimes to what comes immediately before. Sometimes dashes are paired—as in the first example below—and sometimes they are not.

> A Wisconsin man traveling on horseback had the lower parts of his boots—brand-new ones, be it noted—eaten by wolves, but managed to save his toes.
>
> —Richard Erdoes

> I think this is the most extraordinary collection of human talent, of human knowledge, that has ever been gathered at the White House—with the possible exception of when Thomas Jefferson dined alone.
>
> —John F. Kennedy

On the typewriter the dash is made with two hyphens in a row. There is no space between the hyphens and no space between the dash and the word on either side of it, nor is there any other mark of punctuation on either side of the dash. Handwritten and typeset dashes are single, unbroken lines about as wide as a capital *M*.

```
Coca-Cola, potato chips, and brevity--these are the marks of
a good study session in the dorm.
```

Often the dash sets off nouns placed for special emphasis at the beginning of a sentence and then summarized by a pronoun after the dash, as you see in the sentence above. The dash sometimes can set off an independent clause within a sentence. In such sentences, the content of the set-off independent clause is not essential to the main assertion of the sentence. It is added information.

> Love, with Chaucer, is something tender and vulnerable—it must be protected from the sniggers of a callous world, from the cynicism bred by casual conquest, from the damage done by blurted-out ugly words.
>
> —HANS P. GUTH

When used in pairs, dashes serve to separate parenthetical statements more closely related to the sentence than parentheses would allow but less closely related than a pair of commas would imply (see 22c).

> What she gets—and enjoys—from me is a youthful perspective.
>
> —JUDITH VIORST

> Age groups and the part they have played in American culture—or indeed in any culture—are a subject that has seldom been thoroughly discussed.
>
> —MALCOLM COWLEY

Overuse of the dash can distract readers. You should use the dash only for special emphasis.

26b Using Colons

Use the colon (:) to link independent clauses, to introduce direct quotations and lists, and to set off words and phrases at the end of a sentence. The colon also separates titles and subtitles and the numbers of chapters and verses of the Bible, and it is used in other specialized situations.

The colon links independent clauses when the second clause restates or elaborates on the first. Use it when you want to emphasize the second clause.

Mau Mau emerged as a secret society as a result of a prolonged breakdown of Kikuyu tribal life under European influence: the name is a corruption of '*Uma Uma*' (Out! Out!)—given as a warning when police were approaching.

—PENELOPE MAUNSELL

Until recently, women in Switzerland had an overwhelming political disadvantage: they could not vote.

Of this I am sure: Martin will arrive late, talk loudly, and eat too much.

Instead of a comma, you can use a colon as a more formal way of introducing a direct quotation. The use of the colon before a direct quotation adds additional separation between your statement and the quotation.

"Don't speak of it," she said in a reciting voice and choosing her words sadly and carefully: "It was a stroke."

—V. S. PRITCHETT

Later she recalled the hours Faulkner spent helping her to recover hope: "He kept me alive," she said.

—DAVID MINTER

Colons are often used to introduce **block quotations,** which are set off from regular text by spaces and indents, especially if the introduction previews the quotation.

Dickens had contempt for lazy people. Some of his worst characters are those who lie about, waiting for others to wait on them. Here is the way he introduces Mrs. Witterly in *Nicholas Nickleby:*

> The lady had an air of sweet insipidity, and a face of engaging paleness; there was a faded look about her, and about the furniture, and about the house altogether. She was reclining on the sofa in such a very unstudied attitude that she might have been taken for an actress all ready for the first scene in a ballet, and only waiting for the drop curtain to go up.

Colons also introduce itemized lists.

During its first four years the Virginia venture had failed to meet three basic needs: political stability, economic prosperity, and peaceful Indian relations.

—ALDEN T. VAUGHAN

The colon *cannot* be used to introduce a simple series. To correct the sentence below, remove the colon altogether:

> During its first four years the Virginia venture had failed to meet: political stability, economic prosperity, and peaceful Indian relations.

Some writers capitalize the first letter of the first word after a colon if a complete sentence follows the colon.

> He is kind: Innumerable unknowns in dire need have received financial help from Sinatra.
>
> —ISOBEL SILDEN

By convention, colons separate a main title from the subtitle. The first word of the subtitle is always capitalized.

> *Doing Without: Meeting the Energy Crisis in the 1980s*

Colons intervene between Bible chapters and verses.

> Young writers should take Proverbs 12:1 as a motto.

To indicate the time of day, use a colon between the hour and the minutes.

> He woke up at 6:30 in the morning.

Colons follow salutations in business letters.

> Dear Mr. Clinton:

26c Using Parentheses

Parentheses ((. . .)) always work in pairs. Use them to set off information that breaks the flow of thought within a sentence or a paragraph. Parentheses enclose material that is not as important as material set off by commas or dashes (see 22c, 26a).

> The first money you get for a book will probably be your advance; as a rule, half of that is paid when you sign your contract (or as soon thereafter as the legal department and the accounting department

fill out the appropriate forms), and the other half comes due when you deliver a satisfactory manuscript.

—JUDITH APPLEBAUM and NANCY EVANS

At another barrier a seaman held back Kathy Gilnagh, Kate Mullins, and Kate Murphy. (On the *Titanic* everyone seemed to be named Katherine.)

—WALTER LORD

When parentheses enclose a whole sentence, a period comes after the sentence but before the final parenthesis, as in the second example above. A sentence that appears inside parentheses *within a sentence* is neither capitalized nor closed with a period.

John Henry (he was the man with the forty-pound hammer) was a hero to miners fearing the loss of their jobs to machines.

But a question mark or an exclamation point may follow a parenthetical sentence within a sentence.

John Henry (did he really swing a forty-pound hammer?) was a hero to miners fearing the loss of their jobs to machines.

John Henry (he swung a forty-pound hammer!) was a hero to miners fearing the loss of their jobs to machines.

Parentheses are used to enclose many kinds of numbers within a text. In some forms of annotation (see 33g), parentheses enclose page numbers of a book referred to throughout a paper. Parentheses also enclose cross-references to other parts of a book.

Stevens writes that the demands of their offices turn the best university presidents into machines (43).

Carmichael says that the argument Stevens makes is nonsense because (1) university presidents don't work as well as machines, (2) university presidents don't do any real work at all, and (3) universities would be better off if they were run by faculty committees.

Readers tend to find many parenthetical numbers distracting because the numbers interrupt the flow of thought. If the numbers within parentheses were left out of the example above and the statements set off by commas alone, the passage would be more readable.

26d
Using Brackets

Use brackets to set off material within quoted matter that is not part of the quotation.

> Samuel Eliot Morison has written, "This passage has attracted a good deal of scorn to the Florentine mariner [Verrazzano], but without justice."

In this sentence, a writer is quoting Morison. But Morison's sentence does not include the name of the "Florentine mariner." The writer adds the name—Verrazzano—but places it in brackets so that readers will know the identity of the mariner Morison is talking about.

Sometimes material in brackets explains or corrects something that is quoted.

> Vasco da Gama's man wrote in 1487, "The body of the church [it was not a church but a Hindu shrine] is as large as a monastery."

Brackets are also used around words that you insert within a quotation to make it fit the style or grammar of your sentence.

Full quotation

> I went back to the country and farmed a crop of tobacco with my dad that next year. For all the work I put in I didn't make half as much as I'd been making at the factory, so, after the market closed, I wandered back to town and started looking for another job.
>
> —ANN BANKS

Edited quotation

> Jim Wells came off the farm to work in a cigarette factory in North Carolina during the depression. He was fired because he hit a foreman who mistreated him, and, he said, "I went back to the country and farmed a crop of tobacco with my dad that next year [but] I didn't make half as much as I'd been making at the factory." The only thing he could do was to go back to the city and look for another job.

The bracketed word *but* makes the sentence read smoothly. It eliminates the need for an ellipsis (see 26f).

Brackets may enclose the word *sic* (Latin for "thus") after quoted matter that looks like a mistake. *Sic* lets the reader know that the quotation is presented exactly as it appears in its source and that you, the writer, are aware of the error it contains.

> The dean said, "Those kids is [*sic*] going to get kicked out of school for saying I don't know no [*sic*] grammar."

Brackets are sometimes used to enclose editorial notes, page numbers, or other documentation inserted in a text.

26e
Using Slashes

The slash has very limited uses. As a rule, use the slash only to show divisions between lines of poetry when you quote more than one line of a poem as part of a sentence. Poetry shown as a block quotation replicates the original lines, and does not require slashes.

> Sophocles wrote of the uncertainty of human knowledge: "No man can judge that rough unknown or trust in second sight/For wisdom changes hands among the wise."

Occasionally the slash is used to show that something happened over a couple of calendar years.

> The book sold well in 1988/89.

But it is usually better to use *and* or show inclusive dates with a hyphen.

> The book sold well in 1976 and 1977.
>
> The book sold well in 1988–89.

Some writers use the slash to substitute for the conjunction *or* or as a marker between the words *and* and *or* when the words suggest options.

> The course was offered credit/noncredit.
>
> The winner will be chosen by lot, and he/she will drive a new car home.
>
> You can buy the toaster oven and/or the microwave.

Most writers, however, consider such usage awkward. It is usually better to rephrase the sentence.

> Students who took the course received no grades. If they satisfied the requirements, they got credit; if they did not, they received no penalty.
>
> The winner, to be chosen by lot, will drive a new car home.
>
> You can buy the toaster oven or the microwave, or both.

Do not use a slash to show alternate pronouns. See Chapter 11 for less awkward ways of avoiding bias in writing.

26f
Using Ellipses

If you wish to shorten a passage you are quoting, you may omit some words. To show readers that you have done so, use three spaced periods, called an **ellipsis.**

Full quotation

> In the nineteenth century, railroads, lacing their way across continents, reaching into the heart of every major city in Europe and America, and bringing a new romance to travel, added to the unity of nations and fueled the nationalist fires already set burning by the French Revolution and the wars of Napoleon.

Edited quotation

> In his account of nineteenth-century society, Wilkins argued that "railroads . . . added to the unity of nations and fueled the nationalist fires already set burning by the French Revolution and the wars of Napoleon."

Most writers do not use ellipses to indicate that words have been left out at the beginning or the end of a quotation. Academic writers occasionally use ellipses to show omissions at the beginning or at the end of a quotation. The primary function of the ellipsis is to show that something has been left out of the middle of a quotation.

Ellipsis marks may be used at the end of a sentence if you mean to leave a thought hanging, either in your own prose or in something you are quoting. You do this to suggest that you are not sure how the thought might be ended. If you use an ellipsis at the end of a sentence, add a fourth spaced period.

> Oh God, I'm scared. I wish I could die right now with the feeling I have because I know Momma's going to make me mad and I'm going to make her mad, and me and Presley's gonna fight. . . . "Richard, you get in here and put your coat on. Get in here or I'll whip you."
>
> —DICK GREGORY

The ellipsis should serve only as a means of shortening a quotation, never as a device for changing its fundamental meaning or for creating emphasis where none exists in the original.

■ **Exercise 26.1**

1. Write three sentences using dashes and three using parentheses. What difference, if any, do you find in the effects of using the two punctuation marks?
2. Go to the periodical reading room of your library and look at *Time, Newsweek, Ebony, Sports Illustrated, Popular Mechanics,* or the *New York Times Magazine.* Find sentences that use parentheses and sentences that use the dash. Copy as many of them as you can find. What can you say about the ways these punctuation marks are used?
3. Write a paragraph in which you quote something and insert material within brackets in the quotation. Also delete material and replace it with an ellipsis correctly. Explain what you have done.

■ **Exercise 26.2** Explain the use of dashes and parentheses in the following sentences. Is the punctuation appropriate to the meaning? What other punctuation might serve as an alternative?

1. An air-cooled engine requires no antifreeze in winter (an advantage), but it must be fairly small for the cooling to work (a disadvantage).
2. Diesel engines are fuel efficient and durable—but they are expensive to manufacture.
3. The Ford Motor Company paid workers five dollars a day (people said Henry Ford was undermining capitalism by paying so much) to build the Model T on assembly lines before World War I.
4. The rotary gasoline engine (the first popular model sold in the United States was the Japanese Mazda) was smooth, quiet, and durable, but it burned 15 percent more fuel than conventional engines—a reason for its swift demise.

5. Mechanical automobile brakes operated with springs, levers, and the physical strength of the driver—a strength that might not be sufficient to stop a car hurtling down the highway at forty miles per hour.

26g Using Hyphens

Hyphens are bridges between words. The use of hyphens to form compound words is discussed in 27e.

Hyphens are also used to divide words at the end of lines when the entire word will not fit on a line. Generally, you should avoid breaking words this way because such divisions slow your readers down. Never divide the last word on a page. Leave yourself wide margins, and you will rarely have to divide a word.

When you must break a word, put a hyphen at the end of the first line only, not at the start of the next line. The general rule is to divide words only between syllables. If you are unsure about how to break a word into syllables, consult your dictionary (see p. 200). The following pointers will help you to divide words correctly.

Never divide one-syllable words.

Incorrect

None of us at the dean's luncheon thought that the dean **wo-**
uld arrive in tattered jeans and a torn undershirt.

His weird and uncontrollable **la-**
ugh echoed down the corridor.

Never divide a word if the division leaves only one letter at the end of a line or only one or two letters at the beginning of a line. Avoid breaking such words as *hap·py, could·n't, read·er, o·pen, light·ly,* and *hat·ed.*

26g
-

Incorrect

Lamont Harris wore his new tuxedo to the **o-**
pening of the exhibition.

Naomi Lee Fong, who graduates today, never felt so **hap-**
py in her life before.

Divide compound words into the words that make them up or at the hyphen if the word contains a hyphen. Compound words such as *hard-*

working, rattlesnake, bookcases, and *paperwork* should be broken only between the words that form them: *hard-working, rattle-snake, book-cases, paper-work.* Compound words that already have hyphens, such as *brother-in-law, self-denial, ex-convict,* and *anti-Semitic,* are broken after the hyphens only.

Incorrect

She loves being a detective, but she hates the paperwork.

I gave my old fishing rod to my brother-in-law, and he will sell it at his yard sale.

When two consonants come between vowels in a word you are dividing, make the split between the two consonants. Do not split the two consonants if the division does not reflect pronunciation. In the following words, for example, make the split where the dot appears.

ter·ror run·ning
shel·ter bril·liant

In a word like *respire,* however, you would have to divide the word after the prefix *re* and not between the *s* and the *p,* because the word is pronounced *re·spire* and not *res·pire.*

Avoid confusing word divisions. Sometimes part of a divided word forms a shorter word that can mislead your readers. In such cases, write the complete word or break the word where it will not cause confusion. The table shows some misleading divisions and some possible alternatives.

CONFUSING WORD DIVISIONS

Divisions to avoid	Possible alternatives
a-toll	atoll
at-tire	attire
bar-row	barrow
fat-uous	fatuous
his-torian	histor-ian
im-pugn	impugn
mud-dled	muddled
pig-mentation	pigmen-tation, pigmenta-tion

26g -

Be especially careful if you allow a word-processing program to hyphenate for you. Most computer-controlled hyphenation cannot follow the many subtleties of proper English hyphenation. If you cannot turn the hyphenation function off, go through your essay and check every computer-made end-line hyphenation against your dictionary and the guidelines given here. No doubt you'll find many mistakes.

■ **Exercise 26.3** Show where the following words can be divided if you must hyphenate them at the end of a line. Some words can be divided in more than one place. If a word cannot be divided, put a check alongside it.

1. typewriter
2. grasses
3. record (noun)
4. record (verb)
5. indignation
6. taxed
7. loved
8. pruning
9. roughly
10. England

PART

SIX

UNDERSTANDING MECHANICS

CHAPTER

27

IMPROVING SPELLING

Correct spelling is a sign of literacy. If you misspell words, your readers may understand you, but they will be less likely to respect you. Frequent or even occasional misspellings in your writing can make people believe that you are careless or ignorant, and if that happens, you will have to work twice as hard to make them take you and your thoughts seriously.

This chapter provides some suggestions to help you toward better spelling.

27a
Reading and Pronouncing Carefully

Some common words are frequently misspelled because people misread them or mispronounce them. Of course, pronunciations vary from region to region, and no list can include all mispronunciations that lead to spelling trouble. But if you study the following list, you can train your eye and your ear to spot the parts of common words that often cause spelling errors.

COMMONLY MISPRONOUNCED WORDS

accident**ally**	NOT	acciden**tly**
ari**thm**etic	NOT	arith**e**metic
a**thl**etics	NOT	athe**l**etics
can**di**date	NOT	ca**nn**idate

COMMONLY MISPRONOUNCED WORDS (continued)

chi**mn**ey	NOT	chi**ml**ey
cor**por**ation	NOT	co**per**ation
disas**tr**ous	NOT	disas**ter**ous
drow**ned**	NOT	drowne**ded**
envi**ron**ment	NOT	envi**rer**ment
every**y**body	NOT	**ever**body
every**y**thing	NOT	**ever**thing
Fe**bru**ary	NOT	Feb**u**ary
gen**eral**ly	NOT	gen**r**ally *or* gen**er**ly
gover**nm**ent	NOT	gover**m**ent
heigh**t**	NOT	heigh**th**
hun**dr**eds	NOT	hun**der**eds *or* hu**ner**ds
irr**ele**vant	NOT	irr**eve**lant
la**bora**tory	NOT	la**bra**tory *or* la**ber**tory
li**brar**y	NOT	li**berr**y
lit**era**ture	NOT	lit**ra**ture *or* lit**er**ture
ma**the**matics	NOT	ma**th**matics
mischiev**ous**	NOT	mischiev**ious**
op**tim**ist	NOT	op**tom**ist
peremptory	NOT	**pre**emptory
performance	NOT	**pre**formance
persp**ir**ation	NOT	**pre**sp**er**ation
prescription	NOT	**per**scription
pri**vi**lege	NOT	pri**v**lege
production	NOT	**per**duction
pro**gram**	NOT	prog**rum**
pub**licly**	NOT	publi**cally**
re**pre**sent	NOT	re**per**sent
sop**ho**more	NOT	sop**h**more
stren**gth**	NOT	stre**nth**
stu**dious**	NOT	stud**jous**
temp**era**ment	NOT	temp**er**ment
tem**pera**ture	NOT	tem**per**ture, tem**pra**ture, *or* tem**perchoor**
won**dr**ous	NOT	won**der**ous

Some common plurals my be misspelled because they are mispronounced. Misspelling is especially common in the plurals of words ending in *-ist* or *-est.* The plural of *scientist* is *scientists.* The final combination *ts* sounds like the *tz* in *Ritz* or the *ts* in *fights.* Because this *ts* is difficult for some people to pronounce, they often leave it off, thinking almost unconsciously that the *s* sound in *ist* or *est* is sufficient to make the plural. But the plurals of such words always require a final *-s.* Other words with a difficult *s* sound in the final syllable sometimes trouble writers in forming the plural. Here are some plurals to remember.

COMMONLY PRONOUNCED PLURALS

biologist**s**	disc**s**	nest**s**	rasp**s**
desk**s**	humanist**s**	racist**s**	socialist**s**

27b
Distinguishing Homophones

Be especially careful of words that sound alike or nearly alike but have different meanings and different spellings. These are **homophones.** English has lots of homophones; some of the most frequently used ones are included in the table. Study these words. If you don't immediately recognize the distinctions in meanings, look up pairs (or, in a few cases, triplets and quadruplets) in a dictionary. Also look carefully at these words each time you use one in your writing to make sure you have selected the right one. Keep a list of the homophones that have given you trouble in the past.

COMMON HOMOPHONES

affect, effect	foreword, forward
all, awl	hear, here
complement, compliment	its, it's
council, counsel	lead, led
discreet, discrete	lightening, lightning

COMMON HOMOPHONES (continued)

made, maid
pail, pale
pair, pare
peace, piece
pedal, petal
peer, pier
plain, plane
principal, principle
rain, reign, rein
right, rite, write, wright
role, roll
sea, see
stationary, stationery
straight, strait
than, then
their, there, they're
to, too, two
vain, vane, vein
way, weigh
who's, whose
your, you're

27c
Learning the Principles of Spelling

Some principles of English spelling are so generally true that learning them will help you be a better speller.

Distinguishing Between *ei* and *ie*

When you are deciding between the combinations *ei* and *ie,* consider the previous letter and the sound of the word. When these letters sound like the *ee* in *see,* usually place the *i* before *e.*

believe, relieve, grief, chief, yield, wield

But there are exceptions. When preceded by *c,* the spelling is nearly always *ei.*

receive, deceive, ceiling, conceit

When the sound is like *ay* in *bay* or *May,* the spelling is nearly always *ei.*

neigh, feign, neighbor, weigh

Then there are some renegades.

seize, caffeine, codeine

The familiar jingle is worth recalling: Write *i* before *e* except after *c*, or when sounded like *a* as in *neighbor* and *weigh.* But as for most other words with different sounds, it's best to memorize the spellings.

stein, weird, foreign, height, forfeit, pietism, sierra, pierce, pier, pie, pied, fiery, sieve

■ **Exercise 27.1** Some of the following words are misspelled. Spell them correctly. Put a check by each word in the list that is spelled correctly.

1. friendly
2. weight
3. grievous
4. beleif
5. freight
6. believing
7. conceive
8. liesure
9. frieghten
10. heir

■ **Exercise 27.2** Fill in the blanks in the following words with *ei* or *ie* to make the words correct. Explain the reasons for your choices.

1. s ____ zure
2. rec ____ pt
3. perc ____ vable
4. b ____ ge
5. r ____ n
6. v ____ n
7. d ____ gn
8. hyg ____ ne
9. th ____ f
10. fr ____ ze
11. l ____ n
12. n ____ ther
13. n ____ ce
14. conc ____ t
15. dec ____ t

Adding Suffixes

English builds words and changes the meanings of words by adding **suffixes,** or endings. Here are some general patterns in changes in the spelling of the root word when suffixes are added.

Words ending in a silent *-e*

Before adding the suffix *-ing,* drop a final silent *-e* from the root word.

force/forcing, surprise/surprising, manage/managing, hope/hoping, scare/scaring, come/coming, pave/paving, become/becoming, fume/fuming

There are a few exceptions to this rule.

dye/dyeing (to avoid confusion with *dying*)

hoe/hoeing (to avoid mispronunciation)

shoe/shoeing (to avoid mispronunciation and confusion with *showing*)

A final, silent *-e* on a root word is always dropped before the suffix *-ible.*

force/forcible

Though the silent *-e* of the root is usually dropped before the ending *-able,* the *e* is retained often enough to make this principle uncertain. It is best to memorize the words.

observe/observable, advise/advisable, move/movable (*sometimes* moveable), argue/arguable, debate/debatable

knowledge/knowledgeable, manage/manageable, peace/peaceable, notice/noticeable, change/changeable, embrace/embraceable

A final silent *-e* that is preceded by another vowel is always dropped before a suffix.

argue/argument, true/truly

Words ending in *-y*

When adding the suffix *-ing* to a word ending in *-y*, retain the *-y*.

study/studying, rally/rallying, enjoy/enjoying, cry/crying, ready/readying, steady/steadying, lay/laying

When a final *-y* follows a consonant in the root word, change the *y* to *i* before adding an ending other than *-ing*.

merry/merriment, merriest, merrier
happy/happier, happiness, happiest
rally/rallies, rallied, rallier
supply/supplier, supplies, supplied
pity/pitiless, pitiable, pitiful
mercy/merciful, merciless
kingly/kingliness
ugly/uglier, ugliest, ugliness

When a final *-y* follows a vowel in the root word, keep the *y* when adding an *s* to make the plural of a noun or the third-person singular of a verb.

valley/valleys, defray/defrays, delay/delays, dismay/dismays, enjoy/enjoys, toy/toys, ploy/ploys

Always keep the final *-y* when forming the plural of a person's name.

Joe and Mary Kirby/the Kirbys

To form the past tense of verbs ending in a final *-y* preceded by a vowel, generally keep the final *y* and add the suffix *-ed.*

play/played, dismay/dismayed, enjoy/enjoyed

But there are important exceptions.

pay/paid, say/said, lay/laid

■ **Exercise 27.3** Add the suffix indicated for each of the following words. Be sure to change the spelling of the root word when such a change is appropriate.

1. advance + ing
2. highboy + s
3. learn + able
4. horrify + ing
5. quote + able
6. sally + s
7. sense + ible
8. pray + ed
9. quality + s
10. solicit + ing

Words ending in a consonant

Pay attention to words formed when a suffix that begins with a vowel is added to a root that ends in a consonant. These suffixes are *-ing, -er, -est, -ed, -ence, -ance, -ible, -able,* and *-ened.*

With most words of one syllable ending in a consonant immediately preceded by a vowel, double the final consonant.

grip/gripping, quip/quipped, stun/stunning, quit/quitting, plan/planned, sad/saddest, scar/scarring

If the root word ends with two consecutive consonants or with a consonant preceded by two consecutive vowels, do not double the final consonant before suffixes that begin with vowels.

tight/tighter, stoop/stooping, straight/straightest, sing/singer, deep/deepened, creep/creeping, crawl/crawler

If the root word has more than one syllable, and if the accent of the root falls on the last syllable, usually double the final consonant.

occur/occurrence, refer/referred, rebut/rebutting, concur/concurring

But if the final consonant of the root is preceded by a consonant or by two consecutive vowels, or if the accent shifts from the final syllable of the root when the suffix is added, don't double the final consonant.

depart/departing, ferment/fermenting, repair/repairing, refer/reference

If the final consonant is *-l*, check your dictionary. The increasing preference for the words listed below and others is not to double the final *-l*.

cancel/canceling, pencil/penciling, travel/traveled, unravel/unraveled

And there are, as always, exceptions that have to be memorized.

fit/fitted BUT benefit/benefited
ship/shipping BUT worship/worshiped

This rule sounds so complicated that you may think it better to memorize the spellings of all these words rather than to memorize the rule. But give the rule a try: it does work!

Adding Prefixes

Most standard **prefixes**—letters attached to the beginnings of words that change their meanings—do not require changing the spelling of the prefix or the root word. Before root words beginning with vowels, prefixes ending in vowels sometimes require a hyphen (see 27e).

appear/disappear	create/procreate
eminent/preeminent	satisfy/dissatisfy
operate/cooperate	spell/misspell
usual/unusual	

■ **Exercise 27.4** Use the rules you have learned to add the indicated suffixes to the root words below. Explain why you change some roots to add the suffix and why you leave other roots unchanged. The exercise will help you most if you discuss your choices with other members of the class.

1. attend + ance
2. din + ed
3. strip + ing
4. dine + ing
5. mar + ed
6. despair + ed
7. bob + ing
8. accept + ance
9. dip + er
10. map + ing
11. submit + ing
12. reckon + ed
13. detest + able
14. soon + est
15. omit + ed
16. silly + est
17. depend + ence
18. prefer + ing
19. spot + y
20. star + ing
21. confer + ence
22. pin + ed
23. disdain + ed
24. drown + ing
25. pretend + ed

Forming Plurals

Plurals of nouns are formed according to some general rules. Most nouns simply add a final *-s.*

> grove/groves, boat/boats, cobra/cobras, bank/banks, scientist/scientists, moralist/moralists, gripe/gripes, gasp/gasps, disc/discs

Even acronyms and decades are made plural by the addition of *-s.*

> Some critics say that there have been two **FBIs**—the one before the death of J. Edgar Hoover and the one that came later on.
> The **1890s** are popularly called the Gay Nineties because of the extravagant pleasures of the rich during that decade.

Exceptions based on endings

Nouns ending in certain letters are exceptions to this rule.

When the singular of a noun ends in *-s, -x, -ch,* or *-sh,* add *-es* to form the plural.

> kiss/kisses, Marx/the Marxes, Mr. Jones/the Joneses, church/churches, dish/dishes

If a noun ends in *-y* preceded by a consonant, change the *y* to *i* and add *-es* to form the plural; if the final *y* is preceded by a vowel, keep the *y* and add *-s* to make the plural.

> beauty/beauties, sally/sallies, glory/glories, city/cities, country/coun-

tries, destiny/destinies, crudity/crudities, ray/rays, boy/boys, joy/joys, valley/valleys

When a noun ends in *-o* in the singular, form the plural by adding *-s* or *-es*. The best practice here is to look these plurals up in a dictionary.

hero/heroes, solo/solos, tomato/tomatoes, folio/folios, potato/potatoes, flamingo/flamingos *or* flamingoes, piano/pianos, manifesto/manifestos *or* manifestoes, veto/vetoes

To form the plurals of some nouns ending in *-f*, change the final *f* to *v* and add *-es*. If a silent *e* follows the *f*, also change the *f* to *v*.

leaf/leaves, hoof/hooves, knife/knives, life/lives, wife/wives, self/selves

But many nouns ending in *f* form their plurals by the standard addition of *-s*, and modern practice favors standardizing plurals this way.

chief/chiefs, roof/roofs

Irregular plurals

Some nouns have irregular plurals formed by changes in internal vowels or the addition of endings that don't include *-s*. These are some of the oldest and most familiar words in the English language.

child/children, goose/geese, man/men, woman/women, ox/oxen, tooth/teeth, mouse/mice

Some nouns are the same in the singular and plural.

deer/deer, fish/fish *or* fishes, fowl/fowl *or* fowls, moose/moose

Compound nouns

Compound nouns generally form plurals by the addition of *-s* or *-es*.

babysitter/babysitters, millrace/millraces

But when the first element of the compound is the most important word, the *-s* or *-es* is added to it.

attorney general/attorneys general, mother-in-law/mothers-in-law, father-in-law/fathers-in-law, court-martial/courts-martial, passerby/passersby

Latin and Greek words

Many Latin and Greek words have become part of the English language. To form the plurals of such words with the singular ending *-um* or *-on,* drop these endings and add *-a.*

addendum/addenda, criterion/criteria, datum/data, medium/media, phenomenon/phenomena

Some writers now treat *data* as though it were singular, but the preferred practice is still to recognize that *data* is plural and takes a plural verb.

The data *are* clear on this point: the pass/fail course has become outdated by events.

Like *data,* the word *media* requires a plural verb. *Agenda,* by contrast, is now fully accepted as a singular form.

The plurals of a few nouns ending in *-is* are formed by changing this ending to *-es.*

analysis/analyses, basis/bases, crisis/crises, thesis/theses

A few words with Latin roots ending in a vowel and an *x* may change to *-ices* when the plural is formed.

appendix/appendices, index/indices (math), vortex/vortices

But today *-es* is the preferred form for the plurals of these words.

appendixes, indexes (book), vortexes

A few English words with Latin roots ending in *-us* form their plurals by changing the *-us* to *-i.*

alumnus/alumni, tumulus/tumuli, cumulus/cumuli, hippopotamus/hippopotami *or* hippopotamuses, calculus/calculi, cactus/cacti

Even fewer words with Latin roots ending in *-a* form their plurals by changing the *-a* to *-ae.*

alumna/alumnae

■ **Exercise 27.5** Form the plural of each of the following words. Check your plurals against those given in a dictionary when you have finished. (Chapter 12 discusses how to use a dictionary.)

1. mess
2. harp
3. disco
4. arch
5. banjo
6. hello
7. dodo
8. grief
9. radius
10. buffalo
11. elegy
12. harpy
13. phlox
14. rest
15. antenna
16. handful
17. day
18. money
19. son-in-law
20. sheep
21. cow
22. garnish
23. vertebra
24. rabbi
25. prophecy
26. symposium
27. fungus
28. fascist
29. scientist
30. neurosis
31. rest
32. risk
33. critic
34. soprano
35. locus

27d
Using Lists of Words to Improve Spelling

The following lists of words misspelled in student papers were compiled a few years ago by New York State. Of the more than 31,000 misspelled words gathered by English teachers throughout the country, 407 were misspelled more frequently than others. These words are arranged in categories in descending order of difficulty. Study the list carefully. It will help if you have someone read the words aloud to you so that you can try to spell them without looking at them.

WORDS MOST FREQUENTLY MISSPELLED

Words misspelled 100 times or more

believe
belief

benefit
benefited
beneficial

choose
chose
choice

definite
definitely
definition
define

description
describe

environment

exist
existence
existent

its
it's

lose
losing

necessary
unnecessary

occasion
occur
occurred
occurring
occurrence

perform
performance

personal
personnel

precede

principle
principal

27d
spell

Words misspelled 100 times or more (continued)

privilege

professor
profession

receive
receiving

referring

separate
separation

similar

success
succeed
succession

than
then

their
they're
there

too
two
to

write
writing
writer

Words misspelled 50 to 99 times

accommodate

achieve
achievement

acquire

affect
affective

all right*

among

analyze
analysis

apparent

argument
aguing

began
begin

beginner
beginning

busy
business

category

comparative

conscience
conscientious
conscious

consistent
consistency

control
controlled
controlling

controversy
controversial

criticism
criticize

decision
decided

disastrous

embarrass

equipped
equipment

excellent
excellence

experience

explanation

fascinate

forty
fourth

grammar
grammatically

height

imagine
imaginary
imagination

immediate
immediately

intelligence
intelligent

interest

interpretation
interpret

led

loneliness
lonely

marriage

Negro
Negroes

noticeable
noticing

origin
original

passed
past

possess
possession

prefer
preferred

prejudice

prevalent

probably

proceed
procedure

prominent

* Although some dictionaries accept the spelling *alright,* most list it as nonstandard usage. Most college instructors regard *alright* as a misspelling.

Words Misspelled 50 to 99 times (continued)

psychology
psychoanalysis
psychopathic
psychosomatic

pursue

realize
really

repetition

rhythm

sense

shining

studying

surprise

thorough

tries
tried

useful
useless
using

varies
various

weather
whether

Words Misspelled 40 to 49 times

accept
acceptance
acceptable
accepting

accident
accidentally

acquaint
acquaintance

across

aggressive

appear
appearance

article

athlete
athletic

attended
attendant
attendance

challenge

character
characteristic
characterized

coming

convenience
convenient

difference
different

disappoint

discipline
disciple

dominant
predominant

effect

exaggerate

foreign
foreigners

fundamental
fundamentally

government
governor

hero
heroine
heroic
heroes

humor
humorist
humorous

hypocrisy
hypocrite

incident
incidentally

independent
independence

liveliest
livelihood
liveliness
lives

mere

operate

opinion

opportunity

paid

particular

philosophy

planned

pleasant

possible

practical

prepare

quantity

quiet

recommend

ridicule
ridiculous

speech

sponsor

summary
summed

suppose

technique

transferred

unusual
usually

villain

woman

Words misspelled 30 to 39 times

advice
advise

approach
approaches

author
authority
authoritative

basis
basically

before

careless
careful

carrying
carried
carries
carrier

conceive
conceivable

codemn

consider
considerably

continuous

curiosity
curious

dependent

desirability
desire

efficient
efficiency

entertain

extremely

familiar

finally

friendliness
friend

fulfill

further

happiness

hindrance

influential
influence

knowledge

laboratory

maintenance

ninety

oppose
opponent

optimism

parallel

permanent

permit

physical

piece

propaganda
propagate

relieve

religion

response

satire

significance

suppress

temperament

therefore

together

undoubtedly

weird

where

whose

you're

Words misspelled 20 to 29 times

accompanying
accompanies
accompanied
accompaniment

accomplish

accustom

actually
actuality
actual

adolescence
adolescent

against

amateur

amount

appreciate
appreciation

approximate

arouse
arousing

attack

attitude

boundary

Britain
Britannica

capital
capitalism

certain
certainly

chief

clothes

completely

counselor
counsel
council

curriculum

dealt

Words misspelled 20 to 29 times (continued)

despair
disease
divide
divine
especially
excitable
exercise
expense
experiment
fallacy
fantasy
fantasies
favorite
fictitious
field
financier
financially
forward
guarantee
guaranteed
guidance
guiding
hear
here
huge
hungry
hungrily
hunger
ignorance
ignorant
indispensable
intellect
interfere
interference
interrupt
involve
irrelevant

laborer
laboriously
labor
laid
later
leisure
leisurely
length
lengthening
license
likeness
likely
likelihood
luxury
magazine
magnificent
magnificence
maneuver
mathematics
meant
mechanics
medicine
medical
medieval
miniature
mischief
moral
morale
morally
narrative
naturally
noble
obstacle
omit
peace
perceive
persistent
persuade

pertain
phase
playwright
politician
political
primitive
regard
relative
remember
reminisce
represent
roommate
sacrifice
safety
satisfy
satisfied
scene
schedule
seize
sentence
sergeant
several
shepherd
simply
simple
sophomore
source
story
stories
straight
strength
strict
substantial
subtle
suspense
symbol
synonymous

Words misspelled 20 to 29 times (continued)

tendency	those	vacuum
themselves	thought	view
them	tragedy	whole
theory	tremendous	yield
theories		

27e
Using Hyphens

Hyphens are used to form compound words and to avoid confusion. Hyphens relate both to spelling and to style, and in using hyphens writers often have several options. For example, you could write *life-style* or *life style* or *lifestyle* and be correct in each case. A dictionary is the best help when you are unsure about using a hyphen.

The points below explain the most regular uses of hyphens.

Joining Noun Forms

Often in modern American English, a hyphen joins two nouns to make one compound word. Scientists speak of a *kilogram-meter* as a measure of force, and personnel managers speak of a *clerk-typist,* an employee who does general office work plus typing. The hyphen lets us know that the two nouns work together as one. Here are some other examples.

city-state	scholar-poet
composer-conductor	writer-editor

As compound nouns that once were new constructions come into general use, their hyphens tend to disappear. The nouns come to be written as one word, such as *housefly, firelight, firefight,* and *thundershower.*

A noun can also be linked with an adjective, an adverb, or another part of speech to form a compound noun.

accident-prone	cat-hater
break-in	dog-lover
by-product	first-rate

Hyphens also join nouns designating family relationships and compounds of more than two words.

brother-in-law	mother-in-law	stay-at-home
sister-in-law	father-in-law	stick-in-the-mud

Linking Modifiers to Avoid Confusion

Hyphens often help us sort out modifiers that come before the word they modify. If we say "He was a hard running back," we might mean that he was hard and that he was also a running back. If we say "He was a hard-running back," we mean that he ran hard. If we say "She was a quick thinking person," we might mean that she was quick and that she was also thinking. If we say "She was a quick-thinking person," we mean that she thought rapidly.

Notice that the hyphenated words in these examples employ adverbs (*hard, quick*) that do not end in *-ly*. When adverbs end in *-ly,* they do not require a hyphen if they modify an adjective that in turn modifies a noun.

They explored the **newly discovered** territories.

They endured his **clumsily arrogant** bragging.

Modifiers that are hyphenated when they are placed *before* the word they modify are usually not hyphenated when they are placed *after* the word they modify.

He was a **crisis-and-confrontation** politician.

His politics were a mix of **crisis and confrontation.**

It was a **bad-mannered** reply.

The reply was **bad mannered.**

Attaching Prefixes

Hyphens are used to attach prefixes to some words. Often, for example, a hyphen joins a prefix and a capitalized word.

anti-Semitic, un-American, pre-Columbian

Some prefixes are attached to a few words with hyphens even though the main word is not capitalized.

all-conference, ex-husband, self-interest, vice-president

Most prefixes, however, are not attached by hyphens. The prefix is simply joined to the stem with no punctuation.

antisocial nonjudgmental superpower
atypical postwar undersea
extracurricular preliterate

In some cases hyphens are retained to distinguish meanings or aid pronunciation.

co-op, co-worker, re-cover, re-create

Some proper nouns that are joined to make an adjective are hyphenated.

the Franco-Prussian war, a Mexican-American heritage, the Sino-Japanese agreement

Some numbers are hyphenated.

three-fourths of a gallon, thirty-odd, twenty-five

Often you will encounter variant spellings of the same word. Usually these variants are caused by differences in British and American practice.

plow/pough theater/theatre
center/centre humor/humour

In your own writing you should follow American practice. See Chapter 12, Using the Dictionary.

✓ CHECKLIST 27.1: IMPROVING YOUR SPELLING

- Make yourself realize the importance of good spelling, and resolve to spell correctly.
- Write down every word you misspell. Keep a spelling log or journal. Practice frequently misspelled words over and over again to help fix the correct spelling in your mind and in your fingers. Good spelling is a habit of both mind and hand.
- Pronounce words carefully. Many people misspell words because they pronounce them incorrectly.
- Learn to distinguish homophones—words pronounced alike but with different meanings and spellings. Study these words each time you encounter them to make sure you've used the right one.
- Learn the rules that generally hold for spelling, and learn the exceptions to those rules. Most rules have only a few exceptions. When

you have learned the exceptions, you will find that the rules themselves tend to stay in your mind.

- Try to group your errors. Misspellings often fall into patterns—errors with suffixes or plurals, for example.
- Proofread your writing carefully. Misspellings creep into the prose of the best of writers when they are in a hurry, when they are thinking ahead to their next thought as they write, or when they do not wish to break their train of thought to look up a troublesome word.
- Use your dictionary frequently when you proofread your work. Whenever you wonder about the correctness of your spelling of a word, look it up. Writing continually and using a dictionary continually are two excellent ways to become a good speller.
- Learn to write with a computer, and use the spell checker on your word-processing program. But always remember that your spell checker cannot tell the difference between the meanings of words. If you write "their" when you should write "there," the spell checker cannot help you. Your best habit is always to have a dictionary nearby when you write.

■ **Exercise 27.6** Rewrite the following sentences to correct misspellings. Hyphenate words when necessary.

1. He beleived that the badly damaged plane could land safly.
2. The love them today leave them tomorrow philosophy is probly on the decline becaus people now unnerstan it's hypocricy.
3. His nervous laff was a hinderence to his carreer.
4. She remained an optomist though her experence told her that optomists often have trouble accomodating themselves to a pityless city.
5. He had a tendancy to miss classes as a sophmore, and his teachers were ill mannered enough to tāke attendence.

■ **Exercise 27.7** Add hyphens only where they are needed in the following words and phrases. Defend your choices.

1. an off color remark
2. narrow minded
3. preChristian
4. self motivated
5. her daughter in law
6. a fast sailing ship
7. blue green algae
8. a well meaning act
9. faintly heard whisper
10. king of Austria Hungary

CHAPTER

28

CAPITALIZING CORRECTLY

Capital letters give readers signals about sentence patterns, names, titles, and pronouns. Many rules for use of capitals have been fixed by custom, but the rules change all the time. A standard dictionary is a good guide to capitalization. In most college dictionaries names that should always be capitalized are entered with capitals; all others are entered in lowercase (or small) letters. (Remember that capitalizing a word means that only the first letter in the word is capitalized; all other letters in the word appear in lowercase.)

28a
Capitalizing the First Word of a Sentence

The capital letter at the beginning of a sentence signals the reader that a new unit of thought is about to begin. Together with the punctuation mark at the end of the previous sentence, it makes reading easier.

> Because robots greatly reduce human error, the products they manufacture are of a much more uniform quality. But because they reduce human employment, robots risk eliminating part of the market for which their products are destined.

In sentence fragments used for special effects, capitalize the first word.

> But aside from good hair grooming, they are oblivious to everything but each other. Everybody gives them a once-over. Disgusting! Amusing! How touching!
>
> —Tom Wolfe

> Why did she lie under oath on the witness stand to defend her husband? Because she knew he was innocent? No, because she knew he was guilty.

Some writers who ask a series of questions by using fragments do not capitalize the first word of each fragment.

> How many individuals can we count in society? how many actions? how many opinions?
>
> —RALPH WALDO EMERSON

The more common practice is to capitalize the first word in each fragment that answers a question.

> And what are the fundamentals? Reading? Writing? Of course not!
>
> —SLOAN WILSON

Most writers do not capitalize the first word of an independent clause immediately following a colon.

> If a person suffer much from sea-sickness, let him weigh it heavily in the balance. I speak from experience: it is no trifling evil, cured in a week.
>
> —CHARLES DARWIN

But some writers do capitalize the first word after a colon.

> The answer is another question: How many days must go by before millions of people notice they are not eating?
>
> —*The New York Times*

The first word in an independent clause following a semicolon is never capitalized unless it is a proper noun (see 28c).

> All in all, however, outside support counted for little; the men of the village did the work themselves.
>
> —OSCAR HANDLIN

28b
cap

28b Capitalizing Proper Nouns and Their Abbreviations

Proper nouns are the names of specific people, places, or things, names that set off the individual from the species. Proper nouns include names like *Jane* (instead of the common noun *person*), *France* (instead of the common noun *country*), and *Empire State Building* (instead of the common noun *building*).

The table shows examples of proper nouns.

TYPES AND EXAMPLES OF PROPER NOUNS

Names and nicknames of people

Wolfgang Amadeus Mozart, Ernest Hemingway, Cecil Fielder, Ella Fitzgerald, John F. Kennedy, Sandra Day O'Connor, Ulysses S. Grant, Gore Vidal, Joan Didion, the North Carolina Tarheels

Names of places

France, the United States of America, Tennessee, the Panama Canal, Back Bay, the Mississippi Delta, the North Shore, the Irunia Restaurant, the Sierra Nevada, the Great Lakes

Official names of organizations, organized events, courses

Phi Beta Kappa, the U.S. Department of Defense, the Authors' Guild of America, the University of Notre Dame, Cumberland College, Ford Motor Company, the Roman Catholic Church, the American Red Cross, the Boy Scouts of America, the NCAA, the NAACP, Renaissance Weekend, Rosebowl, Triple Crown, History 351: Old South and Civil War

Days of the week, months, special days

Monday, July, Veterans Day, Christmas, Labor Day, Halloween, Yom Kippur, Earth Day, Pearl Harbor Day, Fourth of July

Ethnic groups, nationalities, and their languages

Greeks, Chinese, Americans, Arabs, Turks; Greek, Chinese, English, Arabic, Turkish

Members of religious bodies and their sacred books and names

Jews, Christians, Baptists, Holy Bible, God, Allah, Hindus, Jesus Christ, Holy Spirit, the Koran, the Torah, Pentecostals, Christian Scientists

Historical events, names of movements, and titles of works
World War II, the Louisiana Purchase, Impressionism, the Bill of Rights, *Moby Dick,* "To Autumn"

Place names of regions are generally capitalized if they are well established, like *the Midwest* and *Central Europe,* but do not capitalize directions, as in *turn south.*

While holidays and names of months and days of the week are capitalized, seasons, such as *summer,* are not.

The words *blacks* and *whites* generally are not capitalized when they are used to refer to ethnic groups, but many writers follow individual choice in this matter. The older and now less favored word *Negro* is capitalized.

Many religious terms such as *sacrament, altar, priests, rabbi, preacher,* and *holy water* are not capitalized. The word *Bible* is capitalized (though *biblical* is not), but it is never capitalized when it is used as a metaphor for an essential book, as in this sentence: "His book *Winning at Stud Poker* was for many years the *bible* of gamblers."

Pronoun references to a deity worshiped by people in the present are sometimes capitalized, although some writers use capitals only to prevent confusion.

> Allah, so Muslims believe, sent Mohammed to deliver **His** word to the world.
>
> God helped Abraham carry out **His** law.

In each of the sentences above, the capitalization of the pronoun *His* helps avoid confusion. If the pronoun were not capitalized, readers might not be able to tell if it referred to Allah or Mohammed in the first sentence, or if the law mentioned in the second sentence was God's or Abraham's.

> God acts for his own purposes and according to his own wisdom.

In this sentence the pronoun *his* is not capitalized, since no confusion would result. You may choose to capitalize the pronoun if you wish.

Pronoun references to deities no longer worshiped are not capitalized.

> Jupiter, the Roman god of thunder and lightning, led a tempestuous love life that often got **him** into deep trouble with **his** wife, Juno.

28b cap

Sometimes words not ordinarily capitalized take capitals when they are used as parts of proper names.

My **aunt** is arriving this afternoon.
My **Aunt Lou** tells fantastic stories that I think she makes up.

I have to go to the **bank** before we leave.
The **Cambridge Bank** is on the corner.

I graduated from **high school** in 1989.
I went to **Lenoir City High School.**

Such appellations as *Mother, Father, Cousin, Brother,* and *Sister* may replace proper names in speech and writing. If you intend to refer to a specific individual, capitalize the word.

I still miss **Mother,** although she has been dead for over a decade.

He supposed that **Grandfather** would come to his aid again, as he had so many times in the past.

But most of the time even these words are not capitalized, since they do not replace a proper name. Whether you capitalize such words depends on your intention.

I asked my **mother** to wake me at 5:00 a.m.

Some titles that may be capitalized before a proper name are often not capitalized when they are used after the name.

Everyone knew that **Governor** Grover Cleveland of New York was the most likely candidate for the Democratic nomination.

The most likely candidate for the Democratic nomination was Grover Cleveland, **governor** of New York.

Writers and editors do not agree on the capitalization of titles. *President of the United States,* or the *President* (meaning the chief executive of the United States), is frequently but not always capitalized. Practice varies with other titles also. Some writers say, "I will speak to the *Governor* about your wish to give him a new Cadillac for his personal use." Others say, "The *governor* of this state received a Cadillac last week from an old political friend and business associate." Most writers say, "The *president* of this university has seventeen honorary degrees." Others will say, "The *President* of this university would rather have a winning football team than seventeen honorary degrees." An internal memorandum circulated among university faculty would probably capitalize references to the president.

In general, editors and writers are tending to capitalize less, but it is still important to be consistent. If you write "the **P**resident of the **U**niversity," you should also write "the **C**hair of the **H**istory **D**epartment." If you write "The **p**resident of the **u**niversity," you should also write "the **c**hair of the **h**istory **d**epartment." And, of course, if you say "the **P**resident of the **U**niversity" in one place, you must capitalize in the same way whenever you write "the **P**resident of the **U**niversity."

Words derived from proper nouns generally keep the capitals of the original words.

Miltonic, Reaganomics, Hodgkin's disease, Hollywoodiana, Siamese cat

When proper names describe or identify common nouns, the nouns that follow are generally not capitalized.

Sanka brand, Russian history, French fries, Pennsylvania-Dutch shoo-fly pie, English literature

Brand names and trademarks are capitalized (Apple computer, Mac II, Big Mac), but some former proper nouns and brand names have become common nouns and no longer require capitalization.

diesel, levis, pasteurization

Use capitals for abbreviations made from capitalized words or for words formed from the initial letters of words in a proper name. These words, called **acronyms,** are discussed in 29b. Acronyms of three or more letters do not generally use periods between the letters.

WAC, FBI, NOW, UNESCO, ANZAC, NCAA, SWAT

Abbreviations used as parts of proper names usually take capitals.

T. S. Eliot; Sammy Davis, Jr.; Maria Lopez, M.D.

28c
Capitalizing Titles of Literary and Art Works

Capitalize the major words of the title of any piece of writing, the title of a work of art or architecture, or the name of a ship. Do not capitalize the articles (*a, an,* and *the*) or prepositions and conjunctions of fewer than five letters unless they begin the title. Capitalize the first word after a colon or semicolon in a title.

Book: *Two Years Before the Mast*

Play: *The Taming of the Shrew*

Architecture: the *Eiffel Tower*

Ship: the *Titanic*

Painting: *Mona Lisa*

Magazine article: "Beating the Market: How to Get Rich on Stocks"

Magazine or journal: *Time*

Essay: "On Old Age"

Poem: "Ode on a Grecian Urn"

Music: "The Star-Spangled Banner"

Note that the preposition *Before* in the first title is capitalized. The general rule is that a preposition or conjunction of five letters or more is capitalized.

✔ CHECKLIST 28.1: USING CAPITALS APPROPRIATELY

As you revise your drafts, check to make sure you are using capital letters appropriately. Look for these instances.

- Sentence conventions
  after periods
  the pronoun *I*
  at the beginning of dialogue and quotations
  sometimes after colons
- Names of people
- Place names and names of areas and regions
- Historical events and movements
- Titles of works of literature, art, music, and architecture
- Names of institutions, groups, and organizations
- Titles of classes
- Names of religions, races, nationalities, and sacred things
- Days, months, holidays
- Names derived from proper nouns

28d
Capitalizing Dialogue and Quotations

When you include spoken dialogue in quotation marks, capitalize the first word.

> "You're going to kill us both!" she shouted.
>
> "Calm down," he shouted back. "I spent just thirty minutes learning to drive this motorcycle, and we're already doing a hundred miles an hour."
>
> She cried, "Help!"

Indirect quotations and questions require no capitals for words attributed to a speaker or writer.

> She said that jazz was one of the many contributions of blacks to world culture.
>
> He asked me which I liked better, bluegrass music without drums and electrically amplified instruments, or the more modern country music that is akin to soft rock.

The first word of quotations from printed sources is capitalized if the quotation is introduced as dialogue.

> Jim, the narrator of *My Antonia,* concludes: "Whatever we had missed, we possessed together the precious, the incommunicable past."

But when a quotation from a printed source is only an element in your sentence, not a sentence on its own, the first word is not capitalized.

> Jim took comfort in sharing with Antonia "the precious, the incommunicable past."

Many authors in earlier centuries and some writers today—especially poets—have used capitals in eccentric ways. If you are quoting a text directly, reproduce the capitalization used in the source, whether or not it is correct by today's standards.

> Sun and moon run together in one of Pyramus's speeches, "Sweet Moon, I thank thee for thy sunny Beams."
>
> —ELIZABETH SEWELL

28e
cap

28e Capitalizing Consistently and Carefully

Use capitals consistently when you have a reason for doing so, but avoid them when they are not necessary. When capital letters are optional, select one system and stick to it. Consistency is important.

Some inexperienced writers are tempted to use capitals for emphasis, and they capitalize too much. Unnecessary capitals may confuse readers or irritate them. In modern prose, the tendency is to use lowercase whenever possible.

■ **Exercise 28.1** Follow the directions in each item below, and write full-sentence responses. Observe the conventions of proper capitalization.

1. Name the professor in your school whose lectures you find most interesting.
2. Name the city and state (or city and country) where you were born.
3. Name a supermarket at which you or your family members buy groceries.
4. What is your favorite season of the year?
5. In what direction must you walk or ride to get to campus?
6. In what region of the country did you grow up?
7. What two academic subjects do you enjoy most?
8. Name a book you enjoyed reading recently.
9. What is your favorite TV show?
10. Name your favorite holiday.
11. What is your favorite flower?
12. What was the name of your high school? (Use the words *high school* immediately after the name of the institution.)

■ **Exercise 28.2** Fill in the correct capital or lowercase letters in the blanks below. Explain your choices.

1. __hen __overnor Blankenship stood on the steps of the state __apitol __uilding and said to the __resident of the __nited __tates, "__he states in the __outh need more of the __overnment's support," my neighbors on Main __treet applauded wildly.
2. __t the __an __iego __oo last summer, I disliked the __onkeys and the __pes because they looked so much like little men and women in a cage, but I was fascinated by the __eptile __ouse, where I saw the __frican __ock __ython as well as the __ndian __obras and the __oa __onstrictor.

3. _f you take _ociology 320, a _ourse in the _ociology of _eligion, you will learn to understand some of the strengths of _rotestantism, _udaism, and _oman _atholicism.

■ **Exercise 28.3** Rewrite the following sentences, using capital and lowercase letters correctly.

1. during Summer i like to visit the Ski Resorts in vermont, where few visitors disturb my meditations among the Fir Trees and the Maples that dot the Landscape.
2. when I was a child, thanksgiving day was one of my favorite holidays, not only because my aunts and uncles always came over for a huge dinner but also because my mother and father took the friday after thanksgiving off and the whole family went shopping at lakeland mall.
3. in your sophomore course in english literature next fall, you may read at least one novel by daniel defoe, whose book *robinson crusoe* is sometimes called the first novel in the english language.
4. when we had our accident, we were taken to memorial hospital on greeley parkway, where a man in a white coat named thomas babington examined us and told us there was nothing wrong with us.
5. later, when i discovered that i had a fractured skull and that my brother had a broken leg, we sued the hospital, but the hospital claimed that mr. babington was only visiting the emergency room that day and was not an employee of memorial hospital at all. he was a chef in a local restaurant.

CHAPTER

29

USING NUMBERS AND ABBREVIATIONS

Variations in the styles of authors, the demands of editors, and the requirements of various kinds of writing make it difficult to fix rules for using numbers and abbreviations. In some newspapers and some magazines, the use of figures to express numbers may be common. In books, figures and abbreviations are less common, at least in the body of a text. In footnotes, bibliographies, scientific or technical reports, letters, charts, tables, and graphs, figures and abbreviations must be used no matter what the publication.

You should use figures sparingly for numbers in standard essays, and you should use abbreviations for words only when convention allows. Spell out most abbreviations when you use them the first time in an essay.

29a Spelling Out Numbers

Spell out numbers up to one hundred and round numbers over one hundred. But when there are a great many numbers and spelled-out numbers would take a great deal of space, use figures, even in the body of an essay.

six cartons BUT 181 cartons

twenty-four dollars BUT $23.88

forty thousand children BUT 39,658 children

three million chickens BUT 4,623 chickens

Try to avoid starting a sentence with a number, but if you must, spell the number out.

29b Using Figures

Use figures for statistical comparisons, for quantitative information, and for dates, times of day, and addresses.

In writing about some subjects, especially technical subjects, numbers are so frequent that you should write them as figures.

> The original plan for the house called for a dining room that would be 18 × 25 feet and a living room that would be 30 × 34 feet with plate-glass windows at each end.

Note that in this example the word *by* in the measurements is also abbreviated as ×.

In nontechnical writing, figures are used to express percentages, but spell out *percent.*

> Nearly 60 percent of those who went to the polls voted to reject the referendum.

Dates that include the year usually appear as figures, but some writers prefer to spell them out.

October 9, 1893	the ninth of October 1893
9 October 1893	October ninth (NOT October 9th)
the 1960s	the nineteen-sixties
1929–1930	from 1929 to 1930

The time of day followed by the abbreviation A.M. or P.M. is always expressed in figures. If you use the less technical forms *in the morning* or *in the evening,* spell out the numbers.

> 6:00 A.M., 6 A.M., 8:15 P.M.
> six o'clock in the morning
> a quarter past eight in the evening

Street and highway numbers almost always appear as figures. When a house number and the number of a street come together in an address, then one of the numbers is written out.

1 Park Avenue	850 Fifteenth Street
Apartment 6J	State Highway 2
Interstate 80	

✓ CHECKLIST 29.1: HANDLING NUMBERS

Your use of spelled-out numbers or figures should be consistent and make the text flow. Ask yourself these questions.

- Are numbers spelled out up to 100?
- Are round or approximate numbers spelled out?
- Do sentences begin with numbers or years?
- Are figures used appropriately in dates, years, times, and addresses?
- If a discussion involves many numbers, statistical comparisons, or quantitative information, are figures used?

29c Spelling Out Words

In formal essay writing, spell out most words rather than abbreviate them.

Spell out unfamiliar abbreviations

Abbreviations may cut down readability, since a general audience may be unfamiliar with them or may not recognize them at all. But in some technical writing such as memos or reports intended for a limited audience, you may use abbreviations that are standard to that audience.

> **Not:** Dr. Ruth and SOL Dean Th. Luciano discussed the std. rules about hab. corp. proceedings in the pol. cts. as they might apply to studs. arrested on DWI charges in the commercial dist. alg. Mass. Ave.
>
> **But:** Dr. Ruth Smith and School of Law Dean Thomas Luciano discussed the standard rules about habeas corpus proceedings in the police courts as they might apply to students arrested on charges of driving while intoxicated in the commercial district along Massachusetts Avenue.

Spell out the names of countries, cities, boroughs, and states and the words *Avenue, Boulevard, Highway, Street, River,* and *Mountains* and words like them used as parts of proper names when they appear in the body of your prose.

> The Catskill Mountains of New York flank the Hudson River to the west.

Veterans Highway crosses Deer Park Avenue.

Cherokee Boulevard in Knoxville, Tennessee, runs by the Tennessee River.

See Chapter 38 for how to treat street and state abbreviations in addresses.

Spell out the names of months and days of the week, and spell out people's names.

In September and October, Charles visits the botanical gardens every Sunday.

Avoid the ampersand

Use an ampersand only if it is part of an official name.

Loneliness and poverty often accompany old age.

The stock index published by Standard & Poors is one of the most important economic documents in America.

The pistol was a Smith & Wesson.

Spell out parts of publications, company names

Spell out the words *pages, chapter, volume,* and *edition* and the names of courses of study, and words such as *company, brothers,* and *incorporated* unless they are abbreviated in official titles.

Chapter 16 presents new developments in open-heart surgery.

The eleventh edition of the Encyclopedia Britannica has thousands of pages without one typographical error.

Freshman Composition 102 is a prerequisite for Communications 201.

You may use abbreviations for *page, chapter,* and *edition* in footnotes, endnotes, and bibliographical references (see Chapter 33).

Use the abbreviation *Inc., Corp., Co.,* or *Bros.* only when it is part of the official title of a company.

His brothers formed a toy company called Kidstuff, Inc., and later changed the name to Goldstein Bros.

Avoid the use of *etc.*

It is almost always better to name the items you intend to blanket under the abbreviation *etc.* than to use the abbreviation as a catchall. If you don't want to make a long list, use *and so on, and so forth, for example,* or *such as.*

> This garden is good for planting lettuce, broccoli, spinach, radishes, onions, and other cool-weather vegetables.
>
> *or*
>
> This garden is good for planting cool-weather vegetables—broccoli and spinach, for example.
>
> *or*
>
> This garden is good for planting vegetables such as lettuce and broccoli.

When you do use *etc.*, do not put the conjunction *and* before it. The abbreviation *etc.* stands for the Latin *et cetera* or *et caetera,* which means "and the rest," so the *and* is included in the abbreviation itself.

29d
Abbreviating Familiar Titles

The general guideline about avoiding abbreviations does not apply to commonly abbreviated titles that always precede the person's name. These include *Mr., Mrs., Ms., Dr., St., the Rev., the Hon., Sen., Rep.,* and *Fr.*

> Fr. Louis joined our monastery twenty years ago.
>
> Mrs. Jean Bascom designed the brick walkway in front of our building.
>
> Dr. Epstein and Dr. Kwang consulted on the operation.
>
> The Rev. Dr. Karl Barth visited Gettysburg, Pennsylvania, shortly before he died.
>
> Mr. Roger Jackson will marry Ms. Joan Wilkerson.

Many women prefer the title *Ms.* instead of *Miss* or *Mrs.* (see Chapter 11). Strictly speaking, *Ms.* is not an abbreviation, since it does not stand for a word. But it is used in the same way *Mr.* and *Mrs.* are used—before a name. The title *Miss* is not an abbreviation, so it is not followed by a period. It always precedes the name.

Some abbreviations are always used after a proper name. Usually they indicate academic or professional degrees or honors. Note that a comma is placed between the name and the abbreviation and that a space follows the comma.

Robert Robinson, Jr.
Kai-y Hsu, Ph.D.
Maria Tiante, M.D.
Elaine Leff, C.P.A., LL.D.
Michael Bartlett, Esq.

But spell out titles used without proper names.

Mr. Carew asked if she had seen the doctor.

Notice that when an abbreviation ends a sentence, the period at the end of the abbreviation itself will serve as the period of the sentence. If a question mark or an exclamation point ends the sentence, you must place such a punctuation mark *after* the period in the abbreviation.

When he was in the seventh grade, we called him "Stinky," but now he is William Percival Abernathy, Ph.D.!

Is it true that he now wants to be called Stanley Martin, Esq.?

29e
Using Acronyms

If you use the name of an agency or an organization frequently in an essay or a report, you may abbreviate it to make the repetition less tedious. Write out the name of the agency or the organization the first time you use it, and give the abbreviation in parentheses.

The Student Nonviolent Coordinating Committee (SNCC) was far to the left of other civil rights organizations, and its leaders often mocked the "conservatism" of Dr. Martin Luther King, Jr. SNCC quickly burned itself out and disappeared, but some scholars now give the organization much credit for some of the progress made in civil rights during those hard years.

Abbreviations of agency names that can be used as nouns or adjectives are called **acronyms.** Some, such as SNCC, are pronounced as words ("snick"). Acronyms of three or more letters generally do not use periods, but if you elect to use them, do so consistently.

CIA, EPA, JFK, NAACP, NASA

Many government agencies are regularly referred to by their acronyms or abbreviations, especially in publications that mention them frequently. Often these abbreviations are so well known that they do not require any explanation.

The FBI entered the case immediately, since under the Lindbergh Act kidnapping is a federal crime.

29f
Using Other Common Abbreviations

Abbreviate words typically used with times, dates, and figures.

6 P.M. OR 6:00 P.M.	A.D. 1066
9:45 AM OR 9:45 A.M.	6000 rpm
498 B.C.	

Note that instead of B.C., many writers now use B.C.E., "Before the Common Era." If a year stands alone, without B.C. or B.C.E., it is assumed to be A.D.

29g
Avoiding Latin Abbreviations

In text, use English translations rather than Latin abbreviations.

compare	cf.
for example	e.g.
and others	et al.
and so on, and so forth, and the rest	etc.
in the same place	ibid.
that is	i.e.

Although new documentation systems for research papers use a minimum of abbreviations, you may come across the Latin abbreviations in your own reading and research. A list of the most familiar abbreviations appears in 33h.

■ **Exercise 29.1** Rewrite the following sentences, using numbers and abbreviations appropriately.

1. Dr. Muscatel's house was on 2d. Ave. near the warehouse of the Ledbetter bros.
2. The dr. got up early every a.m. and stayed in her office in the p.m. until the last patient had left.
3. You could call him in the middle of the night, & the rev. would come to your house in 20 minutes.
4. When you saw him on the st., he always seemed deep in thought.
5. 1936 was the year he moved here, & FDR was Pres. of the USA.

CHAPTER 30

USING ITALICS

Some words and phrases need to be set off as distinctive. The titles of novels you refer to in an essay for an American literature class, for example, need to look different from regular text.

> **Confusing:** Hawthorne's Scarlet Letter set him apart from the New England writers of his day.

The reader who did not know that *The Scarlet Letter* is the title of a novel might think that Hawthorne wrote with red ink or had a correspondent named Scarlet!

To set off certain words and phrases, printers use *italics,* a typeface in which the characters slant to the right. Since most typewriters and many computer printers lack an italic face, and since it is impossible to make italics in handwriting, writers preparing manuscripts underline the words a printer would set in italics. An underline is, in fact, a typesetter's mark indicating that a word or words is to be set in italics.

Handwritten

Katharine Hepburn gives one of her best performances in The African Queen.

Typed

`Katharine Hepburn gives one of her best performances in The African Queen.`

Printed

Katharine Hepburn gives one of her best performances in *The African Queen.*

30a/b
ital

30a
Treating Titles of Works of Art

Underline titles of books, magazines, journals, newspapers, plays, films, artworks, long poems, pamphlets and other short works published separately, and musical works.

> Joan Didion, a former editor of *Vogue* and the *National Review,* received glowing reviews in the *New York Times* for her novel *A Book of Common Prayer.*
>
> Picasso's *Guernica* captures the anguish and despair of violence.
>
> Plays by Shakespeare provide details and story lines for Verdi's opera *Falstaff,* the musical comedy *Kiss Me, Kate* by Cole Porter, and Franco Zeffirelli's film *Romeo and Juliet.*

In book titles, *a, an,* or *the* as a first word is capitalized and underlined, but *the* is not generally treated as part of the title in names of newspapers and periodicals.

Quotation marks distinguish the titles of short works—essays, newspaper and magazine articles and columns, short stories, television and radio programs, short poems, songs, chapters or other book subdivisions. Quotation marks are also used for titles of unpublished works, including student papers, theses, and dissertations (see p. 340).

> Elizabeth Cullinan's "Only Human" appears in a collection of her stories called *Yellow Roses.*

The Bible and other sacred books such as the Koran are exceptions.

> The Book of Ecclesiastes provides some of the most haunting phrases in the Bible.

Do not underline the title of your paper on the title page or place it in quotation marks. These conventions are used to refer to titles in writings about them, not in the writings themselves.

30b
Italicizing Foreign Terms

Underline most foreign words and phrases to indicate italics.

> They are wise to remember, however, one thing. He is Sinatra. The boss. *Il Padrone.*
>
> —GAY TALESE

> *Chota hasari*—the little breakfast—consists of a cup of tea at five-thirty or six in the morning, with possibly some fruit or toast served with it. At eleven or at midday a heavier meal is eaten, *chapatis*—thin unleavened wheat cakes—and curry, with *dal*—a kind of lentil soup—and curds and sweets of some sort.
>
> —SANTHA RAMA RAU

> Memphis, in fact, was definitely the mecca, yardstick and *summum bonum.*
>
> —TERRY SOUTHERN

Many foreign words have become so common in English that everyone accepts them as part of the language, and they require no underlining or italics. Some examples are rigor mortis (Latin), pasta (Italian), sombrero (Spanish), bête noire (French), and festschrift (German). Notice that in the quotation from Terry Southern above, the proper noun Mecca is used as a common noun meaning any place where large numbers of people go to have some uplifting experience (see 28c).

Some foreign words are still borderline, and some writers underline them while others do not. Examples are *ex nihilo* (Latin for "from nothing"), *imprimatur* (Latin for "Let it be printed"), and *Weltanschauung* (German for "world view"). Often the preference of the writer or the need for a special effect dictates the decision to underline or not.

Dictionaries offer some help. By labeling as *French* a phrase like *mise-en-scène,* for example, a dictionary guides your decision to underline. Some dictionaries have special sections headed "Foreign Words." Others italicize foreign words when they appear. But writers must use their own judgment about the borderline words. Here it is good to consider your audience and to try to imagine the expectations that readers may bring to your work. Within an essay, be consistent in italicizing foreign words and phrases that appear more than once.

30c Italicizing Words Used as Words

Underline (to indicate italics) words or phrases you use as words rather than for the meaning they convey.

The use of the word *glide* at the end of the last stanza is effective and gives just the amount of emphasis required at the end of the poem.

—CLEANTH BROOKS AND ROBERT PENN WARREN

And if the word *integration* means anything, this is what it means: that we, with love, shall force our brothers to see themselves as they are, to cease fleeing from reality and begin changing it.

—JAMES BALDWIN

Letters used alone also require underlining to show italics.

The word *bookkeeper* has three sets of double letters: double *o*, double *k*, and double *e*.

Some writers use quotation marks to show that words are being used as words.

When I was in graduate school in the late fifties, "criticism" was still a fighting word.

—GERALD GRAFF

30d
Using Italics for Emphasis

Sometimes writers are tempted to italicize words to show the kind of emphasis they'd make in speaking. Use italics for this purpose only occasionally. Too many italicized words will tire readers; their eyes may leap over the underlined or italicized words—the very opposite effect from what you intended. Too much emphasis may mean no emphasis at all.

Weak: You don't *mean* that your *teacher* told the whole *class* that *he* did not know the answer *himself*?

Revised: Your teacher admitted that he did not know the answer? That is amazing.

An occasional word in italics helps you emphasize a point.

That advertisers exploit women's subordination rather than cause it can be clearly seen now that *male* fashions and toiletries have become big business.

—ELLEN WILLIS

It now seems clear that we are not going to improve instruction by finding *the* method or methods that are good for all peoples.

—K. PATRICIA CROSS

In written dialogue, writers may use italics to emphasize words to show the rhythms of speech used by characters.

The lady, however, regarded it very placidly. "I shouldn't have gone if she *had* asked me."

—HENRY JAMES

As they turned to him, Blackburn said: "Can *you* give *me* a few minutes, Dr. Howe?" His eyes sparkled at the little audacity he had committed, the slightly impudent play with hierarchy.

—LIONEL TRILLING

30e Other Uses of Italics

By convention, the names of ships appear in italics, as do the names of air and space vehicles. The names of trains do not.

I packed my valise, and took passage on an ancient tub called the *Paul Jones* for New Orleans.

—MARK TWAIN

Many style manuals also recommend the use of italics for court cases.

In *Brown* v. *Board of Education of Topeka* (1954), the U.S. Supreme Court ruled that segregation in public schools was unconstitutional.

■ **Exercise 30.1** Underline any words or phrases that require italics in the following sentences.

1. An advertisement in the San Diego Evening Tribune announced a cruise on the Queen Elizabeth II, but after I read Katherine Anne Porter's novel Ship of Fools, a vacation on the sea per se did not interest me.
2. Time reported that Da Vinci's painting The Last Supper had deteriorated seriously from pollution and neglect.
3. The word hopefully is common nowadays, but many people who take writing seriously object to it because they think the words I

30e
ital

hope or we hope or it is hoped usually express the meaning more clearly.

4. By the time the police discovered the body, rigor mortis had set in, and Inspector Michaelson told reporters from the Times and the Globe that death had taken place circa twelve hours before.
5. Russell Baker's column Observer appears in the New York Times several days a week.

■ **Exercise 30.2** Rewrite the following sentences to eliminate excessive emphasis. You may change the wording. You may also change the order of the sentences.

1. Mr. Watt promised that this was *absolutely* the last time that he or *any other* member of his department would even *mention* digging a coal mine in Yellowstone National Park.
2. Who could *possibly* have known that the landing gear *was* defective and that the pilot was *drunk?*
3. The crew of the space shuttle *firmly* believed that the *engineering problems* of the flight were less serious than the *psychological problems* of living so close together under such a demanding routine.
4. *Anyone* desiring to change sections *must* file a form with the registrar *before* Friday afternoon.
5. Do you *really* like *country* music?

✓ CHECKLIST 30.1: SETTING OFF WORDS AND PHRASES

As you revise, look for words and phrases that should be distinguished by italics (underlines) or quotation marks. Be sure they are correctly set off from the rest of your text. Pay attention to the following types of words and phrases.

Titles of published works

- Are the titles of works published separately (including books, magazines, journals, newspapers, plays, films, art works, long poems, pamphlets, and musical works) set off in italics?
- Are the titles of short works, including essays, newspaper and maga-

zine articles and columns, short poems, television programs, songs, chapters and other book subdivisions, set off in quotation marks?

- Are titles of unpublished works set off in quotation marks?

Foreign terms

- Are unusual foreign terms set off in italics?
- Are italics used consistently for these terms?

Words as words

- Are words and letters discussed as such italicized to clarify your meaning?

Emphasis

- Is italic used for emphasis only when absolutely necessary?

PART SEVEN
WRITING A RESEARCH PAPER

PART EIGHT
OTHER WRITING TASKS

BOOK THREE

SPECIAL WRITING TASKS

PART
SEVEN

WRITING A RESEARCH PAPER

CHAPTER

CHAPTER

31

STARTING A RESEARCH PROJECT

Research projects rely on careful investigation of varied sources in the library and elsewhere. These sources include not just the obvious books, periodicals, and reference items but also films, plays, concerts, television programs, videotapes, audiotapes, records, computer programs, microfilms, and microfiches. Anything that can provide accurate information efficiently is a tool in the researcher's hands. Thus, research might include interviews; a reporter digging into corruption among city officials, for example, needs firsthand contact with municipal leaders and their aides. Often research begins with telephone calls and casual conversations with your friends, instructors, or other experts who can help set you on the path to information quickly.

The chapters in this part of the handbook use two student papers as models, tracing their development from selecting a topic, through researching and writing, to preparing the final copy. The final copies of both papers are presented in Chapter 34. One paper is an analysis of short stories by Willa Cather. This paper draws on the documentation methods established by the Modern Language Association of America (MLA) and recommended for research in literature and the humanities. Because the conventions of writing about research vary from discipline to discipline, we also include a paper on a scientific topic, the phenomenon of black holes. This paper draws on the documentation methods established by the American Psychological Association (APA) and recommended for research in the social sciences. The more you know about the conventions of the various disciplines, the easier it will be for you to investigate sources and to present your findings for different courses of study.

Thinking through a research paper is much like thinking through any other written composition, even though research papers differ in content and format from other kinds of papers. The planning guidelines set forth in these chapters should help you produce a successful paper.

31a
Choosing a Topic

Choose a subject that interests you, and develop a limited topic by doing prewriting exercises and using the library. Discuss the topic with friends or your instructor.

Start with a general subject that fits both your own interests and your assignment. Think about various topics within that general area; then discuss them with people you know. Try brainstorming, jotting down ideas in an informal list, asking yourself questions about your subject, writing nonstop, or developing a subject tree (illustrated in 1a).

Prewriting exercises will help you explore what you already know about the subject and identify areas you would like to know more about. See, for example, how developing an informal list helped the writer of the paper on Cather to narrow diffuse ideas to a topic of more manageable proportions.

Informal list

Willa Cather

novel My Antonia my favorite in high school English

realistic picture of life on the frontier

hard existence for women

good descriptive detail

simple writing style, deep feelings though

hard to leave behind your family and move West

read one of Cather's short stories, "Sculptor's Funeral"

good short story writer: picture of the hard life for the artist on the western plains

maybe read some other stories by Cather?

women as central characters? difference of effects of hard life on men and women?

making a new life in a new territory you're not prepared for

dangers of famine, weather, Indians

```
Where and how was Cather educated?

What was her life like as a writer?

What did other writers think of her work? book reviews?

Cather's view of her art? What was she trying to achieve in her
   stories and novels?
```

31a topic

Once you have a preliminary idea for your paper, browse through the library. Check the library catalog, general reference books, and periodical indexes to see what others have written on your topic. Preliminary reading in books and magazines helps you decide on the suitability of your topic and limits and sharpens its focus. This early exploring of books and magazines will also help you develop your topic and organize your later research.

How narrow a topic must you choose? The answer to that question depends on your interests, the nature of the assignment, the required length of the paper, the number and quality of available library materials, and the time you have to do your assignment. But try to narrow your topic as much as possible, because narrow topics allow you to use enough specific examples and details to keep readers interested. In the following examples, note how students narrowed their topics until they reached promising starting points for their papers.

Literature

Short stories
↓
Willa Cather's short stories
↓
The theme of isolation in Cather's short stories
↓
The theme of isolation in two stories by Cather

Astronomy

Current questions about the universe
↓
Black holes
↓
How black holes might be located in space
↓
Various techniques used in the search for black holes

As you do preliminary research, you may discover that you need to limit your topic further. Carefully limiting your topic will help you exclude many fruitless areas before you investigate them. For instance, if the writer of the paper on Cather's stories had not narrowed her topic from the informal list above, she would have wasted time researching Cather's later novels, Cather's views on naturalism in fiction, or the ups and downs of her reputation among critics.

***Readers' Guide,* subject entry**

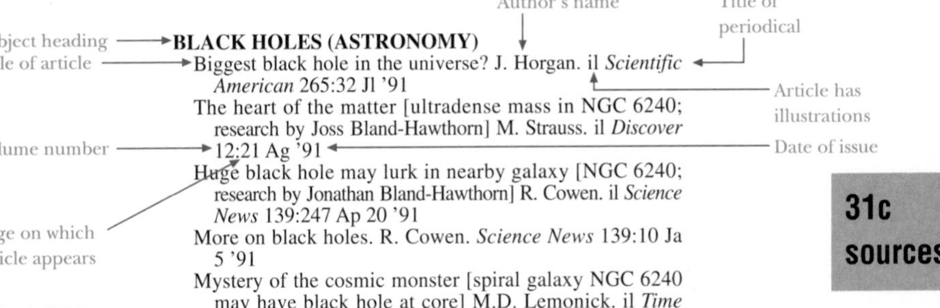

BLACK HOLES (ASTRONOMY)
Biggest black hole in the universe? J. Horgan. il *Scientific American* 265:32 Jl '91
The heart of the matter [ultradense mass in NGC 6240; research by Joss Bland-Hawthorn] M. Strauss. il *Discover* 12:21 Ag '91
Huge black hole may lurk in nearby galaxy [NGC 6240; research by Jonathan Bland-Hawthorn] R. Cowen. il *Science News* 139:247 Ap 20 '91
More on black holes. R. Cowen. *Science News* 139:10 Ja 5 '91
Mystery of the cosmic monster [spiral galaxy NGC 6240 may have black hole at core] M.D. Lemonick. il *Time* 137:74 Ap 22 '91

31c sources

***Readers' Guide,* author entry**

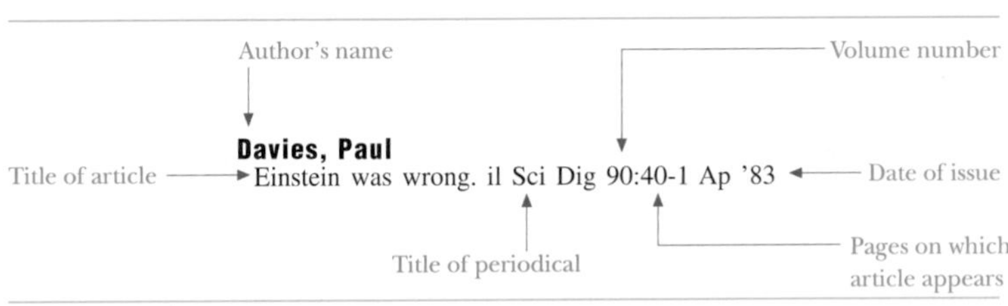

Davies, Paul
Einstein was wrong. il Sci Dig 90:40-1 Ap '83

Other indexes

- *Access* (1975–) bills itself as "the supplementary index to periodicals," meaning that it indexes periodicals not included in *The Readers' Guide* and other general indexes. Even so, *Access* limits itself to the kind of periodical that you might find in a large magazine store.
- *America: History and Life* (1964–), an especially useful index for the research writer investigating any topic dealing with American (including Canadian) history and culture, includes not only citations to articles but also abstracts.
- *The British Humanities Index* (1962–), a British version of *The Readers' Guide,* indexes periodicals published in Great Britain and has a much broader range than its American counterpart because it includes scholarly and professional journals. It succeeds the *Subject Index to Periodicals,* published by the Library Association.

- *Essay and General Literature Index* (1900–) lists essays and articles in essay collections in the humanities and social sciences.
- *Humanities Index* (1974–) includes entries from more than 250 periodicals in archeology, classics, language, literature, history, philosophy, religion, the performing arts, and folklore, arranged by author and subject. Book reviews appear in a separate section at the end.

- *MLA International Bibliography of Books and Articles on the Modern Languages and Literatures,* an annual five-volume bibliography issued by the Modern Language Association, offers a classified list and index by subject of selections on modern languages, literatures, folklore, and linguistics. It draws on hundreds of books and periodicals as well as films, sound recordings, microfilms, and other machine-readable materials.

***MLA International Bibliography*, entry**

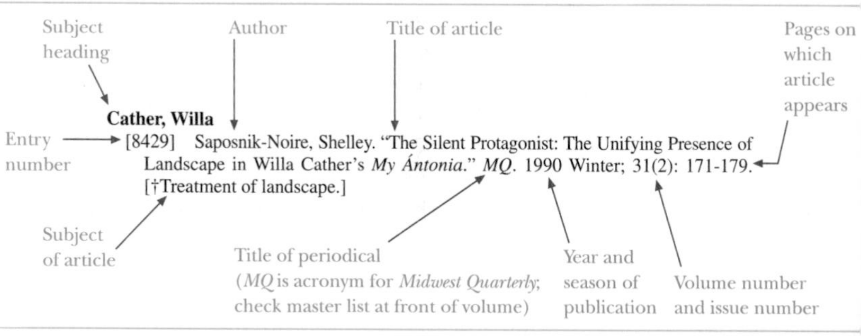

- *The New York Times Index* (1913–), an indispensable resource, includes all stories that have appeared in the *New York Times,* giving the date of each story, the page and column number of the paper, and an abstract of the entry. Cross-references are numerous.
- *Psychological Abstracts* (1927–) abstracts thousands of articles in psychology published every year, making it an excellent tool for any topic with a psychological dimension.
- *Public Affairs Information Service Bulletin* (PAIS) (1915–), listing articles by subject, is a rich resource for almost any topic dealing with politics, economics, international relations, city planning, or other aspects of social or political life.

- *Social Sciences Index* (1974–) covers periodicals in the fields of anthropology, criminology, economics, law, political science, psychology, and sociology, among other areas of interest to social scientists. Here, too, a separate section of book reviews appears in each issue. From 1965 to 1974, the *Humanities Index* and the *Social Sciences Index* were published as the *Social Sciences and Humanities Index.* From 1907 to 1965 the name of the combined index was the *International Index.*

Other indexes to periodical literature deal with specialized fields and include citations to specialized journals. Some articles they list may help you in the later stages of your research, after you have summarized the information about your topic and have developed a general idea of what you want to say about it. Here are a few specialized indexes.

Applied Science and Technology Index (1913–)
Art Index (1929–)
Arts and Humanities Citation Index (1978–)
Biography Index (1947–)
Biological and Agricultural Index (1964–)
Business Periodicals Index (1953–)
Current Index to Journals in Education (1969–)
Education Index (1929–)
Film Literature Index (1973–)
Index to U.S. Government Periodicals (1974–)
Music Index (1949–)
Social Sciences Citation Index (1973–)

Be sure to ask for help from your reference librarian, who will guide you to other indexes for topics dealing with other special fields.

Most periodicals publish their own annual indexes. When you work in a special field, consult the indexes of journals published in the field for articles useful for your research.

Using Standard Reference Books

When you write a research paper, you must do much more than merely repeat information you find in encyclopedias and dictionaries. But it is always a good idea to use such reference works for background information and perhaps for inspiration to guide you to other ways to explore your topic.

General encyclopedias

The reference section of your library will have several encyclopedias. Here are a few standard works you may wish to consult.

Collier's Encyclopedia
Dictionary of American Biography, 20 vols., plus supplements
Dictionary of National Biography, 21 vols., plus supplements (Britain)
Dictionary of American History, 8 vols.
Encyclopaedia Britannica
Encyclopaedia Judaica, 16 vols.
Encyclopaedia of Religion and Ethics, 13 vols.
Encyclopedia Americana
Encyclopedia Canadiana, 10 vols.
Encyclopedia of World Art, 15 vols.
The Golden Bough: A Study in Magic and Religion, edited by Sir James G. Frazer, 13 vols.
Harvard Dictionary of Music
The International Encyclopedia of Film
International Encyclopedia of the Social Sciences, 19 vols.
The McGraw-Hill Dictionary of Art
The McGraw-Hill Encyclopedia of Science and Technology, 15 vols.
New Catholic Encyclopedia, 15 vols.
The New Columbia Desk Encyclopedia
The New Grove Dictionary of Music and Musicians, 20 vols.
The New York Times Film Reviews
The Oxford Classical Dictionary, 2d ed.
The Oxford Dictionary of the Christian Church

Literary research materials

When you write research papers for literature courses, you have a large body of research materials to draw from, including several outstanding works.

- *The Oxford Companion to American Literature,* 4th edition, edited by James D. Hart, offers biographies of American writers and summaries of literary works written in English by Americans. This volume pays little attention to literature not written by U.S. authors, and it ignores Latin American writers.

- *The Oxford Companion to English Literature,* 4th edition, edited by Sir Paul Harvey, presents biographies of British writers and summaries of their important works; it also gives writers' biographies and summarizes plots of European literary works considered influential in Britain and the United States.
- *The Oxford History of English Literature* comes in twelve volumes, each covering a period of literature and written by a distinguished specialist in that field.
- *The Year's Work in English Studies,* published in London annually since 1920, contains graceful, well-written summaries of books and articles published each year in the entire field of English literature.
- *Contemporary Authors* (1962–) is a multivolume series giving short biographies and publication information for twentieth-century writers.
- *Contemporary Literary Criticism* (1976–), another multivolume series, presents excerpts from reviews written by prominent critics of contemporary literature. The series has recently expanded to include film criticism.
- *The Harvard Guide to Contemporary American Writing,* edited by Daniel Hoffmann, 1979, surveys the works of the most prominent recent American writers.

Doing a Computer Search

Automated libraries now can store extensive information on sources and make the information quickly available to researchers. Using electronic reference lists, or **databases,** you can examine bibliographical information as well as abstracts, cross-references, or summaries from hundreds of different sources. Good databases currently are available on the natural, applied, and social sciences, and you can save time by consulting one suited to your topic.

A successful electronic search starts with key words, or **descriptors,** which signal an area of interest and allow the computer to call up the articles. Some databases ask you to specify descriptors by *author, title,* or *subject.* Others allow you to search the entire database for a key word. You should choose the most precise and specific descriptors that you can. A descriptor that is too general will yield hundreds or even thousands of entries. You could spend days going through them all, only to find the vast majority are of no use to you. One way to narrow a search while still using a broad descriptor is to limit it in time. You can start by looking only at the articles published this year, or in the 1990s.

Remember, the computer will look for exactly what you *write,* not necessarily what you mean. For instance, if you are doing a research paper on F. Scott Fitzgerald and your descriptor is *author: Fitzgerald, F. Scott,* you are unlikely to find any references, because Fitzgerald, who died in 1940, hasn't written any articles in a long time. However, you will find many entries under *subject: Fitzgerald, F. Scott* because there are many books and articles about him.

If you have questions about narrowing your field of search, most databases have on-line help. If the computer itself is unable to help you narrow your focus, your librarian can help you select more useful terms. Another approach is to look at a general index, like the *Readers' Guide to Periodical Literature,* under the general heading of your topic to see the various descriptors used there. For instance, the student interested in the general subject of *astronomy* would find seventeen subheadings as useful descriptors.

Database, subject entry

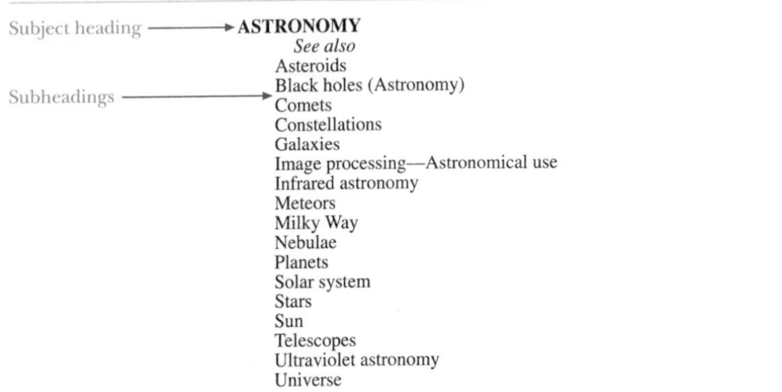

The student researching black holes used the *Wilson Indexes,* a magazine guide of 800 journals and periodicals. Most automated libraries have some computerized periodical index, such as the *Magazine Index, Infotract,* or *Nexis.* Using *astronomy* as a descriptor, the student learned that more than 2,500 entries were available, far too many to be useful. The descriptor *black holes* yielded 303, still too many. The student then chose to look only at articles published in the 1990s. Narrowing the search in this way produced 19 articles.

With most databases, you will be able to print out the titles the computer produces. Before you do, examine the number of citations and the format in which they will appear. You may want to narrow your descriptors further or develop new combinations. You can command the computer to provide simple bibliographical data, or you can request abstracts of articles as well as other relevant material. Ask only for what you need.

Database, sample printout

```
DWIL
SEARCH REQUEST: S=BLACK HOLES
WILSON RECORD-- 17 OF 303 ENTRIES FOUND
             SCREEN 17 OF 303

AUTHORS: CROSSWELL, KEN

ARTICLE TITLE:       THE BEST BLACK HOLE IN THE GALAXY.

SOURCE/DATE:         ASTRONOMY 20:30-7 MAR '92

SPECIAL FEATURES:    IL

SUBJECT DESCRIPTORS: BLACK HOLES(ASTRONOMY)
                     MILKY WAY

               GENERAL SCIENCE INDEX
COMMANDS
HO Holding                I  Index
N  Next record            G  Guide
P  Previous record        H  Help

DWIL
SEARCH REQUEST: K=BLACK HOLES
WILSON RECORD-- 19 OF 303 ENTRIES FOUND
             SCREEN 19 OF 303
AUTHORS: JOHN GRIBBINS

ARTICLE TITLE:       IS NAKEDNESS PERMITTED OUTSIDE
                     THE COSMIC EDEN?

SOURCE/DATE:         NEW SCIENTIST 134:15 APR '92

SPECIAL FEATURES:

SUBJECT DESCRIPTORS: SINGULARITIES (MATHEMATICS)
                     BLACK HOLES (ASTRONOMY)
```


Using Bibliographies and Notes

Look carefully at the scholarly books and articles you consult to find useful bibliographies and notes. References to other books and articles often lead to new and useful sources of information.

In a 1984 collection, *Critical Essays on Willa Cather* by John J. Murphy, the student writing on Cather discovered a three-page list of sources after one of the essays. There she found a reference to an article by Dayton Kohler in a 1947 issue of *College English.* Kohler's point about the effects of the barren landscape of the West on the human spirit helped the writer shape some of her ideas on Cather's stories.

■ **Exercise 31.2*** For any topic you narrowed down in Exercise 31.1, make a list of five indexes that you might use to help you locate articles in periodicals. Use the reference section of your library.

■ **Exercise 31.3*** If your library can do a computer search, make a list of key words relevant to your topic and check the list against the database descriptions. Print out a limited, focused list of sources.

■ **Exercise 31.4*** For any topic you narrowed down in Exercise 31.1, develop at least ten bibliography cards for books, periodicals, and other sources. Be sure to follow either the format suggested by your instructor or the format described in 31c as you copy the required data.

✔ CHECKLIST 31.2: LOCATING SOURCES

After you have decided on your topic, begin the serious search for sources. Here are some places to look.

- the subject catalog of your library catalog
- author entries for authors in the subject catalog, to see if these authors have published related works
- computer databases
- the library stacks where books related to your topic are shelved
- bibliographies and notes in books on your subject
- periodical indexes
- general encyclopedias
- other reference books
- conversations with specialists

CHAPTER 32

PLANNING A RESEARCH PAPER

By this point in your research project, you've concentrated on selecting and narrowing a topic suitable for research and on identifying appropriate libraries, reference tools, and other materials for investigation. Your main tasks now are to shape your thoughts about your topic by exploring some sources and taking notes. You should also develop a flexible plan for your paper. As you read and evaluate what you have read, your topic may change focus or emphasis, and your plan, too, will change. Reading, note taking, and planning will help you produce a well-written paper.

32a Developing a Thesis and a Rough Plan

After prewriting and after limiting your topic, explore some of your resources for information about it. Your purpose at this stage is to develop your ideas about the topic.

Doing research is more than simply gathering information; it is developing something of your own to say about what you have read. Don't worry about the number of people who have already written about your topic. Some careful thought about your resources at this stage will stimulate your own original ideas. As your thoughts take shape, put together a hypothesis and a rough plan. Both will help you concentrate on the topic you expect to develop in your paper.

A **hypothesis** is a debatable assumption that you have to prove. It can be thought of as an educated guess. After some early exploration of your topic, state tentatively what conclusion you expect your research to support. All researchers start with a hypothesis; it guides their investigations, helping them find appropriate sources and rule out others.

	Literature	**Astronomy**
Topic	The theme of isolation in two stories by Cather	Various techniques used in the search for black holes
	↓	↓
Hypothesis	In Cather's stories, characters isolated from familiar surroundings are severely affected physically and spiritually.	Black holes are almost impossible to find, despite astronomers' predictions.

The student writing on Cather noted a remark one critic made about how the American West affected the lives of characters in Cather's novels, especially characters moving to the West from more "civilized" Eastern societies. Was this true about characters in the short stories as well? As the student read Cather's stories and comments about them in secondary sources, she could identify details that seemed to show the effects of separation upon the body and spirit of central characters. Her hypothesis reflects the connection she sees between isolation from familiar worlds and its effects on people.

The student who chose the topic on black holes was struck by researchers' faith in the phenomenon of black holes despite the absence of real physical evidence. Physicists had defined black holes, predicted their presence, and suggested their origins, but no one had reported having found black holes. Could they be found? The student formulated a hypothesis: that black holes were almost impossible to locate.

As you continue reading and exploring, your hypothesis—even your topic itself—may change markedly. Other investigators may have disproved your idea. You may find that what seemed like promising sources offer little or no help. You may discover a new area of thought that reshapes your thinking and pushes you into new territory. At this stage, your hypothesis is tentative, as is your plan for the research paper itself. As your reading continues and your hypothesis becomes more precise, you will refine your thoughts and language and develop a carefully worded thesis for your paper. In the papers on Cather and on black holes (Chapter 34), you can see how the hypotheses changed as the writers thought about their topics during the course of their research.

After you state your hypothesis, sketch a rough plan, a brief list of the headings you intend to cover. The tentative thesis statement and the rough plans that follow guided the writers of the papers on Willa Cather and on black holes.

Literature

Plan: Write about the effects of isolation in Willa Cather's short stories

Tentative thesis: Cather's stories " 'A Death in the Desert' " and "A Wagner Matinee" deal with the theme of isolation.

1. Effects on characters' spirits
2. Effects on their appearance
3. How music is important

Astronomy

Plan: Write about the search for black holes

Tentative thesis: The search for black holes presents complex problems for astronomers today.

1. Definition
2. History of the idea
3. Early search
4. Pulsars
5. Binary stars
6. Current search

These preparatory steps bring your topic into focus for note taking and outlining. Of course, as you continue to read, you will make many changes, both in the thesis and in the rough plan.

■ **Exercise 32.1*** Do some preliminary reading to shape your ideas about the topic that you chose in Exercise 31.1. Then develop a tentative thesis and rough plan to guide your research.

32b Using Primary and Secondary Sources

Read your sources with care, and take careful notes. Most of the sources you will use for a brief research paper will be *secondary,* although you should try to use *primary* sources whenever possible. **Primary sources** include works of literature, such as novels and poems; historical documents, such as diaries, letters, journals, speeches, and autobiographies; and interviews, private conversations, observations, and experiments. **Secondary sources** analyze and comment on other source material. The student writing about Willa Cather could use as a primary source one of Cather's short stories or novels or any of her other published works; as secondary sources, the student could use books or articles written about Cather or her fiction. Among the sources used for this paper, " 'A Death in the Desert' " and "A Wagner Matinee" are primary sources. Secondary sources include an article by Joseph X. Brennan, "Willa Cather and Music," and a book by David Dalches, *Willa Cather: A Critical Introduction.*

32b plan

Write your notes on 3 × 5 inch cards. Put only one idea on each card. Limiting your notes in this way will make it easier for you to organize your materials later (see 32c). Some students prefer larger index cards, but big cards make it tempting to copy down more information and more quotations than you need. Quote directly on your note cards only if you think you may use the quotation in your paper. Summarize or paraphrase many of your sources. Summarizing and paraphrasing force you to absorb the thoughts of your source and to express them in your own words rather than merely repeat them.

A **summary** is a sharply condensed version of an original source in your own words. A summary usually states the thesis briefly and gives the main idea of the original. Your purpose in a summary is to condense important information and to eliminate unessential points. A **paraphrase** is a much fuller summary; it may cite some of the evidence and use some of the words in the original source. A good paraphrase follows the line of reasoning in the original source and the sequence of ideas as well. In both paraphrases and summaries, you must acknowledge your sources.

Do not waste time copying down a long quotation or writing a paraphrase or a summary on a note card. Instead, make a signal card. On a **signal card,** note the page numbers where the information appears and record your thoughts about how a quotation might be used in your paper. Of course, you can't keep library books forever; so when you write signal cards, you should be ready to write your paper. If you think you may not have the book handy when you do write, copy down the material you need, either as a direct quotation or as a paraphrase. Because copying long direct quotations by hand leads to errors, you must proofread such passages with great care.

Copying machines are available in most libraries, and you can copy a page or two from a book or a periodical. (Such copying is strictly regulated by federal copyright laws, and your library may have regulations about the use of copying machines.) Remember that copying the source on a machine is no substitute for reading it. If you are going to use the source in your paper, you must read it carefully and make it part of your own thinking.

Often when you are taking notes, ideas about what you are summarizing, paraphrasing, or copying will occur to you. Be sure your notes distinguish your words and ideas from those of your source. In your paper you will have to identify the sources of all the ideas you have borrowed. If you do not make clear in your notes just whose ideas are whose, you may find yourself committing plagiarism (see 33b). Use parentheses, asterisks, arrows, or some other means to identify your own thoughts in your notes. Also, be careful to note page breaks when a quotation continues to another page. Only a small part of what you record on a note card may appear in the final draft of your paper, and you must be able to report the exact page reference for the quotation you use.

Below is an excerpt from pages 280–81 of Sharon O'Brien's *Willa Cather: The Emerging Voice* (New York: Oxford University Press, 1987) on Cather's "A Wagner Matinee." Various types of note cards prepared from the excerpt follow it. Note that the writer has identified the source at the top of each card in an abbreviated form. (Full bibliographical data will appear on the writer's bibliography cards; see 31c.)

Source

In "A Wagner Matinee," for example, Cather integrates a family story into her fiction: Georgianna and her husband measure off their quarter section of land by tying a cotton handkerchief to a wagon wheel and counting off the revolutions, as had Cather's Aunt Franc and her husband George Cather when they first arrived in Nebraska in the 1880s.[8] In the grim portrayal of Georgianna's Nebraska farm, Cather also drew on her own memories of the difficult transition from Virginia to Nebraska, using her memories of her grandparents' farmhouse in describing Georgianna's bleak environment. Her portrayal of the gifted woman starving for music amid the "silence of the plains" also owes something to her own experience of aesthetic deprivation in Nebraska, a feeling intensified retrospectively when she discovered what her prairie education lacked. As she told Will Owen Jones, the distaste she had felt for Nebraska was because she had been only half nourished there.[9] "The Sculptor's Funeral" also had real-life sources: Cather's witnessing an artist's funeral in Pittsburgh and, on another occasion, seeing the return of a Nebraska boy—in his coffin—to Red Cloud.

But there were dangers in turning from admiration to memory: the risk of punishment and retribution Cather had associated with self-exposure in her first college stories. After "A Wagner Matinee" appeared in *Everybody's Magazine* in 1904, a year before *The Troll Garden,* Cather faced a Nebraska uprising. The resulting controversy over the story was the "nearest she had come to personal disgrace," she told Viola Roseboro later.[10] Like "The Sculptor's Funeral" and Hamlin Garland's *Main-Travelled Roads,* "A Wagner Matinee" portrays the Midwest as a harsh, oppressive, and repressive environment. Family members were particularly insulted by the supposed portrait of Aunt Franc in Georgianna and informed Cather that it wasn't "nice" to say such things in print. Friends and neighbors found the grim depiction of Nebraska unfair, and Cather was even attacked in her hometown paper by her old friend and colleague Will Owen Jones. "If the writers of fiction who use western Nebraska as material would look up now and then and not keep their eyes and noses in the cattle yards," he complained in the *Journal,* "they might be more agreeable company" (*WWC,* p. 254).

In the quotation card below, the exact words of the source are in quotation marks. An arrow distinguishes the writer's thought from that of the source. The summary card highlights the points in the passage that concern the writer of the research paper. Note the many details omitted from the source. On the paraphrase card the notes closely follow the line of reasoning of the original, although the writer has used her own words to restate O'Brien's point. The few words in quotation marks are exact

O'Brien, Cather, p. 281
"Her portrayal of the gifted woman starving for music amid the 'silence of the plains' also owes something to her own experience of aesthetic deprivation in Nebraska, a feeling intensified retrospectively when she discovered what her prairie education lacked.
→ Compare with Gerber and Stouck. This seems to be a major concern of Cather's - artist's survival on the frontier.

Summary card

O'Brien, Cather, p. 281
Cather's own experiences contribute to the grim picture of Aunt Georgianna's Nebraska farm. Cather's own sense of artistic loss and weakness in education influences portrait of talented woman hungering for music on the plains.

Paraphrase card

O'Brien, Cather, p. 281
In "A Wagner Matinee" Cather drew on personal experiences such as measuring off land in Nebraska in the 1880s. Remembering her move from Virginia and the farmhouse of her grandparents in Nebraska, Cather portrayed "Georgianna's bleak environment." The picture of Georgianna and her lack of music on the silent plains relies on Cather's "own experience of aesthetic deprivation in Nebraska" and her sense of what she missed in her prairie education.
→ Where does phrase "silence of the plains" come from? Check stories; also sources at notes 8 and 9.

■ **Exercise 32.2*** Take notes as you read and consult the various sources you have selected for your research. Use the note cards on pages 430 to 431 as models.

32c
plan

32c Organizing Notes

Read and organize your notes carefully and use them to help you focus your ideas and develop your plan. Your tentative thesis and rough plan will guide your reading and note taking and will shape your thoughts about the topic. Your thoughts, in turn, will suggest changes in your thesis and plan. Don't worry if your thesis and plan change many times as you develop your outline, rough drafts, and final draft. Following a preliminary plan too rigidly keeps you from making the major changes in emphasis and organization that later reading and thinking often suggest.

If you have done your research carefully, you will have many note cards on which you have collected quotations, summaries, paraphrases, statistical information, and other data from your sources. Only one idea should appear on each card. Now read your notes over carefully and organize them so that you can develop your paper (see the Topic Summary Guide on the facing page).

In reading through your note cards, you should find that your material falls naturally into subject groups. The headings in your rough plan were your guide for taking and organizing notes from the beginning. By now you have probably clustered related data from various sources around the general headings. Yet as you reread your note cards, you will think of new major headings that bear on your topic and discover some old main headings that do not. You will also think of subheadings that flesh out the main headings.

At this point, you are ready to prepare a formal outline or to write a first draft. First, collect all your note cards, put them in order, and number them consecutively. Now you can prepare a summary guide that tells you, by number, where each note card fits into your plan. See the excerpts from the summary guides developed for the papers we have been tracking.

This kind of guide helps you arrange the note cards according to tentative headings. And because the cards are numbered and each card includes the author's name and the title of the book or the article, you can keep track of your sources as you go along.

This system allows you to experiment. You can group and regroup related data and ideas and shift the order of subject groups around before you make any final decisions. This experimentation also can help you develop your plan by suggesting more effective headings and subheadings.

■ **Exercise 32.3*** Continue reading about your topic and taking notes. Using the rough plan you formulated in Exercise 32.1, develop a more detailed plan.

Literature

TOPIC SUMMARY GUIDE

Headings	Note cards
Music connections	3, 4, 6, 9, 22, 26, 30, 31
Artistic deprivation	1, 7, 12, 13, 14, 28
Physical strain of prairie life	2, 18, 32, 36, 37
Imagery of West	5, 24, 25, 46, 53
Imagery of "civilized" life	19, 59, 63, 64, 65, 68

Astronomy

TOPIC SUMMARY GUIDE

Headings	Note cards
European investigation of black holes	3, 4, 6, 9, 22, 26
Definitions of black holes	1, 7, 12, 13, 14, 28
Finding black holes	2, 18, 32, 36, 37
Interpreting data	30, 31
Key researchers	5, 24, 25, 46, 53
Research methodology	5, 8, 17, 18, 55, 56, 57

✓ CHECKLIST 32.1: PLANNING A RESEARCH PAPER

Planning is crucial to the success of a research paper. Before you begin to write, be sure that you have completed all the planning steps.

- Prepare a preliminary list of sources.
- Develop a hypothesis and tentative thesis.
- Sketch out a rough plan.
- Read your sources.
- Take notes:
  - summarize
  - paraphrase
  - quote (use signal cards).
- Keep track of your sources; make sure that your notes distinguish your ideas from those of your sources.
- Read and organize your notes.

CHAPTER

33

CITING AND DOCUMENTING SOURCES

A research paper requires a thoughtful balance between your own language and the words and sentences you borrow from other sources. Intelligent use of source material is the heart of research writing. As a general rule of thumb, use quotations only when you feel that the original wording will add significantly to your point. Students are often tempted to quote lengthy passages, but this is not a good practice unless you have a clear, specific purpose for doing so. A lengthy passage can be tedious if the reader does not see why you didn't summarize it. Select quotations carefully, and always keep them as short as possible.

To write a paper that does more than simply restate the ideas of others, you must interpret and evaluate source materials, provide commentary to clarify points, and assert your own conclusions. And you must acknowledge every source you use. You need to choose an appropriate and accepted method for citing and documenting materials you use in your paper.

33a Integrating Sources into Your Writing

Integrating source material smoothly into your writing takes thought and care. The thesis of your paper will determine the points you make, but you will be supporting those points with ideas drawn from sources and written in a language and style that may be quite different from your own.

Quoting, Summarizing, and Paraphrasing

Following the methods you used to record your data (see 32b), you could quote the source directly, or you could summarize or paraphrase it. Suppose you wanted to use part of this passage, which appears at the end of the short story "A Wagner Matinee" by Willa Cather. The passage is about Aunt Georgiana, the main character.

Source

The concert was over; the people filed out of the hall chattering and laughing, glad to relax and find the living level again, but my kinswoman made no effort to rise. The harpist slipped its green felt cover over his instrument; the flute players shook the water from their mouthpieces; the men of the orchestra were out one by one, leaving the stage to the chairs and music stands, empty as a winter cornfield.

I spoke to my aunt. She burst into tears and sobbed pleadingly. "I don't want to go, Clark, I don't want to go!"

I understood. For her, just outside the door of the concert hall, lay the black pond with the cattle-tracked bluffs; the tall, unpainted house, with weather-curled boards; naked as a tower, the crook-backed ash seedlings where the dishcloths hung to dry; the gaunt, molting turkeys picking up refuse about the kitchen door.

—WILLA CATHER

One option is to quote the source exactly. You could quote a sentence or two to make your point, or you could present a longer quotation in block form, perhaps an entire paragraph. Either way, you must separate your ideas from those of your source. At the same time, you should blend your own words with the words of the writer you are quoting to produce a smooth and pleasing sentence. Later in this chapter you will learn the mechanics of documenting sources in a variety of citation systems (33d, 33e, 33f, 33g). Here we concentrate on how to make smoother connections between your prose and the prose of your source.

Quotation from source

In the last lines of "A Wagner Matinee" we can see the horrible tragedy of the transplanted artist, as Clark's aunt faces her life back home. Clark explains that "just outside the door of the concert hall, lay . . . the tall, unpainted house, with weather-curled boards" and "the gaunt, molting turkeys picking up refuse about the kitchen door" (115). It is the refuse of Aunt Georgiana's existence.

In this example, the writer uses her source to support the point she's making, the tragedy of the transplanted artist. Quotation marks are placed around each phrase copied from the source. The sentence that includes the quotation starting with "just outside the door of the concert hall" follows smoothly from the sentence before it. The tag "Clark explains that" helps the writer integrate the quoted material with her own writing. The writer uses the conjunction *and* to connect two parts of Cather's sentence that are separated in the original. The spaced periods, called **ellipses** (26f), shorten the quotation. Note how the writer comments on the quotation with her own thoughtful observation: the turkey's refuse is the refuse of Aunt Georgiana's existence. The parenthetical reference "(115)" is to the page number on which the quotation appears in Cather's story. Full documentation appears in the list of works cited (see 33d).

Here is another way the writer could have quoted from her source.

Quotation from source

The final overwhelming images of the story show the utter horror of the transplanted artist:

> For her, just outside the door of the concert hall, lay the black pond with the cattle-tracked bluffs; the tall, unpainted house, with weather-curled boards; naked as a tower, the crook-backed ash seedlings where the dishcloths hung to dry; the gaunt, molting turkeys picking up refuse about the kitchen door.

Here the long quotation supports the point the writer makes in the introductory sentence. Readers will read and see why the writer finds the images overwhelming. This type of long quotation, set apart from the writer's prose by indenting from the left, is called a **block quotation** (see 25a). Use the block form for a quotation of four or more typed lines. Note that quotation marks are not needed.

In the next examples, the author summarizes and paraphrases the source.

Summary

Cather leaves us with a grim picture of the life awaiting Aunt Georgiana when she leaves the concert hall and returns to her bleak homestead on the Nebraska frontier.

Paraphrase

We see a stark, ugly world awaiting Aunt Georgiana. When she returns to her Nebraska homestead from the concert hall, she must face "the black pond" surrounded by bluffs, a weather-beaten farmhouse, small ash trees "where the dishcloths hung to dry," and thin, bony turkeys pecking at garbage outside the kitchen (115).

In the **paraphrase,** which follows the original line of reasoning more closely than the summary (see 32b), the writer uses quotation marks around the phrases from the original.

You must use your judgment about when to use quotation marks for individual words or for brief phrases borrowed from another source. Notice that the words *concert hall* appear in the original story, but in the summary and the paraphrase these words are not enclosed within quotation marks. A good general rule is that when you use three or more consecutive words from another source, you need quotation marks. Keeping this rule in mind will make you think about what you are doing and will help you avoid the unconscious plagiarism that can get you into just as much trouble as the deliberate act (see 33b).

■ **Exercise 33.1** Select a passage from a magazine article or a book, and write a paragraph in which you incorporate elements from the passage into your own writing by following the directions below. Use appropriate citations. Make a copy of the passage to show your instructor.

1. Write a brief summary of the passage as part of a paragraph that might appear in a draft of your paper.
2. Write a short paragraph in which you quote a few lines exactly from the passage.
3. Write a short paragraph in which you paraphrase the passage.

Commenting on Source Material

Although summaries of sources are important elements in most research papers, you should provide more than summaries alone. Readers expect you to guide them by explaining, interpreting, and evaluating source materials. You build paragraphs from quotations, summaries, or paraphrases by giving your own thoughts on your topic.

Extensive research will shape your thoughts and opinions, and as you continue examining different sources, you will formulate new ideas or modify existing ones. Some of your sources may provide conflicting data. Others may simply disagree in their interpretation of facts or even in their definitions of key terms. Still others may offer opinions that challenge what you have read elsewhere. Readers of your paper need your help in sorting out the contradictions and in separating the important ideas from the routine and the facts from the speculations.

Commenting on source material is not easy, but it is important. There are no exact rules to follow. A sensitive researcher learns from experience just when to shed light on a complex point or when to interpret or challenge an important idea. You should respect your sources, of course, but should not be intimidated by them. In citing authorities it is right to question their conclusions, to lay them alongside conclusions drawn by others, or to use them as springboards for your own conclusions. The following examples demonstrate how skilled writers can integrate source material while providing useful commentary on it.

> Cather's debut into fame was noted in volumes concerning American fiction, the first being Grant Overton's *The Women Who Make Our Novels,* issued late in 1918. A literary reporter rather than critic, Overton compiled information about all American female novelists of importance or popularity; but he did not prognosticate which of them, if any, might continue to be read fifty years hence. The order of his chapters was accidental and therefore meaningless; Willa Cather is sandwiched between one Grace S. Richmond, whose books were said to sell "faster than the books of any other American writer," and Clara Louise Burnham, author of "twenty-six books which have sold a half million copies." The thirteen pages Overton granted Cather are devoted largely to a biographical sketch (not always noted for accuracy) and to a summary of her achievement, drawn from reviews; these cover her work from *Alexander's Bridge,* which might have been written by Mrs. Wharton, through the indisputably personal triumph of *My Antonia.* Overton's judgments, reflecting a cross section of others' evalutions, emphasize the significance of Cather's early western experience, her controlled accessibility to it, her fidelity to character, and the esthetic delight furnished by her method.
>
> —PHILIP GERBER

Much more than a summary appears here. Certainly we learn the essence of Overton's entry on Cather and two of her contemporaries. But Gerber's comments and evaluations guide our perceptions. Note how he judges Overton's credentials as a writer about Cather, how he calls the order of chapters in *The Women Who Make Our Novels* meaningless, and how he questions the biographical accuracy in Overton's sketch of Cather. A reader unfamiliar with Overton has not only a summary of his work, but also an assessment of it from Gerber's perspective.

> Two of the shorter pieces in *The Troll Garden,* "A Wagner Matinee" and "The Sculptor's Funeral," take firm grip on the fatality of deprivation which was an inherent part of Miss Cather's native Ne-

> braska material. "A Wagner Matinee" is a bleakly effective *récit,* holding in concentration the terrible spiritual toll taken by frontier life, especially upon women. An old aunt of the narrator, grizzled and deformed, comes to visit her nephew in New York; she had been a music teacher at the Boston Conservatory, and marriage had taken her to a Nebraska homestead fifty miles from a railroad, to live at first in a dugout in a hillside. He takes her to a concert. At the *Tannhäuser* overture, she clutches his coat sleeve. "Then it was I first realized that for her this broke a silence of thirty years; the inconceivable silence of the plains. . . ."
>
> —DOROTHY VAN GHENT

Van Ghent's purpose is to summarize the main action of "A Wagner Matinee," but she provides her own interpretation as well. She classifies the story as a *récit*—a term usually reserved for short novels with simple narrative lines.

In the student's paper on Willa Cather note how the writer comments on source material in this instance, among many others:

> With a brilliant image Cather shows the conflicting forces of past and present in Katharine's life. In the Wyoming house, the music room makes Everett feel that he has stepped into a familiar New York studio almost exactly like his brother's, "so individual and poignantly reminiscent here in Wyoming" (71). As he sits chatting with Katharine, a window blind swinging in the wind reveals "the glaring panorama of the desert--a blinding stretch of yellow, flat as the sea in dead calm" (75). Blinding, yellow, flat, dead: so is Katharine's life away from the East, even in the studio room she has tried so hard to make like Adriance's.

The last sentence interprets for the reader the quotation from Cather's story "A Death in the Desert."

■ **Exercise 33.2** Read the following passage from the book *Sociology* by Paul Horton and Chester Hunt. Write a paragraph or two in which you integrate this source into your prose by quoting and paraphrasing. Provide commentary on the quotations and paraphrases by offering your own clarifications, interpretations, or judgments.

> **Stereotypes.** A *stereotype* is *a group-shared image of another group or category of people.* Stereotypes can be positive (the kindly, dedicated family doctor), negative (the unprincipled, opportunistic politician), or

mixed (the dedicated, fussy, sexless old-maid teacher). Stereotypes are applied indiscriminately to all members of the stereotyped group, without allowance for individual differences. Stereotypes are never entirely untrue, for they must bear *some* resemblance to the characteristics of the persons stereotyped or they would not be recognized. But stereotypes are always distorted, in that they exaggerate and universalize *some* of the characteristics of *some* of the members of the stereotyped group.

Just how stereotypes begin is not known. Once the stereotype has become a part of the culture, it is maintained by *selective perception* (noting only the confirming incidents or cases and failing to note or remember the exceptions), *selective interpretation* (interpreting observations in terms of the stereotype: e.g., Jews are "pushy" while gentiles are "ambitious"), *selective identification* ("they look like school teachers . . ."), and *selective exception* ("he really doesn't act at all Jewish"). All these processes involve a reminder of the stereotype, so that even exceptions and incorrect identifications serve to feed and sustain the stereotype.

—PAUL B. HORTON AND CHESTER L. HUNT

33b
Crediting Sources

You commit **plagiarism** whenever you present words or ideas taken from another person as if they were your own. The easiest way to avoid plagiarism is always to use quotation marks when you quote directly from a source and always to acknowledge a source when you borrow or even allude to someone else's ideas and language, even though you may not have used that person's exact words. Sections 33d, 33e, 33f, and 33g explain accepted methods of documentation and citation.

If you fail to follow these rules for borrowing from other writers, you may be guilty of plagiarism. The most obvious plagiarism is simply **copying,** either word for word or with a few words added or shifted around. Anyone who compares the source and the copy can recognize plagiarism instantly.

Mosaic plagiarism is using words or ideas of others indirectly and failing to credit the source. It may result when a well-meaning, uninformed writer takes bad notes or when a dishonest one deliberately attempts to deceive. Here is an example. The writer has added words and sentences, but anyone who reads the source and the plagiarism can tell that the latter depends entirely on the former.

Source

A territory is an area of space, whether of water or earth or air, which an animal or group of animals defends as an exclusive preserve. The word is also used to describe the inward compulsion in animate beings to possess and defend such a space. A territorial species of animals, therefore, is one in which all males, and sometimes females too, bear an inherent drive to gain and defend an exclusive property.

In most but not all territorial species, defense is directed only against fellow members of the kind. A squirrel does not regard a mouse as a trespasser. In most but not all territorial species—not in chameleons, for example—the female is sexually unresponsive to an unpropertied male. As a general pattern of behavior, in territorial species the competition between males which we formerly believed was one for the possession of females is in truth for possession of property.

—ROBERT ARDREY

Mosaic plagiarism

Territory may be defined as an area of space, water, earth, or air, which animals defend as an exclusive preserve. The word *territory* also describes the inner compulsion in living beings to own and defend such a space. In a territorial species, males and some females are driven to gain and defend their exclusive property against fellow members of the species. The female of most territorial animals is not responsive sexually to a male without property, and the competition between males that we once believed was for the possession of females is really for possession of property.

Plagiarism is a very serious offense. The prose we write ourselves is so individual that when we write something in a striking way or express a new idea, we have produced something that always belongs to us. To call someone else's writing your own is wrong and foolish. The student who plagiarizes can expect a failing grade on the paper and, in many schools, for the whole course. Plagiarism is an honors-code violation and is often grounds for expulsion.

Here is how the writer of the mosaic plagiarism could have avoided it by acknowledging the source of those thoughts, Robert Ardrey.

Revision

Ardrey defines territory as an area "whether of water or earth or air" which animals see as theirs exclusively and which they are driven by an "inward compulsion" to defend against members of their own species. A female in a territorial species is "sexually unresponsive to an unpropertied male." Ardrey believes that males do not compete for females. Instead, "the competition . . . is in truth for possession of property" (3).

You need not attribute information that is common knowledge. If you say that World War II ended in 1945, do not cite the source of your statement, since it is common knowledge. But if you do not know whether information is common knowledge or not, consult your instructor or an expert in the field.

✔ CHECKLIST 33.1: AVOIDING PLAGIARISM

- Always acknowledge your sources.
- Always keep your own notes and comments about a subject separate from the words you copy from other sources. Students sometimes commit plagiarism accidentally because their notes fail to distinguish between what is their own and what they have copied.
- Always use quotation marks when you are quoting directly, even if you choose to quote only a short phrase or clause.
- Even when you are not quoting directly from a source, always be sure to attribute striking ideas to the person who first thought of them.
- Always cite your sources for interpretations, statistical data, and facts that are not common knowledge.

33c Using Various Formats for Documenting Sources

You must acknowledge information, ideas, and words borrowed from others. The format you use for acknowledging your sources may vary, depending on the discipline in which you are doing research. Most up-to-date documentation systems require internal (or parenthetical) citation. With **internal citation,** sources are enclosed in parentheses and are named in brief form directly in the text of the paper instead of in footnotes or in endnotes. This system also requires a list of references or works cited at the end of the paper, where sources are given in full. With **footnotes,** citations, keyed by numbers, appear at the bottom of the page. With **endnotes,** these notes appear at the end of the paper.

Because academic disciplines vary in the precise forms they require for documentation, you must follow the specific format that your instructor requests. Two of the most popular formats are those recommended by the

Modern Language Association of America (MLA) in its *MLA Handbook for Writers of Research Papers* and in its counterpart for scholars, *The MLA Style Manual*; and by the *Publication Manual of the American Psychological Association* (APA). This chapter focuses on these formats. In addition, you will see how to use other parenthetical documentation systems as well as footnotes or endnotes. Your instructor may require the documentation format recommended in the University of Chicago Press's *Chicago Manual of Style* or in Kate L. Turabian's *Manual for Writers of Term Papers, Theses, and Dissertations*. Many other manuals for researchers are also available.

33d Using the MLA Format

Most research papers in the humanities use the MLA format. The main features of this format include parenthetical citations directly in the text, a list of works cited, and, when necessary, explanatory endnotes.

Using Parenthetical References

The MLA system uses an abbreviated format for documentation within the text. (A list of works cited, to be discussed shortly, supplies full publishing data.) A citation in the text typically includes:

- Author's last name
- Location of the material. Usually page numbers alone are enough; in a multivolume source, give the volume number as well. For literary works, you may want to give the act, scene, line, chapter, book, or stanza.

Remember, complete bibliographical information must appear in your list of works cited at the end of the paper. The following model will help you write your own sentences to indicate your sources. The complete entry for Van Ghent's book appears in the list of works cited on p. 509. (The full text from which the quotation in this model internal documentation is taken appears on pages 439–440.)

The key to successful parenthetical documentation is the complete list of works cited at the end of the paper. Every reference you make in your text must correspond to an entry on that list. Information you provide in the parenthetical documentation must match the information on your list of works cited.

Try to be concise and unobtrusive with your parenthetical references. Place them where pauses occur naturally in your sentences and as close as possible to the information you are identifying.

Model internal documentation; MLA format

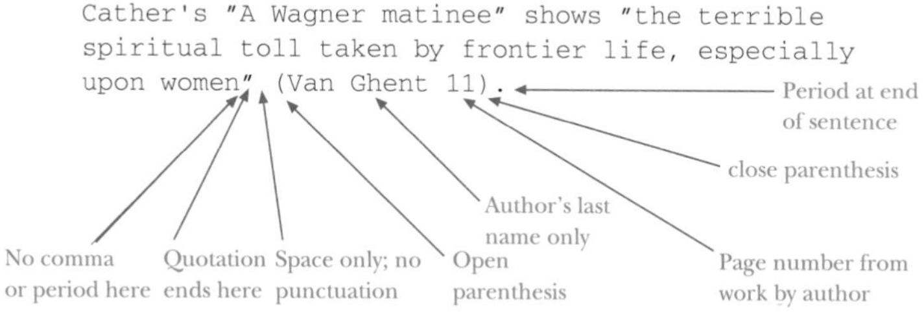

What you include in parentheses and what you include in the accompanying text will reflect your individual style as a writer. Feel free to experiment with different formats for references, remembering that what you include in your text determines what you include in the parenthetical documentation. If you use the author's name in a sentence, do not put that name in parentheses. If you do not name the author in your sentence, name him or her in parentheses.

We cannot show all the stylistic possibilities for internal documentation, but the following examples illustrate the simplest options. Wherever possible, these examples correspond to examples presented in later sections (Preparing a List of Works Cited, p. 450, and Using Footnotes or Endnotes, p. 472).

Parts of single-volume books or articles

Van Ghent believes that "A Wagner Matinee" is a story about "the terrible spiritual toll taken by frontier life, especially upon women" (11).

"A Wagner Matinee," as Van Ghent points out, "is a bleakly effective <u>récit,</u> holding in concentration the terrible spiritual toll taken by frontier life, especially upon women" (11).

In Cather's short story we see how life on the frontier imposes itself on a woman's spirit (Van Ghent 11).

It may be true that some of Cather's writing shows "the fatality of deprivation" (Van Ghent 11), but certainly a story like "A Wagner Matinee" also is a tribute to the power of art in human life.

Van Ghent highlights the bleak, deprived life of Aunt Georgiana (11).

To cite an entire work rather than a part of it, name the author in the text and avoid a parenthetical reference.

Dorothy Van Ghent comments on all of Cather's novels.

An interesting collection of Greek and Roman myths appears in the volume by Mark Morford and Robert Lenardon.

Clifford Morgan, Richard King, and Nancy Robinson have provided a basic text for beginning students of psychology.

Albert Baugh and his colleagues trace the growth and development of English literature from the Middle Ages to the twentieth century.

Multivolume works

In the example below, the number before the colon in parentheses refers to the volume; the number after the colon refers to the page number. The "vii" tells you that the quotation comes from the preface; pagination in the preface or other front matter in a book is generally in lowercase roman numbers.

Sir Thomas Browne's Pseudodoxia Epidemica was "no hasty compilation, but was the product of many years of patient thought, reading, observation, and experiment" (2: vii).

The following parenthetical reference is to an entire volume of a multivolume work and not to any particular part of that volume. Here you use a comma to separate the author's name from the volume number, and you use the abbreviation for *volume.*

Modern readers may be mystified by the range of classical allusions in the Pseudodoxia Epidemica (Browne, vol. 2).

Works cited by title only

For parenthetical references to a work that appears in the list of works cited by title only, use a shortened version of the title. Omit the page number if the article is brief; otherwise include the page number after the title.

Cather had already published The Troll Garden and Song of the Lark, but it was My Antonia that widened her reputation in 1918 ("Cather").

Works by a corporate author

This reference is to *The Humanities in American Life,* prepared by a committee. The committee is listed in the publication as the author.

> In 1980 the Commission on the Humanities recommended that "the humanities, sciences, and technology need to be substantially connected" (21), but we have made little progress toward that goal.

Two or more works by the same author

If you use two or more books by the same author, you'll need to include the title, or a shortened form of it, in parenthetical references to works by this author; otherwise the reader will have no way of knowing which work by that author you are citing. A comma follows the author's name if you use it in the parenthetical reference. If you put the author's name in the text, give only the title and the page reference, as in the second example below. For this example, two of Farrington's books, *The Philosophy of Francis Bacon* and *Aristotle: Founder of Scientific Philosophy,* would appear in the list of works cited.

> Bacon condemned Plato as "an obstacle to science" (Farrington, Philosophy 35).

> Benjamin Farrington points out that Aristotle's father, Nicomachus, a physician, probably trained his son in medicine (Aristotle 15).

Literary works

For classical literary works in several editions, readers find it useful to have more than just page numbers in a reference. Chapter, book, act, scene, line, and stanza numbers make it easier to find materials in any copy of a novel or play. In the parenthetical reference, cite the page number first, then use a semicolon, and then give this information, using accepted abbreviations.

> In the opening sentence of Lord Jim, Conrad shows us the physical power of his hero (3; ch. 1).

> Marlowe says that what set Brown apart from other scoundrels "was the arrogant temper of his misdeeds and a vehement scorn for mankind at large and for his victims in particular" (Conrad 352-53; ch. 38).

More than one work in a single reference

When you cite more than one work in a single parenthetical reference, use semicolons to separate the works. The first two entries in the parenthesis below are to complete articles; the last entry (''Van Ghent 20–21'') is to specific pages in Van Ghent's article. Because a parenthetical reference that is too long will distract readers, you may want to use a footnote or endnote to cite multiple sources.

> Several critics refer to the place of music in Cather's art (Giannone; Brennan; Van Ghent 20–21).

Indirect sources

You should take material from original sources whenever you can. But when the original is unavailable and you have only an indirect source (for example, a published account of someone's spoken comments), use the abbreviation ''qtd. in'' in your parenthetical reference, right before your citation. For this example, the list of works cited would include a reference to Turnball, not to Baker.

> Wolfe was upset at an anonymous criticism of his play The Mountains. He told his teacher at Harvard, George Pierce Baker, that "if I knew who wrote that, I would no longer be responsible for my actions" (qtd. in Turnball 54).

Plays, concerts, films, and television programs

> Linda Lavin's performance in Broadway Bound by Neil Simon pleased most of the New York drama critics.

> In The Unforgiven Clint Eastwood continues to impress audiences with his skills as an actor and a director.

■ **Exercise 33.3** Write a sentence that quotes, summarizes, or paraphrases a portion of each selection below. Within your sentence, provide documentation for the source according to the MLA guidelines. Publishing data appear in parentheses following the quotation; you will not have to use all the information, however.

1. ''When Shakespeare came to London from Stratford-on-Avon, the new poetry, which was to crown the last decades of the sixteenth century and the beginning of the seventeenth, was already established. Its arrival had been announced in 1579 by the publication of Spenser's *The Shepherd's Calendar.*'' (The selection is from *Shakespeare's Songs and Poems,* edited by Edward Hubler. The quotation is from pages xii–xiii. The book was published in 1959 by McGraw-Hill in New York.)

2. "Every summer, one of the nation's longest-running and most hotly contested photo competitions takes place at the offices of Sierra Club Books in San Francisco. Between 50,000 and 100,000 color transparencies are submitted for publication in the four Wilderness calendars, and the flood of entries keeps a small army of freelance photo editors and clerks busy from July to November." (The selection is from an article called "Wilderness Pin-Ups by Sierra Club" by Catherine Kouts in *Publishers Weekly,* vol. 225, no. 17, April 27, 1984, p. 41.)
3. "The Greeks' most important legacy is not, as we would like to think, democracy; it is their mythology. Even though in the second century A.D. a mysterious voice was heard exclaiming 'great Pan is dead,' the Greek gods and many obscure and irrational stories about them lived on in the imaginations of artists and writers, no matter how often or in how many different ways Christians and philosophers tried to dismiss the myths as frivolous or harmful. And even in the twentieth century, when man has acquired greater power than ever before to alter the natural world, the old myths continue to haunt us, not just in the form of nymphs and shepherds on vases or garden statuary, but in many common assumptions about the shape of human experience. The notions—now presumably obsolete—that a man should be active and aggressive, a woman passive and subject to control by the men in her family, are expressed in virtually every Greek myth, even the ones in which the women seek to gain control of their own lives. That the most important phase of a woman's life is the period immediately preceding her marriage (or remarriage) is preserved in the plot of many novels, as is the notion that virginity, or at least celibacy, offers a woman a kind of freedom that she is no longer entitled to when she becomes involved with a man."(The selection is from p. 207 of an article called "Women in Greek Myths" by Mary R. Lefkowitz. The article appears on pp. 207–19 of the Spring 1985 *American Scholar,* vol. 54, no. 2. *The American Scholar* is a journal that numbers pages continuously throughout the annual volume and is published in Washington, D.C., by Phi Beta Kappa.)

Using Explanatory Notes

When you use parenthetical references in your research paper, you can also use footnotes or endnotes to provide additional information that you do not want to include in the text of your paper. In notes, you can provide evaluative comments on your sources or other relevant information that does not fit neatly in your text. Or to avoid the distraction of a long parenthesis including several citations, you can use a note to list multiple citations.

Indicate notes by a raised number in the text. Put your explanatory notes before your list of works cited, on a separate page under the heading "Notes."

Notes to explain

Notes can offer explanations that would be out of place in the text. In the following example, the writer uses a parenthetical reference to cite the page, "(107)," from which she quotes the words "at once pathetic and grotesque." She uses the note to explain information that does not belong in the text itself. In addition, she cites a reference to a critical piece about Cather.

Earlier, when Clark received the letter from Howard announcing Aunt Georgiana's arrival, Clark says that her name called up her figure, "at once pathetic and grotesque" (107).[1]

[1]Cather's family and friends objected to her portrait of Nebraska life when this story first appeared in Everybody's Magazine. A good friend, Will Jones, complained that strangers would always associate Nebraska with Aunt Georgiana's terrible shape, her false teeth, and her yellow skin. Cather denied that she wanted to disparage her homeland but admitted that her family felt insulted: "They had already told her that it was not nice to tell such things" (Woodress 117).

Notes to cite multiple sources

In the example below, the inclusion of seven references in a parenthetical citation in the text would distract readers. The note permits the writer to cite multiple sources without intruding in the text.

Music is a very important element in much of Cather's fiction.[2]

[2]Giannone; Brennan, "Willa Cather"; Brennan, "Music"; Gerber 71-73; Bloom and Bloom 123; Daiches 8; Van Ghent 20-21.

Preparing a List of Works Cited

You must provide a list of works cited for readers of your research paper. A **list of works cited** is an alphabetical list of books, articles, and other sources (such as films, interviews, or dramatic productions) that you consulted in doing your research. All the citations in your paper will be keyed to this list of research materials. (If you use print materials only, your list will be called a **bibliography.**)

If you make bibliography cards carefully (as discussed in 31c), you can produce a list of works cited without much trouble. Each card will have all the data you need to prepare your list for the final draft of your paper.

The following models show you how to document the usual kinds of sources for your research. If you cite some special sources (cartoons, computer programs, musical compositions, works of art), you should consult the *MLA Handbook* itself.

Books and reference works

Model entry (MLA) in a list of works cited; book with one author

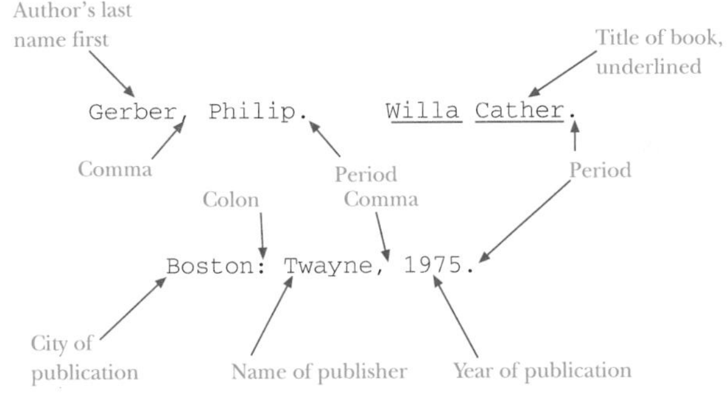

The periods set off three major elements in the entry: the author's name, the title, and the publication data. Note that the MLA style does not include the abbreviation for the state after the city. If the entry requires more than one line, indent the second line and all other lines in the entry five spaces.

Sometimes other facts are required, as in the following example. Note that for ranges of numbers, the MLA system does not repeat the digit for hundreds.

McCray, Curtis L. "Kaptain Kronkite: The Myth of the Eternal
     Frame." Television: The Critical View. Ed. Horace
     Newcomb. 2nd ed. New York: Oxford UP, 1979. 319-33.

McCray is the author of an essay in the second edition of a book edited by Newcomb. Newcomb collected a number of essays and prepared them for publication, hence his designation as editor (Ed.) of the book. The book is in its second edition (2nd ed.), which means that one earlier version exists but that the researcher used the more recent book. Note the short form *Oxford UP* for *Oxford University Press.* Short forms for publisher's names are acceptable.

An anthology The abbreviation *ed.* says that Wolfe is the editor of this collection. If the author is a compiler (of a bibliography, for example) or a translator, use *comp.* or *trans.* after the name.

Wolfe, Don M., ed. American Scene: New Voices. New York: Stuart, 1963.

A book by two or more authors The abbreviation *ed.* here stands for *edition.* An arabic number (with an appropriate suffix to show that the number is ordinal) indicates the edition number. The abbreviation *et al.* is short for the Latin *et alii,* meaning "and others"; when a work has more than three authors, *et al.* replaces the names of all authors but the first. Notice that the name of the first author is the only one that appears last name first.

Morgan, Clifford T., Richard A. King, and Nancy M. Robinson. Introduction to Psychology. 6th ed. New York: McGraw, 1979.

Baugh, Albert C., et al. A Literary History of England. New York: Appleton, 1948.

Van Der Post, Laurens, and Jane Taylor. Testament to the Bushmen. London: Rainbird, 1984.

Two or more books by the same author When you list more than one book by the same author, give the author's name in the first entry only. For each succeeding entry, instead of the author's name type three hyphens and a period, then skip a space and type the title. The hyphens always stand for the author's name exactly as it appears in the entry that comes directly before. (Brooks's name is repeated in the third entry because hyphens would have referred to his name only; he is one of two authors of *Understanding Poetry.*) If the author is an editor, a compiler, or a translator, use a comma after the hyphens and put the correct abbreviation—*ed., comp.,* or *trans.*—before the title. All works listed for the same author appear alphabetically by title.

Brooks, Cleanth. Fundamentals of Good Writing: A Handbook of Modern Rhetoric. New York: Harcourt, 1950.

---. The Hidden God: Studies in Hemingway, Faulkner, Yeats, Eliot, and Warren. New Haven: Yale UP, 1963.

Brooks, Cleanth, and Robert Penn Warren, eds. Understanding Poetry. 3rd ed. New York: Holt, 1960.

Farrington, Benjamin. Aristotle: Founder of Scientific Philosophy. New York: Praeger, 1969.

---. The Philosophy of Francis Bacon. Chicago: U of Chicago P, 1964.

A book with corporate authorship A corporate author might be a commission, committee, or other work by a group whose members aren't identified on the title page as authors.

Commission on the Humanities. The Humanities in American Life: Report of the Commission on the Humanities. Berkeley: U of California P, 1980.

A book with no author's name The citation begins with the title. In the list of works cited, alphabetize the citation by the first word other than an article.

Greece: 1974. Athens: National Tourist Organization of Greece, 1973.

A selection from an anthology Page numbers indicate where the essay being cited appears in the longer work.

Sewell, Elizabeth. "Bacon, Vico, Coleridge, and the Poetic Method." Giambattista Vico: An International Symposium. Ed. Giorgio Tagliacozzo and Hayden V. White. Baltimore: Johns Hopkins P, 1969. 125-36.

A preface, an introduction, a foreword, or an afterword If you are citing one of these elements and not the main work, the name of the writer of the element begins the entry, followed by the name of the element you are citing. Quotation marks or underlining is unnecessary. When the writer of the element is different from the author of the book, use the word *By* after the title and cite the author's full name, first name first. If the writer of the element is the same person who wrote the book, use only the last name after the word *By*. In the first entry, Gardner wrote the foreword; Penrose wrote the book. In the second entry, the writer of the preface is also the author of the book.

Gardner, Martin. Foreword. The Emperor's New Mind. By Roger Penrose. New York: Oxford UP, 1989. v-vii.

Fowles, John. Preface. Islands. By Fowles. Boston: Little, 1978. 1-2.

A work in more than one volume The first entry says that the work is in four volumes and that the researcher used them all. The second entry says that only the second volume was used.

33d
cite

Browne, Thomas. The Works of Sir Thomas Browne. Ed. Geoffrey Keynes. 4 vols. London: Faber, 1928.

Browne, Thomas. The Works of Sir Thomas Browne. Ed. Geoffrey Keynes. Vol. 2. London: Faber, 1928. 4 vols.

An edited book Harris prepared this work of Buck's for publication. The entry indicates that citations in the text of the paper are to Buck's writing. If the citations are to the editor (his introductory comments, for example), his name would begin the entry. See the entry for Gardner, above.

Buck, Pearl. China as I See It. Ed. Theodore F. Harris. New York: Day, 1970.

A translation If your citations are to the translator's comments, and not to the translation itself, use the translator's name to begin the entry. See the entry for Gardner, above.

Maffei, Paolo. Beyond the Moon. Trans. D. J. K. O'Connell. Cambridge: MIT P, 1978.

A publisher's imprint An imprint is the name a publisher sometimes gives to a special group of books to be published under that name. Doubleday, for example, uses the imprint Anchor; Avon uses Camelot; New American Library uses Mentor. When a publisher's imprint appears on the title page, give the imprint name before the publisher's name. Use a hyphen between them.

Lévi-Strauss, Claude. Tristes Tropiques. New York: Pocket-Simon, 1977.

A republished book The original edition appeared in 1959; the writer of the paper used the edition republished by Bantam in 1966.

Knowles, John. A Separate Peace. 1959. New York: Bantam, 1966.

A reference book Material from a well-known reference work such as the *Encyclopedia Britannica* does not require full publication data, but you should note the year of publication. The title in quotation marks is the entry name.

"Black Holes." The New Encyclopedia Britannica: Ready Reference. 1992 ed.

For a signed article in an encyclopedia, include the author's name. Sometimes only initials appear after the article; in that case check the list of initials in the index or in some other volume of the encyclopedia to find out the author's full name.

Moore, Norman. "Hodgkin, Thomas, M.D." Dictionary of National Biography. 1908.
Naylor, John Henry. "Peninsular War." Encyclopedia Britannica: Macropaedia. 1974.

Pamphlets, bulletins, and public documents For a work issued by a government, the name of the government comes first, then the name of the agency. *GPO* is the Government Printing Office.

United States. Congressional Budget Office. Proposition 13: Its Impact on the Nation's Economy, Federal Revenues, and Federal Expenditures. Washington: GPO, 1978.
National Academy of Sciences. Committee on Water, Division of Earth Sciences. Alternatives in Water Management. National Research Council Publication No. 1408. Washington: National Academy of Sciences, 1969.

A work in a series Neither underlined nor in quotation marks, the name of the series appears after the title of the book.

Swimming Medicine IV. International Series on Sports Sciences 6. Baltimore: University Park P, 1978.

Journals, magazines and newspapers

The author's name, the article title, and the publication data are also the main elements in the entry for a journal article. Note that citations include both the title of the article and the title of the journal in which the work appears.

An article in a journal that numbers pages separately in each issue of an annual volume If each issue in a volume is numbered, include the issue number in the citation. Write the volume number, then

Model entry (MLA) in a list of works cited; article in a journal with pages numbered continuously throughout the annual volume

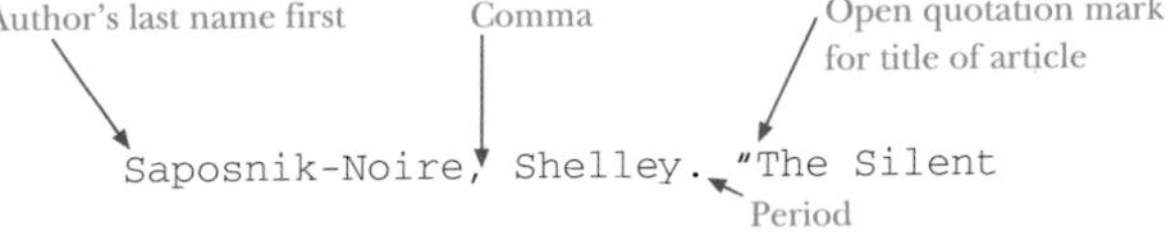

Protagonist: The Unifying Presence of

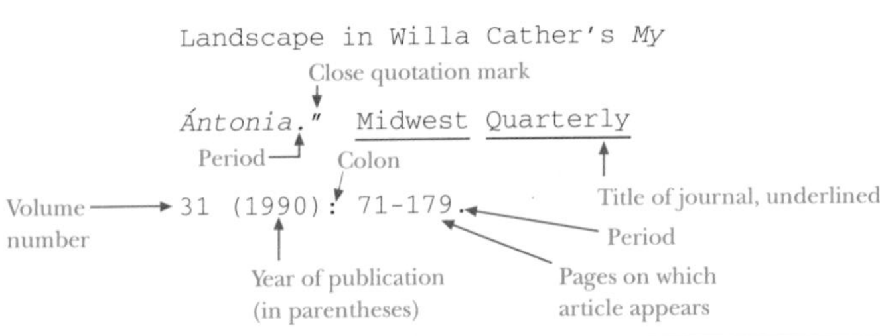

a period, then the issue number. If the journal uses only issue numbers, treat them like volume numbers.

> Jewell, Walter. "The Contribution of Administrative Leadership to Academic Excellence." WPA: Writing Program Administration 3.3 (1980): 9-13.

An article in a monthly or bimonthly magazine Neither volume number nor issue number is needed. Abbreviate the names of months.

> Rees, Martin J. "Black Holes in Galactic Centers." Scientific American Nov. 1990: 56-66.

An article in a weekly or biweekly magazine Include the full date of publication.

Weiss, Rick. "Snakebite Succor: Researchers Foresee Antivenom Improvements." Science News 8 Dec. 1990: 360-63.

An unsigned article in a magazine The citation begins with the title and is alphabetized by the first word other than an article.

"And Now, Robodoc!" Time 23 Nov. 1992: 23.

An article in a daily newspaper For the readers' convenience in locating the article, the section designation *a* appears along with the page number. If an edition is named on the masthead, specify the edition (*natl. ed.* or *late ed.*, for example) after the date. Use a comma between the date and the edition. The plus sign (+) indicates that the article continues, but not on consecutive pages.

Angier, Natalie. "Cheetahs Appear Vigorous Despite Inbreeding." New York Times 10 Nov. 1992: C1+.

Special works

Unpublished dissertations and theses These works are not published, so their titles appear in quotation marks.

Eisenberg, Nora. "The Far Side of Language: The Search for Expression in the Novels of Virginia Woolf." Diss. Columbia U, 1977.

Book reviews Citations to reviews include the name of the reviewer and the name of the author of the work reviewed, as well as the title of the review and the title of the work reviewed.

Kaminer, Wendy. "The Wrong Men." Rev. of In Spite of Innocence: Erroneous Convictions in Capital Cases, by Michael L. Radelet, Hugh Adam Bedau, and Constance E. Putnam. Atlantic Dec. 1992: 147-50.

Material from computer services The following article, originally published in the *Atlantic*, was retrieved from Dialog, one of the computer services available in some libraries.

05049972 DIALOG File 647: MAGAZINE ASAP *This is the FULL TEXT*

A.E. Housman and Willa Cather. (the authors' meeting in 1902)

Sorel, Nancy Caldwell

Atlantic v259 p83(1) July, 1987

SOURCE FILE: MI File 47

CODEN: ATMOA

ARTICLE TYPE: biography

AVAILABILITY: FULL TEXT Online LINE COUNT: 00031

BIOGRAPHEE: Cather, Willa--biography; Houseman, A.E.--biography

DESCRIPTORS: poets--biography; Novelists--biography

A. E. HOUSMAN AND WILLA CATHER

"MANY YEARS AGO when I was very young and foolish" was how Willa Cather would later begin the story. In fact she was nearing thirty that summer of 1902, when, in Europe for the first time, she resolved to call on A. E. Housman. She had been captivated by the bittersweet ballads of A Shropshire Lad; her own first book of poems, April Twilights, would come out the following year. In Housman she saw a kindred spirit. Nature was a malevolent force: certainly in Nebraska that was so. She made the pilgrimage to Shrewsbury and Ludlow and gazed with reverence on Housman's hills. Then, one afternoon in London, her friends Isabelle McClung and Dorothy Canfield in tow, she boarded a bus to Highgate in the firm belief that "if one admired a writer very much one had a perfect right to ring his doorbell."

What she did not anticipate was that the door at 17 North Road would be opened by so cordial a landlady, that they would be so graciously asked inside, and that the poet himself (although shabbily dressed) would descend the stairs open-armed to greet them. But, of course, it was all a mistake. Housman was expecting three Canadian cousins whom he had never met, and he thought--but never mind. Perhaps they would like to come upstairs?

Housman's bachelor rooms were as dog-eared as their inhabitant, who was clearly distressed at facing three strange young ladies (and three yet to come). Willa and Isabelle opened the conversation with the trip to Ludlow. No response. Willa moved on to his poetry and what it meant to her, but from that he visibly retreated. In the uneasy pause that followed, Housman turned to the silent Dorothy (she had neither gone to Ludlow nor read his poetry) and ascertained that she was a scholar of pre-classic Latin--his own field! His reticence vanished. He became absolutely expansive--but neatly deflected every effort to shift the conversation back to poetry.

On the return bus her friends saw that Willa was crying, a fact she never mentioned in later years. By then, she, too, did not suffer fans gladly.

COPYRIGHT The Atlantic Monthly Co. 1987

Cite computer service material as you would cite other print materials, but include a reference to the service at the end of your entry. Provide the publication information given by the service as well as the name of the service and the accession (or identifying) numbers within the service.

Sorel, Nancy Caldwell. "A. E. Housman and Willa Cather." Atlantic July 1987: 83. Dialog file 647, item 05049972.

Recordings The entry starts with the composer, followed by the title of the work. The major performers appear after the word *with*. *Cond.* is an abbreviation for *Conductor* and *Orch.* is an abbreviation for *Orchestra.* LDR-73002 is the catalog number.

Verdi, Giuseppe. La Traviata. With Joan Sutherland, Luciano Pavarotti, and Matteo Manuguerra. Cond. Richard Bonynge. National Philharmonic Orch. and London Opera Chorus. London, LDR-73002, 1981.

Performances: plays, concerts, films, television or radio programs, interviews In the first entry the abbreviation *dir.* is for *director.* The date given is that of the performance cited.

Saks, Gene, dir. Lost in Yonkers. By Neil Simon. With Lucie Arnaz. Richard Rogers Theater. New York. 27 Nov. 1992.

The Mother. By Paddy Chayevsky. Dir. Delbert Mann. Philco Television Playhouse. NBC, 4 Apr. 1954.

Coppola, Francis Ford, dir. Bram Stoker's Dracula. With Gary Oldman, Winona Ryder, Anthony Hopkins, and Keanu Reeves. Columbia, 1992.

Rutter, John, cond. New England Symphonic Ensemble.
Concert. Carnegie Hall, New York. 29 Nov. 1992.

Sills, Beverly. Telephone interview. 6 Dec. 1981.

Final list of works cited

Your list of works cited, placed at the end of your paper, must include data for all the materials you used. A list that also includes data for materials consulted but not cited is headed "Works Consulted." For a sample of a full "Works Cited" list, see pp. 507–509.

✓ CHECKLIST 33.2: PREPARING A LIST OF WORKS CITED, MLA STYLE

- Set up your list on a separate page at the end of your paper.
- Type the title ("Works Cited," "Works Consulted," or "Bibliography") about one inch from the top of the page, and double-space before you type the first entry.
- Arrange all your entries alphabetically according to the author's last name, but do not number them. The author's last name goes first, then the first and middle names.
- If several entries are by the same author, give the author's name in the first entry only. For succeeding entries, replace the author's name with three hyphens, followed by a period.
- List all entries without authors alphabetically according to the first word in the title other than an article.
- Do not separate books from periodicals. Strict alphabetical order guides the arrangement of entries. (For advanced research projects, writers sometimes separate primary from secondary sources.)
- Start the first line of each entry at the left margin. Indent succeeding lines five spaces. Double-space within entries and between them.

Model list of works cited, MLA style (excerpt)

Works Cited

Bloom, Edward A., and Lillian D. Bloom. Willa Cather's Gift of Sympathy. Carbondale: Southern Illinois UP, 1962.

Brennan, Joseph X. "Music and Willa Cather." University Review 31 (1965): 257-64.

---. "Willa Cather and Music." University Review 31 (1965): 175-83.

"Cather." World Scope Encyclopedia. 1955 ed.

Cather, Willa. On Writing. New York: Knopf, 1949.

■ **Exercise 33.4** Using the models in 33d, write correct entries for the following sources to be included in a list of works cited. (You may not need all the data that appear in each group.)

1. *Writing in the Arts and Sciences,* a 1981 textbook published by Winthrop Publishers, Inc., in Cambridge, Massachusetts. The authors, in the order in which they appear on the title page, are Elaine Maimon, Gerald L. Belcher, Gail W. Hearn, Barbara F. Nodine, and Finbarr W. O'Connor.
2. An article by Paul Moses called "Debate Over, Bishops Reach Out," in *Newsday,* a Long Island, New York newspaper. The article appeared on Friday, November 20, 1992, on page 5 and continued on page 41.
3. A book by Stewart C. Easton called *Roger Bacon and His Search for a Universal Science,* published by Greenwood Press of Westport, Connecticut, in 1970.
4. In the quarterly journal *American Scholar,* an essay called "A Culture of One's Own" by Quentin Anderson. The article appeared in Autumn 1992, volume 61, on pages 533–551. *American Scholar* is published by Phi Beta Kappa in Washington, D.C. It is paginated continuously throughout an annual volume.
5. Volume 1 of the two-volume edition of *Joseph Conrad: Life and Letters,* edited by G. Jean-Aubry and published in 1927 by Doubleday in Garden City, New York.

33e cite

■ **Exercise 33.5** Return to Exercise 31.4 and write a list of works cited, including any five sources.

33e Using the APA Format

The *Publication Manual of the American Psychological Association* (APA) provides guidelines for writers of research papers in the social sciences and other academic areas. APA addresses its manual to writers aiming at publication in one of the many APA journals. It recommends that students writing papers in APA style follow supplementary guidelines established by their colleges. If you are told to use the APA *Publication Manual,* check with your instructor for further directions. For example, APA manuscripts submitted for publication require an **abstract,** which is a short, comprehensive summary of the paper. Yet at the instructor's request, many undergraduate papers written in the APA format use an outline instead of an abstract.

Like the MLA, the APA recommends short references documented within the text and a complete list of sources, called **references,** at the end of the paper. The APA parenthetical citation includes the author's last name and the year of publication. In general, page numbers are included only for direct quotations, not paraphrases or summaries.

Using Parenthetical References in the Text

33e cite

Model internal documentation; APA format

```
Periodic emission of radiation from black
holes suggests gravitational collapse is not
as final as once believed (Hawking, 1988).
```

Author's name | Comma | Date of publication | Period

Here are some other examples.

```
Hawking (1988) interprets periodic emission of radiation
from black holes as an indication that gravitational
collapse is not as final as once believed.
```

```
In 1988 Hawking wrote that gravitational collapse may not be
as final as previously believed.
```

Multiple publications in one year

If an author has published more than one work in a single year, these works will appear alphabetically by title in the reference list. For the first work, place an *a* after the year; for the second, place a *b*, and so on. T. G. R. Bower, for example, published two books in 1977, *The Perceptual World of the Child* and *A Primer of Infant Development.* In alphabetical order by title, they are labeled 1977a and 1977b. In the reference below, the writer of the paper calls attention only to *A Primer of Infant Development.*

```
Bower (1977b) discusses the stages of a child's development.
```

Multiple authors

The following examples show how to cite references with multiple authors. In the APA system, if a source has five authors or fewer, cite them all in the first reference. Use an ampersand for *and.* For two authors only, name them both each time you cite their material. For more than two but fewer than six, subsequent references use *et al.* after the first author's name. (As explained earlier, the abbreviation *et al.* is for the Latin phrase *et alii,* meaning "and others." Do not underline the abbreviation. Do not use a period after *et*; do use a period after *al.*) If your source has six authors or more, use *et al.* after the first name each time you cite the work. Use the date in each case.

> Some psychologists see suicide attempts as a gamble (Lester & Lester, 1971).
>
> An important study connects birth order and a child's need to conform (Becker, Lerner, & Carroll, 1966).
>
> Conformity also relates to group pressure (Becker et al., 1966).

Works with no author listed

When the author is unnamed, cite in the text the first few words of the entry that appears in the reference list. Use quotation marks around the title of a chapter or article, and underline the title of a book or periodical. Include the year. Note that the title of an article in the list of references will not appear in quotation marks.

> Women over fifty who are widowed about twelve years report satisfaction and optimism in their lives ("Time Improves," 1992).
>
> In preparing text for publication writers should sketch technical drawings with precision and with symbols clear and consistent with the text (McGraw-Hill Author's Book, 1984).

Page citations

If you want to cite a specific part of your source, put the page number(s) you've taken your information from after the date. Use *p.* and *pp.* as the abbreviations. For ranges of numbers, repeat all digits.

> A six-year-old child who could not speak, Isabelle was "apparently unaware of relationships of any kind" (Mason, 1942, p. 299).

Preparing a List of References

At the end of your paper, beginning on a separate page headed "References," list the sources you cited. Arrange entries alphabetically by author's last name. If two or more works are by the same author, arrange them chronologically by year of publication. If an author has published two or more works in the same year, arrange them alphabetically by title, disregarding articles, and label them *a, b,* and so on, following the year.

Books and reference works

Model entry (APA) in a reference list, book with one author

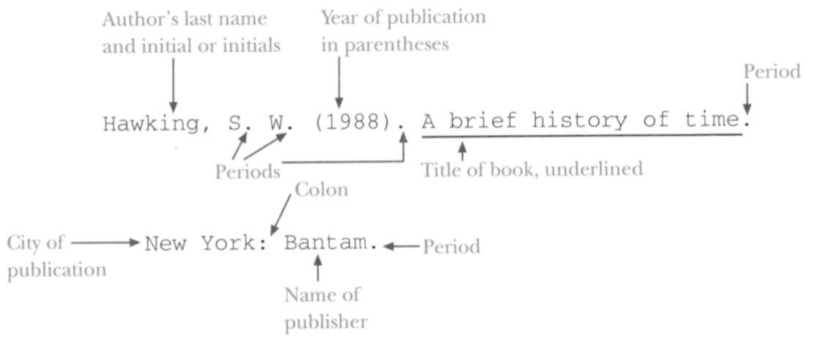

33e cite

Author's last name and initial or initials — Year of publication in parentheses — Period

```
Hawking, S. W. (1988). A brief history of time.
```

Periods — Title of book, underlined — Colon

City of publication → `New York: Bantam.` ← Period

Name of publisher

The periods set off four major elements in the entry: the author's name, the year of publication, the title, and other publication data. Notice that only the first word of the title is capitalized. Proper nouns and the first word of the subtitle, if any, are capitalized too. If the city of publication is not well known or could be confused with another location, give the state or country. For states, use postal abbreviations, not traditional abbreviations. Do not abbreviate *University* in a publisher's name, but give as brief a form of a publisher's name as is intelligible.

A book by two or more authors or editors All authors' or editors' names appear last name first, with commas separating them. Notice that an ampersand is used instead of the word *and.* The abbreviation *Eds.,* in parentheses, says that Lewis and Rosenblum are the editors of this collection.

```
Lester, G., & Lester, D. (1971). Suicide: The gamble with
    death. Englewood Cliffs, NJ: Prentice-Hall.
Lewis, M., & Rosenblum, L. A. (Eds.). (1974). The effect of
    the infant on its caregiver. New York: Wiley.
```

Journals, magazines, newspapers

The author's name, the year of publication, the article title, and other publication date are also the main elements in the entry for a journal

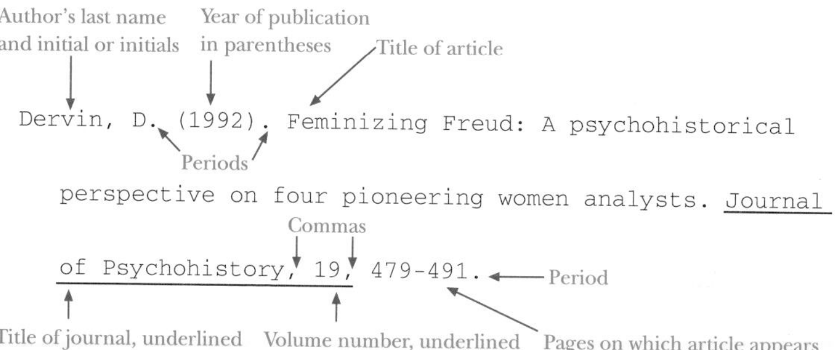

article. Note that citations include both the title of the article and the title of the journal in which the work appears. For the title of the article, only the first word, proper nouns, and the first word of the subtitle, if any, are capitalized. For journal titles, all words except articles, conjunctions, and prepositions of less than four letters are capitalized. Article titles appear without quotation marks. Journal titles are underlined. For page numbers, all digits are repeated.

An article in a journal that numbers pages separately in each issue of an annual volume If each issue in a volume is numbered, include the issue number in the citation. The number 23 after the title is the volume number. The number 3 in parentheses after the volume indicates the issue number.

Labouvie-Vief, G. (1980). Beyond formal operations: Uses and limits of pure logic in life-span development. Human Development, 23 (3), 141-161.

An article in a monthly or bimonthly magazine or daily newspaper A comma separates the year of publication from the month. Use *pp.* to abbreviate *pages* only for magazine and newspaper entries, not for journals. Do not abbreviate months.

Shepard, Nathaniel, Jr. (1981, October 11). Strong gun law sought in Chicago. New York Times, p. 38.

Wang, P. (1992, December). Put your money worries behind you. Money, pp. 76-87.

An article with no author's name The citation begins with the title. In the reference list, alphabetize the citation by the first important word in the title. The reference in the text will be a short version of the title and will appear in quotation marks.

Time improves lives of older widows. (1992-1993, December-January). Modern Maturity, p. 8.

33e cite

Final reference list

The reference list names all sources cited in the text. The list is alphabetical by author, with the exceptions noted above. It begins on a separate page headed "References."

✔ CHECKLIST 33.3: PREPARING A REFERENCE LIST, APA STYLE

- Set up your list on a separate page at the end of your paper.
- Type the title "References" about one inch from the top of the page, and double space before you type the first entry.
- Arrange all entries in alphabetical order according to author's last name. Do not number entries. Do not separate books from periodicals.
- If any authors appear more than once, arrange their entries chronologically, from earliest to latest.
- If any authors have published more than one work in a year, place them alphabetically by title and label them *a, b, c,* and so forth, after the year.
- List entries without authors alphabetically according to the first important word in the title.
- Type the first line of each entry flush with the left margin. Indent three spaces all other lines within each entry. Double-space within entries and between them.

Model APA reference list, APA style (excerpt)

References

Hawking, S. W. (1988). A brief history of time. New York: Bantam.

Lane, E. (1992, November 20). Black hole snapshot: Scientists think that's what Hubble photo may be. Newsday, p. 7.

Wald, R. M. (1992). Space, time, and gravity: The theory of the big bang and black holes. (2nd ed.). Chicago: University of Chicago Press.

■ **Exercise 33.6** Return to Exercise 33.3. Revise your parenthetical documentation according to the APA format, and prepare a reference list for the three sources.

■ **Exercise 33.7** Return to Exercise 31.4. Select any five entries and prepare a reference list according to the APA format.

33f
Comparing the MLA and APA Citation Systems

The MLA and APA systems are the most frequently used research documentation systems in the college curriculum. You should be able to shift from one to the other with a minimum of difficulty as your instructors explain their research paper requirements. You will use the MLA system for courses in humanities, literature, history, religion, communications, and education, among others. Courses in the social sciences—psychology, sociology, political science, economics, statistics, for example—may require the APA system, as may research projects in sciences like biology, chemistry, physics, and geology.

To help you use both systems more easily, we provide on facing pages two text excerpts that are exactly the same. The text and references come from the student paper on black holes. One uses the MLA citation system, and the other uses the APA citation system. Marginal comments indicate important features of each system. In addition, you will find two excerpts from the listed references used in the black holes paper; one excerpt is in MLA style and the other, using the same books and periodicals, is in the APA style. A complete version of the black holes paper in APA style appears in Chapter 34.

MLA Style

If a star's mass is low enough, the star can support itself against gravitational collapse. If not, the gravity continues to shrink the area, which makes the nuclear fuel burn faster and faster. As the fuel becomes exhausted, the star grows colder while the density increases. Jastrow explains what happens next:

Source named in text; no date required

Quotation of four lines or more set up as block quotation and indented ten spaces

> At that point, the mass is so compact that the force of gravity at the surface is billions of times stronger than the force of the sun. The tug of that enormous force prevents the rays of light from leaving the surface of the star. (65)

Specific page citation in parentheses; no abbreviation for *page*

Without the fuel to maintain equilibrium, the star eventually becomes infinitely dense: a black hole!

While gravitational collapse takes place, other strange things happen. As the gravity becomes proportionally more massive, information from the star takes longer and longer to emerge. In a normal star like the sun, light waves are bent by the strong gravitational field. But in a black hole, the gravity is extremely strong; "light cones are bent inward so much that light can no longer escape" (Hawking 87).

Parenthetical citation: author's name and page number without punctuation

This means that as a star collapses it eventually becomes invisible. Worse yet, the dimensions of the star shrink until it becomes a hole not only in space . . . .

Works Cited

Dupree, Andrea K., and Lee Hartman. "Hunting for Black Holes." Natural History Oct. 1979: 30-37.

Hawking, Stephen W. A Brief History of Time. New York: Bantam Books, 1988.

APA Style

Source named in text; date of publication in parentheses

Quotation of forty words or more indented five spaces

Specific page citation—with abbreviation *p.* for "page"—in parentheses

Parenthetical citation: author's name, date, and page number separated by commas

If a star's mass is low enough, the star can support itself against gravitational collapse. If not, the gravity continues to shrink the area, which makes the nuclear fuel burn faster and faster. As the fuel becomes exhausted, the star grows colder while the density increases. Jastrow (1979) explains what happens next:

> At that point, the mass is so compact that the force of gravity at the surface is billions of times stronger than the force of the sun. The tug of that enormous force prevents the rays of light from leaving the surface of the star. (p. 65)

Without the fuel to maintain equilibrium, the star eventually becomes infinitely dense: a black hole!

While gravitational collapse takes place, other strange things happen. As the gravity becomes proportionally more massive, information from the star takes longer and longer to emerge. In a normal star like the sun, light waves are bent by the strong gravitational field. But in a black hole, the gravity is extremely strong; "light cones are bent inward so much that light can no longer escape" (Hawking, 1988, p. 87).

This means that as a star collapses it eventually becomes invisible. Worse yet, the dimensions of the star shrink until it becomes a hole not only in space . . . .

References

Dupree, A. K., & Hartman, L. (1979, October). Hunting for black holes. Natural History, pp. 30-37.

Hawking, S. W. (1988). A brief history of time. New York: Bantam.

Jastrow, R. (1979). Red giants and white dwarfs. New York: Warner.

33f
cite

MLA STYLE HIGHLIGHTS

Form

- Title (Works Cited) centered; no quotation marks, no underlining
- Double space throughout
- Second line of continuing entry indented five spaces
- Periods separate three main elements: author's name, title, publication data. Period completes entire entry.

Elements of Entries

Author. Last name and full first name for authors up to three; for more than three authors, name the first, followed by *et al.* First author listed with last name first, second and third authors listed first name, then last; *and* connects names of final two authors.

Title. Title follows author's name. Titles of articles and chapters are in quotation marks; first letter of all major words is capitalized. Book and periodical titles are underlined; first letter of all major words is capitalized. Book titles are followed by a period, but no mark of punctuation follows a journal title.

Publication data. For books, city of publication, colon, publisher's name (shortened or with appropriate abbreviations), comma, year of publication. For journals with continuous pagination, volume number, year in parentheses, colon, inclusive page numbers. For monthly periodicals, month (abbreviated except May, June, July) and year, colon, inclusive page numbers. For weeklies and dailies, day, month, year, colon, inclusive page numbers. Do not use *p.* or *pp.* Do not repeat digits for hundreds.

APA STYLE HIGHLIGHTS

Form

- Title (References) centered; no quotation marks, no underlining
- Double space throughout
- Second line of continuing entry indented three spaces
- Periods separate four main elements: author's name, year of publication, title, other publication data. Period completes entire entry.

Elements of Entries

Author. Last name first and initials for all authors up through five; for six or more authors, name the first, followed by *et al.* An ampersand (&) connects names of final two authors.

Date. Date, in parentheses, follows author's name. Books require year of copyright. For monthly magazines, year, comma, month. For daily newspapers and weekly and biweekly magazines, year, comma, month, day. Do not abbreviate month.

Title. Title follows date. Book titles are underlined and in lowercase letters, except for first word of title, first word of subtitle (generally after a colon in the title), and proper nouns. Titles of articles and chapters are not underlined or enclosed in quotation marks and follow same guidelines as books for uppercase and lowercase letters. Titles of periodicals are underlined; first letter of all major words is capitalized.

Publication data. For books, city of publication, colon, brief form of publisher's name (but do not abbreviate *university*). For journals with continuous pagination, comma follows journal title, then volume number underlined, comma, inclusive page numbers (no *p.* or *pp.*). For monthly, weekly, daily periodicals, comma follows periodical title, then *p.* (page) or *pp.* (pages), inclusive page numbers. Repeat all digits in ranges.

33g Using Other Systems of Parenthetical References

Your instructor may recommend the number reference system or a full publication data system for citing sources in your paper.

Using the Number System

The number system requires an arabic number for each entry in the list of works cited; these numbers appear in the parenthetical citation, too. A comma separates the number of the entry from the relevant page number, and the entry number is often underlined, as you see below. With such a system, references included in the list of works cited may be arranged in any useful order, such as the order in which the writer cites the references in the text.

```
Hawking is essentially the creator of this definition of
black holes (2, 112).
```

Giving Full Publication Data in Parenthetical References

If you are required to give full parenthetical citation, use square brackets to replace the parentheses you would ordinarily use around city, publisher, and date. Full publication information in parenthetical references is rare; it distracts readers from the text and does not provide for a list of works cited, which readers always find useful. Occasionally, however, you will see this system in a bibliographic study or in a work that cites only a few references.

> Hawking interprets periodic emission of radiation from black holes as an indication that gravitational collapse is not as final as once believed (A Brief History of Time [New York: Bantam, 1988] 112).

33h
cite

33h Using Footnotes or Endnotes

Although internal citation is now much preferred as a system of documentation, many researchers in the past used a system of numbered notes to document their sources accurately. In such a system, notes provide full publishing information.

Footnotes appear at page bottoms, numbered consecutively throughout the paper. **Endnotes** are numbered consecutively at the end of a work. As you do research in older texts, you no doubt will come across footnotes and endnotes.

Below you will find a model footnote entry for a book and a journal article. The entries correspond to the models provided in 33d and are based on the MLA system. In footnotes and endnotes, a comma separates the author's name from the title. Parentheses set off the publication data from the rest of the reference, and, as in bibliographic entries, you can always use the short form of the publisher's name. A period completes the entry. Raised a half space above the line, the number of each note comes after a five-space indentation. Continuing lines of each note are flush with the left margin.

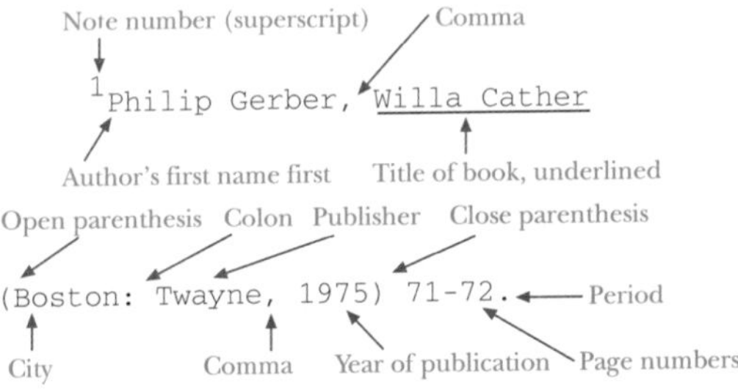

Model footnote or endnote entry, article in a journal with pages numbered continuously throughout an annual volume

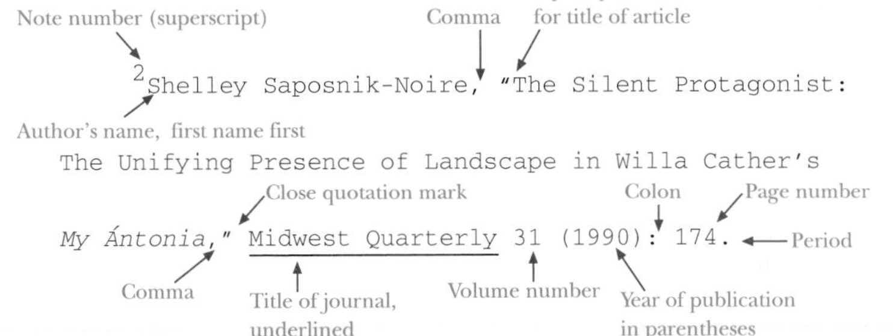

33h cite

Later References to the Same Source

With full publication data in a previous note, writers use a shortened form of citation in each later reference to the source. Generally, these references include only the author's last name and the page number. Although the *MLA Handbook* discourages the use of the Latin abbreviation *ibid.* (for *ibidem,* meaning "in the same place"), the form persists in academic writing. *Ibid.* indicates that the citation appears in exactly the same source as in the preceding note. Capitalize *ibid.* as the first word of the sentence in the note, but do not underline it, and always use a period after the abbreviation. The samples below of first and later citations show both styles.

[1]Bernard Baum, "Willa Cather's Waste Land," South Atlantic Quarterly 48 (1949): 590.

[2]Philip Gerber, Willa Cather (Boston: Twayne, 1975) 71-72.

[3]Baum 593.

[4]Baum.

[5]Gerber 72.

---

[1]Bernard Baum, "Willa Cather's Waste Land," South Atlantic Quarterly 48 (1949): 590.

[2]Ibid. 592.

[3]Philip Gerber, Willa Cather (Boston: Twayne, 1975) 72.

[4]Ibid.

[5]Baum 592.

Abbreviations

The Modern Language Association recommends that writers avoid using some Latin abbreviations that at one time were standard in research papers. You will encounter these abbreviations in your reading, however, and you should know what they mean. The following list includes familiar abbreviations for bibliographical citations, along with some of the short forms of Latin terms you may encounter.

anon.	anonymous
bk., bks.	book(s)
c., ca.	circa (about), used with approximate dates
cf.	*confere* (compare)
ch., chs., chaps.	chapter(s)
col., cols.	column(s)
comp.	compiler, compiled by
cond.	conductor
dir.	director
diss.	dissertation
ed., eds.	edition(s) or editor(s)
et al.	*et alii* (and others)
ff.	and the following pages, as in *pp. 85ff.*
ibid.	*ibidem* (in the same place)
illus.	illustrated by, illustrator, illustration(s)
l., ll.	line(s)
loc. cit.	*loco citato* (in the place cited)
ms, mss	manuscript(s)
n., nn.	note(s), as in *p. 24, n. 2* or *p. 24n*
n.d.	no date (of publication)
no., nos.	number(s)
n.p.	no place (of publication) or no publisher
n. pag.	no pagination
op. cit.	*opere citato* (in the work cited)
orch.	orchestra
p., pp.	page(s)
passim	throughout
pt., pts.	part(s)
qtd.	quoted
q.v.	*quod vide* (which see)
rev.	revision, revised, revised by; or review, reviewed by
rpt.	reprint, reprinted
sc.	scene
sec., secs.	section(s)
st.	stanza
trans.	translator, translated by, translation
univ.	university
vol., vols.	volume(s)

CHAPTER

34

DEVELOPING, WRITING, AND REVISING A RESEARCH PAPER

By this time you are almost ready to begin writing. You have investigated sources and taken careful notes. You can see relations between ideas. You note contradictions and differences of opinion. Your ideas form and re-form; your tentative thesis develops; you read further to explore a point you missed or to check on a point you're not sure of.

You need to think carefully about your thesis now. Your reading and other research should focus your thoughts and allow you to state your point clearly and accurately. You may find that a formal outline helps you organize your paper. A formal outline provides an orderly visual scheme of the paragraphs with main and subordinated points clearly related. From your outline you can write first and subsequent drafts. You will need to revise your research paper several times, paying attention to all the special details of documentation as well as to the general concerns of manuscript preparation. The research papers included in this chapter are models.

34a Revising the Thesis

After studying your rough plan, your tentative thesis, and your notes (which you now have in order), reevaluate your thesis. Here are the tentative theses for the papers on Cather and on black holes. Notice how the writers of these papers continue to refine their theses.

	Literature	**Astronomy**
Tentative thesis	In Cather's stories, characters isolated from familiar surroundings are severely affected physically and spiritually. ↓	Black holes are almost impossible to find, despite astronomers' predictions. ↓
Revised thesis	Cather's " 'A Death in the Desert' " and "A Wagner Matinee" show people who are isolated from familiar environments. ↓	Astronomers are finding it very difficult to discover and investigate black holes. ↓
A second revised thesis	The central characters in Cather's " 'A Death in the Desert' " and "A Wagner Matinee" show the effects of an untamed country on people from a stable, civilized world. ↓	As new ideas evolved about the universe, scientists tried to confirm the existence of black holes, which in the past were only theoretical possibilities. ↓
Final copy	In two particular stories, " 'A Death in the Desert' " and "A Wagner Matinee," the central characters bear the burden of escape and isolation from familiar, stable traditions in a "new country."	But because black holes are impossible by definition to detect directly, the search to confirm their existence is an outstanding instance of theoretical and practical science working together.

■ **Exercise 34.1** Examine the development of topics to thesis statements for the papers on Cather and on black holes (pp. 425–427, 475–476). Comment on the evolution of the theses. What was each writer's original idea? How did it change? How does the final copy reflect the concerns of the writer's early thinking?

■ **Exercise 34.2*** Study your notes, and revise your thesis.

34b
Writing a Formal Outline

Your instructor may require a formal outline, or you may find an outline useful in your efforts to refine your plan. A formal outline gives you an orderly visual scheme of your ideas. As you set down these ideas, use roman numerals for the most important points, capital letters for the next most important points, arabic numbers for supporting points under lettered points, and lowercase letters for the smallest items you include in the outline. Further subordination is possible, but you will rarely need to use as many as four levels. For most papers, two or three levels of subordination will do. The scheme is shown on page 478.

Once you have grouped large, related ideas in your notes, label them with accurate, mutually exclusive, logically arranged headings. Follow your rough plan, but concentrate on making headings sufficient in number and breadth to cover the topic properly.

As you look over these headings, you may see a need for some changes in organization. Make whatever changes you need to shape your ideas, and then fill in supporting information under each major heading. Watch for and delete any overlap or repetition of ideas. Watch for proper sequence of ideas.

All outlines follow the same format, but you can write them as topic outlines or sentence outlines. In a **topic outline,** you write out points as brief capsules of meaning. Each item must communicate an idea, of course, but the items need not be full sentences. In a **sentence outline,**

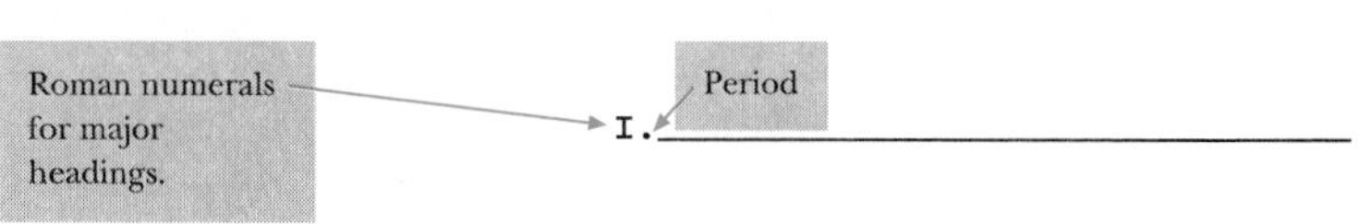
Roman numerals for major headings.
Period
I.

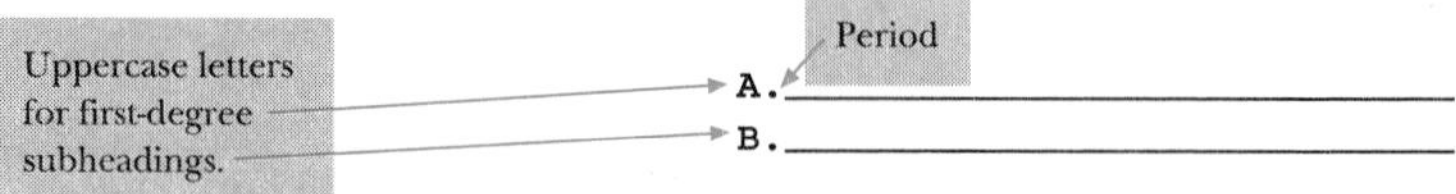
Uppercase letters for first-degree subheadings.
Period
A.
B.

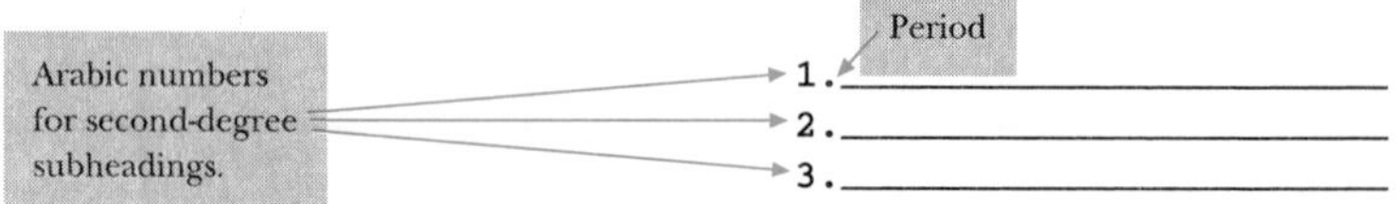
Arabic numbers for second-degree subheadings.
Period
1.
2.
3.

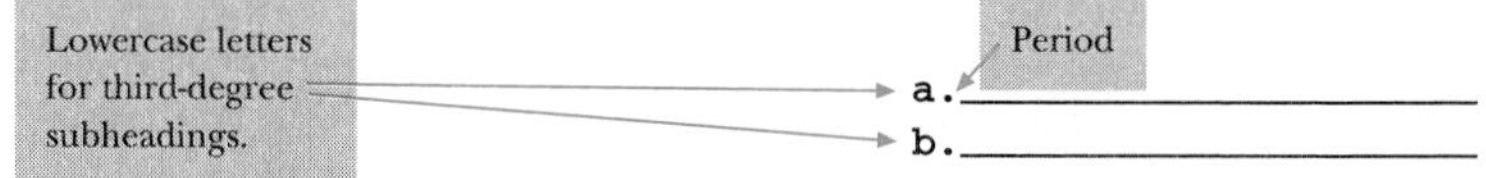
Lowercase letters for third-degree subheadings.
Period
a.
b.

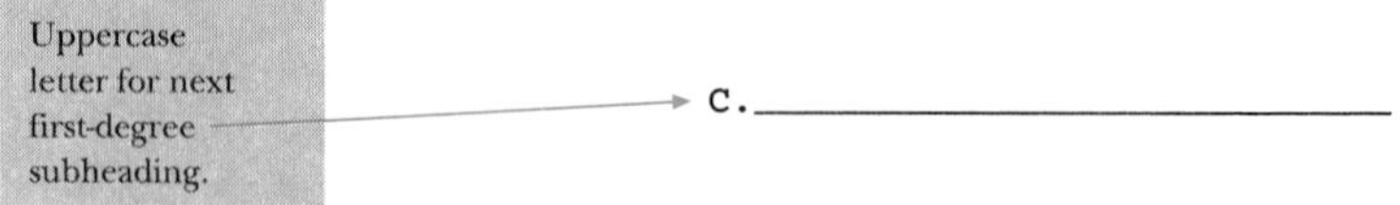
Uppercase letter for next first-degree subheading.
C.

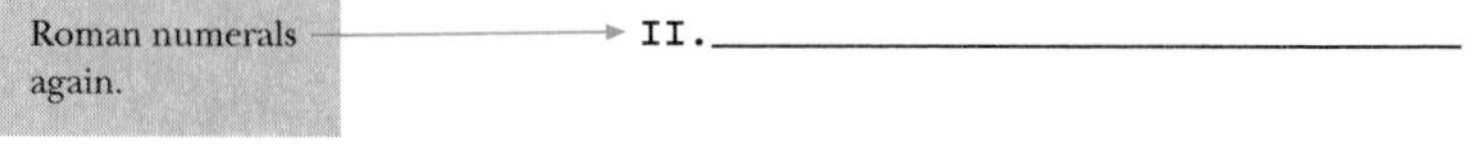
Roman numerals again.
II.

each point appears as a complete grammatical statement, with a subject and a predicate. The sentence outline requires more effort: it asks you to name what you are going to talk about and also to indicate what you are going to say about it. For this reason, a sentence outline may be more productive, but a topic outline can be just as helpful if you think it through just as carefully.

Two rules govern the construction of every formal outline:

1. Every entry requiring division must be divided into at least two parts. When you divide a topic, you must have two or more subheadings under it. If you can come up with only one subpart, incorporate it into the main heading; it belongs there. In short, a *I* requires a *II*; an *A* requires a *B*; a *1* requires a *2*; an *a* requires a *b*.
2. Main headings must be parallel in form, and subheadings under each main heading must be parallel in form.

For the paper on black holes, the student prepared the topic outline on pages 511–512. The sentence outline on pages 486–487 shows you the skeleton of the Cather paper on pages 489–503. Study the outlines carefully and use them as models for form and style.

The rules will help you to construct a clear and useful outline. But remember that you should never be bound to your outline as you write. Feel free to use the ideas that come to all writers, ideas they did not have when they planned their work. In fact, you may prepare the formal outline *after* you write the paper. Every essay that has a logic and structure can be outlined; so you should be able to outline your essay once you have completed it. Then the outline will help you check that you have constructed a logical and clear piece of prose, that you have put everything in its proper place, and that you have developed a thesis in a thoughtful and well-written series of paragraphs leading to a conclusion.

■ **Exercise 34.3** Discuss the strengths and weaknesses in the following outline. Look especially at the relation of the thesis to the points in the outline; look at the main headings and subordinate points; look at the form of the outline, including divisions and the use of numbers and letters. Which points are clear? Which points are not?

34b rev

Outline

Thesis: A study of liberal arts and sciences is valuable for students seeking careers in business.

I. Exclusion of liberal arts and science courses from business curricula
   A. Need for specialized business courses for job training
II. An understanding of people
   A. Value of psychology and sociology
      1. In a study of personality and group dynamics
   B. Value of natural sciences in seeing problems and in stating and in finding solutions to them
   C. Insights into human character from literature
      1. Complete personality studies from fiction
      2. Opportunities to share thoughts of pressured characters
III. Recognition by businesses today of capabilities developing from employees' varied educational backgrounds
   A. Strong qualities of character
   B. Ability to deal with future technologies
IV. Transmission of humanity's cherished values

■ **Exercise 34.4** Examine the outline of the papers on Cather (pages 486–487) and on black holes (pages 511–512). How do the outlines reflect the correct format for formal outlining?

■ **Exercise 34.5*** As your instructor directs, prepare a formal outline for your research paper. Use a *topic* or a *sentence* outline according to your instructor's wishes.

34c
Writing the First Draft

Using your rough plan, your formal outline, and your note cards, write a rough draft of your research paper. This is not final copy, and the point is not to say everything perfectly but simply to flesh out what you have to say. Once you have paragraphs drafted, use them to adjust and refine the rough plan or your formal outline.

At this stage you will have a rough draft but a nearly final outline. Your outline should now be a guide to the next draft, although as new ideas come to you in the process of creating that draft, you may need to refine the outline further. Throughout the writing process, the outline enables you to check the logic of your progress from one point to the next. The outline also helps you check the accuracy and the consistency of your argument and the balance among sections.

As you write your draft, you will be drawing on your note cards. Review 33a, on integrating source material into your own writing. Be sure to acknowledge all sources, using the citation and documentation system your instructor requires. Use the checklist below as a guide.

✓ CHECKLIST 34.1: REVISING A RESEARCH PAPER

Revising is quality control. It may be the most important step you take in turning a good paper into a great one. For a full array of issues to consider as you revise, see Checklist 2.2. Here are some questions to ask yourself about a research paper.

- Is my thesis clear? Does it state accurately the intent of the paper?
- Have I done more than simply summarize other sources? Have I made appropriate commentary on source materials?
- Do my source materials—quotations, summaries, paraphrases—support my points throughout?
- Do my ideas follow logically? Are transitions clear?
- Are all sources clear? Have I always indicated my source of ideas even when paraphrasing or summarizing? Are citations unobtrusive and correctly written?
- Are sources listed with full publication data on a separate page at the end of my paper?

34d Editing the First Draft and Preparing the Final Version

Take the time to polish your prose, also checking carefully for clarity of language and ideas and for conciseness; also check paragraph and sentence structure, grammar, spelling, and mechanics. (Use relevant checklists in Chapters 4–30.) Check the accuracy of quotations, summaries, and paraphrases. Avoid plagiarism by citing sources clearly and consistently (see 33d, 33e, 33f, and 33g). Most instructors ask that you type long papers, and you should follow the guidelines for manuscript preparation carefully (see Checklist 2.3). Handwritten research papers are hard to produce neatly because of their length, and they are difficult to read. If, with your instructor's permission, you choose to write your final copy in longhand, take special pains to produce a neat, clear manuscript.

Number all pages consecutively in the upper right corner, starting with page 1 of the text. Some writers type their last name before the page number in case pages are misplaced. APA style recommends a short form of the title instead of the author's last name. Do not use a period, hyphen, or the word *page* (or the abbreviation *p.*) with the page number. Remember that endnotes and the list of works cited count in the total pagination of your paper. Do not paginate the title page or cover sheet. The outline is paginated with lowercase roman numerals (i, ii, iii).

✓ CHECKLIST 34.2: ASSEMBLING THE FINAL COPY OF A RESEARCH PAPER

As you get ready to submit your research paper, make one final check that all the elements are in order. Final copy for a research paper or a term paper usually includes, in this order:

- Title page. The *MLA Handbook* suggests that the author's name, the class, the date, and so on appear on the first page of the paper, an inch down from the top and an inch from the right. The title is centered, four spaces above the text of the paper. But when formal outlines are required, many instructors prefer a title page. (Sample title pages appear on pp. 485 and 510.) APA recommends a title page.

- Formal outline or abstract.
- The body of the essay.
- Endnotes. If you use parenthetical documentation, endnotes or footnotes will be minimal. If your instructor requires footnotes, place them at the bottom of pages. In APA style endnotes follow the list of references.
- List of works cited (MLA) or references (APA).

34e
Examining Sample Research Papers

The research papers that follow illustrate many of the suggestions made in this chapter. The paper on Willa Cather uses the MLA system of citing sources in the text. Facing page annotations explain essential features of this paper in the MLA format. The paper on black holes uses the APA citation format. Here we provide annotations in the margin in order to point out key elements of an APA style paper. Examine the papers and the explanatory comments, and use them as models whenever you encounter problems in setting up research papers of your own.

■ **Exercise 34.6*** After reading the sample papers and following the guidelines in 34c, prepare the final copy of your research paper. Observe your instructor's specific requirements.

34e
rev

(t-a) Title: one-third down, centered and double-spaced

(t-b) Cather used double quotation marks around the title of the story to show her debt to Robert Browning's poem "A Death in the Desert," which gave Cather her title. The title of the story, then, is written as a quote within a quote.

(t-c) Leave two inches before typing the next line.

(t-d) The writer's name, the instructor's name, the course and section number, and the date the paper is submitted, all centered and double-spaced.

(t-a) Isolation and Escape

in

(t-b) Cather's " 'A Death in the Desert' "

and

"A Wagner Matinee"

(t-c)

by

(t-d) Shirley Hawkins

Mr. C. Prager

English 101, Section 4

April 7, 1990

i

Thesis: The central characters in Willa Cather's stories " 'A Death in the Desert' " and "A Wagner Matinee" show the effects of an untamed country on people from a stable, civilized world.

I. The main characters show the physical burden of living in the barren West.
   A. In " 'A Death in the Desert' " Katharine Gaylord, self-isolated in the Cheyenne of her youth, is dying of tuberculosis.
   B. In "A Wagner Matinee" Aunt Georgiana is a wreck after thirty years on the Nebraska frontier.

II. The characters are also burdened by the toll on their spirits.
   A. Wyoming is for Katharine a spiritual desert.
      1. She misses her former life as a famous singer.
      2. The emptiness of the desert intrudes on the room she modeled after music studios in the East.
      3. She will never return to art.
      4. Her death separates her from art no more surely than did her life.
   B. Georgiana's spirit also suffers the deprivations of frontier life.
      1. In a world of worries about survival she had little opportunity to enjoy the music she has loved so much.
      2. When she returns to Boston, the prairie world is always painfully close.

III. Cather uses music to identify the pain of separation from civilization and life in a primitive setting.

ii

A. For Katharine Gaylord music symbolizes the swift passage of her own life.

1. Both life and artistic achievement are too brief.

2. In a new sonata she recognizes her own personal tragedy of isolation from music.

B. The music Aunt Georgiana hears echoes her particular condition.

1. The overture to *Tannhäuser* reflects her own struggle between art and the frontier.

2. Other selections echo the opposing forces in her life.

IV. Cather acknowledged that the theme of escape ran through her work.

(1-a) The writer's last name and the page number appear near the top of all pages; outline is paginated in roman numerals, and text is page 1; margins are 1 to 1½ inches.

(1-b) Title is centered two inches from the top of the page.

(1-c) *qtd. in Woodress:* the source of the quotation from Fisher is *Willa Cather* by James Woodress (listed among works cited, p. 10 of the essay). As Fisher's original article was not available, the writer used a secondary source.

(1-d) *Gerber, preface:* the quotation appears in the preface, which is unpaginated in Gerber's book (listed among works cited, on p. 10 of the essay).

(1-e) The thesis clearly states the topic. The introduction builds to the thesis. Here is an earlier draft of the student's introduction:

Dorothy Canfield Fisher was a friend of Willa Cather's from college days at the University of Nebraska. She wrote an essay on Cather's works for the New York *Herald Tribune* in 1933. She said: "The one real subject of all her books is the effect a new country—our new country—has on the people transplanted to it from the traditions of a stable, complex civilization" (qtd. in Woodress 247). Fisher was answering complaints by critics about disconnectedness in Cather's novels. But even in Cather's short stories, you can see that Fisher is right. The central characters in the stories generally are hurt by their escape from familiar places to a new one.

(1-f) The words *character* and *story* and the repeated reference to separation connect the paragraphs. The first sentence of this paragraph corresponds to the major heading I in the outline. The rest of this paragraph and the next develop subhead I.A in the outline.

(1-g) The summary gives only essential details to help readers who may not know the story.

(1-a) Hawkins 1

Isolation and Escape in
(1-b) Cather's " 'A Death in the Desert' "
and "A Wagner Matinee"

In a 1933 essay for the New York *Herald Tribune* Dorothy
Canfield Fisher wrote about her friend from college days at the
University of Nebraska. "I offer you a hypothesis about Willa
Cather's work: the one real subject of all her books is the effect a
new country--our new country--has on the people transplanted to it
from the traditions of a stable, complex civilization" (qtd. in
(1-c) Woodress 247). Fisher was addressing complaints by contemporary
critics who saw disconnectedness in Cather's writing, and Fisher
wanted to show that novels like *A Lost Lady* and *Shadows on the Rock*
(1-d) had a common bond (Gerber, preface). But even in Cather's first
collection of short stories, *The Troll Garden*, published in 1905,
(1-e) readers can see that Fisher's comment is valid. In two particular
stories, " 'A Death in the Desert' " and "A Wagner Matinee," the
central characters bear the burden of escape and isolation from
familiar, stable traditions in a "new country."

(1-f) The physical appearance of the main character in each story
shows the strain of the separation she lived through. When we first
see her in " 'A Death in the Desert,' " Katharine Gaylord, a former
(1-g) singer, is dying of lung disease in Cheyenne, Wyoming, the home of
her youth. In the past she had lived in New York and Chicago and had

34e
rev

(2-a) The quotation blends with the writer's own prose. The parenthetical citation indicates that the quoted words appear on page 72 of the collection *The Troll Garden,* abbreviated here as *TG.* The title is required along with Cather's name because the list of works cited contains other works by Cather.

(2-b) The writer has paraphrased from the words Katharine Gaylord speaks in the story. Here is the original source:

Formerly, when it was not *if* I should ever sing Brunnhilde, but quite simply when I *should* sing Brunnhilde, I was always starving myself and thinking what I might drink and what I might not. But broken music boxes may drink whatsoever they list, and no one cares whether they lose their figure.

(2-c) The writer interprets the quotations she has presented.

(2-d) Corresponding to subhead I.B of the outline, this paragraph briefly summarizes important plot elements in "A Wagner Matinee." Note the smooth integration of a quotation from the story in the opening sentence.

(2-e) The page number alone is enough in parentheses here. Readers know that the discussion is still about "A Wagner Matinee."

(2-f) The superscript 1 corresponds to endnote 1 on page 9 of the essay.

traveled throughout Europe with the brilliant yet selfish composer
Adriance Hilgarde, a man she loved deeply without his knowing it.

Now Everett Hilgarde, Adriance's brother and an almost exact
look-alike for the famous musician, observes Katharine, who is being
destroyed by her long illness. Her loose-fitting gown could not
(2-a) hide "the sharp outlines of her emaciated body, but the stamp of her
disease was there; simple and ugly and obtrusive, a pitiless fact
that could not be disguised or evaded" (Cather, *TG* 72). She has
stooped shoulders; she sways unevenly when she walks; and her face
is "older, sadder, softer" (72) than when Everett saw her a long time
(2-b) ago. Self-exiled in the Gaylords' house, Katharine refers to
(2-c) herself as a broken music box (81). Her physical decay reflects her
separation from the lively world of art she once knew.

(2-d) In "A Wagner Matinee" Aunt Georgiana, a former music teacher at
The Boston Conservatory, returns to Boston--"the place longed for
hungrily half a lifetime" (Cather, *TG* 110). For thirty years she
had tended a ranch on the desolate Nebraska frontier. Her nephew
Clark, who spent some of his boyhood years on the farm with her and
(2-e) his uncle Howard, notes her "misshapen figure" (108), her "soiled
linen duster," and her stooped shoulders "now almost bent together
over her sunken chest. . . . She wore ill-fitting false teeth, and
her skin was as yellow as a Mongolian's from constant exposure to a
pitiless wind and to the alkaline water which hardens the most
(2-f) transparent cuticle into a sort of flexible leather" (109).[1]
Earlier, when Clark received the letter from Howard announcing Aunt
Georgiana's arrival, Clark said that her name called up her figure,
"at once pathetic and grotesque" (107). Clark himself knows about

(3-a) The opening sentence corresponds to the major heading II in the outline. The subhead A identifies the character to be discussed here. Second-level subheads 1, 2, 3, and 4 correspond to details introduced and expanded upon in succeeding paragraphs.

(3-b) The quotation card for this source appears below. Note that the writer quotes only the most relevant point and changes the tense of the verb *imposed* so that it fits into her sentence. The brackets show that she supplied the *s.*

Kohler, "WC," 9.
"To a generation coming to maturity between wars Miss Cather already seemed a little old-fashioned. It was true that she did not always flatter the West, and her stories were filled with images of the waste that its barren loneliness imposed upon the human spirit."
*Good statement to support Fisher's point--tough new world's effect on the spirit.

(3-c) Since the sentence identifies Porter as the source, only the page number is required as documentation. For full publishing data, readers can check the list of works cited, where Porter's afterword has a separate entry.

(3-d) This paragraph develops the second-level subhead II.A.1 and II.A.2.

(3-e) The writer interprets and evaluates Cather's image.

(3-f) Here is the signal card that the writer made out and in 4-a below, the quotation from " 'A Death in the Desert' "

Cather, "Death in the Desert," 74-75.
Quote about Everett talking with Katharine - as desert suddenly glares through window -- good to show contrast between two worlds tugging at Katharine.

Hawkins, 3

the pains of that frontier life; when he thinks of corn-husking days on the ranch, he says, "I felt the knuckles of my thumb . . . as though they were raw again" (107).

(3-a) But Cather's stories show more than just the effects of the
untamed West on a person's body. They also show "the waste that its
(3-b) barren loneliness impose[s] upon the human spirit" (Kohler 9). It
is true that for Katharine Gaylord, life in the West has not caused
her bodily pain. Still, her physical condition is a symbol of the
barren life the former artist must live now as she is dying of
tuberculosis. As Katherine Anne Porter says in her 1952 afterword
to *The Troll Garden*, "Wyoming is for her not only an earthly desert
(3-c) but one of the heart, the mind, the spirit" (151). Forced to leave
the life of musical fame that she once had, she is very unhappy, her
brother says, dying "like a rat in a hole, out of her own world, and
she can't fall back into ours" (Cather, *TG* 69).

(3-d) We can see how much that former life meant to Katharine and how
deeply she misses it. It is easier to die in the West, she
maintains: "to go East would be dying twice" (70). It is not that
Wyoming is a new land for her--she grew up there as a child--but it
(3-e) is a land now alien to her spiritual needs. With a brilliant image
Cather shows the conflicting forces of past and present in
Katharine's life. In the Wyoming house, the music room makes
Everett feel that he has stepped into a familiar New York studio
(3-f) almost exactly like his brother's, "so individual and poignantly

(4-a) Note the writer's interpretation. Here is the paragraph from the short story:

34e
rev

"I remember," Everett said seriously, twirling the pencil between his fingers and looking, as he sat with his head thrown back, out under the red window blind which was raised just a little, and as it swung back and forth in the wind revealed the glaring panorama of the desert—a blinding stretch of yellow, flat as the sea in dead calm, splotched here and there with deep purple shadows; and, beyond, the ragged-blue outline of the mountains and the peaks of snow, white as the white clouds.

(4-b) This paragraph develops points II.A.3 and II.A.4 in the outline.

(4-c) The writer has paraphrased Bloom and Bloom:

This avowed hostility between the artist and society gave her the subject for an undergraduate theme, which was published in the *State Journal,* on Thomas Carlyle's fierce withdrawal from social concerns. Later, in " 'A Death in the Desert,' " she further alluded to the alienation as a "long warfare" so futile and enervating that it can only distract the artist's attention from his singular purpose.

(4-d) The opening sentence places the issues of frontier life and artistic fulfillment in a larger critical context and provides a thoughtful bridge to the discussion of "A Wagner Matinee." The parenthetical documentation identifies three critics who have called attention to the issue emphasized here. Full documentation is given in the list of works cited.

(4-e) The point here matches the first-level subhead II.B in the outline.

(4-f) Brief details of the plot explain Aunt Georgiana's reactions in Boston.

Hawkins, 4

reminiscent here in Wyoming" (71). As he sits chatting with
Katharine, a window blind swinging in the wind reveals "the glaring
panorama of the desert--a blinding stretch of yellow, flat as the
(4-a) sea in dead calm" (75). Blinding, yellow, flat, dead: so is
Katharine's life away from the East, even in the studio room she has
tried so hard to make like Adriance's.

(4-b) Only Everett with his tales of city life and, finally (at
Everett's prompting), a letter from Adriance with a copy of a new
sonata he has just written cheer Katharine up somewhat. But it is
very clear from her regular conversations with Everett that her
desperate longing for the art she once knew and her own fate not to
achieve it are the great ironies of the story. When the singer
dies, Cather writes, "the madness of art was over for Katharine"
(4-c) (86). As Bloom and Bloom have noted (151), Cather was fascinated by
the artist isolated from society. In the portrait of Katharine
Gaylord, we see that the singer's death separated her from art no
more surely than the final years of her life.

(4-d) Many critics note Cather's concern with the difficulties an
artist has in leading a satisfying life on the harsh frontier
(Gerber 44; Bloom and Bloom 8; Stouck 299). As with Katharine
(4-e) Gaylord, "the fatality of deprivation" (Van Ghent 11) has a serious
effect on Clark's Aunt Georgiana in "A Wagner Matinee." Yet
Georgiana's circumstances are somewhat different from Katharine's.
Passionate love, not illness, has removed her from the civilized
(4-f) world of Boston. Against her family's wishes, she eloped with a
shiftless village boy who was nine years younger than she
was. Howard led her to the Nebraska homestead, which she did not

34e
rev

(5-a) This paragraph develops the second-level subhead II.B.2 in the outline.

(5-b) Compare the quotation with the paragraph from which it comes. The ellipsis indicates the omission of words that the writer believed were unnecessary for her point.

The concert was over; the people filed out of the hall chattering and laughing, glad to relax and find the living level again, but my kinswoman made no effort to rise. The harpist slipped its green felt cover over his instrument; the flute players shook the water from their mouthpieces; the men of the orchestra went out one by one, leaving the stage to the chairs and music stands, empty as a winter cornfield.

(5-c) The writer's evaluation here emphasizes the importance of the image and justifies the use of the long quotation that follows.

(5-d) This quotation occupies more than four typed lines and therefore is set off from the text as a block quotation. Introduced by a colon, the quotation starts on a new line indented ten spaces from the left margin. Quotation marks are not used, and all lines are double-spaced. As the quotation is part of a single paragraph, no further paragraph indentation is necessary. When a quotation is set off, the parenthetical reference comes after the end mark. (The options of quoting, summarizing, or paraphrasing the original source are discussed in 33a.)

Hawkins, 5

leave for many years. Their lives were always threatened by roving bands of Indians and insufficient supplies. A little parlor organ and church singing provided the only music she heard during all that time. Clark recalls that once, as he practiced at the organ, she told him in a quivering voice, "Don't love it so well, Clark, or it may be taken from you" (Cather, *TG* 110).

(5-a) Unlike Katharine in her permanent exile, Aunt Georgiana returns to her former world of art. Clark takes her to a performance of the symphony orchestra. Here, too, Cather's images weave together the civilized world and the grim prairie. Clark wonders how much of her ability to understand music "had been dissolved in soapsuds or worked into bread or milked in the bottom of the pail" (114). At the end of the concert, Aunt Georgiana sits weeping as the musicians
(5-b) file out, "leaving the stage . . . empty as a winter cornfield"
(5-c) (115). The final overwhelming image of the story shows the utter horror of the transplanted artist:

(5-d)
> For her, just outside the door of the concert hall, lay the black pond with the cattle-tracked bluffs; the tall unpainted house, with weather-curled boards; naked as a tower, the crook-backed ash seedlings where the dishcloths hung to dry; the gaunt, molting turkeys picking up refuse about the kitchen door. (115)

It is the refuse of Aunt Georgiana's existence. Clark realizes that no matter how painful a human life, the soul always can be revived. Yet we must wonder if, in fact, he did a service for his aunt by reawakening her to the joys she had missed for so long. We

(6-a) Note the pair of single quotation marks within the pair of double quotation marks to indicate a quotation within a quotation.

(6-b) The opening sentence corresponds to major heading III in the outline.

(6-c) The superscript 2 corresponds to endnote 2 on page 9 of the essay. It cites seven sources, and, as a parenthetical documentation in the text, would have been too long.

(6-d) The citation indicates a paraphrase. Although the writer's language is original, she nonetheless acknowledges the source of her ideas. Merely changing Brennan's words does not change the fact that the ideas are his. This is what he wrote:

It seems likely, too, that she subscribed to a prevalent nineteenth-century view (one prevalent even yet, for that matter) that music is the supreme art, that the musical experience—in its sensuous immediacy, its emotional intensity and profound spiritual appeal—is the most rapturous, most transcendent, the most certainly ineffable of all aesthetic experiences. In Willa Cather's fiction, at any rate, it is the musical moment which is generally employed to characterize a transcendent rhapsodic emotion that drenches the soul in its intensity but eludes all precise definition.

(6-e) The opening sentence corresponds to outline point III.A. The rest of the paragraph develops outline points III.A.1 and III.A.2.

(6-f) The writer interprets the meaning of the image and relates it to the thesis of the paper.

(6-a) understand, as Clark does at the end, when she "burst into tears and
sobbed pleadingly. 'I don't want to go, Clark, I don't want to
go!' " (115). Yet, of course, go she must.

(6-b) It is obvious that Katharine and Georgiana are both very much
involved in music, and in the two stories, music helps Cather show
how dramatic the separation from civilized society can be for a
person isolated in a primitive setting. Music is a very important
(6-c) element in much of Cather's fiction.[2] Of all the arts, Cather saw
music as the most dynamic form in our culture--even more dynamic
than literature. Through the power of music Cather characterizes an
emotion so powerful that it goes beyond ordinary limits to saturate
(6-d) the human soul (Brennan, "Music" 175).

(6-e) Richard Giannone sees music for Katharine Gaylord in " 'A Death
in the Desert' " as a symbol of how swiftly her life is passing.
Though art is humanity's supreme effort, it is futile, finally,
because life and artistic achievement are so brief (41).
Transplanted now from the life of art, she realizes her dilemma as
she listens to Adriance's composition. As Everett plays the piece,
Katharine recognizes its great tragic themes. Adriance's
achievement prods her own suffering. "This is my tragedy, as I lie
here spent by the racecourse," she proclaims, "listening to the feet
of the runners as they pass me. Ah, God! The swift feet of the
(6-f) runners!" (81). The feet of the runners are elements of that
stable, complex world, to use Fisher's terms again, from which
Katharine was transplanted. Adriance's music tells her of the
"tragedy of the soul" and "the tragedy of effort and failure, the

(7-a) **The opening sentence corresponds to III.B in the outline. The rest of the paragraph expands on III.B.1.**

(7-b) **This paragraph develops point III.B.2 in the outline.**

Hawkins, 7

thing Keats called hell" (Cather, TG 81). It is, of course, Katharine's own failure that she recognizes in the sonata.

(7-a) In "A Wagner Matinee" the musical selections at the concert echo the themes of the story. The first piece Aunt Georgiana hears is the overture to Tannhäuser, one of Wagner's early operas. The overture starts with the Pilgrim's Chorus, the solemn chanting of travelers on their way to Rome (Ewen 673). Giannone says that the motif in this chorus "represents the ecstasy of sacred yearnings" (43). Then the Venusberg motif begins, the music of the sensual, tempting, yet disturbing world of Venus and her followers. Giannone sees this as a contrasting world of profane longings. He points out that in the overture to Tannhäuser, Wagner presents the "struggle between the sacred and profane in man" (43). For Aunt Georgiana, the sacred is her higher yearning for art and music; the profane is the dry prairie in an unfriendly world. The terrible tragedy here, Giannone suggests, is that "in the tug between 'the inconceivable silence of the plains' and 'the little parlor organ,' silence won" (43).

(7-b) Other selections that Aunt Georgiana hears at the matinee, including excerpts from The Flying Dutchman and Tristan and Isolde, similarly reflect the battle between the opposing forces that she so fully embodies. The last piece, Siegfried's funeral march from the Ring cycle, signals the defeat of Wagner's hero, just as it predicts Aunt Georgiana's defeat--her return to Nebraska after the concert ends. Unlike many of Wagner's operas, "A Wagner Matinee" does not end in glory or victory, with good overpowering evil. Art does not

34e
rev

(8-a) The conclusion reminds readers of the introduction and the important point made by Fisher. This paragraph is not simply a restatement of the introductory paragraph. The writer provides interesting background information as she explains Cather's own reaction to her friend's criticism. The conclusion builds further credibility for the thesis of the paper. The writer is implying that even Cather might acknowledge that the two stories treated the lives of women transplanted to a new country from stable societies.

(8-b) The citation "Cather" refers to an encyclopedia entry in the list of works cited.

(8-c) Here the writer draws upon another primary source to make an important point. Note again the smooth integration of source material.

(8-d) The conclusion highlights major points made throughout the research paper.

Hawkins, 8

win (here, nor do sacred yearnings. Nothing redeems Aunt Georgiana's fate (Giannone 45).

(8-a) By 1933, when Dorothy Canfield Fisher was writing her essay for the Tribune, Cather was highly sensitive to comments by critics. Honored for literary accomplishments with the Prix Femina Americain
(8-b) ("Cather"), she nonetheless was attacked by many of her contemporaries (Murphy and Synnott 12-14). After she read a prepublication copy of Fisher's essay, Cather sent her friend a telegram asking her to give up the project. As for Fisher's idea that Cather's fiction deals with the effects of a new country on people removed to it from a civilized world, Cather unhappily "summarized this thesis in one word, 'escape' " (Woodress 247). Yet she recognized that this theme ran through her work. Just a few
(8-c) years later she would write in a letter to The Commonweal, "What has art ever been but escape?" (On Writing 18). In " 'A Death in the Desert' " and "A Wagner Matinee" Cather explores the complex theme of
(8-d) escape by showing artistic women transplanted from civilized societies into hostile worlds.

(9-a) These notes correspond to the superscripts that appear on pages 2 and 6 of the research paper. Notes generally go on a separate page at the end of the text with the word *Notes* centered one inch from the top. Notes are double-spaced and indented five spaces from the left margin. If more than one line is required, subsequent lines are flush with the left margin. Some instructors require the notes to be placed at the bottom of the page on which the matching numeral appears in the text. See 33g.

(9-b) Note the format of the multiple references. The writer separates the references with semicolons. No page numbers follow the first three references because in each case the writer is referring to the whole book or article.

Hawkins, 9

(9-a)

Notes

[1]Cather's family and friends objected to her portrait of Nebraska life when this story first appeared in *Everybody's Magazine*. A good friend, Will Jones, complained that strangers would always associate Nebraska with Aunt Georgiana's terrible shape, her false teeth, and her yellow skin. Cather denied that she wanted to disparage her homeland but admitted that her family felt insulted: "They had already told her that it was not nice to tell such things" (Woodress 117).

(9-b) [2]Giannone; Brennan, "Willa Cather"; Brennan, "Music"; Gerber 71-73; Bloom and Bloom 123; Daiches 8; Van Ghent 20-21.

In this list of works cited, entries are listed alphabetically by author's last name or, as with unsigned works, by the first main word of the title. Books and articles are not separated.

(10-a) A book with two authors. *UP* stands for *University Press.*

34e
rev

(10-b) Three hyphens followed by a period indicate a work by the author of the previous entry. Both citations here are journal articles with pages numbered consecutively throughout an annual volume. The articles are listed alphabetically by the first word of the title.

(10-c) An article in an encyclopedia.

(10-d) A republished book. The date of the original edition is 1905; the date of the current edition is 1971. Also, this NAL book has a special imprint, Plume, which precedes the publisher's name.

(10-e) Standard reference to a book with one author.

(10-f) An entry for an encyclopedia in only one edition. Ewen wrote the particular entry and the rest of the book as well. He is author of the article and author of the encyclopedia. Hence, his name appears in two places.

(10-g) Murphy's complete book is *not* cited in the text of the paper and hence might seem out of place here. However, since the writer of the paper used *two* articles from this anthology, she lists the collection itself and then cites the articles with *cross-references* to this main entry. See 10-i below.

(10-h) Murphy's name is spelled out here as well as in the previous entry. The first entry is a book published under his name alone. If the list included other books by Murphy alone, three hyphens and a period would appear in place of his name in the second and subsequent entries (as in 10-b). The three hyphens, however, stand for only the name or names of authors in the preceding entry. Since the authors of "The Recognition of Willa Cather's Art" are Murphy *and* Synnott, both names are listed.

(10-i) A cross-reference. "Murphy 1–28" refers readers to *Critical Essays on Willa Cather,* the main entry for Murphy. The numbers 1–28 identify the pages on which this essay is found.

Hawkins, 10

(10-a) Works Cited

Bloom, Edward A., and Lillian D. Bloom. *Willa Cather's Gift of Sympathy*. Carbondale: Southern Illinois UP, 1962.

Brennan, Joseph X. "Music and Willa Cather." *University Review* 31 (1965): 257-64.

(10-b) ---. "Willa Cather and Music." *University Review* 31 (1965): 175-83.

(10-c) "Cather." *World Scope Encyclopedia*. 1955 ed.

Cather, Willa. *On Writing*. New York: Knopf, 1949.

(10-d) ---. *The Troll Garden*. 1905. New York. Plume-NAL, 1971.

(10-e) Daiches, David. *Willa Cather: A Critical Introduction*. Ithaca: Cornell UP, 1959.

(10-f) Ewen, David. "Tannhäuser." *The New Encyclopedia of the Opera*. By Ewen. New York: Hill, 1971.

Gerber, Philip L. *Willa Cather*. Boston: Twayne, 1975.

Giannone, Richard. *Music in Willa Cather's Fiction*. Lincoln: U of Nebraska P, 1968.

Kohler, Dayton. "Willa Cather: 1876-1947." *College English* 9 (1947): 8-18.

(10-g) Murphy, John J., ed. *Critical Essays on Willa Cather*. Boston: Hall, 1984.

(10-h) Murphy, John J., and Kevin A. Synnott. "The Recognition of Willa
(10-i) Cather's Art." Murphy 1-28.

(11-a) Porter's afterword, published in 1952, appears in the volume of *The Troll Garden* already cited under Cather's name. The cross-reference "Cather, *Troll Garden*" is used instead of "Cather" because another book by Cather appears in the list.

(11-b) Another cross-reference to Murphy.

(11-c) A book in a series. When the title page indicates that the book is part of a series, put the series name (without quotation marks or underlining) and number before the publishing data.

Hawkins, 11

(11-a) Porter, Katherine Anne. Afterword. 1952. Cather, Troll Garden 134-51.

(11-b) Stouck, David. 1905. "Willa Cather's Last Four Books." Murphy 290-304.

(11-c) Van Ghent, Dorothy. Willa Cather. U of Minnesota Pamphlets on American Writers 36. Minneapolis: U of Minnesota P, 1964.

Woodress, James. Willa Cather. 1970. Lincoln: Bison-U of Nebraska P, 1975.

1

Title

The Continuing Search for Black Holes

Richard Lanier

Ms. J. Clay

English 101.6

November 15, 1993

Name and other information required by instructor

Continuing Search, 2

Thesis: As new ideas evolved about the universe, scientists tried to confirm the existence of black holes, which in the past were only theoretical possibilities.

Topic outline (see 34b)

Letters and arabic numbers for subordinate points

I. Black holes vs. ordinary stars
    A. Definition of black holes
    B. Contrary forces on ordinary stars
        1. Expansion from nuclear burning
        2. Compression from gravity
    C. Theory of formation of black holes
        1. Shrinking gravity's effect on burning fuel
        2. Lack of light
II. History of the search for black holes
    A. Problems in finding them
        1. Their invisibility
        2. Their infinitesimal size
        3. Their place in theories of the universe
    B. Developing ideas through the early 1960s
        1. Einstein's predictions
        2. Later confirmations
III. Modern investigations in physics and astronomy
    A. Discovery of pulsars
    B. Quantum mathematics and black hole possibilities
    C. Idea of binary relationships
IV. Continuing search through X-rays
    A. _Uhuru_ satellite and X-ray detection

Continuing Search, 3

B. X-ray star called V861 Sco

C. Intensive X-ray searches

1. Imaging from Einstein Observatory

2. New information from ROSAT satellite

3. Hubble telescope picture of NGC 4261

V. Hawking's theory and future possibilities for black holes

Short title and page number appear at the top of all pages; margins are 1 to $1\frac{1}{2}$ inches

Continuing Search, 4

Title repeated

The Continuing Search for Black Holes

Introduction builds to thesis

One of the most dramatic and exciting scientific concepts to emerge during the last twenty-five years is the black hole. Scientists suspected the possible existence of black holes in the late 1800s, but it was only in the twentieth century that changes in theoretical physics forced astronomers to start looking for them. So much about black holes runs contrary to our ordinary experience of life that they are difficult to imagine. But because black holes are impossible by definition to detect directly, the search to confirm their existence is an outstanding instance of theoretical and practical science working together.

Thesis: compare with previous versions (see 34a)

Stars, like people, have a life span between birth and death. Unlike people, dying stars can end up in a variety of ways--as supernovas, neutron stars, or pulsars. In all of these cases, they are still objects in the universe and still contribute to the cosmic balance. But some dead stars may become black holes, in which case they are no longer part of the universe at all.

Definition and explanation of black hole

What exactly is a black hole? Black holes are collapsed stars, which "contain the strongest gravitational forces in the known universe" (Shipman, 1980, p. 15). Not all stars are massive enough to collapse. Our own sun, for instance would have to have a mass at least one and one-half times greater with the same volume before a gravitational collapse could begin to take place. In a healthy

Parenthetical citation: author, date, page number. See reference list on p. 15.

Reference to diagram

star, like our sun, the force of gravity is balanced by internal forces, like the gas pressure from nuclear reactions taking place, as shown in Figure 1. As Stephen W. Hawking (1988) points out, this state is similar to a balloon, where the gas inside exerts enough pressure to keep the rubber from collapsing. In a star, super-hot matter is like the gas in a balloon and gravity acts like the rubber

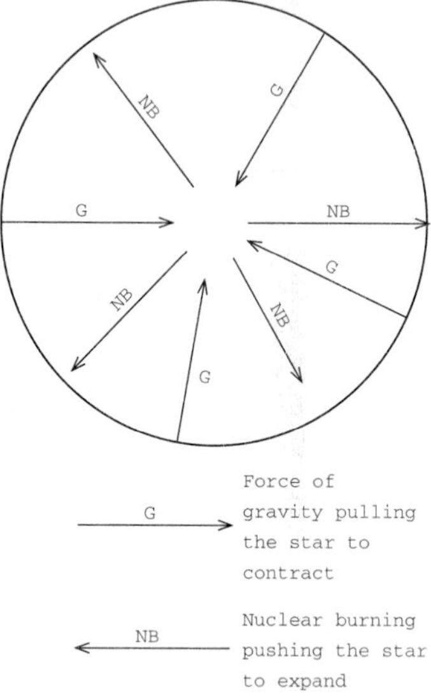

Figure 1. Forces acting on stars.

Citations unnecessary, writer's own words and ideas

coating. When stars get old, their nuclear fuel runs low, and gravity overwhelms the other forces. The star begins to shrink, reducing the volume and forcing the remaining fuel to burn faster. The smaller area makes the remaining matter interact much more intensely than before.

If a star's mass is low enough, the star can support itself against gravitational collapse. If not, the gravity continues to shrink the area, which makes the nuclear fuel burn faster and faster. As the fuel becomes exhausted, the star grows colder while the density increases. Jastrow (1979) explains what happens next:

Quotation of more than forty words double-spaced and set off without quotation marks

> At that point, the mass is so compact that the force of gravity at the surface is billions of times stronger than the force of the sun. The tug of that enormous force prevents the rays of light from leaving the surface of the star. (p. 65)

Without the fuel to maintain equilibrium, the star eventually becomes infinitely dense: a black hole!

Outline point I.C.1

While the gravitational collapse takes place, other strange things happen. As the gravity becomes proportionally more massive, information from the star takes longer and longer to emerge. Eventually the laws governing the normal universe break down in the vicinity of the dying star. In a normal star like the sun, light waves are "bent" by the strong gravitational field. But in a black hole, the gravity is extremely strong; "light cones are bent inward so much that light can no longer escape" (Hawking, 1988, p. 87).

This means that as a star collapses it eventually becomes invisible. Worse yet, the dimensions of the star shrink until it becomes a hole not only in space, but in time as well. Jastrow (1979) describes the process of collapse:

> The star's volume becomes smaller and smaller; from a globe with a two-mile radius it shrinks to the size of a pinhead, then to the size of a microbe, and still shrinking, passes into the realm of distances smaller than any ever probed by man. At all times the star's mass of a thousand trillion trillion tons remains packed into the shrinking volume. But intuition tells us that such an object cannot exist. At some point the collapse must be halted. Yet according to all the laws of twentieth century physics, no force, no matter how powerful, can stop the collapse. (p. 65)

In the late eighteenth century, scientists like Mitchell and Laplace had suggested that a star with sufficiently massive gravity would not allow light to escape and would seem like a dark hole in space (Hawking, 1988). But for nearly one hundred and fifty years, practical scientists refused to accept this conclusion because they knew too little about the nature of light and gravity.

Outline point II.B.1

In the first part of this century, Einstein's Theory of Relativity changed the way people thought about light, gravity, and time. One aspect of his theory was that gravity caused a deformation even of empty space and that this deformation would curve the universe until it folded over on itself. During World War I, a German astronomer named Karl Schwarzschild first formulated the idea of a black hole. He believed that such an object could exist

Citation to encyclopedia article

Superscript 1 corresponds to footnote 1 on page 16 of the essay

if we assume that light is affected by the force of gravity ("Schwarzschild," 1990).[1]

In 1919 Sir Arthur Eddington confirmed Einstein's prediction. During a solar eclipse, Eddington's tests on whether rays of light actually were "twisted" by the gravitational field of the sun offered experimental proof that Einstein's theory was correct (Davies, 1980, p. 135). In the 1920s, one of Eddington's students, Subrahmanyan Chandrasekhar, rediscovered the idea that a star's gravity might be so massive that not even light could escape. The work of Chandrasekhar was very controversial. Eddington and even Einstein could not accept the possibility of such an object.

Article, two authors

In 1939 J. Robert Oppenheimer--later to become famous for his role in creating the atom bomb--and his student Hartland Snyder suggested that a black hole might result from the collapse of enormous, massive stars several times larger than our sun (Dupree & Hartman, 1979). But since no telescope could see these objects if they existed, astronomers pursued other areas of exploration and the whole subject was largely forgotten.

Quotation within a quotation in single quotes

By the 1960s, Schwarzschild, Chandrasekhar, and Oppenheimer had contributed theoretical work that was sound in terms of Einstein's theory, but their notions were contrary to everyday experience and suggested disturbing consequences. No one could resolve the matter, because there are no black holes in our immediate galactic neighborhood. This is a good thing, because, as Wald (1992) points out, "if a black hole were close enough to be 'seen' directly, its gravitational field would be greater than that of the sun" (p. 108).

Outline point III

Only in the last twenty-five years have we developed the practical tools to explore more deeply into the universe and, ultimately perhaps, to confirm black hole theories. In 1967, Jocelyn Bell, an astronomy student at Cambridge, discovered pulsars, objects in the sky that emit regular pulses of energy. At first, Bell believed that she had found alien transmissions, but eventually she realized that pulsars were, in fact, neutron stars. These were stars that had collapsed until the protons, the positively charged particles in atoms, and electrons, which are negatively charged particles, had been forced together to form neutrons, or electrically neutral particles (Thorne, 1977).

The inner space of the atoms in these neutron stars had been so reduced that the stars were only ten miles in diameter, far too small for optical telescopes to reveal. But the neutron stars gave off powerful radio waves, intense radiation created as the compressed atoms collided with each other. Radio telescopes can pick up this radiation, which "sweeps through space like the light from a revolving lighthouse beacon. If the earth happens to lie in the path of the rotating beam, it will receive a sharp burst of radiation once every turn of the pulsar" (Jastrow, 1979, p. 63). This discovery of neutron stars revived interest in the concept of black holes.

Integrated quotation (see 33a)

At the same time, two other Cambridge scientists, Roger Penrose and Stephen Hawking, began contributing new theoretical work to the subject of black holes. Although they did not know it at the time, their work was similar to the predictions of Michell and Laplace. But unlike their predecessors, Penrose and Hawking were armed with quantum mathematics. When they suggested "an event horizon," drawn over the singularity point of a black hole and the normal universe, they had enough calculations to support the idea. Many other scientists began to take the possibility of black holes seriously.

That meant that direct astronomical confirmation might never reveal the existence of a black hole. But because of its massive gravitational field, scientists could detect the effects of black holes without direct evidence by observing the strong gravitational force of a black hole on luminous objects in its immediate vicinity.

Outline point III.C

Astronomers have known for a long time about binary stars (double stars that revolve around each other), and two Russians, Y. B. Zel'dovich and O. K. Guseynov, began compiling a list of stars that were orbiting in pairs with a dark companion. It does not necessarily follow, of course, that a dark companion is a black hole. Zel'dovich and Guseynov's work could also suggest planets. However, astronomers assumed that if the dark companion were a black hole, the star should be losing stellar material into the massive gravitational field. This action is illustrated in Figure 2 with the black hole enlarged in scale compared to the visible star.

In theory, as the stellar gas gets closer to the black hole, it will accelerate until it is traveling at a speed approaching the speed of light (Dupree & Hartman, 1979). When the molecules of gas moving at such a terrific speed collide with each other and with the surface of the black hole itself, the collision should give off enormous quantities of X-rays (Jones, Forman, & Liller, 1974). So a

Article, three authors

Continuing Search, 11

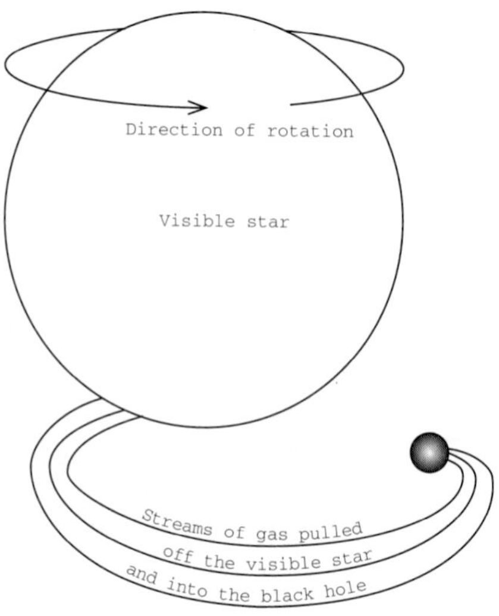

Figure 2. The Pull of stellar gas.

star with an apparent wobble in space, with no detectable partner and giving off huge quantities of X-rays, might be paired with a black hole.

Outline point IV

As a result of this theory, the search to confirm the possible existence of black holes shifted to equipment that detected strong sources of X-ray and radio emissions. Unfortunately, the earth's atmosphere absorbs X-rays. So the search for black holes could not continue until satellites with X-ray telescopes were launched into space.

One of the early probes was the <u>Uhuru</u>, a joint Italian and American satellite launched in 1970. It probed an X-ray source called Cygnus X-1. (Stars are named for the constellations where they are found and according to a system of grid marks set on standard photographs of each segment of the sky.) Initially, the mass of the unseen companion pulling on Cygnus X-1 was estimated to be eight times that of the sun (Thorne, 1977). More recent estimates lower that figure to six (Hawking, 1988), but whichever figure is correct, this mass is too great to be a neutron star. Scientists conclude that the companion in all probability is a black hole.

Outline point IV.B

Another possible location of a black hole is in V861 Sco. The object apears to be connected to a dark companion, and it is curious because it generates a large, luminous ultraviolet flare. William Oegerle and Ronald S. Polidan of Princeton University were intrigued by this flare. Thomson (1979) reported on their findings:

> From the optical properties of V861 Sco, they could determine an orbital period of seven days. They figure that the mass of the primary star is between 20 and 50 times that of the sun. The unseen companion is between 7.5 and 13 solar masses. This rules out a neutron star or a white dwarf. . . . Either ought to have much less mass. It is possible in theory to link the ultraviolet flare with an X-ray flare. X-ray flares are seen in these X-ray binaries and they are explained by changes in the gas flow between the two objects. So it all looks good provided V861 Sco really is the X-ray source. (p. 25)

Ellipsis shows omission

In 1979, the orbiting Einstein Observatory was launched. It

Outline point IV.C.2

conducted an X-ray imaging survey of the sky and identified nearly 60,000 sources of X-ray radiation.

In 1990, the United States, Britain, and Germany launched the ROSAT satellite, the most powerful X-ray telescope yet devised. ROSAT, short for Roentgen Satellite, is named after the discoverer of X-rays. Its mission is to scan the X-ray sources that the Einstein Observatory identified, but with three times the resolution power of that earlier probe. ROSAT has already provided glimpses of another potential black hole, LMC X-1 (Cowen, 1991).

But ROSAT and the Hubble telescope, launched in 1991, have shown the clearest picture to date of what a black hole might look like. Evidence for black holes can be found in many parts of the universe, even in other galaxies like the M51 galaxy which, like our own galaxy, appears to have a massive black hole at its center. According to Rees (1990), black holes may be an integral part of the formation of galaxies themselves. And recently Hubble sent back a picture of what may be a massive black hole in the core of galaxy NGC 4261. Astronomers apparently no longer doubt that there are objects of massive gravitation at work in the universe (Lane, 1992, p. 7).

Commentary on source (see 33a)

Although black holes seem like depressing ends for stars, Stephen Hawking's recent work suggests that they may not be so final after all. As black holes accumulate matter, they may reach a point at which the process of contraction reverses, and a massive disgorging of material may result in quasars, quasi-stellar objects, that appear to be rotating faster than the speed of light. ROSAT reveals dozens of previously unknown quasars, and perhaps as the scientific community digests this information, we may come to understand the relation between quasars and black holes. We may also find that both new theories in physics and new explorations in space once again will lead us to reevaluate our concepts of the way the universe works.

References page for cited works (see 33e)

References

Cowen, R. (1991, June 29). ROSAT revelations. Science News, pp. 408-410.

Davies, P. (1980). The runaway universe. New York: Penguin.

Dupree, A. K., & Hartman, L. (1979, October). Hunting for black holes. Natural History, pp. 30-37.

Hawking, S. J. (1988). A brief history of time. New York: Bantam.

Jastrow, R. (1979). Red giants and white dwarfs. New York: Warner.

Jones, C., Forman, W., & Liller, W. (1974). X-ray sources and their optical counterparts. Sky and Telescope, 48, 289-291.

Lane, E. (1992, November 20). Black hole snapshot: Scientists think that's what Hubble photo may be. Newsday, p. 7.

Rees, M. J. (1990, November). Black holes in galactic centers. Scientific American, pp. 56-66.

Schwarzschild, Karl. (1990). In Encyclopaedia Britannica Micropaedia (Vol. 10, p. 548). New York: Encyclopaedia Britannica.

Shipman, H. L. (1980). Black holes, quasars and the universe (2nd ed). Boston: Houghton Mifflin.

Thomson, D. (1979, July 14). V861 Sco's UV flare. Science News, p. 25.

Thorne, K. S. (1977). The search for black holes. In Cosmology +1 (pp. 66-70). San Francisco: Freeman.

Wald, R. M. (1992). Space, time, and gravity: The theory of the big bang and black holes. (2nd ed). Chicago: University of Chicago Press.

Content footnotes at foot of page where referenced or following list of references.

Continuing Search, 16

Footnotes

[1] In 1798 the French mathematician and astronomer Pierre Simon de Laplace hinted at the possibility of phenomena like black holes, but he never used the term.

PART

EIGHT

OTHER WRITING TASKS

CHAPTER

35

WRITING LOGICAL ARGUMENTS

We argue to persuade others to accept a point of view. In ordinary speech, the word *argument* is often associated with anger and conflict. But in writing, and especially in research papers, *argument* means a conflict of opinions, not of people. The writer of an argumentative paper strives by reason and logic to persuade readers to accept his or her point of view or conclusion. A good argument is carefully stated and well supported by evidence; it makes friends, not enemies.

35a Differentiating Between Argument and Persuasion

Persuasion includes any means by which we get people to do what we want them to do. You can persuade some people to buy a certain brand of beer by showing them funny commercials featuring the beer. You can persuade others to give money to help the homeless by showing them photographs of homeless people living in the streets. You might be able to persuade your parents to lend you the family car for the weekend because you want to go to a party.

Persuasion includes argument. An **argument** is a carefully reasoned conclusion derived from evidence. We make arguments to prove that our point of view is more logical than others. We argue that our interpretation of *Hamlet* or of a short story or novel is the correct one, and we quote from the text to support our conclusion. You want your readers to think through your argument and agree with you. The primary appeal of argument is to reason, to judgment. You evaluate evidence and draw conclusions that seem to be inescapable or at least extremely probable.

The parts of an argument are tightly connected. These logical connections can be built on two kinds of reasoning: inductive and deductive. **Inductive reasoning** moves from particular examples to general truths.

Statistics show that cigarette smokers are ten times more likely than nonsmokers to get lung cancer. The examination of thousands of specific events leads to a general truth: cigarette smoking is dangerous to health. **Deductive reasoning** moves from a general truth we know to a conclusion about a specific instance. Deductive reasoning may start with a general truth that has been proved by induction. Cigarette smoking is dangerous to health; therefore, if you smoke cigarettes, you will probably not live as long as a nonsmoker.

35b Using Inductive Reasoning

The most common way to reason is by induction: we have specific experiences and move from them to general conclusions about what they prove or mean.

Some inductions require rigorous study. Arguments about medical research, for example, often stand on years of experiments. We conclude that cigarette smoking causes lung cancer because the disease is common among heavy cigarette smokers and relatively uncommon among nonsmokers. But we do not know what agent in cigarette smoke causes the cancer, and we cannot observe the smoke acting to make a cancer. Our conclusion is based on *statistics,* a number of instances that seem to have meaning when we construct a generalization that explains them. Some conclusions can be drawn from only one instance. If you accidentally burn yourself with a lighted match, you conclude that matches should be handled with care. You do not have to burn yourself over and over again. The same is true if you slip on an icy sidewalk. You do not have to fall again and again to prove to yourself that ice can be dangerous.

Here an argument based on induction is presented by Jane Brody, nutrition expert for the *New York Times,* writing about cholesterol.

> In a famous study of 12,000 middle-aged men in seven developed countries, Dr. Ancel Keys and his coworkers from the University of Minnesota found that the people of east Finland had the highest death rate from diseases of the coronary arteries—220 per 10,000 men in a five-year period—the highest percentage of saturated animal fats in their diet (22 percent of total calories were saturated fats, mostly from cheese, butter, and milk), and the highest blood cholesterol levels. The United States was not far behind in coronary deaths (185 per 10,000) and blood cholesterol levels.
>
> But in Mediterranean countries like Greece and Italy, where the fat is mostly of vegetable origin and therefore unsaturated and lacking cholesterol, early death from coronary heart disease was far less com-

> mon. And in Japan, where only 10 percent of the diet is fat and most of that is polyunsaturated fat from vegetable sources (only 3 percent of total calories is saturated fat), the cholesterol levels were very low and the death rate from coronary artery disease was only 20 per 10,000.
>
> —JANE BRODY

The conclusion to which this assembled evidence points is that a diet high in cholesterol leads to heart attacks. Here is induction in action.

Inductive arguments begin as people study issues and raise questions that are not easily answered. Often people develop hypotheses or theories to explain the facts and then study the evidence inductively to see if they are true. That is what nutrition experts did in the studies Jane Brody cites.

Gathering Facts

35b argue

Inductive argument always involves a gathering of facts and the drawing of a conclusion from those facts. Here are some simple examples.

Fact	Conclusion
More than one thousand people were vaccinated against smallpox during a great epidemic that swept our state early in the century. Not one of those people got the disease. Not one of the people who did get the disease had been vaccinated.	Vaccinations against smallpox prevented the disease.
My next-door neighbor got into a fight last week with the mail carrier because he said the mail carrier made too much noise walking up on the porch to deliver the mail. The same neighbor was arrested at a high school basketball game Tuesday night because he started a fight with an official over a foul call. He threatened to fight the trash haulers because they made so much noise with his garbage cans, and the paper boy refused to deliver papers anymore after my neighbor yelled at him for being late.	My neighbor has a bad temper.

Making Inferences

An **inference** is a conclusion arrived at through reasoning or implication. When we infer, we use some previous experience or knowledge to make sense of something we observe. If someone smiles at us, we infer friendly feelings because when people have smiled at us in the past, they have been showing friendly feelings. If we wake up in the night and hear a drumming of water on the roof, we infer that it is raining, though we cannot see the rain fall. We have heard rain fall on our roof before, and we recognize the sound when we hear it. If we see fire trucks roaring down the street, their sirens wailing and all the fire fighters looking grim, we assume there is a fire somewhere. Inference is not certainty. A smile may mask evil intent; some practical joker may have turned a hose on our roof; the fire fighters may be going out for coffee. But none of these possibilities is as likely as the expectation we have as a result of our experience. A smile is probably a sign of friendship; water drumming on the roof is probably rain; and the fire trucks screaming down the street are probably going to a fire.

Charles Darwin, the nineteenth-century naturalist, always asked questions as he studied facts. He wondered, for example, how certain plants that grew in ponds and marshes came to be spread across the oceans so that the same varieties grew thousands of miles apart. In his travels he noticed that the types of marsh grass that grew along the shores of North America also grew along the coasts of Europe, yet the animals in these widely separated regions differed considerably. Darwin could understand why aquatic plants (seaweed and so on) might have a wide range. But how did plants with roots in the soil spread around the earth? To solve the problem he made an inference.

> With respect to plants, it has long been known what enormous ranges many fresh-water and even marsh species have, both over continents and to the most remote oceanic islands. This is strikingly illustrated, according to Alph. de Candolle [A French botanist], in those large groups of terrestrial plants, which have very few aquatic members; for the latter seem immediately to acquire, as if in consequence, a wide range. I think favourable means of dispersal explain this fact. I have before mentioned that earth occasionally adheres in some quantity to the feet and beaks of birds. Wading birds, which frequent the muddy edges of ponds, if suddenly flushed, would be the most likely to have muddy feet. Birds of this order wander more than those of any other; and they are occasionally found on the most remote and barren islands of the open ocean; they would not be likely to alight on the surface of the sea, so that any dirt on their feet would not be washed off; and when gaining the land, they would be sure to fly to their natural fresh-water haunts. I do not believe that botanists are aware how charged the mud of ponds is with seeds; I have tried several little experiments, but will here give only the most striking case: I

took in February three tablespoonfuls of mud from three different points, beneath water, on the edge of a little pond: this mud when dried weighed only 6¾ ounces; I kept it covered up in my study for six months, pulling up and counting each plant as it grew; the plants were of many different kinds, and were altogether 537 in number; and yet the viscid mud was all contained in a breakfast cup! Considering these facts, I think it would be an inexplicable circumstance if water-birds did not transport the seeds of fresh-water plants to unstocked ponds and streams, situated at very distant points. The same agency may have come into play with the eggs of some of the smaller fresh-water animals.

—CHARLES DARWIN

Forming Plausible Conclusions

35b argue

Darwin's conclusion is plausible. To say that a conclusion is *plausible* is to say that we can believe it even if we cannot prove it by observation. Most argumentation is based on plausible reasoning rather than on direct observation. When we can observe something directly, we do not have to argue about it.

Induction builds on facts and arrives at an explanation that tries to account for everything we know. But we may lack the key observation that will prove our conclusion beyond all doubt. We can only infer a conclusion. Scientists often make observations of several facts (they usually call these facts *phenomena*) and try to explain them in a logical way. They arrive at a *theory* that explains the facts—an inference, a conclusion that seems to arise naturally from what they know.

An inductive argument proceeds from the gathering of facts and the explanation of how these facts are related. That is, an inductive argument involves analyzing facts and deciding which of them are causes and which of them are effects. Sometimes that analysis leads to an obvious conclusion: cigarette smoking causes lung cancer. But sometimes the conclusions are not so obvious. When a fifty-five-mile-an-hour speed limit was imposed on American highways after the fuel crisis of 1973, traffic fatalities dropped dramatically. Did the lowered speed limit cause this drop? Or did the completion of the American interstate highway system, which occurred about the same time, cause the drop? You must study the issue and gather many data before you can make a compelling argument on either side.

Weighing Possible Conclusions

Inductive arguments may lead to a clearly plausible point of view. For many centuries, no one knew what caused typhoid fever. Once scientists observed under the microscope that the blood of everyone who had typhoid fever contained certain bacteria that were not seen in the blood of people free of the disease, the most plausible inference was that those bacteria caused the disease.

But often in the arguments you make in college papers, in position papers in business or professional life, and in writing about public issues, you discover many plausible sides to an argument. Arguments that have only one side are rarely interesting. So you must assemble the facts and decide what you want to argue. Your decision may depend on how you interpret those facts, or it may depend on what you value in those facts. In either case, you must gather as many factors as you can to be certain that you are being fair to the evidence and let readers know that you know what you are talking about.

✓ CHECKLIST 35.1: APPLYING INDUCTIVE REASONING

- What question do I want to ask of the data?
- Do I have enough specific facts to suggest an answer to the question?
- How are these facts related to one another?
- What answer takes into account the most evidence?
- Can I suggest other plausible answers to the question?
- Have I been fair to the evidence that opposes my answer?

Exercise 35.1 Construct a brief argument from the following group of statements to answer the question, Should the library of Sourmash State University be kept open on Friday nights? Assume that each statement is true; consequently you can use each statement in your argument.

> The administration of Sourmash State University wants to close the school library at 6:00 p.m. on Fridays. Accounts figure that it costs an average of $984.62 for heat, lights, and personnel to keep the library open from 6:00 p.m. until 11:00 p.m. Closing the library will mean a saving of about $10,000 every ten weeks, or about $30,000 during the academic year. An average of five student readers and one professor use the library on Friday night. On the average, ten books were checked out of the library on each of the last ten Fridays that the library was open. "We are trying to save money so student tuitions will not rise," President Vessie Reins told the faculty in explaining the decision to shut the library. One of the students who uses the library every Friday night is senior Helen Walden. Her novel *Late Hours* won the Pulitzer Prize last year and has been translated into

seventeen languages. The one professor who uses the library on Friday nights is Judith Franklin, of the Women's Studies Program. She has completed three volumes of a projected six-volume history of American women writers. Critic and activist Helen Garfield Black says that Franklin's literary history of women writers will change the way literature is taught in American universities for the next century. Should the administration close the library on Friday nights?

35c Using Deductive Arguments

When we reason deductively, we begin with a general truth and use it to give meaning to a fact. A deductive argument is an application of the general to the specific so that a conclusion may be drawn. The general truth is supposedly accepted by everyone likely to be interested in the argument.

Constructing a Syllogism

Deductive reasoning proceeds through a syllogism. In a **syllogism,** the general truth includes the specific case and is the cause of the conclusion. The general truth is called the *major premise,* the specific case is called the *minor premise,* and the conclusion shows what the major premise proves about the minor premise. Here is a standard syllogism.

Major premise: All men are mortal.

Minor premise: Socrates is a man.

Conclusion: Socrates will die.

The general truth accepted by everyone is that all men are mortal. That is, all men will eventually die. No one who reads the argument can deny that assumption. The specific case here is a statement joining Socrates to the general truth by remarking that he is an individual member of the class of beings called men. The conclusion then follows. You can always rephrase a syllogism to use the word *because* or *since* in the statements you make in conclusions derived from the general truth.

All men are mortal; since Socrates is a man, he is mortal.

The major premise in a syllogism is always a broad generalization; the minor premise is always a statement somehow included within the major premise. The conclusion follows necessarily because of the relation of the major premise and the minor premise. Here are more syllogisms based on deductive reasoning:

Major premise: This textbook is revised every three years.

Minor premise: Three years have passed since the last edition of this textbook appeared.

Conclusion: A new edition of this textbook will appear this year.

Major premise: Rain nearly always falls soon after the barometer falls rapidly when the air is warm and moist.

Minor premise: The barometer is falling fast, and the air is muggy and hot.

Conclusion: It is going to rain.

Major premise: Medical research has proved that excessive drinking of alcohol damages the heart, the digestive tract, and other organs of the body, and that heavy drinking is often associated with cancer, insomnia, psychological depression, high blood pressure, and the breakdown of the immune system.

Minor premise: My Aunt Mabel drinks a quart of whiskey a night.

Conclusion: Aunt Mabel will probably not live to a healthy old age.

Major premise: The ability to write well is a great advantage to business and professional people.

Minor premise: I write well.

Conclusion: I have an advantage if I go into business or professional life.

These syllogisms are not quite so solid as the one about Socrates. Socrates has to be mortal because all men eventually die. But Aunt Mabel may live to be ninety-five, and the ability to write well does not guarantee success in business or professional life. When we reason about most subjects to make an argument, the syllogisms we use may not fall together with the certainty of a good key turning a lock. If the major premise is not true, the syllogism will not be true. If the major premise is flawed or not accepted by others, the syllogism built on it will not be convincing.

Major premise: Nonsmokers will never die.

Minor premise: My cousin Horace is a nonsmoker.

Conclusion: Horace will never die.

All people eventually die, whether they smoke cigarettes or not. Although Cousin Horace may live longer than a chain smoker, he will eventually die.

> **Major premise:** First-rate rock composers are much more creative than composers of classical music.
>
> **Minor premise:** John Lennon was a first-rate rock composer.
>
> **Conclusion:** John Lennon was more creative than Beethoven.

The syllogism might stand among people who accept the major premise. But lovers of classical music, especially lovers of Beethoven, would reject the conclusion because they reject the supposed general truth from which the conclusion is drawn. Lovers of the Beatles might accept the syllogism, but it would not convince those on the other side.

Constructing an Argument with Syllogisms

You may find several syllogisms in the same argument. The following paragraph contains two syllogisms.

> In the Declaration of Independence, Thomas Jefferson wrote that people established government and entrusted it with power to preserve their rights to life, liberty, and the pursuit of happiness. A government can legitimately exercise those powers that the people consent to yield to it. The government of King George III of England had not protected those rights; it had, instead, violated them by taking the lives of Americans, by attempting to destroy their liberty, and by making it impossible for them to pursue happiness. Americans did not consent to those actions. Therefore, Jefferson argued, the English government was not a legitimate government; and since it was not a legitimate government, Americans owed it no allegiance. Since they did not owe allegiance to the English government, Americans had a right to abolish it and establish another government in its place.

Here are the syllogisms:

> **Major premise:** Governments, which were established by the people to preserve their rights to life, liberty, and the pursuit of happiness, may legitimately exercise those powers to which the people have consented.
>
> **Minor premise:** The government of King George III had taken actions to which the American people had not consented.
>
> **Conclusion:** King George's government was not legitimate.

Major premise: People have a right to abolish a government that is not legitimate.

Minor premise: King George's government was not legitimate.

Conclusion: Americans had a right to abolish King George's government.

■ **Exercise 35.2** Construct syllogisms from the arguments in the following paragraphs:

1. Universities exist to further the intellectual life of their students and faculty and society at large. The intellectual life is not cheap. It costs money for faculty, money for the buildings where classes are conducted, money for libraries, and money to keep those libraries open at night. Judith Franklin furthers the intellectual life of society every Friday night when she works in the library. The university should support her by keeping the library open so she can work. She is doing what Sourmash University exists to do.
2. Lightning can kill. Bike riders sometimes believe that they are protected from lightning because they are on rubber tires. They think that the rubber protects them by preventing the lightning from running through them into the ground. But that belief is a superstition. Lightning can strike bikers. It kills some cyclists every year. So when a thunderstorm blows up and you are on your bike, seek shelter at once.
3. You can do thousands of things with computers—word processing, complicated math, architectural modeling, graphic design, and more. The more elaborate your computer, the more you can do with it. But the more elaborate your computer, the more it will cost. Most students use their computers only for word processing. Therefore, if you are going to use your computer only to write papers, avoid buying an expensive and elaborate computer.

■ **Exercise 35.3** Study the following syllogisms. Which of them are good syllogisms, and which are bad? What is wrong with the bad ones?

1. **Major premise:** Good teachers always give students good grades.
   Minor premise: I got a bad grade in my writing class.
   Conclusion: I had a bad teacher.
2. **Major premise:** Professional athletes make a lot of money.
   Minor premise: I love basketball.
   Conclusion: I should spend all my time practicing so I can become a professional basketball player.
3. **Major premise:** Taxes are necessary to support state and federal governments.

Minor premise: Taxes on cigarettes provide a substantial proportion of government revenue.
Conclusion: We should encourage people to smoke cigarettes.

4. **Major premise:** Sunburns cause skin cancer.
Minor premise: My skin is very sensitive.
Conclusion: I should avoid sunburn.

Making Assumptions

In making a deductive argument, we often do not spell out the entire syllogism. We assume that the major premise is clear to readers even if we do not state it. We assume that they accept it. Sometimes we call an unexpressed major premise an **assumption.** Here are some examples.

Professor Churl promised us that half our grade would depend on our research paper. We all worked night and day on those papers. I spent every night for three weeks in the library working on mine. But then he said that the term papers were all so good that he would have to give everyone in the class an A if he kept his word. So he counted the term papers as only one-tenth of the grade and said the other nine-tenths would come from the midterm and the final.

Here is the syllogism with the major premise stated.

Major premise: Professors who break their promises to students are unfair.

Minor premise: Professor Churl broke his promise.

Conclusion: Professor Churl was unfair.

Here is another example.

Many American students make a spelling mistake when they form the plurals of words ending in *-est* and *-ist*—words such as *guest, nest, humanist, scientist,* and *colonist.* They do not add a final *s.* The plurals of these words are *guests, nests, humanists, scientists,* and *colonists.* The error seems to come about because these students fail to form the plurals of these words correctly when they speak. It is difficult to make the *s* sound after *-ist,* so many Americans pronounce the singular and the plural the same way. Therefore they spell them the same way. The rule is simple: To make the plural of all words ending in *-est* or *-ist,* add the letter *s.*

Major premise: Mispronunciations may cause misspellings.

Minor premise: Students often mispronounce words such as *guests, nests, humanists, scientists,* and *colonists.*

Conclusion: The mispronunciation causes these plurals to be spelled without the final *s,* as if they were singular nouns.

✓ CHECKLIST 35.2: CONSTRUCTING DEDUCTIVE ARGUMENTS

Constructing a deductive argument requires logic. To be certain your argument is logical, ask yourself these questions.

- Can readers locate the syllogisms in my argument?
- Can readers locate incomplete syllogisms, or assumptions, in my argument?
- Will my major premises be accepted by my readers?
- Will my assumptions in my incomplete syllogisms, or assumptions be accepted by my readers?
- Does each minor premise truly fit its major premise or assumption?
- Do my conclusions follow logically from my major premise and my minor premise?

■ **Exercise 35.4** Find the implied major premise in each syllogism embedded in the following paragraphs.

1. Sylvester Pecks has been campaigning to be elected governor of the state, telling us that he won the Congressional Medal of Honor in Vietnam. He has limped to the platform again and again to tell us how he was wounded in the leg holding his position against overwhelming enemy attack. But now it turns out that he spent the entire Vietnam war in Switzerland acting as a security guard for a girls' school. The headmaster of that school has come forward to tell us that Mr. Pecks broke his leg when he fell through a kitchen window one night as he was making off with steaks from the school's refrigerator. The headmaster has produced medical records from a Swiss hospital to support his claim. Do not vote for Sylvester Pecks.
2. Rattlesnakes abound in the Wyoming countryside around Independence Rock, one of the great landmarks along the old overland trail followed by the pioneers on their way to California and Oregon. Climbing up Independence Rock is a great adventure, and from the top you can see for miles across the rolling prairie.

But be sure you wear tall boots as you walk through the high grass around the rock, and be careful where you put your hands.

3. A recent survey revealed that the average American watches seven hours of television a day. If the average American spent half that much time reading, we would have one of the most knowledgeable citizen bodies in the world. As it is, Americans, entertained by television and neglecting their books, are woefully ignorant of simple facts necessary to understand the world. Another recent survey disclosed that one-third of the students in a large American university could not locate the continent of Europe on a map of the world. Almost half of all Americans claim that they have never read a book through in their lives. Because they watch television and do not read, Americans run the risk of being unable to make policy decisions that may help them survive as a nation.

■ **Exercise 35.5** Write a paragraph in which you imply a major premise to support an argument.

35d Arguing from Authority, Testimony, and Personal Experience

In addition to arguments constructed inductively and deductively you can also build your case on authority, testimony, and personal experience.

Arguing from Authority

If you should write a paper arguing that the characters in Shakespeare's *A Midsummer Night's Dream* are not profound, you may quote the Shakespearean scholar David Young, who has written on that subject and reached a similar conclusion. Young is an authority who strengthens your case because he is known to have studied Shakespeare and to have written a great deal about the plays, especially about the comedies.

Never be afraid to ask for help on a paper. People who have become authorities in their fields usually enjoy talking with students. Are you writing a paper about changes in the countries of Eastern Europe where communist regimes held power for so long? There is probably a professor on your campus who teaches Russian history and who can talk to you about events in Russia and other countries in Eastern Europe. Go talk to that person. He or she can become an authority for your paper.

Any time you quote facts from a book or cite an author's opinion to support your own in an argument paper, you are arguing from authority. (The use of quotations and citations of sources is discussed in 33a.) When you do research, you know enough to be on the lookout for evidence that can give authority to the assertions you make in a paper. But even when you do random reading or when you listen to lectures in other disciplines or watch television or go to the movies, keep your eyes open for materials you can use in your paper.

The following paragraphs present an argument from authority. The historian David McCullough has investigated the recurring attacks of asthma that afflicted young Theodore Roosevelt, later president of the United States. What causes asthma? McCullough believes the disease is at least partly *psychosomatic,* that is, caused by the mental state of the victim rather than by germs, viruses, or some other physical entity. (The nickname *Teedie* in the selection was given young Theodore Roosevelt by his family, and McCullough uses it to indicate the child.)

> In 1864, or two years after the infant Teedie's asthma had begun, a highly important work was published in Philadelphia, a book of 256 pages titled *On Asthma.* The author was an English physician, Henry Hyde Salter, a very keen observer who as the father of an asthmatic child had "experienced the horrors" of the disease. . . . Salter had found no abnormalities in the lungs of his asthmatic patients, no trace of the disease in either the respiratory or circulatory system, and hence concluded that the trouble lay in the nervous system. Asthma, a disease of "the direst suffering," a disease "about whose pathology more various and discrepant ideas prevail than any other," was "essentially a *nervous* disease."
>
> Sudden "mental emotion," Salter said, could bring on an attack and abruptly end one. He did not know why, only what he had observed. He reported on a patient whose attack ceased the moment he saw a fire outside the window and another who had his asthma stop when put on a fast horse. Still other patients found that as soon as they neared the doctor's office, their asthma vanished, "suddenly and without any apparent cause except the mental perturbation at being within the precincts of the physician." The onset of an attack, he noted, was frequently preceded by a spell of depression or "heaviness" (what Teedie called feeling "doleful"), and twenty years in advance of what might be regarded as the first studies in the psychosomatic side of asthma he reported on a small boy who "found his disease a convenient immunity from correction."
>
> "Don't scold me," he would say, if he had incurred his father's displeasure, "or I shall have the asthma." And so he would; his fears were as correct as they were convenient.
>
> —DAVID MCCULLOUGH

Arguing from Testimony and Personal Experience

When we argue from testimony, we say that something happened to us and that this happening proves a point that we wish to make or that it proves our entire argument. Your personal experience may support an argument only if the experience has given you enough information to support generalizations that will help the case you are trying to make. If you have not learned from your experience, your argument may be weakened by inadequate support. Here is an argument from personal experience.

> Disneyland has been criticized for giving a sanitized version of American history, for trivializing international relations and national differences, and for taking all the frightening moments out of fairy tales. But I visited Disneyland with my two children last summer, and we loved it. Yes, it is a form of escapism. But why else do we go to an amusement park? Only a new form of puritanism requires us to be serious every moment about everything. Sometimes we have to relax. And I can't think of a time when I have been happier than I was sitting with my seven-year-old and my five-year-old in Dumbo, the Flying Elephant, circling round and round, suspended over the crowds by the strong steel arms of a friendly Disneyland machine that rotated us in the friendly sunshine.

35e Building a Good Argument

Not every statement can be argued or is worth arguing. Not every statement can stand up in the face of contrary evidence. As you select an argument, be sure you can defend it. As you shape your argument, be sure you present your ideas courteously and without committing common fallacies.

Selecting a Topic

Begin by selecting a topic that is manageable and debatable.

A limited topic

Avoid arguments that are so broad that you can write only a series of assertions. You must gather enough information to know what you are talking about. Topics too broad require more knowledge than you can gather during the term.

You cannot argue in only a few pages that the American government is spending too much money for defense unless you are an expert on the federal budget, particularly on military spending. Even then, you can make that argument work in so short a paper *only* because you are a recognized authority. But you can argue in a brief paper that military spending involves a lot of waste—*if* you can gather evidence of that waste. You can get this information from magazine articles and newspaper stories and from budget hearings recorded in the *Congressional Record.* Many of these sources will be in your school library.

Your argument must be limited enough to state clearly. Your readers must know what you want to prove. Otherwise your argument will be useless.

A topic that lends itself to debate

A strong argument starts with a limited topic that lends itself to debate. If people can take sides on the issue, it's probably a good topic—provided it is limited enough to allow you to know it thoroughly and argue it convincingly. To test a topic for argument, you might ask if anyone cares to debate it.

Statement	**Debatable?**
Shakespeare wrote some interesting plays.	No. Few people would disagree with this topic.
Radio stations should not be allowed by the federal government to play rock music with lyrics that glorify drugs or casual sex.	Yes. Many people think that something should be done to protect young children from such music; others think that a prohibition against such music would violate the First Amendment to the Constitution, with its guarantee of free speech.
Private persons should not be allowed to own pistols.	Yes. Many people, citing the number of murders committed with pistols, think that private ownership of handguns should be banned. Many others believe that such a ban would restrict the freedom of law-abiding gun owners.
We should find a cure for AIDS.	No. AIDS is one of the epidemic diseases of our age, and all serious people believe we should find a cure for it.

Statement	Debatable? *(Con't)*
AIDS victims should be quarantined.	Yes. Many people believe AIDS victims should be kept away from society to protect those who do not have the disease. Others argue that the disease cannot be transferred by casual social contact and that quarantine of its victims would be cruel and inhuman.

Controversy is not essential for good argument. People do not have to be passionate about the subject. But the topic must be debatable. Often controversial topics (such as abortion, welfare, and legalizing drugs) have been argued so much that fresh insights are hard to come by. Do not argue an issue unless you have something new to say about it. It is almost never good to write an argument without reading what other people have written on the subject.

Matters of taste are seldom debatable. It is difficult to argue that a movie or a novel or a short story or a play is good or bad. People often disagree; what seems to be trash to one critic may seem like a masterpiece to another. Many people love the novel *Moby Dick;* others find it boring. Horror movies scare some people; they strike others as silly.

You can argue, however, that a movie or something you read contradicts itself or that it presents stereotypes or that it glorifies violence; you can argue that a movie is complicated, that it addresses this or that issue in society, that it strives for this or that effect. But the simple argument that the movie—or whatever—is ''good'' or ''bad'' will carry little weight.

■ **Exercise 35.6** Which of the following statements would make good arguments? Which cannot be argued in a college paper seven or eight pages long? Write a short paragraph explaining your response to each suggested argument.

1. William Faulkner used descriptions of light in his novels to help emphasize the moods of his characters.
2. Mark Twain's novel *Huckleberry Finn* contains much that can injure the feelings of modern African Americans.
3. The movie *Star Wars* was the most brilliant film ever produced by Hollywood.
4. The movie *Star Wars* uses clichés developed in Hollywood westerns, but reinvents them by transposing them to outer space.
5. Everyone who drives to school would be happier if there were more free parking spaces.

■ **Exercise 35.7** Here are suggested topics for argument papers. Which are debatable, and which are not?

1. The law should ban smoking in all public places.
2. War is one of the great sources of misery in our time.
3. Women in the army should take part in combat.
4. The president of the United States holds great responsibility.
5. A constitutional amendment should outlaw any desecration of the American flag.

Considering Contrary Evidence

The facts rarely line up neatly on one side of any debatable issue. Debatable topics are debatable *because* they have at least two sides. Evidence can be interpreted in different ways. If you are to be fair-minded and reasonable, you must consider the opposing arguments. It is unfair to misquote or misrepresent the opposition. You must think out the opposing point of view as carefully as you can and be sure you represent it correctly.

In dealing with contrary evidence, you have three options: you can point out that it is invalid; you can admit its validity but point out its inferiority; or you can change your mind.

Invalidating contrary evidence

You can argue that the contrary evidence is invalid because it has been misinterpreted by your opponents and that it therefore does not damage your position.

> It is true that keeping the library open on Friday nights costs the university nearly a thousand dollars a week. People who want to close the library argue that all that money will be saved if we take this step. But they have forgotten that when the building is closed, we must pay the salary of a security guard. They have forgotten that even when the building is closed, the lights must be kept on for security, and the heat remains on to protect the books from dampness. They have forgotten that library personnel on duty at night are students working their way through college and that to cut off their pay might be to exclude them from higher education.

Discrediting contrary evidence

You can concede the contrary evidence but argue that your point of view is still superior.

> I do concede that only a handful of people use the library on Friday nights. Although those who want to close the library overestimate the money they would save, I concede that they would indeed save some

money. But why does a university exist? It exists to promote the life of the mind, to expand the intellect and the imagination, to produce knowledge. By keeping the library open on Friday nights, the university confirms these purposes to the handful of people who work there. The books two of these people have written confirm the purposes of the university to the thousands of people who read those books. Through these writers, the university reaches out to readers who can never enter the campus.

The student union is also open on Friday nights. I have checked into the costs of operating the union on those nights. They amount to some six thousand dollars an evening. I am not opposed to keeping the union open on Friday nights. But I do say that a university that saves a little money by closing its library while it keeps open its poolrooms, its bowling alleys, its subsidized soda fountains, and its movie auditorium is selling its soul to the accountants and losing its fundamental purpose.

35e
argue

Acknowledging contrary evidence

Sometimes you may find it effective to develop your argument by the means by which you come to the position. Or, in the course of thinking about your topic, you may change your mind. Chronicling that process is itself a strong argument.

> I once believed in legalizing marijuana. Smoking the weed made people feel good. It seemed to have no harmful effects, and it was not addictive, like alcohol or nicotine. Users said that marijuana did not impair vision or judgment, so drivers high on marijuana could operate cars and trucks in perfect safety. But now a considerable body of research has been built up to prove that marijuana *does* have harmful effects. Smoking marijuana is just as hard on the lungs as smoking tobacco. It does appear to be addictive. And marijuana has been implicated in several private-plane crashes, automobile wrecks, and, recently, train wrecks. It is not the harmless pleasure it once appeared to be, and I now think there are powerful reasons *not* to legalize the drug.

Using a Courteous Tone

Too often, writers of argument papers believe that they can win their argument only by assaulting and insulting everyone who disagrees with them. Fair-minded readers quickly reject writers who argue as though they were at a shouting match. You should learn to argue by friendly persuasion.

It is the fashion today to argue that Machiavelli's *The Prince* is a work of genius and to condemn the critics who have condemned Machiavelli through the centuries. No doubt Machiavelli was a brilliant observer of the sixteenth century and understood the tactics of the petty princes who ruled the Italian city-states. They were immoral men, and Machiavelli described their immorality in elaborate detail. Much of the criticism that has been leveled against Machiavelli through the years should be directed against those princes. He considered himself to be a sort of reporter, describing in great detail how they grasped power and held on to it. One can even argue that like the Christian thinkers of the Middle Ages, Machiavelli believed that human beings were selfish and ignorant, slaves of a flawed human nature.

But despite the brilliance of his observations and the blame that can be placed on the rulers he observed, Machiavelli himself can still be chilling. No particle of sympathy for the victims of those princes penetrates his stately prose. He seems to be above concern for the suffering of the innocent. He was passionately dedicated to building an Italian state strong enough to repel the French, German, and Spanish invaders. But nothing in his writings indicates dedication to human rights or even awareness that human beings have rights. No matter how highly we praise his genius, we must recognize that something is lacking in his spirit.

The tone of the preceding paragraphs does not insult those who have said that Machiavelli was a genius and that he has been judged too harshly by later writers. It makes an argument based on evidence and treats those who have expressed different views gently.

Avoiding Fallacious Reasoning

Some reasoning may appear at first to be logical, but on examination the fallacies or errors in reasoning appear. Certain common fallacies appear again and again in arguments we see in political debate, in advertising, in editorial writing, and indeed in almost every public forum. Learn to recognize the common fallacies and to avoid them in your own writing.

Improper cause and effect

The mere fact that happening *B* occurred after happening *A* is not proof that *A* caused *B*. You must make a stronger connection than mere sequence to establish cause and effect. Many superstitions arise because people make connections between events that have no real relation except that one happened after the other.

> A black cat walked across my path last night, and when I got home, discovered that my house had been robbed. The black cat brought me bad luck.
>
> Since radio, television, and the movies began emphasizing stories about crime, crime has steadily increased; therefore, radio, television, and the movies have been responsible for the increase in the crime rate.

Crime increases for many reasons. We might make the argument if we interviewed several convicted criminals who said they had been motivated by the broadcast media and the movies to commit crime. Or if we could discover a rash of crimes identical to some crime that had been shown in a television story or a movie, we might have some indication that that medium increased the crime rate. But the mere fact that the crime rate rose after such stories became popular in the media is not evidence that the media caused the crimes. We might also discover that the crime rate had increased since television started broadcasting more basketball games. Would you argue that basketball broadcasts had increased crime?

Too little information for generalization

When you engage in inductive reasoning, you gather facts and arrive at generalizations. If you don't gather enough facts, you may make a faulty generalization.

> In many of his novels, William Faulkner wrote about terrible happenings in the American South. Therefore Faulkner must have hated the South.
>
> In his novel *The Turn of the Screw,* Henry James wrote about two ghosts who attempted to corrupt two little children. Therefore James believed in ghosts.
>
> I was in Paris last summer, and a French police officer was very rude to me when I asked him how to find the Louvre Museum. "You are standing next to it," he said. All the French are rude.
>
> My Uncle Herbert smokes two packs of cigarettes a day and is eighty-five years old. Therefore all the talk about the dangers of cigarette smoking is a lie.

Either/or reasoning

Pushing an argument to the extremes weakens it. Don't demand that your readers accept one of two extreme positions.

Either we must stop our children from listening to rock music or civilization will crumble.

Either you buy the new supercharged TurboLemon convertible when our sale ends or you will never have such an opportunity again in your life.

Either people must understand Shakespeare or they cannot consider themselves educated.

The straw man

A *straw man* is a weak or imaginary argument that you attribute to your opponent for the sole purpose of refuting it and seeming to advance your point. This strategy is designed to make readers (or hearers) think the opponent's position is so indefensible that no sensible person could possibly hold back. Often the attack on the straw man is a variation of the either/or fallacy.

Statement: In the United States, prayer in public schools offers many difficulties. It is difficult for sincerely religious people to keep from trying to influence others to accept their point of view. Prayers may easily become sermons. Different people use different forms of prayer. Christians customarily pray with their eyes closed; Jews pray with their eyes open; Americans of some other faiths pray by chanting. Children of various religious backgrounds are forced by law to go to school. But they should not be forced to worship God in a way that contradicts their own beliefs or the beliefs of their parents. The United States is the most religious of all the industrial countries, and we may suggest that religion has flourished here because it has not been forced on anyone. We would do well to ponder this question: Is religion helped by being prescribed by law, no matter how inoffensive the form may seem to those who prescribe it?

Reply: My opponent has questioned the value of prayer in the public schools. Only an atheist would do such a thing. He does not believe in God. He denies that we owe reverence to our Creator. He has blasphemed the Almighty by saying that little children should not pray to Him. It is his kind that will destroy our country, for if we forsake God, God will forsake us. I do not say that he is a Communist, but I say that he is playing into the hands of the Communists by denying God just as they deny God. If you vote for my opponent, my beloved friends, you are voting against religion.

The *ad hominem* argument

An *argumentum ad hominem* is an "attack on the person." The writer (or speaker) avoids the central issue of the opponent's argument and instead attacks the opponent's character.

> My opponent spent an hour last night explaining his economic policies to the nation on television. He advanced columns of figures about jobs and about workers and employment and inflation. He gave us a six-point program that he said would reduce inflation, increase employment, strengthen the dollar, and control the federal deficit. These items were very interesting, but I could not think about them very much because as the cameras zoomed in on him, I realized that he dyes his hair. Now I ask you, what kind of man dyes his hair? Can you believe in such a man? Would any of you women out there marry a man who dyes his hair? People who dye their hair are lying about themselves. And my friends, a man who lies about himself will lie about the budget of the United States. Look at me! I am totally bald. I have an honest, pure-bald head. Look at me, and see a man who believes in the truth. Look at my opponent and see a man who lies about his hair and his age and about anything else that will help him get elected president of the United States.

Begging the question

Begging the question is a fallacy in deductive reasoning that occurs when the person presenting the argument evades or sidesteps the real question by assuming it is established or proved. The person who begs the question states the major premise in such a way that it is a conclusion, without allowing an argument to decide the merits of the case.

> He could not be lying because he is president of the Campus Society for Moral Uplift.

Here is how this statement would be set up in a syllogism.

> **Major premise:** The president of the Campus Society for Moral Uplift cannot tell a lie.
>
> **Minor premise:** He is president of the Campus Society for Moral Uplift.
>
> **Conclusion:** Therefore he cannot tell a lie.

If we accept the major premise, we have no argument. But the major premise begs the question by assuming a perfect correlation between top status in the Campus Society for Moral Uplift and honesty. That correlation cannot be assumed, and the premise is false. Moreover, if the president of the Campus Society for Moral Uplift was charged with lying, the argument should turn on the evidence, not on his position in a campus club.

The red herring

A **red herring** is any issue introduced into an argument that distracts attention from the main issue. People often introduce a red herring when they think they are about to lose an argument. The original red herring was a smoked salt fish with a strong taste and smell. Farmers who wanted to keep fox hunters from galloping across their crops and ruining them would drag a red herring along the edge of their fields to throw the dogs off track.

> That rugged-looking cowboy smokes a famous cigarette in beautiful magazine ads that show stunning color photographs of the American West. You can almost smell the fresh air and feel the glory of space in those ads. You can look at that beautiful scene and that handsome face and know that cigarettes are not nearly as bad for your health as the surgeon general claims they are.

The advertisers of cigarettes know that medical evidence is solidly against smoking. So they present red herrings, beautiful ads that feature beautiful people doing athletic or robust things while they smoke. The ads distract attention from the central issue—whether people should smoke or not.

■ **Exercise 35.8** Read the following sentences, and identify the logical fallacies.

1. Anyone who claims that Americans have the right to burn the flag hates the United States.
2. Forty years ago, when my opponent was a freshman in college, he plagiarized a term paper and had to withdraw from school for a year. That proves he is a dishonest person and does not deserve your vote.
3. If you do not read Plato and Aristotle, you are contributing to the moral laxity of our times.
4. Anyone who thinks Stephen King writes serious novels is a fool.
5. I cannot write about this book because I dislike it so much.
6. I would not want my daughter to be a soldier because it is not ladylike to carry a gun.
7. Religious people are ignorant.
8. Morals have fallen in America because of television.

9. Athletes in television commercials drink beer; so I will drink beer, too.
10. Writing cannot be taught; so I will not take a writing course.

✔ CHECKLIST 35.3: MAKING SOLID ARGUMENTS

As you select your topic for an argument and frame your position, ask yourself these questions to be sure you are on track. Ask yourself these questions again as you revise your first draft, to be sure you are staying on track.

- Is my argument worth making?
- Does anyone dispute my argument?
- Can I make my argument in the space and time I have available?
- Can I develop my argument by reasoning, or can I only assert my opinions?
- Are my inductions logical?
- Are my syllogisms logical?
- Have I considered contrary arguments?
- Have I been courteous to my opponents?
- Are there any logical fallacies in my argument?
- Is my conclusion supported by my evidence?

CHAPTER
36

WRITING ABOUT LITERATURE

Many of your English courses will require you to write about novels, short stories, poems, or plays that you read on your own or that you study and discuss in class. An essay on a literary subject shows your understanding of the work you have read. Such an essay is always critical in the sense that it states your position on, attitude toward, or opinion of the work and provides details to support your point.

36a
Analyzing the Assignment

Your instructor may have a specific goal in asking you to write about a piece of literature. For example, your assignment may be to write about sound images in *The Tempest,* to analyze the theme of Melville's story "Bartleby the Scrivener," to compare two love sonnets by Keats, or to trace the development of a character in a novel. Or your instructor may give a general assignment—to write about a specific literary work or to choose a work on your own and write about it. In these last two cases you have to define the terms of the assignment yourself.

The student whose paper appears at the end of this chapter received this assignment. Read "in Just-" by E. E. Cummings and write an essay of about two or three typed pages that explains the meaning of the poem. The class was studying poetry and had read and discussed some of Cummings's other poems. The text of "in Just-" appears on pages 564–565.

Both specific and open-ended writing assignments about literature almost always require **analysis.** When you analyze something, you scrutinize its parts in order to understand the whole. You look closely at the words and sentences, the motivations and the actions of the characters, the events of the narrative, and the writer's techniques, among other elements. Analysis often involves **interpretation,** an explanation of what you think the work means, and **evaluation,** your opinion and judgment of the literary work. Analysis and interpretation lead to evaluation. You should base your judgments on thorough analysis and careful interpretation.

36b
Reading Actively

Don't write until you've read the work carefully several times. You cannot write a good paper about a work that you have read only once. When you read a text several times, you will begin to notice things that deepen your appreciation and enlarge your understanding of it. That detailed knowledge is a resource that will enable you to write a good paper.

Read actively. If you own the book, underline words and phrases and make notes to yourself in the margin. Some students of literature make their own indexes on the blank pages at the back of a book, especially in longer works. They copy a key phrase and the number of the page on which the phrase appears. They write down the names of characters and the first page on which each character appears. Somethimes they write a short summary of the character's qualities. Summarizing the main events in the plot is a good idea, too. Always record the page numbers in your notes and summaries. Later, when you begin to write about the work, you can find important passages easily.

To read literature actively is to ask questions. Stimulate your mind by posing questions about literary selections and seeking answers to them as you read. When you examine some of the approaches to writing about literature in 36e, you will find questions that will help you understand a novel, short story, poem, or play. Not all the questions will apply to every work. But if you keep them in mind as you read, you will become a more attentive reader, and you will see things in the literature that will help you write about it. Chapters 37 and 39 suggest other ways to read actively.

36c
Developing a Thesis

Follow the guidelines for prewriting presented in Chapter 1 as you prepare to write an essay about a piece of literature. Do brainstorming, make an informal list, or use a rough outline. Keep returning to the literary text as you shape your ideas.

Develop a tentative thesis for your paper. Before you begin writing your thesis statement, look at your assignment again. You may be able to use some of its language in your thesis. For example, if your assignment is to explain how Iago convinces Othello of Desdemona's guilt, your tentative thesis might be, "Iago convinces Othello of Desdemona's guilt by means of carefully developed circumstantial evidence."

See the research paper on Willa Cather in Chapter 34. Willa Cather wrote about harsh and grim life on the Great Plains and how that life deprived people of certain kinds of culture and beauty. You can see how the writer of this paper developed that theme in two of Cather's short stories. This research paper goes beyond a mere summary of the plot.

To develop such themes, you must study a text, think about it, read it again and again, and write down various ideas to try out as paper topics. These ideas may become an informal outline built around a central thesis. You may have to write a draft before your most important idea becomes clear; then you will have to write at least one more draft to develop it.

Use the guidelines in 1f as you formulate your thesis. Remember that your thesis should be flexible and probably will change as you write successive drafts. As with other kinds of writing, the thesis should state a concrete position that you can argue about. Both your topic and your opinion about it should be stated clearly.

The student who wrote about Cummings's poem developed his thesis in three stages.

Tentative thesis	Cummings's "in Just-" is about a group of children who respond to the whistle of the balloonman on a spring afternoon. ↓
Revised 1	In the poem "in Just-" Cummings paints a child's world in the child's own terms. ↓
Revised 2	In the poem "in Just-" E. E. Cummings presents a child's world filled with childhood's delights and dangers. ↓
Final copy	The poem "in Just-" presents an entirely familiar world of children at play in the spring. Yet the poet's unusual use of language shows us the subtle dangers lurking about the delights and pleasures we all associate with childhood.

The tentative thesis is not a thesis at all. It is a summary of the action. It makes no arguable point. The first revised thesis does make an assertion, but it is too broad and not well focused. The second revised thesis makes an arguable assertion that is sufficiently limited for a brief literary paper. For the final copy (pp. 566–71), the student revised the thesis again.

When you write and revise, you must be sure to keep your paper focused on one leading idea. The writer of the paper about Willa Cather in Chapter 34, is not concerned about how Cather got from her birthplace in Virginia to Nebraska. Nor is the writer concerned about the many nineteenth-century stories about artistic young women dying of tuberculosis. These are interesting subjects. They might make interesting topics for other papers. But this paper is about the effect of the vast spaces of the Great Plains and the hardships of life there on two people with a great love of music and the culture that music reflects. The writer would have spoiled the effect if she had been distracted by these other ideas and had neglected her central theme.

36d Considering Audience and Purpose

Your audience for a paper on a literary subject is usually your instructor. In most cases your instructor is familiar with the work he or she has asked you to write about and does not need a detailed plot summary.

Unless your assignment explicitly requires you to do so, avoid writing an extensive plot summary. Of course, you may have to refer to elements in the plot to make your point. But your instructor does not want to read a paper that tells her something she already knows quite well. She wants to see your mind at work. She wants you to think about the piece and to develop ideas that your reading has stimulated in your mind. Write your essay as if both of you know the work and you want to tell her some things you have learned about it.

Your purpose in writing will influence the outcome of your paper. If you are writing an essay with limits defined by your instructor—about two pages (500–750 words), for example—make your point quickly and offer supporting detail and no more. If the assignment is due within a few sessions, you should avoid an overly ambitious plan that draws upon extensive use of secondary sources and other library materials. For brief interpretive essays, most instructors expect you to develop ideas from the primary text itself. If you have been given a substantial amount of time to carry out the assignment, library research is probably a requirement. Chapters 31 through 34 present a research paper on a literary topic and show you how the paper was developed.

36e Considering Approaches to Literary Analysis

You may take any of a variety of approaches when you write about literature and you may ask several kinds of questions as you think about your assignment.

Writing About the Characters

If you decide to focus your essay on character in a work of literature, think about the way the author develops the characters and the relation of character to other aspects of the work, such as plot, structure, and meaning.

Begin by identifying the most important characters in the work. How are they related to each other? How do they relate to each other? Does one character dominate the work, or do several characters share the action equally? What exactly do the characters do? Do they talk more than they act? Do the characters' actions match their talk, or do they talk one way and act another? What do the actions and the talk reveal about the characters? What makes you sympathize with or like one or more of the characters? What makes you unsympathetic toward or dislike one or more of the characters? What moral values do the characters have? How do the characters judge their own situation? What do characters learn in the course of the action? How do characters change? How do what characters learn relate to the work's theme or meaning? If there is a narrator, what additional perspective does this character introduce? For more questions regarding narrators, see below.

Writing About the Plot and Setting

The **plot** is the action of a work; the **setting** is the place and time of the action. Writing about the plot means analyzing the relation of one event to another or the effects of the action on the characters or the effects of the characters on the action. Writing about the setting means trying to present your sense of why the author chose to create the scene as he or she did. The setting involves not only a specific location but also a broader environment of history and geography.

You can raise many questions about plot and setting. How has the author arranged and connected the events? Are the events told in the order in which they occur or in some other order? How does a single important event relate to other events? Where does the action of the work take place? Is there any significance to the setting where the action takes place? What period or periods of time does the work embrace? Why do you suppose the writer set the work in that time? What surprises you in the work? Why are you surprised?

Writing About the Structure of the Work

Literature falls into **genres,** or types. Short stories are one genre. Other genres are plays, poetry, novels, and essays. Screenplays represent a new literary genre. Each genre has a different formal structure. If you decide to focus your essay on the structure of a work of literature, you will need to analyze its elements in light of the expectations of its genre.

Here are some questions to consider. How has the author put the pieces together? How do the various chapters or stanzas or acts relate to each other? What particular chapter or stanza or act stands out for any reason? Why does it stand out? How is the work similar to or different from work in the same literary category, or genre? All poems belong to the genre of poetry, but the structure of a poem by E. E. Cummings is very different from the structure of a poem by John Keats or Thomas Hardy. And, despite similarities, one poem by Cummings is very different from other poems by Cummings. How does the author meet or challenge your expectations for the genre?

Writing About the Tone of the Work

The **tone** is the author's attitude toward the subject. How does the author feel about the characters and their actions, and how does the author make you feel about them? Is the tone impartial, serious, mocking, condemning, playful? What accounts for the author's attitude toward the subject? Why do you think the author wrote the work?

Considering tone usually means considering the speaker, or **narrator,** the person through whose eyes and lips we learn about the events. All narrators have a **point of view,** or perspective. What is the narrator's point of view? Is the story told by a third-person narrator, someone who is not a character in the piece? Or is it told by a first-person narrator? Does the third-person narrator follow one character exclusively, or does the point of view shift from character to character? How much does the narrator know about the characters he or she describes? Are his or her perceptions reliable? How does the narrator's knowledge affect what we as readers know about the action of the work? You never should assume that the narrator in any work is the same as the author of the work. What is the relation between the narrator and the author?

Writing About Language and Style

The **language** comprises the words the writer uses. **Style** includes language as well as sentence structure, usage, and diction. Imagery, figurative language, and symbolism (see Chapter 9 and 36f) contribute to style. Some questions to ask about language and style are:

- Are the words informal, colloquial, formal?
- What kinds of words does the author seem to like?
- Which words does the author repeat frequently?
- Which words seem to have special meaning for the author?
- Where and how has the author used sensory language?
- Are the images original?
- Can you identify a pattern in the uses of imagery?
- How do figurative expressions contribute to the style and meaning of the work?
- Does something in the work appear to stand for something else? That is, does some word, some action, some description or character make you think of something beyond it?
- How are the sentences structured—are they simple or complex, long or short?
- Which sentences do you like and why?
- What special qualities of style do you notice?

✓ CHECKLIST 36.1: CONSIDERING APPROACHES TO LITERARY ANALYSIS

In analyzing a work of literature, consider the following elements. You may decide to concentrate on any one of them, but in doing so, consider their interrelationships.

- the characters
- the plot and/or the setting
- the structure of the work
- the tone of the work
- the language and style of the work

■ **Exercise 36.1** Read "A Rose for Emily," by William Faulkner. Answer in brief paragraphs the following questions about the story.

1. Who is the narrator in the story?
2. Where and when does the story take place?
3. How long a time does the story cover?
4. How old is the narrator?

5. How does Faulkner prepare us for the surprise ending?
6. How is Miss Emily Grierson related to her town?
7. What does Miss Emily say in the story?
8. What do you notice about the style of the work?

36f
Using the Language of Literary Analysis

Literary analysis often involves interpretation and evaluation. As you write about literature, use the language writers and critics use in the study of this art form.

Understanding Key Literary Devices and Terms

Literary critics identify literary devices that have helped writers achieve certain effects. Often these devices help integrate the whole piece for the reader and perhaps reveal an unexpected meaning that makes the text more vivid and more memorable. When you recognize such devices and know their names, you can write about them more effectively and make your papers about literature more interesting. Here are some common literary devices.

Climax

The **climax** of a literary work is that point toward which the entire piece seems to be directed. Usually literary works end shortly after the climax. The problems are resolved or made clear; some point of understanding is reached; the major action of the story takes place.

The climax of Faulkner's "A Rose for Emily" is the point at which the astonished citizens of Miss Emily's little town break into a room of her house after her funeral and discover the corpse of Homer Baron lying in the bed and a strand of Miss Emily's "iron-gray" hair lying on the pillow beside the corpse.

Being able to identify the climax will help you see more clearly all the devices the author is using to keep you reading to see how everything turns out and to see the relation of the various parts of the work to the whole.

Irony

A writer or speaker who uses **irony** means something different from the literal meaning of the words. Sometimes the writer means something entirely opposite from the words in the text. The most famous irony in

English is Jonathan Swift's "A Modest Proposal." Swift, enraged by England's exploitation of Ireland in the eighteenth century, was especially concerned about the neglect of poor Irish children while members of the English upper classes lived in luxury. He wrote:

> I have been assured by a very knowing American of my acquaintance in London, that a young healthy child well nursed is at a year old a most delicious, nourishing and wholesome food, whether stewed, roasted, baked, or boiled, and I make no doubt that it will equally serve in a fricassee, or a ragout.

Swift was not serious about serving little Irish children up for food. But he was serious in his belief that the rich, especially the rich English lords of Ireland, were treating the poor like animals.

Dramatic irony comes from characters in plays, poems, or stories who present or encounter a reality that is the opposite of appearances.

Shakespeare often uses dramatic irony in his plays. Macbeth is told that he will not die until Birnam Wood comes to Dunsinane Castle. He thinks he is secure because he does not believe a forest like Birnam Wood can move; but then Macduff's soldiers cut branches from the trees of Birnam Wood and use them as camouflage to disguise their movements, and so Birnam Wood comes to Dunsinane—and Macbeth is defeated and killed. Dramatic irony is common in all forms of literature.

In all irony, the audience must know that it is irony. In well-done ironic pieces, we know throughout that we are reading something not meant to be taken literally. Inexperienced writers may fail because they know they are writing with irony but do not give their readers any clues. Therefore the readers take their words literally.

Hyperbole

Hyperbole is exaggeration so extravagant that no reasonable person would take it for literal truth.

> The father of this pleasant grandfather, of the neighbourhood of Mount Pleasant, was a horny-skinned, two-legged, money-getting species of spider, who spun webs to catch unwary flies, and retired into holes until they were entrapped. The name of this old pagan's God was Compound Interest. He lived for it, married it, died of it. Meeting with a heavy loss in an honest little enterprise in which all the loss was intended to have been on the other side, he broke something—something necessary to his existence; therefore it couldn't have been his heart—and made an end of his career.
>
> —CHARLES DICKENS, *Bleak House*

Dickens here amuses himself by going back into the genealogy of the Smallweed family, characters in *Bleak House* that Dickens holds up to ridicule. He wants to show us that the entire family of Smallweeds was greedy, heartless, and cruel.

Understatement

Like exaggeration, **understatement** often pops up in ordinary speech, especially in humorous statements intended to defuse a tense situation. Your roommate comes in and starts throwing books against the wall one by one and screaming at the top of his voice because he received a grade of C− on a paper that he was certain would get an A. You say, "I believe you're upset."

Here is Mark Twain describing a celebration of the Fourth of July on an American ship in the Mediterranean during one of his trips to Europe.

> The speeches were bad—execrable, almost without exception. In fact, without *any* exception, but one. Capt. Duncan made a good speech; he made the only good speech of the evening. He said:
>
> "LADIES AND GENTLEMEN:—May we all live to a green old age, and be prosperous and happy. Steward, bring up another basket of champagne."
>
> It was regarded as a very able effort.
>
> —MARK TWAIN, *The Innocents Abroad*

"It was regarded as a very able effort" expresses the enormous relief of the passengers that they were about to be treated to champagne rather than a long speech.

Allusion

When writers make **allusions,** they refer to something indirectly without precisely identifying it. It may be a literary work, a historical event, a work of art, a person, or something else. In writing papers about literature, you should be especially interested in allusions to other written works.

> Methought I saw my late espousèd saint
> Brought to me like Alcestis from the grave
> Whom Jove's great son to her glad husband gave,
> Rescued from death by force, though pale and faint.
>
> —JOHN MILTON, "On His Dead Wife"

At the beginning of this famous sonnet, Milton alludes to the classical myth of Alcestis, the wife of King Admetus of Thessaly. She sacrificed her life to save her husband, and later Zeus (or Jove, as the Romans called him) permitted Hercules to go down into the realm of the dead and bring her back to her husband. Milton also alluded frequently to the Bible.

An allusion can often be used as the topic of a paper about literature because the allusion may provide a key to understanding the work. In poetry particularly, an allusion may give the key to the entire work.

Recognizing Symbols and Images

Fiction writers, dramatists, and poets sometimes use language that makes us think both of the literal truth they are describing and of something beyond that truth. The reverberations that symbols set up broaden and intensify the meaning of the literary work.

To find images and symbols in literature, you must read the text carefully and look closely at individual words to see what special meanings the writer may have poured into them. Look especially at words that are frequently repeated. You must also be well read and familiar with the cultural context of the work.

> Still falls the Rain—
> Dark as the world of man, black as our loss—
> Blind as the nineteen hundred and forty nails
> Upon the Cross.
>
> —EDITH SITWELL, "Still Falls the Rain"

The English poet Edith Sitwell wrote these lines about the German air raids over London in 1940, early in World War II. We may see in the image of the cross the suffering of innocent humankind from war throughout the 1,940 years since Christ.

COMMON LITERARY DEVICES

Climax	The point toward which the entire piece is directed.
Irony	The use of words to express a meaning opposed to the literal meaning.
Dramatic irony	The use of characters who present or encounter a reality that is the opposite of appearances.
Hyperbole	Exaggeration so extravagant that no one would mistake it for the literal truth.
Understatement	A moderate statement in ironic contrast to what the situation warrants.
Allusion	An incidental, indirect reference to someone or something.
Symbols and images	Language that suggests or stands for something beyond its literal meaning.

■ **Exercise 36.2** Read the poems "Richard Cory," by Edwin Arlington Robinson; "Ozymandias," by Percy Bysshe Shelley; and "Death and Co.," by Sylvia Plath. See how many literary devices you can find in each poem.

36g
Writing About Literature: A Sample Paper

Use your prewriting to guide you as you develop the first and later drafts of your essay on a literary topic. Be prepared to revise your thesis as your ideas take shape. Return often to the work you are writing about.

Write your essay as you would an essay on any topic. Write an introduction followed by paragraphs that support your points with specific details. Make your conclusion a natural ending.

One further point: Write about your literary topic in the present tense. The convention in discussing literature and other works of art is to assume that the work "happens" each time it is read, viewed, heard, or studied. Notice in the student paper that follows how the writer uses the present tense to describe what Cummings achieves in his poem: "Cummings *uses* words and images that reflect a child's perception of the world"; "But beneath this simple word *is* a much more complex one"; "the poet *raises* the questions but *provides* no definite answers."

The following essay about a literary subject was written in response to the assignment asking for an analysis of E. E. Cummings's poem "in Just-." The full text of the poem appears below.

in Just-
spring   when the world is mud-
luscious the little
lame balloonman

whistles   far   and wee

and eddieandbill come
running from marbles and
piracies and it's
spring

when the world is puddle-wonderful

the queer
old balloonman whistles
far   and   wee
and bettyandisbel come dancing

from hop-scotch and jump-rope and

it's
spring
and
   the

        goat-footed

balloonMan   whistles
far
and
wee

✔ CHECKLIST 36.2: REVISING AN ESSAY ABOUT LITERATURE

As you revise your essay about literature, attend to all the concerns that have been emphasized in this handbook. Review Checklist 2.2 and 34.1 in particular. Then ask yourself these questions.

- Did I examine the assignment carefully?
- Did I read and reread the literary work actively so that I understand it well?
- Did I do prewriting to develop my ideas on the work?
- Did I state my thesis as a hypothesis that I can argue intelligently?
- Did I offer specific details to support my thesis?
- Did I quote accurately? Did I enclose in quotation marks any exact words that I used from the literary work?
- Did I avoid extensive plot summaries?
- Did I demonstrate my understanding of the work by analyzing it carefully? Did I address literary terms and devices, where appropriate?
- Did I consider my audience and purpose?

(1-a) The short introduction states the thesis succinctly. Compare this final thesis with the tentative and revised theses on page 555.

(1-b) The writer analyzes the language and draws details from the poem. Note the quotation marks enclosing words quoted from the poem and the slash indicating the end of one line and the beginning of the next. See 26e.

(1-c) Note that the writer offers no summary of the poem, as none is needed to understand this essay, but does express his own thinking about the poem.

(1-d) "But" and "this simple world" connect this paragraph with the preceding one.

Delights and Dangers of Childhood

E. E. Cummings's poems show an inventive, playful use of words and sentence structure to force readers to consider common ideas and
(1-a) feelings in a new context. The poem "in Just-" presents an entirely familiar world of children at play in the spring. Yet the poet's unusual use of language shows us the subtle dangers lurking about the delights and pleasures we all associate with childhood.

Cummings uses words and images that reflect a child's perception of the world. He calls the world "mud-luscious" and "puddle-wonderful." With those phrases we can feel a child's delight at springtime. The games abandoned at the balloonman's call--
(1-b) "marbles and / piracies" and "hop-scotch and jump-rope"--accurately show us children at play. Cummings runs the names of the children together on the page so that we hear them just as children would say
(1-c) them, "eddieandbill" and "bettyandisbel." In addition, the balloonman "whistles far and wee," a child's excited expression certainly. The words "it's spring" are repeated twice, again to show the innocent excitement of youngsters outdoors after the spring rain.

(1-d) But beneath this simple world is a much more complex one. The balloonman has a peculiar, ominous power over the children. They stop everything, running and dancing to see him. On one level, of course, it is not surprising for children to greet a neighborhood visitor who sells balloons. Yet Cummings calls him "lame," "queer,"

(2-a) By explaining the allusion to the satyrs, the writer enriches our understanding of the poem.

(2-b) The writer comments on structure. Any phrase repeated in a short poem demands consideration. The writer makes an interesting point about the phrase "far and wee."

(2-c) Again, an explanation of an allusion puts the poem in a broader context.

(2-d) The writer offers his view of the theme of the poem. Clearly he reached this conclusion after considering many elements of the poem, such as language, style, character, and setting.

(2-e) Analyzing a key phrase, and relating it to the structure of the poem, is a good strategy here.

Singh, 2

and "goat-footed." In Greek mythology, the satyrs, creatures who
(2-a) enjoyed wild merrymaking, were humanlike gods with goats' features.
By alluding to the satyrs, the poet implies something sinister.

The phrase for the sound of the balloonman's whistle, "far and
(2-b) wee," which is used three times in this poem of twenty-four very
short lines, also suggests something unusual, even dangerous. Why
"far"? Will the sound transport the children far away? Can children
far away hear it? Although Cummings's piper is more contemporary--he
uses a whistle instead of a flute--the poet certainly is alluding
(2-c) here to the Pied Piper of Hamelin, who enchanted all the children
with his magic flute and lured them away from their town.

In a sense, then, the poem may be viewed as a story of the loss
(2-d) of innocence awaiting children as they grow up. In a secure world of
play there are no troubles. But evil and danger are imminent, maybe
even necessary for passage into adulthood. These ideas help call
(2-e) attention to the phrase "in Just-" / spring." (Cummings probably used
an uppercase letter for the *j* in *Just* for emphasis. The only other
capital letter in the poem is for the word *Man* in *balloonMan*, when
the word appears for the third time. Even the children's names are
set in lowercase letters.)

Does the word *Just* mean "only," suggesting that spring alone, the season of growth and renewal, is the time of joy in a child's life? Or is the message darker, perhaps even ironic? If spring is "just," meaning fair or honorable, where is the justice in children (or their childhoods) being stolen away? Perhaps Cummings is saying

(3-a) **The questions are interesting, especially in light of the writer's conclusion: "the poet raises the questions but provides no definite answers."**

Singh, 3

that spring is not just at all, that its delights are merely seductions. What makes the poem so compelling and provocative is

(3-a) that the poet raises the questions but provides no definite answers.

CHAPTER
37

WRITING ACROSS THE CURRICULUM

Most college courses require writing—short papers, research papers, reports, perhaps even journals that may give an account of your reading and your thoughts about it. The advice we give in this handbook will help you in all these writing assignments.

But different courses have different requirements for writing. A physics professor may ask you to write a lab report describing an experiment demonstrating the forces that operate on a moving body, such as a ball rolling down an inclined plane. A biology course may require you to write a lab report on cell division in a Petri dish. A business course might concentrate on case studies and reports. A history professor may ask you to relate the events that led to the outbreak of the first World War or to explain the thought of an important woman in history or to discuss a controversy among historians. A philosophy course may require a number of short papers developing abstract concepts or steps in logic. An economics professor may ask you to write a paper explaining the ripple effects that sweep through an economy from a change in the minimum wage law or the tax structure. In all these disciplines you may be asked to write reports that show that you have read and understood assigned books and articles.

These different kinds of papers require the same prewriting techniques, the drafting, the revising, and the proofreading that are the subject of this handbook. This chapter suggests ways you can apply these techniques in writing across the curriculum.

✔ CHECKLIST 37.1: UNDERSTANDING THE WRITING ASSIGNMENT

Your instructors are the authorities for what you write in college courses. Listen carefully to what they tell you, and follow their instructions. If they give you written handouts to guide your work, read them carefully. If they do not provide handouts, perhaps you should request them.

For each writing assignment, be sure you understand its purpose and elements as well as the mechanics of length and date due. Consider these questions.

- Does the assignment call for a report or an essay? That is, does the assignment require you primarily to assemble information, or does it require you to collect information and interpret it?
- What are the key words in the assignment? *discuss,* explain, *compare,* evaluate; *why, when, who, where, what.* How do these key words define what you must write?
- How long will the paper be?
- What is the deadline for the assignment?
- Where will you find the evidence to help you write the assigned paper? The library? By observation or field trip? By experiment in the laboratory?
- Will your paper have parenthetical references and a list of works cited or references, or will it be sufficient to mention your few sources in the text?
- Will your instructor look at a draft of the paper before you hand in the final copy?
- Will your instructor let you work on the paper with another student in the class?
- What information from other courses or disciplines will help you write this paper?
- Have you had any personal experiences that may help make the points you want to make in the paper?

37a
Reading Actively

Good writing begins with active reading. Study every subject and course you take in college with an active and critical mind. Don't be passive. Don't accept everything you read merely because it is on the page. Don't accept everything you hear merely because a college professor said it. Ask yourself why people write things, say things, demonstrate things. Ask what your own observations mean.

Read, observe, think, and write with questions in mind. Compare data. Be skeptical. Don't be content with reading one source. Read several sources for the same subject and compare them. How different are histories about Martin Luther written by Catholics, Protestants, Jews, and those with no religion at all? How do astronomers and other scientists differ in their thinking about black holes? How different are the views of women about the works of Ernest Hemingway from the views of men? How does gender shape literature and affect literary criticism?

Try to read as though you were a detective in a mystery novel trying to make all the evidence add up to something. Ask if there is any reason you should *not* believe something you see in a film or hear on tape or read in a book or article. Ask yourself about the motives of writers. What biases do they have? What are they trying to prove? Can you tell if they are not giving you all the information you need? Have they not thought to ask questions that you can ask of their material?

37a curric

Thinking Critically

To write a good paper, you must engage your mind with your subject. That is thinking critically. To think critically is to ask questions about everything you read and to look for meanings that aren't immediately obvious. The critical thinker reads between the lines of texts, considers motives, ponders biases, asks what else needs to be known before a judgment can be made. Such thinkers never take anything for granted. They never read passively. They read and listen and observe skeptically—not out of an angry spirit of contrariness but out of curiosity and a desire to get to the bottom of things.

Drawing Inferences

When you read actively and think critically, you make connections. You connect elements of the work you are reading. You connect ideas from the work with facts you already know and ideas that grow out of them. You put facts and ideas together to draw inferences (see 35b).

An **inference** is not a bare opinion. It is a plausible judgment arrived at by comparing something we are studying with something else we know. An inference is believable on the basis of the evidence, but it often cannot be proved beyond the shadow of a doubt. When you draw inferences in a paper, you put texts and observations in a larger context. You provide meaning. You explain things.

According to an old legend, Sir Isaac Newton observed an apple fall while he sat in a garden in England. He asked himself what force made the apple fall. In pondering this question—or one like it—he inferred that bodies attracted each other by a force called *gravity,* which meant only "the quality of being heavy." No one has ever been able to explain this force. But Newton was able to describe it mathematically and to demonstrate that it was constant throughout the universe, at least as far as it was possible to observe it in his day.

Newton's original inference was very simple—a force exists in bodies that causes them to attract each other. Your inferences may also be simple, but they can lead to interesting arguments that suggest relationships among different pieces of evidence.

Relationships and motives can be very complex. In an American history course you might want to write a paper on the concept of states rights held by political figures in the southern United States long before the Civil War. They seem to have been sincere in their belief that the federal government had no right to coerce the people of Georgia or Mississippi to do anything they did not want to do. But did states rights have any content other than the right to deprive black citizens of civil rights given all Americans by the U.S. Constitution? Could any issue besides race have caused the Civil War? Did southern politicians ever make another important case that might have defined states rights? These are complicated questions that can be approached by trying to infer the real meaning of texts behind the words.

Like Newton, you begin with a fundamental question and expand it into a wide investigation of related questions. You cannot answer these questions off the top of your head. You must read carefully and widely. You must move back and forth between evidence and inference to establish the basis for your conclusions.

■ **Exercise 37.1** Study the following text, and show where the writer is reporting information. Where is this writer drawing an inference and expressing an opinion?

> Arthur M. Schlesinger was for many years regarded as one of the great liberal historians of our times. He wrote three admiring books on Franklin D. Roosevelt's New Deal and another book about the administration of John F. Kennedy in whose administration he served. Both these men were heroic figures to him, as was Woodrow Wilson, the president of the United States during World War I.
>
> Yet it is curious to see how little discussion Schlesinger gives to racism in the United States in the first volume of his three books on the New Deal, *The Crisis of the Old Order,* published in 1957. That was three years after the Supreme Court outlawed racial segregation in the public schools, two years after the Reverend Martin Luther King, Jr., had led blacks in Montgomery, Alabama, to victory over segregation in the city's bus system. It was at a time when racial discrimination was being talked about all over the country.

> Yet except for a brief discussion of the revival of the Ku Klux Klan during and after World War I, Schlesinger hardly speaks of racism at all. The word "Negro"—the word commonly used to describe black Americans in 1957—does not appear in his index. He expresses his approval of Woodrow Wilson for Wilson's plan for a League of Nations. But as president of the United States, Woodrow Wilson introduced racial segregation into the Federal Civil Service, including the United States Post Office. Schlesinger passes that fact over in silence. It is as if Schlesinger simply did not think matters of race were important enough to mention. Or it may be that he did not want to say anything bad about politicians he regarded as liberal and heroic—including Woodrow Wilson. Therefore, it seems, Schlesinger praises them and remains silent about their vices.
>
> —DICK CURRY

■ **Exercise 37.2** Now that you have had some practice in looking at a text where inferences are made, read carefully the following excerpt from a book by William J. Bennett, who was secretary of education under President Ronald Reagan. Read the text, and write down all the questions you can think of about it. Then look at the questions that we have provided. How do your questions compare with ours?

> A third key education reform is parental choice—full, unfettered choice over which schools their children will attend. In a free market economy, those who produce goods and services are ultimately answerable to the consumer; if quality is shoddy, the consumer will buy someone else's product. It doesn't work that way in public education, though. Even when armed with adequate information about school quality (which they rarely have), parents in most places around the country are not permitted to transfer their children from a bad school to a good one.
>
> In a sharp break with my predecessor, Terrel H. Bell, I immediately voiced strong support for vouchers and tuition tax credits when I became Secretary of Education. "The idea of choice is an idea whose time has come," I said at a news conference announcing our proposal. The proposal urged that the federal Chapter I program (compensatory education for the disadvantaged) be administered through vouchers (averaging $600 each) in order to give students from less fortunate environments the chance to choose private schools, too. As I told the National Catholic Educational Association in 1985: "All parents, regardless of income, should be able to choose places where

> they know their children will learn. And they should be able to choose environments where their own values will be extended instead of lost. It's possible that there are some public schools nobody would choose. They are so bad that they might suddenly find themselves without any students. But I have no idea why we should be interested in protecting schools like that from competition—or any schools from competition. Our worst schools are non-competitive schools, and that's no coincidence."
>
> —WILLIAM J. BENNETT, *The Devaluing of America*

If you are writing about Bennett's remarks for a course in sociology or political science or education, here are some questions you might ask as a prewriting exercise to help you write a paper about his views.

1. Does Bennett approve of our present public school system?
2. What does he think will happen if competition is introduced into the public school system?
3. How many poor children might choose a private school if they received vouchers worth $600 each from the federal government?
4. Will $600 pay the tuition at a private school?
5. How does Bennett's proposal relate to the idea of separation of church and state?
6. Who are the people most likely to oppose or support Bennett's proposals?

All these questions require further research. But by asking them and others, you are reading actively, thinking critically, drawing inferences, and on your way to writing a paper about Bennett's proposals.

37b Approaching Texts Critically

All disciplines require you to write about **texts,** either written texts or the "texts" that you observe in the area you are studying. A motion picture can be a "text"; so can a balance sheet or a dissected frog. A painting, a sculpture, a building, a billboard, a television commercial, an athletic uniform, or even a whole city can also be a text in this definition. All these objects present us with different meanings, some obvious, some obscure. As you write about texts, you discover relationships and learn to ask questions that help you understand not only the subject you are investigating but the nature of truth itself.

When you prepare to write in any college class, first consider your texts. Approach your writing assignment by focusing first on these texts. You may wish to do as many writers do and use a notebook to collect your thoughts.

Summarizing and Interpreting

Begin by writing a one-page interpretive summary of the text. Write on one page a brief statement of what is in the book, the article, the short story, the poem, the letter, or whatever written text you have before you. If the text is a painting, a building, a tool, a specimen, or some other meaningful object, describe it briefly. You will find that the effort to describe physical objects helps you see them better. Then try to say what you think the text means. How does it fit with the other information you have about your subject? How do you think you can use the text as you write about it?

If you are writing about a written text, choose a passage that has a special resonance to you, something that you notice, that seems to speak out. We all read things now and then that make us say suddenly, "That's great!" Or we read sentences that convey some thought that we have been groping for ourselves. These meaningful passages can be the basis of interesting structural and thematic discussions. It is always good to look for sentences that hold the key to the meaning of the entire text.

If your text is an object such as a work of art, describe the part of it that stands out to you. If you are looking at a painting of a human figure in an art history course, you may decide whether the face is individual, realistic, abstract, or idealized. Does the face look serene, troubled, loving, angry, determined? Try to decide why the face makes such an impression on you. Speculate on the painter's intention in portraying the face in that way.

In a geology course, you may be on a field trip to study the effects of glaciation, and your "text" may be a landscape with rounded valleys and rocky mountainsides that show the effects of glaciers scraping along the ridges.

Examining Premises and Contradictions

Every text makes some assumptions and contains some inherent contradictions. Pick out the contradictions you see or infer, and try to decide how important they are. For example, isn't it odd that in Shakespeare's *Henry V* the English victory at Agincourt causes the slaughter of several thousand Frenchmen and yet immediately after it King Henry marries the princess of France, Katherine, who seems to love him? What does that seeming contradiction mean?

Perhaps your text is a document. In a political science class, you might be asked to write about the Constitution. What are its assumptions? What are its contradictions? The Declaration of Independence, for example, had stated that "all men are created equal." How did it happen, then, that the Constitution acknowledged slavery? The Fourteenth Amendment, passed in 1868, affirmed that all persons born or naturalized in the United States are citizens. How did it happen, then, that women were not allowed to vote in federal elections until 1920? Examining assumptions and contradictions can often point you straight at the heart of crucial social problems.

For a visual text, ask similar questions. What purpose is served in nature by having a frog's front legs so small compared to the back legs? Why did Picasso paint figures with the faces flattened out and the eyes in the wrong places? Why do medieval paintings show the birth of the Virgin Mary taking place in great castles when according to the New Testament she and her husband Joseph were poor people? Why do advertisers make beer commercials so funny? Why do advertisements for cigarettes show young, healthy people smoking in scenic outdoor settings?

Uncovering Sources

Where did the writer get his or her information? How does the writer use these sources? In formal academic essays, the sources are clearly stated. It's often fascinating to see how a writer uses primary sources to produce a secondary source.

But how do poets get their information? Where does Toni Morrison get the material for her fiction? Where did the ideas for the Constitution come from? What are the sources a historian uses to write about the assassination of John F. Kennedy?

The same questions can be asked of visual objects. How did a photographer take pictures of starving people in Somalia? Did she stand close up to these dying people, or did she stand off at a distance and shoot with a telephoto lens?

What are the impressions of nature we get from the wildlife photography we see so frequently on television? What is the significance of some of the images of science writing—the web of life, the chain reaction in atomic explosions?

How may a photograph of political figures have been cut to eliminate some of them and emphasize others? Why do photographs of Franklin Roosevelt show him sitting down or focus only on his face above a podium?

What subjects did a nineteenth-century French painter choose? Did he paint inside or outside? Why did he paint the same subjects again and again?

What are the sources for a work of music? Has the composer used folk songs, national anthems, or works of other composers?

Analyzing Images and Implications

Images are easy to identify in literary works. The sun and the moon recur in images throughout Shakespeare's plays. But images recur in all kinds of prose. Why do pronouncements from presidents and other government officials so often use images taken from war? Why do some public figures use images from sports? Why, in traditional English, were ships and countries described as *she?* Why do the British have a *mother country* and the Germans a *fatherland?* Think about images in the texts you study and the language you use and try to understand what they seem to imply.

Visual objects also convey images. Why do churches have steeples? Why are women in sculptures of the nineteenth and twentieth centuries so often presented bare-breasted or even nude, while male statues usually have their private parts covered up? Why do women's fashions often emphasize their bodies, while men's fashions obscure their bodies? But in Henry VIII's day male fashions highlighted male bodies—why? Why are American and British graveyards so often laid out like parks with grassy lawns and great trees, while southern European graveyards are often cramped and treeless, the tombs pushed up against one another, and scarcely ever shaded by trees? Why do presidential candidates now present themselves to be photographed in running shorts or in otherwise informal dress, while presidential candidates of an earlier time were nearly always photographed in suits and ties? Why are Coke bottles subtly shaped like the female body? What does the female body have to do with advertising and sales? What does that say about American culture? A photograph of a Yoruba dancer in Africa shows him wearing a painted mask. What possible meaning can the mask have? Why have Chinese artists been so fascinated with dragons? What can the smears of color in a Mark Rothko painting signify?

Images convey meaning. Notice them and write about them. Sometimes meaning is conveyed not so much by imagery as by implication. Write about meanings that may not be obvious but seem to be implied. What does it mean when so many people who commit crimes now claim that they are the real victims: "I sexually harassed various female employees in my office because I was a victim of alcoholism, and I could not help myself?" What does it mean when a government official uses the passive voice, saying something like this: "Mistakes have been made. Money has been lost. Perhaps crimes have been committed. The matter is under investigation."

Why did athletic teams once commonly name themselves "Redskins," "Indians," "Braves," and "Seminoles"? Why is so much glass used in modern high-rise architecture?

Texts have their mysteries, their secrets, their conundrums that no interpreter can ever quite tease out. The silences of a text are often as provocative as its words. When you write about the things you do not understand, you often discover that others find those passages mysterious. And you may discover their meaning, too.

Making Comparisons

Compare one text to other texts by the same writer, artist, scientist, architect, or thinker. Compare one situation to another. Compare one time period to another. Compare one person to one or more other persons. Compare the work of one scientist to that of another. Compare different paintings by the same artist. Compare the same subject as it was painted by several artists.

Always be sure your comparisons are instructive, that they genuinely add to knowledge about an important subject. A recent article in the *New Yorker* compared Margaret Mitchell's *Gone With the Wind* with the "plantation novels" that came before it and with the racism of movies such as *Birth of a Nation.* The comparison was illuminating.

Don't fall into the error of the writer who once compared the sea and the desert: They are both big, they are inhospitable to human beings, but there is a lot more going on under the surface than you may think. Anyone must ask in reading such a comparison, "So what?" When you do any kind of writing—but especially when you compare one thing with another—ask yourself, "So what?" What does it matter? What value is there to the comparison?

■ **Exercise 37.3** Read ten pages in one of the books or articles you are studying in a course you are taking. Subject those ten pages to the approaches described in this section. Summarize them briefly, pick out a sentence or two that seems especially important, look for assumptions and contradictions, find the sources. Are there any images in the text? If so, what impression do they convey? What is implied in the text? What don't you understand about it? Is it useful to compare this text with another? Now consider how these approaches would help you write about the text for a class writing assignment. Sketch a brief outline for a paper.

✓ CHECKLIST 37.2: WHAT IS A TEXT?

Expand your notion of *text.* Think of texts as literary works but also as documents, films, works of art, musical scores, artifacts, objects, substances, specimens. By expanding your notion of text, you can approach writing assignments in any discipline as you would approach a writing assignment about a work of literature. Follow these steps.

- Write a one-page interpretive summary or description.
- Select passages or elements that attract your attention.
- Examine premises and contradictions.
- Look for sources.
- Analyze images.
- Explore implications.
- Identify what you don't understand and ask why.
- Compare the text with others.

37c Using Evidence

All writing assignments, in every discipline, depend on evidence. Unless you are a well-known expert in the field you are writing about, your bare opinion will not count for anything with your readers. You must provide reasons for them to accept your point of view. Instructors in all your college courses want you to support your opinions with evidence that places you solidly within the **discourse community** of the discipline they teach. You must be able to support your writing with evidence that those who know the discipline will find plausible.

Like texts, evidence need not be limited to literary works or documents. Evidence can be letters you find in a library, observations you make on field trips, experiments, interviews, statistical tables, and public opinion polls. If you dissect a frog in a biology laboratory, you observe the evidence of the frog's body.

Distinguishing Primary and Secondary Sources

Most sources of evidence are classified as *primary* or *secondary*. Be sure you understand the difference.

Primary sources

Primary sources are the fundamental building blocks of research. They provide the most direct information because they are the sources nearest to your subject. Primary sources may come from the era you are writing about. Often they come from the person you write about or the people who knew the person.

For example, if you write about how President Woodrow Wilson installed racial segregation in the U.S. Civil Service, your primary sources would include the Wilson Papers edited in many volumes by Arthur Link and others at Princeton University Press. These papers include almost everything Wilson wrote that has survived, including speeches, letters, memos, articles, lecture notes, and others. Books Wilson published are not included in the Wilson Papers because they are available in libraries. But these books would also be primary sources for Wilson's thought. Primary sources might also include the correspondence and diaries of people who had had conversations with him or who had observed him during his lifetime. Primary sources for this writing assignment would also include government documents.

Primary sources for a study of crime in your town would include police reports, court reports, and statistics compiled by various law-enforcement agencies. They might also include records of conversations with or writing by convicted criminals, by those who have been accused of crime, or by victims of crime, by police officers, and by others somehow directly connected with crime and its causes and effects.

The primary sources for a topic in astronomy would include data gathered by astronomers from their observations of stars and planets or other phenomena of the universe. The primary sources of a topic in medical science might be statistics on the spread of a disease such as AIDS or cancer or the common cold. They might also include direct microscopic examination of agents that cause these diseases or of the bodily tissue that they affect.

Secondary sources

Secondary sources are reports and essays written about primary sources. Many people have written about Woodrow Wilson, segregation, crime, astronomy, and disease. A biography of Wilson is a secondary source. So is an article about Wilson in a historical journal. A history of segregation such as C. Vann Woodward's *The Strange Career of Jim Crow* is a secondary source. An essay on Shakespeare's play *Romeo and Juliet* by G. Blakemore Evans is a secondary source for the play.

Secondary sources in the sciences are somewhat more difficult to define. An essay written by a scientist presenting research methods and results is a primary source. But an essay written by a scientist such as Stephen J. Gould about the research of others is a secondary source—a very fine one. Secondary sources convey important information, and they may include arguments or opinions by scholars and others. An essay you write about a scientific subject is a secondary source.

When you use secondary sources, try to discover how reliable they are. A documentary or film that interprets a historical event is a secondary source, as it compiles primary sources—photographs, original footage—to present a point of view. The celebrated documentary by Ken Burns on the Civil War presents many extraordinary images and texts from that tragic conflict. Millions of Americans saw it. But it contains many errors—

such as Abraham Lincoln's age when he died. Do not assume that facts presented in secondary sources are true. Before you use facts, try to verify them in primary or other secondary sources.

A much different example is the 1991 motion picture *JFK* directed by Oliver Stone. It claims that President John F. Kennedy's assassination in 1963 was the work of a conspiracy of government officials who wanted Kennedy out of the way so they could send more American troops to Vietnam. Stone's film suppresses a great deal of evidence that runs counter to his point of view, and it uses evidence in an imbalanced way to make it support his conspiracy theory. No reputable historian of the assassination has taken the movie seriously. You should not use such questionable sources as authority in your writing.

All secondary sources are to some degree unreliable. All are subject not only to human error but to the frames of mind of those who created them. Read secondary sources actively and critically, and try to find out something about the writers, their use of evidence, their points of view, and their reputation among experts in the field.

37c
curric

Secondary sources that become primary sources

Whether a source is primary or secondary may depend on your topic. For example, if you write an essay on changing ways that American movies have portrayed the family, the primary source for your paper will be the movies themselves. You may use a videocassette recorder to look at dozens of movies and to make your judgments. Your secondary sources will be essays by critics who have written about those movies and by scholars who have studied the family in the United States.

But if your topic is film criticism, what people have written about movies becomes your primary source. Perhaps you are writing about *Casablanca.* Because your topic is not the movie but what writers have said about it, your primary sources are the reviews that were published in 1942, when the movie came out, as well as what later scholars and other writers have said about the film.

Why Primary Sources Are Best

Always use primary sources when you can. They grant your writing an authority that secondary sources alone can seldom bring to your work. Use your library; look at videos and documentaries; listen to oral history tapes; interview people; conduct polls or experiments. Use as many different kinds of primary sources as possible.

By using primary sources, your facts are likely to be accurate and convincing. Your study of primary sources may actually reveal something new or show that a secondary source is wrong. For example, Longfellow's poem on the midnight ride of Paul Revere is a secondary source for the first battle of the American Revolution, but it is so familiar to every American that its recounting of events is often taken as fact. According to the poem Paul Revere was in Boston, knowing that the British were about to send troops to destroy the weapons and supplies the citizens of Massachusetts had been collecting to oppose British rule. Longfellow has Revere telling a friend to post lanterns in the steeple of Old North Church to signal whether the British were going to march out of Boston by land or be transported by boats over the Back Bay. If they were going by land, they would have been taking the road to Worcester. If they were ferried across the Back Bay, they would have been going to Concord. Then Revere has a friend row him across the Charles River where he waits for the lanterns to be hung. So Longfellow has Revere say:

> He said to his friend, "If the British march
> By land or sea from the town tonight,
> Hang a lantern aloft in the belfry arch
> Of the North Church tower as a signal light,—
> One if by land and two, if by sea;
> And I on the opposite shore will be,
> Ready to ride and spread the alarm
> Through every Middlesex village and farm."

But when we look at Revere's own story of what happened that night, we discover that there were other riders across the Charles River and the Back Bay and that Revere had the lanterns posted before he was himself rowed across to ride out through the countryside. Revere also explains that he was captured near Lexington and that, although he got away from the British, he was not able to ride on into Concord to spread the alarm.

You may not be tempted to use poetry as a source for historical fact, but keep in mind that although historians claim no "poetic license," they are neither infallible nor free of bias. Using primary sources allows you to bypass one layer of potential error.

37d Writing for Academic Disciplines

Like reading actively and thinking critically, writing makes connections. Each sentence, each paragraph, each section draws on what you know, what you can prove, what you infer. Each builds on what you have written and looks to what you will write next. As you write, you put facts and thoughts together and establish relations between them. The very act of writing helps you organize knowledge and present it in a form that not only communicates with other readers but also helps you see connections and meaning in what you know.

College writing across the curriculum demands similar techniques and approaches. But the form that writing takes can differ significantly from one discipline to another. This chapter concludes with explanations and examples of some types of writing you may be asked to do in college classes. In other chapters we have already covered formal arguments, interpretive essays, and research papers (see Chapters 1 and 31–34), so here we will look only at reports, summaries or abstracts, lab reports, case studies, and position papers.

Writing a Report

37d curric

The **report** provides information in a readable form and does not emphasize original thinking by the author. A report may be a summary of reading or a description of an experiment done in the laboratory. It may be a description of a painting or of a field trip.

An instructor may assign a report to be sure that you have done the required reading and that you know how to draw the information in these texts together into a coherent whole. If you are on a field trip in an archeology or geology or anthropology course, you may collect information and write it up as a report.

Reports thus use both primary and secondary sources. They may include interpretation, but usually do so by quoting recognized authorities in a particular field. The writer does not express an opinion in his or her own voice; rather, the writer will say something like this:

> The historian David Sacks says that Bristol was the most important English port for commerce with the New World during the seventeenth and eighteenth centuries.

The student writer of the report would not give his or her own answer to the question, "What makes Ross run?" Instead, the student quotes an authority:

> When Ross Perot re-entered the 1992 presidential campaign, the *New York Times* writer Michael Kelly asked, "What makes Ross run?" The answer, Kelly said, was simple. "The point is to gain attention."

A report may examine two sides of a question. In 1992, for example, some nutritionists published their opinion that cow's milk is bad for people because it has many risky side effects for some human beings. Other medical authorities said nonsense, that milk is an excellent food and that the nutritionists opposed to milk were in reality trying to get Americans to become vegetarians. The controversy went on for several weeks in the media, both in magazines and newspapers and on television.

A person writing a report on the argument would try to tell both sides of the story as fairly as possible and would not overtly favor one side or another. Objectivity is one of the primary qualities of the report. When you write a report, you do not express your own opinion. You let readers make up their own minds.

Preparing Summaries or Abstracts

Summaries or **abstracts,** as they are called in some disciplines, are valuable ways of extracting important information. The writer must choose the most important information and ideas and present them in a summary form, often in a single paragraph. As summaries and abstracts are usually based on a single text, they use a primary source or a secondary source, but not both. Some research papers, especially in the sciences, require that an abstract be submitted with the paper.

An abstract of an article is a summary that allows a researcher to decide quickly whether or not to read the whole work. Published abstracts usually appear at the beginning or the end of the articles they summarize. You can use abstracts to file information you collect during your research. Here is a sample abstract.

Abstract

> As an unmarried daughter of the provincial upper bourgeoisie, Catherine des Roches (1542–1587) would have encountered pressure to conform to the expectation that she marry. Instead, she chose a studious life of learning and the companionship of her scholarly mother. Included among her extensive published writings is her paraphrase of the Song of the Valiant Woman from Prov. 31:10–31 in which she justifies her unusual career. This study analyzes how des Roches adapted a popular religious text to validate her choice of life-style, and to critique the humanistic/Reformed imperative that women of her class seek an authoritative identity solely within the home.

Writing Lab Reports

A **lab report** is a report of an experiment you do in a laboratory as part of a science course. The lab report describes the materials you use in the experiment, narrates the process of the experiment from start to finish, and gives its results.

The lab report allows your instructor to see if you have done the experiment correctly. The structure required by the report helps train your mind in the orderly methods and precise observations on which good science depends.

Lab reports are based on observation; the experiment is the primary "text." No secondary sources are consulted. Lab reports differ from one discipline to another. In a chemistry or a biology or a physics course, you may be asked to make an experiment in the laboratory and to report the steps you take and the results you get. You will take careful note of the quantities you use, the times involved in the various steps, and the precise results of the experiment.

Here is an example of a lab report in an introductory physics class.

Lab Report

Physics 221

Object of the Experiment: To demonstrate the transfer of energy in moving bodies that collide with one another.

Materials for the Experiment: A baseball, a basketball, and a flat floor.

The Experiment: I held a basketball four feet from the floor in one hand and with the other hand I held a baseball on top of the basketball so that the baseball rested on the basketball. Quickly removing the hand supporting the basketball, I let the two balls fall together on the floor, the baseball atop the basketball. When the basketball struck the floor, it did not bounce. But the baseball on top of it rebounded about sixteen feet in the air. I repeated this experiment several times, and the results were the same each time.

The principles of physics illustrated by the experiment are the conservation of energy and the conservation of momentum. The law of the conservation of energy holds that although energy can be transferred, it cannot be created or destroyed; the law of the conservation of momentum holds that for every action there is an equal reaction. Energy is defined as the ability of a body to do work; momentum is defined as velocity times mass.

The basketball is approximately three times as heavy as the baseball. Their mass thus adds up to a factor of four. When the basketball and the baseball are held four feet above the floor, they represent potential energy--a potential to do work. When they are dropped together, they fall at the same velocity towards the floor. When the basketball strikes the floor, it rebounds according to the law of the conservation of momentum that for every action there is an equal reaction. In the instant of impact, it is traveling upward while the baseball is traveling downward, and they are traveling at the same rate of speed. The basketball rebounds from the baseball, but since it cannot move through the floor, and since it is the heavier object, all the energy of its fall is transferred back to the baseball by the law of the conservation of momentum. When a heavy object collides with an object one-third its weight, all the energy is transferred to the lighter object. Since the balls were held four feet above the ground, and since the mass of the basketball represents three and the mass of the baseball represents one, there is a total mass of four. Since the basketball cannot move, the total energy of the falling mass, four, is transferred to the baseball, which bounces four times as high as the distance the baseball and the basketball were held off the floor. By the law of the conservation of energy, the potential energy of the baseball at the height of its trajectory thus is the total of the potential energy of baseball and basketball together at the start of the experiment.

In geology or botany courses, a lab report may involve identifying specimens of rocks or plants. In such a report, you will note the various qualities of the specimens and key them to a handbook. Your report will describe the step-by-step progress of your identification.

Writing Case Studies

Case studies are narratives that describe situations or problems that require a decision. Case studies are presented as instructional devices in education and psychology classes, in law schools and business schools, and in workshops for management training.

Case studies used for instruction are usually based on real situations and presented objectively so that students can analyze the case and select a solution they can describe and justify. Students generally write up their solutions in the form of an argument (see 37d).

Here is a sample case study that might be used in an education course.

A Case Study

Disruption in the Classroom

The Complaint

Jack B. is a fifth-grade student in the Sunnybrook School. He is white, middle-class, somewhat small for his age and according to his test scores, of high intelligence, though his grades have always been low. He has been a terror to his teachers since he was in first grade. He often disrupts class by throwing books, picking fights with other children both male and female, and by shouting out "Hail Columbia!" while the teacher is going over lessons with the class.

One day when the teacher had a small bouquet of flowers in a vase on her desk, Jack walked up to sharpen a pencil and snatched up the flowers and poured them on the head of a larger boy who was reading a book on the front row. The boy so abused stood up and struck Jack in the face, bloodying his mouth. The teacher separated them with difficulty, and Jack's mother was called to the school and asked to take him home for the day.

The next day instead of shouting "Hail Columbia" during lessons, Jack shouted, "I'm flower champion of the world." He began tearing pages out of one of his textbooks. Again his mother was called to school and asked to take him home for the day.

These disruptions have gone on for five years.

Personal History

Jack's father and mother were divorced when he was two years old, and his father left the state. Jack has not seen him since, and the father provides no support for him. Jack is an only child. His mother is a successful lawyer, expert in contracts and bankruptcy, with an income that allows her to own a large house with a swimming pool and a live-in maid who takes care of Jack through the day. The mother works long hours and often comes home late at night while Jack is in bed. His mother's parents live on a farm in another state. Jack visits them in the summertime, rides horses, watches his grandfather milk cows, and goes out into the fields when hay is cut. He is happy on the farm and never wants to return to the city at the end of the summer.

Jack has few friends because he is so quarrelsome. He spends a great deal of time alone in his room when he is at home. On weekends he sometimes goes with his mother to movies and likes violent films. He likes to sing, and he collects compact disks and sings along with the vocalists. Sometimes his mother takes him to concerts. He likes all kinds of music but especially loves blues and rock. Even in a classical music concert he sits very still and listens with close attention.

Conceptionalization and Treatment

Jack's problems seem to be related to loneliness. He has never known his father, and he scarcely knows his mother. They spend very little time together. His love for music seems to be an example of

A Case Study, 3

music having power to tame the most savage soul. His outbursts in school seem to get attention--any attention by any way, even if the attention he gets is negative. He has not been around other children very much and has very little sense of how to relate to them.

The counselor requested a series of interviews with Jack's mother and discussed several possibilities for treatment. One was that the mother make an adjustment in her own life to give more time to Jack. She has promised that she will try, but she worries that as a single parent, she has financial responsibilities that must be met, and she is afraid that if she gives up income today, she may not have anything to live on at some later time when some accident might deprive her of a job.

The counselor has made an effort to persuade her to discuss these fears with a skilled therapist; it seems that these fears are unwarranted. Perhaps treatment of the mother's anxiety over money will lead to her willingness to work less and to spend more time with Jack.

The counselor has also persuaded Jack to enroll in a children's chorus after school. He is one of the youngest members, but the chance to sing every day has made him much happier. He has met other children who love to sing, and he has made some friends among them.

Jack has also been enrolled in a Saturday swimming group that helps drain off some of his excess energy. The counselor has found a college student on a nearby campus to be Jack's "big brother." The two of them go to the movies and to other functions together, and Jack seems to have developed a real trust in him.

Prognosis

At this moment the prognosis seems borderline hopeful. Jack's mother has promised she will spend more time with her son, although as yet she has continued to postpone reducing her time at the office. Jack has several friends in the chorus and at the swimming pool where he goes on Saturday, and his "big brother" notes an improvement in Jack's social skills. Jack's teachers report that he seems quieter, happier, less intent on disruption. But he still sometimes breaks out into song or irrelevant talk in class.

Discussion

This seems to be a straightforward case, but one with no easy solution. Jack's loneliness would be solved if he had a brother or sister or if his mother could stay home with him more. His new friends at the pool and in the chorus are not sure about him. One of them says Jack is too "clingy." That is, he wants to be with the friend all the time. The main task is to give Jack a feeling of companionship and belonging, to provide a sense of worth that will allow him to be quiet in the proper places for silence. The counselor at the school is looking carefully at the situation.

Writing Short Position Papers

Short papers that respond to reading assignments or to problems posed in a class are sometimes called **position papers.** This type of writing is often required in college ethics courses. The instructor poses an ethical problem: Suppose a bank robber has taken a hostage during a failed robbery and threatens to shoot the hostage if he is not allowed to go free. Would it be ethical for authorities to lie to the terrorist to rescue the hostage?

Because position papers ask for a response to a situation, they have no primary sources. But the student may elect to buttress his or her response by reference to or quotation from authorities. These would serve as secondary sources.

Position papers are usually no more than two pages long. You must get right to the point, explain the problem, give your solution to it, and stop.

CHAPTER

38

WRITING IN THE WORKPLACE

Whenever you send out a business letter, a job application, a memo, or a résumé, you can expect to be judged on the form of what you have written as well as on the content. If you misspell words, type over errors without first removing them, or leave smudges and stains on what you send out, you can expect readers to conclude that you are sloppy and careless in your work. If you do not use the standard business forms, readers will assume you do not know how to use them. If you do not communicate information in a clear and structured way, readers will think you are disorganized. But if your business correspondence is written clearly, directly, and neatly, your business audience will be inclined to take you seriously.

This chapter examines some of the kinds of writing common in the workplace. In addition to business letters and memos, we present some advice for preparing a résumé and applying for a job.

38a
Following Accepted Standards for a Business Letter

In the block style, the major parts of the letter are set flush with the left margin. Do not indent for paragraphs. Indicate paragraphs by leaving a line of space between the last line of one paragraph and the first line of the next.

Letterhead stationery

If you are writing for a business firm or a professional organization, you will probably use stationery with a printed letterhead at the top. The letterhead will give the name of the firm, its address, and often some sort of advertising slogan. You begin such letters with the date, written a couple of spaces under the letterhead. You may center the date, or you may move it to the right or left side of the page.

Space down three or four lines, and type the name and address of the person to whom you are sending the letter. The address of the recipient of your letter is called the **inside address.** Space down two lines and type the salutation. Skip a line, and begin your first paragraph. Do not indent the paragraph. Unlike student papers submitted to college instructors, business letters are single spaced. At the end of the paragraph, skip another line and begin the next paragraph.

When you have finished the letter, double space and type the complimentary close, again starting flush with the left margin. Space down four lines and type your name. If you have a title, write it just under your typed name. Sign your name with a pen in the space between the complimentary close and your typed name.

If you enclose anything with the letter, space down another two lines and write "Enclosure" or "Enclosures" flush with the left margin.

A sample business letter on letterhead stationery, typed in the block format form, is shown on page 597.

Stationery without a letterhead

If you write to a business or to an institution as an individual, not as a representative of an organization, type your letter on unlined, sturdy bond paper, $8\frac{1}{2} \times 11$ inches. Type your own address at the top of the page, starting in the center. Put the date under your address. Then follow the instructions given above for using letterhead stationery.

Modified Block Style

In the block format, every line of the letter except the heading begins flush with the left margin. This format is common in business writing because it is efficient. Word processing programs on computers can be set up to produce the block format automatically, and the writer can move swiftly through the letter.

Some businesses prefer the modified block format. The only difference here is that the complimentary close is centered and the first letter of the typed name of the letter writer is placed four lines directly under the first letter of the typed complimentary close.

Address and Salutation

For the inside address, include the title of the addressee—the person to whom you are writing. The title may appear immediately after the name, or it can be put beneath the name.

International Automobile

3821 Oceanside Drive • Bancroft, Idaho 83217 • Telephone: 208-489-0199

Dealers in Antique Car Replacement Parts

July 29, 1994

Ms. Lenore P. Raven, President
Nevermore Antique Car Restorations, Inc.
35 Oak Street
Belmont, Massachusetts 02178

Dear Ms. Raven:

Thank you for your letter of July 14 inquiring about parts for the standard six-cylinder 1948 Chevrolet Fleetmaster engine. I am happy to tell you that we do carry pistons, rods, and crankshafts for that engine. I am enclosing a price list for the various parts. Shipping charges are included in the prices. We ship by United Parcel Service on the day orders are received. We can arrange overnight delivery at an additional charge.

We accept payment by Visa, MasterCard, or American Express, or money order or certified check.

Thank you for thinking of International Automobile.

Yours sincerely,

Roderick Usher

Roderick Usher
President and General Manager

Enclosure

28 Horseshoe Lane
Fair Hills, New York 10020
March 15, 1994

Mr. Basil Carmine
Ajax Industrial Chemicals
3939 Gentilly Boulevard
New Orleans, Louisiana 70126

Dear Mr. Carmine:

Last week I bought a fifty gallon drum of your industrial strength floor cleanser for my automotive repair business. According to your advertisement in the February Mechanic's Companion, your cleanser, Wipe Out, is guaranteed to remove all oil and grease from garage floors.

I carefully followed your directions in applying the cleanser. I spread the powder over the grease and oil stains on the floor of my establishment and hosed down the powder with water. You can imagine my astonishment when your cleanser began to boil violently and to give off thick red fumes that forced us to evacuate the building.

When we were finally able to reenter the building the next day, we discovered that Wipe Out had eaten large holes in the concrete floor underneath the stains.

I have discussed the situation with my lawyer, Rosalyn East, of East, Burns, and Tavern, and she has advised me to ask you to pay for repairs. Several reputable contractors are preparing estimates, which I shall forward to you.

If you are unwilling to pay for the repairs, we shall have no recourse but to sue you and your firm under state and federal laws regulating interstate commerce and false and misleading advertising. I hope that a lawsuit will not be necessary. And I look forward to your reply.

Yours sincerely,

Glenda Ruby

Glenda Ruby
President, Southside Garage, Inc.

Ms. Glenda Ruby
President, Southside Garage, Inc.
28 Horseshoe Lane
Fair Hills, New York 10020
or
Ms. Glenda Ruby, President
Southside Garage, Inc.

Never abbreviate titles. Do not write:

Ms. Glenda Ruby, Pres.

Mr. Sylvan Glade, Asst. Mgr.

Instead, write:

Ms. Glenda Ruby, President

Mr. Sylvan Glade, Assistant Manager

Some titles ordinarily are placed before the name in the inside address, and some of these titles can be abbreviated:

Dr. Ishmael Romer
Dean Ivy Wallace
Bishop Bernard Law
The Rev. Hiram Welch
Captain Jennifer Jones
Sister Mary Annunciata

The salutation, always followed by a colon in a business letter, greets the person who receives the letter. It is placed flush with the left margin, below the inside address and separated from the inside address by a double space.

Use the addressee's last name in the salutation. Do not address the person by his or her first name unless you are very good friends. Never address by first name a person you have not met or one you know only slightly.

Always say "Dear ______." Do not say "Hi," "Hi there," "Greetings," or anything else that attempts to be cute. The conventions of business writing require the traditional salutation.

Use *Messrs.* (the abbreviated plural of the French *Monsieur*) when you address more than one man. When the addressees are two or more women, use *Mmes.* (the abbreviation of *Mesdames*).

Here are some sample salutations acceptable to most people.

Dear Ms. Ruby:
Dear Dr. Farnsworth:
Dear Messrs. Doolittle and Kreisburg:
Dear Mmes. Cohen and Grey:
Dear Miss Williams:

To avoid unnecessary reference to marital status, many writers favor *Ms.* as a title for women (see 29d). This usage has won wide acceptance, and many women prefer it. However, *Miss* and *Mrs.* are still acceptable, and you should use one of these forms of address if you know that the person you are addressing prefers it. Note whether she has indicated any preference by the way she has typed her name on any letter she has written to you or on the envelope. If she has supplied no clue, use *Ms.*

In writing to business organizations or to someone whose name you do not know, use one of the following kinds of salutation.

Dear Registrar:
Dear American Express:
Dear Sir or Madam:
Dear Sir:
Dear Madam:
Gentlemen:
Mesdames:
Dear Colleagues:
To whom it may concern:

A good dictionary will provide correct forms of addresses and salutations in the special cases of elected government officials, judges and justices, religious leaders, military personnel, and others.

The Body of the Letter

Get to the point quickly, and let your reader know what you want. Business letters are like college papers: they should have a thesis. You write a letter to get the recipient to do something or to believe something. You do not write a business letter to ramble on about all sorts of things that may be on your mind. You may write a business letter to apply for a job, to report on something you have done, to request information, to complain, to apologize, to ask advice, to give information, to develop a plan, or for many other reasons. You should make your purpose clear within the first two sentences of your letter.

Dear Mr. Armstrong:

As president of the Environmental Coalition, I am sending you this letter by certified mail to inform you that we are suing you in federal court to shut down your factory on the Hiwassee River. I have written you several times on this matter, but you have not responded. In the meantime, the pollutants from your factory continue to kill fish by the thousands. So we have no recourse but to sue, and we have taken the first steps to get our suit before the court. You will be hearing from the court and from our lawyers shortly.

Dear Dr. Farnsworth:

I would like to apply for the job of dental hygienist that you have advertised in today's *Morning Bugle.* I worked as a hygienist for ten years in Dallas, Texas, before my wife was transferred here by her business. I am enclosing my résumé, and I would welcome an opportunity to talk with you about the position.

Business people do not have time to study a letter in search of the writer's meaning. They want to know right away what the writer wants of them. You should express that purpose as quickly and as directly as possible. Practice getting to the point as quickly as you can.

Style and tone

Many people think that a good business letter must be bland and impersonal or that the writer must use complicated language to impress the recipient. Less frequently, they think they must use slang or other informal language to attract attention. In fact, a business letter should be simple and direct. It should be natural and courteous, neither too formal nor too informal. It should not contain slang or jargon. Study these examples.

Unnatural: I want to take this opportunity to inform you of the important fact that I am most seriously interested in the announcement of the accounting job that you advertised last week.

Too informal: The accounting job you guys are offering in the latest *Daily Snort* sounds like a real grabber. Count me in. I look forward to pressing the flesh and to throwing all the facts on the table.

Natural: I want to apply for the accounting job you announced in today's *Times-Standard.*

Unnecessarily complex: In your recent communication dated March 16, you asked us to enumerate, categorize, and prioritize the need-based scholarship applicants eligible for financial aid under Title 6 of the Federal Grants Act of 1987. We are able to report that we have now enumerated, categorized, and prioritized the need-based scholarship applicants eligible for financial aid.

Simple and direct: In your letter of March 16, you asked us to count the students who need financial aid, to classify them according to the sort of help they need, and to decide which of them should have preference. Here are our findings.

Length

Whenever possible, keep a business letter to one page. Longer letters burden the people who must read them. They often obscure your meaning. Since business letters almost always ask for some action on the part of the recipient, you may feel that you have to argue your case at length. Sometimes you do indeed have to write a longer letter. But it is usually much better to make your request clearly, briefly give reasons for your request, and close as quickly as possible. Readers of business letters appreciate brevity and clarity.

Final paragraphs

Having stated or explained your business, say clearly what you want the recipient to do next. You may be ordering merchandise; you may be asking for information; you may be requesting agreement; you may be asking for a proposal; you may be asking how a complaint will be met; you may be asking for a response to a report. Most business letters expect a response, and you should spell out clearly what sort of response you expect. Do you want the person to telephone you? Do you want to meet with the person? Do you want a report? Do you want a replacement for faulty merchandise?

Now and then you may not need a response to the letter. You may, for example, acknowledge receipt of a report and thank the writer for her hard work in putting together information you have requested. You do not expect the recipient to respond to a thank-you note.

You should always maintain a courteous and businesslike tone in your letters, but avoid clichés. Don't end your letters with a worn-out expression of gratitude such as "Thank you for your time," "Thank you for your consideration of this request," or "I await the courtesy of a reply." If you write in a friendly tone, you can close the letter immediately after you have stated your business and no one will accuse you of discourtesy. If you want to thank your recipient for something specific, you can do that. The writer of the preceding letter closed with a friendly expression of expectation. You can often close with a pleasant word about future relations. But avoid formula closings.

DUNHAM ENGINEERING

31 Pine Crest Industrial Park
Atlanta, Georgia 30375

November 21, 1994

Mr. Michael Elia, President
Rocky Mountain Scenic Railroad, Inc.
1313 Grand View Street
Boulder, Colorado 80832

Dear Mr. Elia:

I want to arrange a day-long scenic excursion on your railroad for approximately a thousand people on Saturday, May 6, 1995. At that time, the National Association of Subdivision Engineers will be having its annual convention in Denver. We are sure to have at least a thousand people who would enjoy such a trip. We would like to leave around 9:00 A.M. and to return to Boulder around 2:30 or 3:00 P.M. We would like to charter our own train, and we would like to stop for a picnic lunch in the middle of the day.

Please let me know if your line is available for such a trip, and, if it is, quote me your group rates. Please tell me also if you are able to provide the lunch or if we should arrange to have it catered by another firm.

Many people have spoken to me of the beauty of your rail route and the courtesy of your service. I look forward to an enjoyable day on your line.

Yours sincerely,

David Dunham

David Dunham
President

✓ CHECKLIST 38.1: WRITING A BUSINESS LETTER

Business correspondence is to the point. Be sure business letters include the following:

- Return address
- Date
- Recipient's address
- Salutation
- Body
  - In the first sentence, give the purpose of the letter.
  - Tell the recipient what you want.
  - Give brief reasons for what you want.
  - Tell what the recipient can do next.
  - Close the letter.
- Complimentary close
- Signature and typed name

Closing and Signing the Letter

Letters usually close with one of the endings below. A capital letter always starts the first word of the complimentary close; a comma always follows the complimentary close.

Yours truly,	Sincerely,
Very truly yours,	Sincerely yours,
Yours very truly,	Yours sincerely,
Cordially,	Cordially yours,
Respectfully,	Respectfully yours,
Regards,	Best regards,

The signature appears in a four-line space between the complimentary close and the typed name of the writer. Most writers avoid adding a professional title (such as attorney-at-law) or a degree (such as Ph.D.) after their typed name. However, to indicate their official capacity, writers who have a business title often use it.

Sincerely yours,	Very truly yours,
Carolyn Garfield Marketing Manager	W. Prescott Blast Dean of the Faculty

Addressing the Envelope

Address the envelope to include all essential information required for postal delivery. The address centered on the envelope is the same as the inside address; the return address in the upper left of the envelope includes the sender's name and address. Write out all words according to standard practice (see 29c), although you may elect to use either conventional or postal abbreviations for the names of states.

```
Julie Holden
3200 Lake View Drive
State College, PA 16801

                    Ms. Delores Smith
                    Personnel Manager
                    Farm Journal, Inc.
                    230 West Washington Square
                    Philadelphia, PA 19105
```

Fold $8\frac{1}{2} \times 11$ stationery in thirds so that it fits a standard $4 \times 9\frac{1}{2}$ envelope. Fold the bottom third up, then the top third down, leaving about a quarter inch between the top edge of the paper and the bottom fold so that your recipient can open the letter easily. For smaller business envelopes, fold standard paper in half from the bottom up; then fold the paper in thirds, left side first, right side over left.

■ **Exercise 38.1** Write a letter to a local business requesting a catalog or other information you'd like to have. Use the Yellow Pages of your phone book or your school newspaper as a source of names and addresses. Pay close attention to correct format of the letter and the envelope.

38b
Writing a Memo

Modern business runs on **memos**—memorandums or short communications exchanged within an office or between offices in the same firm. As the name indicates, *memo* usually refers to something that should be remembered by people on the staff. Most conferences in a well-run business result in a memo that records what was decided. Supervisors in such businesses use memos to make announcements. Memos are usually kept on file. They are often used to trace the development of policy.

A good memo has many of the qualities of the business letter. But since the memo usually goes out to several people—perhaps hundreds of people—at once, it usually lacks some of the personal conventions of letters.

Formatting a Memo

Memos are intended for quick reading. The first four lines show the date and a summary of essential information introduced by key words:

To:

From:

Subject:

A memo begins with a date in the upper right corner of the page. But instead of the salutation "Dear Ms. Adams," the memo begins with a general address, usually preceded by *To* followed by a colon. The recipients are assumed to be within the organization, so the memo does not include an inside address other than the classification of the people who are to receive the memo.

The memo does not have a complimentary close, and it usually does not have a signature. Instead, the name of the writer of the memo appears after *From* followed by a colon. The writer's initials are then written by hand next to the name. The writer's title may or may not appear on the memo.

A good memo announces the subject on a third line after the word *Subject* followed by a colon. See sample standard headings (page 607).

March 21, 1993

To: All the staff
From: RCM RCM
Subject: Midterm grades

November 28, 1992

To: All coaches
From: Jack Booster, president of the
university JB
Subject: The upcoming NCAA investigation
of our athletic program

January 7, 1993

To: Department supervisors
From: Michele Johnson, Affirmative Action
Officer MJ
Subject: Affirmative Action guidelines

July 29, 1994

To: All members of the staff
From: LB LB
Subject: Dental care

We have made arrangements with the North Slope Community Health Group for complete dental care for employees of the company and their families. Your cost will be a $5.00 monthly fee that will be added to the medical insurance deduction in your paycheck. The company will defray all other costs for each employee enrolled in the dental plan.

The enclosed brochure from the North Slope Community Health Group will answer many of your questions about the plan. If you have further questions, please call Dr. Jerry Pullem at North Slope at 524-7529.

You must enroll in the plan by September 30. If you wish to enroll, please sign the enclosed form and return it to me. Your payroll deduction will begin with your October paycheck.

Composing the Body of a Memo

Like a good business letter, a good memo should be brief and to the point. It should treat only one subject. It should be clear. If some response is required, the expected response should be spelled out. The memo does not have a complimentary close or a signature at the bottom. Study the sample memo on page 607.

38c
Applying for a Job

Some of the most important writing you may ever do is applying for a job. Be sure your résumé and cover letter reflect you, and all you have learned in your writing course, at your best.

Preparing a Résumé

A standard **résumé** presents an overview of your education, your work experience, your interests, and other pertinent personal data. Formats for résumés vary. Some are in the form of paragraphs, giving full information about past experience relevant to the job for which the writer is applying. Others are brief summaries. All good résumés include the information potential employers need to know about their workers.

As the sample shows, you should type your résumé and lay it out attractively. Be sure entries are parallel and that all spacing and capitalization are consistent. Be sure to proofread your résumé carefully, and have someone else proofread it for you, too. A mistake in a résumé can cost you an interview—or a job. Because a brief résumé helps a prospective employer evaluate your record quickly, you should try to keep your presentation to a single page. Do not inflate your résumé with unnecessary details in an effort to make it seem more impressive than it really is. If you are just starting a career, no one will expect you to be rich in experience and skills.

- **Personal data.** Give your name, current address, home address (if it is different from your current address), zip code, and telephone number with the area code. Mention any special abilities, such as fluency with languages other than English or experience in using business machines or computers. Mention any travels that might be relevant to the job.

- **Career objective.** Express your interest in a specific kind of position by stating your immediate and perhaps also your long-range objectives realistically.
- **Education.** List the schools you attended, beginning with high school. Start with your most recent school and work backward. Give your dates of attendance and the degrees you received. Include any honors or awards you won, your major, and any courses you think qualify you especially for the job you are seeking.
- **Work experience.** List the jobs you have held, the dates of your employment, the names of your supervisors, and a brief description of your duties. Again, start with the most recent job and work backward.
- **Special interests.** To reveal details about yourself as an individual, you may wish to include information about hobbies, membership in clubs and organizations, volunteer work, or any special talents you have. Be sure to mention interests that might be useful in the job you are applying for. If you have won any awards, you might want to mention them, too.
- **References.** Give the names, addresses, and telephone numbers of people who will attest to your character and skill as a student and a worker. Be sure to ask permission from anyone you list as a reference, and be sure to select people who know you well and will write or speak strongly in your behalf. People you use as references should write directly to the prospective employer, or they may expect to receive a phone call from the prospective employer. You may send copies of letters that you have received in the past, commending you for your work, and sometimes you may send letters of recommendation that you have solicited from various people. But some employers tend to disregard such letters, preferring instead those written directly to the employer in your behalf.

Preparing a Cover Letter

When you send your résumé to a prospective employer, enclose a letter that catches attention by its careful statement of your qualifications. Among the scores of responses a personnel director receives after a job is advertised, your letter must stand out if you are to receive the consideration you want. Yet your letter must not violate the conventions of courtesy and restraint that have developed in business correspondence over the centuries. You are best served if you present your strongest qualifications clearly, briefly, and carefully.

Julie Holden

Current address
8200 Beaver Avenue
State College, PA 16801
Tel.: (814) 998-0004

Home address
R.D. 2, Box 9
Manheim, PA 17545
Tel.: (717) 777-7888

Career objective
A position of responsibility on the editorial staff of a magazine or publishing firm.

Education
1989-1993
The Pennsylvania State University, B.A. in English (June 1993).
Grade point average: 3.25 of 4.0. Honors: Dean's List.
Major courses: Article Writing, News Reporting, Magazine Journalism, Style Problems, Sociology, Rural Community Services.

1986-1989
Central High School, Manheim, Pennsylvania

Experience
Summers of 1991 and 1992
Clerical assistant at Central High School under the supervision of Mr. Horace K. Williams, Manheim, Pennsylvania. Duties included microfilming, typing, and filing.

Summers of 1989 and 1990
Farmhand on the Schwarzmuller Dairy Farm under the supervision of Mr. Robert Wilkes, Manheim, Pennsylvania. Duties included field work (operating tractors and implements) and barn work (feeding and cleaning).

Special interests
Painting, photography, gardening, macramé.

References
Professor Carolyn Eckhardt
Department of English
The Pennsylvania State University
University Park, PA 16802
Phone: (814) 987-2268

Mr. Horace K. Williams
Guidance Counselor
Central High School
Manheim, PA 17545
Phone: (717) 998-8768

Route 2, Box 9
Manheim, Pennsylvania 17545
February 22, 1994

Ms. Delores Smith
Personnel Manager
Farm Journal, Inc.
230 West Washington Square
Philadelphia, Pennsylvania 19105

Dear Ms. Smith:

I would like very much to become an editorial assistant at Farm Journal. My four years of education at the Pennsylvania State University and my twenty years' experience as the daughter of a farming couple have given me the knowledge and background necessary to do this job.

Like many of your readers, I was born and raised on a farm. I have planted corn, mowed hay, and delivered calves. I share with your readers an appreciation of farm life and an understanding of the independent farmer's problems.

As you will see from my résumé, I am graduating from the university in June with a bachelor of arts degree and a double major in English and sociology. In my classes I have practiced and refined my knowledge of writing and editing and have studied the problems of producing magazines. Now I would like to apply what I have learned.

I will be in Philadelphia the week of March 21. If we could arrange for an interview on the morning of March 23, I would be most grateful. I will call you before that day to see if it is convenient or to see if we can make an appointment at another time.

I look forward very much to meeting you.

Sincerely,

Julie Holden

Julie Holden

Encl.

Because a job-application letter is usually accompanied by a full résumé, you do not need to list educational background, work experience, and other interests. Instead, use the letter to highlight the special talents you bring to the position. Make your letter specific. Don't be satisfied with saying, "I have had much valuable experience that will help me do this job."

The letter reproduced on page 611 is forceful and concise. Note that each paragraph serves a specific function. The first states the writer's purpose in sending the letter. The second describes how the writer's background would help her do the job well. The third paragraph explains how the writer's education has prepared her for this job. The last paragraph asks for an interview. Everything is to the point.

■ **Exercise 38.2** Prepare a résumé that highlights your education and job experience as well as other key information shown in the sample on page 610 and the Checklist below.

✓ CHECKLIST 38.2: PREPARING A RÉSUMÉ

Your résumé is an important document you will have throughout your working life. You will need a résumé for applying for student work-study programs, part-time jobs, summer jobs, and your first job upon graduation. Here are some things to include and attend to.

A résumé should include:

- personal data
- career objective
- education
- work experience
- special interests
- references

Be sure your résumé is:

- attractively laid out
- consistent in format and wording
- error free

CHAPTER

39

IMPROVING STUDY TECHNIQUES

Develop your study skills by applying techniques for improving your comprehension and retention of what you read. Learn to take useful notes when you read and when you listen to lectures. Studying is an active, continual process that requires planning, repetition, and *writing* to help you remember and use information.

39a Planning

Develop a realistic weekly plan for studying. Consider all the demands on your time—eating, sleeping, attending classes, doing homework, exercising, socializing, commuting, watching television—and set aside time for studying. Some students make a weekly chart of their activities. If you do block in regular activities and study time on a calendar, leave a number of free periods so that you have time for relaxing and for making adjustments. When exams or special projects come up, for example, you'll need blocks of time over several days, even weeks, to complete work on time. Try to avoid cramming for tests, because the stress it produces prevents deep learning and memory. If you must cram, try to outline the major points you need to cover and concentrate on learning the central ideas and facts.

39b Reading Actively

You can improve your ability to learn and retain material by approaching your reading with a clear plan and by taking various kinds of notes.

Surveying

Scanning the text for information without reading every word gives you an outline of the material so that you can focus on what you are about to read. When you survey a book, look for chapter titles and subtitles, headings and subheadings, charts, graphs, illustrations, and words in boldface or italics. Skim the opening and closing paragraphs of a chapter or of chapter sections. Surveying of this kind can give you the sense of a book very quickly.

Questioning

Once you have looked through the material, jot down some questions about it. Writing will help make things stick in your mind, and your written questions will provide a good short review. It is always better to write your own questions, but if there are questions at the end of a chapter, let them guide your reading.

Keeping questions in mind as you read will get you actively involved in the material at hand. Your reading now has a purpose: you are trying to find answers to your questions.

Summarizing

Learn how to make summaries. When you read, try to summarize every paragraph by composing a simple, short sentence. Put the author's thoughts into your own words. Don't try to duplicate the style of the book or article you are reading. Putting somebody else's ideas into your own words is a good way of making sure you truly know those ideas.

Underlining has several disadvantages. Obviously, you cannot underline in a library book. If you underline material, you will have to own the book. Underlining is also a passive approach. When students come back to passages they have underlined, they often cannot remember why they underlined them in the first place. Most people underline too much, and the result is boring and confusing. Underlining is never as effective as writing a short summary sentence for each paragraph or each page. A summary sentence ensures that you will reconsider the thoughts in the book, translate them into your own words, and put them on paper.

Comparing

You can also help retain information by looking for the same topic or closely related information in another source. Your instructor may require you to buy one or more books for the course, and you should read these books and make notes about them. But it is also an excellent idea to look up the topics in some of the many reference books available in the library. Try an encyclopedia, various dictionaries, and other reference books your librarian can help you find. (Many of these reference books are listed in 31c of this handbook.)

When you read the same information presented in slightly different ways, you will find that each source has some detail the others do not have. Variety in your learning can be a wonderful help in remembering. If you have taken careful notes on the various things you have read, you should remember more easily.

Analyzing

Another required skill is the ability to analyze, to tell what things mean, to discover how they fit with other things you know. Here again, writing will help you to study. Many instructors advise students to keep a notebook in which they jot down their notes from sources on one page and their thoughts about those notes on a facing page. If you ask yourself questions about the things you put down, you will develop your analytical powers. Pay attention to your own feelings. Do you like a book? Make yourself set down reasons why you like it. Do you dislike a book? Again, write down the reasons for your preference. Whether you feel interested, bored, repelled, or excited, ask yourself what there is in the book (or movie or whatever else you may be studying) that arouses such feelings. Then write your reasons down. You do not have to like a work of literature or art or history merely because someone else does. But you should be able to justify your opinions to others and to yourself. As you get into the habit of writing down these justifications, you will find your analytical ability steadily improving.

Expanding Your Vocabulary

With the aid of a dictionary, keep a written record of new words; write them on index cards or in a notebook. Include correct spelling, pronunciation clues, clear definitions that you write yourself, and a phrase or a sentence using the word properly. Arrange the words in related groups to help yourself study (business words, economics words, psychology words, literature words, and so on). Incorporate any new words into your speaking and writing vocabulary. Here is an example:

```
puerile (PYOO ar il)
juvenile in a bad sense. People who are puerile are not just
children; they are childish. He was puerile when he refused to
let her name appear before his on the program for the play.
```

Reviewing

Immediately after you finish reading, and at convenient intervals thereafter, look over the questions, notes, summaries, or outlines you have created from your reading. Don't try to read every word of the original material in the book or article every time you review. Skim over it. You will learn better from many rapid readings than from one or two slow readings. Skimming will help you get the shape of the material in your mind. As you study your own notes, you will recall many of the supporting details.

Use your written work to help you complete your assignments. It often helps if you close the book, put away your notes, and try to jot down from memory a rough outline of what you are studying. The more ways you can write about material you are learning, the more effectively you will learn it.

39c Taking Notes

Taking good notes requires practice. Some students tape-record lectures so they can listen again to what the instructor has said. But even if you have a tape recorder and the instructor is willing to be recorded, good notes can still help you understand and remember the lecture.

Never try to write down everything you hear in the lecture as it is going on. Unless you know shorthand, you cannot write as fast as a person speaks, and while you are struggling to get a sentence down, the lecturer will have gone on to another point. In your haste, you may garble both what has been said and what is being said.

Your best bet is to write down words, phrases, and short sentences. Use these jottings to stimulate your memory later on. As soon as possible after the lecture is over, take your notes to a quiet place and try to write down as much of the lecture as you can remember. If you do this regularly, you probably will find yourself remembering more and more of each lecture.

Once you have written up your notes, compare what you have with the notes taken by another member of the class. If four or five of you get together to share your notes, you will each acquire an amazingly complete set, and in your discussions of gaps and confusions, you will further your learning.

Don't try to sit for hours without a break. Get up every forty-five minutes or so and walk around the room and stretch. Then sit back down quickly and go to work again. Taking a break will relax your body and perhaps stimulate your mind to some new thought that you can use when you start studying again.

For the sake of good order, don't keep your notes for all of your courses in one notebook. You can keep track of your notes much more easily by using a separate notebook for each course. At graduation, you will have an orderly record of your college education.

✔ CHECKLIST 39.1: IMPROVING STUDY TECHNIQUES

Consider these techniques to help you learn and retain what you have learned.

- Plan a reasonable study schedule; don't get caught having to cram.
- Survey each text chapter before you read it.
- Take advantage of chapter outlines and summaries, time lines, key words, discussion questions, and other study devices your textbooks may provide.
- Make up questions so that you can read with a purpose.
- Summarize rather than underline.
- Consult a variety of sources.
- Analyze what you read.
- Look up and learn unfamiliar words.
- Use a separate notebook for each course.
- Take notes in class quickly; then rewrite and summarize your notes as soon after class as possible.
- Review your notes and reading assignments.
- Compare your notes with classmates; set up a study group for sharing notes and discussing issues as well as anticipating assignments and test questions.

CHAPTER 40

WRITING AN ESSAY EXAM

Most college courses require students to write a midterm and a final examination and perhaps other exams as well. The pressure of time during an examination makes this kind of writing especially challenging, but essay examinations call for the same skills demanded by other kinds of writing. Here are some points to note.

40a Preparing for the Exam

In some ways, preparing for an essay exam is like preparing for any writing assignment. Use the prewriting techniques described in Chapter 1 as you think about the material you will be tested on. Jot down ideas, ask the journalist's questions, draw a subject tree to tie facts and ideas together.

Reviewing Notes

If you have taken adequate notes on lectures and assigned readings (Chapter 39), preparing for the exam should not be overwhelming. Read your text summaries, the notes you have written in the margins of your text, and in your course notes. Underline key words and phrases. Develop outlines. Your goal should be to highlight the major concepts and details the exam is likely to cover.

Anticipating Questions

Imagine that you are the instructor, and write out the questions that you would give. Merely writing questions down helps you organize your mind to answer them. You will often be surprised at how close you can come to the questions that appear on the examination.

40b
Taking the Exam

Be sure to give yourself every advantage in taking an essay exam—or any exam for that matter. Arrive early; don't put yourself under extra pressure by being late. Bring all the supplies you will need—pens, pencils, erasers, paper, bluebooks.

Reading the Questions

When the examination is before you, read it through carefully and spend a minute or two thinking about it. You may find that a later question reminds you of information that is useful for an earlier question. Be sure you understand exactly what each question is asking you to do. Most essay questions contain a cue word that indicates exactly what you are supposed to do: *describe, identify, compare, contrast, explain, analyze,* and so on. A great many students go wrong on exams because they read the questions hastily and misunderstand them, not responding to the cues in the question.

Outlining Responses

Next, jot down a few words to help guide your answer. They will provide a brief outline for you to use in developing your answer, and they will nearly always stimulate your mind to think more clearly about the question. The two or three minutes you spend reading the question and writing down words to help you answer it will save you much time in the actual writing. Suppose you have a question such as this.

> What were the major causes of World War I? Which of these causes do you think was most important in the conflict that broke out in the summer of 1914? Justify your opinion.

Look at the question carefully: it is really *two* questions. The first one requires you to name several causes of World War I. The second requires you to make a choice among the causes you have named, and then to give reasons for your answer.

Once you understand the question, you are ready to start jotting down words and phrases to help form your answer. You begin by asking yourself who took part in the war as it developed in the summer of 1914—information you should remember readily if you have taken careful notes from your lectures and your reading. You remember that Germany and Austria-Hungary stood on one side and that against those two powers stood Serbia, Russia, Belgium, France, and Great Britain. Then you write phrases like these:

Russia vs. Austria-Hungary in the Balkans/Sarajevo
Germany vs. France and England; Alsace-Lorraine/naval race
Germany vs. Russia; Germans fear Russians; Schlieffer Plan
Neutral Belgium in the way of German army
Most important cause: German fear of Russia

Beginning to Write

With these notes before you, you can begin to write. Although you should not waste time restating the essay question in a formulaic manner, often you can use part of the language provided in the question to begin your answer. A well-constructed essay question is often packed with information, and you can borrow from the question as you frame your response. Look at some typical essay questions and the opening sentences students wrote on their examinations.

Course	Question	Response
Marketing	Explain the general selling process that many salespeople use as they sell a product.	Although the selling process varies from person to person, most salespeople follow a general and definable process as they sell products.
Biology	Give a biological definition of aging, and show how the rates of aging vary among animal species.	Any biological definition of aging must begin with a consideration of genetics, which provides the basis of maximum life expectancies among animal species.

Economics	Explain how Keynesian economists attempt to achieve a stable economy through monetary policy.	The goal of monetary policy is economic stability, and Keynesians see monetary policy as moving through a complicated system of causes and effects.
Psychology	Identify the hierarchy (ladder) of needs that, according to Maslow, lead to self-actualization, and explain the elements in the hierarchy.	Abraham Maslow identified a hierarchy of five general needs leading to self-actualization.
Philosophy	Define metaphysics, and explain how Bergson took a new look at the concept handed down from Aristotle.	From classical Greece onward, human beings have sought knowledge for its own sake: "All men by nature desire to know," writes Aristotle in his *Metaphysics.* But Henri Bergson, a twentieth-century philosopher, looked at the concept anew and pointed out that we are using the wrong methods to discover answers to a key metaphysical question: What is there? or What is real?

Justifying Opinions with Concrete Details

Many responses to essay questions are so vague and general that instructors wonder whether the students who wrote them ever came to class. A good answer mentions names, dates, facts, and specific details. A good answer also carries an argument and makes a point—just as any other good piece of writing does. Your first paragraph, even your first sentence, should provide a clear statement of your thesis. Lay out the structure of your essay in the introduction. The reader of an essay exam wants to know immediately what you intend to prove and how you intend to prove it.

A good answer to the question about World War I might read something like this.

> In the summer of 1914, Europe was an arena of peoples who hated each other. The Germans hated the English because the English had a great empire and they themselves had little. The English hated the Germans because, since 1896, the Germans had been building a huge navy under the goading of the German Kaiser, Wilhelm II. The British believed that this German navy was to be used against them, and when the Kaiser sided with Britain's enemies in the Boer War, the British people saw their darkest suspicions confirmed.
>
> The French hated the Germans because the Germans had annexed the French territories of Alsace and Lorraine after the Franco-Prussian War of 1870-1871; the French wanted their land back and spoke continually of "revenge." The Germans heard that talk about revenge and hated the French for not adjusting to the new reality of Europe, which in the German view meant German domination of the continent.

The writer establishes her thesis in the first sentence. She proposes the theory that national hatreds were a major cause of World War I by giving specific reasons for each country's hatred of another country, including appropriate names and dates.

Reviewing and Improving Your Answer

Once you have written your response, read it over. Though you cannot rewrite it, you can often improve it by making minor corrections and additions. You were probably writing fast. If you left words out or misspelled them, make corrections now.

As you review, look especially for ways to strengthen general statements by making them more specific. Simply adding a name, a date, or a factual detail may transform a vague claim into a specific reference that will demonstrate knowledge of the subject.

Vague: Though others flew before them, the Wright brothers are credited as the first to fly.

Specific: Because their powered flights of December 17, 1903, were recorded by witnesses and photographs, the Wright Brothers are credited as the first to fly.

Vague: Time is an interesting concept in Faulkner's "A Rose for Emily."

Specific: In Faulkner's "A Rose for Emily" we have a narrator who seems to be older than Miss Emily Grierson and lives longer than she does. Who is this narrator? How is the narrator related to time?

Vague: John Donne's poem "Death Be Not Proud" ends up being hopeful.

Specific: John Donne's poem "Death Be Not Proud" addresses Death as a person and exalts human nature by condemning the traditional claim that Death finally triumphs over humankind.

■ **Exercise 40.1** Compare the list of questions on pages 620–621 with the opening sentence responses by student writers. What elements have the writers repeated from the question? What elements of their own have they introduced to establish a thesis?

✔ CHECKLIST 40.1: TAKING AN ESSAY EXAM

Doing well on an essay exam requires more than knowing the material. You also must organize it and write about it within a strict time limit. Here are some tips.

- Read the entire exam.
- Be certain you understand every question and are aware of all their parts.
- Make brief notes outlining your response to each question.
- Begin writing, working your thesis sentence into the first paragraph of your answer.
- Back up your generalizations with concrete details.
- When you have finished writing, read the question again to be sure that you have answered all its parts.
- Review, correct, and strengthen your answer.

40c
Writing an Essay Exam: A Sample Answer

The following essay was written in response to an examination question in an introduction to psychology course. The question was "Identify the hierarchy (ladder) of needs that, according to Maslow, lead to self-actualization, and explain the elements in the hierarchy."

■ **Exercise 40.2** Evaluate the student essay on the hierarchy of needs. What are its strengths? Weaknesses? Has the writer answered the question?

■ **Exercise 40.3** Select an essay-type question from the exercises in the textbook of any course you are currently taking. Following the recommendations in this chapter, write a draft response to the question. Share your essay with others in your writing class or with your writing instructor.

Opening paragraph
1. States thesis
2. Repeats key words from question

Abraham Maslow identified a hierarchy of five general needs leading to self-actualization. Arranged from lowest to highest, these needs, Maslow says, must be satisfied in order, with self-actualization the last (and most difficult) to achieve.

Specific details that identify the elements of the hierarchy

The first need on the ladder of needs is <u>physiological</u>. This need includes hunger, thirst, sex--survival, in general. Second is the <u>safety</u> need, such as stability, security, and order. Third is <u>love</u> needs and belongingness; this includes needs for identification, affiliation, and the all-important affection. The fourth needs to be met before the final need of self-actualization are <u>esteem</u> needs, including the needs for success, self-respect, and prestige.

Examples continue identification and provide analysis

To explain the needs hierarchy, psychologists often provide the example of a starving man. That person is concerned only with obtaining food for today. He doesn't think about tomorrow (the safety need) until he is assured that his most basic physiological need (hunger) is met. When today's meal is certain, he can plan for meeting his physiological needs regularly and can concern himself with safety needs, next in the hierarchy. Those needs met, he can address belonging and love needs. At each rung on the ladder of motives we see the same set of priorities. When all other needs are met, people can strive to do what they enjoy and succeed at and thus become self-actualizing, that is, satisfying the need to realize potential and latent abilities.

New paragraph: new point in explanation

Unfortunately, most people do not become self-actualizing. They get stuck on one of the steps of the ladder and do not move ahead. Despite noticeable examples of hunger throughout the world,

Name of Article, 2

most societies do provide an environment in which basic physiological needs can be met, and so most of us move up the ladder to safety needs. These hold most of our attention throughout life. We become intensely focused for example, on job security or the need for protection against crime. Only when we can assure the continued atmosphere of safety do we strive for love and then esteem.

Further points in analysis

Of course, any discussion of the needs hierarchy is of necessity oversimplified. In truth people easily fall back to lower rungs on the ladder when conditions in their lives or environment change. War, for example, with its threats to life and its deprivations can thrust a person already meeting belonging needs into a preoccupation with physiological needs (finding food), which have a much lower order in the hierarchy. Additionally, we often try to meet two different needs at the same time--for instance physiological and safety or belongingness and esteem. Because, according to Maslow, higher level needs can be fulfilled only when lower needs are met, the higher order motives (including self-actualization) often go unrealized. When people cannot achieve the higher rungs on Maslow's ladder, they can grow frustrated and conflicted.

Short summary paragraphs

The needs hierarchy and the various elements in each category provide a helpful method for understanding human motivation and conflict.

CHAPTER

41

USING A WORD PROCESSOR

By all means learn to use computers and word-processing programs before you leave college. The computer has become a standard medium of communication. Word-processing programs enable you to make sweeping revisions or small changes with relative ease. They are fun to use, and they often give writers a sense of control over their work which they lacked when they were doing everything with a pencil or even with a typewriter.

Choose a word-processing program that you can learn easily and that someone you know is using successfully. Manuals are notorious for poor writing. If you cannot understand the manual, you can always consult a friend who knows the program.

Learn to compose at a keyboard. It is a much faster and more convenient way of writing than longhand. To use a computer, you must be able to use a keyboard, so if you don't know how to type, take the time to learn.

Computers eliminate much of the physical labor of writing, but you still have to work hard. No computer can think for you or tell you what you ought to say. But the computer, a good word-processing program, and a printer will make some of your choices easier. Revision becomes much easier, and as we have said so frequently, revision is the heart of writing. A computer is useful to a writer in a variety of ways: you can use it to take notes, to store data, and to create outlines as well as to write and revise your papers and prepare the final copy.

41a
Taking Notes and Storing Data

You can make many of your notes with a computer and a word processor. Book stands that hold books open and upright beside the keyboard are available in office supply shops and many campus bookstores.

Taking notes on a computer gives you several advantages. You can find them quickly by using the *search* command on your word-processing program. For example, suppose you are reading stories by the writer Peter Taylor for a literature paper on his work and you notice how often he mentions mirrors. You think you might mention that detail, perhaps even make a paper out of it. But you don't yet know. So you make this note.

> The person in the mirror now eyed him curiously, even incredulously, and momentarily he resented the intrusion of this third, unfamiliar person on the scene, a person who, so to speak, ought still to have been asleep beside his wife back there in the family's guest room.
>
> —"At the Drug Store," *The Collected Stories of Peter Taylor* (New York: Penguin Books, 1986), p. 117

You might want to add a thought of your own about the use of the mirror in this passage. When you have made several dozen notes, you may want to recover all those places where Taylor mentions a mirror. All you have to do is command your word processor to search for the word *mirror.* It is a much faster process than keeping notes on 3 × 5 cards and having to shuffle through them when you sit down to work on your paper.

In making notes, you may make a file in which you put the full bibliographical information for every source you consult. If in that file you have the full information for *The Collected Stories of Peter Taylor,* you need type only *Taylor* and a page number with your note on mirrors. All good word-processing programs have another feature you can use in your writing. By using only a few keystrokes, you can copy quotations from your note file into the body of the paper you are writing. Not only is the process much easier than typing the quotation over again; it also cuts down your chances of making a copying error.

In taking notes with a computer, you should avoid the temptation to take too many notes or to copy too much *verbatim* (word for word) from the source. You should summarize most information, perhaps using only sentence fragments or abbreviated sentences. So, for the quotation above, you might write:

> Taylor, mirrors, p. 117, *Collected Stories*

Then your computer file serves as an annotated index of your sources. Seeing the word *mirrors* on your computer, you can pick up the book of short stories and turn quickly to the passage. It is always a good idea to make comments on the notes you take. Your thoughts as you write the note should also go into your computer file, marked in some clear way that allows you to distinguish between what you are thinking and what you are seeing in the source.

Avoid taking so many notes that doing the research becomes a substitute for writing the paper. Many writers, both experienced and inexperienced, take so many notes and do so much research that they never get around to writing.

You can set up a separate computer file for each set of notes—a file for English literature, another for history, another for chemistry, and so on. You can set up a bibliography file, listing the various books and articles you use in a research project. You can make a directory that might, for example, combine all the files of notes made in various English courses you have taken in college. You can add files and notes throughout your formal education and afterward.

41b
Creating Outlines

The same features that make a word-processing program a good note file can also help you in outlining a paper. You can construct an outline on your word processor and then move the various parts around easily to achieve a more effective organization. As you work, you can gradually fill in your outline, using sample sentences and paragraphs that you can later fit into your paper. You can try out introductions and conclusions to see which of them best express your purposes.

If you have consulted several sources, you can often put your paper together by transferring notes from your note file to the place where you think they ought to fit in your outline. You can try different arrangements and experiment with different organizations. You can save the various versions of your expanded outlines, print them out, and compare them to see which seems to suit your purposes best.

Some word-processing programs now have built-in outlining functions, and some outlining programs with special functions are on the market. These outliners allow you to put your final paper together easily from an extended outline merely by pressing a few function keys. But by using the *search* and *copy* functions of any program, you can use it as an outliner.

If you use the computer to outline and to arrange your notes in organized blocks, you will see more clearly that writing is seldom a linear process in which one sits down and starts writing a paper from the beginning and goes straight through to the end. Writing is nearly always a process by which the writer brings chunks of material together and then blends them into a whole.

41c
Writing and Revising the Paper

Computers permit you to write more quickly than by hand or typewriter. But be careful. Sometimes your fingers can fly faster than your brain can think. Unless you write carefully, you may spend all the time you thought you saved in revising.

Revising

When you have used a computer for a while, you will learn to revise on the screen, inserting here, deleting there. But you should always print your work out and read it on paper, at least for the final run-through. Read with a pencil in hand to mark those places where you want to revise.

Be sure to give special attention to two errors common in word processing. One is deleting too much; the other is not deleting enough.

Often a writer will produce a sentence like this:

> Mr. Harrington, who has been convicted of car theft, said that his criminal record had nothing to do with his present effort to become city fire inspector, since cars had nothing to do with city buildings.

The writer, looking at this long sentence, naturally thought of ways of shortening it. And so he deleted some words. But as people often do in using computers, he deleted too much.

> Mr. Harrington, of car theft, said that his criminal record had nothing to do with his present effort to become city fire inspector, since cars had nothing to do with city buildings.

He had to insert a word he had accidentally deleted:

> Mr. Harrington, convicted of car theft, said that his criminal record had nothing to do with his present effort to become city fire inspector, since cars had nothing to do with city buildings.

Another error is failure to delete enough. A writer wrote this:

> Custer seemed to think that a dramatic victory over the Sioux Indians in 1876 would make him a national hero and might make him president in the election later that year.

In looking at her sentence, the writer decided to revise and came up with this:

> Custer seemed to think that a slaughtering the Sioux Indians would make him a national hero and might make him president in the election later that year.

The writer decided to make Custer's intentions more vivid by changing "a dramatic victory over" to "slaughtering." So she deleted and inserted. But she has not deleted the article *a,* thus leaving the sentence confused. It should be this:

> Custer seemed to think that slaughtering the Sioux Indians would make him a national hero and might make him president in the election later that year.

Computers allow you to move groups of words or, indeed, whole pages from one part of your essay to another by using a few function keys. You can try out a great many forms for the information you present. But you need to make the parts you move fit into their new spot. Read your work over again to be sure that you have not moved something without proper regard for the new context or that you have not left a noticeable hole in the place where the moved text was originally located. Working on a computer grants marvelous efficiency to the writing process. But it does not take away the requirement of any writer to read the text again and again and again to see that everything hangs together as it should.

Keep your successive drafts, on either backup disks or printouts or both. You may decide that you want to return to an earlier version of a sentence or a paragraph.

Checking for Repetitions

All writers have certain words or expressions they like and therefore tend to use too often. If you think you have used some stylistic mannerism too frequently, use the *search* function on the word-processing program to see how many times you have used it in your paper. For example, you may like the word *doggedly.* Search your paper to see how many times you have used it. If you have used it more than once, you should probably find a synonym.

Sometimes, especially in a long paper, you may repeat information unnecessarily. If you write a paper about southern literature, you might mention Peter Taylor as someone whose writing has little to do with the agrarian tradition of much southern writing. Suppose you are writing and think you may have said that earlier. It's easy to search for *Taylor* in your preceding text to see if you have given the information before.

You can apply the recommendations of this handbook by searching in your writing for words and usages we have warned you against. Are you afraid that you have used needless intensifiers such as *absolutely, definitely,* and *incredibly?* Search for them on the computer and decide if you want to eliminate them. Do you think you may have overused modifiers such as *very, rather,* and *really?* Search for them on the computer, and see if you can eliminate them where they turn up.

Checking Spelling

Many word-processing programs come with dictionaries that allow you to check the spellings of words in your text. These dictionaries are usually smaller than standard desk dictionaries. Most collegiate desk dictionaries list about 150,000 words; a dictionary on a word-processing program usually has around 50,000 words. Geographical, biographical, and specialized names and terms are not usually included in a computer dictionary, but you can add them to the dictionary.

The computer dictionary, often called a *spell checker,* is usually activated when one or more function keys are pressed while the cursor is on the word whose spelling you wish to examine. The computer will usually give you a message telling you whether the word is in the computer's dictionary. If it *is* in the dictionary, you may assume only that the word exists in English. You may need to check the entry in your desk dictionary to be sure you have got the word you want. **Homophones**—words pronounced alike but with different meanings—can trip you up (see 27b). Your computer spell checker may tell you *there* is spelled correctly, but if you meant *they're* or *their,* you've still spelled the word wrong. If the word is *not* in the dictionary as you have spelled it, either you have misspelled it or the computer dictionary does not include it. You might get a message, for example, that the word *dilettante* is not in your computer's dictionary. But on consulting your desk dictionary, you discover that you have spelled the word correctly! So you should never depend on the computer dictionary alone; use it in conjunction with a good desk dictionary.

Some dictionary programs can be set to work as you are typing. A quiet buzzer sounds each time you type a word not in the computer's dictionary. Such a function not only helps you with your spelling but also warns you against typographical errors. The computer will buzz if you misspell the word *believe* by writing "beleive." It will also buzz if you reverse letters in the word *the* so that you get "teh." The computer dictionary can be a valuable aid in proofreading.

41d
Preparing the Final Copy

Computers make life easier for writers but sometimes harder for readers. Be sure you do not let technology burden your readers. You can be courteous in the kind of printer you use for your final drafts and in the way you manage computer paper.

Selecting a Printer and Paper

Computer printers are of three main types. Laser printers are fast, and they have the clearest typeface. Letter-quality printers are heavy and slow, but they also have an excellent typeface, comparable to that of a good electric typewriter. Dot-matrix printers are perhaps the most common and reliable printers generally available. They make characters out of combinations of little dots; the dots are pressed onto the paper by tiny wires pushed through an inked ribbon, and the effect is like the appearance of the lights that form letters and numbers within a square on a scoreboard.

Dot-matrix type has improved dramatically over the years, but some models still make characters that are difficult to read. If you use a dot-matrix printer, be sure that it makes letters with true descenders. That is, the *g, j, p, q,* and *y* should have tails that come below the baseline of the rest of the type. The dots should also be close enough together to make legible letters. Before you use or buy a dot-matrix printer, look at a document that printer has produced. Can you read the document without being distracted by the type? If you have any doubts, find another printer.

Beware of printers that work with thermal-sensitive paper. These printers are often advertised as needing no ribbon; they make an impression by applying heat to treated paper. Such printers are fast and quiet. But often the type fades quickly as chemical changes take place in the paper. You can write something on thermal-sensitive paper and discover in a few months that you have nothing but blank sheets in your file! (Always be careful around any kind of dot-matrix printer; in operation, the printing head is extremely hot and can cause severe burns.)

Be sure the ribbon on your printer is dark enough to provide legible copy. The ribbons on dot-matrix printers wear out rapidly. A faint, scarcely legible type in dot matrix can make life even more difficult for a hard-pressed instructor.

Computer paper may be fed into the printer on a continuous roll. A perforated strip on each side allows a tractor feed to roll the paper line by line into the printer so that the paper does not wrinkle or twist on the roller. When you hand in your paper, be sure to tear off the perforated strip that has been used by the tractor feed. Be sure, too, to separate the pages. Don't hand in a continuous roll of printed pages! Instructors become justifiably annoyed if they have to separate individual sheets and put a student's work together before they can read and grade it.

Computer paper is notoriously poor in quality. Nearly all computer printers, however, will accept ordinary white bond paper. Although you must feed bond paper into some printers one sheet at a time, the greatly improved appearance justifies the extra effort.

Formatting the Document

Formatting a computer document involves laying out pages by adjusting the margins and line spacing, placing material (including page numbers) at the head and the foot of each page, setting the number of lines of type that will appear on a page, and determining the positions of the subheads.

In word processing, as in typing, take care to provide good margins—usually an inch and a half on the left side and at least an inch at the top, the right side, and the bottom. A little practice with your computer and your word-processing program should make it easy for you to set these margins. With most word-processing programs, you can justify the right margin. However, unless your word-processing program and your printer will do proportional spacing, it's always better to leave your right margin unjustified.

Always number your pages. Word-processing programs can set numbers at the top or the bottom of each page, and they can enter the number or set it on the right or left side. It's usually a good idea to number pages at the top. Page numbers are usually set as headers or footers. A *header* is a line of type that goes across the top of every page; a *footer* is a line of type that goes across the bottom of every page. You can add other information as well—the title of your paper, your last name, the date. It's generally good to keep headers and footers simple so they will not distract from the body of the text. Headers and footers should be separated from the body of the text by one line of space if the text is single-spaced and by two lines of space if the text is double-spaced.

All student papers should be double-spaced. When you prepare the computer to paginate, you must tell it how many lines to put on a page. If you double-space on $8\frac{1}{2} \times 11$ paper, you will usually have a header with a page number and about 27 lines of text. A page that ends with a subhead, with the material that the subhead introduces on the next page, looks imbalanced. Consult your program manual to find out how to make the computer move your heading to the top of the next page, where it belongs. Every time you repaginate your text after inserting or deleting material, check through your work to be sure you have not pulled or pushed a subhead to the bottom of a page.

Don't overuse the variety of typefaces your computer or printer may offer you. Boldface and italic are the only special typefaces you need for most work. Avoid eccentric typefaces. Never turn in papers written in a script or gothic typeface.

41e Housekeeping

Computer data are stored by means of electric impulses that are translated onto disks by much the same sort of process that makes tape recordings. Small disks, measuring either $3\frac{1}{2}$ inches or $5\frac{1}{4}$ inches across, are called *floppies* and can be carried around and used in various compatible computers. Hard disks with vast storage capacities are sealed and fixed in the computer and are not intended to be moved from computer to computer.

All these disks are extremely fragile. Floppies can be ruined if they are placed too close to the speakers of a stereo set or even too close to the video monitor of the computer itself. Floppies are also sensitive to dust, to cracker crumbs, to fingerprints, to spilled coffee, and to anything else that touches the magnetic surface. Hard disks are sealed against dust and may give good service for several thousand hours. But all hard disks fail eventually. The failure comes suddenly, without warning. The hard disk simply fails to record data or to give data back to the computer screen.

Once a disk is ruined, the data you have put on it—a copy of your research paper, for example—may be gone forever. And even if you can retrieve the data by some of the technology now available, the process is time consuming and sometimes expensive.

So you should always make backup copies of your work. That means that you should copy the work on one disk to another amd keep the two disks in separate places so that if something happens to one, you will not lose your data. If you are using a hard disk, back your work up on floppies. If your computer fails, you can take your floppies to another compatible computer and go back to work with a minimum of lost time and with no lost data. Whenever you can do so, it's a good idea to print your work out at the end of a session with the computer. Printing the work out takes more time than making a backup disk. If you have a printed copy of your work, you may suffer the inconvenience of having to type it over again to store it on a disk. But at least you have your work.

✓ CHECKLIST 41.1: WRITING WITH A WORD PROCESSOR

Using a word processor may make writing easier, but it sometimes makes revising harder. Word processors can lull you into thinking your paper is better than it is. Always print out a draft, and revise it in the old-fashioned way—in pencil. When you return to the keyboard, keep these cautions and functions in mind.

- Revise carefully to be sure you delete neither too little nor too much and that you insert or move text to the right place.
- Use the *search* function to prevent repetitions.
- Use the spell checker to check your spelling; then confirm any word you're still uncertain of in your desk dictionary.
- Select a printer and typeface that are easy to read.
- Format your document with your readers in mind.
- Back up everything.

ESL APPENDIX

ESL 1

Subjects: Subject Pronouns

In some languages the subject pronoun can be omitted if the reference to a preceding noun is clear. In English, such pronouns must always be included:

No: My sister lives in Woodland. Is a small city.
Yes: My sister lives in Woodland. *It* is a small city.

No: My brother has a large practice. It is a dentist.
Yes: My brother has a large practice. *He* is a dentist.

No: The peony bloomed. Is a beautiful flower.
Yes: The peony bloomed. *It* is a beautiful flower.

ESL 2

Subjects: Prepositional Phrases

A prepositional phrase cannot be used as the subject of a sentence. Use a noun or add a subject pronoun after the prepositional phrase:

No: In my town is very safe.
Yes: My town is very safe.
In my town it is very safe.

No: With my sister go to school.
Yes: I go to school with my sister.
With my sister, I go to school.

No: In the house is warm.
Yes: It is warm in the house.
In the house it is warm.

ESL 3

Subjects: *It* and *There* in Deferred Subjects

In some languages, you can omit *it* or *there* as a subject and still have a complete sentence. In English, these words must always be included.

No: Is not good to miss class.
Are many reasons to get to class on time, too.

Yes: It is not good to miss class.
There are many reasons to get to class on time, too.

ESL 4

Verbs: Phrasal Verbs

Some English verbs combine with adverbs or prepositions (called particles) to form two- and three-word *phrasal verbs* with new and different meanings. The words that make up phrasal verbs often have different meanings in combination than they do separately. The meaning of *put up with* (to tolerate or endure), for example, is different from the individual meanings of *put* or *up* alone.

Phrasal verbs are used more in conversation and informal writing than in academic writing. They are common in idiomatic expressions, often follow no general rules, and must usually be learned or looked up in a dictionary. They are also easy tests of fluency in speaking and writing.

Mistakes in choice of particle and placement of parts of the phrasal verb can destroy or change meaning. To avoid such mistakes, keep these points in mind:

- Phrasal verb particles, unlike prepositions that follow verbs, cannot be separated and moved to other parts of the sentence. The entire phrasal verb may come at the end of the sentence, as in "What time did you *get in?*" (What time did you arrive?)

(continues on next page)

ESL 4 (continued)

- Phrasal verbs can be transitive or intransitive, and some have both transitive and intransitive forms. For instance, *wake up* can be used in the following ways:

  It's time to *wake up.*
  Please *wake* me *up* at 6:00.

- Some verbs and prepositional phrases cannot be separated by other words; some can be. There is no general rule.

  "*Look* the word *up*" is correct.
  "*Look* the child *after*" is wrong. It must be "*Look after* the child."

- Objects of transitive phrasal verbs that cannot be separated should follow the complete verb, as in "*Look over* the assignment."
- Noun objects of phrasal verbs that can be separated can be placed after the verb, or between verb and particle(s), as in "*Hand in* the test" or "*Hand* the test *in*."
- Pronoun objects always come between verb and particle(s), as in "*Look* him *over.*"

Common Phrasal Verbs

ask out	drop in	go out (with)
break down	drop off	go over
break up (with)	drop out (of)	grow up
bring up	figure out	hand in
burn down	fill in	hand out
burn out	fill up	hang out
burn up	find out	hang up
call back	get along (with)	have on
call in	get away (from)	help out
call off	get away (with)	keep on
call up	get back	keep out
catch up (with)	get in	keep out (of)
check in	get on (with)	keep up (with)
check out	get out	leave out
check up (on)	get over	look after
come out	get up	look into
cross out	give back	look out (for)
cut out	give in	look over
cut up	give up	look up

ESL 4 (continued)

make up (with)	shut off	try on
pass out	shut up	try out (for)
pick out	speak out	tune in (to)
pick up	speak up	tune up
put away	stand up (for)	turn down
put back	stay up	turn in
put off	take after	turn off
put on	take care (of)	turn on
put out	take in	turn out
put up (with)	take off	turn up
quiet down	take out	wake up
run across	take over	watch out (for)
run into	tear down	wear out
run out (of)	tear up	wrap up
show off	think over	use up
show up	throw up	

ESL 5

Verbs: Nonprogressive Verbs

Stative verbs are verbs that do not denote action. Instead they express a mental or emotional state or describe some property of their subject. These verbs do not take the progressive form:

> *No:* I am preferring Beethoven's piano sonatas to any of his other works.
> *Yes:* I prefer Beethoven's piano sonatas to any of his other works.

Certain verbs are always stative:

> know, realize, understand, recognize, suppose, imagine, doubt, remember, forget, want, need, prefer, mean, love, like, hate, fear, envy, mind, care, possess, own, belong, seem

Other verbs are sometimes active, depending on the intended meaning:

> be, have, taste, smell, hear, sound, feel, see, look, appear, weigh, cost

Juan's drawings *looked* very professional.
While the committee *was looking* at Juan's drawings, the room became silent.

ESL 6

Verbs: Errors in the Use of Verbs

With do in negatives and questions: Using third-person singular and past tense endings is incorrect.

No: I didn't understood the assignment.
Yes: I didn't understand the assignment.

With auxiliaries: Using third-person singular and past tense endings with verbs following *can* and *may* is incorrect.

No: Mai can helps you with your homework.
Yes: Mai can help you with your homework.

With verb endings for infinitives: Using third-person singular and past tense endings with infinitives used as objects is incorrect.

No: Karl liked to studied in the library.
Yes: Karl likes to study in the library.
Karl liked to study in the library.

ESL 7

Verbs: Gerunds and Infinitives

Gerunds and infinitives can be objects or complements of verbs. Some verbs must be followed by infinitives; some verbs must be followed by gerunds; some verbs can be followed by either form.

Infinitives as objects of verbs often give a sense of purpose or signify that something is expected or anticipated. Gerunds as objects of verbs indicate that something is known or real. So all of these are correct:

I like to swim. I like swimming. I enjoy swimming.

And these are not correct:

I enjoy to swim. I wanted going to the movies.

Deciding which form to use can be a problem in English, since the choice depends on both the meaning and the particular verb.

Here are some techniques to help avoid mistakes:

- An infinitive shows action after the time of the main verb: "I forgot to hand in that paper."
- A gerund indicates action before the time of the verb: "I forget handing in that paper."

- An infinitive indicates an effort: "Try to make an outline before you write your essay."
- A gerund indicates an experiment: "Try making an outline before you write your essay."
- An infinitive indicates a purpose: "I stopped to talk to the teacher after class." "I stopped talking to the teacher after he insulted me."

Here are some common verbs and their complements:

- These common verbs are followed by infinitives:

advise	encourage	make	refuse
agree	expect	mean	remind
allow	fail	need	request
appear	forbid	offer	require
ask	go (purpose)	order	see (purpose)
cause	hear	permit	seem
command	hesitate	persuade	teach
compel	hope	plan	tell
consent	instruct	prepare	trust
dare	intend	pretend	wait
decide	invite	promise	want
deserve	learn	propose	warn

- These common verbs are followed by gerunds:

admit	discuss	imagine	quit
advise	dislike	keep (on)	recall
appreciate	encourage	mention	require
avoid	enjoy	mind	resent
can(not) help	excuse	miss	resist
consider	feel like	object to	risk
delay	finish	postpone	suggest
deny	forbid		

- These verbs can be followed by an infinitive or a gerund with little or no difference in meaning. Generally, an infinitive expresses an action, a gerund expresses a process.

attempt	can(not) stand	like	see
begins	continue	love	stand
can(not) bear	hate	prefer	start

- A few verbs can take either an infinitive or a gerund depending on the meaning.

remember, forget, regret

ESL 8

Verbs: Sequence of Tenses in Conditional Sentences

Verb forms in conditional sentences with *if* or *unless* present special problems. There are three basic kinds of conditional sentences: factual, predictive, and imaginative. Each has different rules.

Purpose of Sentence	*Time of Occurrence*
To state a general truth (factual)	present
To describe habitual action (factual)	present
	past
To express an inference (predictive)	present
	past
Make a promise or prediction (predictive)	future
To describe an event that is possible but not likely, or one that is not possible (imaginative)	present
	past

ESL 8 (continued)

Verb Form in If Clause	*Verb Form in Independent Clause*
If people lack social ties,	they become depressed.
If Rosa is lonely,	she goes to the Student Union.
If Rosa was lonely,	she called her mother.
	present or must + verb stem
If Milna is in bed early,	she must be sick.
	past or must + present perfect
If her light was on,	she must have been awake.
If my symptoms get worse,	I'll call the doctor.
Unless you study,	you'll get poor grades.
past (plural form of be)	*would + stem*
If I studied harder,	I would get all A's.
If I were a genius,	I wouldn't have to study.
past perfect	*would + present perfect*
If I had studied harder,	I would have aced that test.
If I had been a genius,	life would have been easier.

ESL 9

Objects: Position of Indirect Object

An indirect object can also be placed after a direct object. When this happens, it becomes part of a prepositional phrase. The preposition *for* is used after verbs such as *make* and *sing,* which suggest an action on someone or something else's behalf; *to* is used following verbs such as *give* and *tell,* which may imply a transaction between two individuals. A very few verbs, such as *ask* and *demand,* take the preposition *of.*

Usually, either position is acceptable:

Rogelio made *me* a copy of his notes.
Rogelio made a copy of his notes *for me.*

Here are some exceptions:

If the direct object is a pronoun, the indirect object must be placed in a prepositional phrase.

I gave them back *to him* the following day.

The same rule holds if either the direct or the indirect object has lengthy modifiers:

The instructor provided extra time *for all the students who needed help.*

The indirect object must not be expressed in a prepositional phrase following verbs like *cost* and *charge:*

The company charged *us* extra for the duplicates.

The trip cost *the family* a great deal of money.

ESL 10

Nouns: Types of Nouns

Nouns are names of persons, places, things, ideas, actions, and states of existence. Any word can be a noun if in a given context it can be given a name. There are several types of nouns in English, and some of the types overlap. Here is a brief list of the types, with definitions and some examples.

From the point of view of grammar and correct usage, collective nouns and the count/noncount (mass) categories are the most complicated and need special attention [see ESL 11, Count and Noncount (Mass) Nouns].

Type	*Function*	*Examples*
common nouns	name things according to a general class	desk, street, tractor, teacher
proper nouns	name specific people, places, things; capitalized	George Washington, Italy, the White House
concrete nouns	name entities we know from our own experience	tree, house, computer, highway, dog, cat
abstract nouns	name entities that we do not know except mentally, like ideas and states of existence	friendship, ambition, haste, serenity, happiness, life, death
collective nouns	name groups; can be singular or plural	team, crew, audience, class, government
count nouns	name entities that can be counted as individual units	friend, apple, lake, room, desk, shoe
noncount (mass) nouns	name entities that cannot be counted as individual units	sugar, rice, water, life, peace

ESL 11

Nouns: Count and Noncount (Mass) Nouns

Two types of nouns can cause difficulty because of a feature called *countability:*

Count nouns name items that can be counted as individual units.

Noncount or mass nouns name items that cannot be counted.

Here are some familiar categories of mass or noncount nouns:

- Groups/substances consisting of similar items: furniture, machinery, rice, flour, sugar
- Fluids and gases: water, milk, air, hydrogen, ozone
- Games: chess, tag, hide-and-seek, mah-jongg
- Substances: wood, metal, cotton, wool, velvet, leather
- Abstractions: life, death, beauty, peace, cooperation, ignorance, serenity
- Nouns formed from verbs: swimming, skiing, eating, seeing, walking, running

To use these nouns correctly, several points of grammar are important:

- Noncount or mass nouns cannot be made plural; count nouns can be:

  I drink water every day.
  I broke two glasses today.

ESL 11 (continued)

- Noncount or mass nouns take the third-person singular verb:

  Water is good for you.
  The machinery needs repair.
  The sand is soft.

- A few nouns can be either count or noncount depending on emphasis. If the focus is on a concrete example, they are count; if the focus is on a class, they are noncount.

  Dieters should avoid recipes that contain egg. [noncount; mass]

  That recipe calls for three eggs. [count; concrete]

- Count and noncount nouns use different articles or determiners:

  With count nouns: a/an, many/few/a, few/each/every/several

  With noncount nouns: much/little/a little

  With both types: all, some, any, a lot of/ lots of, plenty, none of

  Here are some examples:

  I have many friends in New York. [count]

  We wished them much happiness in the future. [noncount]

  They have some apples and some sugar. [both]

Determiners: Using Articles Correctly

One of the easiest tests of a fluent, idiomatic speaker or writer of English is correct use of articles—*an/an* and *the*. In English, deciding whether to use an article and which article to use is sometimes difficult.

Articles (or determiners) are usually divided into two categories: definite or specific (*the*), and indefinite or nonspecific (*an/an, some,* no article). To avoid errors, think in terms of four choices: *a/an, the, some,* or no article.

Here are some guidelines and examples to help in making the choice.

DEFINITE Use *the* with:

1. Common nouns, singular or plural, and noncount nouns that are specific because:

   The noun has been mentioned previously:
   The college is building *the library.*

   The noun is identified by a modifier:
   The new library will be much better.

   The item is known to your reader/listener:
   Your school has *the best library.*

   The item is unique:
   The computer index is extremely helpful.

2. Singular common count nouns that are used to represent a class of things or people:

   Our library has a good book on *the* panda.

3. Plural proper nouns or proper nouns that name oceans or rivers, a geographical region, an organization or federation, or a newspaper:

   The Smiths are both librarians.
   They sailed *the Atlantic.*
   Cartier explored *the Northeast.*
   New atlases do not list *the Soviet Union.*
   The President's commission will present its report.
   The Atlanta Constitution is a good paper.

INDEFINITE Use *a/an* with:

1. Singular countable common nouns that are nonspecific because:

- There has been no previous mention:
  I have *a study carrel* in the library.
- There is no restricting modifier:
  There is *a copy machine* on the first floor.
- Identity is not important to the context:
  The change machine can change *a dollar.*

2. Singular countable nouns that are generic:

A computer is *an electronic tool.*

INDEFINITE Use *some* with:

Plural or noncount nouns that refer to a specifiable quantity.

I have *some change* for the copy machine.
Bring *some money.*

INDEFINITE Use no article with:

1. Plural or noncount common nouns that are nonspecific because:

- There is no previous mention:
  There are *pens* for sale.
- There is no restricting modifier:
  There are *computer terminals* on every floor.
- Quantity and identity are not important:
  The reference librarian has *scratch paper.*

2. Plural nouns used in an abstract or generic sense:

Carrels are enclosed study cubicles.

3. Singular proper nouns that name a person, a single country/city/continent/a mountain/lake/bay or a disease:

Newsweek is a popular weekly.
Lake Baikal in *Siberia* is very polluted.
Some of the patients have *diabetes.*

ESL 13

Adjectives: Adjective Placement

Where to place adjectives can sometimes be a source of confusion. In general, single-word adjectives should precede the noun they modify, and phrases or clauses that function as adjectives should follow the noun.

No: She had brown hair and curly.
Yes: She had brown, curly hair.
She had hair that was brown and curly.

When several single-word adjectives precede the noun, follow this order:

DETERMINER	QUALITY	SIZE	AGE	SHAPE
two	priceless	little	old	round

PARTICIPLE	COLOR	ORIGIN	NOUN	NOUN
handmade	blue	Swedish	wine	glasses

ESL 14

Adverbs: Placement of Adverbs and Adverbials

The placement of adverbs and adverbials (phrases that can function as adverbs) can present problems in speaking or writing English. These two general rules are reliable guides to correct, idiomatic expression:

1. Never put an adverb or adverbial between the verb and its object:

No: Dr. Sanders gave *this morning* a memorable lecture.
Yes: Dr. Sanders gave a memorable lecture *this morning.*

ESL 14 (continued)

2. When a sentence contains a series of adverbs or adverbials following the verb, the usual order is manner, place, time:

   The students sat attentively [manner] at their desks [place] until class was over [time].

Other placement rules:

1. Indefinite adverbs and adverbials of frequency (*sometimes, occasionally, seldom*) appear in the middle (before the verb, or between the auxiliary and main verb):

   We *seldom* go to the movies.
   We have *seldom* seen them on campus.

2. Definite adverbs and adverbials of frequency (*every, once*) appear in initial or first position:

   Every Thursday we have a seminar.
   Once a year, I go home for a visit.

3. Adverbs and adverbials of place (*at school, on the corner*) and manner (*slowly, anxiously, confidently, with a smile*) go in initial or final position.

   Let's meet *at school.*
   They walked *slowly.*

4. Adverbs and adverbials of time (*lately, early, recently*) go in initial or final position:

   Lately it's been raining a lot.
   It's been raining a lot *lately.*
   Can you come *early*?

5. Adverbs and adverbials of direction (*to the market, in the east*) go only in final position:

   The sun rises *in the east.*
   The vendors are on their way *to the market.*

ESL 15

Prepositions: Choosing the Correct Preposition

English has more prepositions than many other languages, and there is much overlap in their use and meaning.

Prepositions of space and time, like *at, on, in, into, onto,* and *to,* are the most easily confused. This is because they are used not according to the noun that is the object, but according to the aspect of space and time that is emphasized, and/or the degree of precision needed:

at 8 P.M. (exact)
in the evening (indefinite)

Many other common prepositions, like *above* and *under,* have stable meanings that can be checked in a dictionary. Choosing the correct preposition in these cases is usually not a problem. But for the difficult ones, those that can shift the meaning of a phrase, the dictionary is not always enough. Here are some additional hints to help you avoid errors:

- If the preposition is part of a verb phrase, check the phrasal verbs list in ESL 4. It lists the common verb-preposition combinations and their meanings. Such combinations are frequent in English, particularly in everyday conversation and writing.
- The table below presents rules governing the use of prepositions of space and time, along with examples that show which preposition to use in which situation.

SPACE

A Point		*A Surface*		*Enclosed*	
LOCATIONAL					
at	at the car at the library at 20 Oak Street	*on*	on the car on the floor on Oak Street	*in*	in the car in the lobby in the gray house
DIRECTIONAL					
to	to the car	*onto*	onto the floor	*into*	into the house

ESL 15 (continued)

TIME

	Point		*Day*		*Period or Unspecified*
at	at 10:00	*on*	on Monday	*in*	in May
	at Christmas (season)		on May 1		in spring
	at New Year		on Christmas (day)		in 1992
					in the morning/ evening

ESL 16

Participles: Confusion of Past and Present Participles

Differences in meaning between the present participle and the past participle forms of verbs that describe states of mind such as *bore, excite, interest, annoy, challenge,* and *fascinate* can sometimes cause problems. Remember that a present participle describes an experience or a person causing that experience. A past participle describes a person's response to an experience. Here are some examples of correct and incorrect expressions:

No: The lecture was very bored because I am not interesting in biochemistry.

Yes: The lecture was very boring because I am not interested in biochemistry.

No: Jack was annoying when Mary was not exciting at his award.

Yes: Jack was annoyed when Mary was not excited at his award.

ESL 17

Clauses: Mixed Subordination and Coordination

Two clauses can be connected by either a subordinating clause or a coordinating conjunction, but not by both:

No: Although Hang felt sick, *but* he still went to his math class.
Yes: Although Hang felt sick, he still went to his math class.
Hang felt sick, *but* he still went to his math class.

No: Even though he said we would go, *but* it rained.
Yes: Even though he said we would go, it rained.
He said we would go, *but* it rained.

No: If you would like to attend the concert, *and so* would I.
Yes: You would like to attend the concert, *and so* would I.
If you would like to attend the concert, *so* would I.

ESL 18

Clauses: Relative Pronouns and Adjective Clauses

Adjective clauses modify a noun or a pronoun. A relative pronoun (*who, whom, which, that*) is used to connect the clause to the word it modifies. When and how to use these pronouns is often a source of difficulty. Here are some general guidelines.

When the relative pronoun is the subject of the clause, it must always be included.

My cousin *who* lives in St. Louis is very rich.

When the relative pronoun is the object of the clause, it can be omitted. Both of these examples are correct:

The house my cousin lives in is very big.
The house *that* my cousin lives in is very big.

ESL 19

Clauses: Special Problems in Forming Adjective Clauses

The relative pronouns *who/whom, that,* and *which* function not only as subordinators but as the subject or object in the adjective clauses they introduce.

- These adjective clauses should not include additional subject or object pronouns.

  OBJECT
  No: Tina saw two dresses at the mall *that she liked them.*
  Yes: Tina saw two dresses at the mall *that she liked.*

  SUBJECT
  No: She bought the dress *that it was more expensive.*
  Yes: She bought the dress *that was more expensive.*

- The relative pronouns that introduce adjective clauses must always refer to a noun in the main clause.

  No: Carlos threw the ball to *who* was at first base.
  Yes: Carlos threw the ball to *the player who* was at first base.

- Adjective clauses always immediately follow the noun they modify in the main clause.

  No: Mai's cousin plays the piano very well *who lives in Pittsburgh.*
  Yes: Mai's cousin *who lives in Pittsburgh* plays the piano very well.

ESL 20

Dictionaries: Choosing Word Reference Books

A good dictionary designed specifically for second-language students is the best source of information about word meanings. Such dictionaries will help you avoid several common problems.

- Ordinary dictionaries frequently define difficult words with other difficult words. In the American Heritage Dictionary, for example, the word *haze* is defined as "Atmospheric moisture, dust, smoke, and vapor suspended to form a partially opaque condition." An ESL dictionary defines it more simply as "A light mist or smoke."
- Bilingual or "translation" dictionaries frequently oversimplify word meanings. They give synonyms that do not reflect multiple meanings of words. As a result, a writer seeking to use *fresh* in an abstract sense might choose *green,* which in this meaning is not a synonym. For example,

  TV reporters are always in search of *green* news to attract viewers.

- Thesauruses and abridged dictionaries also do not show shades of meaning. For example, if you were looking for a synonym for the word *way,* you might find *direction* and use it in this non-idiomatic fashion:

  Because of my limited English, math class is hard. I often solve problems in the wrong *direction.*

GLOSSARY OF USAGE

Although the meanings of words often change through the years, clear communication is enhanced when these changes take place slowly and meanings are kept as constant as possible. The following words and expressions are often misused or used in nontraditional ways. Studying this list will help you improve your vocabulary and your precision in the use of words.

Accept/Except *Accept* is a verb meaning "to receive willingly"; *except* is a preposition meaning "but."

Please *accept* my apologies.
Everyone *except* Carlos saw the film.

Advice/Advise *Advice* is a noun; *advise* is a verb. The *c* in *advice* is pronounced like the *c* in *certain;* the *s* in *advise* is pronounced like the last *s* in *surprise.*

I took his *advice* about buying stock, and I lost a fortune.
I *advise* you to disregard his *advice.*

Affect/Effect The verb *affect* means "to impress, to move, to change"; the noun *effect* means "result"; the verb *effect* means "to make, to accomplish"; the noun *affect,* meaning "a feeling or an emotion," is used in psychology.

Inflation *affects* our sense of security.
Inflation is one of the many *effects* of war.
Inflation has *effected* many changes in the way we spend money.
To study *affect,* psychologists probe the unconscious.

Ain't *Ain't* is an eighteenth-century contraction that has become a sign of illiteracy and ignorance; it should not be used in formal writing or speech.

All/All of; More/More of; Some/Some of Except before some pronouns, the *of* in these constructions can usually be eliminated.

All France rejoiced.

Some students cut class.

All of us wish you well. [The pronoun *us* requires the *of* before it here.]

All right/Alright The spelling *alright* is an alternate, but many educated readers still think it is incorrect in standard written English.

I told him it was *all right* to miss class tomorrow.

All together/Altogether *All together* expresses unity or common location; *altogether* means "completely," often in a tone of ironic understatement.

At the Imitators-of-Elvis national competition, it was *altogether* startling to see a swarm of untalented, loud young men with their rhinestones, their dyed and greased hair, and their pretensions, gathered *all together* on a single stage.

Allusion/Illusion An *allusion* is an indirect reference to something; an *illusion* is a fantasy that may be confused with reality.

He wrote to her of an "empty house," an *allusion* to their abandoned love affair.

They nourished the *illusion* that they could learn to write well without working hard.

Almost/Most *Almost,* an adverb, means "nearly"; *most,* an adjective, means "the greater part of." Do not use *most* when you mean *almost.*

He wrote her about *almost* [NOT *most*] everything he did.

He told her about *most* things he did.

A lot *A lot* used as a synonym for *many* is always two words.

She had *a lot* of reasons for disliking Carmichael.

Among/Between *Between* expresses a relation of two nouns; *among* expresses a relation involving more than two.

The distance *between* Boston and Knoxville is a thousand miles.

The desire to quit smoking is common *among* people who have smoked for a long time.

But throughout the history of English, *between* has sometimes been used with more than two nouns. It often has the sense of "within."

He covered the space *between* the four corners of his yard with concrete.

Between is sometimes used for more than two when each noun is considered individually.

The treaty that was signed was *between* the United States, Israel, and Egypt. [Each country signed the treaty individually.]

Between usually expresses a more precise relation, and *among* is more general.

Amount/Number Things measured in *amounts* usually cannot be thought of as having any individual identity; things measured in *numbers* can be sorted out and counted separately.

The *amount* of oil left underground in the United States is a matter of dispute.

But the *number* of oil companies losing money is tiny.

Anxious/Eager Careful writers distinguish between these two words when they are used to describe feelings about something that is going to happen. *Anxious* means "fearful"; *eager* signals strong interest or desire.

I am *anxious* when I visit the doctor.

I am *eager* to get out of the hospital.

Anymore/Any more *Anymore* is an adverb always used after a negation; *any more* can be an adjective and a pronoun or noun, or it can be an adverb and an adjective.

I don't enjoy dancing *anymore.*

I can't stand *any more.*

I don't want *any more* peanut butter.

Anyone/Any one; Anybody/Any body; Everyone/Every one; Everybody/Every body *Anyone, anybody, everyone,* and *everybody* are indefinite pronouns; when the pronoun *one* or the noun *body* is modified by the adjectives *any* and *every,* the words remain distinct in space and spelling.

Anybody can make a mistake.

A good murder mystery accounts for *every body* that turns up in the story.

The Scots always thought that *any one* of them was worth three of the enemy.

Anyone can see that this book is complicated.

Apt/Liable/Likely *Apt* means that someone has a special talent for doing something; *liable* means having legal responsibility; *likely* conveys a general expectation or consequence.

The president is an *apt* negotiator.

If my singing breaks your chandelier, I am *liable* for damages.

People who picnic in the woods are *likely* to get poison ivy.

As Do not use *as* as a synonym for *since, when,* or *because.*

UNCLEAR: I told him that he should visit Alcatraz *as* he was going to San Francisco.

BETTER: I told him that he should visit Alcatraz *since* he was going to San Francisco.

UNCLEAR: *As* I complained about the meal, the cook said he didn't like to eat there himself.
BETTER: *When* I complained about the meal, the cook said he didn't like to eat there himself.

UNCLEAR: *As* American Indians fought as individuals and not in organized groups, no wagon train in the history of the West ever had to circle up and fight off a mass attack by an Indian tribe.
BETTER: *Because* American Indians fought as individuals and not in organized groups, no wagon train in the history of the West ever had to circle up and fight off a mass attack by an Indian tribe.

As/Like In formal writing, avoid the use of *like* as a conjunction. Although this usage is becoming more common even among the educated, it still irritates so many people that you would be wise to avoid it.

NOT: He sneezed *like* he had a cold.
BUT: He sneezed *as if* he had a cold.

Like is perfectly acceptable as a preposition that introduces a comparison.

He rode his horse *like* a cavalry soldier.
The peas were *like* bullets.
At the closing bell, the children scattered from the school *like* leaves before the wind.

It is not necessary to substitute *as* for *like* any time *like* is followed by a noun unless the noun is the subject of a dependent clause.

She enjoyed tropical fruits *like* pineapples, bananas, oranges, and mangoes.
They did the assignments uncomplainingly, *as* they would have done nothing, uncomplainingly, if I had assigned them nothing.

It is now acceptable to use *like* before a noun when a verb is implied afterward.

She wants to sing *like* a bird.
He ran across the stage *like* a horse.

At Avoid the use of *at* as a false particle to complete the notion of *where.*

NOT: Where is Carmichael *at*?
BUT: Where is Carmichael?

Awful/Awfully Use *awful* and *awfully* only to convey the emotion of terror or wonder (awe-full).

The vampire flew out the window with an *awful* shriek.

Careful writers avoid the use of *awful* and *awfully* when they mean *very* or *extremely*.

Awhile/A while *Awhile* is an adverb; *a while* is an article and a noun.

Many authors are unable to write anything else for *a while* after they publish their first novel.
Stay *awhile* with me.

Being as/Being that These terms should not be used as synonyms for *since* or *because.*

NOT: *Being as* the mountain was there, we had to climb it.
BUT: *Because* the mountain was there, we had to climb it.

Beside/Besides *Beside* is a preposition meaning "next to" or "apart from"; *besides* is both a preposition and an adverb meaning "in addition to" or "except for."

The ski slope was *beside* the lodge.
She was *beside* herself with joy.
Besides a bicycle, he needed a tent and a pack.

Better Avoid using *better* in expressions of quantity.

Crossing the continent by train took more than [NOT *better than*] four days.

But that/But what Avoid writing these phrases when you mean *that* in expressions of doubt.

NOT: I have no doubt *but that* you can learn to write well.
BUT: I have no doubt *that* you can learn to write well.

NOT: I doubt *but what* any country music singer and writer has ever had the genius of Hank Williams.
BUT: I doubt *that* any country music singer and writer has ever had the genius of Hank Williams.

Can't hardly This is a double negative that is ungrammatical and self-contradictory.

NOT: I can't hardly understand algebra.
BUT: I can hardly understand algebra.
I can't understand algebra.

Case/Instance/Line These words are often used in expressions that can be revised, made more clear, or shortened.

NOT: In Murdock's case, I had to decide if he was telling the truth.
BUT: I had to decide if Murdock was telling the truth.

NOT: In that instance, Murdock lied.
BUT: Murdock lied.
Murdock lied then, but he told the truth the rest of the time.

NOT: Along that line, Murdock lied.
BUT: Murdock lied when he said he was allergic to cats.

In many sentences, the use of *in that instance* or *along that line* or some other similar phrase keeps writers from being specific and their prose from being lively.

Censor/Censure To *censor* is to keep a part or all of a piece of writing, a film, or some other form of communication from reaching its intended audience; to *censure* is to scold or condemn someone. Sometimes the censure is a formal act; sometimes it is a personal expression.

The Chinese government *censors* newspapers.

The House of Representatives *censured* Representative Larsonee for stealing from the Post Office.

Compare with/Compare to When you wish to stress either the similarities or the dissimilarities between two things, use *compare to;* when you wish to stress both similarities and differences, use *compare with.*

She compared his singing to the croaking of a wounded frog.

Compared to driving a motorcycle, driving a sportscar is safer.

He compared Omaha with San Francisco.

The use of *compared with* means that he found some things alike in Omaha and San Francisco and some things that were not alike, and that he mentioned both the similarities and dissimilarities.

Complement/Compliment A *complement* is something added to something else to complete it. A *compliment* is an approving remark. *Complimentary* is an adjective referring to something freely given, as approval or a favor.

He considers sauerkraut a perfect *complement* to hot dogs.

She received many *compliments* on her bulldozer.

All veterans received *complimentary* tickets.

His remarks were *complimentary.*

Convince/Persuade *Convince* usually means to win someone over by means of argument; *persuade* means to move so some form of action or change by argument or by some other means. *Convince* should always take *that* with a clause; *persuade* is followed by *to.*

The experiment *convinced* him *that* light was subject to gravity.

The television images of people dying in Bosnia *persuaded* the president *to* send help from the United States.

Could of/Should of/Would of These are ungrammatical forms of *could have, should have,* and *would have.* Avoid them and use the proper forms.

Differ from/Differ with *Differ from* expresses a lack of similarity; *differ with* expresses disagreement.

The ancient Greeks *differed* less *from* the Persians than we often think.

Aristotle *differed with* Plato on some important issues in philosophy.

Different from/Different than The idiom is *different from.* Careful writers avoid *different than.*

The east coast of Florida is *different from* the west coast.

Disinterested/Uninterested To be *disinterested* is to be impartial; to be *uninterested* is to have no concern about something, to pay no attention, to be bored.

We expect members of a jury to be *disinterested.*
Most people nowadays are *uninterested* in philosophy.

Don't/Doesn't *Don't* is the contraction for *do not; doesn't* is the contraction for *does not.*

You *don't* know what you're talking about.
He *doesn't* either.

Some American speakers say *he don't* and *she don't,* but such usage is nonstandard and should be avoided.

Due to/Because *Due to* is an overworked, wordy, and often confusing expression when it is used to show cause.

WORDY: Due to the fact that I was hungry, I ate too much.
BETTER: Because I was hungry, I ate too much.

Most writers accept the causative use of *due to* in short phrases, such as "His failure was *due to* laziness." But such constructions can be vague and confusing. Whose laziness? His or someone else's? The sentence does not tell us. What about a sentence like this one: "Their divorce was due to infidelity." Whose infidelity? Were both partners unfaithful? Sentences that include an agent are almost always clearer and more vigorous.

He failed because he was lazy.
His unfaithfulness to her caused their divorce.

A good rule of thumb is to use *due to* only in expressions of time in infinitive constructions or in other contexts where the meaning is scheduled.

The plane is *due to* arrive at five o'clock.
He is *due to* receive a promotion this year.

Each and every Use one or the other but not both.

Every cow came in at feeding time.
Each bale has to be put in the barn loft.

Eager/Anxious *See* Anxious/Eager.

Either . . . or/Neither . . . nor Always singular when followed by a singular noun or pronoun.

Neither Kant *nor* Hegel enjoys much popularity today.
When things get calm, *either* he *or* she starts a fight.

Either has an intensive use that *neither* does not, and when it is used as an intensive, *either* is always negative.

She told him she wouldn't go *either.*

Eminent/Imminent/Immanent *Eminent* means "exalted," "celebrated," "well known"; *imminent* means "about to happen" or "about to come"; *immanent* refers to something invisible spread everywhere through the visible world.

Many *eminent* Victorians were melancholy and disturbed.
In August 1939 Europeans sensed that war was *imminent.*

Medieval Christians believed that God's power was *immanent* through the universe.

Enthused/Enthusiastic Most writers and editors prefer the word *enthusiastic.*

The secretary of the interior was *enthusiastic* about the plans to build a high-rise condominium in Yosemite National Park.

Etc. This is a Latin abbreviation for *et cetera,* meaning "and others" or "and other things." Since the *and* is included in the abbreviation, you should not write *and etc.* In a series, a comma comes before *etc.* just as it would come before the coordinating conjunction that closes the series.

Everyone/Every one *See* Anyone/Any one.

Except/Accept *See* Accept/Except.

Expect/Suppose *Expect* means "hope" or "anticipate"; *suppose* means "presume."

I *expect* a good grade on my essay.
I *suppose* that he lost money on the horses.

Farther/Further *Farther* is used for geographical distances. *Further* means "in addition" when geography is not involved.

Ten miles *farther* on is a hotel.
He said *further* that he was annoyed with the play, the actors, and the dog that bit him on stage.
The Department of State hired a new public relations expert so that *further* disasters could be more carefully explained to the press.

Fewer/Less *Fewer* is the adjective for groups or collections whose parts can be counted individually; *less* as an adjective is used for things in bulk not commonly considered collections of individual entities.

Fewer people were at commencement this year.
Your argument has *less* substance than you think.

Flaunt/Flout *Flaunt* means "to wave, to show publicly" with a delight tinged with pride and even arrogance; *flout* means "to scorn" or "to defy," especially in a public way, seemingly without care for the consequences.

He *flaunted* his wealth by wearing overalls lined with mink.
He *flouted* the traffic laws by speeding, driving on the wrong side of the road, and running through a red light.

Former/Latter These words can refer only to one of two persons or things—in sequence, named first, named last.

John saw *Star Wars* and *The Empire Strikes Back.* He liked the former better than the latter.

If you are speaking of three or more things, use *first* and *last.*

Guy's closest friends were Paul, Curtis, and Ricco. The first was Greek, the second was English, and the last was Italian.

Get *Get* is one of the most flexible verbs in English. But in formal writing, you should avoid some of its more colloquial uses, as in *get with it, get it all together, get-up-and-go, get it, get me,* and *that gets me.*

Good/Well *Good* is an adjective; *well* is an adverb except when it refers to good health, in which case it is an adjective. Avoid confusing them.

I felt *good* after the doctor told me that I looked *well.*

She did *well* on the exam.

Half/Half a/A half of Write *half, a half,* or *half a,* but not *a half a, a half of,* or *half of.*

Half the baseball players went out on strike.

Half a loaf is better than none unless you are on a diet.

I want *a half*-dozen eggs to throw at the candidate.

Hanged/Hung People are *hanged* by the neck until dead; pictures and all other things that can be suspended are *hung.*

Hopefully Since the 1960s, *hopefully* has come into common use as an adverb modifying an entire sentence. Many careful writers and speakers object to *hopefully* as a modifier of an entire sentence because it does not specify who has the hope.

Hopefully Franklin will play poker tonight.

Who has the hope, Franklin or the other players who hope to win his money? Or perhaps the hope is held by someone who yearns for Franklin to be out of the house this evening.

Franklin *hopes* to play poker tonight.

All his gambling friends *hope* that Franklin will play poker with them tonight.

I *hope* Franklin is going to play poker tonight.

If . . . then Avoid the common redundancy that results when you use these words in tandem.

REDUNDANT: *If* I get my license, *then* I can drive a cab.

BETTER: If I get my license, I can drive a cab.

Once I get my license, I can drive a cab.

Imply/Infer To *imply* means to suggest something without stating it directly; to *infer* means to draw a conclusion from evidence.

By pouring hot coffee on his head, she *implied* that he should stop singing.

When she dozed off in the middle of his declaration of love for her, he *inferred* that she was not going to marry him.

In/In to/Into *In* refers to a location inside something; *in to* refers to motion with a purpose; *into* refers to movement from outside to inside or from separation to contact.

Charles kept a snake *in* his room.

The dorm supervisor came *in to* kill it.

The snake escaped by crawling *into* the drain.
The supervisor ran *into* the wall, and Charles got *into* trouble.

Incredible/Incredulous The *incredible* cannot be believed; the *incredulous* do not believe. Stories and events may be *incredible;* people are *incredulous.* Avoid using *incredible* and *incredibly* so loosely that your reader can tell that you were too lazy to think of a more precise and more vivid word.

Our *incredible* journey began with a bomb threat and ended with a robbery.
The audience was *incredulous* at his bizarre tale of why his shirt and trousers were torn.

Individual/Person Avoid the use of *individual* as a pompous synonym for *person,* and avoid using *individuals* when *people* will do. *Individual* as either a noun or an adjective should be used only to show a contrast between a person or a single entity and the group. Even then, *person* or one of its cognates may often be used.

The Bill of Rights guarantees *individual* liberties.
OR: The Bill of Rights guarantees *personal* liberties.
The speech was directed to every *person* in the square.
BUT: One of the oldest political questions is the relation between the *individual* and society.

Inside of/Outside of The *of* is unnecessary.

He was *inside* the house watching the pro football game on television.
She was *outside* the house mowing the lawn.

Irregardless This is a nonstandard form of *regardless.* The construction *irregardless* is a double negative, since both the prefix *ir-* and the suffix *-less* are negatives.

It's/Its *It's* is usually the contraction for *it is* but sometimes for *it has; its* is a possessive pronoun.

It's clear that *its* paint is peeling.
It's often been said that spelling is difficult.

Kind/Kinds *Kind* is a singular form and must take singular verbs and modifiers.

This kind of house *is* easy to build.
These kinds are better than those kinds.

Kind, sort, and *type* are often overused in writing. Try to do without them unless the classification they imply is necessary.

AWKWARD: She was a happy kind of person.
BETTER: She was a happy person.

Lie/Lay *Lie* means "to recline"; *lay* means "to place." Part of the confusion in the way we use *lie* and *lay* comes because the principal parts of the verbs are confusing. Study the following sentences.

INTRANSITIVE: I am going to *lie* down to sleep.
TRANSITIVE: He said he would *lay* the clothes carefully on the bed.
PRESENT: I often *lie* awake at night.
PAST: He *lay* on his stomach for a long time and listened intently.
PAST PARTICIPLE: He had *lain* there for an hour before he heard the horses.

PRESENT: He will *lay* the bricks in a straight line.
PAST: She *laid* her book on the steps and left it there.
PAST PARTICIPLE: He had *laid* away money for years to prepare for his retirement.

Literally *Literally* indicates that an expression often used in a figurative way is to be taken as true in this case.

Literally thousands of people gathered for the funeral.

The writer knows that *thousands* is sometimes used to mean merely "a great crowd." He wants people to know that if they counted the crowd at the funeral, they would number thousands. *Literally* is often incorrectly used as an intensive adverb. Avoid this usage, which can sound misleading or even ridiculous.

He *literally* scared Grandpa to death.
His blood *literally* boiled.
Her eyes *literally* flashed fire.

Maybe/May be *Maybe* is an adverb meaning "perhaps"; *may be* is a verb meaning "is possible."

Maybe he can get a summer job selling dictionaries.
That *may be* a problem because he doesn't know how to use one.

Moral/Morale The noun *moral* means "lesson," especially a lesson about standards of behavior or the nature of life; the noun *morale* means "attitude" or "mental condition."

The *moral* of the story is that to have a friend you must be a friend.
Morale dropped sharply among the students when they discovered that they would be penalized for misspelling words.

More important/More importantly The correct idiom is *more important,* not *more importantly.*

More important, if Jackson had not won the Battle of New Orleans, the city might have remained in British hands.

Myself (Himself, Herself, etc.) Pronouns ending with *-self* are reflexive, referring to the noun or pronoun that is the subject of a sentence, or intensive, stressing the noun or pronoun that serves as the antecedent.

Hercules hurt *himself* when he cleaned the stables.
Standing in the doorway was Count Dracula *himself* with a silver goblet in his hand.

When you are unsure whether to use *I, me, she, her, he,* or *him* in a compound subject or object, you may be tempted to substitute one of these pronouns. Don't do it.

NOT: The quarrel was between him and *myself.*

BUT: The quarrel was between him and me.

Nohow/Nowheres These words are nonstandard for *anyway, in no way, in any way, in any place,* and *in no place.* Don't use these words in writing.

Of/Have *See* Could of/Should of/Would of.

Off of Omit the *of.*

He knocked the hide *off* the ball.

She took the painting *off* the wall.

Parameter/Perimeter *Parameter* is a mathematical term referring to an arbitrary constant or an independent variable; *perimeter* means "limit."

The *parameters* were set to give the standard deviation from many distributions.

The *perimeters* of his biography of Theodore Roosevelt were set by Roosevelt's birth and death.

Parameter can sometimes be used correctly outside mathematics or computer science to mean some constant whose value varies, allowing us to measure other variables by it.

Because religion is a *parameter* of human life in all times and places, its effects on the relation between family and society may readily be observed.

Plus Avoid using *plus* as a substitute for *and.*

SUBSTANDARD: He had to walk the dog, wash the dishes, and take out the garbage, *plus* he had to write a book.

STANDARD: He had to walk the dog, wash the dishes, take out the garbage, and write his book.

Practicable/Practical *Practicable* is an adjective applied to things that can be done; practical means "sensible."

A space program that would land human beings on Mars is now *practicable,* but the journey would take a long time.

Many people don't think such a journey is *practical.*

Previous to/Prior to Avoid these wordy and somewhat pompous substitutes for *before.*

Principal/Principle *Principal* is an adjective meaning "first in importance" or a noun referring to the highest office in an organization or a capital sum that collects interest; *principle* is a noun referring to a standard for life, thought, or morals or the underlying unity that joins distinct phenomena.

The *principal* objection to our school's *principal* is that he had no *principles* in handling the endowment, investing it in the company owned by his wife.

Real/Really Avoid the use of *real* when you mean *very.*

The cake was *very* good.

It is grammatically correct to use *really* for the adverb *very,* but *really* is overworked nowadays and should be given a rest, especially because it rarely adds anything worthwhile to a sentence. The overuse of *really* makes you sound insincere, as if you were trying to convince somebody of something without having any evidence at your command.

Reason is because This is a redundant expression.

The reason he fell on the ice is *that* he cannot skate.

Relation/Relationship A short while ago *relationship* was most commonly used for "blood kin." Now it has almost replaced *relation. Relationship* is called a "long variant" of *relation* by H. W. Fowler, a great authority on the English language. It says nothing that *relation* does not say, but often writers use it because it lets them imagine that they are saying much more than they are.

Respective The word is almost always unnecessary in constructions like the following, and you can usually leave it out.

Charles and Robert brought in their *respective* assignments.

Set/Sit *Set* is usually a transitive verb, taking a direct object, meaning "to establish" or "to place"; *sit* is usually intransitive, meaning "to place oneself in a sitting position." The principal parts of *set* are *set, set,* and *set.* The principal parts of *sit* are *sit, sat,* and *sat.*

DiMaggio *set* the standard of excellence in fielding.

The dog *sat* on command.

Occasionally *set* can be intransitive and *sit* transitive.

The concrete took a while to *set.*

He *sits* his horse like a champion.

Shall/Will Not long ago, *shall* was the standard first-person future of the verb *to be* when a simple statement of fact was intended; *will* was the future for the second and third persons. But to say *I will, you shall, she shall,* or *they shall* implied a special determination to accomplish something.

I *shall* be forty-eight on my next birthday.

I *will* eat these cursed beets because they are good for me.

Now the distinction is blurred in the United States, although it is still observed in Britain. Most writers use *will* as the ordinary future tense for the first person.

We *will* come to New York next week.

Shall is still used in a few emphatic constructions in the second and third person.

They *shall* not pass.

You may take my life, but you *shall* not rob me of my dignity.

Some Avoid the use of the adjective *some* in place of the adverb *somewhat.*

He felt *somewhat* better after a good night's sleep.

Somewheres Don't use this nonstandard form for *somewhere.*

Sure Avoid confusing the adjective *sure* with the adverb *surely.*

The hat she wore on the streetcar was *surely* bizarre.

Sure and/Sure to *Sure and* is often used colloquially.

NONSTANDARD: Be *sure and* get to the wedding on time.

In formal writing, *sure to* is preferred.

Be *sure to* get to the wedding on time.

That/Which A few writers use *that* as a restrictive pronoun to introduce restrictive clauses and *which* to introduce nonrestrictive clauses.

The bull *that* escaped ran through my china shop, *which* was located on the square.

This distinction has never been so widely observed or respected that it can be considered a rule of grammar. The distinction offers no help for restrictive and nonrestrictive phrases or for *who* and *whom* clauses, which can be restrictive or nonrestrictive. The best rule is to set off the nonrestrictive elements with commas and to avoid using commas with restrictive elements.

Their/There/They're *Their* is a possessive pronoun; *there* is an adverb of place; *they're* is a contraction of *they are.*

They gave *their* lives.

She was standing *there.*

They're reading more poetry than they once did.

This here/These here/That there/Them there Avoid these nonstandard forms.

Try and/Try to *Try to* is the preferred form.

Try to understand.

Use/Utilize *Utilize* seldom says more than *use,* and simpler is almost always better.

We must learn how to *use* computers.

Verbally/Orally To say something *orally* is to say it aloud; to say something *verbally* is to use words. Many people confuse the two terms today, using *verbally* when they should use *orally.*

We agreed *orally* to get married, but when I asked her to confirm our engagement in writing, she refused.

His eyes displayed anger, but *verbally* he said only that he was disappointed.

Wait for/Wait on People *wait for* those who are late; they *wait on* tables.

Wait for me.

Steve *waited on* four tables at the diner.

Which/Who/Whose *Which* is used for things, *who* and *whose* for people.

The plane, *which* was late, brought the team home from California.

My lost fountain pen was found by a man *who* had never seen one before, *whose* whole life had been spent with ballpoints.

But *whose* is increasingly being used for things in constructions where *of which* would be awkward.

The cathedral, *whose* towers could be seen from miles away, seemed to shelter its city.

GLOSSARY OF GRAMMATICAL TERMS

Grammar is the science of the English language; studying grammar helps us analyze and talk about everyday spoken and written communication. This handbook does not provide a comprehensive course in grammar but instead offers a general introduction to the scientific study of our language (see Chapters 13–20). The terms and definitions below expand some of the concepts introduced earlier.

Absolute phrase A phrase made up of a noun or pronoun and a participle, extending the statement made by the sentence and modifying the sentence as a whole, not a particular element in it.

The sun rose at six o'clock, *its red light throwing long shadows in the forest.*

When the participle is some form of the verb *to be,* it is often omitted.

He flung the ball from center field, *his throw* [being] *like a bullet.*

Absolutes are common in modern English style; they allow compression of action and provide variety in sentences.

Abstract noun A noun that does not call up a concrete memory involving sensual experience. Examples: *relation, idea, thought, strength, matter, friendship, experience, enmity.* An abstract noun refers to some quality *abstracted,* or drawn, from many different experiences, and it may be used to name many different kinds of experiences. Abstract nouns require the help of concrete nouns if they are to make sense.

Acronym A noun made of the initials of an organization and sometimes pronounceable as if it were a word. Familiar acronyms include FBI (Federal Bureau of Investigation), CREEP (Committee to Re-elect the President), SNCC (Students Nonviolent Co-ordinating Committee), and HEW (Department of Health, Education, and Welfare). The forms of acronyms usually do not change, but the possessive case and the plural are formed in the same way as those of other nouns.

SNCC's first leader was Bob Moses.

Active voice The voice of a verb used to report that the subject does something.

The guitar player *sang* tenor.

The active voice always makes a stronger sentence than the passive voice.

Adjectival Any word or group of words (a phrase or a clause) that can be used as an adjective to modify a noun or pronoun. In the following examples, the adjectival words are in italics:

my book, *your* picture, *his* anger, *her* success

She painted the house *next door.*

The table *in the corner* belonged to me.

Writers *who write truly* always have readers.

Adjective Word that modifies a noun or pronoun by describing some quality.

The *red* coat; the *blue* book

Adjectives can come before or after a noun:

The roof of the *old red* barn collapsed.

The barn—*old, weather-beaten,* and *abandoned*—finally collapsed in the last snow.

Adjectives can also come after a verb when they modify the subject. In this position they are *predicate adjectives.*

The barn was *red.*

Adjectives often change form to show comparison.

Her car is *big.*

Jack's car is *bigger.*

My car is *biggest* of all, and I can't afford to drive it.

She bought an *expensive* meal at the Ritz.

She bought a *more expensive* meal at the Algonquin.

But she bought her *most expensive* meal at Tommy's Lunch, since it gave her food poisoning and put her in the hospital for a week.

Adjective clause Clause used to modify a noun or pronoun.

The car *that I drove then* appears in these old snapshots.

Adjective phrase A phrase such as a prepositional phrase that modifies a noun or pronoun.

He came to the end *of the road.*

Adverb Word commonly used to modify a verb, an adjective, or another adverb. Increasingly in modern English, adverbs are being used to modify whole sentences, though here the effect may be confusing. Adverbs tell us *when, where, why, how, how often, to what degree.*

They left *yesterday.*
The sun was *insufferably* hot.
The *more frequently* used room deteriorated *more seriously.*
Happily, the car hit the wall before it could hit me.

Adverbial, adverbial clause, adverbial phrase A clause or phrase that acts as an adverb, usually modifying a verb in another clause but sometimes modifying an adjective or another adverb.

Adverbial clauses often begin with words like *when, because, although, since, if, whether, after,* and *before.*

After he lost at Gettysburg, Lee knew he could not invade the North again.
We often think that women's fashions in the nineteenth century were dull *because we see them only in black-and-white photographs.*

Any phrase used as an adverb is an adverbial phrase. The most common adverbial phrase is the prepositional phrase.

You may find me *at home* this evening.
We groped around *in the dark.*

Adverbial is a word sometimes used to describe a phrase or a clause that acts as an adverb. Sometimes nouns are pressed into service as adverbials.

Many Americans go to church *Sundays.*
We plan to go *home* for Thanksgiving.

Agreement between pronouns and antecedents A matching in number and gender between pronouns and the nouns to which they refer.

Most *Americans* pay too little attention to *their* bodies.
Emma Bovary hated *her* dull life in *her* little town.
Flaubert created in her *his* greatest character.
Anyone dropping a course needs the signature of *his* or *her* faculty advisor.

Agreement between subjects and verbs A matching in number between subjects and verbs. A singular subject must take a singular verb; a plural subject must take a plural verb.

The *general* over all the armies *was* Eisenhower.
The *horses run* nearly every day at Suffolk Downs.
Lee Ann and *Tommy are playing* in the snow.

The greatest trouble in agreement between subjects and verbs usually comes in the third person singular, where *s* or *es* is added to the dictionary form of the verb.

She dances with grace and strength.
He yearns to return to the South.

The common contractions *don't* and *doesn't* give particular difficulty. Remember that *doesn't* is used in the third person singular in the present tense; *don't* is used in all other forms of the present tense:

It *doesn't* matter now.
They *don't* believe us.

She *doesn't* live here any more.

Appositive A noun or noun phrase that identifies another noun or pronoun, usually by naming it again in different words. Appositives usually come after the nouns they identify.

This is my brother *John.*

They loved Chinese food—*tofu, rice, and sweet-and-sour sauces.*

Clarence Penn, *the children's leader at the YMCA,* loved to lead hikes.

Notice that the appositives have the same relation to the rest of the sentence as the nouns they identify. You can leave out either the appositive or the noun identified by the appositive and have a grammatically complete sentence.

The children's leader at the YMCA loved to lead hikes.

Article The *indefinite articles* are *a* and *an;* the *definite* article is *the.* An article (sometimes called a *determiner*) sets off a noun or noun substitute in a sentence or phrase.

a broken toy

an unsettling thought

the treehouse

Auxiliary (helping) verb A verb used to help form the proper tense of another verb in a clause. Common helping verbs are *am, is, are, was, be, been, being, were, do, did, does, have, has, had, shall, will, may, might, can, could, would, should, must,* and *ought.* (*See also* Verb.)

He *had been* sleeping before the earthquake hit.

Rock music *must* have some strange power over children.

They *have* invited Norman to the party, but he *has* not yet accepted.

She *should have been* studying but instead she *was* watching television.

Biased writing Writing that fosters stereotypes or that demeans, ignores, or patronizes people on the basis of gender, age, religion, country of origin, physical abilities, sexual preference, or any other human attribute.

Case Form of a noun or pronoun that shows a grammatical relation to some other part of the sentence. English has only three cases: the *subjective* (or *nominative*), the *possessive* (or *genitive*), and the *objective* (or *accusative*). Only pronouns change form from the nominative in both the possessive and the objective case. Nouns commonly change form only in the possessive.

To form the possessive of a singular noun, add *'s.* For nouns ending in *s,* some writers add only an apostrophe, others add *'s.*

Erasmus/Erasmus', Dick/Dick's, Germany/Germany's

Some pronouns have different forms of all three cases.

Nominative	*Possessive*	*Objective*
I	my/mine	me
who	whose	whom
we	our/ours	them
they	their/theirs	them
he	his	him

Some pronouns have only two forms.

Nominative	*Possessive*	*Objective*
you	your/yours	you
it	its	it
she	her/hers	her

Clause A group of grammatically related words that includes a subject and a predicate. An *independent* (or *main*) clause may stand alone as a sentence; a *dependent* (or *subordinate*) clause acts as a noun, an adjective, or an adverb for some element of another clause. Independent clauses are sometimes called *main clauses;* dependent clauses are sometimes called *subordinate clauses.*

He thought his book was a failure *because it lost money.*

The independent clause (beginning with "He thought") can stand alone as a sentence, the dependent clause (in italics) acts as an adverb modifying the verb *was* in the independent clause.

Clustering Tying together various related ideas; can be done by drawing a subject tree.

Collective noun A noun naming a group of people or things. In American English it is usually considered a grammatical singular. (*See also* Noun.)

The *team* was upset because of the penalty.
The *government* is the plaintiff in the case.
The *majority* is opposed to the measure.

Comma splice The misuse of a comma to join two independent clauses without the help of a coordinating conjunction. You can mend a comma splice by using a coordinating conjunction or by replacing the comma with a semicolon.

COMMA SPLICE: They gathered the wood, she built the fire.
REVISED: They gathered the wood; she built the fire.
They gathered the wood, and she built the fire.

Common noun A noun that is not specific enough to be capitalized within a sentence. Common nouns are words like *desk, typewriter, chair, aircraft, automobile, glue, cow,* and *football.* (*See also* Noun.)

Comparative degree *See* Comparison.

Comparison Adjectives and adverbs can make comparisons. They indicate degrees by changing form or adding words.
The *positive degree* is the form that makes no comparison: *swift, quickly.*
The comparative degree compares no more than two things: a *swifter* boat, runs *more quickly*. Form the comparative degree by adding *-er* to the modifier or by using the word *more* or *less* before the modifier.
The *superlative degree* compares three or more things: the *swiftest* boat, runs *most quickly*. Form the superlative degree by adding *-est* to the modifier or by using the word *most* or *least* before the modifier. Exceptions exist, of course:

Positive	*Comparative*	*Superlative*
good	better	best
bad	worse	worst

Complement A word or group of words that extends or completes the meaning of some other elements in a clause.
A *subject complement* usually follows the verb but adds something to the meaning of the subject. Subject complements can be nouns or adjectives:

Her work was her *life.* [The noun *life* defines the subject, *work.*]

Her work was *difficult.* [The adjective *difficult* modifies the subject, *work.*]

An *object complement* follows immediately after the direct object of a verb or another object in the sentence and extends or completes the meaning of the object.

I wrote a letter to my sister *Nancy*. [*Nancy* is the complement of the object of the preposition, *sister.*]

The university named her *president* last week. [*President* is the complement of the direct object, *her.*]

A *verb complement* can be the direct or indirect object of the verb: it can receive the action of the verb or show for whom or to whom the action is conveyed.

He raised *money* for the campaign. [Direct object, *money.*]

He gave *me* the money. [Indirect object, *me.*]

Complete predicate The predicate, together with all the words that help make it a statement about the subject. (*See also* Predicate.)

Complete subject The subject and the words that describe it. (*See also* Subject.)

Complex sentence A sentence with an independent clause and at least one dependent clause. (*See also* Sentence.)

If you want to write well, you must work hard.
Because she worked hard, she received a promotion.
Although he hates exercise, he ran six miles every morning.

Compound sentence A sentence with at least two independent clauses joined by a comma and a coordinating conjunction or by a semicolon or a colon. (*See also* Sentence.)

We faced strong opposition, but we won.
She washed the clothes; he did the dishes.
Their point was this: men and women should receive equal pay for equal work.

Compound subject Two or more subjects connected by a conjunction. (*See also* Subject.)

Compound-complex sentence A sentence that has at least two independent clauses and at least one dependent clause. (*See also* Sentence.)

The Russians declared war on Germany, and the Germans invaded Belgium because a Serbian killed an Austrian prince.

Conditional mood *See* Mood.

Conjugation A listing of the various forms of a verb to show tense, person, number, voice, and mood.

Conjunction Word that joins elements of sentences to one another. *Coordinating conjunctions* (*and, but, or, nor, for,* and sometimes *so* and *yet*) can join independent clauses. *And,* the most frequently used coordinating conjunction, can be used to join many different elements in a sentence, but all the elements joined by *and* must be grammatically equal. That is, you should not write a sentence like this one: "The house was large, old, and it had not been painted in years." Revise it: "The house was large, old, and weather-beaten."

Subordinating conjunctions (or *subordinators*) mark a dependent clause to come. Example: *although, after, because, when, before.*

Conjunctive adverbs connect ideas between clauses. Examples are *however, nevertheless, moreover, indeed, in fact,* and *as a result.* Conjunctive adverbs are not strong enough to join two clauses without the help of a strong punctuation mark such as the semicolon, as in this sentence: "The sea voyage was long and difficult; however, Darwin seemed to enjoy it." Conjunctive adverbs may be used to begin a sentence to indicate a strong relation between that sentence and the one immediately before it.

Another way is not inevitable. Indeed, nothing in human life is inevitable except death.

Connotation The traditional collection of associations that surround the use of a word. If I say, "I *demand* an answer," the connotation is much less friendly than if I say, "I *request* an answer." If I say, "The orchestra *slogged through* Beethoven's Third Symphony," the impression is much less flattering to the orchestra than if I say, "The orchestra *marched* through Beethoven's Third."

Contraction A shortened word or group of words formed when some letters or sounds are omitted and replaced by an apostrophe. Contractions include forms such as *doesn't* for *does not, can't* for *cannot,* and *won't* for *will not.* Contractions are common in informal speech and writing; they are generally not used in formal writing. You may find contractions in a magazine article; you will probably not find them in a textbook.

Coordinating conjunction *See* Conjunction.

Coordination A grammatical structure that joins sentence elements so that they are of equal importance.

They flew, but we drove.
The bird tumbled from its perch and did a flip.

Correlative conjunctions Conjunctions, used in pairs, that connect sentence elements of equal value. Examples: *both . . . and, either . . . or, neither . . . nor, not only . . . but also.* (*See also* Conjunction.)

Count noun *See* Noun.

Dangling modifier An adjectival element, often at the beginning of a sentence, which does not correctly modify the grammatical subject.

DANGLING MODIFIER: *Crushed by the debt on her credit cards,* it was difficult for her to understand that she was making $40,000 a year and was still broke.

REVISED: Crushed by the debt on her credit cards, she could hardly understand that she was making $40,000 a year and that she was still broke.

Declarative sentence A sentence that makes a statement. Some writers define a *declarative sentence* as a sentence that begins with the subject followed by a verb without any intervening phrases or clauses.

Declension A table of all the forms of a noun or pronoun, showing the various cases. In English, a declension includes the forms of the nominative, the possessive, and the objective in the singular and the plural.

Degree *See* Comparison.

Demonstrative pronoun *See* Pronoun.

Denotation Primary meaning(s) of a word; the strict dictionary definition.

Dependent clause *See* Clause.

Determiner *See* Article.

Diagramming A pictorial method of showing relationships among various grammatical parts of a sentence.

Direct and indirect quotation In a *direct quotation,* the exact words of a source are given within quotation marks.

> The chair of the board said today, "I will not permit that no-good turkey of a president to dictate to this corporation."

In an *indirect quotation,* the sense of what has been said is given in a paraphrase; the exact words of the source are not used.

> The chair of the board declared that he would not allow the president to tell the corporation what to do.

Direct object *See* Object.

Discourse community A group with certain interests, knowledge, and expectations and with certain conventional ways of communicating with one another, such as baseball fans or biologists.

Double negative A substandard construction that makes a negative statement by using two negative forms. A double negative can be a single word such as the nonstandard *irregardless* (which has a negative form, *ir-*, at the beginning and another negative form, *-less,* at the end). A double negative is more commonly two negative words, as in this sentence: "I *don't* have *no* reason to go there." To correct the sentence, remove one of the negatives: "I *don't* have a reason to go there," or "I have *no* reason to go there." A common double negative is the phrase *can't hardly,* as in the sentence "I *can't hardly* do that assignment." The sentence should read, "I *can hardly* do that assignment."

Ellipsis An omission from within a direct quotation, marked by three spaced dots made with the period on the typewriter. You should mark an ellipsis by making a space after the last word you quote; setting a period after the space; making another space, another period, another space, a third period, and another space; and then typing the first word of the quotation beyond the omitted material.
A sentence from David McCullough's *Mornings on Horseback:*

> He must bide his time, maintain perfect decorum and silence, and so passive a role did not sit at all well with him.

The sentence quoted with an ellipsis:

> "He must bide his time, . . . and so passive a role did not sit at all well with him," McCullough said.

Notice that the comma after *time* is included before the ellipsis marks.

Elliptical construction A sentence construction in which words have been left out but are clearly understood.

[what is] *More important,* we learned to write well.
They are older *than she* [is old].
We enjoyed France more than [we enjoyed] *Switzerland.*

Exclamatory sentence A sentence that expresses strong emotion and ends with an exclamation point.

Expletive The use of *there, here,* or *it* as the grammatical subject of a sentence, followed by a form of *to be.*

We saw that *there were* feathers beneath the fence.
"*Here are* footsteps in the mud!" she exclaimed.
It was only Lucinda the cat who had torn a pillow to shreds.

When *it* is used as an expletive, this pronoun is the grammatical subject of a clause.

It is said that his grandfather did time in prison.
It was all a mystery, and we were baffled.

Expository writing Writing that presents, develops, and discusses ideas, rather than telling a story or describing how things look.

Fragment *See* Sentence fragment.

Free modifier A modifier, usually in the form of the present or past participle or participial phrase, that serves as an adjective modifying the subject but appearing after the verb. Free modifiers may be multiplied almost infinitely without confusing the sentence.

Hank Williams began his country music career as a young boy in Alabama, *playing* nightclubs called blood buckets, *writing* songs in cars between engagements, *drinking* too much whiskey, *making* his way painfully to the Grand Ole Opry and national fame.

Free writing Writing nonstop for a stated time period, without any attention to coherence or organization to get ideas on paper and stimulate thinking.

Future perfect tense *See* Tense.

Future tense *See* Tense.

Gender Sexual reference in grammar. Nouns and pronouns can have a masculine, feminine, or neuter *gender.* Many writers now make a special effort to use nouns that do not specify gender when both males and females may be included in the noun: *police officer* rather than *policeman, chair* or *chairperson* rather than *chairman, flight attendant* rather than *stewardess.*

Genitive case *See* Case.

Gerund The present participle of a verb (with the ending *-ing*) used as a noun.

Bicycling is my favorite exercise.

Helping verb *See* Auxiliary verb.

Idiom A word or expression that conveys a meaning established by custom and usage rather than by the literal definition. According to American English idiom, *making out* with someone is different from *making up* with that person. If you say you are *burned out* at your job, you are saying something different from what you mean if you say you are *burned up* at your boss.

Imperative mood *See* Mood.

Imperative sentence A sentence that gives a command or makes a request.

Indefinite pronoun A pronoun (such as *anybody* or *everybody*) that does not require an antecedent noun or pronoun, although it may refer to a noun or pronoun that comes after it in a sentence or a paragraph. (*See also* Pronoun.)

Independent clause *See* Clause.

Indicative mood *See* Mood.

Indirect object Noun or pronoun placed before a direct object and used to show for whom or to whom the action is conveyed by the verb. (*See also* Object.)

Indirect quotation *See* Direct and indirect quotation.

Infinitive A verbal in the form of the simple present and usually marked by the infinitive marker *to.* Infinitives can be used as nouns or adjectives or adverbs.

NOUN: *To die* may not be the worst thing one can do.
ADJECTIVE: She believed she had many books *to write.*
ADVERB: Most Americans are willing *to work.*

Inflection Changes in nouns, pronouns, verbs, adjectives, and adverbs that make these words serve various functions in sentences. The inflections of nouns and pronouns are called *declensions,* the inflections of verbs are called *conjugations,* and the inflections of adverbs and adjectives are called *comparisons.*

Intensive pronoun *See* Pronoun.

Interjection A part of speech used to express sudden or strong feeling.

Ouch! That hurts!
Hey! You can't do that to me!

Interrogative pronoun *See* Pronoun.

Interrogative sentence A sentence that asks a question and that ends with a question mark.

Intransitive verb Verb that reports an act or a state of being and does not take a direct object. Intransitive verbs that join a subject with a subject complement are called *linking verbs.* (*See also* Verb.)

Jack *ran* all the way home.
He *was* sick all that week.
She *had been* an architect in Missouri.

Inverted object A direct object that comes before the subject in a sentence, used only occasionally for sentence variety.

Whiskey he drank by the barrel.

Inverted sentence A sentence in which the subject comes after the verb. The most common inverted sentences begin with the adverb *there:*

There is something in what you say.
Ding, ding, ding went the bell.
Far, far away sounded the trumpets against the hills.

Irregular verb A verb whose simple past and past participle are not formed with the addition of the suffix *-ed.* These are verbs such as *come/came/come; think/thought/thought;* and *sit/sat/sat.*

Linking verb A verb that joins a subject to its complement. The most common linking verbs are forms of the verb *to be,* but all the verbs of sense are also linking verbs, so you should follow them with an adjective form:

I felt bad because he disliked my play.
The spring rain smelled good.

Mass noun *See* Noun.

Misplaced modifier Phrase or clause misplaced in the sentence so that it modifies the wrong thing.

Mrs. Hotchkiss, who loved Indian customs, served the Thanksgiving turkey in a sari and sandals.

Modifier Any word or group of words used as an adjective or adverb to qualify another word or group of words. The *red* truck is set off from trucks that are not red, and the horse *in the field* is set off from horses not in the field. (*See also* Misplaced modifier, Nonrestrictive modifier, Restrictive modifier.)

Mood The form of a verb that shows whether the writer or speaker thinks the action reported is true, false, or desirable.
The *indicative mood* reports actions that the writer assumes to be true:

Cat books now *crowd* the best-seller list.

The *subjunctive mood* reports actions that the writer assumes are untrue or at least uncertain:

If I *were* rich, I would do nothing but farm.

The subjunctive mood can report actions or states that may not be true but that the writer thinks are desirable:

Let justice roll down like waters and righteousness as a mighty stream.

The *imperative mood* expresses a command or a request for an action that the writer or speaker thinks is desirable.

Get out of here!

Bring the books with you when you come.

The *conditional mood* expresses what might be true or false under certain circumstances.

If Betty *is* right, Bob *is* in trouble.

If Betty *were* here, she *could explain* what happened.

Nonrestrictive modifier A clause or phrase that adds to the description of the word it modifies without being essential to the core assertion of the sentence. Nonrestrictive modifiers are usually set off by commas from the word they modify.

Faulkner, *who never finished college,* became one of America's greatest writers.

He ran toward the sound of the train, *stumbling in the tall grass, laughing, longing to see the locomotive and the engineer.*

The DC-3, *one of the most durable aircraft ever built,* still flies the skies in some parts of the world.

Noun Nouns are names of persons, places, things, ideas, actions, and states of existence. Any word can be a noun if in a given context it can be a name. A sure test for a noun is whether it can have one of the articles—*a, an,* or *the*—placed before it. The plurals of nouns are usually formed with the additions of *-s* or *-es,* but there are exceptions: sheep/*sheep,* child/*children,* and man/*men.*

Common nouns name things according to a general class: *desk, street, tractor, welder. Proper nouns* name specific people, places, or things and are spelled with initial capital letters: *Italy, the Department of Agriculture, Abraham Lincoln. Abstract nouns* name entities that lack any specific associations with sense experience: *friendship, ambition, relationship, haste, details. Concrete nouns* name entities that we may recall from our own sense experience: *wood, house, computer, cigar, highway, truck stop, bulldozer. Collective nouns* name groups: *team, crew, church, synagogue, audience, department. Count nouns* name entities that can be counted as individual units. *Mass nouns* name entities that cannot be separated and counted as individual units.

The categories of nouns may overlap. The collective noun *community* is also an abstract noun, since the idea of community is abstracted from our observations of people acting together. *George Washington* is a proper noun, since the name refers to a specific person and is capitalized; but it is also a concrete noun, since the man George Washington was a person whom we can identify by his picture and by works that have been written about him.

Noun clause A dependent clause used as a noun.

They told me *where we would meet in Athens.*

Number The form of a noun, verb, or pronoun that indicates singular or plural.

Object A noun or pronoun that receives the action reported by a verb, a preposition, or a verbal. (Verbals are infinitives, participles, and gerunds.) Objects usually come after the element that conveys action to them. A *direct object* receives the action of a verb (or a verbal) and generally follows the verb in a sentence.

Politicians must raise *money* to be elected.

An *indirect object* is a noun or pronoun placed before a direct object and used to show for whom or to whom the action is conveyed by the verb.

He promised *me* a hot cup of coffee.

Infinitives and verbals may take objects too.

We hoped to give her the *victory.*

Pushing *the couch,* she injured her back.

Prepositions always take objects.

They swam across the *river* together.

Object complement A word or group of words appearing after an object in a sentence and further defining that object.

He named his son *Tsang-Jou.*

They called the storm a *hurricane.*

Objective case Any noun or noun substitute is in the objective case when it is a direct object, an indirect object, or the object of a preposition or verbal. (*See* Case.)

Parenthetical element An element not essential to the main assertion of the sentence. If a parenthetical element represents a large interruption of the flow of a sentence, it may be placed within parentheses or dashes. Nonrestrictive modifiers are sometimes called parenthetical, since their removal does not destroy or confuse the main assertion of the sentence. Some words and expressions such as *incidentally* and *to be sure* are also considered parenthetical.

Herbert Hoover detested Franklin Roosevelt (Hoover would scarcely speak to him during Roosevelt's inaugural in 1932) and went on denouncing the New Deal for years.

He disliked the country—its loneliness appalled him—and he refused to visit it, even to ski or picnic or hike.

Participial phrase *See* Phrase.

Participle *See* Past participle and Present participle.

Parts of speech The names given to words to describe the role they play in communication. The eight parts of speech are noun, pronoun, verb, adjective, adverb, preposition, conjunction, and interjection.

Passive voice Form of a verb phrase that causes the subject of a clause to be acted upon. The passive is always made with some form of the verb *to be* and a past participle. (*See* Active voice; Voice.)

Lincoln *was elected* President in 1860.

The houses on the hill *were* all *built* alike.

Past participle The third principal part of a verb, the form of a verb used with the helping verbs *have* and *had.* It usually ends in *-ed,* but irregular verbs have different endings. The past participle finds common use as an adjective.

The hymn, *sung* by the mighty choir, rolled out into the night.

Their *worn* faces showed the futility of their effort.

The past participle, used with some form of the verb *to be,* is necessary to the passive voice.

The azaleas *were dug up and taken* from the garden before dawn.

Person The form of a pronoun that tells whether someone or something speaks. (*I, me, we, our*), is spoken to (*you, your*), or is spoken about (*he, she, it, their, them*). Verbs also change to show person in some tenses, especially in the third person singular.

FIRST PERSON: *I cry* (or *we cry*) at sad movies.

SECOND PERSON: *You cry* at sad movies.

THIRD PERSON: *He cries* (or *they cry*) at sad movies.

Personal pronoun *See* Pronoun.

Phrasal verb Verb combined with an adverb or preposition to express a new or different meaning. *Put up with,* for example, has a different meaning from *put* or *up* alone.

Phrase A group of related words that has neither subject nor predicate, and that serves as a part of speech in a sentence.

VERB PHRASE: We *are toiling* in the vineyard.

PREPOSITIONAL PHRASE: We must work *until sunset.*

PARTICIPIAL PHRASE: *Leaping the fence,* the horse carried me swiftly to safety in the woods.

INFINITIVE PHRASE: Lyndon Johnson yearned *to be somebody important.*

GERUND PHRASE: *Walking the dog* was his only exercise. [noun]

ABSOLUTE PHRASE: The car crashed through the house, *the front wheels coming to rest on the living room sofa.*

Positive degree *See* Comparison.

Possessive case The form of a noun or pronoun that indicates possession or a special relation. Some pronouns can only indicate possession—*my, mine, our, ours, your, yours, their.* The possessive of nouns (singular or plural) and some pronouns is formed by an apostrophe and an *-s* added at the end—*anybody's, everyone's, Gertrude's, Hubert's, women's* bank, *children's* toys. The possessive of nouns ending in *-s* (singular or plural) is generally formed by the addition of an apostrophe alone—*James', Erasmus',* the class' responsibility, the *states'* governors. Some writers prefer to add *'s* even to those nouns that end in *-s* in the singular—*James's, Erasmus's.* (*See also* Case.)

Possessive pronoun *See* Pronoun.

Predicate Everything in a clause or sentence besides the subject and its immediate adjectives. The predicate declares something about the subject. The *complete predicate* includes everything in the sentence but the subject cluster; the *simple predicate* includes only the verb or verb phrase. In this example *the complete predicate, including the simple predicate, is in italics.*

> The art of the late twentieth century *has departed from all the rules that supposedly guided both painting and sculpture for centuries.*

Predicate adjective An adjective that comes after a verb and modifies the subject. (*See* Complement.)

> She was *dignified.*

Predicate noun A noun that comes after the verb and helps to identify the subject of the sentence. (*See* Complement.)

> Ms. Smythe was an *architect.*

Prefix A letter or a group of letters, often derived from Latin or Greek, added to the beginning of a word to form another word. Common prefixes are *dis-, ir-, un-,* and *a-,* implying some kind of negation, as in *disbelief, irreplaceable, unreliable,* and *asymmetrical; ad-* means something added or joined to something else, as in *admixture.*

Preposition A word that does not change its form and that, by joining with a noun object, brings the noun into the sentence to act as an adjective or adverb. Common prepositions are *about, above, across, after, against, outside, toward,* and *within.* A preposition and its object, the noun or pronoun, make a *prepositional phrase,* and the prepositional phrase almost always serves as an adjective or an adverb in the sentence where it is found.

Prepositional phrase *See* Phrase.

Present participle The form of a verb that ends with *-ing.* With the aid of auxiliary verbs, the present participle forms the progressive of the various verb tenses. Standing by itself, the present participle can be an adjective or an adverb.

> ADJECTIVES: *Staggering* and *shouting,* he protested his innocence.
> ADVERB: They went *singing* through the streets at Christmas.

Present perfect tense *See* Tense.

Present stem The present stem of every English verb except *to be* is the form used with the personal pronoun *I* in the present tense (I *go,* I *stop*). It is also the form of the infinitive (*to go, to stop*). The simple past of a regular verb is formed by the addition of *-ed* or *-d* to the present stem, and the present participle is formed by *-ing* added to the present stem. If the present stem ends in *-e,* that letter is almost always dropped before *-ing* is added. Dictionaries list words in alphabetical order according to the spelling of the present stem; so the present stem is sometimes called the *dictionary form* of the verb.

Present tense *See* Tense.

Prewriting The first step in the writing process: preparation for writing. It can involve thinking and learning about your topic, jotting down ideas, asking the journalist's questions, free writing, clustering, and researching.

Principal parts of a verb The present stem, the simple past, and the past participle of a verb. The various tenses of verbs are formed from their principal parts.

PRESENT STEM: smile, do
SIMPLE PAST: smiled, did
PAST PARTICIPLE: smiled, done

Progressive tense *See* Tense.

Pronoun A word used in place of a noun. Many pronouns have an antecedent that comes before them either in the sentence where they are found or in an earlier sentence. But some pronouns such as *I, you, we, anybody,* and *everyone* may lack a formal antecedent, and sometimes the noun to which a pronoun refers may follow the pronoun in the text. Pronouns are generally classified in the following ways:

PERSONAL: I, you, we, they, he, she, our
RELATIVE: who, whom, which, that
INTERROGATIVE: who? which? what?
DEMONSTRATIVE: this, that, these, those
INDEFINITE: anybody, anyone, everyone, everybody
POSSESSIVE: my, mine, your, her, his, its, our, their
REFLEXIVE: myself, yourself, oneself
INTENSIVE: myself, yourself, oneself

The difference between reflexive and intensive pronouns depends on how they are used in a sentence. Their forms are the same. If the subject is in the same person as the pronoun and acts on it, the pronoun is reflexive, as in the sentence *I did all the damage to myself.* But if the pronoun serves to make a statement much more emphatic than it would be without the pronoun, we say that it is intensive, as in this sentence: *I said it myself.*

Proper noun *See* Noun.

Quotation *See* Direct and indirect quotation.

Reflexive pronoun *See* Pronoun.

Regular verb A verb whose simple past and past participle are both formed by the addition of *-ed* to the present stem: *play/played/played.* (*See also* Irregular verb.)

Relative pronoun *See* Pronoun.

Restrictive modifier A modifying element that defines or restricts the element it modifies, so that its removal from a sentence would confuse the sense of the main assertion.

> The bicycle *that I rode to the coast* had eighteen speeds.
> The man *in the gray suit and white hat* held the gun.
> The woman *who spoke* allayed the fears of the crowd.

Rhetorical question A question asked so that the writer or speaker may provide an answer or may demonstrate to the audience that the answer is obvious. The rhetorical question is often a convenient device for getting into a subject or for shifting emphasis within an essay. It should not be overused.

> How long are we going to let a government of the people be the chief destroyer of the people's land?
> How can we explain the seeming shift between Thomas More's early humanism and his later fury toward the Protestants?

Run-on sentence Two independent clauses run together with no punctuation to separate them. (*See also* Sentence.)

> Scientists, grammarians, and artists are all alike in one respect they depend on the work of others like themselves.
> I rose to applaud the mayor's speech then I tripped over the woman's handbag.

Sentence A statement, question, or command made by a grammatical union between a subject and a predicate. The subject must be a noun or noun substitute, and the predicate must include a verb. The subject controls the verb, and the subject and the verb must agree in number. In a sentence that is not a command, the predicate makes a statement about the subject. In a question, the statement is made in the form of an inquiry that asks to know if the statement is true.

> The personal computer *will soon become as common in the American home as the sofa in the living room.*
> *Will* the personal computer *soon become as common in the American home as the sofa in the living room?*

Sentence fragment A group of words that begins with a capital letter and ends with a closing mark of punctuation, but does not include a subject in grammatical union with a predicate. Correct a sentence fragment by giving it a subject or predicate (or both, when necessary) or by adding it to the sentence that comes directly before or after it.

FRAGMENT: The telephone dropped. *Onto the floor.*
Working at her desk. She suffered terribly.
Dr. Leyton introduced the visiting surgeon. *Who spoke formally without looking up from her notes.*

REVISED: The telephone dropped. It fell to the floor.
Working at her desk, she suffered terribly.
Dr. Leyton introduced the visiting surgeon, who spoke formally without looking up from her notes.

Simple predicate The word (or words) that reports or states a condition, with all the describing words removed; the verb.

Simple sentence A sentence with only one clause.

An orange sun dropped below the horizon.

Bob and Ray amused radio audiences for many years and helped define a new age of American comedy.

Some simple sentences are not very simple.

Catherine arrived in England in 1501 and immediately encountered the English hatred of foreigners, a hatred shown in the scorn heaped on her retainers; in the bitter stinginess of her royal father-in-law, Henry VII; and in the indifference of those around her to her comfort and even to her dignity.

Simple subject The word(s) that serve as the focus of the sentence.

Subject The noun or noun substitute about which the predicate of a clause or sentence makes its statement. The *simple subject* is the noun or noun substitute; the *complete subject,* or the *subject cluster,* includes all the immediate modifiers of the subject.

The absurd and angry group that assembled in a beer hall in Munich that night in 1923 was to create, a decade later, the most bloody revolution in German history.

A *compound subject* is two or more subjects connected by a conjunction.

Subject complement *See* Complement.

Subjective case *See* Case.

Subjunctive mood *See* Mood.

Subordinate clause *See* Clause.

Subordinating conjunction *See* Conjunction.

Subordination The act of placing some elements in sentences in a dependent relation with others so that readers will know what is important and what is not. So-called choppy sentences are usually sentences without adequate subordination.

The hunters walked for miles.

They did not know where they were going.

They had never been in the woods before.

Suffix An ending that changes the meaning of the word to which it is attached. The suffixes in the following words are in italics:

care/care*less,* delight/delight*ful,* boy/boy*ish,* visual/visual*ize*

Superlative degree *See* Comparison.

Syntax The part of grammar that defines the relations between sentences and between parts of sentences. In English syntax, the subject usually comes before the verb; prepositional phrases include a preposition and a noun or noun substitute that acts as the object of the preposition; and clauses serve as nouns, adjectives, or adverbs.

Tense The form of a verb that indicates time, whether present, past, or future. The *simple tenses* include the present, the past, and the future.

PRESENT: I *speak,* she *laughs*

PAST: I *spoke,* she *laughed*

FUTURE: I *shall* (or *will*) *speak,* she *will laugh*

The *perfect tenses* indicate time previous to the simple tenses. Perfect tenses are formed with the past participle and an auxiliary verb, *have* or *had.*

PRESENT PERFECT: I *have spoken,* she *has spoken*

PAST PERFECT: I *had spoken,* she *had spoken*

FUTURE PERFECT: I *shall have spoken,* she *will have spoken*

The *progressive tense* indicates continuing action. It is formed with the present participle and a form of the verb *to be* as auxiliary.

PRESENT PROGRESSIVE: I *am speaking.*

PAST PROGRESSIVE: She *was speaking.*

PAST PERFECT PROGRESSIVE: They *had been speaking.*

Tone The writer's attitude toward the subject—how the writer feels about characters and their actions, and how the writer makes the reader feel about them; the writer's perspective or point of view.

Transitive verb A verb that conveys action from a subject to a direct object. (*See* Verb.)

He *walked* his dog late last night.

She *bought* a new tennis racket.

Verb A word that reports an action or a condition; a word that makes an assertion. *Main verbs* combine with *helping verbs* to form the various tenses. *Intransitive verbs* report that the subject acts or exists in a certain condition; these verbs do not take a direct object. *Transitive verbs* carry action from the subject to an object. A verb can be transitive or intransitive, depending on its use in the sentence. *Linking verbs* join a subject with a complement, either a noun or an adjective. *Phrasal verbs* are combinations with an adverb or preposition that express a new or different meaning.

Jackson *smoked.* [intransitive]
Jackson *smoked* a pipe. [transitive; *pipe* is a direct object]

Verbal Word formed from a verb that does not function as a verb. Verbals are gerunds, participles, and infinitives. A verbal cannot make an assertion about a subject by itself.

Verb complement A direct or indirect object. (*See* Object.)

Verb phrase A main verb and its helping or auxiliary verbs. A verb phrase gives a complete statement of tense.

I *am helping* with the project.
He *had been seen* in the vicinity.

Voice The form of a verb used to indicate whether the subject does the acting (*active*) or is acted upon (*passive*).

ACTIVE VOICE: Ramon García *hit* the ball out of the park.
PASSIVE VOICE: A ball *was hit* out of the park by Ramon García.

Word order Most English sentences begin with the subject, or with an adverb or adverbial. The subject usually comes before the verb. The direct object usually comes after the verb. An indirect object always comes between the verb and the direct object. Most adjectives come immediately before or after the noun or noun substitute they modify. Predicate adjectives or subject complements modify the subject of a clause but come after the verb. Adverbs may be separated from the word or phrase they modify.

ACKNOWLEDGMENTS

Carl Bereiter. Excerpt from "Genetics and Educability," from *Disadvantaged Child,* vol. 3, edited by Jerome Hellmuth. Reprinted with permission from Brunner/Mazel, Inc.

Jane Brody. Excerpt reprinted from *Jane Brody's Nutrition Book* by Jane Brody, by permission of W. W. Norton & Company. Copyright © 1981 by Jane E. Brody.

E. E. Cummings. "in Just-" is reprinted from *Tulips & Chimneys* by E. E. Cummings, edited by George James Firmage, by permission of Liveright Publishing Corporation. Copyright 1923, 1925 and renewed 1951, 1953 by E. E. Cummings. Copyright © 1973, 1976 by the Trustees for the E. E. Cummings Trust. Copyright © 1973, 1976 by George James Firmage.

Tom Cuthbertson. Excerpt from *Anybody's Bike Book* by Tom Cuthbertson. Copyright © 1979. Used with permission of Ten Speed Press, Box 7123, Berkeley, CA 94707.

Richard D. Daugherty. Excerpt from "People of the Salmon," from *America in 1942: The World of the Indian Peoples before the Arrival of Columbus,* edited by Alvin M. Josephy, Jr., Alfred A. Knopf, Inc., 1992. Reprinted by permission of the author.

Joan Didion. Excerpt from "Some Dreamers of the Golden Dream" from *Slouching Towards Bethlehem* by Joan Didion. Copyright © 1966, 1968 by Joan Didion. Reprinted by permission of Farrar, Straus & Giroux, Inc.

Rachel G. Fuchs and Leslie Page Moch. Excerpt from "Pregnant, Single and Far from Home: Migrant Women in Nineteenth-Century Paris," in *American Historical Review,* vol. 95, no. 4, October 1990. Reprinted by permission.

Philip Gerber. Excerpt from *Willa Cather* by Philip Gerber. Copyright 1975 and reprinted with the permission of Twayne Publishers, a division of G. K. Hall & Co., Boston.

Paul B. Horton and Chester L. Hunt. Excerpt from *Sociology*, 6th ed., by Paul B. Horton and Chester L. Hunt. Copyright © 1984. Reprinted by permission of McGraw-Hill, Inc.

Nathan Irvin Huggins. Excerpt from *Black Odyssey* by Nathan Irvin Huggins. Copyright © 1977 by Nathan Irvin Huggins. Reprinted by permission of Pantheon Books, a Division of Random House, Inc.

Roy S. Johnson. Excerpt from the following article is reprinted courtesy of *Sports Illustrated* from the April 30, 1992 issue. Copyright © 1992, Time Inc. "None of Our Business: Arthur Ashe Is a Public Figure, but the Media Had No Right to Make His Illness a Public Matter" by Roy S. Johnson. All Rights Reserved.

Martin Luther King, Jr. Excerpt from "Letter from Birmingham Jail" from *Why We Can't Wait* by Martin Luther King, Jr. Reprinted by arrangement with the Heirs of the Estate of Martin Luther King, Jr., c/o Joan Daves Agency as agent for the Proprietor. Copyright 1963 by Dr. Martin Luther King, Jr. Copyright renewed 1991 by Coretta Scott King.

Maxine Hong Kingston. Excerpt from *The Woman Warrior: Memoirs of a Girlhood among Ghosts.* Reprinted by permission of Alfred A. Knopf, Inc.

David McCullough. Excerpt from *Mornings on Horseback* by David McCullough. Copyright © 1981 by David McCullough. Reprinted by permission of Simon & Schuster, Inc.

N. Scott Momaday. Excerpt from "The Becoming of the Native: Man in America before Columbus," from *America in 1492: The World of the Indian Peoples before the Arrival of Columbus,* edited by Alvin M. Josephy, Jr., Alfred A. Knopf, Inc., 1992. Reprinted by permission of the author.

The New Yorker. Two excerpts from "Talk of the Town" March 30, 1992 and April 6, 1992. Copyright © 1992; The New Yorker Magazine. Reprinted by permission; © The New Yorker Magazine, Inc.

Sharon O'Brien. Excerpts from *Willa Cather: The Emerging Voice* by Sharon O'Brien. Copyright © 1986 by Oxford University Press, Inc. Reprinted by permission.

Nell Irvin Painter. Excerpt from *Standing at Armageddon: The United States 1877-1919* by Nell Irvin Painter, W. W. Norton & Company, Inc., 1987.

Random House Webster's College Dictionary. Definition of the word "compare" and note on the word "lady" from *Random House Webster's College Dictionary* by Random House, Inc. Reprinted by permission of Random House, Inc. and McGraw-Hill, Inc.

Chet Raymo. Excerpt from "Science Musings," in *The Boston Globe,* January 19, 1987. Reprinted by permission of the author.

Reader's Guide to Periodical Literature. Entry for "Black Holes." Copyright © 1982 by the H. W. Wilson Company. Material reproduced by permission of the publisher.

Bernard Reich. Excerpt from "Themes in the History of the State of Israel," in *American Historical Review,* vol. 96, no. 5, December 1991. Reprinted by permission.

Jim Robbins. Excerpt from "Care for a Little Hellish Relish? Or Try a Hotsicle," in *Smithsonian*, January 1992. Reprinted by permission.

David Roberts. Excerpt from "Together, Scientists and Indians Explore the Conundrums of Casa Malpais," in *Smithsonian*, March 1992. Reprinted by permission.

Peter Mark Roget. "Humorist" from *Roget's International Thesaurus*, Fourth Edition, by Peter Mark Roget. Copyright © 1977 by Harper & Row Publishers, Inc. Reprinted by permission of HarperCollins Publishers.

Robert A. Rosenstone. Excerpt from "JFK: Historical Fact/Historical Film," in *American Historical Review*, vol. 97, no. 2, April 1992. Reprinted by permission.

Berton Roueche. Excerpt from "A Walk Along the Towpath" from *What's Left* by Berton Roueche. Reprinted by permission of Harold Ober Associates Incorporated. First published in *The New Yorker*. Copyright © 1962 by Berton Roueche. Copyright renewed 1990 by Berton Roueche.

Youngju Ryu. Excerpt from "Five Heroines for a Hard City," in *The New York Times*, April 4, 1992. Copyright © 1992 by the New York Times Company. Reprinted by permission.

Nancy Caldwell Sorel. Excerpt from "A. E. Housman and Willa Cather." Originally published in the July 1987 issue of *The Atlantic Monthly*.

E. M. Swift. Excerpt from the following article is reprinted courtesy of *Sports Illustrated* from the March 2, 1992 issue. Copyright © 1992, Time Inc. "Women of Mettle" by E. M. Swift. All Rights Reserved.

Lewis Thomas. Excerpt from "On Meddling," from *The Medusa and the Snail* by Lewis Thomas. Copyright © 1974, 1975, 1976, 1977, 1978, 1979 by Lewis Thomas. Used by permission of Viking Penguin, a division of Penguin Books USA Inc.

Wilcomb E. Washburn. Excerpt reprinted with the permission of Charles Scribner's Sons, an imprint of Macmillan Publishing Company from *Red Man's Law/White Man's Law* by Wilcomb E. Washburn. Copyright © 1971 Wilcomb E. Washburn.

Time. Excerpt from "Will Japan's Slump Stifle a U.S. Recovery?" in *Time*, March 23, 1992. Copyright 1992 Time Inc. Reprinted by permission.

INDEX

Each page number consists of two elements: the first element is either a chapter number and section letter (e.g., 17a) or an appendix abbreviation (e.g., ESL refers to the ESL Appendix, GU refers to the Glossary of Usage, and GT refers to the Glossary of Grammatical Terms); the second element after the colon refers to the page number(s) of the citation. Separate citations are indicated by semicolons. For example, 31c: 419–420 means that the entry is in chapter 31, section c, pages 419–420.

ESL APPENDIX